Lecture Notes in Computer Science 3821

Commenced Publication in 1973
Founding and Former Series Editors:
Gerhard Goos, Juris Hartmanis, and Jan van Leeuwen

T02223925

R. Ramanujam   Sandeep Sen (Eds.)

FSTTCS 2005:
Foundations of
Software Technology
and Theoretical
Computer Science

25th International Conference
Hyderabad, India, December 15-18, 2005
Proceedings

 Springer

Volume Editors

R. Ramanujam
The Institute of Mathematical Sciences
CIT Campus, Taramani, Chennai 600 113, India
E-mail: jam@imsc.res.in

Sandeep Sen
Indian Institute of Technology, Kharagpur 721302, India
E-mail: ssen@cse.iitkgp.ernet.in

Library of Congress Control Number: 2005937124

CR Subject Classification (1998): F.3, D.3, F.4, F.2, F.1, G.2

ISSN   0302-9743
ISBN-10   3-540-30495-9 Springer Berlin Heidelberg New York
ISBN-13   978-3-540-30495-1 Springer Berlin Heidelberg New York

Springer is a part of Springer Science+Business Media

springeronline.com

© Springer-Verlag Berlin Heidelberg 2005
Printed in Germany

Typesetting: Camera-ready by author, data conversion by Boller Mediendesign
Printed on acid-free paper   SPIN: 11590156   06/3142   5 4 3 2 1 0

Preface

This year marks a milestone in the history of FST&TCS, which first took place in 1981. We would like to take this opportunity to express our appreciation of the foresight and commitment to excellence shown by the early organizers of the conference. The conference is now organized by IARCS (Indian Association for Research in Computing Science), and the conference has been the foundation on which the IARCS community has been built.

To commemorate the *Silver Jubilee* of FST&TCS, we had an extra day to accommodate special sessions and a larger number of invited speakers. As in previous years, we were fortunate to have a number of highly eminent researchers giving plenary talks. It gives us great pleasure to thank Manindra Agrawal, Tom Henzinger, Russell Impagliazzo, Raimund Seidel, Natarajan Shankar, Joel Spencer and Igor Walukiewicz for agreeing to give talks and for contributing to this volume.

This year's conference attracted 167 submissions with authors from 29 countries. Except for some papers which were deemed to be out of scope by the Program Committee (PC), each submission was reviewed by at least three members of the PC, with help from many external reviewers. With 466 reviews at hand, the PC deliberated for more than two weeks before finally selecting the 38 papers included in this volume. We thank all the reviewers for their invaluable help. The PC members put in a great deal of hard work to select the best papers from the submissions. We express our gratitude to all PC members for doing an excellent job. Special thanks are due to Kamal Lodaya for managing the conference software as well.

FST&TCS included two pre-conference workshops: one on *Algorithms in Networking* coordinated by Amit Kumar (IIT Delhi) and Aravind Srinivasan (University of Maryland), and another on *Software Verification* coordinated by P. Madhusudan (University of Illinois at Urbana Champaign) and Sriram Rajamani (Microsoft Research). We thank the organizers as well as the speakers at the workshops for contributing so significantly to the program.

The conference was held at the International Institute of Information Technology, Hyderabad, and the satellite workshops at the adjoining campus of the University of Hyderabad. We thank the Organizing Committee for taking on the responsibility. We gratefully acknowledge the infrastructural help provided by our institutes, the Institute of Mathematical Sciences, Chennai, and the Indian Institute of Technology, Kharagpur.

We thank Springer for their continued support of FST&TCS over the years in publishing the proceedings.

December 2005

R. Ramanujam and Sandeep Sen
Co-chairs, Program Committee,
FST&TCS 2005

25 Years of FST&TCS

This Conference ... is the first of its kind being held in India and it is hoped that this would be the start of a series of such conferences to serve as a forum for discussing at an advanced level ...

Thus began the foreword to the proceedings of FST&TCS 1981. The conference aimed to provide a forum for computer science in India, a window to the rest of the world and, above all, a challenging environment in which critical analysis would ensure that high quality was scrupulously maintained. FST&TCS has fulfilled these early hopes, and may also claim to have set a standard for other computer science conferences in the region.

In 1981, there were many unknowns and neither the financial requirements nor participation from peers was assured. R. Narasimhan of Tata Institute of Fundamental Research (TIFR) provided unstinted support in all forms including funds and encouragement. Robin Milner looked past our shaky start (with flaky microphones and a projector that worked some of the time) and urged us to persevere. Maurice Nivat, the Keynote Speaker of FST&TCS 1981 and also Editor-in-Chief of the journal Theoretical Computer Science at that time, offered to bring out special issues of the journal from selected papers from the conference: this brought academic rigor as well as international visibility. From 1984 onwards, the proceedings have been published in the LNCS series by Springer. Many distinguished computer scientists have been invited speakers and have also contributed as reviewers.

Over the years, the series has redefined its goals. The focus has moved away from some of the areas that were seen as important 20 years ago. There is today altogether less focus on software technology and a great deal more on foundations. FST&TCS has also been an important step in the growth of many careers in India: many of the research students who hesitatingly submitted papers and even more hesitatingly presented them are now senior computer scientists with established reputations. In many ways, the maturing of FST&TCS has mirrored the maturing of computer science in India. The satellite workshops of the conference on state-of-the-art topics and special tutorial workshops have greatly helped to further research in India, especially for graduate students whose ability to travel abroad for conferences is limited.

Finally, we must thank all those (from India and abroad) who submitted papers, for sharing with us the belief that a conference like this was worth having and long overdue.

Thus ended the preface in 1981 and initiated the long journey that has taken us to 2005 with no fears of faltering.

December 2005

Mathai Joseph and R.K. Shyamasundar
Editors, FST&TCS 1981 Proceedings

CALL FOR PAPERS
Conference on
FOUNDATIONS OF SOFTWARE TECHNOLOGY
and
THEORETICAL COMPUTER SCIENCE
Sponsored by
National Centre for Software Development and Computing Techniques (NCSDCT)

December 11-12, 1981 Bangalore, India

Contributed papers are invited for the first conference scheduled to be held at
The Indian Institute of Science, Bangalore, India.

Topics : The following list of possible topics illustrate the intended scope of the conference :

Foundations of Software Technology: programming methodology, program correctness, programming languages (design, implementation, environment), operating systems, abstract software specifications.

Theoretical Computer Science : complexity of algorithms, automata theory, formal languages, theory of computation.

The conference is being organized to provide a forum for discussion at an advanced level of research topics of current interest in the areas indicated above. The conference will provide an opportunity to staff members and advanced level research students in institutions in India that have specialized post-graduate computer science programmes, for presenting their ongoing research work and plan future research/teaching activities.

The technical contents of the conference will be planned and organized by a committee comprising :

Dr. M. Joseph (NCSDCT, Bombay)
Dr. R. K. Shyamasundar (NCSDCT, Bombay)
Prof. S. V. Rangaswamy (IISc, Bangalore)
Prof. C. R. Muthukrishnan (IIT, Madras)
Prof. S. L. Mehndiratta (IIT, Bombay)
Prof. S. Maheswari (IIT, Delhi)
Prof. K. V. Nori (IIT, Kanpur)
Prof. Rani Siromoney (Madras Christian College, Madras)

Submission of Papers : Authors are requested to inform
Dr. R. K. Shyamasundar
NCSDCT
Tata Institute of Fundamental Research
Homi Bhabha Road, Bombay 400 005, India
of their intent to present a paper with a 200 words abstract before **May 15, 1981.**

Two copies of the complete version of the paper must be sent to the same address as above before **July 31, 1981.**

Authors will be notified of acceptance/rejection by **September 15, 1981.**

Organization

The 25th (*Silver Jubilee*) FST&TCS conference was held at the International Institute of Information Technology, Hyderabad during December 15–18, 2005. The associated workshops were held at the University of Hyderabad, India on December 13 and December 14, 2005.

Program Committee

Luca Aceto, *Aalborg/Reykjavik University*
Mikhail Atallah, *Purdue University*
Anuj Dawar, *Cambridge University*
Paul Gastin, *École Normale Supérieure de Cachan*
Dimitra Giannakopoulou, *NASA Ames Research Center*
Sudipto Guha, *University of Pennsylvania*
Venkatesan Guruswami, *University of Washington*
Sariel Har Peled, *University of Illinois at Urbana-Champaign*
Samir Khuller, *University of Maryland*
Amit Kumar, *Indian Institute of Technology Delhi*
Kamal Lodaya, *Institute of Mathematical Sciences, Chennai*
P. Madhusudan, *University of Illinois at Urbana-Champaign*
Yossi Matias, *Tel Aviv University*
Anca Muscholl, *Université Paris 7*
Tobias Nipkow, *Technische Universität München*
Greg Plaxton, *University of Texas at Austin*
Sanjiva Prasad, *Indian Institute of Technology Delhi*
Jaikumar Radhakrishnan, *TIFR, Mumbai and TTI-C, Chicago*
G. Ramalingam, *IBM Research*
Rajeev Raman, *University of Leicester*
R. Ramanujam, *Institute of Mathematical Sciences, Chennai (Co-chair)*
Mark Reynolds, *University Western Australia, Perth*
Sandeep Sen, *Indian Institute of Technology Kharagpur (Co-chair)*
Santosh Vempala, *Massachusetts Institute of Technology*

Local Organizing Committee

R.K. Bagga, *IIIT, Hyderabad*
R. Govindarajulu, *IIIT, Hyderabad*
Prosenjit Gupta, *IIIT, Hyd. (Chair)*
H. Mohanty, *Univ. of Hyderabad*

Atul Negi, *Univ. of Hyderabad*
Arun K. Pujari, *Univ. of Hyderabad*
Kannan Srinathan, *IIIT, Hyderabad*
V.Ch. Venkaiah, *IIIT, Hyderabad*

Referees

Parosh Abdulla	Ewen Denney	Sanjiv Kapoor
Bharat Adsul	Alin Dobra	Deepak Kapur
Klaus Aehlig	Bruce Donald	Srinivas Kashyap
Pankaj Agarwal	Gilles Dowek	Krishnaram Kenthapadi
Rajeev Alur	Alon Efrat	Delia Kesner
Boris Aronov	Zoltán Ésik	Astrid Kiehn
Christel Baier	François Fages	David Kirkpatrick
Mohua Banerjee	Tomás Feder	Vladlen Koltun
Paul Beame	Kaspar Fischer	Stefan Kreutzer
Arnold Beckmann	Lance Fortnow	M.R.K. Krishna Rao
Eli Ben-Sasson	Cédric Fournet	Karl Krukow
Béatrice Bérard	Martin Fränzle	Michal Kunc
Mark de Berg	Tim French	Orna Kupferman
Binay Bhattacharya	Nicola Galesi	Dietrich Kuske
Bruno Blanchet	Naveen Garg	Salvatore La Torre
Mikolaj Bojanczyk	Rahul Garg	V.S. Lakshmanan
Benedikt Bollig	Blaise Genest	Ralf Lämmel
Ahmed Bouajjani	Thomas Genet	Cosimo Laneve
Patricia Bouyer	Hugo Gimbert	François Laroussinie
Guillaume Brat	Leslie Goldberg	Martin Leucker
Mario Bravetti	Dimitar Guelev	Jean-Jacques Lévy
Michele Bugliesi	Rachid Guerraoui	Nutan Limaye
Andrei Bulatov	Vladimir Gurvich	Christof Löding
Franck Cassez	Stefan Haar	Markus Lohrey
Ilaria Castellani	Boulos Harb	Alessio Lomuscio
Rohit Chadha	Ramesh Hariharan	Etienne Lozes
Amine Chaieb	Rafi Hassin	Meena Mahajan
Supratik Chakraborty	Nevin Heintze	Mohammad Mahdian
Timothy M. Chan	Tom Henzinger	Narciso Martí-Oliet
Krishnendu Chatterjee	Miki Hermann	Jean Mayo
Soma Chaudhuri	Thomas Hildebrandt	Richard Mayr
Chandra Chekuri	John Hitchcock	David McAllester
Meir Cohen	Michael Hoffmann	Ron van der Meyden
Hubert Comon	Lisha Huang	Gatis Midrijanis
Graham Cormode	Joe Hurd	Peter Bro Miltersen
Giovanna D'Agostino	Hans Hüttel	Alexandre Miquel
Deepak D'Souza	Anna Ingólfsdóttir	Bud Mishra
Victor Dalmau	Radu Iosif	Mike Mislove
Anupam Datta	François Irigoin	Joseph S.B. Mitchell
Rowan Davies	Franjo Ivančić	Mark Moir
Kalyanmoy Deb	Radha Jagadeesan	Larry Moss
Carole Delporte-Gallet	Kamal Jain	Asish Mukhopadhyay
Stéphane Demri	David Janin	Madhavan Mukund
X. Deng	Marcin Jurdziński	Andrzej Murawski

S. Muthukrishnan
K. Narayan Kumar
Rolf Niedermeier
Susana Nieva Soto
Yoshio Okamoto
S.P. Pal
Vinayaka Pandit
Paritosh Pandya
Amit Paradkar
Frank Pfenning
Reinhard Pichler
Val Pinciu
Amir Pnueli
Teresa Przytycka
Shaz Qadeer
Balaji Raghavachari
Sriram Rajamani
Edgar Ramos
Jean-François Raskin
Julian Rathke
Anders P. Ravn
Noam Rinetzky
Grigore Rosu
Tim Roughgarden
Yogish Sabharwal
Prahlad Sampath

Rahul Santhanam
Sudeshna Sarkar
Jayalal Sarma
Alan Schmitt
Gerardo Schneider
Philippe Schnoebelen
Falk Schreiber
Stefan Schwoon
Carsten Schürmann
Luc Segoufin
Géraud Sénizergues
Peter Sewell
Natarajan Shankar
Priti Shankar
Nikolay V. Shilov
Janos Simon
Sunil Simon
Aravinda Sistla
Milind Sohoni
Maria Sorea
Christoph Sprenger
Jiri Srba
Frank Stephan
Colin Stirling
C.R. Subramanian
S.P. Suresh

Fabien Tarissan
David Teller
Denis Thérien
P.S. Thiagarajan
Mitul Tiwari
Tayssir Touili
Stavros Tripakis
Kasturi Varadarajan
Moshe Vardi
Vinodchandran Variyam
Björn Victor
Mitchell Wand
Pascal Weil
Jennifer Welch
Ryan Williams
James Worrell
Bożena Woźna
Hiroaki Yamamoto
Noson S. Yanofsky
Nobuko Yoshida
Francesco Zappa Nardelli
Marc Zeitoun
Lisa Zhang
Wiesław Zielonka

Table of Contents

Semiperfect-Information Games

Krishnendu Chatterjee[1] and Thomas A. Henzinger[1,2]

[1] University of California, Berkeley, USA
[2] EPFL, Switzerland
{c_krish,tah}@eecs.berkeley.edu

Abstract. Much recent research has focused on the applications of games with ω-regular objectives in the control and verification of reactive systems. However, many of the game-based models are ill-suited for these applications, because they assume that each player has complete information about the state of the system (they are "perfect-information" games). This is because in many situations, a controller does not see the private state of the plant. Such scenarios are naturally modeled by "partial-information" games. On the other hand, these games are intractable; for example, partial-information games with simple reachability objectives are 2EXPTIME-complete.

We study the intermediate case of "semiperfect-information" games, where one player has complete knowledge of the state, while the other player has only partial knowledge. This model is appropriate in control situations where a controller must cope with plant behavior that is as adversarial as possible, i.e., the controller has partial information while the plant has perfect information. As is customary, we assume that the controller and plant take turns to make moves. We show that these *semiperfect-information turn-based games* are equivalent to *perfect-information concurrent games*, where the two players choose their moves simultaneously and independently. Since the perfect-information concurrent games are well-understood, we obtain several results of how semiperfect-information turn-based games differ from perfect-information turn-based games on one hand, and from partial-information turn-based games on the other hand. In particular, semiperfect-information turn-based games can benefit from randomized strategies while the perfect-information variety cannot, and semiperfect-information turn-based games are in NP ∩ coNP for all parity objectives.

1 Introduction

Games on graphs. Games played on graphs play a central role in many areas of computer science. In particular, when the vertices and edges of a graph represent the states and transitions of a reactive system, then the synthesis problem (Church's problem) asks for the construction of a winning strategy in a game played on a graph [2,17,16,15]. Game-theoretic formulations have also proved useful for the verification [1], refinement [11], and compatibility checking [6] of reactive systems. Games played on graphs are dynamic games that proceed for

R. Ramanujam and S. Sen (Eds.): FSTTCS 2005, LNCS 3821, pp. 1–18, 2005.

an infinite number of rounds. In each round, the players choose moves; the moves, together with the current state, determine the successor state. An outcome of the game, called a *play*, consists of the infinite sequence of states that are visited.

Strategies and objectives. A strategy for a player is a recipe that describes how the player chooses a move to extend a play. Strategies can be classified as follows: *pure* strategies, which always deterministically choose a move to extend the play, vs. *randomized* strategies, which may choose at a state a probability distribution over the available moves; *memoryless* strategies, which depend only on the current state of the play, vs. *memory* strategies, which may depend on the history of the play up to the current state. Objectives are generally Borel measurable functions [14]: the objective for a player is a Borel set B in the Cantor topology on S^ω (where S is the set of states), and the player satisfies the objective iff the outcome of the game is a member of B. In verification, objectives are usually ω-*regular languages*. The ω-regular languages generalize the classical regular languages to infinite strings; they occur in the low levels of the Borel hierarchy (they lie in $\Sigma_3 \cap \Pi_3$) and they form a robust and expressive language for determining payoffs for commonly used specifications. The simplest ω-regular objectives correspond to "safety" (the closed sets in the topology of S^ω) and "reachability" (the open sets).

Classification of games. Games played on graphs can be classified according to the knowledge of the players about the state of the game, and the way of choosing moves. Accordingly, there are (a) *perfect-information* games, where each player has complete knowledge about the history of the play up to the current state, and (b) *partial-information* (or *incomplete-information*) games, where a player may not have complete knowledge about the current state of the game and the past moves played by the other player. According to the way of choosing moves, the games on graphs can be classified into *turn-based* and *concurrent* games. In turn-based games, in any given round only one player can choose among multiple moves; effectively, the set of states can be partitioned into the states where it is player 1's turn to play, and the states where it is player 2's turn. In concurrent games, both players may have multiple moves available at each state, and the players choose their moves simultaneously and independently.

Perfect-information versus partial-information games. The perfect-information turn-based (**PT**) games have been widely studied in the computer-science community, and also have deep connections with mathematical logic. For the algorithmic analysis of **PT** games with ω-regular objectives see, for example, [9,10,19,12,20]. On the other hand, the perfect-information concurrent (**PC**) games (also known as Blackwell games) have been studied mainly in the game-theory community. Only recently has the algorithmic analysis of **PC** games caught interest [7,5,8,3]. It is, however, the *partial-information* games which provide the most natural framework for modular verification and control. In practice, a process or a controller does not have access to the internal or private variables of the other processes or the plant, and partial-information games are the adequate model for such scenarios. Nonetheless, partial-information games have received little attention in computer science, perhaps be due to the high computational complexity of such games. Reif [18] showed that the decision problem for partial-information turn-based games, even for simple reachability objectives, is 2EXPTIME-complete (the same problem can be solved in linear time for **PT** games, and lies in NP $\cap$ coNP for **PC** games [4]).

Semiperfect-information turn-based games. In this paper, we study a subclass of partial-information turn-based games, namely, the *semiperfect-information* turn-based (**ST**) games, where one player (player 1) has incomplete knowledge about the state of the game and the moves of player 2, while player 2 has complete knowledge about the state and player 1 moves. The semiperfect-information games are asymmetric, because one player has partial information and the other player has perfect information. These games provide a better model for controller synthesis than the perfect-information games. In controller synthesis, the controller cannot observe the private variables of the plant and hence has limited knowledge about the state of the game. However, the controller ought to achieve its objective against *all* plant behaviors, and this unconditionally adversarial nature of the plant is modeled most adequately by allowing the plant to have complete knowledge about the game.

Semiperfect-information versus perfect-information games. The **ST** games differ considerably from the **PT** games. In the case of **PT** games, for every Borel objective Φ for player 1 and complementary objective $\overline{\Phi}$ for player 2, the determinacy result of Martin [13] establishes that for every state in the game graph, either player 1 has a pure strategy to satisfy the objective Φ with certainty against all strategies of player 2; or player 2 has a pure strategy to satisfy the objective $\overline{\Phi}$ with certainty against all strategies of player 1. We show that, in contrast, in **ST** games, in general the players cannot guarantee to win with certainty, and randomized strategies are more powerful than pure strategies.

Example 1 (ST games). Consider the game shown in Fig. 1. The game is a turn-based game, where the $\square$ states are player 1 states (where player 1 moves), and the $\diamond$ states are player 2 states (where player 2 moves); we will follow this convention in all figures. The game is a semiperfect-information game, as player 1 cannot distinguish between the two states in $P_1 = \{ s_1, s_2 \}$. Informally, if the current state of the game is in P_1, then player 1 knows that the game is in P_1 but does not know whether the current state is s_1 or s_2. At state s_0 player 2, can choose between s_1 and s_2, which is indicated by the edge from s_0 to P_1. The objective for player 1 is to reach the state s_3, and the set of available moves for player 1 at the states in P_1 is $\{ a, b \}$. Consider a pure strategy σ for player 1. Consider the counter-strategy π for player 2 as follows: each time player 1 plays move a, player 2 places player 1 at state s_2 in the previous round, and the play reaches s_0; and each time player 1 plays move b, player 2 places player 1 at state s_1 in the previous round, and the play again reaches s_0. Hence for every pure strategy σ for player 1 there is a counter-strategy π for player 2 such that the state s_3 is never reached.

Now consider a randomized memoryless strategy σ_m for player 1 as follows: σ_m plays the moves a and b each with probability $1/2$. Given any strategy π for player 2, every time P_1 is reached, it reaches s_3 with probability $1/2$ and goes

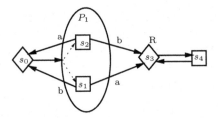

Fig. 1. A semiperfect-information turn-based game.

back to s_0 with probability $1/2$. Hence state s_3 is reached with probability $1/2$ for each visit to P_1, and thus s_3 is eventually reached with probability 1. Given the strategy σ_m, consider a counter-strategy π for player 2 which always places player 1 at state s_1 every time the play reaches s_0. Given the strategies σ_m and π, there exist paths that never reach s_3; however, the measure for the set of those paths is 0. Hence, although player 1 can win with probability 1 from state s_0, she cannot win with certainty. ∎

Semiperfect-information versus partial-information games. The class of **ST** games is considerably simpler than the full class of partial-information turn-based games. While the decision problem for partial-information turn-based games with reachability objectives is 2EXPTIME-complete, we show that for **ST** games the corresponding decision problem is in NP ∩ coNP for reachability and also for general parity objectives (the parity objectives are a canonical representation for ω-regular objectives). This shows that the **ST** games can be solved considerably more efficiently than general partial-information turn-based games.

Outline of our main results. We show that though **ST** games differ from **PT** games, there is a close connection between **ST** (turn-based) games and **PC** (concurrent) games. In fact, we establish the equivalence of **ST** games and **PC** games: we present reductions of **ST** games to **PC** games, and vice versa. The **PC** games have been proposed as a framework for modeling synchronous interactions in reactive systems [7,1]. Our reductions show that such games also provide a framework for analyzing **ST** games. We obtain several results on **ST** games from the equivalence of **ST** games and **PC** games. The main results are as follows:

- The *optimum value* for a player for an objective Φ is the maximal probability with which the player can ensure that Φ is satisfied. We establish the quantitative determinacy for **ST** games with arbitrary Borel objectives: for all **ST** games with objective Φ for player 1 and complementary objective $\overline{\Phi}$ for player 2, the sum of the optimum values for the players at all states is 1.
- The optimum values of **ST** games with parity objectives can be approximated, for any given error bound, in NP ∩ coNP. We give an example showing that the optimum values may be irrational in **ST** games with reachability objectives; this indicates that optimum values can only be approximated.

– We analyze, for various classes of parity objectives, the precise memory requirements for strategies to ensure the optimal values of **ST** games within a given error bound.

2 Definitions

In this section we define semiperfect-information turn-based games, strategies, objectives, and values in such games. We later define perfect-information concurrent games and the corresponding notion of strategies, objectives, and values.

2.1 Semiperfect-Information Turn-Based Games

A *turn-based game* is played over a finite state space by two players (player 1 and player 2), and the players make moves in turns. In games with *perfect information* each player has complete knowledge about the state and the sequence of moves made by both players. In contrast, in games with *semiperfect information* player 1 has partial knowledge about the state and the moves of player 2, whereas player 2 has complete knowledge about the state and the moves of player 1.

Turn-based game structures. A turn-based game structure $G = ((S_1, S_2), \approx, M, \Gamma_1, \Gamma_2, \delta)$ is a tuple with the following components:

1. Two finite, disjoint sets S_1 and S_2 of states. The state space S of the game structure is their union, i.e., $S = S_1 \cup S_2$. The states in S_1 are player 1 states and the states in S_2 are player 2 states.
2. An equivalence relation $\approx$ on S. The restriction of $\approx$ to S_1 induces a partition $\mathcal{P}_1$ of the set S_1 of player 1 states, and the restriction of $\approx$ to S_2 induces a partition $\mathcal{P}_2$ of S_2. Let $\mathcal{P} = \mathcal{P}_1 \cup \mathcal{P}_2$ be the corresponding partition of the entire state space S.
3. A finite set M of moves for the two players.
4. Two functions $\Gamma_1 \colon S_1 \to 2^M \setminus \emptyset$ and $\Gamma_2 \colon S_2 \to 2^M \setminus \emptyset$. Each function Γ_i, for $i = 1, 2$, assigns to every state $s \in S_i$ a nonempty set $\Gamma_i(s) \subseteq M$ of moves that are available to player i at state s.
5. Two functions $\delta_1 \colon S_1 \times M \to S_2$ and $\delta_2 \colon S_2 \times M \to S_1$. The transition function δ_1 for player 1 gives for every state $s \in S_1$ and available move $a \in \Gamma_1(s)$ a successor state $\delta_1(s, a) \in S_2$. The transition function δ_2 for player 2 gives for every state $s \in S_2$ and move $b \in \Gamma_2(s)$ a successor state $\delta_2(s, b) \in S_1$.

Semiperfect-information turn-based games. In semiperfect-information turn-based (**ST**) games player 1's view of the game structure is only partial: player 1 knows the $\approx$-equivalence class of the current state, but not the precise state in that class. We formalize this by separating the visible and invisible parts of player 2's moves and transitions.

– The move assignment Γ_2 for player 2 consists of two parts: Γ_2^{vis} assigns to every state $s \in S_2$ a nonempty set $\Gamma_2^{\mathrm{vis}}(s) \subseteq M$ of available *visible* moves for player 2 at state s; and Γ_2^{inv} assigns to every equivalence class $P \in \mathcal{P}_1$

a nonempty set $\Gamma_2^{\text{inv}}(P) \subseteq M$ of available *invisible* moves for player 2 at P. Intuitively, player 1 can observe the set of visible moves of player 2, but she cannot observe the invisible moves of player 2.

- The transition function δ_2 for player 2 consists of two parts: the *visible* transition function $\delta_2^{\text{vis}} \colon S_2 \times M \to \mathcal{P}_1$ gives for every state $s \in S_2$ and move $a \in \Gamma_2^{\text{vis}}(s)$ a successor class $\delta_2^{\text{vis}}(s, a) \in \mathcal{P}_1$; and the *invisible* transition function $\delta_2^{\text{inv}} \colon \mathcal{P}_1 \times M \to S_1$ gives for every equivalence class $P \in \mathcal{P}_1$ and move $a \in \Gamma_2^{\text{inv}}(P)$ a successor state $\delta_2^{\text{inv}}(P, a) \in P$.

Note that the definition of **ST** games reduces to classical perfect-information turn-based games if $\approx$ is equality, i.e., if each equivalence class of $\approx$ is a singleton.

Example 2 (Games with variables). A game with variables between player 1 and player 2 consists of a four-tuple $(V_1^{\text{pvt}}, V_1^{\text{pub}}, V_2^{\text{pvt}}, V_2^{\text{pub}})$ of boolean variables. The set V_i^{pvt}, for $i = 1, 2$, is the set of *private* variables for player i, which player i can observe and update, but the other player can neither observe nor update. The set V_i^{pub} is the set of *public* variables for player i, which both players can observe but only player i can update. A state of the game is a valuation of all variables in $V = V_1^{\text{pvt}} \cup V_1^{\text{pub}} \cup V_2^{\text{pvt}} \cup V_2^{\text{pub}}$. Player 1 and player 2 alternately update the variables in $V_1 = V_1^{\text{pvt}} \cup V_1^{\text{pub}}$ and in $V_2 = V_2^{\text{pvt}} \cup V_2^{\text{pub}}$, respectively. For player 1, a nondeterministic update function u_1 is given by its private component $u_1^{\text{pvt}} \colon [V_1 \cup V_2^{\text{pub}}] \to 2^{[V_1^{\text{pvt}}]}$ and its public component $u_1^{\text{pub}} \colon [V_1 \cup V_2^{\text{pub}}] \to 2^{[V_1^{\text{pub}}]}$, where $[U]$ is the set of valuations for the variables in U. The nondeterministic player 2 update function is given similarly. We consider the special case that $V_1^{\text{pvt}} = \emptyset$, i.e., player 1 has no private variables, and hence player 2 has complete knowledge of the state. This special class of games with variables can be mapped to **ST** games as follows:

- Two states are equivalent if they agree on the valuation of the variables in $V_1^{\text{pub}} \cup V_2^{\text{pub}}$. This defines the equivalence relation $\approx$.
- The update function u_1^{pub} is represented by the move assignment Γ_1 and transition function δ_1 for player 1. The update function u_2^{pub} is represented by the visible move assignment Γ_2^{vis} and visible transition function δ_2^{vis} for player 2. The update function u_2^{pvt} is represented by the invisible move assignment Γ_2^{inv} and invisible transition function δ_2^{inv} for player 2.

These games provide a model for controller synthesis: player 1 is the controller and player 2 represents the plant. The private plant state is unknown to the controller, but the plant has complete knowledge about the state. If both V_1^{pvt} and V_2^{pvt} are empty, we have perfect-information turn-based games. ∎

Remarks. For technical and notational simplicity we make two simplifying assumptions. First, we assume that for all equivalence classes $P \in \mathcal{P}_1$, if $s, s' \in P$, then $\Gamma_1(s) = \Gamma_1(s')$, i.e., player 1 has the same set of moves available in all states of an equivalence class. This restriction does not cause any loss of generality. Suppose that choosing a move $a \notin \Gamma_1(s)$ at a state s causes player 1 to lose immediately. For $P \in \mathcal{P}_1$, if the sets of available moves are not identical for all states $s \in P$, let $A = \bigcup_{s \in P} \Gamma_1(s)$. Then the equivalence class P can be replaced by P' such that the sets of states in P and P' are the same, and the set of available moves for all states in P' is A. For a state $s \in P$ and a move $a \in A$ with $a \notin \Gamma_1(s)$, in the new equivalence class P', the successor state $\delta_1(s, a)$ is losing for player 1.

Second, we assume that for all equivalence classes $P \in \mathcal{P}_1$ and all states $s \in P$, there exists a move $a \in \Gamma_2^{\mathrm{inv}}(P)$ such that $\delta_2^{\mathrm{inv}}(P, a) = s$. In other words, in each equivalence class P player 2 has the choice to move to any state in P. Hence, if $P = \{s_1, \ldots, s_k\}$, then $\Gamma_2^{\mathrm{inv}}(P) = \{1, \ldots, k\}$ and $\delta_2^{\mathrm{inv}}(P, j) = s_j$ for all $j \in \{1, \ldots, k\}$. In games with variables, this corresponds to the assumption that player 2 can update the variables in V_2^{pvt} in all possible ways, i.e., player 1 has no knowledge about the moves of player 2. We now argue that also this restriction does not result in a loss of generality in the model. Given a **ST** game structure G, suppose that for some state $s \in S_2$, the possible transitions to states in an equivalence class $P \in \mathcal{P}_1$ target a strict subset $Z \subsetneq P$. We transform the game structure G as follows: (a) add a copy of the subset Z of states; (b) the states in the copy Z are player 1 states and Z is an equivalence class; (c) the visible transition of player 2 goes from state s to Z instead of P; and (d) the transition function for player 1 for the states in Z follow the transition function for the corresponding states of the original structure G. Observe that the number of subsets of states that are added by this transformation is bounded by the size of the transition function of the original game structure. Hence the blow-up caused by the transformation, to obtain an equivalent **ST** game structure that satisfies the restriction, is at worst quadratic in the size of the original game structure.

Notation. The *partial-information* (or *hiding*) function $\rho \colon S \to \mathcal{P}$ maps every state $s \in S$ to its equivalence class, i.e., $\rho(s) = P \in \mathcal{P}$ if $s \in P$. The set E of *edges* is defined as follows:

$$E = \{\, (s, s') \mid s \in S_1, s' \in S_2, (\exists a \in \Gamma_1(s))(\delta_1(s, a) = s') \,\}$$
$$\cup \{\, (s, s') \mid s \in S_2, s' \in S_1, (\exists a \in \Gamma_2^{\mathrm{vis}}(s))(\delta_2^{\mathrm{vis}}(s, a) = P \text{ and } s' \in P) \,\}.$$

A *play* $\omega = \langle s_0, s_1, s_2, \ldots \rangle$ is an infinite sequence of states such that for all $j \geq 0$, we have $(s_j, s_{j+1}) \in E$. We denote by Ω the set of all plays. Given a finite sequence $\langle s_0, s_1, \ldots, s_k \rangle$ of states, we write $\rho(\langle s_0, s_1, \ldots, s_k \rangle)$ for the corresponding sequence $\langle \rho(s_0), \rho(s_1), \ldots, \rho(s_k) \rangle$ of equivalence classes. The notation for infinite sequence of states is analogous.

For a countable set A, a *probability distribution* on A is a function $\mu \colon A \to [0, 1]$ such that $\sum_{a \in A} \mu(a) = 1$. We denote the set of probability distributions on A by $\mathcal{D}(A)$. Given a distribution $\mu \in \mathcal{D}(A)$, we denote by $\mathrm{Supp}(\mu) = \{x \in A \mid \mu(x) > 0\}$ the support of μ.

Strategies. A strategy for player 1 is a recipe of how to extend a play. Player 1 does not have perfect information about the states in the play; she only knows the sequence of equivalence classes where the given play has been. Hence, for a finite sequence $\langle s_0, s_1, \ldots, s_k \rangle$ of states representing the history of the play so far, the view for player 1 is given by $\rho(\langle s_0, s_1, \ldots, s_k \rangle)$. Given this view of the history, player 1's strategy is to prescribe a probability distribution over the set of available moves. Formally, a *strategy σ for player 1* is a function σ: $\rho(S^* \cdot S_1) \to \mathcal{D}(M)$, such that for all finite sequences $\langle s_0, s_1, \ldots, s_k \rangle$ of states such that $s_k \in S_1$, and for all moves $a \in M$, if $\sigma(\rho(\langle s_0, s_1, \ldots, s_k \rangle))(a) > 0$, then $a \in \Gamma_1(s_k)$. The strategy σ for player 1 is *pure* if for all $\langle s_0, s_1, \ldots, s_k \rangle$ such that $s_k \in S_1$, there is a move $a \in \Gamma_1(s_k)$ with $\sigma(\rho(\langle s_0, s_1, \ldots, s_k \rangle))(a) = 1$, i.e., for all histories the strategy deterministically chooses a move. The strategy σ is *memoryless* if it is independent of the history of the play and only depends on the current state. Formally, a memoryless strategy σ for player 1 is a function σ: $\rho(S_1) \to \mathcal{D}(M)$. A strategy is *pure memoryless* if it is both pure and memoryless, i.e., it can be represented as a function $\sigma: \rho(S_1) \to M$.

A strategy for player 2 is a recipe for player 2 to extend the play. In contrast to player 1, player 2 has perfect information about the history of the play and precisely knows every state in the history. Given the history of a play such that the last state is a player 2 state, player 2 chooses a probability distribution over the set of available visible moves to select an equivalence class $P \in \mathcal{P}_1$, and also chooses a probability distribution over the set of available invisible moves to select a state in P. Formally, a *strategy π for player 2* consists of two components:

- a function $\pi^{\mathrm{vis}}: S^* \cdot S_2 \to \mathcal{D}(M)$ such that for all $\langle s_0, s_1, \ldots, s_k \rangle$ with $s_k \in S_2$, if $\pi^{\mathrm{vis}}(\langle s_0, s_1, \ldots, s_k \rangle)(a) > 0$, then $a \in \Gamma_2^{\mathrm{vis}}(s_k)$;
- a function $\pi^{\mathrm{inv}}: S^* \cdot S_2 \cdot \mathcal{P}_1 \to \mathcal{D}(M)$ such that for all $\langle s_0, s_1, \ldots, s_k, P_{k+1} \rangle$ with $s_k \in S_2$ and $P_{k+1} \in \mathcal{P}_1$, if $\pi^{\mathrm{inv}}(\langle s_0, s_1, \ldots, s_k, P_{k+1} \rangle)(a) > 0$, then $a \in \Gamma_2^{\mathrm{inv}}(P_{k+1})$.

The strategy π for player 2 is *pure* if both component strategies π^{vis} and π^{inv} are pure. Similarly, the strategy π is *memoryless* if both component strategies π^{vis} and π^{inv} are memoryless; and it is *pure memoryless* if it is pure and memoryless. We denote by Σ and Π the sets of strategies for player 1 and player 2, respectively. We write Σ^P, Σ^M, and Σ^{PM} for the sets of pure, memoryless, and pure memoryless strategies for player 1, respectively. The analogous classes of strategies for player 2 are defined similarly.

Objectives. We specify objectives for the two players by providing sets $\Phi_i \subseteq \Omega$ of *winning plays* for each player i. In this paper we study only zero-sum games, where the objectives of the two players are strictly competitive. In other words, it is implicit that if the objective of one player 1 is Φ_1, then the objective of player 2 is $\Phi_2 = \Omega \setminus \Phi_1$. In the case of semi-perfect information games, the objective Φ_1 of player 1 is specified as a subset of $\mathcal{P}^\omega$, rather than an arbitrary subset of S^ω; this is because player 1 cannot distinguish between the states of an equivalence class. In the setting of games with variables (Example 2), this means that the objective of player 1 gives a property of the traces over the public variables of both players. Given an objective $\Phi \subseteq \mathcal{P}^\omega$, we write $\Omega \setminus \Phi$, short for the complementary objective $\{\rho(\omega) \mid \omega \in \Omega\} \setminus \Phi$.

A general class of objectives are the Borel objectives [13]. A *Borel objective* $\Phi \subseteq \mathcal{P}^\omega$ is a Borel set in the Cantor topology on $\mathcal{P}^\omega$. In this paper we consider ω-*regular objectives* [19], which lie in the first $2\frac{1}{2}$ levels of the Borel hierarchy. The ω-regular objectives, and subclasses thereof, can be specified in the following forms. For a play $\omega = \langle s_0, s_1, s_2, \ldots \rangle \in \Omega$, we define $\mathrm{Inf}(\rho(\omega)) = \{ \rho(s) \in \mathcal{P} \mid s_k = s$ for infinitely many $k \geq 0 \}$ to be the set of equivalence classes that occur infinitely often in ω.

- *Reachability and safety objectives.* Given a set $T \subseteq \mathcal{P}$ of "target" equivalence classes, the reachability objective requires that some equivalence class in T be visited. The set of winning plays is $\mathrm{Reach}(T) = \{ \rho(\omega) \mid \omega = \langle s_0, s_1, s_2, \ldots \rangle \in \Omega$, and $\rho(s_k) \in T$ for some $k \geq 0 \}$. Given a set $F \subseteq \mathcal{P}$, the safety objective requires that only equivalence classes in F be visited. Thus, the set of winning plays is $\mathrm{Safe}(F) = \{ \rho(\omega) \mid \omega = \langle s_0, s_1, s_2, \ldots \rangle \in \Omega$, and $\rho(s_k) \in F$ for all $k \geq 0 \}$.
- *Büchi and coBüchi objectives.* Given a set $B \subseteq \mathcal{P}$ of "Büchi" equivalence classes, the Büchi objective requires that B is visited infinitely often. Formally, the set of winning plays is $\mathrm{Büchi}(B) = \{ \rho(\omega) \mid \omega \in \Omega$ and $\mathrm{Inf}(\rho(\omega)) \cap B \neq \emptyset\}$. Given $C \subseteq \mathcal{P}$, the coBüchi objective requires that all equivalence classes that are visited infinitely often, are in C. Hence, the set of winning plays is $\mathrm{coBüchi}(C) = \{ \rho(\omega) \mid \omega \in \Omega$ and $\mathrm{Inf}(\rho(\omega)) \subseteq C \}$.
- *Parity objectives.* For $c, d \in \mathbb{N}$, let $[c..d] = \{ c, c+1, \ldots, d \}$. Let $p \colon \mathcal{P} \to [0..d]$ be a function that assigns a *priority* $p(P)$ to every equivalence class $P \in \mathcal{P}$, where $d \in \mathbb{N}$. The *even-parity objective* is defined as $\mathrm{Parity}(p) = \{ \rho(\omega) \mid \omega \in \Omega$ and $\min\left(p(\mathrm{Inf}(\rho(\omega)))\right)$ is even$\}$, and the *odd-parity objective* is $\mathrm{coParity}(p) = \{ \rho(\omega) \mid \omega \in \Omega$ and $\min\left(p(\mathrm{Inf}(\rho(\omega)))\right)$ is odd $\}$. Note that for a priority function $p \colon \mathcal{P} \to \{ 0, 1 \}$, the even-parity objective $\mathrm{Parity}(p)$ is equivalent to the Büchi objective $\mathrm{Büchi}(p^{-1}(0))$, i.e., the Büchi set consists of the equivalence class with priority 0.

We say that a play ω *satisfies* an objective $\Phi \subseteq \mathcal{P}^\omega$ if $\rho(\omega) \in \Phi$. Given a state $s \in S$ and strategies $\sigma \in \Sigma, \pi \in \Pi$ for the two players, the *outcome* of the game is a probability distribution over the set Ω of plays, and every Borel objective Φ is a measurable subset. The probability that the outcome of the game satisfies the Borel objective Φ starting from state s following the strategies σ and π is denoted $\mathrm{Pr}_s^{\sigma,\pi}(\Phi)$.

Values of the game. Given an objective Φ for player 1 and a state s, the maximal probability with which player 1 can ensure that Φ is satisfied from s, is called the *value* of the game at s for player 1. Formally, we define the value functions $\langle\!\langle 1 \rangle\!\rangle_{val}$ and $\langle\!\langle 2 \rangle\!\rangle_{val}$ for players 1 and 2 as follows: $\langle\!\langle 1 \rangle\!\rangle_{val}(\Phi)(s) = \sup_{\sigma \in \Sigma} \inf_{\pi \in \Pi} \mathrm{Pr}_s^{\sigma,\pi}(\Phi)$; and $\langle\!\langle 2 \rangle\!\rangle_{val}(\Omega \backslash \Phi)(s) = \sup_{\pi \in \Pi} \inf_{\sigma \in \Sigma} \mathrm{Pr}_s^{\sigma,\pi}(\Omega \backslash \Phi)$. A strategy σ for player 1 is *optimal* from state s for objective Φ if $\langle\!\langle 1 \rangle\!\rangle_{val}(\Phi)(s) = \inf_{\pi \in \Pi} \mathrm{Pr}_s^{\sigma,\pi}(\Phi)$. The strategy σ for player 1 is ε-*optimal*, for a real $\varepsilon \geq 0$, from state s for objective Φ if $\inf_{\pi \in \Pi} \mathrm{Pr}_s^{\sigma,\pi}(\Phi) \geq \langle\!\langle 1 \rangle\!\rangle_{val}(\Phi)(s) - \varepsilon$. The optimal and ε-optimal strategies for player 2 are defined analogously.

Sure, almost-sure, and limit-sure winning strategies. Given an objective Φ, a strategy σ is a *sure* winning strategy for player 1 from a state s for Φ if for every strategy π of player 2, every play ω that is possible when following the strategies σ and π from s, belongs to Φ. The strategy σ is an *almost-sure* winning strategy for player 1 from s for Φ if for every strategy π

of player 2, $\Pr_s^{\sigma,\pi}(\Phi) = 1$. A family $\Sigma^{\mathcal{C}}$ of strategies is *limit-sure* winning for player 1 from s for Φ if $\sup_{\sigma \in \Sigma^{\mathcal{C}}} \inf_{\pi \in \Pi} \Pr_s^{\sigma,\pi}(\Phi)(s) = 1$. See [7,5] for formal definitions. The sure, almost-sure, and limit-sure winning strategies for player 2 are defined analogously. The sure winning set $\langle\langle 1 \rangle\rangle_{sure}(\Phi)$, the almost-sure winning set $\langle\langle 1 \rangle\rangle_{almost}(\Phi)$, and the limit-sure winning set $\langle\langle 1 \rangle\rangle_{limit}(\Phi)$ for player 1 for objective Φ are the sets of states from which player 1 has sure, almost-sure, and limit-sure winning strategies, respectively. The sure winning set $\langle\langle 2 \rangle\rangle_{sure}(\Omega \setminus \Phi)$, the almost-sure winning set $\langle\langle 2 \rangle\rangle_{almost}(\Omega \setminus \Phi)$, and the limit-sure winning set $\langle\langle 2 \rangle\rangle_{limit}(\Omega \setminus \Phi)$ for player 2 are defined analogously.

Observe that the limit-sure winning set is the set of states with value 1, which is the classical notion of *qualitative* winning. It follows from the definitions that for all game structures and all objectives Φ, we have $\langle\langle 1 \rangle\rangle_{sure}(\Phi) \subseteq \langle\langle 1 \rangle\rangle_{almost}(\Phi) \subseteq \langle\langle 1 \rangle\rangle_{limit}(\Phi)$ and $\langle\langle 2 \rangle\rangle_{sure}(\Omega \setminus \Phi) \subseteq \langle\langle 2 \rangle\rangle_{almost}(\Omega \setminus \Phi) \subseteq \langle\langle 2 \rangle\rangle_{limit}(\Omega \setminus \Phi)$. Computing sure, almost-sure, and limit-sure winning sets and strategies is referred to as the qualitative analysis of games; computing values, as the quantitative analysis.

Sufficiency of a family of strategies. Given a family $\Sigma^{\mathcal{C}}$ of player 1 strategies, we say that the family $\Sigma^{\mathcal{C}}$ *suffices* with respect to an objective Φ on a class $\mathcal{G}$ of game structures for

- *sure winning* if for every game structure $G \in \mathcal{G}$ and state $s \in \langle\langle 1 \rangle\rangle_{sure}(\Phi)$, there is a player 1 sure winning strategy $\sigma \in \Sigma^{\mathcal{C}}$ from s for Φ;
- *almost-sure winning* if for every structure $G \in \mathcal{G}$ and state $s \in \langle\langle 1 \rangle\rangle_{almost}(\Phi)$, there is a player 1 almost-sure winning strategy $\sigma \in \Sigma^{\mathcal{C}}$ from s for Φ;
- *limit-sure winning* if for every structure $G \in \mathcal{G}$ and state $s \in \langle\langle 1 \rangle\rangle_{limit}(\Phi)$, $\sup_{\sigma \in \Sigma^{\mathcal{C}}} \inf_{\pi \in \Pi} \Pr_s^{\sigma,\pi}(\Phi) = 1$;
- *ε-optimality*, for $\varepsilon \geq 0$, if for every game structure $G \in \mathcal{G}$ and state s of G, there is a player 1 strategy $\sigma \in \Sigma^{\mathcal{C}}$ such that $\langle\langle 1 \rangle\rangle_{val}(\Phi)(s) - \varepsilon \leq \inf_{\pi \in \Pi} \Pr_s^{\sigma,\pi}(\Phi)$. Sufficiency for optimality is the special case of sufficiency for ε-optimality with $\varepsilon = 0$.

Theorem 1 (Perfect-information turn-based games). *The following assertions hold for all perfect-information turn-based (PT) games:*

1. *[13] For all Borel objectives Φ, the sets $\langle\langle 1 \rangle\rangle_{sure}(\Phi)$ and $\langle\langle 2 \rangle\rangle_{sure}(\Omega \setminus \Phi)$ form a partition of the state space.*
2. *[13] The family Σ^P of pure strategies suffices for sure winning with respect to all Borel objectives.*
3. *[9] The family Σ^{PM} of pure memoryless strategies suffices for sure winning with respect to all parity objectives.*

It follows from Theorem 1 that in the case of **PT** games the values can be either 1 or 0. We show that, in contrast, **ST** games can have values other than 1 and 0. Example 1 shows that in general we have $\langle\langle 1 \rangle\rangle_{sure}(\Phi) \subsetneq \langle\langle 1 \rangle\rangle_{almost}(\Phi)$ in **ST** games, even for reachability objectives Φ. The next example shows that in general $\langle\langle 1 \rangle\rangle_{almost}(\Phi) \subsetneq \langle\langle 1 \rangle\rangle_{limit}(\Phi)$ in **ST** games, again for reachability objectives Φ. We also show that sure determinacy (Part 1 of Theorem 1) does not

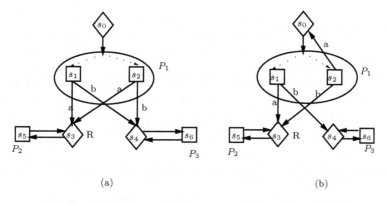

(a)   (b)

Fig. 2. Values and limit-sure winning states in **ST** games.

hold for **ST** games, and that randomized strategies are more powerful than pure strategies in **ST** games.

*Example 3 (Values and limit-sure winning in **ST** games).* Consider the two games shown in Fig. 2(a) and Fig. 2(b). The two state partitions for player 1 are $\mathcal{P}_1^a = \mathcal{P}_1^b = \{\, P_1, P_2, P_3 \,\}$ with $P_1 = \{\, s_1, s_2 \,\}$, $P_2 = \{\, s_5 \,\}$, and $P_3 = \{\, s_6 \,\}$. In both games, the set of moves available to player 1 in $P_1 = \{\, s_1, s_2 \,\}$ is $\{\, a, b \,\}$. The transitions are shown in the figures. The game starts at the state s_0 and the objective for player 1 is to reach the state s_3, i.e., Reach($\{\, s_3 \,\}$).

Values. Consider the game shown in Fig. 2(a). For every pure strategy $\sigma \in \Sigma^P$ for player 1, consider a counter-strategy π for player 2 as follows: if player 1 chooses move a, then player 2 places player 1 at state s_2; and if player 1 chooses move b, then player 2 places player 1 at state s_1. Hence the game reaches s_4 and player 1 looses. The player 1 strategy $\sigma \in \Sigma^M$ that plays move a and b with probability $1/2$, reaches state s_3 with probability $1/2$ against all strategies for player 2. For every player 1 strategy σ that chooses move a with greater probability than move b, the counter-strategy for player 2 places player 1 at state s_2; and for every player 1 strategy σ that chooses move b with greater probability than move a, the counter-strategy for player 2 places player 1 at state s_1. It follows that the value for player 1 at state s_0 is $1/2$. Thus the sure-determinacy result for **PT** games does not extend to **ST** games.

Limit-sure winning. Consider the game shown in Fig. 2(b). For $\varepsilon > 0$, consider the memoryless player 1 strategy $\sigma_\varepsilon \in \Sigma^M$ that plays move a with probability $1 - \varepsilon$, and move b with probability ε. The game starts at s_0, and in each round, if player 2 chooses state s_2, then the game reaches s_3 with probability ε and comes back to s_0 with probability $1 - \varepsilon$; whereas if player 2 chooses state s_1, then the game reaches state s_3 with probability $1 - \varepsilon$ and state s_4 with probability ε. Hence, given the strategy σ_ε for player 1, the game reaches s_3 with probability at least $1 - \varepsilon$ against all strategies π for player 2. Therefore $s_0 \in \langle\!\langle 1 \rangle\!\rangle_{limit}$(Reach($\{\, s_3 \,\}$)). However, we now argue that

$s_3 \notin \langle\!\langle 1 \rangle\!\rangle_{almost}(\text{Reach}(\{ s_3 \}))$, and thus also $s_0 \notin \langle\!\langle 1 \rangle\!\rangle_{sure}(\text{Reach}(\{ s_3 \}))$. To prove this claim, given a strategy σ for player 1, consider the following counter-strategy π for player 2: for $k \geq 0$, in round $2k + 1$, if player 1 plays move a with probability 1, then at round $2k$ player 2 chooses state s_2 and ensures that s_3 is reached with probability 0, and the game reaches s_0 in round $2k + 2$; otherwise, if player 1 plays move b with positive probability in round $2k + 1$, then player 2 in round $2k$ chooses state s_1, and the game reaches s_4 with positive probability. It follows that $s_0 \notin \langle\!\langle 1 \rangle\!\rangle_{almost}(\text{Reach}(\{ s_3 \}))$. $\blacksquare$

2.2   Perfect-Information Concurrent Games

In contrast to turn-based games, where the players make their moves in turns, in concurrent games both players choose their moves simultaneously and independently of each other.

Perfect-information concurrent game structures. A perfect-information concurrent (**PC**) game structure $G = (S, M, \Gamma_1, \Gamma_2, \delta)$ is a tuple that consists of the following components:

- A finite state space S and a finite set M of moves.
- Two move assignments $\Gamma_1, \Gamma_2 \colon S \to 2^M \setminus \emptyset$. For $i = 1, 2$, the move assignment Γ_i associates with each state $s \in S$ a nonempty set $\Gamma_i(s) \subseteq M$ of moves available to player i at state s.
- A deterministic transition function $\delta \colon S \times M \times M \to S$ which gives the successor state $\delta(s, a, b)$ from state s when player 1 chooses move $a \in \Gamma_1(s)$ and player 2 chooses move $b \in \Gamma_2(s)$.

Strategies, objectives, and values. A strategy σ for player 1 is a function $\sigma \colon S^+ \to \mathcal{D}(M)$ such that for all $\langle s_0, s_1, \ldots, s_k \rangle$ if $\sigma(\langle s_0, s_1, \ldots, s_k \rangle)(a) > 0$, then $a \in \Gamma_1(s_k)$. The strategies for player 2 are defined similarly. The classes of pure, memoryless, and pure memoryless strategies are defined as in the case of **ST** games. The definitions for objectives and values are also analogous to the definitions for **ST** games. Concurrent games satisfy a quantitative version of determinacy formalized in the next theorem.

Theorem 2 (Quantitative determinacy [14]). *For all* **PC** *games, Borel objectives* Φ, *and states* s, *we have* $\langle\!\langle 1 \rangle\!\rangle_{val}(\Phi)(s) + \langle\!\langle 2 \rangle\!\rangle_{val}(\Omega \setminus \Phi)(s) = 1$.

3   Equivalence of ST Games and PC Games

In this section we show the equivalence of **ST** games and **PC** games. We first present a reduction from **ST** games to **PC** games.

From ST games to PC games. Consider an **ST** game structure $G = ((S_1, S_2), \approx, M, \Gamma_1, \Gamma_2, \delta)$. We construct a **PC** game structure $\alpha(G) = (\widehat{S}, \widehat{M}, \widehat{\Gamma}_1, \widehat{\Gamma}_2, \widehat{\delta})$ as follows:

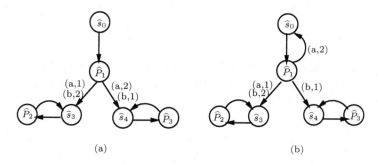

Fig. 3. PC games for the **ST** games of Fig. 2.

– *State space.* Let $\widehat{S} = \{\, \widehat{s} \mid s \in S_2 \,\} \cup \{\, \widehat{P} \mid P \in \mathcal{P}_1 \,\}$. For a state $s \in S$, we write $\alpha(s)$ for $\widehat{\rho(s)} \in \widehat{S}$, i.e., if $s \in S_2$, then $\alpha(s) = \widehat{s}$; and if $s \in S_1$ and $s \in P \in \mathcal{P}_1$, then $\alpha(s) = \widehat{P}$. Also, given a state $\widehat{s} \in \widehat{S}$, we define a map $\beta(\widehat{s})$ as follows: if $s \in S_2$ and $\alpha(s) = \widehat{s}$, then $\beta(\widehat{s}) = s$; else $\beta(\widehat{s}) = s'$ for some $s' \in P$ with $\widehat{s} = \widehat{P}$.

– *Move assignments.* For every state $s \in S_2$, let $\widehat{\Gamma}_2(\widehat{s}) = \Gamma_2^{\mathrm{vis}}(s)$ and $\widehat{\Gamma}_1(\widehat{s}) = \{\bot\}$. For every equivalence class $P \in \mathcal{P}_1$ with $P = \{\, s_1, \ldots, s_k \,\}$, let $\widehat{\Gamma}_1(\widehat{P}) = \Gamma_1(s_1)$ and $\widehat{\Gamma}_2(\widehat{P}) = \Gamma_2^{\mathrm{inv}}(P) = \{\, 1, \ldots, k \,\}$. Let $\widehat{M} = \bigcup_{\widehat{s} \in \widehat{S}} \left(\widehat{\Gamma}_1(\widehat{s}) \cup \widehat{\Gamma}_2(\widehat{s})\right)$.

– *Transition function.* For every state $\widehat{s} \in \widehat{S}$ and all moves $(a, b) \in \widehat{\Gamma}_1(\widehat{s}) \times \widehat{\Gamma}_2(\widehat{s})$, let

$$
\widehat{\delta}(\widehat{s}, a, b) = \begin{cases} \alpha(\delta_2^{\mathrm{vis}}(\beta(\widehat{s}), b)) & \text{if } \beta(\widehat{s}) \in S_2, \\ \alpha(\delta_1(s_b, a)) & \text{if } \widehat{s} = \widehat{P} \text{ for } P = \{\, s_1, \ldots, s_k \,\} \in \mathcal{P}_1. \end{cases}
$$

Intuitively the concurrent state $\widehat{P}$ captures the following idea: player 2 chooses the move $b \in \Gamma_2^{\mathrm{inv}}(P)$ to place player 1 at the state $s_b \in P$; and player 1 chooses a move from $\Gamma_1(s)$ for $s \in P$. The joint moves a for player 1 and b for player 2, together with the player 1 transition function δ_1, determines the transition function $\widehat{\delta}$ of the concurrent game.

Example 4. Fig. 3 shows the **PC** game structures that correspond to the **ST** game structures of Fig. 2, mainly illustrating the reduction for the equivalence class $\mathcal{P}_1 = \{\, s_1, s_2 \,\}$. ∎

Strategy maps. Let $\widehat{\Sigma}$ and $\widehat{\Pi}$ be the sets of player 1 and player 2 strategies in the game structure $\alpha(G)$. Given two strategies $\sigma \in \Sigma$ and $\pi \in \Pi$ in the **ST** structure G, we define corresponding strategies $\alpha(\sigma) \in \widehat{\Sigma}$ and $\alpha(\pi) \in \widehat{\Pi}$ in the **PC** structure $\alpha(G)$ as follows:

$$
\alpha(\sigma)(\langle \widehat{s}_0, \widehat{s}_1, \ldots, \widehat{s}_k \rangle) = \begin{cases} \text{play } \bot \text{ with probability } 1 & \text{if } \beta(\widehat{s}_k) \in S_2, \\ \sigma(\rho(\langle \beta(\widehat{s}_0), \beta(\widehat{s}_1), \ldots, \beta(\widehat{s}_k) \rangle)) & \text{otherwise;} \end{cases}
$$

$$\alpha(\pi)(\langle \widehat{s}_0, \widehat{s}_1, \ldots, \widehat{s}_k \rangle) = \begin{cases} \pi^{\mathrm{vis}}(\langle \beta(\widehat{s}_0), \beta(\widehat{s}_1), \ldots, \beta(\widehat{s}_k) \rangle) & \text{if } \beta(\widehat{s}_k) \in S_2, \\ \pi^{\mathrm{inv}}(\langle \beta(\widehat{s}_0), \beta(\widehat{s}_1), \ldots, \rho(\beta(\widehat{s}_k)) \rangle) & \text{otherwise.} \end{cases}$$

Similarly, given strategies $\widehat{\sigma} \in \widehat{\Sigma}$ and $\widehat{\pi} \in \widehat{\Pi}$ for the two players in the concurrent structure $\alpha(G)$, we define corresponding strategies $\beta(\widehat{\sigma}) \in \Sigma$ and $\beta(\widehat{\pi}) \in \Pi$ in the turn-based structure G as follows:

$$\beta(\widehat{\sigma})(\rho(\langle s_0, s_1, \ldots, s_k \rangle)) = \widehat{\sigma}(\langle \alpha(s_0), \alpha(s_1), \ldots, \alpha(s_k) \rangle) \quad \text{if } s_k \in S_1;$$
$$\beta(\widehat{\pi})^{\mathrm{vis}}(\langle s_0, s_1, \ldots, s_k \rangle) = \widehat{\pi}(\langle \alpha(s_0), \alpha(s_1), \ldots, \alpha(s_k) \rangle) \quad \text{if } s_k \in S_2;$$
$$\beta(\widehat{\pi})^{\mathrm{inv}}(\langle s_0, s_1, \ldots, s_k, P_{k+1} \rangle) = \widehat{\pi}(\langle \alpha(s_0), \alpha(s_1), \ldots, \alpha(s_k), \widehat{P}_{k+1} \rangle).$$

Given an objective $\Phi \subseteq \mathcal{P}^\omega$ for the **ST** game structure G, we denote by $\alpha(\Phi) \subseteq \widehat{S}^\omega$ the corresponding objective for the **PC** game structure $\alpha(G)$, which is formally defined as $\alpha(\Phi) = \{ \langle \widehat{s}_0, \widehat{s}_1, \widehat{s}_2, \ldots \rangle \mid \rho(\langle \beta(\widehat{s}_0), \beta(\widehat{s}_1), \beta(\widehat{s}_2), \ldots \rangle) \in \Phi \}$.

Lemma 1 (ST games to PC games). *For all **ST** game structures G with Borel objectives Φ,*

1. *for all player 1 strategies σ and player 2 strategies π in G, and for all states s of G, we have $\mathrm{Pr}_s^{\sigma,\pi}(\Phi) = \mathrm{Pr}_{\alpha(s)}^{\alpha(\sigma),\alpha(\pi)}(\alpha(\Phi))$;*
2. *for all player 1 strategies $\widehat{\sigma}$ and player 2 strategies $\widehat{\pi}$ in the **PC** game structure $\alpha(G)$, and all states $\widehat{s}$ of $\alpha(G)$, we have $\mathrm{Pr}_{\widehat{s}}^{\widehat{\sigma},\widehat{\pi}}(\alpha(\Phi)) = \mathrm{Pr}_{\beta(\widehat{s})}^{\beta(\widehat{\sigma}),\beta(\widehat{\pi})}(\Phi)$.*

From PC games to ST games. Consider a **PC** game structure $G = (S, M, \Gamma_1, \Gamma_2, \delta)$. We construct an **ST** game structure $\gamma(G) = ((\widetilde{S}_1, \widetilde{S}_2), (\widetilde{\mathcal{P}}_1, \widetilde{\mathcal{P}}_2), \widetilde{M}, \widetilde{\Gamma}_1, \widetilde{\Gamma}_2, \widetilde{\delta})$ as follows:

Every state $s \in S$ with $\Gamma_1(s) = A$ and $\Gamma_2(s) = \{1, \ldots, k\}$ is replaced by a gadget consisting of a player 2 state $\widetilde{s}$ with an edge to an equivalence class $\widetilde{P} \in \widetilde{\mathcal{P}}_1$ such that $\widetilde{P} = \{\widetilde{s}_1, \ldots, \widetilde{s}_k\}$ and

1. $\widetilde{\Gamma}_2^{\mathrm{vis}}(\widetilde{s}) = \{b\}$, $\widetilde{\Gamma}_2^{\mathrm{inv}}(\widetilde{P}) = \{1, \ldots, k\}$, and $\widetilde{\Gamma}_1(\widetilde{s}_j) = A$ for all $\widetilde{s}_j \in \widetilde{P}$;

2. $\widetilde{\delta}_2^{\mathrm{vis}}(\widetilde{s}, b) = \widetilde{P}$, $\widetilde{\delta}_2^{\mathrm{inv}}(\widetilde{P}, j) = \widetilde{s}_j$, and $\widetilde{\delta}_1(\widetilde{s}_j, a) = \gamma(\delta(s, a, j))$, where given a state $s \in S$, we denote by $\gamma(s)$ the state $\widetilde{s} \in \widetilde{S}_2$.

For a state pair $(\widetilde{s}, \widetilde{s}') \in \widetilde{S}^2$, let $\lambda(\widetilde{s}, \widetilde{s}')$ be the state $s \in S$ with $\gamma(s) = \widetilde{s}$.

Example 5. Consider the **PC** game shown in Fig. 4(a). The set of available moves for player 1 at the states s_2 and s_3 is $\{a, b\}$, and for player 2, it is $\{1, 2\}$. Fig. 4(b) shows an equivalent **ST** game, illustrating the translation of the concurrent states s_2 and s_3. ∎

Given an objective $\Phi \subseteq S^\omega$ for the **PC** game structure G, we define the corresponding objective $\gamma(\Phi) \subseteq \widetilde{\mathcal{P}}^\omega$ for the **ST** game structure $\gamma(G)$ as $\gamma(\Phi) = \{ \rho(\langle \widetilde{s}_0, \widetilde{s}_1, \widetilde{s}_2, \ldots \rangle) \mid \langle \lambda(\widetilde{s}_0, \widetilde{s}_1), \lambda(\widetilde{s}_2, \widetilde{s}_3), \ldots \rangle \in \Phi \}$. Similar to the previous reduction, there exist simple translations $\gamma \colon \Sigma \to \widetilde{\Sigma}$ and $\gamma \colon \Pi \to \widetilde{\Pi}$ mapping strategies in the game structure G to strategies in $\gamma(G)$, and reverse translations $\lambda \colon \widetilde{\Sigma} \to \Sigma$ and $\lambda \colon \widetilde{\Pi} \to \Pi$ mapping strategies in $\gamma(G)$ to strategies in G such that the following lemma holds.

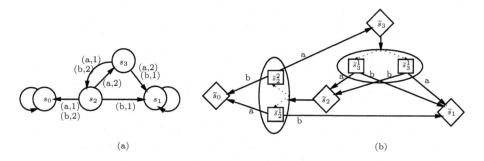

Fig. 4. A **PC** game with irrational values and the corresponding **ST** game.

Lemma 2 (PC games to ST games). *For all **PC** game structures G with Borel objectives Φ,*

1. *for all player 1 strategies σ and player 2 strategies π in G, and for all states s of G, we have $\Pr_s^{\sigma,\pi}(\Phi) = \Pr_{\gamma(s)}^{\gamma(\sigma),\gamma(\pi)}(\gamma(\Phi))$;*
2. *for all player 1 strategies $\tilde{\sigma}$ and player 2 strategies $\tilde{\pi}$ in the **ST** game structure $\gamma(G)$, and for all states $\tilde{s}$ of $\gamma(G)$, we have $\Pr_{\tilde{s}}^{\tilde{\sigma},\tilde{\pi}}(\gamma(\Phi)) = \Pr_{\lambda(\tilde{s},\tilde{s})}^{\lambda(\sigma),\lambda(\pi)}(\Phi)$.*

The following theorem follows from Lemma 1 and Lemma 2.

Theorem 3 (Equivalence of ST and PC games).

1. *For every **ST** game structure G, there is a **PC** game structure $\alpha(G)$ such that for all Borel objectives Φ and all states s of G, we have $\langle\!\langle 1 \rangle\!\rangle_{val}(\Phi)(s) = \langle\!\langle 1 \rangle\!\rangle_{val}(\alpha(\Phi))(\alpha(s))$.*
2. *For every **PC** game structure G, there is an **ST** game structure $\gamma(G)$ such that for all Borel objectives Φ and all states s of S, we have $\langle\!\langle 1 \rangle\!\rangle_{val}(\Phi)(s) = \langle\!\langle 1 \rangle\!\rangle_{val}(\gamma(\Phi))(\gamma(s))$.*

*Example 6 (**ST** games with irrational values).* Consider the **PC** game shown in Fig. 4(a). The objective of player 1 is to reach the state s_0. Recall that the set of available moves for player 1 at the states s_2 and s_3 is $\{a,b\}$, and for player 2, it is $\{1,2\}$. Let the value for player 1 at state s_2 be x. The player 1 strategy σ that plays the moves a and b with probability $1/2$ at s_3 ensures that the value for player 1 at state s_3 is at least $x/2$. Similarly, the player 2 strategy π that plays the moves 1 and 2 with probability $1/2$ at s_3 ensures that the value for player 1 at state s_3 is at most $x/2$. Hence, the value for player 1 at state s_3 is $x/2$. It follows from the characterization of the values of concurrent games as fixpoints of values of matrix games [8] that

$$x = \min\max \begin{bmatrix} 1 & \frac{x}{2} \\ 0 & 1 \end{bmatrix}$$

where the operator min max denotes the optimal value in a matrix game. The solution for x is achieved by solving the following optimization problem:

minimize x subject to $c + ((1 - c) \cdot x)/2 \leq x$ and $1 - c \leq x$.

Intuitively, c is the probability to choose move a in an optimal strategy. The solution to the optimization problem is achieved by setting $x = 1 - c$. Hence, $c + (1 - c)^2/2 = (1 - c)$, which implies $(1 + c)^2 = 2$. Since c must lie in the interval $[0, 1]$, we conclude that $c = \sqrt{2} - 1$. Thus the value for player 1 at state s_2 is $x = 2 - \sqrt{2}$. By Theorem 3 it follows that the player 1 value at state $\tilde{s}_3$ is also $x/2$, which is irrational. ∎

Values and determinacy of ST games. Example 3 shows that the sure determinacy of **PT** games does not extend to **ST** games. Example 6 shows that the values in **ST** games can be irrational even for reachability objectives. Theorem 2 and Theorem 3 establish the quantitative determinacy for **ST** games.

Corollary 1 (Values and determinacy of ST games).

1. There exists an **ST** game with a reachability objective Φ and a state s such that $s \notin (\langle\!\langle 1 \rangle\!\rangle_{sure}(\Phi) \cup \langle\!\langle 2 \rangle\!\rangle_{sure}(\Omega \setminus \Phi))$.
2. There exists an **ST** game with a reachability objective Φ and a state s such that the value $\langle\!\langle 1 \rangle\!\rangle_{val}(\Phi)(s)$ for player 1 at s for Φ is irrational.
3. For all **ST** games, all Borel objectives Φ, and all states s, we have $\langle\!\langle 1 \rangle\!\rangle_{val}(\Phi)(s) + \langle\!\langle 2 \rangle\!\rangle_{val}(\Omega \setminus \Phi)(s) = 1$.

Computational complexity of ST games. The result of [18] shows that computing sure winning sets in the general case of partial-information turn-based games, which correspond to games with variables (Example 2) where all four variable sets V_1^{pvt}, V_1^{pub}, V_2^{pvt}, and V_2^{pub} are nonempty, is 2EXPTIME-complete for reachability objectives. Even in the simpler case when $V_1^{pub} = \emptyset$ or $V_2^{pub} = \emptyset$, the problem is still EXPTIME-complete. We show that **ST** games, which correspond to the subclass of games with variables with $V_1^{pvt} = \emptyset$, can be solved considerably more efficiently. The approach to solve a **ST** game by a reduction to an exponential-size **PT** game, using a subset construction, only yields the sure winning sets. However, solving **ST** games by our reduction to **PC** games allows the arbitrarily precise and more efficient computation of values.

Corollary 2 (Complexity of ST games). For all **ST** games, all parity objectives Φ, and all states s,

1. whether $s \in \langle\!\langle 1 \rangle\!\rangle_{sure}(\Phi)$ or $s \in \langle\!\langle 1 \rangle\!\rangle_{almost}(\Phi)$ or $s \in \langle\!\langle 1 \rangle\!\rangle_{limit}(\Phi)$ can each be decided in NP ∩ coNP;
2. for all rational constants r and $\varepsilon > 0$, whether $\langle\!\langle 1 \rangle\!\rangle_{val}(\Phi)(s) \in [r - \varepsilon, r + \varepsilon]$ can be decided in NP ∩ coNP.

Proof. For all **ST** games the reduction to **PC** games is achieved in linear time. The complexity for computing qualitative winning sets (Part 1 of the corollary) follows from the results of [5]. The complexity for approximating values (Part 2) follows from the results of [3]. ∎

Table 1. Family of strategies for various objectives, where Σ^{PM} denotes the family of pure memoryless strategies, Σ^{M} denotes the family of randomized memoryless strategies, and Σ^{HI} denotes the family of randomized history-dependent, infinite-memory strategies.

objective	sure	almost-sure	limit-sure	ε-optimal
safety	Σ^{PM}	Σ^{PM}	Σ^{PM}	Σ^{M}
reachability	Σ^{PM}	Σ^{M}	Σ^{M}	Σ^{M}
coBüchi	Σ^{PM}	Σ^{M}	Σ^{M}	Σ^{M}
Büchi	Σ^{PM}	Σ^{M}	Σ^{HI}	Σ^{HI}
parity	Σ^{PM}	Σ^{HI}	Σ^{HI}	Σ^{HI}

Sufficiency of strategies for ST games. Our reduction of **ST** games to **PC** games and the characterization of memory requirements for **PC** games with parity objectives [5,3] gives the following corollary.

Corollary 3 (ε-optimal strategies for ST games). *The most restrictive family of strategies that suffices for sure, almost-sure, and limit-sure winning, and for ε-optimality with $\varepsilon > 0$, for **ST** games with respect to different classes of parity objectives is given in Table 1.*

4   Conclusion

We introduced and analyzed **ST** (semiperfect-information turn-based) games, the subclass of partial-information turn-based games where one player has partial knowledge about the state of the game and the other player has complete knowledge. These games provide a better model for controller synthesis than **PT** (perfect-information turn-based) games, by allowing the plant to have private variables that are inaccessible to the controller, and they can be solved at much lower computational costs than the full class of partial-information turn-based games. We established the equivalence of **ST** games and **PC** (perfect-information concurrent) games and thus precisely characterize the class of **ST** games.

Semiperfect-information turn-based stochastic games. The class of **ST** *stochastic* games is the generalization of **ST** games where the transition function is probabilistic rather than deterministic. Similarly, the **PC** stochastic games are the generalization of **PC** games with probabilistic transition functions. The equivalence of **ST** games and **PC** games extends to the stochastic case in a straight-forward manner, i.e., the **ST** stochastic games can be reduced to **PC** stochastic games, and vice versa. The reductions are similar to the reductions for the nonstochastic case. Consequently, results analogous to Theorem 3, Corollary 1, Corollary 2, and Corollary 3 follow for **ST** stochastic games.

Acknowledgments. This research was supported in part by the AFOSR MURI grant F49620-00-1-0327 and the NSF ITR grant CCR-0225610.

References

1. R. Alur, T.A. Henzinger, and O. Kupferman. Alternating-time temporal logic. *Journal of the ACM*, 49:672–713, 2002.
2. J.R. Büchi and L.H. Landweber. Solving sequential conditions by finite-state strategies. *Transactions of the AMS*, 138:295–311, 1969.
3. K. Chatterjee, L. de Alfaro, and T.A. Henzinger. The complexity of quantitative concurrent parity games. In *SODA 06*. ACM Press, 2006.
4. K. Chatterjee, R.Majumdar, and M. Jurdziński. On Nash equilibria in stochastic games. In *CSL 04*, volume 3210 of *LNCS*, pages 26–40. Springer, 2004.
5. L. de Alfaro and T.A. Henzinger. Concurrent omega-regular games. In *LICS 00*, pages 141–154. IEEE Computer Society Press, 2000.
6. L. de Alfaro and T.A. Henzinger. Interface theories for component-based design. In *EMSOFT 01*, volume 2211 of *LNCS*, pages 148–165. Springer, 2001.
7. L. de Alfaro, T.A. Henzinger, and O. Kupferman. Concurrent reachability games. In *FOCS 98*, pages 564–575. IEEE Computer Society Press, 1998.
8. L. de Alfaro and R. Majumdar. Quantitative solution of omega-regular games. In *STOC 01*, pages 675–683. ACM Press, 2001.
9. E.A. Emerson and C. Jutla. The complexity of tree automata and logics of programs. In *FOCS 88*, pages 328–337. IEEE Computer Society Press, 1988.
10. E.A. Emerson and C. Jutla. Tree automata, mu-calculus, and determinacy. In *FOCS 91*, pages 368–377. IEEE Computer Society Press, 1991.
11. T.A. Henzinger, O. Kupferman, and S. Rajamani. Fair simulation. *Information and Computation*, 173:64–81, 2002.
12. M. Jurdzinski. Small progress measures for solving parity games. In *STACS 00*, volume 1770 of *LNCS*, pages 290–301. Springer, 2000.
13. D.A. Martin. Borel determinacy. *Annals of Mathematics*, 102:363–371, 1975.
14. D.A. Martin. The determinacy of Blackwell games. *The Journal of Symbolic Logic*, 63:1565–1581, 1998.
15. R. McNaughton. Infinite games played on finite graphs. *Annals of Pure and Applied Logic*, 65:149–184, 1993.
16. A. Pnueli and R. Rosner. On the synthesis of a reactive module. In *POPL 89*, pages 179–190. ACM Press, 1989.
17. P.J. Ramadge and W.M. Wonham. Supervisory control of a class of discrete-event processes. *SIAM Journal of Control and Optimization*, 25:206–230, 1987.
18. J.H. Reif. Universal games of incomplete information. In *STOC 79*, pages 288–308. ACM Press, 1979.
19. W. Thomas. Languages, automata, and logic. In *Handbook of Formal Languages*, volume 3, chapter 7, pages 389–455. Springer, 1997.
20. J. Vöge and M. Jurdziński. A discrete strategy improvement algorithm for solving parity games. In *CAV 00*, volume 1855 of *LNCS*, pages 202–215. Springer, 2000.

Computational Complexity Since 1980

Russell Impagliazzo*

Department of Computer Science
University of California, San Diego
La Jolla, CA 92093-0114
russell@cs.ucsd.edu

1   Introduction

The field of computational complexity is reaching what could be termed middle age, with over forty years having passed since the first papers defining the discipline. With this metaphor in mind, the early nineteeneighties represented the end of adolescence for the area, the time when it stopped wondering what it would be when it grew up. During the childhood period of the sixties, research centered on establishing the extent to which computational complexity, or the inherrent computational resources required to solve a problem, actually existed and was well-defined.

In the early seventies, Cook (with contributions from Edmonds, Karp and Levin) gave the area its central question, whether P equals NP. Much of this decade was spent exploring the ramifications of this question. However, as the decade progressed, it became increasingly clear that $Pvs.NP$ was only the linking node of a nexus of more sophisticated questions about complexity. Researchers began to raise computational issues that went beyond the time complexity of well-defined decision problems by classical notions of algorithm.

Some of the new questions that had arisen included:

- Hardness of approximation: To what extent can NP-hardness results be circumvented? More precisely, which optimization problems can be efficiently solved approximately?
- Average-case complexity: Does NP-hardness mean that intractible instances of a problem actually arise? Or can we devise heuristics that solve typical instances? Which problems can be solved on "most" instances?
- Foundations of cryptography: Can computational complexity be used as a foundation for cryptography? What kind of computational hardness is needed for such a cryptography? ([DH], [RSA])
- Power of randomness: What is the power of randomized algorithms? Should randomized algorithms replace deterministic ones to capture the intuitive notion of efficient computation? ([Ber72],[Rab80], [SS79], [Sch80], [Gill]).

* Research supported by NSF Award CCF0515332, but views expressed here are not endorsed by the NSF.

- Circuit complexity: Which problems require many basic operations to compute in non-uniform models such as Boolean or arithmetic circuits? How does the circuit complexity of problems relate to their complexity in uniform models?
- Constructive combinatorics: Many mathematically interesting objects, such as from extremal graph theory, are proved to exist non-constructively, e.g., through the probabilistic method. When can these proofs be made constructive, exhibiting explicit and easily computable graphs or other structures with the desired properties?

This is a very incomplete list of the issues that faced complexity theory. My choice of the above topics is of course biased by my own research interests and by the later history of the area. For example, at the time, any list of important areas for complexity would include time-space tradeoffs and parallel computation, which I will have to omit out of my own concerns for time and space. However, it is fair to say that all of the topics listed were and remain central questions in computational complexity.

It is somewhat sad that we still do not know definitive answers to any of these questions. However, in the last twenty-five years, a number of significant and, at the time, highly counter-intuitive, connections have been made between them. The intervening period has made clear that, far from being six independent issues that will be addressed separately, the questions above are all interwoven to the point where it is impossible to draw clear boundaries between them. This has been established both by direct implications (such as, "If any problem in E requires exponential circuit size, then $P = BPP$") and by the transferance of issues and techniques that originated to address one question but ended up being a key insight into others.

In the following, we will attempt to trace the evolution of some key ideas in complexity theory, and in particular highlight the work linking the above list of questions. Our central thesis is that, while the work of the sixties showed that complexity theory is a well-defined field of mathematics, and that of the seventies showed how important this field is, the work since then has demonstrated the non-obvious point that complexity theory is best tackled as a single, united field, not splintered into specialized subareas. Of course, due to the clarity of hindsight, we may be biased in picking topics that support this thesis, but we feel that the existence of so many interrelated fundamental questions is prima facia evidence in itself.

2   Some Key Techniques in Complexity

A common complaint about complexity theory used to be that complexity theorists took an *ad hoc* approach to their field, rather than developing a set of unifying and deep techniques. We will attempt to show that this complaint, if it were ever true, is obsolete. In particular, we will trace a few fundamental technical approaches that have evolved to become essential tools that span complexity.

1. Arithmetization Complexity studies mainly Boolean functions, with discrete zero-one valued inputs and outputs. In essence, arbitrary Boolean functions are just strings of bits, and hence have no fundamental mathematical properties. The technique of arithmetization is to embed or interpolate a Boolean function within a algebraic function, such as a polynomial. This can be used algorithmically (to perform operations on functions), or conceptually (to reason about the nature of functions computable with low complexity).

   While introduced as a tool for proving lower bounds on circuits, arithmetization has evolved into a fundamental approach to complexity, and is now essential in the study of interactive proofs, hardness of approximation, learning theory, cryptography, and derandomization.

2. Error-correcting codes As mentioned before, a Boolean function can be identified with a string of bits. The process of arithmetization became understood as computing a code on this string, to obtain a version of the function that codes the original function redundantly. Many of the applications of arithmetization are in fact consequences of the good error-correction properties of this coding. This made decoding algorithms of various kinds essential to complexity.

3. Randomness Complexity theorists frequently view the hardness of a problem as a contest between a solver (trying to solve instances of the problem) and an unknown adversary, trying to create intractible instances. Game theory suggests that the best strategies for such a game might have to be randomized. Perhaps this is one reason why randomness plays such a huge role in complexity. In any case, randomized computation has become the default model for reasoning in complexity, even when reasoning about deterministic algorithms or circuits.

4. Pseudo-randomness and computational indistinguishability The flip side of randomness is pseudo-randomness. As mentioned earlier, randomness often comes into the arguements even when we want to reason about deterministic computation. We then want to eliminate the randomness. When does a deterministic computation look "random enough" that it can be safely substituted for the randomness in a computation? More generally, when do two distributions look sufficiently "similar" that conclusions about one can be automatically tranferred to another? The core idea of computational indistinguishablity is that, when it is computationally infeasible to tell two distributions apart, then they will have the same properties as far as efficient computation is concerned. This simple idea originating in cryptography has percolated throughout complexity theory. Different contexts have different answers to what is "random enough", based on the type of computation that will be allowed to distinguish between the two.

5. Constructive extremal graph theory Randomness had a similar role in combinatorics. In particular, randomly constructed graphs and other structures often had desireable or extreme combinatorial properties. This raised the challenge of coming up with specific constructions of structures with similar properties. This can be thought of as particular cases of derandomization, which links it to the previous topic. In fact, there are connections both

ways: "derandomizing" the probabilistic constructions of extremal graphs gives new constructions of such graphs; constructions of such graphs give new ways to derandomize algorithms.

3   The Challenges to Complexity as of 1980

During the 1970's, it became clear (if it wasn't already) that the field had to go beyond deterministic, worst-case, time complexity, and beyond techniques borrowed from recursion theory. "Traditional" complexity was challenged by the following results and issues:

Circuit complexity Circuit complexity, the number of Boolean operations needed to compute functions, was a major impetus to much foundational work in complexity. Riordan and Shannon ([RS]) had introduced circuit complexity in 1942, and had shown, non-constructively, that most Boolean functions require exponential circuit size. However, there were no natural functions that were known to require large circuits to compute. The first challenge that lay before complexity theory was to find examples of such functions.

A related challenge is the circuit minimization problem. This is circuit complexity viewed algorithmically: given a Boolean function, design the circuit computing the function that uses the minimum number of gates. This seems harder than proving a lower bound for a specific function, since such an algorithm would in some sense characterize what makes a function hard. In his Turing Award lecture ([K86]), Karp reports that it was in attempting to program computers to solve circuit minimization that he became aware of the problem of exponential time. In the Soviet Bloc, Yablonski ([Yab]) was motivated by this problem to introduce the notion of *perebor*, usually translated as "brute-force search". (Unfortunately, he also falsely claimed to have proved that *perebor* was necessary for this problem.)

There was much work in circuit complexity before 1980; see [We87] for references. However, for natural Boolean functions, the hardness results were relatively minor, in the sense of proving only small polynomial bounds on circuit size, and only for restricted models. Even now, no one knows any super-linear bound for a function computable in strictly exponential ($2^{O(n)}$) time. (It is possible to simply define a Boolean function as "The lexicographically first Boolean function that requires exponential circuit size". This function will be in the exponential hierarchy, so functions hard for EH will require exponential size circuits. In his 1974 thesis, Stockmeyer gave a specific function, true sentences of weak monadic second-oder theory of the natural numbers with successor, whose circuit size is almost the maximum possible. However, the proof is by showing that this function is hard for EXPSPACE. To make the lower bound challenge precise, we can formalize a "natural" function as one that has reasonably low uniform complexity.)

Cryptography In [DH], Diffie and Hellman pointed towards basing cryptography on the inherrent computational intractability of problems. Shortly afterwards, [RSA] gave a suggestion of a public-key cryptosystem based on the intractibility of factoring. This raised the question, how hard are factoring and other number-theoretic problems? Are they NP-complete? More importantly, is it relevant whether they are NP-complete? One of the main challenges of cryptography is that, while intractibility is now desireable, hardness is no longer simply the negation of easiness. In particular, worst-case hardness is not sufficient for cryptography; one needs some notion of *reliable hardness*. While [DH] discusses the difference between worst-case and average-case complexity, a formal notion was not fully described. The challenge presented to complexity-theory circa 1980 was to clarify what kinds of hardness constituted useful hardness for cryptography, and what kinds of evidence could be used to argue that specific problems had such hardness.

Randomized algorithms A phenomenon that arose during the 1970's was the use of random choices in designing efficient algorithms. In 1972, Berlekamp gave a probabilistic algorithm to factor polynomials ([Ber72]). Later, Solovay and Strassen [SS79] and Rabin [Rab80] gave such algorithms for the classical problem of primality. A third example was the Schwartz-Zippel polynomial-identity testing algorithm ([Sch80], [Zip79]). Another interesting randomized algorithm was given in [AKLLR], where it is shown that a sufficiently long random walk in an undirected graph visits all nodes within the connected component of the starting node. This shows reachability in undirected graphs can be computed in logarithmic space by a randomized algorithm.

These algorithms presented a challenge to the then recently adopted standard that (deterministic) polynomial-time captured the intuitive notion of tractible computation, the so-called time-bounded Church's Thesis. Should deterministic or randomized polynomial time be the default standard for efficient computation? This question was formalized by Gill ([Gill]), who defined the now standard complexity classes corresponding to probabilistic algorithms with different error conditions, $P \subseteq ZPP \subseteq RP \subseteq BPP \subseteq PP \subseteq PSPACE$. Of course, it could be that the above notions are identical, that $P = ZPP = RP = BPP$. Unlike for P vs NP, there was no consensus about this. On the one hand, in his 1984 NP-completeness column ([J84]), Johnson refers to the above containments and states "It is conjectured that all of these inclusions are proper." In contrast, Cook in his 1982 Turing Award lecture ([C83]) says, "It is tempting to conjecture yes [that $RP = P$] on the philisophical grounds that random coin tosses should not be of much use when the answer sought is a well-defined yes or no." (It should be noted that neither is willing to actually make a conjecture, only to discuss the possibiltiy of conjectures being made.)

If the two models are in fact different, then it still needs to be decided which is the right model of computation. If one is interested in computation possible within the physical world, this then becomes a question of whether random bits are physically obtainable. Of course, quantum mechanics suggests that the universe is inherrently probabilistic. (We can knowingly realize the genie that this consideration will eventually let out of the bottle.) However, this does not mean that fair random bits are physically obtainable, another question which will grow in importance.

Random-like graphs and structures Meanwhile, in combinatorics, randomness has long played a role in showing that objects exist non-constructively. Erdos's *probabilistic method* is perhaps the most important tool in the area. In particular, there are certain very desireable properties of graphs and other structures which hold almost certainly under some simple probability distribution, but where no specific, constructive example is known. For example, random graphs were known to be good expanders and super-concentrators. Deterministic constructions could come close to the quality of random graphs ([GG]) but didn't match them.

If we use the standard for "constructive" as polynomial-time computable (in the underlying size), these properties of random graphs can be thought of as examples of the power of randomized algorithms. A coin-tossing machine can easily construct graphs with these properties, but no deterministic machine was known to be able to. More subtly, question of whether randomized algorithms can be derandomized can be viewed as a special case of the construction of "quasi-random objects". Let $S = \{x_1, ..x_m\}$ be a (multi)-set of n bit strings. We call S an n, s *hitting set* if for any circuit C with n inputs and at most s gates, if $Prob_x[C(x) = 1] > 1/2$ then $\exists i, C[x_i] = 1$. In other words, a hitting set can produce witnesses of satisfiability for any circuit with ample numbers of such witnesses. Adleman ([Adl78]) proved that RP had small circuits by giving a construction via the probabilistic method of a small ($m = poly(n, s)$) hitting set. If we could deterministically produce such a set, then we could simulate any algorithm in RP by using each member of the hitting set (setting s equal to the time the randomized algorithm takes and n as the number of random bits it uses) as the random choices for the algorithm. We accept if any of the runs accepts. (More subtly, it was much later shown in [ACRT] that such a hitting set could also derandomize algorithms with two-sided error, BPP.)

A similar notion was introduced by [AKLLR]. A n node *universal traversal sequence* is a set of directions to take so that following them causes a walk in any n-node undirected graph to visit the entire connected component of the starting place. They showed that random sequences of polynomial length were universal. Constructing such a sequence would place undirected connectivity in L. Heintz and Schnorr HS introduced the notion of *perfect test set*, a set of input sequences to an arithmetic circuit one of which would disprove any invalid polynomial identity. They showed a probabilistic construction (for identities over any field, and whose size is independent of the field size.)

In fact, we can also view the problem of constructing a hard function for circuit complexity as another example of making the probabilistic method constructive. Riordan and Shannon's proof established that almost all functions require exponential circuit complexity. If we construct such a function in polynomial-time (in, say, its truth-table size, 2^n), this would produce a hard function in E.

To close the circle, observe that constructing a polynomial-size hitting set would also produce a hard function. Let $S(n, s) = \{x_1, .. x_m\}$ be a hitting set constructed in poly(s) time. Then let $k = \log m + 1 = O(\log s)$ and define a Boolean function $f(y)$ on k bit inputs by: $f(y) = 1$ if and only if y is not a prefix of any x_i. With the choice of k as above, $f(y) = 1$ with probability at least $1/2$, so if C computed f with less than s gates, $C'(y_1..y_n) = C(y_1..y_k)$ would have to be 1 for some x_i in S, which contradicts the definition of f. f is computable in time $poly(s) = 2^{O(k)}$, so $f \in E$ and requires $s = 2^{\Omega(k)}$ circuit complexity. This simple proof does not seem to appear in print until the late nineties. However, the analagous result for aritmetic circuit complexity (a perfect hitting set construction implies an arithmetic circuit lower bound) is in [HS].

4   Meeting the Challenges

We can see that even before 1980, there were a number of connections apparrent between these questions. As complexity went forward, it would discover more and deeper connections. In the following sections, we will attempt to highlight a few of the discoveries of complexity that illustrate both their intellectual periods and these connections.

5   Cryptography, the Muse of Modern Complexity

As mentioned earlier, the growth of modern cryptography motivated a new type of complexity theory. In fact, many of the basic ideas and approaches of modern complexity arose in the cryptographic literature. Especially, the early 1980's were a golden age for cryptographic complexity.

Complexity theory and modern cryptography seemed a match made in heaven. Complexity theorists wanted to understand which computational problems were hard; cryptographers wanted to use hard problems to control access to information and other resources. At last, complexity theorists had a reason to root for problems being intractible! However, it soon became clear that cryptography required a new kind of complexity. Some of the issues complexity was forced to deal with were:

Reliable intractibility: Complexity theory had followed algorithm design in taking a conservative approach to definitions of tractibility. A problem being tractible meant that it was reliably solved by an algorithm that always ran quickly and always produced the correct result. This is a good definition of "easy computational problem". But the negation of a conservative definition of "easy" is a much too liberal to be a useful notion of "hard", especially when even occasional easy instances of a problem would compromise security completely. To handle this, complexity theory had to move beyond worst-case complexity to an understanding of distributional or average-case complexity. Once complexity moved to the average-case, it was necessary

Randomized computing: A deterministic algorithm is equally accessible to everyone, intended user and attacker alike. Therefore, cryptographic problems must be generated randomly. This made randomized computation the default model for cryptography. Randomized algorithms moved from being viewed as an exotic alternative to the standard model.

Going beyond completeness: Most of the computational problems used in cryptography fall within classes like $NP \cap Co - NP$ or UP that do not seem to have complete problems. Cryptosystems that were "based" on NP-complete problems were frequently broken. This had to do with the gap between worst-case and average-case complexity. However, even after Levin introduced average-case complete problems ([Lev86]), it was (and is) still unknown whether these can be useful in cryptography. Complexity theory had to have new standards for believable intractibility that were not based on completeness.

Adversaries and fault-tolerant reductions: While the notion of completeness was not terribly helpful, the notion of reduction was essential to the new foundations for cryptography. However, it needed to be dramatically altered. When talking about reductions between average-case problems, one needed to reason about oracles that only solved the problem being reduced to some fraction of the time (while believing that no such oracles actually are feasible). Since we don't know exactly what function this oracle performs the rest of the time, it seems the only safe approach is to view the oracle as being created by an "adversary", who is out to fool the reduction. Thus, what is needed is a fault-tolerant approach to reductions, where the small fraction of true answers can be used despite a large fraction of incorrect answers. This would link cryptography with other notions of fault-tolerant computation, such as error-correcting codes.

Computation within an evolving social context: In traditional algorithm design, and hence traditional complexity, the input arrived and then the problem had to be solved. In cryptography, there had to be communication between the parties that determined what the problem to be solved was. Cryptography was in essence social and interactive, in that there was almost always multiple, communicating parties performing related computations. In particular, this meant that an attacker could partially determine the instance of the problem whose solution would crack the system. Complexity theory had to go beyond reasoning about the difficulty of solving problems to understand the difficulty of breaking protocols, patterns of interleaving communication and computation.

In retrospect, it is astonishing how quickly a complexity-theoretic foundations for cryptography that addressed all of these issues arose. Within a decade of Diffie and Hellman's breakthrough paper, complexity-based cryptography had established strong, robust definitions of security for encryption and electronic signatures, and had given existence proofs that such secure cryptographic functions existed under reasonable assumptions. Moreover, complexity-theoretic cryptography unleashed a wave of creativitiy, that encompassed such avant garde notions as oblivious transer, zero-knowledge interactive proofs, and secure distributed "game" playing, aka, "mental poker". Complexity would never be the same.

We'll look at some landmark papers of 80's cryptography, that were not only important for their role in establishing modern cryptography, but introduced fundamental ideas and tools into general complexity theory.

5.1   Cryptographic Pseudo-randomness

In 1982, Blum and Micali ([BM]) introduced the notion of cryptographic pseudorandomness. Shortly thereafter, Yao ([Yao82]) strengthened their results considerably and explored some of the ramifications of this concept. Together, these two papers presented a dramatic rethinking of information theory, probability, and the likely power of randomized algorithms in the face of complexity theory. (In addition, of course, they gave cryptography one of its most important tools.)

Blum and Micali's paper introduced what would become the gold standard for "hard" Boolean function, unpredictability. A function b is computationally unpredictable (given auxilliary information f) if, over choice of a random x, the probability that an adversary, given $f(x)$, can predict $b(x)$ is only negligibly more than a random coin toss. Intuitively, this means that b *looks like* a random coin to any feasible adversary, and this intution can frequently be made formal.

Blum and Micali give an example of such a function, assuming the difficulty of finding discrete logarithms. The bit they show is hard, is, given $g^x mod p$, determine whether x mod $p - 1 \leq (p - 1)/2$. Let's call this function $b(x)$. The way they prove that $b(x)$ is unpredictable is also, in hindsight, prescient. In fact, a recent paper by Akavia, Goldwasser, and Safra ([AGS]) gives the modern insight into why this bit is hidden. There argument combines the random self-reducibility of the discrete logarithm and a *list-decoding algorithm* for a simple *error-correcting code*. The original proof of Blum and Micali is close in spirit, but also uses the ability to take square roots mod p, so the corresponding code would be more complex. First, we observe that, given $g, g^x mod p$, and z_1, z_2, we can compute $(g^x)^{z_1} g^{z_2} = g^{xz_1 + z_2 mod p - 1}$. This means that a predictor for $b(x)$ given g^x also gives us a predictor for $b(xz_1 + z_2 mod p - 1)$. Consider the exponentially long code $C(x)$ that maps x to the sequence $b(xz_1 + z_2)$ for each $z_1, z_2 \in Z_{p-1}$. Note that for $x - y$ relatively prime to $p - 1$ and random z_1, z_2, $xz_1 + z_2$ and $yz_1 + z_2$ take on all possible pairs of values mod each odd prime factor of $p - 1$. It follows that $C(x)$ and $C(y)$ will be almost uncorrelated, so the code has large distance, at least for almost all pairs.

A predicting algorithm $P(g^r)$, which guesses $b(r)$ given g^r with probability $1/2 + \epsilon$ determines the flawed code word $\overline{C}$ where $\overline{C}_z = P(g^{xz})$ which has relative hamming distance $1/2 - \epsilon$ from C. Is that enough information to recover the message x? Not completely, but it is enough to recover a polynomial number of possible x's, and we can then exponentiate each member of this list and compare to g^x to find x. The final step is to do this *list-decoding* algorithmically. However, since the code-word itself is exponentially long, we can only afford to look at the code in a small fraction of positions. This means that we need a *local list decoding* algorithm for this code, one that produces such a list of possible messages using a polynomial (or poly-log in the size of the code word) number of random access queries to bits of the codeword. [AGS] provide such an algorithm. The original proof of Blum and Micali would provide such an algorithm for a more complex code. Locally-decodeable error-correcting codes of various kinds will arise repeatedly in different guises, before finally being made explicit in the PCP constructions. Intuitively, they arise whenever we need to use an adversarial oracle only correlated with a function to compute a related function reliably. The oracle will correspond to a corrupted code-word, and the message will correspond to the related function.

Yao's sequel paper (citeYao82) is perhaps even more prescient. First, it shows that the unpredictibility criterion of Blum and Micali is equivalent to a *computational indistinguishability* criterion. Two computational objects (strings, functions, or the like) are computationally indistinguishable, informally, if no feasible algorithm, given a random one of the two objects, can determine which object it has been given significantly better than random guessing. Thus, it is a type of computational Turing test: if no feasible algorithm can tell two things apart, for purposes of effective computation, they are the same. This notion, implicit in Yao's paper, and made explicit in the equally revolutionary [GMR], is indespensible to modern complexity. The proof of equivalence also introduced the hybrid method, of showing two objects are indistinguishable by conceptualizing a chain of objects, each indistinguishable from the next, that slowly morph one object into another.

Second, this paper introduces the possibility of *general derandomization* based on a hard problem. This is the use of sufficiently hard problems to transform randomized algorithms into deterministic ones. What makes this counter-intuitive is that intractibility, the *non-existence* of algorithms, is being used to design algorithms! However, once that logical leap is made, derandomization results make sense. Yao proved that a Blum-Micali style pseudo-random generator transforms a relatively small number of random bits into a larger number of bits computationally indistinguishable from random bits. Thus, these pseudo-random bits can replace truly random bits in any algorithm, without changing the results, giving a randomized algorithm that uses far fewer random bits. The algorithm can then be made deterministic at reduced cost by exhaustive search over all possible input sequences of bits to the pseudo-random generator. There was one caveat: to derandomize algorithms in the worst-case, Yao needed the generator to be secure against small circuits, not just feasible algorithms. This was due to the fact that the randomized algorithm using pseudo-random bits might only be incorrect on a vanishingly small fraction of inputs; if there were no way to locate a fallacious input, this would not produce a distinguishing test. However, such inputs could be hard-wired into a circuit.

In fact, the set of possible outputs for a pseudo-random generator in Yao's sense is a *small discrepancy set*, in that, for any small circuit, the average value of the circuit on the set is close to its expected value on a random input. This implies that it is also a hitting set, and we saw that such a set implies a circuit lower bound. So it seems for a Yao-style derandomization, assuming hardness versus circuits is necessary. But this leaves open whether other types of derandomization could be performed without such a hardness assumption.

A third basic innovation in Yao's paper was the xor lemma, the first of a class of *direct product results*. These results make precise the following intuition: that if it is hard to compute a function b on one input, then it is harder to compute b on multiple unrelated inputs. In particular, the *xor* lemma says that, if no small circuit can compute $b(x)$ correctly for more than a $1 - \delta$ fraction of x, and $k = \omega(\log n/\delta)$, then no small circuit can predict $b(x_1) \oplus ...b(x_k)$ with probability $1/2 + 1/n^c$ over random sequences $x_1...x_k$. There are a huge number of distinct proofs of this lemma, and each proof seems to have applications and extensions that others don't have. Ironically, the most frequently proved lemma in complexity was stated without proof in Yao's paper, and the first published proof was in [Lev87].

Again invoking hindsight, as suggested in [Tre03] and [I03], we can view the xor lemma as a result about *approximate local list decoding*. Think of the original function b as a message to be transmitted, of length 2^n, whose x'th bit is $b(x)$. Then the code $H_k(b)$ (which we'll call the k-sparse Hadamard code) is the bit sequence whose $(x_1, ..x_k)$th entry is $b(x_1) \oplus b(x_2)... \oplus b(x_k)$. In the xor lemma, we are given a circuit C that agrees with $H_k(b)$ on $1/2 + \epsilon$ fraction of bit positions, and we wish to reconstruct b, except that we are allowed to err on a δ fraction of bit positions. This allowable error means that we can reduce the traditional error correction goal of recovering the message to the weaker condition of recovering a string that agrees with the message on all but a δ on bits. In fact, it is easy to see that it will be information-theoretically impossible to avoid a $\Omega(\log 1/\epsilon/k)$ fraction of mistakes, and even then, it will only be possible to produce a list of strings, one of which is this close to the message. Fortunately, this weaker goal of approximately list decoding the message is both possible and sufficient to prove the lemma. Each member of the list of possible strings produced in a proof of the xor lemma can be computed by a relatively small circuit (using C as an oracle), and one such circuit is guaranteed to compute b with at most a δ fraction of errors, a contradiction. This description of what a proof of the xor lemma is also gives an indication of why we need so many different proofs. Each proof gives a slightly different approximate list decoding algorithm, with different trade-offs between the relevant parameters, ϵ, δ, the total time, and the size of the list produced. (The logarithm of the size of the list can be viewed as the non-uniformity, or number of bits of advice needed to describe which circuit to use.)

Finally, Yao's paper contains a far-reaching discussion of how computational complexity's view of randomness differs from the information-theoretic view. For example, information theoretically, computation only decreases randomness, whereas a cryptographic pseudo-random generator in effect increases computational randomness.

An important generalization of cryptographic pseudo-random generator was that of *pseudo-random function generator* introduced by Goldreich, Goldwasser, and Micali ([GGM]), who showed how to construct such a function generator from any secure pseudo-random generator. A pseudo-random function generator can be thought of as producing an exponentially long pseudo-random string. The string is still computable in polynomial-time, in that any particular bit is computable in polynomial time. It is indistinguishable from random by any feasible adversary that also has random access to its bits. Luby and Rackoff ([LR]) showed that a pseudorandom function generator could be used to construct a secure block cipher, the format for conventional private-key systems. It is ironic that while public-key encryption motivated a complexity based approach to cryptography, the complexity of private-key cryptography is well understood (combining the above with [HILL]), but that of public-key cryptography remains a mystery ([IR], [Rud91]).

Skipping fairly far ahead chronologically, there is one more very important paper on pseudo-randomness, by Goldreich and Levin ([GL89]). This paper shows how to construct a unpredictable bit for any one-way function. Like Blum and Micali's, this result is best understood as a list-decoding algorithm. However, without knowing any properties of the one-way function, we cannot use random self-reducibility to relate the hidden bit on one input to a long code-word. Instead, [GL89] use a randomized construction of a hidden bit. Technically, they define $f'(x, r) = f(x), r$ as a padded version of one-way function f, and define $b(x, r)$ as the parity of the bits in x that are 1 in r, or the inner product mod 2 of x and r. Thus, fixing x, a predictor for $b(x, r)$ can be thought of as a corrupted version of the *Hadamard code* of x, $H(x)$, an exponentially long string whose r'th bit is $< x, r >$, the inner product of x and r mod 2. Their main result is a local list-decoding algorithm for this code, thus allowing one to reconstruct x (as one member of a list of strings) from such a predictor. The claimed result then follows, by simply comparing $f(x)$ with $f(y)$ for each y on the list. More generally, this result allows us to convert a secret string x (i.e., hard to compute from other information) to a pseudo-random bit, $< x, r >$, for a randomly chosen r.

5.2   Interactive Proofs

A second key idea to arise from cryptography grew out of thinking about computation within the context of protocols. Security of protocols was much more complex than security of encryption functions. One had to reason about what an adversary could learn during one part of a protocol and how that affected the security of later parts. Frequently, an attacker can benefit by counter-intuitive behaviour during one part of a protocol, so intuition about "sensible" adversaries can be misleading. For example, one way for you to convince another person of your identity is to decrypt random challenges with your secret key. But what if instead of random challenges, the challenges were chosen in order to give an attacker (pretending to question your identity) information about your secret key? For example, using such a chosen cyphertext attack, one can easily break Rabin encryption. To answer such questions, Goldwasser, Micali, and Rackoff ([GMR]) introduced the concept of *the knowledge leaked by a protocol*. Their standard for saying that a protocol only leaked certain knowledge was *simuability*: a method should exist so that, with the knowledge supposed to be leaked, for any strategy for the dishonest party, the dishonest party could produce transcripts that were indistinguishable from participating in the protocol *without further interaction with the honest party*. This meant that the knowledge leaked is a cap on what useful information the dishonest party could learn during the protocol.

In addition, [GMR] looked at a general purpose for protocols: for one party to prove facts to another. NP can be characterized as those statements which a prover of unlimited computational power can convince a skeptical polynomial-time verifier. If the verifier is deterministic, there is no reason for the prover to have a conversation with the verifier, since the prover can simulate the verifier's end of the line. But if verifiers are allowed to be randomized, as is necessary for zero-knowledge, then it makes sense to make such a proof interactive, a conversation rather than a monologue. [GMR] also defined the complexity classes IP of properties that could be proved to a probabilistic verifier interactively. Meanwhile, Babai (in work later published with Moran, [BMor]) had introduced a similar but seemingly more limited complexity class, to represent probabilistic versions of NP. Goldwasser and Sipser ([GS]) eventually proved that the two notions, IP and AM, were equivalent.

Once there was a notion of interactive proof, variants began to appear. For example, Ben-Or, Goldwasser, Micali and Wigderson ([BGKW]) introduced multiple prover interactive proofs (MIP), where non-communicating provers convinced a skeptical probabilistic verifier of a claim. Frankly, the motivation for MIP was somewhat weak, until Fortnow, Rompel and Sipser showed that MIP was equivalent to what would later be known as probabilistically checkable proofs. These were languages with exponentially long (and thus too long for a verifier to look at in entirety) proofs, where the validity of the proof could be verified with high probability by a probabilistic polynomial-time machine with random access to the proof. Program checking ([BK], [BLR], [Lip91]) was a motivation for looking at interactive proofs from a different angle. In program checking, the user is given a possibly erroneous program for a function. Whatever the program is, the user should never output an incorrect answer (with high probability), and if the program is correct on all inputs, the user should always give the correct answer, but the user may not output any answer if there is an error in the program. The existence of such a checker for a function is equivalent to the function having an interactive proof system where the provers strategy can be computed in polynomial-time with an oracle for the function. A simple "tester-checker" method for designing such program checkers was described in [BLR], which combined two ingredients: random-self reducibility, to reduce checking whether a particular result was fallacious to checking whether the program was fallacious for a large fraction of inputs; and downward self-reducibility, to reduce checking random inputs of size n to checking particular inputs of size $n - 1$.

6   Circuit Complexity and Arithmetization:

The history of circuit complexity is one of dramatic successes and tremendous frustrations. The 1980's were the high point of work in this area. The decade began with the breakthrough results of [FSS, Aj83], who proved super-polynomial lower bounds on constant-depth unbounded fan-in circuits. For a while subsequently, there was a sense of optimism, that we would continue to prove lower bounds for broader classes of circuits until we proved $P \neq NP$ via lower bounds for general circuits. This sense of optimism became known as the Sipser program, although we do not believe Sipser ever endorsed it in writing. With Razborov's lower bounds for monotone circuits ([Raz85]), the sense that we were on the verge of being able to separate complexity classes became palpable. Unfortunately, the switching lemma approach seemed to be stuck at proving better lower bounds for constant depth circuits ([Yao85, Has86]) and the monotone restriction seemed essential, since, in fact, similar monotone lower bounds could be proved for functions in P ([Tar88]). While there have been numerous technically nice new results in circuit complexity, it is fair to say that there have been no real breakthroughs since 1987. This lack of progress is still a bitter disappointment and a mystery, although we will later see some technical reasons why further progress may require new techniques.

However, in its death, circuit complexity bequeathed to us a simple technique that has gone on to produce one amazing result after another. This technique is arithmitization, conceptually (or algorithmically) interpolating a Boolean function into a polynomial over a larger field. Actually, it is more correct to say this technique was rediscovered at this time. Minsky and Pappert had used a version of arithmitization to prove lower bounds on the power of perceptrons, majorities of circuits that depended on small numbers of inputs ([MP]); their aim was to understand the computational power of neurons. Also, some papers on using imperfect random sources ([CGHFRS]) used similar ideas. However, it was Razborov ([Raz87]) and Smolensky ([Smol87]) that really showed the power and beauty of this idea. The result they proved seems like a small improvement over what was known. Parity was known not to be computable with small constant-depth circuits; what if we allowed parity as a basic operation? Razborov and Smolensky proved that adding parity gates, or, more generally, counting modulo any fixed prime, would not help compute other fundamental functions, like majority or counting modulo a different prime. This is a technical improvement. The revolution was in the simplicity of the proof. They showed how to approximate unbounded fan-in Boolean operations with low degree polynomials over any finite field. Each such gates then contributed a small amount to the error, and each layer of such gates, a small factor to the degree. Choosing the field of characteristic equal to the modular gates in the circuit, such gates had no cost in error or degree, translating directly to linear functions. An equally elegant argument showed that counting modulo another prime was in some sense "complete" over all functions for having small degree approximations, which led to a contradiction via a counting argument.

A direct use of the ideas in these papers is part of Toda's Theorem, that $PH \subseteq P^{\#P}$ ([Toda]). The polynomial hierarchy has the same structure as a constant-depth circuit, with existential quantifiers being interpretted as "Or" and universal as "And". A direct translation of the small degree approximation of this circuit gives a probabilistic algorithm that uses modular counting, i.e., an algorithm in $BPP^{\oplus P}$. The final step of Toda's proof, showing $BPP^{\oplus P} \subseteq P^{\#P}$, also uses arithimetization, finding a clever polynomial that puts in extra 0's between the least significant digit and the other digits in the number of solutions of a formula.

The power of arithimetization is its generality. A multilinear polynomial is one where, in each term, there is no variable raised to a power greater than one, i.e., it is a linear combination of products of variables. Take any Boolean function and any field. There is always a unique multilinear polynomial that agrees with the function on $0, 1$ inputs. We can view the subsequent "multi-linearization" of the function as yet another error-correcting code. The message is the Boolean function, given as its truth table, and the code is the sequence of values of the multi-linearization on all tuples of field elements. (This is not a binary code, but we can compose it with a Hadamard code to make it binary.) Beaver and Feigenbaum ([BF90]) observed that every multilinear function is random-self-reducible, by interpolating its values at $n+1$ points along a random line passing through the point in question. This can be viewed as a way to locally error correct the code, when there is less than a $1/(n + 1)$ fraction of corruptions in the code word. Lipton ([Lip91]) made the same observation independently, and observed that the permanent function, which is complete for $\#P$, is already multi-linear. Thus, he concluded, if $BPP \neq \#P$, then the permanent is hard in the average-case (with non-negligible probability.) Since the multi-linearization can be computed in logspace given the truth table for the function, $PSPACE$, EXP and similar classes are closed under multi-linearization. Therefore, the same conclusion holds for these classes and their complete problems.

These observations about the complexity of multi-linear functions are relatively straight-forward, but they would soon lead to deeper and deeper results.

7   The Power of Randomized Proof Systems

The most stunning success story in recent complexity is the advent of hardness of approximation results using probabilistically checkable proofs. The most surprising element of this story is that it was surprising. Each move in the sequence of papers that produced this result was almost forced to occur by previous papers, in that each addressed the obvious question raised by the previous one. (Of course, much work had to be done in finding the answer.) But no one had much of an idea where this trail of ideas would end until the end was in sight. We will not be able to present many technical details of this series of results, but we want to stress the way one result built on the others. The following is certainly not meant to belittle the great technical achievments involved, but we will have to slur over most of the technical contributions.

The ideas for the first step were almost all in place. As per the above, we all knew the permanent was both random-self-reducible and downward self-reducible. [BLR] had basically shown that these two properties implied a program checker, and hence membership in IP. However, it took [LFKN92] to put the pieces together, with one new idea. The random self-reducibility of the permanent reduces one instance to several random instances, and the downward self-reducibility to several smaller instances. The new idea involved combining those several instances into one, by finding a small degree curve that passed through them all. The prover is asked to provide the polynomial that represents the permanent on the curve, which must be consistent with all of the given values, and is then challenged to prove that the formula given is correct at a random point. This gave the result that $PH \subseteq P^{\#P} \subseteq IP$. What made this result exciting is that few had believed the inclusion would hold. The rule of thumb most of us used was that unproven inclusions don't hold, especially if there are oracles relative to which they fail, as in this case ([AGH]).

The next obvious question, was this the limit of IP's power? The known limit was $PSPACE$, and many of the techniques such as random-self reduction and downwards self-reduction were known to hold for $PSPACE$. So we were all trying to prove $IP = PSPACE$, but Adi Shamir ([Sha92]) succeeded. His proof added one important new element, degree reduction, but it was still similar in concept to [LFKN92]. Once the power of IP was determined, a natural question was to look at its generalizations, such as multi-prover interactive proofs, or equivalently, probabilistically checkable proofs of exponential length. Since such a proof could be checked deterministically in exponential time, $MIP \subseteq NEXP$. [BFL91] showed the opposite containment, by a method that was certainly more sophisticated than, but also clearly a direct descendent of, Shamir's proof.

Now, most of the [BFL91] proof is not about $NEXP$ at all; it's about 3-SAT. The first step they perform is reduce the $NEXP$ problem to a locally defineable 3-SAT formula. Then they arithmetize this formula, getting a low degree polynomial that agrees with it on Boolean inputs. They also arithmetize a presumed satisfying assignment, treated as a Boolean function from variable names to values. Using the degree reduction method of Shamir to define intermediate polynomials, the prover then convinces the verifier that the polynomial, the sum of the unsatisfied clauses, really has value 0. There was only one reason why it couldn't be interpreted as a result about NP rather than $NEXP$: the natural resource bound when you translate everything down an exponential is a verifier running in poly-logarithmic time. Even if such a verifier can be convinced that the given string is a valid proof, how can she be convinced that it is a proof of the given statement (since she does not have time to read the statement)? [BFLS91] solved this conundrum by assuming that the statement itself is arithmetized, and so given in an error-corrected format.

However, later work has a different interpretation. We think of the verification as being done in two stages: in a pre-processing stage, the verifier is allowed to look at the entire input, and perform arbitrary computations. Then the prover gives us a proof, after which the probabilistic verifier is limited in time and access to the proof. When we look at it this way, the first stage is a traditional reduc-tion. We are mapping an instance of 3-SAT to an instance of the problem: given the modified input, produce a proof that the verifier will accept. Since the verifier always accepts or rejects with high probability, we can think of this latter prob-lem as being to distinguish between the existence of proofs for which almost all random tapes of the verifier lead to acceptance, and those where almost all lead to rejection. In other words, we are reducing to an approximation problem: find a proof that is approximately optimal as far as the maximum number of random tapes for which the verifier accepts. So in retrospect, the connection between probabilistically checkable proofs and hardness of approximation is obvious. At the time of [FGLSS], it was startling. However, since [PY88] had pointed to the need of a theory of just this class of approximation problems, it also made it obvious what improvements were needed: make the number of bits read con-stant, so the resulting problem is $MAX - kSAT$ for some fixed k, and make the number of random bits used $O(\log n)$ so the reduction is polynomial-time, not quasi-polynomial. The papers that did this ([AS98, ALM$^+$98]) are tours de force, and introduced powerful new ways to use arithmetization and error-correction.

They were followed by a series of papers that used similar techniques tuned for various approximation problems. For many of these problems, the exact threshold when approximation became hard was determined. See e.g., [AL] for a survey. This area remains one of the most vital in complexity theory. In ad-dition to more detailed information about hardness of approximation, the PCP theorem is continually revisited, with more and more of it becoming elementary, with the most elegant proof so far the recent work of Dinur ([D05]).

8   The Combinatorics of Randomness

As mentioned earlier, many problems in constructive extremal combinatorics can be viewed as derandomizing an existence proof via the probabilistic method. However, it became clear that solving such construction problems also would give insight into the power of general randomized algorithms, not just the specific one in question. For example, Karp, Pippenger, and Sipser ([KPS]) showed how to use constructions of expanders to decrease the error of a probabilistic algorithm without increasing the number of random bits it uses. Sipser ([Sip88]) shows how to use a (then hypothetical) construction of a graph with strong expansion properties to either get a derandomization of RP or a non-trivial simulation of time by space. Ajtai, Komlos and Szemeredi ([AKS87]) showed how to use constructive expanders to simulate randomized logspace algorithms that use $O(\log^2 n/\log\log n)$ random bits in deterministic logspace.

Later, results began to flow in the other direction as well. Solutions to prob-lems involving randomized computation lead to new constructions of random-like graphs. A basic question when considering whether randomized algorithms are the more appropriate model of efficient computation is, are these randomized algorithms physically implementable? Although quantum physics indicates that we live in a probabilistic world, nothing in physics guarantees the existence of unbiased, independent coin tosses, as is assumed in designing randomized algorithms. Can we use possibly biased sources of randomness in randomized algorithms? Van Neummann ([vN51]) solved a simple version of this problem, where the coin tosses were independent but had an unknown bias; this was generalized by Blum ([B86]) to sequences generated by known finite state Markov processes with unknown transition probabilities. Santha and Vazirani ([SV]) proved that from more general unknown sources of randomness, it is impossible to obtain unbiased bits. (Their source was further generalized by [Z90] to sources that had a certain *min-entropy* k, meaning no one string is produced with probability greater than 2^{-k}. However, there were some loopholes: if one is willing to posit two independent such sources, or that one can obtain a logarithmic number of truly random bits that are independent from the source, it is then (information-theoretically) possible to extract nearly k almost unbiased bits from such a source. For the purpose of a randomized algorihtm, it is then possible to use the source to simulate the algorithm by trying all possible sequences in place of the "truly random one". The idea of such an extractor was implicit in [Z90, Z91], and then made explicit by Nisan and Zuckerman ([NZ]).

We can view such an extractor as a very uniform graph, as follows. Let n be the number of bits produced by the source, s the number of random, k the min-entropy guarantee, and m the length of the nearly unbiased string produced, so the extractor is a function $Ext : \{0,1\}^n \times \{0,1\}^s \leftarrow \{0,1\}^m$. View this function as a bipartite graph, between n bit strings and m bit strings, where $x \in \{0,1\}^n$ and $y \in \{0,1\}^m$ are adjacent if there is an $r \in \{0,1\}^s$ with $Ext(x,r) = y$. Since the extractor, over random r, must be well-distributed when x is chosen from any set of size at least 2^k, this means that the number of edges in the graph between any set of nodes on the left of size 2^k or greater and any set of nodes on the right, is roughly what we would expect it to be if we picked $D = 2^s$ random neighbors for each node on the left. Thus, between all sufficiently large sets of nodes, the numbers of edges looks like that in a random graph of the same density. Using this characterization, Nisan and Zuckerman used extractors to construct better expanders and superconcentrators.

While we will return to extractors when we discuss hardness vs. randomness results, some of the most recent work has shown connections between randomized algorithms and constructions of random-like graphs in suprising ways. For example, the zig-zag product was introduced by Reingold, Vadhan and Wigderson to give a modular way of producing expander graphs. Starting with a small expander, one can use the zig-zag and other graph products to define larger and larger constant degree expanders. However, because it is modular, products make sense starting with an arbitrary graph. Reingold showed, in effect, that graph products can be used to increase the expansion of graphs without changing their connected components. He was able to use this idea to derandomize [AKLLR] and give the first logspace algorithm for undirected graph reachability.

A different connection is found in [BKSSW], where a new construction of bipartite Ramsey graphs (which have no large complete or empty bipartite subgraphs) used techniques from [BIW], where a method was given for combining multiple independent sources into a single almost unbiased random output. That method was itself based on results in combinatorics, namely results in additive number theory due to Bourgain, Katz, and Tao ([BKT], and Konyagin ([Kon]).

9   Converting Hardness to Pseudorandomness

As we saw earlier, Yao showed that a sufficiently hard cryptographic function sufficed to derandomize arbitrary algorithms. Starting with Nisan and Wigderson ([NW94]), similar results have been obtained with a weaker hardness condition, namely, a Boolean function f in E that has no small circuits computing it. What makes this weaker is that cryptographic problems need to be sampleable with some form of solution, so that the legitimate user creating the problem is distinguished from the attacker. Nisan and Wigderson's hard problem can be equally hard for all.

To derandomize an algorithm A, it suffices to, given x, estimate the fraction of strings r that cause probabilistic algorithm $A(x, r)$ to output 1. If A runs in $t(|x|)$ steps, we can construct an approximately $t(|x|)$ size circuit C which on input r simulates $A(x, r)$. So the problem reduces to: given a size t circuit $C(r)$, estimate the fraction of inputs on which it accepts. Note that solving this circuit-estimation problem allows us to derandomize $Promise - BPP$ as well as BPP, i.e., we don't use a global guarantee that the algorithm either overwhelmingly accepts or rejects *every instance*, only that it does so *on the particular instance that we are solving*.

We could solve this by searching over all 2^t t-bit strings, but we'd like to be more efficient. Instead, we'll search over a specially chosen small *low discrepancy set* $S = \{r_1, ... r_m\}$ of such strings, as defined earlier. The average value over $r_i \in S$ of $C(r_i)$ approximate the average over all r's for any small circuit C. This is basically the same as saying that the task of distinguishing between a random string and a member of S is so computationally difficult that it lies beyond the abilities of size t circuits. We call such a sample set *pseudo-random*. Pseudo-random sample sets are usually described as the range of a function called a *pseudo-random generator*. For cryptographic purposes, it is important that this generator be easily computable, say polynomial-time in its output length. However, for derandomization, we can settle for it to be computable in $poly(m)$ time, i.e., in exponential time in its input size. Since such a slow process is hardly describable as a generator, we will avoid using the term, and stick to low discrepancy set.

We will take an algorithmic point of view, where we show explicitly how to construct the discrepancy from the truth table of a hard function f. To show the relationship, we will denote the set as S_f.

9.1   The Standard Steps

The canonical outline for constructing the low discrepancy set from f was first put together in [BFNW93]; however, each of their three steps was at least implicit in earlier papers, two of which we've alredy discussed. Later constructions either improve one of the steps, combine steps, or apply the whole argument recursively. However, a conceptual break-through that changed the way researchers looked at these steps is due to [Tre01] and will be explored in more detail in the next subsection.

1. Extension and random-self-reduction. Construct from f a function $\hat{f}$ so that, if $\hat{f}$ has a circuit that computes its value correctly on *almost all* inputs, then f has a small circuit that is correct on *all* inputs. This is usually done by the multilinearization method of [BF90] or variants, that we discussed previously in the context of arithmetization. However, the real need here is that $\hat{f}$ be a *locally decodeable error-correcting code* of message f. Then, if we have a circuit that computes $\hat{f}$ *most of the time*, we can view it as a corrupted code word, and "decode" it to obtain a circuit that computes f *all of the time*.
   The key to efficiency here is to not make the input size for $\hat{f}$ too much larger than that for f, since all known constructions for S_f depend at least exponentially on this input size. This corresponds to a code with as high a rate as possible, although inverse polynomial rate is fine here, whereas it is terrible for most coding applications.

2. Hardness Amplification: From $\hat{f}$, construct a function $\overline{f}$ on inputs of size $\overline{\eta}$ so that, from a circuit that can predict $\overline{f}$ with an ϵ advantage over guessing, we can construct a circuit that computes $\hat{f}$ on almost all inputs.
   The prototypical example of a hardness amplification construction is the exclusive-or lemma [Yao82, Lev86], that we have discussed. Here $\overline{f(y_1 \circ y_2 ... \circ y_k)} = \hat{f}(y_1) \oplus \hat{f}(y_2) ... \oplus \hat{f}(y_k)$. As mentioned earlier, the generalization is to use any *approximate local list decodeable* code. Again, the key to efficiency is to minimize the input size, which is the same as maximizing the rate of the code. This is rather tricky, since direct products seem to need multiple inputs. [I95, IW97] solve this by using correlated inputs that are still "unrelated" enough for a direct product result to hold.

3. Finding quasi-independent sequences of inputs. Now we have a function $\overline{f}$ whose outputs are almost as good as random bits at fooling a size-limited guesser. However, to determine a t bit sequence to put in S, we need t output bits that look mutually random. In this step, a small sets of input vectors V is constructed so that for $(v_1, ...v_t) \in_U V$, guessing $\overline{f}$ on v_i is hard and in some sense independent of the guess for v_j.
   Then the sample set will be defined as: $S = \{(\overline{f}(v_1), ...\overline{f}(v_t)) | (v_1, ...v_t) \in V\}$
   The classical construction for this step is from [NW94]. This construction starts with a *design*, a family of subsets $D_1, ..D_t \subseteq [1, ..\mu], |D_i| = \overline{\eta}$, and $|D_i \cap D_j| \le \Delta$ for $i \ne j$. Then for each $w \in \{0,1\}^\mu$ we construct $v_1, ...v_t$, where v_i is the bits of w in D_i, listed in order. Intuitively, each v_i is "almost independent" of the other v_j, because of the small intersections. More precisely, if a test predicts $\hat{f}(v_i)$ from the other v_j, we can restrict the parts of w outside D_i. Then each restricted v_j takes on at most 2^Δ values, but we haven't restricted v_i at all. We can construct a circuit that knows these values of $\hat{f}$ and uses them in the predictor.

The size of S_f is 2^μ, so for efficiency we wish to minimize μ. However, our new predicting circuit has size $2^\Delta poly(t)$, so we need $\Delta \in O(\log t)$. Such designs are possible if and only if $\mu \in \Omega(\bar{\eta}^2/\Delta)$. Thus, the construction will be poly-time if we can have $\bar{\eta} = O(\eta) = O(\log t)$.

[BFNW93] use this outline to get a *low-end* hardness-randomness tradeoff, meaning the hardness assumption is relatively weak and so is the derandomization result. They prove that, if there's a function in EXP that requires more than polynomial-sized circuit size, then (promise)-BPP problems are solvable in deterministic sub-exponential time. [IW97] prove a pretty much optimal *high-end* hardness-randomness tradeoff. If there is an $f \in E$ that requires exponential-sized circuit size, then (promise)-$BPP = P$. [STV01] obtains a similar high-end result, but combines the first two steps into a single step by using algebraic *local list-decodeable codes* directly, rather than creating such a code artificially by composing a local decodeable code for low noise (multivariate extension, etc.) with a local approximately list-decodeable code for high noise (xor lemma).

9.2   Extractors and Hardness Vs. Randomness

At this point, Trevisan ([Tre01]) changed our perspective on hardness vs. randomness and extractors entirely. He observed that these two questions were *fundamentally identical*. This observation allowed ideas from one area to be used in the other, which resulted in tremendous progress towards optimal constructions for both.

Look at any hardness to randomness construction. From a function f we create a set S_f. If we have a test T that distinguishes a random element of S_f from random, then there is a small circuit using T as an oracle that computes f. Look at the extractor that, treats the output of the flawed source as f and uses its random seed to pick an element of S_f. If the resulting distribution were not close to random, there would be a test T that would be far from random for many S_f's from our source. Then each such f would be computable by a small circuit using T as an oracle. Since there are not many such circuits, there must be such an f with a relatively high probability of being output from the source. Contrapositively, this means that any sufficiently high min-entropy source the extracted string will be close to random.

Trevisan used this observation to use variants of the [BFNW93] and [IW97] as new constructions of extractors with better parameters than previous ones. This started a flurry of work culminating in asymptotically optimal extractors ([SU01]) for all min-entropies and optimal hardness-randomness constructions for all hardness functions ([Uma02]).

10   Hardness from Derandomization

Recently, derandomization has caused our supply of natural examples where randomness seems to help to dwindle. For example, Agrawal, Kayal, and Saxena ([AKS02]) have come up with a deterministic polynomial-time algorithm for primality, and Reingold has a deterministic logspace algorithm for undirected connectivity. Is it possible that we can simply derandomize all probabilistic algorithms without any complexity assumptions?

In particular, are circuit lower bounds necessary for derandomization? Some results that suggested they might not be are [IW98] and [Kab01], where average-case derandomization or derandomization vs. a deterministic adversary was possible based on a uniform or no assumption. However, intuitively, the instance could code a circuit adversary in some clever way, so worst-case derandomization based on uniform assumptions seemed difficult. Recently, we have some formal confirmation of this: Proving worst-case derandomization results automatically prove new circuit lower bounds.

These proofs usually take the contrapositive approach. Assume that a large complexity class has small circuits. Show that randomized computation is unexpectedly powerful as a result, so that the addition of randomness to a class jumps up its power to a higher level in a time hierarchy. Then derandomization would cause the time hierarchy to collapse, contradicting known time hierarchy theorems.

An example of unexpected power of randomness when functions have small circuits is the following result from [BFNW93]:

Theorem 1. *If $EXP \subseteq P/poly$, then $EXP = MA$.*

This didn't lead directly to any hardness from derandomization, because MA is the probabilistic analog of NP, not of P. However, combining this result with Kabanet's easy witness idea ([Kab01]), [IKW01] managed to extend it to $NEXP$.

Theorem 2. *If $NEXP \subseteq P/poly$, then $NEXP = MA$.*

Here, MA is the class of problems with non-interactive proofs certifiable by a probabilistic polynomial-time verifier. It is easy to show that derandomizing $Promise - BPP$ collapses MA with NP. It follows that full derandomization is not possible without proving a circuit lower bound for $NEXP$.

Corollary 1. *If $Promise - BPP \subseteq NE$, then $NEXP \not\subseteq P/poly$.*

Kabanets and Impagliazzo [KI] used a similar approach to show that we cannot derandomize the classical Schwartz-Zippel ([Sch80] [Zip79]) algorithm for polynomial identity testing without proving circuit lower bounds. Consider the question: given an arithmetic circuit C on n^2 inputs, does it compute the permanent function? This problem is in BPP, via a reduction to polynomial identity testing. This is because one can set inputs to constants to set circuits that should compute the permanent on smaller matrices, and then use the Schwartz-Zippel test ([Sch80], [Zip79]) to test that each function computes the expansion by minors of the previous one. Then assume $Perm \in AlgP/poly$. It follows that $PH \subseteq P^{Perm} \subseteq NP^{BPP}$, because one could non-deterministically guess the algebraic circuit for Perm and then verify one's guess in BPP. Thus, if $BPP = P$ (or even $BPP \subseteq NE$) and $Perm \in AlgP/poly$, then $PH \subseteq NE$. If in addition,

$NE \subseteq P/poly$, we would have $Co - NEXP = NEXP = MA \subseteq PH \subseteq NE$, a contradiction to the non-deterministic time hierarchy theorems. Thus, if $BPP \subseteq NE$, either $Perm \notin AlgP/poly$ or $NE \not\subseteq P/poly$. In either case, we would obtain a new circuit lower bound, although it is not specified whether the bound is for Boolean or arithmetic circuits.

Thus, the question of derandomization and circuit lower bounds are inextricably linked. We cannot make substantial progress on one without making progress on the other.

11 Natural Proofs

If we cannot eliminate the need for circuit lower bounds, can we prove them? Why did circuit complexity fizzle in the late 80's?

The natural proofs paradigm of Razborov and Rudich ([RR97]) explains why the approaches used then died out, and give us a challenge to overcome in proving new lower bounds. An informal statement of the idea of natural proofs is that computational hardness might also make it hard to prove lower bounds. When we prove that a function requires large circuits, we often characterize what makes a function hard. In other words, insight into an existence of hard functions often gives us insight into the computational problem of recognizing hard functions. On the other hand, if cryptographic pseudo-random function generators can be computed (in a class of circuits), then it is computationally hard to recognize hard functions reliably. By definition, a pseudo-random function is easy to compute any bit, for an algorithm knowing the seed (also called the key). Thus, hardwiring the key, each such function has low complexity. However, random functions have high complexity. If we could reliably, given the truth table of functions, compute their complexity, this would give a way to distinguish between pseudo-random functions and truly random functions, contradicting the definition of pseudo-randomness. Unfortunately, for almost all circuit classes where we don't have lower bounds, there are plausibly secure pseudorandom function generators computable in the class. That means that our lower bounds for these classes will either have to be less constructive (not giving an effective characterization), or tailored to a specific hard function and so not give a general classification of hard functions.

Optimistically, there is no known analog of natural proofs for arithmetic circuits. Maybe we (as Valliant suggests in [Val92]) should strive for arithmetic circuit lower bounds first, before tackling Boolean circuits.

12 Conclusion

Recently, I told a long-time friend who isn't a mathematician what I was working on. His shocked reply was that that was the exact same topic I was working on my first month of graduate school, which was very close to the truth. The classical challenges that have been with us for over two decades remain. We know so much more about the questions, but so little about the answers. (Of course,

I have shortchanged the genuinely new areas of complexity, such as quantum complexity, in my pursuit of links with the past.)

The more we study these problems, the closer the links between them seem to grow. On the one hand, it is hard to be optimistic about our area soon solving any one of these problems, since doing so would cut through the Gordian knot and lead to progress in so many directions. It seems that randomness does not make algorithms more powerful, but that we need to prove lower bounds on circuits to establish this. On the other hand, it seems that if cryptographic assumptions hold, proving circuit lower bounds is difficult.

On the other hand, it is hard to be pessimistic about an area that has produced so many fascinating and powerful ideas. It is hard to be pessimistic when every year, substantial progress on another classical complexity progress is made. There are no safe bets, but if I had to bet, I would bet on the longshots. The real progress will be made in unexpected ways, and will only be perfectly reasonable in hindsight.

References

[Adl78]   L. Adleman Two Theorems on Random Polynomial Time. *FOCS*, 1978, pp. 75-83.

[AGH]   W. Aiello, S. Goldwasser, and J. Hstad, On the power of interaction. *Combinatorica*, Vol 10(1), 1990, pp. 3-25.

[AKS02]   M. Agrawal, N. Kayal, and N. Saxena, Primes is in *P*. *Annals of Mathematics*, Vol. 160, No. 2, 2004, pp. 781-793.

[Aj83]   M. Ajtai. $\Sigma_{1,1}$ formulas on finite structures. *Annals of Pure and Applied Logic*, 1983

[AKS87]   M. Ajtai, J. Komlos, and E. Szemeredi, Deterministic Simulation in LOGSPACE. *19'th STOC*, 1987, pp. 132-140.

[AGS]   A. Akavia, S. Goldwasser, and S. Safra, Proving Hard-core Predicates Using List Decoding. *FOCS*, 2003, pp. 146-156.

[AKLLR]   R. Aleliunas, R. Karp, R. Lipton, L. Lovasz, and C. Rackoff, Random Walks, Universal Traversal Sequences, and the Complexity of Maze Problems *20th FOCS*, 1979, pp. 218-223.

[ACR98]   A.E. Andreev, A.E.F. Clementi, and J.D.P. Rolim. A new general derandomization method. *Journal of the Association for Computing Machinery*, 45(1):179–213, 1998. (preliminary version in ICALP'96).

[ACRT]   A. Andreev, A. Clementi, J. Rolim, and L. Trevisan, "Weak random sources, hitting sets, and BPP simulation", *38th FOCS*, pp. 264-272, 1997.

[AL]   S. Arora and C. Lund, Hardness of Approximations In, *Approximation Algorithms for NP-hard Problems*, D. Hochbaum, editor, PWS Publishing, 1996.

[ALM⁺98]   S. Arora, C. Lund, R. Motwani, M. Sudan, and M. Szegedy. Proof verification and the hardness of approximation problems. *Journal of the Association for Computing Machinery*, 45(3):501–555, 1998. (preliminary version in FOCS'92).

[AS97]   S. Arora and M. Sudan. Improved low-degree testing and its applications, In *Proceedings of the Twenty-Ninth Annual ACM Symposium on Theory of Computing*, pages 485–495, 1997.

[AS98]   S. Arora and S. Safra. Probabilistic checking of proofs: A new charac-
            terization of NP. *Journal of the Association for Computing Machinery*,
            45(1):70–122, 1998. (preliminary version in FOCS'92).

[BFLS91]   L. Babai, L. Fortnow, L. A. Levin, M. Szegedy, Checking Computations
            in Polylogarithmic Time 23rd STOC, 1991, pp. 21-31

[BFL91]   L. Babai, L. Fortnow, and C. Lund. Non-deterministic exponential time
            has two-prover interactive protocols. *Computational Complexity*, 1:3–40,
            1991.

[BFNW93]   L. Babai, L. Fortnow, N. Nisan, and A. Wigderson. BPP has subexpo-
            nential time simulations unless EXPTIME has publishable proofs. *Com-
            plexity*, 3:307–318, 1993.

[BMor]   L. Babai and S. Moran Arthur-Merlin games: a randomized proof system,
            and a hierarchy of complexity class *JCSS*, Vol 36, Issue 2, 1988, pp.
            254-276.

[BIW]   B. Barak, R. Impagliazzo, and A. Wigderson, Extracting Randomness
            Using Few Independent Sources, *45th FOCS*, 2004, pp. 384-393.

[BKSSW]   B. Barak, G. Kindler, R. Shaltiel, B. Sudakov, and A. Wigderson, Sim-
            ulating independence: new constructions of condesnsors, ramsey graphs,
            dispersers and extractors. *37th STOC*, 2005, pp. 1-10.

[BF90]   D. Beaver and J. Feigenbaum. Hiding instances in multioracle queries.
            In *Proceedings of the Seventh Annual Symposium on Theoretical Aspects
            of Computer Science*, volume 415 of *Lecture Notes in Computer Science*,
            pages 37–48, Berlin, 1990. Springer Verlag.

[BGKW]   M. Ben-Or, S. Goldwasser, J. Kilian, and A. Wigderson Multi-Prover
            Interactive Proofs: How to Remove Intractability Assumptions. *STOC*,
            1988, pp. 113-131.

[Ber72]   E.R. Berlekamp. Factoring Polynomials. *Proc. of the 3rd Southeastern
            Conference on Combinatorics, GRAPH THEORY AND COMPUTING*
            1972, pp. 1-7.

[B86]   M. Blum Independent Unbiased Coin Flips From a Correlated Biased
            Source: a Finite State Markov *Combinatorica*, Vol. 6, No. 2, 1986, pp.
            97-108. Chain FOCS 1984: 425-433

[BK]   M. Blum and S. Kannan, Designing Programs That Check Their Work.
            STOC, 1989, pp. 86-97.

[BLR]   M. Blum, M. Luby, and R. Rubinfeld Self-Testing/Correcting with Ap-
            plications to Numerical Problems. *J. Comput. Syst. Sci.* Vol 47(3), 1993,
            pp. 549-595.

[BM]   M. Blum and S. Micali. "How to Generate Cryptographically Strong Se-
            quences of Pseudo-Random Bits", *SIAM J. Comput.*, Vol. 13, pages 850–
            864, 1984.

[BKT]   J. Bourgain, N. Katz, and T. Tao, A sum-product estimate in finite fields,
            and applications *Geometric and Functional Analysis*, Vol. 14, 2004, pp.
            27-57.

[DH]   W. Diffie and M. Hellman, New Directions in Cryptography, *IEEE Trans-
            actions on Information Theory*, Vol. IT-22, No. 6, 1976, pp. 644-654.

[CGHFRS]   B. Chor, O. Goldreich, J. Hstad, J. Friedman, S. Rudich, R. Smolensky
            The Bit Extraction Problem of t-Resilient Functions. *FOCS*, 1985, pp.
            396-407.

[C83]   S. Cook, An Overview of Computational Complexity. *Communications
            of the ACM*, Volume 26, Number 3, pp. 401-407.

[D05]   I. Dinur, The PCP Theorem by gap amplification. ECCC tech. report TR05-046, 2005.

[FGLSS]   U. Feige, S. Goldwasser, L. Lovasz, S. Safra, and M. Szegedy, Approximating Clique is Almost NP-complete. *FOCS*, 1991, pp. 2-12.

[For01]   L. Fortnow. Comparing notions of full derandomization. In *Proceedings of the Sixteenth Annual IEEE Conference on Computational Complexity*, pages 28–34, 2001.

[FSS]   M. Furst, J. B. Saxe, and M. Sipser. Parity, Circuits, and the Polynomial-Time Hierarchy. *Mathematical Systems Theory*, 17(1), 1984, pp. 13-27.

[GG]   O. Gabber and Z. Galil. Explicit Constructions of Linear-Sized Superconcentrators. *J. Comput. Syst. Sci.* Vol. 22(3), 1981, pp. 407-420.

[Gill]   J. Gill. Computational complexity of proabilistic Turing machines. *SIAM J. Comput.*, Vol. 6, 1977, pp. 675-695.

[GL89]   O. Goldreich and L.A. Levin. "A Hard-Core Predicate for all One-Way Functions", in *ACM Symp. on Theory of Computing*, pp. 25–32, 1989.

[GGM]   O. Goldreich, S. Goldwasser, and S. Micali. How to construct random functions. *J. ACM*, Vol. 33(4), 1986, pp. 792-807.

[GS]   S. Goldwasser and M. Sipser, Private Coins versus Public Coins in Interactive Proof Systems *STOC*, 1986, pp. 59-68.

[GMR]   S. Goldwasser, S. Micali, and C. Rackoff The Knowledge Complexity of Interactive Proof Systems. *SIAM J. Comput.* 18(1), 1989, pp. 186-208.

[Has86]   J. Hstad Almost Optimal Lower Bounds for Small Depth Circuits. *STOC*, 1986, pp. 6-20.

[HILL]   J. Hstad, R. Impagliazzo, L. A. Levin and M. Luby. A Pseudorandom Generator from any One-way Function. *SIAM J. Comput.*, 28(4), 1999, pp. 1364-1396.

[HS]   J. Heintz and C.-P. Schnorr. Testing Polynomials which Are Easy to Compute. *STOC*, 1980, pp. 262-272.

[I95]   R. Impagliazzo, "Hard-core Distributions for Somewhat Hard Problems", in *36th FOCS*, pages 538–545, 1995.

[I03]   R. Impagliazzo. Hardness as randomness: a survey of universal derandomization. CoRR cs.CC/0304040, 2003.

[IKW01]   R. Impagliazzo, V. Kabanets, and A. Wigderson. In search of an easy witness: Exponential time vs. probabilistic polynomial time. In *Proceedings of the Sixteenth Annual IEEE Conference on Computational Complexity*, pages 1–11, 2001.

[IR]   R. Impagliazzo and S. Rudich Limits on the Provable Consequences of One-Way Permutations. *STOC*, 1989, pp. 44-61.

[IW97]   R. Impagliazzo and A. Wigderson. P=BPP if E requires exponential circuits: Derandomizing the XOR Lemma. In *Proceedings of the Twenty-Ninth Annual ACM Symposium on Theory of Computing*, pages 220–229, 1997.

[IW98]   R. Impagliazzo and A. Wigderson. Randomness vs. time: Derandomization under a uniform assumption. In *Proceedings of the Thirty-Ninth Annual IEEE Symposium on Foundations of Computer Science*, pages 734–743, 1998.

[J84]   D. Johnson, The NP-completeness column: An ongoing guide. (12th article) *Journal of Algorithms*, Vol. 5, 1984, pp. 433-447.

[Kab01]   V. Kabanets. Easiness assumptions and hardness tests: Trading time for zero error. *Journal of Computer and System Sciences*, 63(2):236–252, 2001. (preliminary version in CCC'00).

[Kab02]   V. Kabanets. Derandomization: A brief overview. *Bulletin of the European Association for Theoretical Computer Science*, 76:88–103, 2002. (also available as ECCC TR02-008).

[KI]   V. Kabanets and R. Impagliazzo, Derandomizing Polynomial Identity Tests Means Proving Circuit Lower Bounds *Computational Complexity*, Vol. 13, No. 1-2, 2004, pp. 1-46.

[Kal92]   E. Kaltofen. Polynomial factorization 1987–1991. In I. Simon, editor, *Proceedings of the First Latin American Symposium on Theoretical Informatics*, Lecture Notes in Computer Science, pages 294–313. Springer Verlag, 1992. (LATIN'92).

[K86]   R. M. Karp. Combinatorics, Complexity, and Randomness. *Commun. ACM*, Vol. 29(2), 1986, pp. 97-109.

[KL]   R. M. Karp and R. J. Lipton, "Turing Machines that Take Advice", *L'Ensignment Mathematique*, 28, pp. 191–209, 1982.

[KPS]   R. M. Karp, N. Pippenger, and M. Sipser, A time randomness tradeoff *AMS Conference on Probabilistic Computational Complexity*, 1985.

[Kon]   S. Konyagin, A sum-product estimate in fields of prime order Arxiv technical report 0304217, 2003.

[Lev87]   L. A. Levin, One-Way Functions and Pseudorandom Generators. *Combinatorica*, Vol. 7, No. 4, pp. 357–363, 1987.

[Lev86]   L. A. Levin, Average Case Complete Problems. *SIAM J. Comput.* Vol. 15(1), 1986, pp. 285-286.

[Lip91]   New directions in testing. Distributed Computing and Cryptography, 1991.

[LR]   M. Luby and C. Rackoff How to Construct Pseudorandom Permutations from Pseudorandom Functions. *SIAM J. Comput.* 17(2), 1988, pp. 373-386.

[LFKN92]   C. Lund, L. Fortnow, H. Karloff, and N. Nisan. Algebraic methods for interactive proof systems. *Journal of the Association for Computing Machinery*, 39(4):859–868, 1992.

[Lip91]   R. Lipton. New directions in testing. In J. Feigenbaum and M. Merrit, editors, *Distributed Computing and Cryptography*, pages 191–202. DIMACS Series in Discrete Mathematics and Theoretical Computer Science, Volume 2, AMS, 1991.

[MP]   M. Minsky and S. Pappert, *Perceptrons: An Introduction to Computational Geometry*, MIT Press, Cambridge, MA, 1969. (Expanded edition, 1988.)

[NW94]   N. Nisan and A. Wigderson. Hardness vs. randomness. *Journal of Computer and System Sciences*, 49:149–167, 1994.

[NZ]   N. Nisan and D. Zuckerman. Randomness is Linear in Space. *JCSS*, Vol 52, No. 1, 1996, pp. 43-52.

[Pap94]   C.H. Papadimitriou. *Computational Complexity*. Addison-Wesley, Reading, Massachusetts, 1994.

[PY88]   C.H. Papadimitriou and M. Yannakakis. Optimization, Approximation, and Complexity Classes *STOC*, 1988, pp. 229-234. *Computational Complexity*. Addison-Wesley, Reading, Massachusetts, 1994.

[Rab80]   M. O. Rabin. Probabilistic Algorithm for Testing Primality. *Journal of Number Theory*, 12:128–138, 1980.

[Raz85]   A.A. Razborov, Lower bounds for the monotone complexity of some Boolean functions, *Doklady Akademii Nauk SSSR*, Vol. 281, No 4, 1985, pages 798-801. English translation in *Soviet Math. Doklady*, 31:354-357, 1985.

[Raz87]   A.A. Razborov, Lower bounds on the size of bounded-depth networks over a complete basis with logical addition. *Mathematicheskie Zemetki*, Vol. 41, No 4, 1987, pages 598-607. English translation in Notes of the Academy of Sci. of the USSR, 41(4):333-338, 1987.

[RR97]   A.A. Razborov and S. Rudich. Natural proofs. *Journal of Computer and System Sciences*, 55:24–35, 1997.

[RS]   J. Riordan and C. Shannon, The Number of Two-Terminal Series-Parallel Networks. *Journal of Mathematics and Physics*, Vol. 21 (August, 1942), pp. 83-93.

[RSA]   R. Rivest, A. Shamir, and L. Adleman, A Method for Obtaining Digital Signatures and Public-Key Cryptosystems, *Communications of the ACM*, Vol.21, No. 2, 1978, pp.120-126.

[Rud91]   S. Rudich The Use of Interaction in Public Cryptosystems. *CRYPTO*, 1991, pp. 242-251.

[SV]   M. Santha and U. V. Vazirani, Generating Quasi-Random Sequences from Slightly Random Sources, *25th FOCS*, 1984, pp. 434-440.

[Sch80]   J.T. Schwartz. Fast probabilistic algorithms for verification of polynomial identities. *Journal of the Association for Computing Machinery*, 27(4):701–717, 1980.

[SU01]   R. Shaltiel and C. Umans. Simple extractors for all min-entropies and a new pseudo-random generator. In *Proceedings of the Forty-Second Annual IEEE Symposium on Foundations of Computer Science*, pages 648–657, 2001.

[Sha92]   A. Shamir. IP=PSPACE. *Journal of the Association for Computing Machinery*, 39(4):869–877, 1992.

[Sip88]   M. Sipser Extractors, Randomness, or Time versus Space. *JCSS*, vol 36, No. 3, 1988, pp. 379-383.

[Smol87]   R. Smolensky, Algebraic Methods in the Theory of Lower Bounds for Boolean Circuit Complexity. *STOC*, 1987, pp. 77-82.

[SS79]   R. Solovay and V. Strassen, A fast Monte Carlo test for primality *SIAM Journal on Computing* 6(1):84-85, 1979.

[STV01]   M. Sudan, L. Trevisan, and S. Vadhan. Pseudorandom generators without the XOR lemma. *Journal of Computer and System Sciences*, 62(2):236–266, 2001. (preliminary version in STOC'99).

[Sud97]   M. Sudan. Decoding of Reed Solomon codes beyond the error-correction bound. *Journal of Complexity*, 13(1):180–193, 1997.

[Tar88]   É. Tardos The gap between monotone and non-monotone circuit complexity is exponential. *Combinatorica* 8(1), 1988, pp. 141-142.

[Toda]   S. Toda, "On the computational power of PP and $\oplus P$", in *30th FOCS*, pp. 514–519, 1989.

[Tre01]   L. Trevisan. Extractors and pseudorandom generators. *Journal of the Association for Computing Machinery*, 48(4):860–879, 2001. (preliminary version in STOC'99).

[Tre03]   L. Trevisan, List Decoding Using the XOR Lemma. Electronic Colloquium on Computational Complexity tech report 03-042, 2003.

[Uma02]   C. Umans. Pseudo-random generators for all hardnesses. In *Proceedings of the Thirty-Fourth Annual ACM Symposium on Theory of Computing*, 2002.

[Val92]   L. Valiant. Why is Boolean complexity theory difficult? In M.S. Paterson, editor, *Boolean Function Complexity*, volume 169 of *London Math. Society Lecture Note Series*, pages 84–94. Cambridge University Press, 1992.

[vN51]   J. von Neumann, Various Techniques Used in Relation to Random Digits *Applied Math Series*, Vol. 12, 1951, pp. 36-38.

[We87]   I. Wegener *The Complexity of Boolean Functions.* Wiley-Teubner, 1987.

[Yab]   S. Yablonski, The algorithmic difficulties of synthesizing minimal switching circuits. *Problemy Kibornetiki 2*, 1959, pp. 75-121.

[Yao82]   A.C. Yao. Theory and applications of trapdoor functions. In *Proceedings of the Twenty-Third Annual IEEE Symposium on Foundations of Computer Science*, pages 80–91, 1982.

[Yao85]   A.C. Yao. Separating the Polynomial-Time Hierarchy by Oracles. *FOCS*, 1985, pp. 1-10.

[Zip79]   R.E. Zippel. Probabilistic algorithms for sparse polynomials. In *Proceedings of an International Symposium on Symbolic and Algebraic Manipulation (EUROSAM'79)*, Lecture Notes in Computer Science, pages 216–226, 1979.

[Z90]   D. Zuckerman, General Weak Random Sources *31st FOCS*, 1990, pp. 534-543.

[Z91]   D. Zuckerman, Simulating BPP Using a General Weak Random Source, *FOCS*, 1991, pp. 79-89.

Developments in Data Structure Research During the First 25 Years of FSTTCS

Raimund Seidel

Universität des Saarlandes
Fachrichtung Informatik
Im Stadtwald
D-66123 Saarbrücken, Germany
rseidel@cs.uni-sb.de

Abstract. We survey and highlight some of the developments in data structure research during the time of the first 25 years of the FSTTCS conference series.

1 Introduction

When Sandeep Sen, co-chairman of FSTTCS 2005, kindly invited me to give a plenary talk at this conference and suggested as topic "the development of data structure research during the last 25 years," (i.e. during the lifetime of the FSTTCS conference series) I felt honored — and challenged. So much has happened in data structures during this time! A recent "handbook"[1] on this subject contains about 60 articles spread over about 1400 pages, and still those articles are just surveys that for the most part cannot claim complete coverage. How could I make a selection of topics to present from such a large body of work? How could I do justice to all the neat and interesting ideas developed in this area? How could I do justice to all the authors who have come up with those ideas? How can I do all this and stay within one hour of presentation time, or a few pages of conference proceedings text?

I had to make a few decisions: First, this talk (article) is intended explicitly for the non-experts, for researchers whose main interests lie outside the area of data structures, algorithms, and their performance analysis. Second, in this talk (article) I will try to convey only the main ideas that have been developed over approximately the last 25 years and I will talk about very few definite data structures explicitly. When I say "main ideas" I should correct this immediately to "what I consider to be main ideas." The selection is certainly affected by my personal preferences and my own research topics. Surely some of my colleagues would present a different selection of ideas and topics, although I hope there still would be some large agreement. Third, I forego any claim to any completeness; many topics and I ideas I will not cover at all (data structures for string manipulations or for graphs, to name a few).

It is my hope that non-experts will be able to walk away from this talk not just with some data structuring buzzwords, but with sufficient meaning and

R. Ramanujam and S. Sen (Eds.): FSTTCS 2005, LNCS 3821, pp. 48–59, 2005.

interpretation attached to those words, so that it will be possible to strike the right connections and associations to the data structuring world in case the need to do so arises.

2   Amortization

Amortization was initially just a new convenient way of talking about and describing the performance of some data structures. In time this way of thinking influenced the way how new data structures were designed, paving the way for structures like splay trees [2], Fibonacci heaps [3], and many others.

Consider a data structure with two operations, say, query and insert. The traditional way of describing the performance characteristics of such a structure would be in terms of the following three quantities:

$S(n)$ the space needed in the worst case when the structure holds at most n items;

$Q(n)$ the time a query needs in *the worst case* when the structure holds at most n items;

$I(n)$ the time an insertion needs in *the worst case* when the structure holds at most n items;

Let us forget about the space bound $S(n)$ for the time being. In this setup any sequence of m_I insert operations interspersed with m_Q query operations is guaranteed to take time at most

$$m_I I(n) + m_Q Q(n),$$

assuming that the maximum number of items in the data structure at any point is n. However, this may be a very pessimistic bound. If for instance most insertions take only $O(1)$ time and very rarely some insertion takes $O(n)$ time, then in this setup one needs to put $Q(n) = O(n)$ and one gets an $O(m_I \cdot n)$ upper bound for the total insertion cost in the sequence, although the true total cost may be much lower, due to the infrequency of expensive insertions[1] .

Consider the following example, which will be used in several sections: We want to maintain a set A of keys from an ordered universe under insert operations and membership queries. We will do this in the following non-standard way. We partition A into disjoint subsets whose sizes are distinct powers of 2 (the binary representation of $n = |A|$ yields those subset sizes). Each of those subsets we store in a sorted array. Thus such a subset of size 2^k can be queried for membership in $O(k)$ time via binary search. A membership query in the entire set can then be realized by querying in each of the subsets leading to a worst case time bound for the entire query of

$$Q(n) = \sum_{0 \le k \le \log_2 n} O(k) = O(\log^2 n).$$

---

[1] We use the word "cost" here as synonymous with the word "time." See the "bank account method" below for more about this correspondence.

How do we realize insertions? When inserting element x we first create a new subset of size $2^0 = 1$ holding just x, and then as long as we have two subsets of the same size in the partition, we join them to one of double size (each of those "joins" amounts to merging two sorted arrays into one and can be done in linear time). Note that with this strategy inserting an element into a set of even size takes only $O(1)$ time, since no merging needs to be done at all, whereas inserting an element into a set of size $n = 2^\ell - 1$ will take $O(n)$ time. Thus most insertions (at least half of them) are very cheap, whereas some are very expensive.

But it is quite easy to see (and we'll sketch three proofs below) that any sequence of $m_I = n$ insertions into an initially empy set will take time $O(n \log n)$ overall. Thus the "average" insertion cost is actually only $O(\log n)$, where the average is taken over the sequence of operations.

We say that a data structure has *amortized* query performance $Q_A(n)$ and *amortized* insertion performance $I_A(n)$ if for every m_Q and m_I every sequence of m_I insertions interspersed with m_Q queries takes total time at most

$$m_Q Q_A(n) + m_I I_A(n),$$

where n is the maximum size of the data structure[2]. This definition can be generalized in an obvious way if there are further operations on the data structure, like deletions, etc.

Thus amortized complexity of an operation is its worst case average cost, where the average is taken over a sequence of operations. In our running example we have

$$Q_A(n) = O(\log^2 n) \qquad \text{and} \qquad I_A = O(\log n).$$

The bound for $Q_A(n)$ is clear, since obviously worst case complexity is always an upper bound to amortized complexity. For the the second bound we now sketch three proof methods.

Aggregate Method: We try to argue holistically. In a sequence of n insertions into an initially empty set our method will cause $\lfloor n/2^k \rfloor$ merges producing arrays of size 2^k. Each such merge costs time $O(2^k)$. Thus the total cost will be

$$\sum_{k>0} \lfloor n/2^k \rfloor O(2^k) = O(n \log n).$$

Bank Account Method: We conceptually equate time and money. Money can be stored for later use, which is easier to imagine than "storing time" for later use. Each constant time primitive operation thus costs money, say one dollar. Each insertion operation brings $\lfloor \log_2 n \rfloor$ dollars into the system that are conceptually kept in a "bank account" at the inserted key. In every merge operation every involved key pays one dollar from its account to defray the time costs of this merge. Since every key can be involved in at most $\lfloor \log_2 n \rfloor$ merges (the size of its containing array doubles every time) no account will ever be overdrawn and the $n \lfloor \log_2 n \rfloor$ dollars brought into the system in total can pay for

---

[2] In some cases, like when not starting with an empty structure, one needs to relax the conditions, and require this to be true only for sufficiently large m_Q and m_I.

all primitive operations. The amortized time of an insertion operation can now be measured by the amount of money it has to bring into the system, which in our example is $O(\log n)$.

Potential Method: One defines a "potential function" Φ mapping the state of the data structure to a real number. Let Φ_i denote the value of Φ after the i-th insertion, and let a_i be the *actual* cost of the i-th insertion. Now suppose we can prove that for every i we have

$$a_i + \Phi_i - \Phi_{i-1} \leq f(n).$$

Then we have

$$\left(\sum_{1 \leq i \leq n} a_i\right) + (\Phi_n - \Phi_0) = \sum_{1 \leq i \leq n} (a_i + \Phi_i - \Phi_{i-1}) \leq n \cdot f(n),$$

and therefore

$$\sum_{1 \leq i \leq n} a_i \leq n \cdot f(n) - (\Phi_n - \Phi_0).$$

If in addition $\Phi_i > \Phi_0$ holds for all i, then this last inequality implies that the total sum of all n actual insertion times is upper bounded by $n \cdot f(n)$, which means $f(n)$ is an upper bound to the amortized insertion cost.

The potential method relies heavily on a clever choice of a potential function Φ. In the case of our example we can choose

$$\Phi = \sum_{k: \text{ there is a subset of size } 2^k} (\log_2 n - k) \cdot 2^k$$

and the desired $O(\log n)$ amortized insertion complexity bound can be shown to follow. This is not surprising since the chosen potential function is essentially the sum of all the bank accounts of the previous method. Such a transfer of view is always possible. However, there are situations, as for instance with splay trees, where the myopic view of individual bank accounts is inadequate and a global view in form of a potential function makes amortized analysis much easier.

Amortization has proven to be an extremely useful way of looking at data structures. Although it had been used implicitly before, this way analyzing data structure was made explicit only in the mid 80's, see for instance the article of Tarjan [4]. By now the concept is treated already in many textbooks.

3   Automatic Dynamization

There are situations where it is easy to build a static data structure for some query problem that admits fast querying, but that does not readily admit fast updates. Inserting a new item into the structure or deleting an existing item may be as expensive as rebuilding the entire structure from scratch. In the early 80's there was considerable research in designing more or less automatic ways that create out of a static data structure, i.e. one that does not easily admit updates, a dynamic data structure, i.e. one that admits insertions and deletion [5,6].

These methods apply mostly to data structuring problems that are in some sense *decomposable*, i.e. the answer to a query to the entire set can be cheaply obtained from the answers to queries to some collection of subsets. This is for instance true for the set membership problem, the example in the previous section: $x \in A$ iff $x \in A_j$ for some $j \in J$, provided $\bigcup_{j \in J} A_j = A$. For such decomposable problems a natural way to make a static data structure dynamic is to break the problem into disjoint blocks, perform a query by making queries in each of the blocks and combining the answers, and to perform an update by rebuilding the data structure for just one block (or few blocks). For the querying strategy it is advantageous to have few blocks, for the updates it is advantageous to have small blocks.

There are two ways to reconcile the "small" and "few" requirements. The first is the so-called equal block method, which keeps all blocks of approximately the same size. The second is the so-called logarithmic block method, which keeps blocks of different sizes, say all have size a power of two and no two blocks have the same size.

As an example for the **equal block method** consider nearest neighbor searching in the plane: One is to store a set P of n sites in the plane, so that given a query point q in the plane one can determine quickly its nearest site, i.e. the site $p \in P$ that is closest to q. For the static case there is a classic solution via so-called Voronoi diagrams and planar subdivision search, which has preprocessing time $O(n \log n)$, space usage $O(n)$, and query time $O(\log n)$. This method can be dynamized by breaking P into about $n^{1/2}$ blocks, each containing about $n^{1/2}$ sites. A query can now be performed by querying in each of the $n^{1/2}$ blocks, yielding an $O(n^{1/2} \log n)$ query time overall. An insertion of a new site p can be performed by rebuilding the static data structure for the smallest block (but now including p). Similarly the deletion of site p can be performed by rebuilding the structure for the block that contains p (but now without p). This yields an update time of $O(n^{1/2} \log n)$. Some additional care needs to be taken to ensure that the blocks stay of about the same size. Note the possible tradeoff between query time and update time depending on the number of blocks.

An example for the **logarithmic block method** was given in the previous section, where the data structure "sorted array" was dynamized: The idea is to break the problem into a logarithmic number of blocks whose sizes are distinct powers of two. Inserting a new element works by first creating an additional block of size 1 for the new element, and then, as long as there are two block of the same size 2^k destroying them and building from scratch a data structure for the union of those two blocks, which has size 2^{k+1}. A construction time of $O(n \log n)$ and query time $O(\log n)$ for a static problem then yields a worst case query time of $O(\log^2 n)$ and amortized insertion time of $O(\log^2 n)$ for the dynamic problem (if no deletions are allowed). Note that these bounds also apply to the nearest neighbor searching problem of the previous paragraph. A speedup of the insertion time is possible if the data structure for the union of two equal sized blocks can be constructed from the data structures of the individual blocks in a faster manner than brute-force new construction from scratch. This is easily seen to be the case in the set membership example of the previous section (merging two sorted list into a single sorted list can be done in linear time), it happens to be the case for the nearest neighbor searching problem also (see [7]).

In general the logarithmic block method does not admit easy deletions: If the element to be deleted happens to be in the largest block, and the only way to achieve the deletion is to rebuild the data structure for the largest block from scratch without the deleted element, then such a delete operation is expensive indeed. This applies to our nearest neighbor searching example. However, for the set membership example so-called weak deletions are possible. The simple idea is to mark elements as deleted, without actually removing them from the data structure. This is obviously possible in our set memberhip example, and does not hurt the insertion and query time (and space requirements) too much, as long as not too many, say, more than half of the elements are marked as deleted. What should one do in that case? Simply rebuild the entire structure from scratch, of course without the deleted elements. In our example of the set membership problem this actually yields a logarithmic amortized deletion time.

A detailed study of those issues can be found in Overmars' book [6], which also discusses other general ideas, like e.g. turning the outlined general amortized bounds into worst case bounds. Although the techniques of automatic dynamization are for the most part not particularly deep or difficult, they can be very useful and in many cases lead to quick and dirty solutions that are surprisingly efficient.

4   Fractional Cascading

A sorted list L of $\ell = |L|$ reals breaks the real line into $\ell + 1$ intervals. Assume that some "answer" is associated with each of those intervals, and consider the query problem, where given a query number q one would like to determine the "answer" associated with the interval that contains q. Using binary search such a query problem can easily be solved in logarithmic query time using linear space.

Now suppose we have m such sorted lists $L_1, \ldots, L_m$ and for a given query number q the containing interval and its associated answer is to be found and reported for every one of those m lists. A natural and straightforward solution is to perform independent binary searches in each of those lists, yielding a query time of $O(m \log \ell)$ using space $O(N)$, where $N = \sum_{1 \le i \le m} \ell_i$ and $\ell = \max_i \ell_i$. Another approach would be to combine the m lists into one list L of size N and storing with each of the $N+1$ intervals the sequence of m answers, one from each L_i. This results in faster query time of $O(\log N + m)$ (the summand m accounts the reporting of the m answers), but in a space requirement of $O(Nm)$.

Is there a way of achieving $O(\log N + m)$ query time, using just $O(N)$ space? *Fractional cascading* provides a positve answer to this question. The basic idea is as follows: Set $L'_m = L_m$, and for $k = m-1$ down to 1 obtain list L'_k by inserting, say, every fourth element of L'_{k+1} into L_k. If you now know the placement of a query point q in list L'_k, then you know q's placement in L_k and moreover it just takes a constant number of additional comparisons to find q's placement in L'_{k+1} (after all, there at most 4 possible choices of intervals). This of course assumes appropriate "bridging" information, which however is not too hard to achieve.

A query can now indeed by answered in time $O(\log N + m)$: In $O(\log N)$ time find the placement of q in L'_1, from this find in constant time the proper placement of q in L_1 and also the placement of q in L'_2, and then iterate.

The space requirement is proportional to $\sum_{1 \leq k \leq m} |L'_k|$. Since

$$\sum_{1 \leq k \leq m} |L'_k| = |L_m| + \sum_{1 \leq k < m} (|L_k| + |L'_{k+1}|/4) \leq \sum_{1 \leq k \leq m} |L_k| + \sum_{1 \leq k \leq m} |L'_k|/4$$

we obtain

$$\sum_{1 \leq k \leq m} |L'_k| \leq= (4/3) \cdot \sum_{1 \leq k \leq m} |L_k| = O(N),$$

and hence the space requirement is indeed $O(N)$.

The observant reader will surely have noticed one application of fractional cascading: We can apply it to our solution to the set membership problem. Since m, the number of lists, there is $O(\log n)$ and N, the sum of the list sizes, is n, we obtain an $O(\log n)$ worst case time bound for querying in this structure, improving upon the $O(\log^2 n)$ bound that we had established so far. If a little bit of care is taken, then the logarithmic amortized time bounds for insertions and deletions that we have established already can be maintained in the presence of fractional cascading also.

This basic idea of fractional cascading can be generalized to situations where the lists are not just arranged in a linear sequence but where lists are associated to the nodes of a directed acyclic graph and one wishes to query in all lists along some directed path in the graph. Fractional cascading has a surprising number of applications, in particular in computational geometry. It was originally proposed by Chazelle and Guibas [8,9], although some similar ideas had appeared before (see e.g. [10]). For further work see for instance [11,12].

5   Persistence

Imagine a data structure undergoing a sequence of updates, each generating a new, current version of the data structure. What does one need to do so that any point in time one can perform a query in one of the *previous* versions of the data structure. Such a data structure is called *persistent* (in contrast to *ephemeral*). Generating an entirely new structure with every update certainly would allow such queries in the past to be performed efficiently. However, the update costs, and maybe more importantly, the space costs would be formidable. So the question is how should the various versions of the data structure be related, what substructures should they share, so that fast queries in the past are possible but the overall additional cost in update time and space usage is small.

For our example of section 2 for the set membership problem (without fractional cascading) there is a rather straightforward solution to this problem: simply keep around any sorted array that is ever created. With proper book keeping queries of past versions can then be performed easily, and still in $O(\log^2 n)$ time. The amortized insertion cost is still $O(\log n)$, just the space usage increases from $O(n)$ to $O(n \log n)$. An interesting question now is whether something like this can be achieved without the increase in space costs.

A quite general positive answer to this question was produced by Driscoll et al. [13] for the case when the data structures can be modelled as graphs. For the sake of definiteness it may be best to think about balanced search trees. One way of making such a search tree persistent is the following: all that essentially changes in a search tree during an update is a path from the root to some treenode. So just create a new copy of this path and share the subtrees that are to hang off this path with the previous structures. If one wants to perform a query in a past version then simply locate the appropriate past root node r and start the usual tree search from there. So the query time does not change at all (except for the additional time to identify r). However the space usage will go up by a logarithmic factor since with every update $O(\log n)$ new nodes need to be created for the new path.

In contrast to this *path copying* method there is also another method that is sometimes referred to as *fat node method*. Every pointer field is now replaced by an array of pointers, where each enry is endowed with time-stamps telling at which point in time this particular pointer was valid. If during a tree update a pointer is to be changed to a new target, this is achieved by adding a new entry to the corresponding array, together with the appropriate time stamp information. The total space that is used by this method is proportional to the total number of pointer changes during all the updates. There are balancing scheme for search trees that guarantee a constant number of pointer changes per update (either in the amortized or the expected sense). Using such a balancing scheme the total space for this fat node persistent structure is proportional to the size of the ephemeral structure plus the number of update operations, which is the best what we can hope for. However, the query time bound may increase by a factor of $O(\log m)$, where m is the number of updates. Why? When we want to follow a pointer during a query we first need to identify the time-correct version of this pointer, which we can only do by (binary) searching the array of the corresponding pointer field. Thus the cost of following one pointer is not constant any more, but logarithmic.

Driscoll et al. invented an interesting way of combining the path copying and the fat node method. The idea is to grow nodes only to some constant "fatness," and after that split the node. This is somewhat reminiscent of fractional cascading. Interestingly this simple idea suffices to create a persistent search tree with logarithmic update time, logarithmic query time in the presence and the past, and only linear space usage.

There are additional research issues regarding persistence [14], for instance the idea of allowing not just queries but also updates in the past (so-called full persistence). This immediately causes the phenomenon of non-linear time, i.e. time is not a total order any more, but a partial order, and it becomes difficult to specify for queries in the past which "past" is actually intended. One of the most outstanding applications of persistent search trees is so-called planar point location [15].

6   Randomization

25 years ago randomization was not particularly prevalent in computer science. Nowadays it is ubiquitous and appears in almost all subfields of computing, especially in algorithms, and of course in data structures. There is a multitude of data structures that rely on randomization, especially in comptuational geometry. We will discuss only two particularly simple randomized data structure, which as Ketan Mulmuley pointed out in his book [16] exemplify two particular approaches to applying randomization. Both of these data structures realize the abstract data type "sorted sequence." The first one are so-called skip lists [17], the second one are randomized search trees [18], also sometimes called treaps.

Skip lists: Consider a sorted sequence S of n keys stored in a singly linked list L_0. Searching for a key in L_0 would take time $O(n)$ in the worst case. To speed this up take a random sample of expected pn elements of S (p some constant between 0 and 1), and arrange them in sorted order in a simply linked list L_1. Connect the elements of L_1 to the corresponding element in L_0. Now consider a search for some key x: first search for it in L_1; if you find it there, you are done; if you don't find it you identify two consecutive nodes u and v in L_1 whose keys span an interval that contains x; the expected number of nodes in L_0 between the nodes corresponding to u and v is $1/p - 1 = O(1)$. Thus after having "located" x in L_1 it only takes expected constant additional effort to locate x in L_0. How do you locate x in L_1? If L_1 has constant size, then by sequential search, otherwise you apply the same sampling method recursively.

Thus skip lists can be viewed as a logarithmic height tower of coarser and coarser random samples, and a search starts at the coarsest level and repeatedly descends to the next finer level with constant expected effort, resulting in an $O(\log n)$ expected overall search effort. This approch has been transferred to many other query problems, e.g. [19]. Skip lists allow various update operations with similarly fast expected performance. They admit rather simple implementations.

Randomized Search Trees: It is well known that if a sequence of n keys is inserted in an initially empty binary search tree via the usual insertion algorithm and this sequence is in random order, then the resulting tree can be expected to be reasonably balanced. How can this "random insertion order" be simulated for every order? Imagine that in the above setup every inserted key stores with it also its insertion time. It can easily be seen that now the resulting tree must be a min-heap with respect to the insertion times and a search tree with respect to the keys. Now consider a set S of items, each being a pair *(key,priority)*. Define the treap for S to be a tree T with one node for eash item in S, so that T is a search tree with respect to the keys and a heap with respect to the priorities. Update operations for such a treap can easily be designed. For storing a set K of keys in a treap I have the freedom to choose for each key a priority. If I choose this to be a random number, then in effect this approach simulates the "random insertion order" that we talked about, irrespective of the order in which the keys in K are actually inserted in to the treap.

For just about every binary search tree operation thinkable randomized search trees match the best worst case performance of any tree strategy in terms of their expected performance. Randomized search trees are easy to implement and it is even possible to do this without using space to store priorities.

7   Hashing

Hashing is a well-known class of methods for realizing a dictionay abstract data type. Already a few years before the first FSTTCS conference Carter and Wegmann [20] came up with the concept of *universal hashing*, which allowed to do hashing with probabilistic performance guarantees that were not based on assumed input distributions but only rested on the assumption that random numbers can be fairly generated. Universal hashing achieves constant expected time lookup and update operations, however the worst case is essentially logarithmic with high probability. During the first years of the FSTTCS conference series Fredman, Komlós, and Szemerédi [21] gave an ingenious construction that showed that using universal hashing it was possible to do "perfect" hashing. This hashing is perfect in the sense that worst case lookup time is constant and the space usage is linear. However, this worked only for the static case where a table could be built once and for all and no updates would happen. Later Dietzfelbinger et al. [22] by judicious application of automatic dynamization techniques showed that perfect hashing could be made dynamic. However, their method is not exactly simple or simple to implement.

A very interesting recent development is the notion of "cuckoo hashing" proposed by Pagh and Rodler [23] which promises to be a substantially simpler realization of dynamic perfect hashing. The idea is to use two hash functions h_1 and h_2, and each key x is stored either in location $h_1(x)$ or $h_2(x)$. This immediately gurantees constant lookup time, since at most two table locations need to be checked. The same holds for deletions. Insertions proceed by possibly repeatedly "bumping" elements already stored in the table and moving them to their other possible location. Pagh and Radler can show that if the load factor is not too high and the hash functions are truly random, then the expected insertion time is constant also. It is an interesting open problem to replace this perfect randomness requirement on the hash functions by something more reasonable.

8   Transdichotomy

The word "transdichotomy" refers to going beyond the usual binary comparisons that are typically used in searching or priority data structures. The term was introduced by Fredman and Willard in their seminal paper [24]. The main idea is to exploit the parallelism that is inherent in operations that act in constant time on words that contain many bits. A bitwise OR operation of two 64 bit words can for instance really be viewed as 64 operations on 1 bit words done in parallel, or also as 8 operations on 8 bit words. With this insight it is for instance not too hard to come up with a way of doing binary search in a sequence of 8 ordered 7-bit numbers in essentially a single 64-bit word operations. This idea requires that we deal with relatively short strings, however typically input strings are about word sized. Fortunately a number of "range reduction" mechanisms have been developed that allow to transform problems on long bitstrings to problems on short bitstrings. The oldest nontrivial reduction of this kind was developed by van Emde Boas [25].

Considerable progress has been made in this area during the last years. For instance, it was shown that in an ordered dictionary a worst case search cost and amortized update cost of $O(\sqrt{\log n / \log \log n})$ is possible and even a matching lower bound was shown. We refer the reader to the survey article [26] for further details in this fascinating area.

9 Implementations

The last 25 years have seen a tremendous effort transferring the theoretical insights in data structure research to actual implementations. The most prominent of these projects, at least from the theoreticians point of view, may have been the LEDA project [27], since it has been a very long term project driven by theory research and in turn driving some of that research. However, this is not the place to either list all such systems or dwell on their virtues and vices. We simply refer the reader to the repository `http://www.cs.sunysb.edu/~algorith/` maintained by Steven S. Skiena at SUNY Stony Brook.

10 Conclusions

There are many topics in data structures that we have not touched such as succinct data structures, external data structure, cache oblivious ones, kinetic data structures, competitive analysis, data structures for geometric problems, and so on. All of those areas have taken tremendous strides in the last 25 years. It will be interesting to see what the developments will take place until the 50th FSTTCS.

References

1. Mehta, Sahni, eds.: Handbook of Data Structures and Applications. Chapman & Hall/CRC (2005)
2. Sleator, D.D., Tarjan, R.E.: Self-adjusting binary search trees. J. ACM **32** (1985) 652–686

3. Fredman, M.L., Tarjan, R.E.: Fibonacci heaps and their uses in improved network optimization algorithms. J. ACM **34** (1987) 596–615
4. Tarjan, R.E.: Amortized computational complexity. SIAM Journal on Algebraic and Discrete Methods **6** (1985) 306–318
5. Bentley, J.L., Saxe, J.B.: Decomposable searching problems i: Static-to-dynamic transformation. J. Algorithms **1** (1980) 301–358
6. Overmars, M.H.: The design of dynamic data structure. Volume 156 of LNCS. Springer Verlag (1983)
7. Kirkpatrick, D.G.: Efficient computation of continuous skeletons. In: FOCS. (1979) 18–27
8. Chazelle, B., Guibas, L.J.: Fractional cascading: I. a data structuring technique. Algorithmica **1** (1986) 133–162
9. Chazelle, B., Guibas, L.J.: Fractional cascading: Ii. applications. Algorithmica **1** (1986) 163–191
10. Cole, R.: Searching and storing similar lists. J. Algorithms **7** (1986) 202–220
11. Sen, S.: Fractional cascading revisited. J. Algorithms **19** (1995) 161–172
12. Mehlhorn, K., Näher, S.: Dynamic fractional cascading. Algorithmica **5** (1990) 215–241
13. Driscoll, J.R., Sarnak, N., Sleator, D.D., Tarjan, R.E.: Making data structures persistent. J. Comput. Syst. Sci. **38** (1989) 86–124
14. Sarnak, N.: Persistend Data Structures. PhD thesis, New York University (1986)
15. Sarnak, N., Tarjan, R.E.: Planar point location using persistent search trees. Commun. ACM **29** (1986) 669–679
16. Mulmuley, K.: Computational Geometry: An Introduction through Randomized Algorithms. Prentice Hall (1993)
17. Pugh, W.: Skip lists: A probabilistic alternative to balanced trees. Commun. ACM **33** (1990) 668–676
18. Seidel, R., Aragon, C.R.: Randomized search trees. Algorithmica **16** (1996) 464–497
19. Eppstein, D., Goodrich, M.T., Sun, J.Z.: The skip quadtree: a simple dynamic data structure for multidimensional data. In: Symposium on Computational Geometry. (2005) 296–305
20. Carter, J.L., Wegman, M.N.: Universal classes of hash functions. JCSS **18** (1979) 143–154
21. Fredman, M.L., Komlós, J., Szemerédi, E.: Storing a sparse table with 0(1) worst case access time. J. ACM **31** (1984) 538–544
22. Dietzfelbinger, M., Karlin, A.R., Mehlhorn, K., auf der Heide, F.M., Rohnert, H., Tarjan, R.E.: Dynamic perfect hashing: Upper and lower bounds. SIAM J. Comput. **23** (1994) 738–761
23. Pagh, R., Rodler, F.F.: Cuckoo hashing. J. Algorithms **51** (2004) 122–144
24. Fredman, M.L., Willard, D.E.: Trans-dichotomous algorithms for minimum spanning trees and shortest paths. J. Comput. Syst. Sci. **48** (1994) 533–551
25. van Emde Boas, P.: Preserving order in a forest in less than logarithmic time and linear space. Inf. Process. Lett. **6** (1977) 80–82
26. Andersson, A.: Searchin dn priority queues in $o(\log n)$ time. In Mehta, Sahni, eds.: Handbook of Data Structures and Applications. Chapman & Hall/CRC (2005)
27. Mehlhorn, K., Näher, S.: Leda: A platform for combinatorial and geometric computing. Commun. ACM **38** (1995) 96–102

Inference Systems for Logical Algorithms*

Natarajan Shankar

Computer Science Laboratory
SRI International
Menlo Park CA 94025 USA
shankar@csl.sri.com
http://www.csl.sri.com/~shankar/
Phone: +1 (650) 859-5272 Fax: +1 (650) 859-2844

Abstract. Logical algorithms are defined in terms of individual computation steps that are based on logical inferences. We present a uniform framework for formalizing logical algorithms based on inference systems. We present inference systems for algorithms such as resolution, the Davis–Putnam–Logemann–Loveland procedure, equivalence and congruence closure, and satisfiability modulo theories. The paper is intended as an introduction to the use of inference systems for studying logical algorithms.

1 Introduction

Automated reasoning is an established branch of computing with many noteworthy contributions. It is also a vast subject so that even the two massive volumes of *The Handbook of Automated Reasoning* [RV01] do not succeed in capturing the breadth of the subject. Recently, automated reasoning technology has not only witnessed dramatic improvements in efficiency and functionality, it has also found a wide range of applications in solving open mathematical problems, hardware and software verification, program analysis, and constraint solving. We briefly survey some of the recent developments focusing on logical algorithms in which individual computation steps can be seen as logical inferences. Such logical algorithms are given uniform presentations and proofs in terms of inference systems which are used to clearly separate the logic behind the algorithm from the computational details. Inference systems also make it easy to explore inference strategies, optimizations, extensions such as proof and witness generation, and also composition mechanisms.

The development of metamathematics [Kle52] in the first half of the twentieth century coupled with the growth of computer technology in the late 1940s and 1950s laid the foundation for the development of automated reasoning. The significant landmarks in the first twenty-five years of the field include

– 1954: Martin Davis' implementation of Presburger's decision procedure for the first-order theory of addition over the integers [Dav57].

---

* This research was supported NSF Grants CCR-ITR-0326540 and CCR-ITR-0325808.

R. Ramanujam and S. Sen (Eds.): FSTTCS 2005, LNCS 3821, pp. 60–78, 2005.

- 1956: Newell, Shaw, and Simon's Logic Theorist program which introduces key techniques such as substitution, forward and backward chaining, and subgoaling [NSS57].
- 1960: Davis and Putnam's search procedure for propositional satisfiability. The practical variant of this procedure due to Davis, Logemann, and Loveland is still the basis of most modern satisfiability solvers [DP60a, DLL62].
- 1962: McCarthy's proposal of automated proof checking as a basic challenge [McC62].
- 1963: Robinson's resolution principle for proof search in first-order logic [Rob65a].
- 1965: Various strategies for resolution proof search such as hyper-resolution [Rob65b] and set of support [WRC65].
- 1966: Knuth and Bendix's completion procedure solving word problems in an equational theory by transforming the theory into a confluent and terminating rewrite system [KB70].
- 1966: Buchberger's method for constructing a Gröbner basis for computing membership in a polynomial ideal [Buc76].
- 1970: de Bruijn's Automath framework for proof checking![dB80].
- 1971: The invention of logic programming based on resolution applied to Horn clauses by Kowalski and Colmerauer [Coh88].
- 1972: Milner's LCF framework [GMW79] for automated proof checking which is at the foundation of a number of current systems including HOL [GM93], HOL Light [Har96], Coq [Tea05], Isabelle [Pau94], Lego [LP92], and Nuprl [CAB+86].
- 1973: Boyer and Moore's induction theorem prover [BM79] which has since evolved into Thm, Nqthm, and now ACL2 [KMM00].
- 1977: Bledsoe's critique of resolution theorem proving and espousal of an alternative approach based on "natural deduction" [Ble77].
- 1977: Kozen and Shostak's congruence closure algorithm [Koz77, Sho78] for deciding uniform word problems in the theory of equality, and subsequent optimization by Downey, Sethi, and Tarjan [DST80].
- 1979: Nelson and Oppen's method [NO79] for combining ground decision procedures, and subsequent specialization by Shostak [Sho84] to solvable and canonizable theories.

In the last twenty five years, there has been an explosion of work in the construction of theorem-proving systems. Some of these, such as McCune's Otter and EQP, have been used to solve open problems in certain branches of mathematics [McC97]. The TPTP problem repository [SS98] and the CASC competition held at the Conference on Automated Deduction have made it possible to evaluate theorem proving software and quantify progress. The degree and efficiency of automation has been greatly increased through powerful indexing techniques, the combination of different techniques such as model checking, induction, and rewriting,

In the rest of the paper, we describe a framework for presenting and reasoning about logical algorithms called inference systems. We introduce the inference systems framework in Section 2. Examples of inference systems for propositional satisfiability are presented in Section 3. Systems for reasoning about equality are covered in Section 4. We focus on the combination of theory-based constraint solving and satisfiability in Section 5. Future work and conclusions are summarized in Section 6. The paper is a tutorial introduction to some key logical algorithms and the inference systems framework for describing and studying these algorithms.

2   Inference Systems

An inference structure is a pair $\langle \Psi, \vdash \rangle$ consisting of a set of logical states Ψ and a binary inference relation $\vdash$ on logical states. If $\psi \vdash \theta$ holds, then ψ is the *premise* state and θ is the *conclusion* state. Corresponding to an inference system, there is a set of models $\mathcal{M}$, so that when $M \models \psi$, the model M from $\mathcal{M}$ satisfies ψ. If there is a model $M \in \mathcal{M}$ such that $M \models \psi$, then ψ is said to be *satisfiable*. If ψ is satisfiable iff θ is satisfiable, then ψ and θ are *equisatisfiable*. An inference relation $\vdash$ is said to be *conservative* if ψ and θ are equisatisfiable whenever $\psi \vdash \theta$.[1]

The inference relation $\vdash$ is said to be *well-founded* if there are no infinite sequences of the form $\langle \psi_i | i \geq 0 \rangle$ such that $\psi_i \vdash \psi_{i+1}$ for $i \geq 0$. An inference structure with a well-founded inference relation is said to be *progressive*. Given an inference structure $\langle \Psi, \vdash \rangle$, a state $\psi \in \Psi$ is *reducible* if there is a $\theta \in \Psi$ such that $\psi \vdash \theta$. Otherwise, ψ is said to be *irreducible*. There is a special state $\perp$ in Ψ that is unsatisfiable and irreducible. An inference structure is *canonizing* if every irreducible state different from $\perp$ is satisfiable. An *inference system* is an inference structure that is conservative, progressive, and canonizing.

With respect to an inference system $\langle \Psi, \vdash \rangle$, the operation *satisfiable*(ψ) takes a state ψ and returns $\perp$ if it is unsatisfiable, and $\top$, otherwise.

$$satisfiable(\perp) = \perp$$
$$satisfiable(\psi) = satisfiable(\psi'), \text{ where } \psi \vdash \psi'$$
$$satisfiable(\psi) = \top, \text{ otherwise.}$$

If $\mathcal{I}$ is an inference system $\langle \Psi, \vdash \rangle$, then we write *satisfiable*$_\mathcal{I}(\psi)$ to identify the set of states and the inference relation.

Theorem 1. *If the inference relation $\vdash$ is decidable, then an inference system $\langle \Psi, \vdash \rangle$ yields a decision procedure for satisfiability.*

Proof. The procedure *satisfiable* is terminating since in the recursive call ψ' is smaller than ψ according to a well-founded ordering, namely $\vdash$.

Then, by well-founded induction, we can prove that *satisfiable*$(\psi) = \top$ iff ψ is satisfiable. In the base case, when ψ is irreducible, by canonicity, ψ is satisfiable

---

[1] Most of the inference systems we present are *strongly conservative* in that each inference step actually preserves models rather than just satisfiability.

iff $\psi \neq \perp$. In the induction step, by conservativity, ψ and ψ' are equisatisfiable, and by the induction hypothesis, $satisfiable(\psi') = \top$ iff ψ' is satisfiable. $\blacksquare$

An inference state ψ is typically of the form $\kappa_1 | \ldots | \kappa_n$ for *configurations* κ_i and $0 \leq n$. A model $M \in \mathcal{M}$ satisfies $\kappa_1 | \ldots | \kappa_n$ iff there is an i, $1 \leq i \leq n$, such that $M \models \kappa_i$. The $|$ operator is associative and commutative. The state $\perp$ can be defined as the empty set of configurations, but there is also a special unsatisfiable configuration $\perp$ such that $\perp|\psi = \psi$. A configuration typically includes a set of formulas along with other, possibly non-logical, information needed to define the valid inference steps. Such a configuration is satisfied by M if each associated formula is satisfied by M. The inference relation must be *monotonic* so that if $\psi \vdash \theta$, the $\psi|\psi' \vdash \theta|\psi'$. Many inference systems are *local*: $\psi \vdash \psi'$ iff for some $\kappa \in \psi$, $\kappa \vdash \theta$, and $\psi' = (\psi - \{\kappa\})|\theta$.

We can now examine some examples of decision procedures given in the form of inference systems. Inference structures are defined by specifying the well-formed set of logical states Ψ and a set of inference rules, each of the form $\frac{\Phi_1}{\Phi_2}$. An inference step $\psi_1 \vdash \psi_2$ holds if ψ_1 is an instance of Φ_1 obtained by substituting syntactic expressions of the appropriate type for the metavariables, and ψ_2 is the corresponding instance of Φ_2. If the inference structure given by the inference rules is progressive, conservative, and canonizing, then it is an inference system.

3 Propositional Satisfiability

Given a set of propositional variables P, a propositional formula ϕ has the syntax

$$\phi := P \mid \neg\phi \mid \phi_1 \vee \phi_2 \mid \phi_1 \wedge \phi_2 \mid \phi_1 \supset \phi_2$$

The interpretation is as expected with each model M mapping formulas to $\{\top, \perp\}$. We present two styles of propositional inference systems: resolution and the Davis–Putnam–Logemann–Loveland (DPLL) procedure [DP60b, DLL62]. We do not examine proof construction for these propositional inference systems since their inference rules can already be seen as proof rules. For example, the resolution calculus is one where the sequents contain only literals and cut is the only inference rule. The **DPLL** inference system corresponds to a one-sided sequent calculus on clauses with the cut rule.

3.1 Resolution

Many proof search procedures are based on the resolution rule of inference. Though resolution is not an effective method for propositional satisfiability, it is quite powerful as a first-order proof search method. We focus on the propositional case and present an inference system for ordered resolution. Here each configuration is a finite set of clauses, and each clause is a (possibly empty) disjunction of literals, where each literal is either a positive atom p or a negative atom $\neg p$. The complement $\bar{l}$ of a literal l is defined so that $\bar{p} = \neg p$ and $\overline{\neg p} = p$. Since we interpret the configuration as the conjunction of its clauses, we

Res	$\dfrac{\Gamma, l \vee C_1, \bar{l} \vee C_2}{\Gamma, l \vee C_1, \bar{l} \vee C_2, C_1 \vee C_2}$	$\begin{array}{l} C_1 \vee C_2 \notin \Gamma \\[4pt] C_1 \vee C_2 \text{ is not tautological} \end{array}$
Contrad	$\dfrac{\Gamma}{\bot}$ if $p, \neg p \in \Gamma$ for some p	

Fig. 1. Ordered Resolution Inference System **ORes**

are essentially assuming that the input is given in conjunctive normal form. We assume an ordering $\succ$ on atoms so that each clause is sorted in decreasing order of the atoms appearing in the literals. This means the head literal l of a clause $l \vee C$ is the maximal literal. Any tautological clauses of the form $l \vee \neg l \vee A$ are automatically deleted from the clause set. Also, duplicate literals in a clause are eliminated so that $l \vee l \vee C$ is simplified to $l \vee C$. The inference structure **ORes** for ordered resolution is specified by the inference rules Figure 1 so that a state consists of a set of clauses, and each inference step $\psi_1 \vdash \psi_2$ must be an instance of an inference rule in Figure 1.

Theorem 2. *The **ORes** inference structure is a local inference system.*

Proof. Each of the rules in **ORes** has exactly one premise and one conclusion configuration. Conservativity is easily established for these rules since any model of the premise clauses satisfies the conclusion clauses and vice-versa. The progressiveness property follows easily since there are only a bounded number of distinct clauses in a given set of atoms, and each resolution step generates a new clause.

To show that the inference rules are canonizing, we construct a model M satisfying a given irreducible, non-$\bot$ state Γ. Assume that the configuration contains n distinct atoms ordered as $p_1, \ldots, p_N$, and define M as M_N, where each M_i provides a truth assignment for the atoms $p_1, \ldots, p_i$ such that all the clauses in Γ in these atoms are satisfied. First, define $M_0 = \emptyset$. Then, assuming the induction hypothesis that M_i satisfies all the clauses in Γ made up of atoms from $p_0, \ldots, p_i$, we can construct M_{i+1} as follows. If p_{i+1} is the maximal literal in a clause $p_{i+1} \vee C$ and $\neg p_{i+1}$ occurs as the maximal literal in $\neg p_{i+1} \vee D$, then by the **Res** rule, the clause $C \vee D$ occurs in Γ or is tautological. In either case, if $M_i \models C$, then let $M_{i+1} = M_i\{p_{i+1} \to \bot\}$. Otherwise, if $M_i \models D$, then let $M_{i+1} = M_i\{p_{i+1} \to \top\}$. Note that M_{i+1} satisfies all the clauses in the atoms $p_1, \ldots, p_{i+1}$. If $\neg p_{i+1}$ does not occur as the maximal literal in any clause in Γ, then we define M_{i+1} as $M_i\{p_{i+1} \to \top\}$ so that M_{i+1} clearly satisfies all the clauses in the atoms $p_1, \ldots, p_{i+1}$. Similarly, if p_{i+1} does not occur as the maximal literal, then we define M_{i+1} as $M_i\{p_{i+1} \to \bot\}$. Clearly, M_N then satisfies Γ. ∎

The **Ores** system can be used to demonstrate the unsatisfiability of the same example as in the previous subsection with $p \succ q$.

$$\dfrac{\overbrace{p \vee q, \neg p \vee q, p \vee \neg q, \neg p \vee \neg q}^{\Gamma}}{\dfrac{\dfrac{q, \Gamma}{\neg q, q, \Gamma}}{\bot}}$$

$\quad$ Res

$\quad$ Contrad

$\quad$ Res

There are many variants of the resolution system above. One important optimization is the subsumption rule. Given a clause C, let $lits(C)$ represent the set of literals that are disjuncts of C.

$$\boxed{\mathbf{Sub}\left|\dfrac{C, C', \Gamma}{C, \Gamma}\quad lits(C) \subset lits(C')\right.}$$

If we add this rule to the **ORes** inference system, we lose progressiveness. However, if we also strengthen the **Res** rule so that it never introduces a subsumed clause to the conclusion state, then progressiveness is maintained as in the proof of Theorem 2.

$$\boxed{\mathbf{Res}\left|\dfrac{\Gamma, l \vee C_1, \bar{l} \vee C_2}{\Gamma, l \vee C_1, \bar{l} \vee C_2, C_1 \vee C_2}\quad \text{for all } C \in \Gamma : lits(C) \nsubseteq lits(C_1 \vee C_2)\right.}$$

The canonicity argument in the proof of Theorem 2 does need to be revised since when $p_{i+1} \vee C$ and $\neg p_{i+1} \vee D$ are in Γ, we can only infer that either $C \vee D$ is tautological or some clause subsuming $C \vee D$ also appears in Γ. However, this is sufficient for completing the proof as given.

There are many variants of resolution which can also be similarly presented within the inference system framework, but we omit these from the present description.

3.2   The Davis-Putnam-Logemann-Loveland Procedure

The original Davis–Putnam procedure [DP60a] for propositional satisfiability contained a resolution rule that proved to be expensive in terms of space usage. Since this rule was redundant, it was dropped to obtain the Davis–Putnam–Logemann–Loveland (DPLL) procedure [DLL62]. DPLL employs the same representation as resolution but instead of deriving new clauses, it searches for a satisfying truth assignment. The inference system shown in Figure 2 is a simplified form of the DPLL procedure. The **Split** rule splits a single configuration Γ into two configuration l, Γ and $\bar{l}, \Gamma$. Since any unit clause, that is a clause consisting of a single literal, must be satisfied for the configuration to be satisfied, the corresponding truth assignment is propagated. The **Unit** rule is a form of resolution where one of the participating clauses is a unit clause.

Split	$$\dfrac{\Gamma}{p,\Gamma \mid \neg p,\Gamma}\quad p,\neg p \notin \Gamma, p \text{ occurs in } \Gamma$$
Contrad	$$\dfrac{\Gamma,\bar{l},l}{\bot}$$
Unit	$$\dfrac{\Gamma,C \vee \bar{l},l}{\Gamma,C,l}\quad C \text{ nonempty}$$

Fig. 2. A Simplified DPLL Inference System **DPLL**

Theorem 3. *The **DPLL** inference structure is a local inference system.*

Proof. The **DPLL** rules are clearly conservative.

The inference rules yield a progressive system. Assume without loss of generality that the atoms appearing in the formulas are chosen from $p_0,\ldots,p_{N-1}$ and that $U(\Gamma)$ is the number of distinct unit clauses occurring in the clause set Γ. Let $m_1(\Gamma) = 2*N - |U(\Gamma)|$ and $m_2(\Gamma) = \Sigma_{C\in\Gamma}|lits(C)|$. In each inference step, $\Gamma \vdash (\Gamma_1|\ldots|\Gamma_n)$, either $m_1(\Gamma_i) < m_1(\Gamma)$ or $n = 1$, $m_1(\Gamma_1) = m_1(\Gamma)$, and $m_2(\Gamma_1) < m_2(\Gamma)$.

The canonicity of the inference rules is established by arguing that when none of the inference rules is applicable, either the state is $\bot$ or is a state containing configurations that consist solely of unit clauses. Since **Contrad** rule is inapplicable, each of these configurations is satisfiable. ∎

We illustrate the **DPLL** inference system on the same example as before. Here, the unit propagation steps are executed to completion as **Unit*** following each **Split** step.

$$
\begin{array}{c}
\overbrace{p \vee q, \neg p \vee q, p \vee \neg q, \neg p \vee \neg q}^{\Gamma}\\
\hline
p,\Gamma \mid \neg p,\Gamma\\
\hline
p,q,\neg q, p \vee q, p \vee \neg q \mid \neg p,\Gamma\\
\hline
\bot \mid \neg p,\Gamma\\
\hline
\neg p, q, \neg q, \neg p \vee q, \neg p \vee \neg q\\
\hline
\bot
\end{array}
\quad
\begin{array}{l}
\text{Split}\\[4pt]
\text{Unit}^*\\[4pt]
\text{Contrad}\\[4pt]
\text{Unit}^*\\[4pt]
\text{Contrad}
\end{array}
$$

The **Delete** rule shown below is not needed for completeness but is useful for discarding clauses that are already satisfied by any truth assignment satisfying the unit clauses in the configuration.

Delete	$$\dfrac{l, l \vee C, \Gamma}{l,\Gamma}$$

3.3   Conflict-Directed Backjumping

Implementations of **DPLL** typically follow a depth-first strategy. The configuration is split into the clause set G and the partial assignment κ. Following an application of the **Split** rule, one of the configurations (i.e., branches), say $G; \kappa, p$ is explored completely before the other branch is considered. For the chosen branch of the **Split** rule, the **Unit** rule is applied exhaustively (unit propagation), unless a contradiction (conflict) is found. If a conflict is reached as a result of splitting $G; \kappa$ to obtain $G; \kappa, p$, then a conflict clause C is constructed so that $G \cup \overline{C}$ is unsatisfiable, where $\overline{C} = lits(C)$ and $\overline{M} = \{\overline{l} | l \in M\}$ for a set of literals M. The conflict clause is used to *backjump* to $G, C; \kappa'$ where κ' extends a prefix of κ with additional unit clauses derived using C. The addition of conflict clauses together with backjumping can simulate backtracking.

Conflict-directed backjumping can be captured within a *non-local* inference system. The inference rules **DPLL(CDB)** for DPLL augmented with conflict-directed backjumping are shown in Figure 3. Each configuration in the state is represented as a pair of the clause set G and the decision configuration κ. Since the clause set G is shared by all of the configurations, the state is represented as $G \otimes (\kappa_1 | \ldots | \kappa_n)$ abbreviating $G; \kappa_1 | \ldots | G; \kappa_n$. Each κ_i is a sequence of the form $P_0; P_1; \ldots; P_m$, where each P_j is itself a sequence of literals. The set P_0 consists of the unit consequences of the input clauses, whereas each sequence P_i for $1 \leq i \leq m$ consists of the decision literal followed by the unit consequences. If for $1 \leq i \leq n$, each P_i is nonempty, then the corresponding sequence of decision literals is represented as $\langle P_1(0), \ldots, P_n(0) \rangle$. The sequence κ is overloaded to also represent the set of literals appearing in it, as is also done with a sequence element P. Given κ of the form $P_0; \ldots; P_n$ and a sequence Q of literals, $\kappa \circ Q$ represents $P_0; \ldots; (P_n \circ Q)$, where $P_n \circ Q$ is the result of concatenating the sequences P_n and Q.

For a set of clauses G and a set of literals L, the sequence of unit clauses implied by $G; L$ is written as $UC(G; L)$ is defined to return the smallest set of literals M so that for any clause $C \in G$, $k = |lits(C) - (\overline{L} \cup \overline{M})|$, $k \neq 1$. Clearly, $L \cap M = \emptyset$. Let $\mathbf{M}$ represent a sequence of the elements in the set of literals M. Note that $UC(G; L)$ can be computed using an auxiliary inference system using the **Unit** rule from Figure 2. We write $\kappa' \sqsubseteq \kappa$ if κ' is a prefix of κ. Let N be the number of distinct atoms in the input clause set G_0. Given a sequence κ of the form $P_0, P_1; \ldots; P_N$, define $m_3(\kappa)$ and $m_4(\kappa)$ as follows.

$$m_3(P_0; \ldots; P_N) = (2 * N + 1)^N * |P_0| + \ldots + (2 * N + 1)^{(N-i)} * |P_i| + \ldots |P_N|$$
$$m_4(\kappa) = (2 * N + 1)^{N+1} - m_3(\kappa)$$

For example, if $k = 3$ and $\kappa = \langle \rangle; \langle p_1 \rangle; \langle \neg p_2 \rangle; \langle p_3, \neg p_1 \rangle$, then $m_3(\kappa) = 49 + 7 + 2 = 58$ $m_4(\kappa) = 2401 - 58 = 2343$. If κ is of the form $P_0; P_1; \ldots; P_i$ for some $i < N$, then $\hat{\kappa}$ is the result of padding κ with a suffix sequence $N - i$ empty sets. We write $\kappa \prec \kappa'$ if $\kappa = P_0; P_1; \ldots; P_m$ and $\kappa' = P_0'; P_1'; \ldots; P_m'$ where $P_i(0) = P_i'(0)$ for $1 \leq i \leq m$, $\kappa \subseteq \kappa'$, and $m_3(\hat{\kappa}) < m_3(\hat{\kappa'})$.

The inference rules in Figure 3 use the **ORes** inference system and unit closure as auxiliary systems. The **Split** rule is as in **DPLL**, whereas the unit

Split	$$\dfrac{G \otimes (\kappa|\psi)}{G \otimes (\kappa; \langle p \rangle|\kappa; \langle \neg p \rangle|\psi)} \quad \begin{array}{l} p \text{ occurs in } G \\ p, \neg p \notin \kappa \end{array}$$
Unitclose	$$\dfrac{G \otimes (\kappa|\psi)}{G \otimes (\kappa \circ \boldsymbol{Q}|\psi)} \quad \text{for } Q = UC(G; \kappa) \neq \emptyset$$
Backjump	$$\dfrac{G \otimes (\kappa|\psi)}{(G, C) \otimes (\kappa' \circ \boldsymbol{Q}|\psi)} \quad \begin{array}{l} \kappa' \sqsubseteq \kappa, \\ Q = UC(G, C; \kappa') \neq \emptyset \\ satisfiable_{\mathbf{ORes}}(G \cup \overline{C}) = \bot \end{array}$$
Delete	$$\dfrac{(G, C) \otimes \psi}{G \otimes \psi} \quad \text{if } satisfiable_{\mathbf{ORes}}(G \cup \overline{C}) = \bot$$
Subsume	$$\dfrac{G \otimes (\kappa|\psi)}{G \otimes \psi} \quad \text{if for some } \kappa' \in \psi, \kappa \prec \kappa'$$
Contrad	$$\dfrac{G \otimes (\kappa|\psi)}{G \otimes \psi} \quad p, \neg p \in G; \kappa \text{ for some } p$$

Fig. 3. The Inference Rules for **DPLL(CDB)**

propagation steps are packaged into the **Unitclose** rule. The backjumping rule **Backjump** augments G with a lemma clause C while replacing κ with a prefix κ' together with new unit clauses Q derived from G, C and κ'. The **Delete** rule drops a clause that is known to be derivable from the others in G, whereas the **Subsume** rule drops a decision configuration that is already derivable from another configuration.

Theorem 4. *The inference structure **DPLL(CDB)** is an inference system.*

Proof. The inference rules of **DPLL(CDB)** are conservative. Any model of $G \otimes (\kappa_1| \ldots |\kappa_n)$ is a model of G since each model of G is a model of some κ_i. In each inference step $G \otimes \psi \vdash G' \otimes \psi'$, we have that $G \iff G'$ so that any model of G' is a model of G and vice-versa.

The progressiveness property holds since each inference step from $G; \psi$ to $G'; \psi'$ either deletes an element κ of ψ to possibly replace it with a zero or more configurations $\kappa_1, \ldots, \kappa_n$ such that $m_4(\hat{\kappa}_i) < m_4(\hat{\kappa})$ for $1 \leq i \leq n$, or ψ is held fixed and $|G'| < |G|$.

Canonicity also holds: when no further rules are applicable to a state $G \otimes (\kappa_1| \ldots |\kappa_n)$, then the literals in any of the κ_i yield a satisfying assignment for G. ∎

Nieuwenhuis, Oliveras, and Tinelli [NO05] give a formal presentation of the DPLL procedure with conflict-directed backjumping and lemma deletion in a form that is quite close to the usual depth-first search implementation. Our presentation uses the more general framework of inference systems. The depth-first search approach can be simulated by **DPLL(CDB)** using a strategy where

Split is always followed by **Unitclose** on the chosen branch, **Backjump** is always followed by **Subsume** steps to delete all configurations that are subsumed by the newly created one, and by restricting the application of the **Contrad** rule to the case where there is a singleton configuration κ in ψ of the form P_0.

4   Propagating Equality

We first consider an inference system for checking satisfiability with respect to equivalence constraints. These constraints are in the form of equalities and disequalities between variables. The equivalence constraints can be compiled into a union-find data structure that can be used to determine if any of the disequality constraints is contradicted. This basic inference system is extended to equality/disequality constraints over terms using the congruence closure algorithm.

4.1   Equivalence Constraints

Maintaining equivalence classes is a basic operation in many applications of computing. We present an inference system based on the union-find algorithm.

Assume an order $\leq$ over the set of variables. The state contains the input Γ which consists of equalities and disequalities between variables, and the *find* structure F which is a finite set of equalities between variables. The find structure F should be functional, that is, if $x = y$ and $x = y'$ in F, then $y \equiv y'$. A functional equality set can be used as a lookup table so that $F(x) = y$ if $x = y \in F$, and $F(x) = x$ if there is no y such that $x = y \in F$. The equality set F should also be acyclic so that the iterated closure of the lookup operation can be defined as follows.

$$F^*(x) = \begin{cases} x, & \text{if } F(x) \equiv x \\ F^*(F(x)), & \text{otherwise.} \end{cases}$$

For example, if F is $\{x = y, y = z, u = v\}$, then $F^*(x) = z$. Thus, for any x, $F^*(x)$ is the canonical representative of its equivalence class. The union operation merges two distinct equivalence classes by mapping the canonical representative of one class to that of the other.

$$union(F)(x, y) = F \cup \{x' = y'\}, \text{ where } x' \equiv F^*(x) \not\equiv F^*(y) \equiv y'$$

The inference system for equivalence is shown in Figure 4. Each configuration has the form $G; F; D$ where G contains the unprocessed inputs, F contains the find structure, and D contains the disequalities processed from the input. The **Delete** rule discards a redundant input equality. The **Merge** rule merges two distinct equivalence classes. The **Diseq** rule transfers a disequality from G to D. The **Contrad** rule is triggered when there is an input disequality constraint $x \neq y$ for x and y in the same equivalence class.

Theorem 5. *The inference structure **Eq** is an inference system.*

Delete	$\dfrac{x = y, G; F; D}{G; F; D}$ if $F^*(x) \equiv F^*(y)$
Merge	$\dfrac{x = y, G; F; D \quad \text{if } F^*(x) \not\equiv F^*(y)}{G; F'; D \qquad F' = union(F)(x,y)}$
Diseq	$\dfrac{x \neq y, G; F; D}{G; F; x \neq y, D}$
Contrad	$\dfrac{G; F; x \neq y, D}{\bot}$ if $F^*(x) = F^*(y)$

Fig. 4. An Inference System **Eq** for Equivalence

Proof. Since each rule application processes an input constraint, the progressiveness of the rules is straightforward. The rules yield a conservative inference structure since $F \implies x = F(x)$ and $F \implies x = F^*(x)$. The canonicity is established through the construction of a term model corresponding to an irreducible state so that each variable is mapped to its canonical representative $F^*(x)$. ∎

As an illustration of the **Eq**, we demonstrate the unsatisfiability of the formulas $x = y, u = v, x \neq z, z = y$.

$$\cfrac{\cfrac{\cfrac{\cfrac{x = y, u = v, x \neq z, z = y; \emptyset; \emptyset}{u = v, x \neq z, z = y; x = y; \emptyset}\ \text{Merge}}{x \neq z, z = y; x = y, u = v; \emptyset}\ \text{Merge}}{\cfrac{z = y; x = y, u = v; x \neq z}{\emptyset; x = y, u = v, z = y, x \neq z}\ \text{Diseq}}\ \text{Merge}}{\bot}\ \text{Contrad}$$

The construction of proofs corresponding to unsatisfiable inputs is carried out by tracking the input corresponding to each entry in F. For this purpose, we number the inputs so that the i'th input has the form $x =_{\langle i \rangle} y$ if it is an equality or $x \neq_{\langle i \rangle} y$ in the case of a disequality. Then the equality $y =_{\langle -i \rangle} x$ represents an application of the symmetry rule to $x =_{\langle i \rangle} y$. A sequence of positive and negative indices $x =_{\langle i_1, i_2, \ldots \rangle} y$ represents a series of applications of transitivity. Given input G of the form $x_1 =_{\langle 1 \rangle} y_1, \ldots, x_n =_{\langle n \rangle} y_n$, the judgment $G \models x =_\sigma y$ represents a proof:

- Either σ is empty and $x \equiv y$, or
- σ is of the form $j; \sigma'$ for $j > 0$ and input j is of the form $x =_{\langle j \rangle} z$ for some z, and $G \models z =_{\sigma'} y$, or $j = -j'$ for $j' > 0$, and input j' is of the form $z =_{\langle j' \rangle} x$, and $z =_{\sigma'} y$.

A slight modification of the **Eq** inference system makes it easy to maintain such proofs. Define $F\langle x \rangle$ to return an equality set equivalent to F in which x is the root of its equivalence class.

$$F\langle x\rangle = \begin{cases} F'\langle y\rangle, \\ \text{where } F' = (F - \{x =_{\langle i\rangle} y\}) \cup \{y =_{\langle -i\rangle} x\}, \text{ and } y \equiv F(x) \not\equiv x \\ F, \text{ otherwise.} \end{cases}$$

The union operation can then be redefined as below so that each equality in the find structure corresponds directly to an input equality constraint or its inverse.

$$union(F)(x =_{\langle i\rangle} y) = F\langle x\rangle \cup \{x =_{\langle i\rangle} x\}$$

Let G_0 represent the input component in the initial state ψ_0 of an inference, then in every state ψ of the form $G; F; D$ reachable from ψ_0 by valid inference steps, and form $x =_{\langle j\rangle} y \in F$, $G_0 \models x =_{\langle j\rangle} y$. In order to prove that $x = F^*(x)$, we define $\Pi^*(x)$ as follows.

$$\Pi^*(x) = \begin{cases} \langle\rangle, \text{ if } F(x) \equiv x \\ j; \Pi^*(y), \text{ if } x =_{\langle j\rangle} y \in F \end{cases}$$

Note that $G_0 \models x =_{\Pi^*(x)} F^*(x)$ for each state $G; F; D$ reachable from $G_0; \emptyset; \emptyset$ by means of valid inference steps in **Eq**. Then, whenever $F^*(x) \equiv F^*(y)$, we have $G_0 \models x_{\Pi^*(x);(\Pi^*(y))^-} y$, where $(\sigma)^-$ is the sequence obtained by negating each element of σ. Similarly $G_0 \vdash \perp_{j;\sigma}$ represents a proof contradiction if for some $x, y, x \neq_{\langle j\rangle} y \in G_0$ and $G_0 \models x =_\sigma y$.

The example above can now be repeated with proof annotations.

$$\frac{\dfrac{\dfrac{\dfrac{\dfrac{x =_{\langle 1\rangle} y, u =_{\langle 2\rangle} v, x \neq_{\langle 3\rangle} z, z =_{\langle 4\rangle} y; \emptyset; \emptyset}{u =_{\langle 2\rangle} v, x \neq_{\langle 3\rangle} z, z =_{\langle 4\rangle} y; x =_{\langle 1\rangle} y; \emptyset} \text{ Merge}}{x \neq_{\langle 3\rangle} z, z = \langle 4\rangle y; x =_{\langle 1\rangle} y, u =_{\langle 2\rangle} v; \emptyset} \text{ Merge}}{z =_{\langle 4\rangle} y; x =_{\langle 1\rangle} y, u =_{\langle 2\rangle} v; x \neq_{\langle 3\rangle} z} \text{ Diseq}}{\emptyset; x =_{\langle 1\rangle} y, u =_{\langle 2\rangle} v, z =_{\langle 4\rangle} y, x \neq_{\langle 3\rangle} z} \text{ Merge}}{\perp_{3;\langle 1,-4\rangle}} \text{ Contrad}$$

The proofs generated are irredundant in the sense that no premise that is used in a proof can be omitted, but these proofs are not minimal since the **Delete** rule discards inputs that might yield shorter proofs. The above proof construction is based on the proof-producing algorithms of de Moura, Rueß, and Shankar [dMRS04] and Nieuwenhuis and Oliveras [NO05].

4.2 Congruence Closure

The inference system **Eq** can be extended to checking satisfiability on equality and disequality constraints over terms. Here, in addition to the reflexivity, symmetry, and transitivity rules for equality, we also have a congruence rule for inferring $f(a_1, \ldots, a_n) = f(b_1, \ldots, b_n)$ from $a_i = b_i$ for $1 \leq i \leq n$.

The inference system **CC** is based on the congruence closure algorithm. The state now contains the set of input constraints G, the find equalities F, and

Delete	$\dfrac{x = y, G; F; D; U}{G; F; D; U}$ if $F^*(x) \equiv F^*(y)$
Abstract	$\dfrac{G[f(x_1, \ldots, x_n)]; F; D; U}{G[x]; F; D; x = f(x_1, \ldots, x_n), U}$ $\quad x \notin vars(G; F; D; U)$
Congruence	$\dfrac{G; F; D; U}{G; F'; D; U}$ $\begin{array}{l} x = f(x_1, \ldots, x_n) \in U, \\ y = f(y_1, \ldots, y_n) \in U, \\ F^*(x_i) \equiv F^*(y_i), \text{ for } 1 \leq i \leq n \\ F^*(x) \not\equiv F^*(y) \\ F' = union(f)(x, y) \end{array}$
Merge	$\dfrac{x = y, G; F; D; U}{G; F'; D; U}$ $\begin{array}{l} \text{if } F^*(x) \not\equiv F^*(y) \\ F' = union(F)(x, y) \end{array}$
Diseq	$\dfrac{x \neq y, G; F; D; U}{G; F; x \neq y, D; U}$
Contrad	$\dfrac{G; F; x \neq y, D; U}{\perp}$ if $F^*(x) \equiv F^*(y)$

Fig. 5. An Inference System **CC** for Congruence

a term map U that is a set of equalities of the form $x = f(x_1, \ldots, x_n)$. In addition to the **Delete, Merge, Diseq**, and **Contrad** rules from the **Eq** system, the **CC** inference system contains two rules for treating terms and inferring equality by congruence. The rule **Abstract** replaces a *flat* subterm of the form $f(x_1, \ldots, x_n)$ in the input G by a fresh variable x while adding $x = f(x_1, \ldots, x_n)$ to U. The **Congruence** rule merges x and y in F when $x = f(x_1, \ldots, x_n)$ and $y = f(y_1, \ldots, y_n)$ appear in U and x_i and y_i are in the same equivalence class as partitioned by F.

Theorem 6. *The* **CC** *inference structure is an inference system.*

Proof. Each rule in **CC** either decreases the size of the input G or preserves the size of the input while decreasing the number of distinct equivalence classes in the variables occurring in the premise state. Hence, the inference structure is progressive.

The conservativeness can be easily checked for each rule in **CC**.

The canonicity of **CC** follows from the construction of a term model M so that for each variable x, $M(x) = F^*(x)$, and for a term $f(a_1, \ldots, a_n)$, $M(f(a_1, \ldots, a_n)) = F^*(x)$ if $M(a_i) = M(x_i)$ for $1 \leq i \leq n$ and $x = f(x_1, \ldots, x_n) \in U$. Otherwise, $M(f(a_1, \ldots, a_n)) = f(M(a_1), \ldots, M(a_n))$. ∎

As an example of the inference system, consider the input $x = f(y), y = f(x), f(f(y)) \neq f(x)$.

$$\frac{\frac{\frac{\frac{\frac{\frac{\frac{x = f(y), y = f(x), f(f(y)) \neq y); \emptyset; \emptyset; \emptyset}{x = u_1, y = f(x), f(u_1) \neq y; \emptyset; \emptyset; u_1 = f(y)} \text{ Abstract}}{y = f(x), f(u_1) \neq y; x = u_1; \emptyset; u_1 = f(y)} \text{ Merge}}{y = u_2, f(u_1) \neq y; x = u_1; \emptyset; u_1 = f(y), u_2 = f(x)} \text{ Abstract}}{f(u_1) \neq y; x = u_1, y = u_2; \emptyset; u_1 = f(y), u_2 = f(x)} \text{ Merge}}{u_3 \neq y; x = u_1, y = u2; \emptyset; u_1 = f(y), u_2 = f(x), u_3 = f(u_1)} \text{ Abstract}}{\emptyset; x = u_1, y = u2; u_3 \neq y; u_1 = f(y), u_2 = f(x), u_3 = f(u_1)} \text{ Diseq}}{\emptyset; x = u_1, y = u2, u_3 = u_2; u_3 \neq y; u_1 = f(y), u_2 = f(x), u_3 = f(u_1)} \text{ Congruence}}{\bot} \text{ Contrad}$$

Proof construction for **CC** is an extension of that from **Eq** where the equalities in F are justified either by an input equality in the case of the **Merge** rule, or by congruence in the case of the **Congruence** rule. In the above example, if the inputs are numbered as $x =_{\langle 1 \rangle} f(y), y =_{\langle 2 \rangle} f(x), f(f(y)) \neq_{\langle 3 \rangle} f(x)$, the proof of the contradiction is $3; \langle C(f)(\langle -1 \rangle), 2\rangle$. The inference system **CC** is a variant of the abstract congruence closure algorithms of Kapur [Kap97] and Bachmair, Tiwari, and Vigneron [BTV03].

5 Satisfiability Modulo Theories

The inference systems for equality presented in Section 4 check the satisfiability of conjunctions of literals. Similar inference systems can be given for ordering constraints, arithmetic equality and inequality constraints, arrays, and recursive datatypes. These inference systems can be designed to generate proofs of unsatisfiability, *explanations* identifying the input formulas that are relevant to the proof of unsatisfiability, and implied equalities between variables. The generation of implied equalities between variables is not relevant for satisfiability within a single theory, but is needed for composing inference systems for different theories. Typical constraints arising in embedded uses of decision procedures in verification, type checking, and translation validation, involve a mix of theories such as equality over uninterpreted terms, arrays, arithmetic equalities and inequalities, and recursive datatypes. Such combination decision procedures were first developed by Shostak [Sho79, Sho84] and Nelson and Oppen [NO79], and have been the target of active research in recent years. The theory of modular inference systems, and their composition and refinement, is developed in detail elsewhere [GRS04].

The inference systems for theories discussed above can be used to check the satisfiability of conjunctions of literals of the form $l_1, \ldots, l_n$ in a theory or a union of theories, and can be used as an auxiliary inference system in deciding the validity of quantifier-free formulas. To check the satisfiability of existentially quantified formulas in a theory the **DPLL** inference system can be enhanced with calls to a theory-specific decision procedure for this purpose. Augmenting **DPLL** with theory satisfiability for a theory T is simply a matter of adding the following rule

Lemma	$\dfrac{\Gamma}{\Gamma, l_1 \vee \ldots \vee l_n}$	if $satisfiable_T(\overline{l_1}, \ldots, \overline{l_n}) = \bot,$ and for all $C \in \Gamma,\ lits(C) \not\subseteq \{l_1, \ldots, l_n\}$ where l_i or $\overline{l_i}$ occurs in Γ, for $1 \le i \le n$

Let **DPLL(L)** label the inference rules obtained by adding the **Lemma** rule to the **DPLL** rules.

Theorem 7. *The **DPLL(L)** inference structure is an inference system.*

Proof. For progressiveness, observe that given an input set of clauses, there is a bound on the number of lemma clauses that can be generated since there are at most 3^N clauses in N distinct atoms. In each application of a **DPLL(L)** rule, either the number of missing clauses in Γ, that is $3^N - |\Gamma|$, decreases (in the case of the **Lemma** rule) or it stays the same and the termination argument from the proof of Theorem 3 can applied.

Since each added lemma clause is valid in all models, the **Lemma** rule is conservative.

For canonicity, given an irreducible non-$\bot$ state Γ, let $units(\Gamma)$ be the set of unit literals in Γ. Then, clearly $satisfiable_T(units(\Gamma))$ since otherwise, the negation of $units(\Gamma)$ would be a lemma clause and a contradiction would have been established by the **Unit** and **Contrad** rules. The entire state Γ is then satisfiable: each clause contains at least one literal that appears in $units(\Gamma)$. ∎

A naïve application of the **Lemma** rule would be horribly inefficient. In the *eager* strategy, the lemmas are enumerated and the **Lemma** rule is invoked on these enumerated lemmas prior to any other rule application. This approach is viable when there are efficient ways of enumerating the valid lemmas without generating and testing them. The *lazy* strategies invoke the **Lemma** rule as needed for refining the **Contrad**, **Unit**, and **Split** rules. the following instance of the **Lemma** is sufficient for completeness.

ContradLemma	$\dfrac{\Gamma}{C, \Gamma}$	$C \equiv l_1 \vee \ldots \vee l_n,$ $\overline{C} \subseteq units(\Gamma),$ $satisfiable_T(\overline{C}) = \bot$

The system with the **ContradLemma** rule is sound and complete, but requires an exhaustive enumeration of the truth assignments to the atoms through the **Split** rule. The **Unit** can be similarly strengthened with a **UnitLemma** rule, which also helps avoid needless applications of **Split**.

UnitLemma	$\dfrac{\Gamma}{l \vee C, \Gamma}$	$\overline{C} \subseteq units(\Gamma),$ $satisfiable_T(\{\overline{l}\} \cup \overline{C}) = \bot,$ $l \notin units(\Gamma),$ $\overline{l}$ occurs in Γ

The **UnitLemma** rule can be used together with the **Unit** and **Delete** rules to assign truth values to literals appearing clauses. Similarly, splitting on literals that are implied by the unit clauses in the configuration, can be avoided. In the

ContradLemma and **UnitLemma** rules, the subset $\overline{C}$ of $units(\Gamma)$ is obtained from the explanation generated from the contradiction.

The combination of **DPLL(CDB)** and the **Lemma** rule is not progressive due to the possible deletion of added lemmas by the **Delete** rule. However, the **Backjump** rule can be modified to add lemma clauses that are derived using **ORes** or theory satisfiability, and the same termination argument as Theorem 4 holds. Nieuwenhuis, Oliveras, and Tinelli [NO05] give a related treatment of theory-based extensions of DPLL.

6 Conclusions

Logical algorithms use inference as the basic computing mechanism. Many general-purpose algorithms are instances of logical algorithms. These include a number of decision algorithms as well as those for maintaining equivalence classes, and computing transitive closures and shortest paths. Logical algorithms can be described in terms of inference systems given by an inference relation on logical states. The inference system paradigm has the advantage of separating concerns between the logical correctness of the inference steps, the best strategies for applying these inferences, and the efficient implementation of each inference step. The logical correctness is preserved regardless of the strategy. The efficient application of inferences relies on the use of suitable representations of the logical state. The inference systems presentation is also useful in computing additional useful information in the form of proofs, explanations, and models. Inference systems can also be systematically composed in various ways while preserving the relevant logical properties. We have sketched the basic inference system paradigm and shown a few basic examples as a step toward a more comprehensive catalog of inference systems. These examples already weave together the different strands of early work including propositional satisfiability, proof checking, and decision procedures. A great deal more work is needed to understand how such high-level algorithmic descriptions can be systematically optimized to yield efficient implementations.

Acknowledgments. Alan Bundy's encouraging remarks during the *Calculemus* workshop at Newcastle, England in July 2005 stimulated the writing of this paper. The material presented here is based on a course entitled *Little Engines of Proof* taught together with Leonardo de Moura, Harald Rueß, and Ashish Tiwari at Stanford University during Fall 2003. Leonardo and Ashish provided valuable feedback on early versions, as did Sam Owre and Bruno Dutertre.

References

[Ble77]   W. W. Bledsoe. Non-resolution theorem proving. *Artificial Intelligence*, 9:1–36, 1977.

[BM79]   R. S. Boyer and J S. Moore. *A Computational Logic*. Academic Press, New York, NY, 1979.

[BTV03]   Leo Bachmair, Ashish Tiwari, and Laurent Vigneron. Abstract congruence closure. *Journal of Automated Reasoning*, 31(2):129–168, 2003.

[Buc76]   B. Buchberger. A theoretical basis for the reduction of polynomials to canonical forms. *ACM SIGSAM Bulletin*, 10(3):19–29, 1976.

[CAB⁺86] R. L. Constable, S. F. Allen, H. M. Bromley, W. R. Cleaveland, J. F. Cremer, R. W. Harper, D. J. Howe, T. B. Knoblock, N. P. Mendler, P. Panangaden, J. T. Sasaki, and S. F. Smith. *Implementing Mathematics with the Nuprl Proof Development System*. Prentice Hall, Englewood Cliffs, NJ, 1986.

[Coh88]   Jacques Cohen. A view of the origins and development of prolog. *Communications of the ACM*, 31(1):26–36, 1988.

[Dav57]   M. Davis. A computer program for Presburger's algorithm. In *Summaries of Talks Presented at the Summer Institute for Symbolic Logic, 1957*. Reprinted in Siekmann and Wrightson [SW83], pages 41–48.

[dB80]   N. G. de Bruijn. A survey of the project Automath. In *To H. B. Curry: Essays on Combinatory Logic, Lambda Calculus and Formalism*, pages 589–606. Academic Press, 1980.

[DLL62]   M. Davis, G. Logemann, and D. Loveland. A machine program for theorem proving. *Communications of the ACM*, 5(7):394–397, July 1962. Reprinted in Siekmann and Wrightson [SW83], pages 267–270, 1983.

[dMRS04] Leonardo de Moura, Harald Rueß, and Natarajan Shankar. Justifying equality. In *Proceedings of PDPAR '04*, 2004.

[DP60a]   M. Davis and H. Putnam. A computing procedure for quantification theory. *Journal of the ACM*, 7:201–215, 1960.

[DP60b]   M. Davis and H. Putnam. A computing procedure for quantification theory. *JACM*, 7(3):201–215, 1960.

[DST80]   P. J. Downey, R. Sethi, and R. E. Tarjan. Variations on the common subexpressions problem. *Journal of the ACM*, 27(4):758–771, October 1980.

[GM93]   M. J. C. Gordon and T. F. Melham, editors. *Introduction to HOL: A Theorem Proving Environment for Higher-Order Logic*. Cambridge University Press, Cambridge, UK, 1993.

[GMW79]   M. Gordon, R. Milner, and C. Wadsworth. *Edinburgh LCF: A Mechanized Logic of Computation*, volume 78 of *Lecture Notes in Computer Science*. Springer-Verlag, 1979.

[GRS04]   H. Ganzinger, H. Rueß, and N. Shankar. Modularity and refinement in inference systems. Technical Report CSL-SRI-04-02, SRI International, Computer Science Laboratory, 333 Ravenswood Ave, Menlo Park, CA, 94025, January 2004. Revised, August 2004.

[Har96]   John Harrison. HOL Light: A tutorial introduction. In *Proceedings of the First International Conference on Formal Methods in Computer-Aided Design (FMCAD'96)*, volume 1166 of *Lecture Notes in Computer Science*, pages 265–269. Springer-Verlag, 1996.

[Kap97]   Deepak Kapur. Shostak's congruence closure as completion. In H. Comon, editor, *International Conference on Rewriting Techniques and Applications, RTA '97*, number 1232 in Lecture Notes in Computer Science, pages 23–37, Berlin, 1997. Springer-Verlag.

[KB70]   D. E. Knuth and P. Bendix. Simple word problems in universal algebras. In J. Leech, editor, *Computational Problems in Abstract Algebras*, pages 263–297. Pergamon Press, Oxford, 1970.

[Kle52]   S. C. Kleene. *Introduction to Metamathematics*. North-Holland, Amsterdam, 1952.

[KMM00]   Matt Kaufmann, Panagiotis Manolios, and J Strother Moore. *Computer-Aided Reasoning: An Approach*, volume 3 of *Advances in Formal Methods*. Kluwer, 2000.

[Koz77]   Dexter Kozen. Complexity of finitely presented algebras. In *Conference Record of the Ninth Annual ACM Symposium on Theory of Computing*, pages 164–177, Boulder, Colorado, 2–4 May 1977.

[LP92]   Z. Luo and R. Pollack. The LEGO proof development system: A user's manual. Technical Report ECS-LFCS-92-211, University of Edinburgh, 1992.

[McC62]   J. McCarthy. Computer programs for checking mathematical proofs. In *Recursive Function Theory, Proceedings of a Symposium in Pure Mathematics*, volume V, pages 219–227, Providence, Rhode Island, 1962. American Mathematical Society.

[McC97]   W. W. McCune. Solution of the Robbins problem. Available from ftp://info.mcs.anl.gov/pub/Otter/www-misc/robbins-jar-submitted.ps.gz, 1997.

[NO79]   G. Nelson and D. C. Oppen. Simplification by cooperating decision procedures. *ACM Transactions on Programming Languages and Systems*, 1(2):245–257, 1979.

[NO05]   Robert Nieuwenhuis and Albert Oliveras. Proof-Producing Congruence Closure. In Jürgen Giesl, editor, *Proceedings of the 16th International Conference on Term Rewriting and Applications, RTA'05 (Nara, Japan)*, volume 3467 of *Lecture Notes in Computer Science*, pages 453–468. Springer, 2005.

[NSS57]   A. Newell, J. C. Shaw, and H. A. Simon. Empirical explorations with the logic theory machine: A case study in heuristics. In *Proc. West. Joint Comp. Conf.*, pages 218–239, 1957. Reprinted in Siekmann and Wrightson [SW83], pages 49–73, 1983.

[Pau94]   Lawrence C. Paulson. *Isabelle: A Generic Theorem Prover*, volume 828 of *Lecture Notes in Computer Science*. Springer-Verlag, 1994.

[Rob65a]   J. A. Robinson. A machine-oriented logic based on the resolution principle. *Journal of the ACM*, 12(1):23–41, 1965.

[Rob65b]   J.A. Robinson. Automatic deduction with hyper-resolution. *International Journal of Computational Mathematics*, 1:227–234, 1965.

[RV01]   A. Robinson and A. Voronkov, editors. *Handbook of Automated Reasoning*. Elsevier Science, 2001.

[Sho78]   Robert E. Shostak. An algorithm for reasoning about equality. *Communications of the ACM*, 21(7):583–585, July 1978.

[Sho79]   Robert E. Shostak. A practical decision procedure for arithmetic with function symbols. *Journal of the ACM*, 26(2):351–360, April 1979.

[Sho84]   Robert E. Shostak. Deciding combinations of theories. *Journal of the ACM*, 31(1):1–12, January 1984.

[SS98]   G. Sutcliffe and C.B. Suttner. The TPTP Problem Library: CNF Release v1.2.1. *Journal of Automated Reasoning*, 21(2):177–203, 1998.

[SW83]   J. Siekmann and G. Wrightson, editors. *Automation of Reasoning: Classical Papers on Computational Logic, Volumes 1 & 2*. Springer-Verlag, 1983.

[Tea05]   Coq Development Team. The Coq proof assistant reference manual, version 8.0. Technical report, INRIA, Rocquencourt, France, January 2005.

[WRC65]   L. Wos, G.A. Robinson, and D. Carson. Efficiency and completeness of the set of support strategy in theorem proving. *Journal of the ACM*, 12(4):536–541, 1965.

From Logic to Games

Igor Walukiewicz

CNRS
LaBRI, Université Bordeaux-1
351, Cours de la Libération, 33 405, Talence
France

1 Introduction

The occasion of 25th jubilee of FSTCS gives an opportunity to look a bit further back then one normally would. In this presentation we will look at some developments in what is called formal verification. In the seventies logics occupied a principal place: Hoare logic [43], algorithmic logic [38], dynamic logic [41, 42], linear time temporal logic [55]. With a notable exception of the last one, these formalisms included programs into syntax of the logic with an idea to reduce verification to validity checking. Temporal logic was the first to advocate externalization of modeling of programs and passing from validity checking to model checking. Since the eighties, this view became predominant, and we have seen a proliferation of logical systems. We have learned that game based methods not only are very useful but also permit to abstract from irrelevant details of logical formalisms. At present games themselves take place of specification formalisms.

Roughly, model-checking can be seen as a discipline of verifying properties of labelled graphs. So, we are interested in formalisms for specifying graph properties. This formulation is misleadingly simple at the first sight. Observe, for example, that almost all the richness of first-order logic already appears over graph models, i.e., models with one binary relation. Thus, the goal is to get formalisms that are expressive and at the same time have decidable model-checking problem (and preferably with low computational complexity).

The foundations of the discipline were ready before 1980-ties. Automata theory existed already for a long time[71]. Büchi and Rabin have shown decidability of monadic second-order (MSO) theories of sequences [16] and trees [70], respectively. Martin has proven determinacy of Borel games [56]. Manna and Pnueli have already proposed a new way of looking at program verification using linear time temporal logic. Kamp's theorem gave equivalence of LTL with first-order logic over sequences [46].

Nevertheless, it is fair to say that a quarter of a century ago, at the beginning of 80-eighties, the next important period in the development of the field took place. In a relatively short interval of time a big number of significant concepts have been born. Emerson and Clarke introduced CTL and the branching/linear time distinction was clarified [25, 52]. Kozen defined the μ-calculus [48], the logic that will later bring games to the field. Independently, Büchi [17], and Gurevich and Harrington [40], arrive at understanding that the cornerstone of Rabin's

R. Ramanujam and S. Sen (Eds.): FSTTCS 2005, LNCS 3821, pp. 79–91, 2005.

decidability result for MSO theory of trees is a theorem about existence of some special strategies, now called finite memory, in some class of games. A bit later, Street and Emerson [77, 78] developed techniques to attack satisfiability problem for the μ-calculus. Around 1980 a concept of alternation was born [23]. These have given later rise to alternating automata [63] and finally to understanding that these are essentially the same as the μ-calculus.

In what follows we will give a brief introduction to the concepts described above. This will bring us in a position to discuss open problems and directions for future research. Present note is not meant to be a comprehensive survey of the discipline. Citations and results are merely chosen to demonstrate development of some lines of research, there is by far not enough place to present all important accomplishments of the field.

2   The Concepts

We need to start with presentation of some basic concepts. From 25 years perspective it is clear that they where very influential in development of the theory. The μ-calculus turned out to be important because of its purity, its expressive power and because of technical problems posed by the fixpoint operator. Old methods, like construction of syntactic models from consistent sets of formulas, are not applicable to the μ-calculus. New techniques were required, and this is where automata theory and game theory came to rescue.

2.1   The μ-Calculus

Formulas of the μ-calculus over the sets $Prop = \{p_1, p_2, \ldots\}$ of *propositional constants*, $Act = \{a, b, \ldots\}$ of *actions*, and $Var = \{X, Y, \ldots\}$ of *variables*, are defined by the following grammar:

$$F := Prop \mid \neg Prop \mid Var \mid F \vee F \mid F \wedge F \mid$$
$$\langle Act \rangle F \mid [Act]F \mid \mu Var.F \mid \nu Var.F$$

Note that we allow negations only before propositional constants. This is not a problem as we will be interested in *sentences*, i.e., formulas where all variables are bound by μ or ν. In the following, $\alpha, \beta, \ldots$ will denote formulas.

Formulas are interpreted in *transition systems*, these are of the form $\mathcal{M} = \langle S, \{R_a\}_{a \in Act}, \rho \rangle$, where: S is a nonempty set of *states*, $R_a \subseteq S \times S$ is a binary relation interpreting the action a, and $\rho : Prop \rightarrow \mathcal{P}(S)$ is a function assigning to each propositional constant a set of states where this constant holds.

For a given transition system $\mathcal{M}$ and an *assignment* $V : Var \rightarrow \mathcal{P}(S)$, the set of states in which a formula α is true, denoted $\| \alpha \|_V^{\mathcal{M}}$, is defined inductively as follows:

$$\| p \|_V^{\mathcal{M}} = \rho(p) \qquad \| \neg p \|_V^{\mathcal{M}} = S - \rho(p)$$

$$\| X \|_V^{\mathcal{M}} = V(X)$$

$$\| \langle a \rangle \alpha \|_V^{\mathcal{M}} = \{s : \exists s'.R_a(s,s') \wedge s' \in \| \alpha \|_V^{\mathcal{M}}\}$$

$$\| \mu X.\alpha(X) \|_V^{\mathcal{M}} = \bigcap \{S' \subseteq S : \| \alpha \|_{V[S'/X]}^{\mathcal{M}} \subseteq S'\}$$

$$\| \nu X.\alpha(X) \|_V^{\mathcal{M}} = \bigcup \{S' \subseteq S : S' \subseteq \| \alpha \|_{V[S'/X]}^{\mathcal{M}}\}$$

We have omitted here the obvious clauses for boolean operators and for $[a]\alpha$ formula. We will omit V in the notation if α is a sentence and will sometimes write $\mathcal{M}, s \vDash \alpha$ instead of $s \in \| \alpha \|^{\mathcal{M}}$.

The *model-checking problem for the μ-calculus* is: given a sentence α and a finite transition system $\mathcal{M}$ with a distinguished state s^0 decide if $\mathcal{M}, s^0 \vDash \alpha$.

2.2   Games

A *game* G is a tuple $\langle V_E, V_A, T \subseteq (V_E \cup V_A)^2, Acc \subseteq (V_E \cup V_A)^\omega \rangle$ where Acc is a set defining the *winning condition* and $\langle V_E \cup V_A, T \rangle$ is a graph with the vertices partitioned into those of Eve and those of Adam. We say that a vertex v' is a *successor* of a vertex v if $T(v, v')$ holds.

A *play* between Eve and Adam from some vertex $v \in V = V_E \cup V_A$ proceeds as follows: if $v \in V_E$ then Eve makes a choice of a successor, otherwise Adam chooses a successor; from this successor the same rule applies and the play goes on forever unless one of the parties cannot make a move. The player who cannot make a move looses. The result of an infinite play is an infinite path $v_0 v_1 v_2 \ldots$ This *path is winning* for Eve if it belongs to Acc. Otherwise Adam is the winner.

A *strategy* σ for Eve is a function assigning to every sequence of vertices $\boldsymbol{v}$ ending in a vertex v from V_E a vertex $\sigma(\boldsymbol{v})$ which is a successor of v. A *play respecting* σ is a sequence $v_0 v_1 \ldots$ such that $v_{i+1} = \sigma(v_i)$ for all i with $v_i \in V_E$. The *strategy* σ *is winning for Eve* from a vertex v iff all the plays starting in v and respecting σ are winning. A *vertex is winning for Eve* if there exists a strategy winning from it. The strategies for Adam are defined similarly. Usually we are interested in *solving games*, i.e., deciding which vertices are winninng for Eve and which for Adam.

A *strategy with memory M* is a triple:

$$c : M \times V_E \to \mathcal{P}(V), \quad up : M \times V \to M, \quad m_0 \in M$$

The role of the initial memory element m_0 and the memory update function up is to abstract some information from the sequence $\boldsymbol{v}$. This is done by iteratively applying up function:

$$up^*(m, \varepsilon) = m \quad \text{and} \quad up^*(m, \boldsymbol{v}v) = up^*(up(m, \boldsymbol{v}), v)$$

This way, each sequence $\boldsymbol{v}$ of vertices is assigned a memory element $up^*(m_0, \boldsymbol{v})$. Then the choice function c defines a strategy by $\sigma(\boldsymbol{v}v) = c(up^*(m_0, \boldsymbol{v}), v)$. The strategy is *memoryless* iff $\sigma(v) = \sigma(w)$ whenever v and w end in the same vertex; this is a strategy with a memory M that is a singleton.

In most of the cases here the winning conditions $Acc \subseteq V^\omega$ will be *Muller conditions*: that is, there will be a colouring $\lambda : V \rightarrow$ *Colours* of the set of vertices with a finite set of colours and a set $\mathcal{F} \subseteq \mathcal{P}(\textit{Colours})$ that define the winning sequences by:

$$v \in Acc \quad \text{iff} \quad \text{Inf}_\lambda(v) \in \mathcal{F}$$

where $\text{Inf}_\lambda(v)$ is the set of colours appearing infinitely often on v.

An important special case is a *parity condition*. It is a condition determined by a function $\Omega : V \rightarrow \{0, \dots, d\}$ in the following way:

$$Acc = \{v_0 v_1 \dots \in V^\omega : \limsup_{i \to \infty} \Omega(v_i) \text{ is even}\}$$

Hence, in this case, the colours are natural numbers and we require that the biggest among those appearing infinitely often is even. This condition was discovered by Mostowski [60] and is the most useful form of Muller conditions. It is the only Muller condition that guarantees existence of memoryless strategies [33, 61, 58]. It is closed by negation (the negation of a parity condition is a parity condition). It is universal in the sense that very game with a Muller condition can be reduced to a game with a parity condition [60].

2.3   Between Games and Formulas

The truth of a given formula in a given model can be characterized by games. To see this, consider the task of checking if a propositional formula (in a positive normal form) is true in a given valuation. If the formula is a disjunction then Eve should choose one of the disjuncts that she believes is true; if it is a conjunction then Adam should choose one of the conjuncts he believes is false. The game continues until it arrives at a literal (a proposition or its negation). Eve wins iff the literal is true in the valuation fixed at the beginning. It is easy to see that Eve has a winning strategy in this game iff the initial formula is true in the valuation.

Observe that we can define a similar game for almost any logic, just using directly the clauses defining its semantics. For example, for first-order logic Eve would choose in the case of disjunction and existential quantifier, and Adam in the case of conjunction and universal quantifier. This view is of course well known. The reason why it is not used too much in the context of first-order logic is that the game becomes quite complicated. One can consider Ehrenfeucht-Fraïssé games as a way of hiding these complications at the cost of limiting the scope of applicability of the concept.

While it is clear how to define game rules for disjunction, conjunction, and most other cases, it is much less clear what to do with fixpoints. The best we can do when we want to see if a formula $\mu X.\alpha(X)$ holds is to check if its unwinding $\alpha(\mu X.\alpha(X))$ holds. Such an unwinding rule introduces potential of infinite plays as for $\mu X.X$. The other problem is that for the greatest fixpoint $\nu X.\alpha(X)$ we cannot do better but suggest the same rule. One of the most important developments in these 25 years is to admit infinite plays and to realize that fixpoints give rise to a parity condition on infinite plays: least fixpoints are given odd ranks, greatest fixpoints even ranks, and the exact value of the rank depends on the nesting depth (see [76] for details).

Summarizing, one can look at the formula as a kind of schema that when put together with a model defines a game. Observe that a schema by itself does not define a game directly; putting it differently, the satisfiability question requires more than just examining the structure of the formula. We see the same phenomenon in a formalism of alternating automata. It is a very beautiful fact that the to formalisms agree. Actually it is one of the cornerstones of the whole theory.

2.4   Alternating Automata

An *alternating automaton* on on transition systems is a tuple:

$$\mathcal{A} = \langle A, P, Q^\exists, Q^\forall, q^0, \delta : Q \times \mathcal{P}(P) \to \mathcal{P}(A \times Q), Acc \rangle$$

where $A \subseteq Act \cup \{id\}$, $P \subseteq Prop$ are finite set of actions and propositions, respectively, relevant to the automaton. Set Q is a finite set of states partitioned into existential, $Q^\exists$, and universal, $Q^\forall$ states. State $q^0 \in Q$ is the initial state of the automaton and δ is the transition function that assigns to each state and label, which is valuation relevant propositions, a set of possible moves. An intuitive meaning of a move $(a, q') \in A \times Q$ is to move over an edge labelled a and change the state to q'. The action id is a self-loop permitting to stay in the same node. Finally, $Acc \subseteq Q^\omega$ is an acceptance condition.

The simplest way to formalize the notions of a run and of an acceptance of an automaton is in terms of games. Given an automaton $\mathcal{A}$ as above and a transition system $\mathcal{M} = \langle S, \{R_a\}_{a \in Act}, \rho \rangle$ we define the *acceptance game* $G(\mathcal{A}, P) = \langle V_E, V_A, T, Acc_G \rangle$ as follows:

- The set of vertices for Eve is $(Q^\exists \times S)$.
- The set of vertices for Adam is $(Q^\forall \times S)$.
- From each vertex (q, s), for every $(a, q') \in \delta(q, \lambda(s))$ and $(s, s') \in R_a$ we have an edge in T to (q', s'); we assume that R_{id} is the identity relation on states.
- The winning condition Acc_G consists of the sequences:

$$(q_0, s_0)(q_1, s_1) \ldots$$

such that the sequence $q_0, q_1 \ldots$ is in Acc, i.e., it belongs to the acceptance condition of the automaton.

Let us see how to construct an automaton equivalent to a sentence α of the μ-calculus (we do not admit free variables in α). The states of the automaton $\mathcal{A}_\alpha$ will be the subformulas of the formula α plus two states $\top$ and $\bot$. The initial state will be α. The action and proposition alphabets of $\mathcal{A}_\alpha$ will consist of the actions and propositions that appear in α. The transitions will be defined by:

- $\delta(p, v) = \top$ if $p \in v$ and $\bot$ otherwise;
- $\delta(\beta_1 \vee \beta_2, v) = \delta(\beta_1 \wedge \beta_2, v) = \{(id, \beta_1), (id, \beta_2)\}$;
- $\delta(\langle a \rangle \beta, v) = \delta([a]\beta, v) = \{(a, \beta)\}$;
- $\delta(\mu X.\beta(X), v) = \delta(\nu X.\beta(X), v) = \{(id, \beta(X))\}$;
- $\delta(X, v) = \{(id, \beta(X))\}$.

The symbols in the last rule demand some explications. Here X is a variable and $\beta(X)$ is the formula to which it is bound, i.e., we have $\mu X.\beta(X)$ or $\nu X.\beta(X)$ in α. We can suppose that X is bound precisely once in α as we can always rename bound variables.

Observe that the rules for conjunction and disjunction are the same. The difference is that a disjunction subformula will be an existential state of $\mathcal{A}_\alpha$ and the conjunction subformula an universal one. Similarly for $\bot$, $\top$ as well as for $\langle a \rangle$ and $[a]$ modalities. This means, in particular, that $\top$ is an accepting state as there are no transitions from $\top$ and Adam looses immediately in any position of the form $(\top, s)$.

It remains to define the acceptance condition of $\mathcal{A}_\alpha$. It will be the parity condition where all the subformulas but variables have rank 0. To define the rank of a variable X we look at the formula it is bound to. If it is $\mu X.\beta(X)$ then the rank of X is $2d + 1$ where d is the nesting depth of $\mu X.\beta(X)$. If it is is $\nu X.\beta(X)$ then it is $2d$. For the precise definition of the nesting depth we refer the reader to [4], here it suffices to say that the principle is the same as for quantifier depth in first-order logic.

We will not discuss here, not too difficult, proof that this construction gives indeed an automaton equivalent to the formula. What is worth pointing out is that the translation in the other direction is also possible. From a given alternating automaton one can construct an equivalent formula of the μ-calculus. This equivalence is a very good example of a correspondence between formula and diagram based formalisms as advocated by Wolfgang Thomas [79]. The μ-calculus is compositional, it permits doing proofs by induction on the syntax. Automata are better for algorithmic issues and problems such as minimization.

The last remark we want to make here is about satisfiability. The above reduction shows that the satisfiability question for the μ-calculus can be solved via emptiness problem for alternating automata. This in turn requires transformation of alternating to nondeterministic automata or in other words, elimination of universal branching. When we look back we can see that this is an universal phenomenon that appears even in the case of propositional logic.

3   Perspectives

One of the obvious problems that resisted over the last 25 years is the model checking problem for the μ-calculus. Equivalently, it is the problem of solving parity games. In this formulation it is a, potentially simpler, instance of the problem of solving stochastic games [44] which complexity is open for quite some time. There are at least two directions of research that are connected to this problem and that are also interesting in their own right.

One direction is to find polynomial-time algorithms for some restricted classes of games. For example, for any constant, games whose graphs have tree-width bounded by this constant can be solved in polynomial time [68]. Recently, a new graph complexity measure, called entanglement, has been proposed and the same result for graphs of bounded entanglement has been proved [8]. In the future it would be interesting to consider the case of clique-width. Tree-width is connected to MSO logic where quantification over transitions is permitted. It is known that in this logic each μ-calculus formula is equivalent to a formula of quantifier depth 3. Clique-width [27] is linked to MSO logic where only quantification over states is permitted. In this case it is open whether a finite number of quantifier alternations suffices to capture the whole μ-calculus.

The other direction is to consider the model-checking and game solving problems for graphs represented implicitly. A simple example is a graph represented as a synchronized product of transition systems. In this case even alternating reachability is EXPTIME-complete (see [30] for more detailed analysis) but the model-checking problem for the whole μ-calculus stays also in EXPTIME. The other possibility is to consider configuration graphs of some type of machines. In recent years pushdown graphs, i.e., graphs of configurations of pushdown machines have attracted considerable attention [62, 9, 34, 50, 74, 83]. One research direction is to find interesting and decidable classes of properties of pushdown systems [11, 36, 75]. The other direction is to go forward to more complicated cases like higher order pushdowns [18, 19], higher order recursive program schemes [45, 47] or pushdowns with parallel composition [10]. The biggest challenge here is to push the decidability frontier.

The understanding that the μ-calculus corresponds exactly to games with parity conditions suggest to look for other winning conditions with interesting properties. For finite Muller conditions we know how to calculate a memory required to win [32]. Recently, more general winning conditions were investigated as for example Muller conditions over infinite number of colours [39]. A particular case of such a condition is when colours are natural numbers and the winner is decided by looking at the parity of the smallest number appearing infinitely often (additionally we can assume that Eve wins if there is no such number). It turns out that this infinite kind of a parity condition is the only type of infinite Muller condition that guarantees the existence of memoryless strategies in all games. It is important to add that for this result to hold all positions of the game need to have a colour assigned. If we permit partial assignments of colours or put coloring on edges of the game graph and not on positions then only ordinary (i.e. finite) parity conditions admit memoryless strategies [26]. In the recent paper [37] this later result is extended to include also quantitative conditions such as mean or discounted pay-off.

While we know already a great deal about the μ-calculus itself [4], there still remains a lot to explore. One of the obvious research topics suggested by the syntax of the logic is that of the alternation hierarchy of fixpoint operators. Curiously, as the translation presented above shows, the alternation depth of the formula corresponds to the size of a parity condition in the equivalent alternating automaton. Thus, one can equivalently study the later hierarchy. The infiniteness of the hierarchy for the μ-calculus was shown by Bradfield [14] and for alternating tree automata independently by Bradfield [15] and Arnold [3]. It is worth noting that hierarchy questions for nondeterministic tree automata were solved ten years earlier by Niwiński [64], and for the even simpler case of deterministic automata, another ten years back by Wagner [82]. (As a side remark let us mention that quite recently Arnold and Santocanale has shown a surprising behaviour of diagonal classes [5].) Once the basic hierarchy questions are resolved, the next challenge is to provide algorithms for determining the level in the hierarchy of a given recognizable language. The first step was to give a polynomial time algorithm for computing the level in the hierarchy of deterministic automata [65]. Next, Urbański [80] has shown that it is decidable if a deterministic Rabin tree automaton is equivalent to a nondeterministic Büchi one. Actually, the problem is also in PTIME [66]. More recently [67], the case of deterministic tree automata was completely solved. There are forbidden pattern characterizations for all the levels of the hierarchy of nondeterministic automata; that is, given a deterministic automaton one can tell by examining its structure to which level of the hierarchy of nondeterministic automata it belongs to. This also solves the problem for levels of alternating automata hierarchy as all deterministic languages are recognizable by co-Büchi alternating automata. The challenge for the future is to calculate hierarchy levels for nondeterministic automata.

There are numerous other directions of active research. We will describe just three more very briefly here, referring the reader to the cited papers for details.

Games as well as logics and automata can be augmented with real-time. While real-time automata are around for some time now [2], there is no standard logic for real-time. This is partially due to the fact that timed-automata are not closed under complement and it is difficult to decide on some other good class of real-time properties. Also quantitative reachability problems, like minimizing reachability cost, appear to be interesting [1, 12, 21].

The rules of playing games may be extended [28]: one may allow concurrent moves when two players choose moves independently and the game proceeds to the state that is a function of the two choices. An example of "paper, scissors, stone" game shows that randomized strategies are sometimes necessary to win in such games. This means that now a player does not win for sure, but only with certain probability; the maximal such probability is called the value of the player. Another extension is to allow randomized positions where a successor is chosen randomly with respect to some probability distribution. The quantitative determinacy result of Martin [57] states that in every game with concurrent moves and randomized positions the values for Eva and Adam sum up to 1. In [28] de Alfaro and Majumdar show how to calculate the values of a game using appropriate extension of the μ-calculus. It can also happen that the objectives of the two players are not antagonistic, in this case we talk about Nash equilibria rather than values of games. Recently [24], Chatterjee has shown how to calculate

Nash equilibria for a very general class of concurrent, stochastic, nonzero-sum, infinite games.

Finally, each of these game models can be applied to synthesis [69, 72, 49, 20]. The synthesis problem is to construct a system from a given specification. It is often solved by reduction to the problem of finding a strategy in some game [6]. If the problem mentions real-time then the game will have real-time constraints [7, 29, 31, 13, 22]. If the problem concerns distributed setting then either the reduction or the game model will have to take it into account [73, 53, 54, 51, 59, 35]. The number of choices is truly overwhelming and we need to understand much better in what cases synthesis is feasible.

References

[1] R. Alur, M. Bernadsky, and P. Madhusudan. Optimal reachability for weighted timed games. In *ICALP*, volume 3124 of *Lecture Notes in Computer Science*, pages 122–133, 2004.

[2] R. Alur and P. Madhusudan. Decision problems for timed automata: A survey. In *Formal Methods for the Design of Real-Time Systems*, volume 3185 of *Lecture Notes in Computer Science*, pages 1–24, 2004.

[3] A. Arnold. The mu-calculus alternation-depth hierarchy is strict on binary trees. *RAIRO–Theoretical Informatics and Applications*, 33:329–339, 1999.

[4] A. Arnold and D. Niwiski. *The Rudiments of the Mu-Calculus*, volume 146 of *Studies in Logic*. North-Holland, 2001.

[5] A. Arnold and L. Santocanale. Ambiguous classes in the games mu-calculus hierarchy. In *FOSSACS 03*, volume 2620 of *Lecture Notes in Computer Science*, pages 70–86, 2003.

[6] A. Arnold, A. Vincent, and I. Walukiewicz. Games for synthesis of controllers with partial observation. *Theoretical Computer Science*, 303(1):7–34, 2003.

[7] E. Asarin, O. Maler, A. Pnueli, and J. Sifakis. Contrloller synthesis for timed automata. In *Proc. IFAC Symp. System Structure and Control*, pages 469–474, 1998.

[8] D. Berwanger and E. Grädel. Entanglement - a measure for the complexity of directed graphs with applications to logic and games. In *LPAR 2004*, volume 3452 of *Lecture Notes in Computer Science*, pages 209–223, 2004.

[9] A. Bouajjani, J. Esparza, and O. Maler. Reachability analysis of pushdown automata: Applications to model checking. In *CONCUR'97*, volume 1243 of *Lecture Notes in Computer Science*, pages 135–150, 1997.

[10] A. Bouajjani, M. Mueller-Olm, and T. Touili. Regular symbolic analysis of dynamic networks of pushdown systems. In *CONCUR'05*, volume 3653 of *Lecture Notes in Computer Science*, 2005.

[11] A. Bouquet, O. Serre, and I. Walukiewicz. Pushdown games with the unboundedness and regular conditions. In *FSTTCS'03*, volume 2914 of *Lecture Notes in Computer Science*, pages 88–99, 2003.

[12] P. Bouyer, F. Cassez, E. Fleury, and K. G. Larsen. Optimal strategies in priced timed game automata. In *FSTTCS*, Lecture Notes in Computer Science, 2004.

[13] P. Bouyer, D. D'Souza, P. Madhusudan, and A. Petit. Timed control with partial observability. In *CAV'03*, volume 2725 of *Lecture Notes in Computer Science*, pages 180–192, 2003.

[14] J. Bradfield. The modal mu-calculus alternation hierarchy is strict. *Theoretical Computer Science*, 195:133–153, 1997.

[15] J. Bradfield. Fixpoint alternation: Arithmetic, transition systems, and the binary tree. *RAIRO–Theoretical Informatics and Applications*, 33:341–356, 1999.

[16] J. R. Büchi. On the decision method in restricted second-order arithmetic. In *Proc. Internat. Congr. on Logic, Methodology and Philosophy of Science*, pages 1–11. Stanford Univ. Press, 1960.

[17] J. R. Buchi. State strategies for games in $F_{\sigma\delta} \cap G_{\delta\sigma}$. *Journal of Symbolic Logic*, 48:1171–1198, 1983.

[18] T. Cachat. Symbolic strategy synthesis for games on pushdown graphs. In *ICALP'02*, volume 2380 of *Lecture Notes in Computer Science*, pages 704–715, 2002.

[19] T. Cachat. Uniform solution of parity games on prefix-recognizable graphs. In A. Kucera and R. Mayr, editors, *Proceedings of the 4th International Workshop on Verification of Infinite-State Systems*, volume 68 of *Electronic Notes in Theoretical Computer Science*. Elsevier Science Publishers, 2002.

[20] C. G. Cassandras and S. Lafortune. *Introduction to Discrete Event Systems*. Kluwer Academic Publishers, 1999.

[21] F. Cassez, A. David, E. Fleury, K. G. Larsen, and D. Lime. Efficient on-the-fly algorithms for the analysis of timed games. In *CONCUR'05*, Lecture Notes in Computer Science, 2005.

[22] F. Cassez, T. Henzinger, and J. Raskin. A comparison of control problems for timed and hybrid systems. In *Hybrid Systems Computation and Control (HSCC'02)*, number 2289 in Lecture Notes in Computer Science, pages 134–148, 2002.

[23] A. K. Chandra, D. C. Kozen, and L. J. Stockmeyer. Alternation. *Journal of the Association of Computing Machinery*, 28(1):114–133, 1981.

[24] K. Chatterjee. Two-player nonzero-sum omega-regular games. In *CONCUR'05*, Lecture Notes in Computer Science, 2005.

[25] E. Clarke and E. Emerson. Design and synthesis of synchronization skeletons using branching time temporal logic. In *Workshop on Logics of Programs*, volume 131 of *Lecture Notes in Computer Science*, pages 52–71. Springer-Verlag, 1981.

[26] T. Colcombet and D. Niwiński. On the positional determinacy of edge–labeled games. Submitted, 2004.

[27] B. Courcelle and P. Weil. The recognizability of sets of graphs is a robust property. To appear in Theoretical Computer Science, http://www.labri.fr/Perso/~weil/publications/.

[28] L. de Alfaro. Quantitative verification and control via the mu-calculus. In *CONCUR'03*, volume 2761 of *Lecture Notes in Computer Science*, pages 102–126, 2003.

[29] L. de Alfaro, M. Faella, T. A. Henzinger, R. Majumdar, and M. Stoelinga. The element of surprise in timed games. In *CONCUR'03*, volume 2761 of *Lecture Notes in Computer Science*, pages 142–156, 2003.

[30] S. Demri, F. Laroussinie, and P. Schnoebelen. A parametric analysis of the state exposion problem in model checking. In *STACS'02*, volume 2285 of *Lecture Notes in Computer Science*, pages 620–631, 2002.

[31] D. D'Souza and P. Madhusudan. Timed control synthesis for external specifications. In *STACS'02*, volume 2285 of *Lecture Notes in Computer Science*, pages 571–582, 2002.

[32] S. Dziembowski, M. Jurdzinski, and I. Walukiewicz. How much memory is needed to win infinite games. In *LICS*, pages 99–110, 1997.

[33] E. A. Emerson and C. S. Jutla. Tree automata, mu-calculus and determinacy. In *Proc. FOCS'91*, pages 368–377, 1991.

[34] J. Esparza and A. Podelski. Efficient algorithms for pre star and post star on interprocedural parallel flow graphs. In *POPL'00: Principles of Programming Languages*, 2000.

[35] B. Finkbeiner and S. Schewe. Uniform distributed synthesis. In *LICS05*, 2005.

[36] H. Gimbert. Parity and explosion games on context-free graphs. In *CSL'04*, volume 3210 of *Lecture Notes in Computer Science*, pages 56–70, 2004.

[37] H. Gimbert and W. Zielonka. When can you play positionally? In *MFCS'04*, volume 3153 of *Lecture Notes in Computer Science*, 2004.

[38] G.Mirkowska and A.Salwicki. *Algorithmic Logic*. D.Reidel PWN, 1987.

[39] E. Grädel and I. Walukiewicz. Positional determinacy of infnite games, 2004. Submitted.

[40] Y. Gurevich and L. Harrington. Trees, automata and games. In *14th ACM Symp. on Theory of Computations*, pages 60–65, 1982.

[41] D. Harel. Dynamic logic. In *Handbook of Philosophical Logic Vol II*, pages 497–604. D.Reidel Publishing Company, 1984.

[42] D. Harel, D. Kozen, and J. Tiuryn. *Dynamic Logic*. MIT Press, 2000.

[43] C. A. R. Hoare. An axiomatic basis for computer programming. *Communications of the ACM*, 12:576–585, 1969.

[44] A. Hoffman and R. Karp. On nonterminating stochastic games. *Management Science*, 12:369–370, 1966.

[45] C.-H. L. O. K. Aehlig, J. G. de Miranda. The monadic second order theory of trees given by arbitrary level-two recursion schemes is decidable. In *TLCA'05*, volume 3461 of *Lecture Notes in Computer Science*, pages 39–54, 2005.

[46] H. Kamp. *Tense Logic and the Theory of Linear Order*. PhD thesis, University of California, 1968.

[47] T. Knapik, D. Niwinski, P. Urzyczyn, and I. Walukiewicz. Unsafe grammars and panic automata. In *ICALP'05*, volume 3580 of *Lecture Notes in Computer Science*, pages 1450–1461, 2005.

[48] D. Kozen. Results on the propositional mu-calculus. *Theoretical Computer Science*, 27:333–354, 1983.

[49] R. Kumar and V. K. Garg. *Modeling and control of logical discrete event systems*. Kluwer Academic Pub., 1995.

[50] O. Kupferman and M. Vardi. An automata-theoretic approach to reasoning about infinite-state systems. In *Proceedings of CAV'00*, volume 1855 of *Lecture Notes in Computer Science*, pages 36–52. Springer Verlag, 2000.

[51] O. Kupferman and M. Vardi. Synthesizing distributed systems. In *Proc. 16th IEEE Symp. on Logic in Computer Science*, 2001.

[52] L. Lamport. "sometime" is sometimes "not never" – on the temporal logic of programs. In *POPL'80*, pages 174–185, 1980.

[53] P. Madhusudan. *Control and Synthesis of Open Reactive Systems*. PhD thesis, University of Madras, 2001.

[54] P. Madhusudan and P. Thiagarajan. A decidable class of asynchronous distributed controllers. In *CONCUR'02*, volume 2421 of *Lecture Notes in Computer Science*, 2002.

[55] Z. Manna and A. Pnueli. Verification of the concurrent programs: the temporal framework. In R.Boyer and J.Moore, editors, *The Correctness Problem in Computer Scince*, pages 215–273. Academic Press, 1981.

[56] D. Martin. Borel determinacy. *Ann. Math.*, 102:363–371, 1975.

[57] D. Martin. The determinacy of Blackwell games. *The Journal of Symbolic Logic*, 63(4):1565–1581, 1998.

[58] R. McNaughton. Infinite games played on finite graphs. *Ann. Pure and Applied Logic*, 65:149–184, 1993.

[59] S. Mohalik and I. Walukiewicz. Distributed games. In *FSTTCS'03*, volume 2914 of *Lecture Notes in Computer Science*, pages 338–351, 2003.

[60] A. W. Mostowski. Regular expressions for infinite trees and a standard form of automata. In *Fifth Symposium on Computation Theory*, volume 208 of *LNCS*, pages 157–168, 1984.

[61] A. W. Mostowski. Games with forbidden positions. Technical Report 78, University of Gdansk, 1991.

[62] D. Muller and P. Schupp. The theory of ends, pushdown automata and second-order logic. *Theoretical Computer Science*, 37:51–75, 1985.

[63] D. Muller and P. Schupp. Alternating automata on infinite trees. *Theoretical Computer Science*, 54:267–276, 1987.

[64] D. Niwiński. On fixed-point clones. In *Proc. 13th ICALP*, volume 226 of *LNCS*, pages 464–473, 1986.

[65] D. Niwiński and I. Walukiewicz. Relating hierarchies of word and tree automata. In *STACS'98*, volume 1373 of *Lecture Notes in Computer Science*. Springer-Verlag, 1998.

[66] D. Niwiński and I. Walukiewicz. A gap property of deterministic tree languages. *Theoretical Computer Science*, 303(1):215–231, 2003.

[67] D. Niwiński and I. Walukiewicz. Deciding nondeterministic hierarchy of deterministic tree automata. *Electr. Notes Theor. Comput. Sci.*, 123:195–208, 2005.

[68] J. Obdrzalek. Fast mu-calculus model checking when tree-width is bounded. In *CAV'03*, volume 2725 of *Lecture Notes in Computer Science*, pages 80–92, 2003.

[69] A. Pnueli and R. Rosner. On the synthesis of a reactive module. In *Proc. ACM POPL*, pages 179–190, 1989.

[70] M. Rabin. Decidability of second-order theories and automata on infinite trees. *Trans. Amer. Math. Soc.*, 141:1–35, 1969.

[71] M. O. Rabin and D. Scott. Finite automata and their decision problems. *IBM Journal of Research and Development*, pages 114–125, 1959. Reprinted in Sequential machines (editor E. F. Moore), Addison-Wesley, Reading, Massachusetts, 1964, pages 63-91.

[72] P. J. G. Ramadge and W. M. Wonham. The control of discrete event systems. *Proceedings of the IEEE*, 77(2):81–98, 1989.

[73] K. Rudie and W. Wonham. Think globally, act locally: Decentralized supervisory control. *IEEE Trans. on Automat. Control*, 37(11):1692–1708, 1992.

[74] O. Serre. Note on winning positions on pushdown games with ω-regular conditions. *Information Processing Letters*, 85:285–291, 2003.

[75] O. Serre. Games with winning conditions of high Borel complexity. In *ICALP'04*, volume 3142 of *Lecture Notes in Computer Science*, pages 1150–1162, 2004.

[76] C. Stirling. *Modal and Temporal Properties of Processes*. Texts in Computer Science. Springer, 2001.

[77] R. S. Streett and E. A. Emerson. The propositional mu-calculus is elementary. In *ICALP*, volume 172 of *Lecture Notes in Computer Science*, pages 465–472, 1984.

[78] R. S. Streett and E. A. Emerson. An automata theoretic procedure for the propositional mu-calculus. *Information and Computation*, 81:249–264, 1989.

[79] W. Thomas. Logic for computer science: The engineering challenge. volume 2000 of *Lecture Notes in Computer Science*, pages 257–267, 2002.

[80] T. Urbański. On deciding if deterministic Rabin language is in Büchi class. In *ICALP'00*, volume 1853 of *Lecture Notes in Computer Science*, pages 663–674, 2000.

[81] M. Y. Vardi and P.Wolper. Automata theoretic techniques for modal logics of programs. In *Sixteenth ACM Symposium on the Theoretical Computer Science*, 1984.

[82] K. Wagner. Eine topologische Charakterisierung einiger Klassen regulärer Folgenmengen. *J. Inf. Process. Cybern. EIK*, 13:473–487, 1977.

[83] I. Walukiewicz. Pushdown processes: Games and model checking. *Information and Computation*, 164(2):234–263, 2001.

Proving Lower Bounds Via Pseudo-random Generators

Manindra Agrawal

Department of Computer Science
Indian Institute of Technology, Kanpur
manindra@iitk.ac.in

Abstract. In this paper, we formalize two stepwise approaches, based on *pseudo-random generators*, for proving P $\neq$ NP and its arithmetic analog: *Permanent requires superpolynomial sized arithmetic circuits*.

1   Introduction

The central aim of complexity theory is to prove lower bounds on the complexity of problems. While the relative classification of problems (via reductions) has been very successful, not much progress has been made in determining their absolute complexity. For example, we do not even know if NE admits nonuniform NC^1 circuits.

Initial attempts (in 1970s) to prove lower bounds centered on using the diagonalization technique that had proven very useful in recursion theory. However, a series of relativization results soon showed that this technique cannot help in its standard guise [6]. Very recently, the technique has been used to prove certain simultaneous time-space lower bounds [7], however, its usefulness for single resource lower bounds remains unclear.

In the 1980s, the results of Razborov [15] (lower bounds on monotone circuits) and Håstad [8] (lower bounds on constant depth circuits) gave rise to the hope of proving lower bounds via combinatorial arguments on boolean circuit model of complexity classes. However, there was little progress since mid-80s and ten years later Razborov and Rudich [16] explained the reason for this: they showed that combinatorial arguments used for previous lower bounds cannot be extended to larger classes.

Over the last ten years, a new paradigm is slowly emerging that might lead us to strong lower bounds: *pseudo-random generators*. These were introduced in 1980s by Yao [22], Blum, and Micali [4], Nisan and Wigderson [14] to formulate the hardness of cryptographic primitives (in the first two references) and to derandomize polynomial-time randomized algorithms (in the last reference).

It was known from the beginning that existence of pseudo-random generators implies lower bounds on boolean circuits. In fact, they can be viewed as a strong form of diagonalization. Attempts were then made to prove the other (and seemingly more interesting) direction: lower bounds on boolean circuits imply existence of pseudo-random generators. This was achieved after a lot of effort:

R. Ramanujam and S. Sen (Eds.): FSTTCS 2005, LNCS 3821, pp. 92–105, 2005.

Håstad, Impagliazzo, Levin and Luby [9] showed that pseudo-random generators of *polynomial stretch* are equivalent to *one-way functions*, Impagliazzo and
Wigderson [10] showed that pseudo-random generators of *exponential stretch* are
equivalent to hard sets in E.

Some recent advances suggest that the first (and easier) direction of the above
equivalence may in fact hold the key to obtaining lower bounds. Very recently,
Omer Reingold used expander graphs (these are one of the fundamental tools in
derandomization) to search in an undirected graph using logarithmic space [17].
This proves SL = L, resolving the complexity of the class SL. Although Reingold's result does not yield a pseudo-random generator or a lower bound, it
suggests that one can do derandomization without appealing to lower bounds,
and a strong enough derandomization will result in a lower bound.

Lower bounds for arithmetic circuits have also been investigated, but again,
without much success. It appears that obtaining lower bounds for these circuits should be easier than boolean circuits since boolean circuits can simulate
arithmetic circuits but not vice versa. Kabanets and Impagliazzo [11] have recently observed a connection between lower bounds on arithmetic circuits and
derandomizations of *polynomial identity testing problem* (given a multivariate
polynomial computed by an arithmetic circuit, test if it is identically zero). This
connection, however, is not as tight as for boolean circuits. For these circuits too
there is some evidence that proving lower bounds via derandomization might
work: the primality testing algorithm of Agrawal, Kayal, Saxena [2] essentially
derandomizes a certain polynomial identity.

Admittedly, the evidence for the success of "pseudo-random generator" approach is weak: neither Reingold's result nor the primality testing algorithm
yield a lower bound (the AKS "derandomization" works only for a problem, not
a class). However, this is one of the, if not the, most promising approach that
we have presently for obtaining boolean and arithmetic circuit lower bounds
and so needs to be investigated seriously. In this article, we formulate, based
on pseudo-random generators, stepwise approaches to resolve two of the most
important conjectures in complexity theory: P ≠ NP and its arithmetic analog
Permanent requires superpolynomial-sized arithmetic circuits. For arithmetic circuits, the result of Kabanets and Impagliazzo is not strong enough to show that
derandomization implies second conjecture. To make it work, we define pseudo-
random generators for arithmetic circuits and show that certain generators imply
the desired lower bound on arithmetic circuits.

2   Pseudo-random Generators for Boolean Circuits

Let $\mathcal{C}(s(n), d(n))$ denote the class of circuits of size $s(n)$ and depth $d(n)$ on inputs
of size n. We will assume that all our circuits are *layered* with layers alternating
between AND and OR gates.

We begin with the definition of a pseudo-random generator for boolean circuits.

Definition 21 Function f, $f : \{0,1\}^* \mapsto \{0,1\}^*$, is a $(\ell(n), n)$-*pseudo-random generator against* $\mathcal{C}(s(n), d(n))$ if:

- $f(\{0,1\}^{\ell(n)}) \subseteq \{0,1\}^n$ with $\ell(n) < n$ for all n.
- For any circuit $C \in \mathcal{C}(s(n), d(n))$,

$$\left| \Pr_{x \in \{0,1\}^n}[C(x) = 1] - \Pr_{y \in \{0,1\}^{\ell(n)}}[C(f(y)) = 1] \right| \leq \frac{1}{n}.$$

The difference between output and input length of a pseudo-random generator, $n - \ell(n)$, is called the *stretch* of the generator. A simple counting argument shows that there exist $(O(\log s(n)), n)$-pseudo-random generators against $\mathcal{C}(s(n), d(n))$:

Define f by randomly assigning strings of length n for inputs of size $4 \log s(n)$. Let y be a string of size $4 \log s(n)$. For a circuit $C \in \mathcal{C}(s(n), d(n))$ with input size n, define random variable Y to be $C(f(y))$. The expected value of Y is precisely the fraction of strings accepted by C. We have $s^4(n)$ such independent random variables with the same expected value. Hence, by Chernoff's bound, the probability that the average of these variables differs from the expectation by more than $\frac{1}{n}$ is less than $\frac{1}{2^{s^3(n)}}$. Since there are less than $2^{s^2(n)}$ circuits of size $s(n)$, most of the choices of f will be pseudo-random.

It is also easy to see (via a similar counting argument) that $(o(\log s(n)), n)$-pseudo-random generators cannot exist against $\mathcal{C}(s(n), d(n))$. This motivates the following definition.

Definition 22 A $(O(\log s(n)), n)$-pseudo-random generator against $\mathcal{C}(s(n), d(n))$ is called an *optimal* pseudo-random generator against $\mathcal{C}(s(n), d(n))$.

So far, we have not examined the computability aspect of pseudo-random generators. It is easy to see that optimal pseudo-random generators against $\mathcal{C}(s(n), d(n))$ can be computed in time $O(2^{s^2(n)})$. To make the notion interesting, we need to compute them faster. There are two ways in which the time complexity of a generator can be measured: as a function of output size or as a function of input size. We choose to express it in terms of input size.

Definition 23 A $(\ell(n), n)$-pseudo-random generator f against $\mathcal{C}(s(n), d(n))$ is $t(m)$-*computable* if there is an algorithm running in time $t(m)$ that on input (y, i) with $|y| = m = \ell(n)$ and $1 \leq i \leq n$, outputs i^{th} bit of $f(y)$.

In the above, we have defined the complexity of f slightly differently – usually it is defined to be the complexity of computing the entire $f(y)$. Our definition has an advantage when both $\ell(n)$ and $t(\ell(n))$ are substantially smaller than n. In that case, the first few bits of f can be computed very quickly and this fact would be useful later.

3   Boolean Circuit Lower Bounds Via Pseudo-random Generators

A $(\ell(n), n)$-pseudo-random generator against $\mathcal{C}(s(n), d(n))$ that is $2^{O(m)}$-computable yields a lower bound on $\mathcal{C}(s(\ell^{-1}(n)), d(\ell^{-1}(n)))$.

Theorem 31 ([14]) *Let f be a $t(m)$-computable $(\ell(n), n)$-pseudo-random generator against $\mathcal{C}(s(n), d(n))$. Then there is a set in $\mathrm{Ntime}(t(m) \cdot m) \cap \mathrm{Dtime}(t(m) \cdot 2^m)$ that cannot be accepted by any circuit family in $\mathcal{C}(s(\ell^{-1}(n)), d(\ell^{-1}(n)))$.*

Proof. Define a set A as follows:

> On input x, $|x| = m = \ell(n) + 1$ for some n, find if there exists a y, $|y| = \ell(n)$ such that x is a prefix of $f(y)$. If yes, accept otherwise reject.

The set A is in $\mathrm{Ntime}(t(m) \cdot m)$: guess a y of size $m - 1$ and compute first m bits of $f(y)$. The set of also in $\mathrm{Dtime}(t(m) \cdot 2^m)$: for every y of size $m - 1$ compute the first m bits of $f(y)$ and check if any matches.

Suppose there is a circuit family in $\mathcal{C}(s(\ell^{-1}(n)), d(\ell^{-1}(n)))$ that accepts A. Fix an input size $m = \ell(n) + 1$ for some n and consider the corresponding circuit C from the family. Construct a new circuit, say D, on input size n as follows. Circuit D simply simulates circuit C on the first m bits of its input (ignoring the remaining bits). By the definition of A, it follows that for every y, $|y| = m - 1$, $f(y)$ is accepted by D. In addition, circuit D rejects at least half of its inputs (because the number of prefixes of m bits of $f(y)$'s is at most 2^{m-1}). Circuit D is in $\mathcal{C}(s(n), d(n))$ since the input size has grown from m (for circuit C) to n (for circuit D). Therefore,

$$\left| \Pr_{x \in \{0,1\}^n}[D(x) = 1] - \Pr_{y \in \{0,1\}^{m-1}}[D(f(y)) = 1] \right| \leq \frac{1}{n}.$$

However, the first probability is less than $\frac{1}{2}$ while the second is 1 as argued above. This is a contradiction.   □

For optimal generators, we get the following corollary.

Corollary 32 *Let f be a $t(m)$-computable optimal pseudo-random generator against $\mathcal{C}(s(n), d(n))$. Then there is a set in $\mathrm{Ntime}(t(m) \cdot m) \cap \mathrm{Dtime}(t(m) \cdot 2^m)$ that cannot be accepted by any circuit family in $\mathcal{C}(2^{\epsilon n}, d(s^{-1}(2^{\epsilon n})))$ for some $\epsilon > 0$.*[1]

As of now, the best pseudo-random generator known is the following.

Lemma 33 ([8, 14]) *For any $d > 0$, there exists a $m^{O(1)}$-computable $(\log^{O(d)} n, n)$-pseudo-random generator against $\mathcal{C}(n, d)$, the class of size n, depth d circuits.*

---

[1] The converse of this corollary was shown by Impagliazzo and Wigderson [10].

The above generator is constructed by taking Håstad's lower bound [8] on constant-depth circuits and applying Nisan-Wigderson's construction [14] of pseudo-random generators on it. This generator is clearly not an optimal generator, but comes close – its input length is $\log^{O(d)} n$ instead of $O(\log n)$. If one can reduce the input length to, say, $O(t(d) \log n)$ for any function $t(\cdot)$, then we get an optimal generator. This is our first step:

Step 1. *Obtain a $2^{O(m)}$-computable optimal pseudo-random generator against $\mathcal{C}(n, d)$ for each $d > 0$.*

Such generators will already yield an interesting lower bound.

Lemma 34 *If there exists a $2^{O(m)}$-computable optimal pseudo-random generator against $\mathcal{C}(n, d)$ then there is a set in E that cannot be accepted by any circuit family in $\mathcal{C}(2^{\epsilon n}, d)$ for some $\epsilon > 0$.*

Proof. Direct from Corollary 32.   □

It is worth mentioning at this point that exponential lower bounds are not known even for *depth three* circuits! The above lemma implies another lower bound:

Corollary 35 *If there exists a $2^{O(m)}$-computable optimal pseudo-random generator against $\mathcal{C}(n, d)$ then there is a set in E that cannot be accepted by a non-uniform semiunbounded circuit family of size $n^{d-\epsilon}$, depth $(d - \epsilon) \log n$ for any $\epsilon > 0$.*

Proof. Take any size $n^{d-\epsilon}$, depth $(d - \epsilon) \log n$ (for some $\epsilon > 0$) circuit C on n inputs with unbounded fanin OR-gates. The circuit can be converted into a subexponential size depth d circuit as follows. Cut C into $\frac{d}{2}$ layers of depth $\frac{2(d-\epsilon)}{d} \log n$ each. In each layer, write each topmost gate as OR-of-ANDs of bottommost gates. A direct counting shows that each such OR-of-ANDs will have $O(n^{2dn^{1-\frac{\epsilon}{d}}})$ gates. There are at most $n^{d-\epsilon}$ OR-of-ANDs, and therefore, the size of the resulting circuit is at most $2^{O(\log n \cdot n^{1-\frac{\epsilon}{d}})} = 2^{o(n)}$. The depth of the circuit is d. The existence of a $2^{O(m)}$-computable optimal pseudo-random generator against $\mathcal{C}(n, d)$ implies the existence of a set A in E that cannot be accepted by any family of circuits from $\mathcal{C}(2^{\delta n}, d)$ for suitable $\delta > 0$ by the above lemma. This means that circuit C cannot accept $\{A\}_{=n}$.   □

By improving the complexity of the generator, we can get a better lower bound. This is our second step:

Step 2. *Obtain a $m^{O(1)}$-computable optimal pseudo-random generator against $\mathcal{C}(n, d)$ for each $d > 0$.*

The better time complexity of the generator implies that the set A will now belong to the class NP instead of E. Thus we get:

Corollary 36 *If there exists a $m^{O(1)}$-computable optimal pseudo-random generator against $C(n, d)$ then there is a set in NP that cannot be accepted by a non-uniform semiunbounded circuit family of size $n^{d-\epsilon}$, depth $(d - \epsilon) \log n$ for any $\epsilon > 0$.*

The next aim is to construct an optimal pseudo-random generator against a larger class of circuits: class of logarithmic depth circuits of fanin two, i.e., NC^1. This class contains constant depth circuits and is only "slightly higher" (although *no* lower bounds are known for this class).

Step 3. *Obtain a $m^{O(1)}$-computable optimal pseudo-random generator against $C(n, \log n)$.*

This generalization improves the lower bound *substantially*.

Lemma 37 *If there exists a $m^{O(1)}$-computable optimal pseudo-random generator against $C(n, \log n)$ then there is a set in NP that cannot be accepted by any non-uniform family of sublinear depth and subexponential size circuits.*

Proof. Directly from Corollary 32.   □

The last step is to push the class of circuits further up to all polylog depth circuits, i.e., the class NC. This class is believed to be substantially smaller than the class of all polynomial sized circuits.

Step 4. *Obtain a $m^{O(1)}$-computable optimal pseudo-random generator against $C(n, \log^{O(1)} n)$.*

The following lemma follows immediately.

Lemma 38 *If there exists a $m^{O(1)}$-computable optimal pseudo-random generator against $C(n, \log^{O(1)} n)$ then there is a set in NP that cannot be accepted by any non-uniform family of polynomial depth and subexponential size circuits.*

As a corollary of above, we have:

Corollary 39 *If there exists a $m^{O(1)}$-computable optimal pseudo-random generator against $C(n, \log^{O(1)} n)$ then $P \neq NP$.*

4   Pseudo-random Generators for Arithmetic Circuits

Lower bounds for arithmetic circuits are even less understood than boolean circuits. For example, we do not even know lower bounds on depth four arithmetic circuits. Mulmuley and Sohoni [12] have been trying to use algebraic geometric techniques for proving arithmetic circuit lower bounds. Here, we formulate an alternative way using pseudo-random generators.

Let $\mathcal{A}(n, F)$ be the class of arithmetic circuits over field F such that any circuit $C \in \mathcal{A}(n, F)$ has n addition, subtraction, and multiplication gates over the field F. We assume that all arithmetic circuits are *layered* and the layers alternate between multiplication and addition/subtraction gates. Circuit C has at most n input variables and computes a polynomial over F of degree at most 2^n. Note that the number of input variables for arithmetic circuit is not as important parameter as for boolean circuits. Even single variable circuits can compute very complex polynomials. Kabanets and Impagliazzo [11] showed a connection between *polynomial identity testing* and lower bounds on arithmetic circuits. They proved that if there is a polynomial-time deterministic algorithm for verifying polynomial identities then NEXP cannot have polynomial-sized arithmetic circuits. They also proved a partial converse: if Permanent cannot be computed by polynomial-sized arithmetic circuits, then polynomial identity testing can be done in subexponential time.

We make this relationship between identity testing and lower bounds stronger via an appropriate notion of pseudo-random generator against arithmetic circuits.

Definition 41 Function $f : \mathbb{N} \mapsto (F[y])^*$ is a $(\ell(n), n)$-*pseudo-random generator* against $\mathcal{A}(n, F)$ if:

- $f(n) \in (F[y])^{n+1}$ for every $n > 0$.
- Let $f(n) = (f_1(y), \ldots, f_n(y), g(y))$. Then each $f_i(y)$ as well as $g(y)$ is a polynomial of degree at most $2^{\ell(n)}$.
- For any circuit $C \in \mathcal{A}(n, F)$ with $m \leq n$ inputs:
  $C(x_1, x_2, \ldots, x_m) = 0$ iff $C(f_1(y), f_2(y), \ldots, f_m(y)) = 0 \pmod{g(y)}$.

A direct application of Schwartz-Zippel lemma [18, 23] shows that there always exist $(O(\log n), n)$-pseudo-random generators against $\mathcal{A}(n, F)$:

> For every $n > 0$, define $f(n)$ to be the sequence $(f_1(y), f_2(y), \ldots, f_n(y), g(y))$ where each $f_i(y)$ is a random degree $n^3 - 1$ polynomial and $g(y)$ is an irreducible polynomial of degree n^3 over F. In addition, if F is infinite, all these polynomials have coefficients bounded by 2^n. Let $C \in \mathcal{A}(n, F)$ compute a non-zero polynomial on $m \leq n$ variables. Let $\hat{F}$ be the extension field $F[y]/(g(y))$. Polynomial $f_i(y)$ can be thought of as a random element of the field $\hat{F}$. Now by Schwartz-Zippel lemma, the probability that $C(f_1(y), f_2(y), \ldots, f_m(y)) = 0 \pmod{g(y)}$ is at most $\frac{\deg C}{2^{n^3}} \leq \frac{1}{2^{n^3-n}}$ since $\deg C \leq 2^n$. Since there are at most 2^{n^2} circuits of size n, the probability that the generator fails against any such circuit is at most $\frac{1}{2^{n^3-n^2-n}}$. Therefore, most of the choices of f are pseudo-random.

As in the case of boolean circuits, we call such generators *optimal* pseudo-random generators. There are, however, a few of crucial differences between the boolean and arithmetic cases. Firstly, the pseudo-random generator against arithmetic circuits does not approximate the number of zeroes of the polynomial computed by the circuit. Secondly, it computes a polynomial for each input instead of a bit value and a moduli polynomial. Finally, it outputs only *one* sequence of $n + 1$ polynomials as opposed to a polynomial number of strings of length

n in the boolean case. The degree of each output polynomial is $2^{\ell(n)}$ which equals $n^{O(1)}$ for optimal generator. Therefore, the time needed to compute such a generator is $2^{\Omega(\ell(n))}$ ($= n^{\Omega(1)}$ for optimal case). This can be exponentially larger than the input size of the generator. Hence we do not have as much freedom available to vary the time complexity of the generator. This motivates the following definition.

Definition 42 A $(\ell(n), n)$-pseudo-random generator f against $\mathcal{A}(n, F)$ is *efficiently computable* if $f(n)$ is computable in time $2^{O(\ell(n))}$.

This definition of pseudo-random generators is the right one from the perspective of derandomization of identity testing.

Theorem 43 *Suppose there exists an efficiently computable $(\ell(n), n)$-pseudo-random generator against $\mathcal{A}(n, F)$. Then polynomial identity testing can be done deterministically in time $n \cdot 2^{O(\ell(n))}$.*

Proof. Let $C \in \mathcal{A}(n, F)$ be a circuit of size n computing a possible identity over F on $m \leq n$ variables. Then $C(f_1(y), f_2(y), \ldots, f_m(y)) \pmod{g(y)}$ can be computed in time $2^{O(\ell(n))}$: each $f_i(y)$ and $g(y)$ is of degree $2^{O(\ell(n))}$ and can be computed in the same time; and then the circuit C can be evaluated modulo $g(y)$ in $n \cdot 2^{O(\ell(n))}$ time. $\square$

Corollary 44 *Suppose there exists an efficiently computable optimal pseudo-random generator against $\mathcal{A}(n, F)$. Then polynomial identity testing can be done in P.*

A further evidence of "correctness" of the definition is provided by the AKS primality test [2] which can be viewed as derandomization of a specific identity. The identity is $C(x) = (1 + x)^n - x^n - 1$ over Z_n and, as shown in [1], the function $f(n) = (x, g(x))$ with

$$g(x) = x^{16 \log^5 n} \cdot \prod_{r=1}^{16 \log^5 n} \prod_{a=1}^{4 \log^4 n} ((x - a)^r - 1)$$

($g(x)$ is of degree $O(\log^{14} n)$) is an efficiently computable optimal "pseudo-random generator" against $C(x) \in \mathcal{A}(O(\log n), Z_n)$ (it is not really a pseudo-random generator since it works only against a subset of circuits in $\mathcal{A}(O(\log n), Z_n)$).

5   Arithmetic Circuit Lower Bounds Via Pseudo-random Generators

As in the case of boolean circuits, an efficiently computable pseudo-random generator implies a lower bound:

Theorem 51 *Let f be an efficiently computable $(\ell(n), n)$-pseudo-random generator against $\mathcal{A}(n, F)$. Then there is a multilinear polynomial computable in time $2^{O(\ell(n))}$ that cannot be computed by any circuit family in $\mathcal{A}(n, F)$.*[2]

Proof. For any $m = \ell(n)$, define polynomial $q(x_1, x_2, \ldots, x_{2m})$ as:

$$q(x_1, x_2, \ldots, x_{2m}) = \sum_{S \subseteq [1,2m]} c_S \cdot \prod_{i \in S} x_i.$$

The coefficients c_S satisfy the condition

$$\sum_{S \subseteq [1,2m]} c_S \cdot \prod_{i \in S} f_i(y) = 0$$

where $f(n) = (f_1(y), f_2(y), \ldots, f_n(y), g(y))$. Such a q always exists as the following argument shows.

The number of coefficients of q are exactly 2^{2m}. These need to satisfy a polynomial equation of degree at most $2m \cdot 2^m$. So the equation gives rise to at most $2m \cdot 2^m + 1$ homogeneous constraints on the coefficients. Since $(2m \cdot 2^m + 1) < 2^{2m}$ for $m \geq 3$, there is always a non-trivial polynomial q satisfying all the conditions.

The polynomial q can be computed by solving a system of $2^{O(m)}$ linear equations in $2^{O(m)}$ variables over the field F. Each of these equations can be computed in time $2^{O(m)}$ using computability of f. Therefore, q can be computed in time $2^{O(m)}$. Now suppose q can be computed by a circuit $C \in \mathcal{A}(n, F)$. By the definition of polynomial q, it follows that $C(f_1(y), f_2(y), \ldots, f_{2m}(y)) = 0$. The size of circuit C is n and it computes a non-zero polynomial. This contradicts the pseudo-randomness of f. □

As in the case of boolean circuits, optimal pseudo-random generators against constant depth arithmetic circuits is our first goal.

Step 1. *Obtain an efficiently-computable optimal pseudo-random generator against size n arithmetic circuits of depth d over F for each $d > 0$.*

And exactly as in the boolean case, we get a lower bound on log-depth polynomial size circuits with unbounded fanin addition gates.

Lemma 52 *If there exist efficiently-computable optimal pseudo-random generators against size n arithmetic circuits of depth d over F then for there exists a multilinear polynomial computable in E that cannot be computed by a nonuniform family of circuits with unbounded fanin addition gates of size $n^{d-\epsilon}$, depth $(d - \epsilon) \log n$ for any $\epsilon > 0$.*

---

[2] A partial converse of this theorem can also be shown: if there exists a polynomial computable in time $2^{O(\ell(n))}$ that cannot be computed by a circuit family in $\mathcal{A}(n, F)$ then there exists an efficiently computable $(\ell^2(n), n)$-pseudo-random generator against the class of size n circuits over F whose degree is bounded by n.

Proof. A size $n^{d-\epsilon}$, depth $(d - \epsilon) \log n$ arithmetic circuit with unbounded fanin addition gates can be translated, exactly as in proof of Lemma 35, to a subexponential sized depth d circuit. The optimal pseudo-random generator against depth d circuits gives the lower bound. □

The class of arithmetic branching programs is equivalent to the class of polynomials computed by determinants of a polynomial sized matrix [21, 19, 5]. Also, polynomial-sized arithmetic formulas can be expressed as polynomial sized arithmetic branching programs. We get a much stronger lower bound by generalizing the pseudo-random generator to work against polynomial sized branching programs.

Step 2. *Obtain an efficiently-computable optimal pseudo-random generator against size n arithmetic branching programs over F.*

This step nearly achieves our final goal.

Lemma 53 *If there exist efficiently-computable optimal pseudo-random generators against size n arithmetic branching programs over F then there exists a multilinear polynomial computable in E that (1) cannot be expressed as the determinant of a subexponential sized matrix and (2) cannot be computed by a $2^{o(\frac{n}{\log n})}$-sized arithmetic circuit.*

Proof. The first part follows directly from Theorem 51 translated for arithmetic branching programs. For the second part, recall that the polynomial q is multilinear and so has polynomial degree. In [20] it is shown that arithmetic circuits of size N and degree D can be transformed to arithmetic circuits of size $N^{O(1)}$ with depth $O(\log N \log D)$. Further, a circuit of depth $O(\log N \log D)$ can be expressed as determinant of a matrix of size $2^{O(\log N \log D)} = N^{O(\log D)}$. Using the lower bound of first part, it follows that the polynomial q cannot be computed by arithmetic circuits of size $2^{o(\frac{n}{\log n})}$. □

To obtain a lower bound on permanent, we need to improve the time complexity of polynomial q. Suppose that each coefficient c_S of the polynomial q can be computed by a #P-function (this will require that all coefficients of each polynomial in $f(n)$ to be computed by a #P-function). Then it follows that the polynomial q can be expressed as permanent of a matrix of size polynomial in m (because permanent captures #P-computations). Let us call such a generator #P-computable.

Step 3. *Obtain a #P-computable optimal pseudo-random generator against size n arithmetic branching programs over F.*

Corollary 54 *If there exists an efficiently-computable optimal pseudo-random generator against size n arithmetic branching programs over F then the permanent of a $n \times n$ matrix over F (1) cannot be expressed as the determinant of a subexponential-sized matrix over F, (2) cannot be computed by a $2^{o(\frac{n}{\log n})}$-sized arithmetic circuit.*

Of course, the above step cannot be carried out for fields of characteristic two where permanent is equal to the determinant.

6   Will This Approach Work?

In the sequence of steps proposed to prove arithmetic and boolean circuit lower bounds, perhaps the most important one is step 1. Achieving this step will, besides providing strong lower bounds for the first time, will establish the correctness of the approach and increase the possibility that remaining steps can also be achieved.

In this section, we discuss some potential candidates to achieve Step 1 for both boolean and arithmetic circuits.

6.1   Step 1 for Boolean Circuits

Hitting set generators are a weaker form of optimal pseudo-random generators. The difference is that for a circuit C that accepts at least half of its inputs, a hitting set generator is required to generate at least one input x to C such that $C(x) = 1$. (As opposed to this, pseudo-random generators are required to generate appoximately $\Pr_x[C(x) = 1]$ fraction of x's on which $C(x) = 1$.) Both hitting set generators and optimal pseudo-random generators against $\mathcal{C}(s(n), d(n))$ have input of size $O(\log s(n))$.

The proof of Theorem 31 shows that efficiently computable hitting set generators are sufficient to obtain lower bounds. Coupled with the result of [10], this implies that efficiently computable hitting set generators and efficiently computable optimal pseudo-random generators are equivalent.

Let $f : \{0,1\}^{O(\log n)} \mapsto \{0,1\}^n$ be any $\frac{1}{n^{2d}}$-*biased*, $2 \log n$-*wise indepen-dent* generator. In other words, any $2 \log n$ output bits of f, on a random input, are nearly independent (with a bias of at most $\frac{1}{n^{2d}}$). There exist several constructions of such generators [13, 3]. We take one from [3]. Define $f_{B,d}$, $f_{B,d} : \{0,1\}^{(4d+4)\log n} \mapsto \{0,1\}^n$, as:

$$f_{B,d}(x, y) = (x^0 \cdot y)(x^1 \cdot y) \cdots (x^{n-1} \cdot y)$$

where $|x| = |y| = (2d + 2) \log n$, x^i is computed in the field $F_{n^{2d+2}}$ treating x as an element of the field, and '$\cdot$' is inner product modulo 2. It is shown in [3] that $f_{B,d}$ satisfies the required independence property.

Functions $f_{B,d}$ can easily shown to be $m^{O(1)}$ computable. We can prove the following about function $f_{B,2}$:

Lemma 61 *Function $f_{B,2}$ is a hitting set generator against depth 2, size n boolean circuits.*

Proof. Without loss of generality, consider a depth 2, size n circuit C that is an OR-of-ANDs and accepts at least half fraction of inputs. Delete all the AND gates from C of fanin more than $2 \log n$. Let the resulting circuit be C'. Any input accepted by circuit C' is also accepted by C and the fraction of inputs accepted by C' is at least $\frac{1}{2} - \frac{1}{n}$ (a deleted AND gate outputs a 1 on at most $\frac{1}{n^2}$ inputs and there are at most n deleted AND gates). Consider any surviving AND gate in the circuit. Its fanin is at most $2 \log n$. Therefore, it outputs a 1 on at least $\frac{1}{n^2}$ inputs. Since the output of $f_{B,2}$ is $2 \log n$-wise independent with a bias of at most $\frac{1}{n^4}$, the probability that this AND gate will output a 1, when given $f_{B,2}$ as input, is at least $\frac{1}{n^2} - \frac{1}{n^4} > 0$. Hence $f_{B,2}$ is a hitting set generator against C.

About lemma and Lemma 35 together show that:

Corollary 62 *There is a set in* NP *that cannot be accepted by semiunbounded circuits of size $n^{2-\epsilon}$ and depth $(2 - \epsilon) \log n$ for any $\epsilon > 0$.*

In fact, using a different definition for $f_{B,2}$ from [3] can bring the complexity of the hard set down to SAC^1 from NP. This implies that $f_{B,d}$ *cannot be a* hitting set generator for all d (because SAC^1 circuits can be transformed to subexponential sized constant depth circuits as observed earlier). However, it appears that a combination of $f_{B,d}$ with other derandomization primitives can result in hitting set generators for higher depths.

6.2   Step 1 for Arithmetic Circuits

We need to weaken the definition of pseudo-random generators for arithmetic circuits too.

Definition 63 Function $f : \mathbb{N} \times \mathbb{N} \mapsto (F[y])^*$ is a *hitting set generator* against $\mathcal{A}(n, F)$ if:

- $f(n, k) \in (F[y])^{n+1}$ for every $n > 0$ and $1 \le k \le n^{O(1)}$.
- Let $f(n, k) = (f_{1,k}(y), \ldots, f_{n,k}(y), g_k(y))$. Then each $f_{i,k}(y)$ as well as $g_k(y)$ is a polynomial of degree at most $n^{O(1)}$.
- For any circuit $C \in \mathcal{A}(n, F)$ with $m \le n$ inputs:
  $C(x_1, x_2, \ldots, x_m) = 0$ iff for every k, $1 \le k \le n^{O(1)}$,

$$C(f_{1,k}(y), f_{2,k}(y), \ldots, f_{m,k}(y)) = 0 \ (\mathrm{mod} \ g_k(y)).$$

It is easy to see that a complete derandomization of identity testing can also be done by an efficiently computable hitting set generator. By slightly modifying the definition of polynomial q in the proof of Theorem 51, a similar lower bound can be shown too (q will now need to satisfy $n^{O(1)}$ polynomial equations of degree $n^{O(1)}$ instead of just one; this still translates to $n^{O(1)}$ homogeneous constraints on the coefficients of q).

Define function $f_{A,d}$ as:

$$f_{A,d}(n, k) = (y^{k^0}, y^{k^1}, \ldots, y^{k^{n-1}}, y^r - 1)$$

where $r \ge n^{4d}$ is a prime and $1 \le k < r$.

Function $f_{A,d}$ is easily seen to be $n^{O(1)}$ computable. Polynomial q, defined for function $f_{A,d}$, can be computed in PSPACE (it is not clear how to compute q in #P). We can prove the following about function $f_{A,2}$:

Lemma 64 *Function $f_{A,2}$ is a hitting set generator against size n, depth 2 arithmetic circuits.*

Proof. Consider a size n, depth 2 arithmetic circuit C computing a non-zero polynomial. If C has a multiplication gate at the top, then it will be non-zero on any sequence $f_{A,2}(n, k)$ such that $k^i \neq k^j \pmod{r}$ for $1 \leq i < j < n$. Most of the k's (e.g., any k which is a generator for F_r^*) have this property.

Now consider C with an addition gate at the top. C then computes a polynomial of degree up to n with at most n non-zero terms. Let t_1 be the first term of this polynomial (under some ordering) and let t_j be any other term. Then the number of k's for which $t_1 = t_j \pmod{y^r - 1}$ under the substitution of variables according to $f_{A,2}(n, k)$ is at most $n - 1$. So the number of k's for which $t_1 = t_j \pmod{y^r - 1}$ for *some* j is at most n^2. As total number of k's is n^4, there exist k's for which $t_1 \neq t_j \pmod{y^r - 1}$ for any $j > 1$ under the substitution $f_{A,2}(n, k)$. C evaluates to a non-zero polynomial modulo $y^r - 1$ on such inputs.

Using Lemma 52, this results in:

Corollary 65 *There is a multilinear function computable in* PSPACE *that cannot be computed by circuits with unbounded fanin addition gates of size $n^{2-\epsilon}$ and depth $(2 - \epsilon) \log n$ for any $\epsilon > 0$.*

We conjecture that above lemma holds for all depths:

Conjecture. *Function $f_{A,d}$ is a hitting set generator against depth d, size n arithmetic circuits for every $d > 0$.*

It is to be hoped that the next twenty five years will be more fruitful for lower bounds than the previous ones. One might even hope that all the proposed steps will be achieved answering two of the most fundamental questions in complexity theory.

References

[1] Manindra Agrawal. On derandomizing tests for certain polynomial identities. In *Proceedings of the Conference on Computational Complexity*, pages 355–362, 2003.

[2] Manindra Agrawal, Neeraj Kayal, and Nitin Saxena. PRIMES is in P. *Annals of Mathematics*, 160(2):781–793, 2004.

[3] N. Alon, O. Goldreich, J. Håstad, and R. Peralta. Simple constructions of almost k-wise independent random variables. In *Proceedings of Annual IEEE Symposium on Foundations of Computer Science*, pages 544–553, 1990.

[4] M. Blum and S. Micali. How to generate cryptographically strong sequences of pseudo-random bits. *SIAM Journal on Computing*, 13:850–864, 1984.

[5] C. Damm. DET=L$^{\#l}$. Technical Report Informatik-preprint 8, Fachbereich Informatik der Humboldt Universität zu Berlin, 1991.

[6] L. Fortnow. The role of relativization in complexity theory. Bulletin of the European Association for Theoretical Computer Science, 1994. Complexity Theory Column.

[7] L. Fortnow. Time-space tradeoffs for satisfiability. J. Comput. Sys. Sci., 60(2):337–353, 2000.

[8] J. Håstad. Computational limitations on small depth circuits. PhD thesis, Massachusetts Institute of Technology, 1986.

[9] J. Håstad, R. Impagliazzo, L. Levin, and M. Luby. A pseudo-random generator from any one-way function. SIAM Journal on Computing, pages 221–243, 1998.

[10] R. Impagliazzo and A. Wigderson. P = BPP if E requires exponential circuits: Derandomizing the XOR lemma. In Proceedings of Annual ACM Symposium on the Theory of Computing, pages 220–229, 1997.

[11] Valentine Kabanets and Russell Impagliazzo. Derandomizing polyonmial identity tests means proving circuit lower bounds. In Proceedings of Annual ACM Symposium on the Theory of Computing, pages 355–364, 2003.

[12] K. Mulmuley and M. Sohoni. Geometric complexity theory I: An approach to the P vs. NP and other related problems. SIAM Journal on Computing, 31(2):496–526, 2002.

[13] J. Naor and M. Naor. Small-bias probability spaces: Efficient constructions and applications. In Proceedings of Annual ACM Symposium on the Theory of Computing, pages 213–223, 1990.

[14] N. Nisan and A. Wigderson. Hardness vs. randomness. J. Comput. Sys. Sci., 49(2):149–167, 1994.

[15] A. Razborov. Lower bounds for the monotone complexity of some boolean functions. Doklady Akademii Nauk SSSR, 281(4):798–801, 1985. English translation in Soviet Math. Doklady, 31:354-357, 1985.

[16] A. Razborov and S. Rudich. Natural proofs. In Proceedings of Annual ACM Symposium on the Theory of Computing, pages 204–213, 1994.

[17] O. Reingold. Undirected s-t-connectivity in logspace. In Proceedings of Annual ACM Symposium on the Theory of Computing, pages 376–385, 2005.

[18] J. T. Schwartz. Fast probabilistic algorithms for verification of polynomial identities. J. ACM, 27(4):701–717, 1980.

[19] S. Toda. Counting problems computationally equivalent to the determinant. manuscript, 1991.

[20] L. Valiant, S. Skyum, S. Berkowitz, and C. Rackoff. Fast parallel computation of polynnomials using few processors. SIAM Journal on Computing, 12:641–644, 1983.

[21] V Vinay. Counting auxiliary pushdown automata and semi-unbounded arithmetic circuits. In Proceedings of the Structure in Complexity Theory Conference, pages 270–284. Springer LNCS 223, 1991.

[22] A. C. Yao. Theory and applications of trapdoor functions. In Proceedings of Annual IEEE Symposium on Foundations of Computer Science, pages 80–91, 1982.

[23] R. E. Zippel. Probabilistic algorithms for sparse polynomials. In EUROSCAM'79, pages 216–226. Springer LNCS 72, 1979.

Erdős Magic

Joel Spencer

Courant Institute of Mathematical Sciences
New York
joel.spencer@cims.nyu.edu

Abstract. The *Probabilistic Method* ([AS]) is a lasting legacy of the late Paul Erdős. We give two examples - both problems first formulated by Erdős in the 1960s with new results in the last decade and both with substantial open questions. Further in both examples we take a Computer Science vantagepoint, creating a probabilistic algorithm to create the object (coloring, packing, respectively) and showing that with positive probability the created object has the desired properties.

- Given m sets each of size n (with an arbitrary intersection pattern) we want to color the underlying vertices Red and Blue so that no set is monochromatic. Erdős showed this may always be done if $m < 2^{n-1}$ (proof: color randomly!). We give an argument of Srinivasan and Radhakrishnan ([RS]) that extends this to $m < c2^n \sqrt{n/\ln n}$. One first colors randomly and then recolors the blemishes with a clever random sequential algorithm.
- In a universe of size N we have a family of sets, each of size k, such that each vertex is in D sets and any two vertices have only $o(D)$ common sets. Asymptotics are for fixed k with $N, D \to \infty$. We want an asymptotic packing, a subfamily of $\sim N/k$ disjoint sets.
  Erdős and Hanani conjectured such a packing exists (in an important special case of asymptotic designs) and this conjecture was shown by Rödl. We give a simple proof of the author ([S]) that analyzes the random greedy algorithm.

Paul Erdős was a unique figure, an inspirational figure to countless mathematicians, including the author. Why did his view of mathematics resonate so powerfully? What was it that drew so many of us into his circle? Why do we love to tell Erdős stories? What was the magic of the man we all knew as Uncle Paul?

References

[AS] Alon, Noga and Spencer, Joel, *The Probabilistic Method, Second Edition*, John Wiley & Sons, 2000.
[RS] Radhakrishnan, J. and Srinivasan, A., Improved bounds and algorithms for hypergraph two-coloring, *Random Structures and Algorithms*, **16**, 4-32, 2000.
[S]   Spencer, J., Asymptotic Packing via A Branching Process, *Random Structures and Algorithms*, **7**, 167-172, 1995.

R. Ramanujam and S. Sen (Eds.): FSTTCS 2005, LNCS 3821, pp. 106–106, 2005.
© Springer-Verlag Berlin Heidelberg 2005

No Coreset, No Cry: II*

Michael Edwards and Kasturi Varadarajan

Department of Computer Science
The University of Iowa
Iowa City, IA 52242-1419
[mcedward,kvaradar]@cs.uiowa.edu

Abstract. Let P be a set of n points in d-dimensional Euclidean space, where each of the points has integer coordinates from the range $[-\Delta, \Delta]$, for some $\Delta \geq 2$. Let $\varepsilon > 0$ be a given parameter. We show that there is subset Q of P, whose size is polynomial in $(\log \Delta)/\varepsilon$, such that for any k slabs that cover Q, their ε-expansion covers P. In this result, k and d are assumed to be constants. The set Q can also be computed efficiently, in time that is roughly n times the bound on the size of Q. Besides yielding approximation algorithms that are linear in n and polynomial in $\log \Delta$ for the k-slab cover problem, this result also yields small coresets and efficient algorithms for several other clustering problems.

1 Introduction

A slab in $\Re^d$ is specified by a hyperplane h and a real number $r \geq 0$: $\mathrm{Slab}(h, r)$ is the set of points at distance at most r from h. The *width* of such a slab is $2r$. Note that such a slab can be viewed as the set of points enclosed between two parallel hyperplanes at distance $2r$ apart. For an $\varepsilon \geq 0$, the ε-expansion of $\mathrm{Slab}(h, r)$ is $\mathrm{Slab}(h, r(1 + \varepsilon))$; note that its width is $2r(1 + \varepsilon)$.

For an integer $k \geq 1$ and a parameter $0 < \varepsilon < 1$, a (k, ε) (multiplicative) coreset of a point set $P \subseteq \Re^d$ is a subset $Q \subset P$ such that given any k slabs that cover Q, the ε-expansion of the k slabs covers P. (A set of k slabs is said to cover a point set if the point set is contained in the union of the k slabs.)

A $(1, \varepsilon)$ coreset for any set of n points $P \subseteq \Re^d$ of size $O(1/\varepsilon^{(d-1)/2})$ exists, and can be computed in $O(n)$ time [3,4,1,5]. (We are ignoring constants in the running time that depend on ε. Throughout this paper, d will be treated as a constant.) Such a coreset immediately implies a linear time algorithm for computing an approximately minimum width slab enclosing P. Moreover, a $(1, \varepsilon)$ coreset automatically implies a small $(1, \varepsilon)$ coreset of other kinds, obtained essentially by replacing 'slab' in the definition above by 'ball', 'cylinder', 'spherical shell', 'cylindrical shell', etc. [1]. One immediately obtains linear-time approximation algorithms for various extent measure problems, such as finding the minimum-width slab, cylinder, spherical shell, cylindrical shell, etc. enclosing a point set. Furthermore, a small $(1, \varepsilon)$ coreset also yields small coresets corresponding to

* This work was partially supported by NSF CAREER award CCR 0237431

such extent measure problems for points with algebraic motion [1]. This pleasant state of affairs continues to persist if we want to handle a few outliers [8].

It is therefore natural to ask if small (k, ε) coresets exist, for $k \geq 2$. We are asking, informally, if the pleasant state of affairs for the one cluster case also holds for the multiple cluster case. Answering this question in the negative, Har-Peled [7] gave an example of a point set $P \subset \Re^2$ for which any $(2, 1/2)$ coreset has size at least $|P| - 2$. In other words, the coreset needs to contain nearly all the points. This is unfortunate, since a small coreset would yield small coresets for several clustering problems. (Nevertheless, small coresets exist for the k balls case [7], and small coresets of a weaker type exist for the k cylinders case [2]. These are the exceptions.)

Har-Peled's construction, when embedded on an integer grid, uses coordinates that are exponentially large in the number of input points. In this paper, we ask whether small coresets exist if the coordinates are reasonably small. The main result of this paper is the following theorem, which answers the question in the affirmative.

Theorem 1. *Let P be any set of n points in $\Re^d$, with the co-ordinates of each point in P being integers in the range $[-\Delta, \Delta]$, where $\Delta \geq 2$. For any integer $k \geq 1$, and $0 < \varepsilon < 1$, there is a (k, ε) coreset of P with at most $(\log \Delta/\varepsilon)^{f(d,k)}$ points, where $f(d, k)$ is a function of only d and k. Such a coreset can be constructed in $n(\log \Delta/\varepsilon)^{f(d,k)}$ time.*

We remark that k and d are treated as constants in the big-O notation.

Evidently, the theorem implies an algorithm whose running time is linear in n and polynomial in $\log \Delta$ (ignoring 'constants' that depend on ε, d, and k) for computing k slabs of width $(1 + \varepsilon)r^*$ that cover P, where r^* is the smallest number such that k slabs of width r^* cover P. (That is, r^* is the width of the optimal k-slab cover of P.) Such an algorithm is obtained by computing a (k, ε) coreset of P, computing an optimal k-slab cover for the coreset, and taking their ε-expansion. (An algorithm that is more efficient in terms of the hidden constants can be obtained, if really needed, by working through the proof of Theorem 1.)

The theorem also holds if we replace 'slab' in the definition of a (k, ε) coreset by an 'ℓ-cylinder', where an ℓ-cylinder is the set of points within a certain distance from an ℓ-dimensional flat (affine subspace of dimension ℓ). The proof readily carries over to this case. Consequently, we also obtain efficient algorithms for approximating the k-ℓ-cylinder cover of the point set P.

Other consequences for clustering follow from Theorem 1 using the machinery developed in Agarwal et al. [1]. We give two illustrative examples. An annulus in $\Re^2$ is the set of points between two concentric circles, and its width is the difference between the two radii. An ε-expansion of an annulus is defined accordingly. Let P be a set of points in $\Re^2$ with integer coordinates in the range $[-\Delta, \Delta]$, and let $k \geq 1$ be an integer and $0 < \varepsilon < 1$ be a parameter. We can compute, in linear time, a subset $Q \subset P$ of $(\log \Delta/\varepsilon)^{g(k)}$ points such that for any k annuli that cover Q, their ε-expansion covers P. Here, g is only a function of k.

The second example concerns moving points [6]. Let $P = \{p_1, \ldots, p_n\}$ be a set of points moving linearly in $\Re^2$, where the position of point p_i at time t is given by $p_i[t] = a_i + b_i t$, where $a_i, b_i \in \Re^2$ have integer coordinates in the range $[-\Delta, \Delta]$. Let $P[t] = \{p_1[t], \ldots, p_n[t]\}$ denote the point set at time t. Let $k \geq 1$ be an integer and $0 < \varepsilon < 1$ be a parameter. We can compute, in linear time, a subset $Q \subset P$ of size $(\log \Delta/\varepsilon)^{g(k)}$ such that for any time t, and any k balls that cover $Q[t]$, their ε-expansion covers $P[t]$. These examples by no means exhaust the consequences. For instance, we can replace linear motion by quadratic motion and balls by slabs in the second example.

In summary, small coresets do exist for the multiple cluster case, provided we are willing to expand our definition of 'small' in a reasonable way.

Technique. The proof of Theorem 1 builds (k, ε) coresets from $(k - 1, \varepsilon)$ coresets. The idea is to add to the coreset a subset Q' composed of $(k - 1, \varepsilon)$ coresets of a small number of appropriately chosen subsets of P. The subset Q' will have the property that for any set of k slabs, the points of Q' contained in the k'th slab tell us approximately which subset of P is contained in the k'th slab. We are then left with the problem of adding a $(k - 1, \varepsilon)$ coreset for the remainder of P. The cases where Q' fails to give us such meaningful information are precisely those where the k'th slab plays no essential role – the ε-expansion of the first $k - 1$ slabs covers P. Crucial to the entire construction is an idea from [3], which says, in a technical sense that is convenient to us, that in order to know the shape of a cluster, it is sufficient to know its d principal dimensions.

Is bounded spread enough? We modify the construction of Har-Peled [7] to show that merely assuming bounded spread is not enough to obtain a coreset of the type obtained in Theorem 1. The point set is $P = \{p_1, \ldots, p_n\}$ in $\Re^3$, where $p_i = (1/2^{n-i}, 1/2^{i-1}, i - 1)$. The spread of this point set, that is, the ratio of the maximum to minimum interpoint distance, is clearly $O(n)$. We claim that any $(2, 1/2)$ coreset for this point set must include each p_i, for $1 \leq i \leq n$, and must consequently have all the points. Suppose, to the contrary, that there is such a coreset without p_i. Then the slab $\mathrm{Slab}(h_1, 1/2^{n-(i-1)})$, where h_1 is the hyperplane $x = 0$, covers the points $p_1, \ldots, p_{i-1}$, and the slab $\mathrm{Slab}(h_2, 1/2^i)$, where h_2 is the hyperplane $y = 0$, covers the points $p_{i+1}, \ldots, p_n$. Therefore the two slabs cover the coreset points. But evidently a $1/2$-expansion of these two slabs does not cover p_i, a contradiction.

In Section 2, we establish some geometrical facts needed in Section 3, where we prove Theorem 1. We omit from this version the proofs for the consequences of Theorem 1 claimed above. These consequences follow, with some care, via the arguments used for the one cluster case in [1].

2   Preliminaries

For any subset $V = \{v_1, \ldots, v_\ell\}$ of points in $\Re^d$, let

$$\mathrm{Aff}(V) = \{a_1 v_1 + \cdots + a_\ell v_\ell \mid a_1 + \cdots a_\ell = 1\}$$

be the *affine subspace* or *flat* spanned by them. If $\mathrm{Aff}(V)$ has dimension t, then it is called a t-flat.

Let $\text{proj}(q, F)$ denote the closest point on flat F to a point q, and let $\text{dist}(q, F)$ denote the diatance between q and $\text{proj}(q, F)$.

For any subset $V = \{v_1, \ldots, v_\ell\}$ of points in $\Re^d$, let

$$\text{conv}(V) = \{a_1 v_1 + \cdots + a_\ell v_\ell \mid a_1, \ldots, a_\ell \geq 0, a_1 + \cdots a_\ell = 1\}$$

be the *convex hull* of V.

Let $\mathcal{D}$ denote the points in $\Re^d$ with integer co-ordinates in the range $[-\Delta, \Delta]$. The following proposition is well known.

Proposition 1 *There exists a constant $c_d > 0$, depending only on the dimension d, such that for any subset $V \subseteq \mathcal{D}$ and point $q \in \mathcal{D}$, $\text{dist}(q, \text{Aff}(V))$ is either 0 or a number in the range $[c_d/\Delta^d, 4d\Delta]$.*

Lemma 1. *There exists a constant c'_d, depending only on the dimension, for which the following is true. Let $v_0, \ldots, v_t$ be any set of points, where $t \leq d$. For $1 \leq i \leq t$, let u_i denote the vector $v_i - \text{proj}(v_i, \text{Aff}(\{v_0, \ldots, v_{i-1}\}))$, and suppose that $\|u_i\| > 0$. Suppose that for every $i \geq 1$ and $j \geq i$, we have $\text{dist}(v_j, \text{Aff}(\{v_0, \ldots, v_{i-1}\})) \leq 2\|u_i\|$. Then the t-simplex $\text{conv}(\{v_0, \ldots, v_t\})$ contains a translate of the hyper-rectangle*

$$\{c'_d(a_1 u_1 + a_2 u_2 + \cdots + a_t u_t) \mid 0 \leq a_i \leq 1\}.$$

Proof. This is the central technical lemma that underlies the algorithm of Barequet and Har-Peled [3] for computing an approximate bounding box of a point set. For expository purposes, we sketch a proof. We may assume without loss of generality that v_0 is the origin, and $u_1, \ldots, u_t$ are multiples of the first t unit vectors in the standard basis for $\Re^d$. Scale the first t axes so that $u_1, \ldots, u_t$ map to unit vectors. The conditions of the lemma ensure that the images $v'_0, \ldots, v'_t$ of $v_0, \ldots, v_t$ lie in the " cube "

$$C = \{(x_1, \ldots, x_d) \mid -2 \leq x_i \leq 2 \text{ for } i \leq t, x_i = 0 \text{ for } i > t\},$$

and the (t-dimensional) volume of $\text{conv}(\{v'_0, \ldots, v'_t\})$ is at least $1/t!$, which is at least $\frac{1}{4^d d!}$ of the volume of C. It follows (see Lemma 3.5 of [3]) that there exists $c'_d > 0$, depending only on d, such that a translate of $c'_d C$ is contained in $\text{conv}(\{v'_0, \ldots, v'_t\})$. Scaling back gives the required hyper-rectangle. $\square$

It is worth stating that under the conditions of Lemma 1, the set $\{v_0, \ldots, v_t\}$ is contained in the hyperrectangle

$$v_0 + \{(a_1 u_1 + a_2 u_2 + \cdots + a_t u_t) \mid -2 \leq a_i \leq 2\}.$$

3   The Coreset Construction

In this section, we describe our algorithm for constructing a (k, ε) coreset for any given subset of $\mathcal{D}$, for $k \geq 2$. Our construction is inductive and will assume an algorithm for constructing a $(k-1,\varepsilon)$ coreset for any given subset of $\mathcal{D}$. As the base case, we know that a $(1,\varepsilon)$ coreset of size $O(1/\varepsilon^{d-1})$ for any subset $P' \subset \mathcal{D}$ can be constructed in $O(|P'|+1/\varepsilon^{d-1})$ time [1]. Let λ denote the smallest integer that is at least $\log_2 \frac{4d\Delta}{c_d/\Delta^d}$, where $c_d > 0$ is the constant in Proposition 1. Note that $\lambda = O(\log \Delta)$.

Let $P \subset \mathcal{D}$ be the point set for which we wish to construct a (k,ε) coreset. Our algorithm can be viewed as having $d+1$ levels. At level t, we do some work corresponding to each instantiation of the variables $v_0, \ldots, v_t$. Let Q denote the final coreset that the algorithm returns; Q is initialized to be the empty set.

We construct a $(k-1,\varepsilon)$ coreset K of the point set P and add K to Q. Each point in K is a choice for the variable v_0. For each choice of v_0 from K, we proceed to Level 0 with the point set $P[v_0] = P$.

Level 0: Suppose we have entered this level with $\{v_0\}$ and $P[v_0]$. We partition $P[v_0]$ into $\lambda+1$ buckets. The 0'th bucket $B_0[v_0]$ contains just v_0 and for $1 \le i \le \lambda$, the i'th bucket $B_i[v_0]$ contains all points $p \in P[v_0]$ such that $c_d 2^{i-1}/\Delta^d \le \mathrm{dist}(p, \mathrm{Aff}(\{v_0\})) < c_d 2^i/\Delta^d$. (Note that $\mathrm{Aff}(\{v_0\})$ simply consists of the point v_0.) By Proposition 1, we do indeed have a partition of $P[v_0]$. For each $1 \le i \le \lambda$, we construct a $(k-1,\varepsilon)$ coreset $K_i[v_0]$ of $B_i[v_0]$ and add $K_i[v_0]$ to Q.

Each point in $\bigcup_{i=1}^{\lambda} K_i[v_0]$ is a choice for v_1. If v_1 is chosen from $K_j[v_0]$, we enter Level 1 with $\{v_0, v_1\}$ and the corresponding set $P[v_0, v_1] = \bigcup_{i=0}^{j} B_i[v_0]$. Note that for any $p \in P[v_0, v_1]$, we have $\mathrm{dist}(p, \mathrm{Aff}(v_0)) \le 2\mathrm{dist}(v_1, \mathrm{Aff}(v_0))$.

Level 1: Suppose we have entered this level with $\{v_0, v_1\}$ and $P[v_0, v_1]$. We partition $P[v_0, v_1]$ into $\lambda+1$ buckets. The 0'th bucket $B_0[v_0, v_1]$ contains all the points of $P[v_0, v_1]$ that lie on $\mathrm{Aff}(\{v_0, v_1\})$. (Note that $\mathrm{Aff}(\{v_0, v_1\})$ is simply the line through v_0 and v_1.) For $1 \le i \le \lambda$, the i'th bucket $B_i[v_0, v_1]$ contains all points $p \in P[v_0, v_1]$ such that $c_d 2^{i-1}/\Delta^d \le \mathrm{dist}(p, \mathrm{Aff}(\{v_0, v_1\})) < c_d 2^i/\Delta^d$. By Proposition 1, we do indeed have a partition of $P[v_0, v_1]$.

Let $u_1 = v_1 - \mathrm{proj}(v_1, \mathrm{Aff}(\{v_0\}))$. Cover the "rectangle"

$$R[v_0, v_1] = v_0 + \{a_1 u_1 | -2 \le a_1 \le 2\}$$

by $O(1/\varepsilon)$ copies of translates of the scaled down rectangle

$$R'[v_0, v_1] = \{\frac{\varepsilon}{2} c_d' a_1 u_1 | 0 \le a_1 \le 1\}.$$

Here, $c_d' > 0$ is the constant in Lemma 1. Note that the bigger rectangle $R[v_0, v_1]$ lies on $\mathrm{Aff}(\{v_0, v_1\})$ and contains $B_0[v_0, v_1]$. For each of the $O(1/\varepsilon)$ copies of $R'[v_0, v_1]$, we compute a $(k-1,\varepsilon)$ coreset of the points of $B_0[v_0, v_1]$ contained in that copy, and add all these coreset points to Q.

For each $1 \le i \le \lambda$, we construct a $(k-1,\varepsilon)$ coreset $K_i[v_0, v_1]$ of $B_i[v_0, v_1]$ and add $K_i[v_0, v_1]$ to Q. Each point in $\bigcup_{i=1}^{\lambda} K_i[v_0, v_1]$ is a choice for v_2. If v_2 is chosen from $K_j[v_0, v_1]$, we enter Level 2 with $\{v_0, v_1, v_2\}$ and the corresponding set $P[v_0, v_1, v_2] = \bigcup_{i=0}^{j} B_i[v_0, v_1]$. Note that for any $p \in P[v_0, v_1, v_2]$, we have $\mathrm{dist}(p, \mathrm{Aff}(v_0, v_1)) \le 2\mathrm{dist}(v_2, \mathrm{Aff}(v_0, v_1))$.

Level t $(2 \le t < d)$: Suppose we have entered this level with $\{v_0, \ldots, v_t\}$ and $P[v_0, \ldots, v_t]$. We partition $P[v_0, \ldots, v_t]$ into $\lambda+1$ buckets. The 0'th bucket

$B_0[v_0, \ldots, v_t]$ contains all the points of $P[v_0, \ldots, v_t]$ that lie on $\mathrm{Aff}(\{v_0, \ldots, v_t\})$. For $1 \leq i \leq \lambda$, the i'th bucket $B_i[v_0, \ldots, v_t]$ contains all points $p \in P[v_0, \ldots, v_t]$ such that $c_d 2^{i-1}/\Delta^d \leq \mathrm{dist}(p, \mathrm{Aff}(\{v_0, \ldots, v_t\})) < c_d 2^i/\Delta^d$. By Proposition 1, we do indeed have a partition of $P[v_0, \ldots, v_t]$.

For $1 \leq i \leq t$, let u_i denote the vector $v_i - \mathrm{proj}(v_i, \mathrm{Aff}(\{v_0, \ldots, v_{i-1}\}))$. Cover the rectangle

$$R[v_0, \ldots, v_t] = v_0 + \{a_1 u_1 + a_2 u_2 + \cdots + a_t u_t| -2 \leq a_i \leq 2\}$$

by $O(1/\varepsilon^t)$ copies of translates of the scaled down rectangle

$$R'[v_0, \ldots, v_t] = \{\frac{\varepsilon}{2} c'_d (a_1 u_1 + a_2 u_2 + \cdots + a_t u_t)|0 \leq a_i \leq 1\}.$$

Note that the bigger rectangle $R[v_0, \ldots, v_t]$ lies on $\mathrm{Aff}(\{v_0, \ldots, v_t\})$ and contains $B_0[v_0, \ldots, v_t]$. For each of the $O(1/\varepsilon^t)$ copies of $R'[v_0, \ldots, v_t]$, we compute a $(k-1, \varepsilon)$ coreset of the points of $B_0[v_0, \ldots, v_t]$ contained in that copy, and add all these coreset points to Q.

For each $1 \leq i \leq \lambda$, we construct a $(k-1, \varepsilon)$ coreset $K_i[v_0, \ldots, v_t]$ of $B_i[v_0, \ldots, v_t]$ and add $K_i[v_0, \ldots, v_t]$ to Q. Each point in $\bigcup_{i=1}^{\lambda} K_i[v_0, \ldots, v_t]$ is a choice for v_{t+1}. If v_{t+1} is chosen from $K_j[v_0, \ldots, v_t]$, we enter Level $t+1$ with $\{v_0, \ldots, v_t, v_{t+1}\}$ and the corresponding set

$$P[v_0, \ldots, v_t, v_{t+1}] = \bigcup_{i=0}^{j} B_i[v_0, \ldots, v_t].$$

Note that for any $p \in P[v_0, \ldots, v_{t+1}]$, we have

$$\mathrm{dist}(p, \mathrm{Aff}(v_0, \ldots, v_t)) \leq 2\mathrm{dist}(v_{t+1}, \mathrm{Aff}(v_0, \ldots, v_t)).$$

Level d: Suppose we entered this level with $\{v_0, \ldots, v_d\}$ and $P[v_0, \ldots, v_d]$. For $1 \leq i \leq d$, let u_i denote the vector $v_i - \mathrm{proj}(v_i, \mathrm{Aff}(\{v_0, \ldots, v_{i-1}\}))$. Cover the rectangle

$$R[v_0, \ldots, v_d] = v_0 + \{a_1 u_1 + a_2 u_2 + \cdots + a_d u_d| -2 \leq a_i \leq 2\}$$

by $O(1/\varepsilon^d)$ copies of translates of the scaled down rectangle

$$R'[v_0, \ldots, v_d] = \{\frac{\varepsilon}{2} c'_d (a_1 u_1 + a_2 u_2 + \cdots + a_d u_d)|0 \leq a_i \leq 1\}.$$

Note that the bigger rectangle contains $P[v_0, \ldots, v_d]$. For each of the $O(1/\varepsilon^d)$ copies, we compute a $(k-1, \varepsilon)$ coreset of the points of $P[v_0, \ldots, v_d]$ contained in that copy, and add all these coreset points to Q.

This completes the description of the algorithm for computing Q.

Running Time and Size

Let $S(k)$ be an upper bound on the size of a (k, ε) coreset of any subset of points from $\mathcal{D}$ computed by our algorithm. We derive a bound for $S(k)$, for $k \geq 2$, using a bound for $S(k-1)$, noting that $S(1) = O(1/\varepsilon^{d-1})$.

There are $S(k-1)$ choices for v_0. For a choice of v_0, there are $O(\log \Delta)S(k-1)$ choices of v_1. For a given choice of $v_0, \ldots, v_t$ $(1 \leq t \leq d-1)$, there are $O(\log \Delta)S(k-1)$ choices of v_{t+1}. Thus for $0 \leq t \leq d$, we may bound the number of choices $v_0, \ldots, v_t$ by $O(\log^d \Delta (S(k-1))^{d+1})$. For each choice of $v_0, \ldots, v_t$, we compute $(k-1, \varepsilon)$ coresets $O(\log \Delta + 1/\varepsilon^d)$ times. We therefore have

$$S(k) \leq O\left(\left(\frac{\log \Delta}{\varepsilon}\right)^{d+1}\right) \times (S(k-1))^{d+2}.$$

The bound in Theorem 1 on the size of Q follows from this.

A similar analysis bounds the running time.

Proof of Coreset Property

Let $S_1, \ldots, S_k$ be any k slabs that cover Q. We argue that an ε-expansion of the slabs covers P. Suppose the last slab S_k contains no point from $K \subset Q$. Then since K is a $(k-1, \varepsilon)$ coreset for P, and the first $k-1$ slabs $S_1, \ldots, S_{k-1}$ cover K, their ε-expansion covers P and we are done. Let us therefore assume that there is some $v_0 \in K$ that is contained in S_k. We now need to argue that an ε-expansion of $S_1, \ldots, S_k$ covers $P[v_0] = P$.

Stage 0: Let $j \geq 1$ be the largest integer such that S_k contains some point from $K_j[v_0]$. If no such j exists, let $j = 0$. The sets $K_i[v_0]$, $j+1 \leq i \leq \lambda$, are contained in the first $k-1$ slabs $S_1, \ldots, S_{k-1}$. Thus an ε-expansion of these slabs covers $B_i[v_0]$, $j+1 \leq i \leq \lambda$. If $j = 0$, we are done, since $B_0[v_0] = \{v_0\}$ is contained in S_k, and all points in $P[v_0] = \bigcup_{i=0}^{\lambda} B_i[v_0]$ are covered by an ε-expansion of the slabs.

So let us assume that $j \geq 1$. Let $v_1 \in K_j[v_0]$ be a point contained in S_k. We now need to argue that an ε-expansion of $S_1, \ldots, S_k$ covers $P[v_0, v_1] = \bigcup_{i=0}^{j} B_i[v_0]$.

Stage 1: First consider the point set $B_0[v_0, v_1]$ that lies on $\mathrm{Aff}(\{v_0, v_1\})$. Let us consider the points of $B_0[v_0, v_1]$ contained in one of the $O(1/\varepsilon)$ copies ρ of $R'[v_0, v_1]$. Since a $(k-1, \varepsilon)$ coreset of these points has been added to Q, these points will be covered by an ε-expansion of the first $k-1$ slabs if the slab S_k does not intersect ρ. So let us assume that S_k does intersect ρ. Since S_k contains v_0, v_1, by Lemma 1, it contains a rectangle that is a translate of a scaling of $R'[v_0, v_1]$ by a factor of $2/\varepsilon$. So this copy ρ of $R'[v_0, v_1]$ is contained in a slab 'parallel' to S_k (the hyperplane defining the two slabs are parallel) but whose width is $\varepsilon/2$ of the width of S_k. Since S_k intersects ρ, we may conclude that an ε-expansion of S_k covers ρ.

We have just argued that the point set $B_0[v_0, v_1]$ is covered by an ε-expansion of the k slabs, since each point in $B_0[v_0, v_1]$ is contained in one of the copies of $R'[v_0, v_1]$.

Let $j \geq 1$ be the largest integer such that S_k contains some point from $K_j[v_0, v_1]$. If no such j exists, set $j = 0$. The sets $K_i[v_0, v_1]$, $j + 1 \leq i \leq \lambda$, are contained in the first $k - 1$ slabs $S_1, \ldots, S_{k-1}$. Thus an ε-expansion of these slabs covers $B_i[v_0, v_1]$, $j + 1 \leq i \leq \lambda$.

If $j = 0$, we are done, since all the points in $P[v_0, v_1] = \bigcup_{i=0}^{\lambda} B_i[v_0, v_1]$ are covered by an ε-expansion of the k slabs.

So let us assume that $j \geq 1$. Let $v_2 \in K_j[v_0, v_1]$ be a point contained in S_k. We now need to argue that an ε-expansion of $S_1, \ldots, S_k$ covers $P[v_0, v_1, v_2] = \bigcup_{i=0}^{j} B_i[v_0, v_1]$.

Stage t $(2 \leq t < d)$: We enter this stage to argue that an ε-expansion of the k slabs contains $P[v_0, \ldots, v_t]$, for some choice of $v_0, \ldots, v_t$ that are contained in S_k.

First consider the point set $B_0[v_0, \ldots, v_t]$ that lies on $\mathrm{Aff}(\{v_0, \ldots, v_t\})$. Let us consider the points of $B_0[v_0, \ldots, v_t]$ contained in one of the $O(1/\varepsilon^t)$ copies ρ of $R'[v_0, \ldots, v_t]$. Since a $(k - 1, \varepsilon)$ coreset of these points has been added to Q, these points will be covered by an ε-expansion of the first $k - 1$ slabs if the slab S_k does not intersect ρ. So let us assume that S_k does intersect ρ. Since S_k contains $v_0, \ldots, v_t$, by Lemma 1, it contains a rectangle that is a translate of a scaling of $R'[v_0, \ldots, v_t]$ by a factor of $2/\varepsilon$. So this copy ρ of $R'[v_0, \ldots, v_t]$ is contained in a slab 'parallel' to S_k but whose width is $\varepsilon/2$ of the width of S_k. Since S_k intersects ρ, we may conclude that an ε-expansion of S_k covers ρ.

We have just argued that the point set $B_0[v_0, \ldots, v_t]$ is covered by an ε-expansion of the k slabs, since each point in $B_0[v_0, \ldots, v_t]$ is contained in one of the copies of $R'[v_0, \ldots, v_t]$.

Let $j \geq 1$ be the largest integer such that S_k contains some point from $K_j[v_0, \ldots, v_t]$. If no such j exists, set $j = 0$. The sets $K_i[v_0, \ldots, v_t]$, $j + 1 \leq i \leq \lambda$, are contained in the first $k - 1$ slabs $S_1, \ldots, S_{k-1}$. Thus an ε-expansion of these slabs covers $B_i[v_0, \ldots, v_t]$, $j + 1 \leq i \leq \lambda$.

If $j = 0$, we are done, since all the points in $P[v_0, \ldots, v_t] = \bigcup_{i=0}^{\lambda} B_i[v_0, \ldots, v_t]$ are covered by an ε-expansion of the k slabs.

So let us assume that $j \geq 1$. Let $v_{t+1} \in K_j[v_0, \ldots, v_t]$ be a point contained in S_k. We now need to argue that an ε-expansion of $S_1, \ldots, S_k$ covers $P[v_0, \ldots, v_t, v_{t+1}] = \bigcup_{i=0}^{j} B_i[v_0, \ldots, v_t]$.

Stage d: We enter this stage to argue that an ε-expansion of the k slabs contains $P[v_0, \ldots, v_d]$, for some choice of $v_0, \ldots, v_d$ that are contained in S_k. This argument is identical to the argument given above for $B_0[v_0, \ldots, v_t]$. In fact, $P[v_0, \ldots, v_d]$ may be thought of as $B_0[v_0, \ldots, v_d]$.

We have completed the proof of Theorem 1.

Acknowledgements

We thank Piotr Indyk for suggesting the problem that is addressed in this paper, and Sariel Har-Peled for raising it again. We also thank the reviewers for useful feedback.

References

1. P. K. Agarwal, S. Har-Peled, and K. R. Varadarajan, Approximating extent measures of points, *J. Assoc. Comput. Mach.*, 51 (2004), 606–635.
2. P. K. Agarwal, C. M. Procopiuc, and K. R. Varadarajan, Approximation algorithms for *k*-line center, *Proc. 10th Annu. European Sympos. Algorithms*, 2002, pp. 54–63.
3. G. Barequet and S. Har-Peled, Efficiently approximating the minimum-volume bounding box of a point set in three dimensions, *J. Algorithms*, 38 (2001), 91–109.
4. T. M. Chan, Approximating the diameter, width, smallest enclosing cylinder and minimum-width annulus, *Internat. J. Comput. Geom. Appl.*, 12 (2002), 67–85.
5. T. M. Chan, Faster core-set constructions and data stream algorithms in fixed dimensions, *Proc. 20th Annu. ACM Sympos. Comput. Geom.*, 2004, pp. 152–159.
6. S. Har-Peled, Clustering motion, *Discrete Comput. Geom.*, 31 (2004), 545–565.
7. S. Har-Peled, No coreset, no cry, *Proc. 24th Conf. Found. Soft. Tech. Theoret. Comput. Sci.*, 2004.
8. S. Har-Peled and Y. Wang, Shape fitting with outliers, *SIAM J. Comput.*, 33 (2004), 269–285.

Improved Bounds on the Union Complexity of Fat Objects

Mark de Berg*

Department of Computing Science, TU Eindhoven,
P.O. Box 513, 5600 MB Eindhoven, the Netherlands
mdberg@win.tue.nl.

Abstract. We introduce a new class of fat, not necessarily convex or polygonal, objects in the plane, namely locally γ-fat objects. We prove that the union complexity of any set of n such objects is $O(\lambda_{s+2}(n) \log^2 n)$. This improves the best known bound, and extends it to a more general class of objects.

1 Introduction

The running time of geometric algorithms and the amount of storage used by geometric data structures often depend on the combinatorial complexity of certain geometric structures. Hence, the study of the combinatorial complexity of geometric structures is an important and active area within computational geometry. In this paper we study the combinatorial complexity of the union of a set $\mathcal{F}$ of n objects in the plane. This is relevant because there are many geometric algorithms and data structures whose performance depends on the union complexity of planar objects. Examples are algorithms for hidden-surface removal [12], data structures for ray shooting [3,13], algorithms for computing depth orders [13], and algorithms for motion planning [21,14].

In the worst case the complexity of the union of n constant-complexity objects in the plane can be as high as $\Theta(n^2)$, a bound which is for example achieved by a set of n long and thin rectangles arranged in a grid-like pattern. In many applications, however, one would expect that the objects have some favorable properties and that the union complexity is much lower. One such property that has received considerable attention is *fatness*. Intuitively, an object is called fat if it is not arbitrarily long and skinny—see Section 2 for precise definitions. There are many algorithmic results for fat objects, several of which depend on the union complexity of fat objects in the plane. Hence, the union complexity of fat objects in the plane has been studied extensively.

One of the first results on the union complexity of fat objects was for fat wedges, that is, wedges whose interior angle is bounded from below by a constant. For this case it has been shown [1,9] that the union complexity is $O(n)$.

* MdB was supported by the Netherlands' Organisation for Scientific Research (NWO) under project no. 639.023.301.

R. Ramanujam and S. Sen (Eds.): FSTTCS 2005, LNCS 3821, pp. 116–127, 2005.

Matoušek *et al.* [16] considered the case of fat triangles. A triangle is called δ-*fat* if all of its angles are at least δ for some fixed constant δ. Matoušek *et al.* proved that the union complexity of n such triangles is $O((1/\delta^3)n \log \log n)$. Later this bound was improved by Pach and Tardos [18] to $O((1/\delta \log(1/\delta))n \log \log n)$.

Several people have worked on extending these results to more general types of fat objects, in particular to curved and/or non-convex objects [8,11,10,15] and to higher dimensions [2,17]. The most general result for planar objects to date is by Efrat [8], who considered so-called (α, β)-covered objects—see the next section for a definition. Efrat proved that the union complexity of n constant-complexity (α, β)-covered objects is bounded by $O(\lambda_{s+2}(n) \log^2 n \log \log n)$, where s is the maximum number of intersections between any pair of object boundaries and $\lambda_t(n)$ denotes the maximum length of an (n, t) Davenport-Schinzel sequence; $\lambda_t(n)$ is near-linear for any constant t [19].

We introduce in Section 2 a new class of fat objects in the plane, namely *locally γ-fat objects*. This class is more general than the class of (α, β)-covered objects. We prove that the union complexity of n constant-complexity locally γ-fat objects is $O(\lambda_{s+2}(n) \log^2 n)$, thus not only generalizing the result of Efrat but also slightly improving the bound. Our proof uses a generalization of the so-called Density Lemma [3] to locally γ-fat objects. This powerful tool, which is interesting in its own right, allows us to reduce the problem of bounding the union complexity of locally γ-fat objects to the problem of bounding the union complexity of so-called consistently oriented fat quasi-triangles; these are almost triangular fat shapes with two edges in a fixed orientation. We then give a simple proof that the union complexity of such shapes is $O(\lambda_{s+2}(n) \log^2 n)$. An interesting feature of our proof is that, unlike Efrat's proof, it does not rely on the result of Matoušek *et al.* [16] for fat triangles.

2   Preliminaries

Let $\mathcal{F} := \{o_1, \dots, o_n\}$ be a set of objects in the plane. From now on, we assume that each object is compact, that is, bounded and closed. We also assume that each object has constant complexity; in particular we assume that the boundary of each object consists of $O(1)$ algebraic curves of constant maximum degree. Hence, any two object boundaries intersect at most s times for some constant s.

Fatness and low density. We first define (α, β)-covered objects, as introduced by Efrat [8]. Fig. 1(i) illustrates the definition.

Definition 1 *A planar object o is called (α, β)-covered if for every point p on the boundary of o one can place a triangle t_p with the following properties:*

(i) t_p is contained inside o,
(ii) p is a vertex of t_p,
(iii) t_p is an α-fat triangle, that is, all its angles are at least α,
(iv) the length of each edge of t_p is at least $\beta \cdot diam(o)$, where $diam(o)$ is the diameter of o.

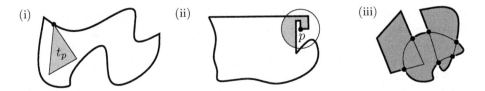

Fig. 1. Illustration of the various definitions.

Next we introduce a new characterization of fatness. Let $area(o)$ denote the area of an object o. Consider an object o and a disk D whose center lies inside o. If o is non-convex $D \cap o$ may consist of several connected components. We define $D \sqcap o$ to be the connected component that contains the center of D.

Definition 2 *Let o be an object in the plane. We say that o is* locally γ-fat *if, for any disk D whose center lies in o and that does not fully contain o in its interior, we have $area(D \sqcap o) \geq \gamma \cdot area(D)$.*

This definition is illustrated in Fig. 1(ii). It is similar to the fatness definition introduced by Van der Stappen *et al.* [20,21], except that we use $area(D \sqcap o)$ instead of $area(D \cap o)$. Thus for convex objects, where $D \sqcap o = D \cap o$, the definitions are identical.

Lemma 3 *Any (α, β)-covered object o is locally γ-fat for some $\gamma = \Omega(\alpha\beta^2)$.*

Proof. Let D be a disk centered at a point $p \in o$ and not containing o in its interior.

First assume $p \in \partial o$. Then there is an α-fat triangle $t_p \subset o$ with p as a vertex all of whose edges have length at least $\beta \cdot diam(o)$. Clearly $D \cap t_p \subset D \sqcap o$. If t_p is not fully contained in D then $area(D \cap t_p) = \Omega(\alpha \cdot area(D))$ because all angles of t_p are at least α. If, on the other hand, $t_p \subset D$ then

$$area(D \sqcap o) \geq area(D \cap t_p) = area(t_p) = \Omega(\alpha \cdot (\beta \cdot diam(o))^2) = \Omega(\alpha\beta^2 \cdot area(D)),$$

where the last equality follows because D does not fully contain o.

Now assume p lies in the interior of o. Let p' be a point on ∂o with minimum distance to p. If $dist(p, p') \geq radius(D)/2$ then $area(D \sqcap o) \geq area(D)/4$. Otherwise, let $D' \subset D$ be the disk with center p' and radius $radius(D)/2$. Now $D' \sqcap o \subset D \sqcap o$, and since $p' \in \partial o$ we have

$$area(D \sqcap o) \geq area(D' \sqcap o) = \Omega(\alpha\beta^2 \cdot area(D')) = \Omega(\alpha\beta^2 \cdot area(D)).$$

$\square$

The reverse is not true: it is not possible to find constants α, β that depend only on γ such that any locally γ-fat object is an (α, β)-covered object. This can be seen in Fig. 1(ii): it is impossible to place a triangle with the point p as a vertex that is relatively large and stays inside the object. (Note that the part of the object sticking out in the top right can be made arbitrarily small without significantly changing the local fatness.)

Besides the concept of fatness, we also need the concept of *density* [4]. For an object o in $\mathbb{R}^2$, we use $size(o)$ to denote the radius of the smallest enclosing disk of o. Note that a locally γ-fat object o in $\mathbb{R}^2$ has area $\Omega(\gamma \cdot size(o)^2)$.

Definition 4 *The* density *of a set S of objects in $\mathbb{R}^2$ is defined as the smallest number λ such that the following holds: any disk $D \subset \mathbb{R}^2$ is intersected by at most λ objects $o \in S$ such that $size(o) \geq size(D)$.*

Notation. We end with some more notation and terminology. We use ∂o to denote the boundary of an object o and we use $\mathcal{U}(S)$ to denote the union of a set S of objects. The union boundary $\partial\mathcal{U}(S)$ of a set S of planar objects consists of maximally connected portions of the boundaries of the objects in S. We call these portions the *edges* of $\mathcal{U}(S)$; the endpoints of these edges are called the *corners* of $\mathcal{U}(S)$.[1] The *(combinatorial) complexity* of $\mathcal{U}(S)$ is defined as the total number of edges and corners of $\mathcal{U}(S)$. For example, the union in Fig. 1(iii) has complexity 12, as it has six corners and six edges. Notice that, up to an additive term equal to the number of objects in S, the complexity of $\mathcal{U}(S)$ is linear in the number of corners. Hence, it suffices to bound that number.

3 The Density Lemma for Locally γ-Fat Objects

In this section we prove a generalization of the Density Lemma [3] to non-convex fat objects. This lemma will enable us to bound the complexity of the union of two unions of fat objects. Recall that by an edge of the union of a set of objects we mean a maximally connected portion of the union boundary that is contributed by a single object.

Lemma 5 [Density Lemma] *Let $\mathcal{F}$ be a set of n locally γ-fat objects, and let $E(\mathcal{F})$ denote the set of edges of the union $\mathcal{U}(\mathcal{F})$. Then the density of $E(\mathcal{F})$ is $O(1/\gamma)$.*

Proof. We proceed in much the same way as in [3]. Let D be a disk, and assume without loss of generality that $size(D) = 1$. Let $E_D \subset E(\mathcal{F})$ be the set of edges $e \in E(\mathcal{F})$ that intersect D and for which $size(e) \geq 1$. We have to show that $|E_D| = O(1/\gamma)$.

We partition the bounding square of D into four unit squares. Together these four squares—the four squares drawn with thick lines in Fig. 2(i)—cover D. Let

---

[1] The boundaries of the objects may contain vertices (breakpoints between adjacent boundary segments or arcs) as well. Such vertices may also show up on the union boundary. These are not corners in our definition and, hence, do not contribute to the complexity. However, their total number is bounded by the total complexity of the objects, so counting them does not change the bounds asymptotically.

S_1 be any one of these squares, and let $E_{S_1} \subset E_D$ denote the edges intersecting S_1. Let S_2 and S_{mid} be squares with the same center as S_1, where S_2 has edge length $\sqrt{2}$ and S_{mid} has edge length $(1 + \sqrt{2})/2$. Thus S_{mid} is midway between S_1 and S_2. Since $size(e_i) \geq 1$ for any $e_i \in E_{S_1}$, such an edge e_i cannot be completely contained in the interior of S_2. Since e_i intersects S_1 be definition, it must therefore cross the square annulus $S_2 \setminus S_1$. In fact, if we cover $S_2 \setminus S_1$ using four (partially overlapping) rectangles —Fig. 2(i) shows one of these rectangles shaded—of size $\sqrt{2}$ by $(\sqrt{2} - 1)/2$, then there must be one such rectangle R crossed by e_i. That is, a portion e_i^* of e_i connects the two longer sides of R—see Fig. 2(ii). We shall bound the number of such edge portions e_i^* for which $\mathcal{U}(\mathcal{F})$

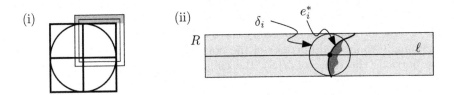

Fig. 2. Illustration for the proof of Lemma 5.

lies locally to the right of e_i^*; the number of edges for which $\mathcal{U}(\mathcal{F})$ lies locally to the left can be bounded similarly. Let p_i^* be a point where e_i^* intersects the line ℓ midway between the two longer sides of R, and let δ_i be the disk centered at p_i^* of radius $(\sqrt{2} - 1)/4$. Let $object(e_i)$ be the object of which e_i is a boundary piece. Because e_i is locally γ-fat, we have

$$area(\delta_i \sqcap object(e_i)) \geq \gamma \cdot \pi((\sqrt{2} - 1)/4)^2.$$

Now consider another edge $e_j \in E_{S_1}$, with a portion e_j^* crossing R and where $\mathcal{U}(\mathcal{F})$ lies locally to the right, and consider a disk δ_j of radius $(\sqrt{2}-1)/4$ centered at a point of $e_j^* \cap \ell$. Then $area(\delta_j \sqcap object(e_j))$ can be bounded as above. Because e_i^* and e_j^* are portions of union edges, they do not intersect any other object (except possibly at their endpoints). It follows that

$$(\delta_i \sqcap object(e_i)) \cap (\delta_j \sqcap object(e_j)) = \emptyset.$$

Since the area of R is $1 - \frac{1}{2}\sqrt{2}$, the number of edge portions we have to count for R for which $\mathcal{U}(\mathcal{F})$ lies locally to the right is at most

$$\frac{1 - \frac{1}{2}\sqrt{2}}{\gamma \cdot \pi((\sqrt{2} - 1)/4)^2} = O(1/\gamma).$$

The lemma follows. $\square$

The Density Lemma allows us to bound the complexity of the combined union of sets of fat objects.

Lemma 6 [Merging Lemma] *Let S_1 and S_2 be sets of constant-complexity objects in the plane such that all objects in S_1 are locally γ_1-fat and all objects in S_2 are locally γ_2-fat. Let U_1 and U_2 denote the complexity of the union of S_1 and S_2, respectively. Then the complexity of $\mathcal{U}(S_1 \cup S_2)$ is $O(U_1/\gamma_2 + U_2/\gamma_1)$.*

Proof. This was already stated for convex objects [3] and the same proof applies if we replace the Density Lemma for convex objects with the more general version above. In short: one can charge any intersection point of the two union boundaries to the smaller of the two involved edges. By the Density Lemma, any edge of $\mathcal{U}(S_1)$ is charged $O(1/\gamma_2)$ times and any edge of $\mathcal{U}(S_2)$ is charged $O(1/\gamma_1)$ times. $\qquad\square$

4   From Locally γ-Fat Objects to Quasi-Triangles

As in most papers on the union complexity of fat objects, we wish to replace our locally γ-fat objects by simpler 'canonical' objects. Let $\mathcal{D}$ be a set of $40/\gamma$ equally spaced orientations, where we assume for simplicity that $40/\gamma$ is an integer. Thus the angle between two consecutive orientations in $\mathcal{D}$ is $\gamma^* := \gamma\pi/20$. We call a direction in $\mathcal{D}$ a *standard direction*. A *quasi-triangle* is an object Δ bounded by two straight edges and one smooth Jordan arc without inflection points.

Definition 7 *A γ-standard quasi-triangle is a quasi triangle Δ such that*

(a) its two edges have standard directions, and their angle inside Δ is between $\pi - 7\gamma^*$ and $\pi - \gamma^*$;

(b) the tangent line at any point of the Jordan arc makes an angle of at least γ^* with the edges of Δ, and the tangent direction along σ does not vary by more than γ^*.

We say that two γ-standard quasi-triangles are consistently oriented *if their edges have the same standard orientations.*

Fig. 3 illustrates this definition. Observe that property (b) implies that any line parallel to one of the two edges of Δ intersects its Jordan arc at most once. Also note that because of property (a) any set of γ-standard quasi-triangles can be partitioned into $O(1/\gamma)$ subsets of consistently oriented γ-standard quasi-triangles. The following lemma follows from the fact that the angles at each

Fig. 3. The standard directions and four consistently oriented γ-standard quasi-triangles.

vertex of a γ-standard quasi-triangle are all at least γ^*—this follows from (b)—
and that the tangent direction along the arc cannot vary too much.

Lemma 8 *A γ-standard quasi-triangle is locally γ'-fat for $\gamma' = \Omega(\gamma)$.*

We now set out to reduce the problem of bounding the union of locally γ-fat
objects to the problem of bounding the union of γ-standard quasi-triangles. We
do this by covering the boundary of each locally γ-fat object using γ-standard
quasi-triangles, as follows.

Let o be a locally γ-fat object. We partition ∂o into a number of *subarcs* by
putting breakpoints on ∂o in two steps. In the first step we put breakpoints at
the following three types of points:

(i) every non-smooth point of ∂o;
(ii) every inflection point of ∂o;
(iii) every smooth point where the tangent line has a standard direction.

Let B_1 be the resulting set of breakpoints. Because o has constant complexity
and there are $O(1/\gamma)$ standard directions, $|B_1| = O(1/\gamma)$. In the second step we
further refine ∂o by putting breakpoints as follows.

(iv) Put a breakpoint at each point $p \in \partial o$ for which there is a breakpoint
$q \in B_1$ such that the line segment pq has a standard direction and $pq \subset o$.

Let B_2 denote the resulting set of breakpoints. We have $|B_2| = |B_1| \cdot O(1/\gamma) =
O(1/\gamma^2)$.

Next, we define a γ-standard quasi-triangle $\Delta(\sigma)$ for each of the $O(1/\gamma^2)$
subarcs σ induced by the set of breakpoints. Let p and q be the endpoints of a
subarc σ. Assume without loss of generality that pq is parallel to the x-axis and
that σ bounds o from above. Let ℓ_p and ℓ_q be the vertical lines through p and q,
respectively. Rotate ℓ_p and ℓ_q in counterclockwise direction around p resp. q
until they have a standard direction. The γ-standard quasi-triangle $\Delta(\sigma)$ is now
formed by σ and two straight edges pr and qr, where r is a point in between ℓ_p
and ℓ_q as specified in the next lemma and illustrated in Fig. 4.

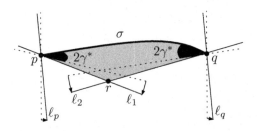

Fig. 4. The γ-standard quasi-triangle $\Delta(\sigma)$ defined for σ.

Lemma 9 *There is a point r below σ and between ℓ_p and ℓ_q such that $\Delta(\sigma)$ is a γ-standard quasi-triangle.*

Proof. Draw a line ℓ_1 through p whose angle with σ at the point p is $2\gamma^*$. Rotate ℓ_1 clockwise until it reaches a standard direction. Similarly, draw a line ℓ_2 through q whose angle with σ at the point q is $2\gamma^*$, and rotate ℓ_2 counterclockwise until it reaches a standard direction. Let r be the intersection point of ℓ_1 and ℓ_2—see Fig. 4. Clearly pr and qr have standard directions and r lies below σ and between ℓ_p and ℓ_q. Moreover, the angles that pr and qr make with σ are at least $2\gamma^*$ and at most $3\gamma^*$. Since the tangent direction along σ does not vary by more than γ^*, this implies that the angle between pr and qr is between $\pi - 7\gamma^*$ and $\pi - \gamma^*$, which establishes property (a).

Property (b) follows because the angles that pr and qr make with σ at p resp. q are at least $2\gamma^*$ and the tangent direction along σ does not vary by more than γ^*. □

Lemma 10 *The γ-standard quasi-triangle $\Delta(\sigma)$ defined above is contained in o.*

Proof. Let x be the lowest point on ℓ_p such that $px \subset o$. Clearly $x \in \partial o$. (Note that it may happen that $x = p$.) Imagine sweeping a segment s from left to right through o, as follows. Start with $s = px$. Move s to the right, keeping it parallel to ℓ_p and keeping its endpoints on ∂o, until s reaches ℓ_q. Note that the upper endpoint of s will move along σ. The lower endpoint of s cannot encounter a breakpoint from B_1 during the sweep, otherwise this breakpoint would have generated a type (iv) breakpoint on σ and σ would not be a subarc. Let σ' be the part of ∂o followed by the lower endpoint of s—see Fig. 5(i). Because there is no breakpoint on σ', we know that σ' does not contain a point where the tangent line has a standard direction. Hence, σ' can cross both pr and qr at most once.

If σ' crosses neither pr nor qr, then $\Delta(\sigma) \subset o$ and we are done, so assume for a contradiction that σ' crosses pr and qr. Take a line through p whose angle with pq is γ^* and a line through p whose angle with pq is γ^*, such that their intersection point r' lies above σ, as in Fig. 5(ii). Consider the 6-gon defined by the following six points: p, r', q, the intersection of the extension of pr with ℓ_q, r, and the intersection of the extension of qr with ℓ_p—see Fig. 5. Then both σ and σ' are contained in this 6-gon. Let w be the distance between ℓ_p and ℓ_q. Using that $\text{angle}(pq, pr') = \text{angle}(pq, qr') = \gamma^*$, and that $\text{angle}(pq, pr) \leq 4\gamma^*$ and $\text{angle}(pq, qr) \leq 4\gamma^*$, one can show that the area of the 6-gon is at most $(9/2)\gamma^* w^2$. Now let D be the disk centered at a point of σ and touching ℓ_p and ℓ_q. Because o is locally γ-fat, we have $D \sqcap o \geq \gamma\pi(w\cos(\gamma^*)/2)^2 \geq 0.24\gamma\pi w^2$. On the other hand, $D \sqcap o$ is contained in the area enclosed by σ and σ'. But this area is at most $(9/2)\gamma^* w^2$, which is a contradiction since $\gamma^* = \gamma\pi/20$.

Now we can reduce the problem of bounding the union complexity of a set of locally γ-fat objects to the problem of bounding the union complexity of a set of locally fat γ-standard quasi-triangles.

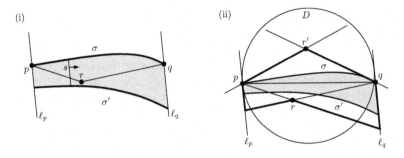

Fig. 5. Illustrations for the proof of Lemma 5.

Proposition 11 *Let $u_\gamma(n)$ denote the maximum complexity of the union of a collection of n consistently oriented γ-standard quasi-triangles. Then the maximum union complexity of any set $\mathcal{F}$ of n locally γ-fat objects is $O((1/\gamma^2) \cdot u_\gamma(n/\gamma^2))$.*

Proof. Replace each $o \in \mathcal{F}$ by a collection $T(o)$ of quasi-triangles as described above. Since we have $\partial o \subset \partial \mathcal{U}(T(o))$ and $\mathcal{U}(T(o)) \subset o$ for each object o, the complexity of $\mathcal{U}(\mathcal{F})$ is no more than the complexity of $\mathcal{U}(\{T(o) : o \in \mathcal{F}\})$.

This gives us a set T of $O(n/\gamma^2)$ γ-standard quasi-triangles. We partition T into $O(1/\gamma)$ subsets T_i of consistently oriented quasi-triangles. Set $n_i := |T_i|$. Every corner of $\mathcal{U}(\mathcal{F})$ will show up either as (i) a corner of $\mathcal{U}(T_i)$ for some i, or (ii) as a corner of $\mathcal{U}(T_i \cup T_j)$ for some pair i, j. The number of corners of type (i) is $\sum_i u_\gamma(n_i) = O(u_\gamma(n/\gamma^2))$. To bound the corners of type (ii) we use the Merging Lemma and Lemma 8, which imply that the complexity of $\mathcal{U}(T_i \cup T_j)$ is $O((u_\gamma(n_i) + u_\gamma(n_j))/\gamma)$. Hence, the total number of type (ii) corners is bounded by

$$\sum_i \sum_j O((u_\gamma(n_i) + u_\gamma(n_j))/\gamma) = \sum_i \{O(1/\gamma) \cdot O(u_\gamma(n_i)/\gamma) + O(u_\gamma(n/\gamma^2)/\gamma)\}$$
$$= O((1/\gamma^2) \cdot u_\gamma(n/\gamma^2))$$

$\square$

5   The Union Complexity of γ-Standard Quasi-Triangles

Let T be a set of consistently oriented γ-standard quasi-triangles. Without loss of generality we assume each $\Delta \in T$ has one edge parallel to the x-axis, and one edge that makes an angle α with the positive x-axis. Recall that $\pi - 7\gamma^* \leq \alpha \leq \pi - \gamma^*$. Set $m := |T|$.

Draw a horizontal line through the horizontal edge and the highest point of every $\Delta \in T$. This partitions the plane into at most $2m + 1$ horizontal strips. Let $\mathcal{T}$ be a balanced binary tree whose leaves correspond to these strips in

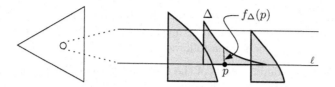

Fig. 6. Illustration for the proof of Lemma 12. For clarity the two straight edges of the quasi triangles are drawn at a right angle (as could be achieved by a suitable transformation) although in fact the angle is almost π.

order. We associate each node ν in $\mathcal{T}$ with the horizontal strip $strip(\nu)$ that is the union of the strips corresponding to the leaves in the subtree rooted at ν. Finally, we associate with each node ν a subset $T(\nu) \subset T$, as follows: $\Delta \in T(\nu)$ if Δ completely crosses the strip of ν but does not completely cross the strip of the parent of ν. (This is equivalent to constructing a segment tree [5] on the projections of the Δ's onto the y-axis, and defining $T(\nu)$ to be the quasi-triangles whose projections are stored in the canonical subset of ν.) We clip each $\Delta \in T(\nu)$ to $strip(\nu)$, so that $T(\nu)$ will only contain the parts of these quasi-triangles lying within $strip(\nu)$. Note that if $N(\Delta)$ is the collection of nodes to which a quasi-triangle Δ is associated, then the clipped pieces of Δ within the strips of the nodes $\nu \in N(\Delta)$ together form Δ. So by assigning Δ to the nodes in $N(\Delta)$ and clipping it, we effectively cut Δ into $|N(\Delta)|$ pieces. Since any Δ is associated to at most two nodes at every level of $\mathcal{T}$—this is a standard property of segment-tree like structures [5]—Δ is cut into $O(\log m)$ pieces. Hence, if we set $m_\nu := |T(\nu)|$ then $\sum_{\nu \in \mathcal{T}} m_\nu = O(m \log m)$.

Lemma 12 *The complexity of $\mathcal{U}(T(\nu))$ is $O(\lambda_{s+2}(m_\nu))$.*

Proof. Let ℓ be the line bounding $strip(\nu)$ from below. For each $\Delta \in T(\nu)$, we define a function $f_\Delta : \ell \to \mathbb{R}$ as follows. Let $l(p)$ be the line through the point p that makes an angle α with the positive x-axis. Then

$$f_\Delta(p) := \text{the length of } l(p) \cap \Delta.$$

Now the boundary of $\mathcal{U}(T(\nu))$ is the upper envelope of the set of functions $\{f_\Delta(p) : \Delta \in T(\nu)\}$—see Fig. 6—which has complexity $O(\lambda_{s+2}(m_\nu))$ [19], where s is the maximum number of intersections between two object boundaries.   □

Next we consider the union of all (clipped) quasi-triangles associated to nodes at a fixed depth in $\mathcal{T}$. Let $N(k)$ denote the nodes of $\mathcal{T}$ at depth k, and define $T(k) := \bigcup_{\nu \in N(k)} T(\nu)$.

Lemma 13 *The complexity of $\mathcal{U}(T(k))$ is $O(\lambda_{s+2}(m))$.*

Proof. The strips of the nodes at a fixed level in the tree are disjoint. Hence, the complexity of $\mathcal{U}(T(k))$ is bounded by the sum of the complexities at each of the nodes $\nu \in N(k)$, which is $\sum_{\nu \in N(k)} O(\lambda_{s+2}(m_\nu))$ by the previous lemma. Since any quasi-triangle can be associated with at most two nodes at any fixed level, we have $\sum_{\nu \in N(k)} m_\nu \leq 2m$. The lemma follows. □

To combine the unions of different levels of the tree we use the following lemma.

Lemma 14 *The set $E(k)$ of boundary edges of $\mathcal{U}(T(k))$ has density $O(1/\gamma^2)$.*

Proof. For $\nu \in N(k)$, let $E(\nu)$ denote the set of boundary edges of $\mathcal{U}(T(\nu))$. Since the strips of the nodes in $N(k)$ are disjoint, we have $E(k) = \cup_{\nu \in N(k)} E(\nu)$.

First we note that, even though the quasi-triangles in $T(\nu)$ are not necessarily fat because they are clipped, the set $E(\nu)$ still has density $O(1/\gamma)$. Indeed, the edges of the union of the unclipped quasi-triangles have density $O(1/\gamma)$ by the Density Lemma; clipping the union to $strip(\nu)$ can only remove or shorten edges, which does not increase the density.

Now consider an edge $e \in E(\nu)$ and let w be the width of $strip(\nu)$. We observe that $size(e) = O(w/\gamma)$, because at any point $p \in e$ the tangent to e makes an angle $\Omega(\gamma)$ with the boundary lines of the strip. Let D be a disk and assume without loss of generality that D has unit radius. We must argue that D is intersected by $O(1/\gamma^2)$ edges $e \in E(k)$ with $size(e) \geq 1$. By the previous observation, we only have to consider edges lying in strips of width $\Omega(\gamma)$. Clearly D can be intersected by only $O(1/\gamma)$ such strips, because the strips in $N(k)$ are disjoint. Since within each strip the density of the boundary edges is $O(1/\gamma)$, the overall density is $O(1/\gamma^2)$. □

We can now prove a bound on the total union complexity of T.

Lemma 15 *The complexity of $\mathcal{U}(T)$ is $O((\lambda_{s+2}(m) \log^2 m)/\gamma^2)$.*

Proof. Consider a corner v of $\mathcal{U}(T)$ that is an intersection point of the boundaries of two quasi-triangles Δ_1 and Δ_2. Let ν_1 be the node such that Δ_1 is associated to ν_1 and the clipped portion of Δ_1 within $strip(\nu_1)$ contains v. Define ν_2 similarly for Δ_2. Let k_1 and k_2 be the depths of ν_1 and ν_2, respectively. If $k_1 = k_2$ then the corner v is already accounted for in the bound $O(\lambda_{s+2}(m))$ on the complexity of $\mathcal{U}(T(k_1))$. To account for the corners v where $k_1 \neq k_2$ we must consider the unions $\mathcal{U}(T(k_1) \cup T(k_2))$ at different depths k_1 and k_2. Since the sets of boundary edges of $\mathcal{U}(T(k_1))$ and $\mathcal{U}(T(k_2))$ have density $O(1/\gamma^2)$ by the previous lemma, we can use Lemma 13 and argue as in the proof of the Merging Lemma to bound the complexity of $\mathcal{U}(T(k_1) \cup T(k_2))$ by $O(\lambda_{s+2}(m)/\gamma^2)$. Because the depth of T is $O(\log m)$ we now have

$$\sum_{k_1} \sum_{k_2} O((\lambda_{s+2}(m))/\gamma^2) = O((\lambda_{s+2}(m) \log^2 m)/\gamma^2),$$

which completes the proof. □

Plugging this result into Proposition 11 we get our main theorem.

Theorem 16 *The union complexity of any set $\mathcal{F}$ of n constant-complexity locally γ-fat objects is $O((1/\gamma^6) \cdot \lambda_{s+2}(n) \log^2 n)$.*

References

1. H. Alt, R. Fleischer, M. Kaufmann, K. Mehlhorn, S. Naher, S. Schirra and C. Uhrig. Approximate motion planning and the complexity of the boundary of the union of simple geometric figures. *Algorithmica* 8:391–406 (1992).
2. B. Aronov, A. Efrat, V. Koltun and M. Sharir. On the union of κ-curved objects in three and four dimensions. In *Proc. 20th ACM Symp. Comput. Geom.*, pages 383–390, 2004.
3. M. de Berg. Vertical ray shooting for fat objects. In *Proc. 21st ACM Symp. Comput. Geom.*, pages 288–295, 2005.
4. M. de Berg, M. Katz, F. van der Stappen, and J. Vleugels. Realistic input models for geometric algorithms. *Algorithmica* 34:81–97 (2002).
5. M. de Berg, M. van Kreveld, M. Overmars, and O. Schwarzkopf. *Computational Geometry: Algorithms and Applications (2nd edition)*. Springer-Verlag, 2000.
6. C.A. Duncan. *Balanced Aspect Ratio Trees*. Ph.D. Thesis, John Hopkins University, 1999.
7. C.A. Duncan, M.T. Goodrich, S.G. Kobourov, Balanced aspect ratio trees: Combining the advantages of k-d trees and octrees, In *Proc. 10th Ann. ACM-SIAM Sympos. Discrete Algorithms*, pages 300–309, 1999.
8. A. Efrat. The complexity of the union of (α, β)-covered objects. *SIAM J. Comput.* 34:775–787 (2005).
9. A. Efrat, G. Rote and M. Sharir. On the union of fat wedges and separating a collection of segments by a line. *Comput. Geom. Theory Appl.* 3: 277–288 (1993).
10. A. Efrat and M. Sharir. The complexity of the union of fat objects in the plane. In *Proc. 13th ACM Symp. Comput. Geom.* pages 104–112, 1997.
11. A. Efrat and M. Katz. On the union of α-curved objects. In *Proc. 14th ACM Symp. Comput. Geom.*, pages 206–213, 1998.
12. M.J. Katz, M. Overmars, and M. Sharir. Efficient output sensitive hidden surface removal for objects with small union size. *Comput. Geom. Theory Appl.* 2:223–234 (1992).
13. M.J. Katz. 3-D vertical ray shooting and 2-D point enclosure, range searching, and arc shooting amidst convex fat objects. *Comput. Geom. Theory Appl.* 8:299–316 (1998).
14. K. Kedem, R. Livne, J. Pach, and M. Sharir. On the union of Jordan regions and collision-free translational motion amidst polygonal obstacles in the plane. *Discr. Comput. Geom.* 1:59–71 (1986).
15. M. van Kreveld. On fat partitioning, fat covering, and the union size of polygons. *Comput. Geom. Theory Appl.* 9:197–210 (1998).
16. J. Matoušek, J. Pach, M. Sharir, S. Sifrony, and E. Welzl. Fat triangles determine linearly many holes. *SIAM J. Comput.* 23:154-169 (1994).
17. J. Pach, I. Safruti and M. Sharir. The union of congruent cubes in three dimensions. *Discr. Comput. Geom.* 30:133–160 (2003).
18. J. Pach and G. Tardos. On the boundary complexity of the union of fat triangles. *SIAM J. Comput.* 31: 1745-1760 (2002).
19. M. Sharir and P.K. Agarwal. *Davenport-Schinzel sequences and their geometric applications*. Cambridge University Press, 1995.
20. A.F. van der Stappen. *Motion planning amidst fat obstacles*. Ph.D. thesis, Utrecht University, Utrecht, the Netherlands, 1994.
21. A.F. van der Stappen, D. Halperin, and M.H. Overmars. The complexity of the free space for a robot moving amidst fat obstacles. *Comput. Geom. Theory Appl.* 3:353–373, 1993.

On the Bisimulation Congruence in χ-Calculus*
(Extended Abstract)

Taolue Chen[1,2**], Tingting Han[2], and Jian Lu[2]

[1] CWI, Department of Software Engineering,
P.O. Box 94079, 1090 GB Amsterdam, The Netherlands
Taolue.Chen@cwi.nl
[2] State Key Laboratory of Novel Software Technology,
Nanjing University, Nanjing, Jiangsu, P.R.China, 210093

Abstract. In this paper, we study weak bisimulation congruences for the χ-calculus, a symmetric variant of the π-calculus. We distinguish two styles of such bisimulation definitions, i.e. "open" and "closed" bisimulation, the difference between which lies in that in open style the equivalence is closed under context in every bisimulation step whereas in closed style the equivalence is closed under context only at the very beginning. As a result, we show that both in labelled and barbed congruence, the open and closed style definitions coincide. Thus all bisimulation congruences collapse into two equivalences, that is, the well-known open congruence and open barbed congruence, which are the same in the strong case, while in the weak case their difference can be reflected by one axiom. The results of this paper close some conjectures in the literatures and shed light on the algebraic theory of a large class of mobile process calculi.

1   Introduction

Over the last decade, various calculi of mobile processes, notably the π-calculus [11], have been the focus of research in concurrency theory. Since 1997, several publications have focused on a class of new calculi of mobile process. These models include χ-calculus [5] due to Fu, update calculus [13] and fusion calculus [14] due to Parrow and Victor with its variants, such as explicit fusion [8], due to Gardner and Wischik. Roughly speaking, in a uniform terminology they are respectively χ-calculus, asymmetric χ-calculus and polyadic χ-calculus.

In the research of algebraic theory for mobile process, bisimulation equivalence is the standard paradigm for behavioral comparison. Comparing to the traditional process calculi, e.g. CCS [10], for mobile processes, there are often

* This work is partially supported by NNSFC (60233010, 60273034, 60403014) and 973 Program of China (2002CB312002).
** Corresponding author. The author is partially supported by the Dutch BSIK/ BRICKS Project (Basic Research in Informatics for Creating the Knowledge Society).

R. Ramanujam and S. Sen (Eds.): FSTTCS 2005, LNCS 3821, pp. 128–139, 2005.

many natural definitions of bisimilarity, which makes the theory much more involved. For example, in the π-calculus, the most well-known of them include late/early bisimulation [11], open bisimulation [15], barbed bisimulation [12], etc. It is widely recognized that a bisimulation equivalence is most useful when it is a *congruence*, i.e. is preserved by the syntactic constructions of the calculus. Unfortunately, in mobile process calculi, most of bisimulation equivalences are not congruences themselves! This gives rise to the problem on how to refine the bisimulation definition and thus obtain a congruence. It is well-known that congruence relations on mobile processes should be closed under *substitution* on names, which gives rise to a choice of whether the requirement of closure under substitution is placed on the *first* step of a bisimulation or on *each* step of the bisimulation. For example, open equivalence [15] is closed under substitution in each bisimulation step, while early, late [11] and barbed equivalences [12] are closed under substitution only in the first step of bisimulation. This distinction makes open bisimulation strictly stronger than the other three (please note that this is only the case in the π-calculus, as the results of this paper will suggest, in the χ-calculus, the situation is quite different).

In the light of the above discussion, we argue that "open" is indeed a *general* definition style while it is not only a *single* or *ad hoc* definition. Let us generalize the above mentioned "substitution" to a broader notion of *context*. Remarkably, there are at least two reasonable ways of ensuring the congruence property:

- Either take the largest congruence that is a bisimulation; this is the "reduction based" equivalence chosen for the ν-calculus in [9] and Abadi and Fournet's work, e.g. [1]. In this paper, we will call it "open" style, following Sangiorgi [15]. This models the situation where environments change during execution (the norm in distributed computation).
- Or take the largest congruence included in the bisimulation; this is the two-stage definition traditionally chosen for CCS and the π-calculus; for symmetry, in this paper, we will call it "closed" style. This models the situation where a sub-program's context is fixed at compile time. They are generally just called "congruence" in the literature on π-calculus, e.g. [11].

We also can study the bisimulation relations in mobile process calculi from another perspective, that is, we can distinguish the labelled and the barbed style. Since we believe this distinction is much more familiar to the readers, we will not explain it further. To summarize, in our opinion, there are actually four key ways to define behavioral equivalences in mobile process calculi: depending on whether the relation is closed under initial contexts ("closed" style) or under subsequently-changing contexts as well (reduction-closed congruence, open style); and orthogonally whether we just observe the channels over which messages are sent (barbed style) or also record the message and the resulting state (labelled style). Clearly, the combinations give rise to (at least) four sensible bisimulation equivalences. Three of them are familiar in the community and have been mentioned above. The remaining one, that is, the combination of "open" and "barbed", is open barbed bisimulation, which is also extensively studied by Sangiorgi and Walker [16] and the first author in [2] in recent days.

So far, most of the bisimulation congruences for χ-calculus, notably [6], are defined in the open style, while in the research on mobile process calculi, the closed style definitions seem to be more standard. In our opinion, this is not very ideal for our understanding of the χ-calculus, the representative of a large class of mobile process calculi. Under such a situation, one of the contributions of this paper is to show how the four standard definitions of bisimulation congruence, familiar from the π-calculus, can be applied to the χ-calculus. Based on it, we study the relationships of these bisimulation equivalences. Intuitively, one might expect the closed and open congruences to generate the same relation, since one could presumably write an initial environment sophisticated enough to model a subsequently-changing environment. Unfortunately, this result does not hold for the (synchronous) π-calculus. Interestingly, if we restrict to the asynchronous π-calculus, the analogous results hold! See Fournet and Gonthier's work [4] for more details and we will discuss it further in Section 5. Now, a natural question is: What's the situation in the χ-calculus? The main contribution of this paper is to provide a systematic investigation on this. We compare the open and closed style bisimulations in the setting of χ-calculus, and study both labelled and barbed versions. Moreover, we focus on the weak version of bisimulation, since it is much more general and difficult. Our results show that for both labelled and barbed bisimulation, the closed and open style definitions coincide. This is mainly, in our point of view, due to the fact that in χ-calculus, we can simulate the notion of substitution through the parallel operator. It is worth pointing out that Fu says ([6], pp. 225): "Our intuition strongly suggests that the barbed bisimilarity and the barbed equivalence, which Parrow and Victor have studied, coincide in the absence of the mismatch operator. But so far we have not been able to formally prove this conjecture." One of the results in this paper confirms Fu's conjecture (see Theorem 2 in Section 4), thus we close this open problem. Moreover, our results also support Fu, Parrow, Victor's general arguments that in χ-like process algebra, open bisimulation is more natural.

We note that in [18] Wischik and Gardner have performed closely related research. However, modulo the differences on the underlying process calculi, there are some dramatic differences: (1) We discuss the weak case of bisimulation, while [18] only considers the strong case. They claim that weak bisimulation congruences have been studied by Fu for the χ-calculus. However, as we have pointed out, this is not the case, since Fu only considers the "open" style relations. Under such a situation, our results can be regarded as the weak counterpart of [18]. Moreover, [18] mentions that "An interesting open problem is to explore such congruences[3] for the explicit fusion calculus ...". We believe the results of the current paper will, at least, shed light on such issues, due to the similarity of χ-calculus and explicit fusion. (2) [18] only proves the coincide of "open" and "closed" (they call them reduction-based and shaped) style for labelled bisimulation. As for the barbed case, they apply Sangiorgi's "stratification" technique [17] to show the coincidence of ground equivalence and barbed equivalence, then they show (trivially) the coincidence of open barbed congruence and open con-

---

[3] Here, they are essentially referring to the weak open congruences studied by Fu.

gruence, thus the result is obtained. This is feasible in the strong case. However, in the weak case, as we will see, labelled bisimulation and barbed bisimulation do not coincide at all! To deal with this, we give a direct proof for the coincide of "open" and "closed" style for barbed bisimulation, which is much more complicated.

We should point out that the bisimulation congruences studied in this paper are all "partial" congruences since they are not closed under summation (technically speaking, they are closed under *context* but fail under *full context*, see Definition 1). Since this problem is common and Milner [10] has provided an elegant way to deal with this, it is not a true drawback. We also note that this is only an extended abstract, since due to space restriction, all the proofs have to be omitted. For more detailed proofs, explanations, remarks, we refer the interested readers to our technical report [3].

The structure of this paper is as follows: Section 2 summarizes some background material on χ-calculus. Section 3 presents the results on label style bisimulation while Section 4 discusses barbed style bisimulations. This paper is concluded in Section 5, where some remarks are also given.

2   Background

In this section, we will review some background material for χ-calculus, we refer the reader to [5] [6] for more details. Let $\mathcal{N}$ be a set of names, ranged over by lower case letters. $\bar{\mathcal{N}}$, the set of conames, denotes $\{\bar{x} \mid x \in \mathcal{N}\}$. The set $\mathcal{N} \cup \bar{\mathcal{N}}$ will be ranged over by α. Let $\bar{\alpha}$ be a if $\alpha = \bar{a}$ and $\bar{a}$ if $\alpha = a$.

We will write $\mathcal{C}$ for the set of χ-processes defined by the following grammar:

$$P := 0 \mid \alpha x.P \mid P|P \mid (\nu x)P \mid [x = y]P \mid P + P \mid !P$$

The intuitional sense is standard. The name x in $(\nu x)P$ is bound. A name is free in P if it is not bound in P. The free names, the bound names and names of P, as well as the notations $fn(P)$, $bn(P)$ and $n(P)$, are used in their standard meanings. In the sequel we will use the functions $fn(-), bn(-)$ and $n(-)$ without explanation. We will adopt the α-convention saying that a bound name in a process can be replaced by a fresh name without changing the syntax of the process. And in any discussion we assume that the bound names of any processes or actions under consideration are chosen to be different from the names free in any other entities under consideration, such as processes, actions, substitutions, and set of names. As a convention, we often abbreviate $\alpha x.0$ simply as αx. Moreover, sometimes a communication needs to carry no parameter when the passed names are unimportant. To model this, we will usually write $\alpha.P$ for $\alpha x.P$ where $x \notin fn(P)$.

A *context* is a process with a hole. Now, we give a formal definition as follows.

Definition 1. Contexts *are defined inductively as follows:*

(i) [] *is a context.*
(ii) If $C[]$ *is a context then* $\alpha x.C[], P|C[], C[]|P, (\nu x)C[], [x = y]C[]$ *are contexts.*

Full contexts *are those contexts that satisfy additionally:*
(iii) If $C[]$ is a context then $P + C[], C[] + P$ are contexts.

The operational semantics is defined by the following labelled transition system:

$$\text{Sqn} \quad \frac{}{\alpha x.P \overset{\alpha x}{\to} P} \qquad\qquad \text{Sum} \quad \frac{P \overset{\lambda}{\to} P'}{P + Q \overset{\lambda}{\to} P'}$$

$$\text{Cmp0} \quad \frac{P \overset{\gamma}{\to} P' \quad bn(\gamma) \cap fn(Q) = \emptyset}{P|Q \overset{\gamma}{\to} P'|Q} \qquad \text{Cmp1} \quad \frac{P \overset{y/x}{\to} P'}{P|Q \overset{y/x}{\to} P'|Q\{y/x\}}$$

$$\text{Cmm0} \quad \frac{P \overset{\alpha(x)}{\to} P' \quad Q \overset{\bar{\alpha}y}{\to} Q'}{P|Q \overset{\tau}{\to} P'\{y/x\}|Q'} \qquad \text{Cmm1} \quad \frac{P \overset{\alpha(x)}{\to} P' \quad Q \overset{\bar{\alpha}(x)}{\to} Q'}{P|Q \overset{\tau}{\to} (\nu x)(P'|Q')}$$

$$\text{Cmm2} \quad \frac{P \overset{\alpha x}{\to} P' \quad Q \overset{\bar{\alpha}y}{\to} Q' \quad x \neq y}{P|Q \overset{y/x}{\to} P'\{y/x\}|Q'\{y/x\}} \qquad \text{Cmm3} \quad \frac{P \overset{\alpha x}{\to} P' \quad Q \overset{\bar{\alpha}y}{\to} Q'}{P|Q \overset{\tau}{\to} P'|Q'}$$

$$\text{Loc0} \quad \frac{P \overset{\lambda}{\to} P' \quad x \notin n(\lambda)}{(\nu x)P \overset{\lambda}{\to} (\nu x)P'} \qquad \text{Loc1} \quad \frac{P \overset{\alpha x}{\to} P' \quad x \notin \{\alpha, \bar{\alpha}\}}{(\nu x)P \overset{\alpha(x)}{\to} P'}$$

$$\text{Loc2} \quad \frac{P \overset{y/x}{\to} P'}{(\nu x)P \overset{\tau}{\to} P'} \qquad\qquad \text{Match} \quad \frac{P \overset{\lambda}{\to} P'}{[x = x]P \overset{\lambda}{\to} P'}$$

$$\text{Rep} \quad \frac{!P|P \overset{\lambda}{\to} P'}{!P \overset{\lambda}{\to} P'}$$

Note that we have omitted all the symmetric rules. In the above rules the letter γ ranges over the set $\{\alpha(x), \alpha x \mid \alpha \in \mathcal{N} \cup \bar{\mathcal{N}}, x \in \mathcal{N}\} \cup \{\tau\}$ of non-update actions and the letter λ over the set $\{\alpha(x), \alpha x, y/x \mid \alpha \in \mathcal{N} \cup \bar{\mathcal{N}}, x \in \mathcal{N}\} \cup \{\tau\}$ of all actions. The symbols $\alpha(x), \alpha x, y/x$ represent restricted action, free action and update action respectively. The x in $\alpha(x)$ is bounded whereas the other names are all free. We refer to [6] for more detailed explanations.

The process $P\{y/x\}$ appearing in the above structured operational semantics is obtained by substituting y for x throughout P. The notion $\{y/x\}$ is an atomic substitution of y for x. A general substitution denoted by σ, σ' etc, is the composition of atomic substitutions. The composition of zero atomic substitutions is an empty substitution, written as $\{\}$ whose effect on a process is vacuous. The result of applying σ to P is denoted by $P\sigma$.

As usual, let $\Rightarrow$ be the reflexive and transitive closure of $\overset{\tau}{\to}$, and $\overset{\tau}{\Rightarrow}$ be the composition $\Rightarrow \overset{\tau}{\to} \Rightarrow$. The relation $\overset{\lambda}{\Rightarrow}$ is the same as $\overset{\lambda}{\Rightarrow}$ if $\lambda \neq \tau$ and is $\Rightarrow$ otherwise. A sequence of names $x_1, \ldots, x_n$ will be abbreviated as $\tilde{x}$; and consequently $(\nu x_1) \ldots (\nu x_n)P$ will be abbreviated to $(\nu \tilde{x})P$. Moreover, we will abuse the notation a little since for a finite name set $N = \{x_1, \ldots, x_n\}$, we will write $(\nu \tilde{N})P$ for $(\nu \tilde{x})P$.

In the rest of this section we state some technical lemmas whose proofs are by simple induction on derivation.

Lemma 1. *The following two properties hold:*

(i) *If $P \xrightarrow{\lambda} P'$, then $fn(P') \subseteq fn(P) \cup bn(\lambda)$.*
(ii) *If $P \xrightarrow{y/x} P'$, then $x \notin fn(P')$.*
(iii) *If $P \Rightarrow P'$, then $P\sigma \Rightarrow P'\sigma$.*
(iv) *If $P \xRightarrow{y/x} P'$, then $P \xRightarrow{x/y} P'\{x/y\}$.*

3   Labelled Bisimulation

In this section, we discuss bisimulation for χ-calculus in the labelled semantics.

3.1   Closed Style Definitions

First, let us see how late bisimulation in π-calculus can be adapted to χ-calculus.

Definition 2. *Let $\mathcal{R}$ be a binary symmetric relation on $\mathcal{C}$. It is called a* late
bisimulation *if whenever $P\mathcal{R}Q$ then the following properties hold:*

(i) *If $P \xrightarrow{\lambda} P'$, where $\lambda = y/x, \tau$ then Q' exists such that $Q \xRightarrow{\hat{\lambda}} Q'$ with $P'\mathcal{R}Q'$.*
(ii) *If $P \xrightarrow{\alpha x} P'$ then Q', Q'' exist such that $Q \Rightarrow\xrightarrow{\alpha x} Q''$, and for every y, $Q''\{y/x\} \Rightarrow Q'$ with $P'\{y/x\}\mathcal{R}Q'$.*
(iii) *If $P \xrightarrow{\alpha(x)} P'$ then Q', Q'' exist such that $Q \Rightarrow\xrightarrow{\alpha(x)} Q''$, and for every y, $Q''\{y/x\} \Rightarrow Q'$ with $P'\{y/x\}\mathcal{R}Q'$.*

Late bisimilarity $\approx_l$ *is the largest late bisimulation.*

Since we are interested in bisimulation congruence, we consider the finer equivalence obtained as bisimilarity.

Definition 3. *P and Q are* late equivalent, *written $P \approx_{cl} Q$, if for any context $C[]$, $C[P] \approx_l C[Q]$.*

In a similar way, we also can adapt early bisimulation to χ-calculus.

Definition 4. *Let $\mathcal{R}$ be a binary symmetric relation on $\mathcal{C}$. It is called an* early
bisimulation *if whenever $P\mathcal{R}Q$ then the following properties hold:*

(i) *If $P \xrightarrow{\lambda} P'$, where $\lambda = y/x, \tau$ then Q' exists such that $Q \xRightarrow{\hat{\lambda}} Q'$ with $P'\mathcal{R}Q'$.*
(ii) *If $P \xrightarrow{\alpha x} P'$ then for every y, Q', Q'' exist such that $Q \Rightarrow\xrightarrow{\alpha x} Q''$, and $Q''\{y/x\} \Rightarrow Q'$ with $P'\{y/x\}\mathcal{R}Q'$.*
(iv) *If $P \xrightarrow{\alpha(x)} P'$ then for every y, Q', Q'' exist such that $Q \Rightarrow\xrightarrow{\alpha(x)} Q''$, and $Q''\{y/x\} \Rightarrow Q'$ with $P'\{y/x\}\mathcal{R}Q'$.*

Early bisimilarity $\approx_e$ *is the largest early bisimulation.*
P and Q are early equivalent, *written $P \approx_{ce} Q$, if for any context $C[]$, $C[P] \approx_e C[Q]$.*

Definition 5. *Let $\mathcal{R}$ be a binary symmetric relation on $\mathcal{C}$. It is called a* ground bisimulation *if whenever $P\mathcal{R}Q$ and $P \xrightarrow{\lambda} P'$ then Q' exists such that $Q \xRightarrow{\hat{\lambda}} Q'$ with $P'\mathcal{R}Q'$.*

Ground bisimilarity $\approx_g$ is the largest ground bisimulation.

Definition 6. *P and Q are* ground equivalent, *written $P \approx_{cg} Q$, if for any context $C[]$, $C[P] \approx_g C[Q]$.*

Remark 1. In the π-calculus, late and early bisimulation, which appeared in the original paper [11], are well-known. In order to obtain a congruence, it is often required that bisimulation should be closed under substitutions, see the corresponding definitions in [11]. Here, in order to reflect our understanding on the "closed" style equivalence, we choose to present it by the notion of *context*. However, this can be simplified in the sense that we provide the following *Context Lemma*. Note that ground bisimulation is not common in research on π-calculus. The main reason is that it is not even closed under the parallel operator (thus it can not be refined to congruence only by requiring closure under substitution), so that is of little sense. Therefore, to obtain a congruence, one has to require closure both under substitution and the parallel operator, which actually will lead to early congruence. Moreover, it is worth pointing out that in the setting of χ-calculus, only requiring closure under substitution is not sufficient! We provide a counterexample to illustrate this. Suppose $P = \bar{a}.\bar{a} + \bar{a} + \bar{a}.[x = y]\bar{a}$, and $Q = \bar{a}.\bar{a} + \bar{a}$. It is not difficult to observe that for any substitution σ, $P\sigma \approx_l Q\sigma$. However, if $R = \langle x|y\rangle$, then $P|R \xrightarrow{\bar{a}} [x = y]\tau|R$. How can $Q|R$ match this transition? Clearly we have only two choices, $Q|R \xrightarrow{\bar{a}} 0|\langle x|y\rangle$ or $Q|R \xrightarrow{\bar{a}} \tau|\langle x|y\rangle$, but in both cases, the bisimulation game fails. Thus, we can conclude that $P|R \napprox_l Q|R$, so $P \napprox_l Q$! That is, if only requiring closure under substitution is required, we would obtain an ill-defined bisimulation relation, since it would not be closed under the parallel operator. Instead, it is interesting and surprising that to require closure under the parallel operator is enough to give rise to a (partial) congruence, since it turns out that the parallel operator can exert a similar effect as substitution.

Lemma 2. *For any processes P and Q, substitution σ, if $P \approx_{\square} Q$, then $P\sigma \approx_{\square} Q\sigma$, where $\square \in \{cg, cl, ce\}$.*

Lemma 3. *(Context Lemma for Labelled Bisimulation) $P \approx_{c\square} Q$, iff for any process $R \in \mathcal{C}$, $P|R \approx_{\square} Q|R$, where $\square \in \{g, l, e\}$.*

Lemma 4. *$\approx_{cl} \subseteq \approx_{ce} \subseteq \approx_{cg}$.*

3.2   Open Style Definitions

Definition 7. *Let $\mathcal{R}$ be a binary symmetric relation on $\mathcal{C}$. It is called an* open congruence *if the following two properties hold:*

(i) $\mathcal{R}$ is a ground bisimulation.
(ii) For any context $C[]$, $(P, Q) \in \mathcal{R}$ implies $(C[P], C[Q]) \in \mathcal{R}$.

P and Q are open congruent, *notation* $P \approx_o Q$, *if there exists some* open congruence $\mathcal{R}$ *such that* $(P, Q) \in \mathcal{R}$.

We present a different form of open congruence.

Definition 8. *([6], Definition 17) Let $\mathcal{R}$ be a binary symmetric relation on $\mathcal{C}$. It is called an* open bisimulation *if whenever $P\mathcal{R}Q$ and $P\sigma \xrightarrow{\lambda} P'$, then Q' exists such that $Q\sigma \xrightarrow{\hat{\lambda}} Q'$ and $(P', Q') \in \mathcal{R}$.*
Open bisimilarity $\approx_{open}$ is the largest open bisimulation.

Clearly, according to Theorem 19 and Theorem 21 of [6], the above definition ($\approx_{open}$) is a rephrase of open bisimulation defined in Definition 7. Precisely, it can be regarded as a characterization of Definition 7, which will smooth the proofs of the results presented in the next section.

3.3   Relationships

As in [6], we first establish a technical lemma about the following general property, which will simplify the proof greatly, though it is very simple and obvious itself.

A weak bisimulation $\approx$ is said to satisfy the *-property if $P \Rightarrow P_1 \approx Q$ and $Q \Rightarrow Q_1 \approx P$ implies $P \approx Q$.

Lemma 5. $\dot{\approx}_g$ *satisfies the *-property.*

Lemma 6. $\approx_o \subseteq \approx_{cl}$.

The following lemma is devoted to stating that ground equivalent is not weaker than open congruence. The main proof idea is to construct a bisimulation relation $\mathcal{S}$ such that $\approx_{cg} \subseteq \mathcal{S}$, and prove that $\mathcal{S}$ is an open congruence. To this end, we need to construct a sophisticated context. Unfortunately, its proof is rather long and can not be presented here because of the space restriction. For more details, see [3].

Lemma 7. $\approx_{cg} \subseteq \approx_o$.

Theorem 1. $\approx_{cl} = \approx_{ce} = \approx_{cg} = \approx_o$.

4   Barbed Bisimulation

In this section, we turn to reduction semantics and barbed style bisimulation whose idea lies in that two processes are regarded as equal if they can simulate each other's communication while maintaining the same ability to communicate through any particular name. As in the previous section, we start from the closed style definition, and then treat the open style one.

Definition 9. *(Barb) A process P is strongly barbed at a, notion $P \downarrow_a$, if $P \xrightarrow{\alpha(x)} P'$ or $P \xrightarrow{\alpha x} P'$ for some P' such that $a \in \{\alpha, \bar{\alpha}\}$. P is barbed at a, written $P \Downarrow_a$, if some P' exists such that $P \Rightarrow P' \downarrow_a$.*

Definition 10. *Let $\mathcal{R}$ be a binary symmetric relation on $\mathcal{C}$. It is called a* barbed *bisimulation if whenever $P \mathcal{R} Q$ then the following two properties hold:*

- *For any name a, if $P \downarrow_a$, then $Q \Downarrow_a$.*
- *If $P \xrightarrow{\tau} P'$ then Q' exists such that $Q \Rightarrow Q'$ with $P' \mathcal{R} Q'$.*

The barbed bisimilarity *$\dot{\approx}_b$ is the largest barbed bisimulation.*

For barbed bisimilarity, we have the following properties.

Lemma 8. *$\dot{\approx}_b$ satisfies the *-property.*

Lemma 9. *For any processes P, Q, R, and name $s \notin fn(P, Q, R)$, if $P|(R + s) \dot{\approx}_b Q|(R + s)$, then $P|R \dot{\approx}_b Q|R$.*

Definition 11. *P and Q are* barbed equivalent, *written $P \approx_{cb} Q$, if for any context $C[]$, $C[P] \dot{\approx}_{cb} C[Q]$.*

We also provide a *Context Lemma* to simplify "any context" in the above definition.

Lemma 10. *(Context Lemma for Barbed Bisimulation)*

$$P \approx_{cb} Q \ iff \ (\nu \tilde{x})(P|R) \dot{\approx}_b (\nu \tilde{x})(Q|R) \ for \ any \ \tilde{x} \in \mathcal{N}, \ process \ R \in \mathcal{C}.$$

Remark 2. The context in Lemma 10 is essential. We can not only require that it is closed by the parallel operator as in Lemma 3, because this is not discriminate enough. The following is a counterexample. Suppose $P = ax|\bar{a}y$ and $Q = ax.\bar{a}y + \bar{a}y.ax$. We can prove that for any process R, $P|R \approx_b Q|R$ (here please note that in our semantics, $ax|\bar{a}y$ has no interaction, i.e. $ax|\bar{a}y \not\xrightarrow{\tau}$). However, $P \not\approx_b Q$, because when they are put the context $(\nu x)[]$, we can distinguish them.

Now, we turn to the "open" style definition.

Definition 12. *Let $\mathcal{R}$ be a binary symmetric relation on $\mathcal{C}$. It is called an* open *barbed congruence if the following two properties hold:*

(i) $\mathcal{R}$ is a barbed bisimulation.
(ii) For any context C, $(P, Q) \in \mathcal{R}$ implies $(C[P], C[Q]) \in \mathcal{R}$.

P and Q are open barbed congruent, *notation $P \approx_{ob} Q$, if there exists some barbed congruence $\mathcal{R}$ such that $(P, Q) \in \mathcal{R}$.*

Note 1. Barbed equivalence is studied in [12], and *open barbed congruence* here is essentially the *barbed congruence* in [6]. Here for a uniform terminology, we follow Sangiorgi and Walker [16].

To characterize open barbed congruence, we borrow an alternative definition from [6].

Definition 13. *([6], Definition 20) Let $\mathcal{R}$ be a binary symmetric relation on $\mathcal{C}$. It is called an* open ba-bisimulation *if whenever $P\mathcal{R}Q$ then for any substitution σ it holds that:*

(i) *If $P\sigma \xrightarrow{\lambda} P'$, where $\lambda = y/x, \tau, \alpha(x)$ then Q' exists such that $Q\sigma \xRightarrow{\hat{\lambda}} Q'$ and $P'\mathcal{R}Q'$.*

(ii) *If $P\sigma \xrightarrow{\alpha x} P'$ then Q' exists such that $P'\mathcal{R}Q'$ and either $Q\sigma \Rightarrow\xrightarrow{\alpha x} Q'$, or $Q\sigma \xrightarrow{\alpha(z)x/z}\Rightarrow Q'$ for some fresh z.*

Open ba-bisimilarity, *denoted $\approx_{open}^{ba}$, is the largest* open ba-bisimulation.

Actually, we have the following lemma. And in the sequel, when we mention open barbed congruence, we will use the form in Definition 13.

Lemma 11. *([6], Theorem 21 (iii))* $\approx_{open}^{ba}=\approx_o$.

Now, we sketch the proof of the main result of this section, that is, the relationship of barbed equivalent and open barbed congruence. First we present a simple result.

Lemma 12. $\approx_{ob}\subseteq\approx_{cb}$.

The following lemma is the most important result of this paper. The main idea of proof is similar to Lemma 7. For more details, see [3].

Lemma 13. $\approx_{cb}\subseteq\approx_{ob}$.

Now, we have the following theorem:

Theorem 2. $\approx_{cb}=\approx_{ob}$.

Naturally, this raises the following problem: does ground congruence ($\approx_{cg}$) coincide with barbed equivalence ($\approx_{cb}$)? This question has also been studied extensively in π-calculus and it turned out to be a very difficult problem. Please see [2][3], among others, for more detailed discussion. Fortunately, now we can solve this problem easily in the setting of χ-calculus. Thanks to Theorem 1 and Theorem 2, clearly we can reduce this problem to the similar problem of open congruence and open barbed congruence, which is much simpler. As [6] shows:

– For the strong case, the two bisimulation equivalences coincide.
– For the weak case, the differences can be characterized by the following axiom, which holds for open barbed congruence while not for open congruence.

Prefix Law: $\alpha(z).(P + \langle x|z\rangle.Q) = \alpha(z).(P + \langle x|z\rangle.Q) + \alpha x.Q\{x/z\} \quad x \neq z$

Now, we can claim that we solve this problem in the χ-calculus completely: In the strong case, barbed equivalence and late equivalence (thus early and ground equivalence) coincide while in the weak case barbed equivalence is *strictly weaker* than the other three.

5   Conclusion

In this paper, we study the bisimilation congruences in χ-calculus. The main contributions and results are as follows:

– We adapt the bisimulation definitions for π-calculus to χ-calculus in a natural way. We find that in χ-calculus, the "open" and "closed" distinction common in π-calculus disappears. Thus we close the conjecture proposed by Fu in [6].
– We show that there are essentially two different bisimulation congruences, i.e. open congruence and open barbed congruence. In the weak case, the difference can be characterized by one axiom. Moreover, if we only consider the strong case, all sensible bisimulation equivalences collapse to just one.
– As a byproduct, we solve the problem of characterizing weak barbed equivalent in χ-calculus. It is essentially Definition 13. Moreover, according to our results, [6] actually gives an axiomatization for this relation.

In short, the key results of this paper can be reflected by the following diagram.

$$\approx_{cl}=\approx_{ce}=\,\approx_{cg}\subset\,\approx_{cb}$$
$$\parallel\quad\parallel$$
$$\approx_{o}\subset\,\approx_{ob}$$

We now present some concluding remarks.

– In this paper, we only consider χ-calculus without mismatch operator [7]. This is not a very serious disadvantage, since besides some technical details, the main results of this paper can be adapted. Here, we would like to mention Fu and Yang's paper [7]. In their paper, open barbed congruence is also studied, and they also mention barbed equivalence ([7], Definition 34). However, they argue that open barbed congruence is contained in barbed equivalence and the inclusion is *strict*. To support this, they invite an example: $P_1 = [x \neq y]\tau.(P + \tau.[x \neq y]\tau.(P + \tau))$ and $P_2 = [x \neq y]\tau.(P + \tau)$, for which they "show" that they are open barbed congruent but not barbed equivalent. In our point of view, this is definitely incorrect since $P_1|\langle x|y\rangle$ and $P_2|\langle x|y\rangle$ are not open barbed congruent. Thus P_1 and P_2 are also not open barbed congruent! Currently we are performing a similar systematic study of χ-calculus with mismatch.
– It is worth emphasizing that the results in this paper have strong implications to other calculi falling into the family of fusion-style mobile calculi. Since all of these calculi share a similar communication mechanism, we believe the results in this paper generally also hold in, among others, update-calculus, fusion calculus, explicit fusion calculus.
– As we have said in Section 1, [4] discusses a similar problem in the setting of asynchronous π-calculus. To prove the analogous result for weak barbed congruences, Fournet and Gonthier actually have to use a *Universal Pi-calculus Machine* for their initial environment, and they use it to simulate the execution of a Gödelized version of a program. This leads to a very long

technical proof. Our proof technique, like that of Fournet and Gonthier, also involves creating an initial sophisticated environment. However, thanks to the mechanism of χ-calculus, our environment is much simpler.

Acknowledgement. We are grateful to Wan Fokkink for his careful reading of a draft of this paper and valuable comments. We also would like to thank the anonymous referees for their excellent criticisms.

References

1. M. Abadi and C. Fournet. Mobile values, new names, and secure communication. In *POPL*, pages 104–115, 2001.
2. T. Chen. *Research on the Theory and Application of Mobile Process Calculi*. Master's thesis, Nanjing University, Nanjing, P.R.China, 2005.
3. T. Chen, T. Han, and J. Lu. On bisimulation congruence in χ-calculus. Technical report, CWI, Amsterdam, The Netherlands. 2005.
4. C. Fournet and G. Gonthier. A hierarchy of equivalences for asynchronous calculi. *J. Log. Algebr. Program.*, 63:131–1739, 2005.
5. Y. Fu. A proof theoretical approach to communication. In P. Degano, R. Gorrieri, and A. Marchetti-Spaccamela, editors, *ICALP*, volume 1256 of *Lecture Notes in Computer Science*, pages 325–335. Springer, 1997.
6. Y. Fu. Bisimulation congruence of chi calculus. *Inf. Comput.*, 184(1):201–226, 2003.
7. Y. Fu and Z. Yang. Understanding the mismatch combinator in chi calculus. *Theor. Comput. Sci.*, 290(1):779–830, 2003.
8. P. Gardner and L. Wischik. Explicit fusions. In M. Nielsen and B. Rovan, editors, *MFCS*, volume 1893 of *Lecture Notes in Computer Science*, pages 373–382. Springer, 2000.
9. K. Honda and N. Yoshida. On reduction-based process semantics. *Theor. Comput. Sci.*, 151(2):437–486, 1995.
10. R. Milner. *Communication and Concurrency*. Prentice Hall, 1989.
11. R. Milner, J. Parrow, and D. Walker. A calculus of mobile process, part I/II. *Inf. Comput.*, 100:1–77, 1992.
12. R. Milner and D. Sangiorgi. Barbed bisimulation. In W. Kuich, editor, *ICALP*, volume 623 of *Lecture Notes in Computer Science*, pages 685–695. Springer, 1992.
13. J. Parrow and B. Victor. The update calculus (extended abstract). In M. Johnson, editor, *AMAST*, volume 1349 of *Lecture Notes in Computer Science*, pages 409–423, 1997.
14. J. Parrow and B. Victor. The fusion calculus: Expressiveness and symmetry in mobile processes. In *LICS*, pages 176–185, 1998.
15. D. Sangiorgi. A theory of bisimulation for the π-calculus. *Acta Inf.*, 33(1):69–97, 1996.
16. D. Sangiorgi and D. Walker. On barbed equivalences in pi-calculus. In *CONCUR*, volume 2154 of *Lecture Notes in Computer Science*, pages 292–304, 2001.
17. D. Sangiorgi and D. Walker. *The π-calculus: a Theory of Mobile Processes*. Cambridge University Press, 2001.
18. L. Wischik and P. Gardner. Strong bisimulation for the explicit fusion calculus. In I. Walukiewicz, editor, *FoSSaCS*, volume 2987 of *Lecture Notes in Computer Science*, pages 484–498. Springer, 2004.

Extending Howe's Method to Early Bisimulations for Typed Mobile Embedded Resources with Local Names

Jens Chr. Godskesen and Thomas Hildebrandt

IT University of Copenhagen, Denmark
{jcg, hilde}@itu.dk

Abstract. We extend Howe's method to prove that *input-early* strong and -delay contextual bisimulations are congruences for the Higher-order mobile embedded resources (*Homer*) calculus, a typed higher order process calculus with active mobile processes, nested locations and local names which conservatively extends the syntax and semantics of higher-order calculi such as Plain CHOCS and HOpi. We prove that the input-early strong and -delay contextual bisimulation congruences are sound co-inductive characterisations of barbed bisimulation congruence and in fact *complete* in the strong case. The extension of Howe's method provides considerably simpler congruence proofs than established previously for similar calculi for mobile processes in nested locations.

1 Introduction

The ability to reason compositionally about the behaviour of processes and compare their behaviour in any context are key issues in semantics. A way to achieve this is to give a co-inductive characterisation of a behavioural congruence, for process calculi typically a notion of barbed bisimulation congruence in terms of a labelled transition bisimulation. In the present paper we study this problem for higher-order process calculi allowing to represent active, copyable (non-linear), objectively mobile processes with local names and nested locations as found in the Seal calculus [1], the M-calculus [2] and its recent successor the Kell calculus [3]. This has proven to be a difficult problem.

Our main contribution is to extend *Howe's method* [4], a classical technique for proving that applicative bisimulation is a congruence, to *early* bisimulations for a core higher-order calculus with local names and static scope, extended with non-linear active process mobility and explicit, nested locations. We call the calculus Homer as short for *Higher-Order Mobile Embedded Resources* [1]. Thereby we also propose a calculus which conservatively extends the standard syntax and semantics of higher-order process calculi such as Plain CHOCS [5] and HOπ [6], which has been one of the main design criteria behind Homer. The result is a calculus with considerable simpler syntax and semantics than present calculi with comparable expressive power.

Active process mobility is introduced in Homer by the prefix $n\langle r\rangle$ denoting a resource r residing at the location (or address) n, which may be *moved* by the complementary prefix, $\overline{n}(x)$, expressed by a reaction rule

$$n\langle r\rangle p \parallel \overline{n}(x)q \searrow p \parallel q[r/x] \ ,$$

---

[1] and reference to the dangerous mobile embedded resources in the legend of Troy.

R. Ramanujam and S. Sen (Eds.): FSTTCS 2005, LNCS 3821, pp. 140–151, 2005.
© Springer-Verlag Berlin Heidelberg 2005

where r is a process and x is a process variable binding any number of occurrences of x in q. The rule complements the usual reaction rule for higher-order process calculi

$$\overline{n}\langle r \rangle p \parallel n(x)q \searrow p \parallel q[r/x] \ ,$$

where the process r is assumed to be *passive*, meaning that it can neither compute internally nor interact with other processes before it has been sent. In the usual way the receiver may activate or forward any number of copies of the process, but once a copy has started computing, it cannot be moved again. This kind of mobility is known as *code mobility* or *passive process* mobility. To allow *active process* mobility the process r in the prefix $n\langle r \rangle$ can perform internal computations, that is $r \searrow r'$ implies $n\langle r \rangle p \searrow n\langle r' \rangle p$ as in [7]. We allow interaction with (arbitrarily) nested active mobile resources by the use of *nested* names as introduced in [8]. For instance, a resource r may be sent to the subaddress *server* : 80 by the reaction

$$\overline{server : 80}\langle r \rangle p \parallel server\langle 80(x)q' \parallel q'' \rangle \searrow p \parallel server\langle q'[r/x] \parallel q'' \rangle \ .$$

Dually, a resource r may be taken from the subaddress *server* : 80 by the reaction

$$server\langle 80\langle r \rangle q' \parallel q'' \rangle \parallel \overline{server : 80}(x)p \searrow server\langle q' \parallel q'' \rangle \parallel p[r/x] \ .$$

As usual we let $(n)p$ denote a process p in which the name n is local with static scope. This provides the means to control access to resources. A standard example is the *perfect firewall equation* [9]: $(n)(n\langle p \rangle) \approx \mathbf{0}$, expressing that a resource computing at a location with *a local name* has no observable behaviour.

When a resource is moved from a location it may be necessary to extend the scope of a name through a location boundary, which we will refer to as *vertical* scope extension. For instance, if the resource r below contains the name n, we will expect the reaction

$$m\langle (n)(m'\langle r \rangle \parallel p) \rangle \parallel \overline{m : m'}(x)q \searrow (n)(m\langle p \rangle \parallel q[r/x]) \tag{1}$$

in which the scope of n is extended. If mobile processes can *not* be copied during computation, such as in the Mobile Ambients calculus [9], vertical scope extension can simply be dealt with in the structural congruence by introducing the equation

$$m\langle (n)p \rangle \equiv (n)m\langle p \rangle \ , \ \text{if } n \neq m \ .$$

However, as also identified in [1,3] this equation is unsound if mobile processes can be copied. If placed in a context with a copying process $(-) \parallel \overline{m}(x)(x \parallel x)$ then the left hand process in (1) above will reduce to $(n)p \parallel (n)p$ while the right hand process will reduce to $(n)(p \parallel p)$, which in general will not be equivalent. The solution taken in Homer is to extend the scope of the name n in the reaction (1) *if and only if* the name n is free in p, which is consistent with the semantics of Plain CHOCS and HOπ. This solution contrasts the more eager solution in [10,3] where the scope of all local names is extended before resources move, i.e. local names will *always* be shared between dynamically created copies of a process.

The vertical scope extension of Homer implies that a context can test if a name is free in a mobile process (see [11] for a detailed discussion). Consequently, any non-trivial congruence must be *well typed*, meaning that related processes r and r' must have

$$
\begin{array}{llll}
(inactive) \ \dfrac{}{0 : \tilde{n}} & (variable) \ \dfrac{}{x : \tilde{n}} & (context) \ \dfrac{}{(-)_{\tilde{n}} : \tilde{n}'} \ \tilde{n} \subseteq \tilde{n}' & (prefix) \ \dfrac{e : \tilde{n}}{\varphi e : \varphi \cup \tilde{n}}
\end{array}
$$

$$
\begin{array}{lll}
(rest) \ \dfrac{F : \tilde{n}}{(n)F : \tilde{n} \setminus n} & (abs) \ \dfrac{p : \tilde{n}}{(x)p : \tilde{n}} & (parallel) \ \dfrac{F : \tilde{n} \quad p : \tilde{n}'}{F \parallel p : \tilde{n} \cup \tilde{n}'}
\end{array}
$$

$$
\begin{array}{ll}
(concretion) \ \dfrac{p' : \tilde{n}' \quad p : \tilde{n}}{\langle p' : \tilde{n}' \rangle p : \tilde{n} \cup \tilde{n}'} & (nesting) \ \dfrac{F : \tilde{n}' \quad p : \tilde{n}}{\varphi \langle F : \tilde{n}' \rangle p : \tilde{n} \cup \tilde{n}' \cup \varphi}
\end{array}
$$

Table 1. Typing rules.

the same set of free names. This means that the firewall equation $(n)(n\langle p \rangle) \approx \mathbf{0}$, will only hold if the process p has no free variables. We remedy this problem by explicitly typing processes by a set of names *including* the usual free names of the process, but allowing additional (unused) names. Interestingly, it turns out that one then also needs to explicitly type all mobile sub resources. We can now state a *well typed firewall equation* as $(n)(n\langle p : \tilde{n} \rangle) : \tilde{m} \approx \mathbf{0} : \tilde{m}$, where $\tilde{n}$ is the type of process p.

The above constructions are the only primitives in Homer. In particular, process passing is the only means of communication, thus, the issue of name passing is separated from process passing. The synchronous π-calculus can in fact be encoded in a (simplified) variant of Homer [12]. The simplicity of the calculus helps us to adapt Howe's method to show that both strong and so called delay *input-early* contextual bisimulation are congruences for Homer. This gives a sound and complete characterisation of strong barbed bisimulation, and a sound characterisation of weak barbed bisimulation. It also helps pinpointing the need for typing processes and mobile sub resources, which is studied in more detail in [13].

2 The Homer Calculus

We assume an infinite set of *names* $\mathcal{N}$ ranged over by m and n, and let $\tilde{n}$ range over finite sets of names. We let δ range over non-empty finite sequences of names, referred to as *paths* and $\bar{\delta}$ denotes *co-paths*. We let φ range over δ and $\bar{\delta}$ and define $\bar{\bar{\delta}} = \delta$. We assume an infinite set of *process variables* $\mathcal{V}$ ranged over by x and y. The sets **p** of *process expressions*, **a** of *abstractions*, and **c** of *concretions* are defined by the grammar:

$$
p ::= \mathbf{0} \mid x \mid \varphi e \mid p \parallel p' \mid (n)p \ , \quad a ::= (x)p \ , \quad c ::= b \mid (n)c \ ,
$$

where $b ::= \langle p' : \tilde{n} \rangle p$ is a basic (unrestricted) concretion and $e ::= a \mid b$. We let **f**, ranged over by f, denote $\mathbf{p} \cup \mathbf{a} \cup \mathbf{c}$. Whenever e denotes a basic concretion we let $\bar{e}$ denote an abstraction, and vice versa.

The constructors are the standard ones from concurrent process calculi, extended with process variables and by *types* $\tilde{n}$. The processes $\bar{\delta}\langle p' : \tilde{n} \rangle p$ and $\delta(x)p$ correspond to sending and receiving processes, except that paths, and not only names, are allowed

$$\varphi(e : \tilde{n}) = \varphi e : \tilde{n} \cup \varphi \qquad F : \tilde{n} \parallel p' : \tilde{n}' = F \parallel p' : \tilde{n} \cup \tilde{n}' \qquad (n)(F : \tilde{n}) = (n)F : \tilde{n} \setminus n$$

$$(y)(p : \tilde{n}) = (y)p : \tilde{n} \qquad \langle p : \tilde{n} \rangle (p' : \tilde{n}') = \langle p : \tilde{n} \rangle p' : \tilde{n} \cup \tilde{n}'$$

$$\varphi \langle F : \tilde{n}' \rangle (p : \tilde{n}) = \varphi \langle F : \tilde{n}' \rangle p : \tilde{n} \tilde{n}' \cup \delta$$

Table 2. Extension of process constructors to typed terms.

as addresses. As explained in the introduction, the new constructs $\delta \langle p' : \tilde{n} \rangle p$ and $\bar{\delta}(x)p$ add active process mobility to the calculus.

The restriction operator (n) binds the name n and (x) binds the variable x. The sets $fn(f)$ and $fv(f)$ of *free names* and *free variables* are defined accordingly as usual, except that $fn(\langle p' : \tilde{n} \rangle p) = \tilde{n} \cup fn(p)$, i.e. the type of a sub-resource defines its free names. We say that a term with no free variables is *closed* and let $\mathbf{f}_c$ ($\mathbf{p}_c$) denote the set of closed terms (processes).

As usual, we let prefixing and restriction be right associative and bind stronger than parallel composition. Often we shall write $\langle p : \tilde{n} \rangle$ instead of $\langle p : \tilde{n} \rangle 0$. For a set of names $\tilde{n} = \{n_1, \ldots, n_k\}$ we let $(\tilde{n})f$ denote $(n_1) \cdots (n_k)f$. We will write n for the set $\{n\}$ and δ for the set of names in δ (or $\bar{\delta}$) when no confusion can occur. We write $f \equiv_\alpha f'$, if f and f' are α-convertible (wrt. both names and variables), and we let $\mathbf{f}_{/\alpha}$ (and $\mathbf{f}_{c/\alpha}$) denote the set of α-equivalence classes of (closed) terms. Likewise we let $\mathbf{p}_{/\alpha}$ (and $\mathbf{p}_{c/\alpha}$) denote the set of α-equivalence classes of (closed) processes. From now on we consider terms up to α-equivalence.

We define a family of type indexed *evaluation contexts* $E_{\tilde{n}}$. They are contexts with no free variables, and whose "hole" is indexed by a type $\tilde{n}$ and is either not guarded by a prefix or guarded by a prefix δ and nested in a concretion, i.e.

$$E_{\tilde{n}} ::= (-)_{\tilde{n}} \mid E_{\tilde{n}} \parallel p \mid (n)E_{\tilde{n}} \mid \delta \langle E_{\tilde{n}} : \tilde{n}' \rangle p \quad , p \in \mathbf{p}_c.$$

The free names of $E_{\tilde{n}}$ are defined similarly as for processes. If the type index of the hole in $E_{\tilde{n}}$ is not important we may write E instead of $E_{\tilde{n}}$.

We let F range over processes, abstractions, concretions, and evaluation contexts. If $F : \tilde{n}$ can be inferred from the rules in Table 1 we say that F is of type $\tilde{n}$. From now on writing $F : \tilde{n}$ we assume F is of type $\tilde{n}$. We can prove a simple kind of subsumption (using α-conversion if needed).

Proposition 1. *(Subsumption)* $F : \tilde{n}$ *implies* $F : \tilde{n}'$ *for all* $\tilde{n}'$ *where* $\tilde{n} \subseteq \tilde{n}'$.

By convenience we extend the process constructors to typed terms as defined in Table 2 (following the rules of Table 1). We let P, A, and C range over the set of typed processes $\mathbf{P}_{/\alpha}$, abstractions $\mathbf{A}_{/\alpha}$, and concretions $\mathbf{C}_{/\alpha}$ up to α-equivalence respectively, and we let T range over $\mathbf{T}_{/\alpha} = \mathbf{P}_{/\alpha} \cup \mathbf{A}_{/\alpha} \cup \mathbf{C}_{/\alpha}$. The closed variants of $\mathbf{T}_{/\alpha}$, $\mathbf{P}_{/\alpha}$, $\mathbf{A}_{/\alpha}$, and $\mathbf{C}_{/\alpha}$ are denoted by $\mathbf{T}_{c/\alpha}$, $\mathbf{P}_{c/\alpha}$, $\mathbf{A}_{c/\alpha}$, and $\mathbf{C}_{c/\alpha}$. Finally, we let $\mathcal{E}_{\tilde{n}}$ range over typed type indexed evaluation contexts and occasionally we leave out the type index writing $\mathcal{E}$ for $\mathcal{E}_{\tilde{n}}$ if the type index is not important.

Whenever $F : \tilde{n}$ then we write $E_{\tilde{n}}(F)$ (or by convenience $E_{\tilde{n}} : \tilde{n}'(F : \tilde{n})$) for the insertion of F in the hole of $E_{\tilde{n}}$. Note that free names of F may get bound by insertion of F in the hole of a context.

Proposition 2. If $E_{\tilde{n}} : \tilde{n}'$ and $F : \tilde{n}$ then $E_{\tilde{n}}(F) : \tilde{n}'$.

Substitution of all free occurrences of a variable x in a typed term T by a typed process P is defined inductively as expected, extending explicit types to include the type of P. The extension of types means that if $f : \tilde{n}[p : \tilde{n}'/x] = f' : \tilde{n}''$ then $\tilde{n}'' = \tilde{n} \cup \tilde{n}'$.

In the remaining part of this paper we consider only a restricted form of concretions on the form $(\tilde{n})\langle p' : \tilde{n}' \rangle p$ where $\tilde{n} \subseteq \tilde{n}'$. These concretions we close by convenience under process operators, hence whenever $c = (\tilde{n})\langle p_1 : \tilde{n}_1 \rangle p$ and assuming $\tilde{n} \cap (fn(p') \cup n \cup \delta) = \emptyset$ (using α-conversion if needed) we write $c \parallel p'$ for $(\tilde{n})\langle p_1 : \tilde{n}_1 \rangle (p \parallel p')$, we write $\delta\langle c : \tilde{n}' \rangle p'$ for $(\tilde{n})\langle p_1 : \tilde{n}_1 \rangle \delta\langle p : \tilde{n}'\tilde{n} \rangle p'$, and we let $(n)c$ denote $(n\tilde{n})\langle p_1 : \tilde{n}_1 \rangle p$ if $n \in \tilde{n}_1$ and otherwise it denotes $(\tilde{n})\langle p_1 : \tilde{n}_1 \rangle (n)p$. We also allow abstractions to be closed under process constructs, hence whenever $a = (x)p$ and assuming $x \notin fv(p')$ we write $a \parallel p'$ for $(x)(p \parallel p')$, $\delta\langle a : \tilde{n} \rangle p'$ for $(x)\delta\langle p : \tilde{n} \rangle p'$, and $(n)a$ for $(x)(n)p$. Finally, we define the *application* of a typed abstraction $A = (x)p : \tilde{n}$ to a typed concretion $C = (\tilde{n}')\langle P \rangle P'$ (assuming that $\tilde{n} \cap \tilde{n}' = \emptyset$) by $A \cdot C = C \cdot A = (\tilde{n}')(p : \tilde{n}[P/x] \parallel P')$.

3   Reaction Semantics

We provide Homer with a reaction semantics as usual defined through the use of evaluation contexts, structural congruence, and reaction rules.

As touched upon in the introduction equivalent processes must have the same free names, this we capture using well typedness. A binary relation $\mathcal{R}$ on $\mathbf{T}_{/\alpha}$ is *well typed* if $f : \tilde{n} \mathcal{R} f' : \tilde{n}'$ implies $\tilde{n} = \tilde{n}'$ and $f : \tilde{n}'' \mathcal{R} f' : \tilde{n}''$ for all $\tilde{n}''$ where $\tilde{n} \subseteq \tilde{n}''$. In the sequel we always assume binary relations on $\mathbf{T}_{/\alpha}$ to be well typed.

We say that a well-typed binary relation $\mathcal{R}$ on $\mathbf{P}_{/\alpha}$ is *substitutive* if $P \mathcal{R} P'$ and $P_1 \mathcal{R} P_1'$ implies $P[P_1/x]\mathcal{R}P'[P_1'/x]$. We also say that $\mathcal{R}$ is *constructor compatible* if $P \mathcal{R} P'$ and $P_1 \mathcal{R} P_1'$ implies $\varphi(x)P \mathcal{R} \varphi(x)P'$, $\varphi\langle P_1 \rangle P \mathcal{R} \varphi\langle P_1' \rangle P'$, $P \parallel P_1 \mathcal{R} P' \parallel P_1'$, and $(n)P \mathcal{R} (n)P'$. A well typed relation $\mathcal{R}$ on $\mathbf{P}_{/\alpha}$ is a *congruence* if it is substitutive and constructor compatible.

Structural congruence $\equiv$ is then the least equivalence relation on $\mathbf{p}_{/\alpha}$ that is a congruence and that satisfies the (usual) monoid rules for $(\parallel, \mathbf{0})$ and scope extension as for the π-calculus. In particular, we do *not* allow vertical scope extension described by Eq.(1) in the introduction.

As Homer permits reactions between a process and an arbitrarily deeply nested subresource, we define a restricted set of evaluation contexts, i.e. a family of *path contexts* $D_{\tilde{n},\gamma}$ indexed by the type $\tilde{n}$ of its hole and a path address $\gamma \in \mathcal{N}^*$ which indicates the path under which the context's 'hole' is found. . We do so conveniently using *multi hole path contexts*. A multi hole path contexts $D_{\tilde{n},\gamma}^{\tilde{n}_1,\ldots,\tilde{n}_k}$ has $k+1$ holes and is also indexed by a sequence of types $\tilde{n}_1,\ldots,\tilde{n}_k$ indexing the auxiliary holes in the context. A multi hole path context is defined inductively by $D_{\tilde{n},\varepsilon}^{\varepsilon} = (-)_{\tilde{n}}$ (where epsilon denotes an empty sequence) and

$$D_{\tilde{n},\delta\gamma}^{\tilde{n}_1,\ldots,\tilde{n}_k} ::= \delta\langle(\tilde{m})(D_{\tilde{n},\gamma}^{\tilde{n}_1,\ldots,\tilde{n}_{k-2}} \parallel (-)_{\tilde{n}_{k-1}}) : \tilde{n}'\rangle(-)_{\tilde{n}_k}$$

$$(react) \quad \overline{\gamma \delta} e \parallel D_{\tilde{n},\gamma}(\delta \overline{e}) : \tilde{n}' \searrow e : \tilde{n}' \cdot D_{\tilde{n},\gamma}(\overline{e}) : \tilde{n}'$$

Table 3. Reaction rule

such that $\gamma \cap \tilde{m} = \emptyset$ and none of the names in $\tilde{m}$ are already bound in $D_{\tilde{n},\gamma}^{\tilde{n}_1,\ldots,\tilde{n}_{k-2}}$, i.e. we assume all names binding the hole of a context are unique. For closed typed processes $p_i : \tilde{n}_i$, $i = 1,\ldots,k$, we write $D_{\tilde{n},\gamma}^{\tilde{n}_1,\ldots,\tilde{n}_k}(p_1,\ldots,p_k)$ for the insertion of p_i in the hole indexed by $\tilde{n}_i$ in the context, resulting in a (single hole) path context $D_{\tilde{n},\gamma}$.

We let $\mathcal{D}_{\tilde{n},\gamma}$ range over well typed (single hole) path contexts. If the indexed path in $\mathcal{D}_{\tilde{n},\gamma}$ is not important we write $\mathcal{D}_{\tilde{n}}$ instead. Finally, we define $\searrow$ as the least binary relation on $\mathbf{P}_{c/\alpha}$ satisfying the (parametrized) reaction rule in Table 3 and closed under structural congruence and all type matching evaluation contexts. By the latter we mean that $p : \tilde{n} \searrow p' : \tilde{n}$ implies $\mathcal{E}_{\tilde{n}}(p) \searrow \mathcal{E}_{\tilde{n}}(p')$ for all $\mathcal{E}_{\tilde{n}}$. Notice, that the evaluation context $\delta \langle E_{\tilde{n}} : \tilde{n}' \rangle p : \tilde{n}''$ enables internal reactions of active resources.

Below we exemplify key ideas of Homer, more examples can be found in [11].

Example: Recursion and replication We may encode recursion (up to weak equivalence) as in [5]. Let $p : \tilde{n}$ and define $rec\, x.p =_{def} (a)(rec^a x.p)$ where $rec^a x.p = \overline{a}\langle r : a\tilde{n}\rangle \parallel r$ for $r = a(x)p[(\overline{a}\langle x : 0\rangle \parallel x) : a/x]$, with $a \notin \tilde{n}$. Then $rec^a x.p \searrow p[rec^a x.p : a\tilde{n}/x]$. One may then encode replication by $!p =_{def} rec\, x.(p \parallel x)$.

Example: Static local name discipline The following example illustrates the importance of explicitly typing of sub resources. Suppose $n \notin \tilde{n}$. Let $p_1 =_{def} \overline{ab}(x)\overline{a}(y)(y \parallel y)$, let $p_2 =_{def} a\langle (n)(b\langle r : n\tilde{n}\rangle \parallel p) : \tilde{n}\rangle$, and let $p_3 =_{def} a\langle (n)(b\langle r : \tilde{n}\rangle \parallel p) : \tilde{n}\rangle$. Then

$$p_1 \parallel p_2 : ab\tilde{n} \searrow (x)\overline{a}(y)(y \parallel y) : ab\tilde{n} \cdot a\langle (n)(\langle r : n\tilde{n}\rangle \parallel p) : \tilde{n}\rangle : ab\tilde{n}$$
$$= (n)(\overline{a}(y)(y \parallel y) \parallel a\langle p : n\tilde{n}\rangle) : ab\tilde{n} \searrow (n)(p \parallel p) : ab\tilde{n}$$

since by convention $a\langle (n)(\langle r : n\tilde{n}\rangle \parallel p) : \tilde{n}\rangle = (n)\langle r : n\tilde{n}\rangle a\langle (0 \parallel p) : n\tilde{n}\rangle$, however

$$p_1 \parallel p_3 : ab\tilde{n} \searrow (x)\overline{a}(y)(y \parallel y) : ab\tilde{n} \cdot a\langle (n)(\langle r : \tilde{n}\rangle \parallel p) : \tilde{n}\rangle : ab\tilde{n}$$
$$= \overline{a}(y)(y \parallel y) \parallel a\langle (n)p : \tilde{n}\rangle : ab\tilde{n} \searrow (n)p \parallel (n)p : ab\tilde{n}$$

because by convention $a\langle (n)(\langle r' : \tilde{n}\rangle \parallel p) : \tilde{n}\rangle = \langle r : \tilde{n}\rangle a\langle (n)(0 \parallel p) : \tilde{n}\rangle$. Hence the scope of n is extended vertically only if n appear in the type of r. Thus, if we did not explicitly type sub resources then (for suitable p) the context $a\langle (n)(b\langle (-)_{n\tilde{n}}\rangle \parallel p)\rangle \parallel p_1$ would violate the typed perfect firewall equation $(m)m\langle q\rangle : n\tilde{n} \approx 0 : n\tilde{n}$, for $m \neq n \in fn(q)$.

4 Transition Semantics

In this section we provide Homer with a labelled transition semantics. We let π range over the set Π of labels which consists of labels of the form τ and φ. The set of free names in π, $fn(\pi)$, are defined as expected. As for the reduction semantics we define the transitions for α-equivalence classes of closed processes. The rules in Table 4 then define a labelled transition system

$$(\mathbf{T}_{c/\alpha}, \longrightarrow \subseteq \mathbf{P}_{c/\alpha} \times \Pi \times \mathbf{T}_{c/\alpha}).$$

$$(prefix) \; \frac{}{\varphi e : \tilde{n} \xrightarrow{\varphi} e : \tilde{n}} \qquad\qquad (sync) \; \frac{p : \tilde{n} \xrightarrow{\varphi} A \quad p' : \tilde{n} \xrightarrow{\bar{\varphi}} C}{p \parallel p' : \tilde{n} \xrightarrow{\tau} A \cdot C}$$

$$(par) \; \frac{p : \tilde{n} \xrightarrow{\pi} T}{p \parallel p' : \tilde{n} \xrightarrow{\pi} T \parallel p' : \tilde{n}} \qquad\qquad (sym) \; \frac{p \parallel p' : \tilde{n} \xrightarrow{\pi} T}{p' \parallel p : \tilde{n} \xrightarrow{\pi} T}$$

$$(rest) \; \frac{p : \tilde{n}n \xrightarrow{\pi} T}{(n)p : \tilde{n} \xrightarrow{\pi} (n)T}, \; n \notin fn(\pi) \qquad (nesting) \; \frac{P \xrightarrow{\pi} T}{\delta\langle P\rangle p : \tilde{n} \xrightarrow{\delta \cdot \pi} \delta\langle T\rangle p : \tilde{n}}$$

Table 4. Transition rules.

The rules are completely standard, except for the handling of typing and interaction with nested resources, which shows in the (*prefix*) and (*nesting*) rules. The (*prefix*) rule expresses that types are preserved by transitions. The (*nesting*) rule takes care of the communication and computation of arbitrarily deeply nested resources. It uses an operation $\delta \cdot (\_)$ formally defined by: $\delta \cdot \tau = \tau$ and $\delta \cdot \delta' = \delta\delta'$. Note that the operation is not defined for $\bar{\delta}$ since it is directed "downward" and thus not visible outside the resource. Since $\delta \cdot \tau = \tau$, the nesting rule implies that $\delta\langle P\rangle p : \tilde{n} \xrightarrow{\tau} \delta\langle T\rangle p : \tilde{n}$, if $P \xrightarrow{\tau} T$.

As explained in the introduction, the action prefixes allow two kinds of movement of resources. Since they are completely dual, they are both treated by the rule (*prefix*) and the synchronisation rule (*sync*). For instance, illustrating also the use of the rule (*nesting*), we have

$$n\langle m\langle P\rangle p : \tilde{n}\rangle p' \parallel \overline{nm}(x)p'' : \tilde{n}' \xrightarrow{\tau} \langle P\rangle n\langle p : \tilde{n}\rangle p' : \tilde{n}' \cdot (x)p'' : \tilde{n}'$$

because $n\langle m\langle P\rangle p : \tilde{n}\rangle p' : \tilde{n}' \xrightarrow{nm} \langle P\rangle n\langle p : \tilde{n}\rangle p' : \tilde{n}'$ and $\overline{nm}(x)p'' : \tilde{n}' \xrightarrow{\overline{nm}} (x)p'' : \tilde{n}'$.

Below we state the correspondence between our reaction and transition semantics.

Proposition 3. $P \searrow P'$ iff $P \equiv \xrightarrow{\tau} \equiv P'$ and $P \downarrow n$ iff $P \xrightarrow{n} C$ for some C.

5   Bisimulation Congruences

Next we consider how to describe congruences as bisimulations. First, we define strong and weak *barbed bisimulation congruences* based on the reduction semantics, and next we define early variants of strong and delay contextual transition bisimulations. We prove that the early transition bisimulations are congruences using a novel extension of Howe's method, based on the approach in [14], and that they are sound (and in the strong case also complete) with respect to barbed bisimulation congruences.

We define weak and strong *barbs* standardly letting $\searrow^*$ be the transitive and reflexive closure of $\searrow$, and choosing barbs similarly to [15,1]

$$P \downarrow n \text{ if } P \equiv (\tilde{n})(n\langle P'\rangle p \parallel p') : \tilde{n}' \text{ and } n \notin \tilde{n}, \qquad \text{and} \qquad P \Downarrow n \text{ if } \exists P \searrow^* P'. P' \downarrow n .$$

In a previous version [11] we show (as in [15,1]) that this choice of barbs is indeed robust. In particular, one could have chosen to observe location paths.

We restrict binary relations $\mathcal{R}$ on $\mathbf{P}_{/\alpha}$ to closed terms by $\mathcal{R}_c = \mathcal{R} \cap \mathbf{P}_{c/\alpha} \times \mathbf{P}_{c/\alpha}$.

Definition 1. A *weak barbed simulation* is a well typed binary relation $\mathcal{R}$ on $\mathbf{P}_{c/\alpha}$ such that whenever $P_1 \mathcal{R} P_2$,

    i) if $P_1 \downarrow n$ then $P_1' \Downarrow n$ *ii)* if $P_1 \searrow P_1'$, then $\exists P_2 \searrow^* P_2'$ such that $P_1' \mathcal{R} P_2'$

$\mathcal{R}$ is a *weak barbed bisimulation* if $\mathcal{R}$ and $\mathcal{R}^{-1}$ are weak barbed simulations. *Weak barbed bisimulation congruence* $\approx_b$ is the largest congruence such that $(\approx_b)_c$ is a weak barbed bisimulation.

We define *strong barbed simulation* similar to above by replacing $\searrow^*$ with $\searrow$ and $q \Downarrow n$ with $q \downarrow n$, and define *strong barbed bisimulation congruence*, $\sim_b$, accordingly.

We define *delay* transitions by $P \Longrightarrow P$ and $P \overset{\pi}{\Longrightarrow} P'$, if $P \overset{\tau}{\Longrightarrow} P'' \overset{\pi}{\longrightarrow} P'$, which compared to weak transitions do not allow τ-transitions after the visible transition.

We extend well typed binary relations $\mathcal{R}$ on $\mathbf{P}_{c/\alpha}$ to open terms the usual way, by defining $p : \tilde{n} \, \mathcal{R}^\circ \, p' : \tilde{n}$ if $p : \tilde{n}[P_1/x_1]\dots[P_k/x_k] \, \mathcal{R} \, p' : \tilde{n}[P_1/x_1]\dots[P_k/x_k]$ for all $P_1,\dots,P_k \in \mathbf{P}_{c/\alpha}$, where $fv(p) = fv(p') = \{x_1,\dots,x_k\}$, i.e. requiring two open terms to be related after substitution with closed resources. Also we extend $\mathcal{R}^\circ$ to typed concretions by $c : \tilde{n} \, \mathcal{R}^\square \, c' : \tilde{n}$ if for all $A, A \cdot c : \tilde{n} \, \mathcal{R}^\circ \, A \cdot c' : \tilde{n}$.

Like in [1] we introduce an (input) *early* delay context bisimulation by

Definition 2. An (input) *early delay context simulation* is a well typed binary relation $\mathcal{R}$ on $\mathbf{P}_{c/\alpha}$ such that $p : \tilde{n} \, \mathcal{R} \, P$ implies

    if $p : \tilde{n} \overset{\tau}{\longrightarrow} P_1$ then $\exists P_2. P \overset{\tau}{\Longrightarrow} P_2$ and $P_1 \mathcal{R} P_2$

    if $p : \tilde{n} \overset{\bar{\delta}}{\longrightarrow} A$ then $\forall C \in \mathbf{C}_{c/\alpha}. \exists A'. P \overset{\bar{\delta}}{\Longrightarrow} A'$ and $A \cdot C \mathcal{R} A' \cdot C$

    if $p : \tilde{n} \overset{\delta}{\longrightarrow} A$ then $\forall C \in \mathbf{C}_{c/\alpha}, \mathcal{D}_{\tilde{n}}. \exists A'. P \overset{\delta}{\Longrightarrow} A'$ and $\mathcal{D}_{\tilde{n}}(A) \cdot C \mathcal{R} \, \mathcal{D}_{\tilde{n}}(A') \cdot C$

    if $p : \tilde{n} \overset{\bar{\delta}}{\longrightarrow} C$ then $\exists C'. P \overset{\bar{\delta}}{\Longrightarrow} C'$ and $C \mathcal{R}^\square C'$

    if $p : \tilde{n} \overset{\delta}{\longrightarrow} C$ then $\exists C'. P \overset{\delta}{\Longrightarrow} C'$ and $\forall \mathcal{D}_{\tilde{n}}. \mathcal{D}_{\tilde{n}}(C) \, \mathcal{R}^\square \, \mathcal{D}_{\tilde{n}}(C')$

$\mathcal{R}$ is an *early delay context bisimulation* if both $\mathcal{R}$ and $\mathcal{R}^{-1}$ are early delay context simulations. Let $\approx_e$ denote the largest early delay context bisimulation. We define *early strong context simulation* by replacing $\Longrightarrow$ with $\longrightarrow$, and let $\sim_e$ denote the largest *early strong context bisimulation*.

Proposition 4. $\sim_b$, $\approx_b$, $\sim_e$, *and* $\approx_e$ *are equivalence relations.*

By defining testing contexts for the different kinds of labels, one can prove that early contextual bisimulation, in the strong case, is in fact complete with respect to barbed bisimulation congruence as stated below. We conjecture that $\approx_e^\circ$ is not complete with respect to $\approx_b$.

Proposition 5. $\sim_b \subseteq \sim_e^\circ$.

$$\dfrac{0 : \tilde{n}\,\mathcal{R}^\circ P}{0 : \tilde{n}\,\mathcal{R}^\blacksquare P} \qquad \dfrac{x : \tilde{n}\,\mathcal{R}^\circ P}{x : \tilde{n}\,\mathcal{R}^\blacksquare P} \qquad \dfrac{p_1 : \tilde{n}\,\mathcal{R}^\blacksquare p_1' : \tilde{n} \quad p_2 : \tilde{n}\,\mathcal{R}^\blacksquare p_2' : \tilde{n} \quad p_1' \parallel p_2' : \tilde{n}\,\mathcal{R}^\circ P}{p_1 \parallel p_2 : \tilde{n}\,\mathcal{R}^\blacksquare P}$$

$$\dfrac{P'\,\mathcal{R}^\blacksquare P'' \quad p' : \tilde{n}\,\mathcal{R}^\blacksquare p'' : \tilde{n} \quad \varphi\langle P''\rangle p'' : \tilde{n}\,\mathcal{R}^\circ P}{\varphi\langle P'\rangle p' : \tilde{n}\,\mathcal{R}^\blacksquare P} \qquad \dfrac{p : \tilde{n}\,\mathcal{R}^\blacksquare p' : \tilde{n} \quad \varphi(x)p' : \tilde{n}\,\mathcal{R}^\circ P}{\varphi(x)p : \tilde{n}\,\mathcal{R}^\blacksquare P}$$

$$\dfrac{p : \tilde{n}n\,\mathcal{R}^\blacksquare p' : \tilde{n}n \quad (n)p' : \tilde{n}\,\mathcal{R}^\circ P}{(n)p : \tilde{n}\,\mathcal{R}^\blacksquare P} \qquad \dfrac{P\,\mathcal{R}^\blacksquare P' \quad p : \tilde{n}\,\mathcal{R}^\blacksquare p' : \tilde{n} \quad \langle P'\rangle p' : \tilde{n}\,\mathcal{R}^\square C}{\langle P\rangle p : \tilde{n}\,\mathcal{R}^\blacksquare C}$$

$$\dfrac{c : \tilde{n}n\,\mathcal{R}^\blacksquare c' : \tilde{n}n \quad (n)c' : \tilde{n}\,\mathcal{R}^\square C}{(n)c : \tilde{n}\,\mathcal{R}^\blacksquare C}$$

Table 5. Howe relation for typed processes and concretions.

We now show the main technical result of the paper, that $\sim_e{}^\circ$ and $\approx_e{}^\circ$ are indeed congruences, by adapting Howe's method to active mobile processes in nested locations. This is in fact a combination of two new results. The first new result is that Howe's method can be extended to *input-early* strong and delay bisimulations, by extending the relation to also cover concretions, despite that it has been considered difficult to extend Howe's method to early bisimulations for higher-order calculi with static scope [14]. The second result is to extend Howe's method to active process mobility in nested locations. We find that the application of Howe's method is considerably simpler than the direct method applied e.g. in [1].

First we define the *Howe-relation* $\mathcal{R}^\blacksquare$ on $\mathbf{P}_{/\alpha} \cup \mathbf{C}_{/\alpha}$, relative to a binary relation $\mathcal{R}$ on $\mathbf{P}_{c/\alpha}$ and as the least relation satisfying the rules in Table 5. Let $\mathcal{R}^\bullet = \mathcal{R}^\blacksquare \cap \mathbf{P}_{/\alpha} \times \mathbf{P}_{/\alpha}$, i.e. the relation restricted to (possibly open) processes. It is easy to prove that if $\mathcal{R}$ is well typed then $\mathcal{R}^\bullet$ and $\mathcal{R}^\blacksquare$ are so too. As in [14] we prove the following properties.

Proposition 6. *Let $\mathcal{R}$ be an equivalence relation on $\mathbf{P}_{c/\alpha}$ then*

1. $\mathcal{R}^\blacksquare$ *is reflexive.*   4. $\mathcal{R}^\bullet$ *is substitutive.*   7. $\mathcal{R}^{\bullet*}$ *is symmetric*
2. $\mathcal{R}^\square \subseteq \mathcal{R}^\blacksquare$.   5. $\mathcal{R}^\bullet$ *is constructor compatible*
3. $\mathcal{R}^\blacksquare\mathcal{R}^\square \subseteq \mathcal{R}^\blacksquare$.   6. $\mathcal{R}^{\bullet-1} \subseteq \mathcal{R}^{\bullet*}$

The key is now to show, since $\sim_e{}^\bullet$ ($\approx_e{}^\bullet$) is a congruence, that $\sim_e{}^\circ = \sim_e{}^\bullet$ ($\approx_e{}^\circ = \approx_e{}^\bullet$).

Next, as a novel contribution of this paper we extend the Howe-relation to path contexts. Let $\mathcal{R}$ be a binary relation on $\mathbf{P}_{c/\alpha}$. We define the Howe-relation $\mathcal{R}^\blacktriangle$ on path context by $D_{\tilde{n},\gamma} : \tilde{n}'\mathcal{R}^\blacktriangle D'_{\tilde{n},\gamma} : \tilde{n}'$ if there exists $D_{\tilde{n},\gamma}^{\tilde{n}_1,\dots,\tilde{n}_k}$ and $p_i : \tilde{n}_i\,\mathcal{R}^\bullet p_i' : \tilde{n}_i$, $i = 1,\dots,k$ such that $D_{\tilde{n},\gamma} : \tilde{n}' = D_{\tilde{n},\gamma}^{\tilde{n}_1,\dots,\tilde{n}_k}(p_1,\dots,p_k) : \tilde{n}'$ and $D'_{\tilde{n},\gamma} : \tilde{n}' = D_{\tilde{n},\gamma}^{\tilde{n}_1,\dots,\tilde{n}_k}(p_1',\dots,p_k') : \tilde{n}'$. Observe that two related path contexts have the same path to their hole which are indexed by the same type, also they restrict their holes by the same names.

In order to establish $\approx_e{}^\circ = \approx_e{}^\bullet$ the method of Howe utilises that $\approx_e{}^\bullet$ satisfies the following bisimulation property. A similar property for $\sim_e{}^\bullet$ is used to prove $\sim_e{}^\circ = \sim_e{}^\bullet$.

Lemma 1. $p : \tilde{n}, P \in \mathbf{P}_{c/\alpha}$ and $p : \tilde{n} \approx_e^{\bullet} P$ implies that if:

$p : \tilde{n} \xrightarrow{\tau} P_1$ then $\exists P_2 . P \xRightarrow{\tau} P_2$ and $P_1 \equiv \approx_e^{\bullet} P_2$

$p : \tilde{n} \xrightarrow{\bar{\delta}} A$ then $\forall C \approx_e^{\blacksquare} C' . \exists A' . P \xRightarrow{\bar{\delta}} A'$ and $A \cdot C \equiv \approx_e^{\bullet} A' \cdot C'$

$p : \tilde{n} \xrightarrow{\delta} A$ then $\forall C \approx_e^{\blacksquare} C', \mathcal{D}_{\tilde{n}} \approx_e^{\blacktriangle} \mathcal{D}'_{\tilde{n}} . \exists A'. P \xRightarrow{\delta} A'$ and $\mathcal{D}_{\tilde{n}}(A) \cdot C \equiv \approx_e^{\bullet} \mathcal{D}'_{\tilde{n}}(A') \cdot C'$

$p : \tilde{n} \xrightarrow{\bar{\delta}} C$ then $\exists C' . P \xRightarrow{\bar{\delta}} C'$ and $C \approx_e^{\blacksquare} C'$

$p : \tilde{n} \xrightarrow{\delta} C$ then $\exists C' . P \xRightarrow{\delta} C'$ and $\forall \mathcal{D}_{\tilde{n}} \approx_e^{\blacktriangle} \mathcal{D}'_{\tilde{n}} . \mathcal{D}_{\tilde{n}}(C) \approx_e^{\blacksquare} \mathcal{D}'_{\tilde{n}}(C')$

Proposition 7. $\sim_e^{\circ}$ and $\approx_e^{\circ}$ are congruences.

From Prop. 3 and from Prop. 7 it follows that $\sim_e^{\circ}$ and $\approx_e^{\circ}$ are sound with respect to barbed and weak barbed bisimulation congruence, respectively.

Proposition 8. $\sim_e^{\circ} \subseteq \sim_b$ and $\approx_e^{\circ} \subseteq \approx_b$.

From Prop. 5 and Prop. 8 we conclude that

Theorem 1. $\sim_e^{\circ} = \sim_b$

In [11] we study late strong and delay contextual bisimulations for (an equivalent) variant of Homer. It turns out that the late strong and delay context bisimulations are in fact *strictly* contained in their corresponding early context bisimulations.

6 Conclusions and Related Work

We presented the calculus Homer, which combines higher-order process passing, local names, nested locations and copyable, active mobile computing resources. We gave reaction and labelled transition semantics as conservative extensions of the standard semantics of a pure process-passing calculi with local names, and presented the first generalisation of Howe's method to a calculus with *active* mobile processes at nested locations and local names, proving that *early* delay (and strong) contextual bisimulation is a congruence and a sound (and complete) characterisation of weak (strong) barbed bisimulation congruence. Finally, we identified the need for typing processes and mobile sub resources with names.

Thomsen [5] and Prasad, Giacalone, and Mishra [16] provides so-called higher-order labelled transition bisimulations for respectively Plain CHOCS and Facile, which are early bisimulations where processes in higher-order labels are required to be bisimilar. Sangiorgi shows in [17] that higher-order bisimulation is too discriminating and presents an elegant, and now classical, solution to the problem using triggered processes and normal bisimulation for the higher-order π-calculus. Jeffrey and Rathke extend in [18] the result to recursive types. Sound and complete characterisations of barbed bisimulation congruence exist for variants of the Ambient calculus [19,20]. However, none of the variants of the Ambient calculs or HOπ (or the first-order π-calculus) allow for *copyable* active mobile processes.

A series of papers, summarised in [1], develop the semantics of the Seal calculus which shares nested locations, objective non-linear mobility and local names with static scoping with Homer. A sound characterisation of reduction barbed bisimulation congruence for the Seal calculus is provided in [1], given by a delay bisimulation as in the present paper. The authors leave important problems open, as e.g. providing a sound and complete characterisation of barbed bisimulation congruence and a deeper understanding of the interrelation between local names and copyable mobile processes. We have contributed to both of these problems by providing a sound and complete characterisation of strong barbed bisimulation congruence and identified the need for typing mobile sub resources if one uses the standard vertical scope extension used in HOπ.

The M-calculus and the Kell calculus of Schmitt and Stefani share with Homer in being based on process passing and process substitution. A sound and complete characterisation of barbed bisimulation congruence has been announced in [3], however, a detailed proof has not been published yet.

None of the congruence proofs for the above mentioned calculi apply the method by Howe. Howe's method was originally introduced for lazy functional programming languages. It has later been applied to the Abadi-Cardelli object calculi by Gordon [21], higher-order functions with concurrent communication (a fragment of Reppy's Concurrent ML) by Jeffrey [22], late bisimulations for local names with static scope by Jeffrey and Rathke [10] and Baldamus and Frauenstein in [14].

A problem left open is to give a sound and complete co-inductive characterisation of an appropriate weak barbed congruence. A delay bisimulation seems to be needed to be able to apply Howe's method and a standard weak barbed bisimulation is unlikely to be included in a delay bisimulation in the higher-order setting.

Another problem is if the trigger, normal and up-to-context bisimulation techniques can be adapted to calculi with non-linear active process mobility and explicit, nested locations. It could provide us with a bisimulation without universal quantification over contexts.

The type system presented is studied in a bigraphical setting in [13]. In [11] the types are represented by a *free name extension* process constructor in some ways dual to the local name operator. Work on more complex type systems for Homer has been initiated in [23], presenting a type system for linear and non-linear mobile resources for an early version of the Homer calculus and is currently being adapted to the present version of Homer.

References

1. Castagna, G., Vitek, J., Nardelli, F.Z.: The Seal calculus. Accepted for publication in *Information and Computation* (2004)
2. Schmitt, A., Stefani, J.B.: The M-calculus: A higher-order distributed process calculus. In: Proceedings of the 30th ACM SIGPLAN-SIGACT symposium on Principles of programming languages (POPL'03). (2003) 50–61
3. Schmitt, A., Stefani, J.B.: The Kell calculus: A family of higher-order distributed process calculi. In: Proceedings of the International Workshop on Global Computing 2004 Workshop (GC 2004). LNCS, Springer Verlag (2004)

4. Howe, D.J.: Proving congruence of bisimulation in functional programming languages. Information and Computation **124** (1996) 103–112

5. Thomsen, B.: Plain CHOCS. A second generation calculus for higher order processes. Acta Informatica **30** (1993) 1–59

6. Sangiorgi, D.: Expressing Mobility in Process Algebras: First-Order and Higher-Order Paradigms. PhD thesis, LFCS, University of Edinburgh (1993)

7. Boudol, G.: Towards a lambda-calculus for concurrent and communicating systems. In Díaz, J., Orejas, F., eds.: Proceedings of Theory and Practice of Software Development (TAPSOFT '89). Volume 351 of LNCS., Springer Verlag (1989) 149–161

8. Godskesen, J.C., Hildebrandt, T., Sassone, V.: A calculus of mobile resources. In: Proceedings of CONCUR'2002. LNCS, Springer (2002)

9. Cardelli, L., Gordon, A.D.: Mobile ambients. In Nivat, M., ed.: Proceedings of FoSSaCS '98. Volume 1378 of LNCS., Springer (1998) 140–155

10. Jeffrey, A., Rathke, J.: Towards a theory of bisimulation for local names. In: Proceedings of LICS '99, IEEE, Computer Society Press (1999) 56–66

11. Hildebrandt, T., Godskesen, J.C., Bundgaard, M.: Bisimulation congruences for homer - a calculus of higher order mobile embedded resources. Technical Report TR-2004-52, IT University of Copehagen, Department of Theoretical Computer Science (2004)

12. Bundgaard, M., Hildebrandt, T., Godskesen, J.C.: A CPS encoding of name-passing in higher-order mobile embedded resources. Journal of Theoretical Computer Science (2005) To appear.

13. Bundgaard, M., Hildebrandt, T.: A bigraphical semantics of higher order mobile embedded resources with local names (2005) submitted for publication.

14. Baldamus, M., Frauenstein, T.: Congruence proofs for weak bisimulation equivalences on higher-order process calculi. Technical Report Report 95–21, Berlin University of Technology, Computer Science Department (1995)

15. Merro, M., Hennessy, M.: Bisimulation congruences in safe ambients. Computer Science Report 2001:05, University of Sussex (2001)

16. Prasad, S., Giacalone, A., Mishra, P.: Operational and algebraic semantics for Facile: A symmetric integration of concurrent and functional programming. In Paterson, M., ed.: Proceedings of the 17th International Colloquium on Automata, Languages and Programming (ICALP'90). Volume 443 of LNCS., Springer Verlag (1990) 765–778

17. Sangiorgi, D.: Bisimulation in higher-order process calculi. Journal of Information and Computation **131** (1996) 141–178 Available as Rapport de Recherche RR-2508, INRIA Sophia-Antipolis, 1995. An early version appeared in *Proceedings of PROCOMET'94*, pages 207–224. IFIP. North Holland Publisher.

18. Jeffrey, A., Rathke, J.: Contextual equivalence for higher-order π-calculus revisited. In Brookes, S., Panangaden, P., eds.: Proceedings of the 19th Conference on Mathematical Foundations of Programming Semantics (MFPS'04). Volume 83 of ENTCS., Elsevier (2004)

19. Merro, M., Nardelli, F.Z.: Behavioural theory for mobile ambients. In: Proceedings of the 3rd International Conference on Theoretical Computer Science (IFIP TCS 2004). (2004)

20. Bugliesi, M., Crafa, S., Merro, M., Sassone, V.: Communication and mobility control in boxed ambients. Journal of Information and Computation (2003)

21. A.D.Gordon: Operational equivalences for untyped and polymorphic object calculi. In: Higher Order Operational Techniques in Semantics, Cambridge University Press (1998)

22. Jefrfrey, A.: Semantics for core concurrent ml using computation types. In: Higher Order Operational Techniques in Semantics, Cambridge University Press (1998)

23. Godskesen, J.C., Hildebrandt, T.: Copyability types for mobile computing resources (2004) International Workshop on Formal Methods and Security.

Approximation Algorithms for Wavelength Assignment

Vijay Kumar[1] and Atri Rudra[2]

[1] Strategic Planning and Optimization Team,
Amazon.com,
Seattle, WA, USA
vijayk@amazon.com

[2] Department of Computer Science and Engineering,
University of Washington,
Seattle, WA, USA
atri@cs.washington.edu

Abstract. Winkler and Zhang introduced the FIBER MINIMIZATION problem in [10]. They showed that the problem is NP-complete but left the question of approximation algorithms open. We give a simple 2-approximation algorithm for this problem. We also show how ideas from the Dynamic Storage Allocation algorithm of Buchsbaum et al. [4] can be used to give an approximation ratio arbitrarily close to 1 provided the problem instance satisfies certain criteria. We also show that these criteria are necessary to obtain an approximation scheme. Our 2-approximation algorithm achieves its guarantee unconditionally.

We also consider the extension of the problem to a ring network and give a $2 + o(1)$-approximation algorithm for this topology. Our techniques also yield a factor-2 approximation for the related problem of PACKING INTERVALS IN INTERVALS, also introduced by Winkler and Zhang in [10].

1 Introduction

The FIBER MINIMIZATION problem on an *optical linesystem* ([10]) relates to the efficient construction of an optical fiber network to meet a specified collection of demands. Consider n links (or edges) connected in a line. Each demand needs to use some consecutive links, and thus the demands can be represented as a set of line intervals. A segment of optical fiber, which is of wavelength μ and spans some consecutive links, can carry a collection of demands such that links required by the demands are contained within the links spanned by the fiber, and no two demands are assigned the same wavelength if there is a link which they both use. The goal is to get a set of fiber segments which can carry all demands such that the total length of fiber used is minimized.

This problem was introduced by Winkler and Zhang in [10]. The problem is motivated by wavelength division multiplexing (WDM), which is used to partition the bandwidth available on an optical fiber into multiple channels using

R. Ramanujam and S. Sen (Eds.): FSTTCS 2005, LNCS 3821, pp. 152–163, 2005.

different wavelengths. These technologies have made very fast all-optical transmission physically possible. See [3,10] for more details on the practical motivations.

1.1 Problem Definition

More formally, consider a linesystem of n links $e_1, e_2, \cdots, e_n$. We represent each demand by $d_j = [l_j, r_j]$ for $l_j \leq r_j$ if it requires the links $e_{l_j}, e_{l_j+1} \cdots, e_{r_j}$; the set of demands is denoted by D. We say demands d_j and $d_{j'}$ intersect (or overlap) if either $l_j \leq l_{j'} \leq r_j$ or $l_{j'} \leq l_j \leq r_{j'}$. A fiber interval f is represented by $f = [l_f, r_f]$ for $l_f \leq r_f$ if it spans the edges $e_{l_f}, e_{l_f+1} \cdots, e_{r_f}$. The goal is to construct a set F of fiber intervals (each capable of carrying μ different wavelengths) of minimum total length $(\sum_{F \ni f=[l_f,r_f]}(r_f - l_f + 1))$ such that D can be packed in F. A packing of D in F is an assignment of each demand $d_j = [l_j, r_j]$ to a fiber $f = [l_f, r_f] \in F$, and a wavelength $\omega \in \{1, \cdots, \mu\}$ within f, such that $[l_j, r_j] \subseteq [l_f, r_f]$ and no two intersecting demands are assigned the same wavelength in the same fiber.

1.2 Previous Work

There is a substantial body of work relating to resource optimization in WDM networks. Most of this work addresses the problem of minimizing the number of wavelengths necessary to satisfy the presented demand for a given network topology. This body of work is too extensive to summarize here — please see [8] for a survey of the field.

In some recent work [2,3,5,9,10] it is sought to more faithfully represent real-world constraints by assuming that fiber has a fixed capacity. Starting with [10] this vein of research aims to optimize the use of fiber. There are different flavors of this problem depending on what the objective function is —

- Minimizing the ratio of the number of fibers deployed to the minimum number of fibers required for any edge [2].
- Minimizing the maximum over all links the the number of fibers used in a link [2,5,6].
- Minimize the total amount of fiber used [3,6].

Much recent work addresses a different flavor of the FIBER MINIMIZATION problem. That version assumes the availability of a device called a *mesh optical add/drop multiplexer* (or MOADM), which allows the signals to moved from one fiber to another as they pass through the nodes in the optical network under consideration. In the presence of MOADMs, the FIBER MINIMIZATION problem becomes "easier" as we are allowed to "break" a demand into segments which span an edge while routing them through the network. For the case of a linesystem, [10] give a polynomial time algorithm to solve this version of the problem. For ring and tree networks, constant-factor approximation algorithms are known [5,9]. Recently, Andrews and Zhang have showed that for general graph topologies, this problem (which they call SUMFIBER-CHOOSEROUTE) is hard to approximate to within a poly-logarithmic factor of the optimal for a general network topology under some complexity assumptions, whether the routing of the demands is performed by the algorithm ([3]), or specified as input ([2]). They also prove ([2]) a similar hardness result under a similar complexity assumption for the problem where the objective function is to minimize the ratio, over all edges, of the number of fibers deployed for that edge to the minimum number of fibers required. These negative results are accompanied in all cases by approximation algorithms with logarithmic approximation ratios.

A related set of problems is tackled in [1], where linesystem design is modeled as a generalized graph coloring problem. A collection of optimal and approximation algorithms are presented for different network scenarios, where the objective is to minimizing costs related to the set of colors employed. It has been pointed out to us that some of their techniques can be employed to substitute Phase 1 of our algorithm in Section 2.

In the setting of [10] where there are no MOADMs, — that is, a demand cannot change fibers at any node — FIBER MINIMIZATION was shown to be NP-complete in [10]. To the best of our knowledge, ours are the first approximation algorithms in this model.

1.3 Our Results

We present polynomial time approximation algorithms for the FIBER MINIMIZATION problem on some simple network topologies.

- In Section 2, we give a 2-approximation algorithm for the FIBER MINIMIZATION problem. This problem is similar to the Dynamic Storage Allocation (DSA) problem in some aspects, and we employ techniques from the DSA literature, such as those of Gergov [7] and Buchsbaum et al. [4], to tackle it (Incidentally, the proof of Theorem 1 has essentially the same structure as the proof — to the best of our knowledge, unpublished — of Gergov's [7] algorithm being a 3-approximation for DSA, and may be interesting on that account).
- We use a result of Buchsbaum et al. [4] to derive an approximation scheme for FIBER MINIMIZATION in Section 3.
- We extend these results to obtain other approximations for related problems. In Section 4 give a factor $2 + o(1)$ approximation algorithm for FIBER MINIMIZATION on a ring.
- We investigate the related problem of PACKING INTERVALS IN INTERVALS — also posed in [10] — in Section 5, and obtain a 2-approximation algorithm.

2 A 2-Approximation Algorithm for FIBER MINIMIZATION

As specified in Section 1.1, the input D to the FIBER MINIMIZATION problem consists of demands d_j, each of which is an interval of the form $[l_j, r_j]$, where

$l_j \leq r_j \in \{1, \cdots, n\}$. For each link e_i, we define $L_D(i) = |\{d_j \in D : i \in [l_j, r_j]\}|$ (WLOG we assume that $L_D(i)$ is a multiple of μ) and $L_D^{max} = \max_i L_D(i)$. The algorithm uses an $L_D^{max} \times n$ matrix H to keep track of wavelength assignments. For each $k \in \{1, \cdots, L_D^{max}\}$, the row H_k is referred to as the kth row and finally would correspond to a wavelength in some fiber interval. We say that link e_i is colored c_i in row k if $H_{k,i} = c_i$. For any row k and color C, we call an interval $[l, r]$ in the kth row a C segment if $H_{k,l-1} \neq C$, $H_{k,r+1} \neq C$ and $\forall i \in [l, r]$, $H_{k,i} = C$.

The algorithm, which we refer to as the **Simple** algorithm, is specified in Figures 1 and 2. In **Phase 1**, the algorithm constructs the matrix H and then derives a "packing" P_D from H. We say that demand $d_j \in D$ is packed in P_D if $\langle j, k \rangle \in P_D$ for some $k \in \{1, \cdots, L_D^{max}\}$. P_D is not a feasible solution since the assignments of some demands overlap, although only to a limited extent. In **Phase 2**, the overlaps are taken care of and a valid packing derived.

2.1   Algorithm Outline

Let us briefly summarize the algorithm before we formally describe it. The basic intuition for the algorithm comes from techniques often used for the Dynamic Storage Allocation (DSA) problem, in particular those used in [7]. FIBER MINIMIZATION has some similarities with DSA, with the important distinction that while the demands in DSA are axis-parallel rectangles, demands in our problem are line intervals.

In a nutshell, this is how the algorithm works. During Phase 1 (Figure 1), each matrix entry $H_{k,i}$ either has the value *red* (which means that no demand can be "placed on e_i" in the kth row), or *green* (which means that at most one demand can be "placed on e_i" in the kth row), or *blue* (which means overlapping demands can be "placed on e_i" in the kth row). Each edge e_i is "alloted" $L_D(i)$ rows, which is why the first $L_D^{max} - L_D(i)$ entries in the ith column of H are colored *red* in Step 2. All other entries are colored *green*. Initially all green segments are "available".

In Step 3, the algorithm iterates over all possible rows and in each iteration looks for an "available" green segment over which some "unpacked" demand can be placed (maybe partially) in the following way: this demand can possibly intersect blue segments in that row but it must not intersect with any other green segment. The placement of a demand can fragment an "available" green segment into smaller "available" green segments (the edges common to the placed demand and the green segment are no longer available). The iteration is complete when no demand can be placed on any available green segment. Edges which were colored blue in the current row or did not have any demand placed on them in the current row are colored blue in the next row. Note that this implies that if an edge becomes blue in one row then it remains blue for all the subsequent iterations (rows). Phase 1 of the algorithm is complete when D_{max} iterations are complete. We will show in Lemma 4 that after the first phase, all demands are "packed".

Further, in Lemma 5 we show that in a blue segment a demand may intersect, if at all, with no more than one other demand. This suggests Phase 2 (Figure 2) of the algorithm where demands are finally packed into fiber intervals. Consider μ consecutive rows and consider maximal intervals of consecutive edges which are not colored red in any of the μ rows. In each such segment, every one of the μ rows has, by Lemma 5, at most two demands conflicting over any particular link. Thus, creating two fiber intervals corresponding to such a segment is sufficient to accommodate all the demands.

The algorithm is more formally described in Figures 1 and 2.

Phase 1

1. $J \leftarrow D$, $P_D \leftarrow \emptyset$.
2. **for** $(k \leftarrow 1; k \leq L_D^{max}; k \leftarrow k + 1)$
      for $(i \leftarrow 1; i \leq n; i \leftarrow i + 1)$
          $H_{k,i} \leftarrow$ *red* if $k \leq L_D^{max} - L_D(i)$; otherwise $H_{k,i} \leftarrow$ *green*.
3. **for** $(k \leftarrow 1; k \leq L_D^{max}; k \leftarrow k + 1)$
    (a) $G \leftarrow \{[l, r] : H_{k,j}$ is green for all $j \in [l, r]; [l, r]$ is maximal$\}$ (G is the set of all maximal green intervals in the kth row)
    (b) **while** $\exists [l, r] \in G$
        i. **if** $\exists d_j = [l_j, r_j] \in J$ such that (d_j is an unpacked demand)
           A. $[l, r] \cap [l_j, r_j] \neq \emptyset$ (d_j intersects $[l, r]$), and
           B. $\forall w \in [l_j, r_j]$, either $w \in [l, r]$ or $H_{k,w} = blue$ (d_j intersects no other interval in G)
        then
           Add $\langle j, k \rangle$ to P_D and for all $i \in [l_j, r_j] \cap [l, r]$ set $H_{k+1,i} \leftarrow green$.
           delete d_j from J
           delete $[l, r]$ from G
           if $l < l_j$ add $[l, l_j]$ to G
           if $r_j < r$ add $[r_j, r]$ to G
        else
           for all $i \in [l, r]$ set $H_{k,i} \leftarrow blue$
           delete $[l, r]$ from G
    (c) **for** $(i \leftarrow 1; i \leq n; i \leftarrow i + 1)$
        if $H_{k,i} = blue$ **then** set $H_{k+1,i} \leftarrow blue$

Fig. 1. Phase 1 of the **Simple** algorithm

2.2   Correctness and Performance

The following three lemmas follow directly from the way the matrix H is manipulated in the algorithm of Figure 1.

Lemma 1. *At the end of Phase 1, if $H_{k,i} =$ green for any k and i, then for all $1 \leq k' < k$, $H_{k',i} =$ green or $H_{k',i} =$ red.*

$F_D \leftarrow \emptyset$.
for $(k = 1; k \leq L_D^{max}; k = k + \mu)$

1. $\forall i \in \{1, \cdots, n\}$, $c[i] \leftarrow black$;
2. $\forall i \in \{1, \cdots, n\}$, if $\exists j \in [k, k + \mu)$ such that $H_{j,i} = red$ then $c[i] \leftarrow red$.
3. for each maximal interval $I = [l, r] \subseteq [1, n]$ such that $i \in [l, r] \Rightarrow c[i] = black$,
   (a) Create two fiber segments $f_1(I)$ and $f_2(I)$ and add them to F_D.
   (b) **for** all $j \in [k, k + \mu)$,
      i. Let $S_j \leftarrow \{d_i : d_i \subseteq I, \langle i, j \rangle \in P_D\}$. Let $s_{j,1}, s_{j,2}, \cdots, s_{j,N}$ be an ordering of S_j such that for any two demands $s_{j,a} = [l_a, r_a]$ and $s_{j,b} = [l_b, r_b]$, $a < b \Rightarrow r_a \leq r_b$.
      ii. **for** $i = 1, 2, \cdots, N$,
         - Assign $s_{j,i}$ the wavelength $j - k + 1$.
         - Assign $s_{j,i}$ the fiber segment $f_2(I)$ if there exists some demand $s_{j,u}$ assigned wavelength $j - k + 1$ and fiber segment $f_1(I)$, such that $s_{j,i} \cap s_{j,u} \neq \emptyset$; otherwise, assign $s_{j,i}$ the fiber segment $f_1(I)$.

Fig. 2. Phase 2 of the **Simple** algorithm

Proof. If $H_{k',i}$ is colored blue, then $H_{j,i}$ gets colored blue for all $j > k'$ due to repeated execution of Step 3(c); in particular $H_{k,i}$ gets colored blue, which contradicts the assumption on $H_{k,i}$ in the lemma. ∎

Lemma 2. *At the end of Phase 1, if $H_{k,i} = $ red for any k and i, then for all $1 \leq k' < k$, $H_{k',i} = $ red.*

Proof. This is ensured by Step 2, where $H_{k,i}$ is colored red for all k less than a certain value. The color red is not employed at any other step in the algorithm; nor is it ever replaced by any other color. ∎

Lemma 3. *At the end of Phase 1, $L_D(i) = |\{k : H_{k,i} \neq$ red $\}|$.*

Proof. This follows from how the coloring decision is made at Step 2, and the fact that the set $\{(k, i) : H_{k,i}$ is $red\}$ is invariant over the later steps of the algorithm. ∎

We now show that all demands in D are "packed" in P_D after Phase 1.

Lemma 4. *At the end of Phase 1, J is empty.*

Proof. Assume that this is not the case, and there is a demand $d_t = [l_t, r_t] \in J$ at the end of Phase 1. One of the following three cases must arise:

- **Case 1:** There is one $i \in [l_t, r_t]$ such that $H_{L_D^{max},i} = $ red. By Lemma 2, for all $k \in [1, L_D^{max}]$, $H_{k,i} = $ red. Lemma 3 implies that $D(i) = 0$, which contradicts the fact that d_t uses link i.
- **Case 2:** There exists $i \in [l_t, r_t]$ such that $H_{L_D^{max},i} = $ green. It follows from Lemmas 1 and 2 and the coloring criterion of Step 2 that for all $k \in \{1, \cdots, L_D^{max} - L_D(i)\}$, $H_{k,i} = $ red; and for all $k' \in \{L_D^{max} - L_D(i) + 1, \cdots, L_D^{max}\}$, $H_{k',i} = $ green.

For each such k', it must be the case that in the k'th iteration of the **for** loop in Step 3, some demand $d_j \ni e_i$ was placed in row k', since otherwise $H_{k',i}$ would have been colored blue at Step 3(b). In all there would be $L_D(i)$ such demands, one for each value of k'. Including them, and including d_t, there are at least $L_D(i) + 1$ demands that use link e_i, which contradicts the definition of $L_D(i)$.

- **Case 3:** For all $i \in [l_t, r_t]$, $H_{L_D^{max},i}$ = blue. We complete the proof by showing that d_t would have been placed by the algorithm in some row. Consider $k^* = \min\{k : \forall j \in [l_t, r_t], H_{k,j} = \text{blue}\}$. By the choice of k^*, there exists an interval $[l, r] \subseteq [l_t, r_t]$ such that in some iteration of the **while** loop of Step 3(b),
  - $[l, r] \in G$, and
  - for all $i \in [l_t, r_t] - [l, r]$, $H_{k^*,i}$ = blue, and
  - for all $j \in [l, r]$, $H_{k^*,j}$ is colored blue by the **else** clause of Step 3(b)(i).

This can only happen when there is no demand d_j which is suitable for placing over $[l, r]$ in row k^*: as indicated by conditions A and B in the **if** statement. However, d_t is precisely such a demand; it is unpacked, it intersects $[l, r]$, and (by the choice of k^*) it does not anymore intersect any other interval in G. Thus, instead of coloring $[l, r]$ blue, d_t should have been placed over it; and this completes our proof by contradiction. ∎

We now show that the packing P_D has a nice property– no link is used by more than two demands that are placed in the same row. In other words, no three demands conflict simultaneously.

Lemma 5. $\forall(i, k)$, $|\{j : \langle j, k \rangle \ni e_i\}| \leq 2$.

Proof. It is easy to see from the way intervals are added to and deleted from G that only one demand is placed on a green segment, that is, demands do not overlap over green segments. Thus, it follows that overlaps can only take place over blue segments (as no demands are placed over red segments).

Consider such a segment $[l, r]$ in row k. Among the demands that are placed over this segment, there can be at most one demand that contains $H[k, l-1]$, and at most one demand that contains $H[k, r+1]$ — that is because both $H[k, l-1]$ and $H[k, r+1]$ are non-blue and thus can not have overlapping demands placed on them. By placement rules [3(b)i.A.] and [3(b)i.B.], no demand is contained within a blue segment. Thus, no more than two demands can be placed over $[l, r]$ in row k. ∎

We next show that Phase 2 outputs a valid solution.

Lemma 6. *Phase 2 (Figure 2) produces a valid packing of D in the set of F_D.*

Proof. Consider a demand $d_i = [l_i, r_i]$. Let d_i be placed in row j where $j \in [(h-1)\mu, h\mu)$ for some j and h — that is, $\langle i, j \rangle \in P_D$.

First of all, let us verify that d_i is assigned a fiber interval in Phase 2. Consider the hth iteration of the **for** loop (Figure 2) in Phase 2. At Step 3(a), an interval $I \ni [l_i, r_i]$ would indeed be created, except if $c[u] = red$ for some $u \in [l_i, r_i]$. Is that possible? For that to be the case, there must exist some $j' \in [(h-1)\mu, h\mu)$ such that $H_{j',u} = red$.

Recall how certain elements of H are colored *red* at Step 2 in Phase 1 (Figure 1). If $H_{j',u}$ is *red*, then $H_{v,u}$ is *red* for all $v \leq L_D^{max} - L_D(u)$, and it is not *red* for any other v. Since $L_D^{max} - L_D(u)$ is a multiple of μ (we have assumed the load at any link to be a multiple of μ), it follows that $H_{v,u}$ is *red* either for all $v \in [(h-1)\mu, h\mu)$, or for none of those values of v. In the latter case, the desired fiber interval I is indeed created; while the former case is easy to rule out, since it implies that $H_{j,u}$ is *red* as well, which is not possible given that $\langle i, j \rangle \in P_D$ and $u \in [l_i, r_i]$ (no d_i can be placed over a *red* interval in Phase 1).

Note that demand d_i is assigned wavelength $j - (h-1)\mu + 1$, and one of the fibers $f_1(I)$ and $f_2(I)$. It remains to be verified that no other demand is assigned the same wavelength and the same fiber. We do this by pointing out that the set of demands that have been assigned wavelength $j - (h-1)\mu + 1$ on $f_1(I)$ or $f_2(I)$ is exactly the set of demands d_k for which $\langle k, j \rangle \in P_D$. This set of demands has been characterized by Lemma 5– any given link is contained in no more than two of these demands. This set of demand can be thought of as a collection of line intervals. Packing them into $f_1(I)$ and $f_2(I)$ without conflict is akin to 2-coloring the corresponding interval graph (whose clique number is 2). It is well-known and easy to see that a legal 2-coloring can be obtained simply by scanning the intervals left-to-right, and greedily assigning them one of two colors. Note that this is precisely what Step 3(b)ii of Phase 2 (Figure 2) attempts to do.   ∎

Let L be defined as $\frac{\sum_{i=1}^{n} L_D(i)}{\mu}$. For any set F of fiber intervals, let L_F be the total length of fiber used in F.

The following lemma shows that F_D is a pretty good solution.

Lemma 7. $L_{F_D} = 2L$.

Proof. Let us denote a fiber interval f by $[l_f, r_f]$, and for any link e_i, let $L_{F_D}(i) = |\{f \in F_D : i \in [l_f, r_f]\}|$. We will prove a stronger claim– for all e_i, $L_{F_D}(i) = 2\frac{L_D(i)}{\mu}$. The lemma follows by summing over all links.

Consider Step 3 of Phase 2 (Figure 2), where fiber intervals are created in pairs ($f_1(I)$ and $f_2(I)$). This step is repeated in the L_D^{max}/μ iterations of the **for** loop. A link e_i will not be contained in these fiber intervals for iterations $1, 2, \cdots, \frac{L_D^{max} - L_D(i)}{\mu}$, and included in both intervals of a pair ($f_1(I)$, $f_2(I)$) in all subsequent iterations. This is because $H_{v,i}$ is *red* for all $v \leq L_D^{max} - L_D(i)$, and not *red* for any other v, as we saw in the proof of Lemma 6. This implies that during the first $\frac{L_D^{max} - L_D(i)}{\mu}$ iterations, $c[i]$ is *red*, and thus the fiber intervals created do not include link e_i. In other words, link e_i is contained in exactly $2\frac{L_D(i)}{\mu}$ fiber intervals.   ∎

Clearly, L is a trivial lower bound on the length of the optimal set of fiber intervals for D. Thus, we have the following result.

Theorem 1. Simple *algorithm is a 2-approximation algorithm for the FIBER MINIMIZATION problem.*   ∎

3   An Approximation Scheme

In this section we employ the *boxing* technique of Buchsbaum et al. [4] to the FIBER MINIMIZATION problem. The application of a result of [4] yields an approximation scheme for our problem. Let us first briefly describe *boxing*, which is applied in [4] to the Dynamic Storage Allocation problem. Let Z be a set of *jobs*, where each job i is a triple of start time l_i, end time r_i and height h_i. To *box* Z means placing the jobs in a box b starting from time $l_b = \min\{l_j : j \in Z\}$, ending at time $r_b = \max\{r_j : j \in Z\}$ and of height $h_b \geq \sum_{j \in Z} h_j$. A *boxing* of Z into a set B of boxes is a partition of Z into $|B|$ subsets, each of which is then boxed into a distinct $b \in B$. At any time t, let $L_Z(t)$ denote $\sum_{j \in Z: l_j \leq t \leq r_j} h_j$, and let $L_B(t) = \sum_{b \in B: l_b \leq t \leq r_b} h_b$.

We will be working with jobs of unit height, for which the algorithm in Section 2.1 of [4] comes with the following performance guarantee:

Theorem 2. *[4] Given a set Z of jobs, each of height 1, an integer box-height parameter H, and a sufficiently small positive ϵ, there exists a set B of boxes, each of height H, and a boxing of Z into B such that for all time t:*
$$L_B(t) \leq (1 + 4\epsilon)L_Z(t) + O(\tfrac{H \log H}{\epsilon^2} \log \tfrac{1}{\epsilon}).$$

The key insight here is that each demand in the FIBER MINIMIZATION problem can be viewed as a job of unit height, and packing of demands into fiber intervals is analogous to the boxing of a collection of jobs. This leads us to the following bound, where $L_F(t)$ denotes as before the number of fibers in F containing the link e_t and $L_D(t)$ denotes the number of demands in D using link e_t.

Lemma 8. *Given a set D of demands and a sufficiently small positive ϵ, there exists a set of fiber intervals F and a packing of the demands of D into F such that for all links e_t:*
$$L_F(t) \leq (1 + 4\epsilon)\frac{L_D(t)}{\mu} + O(\tfrac{\log \mu}{\epsilon^2} \log \tfrac{1}{\epsilon}).$$

Proof. A straightforward reduction maps an instance D of the FIBER MINIMIZATION problem to an instance of boxing. Corresponding to every demand $[l, r]$ in D, let there be a job with a start time of $l - 1$ and end time of r. Each link e_i is mapped to the time interval $[i - 1, i]$, and fiber intervals of wavelength $\mu = H$ map to boxes of height $H = \mu$.

Consider the boxing algorithm in Section 2.1 of [4]. As observed above, a demand $[l, r]$ in D corresponds to a job $(l - 1, r)$ in the DSA setting. Further note that a box of height μ in the DSA setting corresponds to a fiber interval. The set of fiber intervals F and set of demands D map directly to the set B of boxes and set Z of jobs, respectively, in the boxing instance. Observe that $L_D(t) = L_Z(t)$ and $L_F(t) = \frac{L_B(t)}{\mu}$.

The lemma follows directly from an application of Theorem 2 to the boxing instance Z with $H = \mu$. ∎

Noting that $L_F = \sum_{i=1}^{n} L_F(i)$ is the total length of fiber used by the algorithm, and $L_D = \frac{\sum_{i=1}^{n} L_D(i)}{\mu}$, we have

Theorem 3. $L_F \leq (1 + 4\epsilon)L_D + O(n)$ *for sufficiently small positive constant ϵ.*

Proof. Using Lemma 8 and summing over all links. The last term on the right hand side in Lemma 8 is a constant, which leads to the $O(n)$ upon summation. ∎

As in Section 2, we observe that for F^*, the optimal set of fiber intervals, $L_{F^*} \geq L_D$. Thus, algorithm of [4] has a competitive ratio arbitrarily close to 1 provided $L_D = \Omega(n)$.

Next, we look at the $O(n)$ term in Theorem 3 more carefully.

3.1   A Lower Bound

It is easy to see that the $O(n)$ additive term in the statement of Theorem 3 cannot be done away with for any approximation scheme. Consider the set D_{bad} of demands over $2n + 1$ links. D_{bad} contains one copy of demand $[1, 2n + 1]$, and $\mu - 1$ copies each of demands $[1, n + 1]$ and $[n + 1, 2n + 1]$.

Clearly, $L_{D_{bad}} \leq 2n + 2$ while L_{F^*}, the value of the optimal solution, is $3n + 2$. That is, there can be no positive constant $\delta < \frac{1}{2}$ such that $L_{F^*} < (1 + \delta)L_{D_{bad}} + o(n)$ for all n.

4   FIBER MINIMIZATION in a Ring

Next, we look at what is perhaps the most natural generalization of the FIBER MINIMIZATION problem. Ring topologies are very commonly encountered and widely studied in optical routing literature. Consider a ring of n links where each demand d_j in the demand set D is an arc $[l_j, r_j]$ which requires links $e_{l_j}, e_{l_j+1 \bmod(n)}, \cdots, e_{r_j}$. Fiber intervals are now arcs each of which can support μ different wavelengths. The goal is to find the set of fiber arcs with the minimum total length.

The straightforward technique of partitioning an arc coloring problem into two interval coloring problems and taking the union of the two solutions would seem to directly obtain an approximation ratio of twice of that of the approximation ratio for the problem on a line system (that is, a ratio of four in this case). However, a small tweak gives a $(2 + \epsilon)$-approximation ratio algorithm with two invocations of the **Simple** algorithm of Figures 1 and 2. Arbitrarily pick a link e_i and consider the set of demands using link e_i, $D^i = \{d_j \in D : i \in \{l_j, l_j + 1 \bmod(n), \cdots, r_j\}\}$. Now run the **Simple** algorithm on both D^i and $D - D^i$ to get sets of fiber intervals (arcs) F_{D^i} and F_{D-D^i}. Define $F_D = F_{D^i} \cup F_{D-D^i}$. Due to (possible) rounding[3] "errors" we now have for each link e_i, $L_{F_D}(i) \leq 2L_D(i) + 1$. Thus we have:

Theorem 4. *The combined algorithm gives $L_{F_D} \leq 2L_{F_D^*} + n$, where F_D^* is the optimal set of fibers arcs for D.*

---

[3] For each arc e_i at most 2 fiber intervals containing e_i from the two solutions can be merged in the solution for the original problem.

Theorem 4 implies that if $L_{F_D^*} \geq \frac{1}{\epsilon}n$, then the combined algorithm achieves an approximation ratio of $2 + \epsilon$.

The ideas developed in the paper so far can be applied to the related problem of PACKING INTERVALS IN INTERVALS [10].

5   PACKING INTERVALS IN INTERVALS

Winkler and Zhang also introduced the PACKING INTERVALS IN INTER-VALS problem in [10]. Here we are given a set of demands D and a set of fiber intervals F, and the goal is to determine if D can be packed in F. Consider the optimization version of this decision problem. What is the smallest value of μ such that F can accommodate D? Our techniques imply a 2-approximation algorithm for this problem in the following sense:

Theorem 5. *If D can be packed in F using no more than $\frac{\mu}{2}$ wavelengths in each fiber, then there exists an algorithm which can pack D in F utilizing no more than μ wavelengths in each fiber.*

Proof (Sketch): A small modification to the **Simple** algorithm is required. Let F be the set of fiber intervals and for each edge e_i define $L_D(i) = \frac{\mu}{2} |\{f : F \ni f = [l_f, r_f] \text{ and } i \in [l_f, r_f]\}|$. As in Section 2, L_D^{max} is defined as $\max_i L_D(i)$. Run Step 1 and 2 of Figure 1 with these values of $L_D(i)$ and L_D^{max}. Run Step 3 of Figure 1 with the given set of demands D. Execute Phase 2 (Figure 2) using $\frac{\mu}{2}$ in place of μ, and in the output F_D merge each $(f1(I), f2(I))$ pair.

Using arguments similar to ones used to prove Lemma 4, one can show that if D can be packed in F using no more than $\frac{\mu}{2}$ wavelengths in each fiber then J is empty after the execution of Phase 1 . Similarly, analogues of Lemmas 5, 6 and 7 can be proved if the assumption of the theorem statement is valid. The definition of $L_D(i)$ and the fact that the constructed F_D is actually F completes the proof. A detailed proof is omitted due to space restrictions.   ∎

6   Conclusions

We presented a clean 2-approximation algorithm for the FIBER MINIMIZA-TION problem on a linesystem. We also apply techniques from [4] to give an approximation scheme for this problem. Based upon our 2-approximation algorithm, we obtain good approximations for the related problems of FIBER MINIMIZATION on a ring and PACKING INTERVALS IN INTERVALS.

Interesting open problems include investigating the FIBER MINIMIZATION problem on other network topologies, particularly those common in optical fiber networks, such as trees and meshes.

References

1. M. Alicherry and R. Bhatia. Line system design and a generalized coloring problem. In *Proc. of ESA 03*, 2003.

2. M. Andrews and L. Zhang. Wavelength assignment in optical networks with fixed fiber capacity. In *Proc. of ICALP*, 2004.
3. M. Andrews and L. Zhang. Bounds on fiber minimization in optical networks. In *Proc. of IEEE INFOCOM 05*, 2005.
4. A. Buchsbaum, H. Karloff, C. Kenyon, N. Reingold, and M. Thorup. Opt versus load in dynamic storage allocation. In *Proc. of STOC 03*, 2003.
5. C. Chekuri, M. Mydlarz, and F. B. Shepard. Multicommodity demand flow in a tree. In *Proc. of ICALP 03*, 2003.
6. T. Erlebach, A. Pagourtzis, K. Potika, and S. Stefanakos. Resource allocation problems in multifiber WDM tree networks. In *Proc. of the 29th Workshop on Graph Theoretic Concepts in Computer Science*, pages 128–229, 2003.
7. J. Gergov. Algorithms for compile-time memory optimization. In *Proc. of 10th SODA*, 1999.
8. R. Klasing. Methods and problems of wavelength-routing in all-optical networks. In *Tech rep. CS-RR-348, Department of Computer Science, University of Warwick*, 1998.
9. C. Nomikos, A. Pagourtzis, and S. Zachos. Routing and path-multicoloring. *Information Processing Letters*, 2001.
10. P. Winkler and L. Zhang. Wavelength assignment and generalized interval graph coloring. In *Proc. of SODA 03*, 2003.

The Set Cover with Pairs Problem[*]

Refael Hassin and Danny Segev

School of Mathematical Sciences,
Tel-Aviv University, Tel-Aviv 69978, Israel
{hassin, segevd}@post.tau.ac.il

Abstract. We consider a generalization of the set cover problem, in which elements are covered by *pairs of objects*, and we are required to find a minimum cost subset of objects that induces a collection of pairs covering all elements. Formally, let U be a ground set of elements and let S be a set of objects, where each object i has a non-negative cost w_i. For every $\{i, j\} \subseteq S$, let $\mathcal{C}(i, j)$ be the collection of elements in U covered by the pair $\{i, j\}$. The *set cover with pairs* problem asks to find a subset $A \subseteq S$ such that $\bigcup_{\{i,j\} \subseteq A} \mathcal{C}(i, j) = U$ and such that $\sum_{i \in A} w_i$ is minimized.
In addition to studying this general problem, we are also concerned with developing polynomial time approximation algorithms for interesting special cases. The problems we consider in this framework arise in the context of domination in metric spaces and separation of point sets.

1 Introduction

Given a ground set U and a collection S of subsets of U, where each subset is associated with a non-negative cost, the *set cover* problem asks to find a minimum cost subcollection of S that covers all elements. An equivalent formulation is obtained by introducing a *covering function* $\mathcal{C} : S \to 2^U$, that specifies for each member of S the subset of U it covers. Set cover now becomes the problem of finding a subset $A \subseteq S$ of minimum cost such that $\bigcup_{i \in A} \mathcal{C}(i) = U$.

We consider a generalization of this problem, in which the covering function $\mathcal{C}$ is defined for pairs of members of S, rather than for single members. Formally, let $U = \{e_1, \ldots, e_n\}$ be a ground set of elements and let $S = \{1, \ldots, m\}$ be a set of *objects*, where each object $i \in S$ has a non-negative cost w_i. For every $\{i, j\} \subseteq S$, let $\mathcal{C}(i, j)$ be the collection of elements in U covered by the pair $\{i, j\}$. The objective of the *set cover with pairs* problem (SCP) is to find a subset $A \subseteq S$ such that $\mathcal{C}(A) = \bigcup_{\{i,j\} \subseteq A} \mathcal{C}(i, j) = U$ and such that $w(A) = \sum_{i \in A} w_i$ is minimized. We refer to the special case in which each object has a unit weight as the *cardinality SCP* problem.

SCP is indeed a generalization of the set cover problem. A set cover instance with $U = \{e_1, \ldots, e_n\}$ and $S_1, \ldots, S_m \subseteq U$ can be interpreted as an SCP instance by defining $\mathcal{C}(i, j) = S_i \cup S_j$ for every $i \neq j$. Therefore, hardness results regarding set cover extend to SCP, and in particular the latter problem cannot be approximated within a ratio of $(1 - \epsilon) \ln n$ for any $\epsilon > 0$, unless $\text{NP} \subset \text{TIME}(n^{O(\log \log n)})$ [4].

---

[*] Due to space limitations, most proofs are omitted from this extended abstract. We refer the reader to the full version of this paper [8], in which all missing proofs are provided.

R. Ramanujam and S. Sen (Eds.): FSTTCS 2005, LNCS 3821, pp. 164–176, 2005.

1.1   Applications

In addition to studying the SCP problem, we are concerned with developing polynomial time approximation algorithms for interesting special cases, that arise in the context of domination in metric spaces and separation of point sets.

Remote Dominating Set. Let $M = (V, d)$ be a finite metric space, and let $r_1 \leq r_2$ be two *covering radii*. We refer to the elements of $V = \{v_1, \ldots, v_n\}$ as points or vertices, and assume that each $v \in V$ is associated with a non-negative cost c_v. A subset of points $S \subseteq V$ is called a *remote dominating set* if for every $v \in V$ there is a point $u \in S$ within distance r_1 of v, or a pair of points $u_1 \neq u_2 \in S$ within distance r_2 of v each. The remote dominating set problem (RDS) asks to find a minimum cost remote dominating set in M.

RDS can be interpreted as a special case of SCP: The set of elements to cover is V, which is also the set of covering objects, and the collection of points covered by $u \neq v \in V$ is

$$C(u, v) = \{w \in V : \min \{d(u, w), d(v, w)\} \leq r_1 \text{ or } \max \{d(u, w), d(v, w)\} \leq r_2\} \ .$$

When $d(u, v) \in \{1, 2\}$ for every $u \neq v$ and $r_1 = r_2 = 1$, RDS reduces to the standard *dominating set* problem. Therefore, hardness results regarding set cover extend to RDS, as the dominating set problem is equivalent to set cover with regard to inapproximability.

We also consider two special cases of this problem, for which significantly better approximation algorithms are possible. In the *cardinality RDS on a tree* problem, the metric d is generated by a tree $T = (V, E)$ with unit length edges, and the covering radii are $r_1 = 1$ and $r_2 = 2$. In the *cardinality Euclidean RDS* problem, V is a set of points in the plane, and $d(u, v) = \|u - v\|_2$.

Group Cut on a Path. Let $P = (V, E)$ be a path, in which each edge $e \in E$ has a non-negative cost c_e, and let $G_1, \ldots, G_k$ be k *groups*, where each group is a set of at least two vertices. A group G_i is *separated by the set of edges* $F \subseteq E$ if there is a representative $v_i \in G_i$ such that no vertex in $G_i \setminus \{v_i\}$ belongs to the connected component of $P - F$ that contains v_i. The objective of the group cut on a path problem (GCP) is to find a minimum cost set of edges that separates all groups.

Given a GCP instance we may assume without loss of generality that any optimal solution contains at least two edges. This assumption implies that GCP is a special case of SCP: The elements to cover are the groups $G_1, \ldots, G_k$, and the covering objects are the edges. The groups covered by pairs of edges are defined as follows. Let $v_1, \ldots, v_r$ be the left-to-right order of the vertices in G_i, and let $[v_i, v_j]$ be the set of edges on the subpath connecting v_i and v_j. The group G_i is covered by a pair of edges $e' \neq e'' \in E$ if $\{e', e''\} \cap ([v_1, v_2] \cup [v_{r-1}, v_r]) \neq \emptyset$ or if $e' \in [v_{t-1}, v_t]$ and $e'' \in [v_t, v_{t+1}]$ for some $2 \leq t \leq r - 1$.

1.2   Our Results

In Section 2 we study a natural extension of the greedy set cover algorithm [1,11,13] to approximate SCP. We define a class of functions, called *feasible maps*, that assign the elements in U to pairs of objects in the optimal solution, and characterize them by *max* and *mean* properties. We then present a conditional analysis of the greedy algorithm, based on the existence of such maps. Specifically, we prove an approximation guarantee of αH_n for the weighted and cardinality versions of the problem, given the existence of feasible maps whose max and mean are at most α, respectively. We also prove that the unconditional approximation ratio for cardinality SCP is $O(\sqrt{n \log n})$.

We continue the discussion with indications for the hardness of SCP. First, although the set cover problem becomes trivial when each subset contains a single element, we show that the corresponding special case of SCP, where each pair of objects covers at most one element, is at least as hard to approximate as set cover. Second, the analysis of the greedy set cover algorithm in [13] shows that the integrality gap of the natural LP-relaxation of set cover is $O(\log n)$. However, we demonstrate that this property does not extend to SCP, for which the integrality gap is $\Omega(n)$.

As a first attempt at attacking the RDS problem, one might consider using the greedy SCP algorithm. However, we show in Section 3 that the approximation guarantee of this algorithm is $\Omega(\sqrt{n})$, mainly due to the observation that there are instances of RDS in which non-trivial feasible maps do not exist. Nevertheless, we provide a $2H_n$-approximation algorithm that constructs a remote dominating set by approximating two dependent set cover problems.

In Section 4 we proceed to the cardinality RDS problem on a tree $T = (V, E)$. Although this problem can be solved to optimality in $O(|V|^3)$ time using dynamic programming techniques [8], we demonstrate that it can be well approximated much faster. We first show how to map a subset of "problematic" vertices of T to a small collection of pairs in the optimal solution. We then exploit the special structure of this map to present a linear time 2-approximation algorithm, and illustrate that in general graphs this algorithm does not guarantee a non-trivial approximation ratio.

In Section 5 we present a polynomial time approximation scheme for the Euclidean RDS problem. Although we follow the general framework of Hochbaum and Maass for covering and packing problems in Euclidean spaces [10], our analysis is more involved. This is due to the use of two covering radii and the restriction that the set of points we choose must be a subset of V, instead of any set of points in the plane.

Finally, in Section 6 we discuss the hardness of approximating GCP, and in particular prove that this problem is as hard to approximate as set cover. Moreover, we identify the exact point at which GCP becomes NP-hard, by showing that this problem is polynomial time solvable when the cardinality of each group is at most 3, but as hard to approximate as vertex cover when the bound on cardinality is 4. On the positive side, we prove the existence of a feasible map whose max is at most 2. This result enables us to show that the approximation ratio of the greedy SCP algorithm for this special case is $2H_k$, where k is the number of groups to be separated.

2   Set Cover with Pairs

In this section we suggest a natural extension of the greedy set cover algorithm to approximate SCP, and present a conditional analysis based on the existence of a mapping of the elements in U to pairs of objects in the optimal solution, that satisfies certain properties. We then make use of these results to prove an approximation ratio of $O(\sqrt{n \log n})$ for cardinality SCP. We also prove that the special case in which each pair of objects covers at most one element is at least as hard to approximate as set cover, and demonstrate that the integrality gap of the natural LP-relaxation of SCP is $\Omega(n)$.

2.1   A Greedy Algorithm

The greedy SCP algorithm iteratively picks the most cost-effective object or pair of objects until all elements are covered, where cost-effectiveness is defined as the ratio between the objects costs and the number of newly covered elements. Let GR be the set of objects already picked when an iteration begins, where initially $GR = \emptyset$. We define:

1. For every $i \in S \setminus GR$, the current covering ratio of i is

$$\frac{w_i}{|\mathcal{C}(GR \cup \{i\})| - |\mathcal{C}(GR)|} \, .$$

2. For every $i \neq j \in S \setminus GR$, the current covering ratio of $\{i, j\}$ is

$$\frac{w_i + w_j}{|\mathcal{C}(GR \cup \{i, j\})| - |\mathcal{C}(GR)|} \, .$$

In each iteration we augment GR by adding a single object $i \in S \setminus GR$ or a pair of objects $i \neq j \in S \setminus GR$, whichever attains the minimum covering ratio. The algorithm terminates when U is completely covered.

2.2   Conditional Analysis

Let $F \subseteq S$ be a feasible solution, that is, a set of objects that covers the elements of U, and let $P(F) = \{\{i, j\} \subseteq F : i \neq j\}$. A function $\mathcal{M} : U \to P(F)$ is a *feasible map with respect to F* if the pair of objects $\mathcal{M}(e)$ covers e, for every $e \in U$. Given a feasible map $\mathcal{M}$, for every $\{i, j\} \in P(F)$ we use $\mathbb{I}_{\mathcal{M}}(i, j)$ to indicate whether at least one element is mapped to $\{i, j\}$. We define:

$$\max(\mathcal{M}, F) = \max_{i \in F} \sum_{j \neq i} \mathbb{I}_{\mathcal{M}}(i, j) \, , \quad \text{mean}(\mathcal{M}, F) = \frac{1}{|F|} \sum_{i \in F} \sum_{j \neq i} \mathbb{I}_{\mathcal{M}}(i, j) \, .$$

In other words, $\max(\mathcal{M}, F) \leq \alpha$ if each object $i \in F$ belongs to at most α pairs to which elements are mapped. Similarly, $\text{mean}(\mathcal{M}, F) \leq \alpha$ if the average number of pairs, to which elements are mapped, an object belongs to is at most α. Clearly, $\text{mean}(\mathcal{M}, F) \leq \max(\mathcal{M}, F)$.

In Lemma 1 we show that given the existence of a feasible map $\mathcal{M}$ with respect to an optimal solution OPT, for which $\max(\mathcal{M}, \text{OPT}) \leq \alpha$, the greedy SCP algorithm constructs a solution whose cost is within factor αH_n of optimum. In Lemma 2 we show that to obtain an approximation guarantee of αH_n for cardinality SCP, the weaker condition of $\text{mean}(\mathcal{M}, \text{OPT}) \leq \alpha$ is sufficient.

Lemma 1. *If there exists an optimal solution* OPT *and a feasible map* $\mathcal{M}$ *such that* $\max(\mathcal{M}, \text{OPT}) \leq \alpha$, *then* $w(\text{GR}) \leq \alpha H_n \cdot w(\text{OPT})$.

Proof. For every $\{i, j\} \in P(\text{OPT})$, let $\mathcal{M}^{-1}(i, j) = \{e \in U : \mathcal{M}(e) = \{i, j\}\}$. By definition of $\mathcal{M}$, $\{\mathcal{M}^{-1}(i, j) : \{i, j\} \in P(\text{OPT})\}$ is a partition of U. In each iteration of the algorithm, we distribute the cost of the newly picked object or pair of objects among the new covered elements: If x new elements are covered, each such element is charged $\frac{w_i}{x}$ or $\frac{w_i + w_j}{x}$, depending on whether a single object or a pair of objects are picked.

Let $\mathcal{M}^{-1}(i, j) = \{e'_1, \ldots, e'_k\}$, where the elements of $\mathcal{M}^{-1}(i, j)$ are indexed by the order they were first covered by the greedy algorithm, breaking ties arbitrarily. Consider the iteration in which e'_l was first covered. One possibility of the greedy algorithm was to pick $\{i, j\}$ (or if one of i and j was already picked, then take the other one), covering the elements $e'_l, \ldots, e'_k$, and possibly other elements as well. Therefore, each element that was covered in this iteration is charged at most $\frac{w_i + w_j}{k - l + 1}$, and the total cost charged to the elements of $\mathcal{M}^{-1}(i, j)$ satisfies

$$\text{charge}(\mathcal{M}^{-1}(i, j)) = \sum_{l=1}^{k} \text{charge}(e'_l) \leq \sum_{l=1}^{k} \frac{w_i + w_j}{k - l + 1} \leq (w_i + w_j)H_n \ .$$

Since $w(\text{GR})$ is charged to $e_1, \ldots, e_n$, we have

$$w(\text{GR}) = \sum_{j=1}^{n} \text{charge}(e_j)$$

$$= \sum_{\{i,j\} \in P(\text{OPT})} \text{charge}(\mathcal{M}^{-1}(i, j))$$

$$\leq H_n \sum_{\{i,j\} \in P(\text{OPT})} (w_i + w_j)\mathbb{I}_{\mathcal{M}}(i, j)$$

$$= H_n \sum_{i \in \text{OPT}} w_i \sum_{j \neq i} \mathbb{I}_{\mathcal{M}}(i, j)$$

$$\leq \alpha H_n \sum_{i \in \text{OPT}} w_i$$

$$= \alpha H_n \cdot w(\text{OPT}) \ ,$$

where the last inequality holds since $\sum_{j \neq i} \mathbb{I}_{\mathcal{M}}(i, j) \leq \max(\mathcal{M}, \text{OPT}) \leq \alpha$ for every $i \in \text{OPT}$. $\qquad \square$

Lemma 2. *If there exists an optimal solution* OPT *for cardinality SCP and a feasible map* $\mathcal{M}$ *such that* $\text{mean}(\mathcal{M}, \text{OPT}) \leq \alpha$, *then* $|\text{GR}| \leq \alpha H_n \cdot |\text{OPT}|$.

2.3   Approximation Ratio for Cardinality SCP

The conditional analysis in Lemma 2 is based on the existence of a feasible map $\mathcal{M}$ with respect to the optimal solution with small mean$(\mathcal{M}, \text{OPT})$. In Lemma 3 we demonstrate that there are instances of cardinality SCP in which a non-trivial map does not exist, and show that the approximation ratio of the greedy SCP algorithm might be $\Omega(\sqrt{n})$. However, in Theorem 4 we prove that the cardinality of the solution constructed by the greedy algorithm is within factor $\sqrt{2nH_n}$ of the minimum possible.

Lemma 3. *The approximation guarantee of the greedy algorithm for cardinality SCP is $\Omega(\sqrt{n})$.*

Theorem 4. $|\text{GR}| \le \sqrt{2nH_n} \cdot |\text{OPT}|.$

Proof. We first observe that $|\text{GR}| \le 2n$, since in each iteration of the algorithm at least one element is covered using at most two objects. In addition, any feasible map $\mathcal{M}$ with respect to OPT certainly satisfies mean$(\mathcal{M}, \text{OPT}) \le |\text{OPT}|$, since

$$\text{mean}(\mathcal{M}, \text{OPT}) \le \max(\mathcal{M}, \text{OPT}) \le |\text{OPT}| \ .$$

By Lemma 2 we have $|\text{GR}| \le H_n \cdot |\text{OPT}|^2$, and it follows that

$$|\text{GR}| \le \min\left\{2n, H_n \cdot |\text{OPT}|^2\right\} \le (2n)^{\frac{1}{2}} \left(H_n \cdot |\text{OPT}|^2\right)^{\frac{1}{2}} = \sqrt{2nH_n} \cdot |\text{OPT}| \ .$$

$\square$

2.4   The Hardness of SCP: Additional Indications

The Case $|\mathcal{C}(i,j)| \le 1$. The set cover problem becomes trivial when each subset contains a single element. However, in Theorem 5 we prove that SCP remains at least as hard to approximate as set cover when each pair of objects covers at most one element. We refer to this special case as SCP_1.

Theorem 5. *For any fixed $\epsilon > 0$, a polynomial time α-approximation algorithm for SCP_1 would imply a polynomial time $(1 + \epsilon)\alpha$-approximation algorithm for set cover.*

Proof. Given a set cover instance I, with a ground set $U = \{e_1, \ldots, e_n\}$ and a collection $\mathcal{S} = \{S_1, \ldots, S_m\}$ of subsets of U, we construct an instance $\rho(I)$ of SCP_1 as follows.

1. Let $k = \lceil \frac{n}{\epsilon} \rceil$.
2. The set of elements is $\bigcup_{t=1}^{k} \{e_1^t, \ldots, e_n^t\}$.
3. The set of objects is $(\bigcup_{t=1}^{k} \{S_1^t, \ldots, S_m^t\}) \cup \{y_1, \ldots, y_n\}$.
4. For $t = 1, \ldots, k$, $i = 1, \ldots, m$ and $j = 1, \ldots, n$, the pair $\{S_i^t, y_j\}$ covers e_j^t if $e_j \in S_i$.
5. Other pairs do not cover any element.

Let $S^* \subseteq S$ be a minimum cardinality set cover in I. Given a polynomial time α-approximation algorithm for SCP_1, we show how to find in polynomial time a set cover with cardinality at most $(1 + \epsilon)\alpha|S^*|$, for any fixed $\epsilon > 0$.

The construction of $\rho(I)$ guarantees that the collection of objects $\{S_i^t, y_1, \ldots, y_n\}$ covers the set of elements $\{e_j^t : e_j \in S_i\}$, for every $t = 1, \ldots, k$. Therefore, since S^* is a set cover in I, the objects $(\bigcup_{t=1}^k \{S_i^t : S_i \in S^*\}) \cup \{y_1, \ldots, y_n\}$ cover all elements of $\rho(I)$. It follows that $\mathrm{OPT}(\rho(I)) \leq k|S^*| + n$, and we can find in polynomial time a feasible solution $\tilde{S}$ to $\rho(I)$ such that $|\tilde{S}| \leq \alpha(k|S^*|+n)$. Let t' be the index t for which $|\tilde{S} \cap \{S_1^t, \ldots, S_m^t\}|$ is minimized. Then $S' = \{S_i : S_i^{t'} \in \tilde{S} \cap \{S_1^{t'}, \ldots, S_m^{t'}\}\}$ is a set cover in I with cardinality

$$|S'| = \min_{t=1,\ldots,k} |\tilde{S} \cap \{S_1^t, \ldots, S_m^t\}| \leq \frac{|\tilde{S}|}{k} \leq \frac{\alpha(k|S^*| + n)}{k} \leq (1 + \epsilon)\alpha|S^*| .$$

$\square$

Integrality Gap of LP-Relaxation. In contrast with the set cover problem, for which the integrality gap of the natural LP-relaxation is $O(\log n)$ [13], we show in Theorem 6 that the integrality gap of the corresponding relaxation of SCP is $\Omega(n)$.

SCP can be formulated as an integer program by:

$$\text{minimize} \quad \sum_{i \in S} w_i x_i$$

$$\text{subject to} \quad \sum_{\{i,j\}:e \in C(i,j)} y_{\{i,j\}} \geq 1 \quad \forall e \in U \quad (2.1)$$

$$y_{\{i,j\}} \leq x_i \quad \forall i \neq j \in S \quad (2.2)$$

$$x_i, y_{\{i,j\}} \in \{0,1\} \quad \forall i \neq j \in S \quad (2.3)$$

The variable x_i indicates whether the object i is chosen for the cover, whereas $y_{\{i,j\}}$ indicates whether both i and j are chosen. Constraint (2.1) guarantees that for each element $e \in U$ we pick at least one pair of objects that covers it. Constraint (2.2) ensures that a pair of objects cannot cover any element unless we indeed pick both objects. The LP-relaxation of this integer program, (LP), is obtained by replacing the integrality constraint (2.3) with $x_i \geq 0$ and $y_{\{i,j\}} \geq 0$.

Theorem 6. *The integrality gap of* (LP) *is* $\Omega(n)$, *even for cardinality SCP.*

Proof. Consider the instance of cardinality SCP with $U = \{e_1, \ldots, e_n\}$ and $S = \{1, \ldots, 2n\}$. The elements covered by pairs of objects in S are:

1. $C(i, n+1) = C(i, n+2) = \cdots = C(i, 2n) = \{e_i\}$, $i = 1, \ldots, n$.
2. Other pairs do not cover any element.

Since any integral solution must pick the objects $1, \ldots, n$ and at least one of the objects $n + 1, \ldots, 2n$, $|\mathrm{OPT}| \geq n + 1$. We claim that the fractional solution $x_i' = \frac{1}{n}$ and $y_{\{i,j\}}' = \frac{1}{n}$ for every $i \neq j$ is feasible for (LP). Clearly, this solution is non-negative and satisfies constraint (2.2). In addition, $\sum_{\{i,j\}: e \in \mathcal{C}(i,j)} y'_{\{i,j\}} = 1$ for every $e \in U$, since the left-hand-side contains exactly n summands, each of value $\frac{1}{n}$. It follows that the cost of an optimal fractional solution is at most 2, and the integrality gap of (LP) is at least $\frac{n+1}{2}$. □

3 Remote Dominating Set

In the following we show that there are instances of the problem in which a non-trivial map does not exist, and demonstrate that the greedy algorithm might construct a solution for RDS whose cost is $\Omega(\sqrt{n})$ times the optimum. On the positive side however, we provide a $2H_n$-approximation algorithm for RDS that constructs a remote dominating set by approximating two dependent set cover problems.

3.1 The Greedy SCP Algorithm for RDS

According to our interpretation of the RDS problem as a special case of SCP, the greedy algorithm picks in each iteration a single point or a pair of points, whichever attains the minimum ratio of cost to number of newly covered points. By modifying the construction in Lemma 3, we prove in Lemma 7 that the approximation ratio of this algorithm is $\Omega(\sqrt{n})$.

Lemma 7. *The approximation guarantee of the greedy algorithm for RDS is $\Omega(\sqrt{n})$.*

3.2 A $2H_n$-Approximation Algorithm

Despite these negative results regarding the performance of the greedy SCP algorithm for the RDS problem, we show that this problem can still be approximated to within a logarithmic factor. Our algorithm constructs a remote dominating set by approximating two dependent set cover problems, (SC_1) and (SC_2).

For $v \in V$, let $N_v = \{u \in V : d(v, u) \leq r_2\}$. Using the greedy set cover algorithm, we construct an RDS in two phases:

1. We first approximate (SC_1): The set of elements to cover is V; the covering sets are $\mathcal{S} = \{N_v : v \in V\}$; the cost of N_v is c_v. Let S_1 be the cover we obtain. V can now be partitioned into two sets: V_1, points within distance r_1 of some point in S_1 or within distance r_2 of two points in S_1, and $V_2 = V \setminus V_1$.
2. We then approximate (SC_2): The set of elements to cover is V_2; the covering sets are $\mathcal{S} = \{N_v : v \in V \setminus S_1\}$; the cost of N_v is c_v. Let S_2 be the cover we obtain.

Theorem 8. *Let* OPT *be a minimum cost RDS. Then*

1. $S_1 \cup S_2$ *is an RDS.*
2. $c(S_1 \cup S_2) \leq 2H_n \cdot c(\text{OPT})$.

4   Cardinality RDS on a Tree

In this section we consider the minimum cardinality RDS problem on a tree $T = (V, E)$ with unit length edges and covering radii $r_1 = 1$ and $r_2 = 2$. It would be convenient to work directly with the tree representation of the problem, instead of working with the related metric space.

We constructively show that a minimum cardinality dominating set in T is a 2-approximation, by exploiting special properties of a partial map we find. We also prove that this bound is tight, and demonstrate that in general graphs a minimum cardinality dominating set does not guarantee a non-trivial approximation ratio.

4.1   The Existence of Acyclic Mapping Graphs

Let S be an RDS that contains at least two vertices. We denote by $L \subseteq V$ the set of vertices that are not covered by a single vertex in S. In other words, $v \in L$ if there is no vertex in S within distance 1 of v. Given a partial map $\mathcal{M}_L : L \to P(S)$, its *mapping graph* $\mathcal{G}(\mathcal{M}_L)$ is defined by:

1. The set of vertices of $\mathcal{G}(\mathcal{M}_L)$ is S.
2. For $u \neq v \in S$, (u, v) is an edge of $\mathcal{G}(\mathcal{M}_L)$ if there is a vertex $w \in L$ such that $\mathcal{M}_L(w) = \{u, v\}$.

Lemma 9. *There is a partial map $\mathcal{M}_L : L \to P(S)$ whose mapping graph $\mathcal{G}(\mathcal{M}_L)$ is acyclic.*

4.2   A 2-Approximation Algorithm

Based on the existence of a partial map whose mapping graph is acyclic, in Lemma 10 we constructively show that for every remote dominating set S in T there is a dominating set of cardinality at most $2|S| - 1$.

Lemma 10. *Let S be an RDS in T. Then there is a dominating set of cardinality at most $2|S| - 1$.*

A minimum cardinality dominating set D^* in T can be found in linear time [2], and in the special case we consider, this set is also an RDS. Lemma 10 proves, in particular, the existence of a dominating set whose cardinality is at most $2|\text{OPT}| - 1$, where OPT is a minimum cardinality RDS in T. We have as a conclusion the following theorem.

Theorem 11. $|D^*| \leq 2|\text{OPT}| - 1$.

In Lemma 12 we show that the bound given in Theorem 11 is tight, by providing an instance with $|D^*| = 2|\text{OPT}| - 1$. We also demonstrate that in general graphs a minimum cardinality dominating set does not guarantee a non-trivial approximation ratio.

Lemma 12. *There are instances in which $|D^*| = 2|\text{OPT}| - 1$. In addition, when the underlying graph is not restricted to be a tree, there are instances with $|\text{OPT}| = O(1)$ and $|D^*| = \Omega(n)$.*

5 Euclidean RDS

In this section we present a polynomial time approximation scheme for the Euclidean RDS problem, following the general framework suggested by Hochbaum and Maass for covering and packing problems in Euclidean spaces [10]. The unifying idea behind their *shifting* strategy is to repeatedly apply a simple divide-and-conquer approach and select the best solution we find.

To simplify the presentation, we denote by $P = \{p_1, \ldots, p_n\}$ the set of points to be covered, and let $D = r_2$. We also assume that P is bounded in a rectangle I, where the length of the long edge of I is nD. Otherwise, we can partition P into sets for which this property is satisfied, and separately use the algorithm for each set.

The Vertical Partitions. We divide I into pairwise disjoint vertical strips of width D. Given a shifting parameter l, the partition V_0 of I consists of strips of width lD. For every $i = 1, \ldots, l - 1$, let V_i be the partition of I obtained by shifting V_0 to the right over distance iD.

For each partition V_i we define a set of points $\text{OPT}(V_i)$ as follows. For every strip J in the partition V_i, let $\text{OPT}(V_i, J)$ be a minimum cardinality set of points in P that covers the points P_J, where P_J is the set of points in P located in the strip J. Then $\text{OPT}(V_i) = \bigcup_{J \in V_i} \text{OPT}(V_i, J)$. Clearly, $\text{OPT}(V_i)$ is an RDS.

Lemma 13. *Let* OPT *be a minimum cardinality Euclidean RDS, then*

$$\min_{i=0,\ldots,l-1} |\text{OPT}(V_i)| \leq \left(1 + \frac{2}{l}\right) |\text{OPT}| .$$

The Horizontal Partitions. We are now concerned with the problem of finding a small set of points in P that covers P_J, for a given strip J. We divide J into pairwise disjoint horizontal strips of height D. The partition H_0 of J consists of strips of height lD. For every $i = 1, \ldots, l - 1$, let H_i be the partition of J obtained by shifting H_0 up over distance iD.

For each partition H_i we define a set of points $\text{OPT}(H_i)$ as follows. For every strip R in the partition H_i, let $\text{OPT}(H_i, R)$ be a minimum cardinality set of points in P that covers the points P_R, where P_R is the set of points in P located in the strip R. Then $\text{OPT}(H_i) = \bigcup_{R \in H_i} \text{OPT}(H_i, R)$. Clearly, $\text{OPT}(H_i)$ is a set of points in P that covers P_J.

Lemma 14. *Let* OPT^J *be a minimum cardinality set of points in P that covers P_J, then*

$$\min_{i=0,\ldots,l-1} |\text{OPT}(H_i)| \leq \left(1 + \frac{2}{l}\right) |\text{OPT}^J| .$$

Optimal Solution in an $lD \times lD$ Square. Lemmas 13 and 14 show that in order to obtain a polynomial time approximation scheme for Euclidean RDS, it is sufficient to optimally solve the following problem: Given R, an $lD \times lD$ square in I, find a minimum cardinality set of points in P that covers P_R. The next lemma allows us to perform an exhaustive search for an optimal solution to this problem in time $O(n^{O(l^2)})$.

Lemma 15. *There is a set of points $S \subseteq P$, $|S| = O(l^2)$, that covers P_R.*

Theorem 16. *There is a polynomial time approximation scheme for the Euclidean RDS problem.*

6   Group Cut on a Path

In this section we first discuss the hardness of approximating GCP, and prove that this problem is as hard to approximate as set cover. We also identify the exact point at which GCP becomes NP-hard. We then present a simple proof for the existence of a feasible map $\mathcal{M}$ with respect to the optimal solution for which $\max(\mathcal{M}, \text{OPT}) \leq 2$. This result, combined with Lemma 1, enables us to show that the approximation ratio of the greedy SCP algorithm for this special case is $2H_k$.

6.1   Hardness Results

By describing an approximation preserving reduction, we prove in Theorem 17 that GCP is as hard to approximate as set cover. A special case of this reduction also shows that GCP is as hard to approximate as vertex cover even when the cardinality of each group is at most 4. In addition, we prove in Lemma 18 that when the bound on cardinality is 3, the problem is polynomial time solvable.

Theorem 17. *A polynomial time approximation algorithm for the GCP problem with factor α would imply a polynomial time approximation algorithm for the set cover problem with the same factor.*

Note that vertex cover is a special case of set cover in which each element belongs to exactly two sets. Therefore, the proof of Theorem 17 can be modified to show that GCP is as hard to approximate as vertex cover even when the cardinality of each group is at most 4.

Lemma 18. *GCP is polynomial time solvable when $|G_i| \leq 3$ for every $i = 1, \ldots, k$.*

6.2   A Feasible Map with Small Max

Let $F \subseteq E$ be any feasible solution, with $|F| \geq 2$. In Lemma 19 we prove the existence of a feasible map $\mathcal{M} : \{G_1, \ldots, G_k\} \to P(F)$ for which $\max(\mathcal{M}, F) \leq 2$.

Lemma 19. *There is a feasible map $\mathcal{M} : \{G_1, \ldots, G_k\} \to P(F)$ with*

$$\max(\mathcal{M}, F) \leq 2 \ .$$

Let OPT be a minimum cost set of edges that separates $G_1, \ldots, G_k$, and without loss of generality $|\text{OPT}| \geq 2$. The next theorem follows from Lemmas 1 and 19.

Theorem 20. *The greedy SCP algorithm constructs a solution whose cost is at most $2H_k \cdot c(\text{OPT})$.*

7 Concluding Remarks

There is a huge gap between the upper bound for approximating the cardinality SCP problem, that was established in Theorem 4, and the logarithmic lower bound that follows from the observation that SCP contains set cover as a special case. The first, and probably the most challenging, open problem is to obtain either an improved hardness result or an improved approximation algorithm. Another open problem in this context is to provide a non-trivial algorithm for the general problem.

In addition, it would be interesting to study the seemingly simple special case, in which each pair of objects covers at most one element. We proved that this problem is at least as hard to approximate as set cover, but we do not know how to significantly improve the approximation guarantee. Moreover, we consider this case to demonstrate the main difficulty in approximating SCP, as it shows that the objective is to choose a dense set of objects that covers all elements.

We suggest for future research the *partial SCP* problem, a variant of SCP in which we are given an additional parameter k, and the objective is to cover at least k elements with minimum cost. This problem is closely related to the *dense k-subgraph* problem, that required to find in a given graph $G = (V, E)$ a set of k vertices whose induced subgraph has maximum number of edges. This problem is NP-hard, and the currently best approximation guarantee in general graphs is $O(n^{-\delta})$, for some constant $\delta < \frac{1}{3}$, due to Feige, Kortsarz and Peleg [5]. The next theorem relates these problems, and shows that the approximation guarantee of dense k-subgraph can be improved by developing an $o(n^{\delta/2})$-approximation algorithm for partial SCP.

Theorem 21. *A polynomial time $\alpha(k)$-approximation algorithm for partial SCP would imply a randomized polynomial time $\frac{1}{\alpha^2(k^2)(1+\epsilon)}$-approximation algorithm for dense k-subgraph, for any fixed $\epsilon > 0$.*

References

1. V. Chvátal. A greedy heuristic for the set covering problem. *Mathematics of Operations Research*, 4:233–235, 1979.
2. E. J. Cockayne, S. E. Goodman, and S. T. Hedetniemi. A linear algorithm for the domination number of a tree. *Information Processing Letters*, 4:41–44, 1975.
3. E. Dahlhaus, D. S. Johnson, C. H. Papadimitriou, P. D. Seymour, and M. Yannakakis. The complexity of multiterminal cuts. *SIAM Journal on Computing*, 23:864–894, 1994.
4. U. Feige. A threshold of $\ln n$ for approximating set cover. *Journal of the ACM*, 45:634–652, 1998.
5. U. Feige, G. Kortsarz, and D. Peleg. The dense k-subgraph problem. *Algorithmica*, 29:410–421, 2001.
6. N. Garg, V. V. Vazirani, and M. Yannakakis. Primal-dual approximation algorithms for integral flow and multicut in trees. *Algorithmica*, 18:3–20, 1997.
7. S. Guha and S. Khuller. Approximation algorithms for connected dominating sets. *Algorithmica*, 20:374–387, 1998.
8. R. Hassin and D. Segev. The set cover with pairs problem, 2005.
   http://www.math.tau.ac.il/~segevd/Papers/SCP-Jour.pdf.

9. R. Hassin and A. Tamir. Improved complexity bounds for location problems on the real line. *Operations Research Letters*, 10:395–402, 1991.

10. D. S. Hochbaum and W. Maass. Approximation schemes for covering and packing problems in image processing and VLSI. *Journal of the ACM*, 32:130–136, 1985.

11. D. S. Johnson. Approximation algorithms for combinatorial problems. *Journal of Computer and System Sciences*, 9:256–278, 1974.

12. F. T. Leighton and S. Rao. Multicommodity max-flow min-cut theorems and their use in designing approximation algorithms. *Journal of the ACM*, 46:787–832, 1999.

13. L. Lovász. On the ratio of optimal integral and fractional covers. *Discrete Mathematics*, 13:383–390, 1975.

14. P. Slavík. Improved performance of the greedy algorithm for partial cover. *Information Processing Letters*, 64:251–254, 1997.

Non-disclosure for Distributed Mobile Code

Ana Almeida Matos

INRIA Sophia Antipolis

Abstract. This paper addresses the issue of confidentiality and declassification for global computing in a language-based security perspective. The purpose is to deal with new forms of security leaks, which we call *migration leaks*, introduced by code mobility. We present a generalization of the non-disclosure policy [AB05] to networks, and a type and effect system for enforcing it. We consider an imperative higher-order lambda-calculus with concurrent threads and a flow declaration construct, enriched with a notion of domain and a standard migration primitive.

1 Introduction

Protecting confidentiality of data is a concern of particular relevance in a global computing context. When information and programs move throughout networks, they become exposed to users with different interests and responsibilities. This motivates the search for practical mechanisms that enforce respect for confidentiality of information, while minimizing the need to rely on mutual trust. Access control is important, but it is not enough, since it is not concerned with how information may flow between the different parts of a system. Surprisingly, very little research has been done on the control of information flow in networks. In fact, to the best of our knowledge, this work is the first to address the problem in an imperative setting where mobility of resources plays an explicit role.

This paper is about ensuring confidentiality in networks. More specifically, it is about controlling information flows between subjects that have been given different security clearances, in the context of a distributed setting with code mobility. Clearly, in such a setting, one cannot assume resources to be accessible by all programs at all times. In fact, a network can be seen as a collection of sites where conditions for computation to occur are not guaranteed by one site alone. Could these failures be exploited as covert information flow channels? The answer is *Yes*. New security leaks, that we call *migration leaks*, arise from the fact that execution or suspension of programs now depend on the position of resources over the network, which may in turn depend on secret information.

We take a language based approach [SM03], which means that we restrict our concern to information leaks occurring within computations of programs of a given language. These can be statically prevented by means of a type and effect system [VSI96, LG88], thus allowing rejection of insecure programs before execution. As is standard, we attribute security levels to the objects of our language (memory addresses), and have them organized into a lattice [Den76]. Since confidentiality is the issue, these levels indicate to which subjects the contents of an

R. Ramanujam and S. Sen (Eds.): FSTTCS 2005, LNCS 3821, pp. 177–188, 2005.

object are allowed to be disclosed. Consequently, during computation, information contained in objects of "high" security level (let us call them "high objects") should never influence objects of lower or incomparable level. This policy has been widely studied and is commonly referred to as *non-interference* [GM82]. In a more general setting, where the security lattice may vary within a program, *non-disclosure* [AB05] can be used instead.

We consider a calculus for mobility where the notion of location of a program and of a resource has an impact in computations: resources and programs are distributed over computation sites – or *domains* – and can change position during execution; accesses to a resource can only be performed by a program that is located at the same site; remote accesses are suspended until the resources become available. The language of local computations is an imperative λ-calculus with concurrent threads, to which we add a standard migration primitive. We include a flow declaration construct [AB05] for providing the programmer with means to declassify information, that is to explicitly allow certain information leaks to occur in a controlled way (find overviews in [AB05, SS05]). We show that mobility and declassification can be safely combined provided that migrating threads compute according to declared flow policies.

The security properties we have at hand, designed for local computations where the notion of locality does not play a crucial role, are not suitable for treating information flows in a distributed setting with code mobility. In fact, since the location of resources in a network can be itself a source of information leaks, the notion of safe program must take this into account. For this purpose, we extend the usual undistinguishability relation for memories to states that track the positions of programs in a network. Furthermore, it is not reasonable to assume a global security policy that all threads comply to. Admitting that each program has its own security policy raises problems in ensuring that the threads who share resources respect one another's flow policies. For instance, when should one allow "low level" information to be accessed by "high level" readers, if the assignment of the levels 'low' and 'high' were based on different criteria? It turns out that, if the security levels are sets of *principals*, there is a "minimum" security policy that every thread must satisfy, and which we use to conveniently approximate the "intersection" of security policies in any network.

The paper is organized as follows: In the next section we define a distributed calculus with code and resource mobility. In Section 3 we formulate a nondisclosure property that is suitable for a decentralized setting. In Section 4 we develop a type and effect system that only accepts programs satisfying such a property. Finally, we comment on related work and conclude.

2   The Calculus

The design of network models is a whole research area in itself, and there exists a wide spectrum of calculi that focus on different aspects of mobility (see [BCGL02]). We are interested in a general and simple framework that addresses the unreliable nature of resource access in networks, as well as trust concerns that are raised when computational entities follow different security orientations. We then consider a distributed ML-like core language where domains in a network can communicate with each other via mobile threads, in general composed of programs and memory, yet enriched with a flow declaration construct.

In this section we define the syntax and semantics for the calculus at the local and network level. Very briefly, a *network* consists of a number of *domains*, places where local computations occur independently. Threads may execute concurrently inside domains, create other threads, and *migrate* into another domain. They can own and create a *store* that associates values to *references*, which are addresses to memory containers. These stores move together with the thread they belong to, which means that threads and local references are, at all times, located in the same domain. However, a thread need not own a reference in order to access it. Read and write operations on references may be performed if and only if the corresponding memory location is present in the domain (otherwise they are implicitly suspended).

2.1   Syntax

In order to define the syntax of the language we need to introduce the notions of *security level* and of *flow policy* (they are fully explained in Section 3). *Security levels* j, k, l are sets of *principals* (ranged over by $p, q \in \mathcal{P}$). They are apparent in the syntax as they are assigned to references (and reference creators, not to values) and threads (and thread creators). The security level of a reference is to be understood as the set of principals that are allowed to read the information contained in that reference. The security level of a thread is the set of principals that can have information about the location of the thread. We use *flow policies* as in [AB05] for defining a flow declaration construct that enables downgrading computations by encapsulating expressions in a context allowed by the security policy. For now it is enough to know that a flow policy (ranged over by F, G) is a binary relation over $\mathcal{P}$, where a pair $(p, q) \in F$ is denoted $p \prec q$, and is to be understood as "whatever p can read, q can also read".

Names are given to domains ($d \in \mathcal{D}$), threads ($m, n \in \mathcal{N}$) and references (a), which we also call *addresses*. References are lexically associated to the threads that create them: they are of the form $m.u, n.u$, where u is an identifier given by the thread. Thread and reference names can be created at runtime. We add annotations (subscripts) to names: references carry their security level and the type of the values that they can hold (the syntax of types will be defined later, in Section 4), while thread names carry their security level. In the following we may omit these subscripts whenever they are not relevant, following the convention that the same name has always the same subscript.

Threads are named expressions (M^{m_j}), where the syntax of M is given by:

$$
\begin{array}{lll}
\textit{Expressions} & M, N ::= & V \mid x \mid (M\ N) \mid (\text{if } M \text{ then } N_1 \text{ else } N_2) \\
& \mid & (M; N) \mid (\text{ref}_{l,\theta}\ M) \mid (?\ N) \mid (M :=^? N) \mid (\varrho x V) \\
& \mid & (\text{thread}_l\ M) \mid (\text{goto } d) \mid (\text{flow } F \text{ in } M) \\
\textit{Values} & V, W ::= & () \mid m_j.u_{l,\theta} \mid (\lambda x.M) \mid tt \mid ff
\end{array}
$$

The language of expressions is an imperative higher-order λ-calculus with thread creation (thread$_l$ M), migration (goto d) and a flow declaration (flow F in M). The commands (? N) and ($M :=^? N$) correspond to the dereferencing and assignment operations on references, respectively. The different notation is due to the fact that these operations can potentially suspend. The notation follows [Bou04], though here we shall not consider any form of reaction to suspension. The construct ($\varrho x V$), where x is binded in V, is used to express recursive values.

We define stores S that map *references* to values, and pools (sets) P of *threads* (named expressions) that run concurrently. These two sets are part of domains $d[P, S]$, which in turn form networks whose syntax is given by:

$$Networks \ \ X, Y \ldots \ \ ::= \ \ d[P, S] \ \mid \ X \parallel Y$$

Networks are flat juxtapositions of domains, whose names are assumed to be distinct, and where references are assumed to be located in the same domain as the thread that owns them. Notice that networks are in fact just a collection of threads and owned references that are running in parallel, and whose executions depend on their relative location. To keep track of the locations of threads and references it suffices to maintain a mapping from thread names to domain names.

2.2   Semantics

Given a set $\mathcal{D}$ of domain names in a network, and assuming that all threads in a configuration have distinct names, the semantics of the language is operationally defined as a transition system between configurations of the form $\langle T, P, S \rangle$ representing network $d_1[P_1, S_1] \parallel \cdots \parallel d_n[P_n, S_n]$ where:

T is a function from thread names with security level to the domains where they appear, given by $T = \{m_l \mapsto d_1 | M^{m_l} \in P_1\} \cup \cdots \cup \{m_l \mapsto d_n | M^{m_l} \in P_n\}$.
P and S are the (disjoint) unions of all the thread pools, respectively stores, that exist in the network, that is $P = P_1 \cup \cdots \cup P_n$ and $S = S_1 \cup \cdots \cup S_n$.

We call the pair (T, S) the *state* of the configuration. We define $\mathsf{dom}(T)$, $\mathsf{dom}(P)$ and $\mathsf{dom}(S)$ as the sets of decorated names of threads and references that are mapped by T, P and S, respectively. We say that a thread or reference name is fresh in T or S if it does not occur, with any subscript, in $\mathsf{dom}(T)$ or $\mathsf{dom}(S)$, respectively. We denote by $\mathsf{tn}(P)$ and $\mathsf{rn}(P)$ the set of decorated thread and reference names, respectively, that occur in the expressions of P (this notation is extended in the obvious way to expressions). Furthermore, we overload tn and define, for a set R of reference names, the set $\mathsf{tn}(R)$ of thread names that are prefixes of some name in R.

We restrict our attention to *well formed configurations* $\langle T, P, S \rangle$ satisfying the condition for memories $\mathsf{dom}(S) \supseteq \mathsf{rn}(P)$, a similar condition for the values stored in memories obeying $a_{l,\theta} \in \mathsf{dom}(S)$ implies $\mathsf{dom}(S) \supseteq \mathsf{rn}(S(a_{l,\theta}))$, and the corresponding one for thread names $\mathsf{dom}(T) \supseteq \mathsf{dom}(P)$ and $\mathsf{dom}(T) \supseteq \mathsf{tn}(\mathsf{dom}(S))$. We denote by $\{x \mapsto W\}M$ the capture avoiding substitution of W for the free occurrences of x in M. The operation of updating the image of an object z_o to z_i in a mapping Z is denoted $Z[z_o := z_i]$.

In order to define the operational semantics, it is useful to write expressions using evaluation contexts. Intuitively, the expressions that are placed in such contexts are to be executed first.

$Contexts$ $\mathbf{E} ::= [] \mid (\mathbf{E}\ N) \mid (V\ \mathbf{E}) \mid (\text{if } \mathbf{E} \text{ then } M \text{ else } N) \mid (\mathbf{E}; N)$
$\mid (\text{ref}_{l,\theta}\ \mathbf{E}) \mid (?\ \mathbf{E}) \mid (\mathbf{E} :=^? N) \mid (V :=^? \mathbf{E}) \mid (\text{flow } F \text{ in } \mathbf{E})$

Evaluation is *not* allowed under threads that have not yet been created. We denote by $\lceil \mathbf{E} \rceil$ the flow policy that is permitted by the context $\mathbf{E}$. It collects all the flow policies that are declared using flow declaration constructs into one:

$$\lceil [] \rceil = \emptyset, \qquad \lceil (\text{flow } F \text{ in } \mathbf{E}) \rceil = F \cup \lceil \mathbf{E} \rceil,$$
$$\lceil \mathbf{E}'[\mathbf{E}] \rceil = \lceil \mathbf{E} \rceil, \ \textit{if } \mathbf{E}' \textit{ does not contain flow declarations}$$

The transitions of our (small step) semantics are defined between configurations, and are decorated with the flow policy of the context that is relevant to the expression being evaluated (it will be used later to formulate the non-disclosure property). We omit the set-brackets for singletons. We start by defining the transitions of a single thread.

The evaluation of expressions might depend on and change the store, the position of references in the network, and the name of the thread of which they are part. However, there are rules that depend only on the expression itself.

$$\langle T, \mathsf{E}[((\lambda x.M)\ V)]^{m_j}, S \rangle \xrightarrow[\lceil \mathbf{E} \rceil]{0} \langle T, \mathsf{E}[\{x \mapsto V\}M]^{m_j}, S \rangle$$

$$\langle T, \mathsf{E}[(\text{if } tt \text{ then } N_1 \text{ else } N_2)]^{m_j}, S \rangle \xrightarrow[\lceil \mathbf{E} \rceil]{0} \langle T, \mathsf{E}[N_1]^{m_j}, S \rangle$$

$$\langle T, \mathsf{E}[(\text{if } \textit{ff} \text{ then } N_1 \text{ else } N_2)]^{m_j}, S \rangle \xrightarrow[\lceil \mathbf{E} \rceil]{0} \langle T, \mathsf{E}[N_2]^{m_j}, S \rangle$$

$$\langle T, \mathsf{E}[(V; N)]^{m_j}, S \rangle \xrightarrow[\lceil \mathbf{E} \rceil]{0} \langle T, \mathsf{E}[N]^{m_j}, S \rangle$$

$$\langle T, \mathsf{E}[(\varrho x W)]^{m_j}, S \rangle \xrightarrow[\lceil \mathbf{E} \rceil]{0} \langle T, \mathsf{E}[(\{x \mapsto (\varrho x W)\}\ W)]^{m_j}, S \rangle$$

$$\langle T, \mathsf{E}[(\text{flow } F \text{ in } V)]^{m_j}, S \rangle \xrightarrow[\lceil \mathbf{E} \rceil]{0} \langle T, \mathsf{E}[V]^{m_j}, S \rangle$$

The name of the thread is relevant to the rules that handle references: when a reference is created, it is named after the parent thread. Accesses to references can only be performed within the same domain.

$$\langle T, \mathsf{E}[(\text{ref}_{l,\theta}\ V)]^{m_j}, S \rangle \xrightarrow[\lceil \mathbf{E} \rceil]{0} \langle T, \mathsf{E}[m_j.u_{l,\theta}]^{m_j}, S \cup \{m_j.u_{l,\theta} \mapsto V\} \rangle, \ \textit{if } m.u \textit{ fresh in } S$$

$$\langle T, \mathsf{E}[(?\ n_k.u_{l,\theta})]^{m_j}, S \rangle \xrightarrow[\lceil \mathbf{E} \rceil]{0} \langle T, \mathsf{E}[V]^{m_j}, S \rangle, \ \textit{if } T(n_k) = T(m_j) \ \& \ S(n_k.u_{l,\theta}) = V$$

$$\langle T, \mathsf{E}[(n_k.u_{l,\theta} :=^? V)]^{m_j}, S \rangle \xrightarrow[\lceil \mathbf{E} \rceil]{0} \langle T, \mathsf{E}[()]^{m_j}, S[n_k.u_{l,\theta} := V] \rangle, \ \textit{if } T(n_k) = T(m_j)$$

Fresh names are arbitrarily attributed to threads when they are created. The (goto d) statement is used for sending the executing thread to a domain named d (subjective migration). By simply changing the domain that is associated to the migrating thread's name, both the thread and associated store are subtracted from the emitting domain and integrated into the destination domain.

$$\langle T, \{\mathsf{E}[(\text{thread}_l\ N)]^{m_j}\}, S \rangle \xrightarrow[\lceil \mathbf{E} \rceil]{N^{n_l}} \langle T \cup \{n_l \mapsto T(m_j)\}, \{\mathsf{E}[()]^{m_j}\}, S \rangle, \ \textit{if } n \textit{ fresh in } T$$

$$\langle T, \{\mathsf{E}[\text{goto } d]^{m_j}\}, S \rangle \xrightarrow[\lceil \mathbf{E} \rceil]{0} \langle T[m_j := d], \{\mathsf{E}[()]\}, S \rangle$$

Finally, the execution of threads in a network is compositional. The following three rules gather the threads that are spawned into a pool of threads.

$$\cfrac{\langle T, M^{m_j}, S \rangle \xrightarrow[\lceil E \rceil]{0} \langle T', M'^{m_j}, S' \rangle}{\langle T, M^{m_j}, S \rangle \xrightarrow[\lceil E \rceil]{} \langle T', M'^{m_j}, S' \rangle} \quad \cfrac{\langle T, M^{m_j}, S \rangle \xrightarrow[\lceil E \rceil]{N^{n_l}} \langle T', M'^{m_j}, S' \rangle \quad \text{if } N^{n_l} \neq ()}{\langle T, M^{m_j}, S \rangle \xrightarrow[\lceil E \rceil]{} \langle T', \{M'^{m_j}, N^{n_l}\}, S' \rangle}$$

$$\cfrac{\langle T, P, S \rangle \xrightarrow[\lceil E \rceil]{} \langle T', P', S' \rangle \quad \langle T, P \cup Q, S \rangle \text{ is well formed}}{\langle T, P \cup Q, S \rangle \xrightarrow[\lceil E \rceil]{} \langle T', P' \cup Q, S' \rangle}$$

One can prove that the above rules preserve well-formedness of configurations, and that the language of expressions is deterministic up to choice of new names.

3   Decentralized Non-disclosure Policies

We begin this section with the definition of an extended flow relation. A discussion on the implementation and meaning of multiple flow policies follows. We then define the non-disclosure policy for networks and prove soundness of our type system with respect to that property.

3.1   From Flow Relations to Security Lattices

We have mentioned that security levels are sets of principals representing read-access rights to references. Our aim is to insure that information contained in a reference a_{l_1} (omitting the type annotation) does not leak to another reference b_{l_2} that gives a read access to an unauthorized principal p, i.e., such that $p \in l_2$ but $p \notin l_1$. Reverse inclusion defines the allowed flows between security levels, allowing information to flow from level l_1 to level l_2 if and only if $l_1 \supseteq l_2$.

Given a security level l and a flow policy F, the upward closure of l w.r.t. F is the set $\{p \mid \exists q \in l . (q, p) \in F\}$ and is denoted by $l \uparrow_F$. Now denoting the reflexive and transitive closure of F by F^*, we can derive (as in [ML98, AB05]) a more permissive flow relation:

$$l_1 \preceq_F l_2 \overset{\text{def}}{\Leftrightarrow} \forall q \in l_2. \exists p \in l_1 . p \, F^* \, q \quad \Leftrightarrow \quad (l_1 \uparrow_F) \supseteq (l_2 \uparrow_F)$$

This relation defines a lattice of security levels, where meet ($\sqcap_F$) and join ($\sqcup_F$) are given respectively by the union of the security levels and intersection of their upward closures with respect to F:

$$l_1 \sqcap_F l_2 = l_1 \cup l_2 \qquad l_1 \sqcup_F l_2 = (l_1 \uparrow_F) \cap (l_2 \uparrow_F)$$

Notice that $\preceq_F$ extends $\supseteq$ in the sense that $\preceq_F$ is larger than $\supseteq$ and that $\preceq_\emptyset = \supseteq$. We will use this mechanism of extending the flow relation with a flow policy F in the following way: the information flows that are allowed to occur in an expression M placed in a context $E[]$ must satisfy the flow relation $\preceq_{\lceil E \rceil}$.

3.2   The Non-disclosure Policy

In this section we define the non-disclosure policy for networks, which is based on a notion of bisimulation for sets of threads P with respect to a "low" security level. As usual, the bisimulation expresses the requirement that P_1 and P_2 are to be related if, when running over memories that coincide in their low part, they perform the same low changes. Then, if P is shown to be bisimilar to itself, one can conclude that the high part of the memory has not interfered with the low part, i.e., no security leak has occurred. Using the flow policies that were presented earlier, the notion of "being low" can be extended as in [AB05], thus weakening the condition on the behavior of the threads.

As we will see in Section 4, the position of a thread in the network can reveal information about the values in the memory. For this reason, we must use a notion of "low-equality" that is extended to states $\langle T, S \rangle$. The intuition is that a thread can access a reference if and only if it is located at the same domain as the thread that owns it. Threads that own low references can then be seen as "low threads". We are interested in states where low threads are co-located. Low-equality on states is defined pointwise, for a security level l that is considered as low:

$$S_1 =^{F,l} S_2 \quad \overset{\text{def}}{\Leftrightarrow} \quad \forall a_{k,\theta} \in \mathsf{dom}(S_1) \cup \mathsf{dom}(S_2) \; . \; k \preceq_F l \Rightarrow$$
$$a_{k,\theta} \in \mathsf{dom}(S_1) \cap \mathsf{dom}(S_2) \; \& \; S_1(a_{k,\theta}) = S_2(a_{k,\theta})$$

$$T_1 =^{F,l} T_2 \quad \overset{\text{def}}{\Leftrightarrow} \quad \forall n_k \in \mathsf{dom}(T_1) \cup \mathsf{dom}(T_2) \; . \; k \preceq_F l \Rightarrow$$
$$n_k \in \mathsf{dom}(T_1) \cap \mathsf{dom}(T_2) \; \& \; T_1(n_k) = T_2(n_k)$$

We say that two states are low-equal if they coincide in their low part (including their domains). This relation is transitive, reflexive and symmetric.

Now we define a bisimulation for networks, which can be used to relate networks with the same behavior over low parts of the states. In the following we denote by $\twoheadrightarrow$ the reflexive closure of the union of the transitions $\underset{F}{\longrightarrow}$, for all F.

Definition 1 (l-Bisimulation and $\approx_l$). *Given a security level l, we define an l-bisimulation as a symmetric relation $\mathcal{R}$ on sets of threads such that*

$$P_1 \; \mathcal{R} \; P_2 \; \& \; \langle T_1, P_1, S_1 \rangle \underset{F}{\longrightarrow} \langle T_1', P_1', S_1' \rangle \; \& \; \langle T_1, S_1 \rangle =^{F,l} \langle T_2, S_2 \rangle \; \& \; (*) \; implies:$$
$$\exists T_2', P_2', S_2' : \langle T_2, P_2, S_2 \rangle \twoheadrightarrow \langle T_2', P_2', S_2' \rangle \; \& \; \langle T_1', S_1' \rangle =^{\emptyset,l} \langle T_2', S_2' \rangle \; \& \; P_1' \; \mathcal{R} \; P_2'$$

where $(*) = \mathsf{dom}(S_1' - S_1) \cap \mathsf{dom}(S_2) = \emptyset$ and $\mathsf{dom}(T_1' - T_1) \cap \mathsf{dom}(T_2) = \emptyset$. The relation $\approx_l$ is the greatest l-bisimulation.

Intuitively, our security property states that, at each computation step performed by some thread in a network, the information flow that occurs respects the basic flow relation (empty flow policy), extended with the flow policy (F) that is declared by the context where the command is executed.

Definition 2 (Non-disclosure for Networks). *A set P of threads satisfies the non-disclosure policy if it satisfies $P \approx_l P$ for all security levels l.*

The non-disclosure definition differs from that of [AB05] in two points: first, the position of the low threads is treated as "low information"; second, for being independent from a single flow policy – as we have seen, each thread in the network may have its own flow policy.

4   The Type and Effect System

The type and effect system that we present here selects secure threads by ensuring the compliance of all information flows to the flow relation that rules in each point of the program. To achieve this, it constructively determines the *effects* of each expression, which contain information on the security levels of the references that the expression reads and writes, as well as the level of the references on which termination or non-termination of the computations might depend.

A key observation is that non-termination of a computation might arise from an attempt to access a *foreign* reference. In order to distinguish the threads that own each expression and reference, we associate unique identifiers $\bar{m}, \bar{n} \in \mathcal{N}$ to names of already existing threads, as well as to the unknown thread name '?' for those that are created at runtime. It should be clear that information on which the position of a thread n might depend can leak to another that simply attempts to access one of n's references. For this reason, we associate to each thread a security level representing its "visibility" level, since just by owning a low reference, the position of a thread can be detected by "low observers".

Judgments have the form $\Sigma, \Gamma \vdash_G^{\bar{n}_l} M : s, \tau$, where Σ is a partial injective mapping from the set of decorated thread names extended with '?', and the set of decorated thread identifiers. The typing context Γ assigns types to variables. The expression M belongs to the thread that is statically identified by $\bar{n}_l$. The security level l is a lower bound to the references that the thread can own. The flow policy G is the one that is enforced by the context in which M is evaluated. The security effect s has the form $\langle s.r, s.w, s.t \rangle$, where $s.r$ is an upper bound on the security levels of the references that are read by M, $s.w$ is a lower bound on the that are written by M, and $s.t$ is an upper bound on those levels of the references on which the termination of expression M might depend. Finally, τ is the type of the expression, whose syntax is as follows, for any type variable t:

$$\tau, \sigma, \theta \quad ::= \quad t \mid \mathsf{unit} \mid \mathsf{bool} \mid \theta \; \mathsf{ref}_{l, \bar{n}_k} \mid \tau \xrightarrow[\bar{n}_k, G]{s} \sigma$$

As expected, the reference type shows the reference's security level l and the type θ of the value that it points to; now we also add the identifier $\bar{n}$ and security level k of the thread that owns the reference. As for the function type, we have the usual latent parameters that are needed to type the body of the function.

The rules of the type system are shown in Figure 1. Whenever we have $\Sigma; \Gamma \vdash_G^{\bar{n}} M : \langle \bot, \top, \bot \rangle, \tau$, for all $\bar{n}, G$, we simply write $\Sigma; \Gamma \vdash M : \tau$. We also abbreviate meet and join with respect to the empty flow relation ($\sqcap_\emptyset, \sqcup_\emptyset$) by $\sqcap, \sqcup$, and $\langle s.r \sqcup s'.r, s.w \sqcap s'.w, s.t \sqcup s'.t \rangle$ by $s \sqcup s'$. We must now convince ourselves that the type system indeed selects only safe threads, according to the security notion defined in the previous section. We refer the reader to [AB05] for explanations regarding the use of flow policies in the typing rules. The usual intuitions on treating termination leaks can be useful to understand the new conditions regarding migration leaks. In fact, suspension of a thread on an access to an absent reference can be seen as a non-terminating computation that can be unblocked by migration of concurrent threads.

In rule LOC, the identifier of the thread name that owns the reference is obtained by applying Σ to the prefix of the address. In rule REF, the reference

$$[\text{NIL}] \;\; \Sigma; \Gamma \vdash () : \text{unit} \qquad [\text{FLOW}] \;\; \frac{\Sigma; \Gamma \vdash^{\bar{m}j}_{G \sqcup F} M : s, \tau}{\Sigma; \Gamma \vdash^{\bar{m}j}_{G} (\text{flow } F \text{ in } M) : s, \tau}$$

$$[\text{ABS}] \;\; \frac{\Sigma; \Gamma, x : \tau \vdash^{\bar{m}j}_{G} M : s, \sigma}{\Sigma; \Gamma \vdash (\lambda x.M) : \tau \xrightarrow[\bar{m}j, G]{s} \sigma} \qquad [\text{REC}] \;\; \frac{\Sigma; \Gamma, x : \tau \vdash W : \tau}{\Sigma; \Gamma \vdash (\varrho x W) : \tau}$$

$$[\text{VAR}] \;\; \Sigma; \Gamma, x : \tau \vdash x : \tau \qquad [\text{LOC}] \;\; \Sigma; \Gamma \vdash n_k.u_{l,\theta} : \theta \; \text{ref}_{l, \Sigma(n_k)}$$

$$[\text{REF}] \;\; \frac{\Sigma; \Gamma \vdash^{\bar{m}j}_{G} M : s, \theta \quad \begin{array}{c} j \preceq l \\ s.r, s.t \preceq_G l \end{array}}{\Sigma; \Gamma \vdash^{\bar{m}j}_{G} (\text{ref}_{l,\theta} \; M) : s, \theta \; \text{ref}_{l, \bar{m}j}} \qquad [\text{DER}] \;\; \frac{\Sigma; \Gamma \vdash^{\bar{m}j}_{G} M : s, \theta \; \text{ref}_{l, \bar{n}_k}}{\Sigma; \Gamma \vdash^{\bar{m}j}_{G} (? \; M) : s \sqcup \langle l, \top, \bar{t} \rangle, \theta} \; (*)$$

$$[\text{ASS}] \;\; \frac{\Sigma; \Gamma \vdash^{\bar{m}j}_{G} M : s, \theta \; \text{ref}_{l, \bar{n}_k} \quad \Sigma; \Gamma \vdash^{\bar{m}j}_{G} N : s', \theta \quad \begin{array}{c} s.t \preceq_G s'.w \\ s.r, s'.r, s.t, s'.t, j \preceq_G l \end{array}}{\Sigma; \Gamma \vdash^{\bar{m}j}_{G} (M :=^? N) : s \sqcup s' \sqcup \langle \bot, l, \bar{t} \rangle, \text{unit}} \; (*)$$

$$(*) \; \textit{where } \bar{t} = (\text{if } \bar{m} \neq \bar{n} \text{ then } k \sqcup j \text{ else } \bot)$$

$$[\text{BOOLT}] \;\; \Sigma; \Gamma \vdash tt : \text{bool} \qquad [\text{BOOLF}] \;\; \Sigma; \Gamma \vdash ff : \text{bool}$$

$$[\text{COND}] \;\; \frac{\Sigma; \Gamma \vdash^{\bar{m}j}_{G} M : s, \text{bool} \quad \Sigma; \Gamma \vdash^{\bar{m}j}_{G} N_i : s_i, \tau \quad s.r \sqcup s.t \preceq_G s_1.w \sqcup s_2.w}{\Sigma; \Gamma \vdash^{\bar{m}j}_{G} (\text{if } M \text{ then } N_1 \text{ else } N_2) : s \sqcup s_1 \sqcup s_2 \sqcup \langle \bot, \top, s.r \rangle, \tau}$$

$$[\text{APP}] \;\; \frac{\Sigma; \Gamma \vdash^{\bar{m}j}_{G} M : s, \tau \xrightarrow[\bar{m}j, G]{s'} \sigma \quad \Sigma; \Gamma \vdash^{\bar{m}j}_{G} N : s'', \tau \quad \begin{array}{c} s.t \preceq_G s''.w \\ s.r, s''.r, s.t, s''.t \preceq_G s'.w \end{array}}{\Sigma; \Gamma \vdash^{\bar{m}j}_{G} (M \; N) : s \sqcup s' \sqcup s'' \sqcup \langle \bot, \top, s.r \sqcup s''.r \rangle, \sigma}$$

$$[\text{SEQ}] \;\; \frac{\Sigma; \Gamma \vdash^{\bar{m}j}_{G} M : s, \tau \quad \Sigma; \Gamma \vdash^{\bar{m}j}_{G} N : s', \sigma \quad s.t \preceq_G s'.w}{\Sigma; \Gamma \vdash^{\bar{m}j}_{G} (M; N) : s \sqcup s', \sigma}$$

$$[\text{THR}] \;\; \frac{\begin{array}{c} j \preceq_G l \\ \bar{n} \textit{ fresh in } \Sigma \end{array} \quad \Sigma, ? : \bar{n}_l; \Gamma \vdash^{\bar{n}_l}_{G} M : s, \text{unit}}{\Sigma; \Gamma \vdash^{\bar{m}j}_{G} (\text{thread}_l \; M) : \langle \bot, s.w \sqcap l, \bot \rangle, \text{unit}}$$

$$[\text{MIG}] \;\; \Sigma; \Gamma \vdash^{\bar{m}j}_{G} \text{goto } d : \langle \bot, j, \bot \rangle, \text{unit}$$

Fig. 1. Type system

that is created belongs to the thread identified by the superscript of the '$\vdash$'. We check that the security level that is declared for the new reference is greater than the level of the thread. In rule THR, a fresh identifier – image of an unknown thread name represented by '?' – is used to type the thread that is created. The new thread's security level must preserve that of the parent thread.

In rule MIG we add the security level of the thread to the write effect to prevent migrations of threads owning low references to depend on high information. The motivation for this is that the mere arrival of a thread and its references to another domain might trigger the execution of other threads that were suspended on an access to a low reference, as in the following program:

$$d_1[\{(\text{if } (? \; n_1.x_H) \text{ then goto } d_2 \text{ else } ())^{n_1}\}, \{n_1.y_L \mapsto 1\}] \parallel d_2[\{(n_1.y_L :=^? 0)^{n_2}\}, \emptyset]$$

Notice that the rule COND rejects thread n in a standard manner, since $H \not\preceq L$.

In rules DER and ASS, the termination effect is updated with the level of the thread that owns the foreign reference we want to access. Without this restriction, suspension on an access to an absent reference could be unblocked by other threads, as is illustrated by the following example:

$$d[\,(\text{if } a_H \text{ then } (\text{goto } d_1) \text{ else } (\text{goto } d_2))^{m_j}, \{m_j.x_\top \mapsto 42\}\,] \parallel$$
$$\parallel d_1[\,((m_j.x_\top :=^? 0); (n_{1k_1}.y_L :=^? 0))^{n_{1k_1}}, S_1\,] \parallel$$
$$\parallel d_2[\,((m_j.x_\top :=^? 0); (n_{2k_2}.y_L :=^? 0))^{n_{2k_2}}, S_2\,]$$

Then, depending on the value of the high reference a, different low assignments would occur to the low references $n_1.y_L$ and $n_2.y_L$. To see why we can take j for preventing the leak from a_H to $n_1.y_L, n_2.y_L$, notice that (by MIG and COND) $H \preceq j$. The same example can show a potential leak of information about the positions of the threads n_1 and n_2 via their own low variables $n_1.y_L, n_2.y_L$. This also accounts for updating the termination level of the assignments $(m_j.x_\top :=^? 0)$ and $(m_j.x_\top :=^? 0)$ with the security levels k_1 and k_2, respectively.

The previous example shows how migration of a thread can result in an information leak from a high variable to a lower one via an "observer" thread. It is the ability of the observer thread to detect the presence of the first thread that allows the leak. However, one must also prevent the case where it is the thread itself that reveals that information, like in the following simple example:

$$d[\,(n.u_L :=^? 0)^{m_j}, \emptyset\,]$$

This program is insecure if $j \not\preceq L$, and it is rejected by the condition $j \preceq_G l$ in rule ASS. Notice that, in the typing rule, for the cases where $m = n$ the condition is satisfied anyway due to the meaning of j.

We now give a safety property of our type system:

Theorem 1 (Subject reduction). *If* $\Sigma; \Gamma \vdash_G^{\Sigma(m_j)} M : s, \tau$ *and* $\langle T, M^{m_j}, S\rangle$ $\xrightarrow[F]{N^{n_l}} \langle T', M'^{m_j}, S'\rangle$, *then* $\exists s'$ *such that* $\Sigma; \Gamma \vdash_G^{\Sigma(m_j)} M' : s', \tau$, *where* $s'.r \preceq s.r$, $s.w \preceq s'.w$ *and* $s'.t \preceq s.t$. *Furthermore, if* $N^{n_l} \neq ()$, *then* $\exists \bar{n}, s''$ *such that* $\Sigma, ? : \bar{n}_l; \Gamma \vdash_G^{\bar{n}_l} N : s''$, unit *where* $\bar{n}$ *is fresh in* Σ, $j \preceq_G l$ *and* $s.w \preceq s''.w$.

This result states that computation preserves the type of threads, and that as the effects of an expression are performed, the security effects of the thread "weaken". We now state the main result of the paper, saying that our type system only accepts threads that can securely run in a network with other typable threads.

Theorem 2 (Soundness). *Consider a set of threads P and an injective mapping Σ from decorated thread names to decorated thread identifiers, such that* $\text{dom}(\Sigma) = \text{tn}(P)$. *If for all $M^{m_j} \in P$ we have that $\exists \Gamma, s, \tau . \Sigma; \Gamma \vdash_\emptyset^{\Sigma(m_j)} M : s, \tau$, then P satisfies the non-disclosure policy for networks.*

This result is compositional, in the sense that it is enough to verify the typability of each thread separately in order to ensure non-disclosure for the whole network. Having the empty set as the flow policy of the context means that there is no global flow policy that encompasses the whole network. One could easily prove non-disclosure with respect to a certain global flow policy G by requiring the typability of all the threads with respect to G. However, by choosing the empty global flow policy we stress the decentralized nature of our setting.

5   Conclusion and Related Work

To the best of our knowledge, this paper is the first to study insecure information flows that are introduced by mobility in the context of a distributed language with states. We have identified a new form of security leaks, the *migration leaks*, and provided a sound type system for rejecting them. The discussion on related work will focus on type-based approaches for enforcing information flow control policies in settings with concurrency, distribution or mobility.

A first step towards the study of confidentiality for distributed systems is to study a language with concurrency. Smith and Volpano [SV98] proved non-interference for an imperative multi-threaded language. They identified the *termination leaks* that appear in concurrent contexts but that are not problematic in sequential settings. This line of study was pursued by considering increasingly expressive languages and refined type systems [Smi01, BC02, AB05, Bou05]. In the setting of synchronous concurrent systems, new kinds of termination leaks – the *suspension leaks* – are to be handled. A few representative studies include [Sab01, ABC04]. Already in a distributed setting, but restricting interaction between domains to the exchange of values (no code mobility), Mantel and Sabelfeld [SM02] provided a type system for preserving confidentiality for different kinds of channels over a publicly observable medium.

Progressing rather independently we find a field of work on mobile calculi based on purely functional concurrent languages. To mention a few representative papers, we have Honda *et al.*'s work on for π-calculus [HVY00], and Hennessy and Riely's study for the security π-calculus [HR00]. The closest to the present work is the one by Bugliesi *et al.* [CBC02], for Boxed Ambients [BCC01], a purely functional calculus based on the mobility of *ambients*. Since ambient names correspond simultaneously to places of computation, subjects of migration, and channels for passing values, it is hard to establish a precise correspondence between the two type systems. Nevertheless, it is clear that the knowledge of the position of an ambient of level l is considered as l-level information, and that migration is also identified as a way of leaking the positions of ambients, though the dangerous usages of migration are rejected rather differently.

Sharing our aim of studying the distribution of code under decentralized security policies, Zdancewic *et al.* [ZZNM02] have however set the problem in a very different manner. They have considered a distributed system of potentially corrupted hosts and of principals that have different levels of trust on these hosts. They then proposed a way of partitioning the program and distributing the resulting parts over hosts that are trusted by the concerned principals.

Acknowledgments

I would like to thank Gérard Boudol, Ilaria Castellani, Jan Cederquist, Matthew Hennessy, Tamara Rezk and the anonymous referees for insightful comments at different stages of this work. This research was partially funded by the PhD scholarship POSI/SFRH/BD/7100/2001 and by the French ACI Project CRISS.

References

[AB05]   A. Almeida Matos and G. Boudol. On declassification and the non-disclosure policy. In *CSFW*, 2005.

[ABC04]   A. Almeida Matos, G. Boudol, and I. Castellani. Typing noninterference for reactive programs. In *FCS*, volume 31 of *TUCS General Publications*, 2004.

[BC02]   G. Boudol and I. Castellani. Noninterference for concurrent programs and thread systems. *Theoretical Computer Science*, 281(1):109–130, 2002.

[BCC01]   M. Bugliesi, G. Castagna, and S. Crafa. Boxed ambients. In *TACS*, volume 2215 of *LNCS*, 2001.

[BCGL02]   G. Boudol, I. Castellani, F. Germain, and M. Lacoste. Analysis of formal models of distribution and mobility: state of the art. Mikado D1.1.1, 2002.

[Bou04]   G. Boudol. ULM, a core programming model for global computing. In *ESOP*, volume 2986 of *LNCS*, 2004.

[Bou05]   G. Boudol. On typing information flow. In *ICTAC*, LNCS, 2005.

[CBC02]   S. Crafa, M. Bugliesi, and G. Castagna. Information flow security for boxed ambients. In *F-WAN*, volume 66(3) of *ENTCS*, 2002.

[Den76]   D. E. Denning. A lattice model of secure information flow. *Communications of the ACM*, 19(5):236–243, 1976.

[GM82]   J. A. Goguen and J. Meseguer. Security policies and security models. In *Symposium on Security and Privacy*, 1982.

[HR00]   M. Hennessy and J. Riely. Information flow vs resource access in the asynchronous pi-calculus. In *ICALP'00*, volume 1853 of LNCS, 2000.

[HVY00]   K. Honda, V. Vasconcelos, and N. Yoshida. Secure information flow as typed process behaviour. In *ESOP*, volume 1782 of LNCS, 2000.

[LG88]   J. M. Lucassen and D. K. Gifford. Polymorphic effect systems. In *POPL*, 1988.

[ML98]   A. Myers and B. Liskov. Complete, safe information flow with decentralized labels. In *Symposium on Security and Privacy*, 1998.

[Sab01]   A. Sabelfeld. The impact of synchronization on secure information flow in concurrent programs. In *Andrei Ershov International Conference on Perspectives of System Informatics*, 2001.

[SM02]   A. Sabelfeld and H. Mantel. Static confidentiality enforcement for distributed programs. In *SAS*, volume 2477 of LNCS, 2002.

[SM03]   A. Sabelfeld and A. Myers. Language-based information-flow security. *Journal on Selected Areas in Communications, 21(1)*, 2003.

[Smi01]   Geoffrey Smith. A new type system for secure information flow. In *CSFW*, 2001.

[SS05]   A. Sabelfeld and D. Sands. Dimensions and principles of declassification. In *CSFW*, 2005.

[SV98]   G. Smith and D. Volpano. Secure information flow in a multi-threaded imperative language. In *POPL*, 1998.

[VSI96]   D. Volpano, G. Smith, and C. Irvine. A sound type system for secure flow analysis. *Journal of Computer Security*, 4(3), 1996.

[ZZNM02]   S. Zdancewic, L. Zheng, N. Nystrom, and A. C. Myers. Secure program partitioning. *ACM Transactions in Computer Systems*, 20(3):283–328, 2002.

Quantitative Models and Implicit Complexity

Ugo Dal Lago[1] and Martin Hofmann[2]

[1] Dipartimento di Scienze dell'Informazione
Università di Bologna
dallago@cs.unibo.it
[2] Institut für Informatik
Ludwig-Maximilians-Universität, München
mhofmann@informatik.uni-muenchen.de

Abstract. We give new proofs of soundness (all representable functions on base types lies in certain complexity classes) for Elementary Affine Logic, LFPL (a language for polytime computation close to realistic functional programming introduced by one of us), Light Affine Logic and Soft Affine Logic. The proofs are based on a common semantical framework which is merely instantiated in four different ways. The framework consists of an innovative modification of realizability which allows us to use resource-bounded computations as realisers as opposed to including all Turing computable functions as is usually the case in realizability constructions. For example, all realisers in the model for LFPL are polynomially bounded computations whence soundness holds by construction of the model. The work then lies in being able to interpret all the required constructs in the model. While being the first entirely semantical proof of polytime soundness for light logics, our proof also provides a notable simplification of the original already semantical proof of polytime soundness for LFPL. A new result made possible by the semantic framework is the addition of polymorphism and a modality to LFPL thus allowing for an internal definition of inductive datatypes.

1 Introduction

In recent years, a large number of characterizations of complexity classes based on logics and lambda calculi have appeared. At least three different principles have been exploited, namely linear types [3,10], restricted modalities in the context of linear logic [8,1,13] and non-size-increasing computation [9]. Although related one to the other, these systems have been studied with different, often unrelated methodologies and few results are known about relative intentional expressive power. We believe that this area of implicit computational complexity needs unifying frameworks for the analysis of quantitative properties of computation. This would help to improve the understanding of existing systems. More importantly, unifying frameworks can be used *themselves* as a foundation for controlling the use of resources inside programming languages.

In this paper, we introduce a new semantical framework which consists of an innovative modification of realizability. The main idea underlying our proposal

R. Ramanujam and S. Sen (Eds.): FSTTCS 2005, LNCS 3821, pp. 189–200, 2005.

lies in considering bounded-time algorithms as realizers instead of taking plain Turing Machines as is usually the case in realizability constructions. Bounds are expressed abstractly as elements of a monoid. We can define a model for a given (logical or type) system by choosing a monoid flexible enough to justify all the constructs in the system. The model can then be used to study the class of representable functions.

This allows us to give new proofs of soundness (all representable functions on base types lies in certain complexity classes) for Light Affine Logic (LAL, [1]), Elementary Affine Logic (EAL, [5]), LFPL [9] and Soft Affine Logic (SAL, [2]). While being the first entirely semantical proof of polytime soundness for light logics, our proof also provides a notable simplification of the original already semantical proof of polytime soundness for LFPL [9]. A new result made possible by the semantic framework is the addition of polymorphism and a modality to LFPL.

The rest of the paper is organized as follows. This Section is devoted to a brief description of related work and to preliminaries. In Section 2 we introduce length spaces and show they can be used to interpret multiplicative linear logic with free weakening. Sections 3 and 4 are devoted to present instances of the framework together with soundness results for elementary, soft and light affine logics. Section 5 presents a further specialization of length spaces and a new soundness theorem for LFPL based on it.

An extended version of this paper is available [7].

Related-Work. Realizability has been used in connection with resource-bounded computation in several places. The most prominent is Cook and Urquhart work (see [4]), where terms of a language called PV^ω are used to realize formulas of bounded arithmetic. The contribution of that paper is related to ours in that realizability is used to show "polytime soundness" of a logic. There are important differences though. First, realizers in Cook and Urquhart [4] are typed and very closely related to the logic that is being realized. Second, the language of realizers PV^ω only contains first order recursion and is therefore useless for systems like LFPL or LAL. In contrast, we use untyped realizers and interpret types as certain partial equivalence relations on those. This links our work to the untyped realizability model HEO (due to Kreisel [12]). This, in turn, has also been done by Crossley et al. [6]. There, however, one proves externally that untyped realizers (in this case of bounded arithmetic formulas) are polytime. In our work, and this happens for the first time, the untyped realizers are used to give meaning to the logic and obtain polytime soundness as a corollary. Thus, certain resource bounds are built into the untyped realizers by their very construction. Such a thing is not at all obvious, because untyped universes of realizers tend to be Turing complete from the beginning due to definability of fixed-point combinators. We get around this problem through our notion of a resource monoid and addition of a certain time bound to Kleene applications of realizers. Indeed, we consider this as the main innovation of our paper and hope it to be useful elsewhere.

Preliminaries. In this paper, we rely on an abstract computational framework rather than a concrete one like Turing Machines. This, in particular, will simplify proofs.

Let $L \subseteq \Sigma^*$ be a set of finite sequences over the alphabet Σ. We assume a pairing function $\langle \cdot, \cdot \rangle : L \times L \to L$ and a length function $| \cdot | : L \to \mathbb{N}$ such that $|\langle x, y \rangle| = |x| + |y| + cp$ and $|x| \leq length(x)$, where $length(x)$ is the number of symbols in x and cp is a fixed constant. We assume a reasonable encoding of algorithms as elements of L. We write $\{e\}(x)$ for the (possibly undefined) application of algorithm $e \in L$ to input $x \in L$. We furthermore assume an abstract time measure $Time(\{e\}(x)) \in \mathbb{N}$ such that $Time(\{e\}(x))$ is defined whenever $\{e\}(x)$ is and, moreover, there exists a fixed polynomial p such that $\{e\}(x)$ can be evaluated on a Turing machine in time bounded by $p(Time(\{e\}(x)) + |e| + |x|)$ (this is related to the so-called invariance thesis [14]). By "reasonable", we mean for example that for any $e, d \in L$ there exists $d \circ e \in L$ such that $|d \circ e| = |d| + |e| + O(1)$ and $\{d \circ e\}(x) = \{d\}(y)$ where $y = \{e\}(x)$ and moreover $Time(\{d \circ e\}(x)) = Time(\{e\}(x)) + Time(\{d\}(y)) + O(1)$. We furthermore assume that the abstract time needed to compute $d \circ e$ from $\langle d, e \rangle$ is constant. Likewise, we assume that "currying" and rewiring operations such as $\langle x, \langle y, z \rangle \rangle \mapsto \langle \langle y, z \rangle, x \rangle$ can be done in constant time. However, we do allow linear (in $|x|$) abstract time for copying operations such as $x \mapsto \langle x, x \rangle$.

There are a number of ways to instantiate this framework. In the full version of this paper [7], the precise form of the assumptions we make as well as one instance based on call-by-value lambda-calculus are described.

2 Length Spaces

In this section, we introduce the category of length spaces and study its properties. Lengths will not necessarily be numbers but rather elements of a commutative monoid.

A *resource monoid* is a quadruple $M = (|M|, +, \leq_M, \mathcal{D}_M)$ where
(i) $(|M|, +)$ is a commutative monoid;
(ii) $\leq_M$ is a pre-order on $|M|$ which is compatible with $+$;
(iii) $\mathcal{D}_M : \{(\alpha, \beta) \mid \alpha \leq_M \beta\} \to \mathbb{N}$ is a function such that for every α, β, γ

$$\mathcal{D}_M(\alpha, \beta) + \mathcal{D}_M(\beta, \gamma) \leq \mathcal{D}_M(\alpha, \gamma)$$
$$\mathcal{D}_M(\alpha, \beta) \leq \mathcal{D}_M(\alpha + \gamma, \beta + \gamma)$$

and, moreover, for every $n \in \mathbb{N}$ there is α such that $\mathcal{D}_M(0, \alpha) \geq n$.
Given a resource monoid $M = (|M|, +, \leq_M, \mathcal{D}_M)$, the function $\mathcal{F}_M : |M| \to \mathbb{N}$ is defined by putting $\mathcal{F}_M(\alpha) = \mathcal{D}_M(0, \alpha)$. We abbreviate $\sigma + \ldots + \sigma$ (n times) as $n.\sigma$.

Let us try to give some intuition about these axioms. We shall use elements of a resource monoid to bound data, algorithms, and runtimes in the following way: an element φ bounds an algorithm e if $\mathcal{F}_M(\varphi) \geq |e|$ and, more importantly, whenever α bounds an input x to e then there must be a bound $\beta \leq_M \varphi + \alpha$ for the result $y = \{e\}(x)$ and, most importantly, the runtime of that computation must be bounded by $\mathcal{D}_M(\beta, \varphi + \alpha)$. So, in a sense, we have the option of either producing a large output fast or to take a long time for a small output. The "inverse triangular" law above ensures that the composition of two algorithms bounded by φ_1 and φ_2, respectively, can be bounded by $\varphi_1 + \varphi_2$ or a simple modification thereof. In particular, the contribution of the unknown intermediate result in a composition cancels out using that law. Another useful intuition is that $\mathcal{D}_M(\alpha, \beta)$ behaves like the difference $\beta - \alpha$, indeed, $(\beta - \alpha) + (\gamma - \beta) \le \gamma - \alpha$.

A *length space* on a resource monoid $M = (|M|, +, \le_M, \mathcal{D}_M)$ is a pair $A = (|A|, \Vdash_A)$, where $|A|$ is a set and $\Vdash_A \subseteq |M| \times L \times |A|$ is a (infix) relation satisfying the following conditions:
(i) If $\alpha, e \Vdash_A a$, then $\mathcal{F}_M(\alpha) \ge |e|$;
(ii) For every $a \in |A|$, there are α, e such that $\alpha, e \Vdash_A a$;
(iii) If $\alpha, e \Vdash_A a$ and $\alpha \le_M \beta$, then $\beta, e \Vdash_A a$;
(iv) If $\alpha, e \Vdash_A a$ and $\alpha, e \Vdash_A b$, then $a = b$.
The last requirement implies that each element of $|A|$ is uniquely determined by the (nonempty) set of it realisers and in particular limits the cardinality of any length space to the number of partial equivalence relations on L.

A *morphism* from length space $A = (|A|, \Vdash_A)$ to length space $B = (|B|, \Vdash_B)$ (on the same resource monoid $M = (|M|, +, \le_M, \mathcal{D}_M)$) is a function $f : |A| \to |B|$ such that there exist $e \in L \subseteq \Sigma^*$, $\varphi \in |M|$ with $\mathcal{F}_M(\varphi) \ge |e|$ and whenever $\alpha, d \Vdash_A a$, there must be β, c such that:
(i) $\beta, c \Vdash_B f(a)$;
(ii) $\beta \le_M \varphi + \alpha$;
(iii) $\{e\}(d) = c$;
(iv) $Time(\{e\}(d)) \le \mathcal{D}_M(\beta, \varphi + \alpha)$.
We call e a realizer of f and φ a majorizer of f. The set of all morphisms from A to B is denoted as $Hom(A, B)$. If f is a morphism from A to B realized by e and majorized by φ, then we will write $f : A \xrightarrow{e, \varphi} B$ or $\varphi, e \Vdash_{A \multimap B} f$.

Remark 1. It is possible to alter the time bound in the definition of a morphism to $Time(\{e\}(d)) \le \mathcal{D}_M(\beta, \varphi + \alpha)\mathcal{F}_M(\alpha + \varphi)$. This allows one to accommodate linear time operations by padding the majorizer for the morphism. All the subsequent proofs go through with this alternative definition, at the expense of simplicity and ease of presentation,

Given two length spaces $A = (|A|, \Vdash_A)$ and $B = (|B|, \Vdash_B)$ on the same resource monoid M, we can build $A \otimes B = (|A| \times |B|, \Vdash_{A \otimes B})$ (on M) where $\alpha, e \Vdash_{A \otimes B} (a, b)$ iff $\mathcal{F}_M(\alpha) \ge |e|$ and there are f, g, β, γ with

$$\beta, f \Vdash_A a;$$
$$\gamma, g \Vdash_B b;$$
$$e = \langle f, g \rangle;$$
$$\alpha \ge_M \beta + \gamma.$$

$A \otimes B$ is a well-defined length space due to the axioms on M.

Given A and B as above, we can build $A \multimap B = (Hom(A, B), \Vdash_{A \multimap B})$ where $\alpha, e \Vdash_{A \multimap B} f$ iff f is a morphism from A to B realized by e and majorized by α.

Lemma 1. *Length spaces and their morphisms form a symmetric monoidal closed category with tensor and linear implication given as above.*

A length space I is defined by $|I| = \{0\}$ and $\alpha, e \Vdash_A 0$ when $\mathcal{F}_M(\alpha) \geq |e|$. For each length space A there are isomorphisms $A \otimes I \simeq A$ and a unique morphism $A \to I$. The latter serves to justify full weakening.

For every resource monoid M, there is a length space $B_M = (\{0,1\}^*, \Vdash_{B_M})$ where $\alpha, e \Vdash_{B_M} t$ whenever e is a realizer for t and $\mathcal{F}_M(\alpha) \geq |e|$. The function s_0 (respectively, s_1) from $\{0,1\}^*$ to itself which appends 0 (respectively, 1) to the left of its argument can be computed in constant time in our computational model and, as a consequence, is a morphism from B_M to itself.

2.1   Interpreting Multiplicative Affine Logic

We can now formally show that second order multiplicative affine logic (i.e. multiplicative linear logic plus full weakening) can be interpreted inside the category of length spaces on any monoid M. Doing this will simplify the analysis of richer systems presented in following sections. Formulae of (intuitionistic) multiplicative affine logic are generated by the following productions:

$$A ::= \alpha \mid A \multimap A \mid A \otimes A \mid \forall \alpha.A$$

where α ranges over a countable set of atoms. Rules are reported in figure 1. A *realizability environment* is a partial function assigning length spaces (on the

---

Identity, Cut and Weakening.

$$\frac{}{A \vdash A} \; I \qquad \frac{\Gamma \vdash A \quad \Delta, A \vdash B}{\Gamma, \Delta \vdash B} \; U \qquad \frac{\Gamma \vdash A}{\Gamma, B \vdash A} \; W$$

Multiplicative Logical Rules.

$$\frac{\Gamma, A, B \vdash C}{\Gamma, A \otimes B \vdash C} \; L_\otimes \qquad \frac{\Gamma \vdash A \quad \Delta \vdash B}{\Gamma, \Delta \vdash A \otimes B} \; R_\otimes \qquad \frac{\Gamma \vdash A \quad \Delta, B \vdash C}{\Gamma, \Delta, A \multimap B \vdash C} \; L_\multimap \qquad \frac{\Gamma, A \vdash B}{\Gamma \vdash A \multimap B} \; R_\multimap$$

Second Order Logical Rules.

$$\frac{\vdash \Gamma, A[C/\alpha] \vdash B}{\Gamma, \forall \alpha.A \vdash B} \; L^\forall \qquad \frac{\Gamma \vdash A \quad \alpha \notin FV(\Gamma)}{\Gamma \vdash \forall \alpha.A} \; R^\forall$$

Fig. 1. Intuitionistic Multiplicative Affine Logic

---

same resource monoid) to atoms. Realizability semantics $[\![A]\!]_\eta^\mathscr{R}$ of a formula A on the realizability environment η is defined by induction on A:

$$[\![\alpha]\!]_\eta^{\mathscr{R}} = \eta(\alpha)$$
$$[\![A \otimes B]\!]_\eta^{\mathscr{R}} = [\![A]\!]_\eta^{\mathscr{R}} \otimes [\![B]\!]_\eta^{\mathscr{R}}$$
$$[\![A \multimap B]\!]_\eta^{\mathscr{R}} = [\![A]\!]_\eta^{\mathscr{R}} \multimap [\![B]\!]_\eta^{\mathscr{R}}$$
$$[\![\forall\alpha.A]\!]_\eta^{\mathscr{R}} = (|[\![\forall\alpha.A]\!]_\eta^{\mathscr{R}}|, \Vdash_{[\![\forall\alpha.A]\!]_\eta^{\mathscr{R}}})$$

where

$$|[\![\forall\alpha.A]\!]_\eta^{\mathscr{R}}| = \prod_{C \in \mathscr{U}} |[\![A]\!]_{\eta[\alpha \to C]}^{\mathscr{R}}|$$

$$\alpha, e \Vdash_{[\![\forall\alpha.A]\!]_\eta^{\mathscr{R}}} a \iff \forall C.\alpha, e \Vdash_{[\![A]\!]_{\eta[\alpha \to C]}^{\mathscr{R}}} a$$

Here $\mathscr{U}$ stands for the class of all length spaces. A little care is needed when defining the product since strictly speaking it does not exist for size reasons. The standard way out is to let the product range over those length spaces whose underlying set equals the set of equivalence classes of a partial equivalence relation on L. As already mentioned, every length space is isomorphic to one such. When working with the product one has to insert these isomorphisms in appropriate places which, however, we elide to increase readability.

If $n \geq 0$ and $A_1, \ldots, A_n$ are formulas, the expression $[\![A_1 \otimes \ldots \otimes A_n]\!]_\eta^{\mathscr{R}}$ stands for I if $n = 0$ and $[\![A_1 \otimes \ldots \otimes A_{n-1}]\!]_\eta^{\mathscr{R}} \otimes [\![A_n]\!]_\eta^{\mathscr{R}}$ if $n \geq 1$.

3   Elementary Length Spaces

In this section, we define a resource monoid $\mathcal{L}$ such that elementary affine logic can be interpreted in the category of length spaces on $\mathcal{L}$. We then (re)prove that functions representable in EAL are elementary time computable.

A *list* is either *empty* or $cons(n, l)$ where $n \in \mathbb{N}$ and l is itself a list. The sum $l + h$ of two lists l and h is defined as follows, by induction on l:

$$empty + h = h + empty = h;$$
$$cons(n, l) + cons(m, h) = cons(n + m, l + h).$$

For every $e \in \mathbb{N}$, binary relations $\leq_e$ on lists can be defined as follows
- $empty \leq_e l$ for every e;
- $cons(n, l) \leq_e cons(m, h)$ iff there is $d \in \mathbb{N}$ such that
  (i) $n \leq 3^e(m + e) - d$;
  (ii) $l \leq_d h$.

For every e and for every lists l and h with $l \leq_e h$, we define the natural number $\mathcal{D}_e(l, h)$ as follows:

$$\mathcal{D}_e(empty, empty) = 0;$$
$$\mathcal{D}_e(empty, cons(n, l)) = 3^e(n + e) + \mathcal{D}_{3^e(n+e)}(empty, l);$$
$$\mathcal{D}_e(cons(n, l), cons(m, h)) = 3^e(m + e) - n + \mathcal{D}_{3^e(m+e)-n}(l, h).$$

Given a list l, $!l$ stands for the list $cons(0, l)$. The depth $depth(l)$ of a list l is defined by induction on l: $depth(empty) = 0$ while $depth(cons(n, l)) = depth(l) +$

1. $|l|$ stands for the maximum integer appearing inside l, i.e. $|empty| = 0$ and $|cons(n, l)| = \max\{n, |l|\}$. For every natural number n, $[n]_{\mathcal{L}}$ stands for $cons(n, empty)$.

Relation $\leq_0$ and function $\mathcal{D}_0$ can be used to build a resource monoid on lists. $|\mathcal{L}|$ will denote the set of all lists, while $\leq_{\mathcal{L}}, \mathcal{D}_{\mathcal{L}}$ will denote $\leq_0$ and $\mathcal{D}_0$, respectively.

Lemma 2. $\mathcal{L} = (|\mathcal{L}|, +, \leq_{\mathcal{L}}, \mathcal{D}_{\mathcal{L}})$ *is a resource monoid.*

An *elementary length space* is a length space on the resource monoid $(|\mathcal{L}|, +, \leq_{\mathcal{L}}, \mathcal{D}_{\mathcal{L}})$. Given an elementary length space $A = (|A|, \Vdash_A)$, we can build the length space $!A = (|A|, \Vdash_{!A})$, where $l, e \Vdash_{!A} a$ iff $h, e \Vdash_A a$ and $l \geq_{\mathcal{L}} !h$. The construction $!$ on elementary length spaces serves to capture the exponential modality of elementary affine logic. Indeed, the following two results prove the existence of morphisms and morphisms-forming rules precisely corresponding to axioms and rules from **EAL**.

Lemma 3 (Basic Maps). *Given elementary length spaces A, B, there are morphisms:*

$$contr : !A \to !A \otimes !A$$
$$distr : !A \otimes !B \to !(A \otimes B)$$

where $contr(a) = (a, a)$ and $distr(a, b) = (a, b)$

Lemma 4 (Functoriality). *If $f : A \xrightarrow{e, \varphi} B$, then there is ψ such that $f : !A \xrightarrow{e, \psi} !B$*

Elementary bounds can be given on $\mathcal{F}_{\mathcal{L}}(l)$ depending on $|l|$ and $depth(l)$:

Proposition 1. *For every $n \in \mathbb{N}$ there is an elementary function $p_n : \mathbb{N} \to \mathbb{N}$ such that $\mathcal{F}_{\mathcal{L}}(l) \leq p_{depth(l)}(|l|)$.*

We emphasize that Proposition 1 does not assert that the mapping $(n, m) \mapsto p_n(m)$ is elementary. This, indeed, cannot be true because we know **EAL** to be complete for the class of elementary functions. If, however, $A \subseteq \mathcal{L}$ is such that $l \in A$ implies $depth(l) \leq c$ for a fixed c, then $(l \in A) \mapsto p_{depth(l)}(|l|)$ is elementary and it is in this way that we will use the above proposition.

3.1   Interpreting Elementary Affine Logic

EAL can be obtained by endowing multiplicative affine logic with a restricted modality. The grammar of formulae is enriched with a new production $A ::= !A$, while modal rules are reported in figure 2. Realizability semantics is extended by $[\![!A]\!]_\eta^{\mathcal{R}} = ![\![A]\!]_\eta^{\mathcal{R}}$.

Theorem 1. *Elementary length spaces form a model of* **EAL**.

Exponential Rules and Contraction.

$$\frac{\Gamma \vdash A}{!\Gamma \vdash !A} \; P \qquad \frac{\Gamma, !A, !A \vdash B}{\Gamma, !A \vdash B} \; C$$

Fig. 2. Intuitionistic Elementary Affine Logic

Now, consider the formula

$$List_{\mathsf{EAL}} \equiv \forall \alpha.!(\alpha \multimap \alpha) \multimap !(\alpha \multimap \alpha) \multimap !(\alpha \multimap \alpha).$$

Binary lists can be represented as cut-free proofs with conclusion $List_{\mathsf{EAL}}$. Suppose you have a proof $\pi :!^j List_{\mathsf{EAL}} \multimap !^k List_{\mathsf{EAL}}$. From the denotation $[\![\pi]\!]^{\mathscr{R}}$ we can build a morphism g from $[\![List_{\mathsf{EAL}}]\!]^{\mathscr{R}}$ to $B_{\mathcal{L}}$ by internal application to ε, s_0, s_1. This map then induces a function $f : \{0,1\}^* \to \{0,1\}^*$ as follows: given $w \in \{0,1\}^*$, first compute a realizer for the closed proof corresponding to it, then apply g to the result.

Remark 2. Notice that elements of $B_{\mathcal{L}}$ can all be majorized by lists with unit depth. Similarly, elements of $[\![List_{\mathsf{EAL}}]\!]^{\mathscr{R}}$ corresponding to binary lists can be majorized by lists with bounded depth. This observation is essential to prove the following result.

Corollary 1 (Soundness). *Let π be an* EAL *proof with conclusion $!^j List_{\mathsf{EAL}} \multimap !^k List_{\mathsf{EAL}}$ and let $f : \{0,1\}^* \to \{0,1\}^*$ be the function induced by $[\![\pi]\!]^{\mathscr{R}}$. Then f is computable in elementary time.*

The function f in the previous result equals the function denoted by the proof π in the sense of [11]. This intuitively obvious fact can be proved straightforwardly but somewhat tediously using a logical relation or similar, see also [11].

4   Other Light Logics

Girard and Lafont have proposed other refinements of Linear Logic, namely Light Linear Logic and Soft Linear Logic, which capture polynomial time. We have succeeded in defining appropriate reource monoids for affine variants of these logics, too. In this way we can obtain proofs of "polytime soundness" by performing the same realizability interpretation as was exercised in the previous section. These instantiations of our framework are considerably more technical and difficult to find, but share the idea of the EAL interpretation which is why we have decided not to include them in this Extended Abstract. The interested reader may consult the full paper [7].

In the following section, we will elaborate in some more detail a rather different instantiation of our method.

5 Interpreting LFPL

In [9] one of us had introduced another language, LFPL, with the property that all definable functions on natural numbers are polynomial time computable. The key difference between LFPL and other systems is that a function defined by iteration or recursion is not marked as such using modalities or similar and can therefore be used as a step function of subsequent recursive definitions.

In this section we will describe a resource monoid $\mathcal{M}$ for LFPL, which will provide a proof of polytime soundness for that system. This is essentially the same as the proof from [9], but more structured and, hopefully, easier to understand.

The new approach also yields some new results, namely the justification of second-order quantification, a !-modality, and a new type of binary trees based on cartesian product which allows alternative but not simultaneous access to subtrees.

5.1 Overview of LFPL

LFPL is intuitionistic, affine linear logic, i.e., a linear functional language with $\otimes, \multimap, +, \times$. Unlike in the original presentation we also add polymorphic quantification here. In addition, LFPL has basic types for inductive datatypes, for example unary and binary natural numbers, lists, and trees. There is one more basic type, namely $\Diamond$, the resource type.

The recursive constructors for the inductive datatypes each take an additional argument of type $\Diamond$ which prevents one from invoking more constructor functions than one. Dually to the constructors one has iteration principles which make the $\Diamond$-resource available in the branches of a recursive definition. For example, the type $T(X)$ of X-labelled binary trees has constructors **leaf** : $T(X)$ and **node** : $\Diamond \multimap X \multimap T(X) \multimap T(X) \multimap T(X)$. The iteration principle allows one to define a function $T(X) \multimap A$ from closed terms A and $\Diamond \multimap X \multimap A \multimap A \multimap A$. In this paper we "internalise" the assumption of closedness using a !-modality.

5.2 A Resource Monoid for LFPL

The underlying set of $\mathcal{M}$ is the set of pairs (n, p) where $n \in \mathbb{N}$ is a natural number and p is a monotone polynomial in a single variable x. The addition is defined by $(n, p) + (m, r) = (n + m, p + r)$, accordingly, the neutral element is $0 = (0, 0)$. We have a submonoid $\mathcal{M}_0 = \{(n, p) \in \mathcal{M} \mid n = 0\}$.

To define the ordering we set $(n, p) \leq (m, r)$ iff $n \leq m$ and $(r - p)(x)$ is monotone and nonnegative for all $x \geq m$. For example, we have $(1, 42x) \leq (42, x^2)$, but $(1, 42x) \not\leq (41, x^2)$. The distance function is defined by

$$\mathcal{D}_{\mathcal{M}}((n, p), (m, r)) = (r - p)(m).$$

We can pad elements of $\mathcal{M}$ by adding a constant to the polynomial. The following is now obvious.

Lemma 5. *Both $\mathcal{M}$ and $\mathcal{M}_0$ are resource monoids.*

A simple inspection of the proofs in Section 2.1 shows that the realisers for all maps can be chosen from $\mathcal{M}_0$. This is actually the case for an arbitrary submonoid of a resource monoid. We note that realisers of elements may nevertheless be drawn from all of $\mathcal{M}$. We are thus led to the following definition.

Definition 1. *An* LFPL-*space is a length space over the resource monoid $\mathcal{M}$. A morphism from* LFPL *length space A to B is a morphism between length spaces which admits a majorizer from* $\mathcal{M}_0$.

Proposition 2. LFPL *length spaces with their maps form a symmetric monoidal closed category.*

Definition 2. *Let A be an* LFPL *space and $n \in \mathbb{N}$. The* LFPL *space A^n is defined by $|A^n| = |A|$ and $\alpha, e \Vdash_{A^n} a$ iff $\alpha \geq (2n - 1).\beta$ for some β such that $\beta, e \Vdash_A a$.*

So, A^n corresponds to the subset of $A \otimes \ldots \otimes A$ consisting of those tuples with all n components equal to each other. The factor $2n - 1$ ("modified difference") instead of just n is needed in order to justify the linear time needed to compute the copying involved in the obvious morphism from A^{m+n} to $A^m \otimes A^n$.

Let $\mathcal{I}$ be an index set and A_i, B_i be $\mathcal{I}$-indexed families of LFPL spaces. A uniform map from A_i to B_i consists of a family of maps $f_i : A_i \to B_i$ such that there exist α, e with the property that $\alpha, e \Vdash f_i$ for all i. Recall that, in particular, the denotations of proofs with free type variables are uniform maps.

Proposition 3. *For each A there is a uniform (in m, n) map $A^{m+n} \to A^m \otimes A^n$. Moreover, A^1 is isomorphic to A.*

The LFPL-space $\Diamond$ is defined by $|\Diamond| = \{\Diamond\}$ and put $\alpha, d \Vdash_\Diamond \Diamond$ if $\alpha \geq (1, 0)$.

For each LFPL-space A we define LFPL-space $!A$ by $|!A| = |A|$ and $\alpha, t \Vdash_{!A} a$ if there exists $\beta = (0, p) \in \mathcal{M}_0$ with $\beta, t \Vdash_A a$ and $\alpha \geq (0, (x + 1)p)$.

Proposition 4. *There is an* LFPL *space $\Diamond$ and for each* LFPL *space A there is an* LFPL *space $!A$ with the following properties:*
(i) $|!A| = |A|$;
(ii) If $f : A \to B$ then $f : !A \to !B$;
(iii) $!(A \otimes B) \simeq !A \otimes !B$;
(iv) The obvious functions $!A \otimes \Diamond^n \to A^n \otimes \Diamond^n$ are a uniform map.
The last property means intuitively that with n "diamonds" we can extract n copies from an element of type $!A$ and get the n "diamonds" back for later use.

The proof of the last assertion relies on the fact that $(2n - 1, (2n - 1)p) \leq (2n - 1, (x + 1)p)$ for arbitrary n.

Definition 3. *Let T_i be a family of* LFPL *spaces such that $|T_i| = T$ independent of i. The* LFPL *space $\exists i.T_i$ is defined by $|\exists i.T_i| = |T|$ and $\alpha, e \Vdash_{\exists i.T_i} t$ iff $\alpha, e \Vdash_{T_i} t$ for some i.*

Note that if we have a uniform family of maps $T_i \to U$ where U does not depend on i then we obtain a map $\exists i.T_i \to U$ (existential elimination).

Conversely, if we have a uniform family of maps $U_i \to V_{f(i)}$ then we get a uniform family of maps $U_i \to \exists j.V_j$ (existential introduction). We will use an informal "internal language" to denote uniform maps which when formalised would amount to an extension of LFPL with indexed type dependency in the style of Dependent ML [15].

5.3   Inductive Datatypes

In order to interpret unary natural numbers, we define $N = \exists n.N_n$ where

$$N_n = \Diamond^n \otimes \forall\alpha.(\alpha \multimap \alpha)^n \multimap \alpha \multimap \alpha.$$

We can internally define a successor map $\Diamond \otimes N_n \to N_{n+1}$ as follows: starting from $d : \Diamond, c : \Diamond^n$ and $f : \forall\alpha.(\alpha \multimap \alpha)^n \multimap \alpha \multimap \alpha$ we obtain a member of $\Diamond^{n+1}$ (from d and c) and we define $g : \forall\alpha.(\alpha \multimap \alpha)^{n+1} \multimap \alpha \multimap \alpha$ as $\lambda(x^{A\multimap A}, y^{(A\multimap A)^n}).\lambda z^A.x(f\ y\ z)$. From this, we obtain a map $\Diamond \otimes N \to N$ by existential introduction and elimination.

Of course, we also have a constant zero $I \to N_0$ yielding a map $I \to N$ by existential introduction.

Finally, we can define an iteration map $N_n \multimap !(\Diamond \otimes A \multimap A) \multimap A \multimap A$ as follows: Given $(d, f) \in N_n$ and $t :!(\Diamond \otimes A \multimap A)$, we unpack t using Proposition 4 to yield $u \in ((\Diamond \otimes A) \multimap A)^n$ as well as $d \in \Diamond^n$. Feeding these "diamonds" one by one to the components of u we obtain $v \in (A \multimap A)^n$. But then $f\ v$ yields the required element of $A \multimap A$. Existential elimination now yields a single map $N \multimap !(\Diamond \otimes A \multimap A) \multimap A \multimap A$.

In the full version of this paper [7], we also show how to interpret two different kinds of binary trees.

6   Conclusion

We have given a unified semantic framework with which to establish soundness of various systems for capturing complexity classes by logic and programming. Most notably, our framework has all of second-order multiplicative linear logic built in, so that only the connectives and modalities going beyond this need to be verified explicitly.

While resulting in a considerable simplification of previous soundness proofs, in particular for LFPL and LAL, our method has also lead to new results, in particular polymorphism and a modality for LFPL.

The method proceeds by assiging both abstract resource bounds in the form of elements from a resource monoid and resource-bounded computations to proofs (respectively, programs). In this way, our method can be seen as a combination of traditional Kleene-style realisability (which only assigns computations) and polynomial and quasi interpretation known from term rewriting (which only assigns resource bounds). An altogether new aspect is the introduction of more general notions of resource bounds than just numbers or polynomials as formalised in the concept of resource monoid. We thus believe that our methods can also be used to generalise polynomial interpretations to (linear) higher-order.

References

1. Andrea Asperti and Luca Roversi. Intuitionistic light affine logic. *ACM Transactions on Computational Logic*, 3(1):137–175, 2002.
2. Patrick Baillot and Virgile Mogbil. Soft lambda-calculus: a language for polynomial time computation. In *Proceedings of the 7th International Conference on Foundations of Software Science and Computational Structures*, 2004.
3. Stephen Bellantoni, Karl Heinz Niggl, and Helmut Schwichtenberg. Higher type recursion, ramification and polynomial time. *Annals of Pure and Applied Logic*, 104:17–30, 2000.
4. Stephen Cook and Alasdair Urquhart. Functional interpretations of feasible constructive arithmetic. *Annals of Pure and Applied Logic*, 63(2):103–200, 1993.
5. Paolo Coppola and Simone Martini. Typing lambda terms in elementary logic with linear constraints. In *Proceedings of the 6th International Conference on Typed Lambda-Calculus and Applications*, pages 76–90, 2001.
6. John Crossley, Gerald Mathai, and Robert Seely. A logical calculus for polynomial-time realizability. *Journal of Methods of Logic in Computer Science*, 3:279–298, 1994.
7. Ugo Dal Lago and Martin Hofmann. Quantitative models and implicit complexity. Arxiv Preprint. Available from http://arxiv.org/cs.LO/0506079, 2005.
8. Jean-Yves Girard. Light linear logic. *Information and Computation*, 143(2):175–204, 1998.
9. Martin Hofmann. Linear types and non-size-increasing polynomial time computation. In *Proceedings of the 14th IEEE Syposium on Logic in Computer Science*, pages 464–473, 1999.
10. Martin Hofmann. Safe recursion with higher types and BCK-algebra. *Annals of Pure and Applied Logic*, 104:113–166, 2000.
11. Martin Hofmann and Philip Scott. Realizability models for BLL-like languages. *Theoretical Computer Science*, 318(1-2):121–137, 2004.
12. Georg Kreisel. Interpretation of analysis by means of constructive functions of finite types. In Arend Heyting, editor, *Constructivity in Mathematics*, pages 101–128. North-Holland, 1959.
13. Yves Lafont. Soft linear logic and polynomial time. *Theoretical Computer Science*, 318:163–180, 2004.
14. Peter van Emde Boas. Machine models and simulation. In *Handbook of Theoretical Computer Science, Volume A: Algorithms and Complexity*, pages 1–66. Elsevier, 1990.
15. Hongwei Xi and Frank Pfenning. Dependent types in practical programming. In *Proceedings of the 26th ACM SIGPLAN Symposium on Principles of Programming Languages*, pages 214–227, 1999.

The MSO Theory of Connectedly Communicating Processes

P. Madhusudan[1], P.S. Thiagarajan[2], and Shaofa Yang[2]

[1] Dept. of Computer Science, University of Illinois at Urbana-Champaign
madhu@cs.uiuc.edu
[2] School of Computing, National University of Singapore
{thiagu,yangsf}@comp.nus.edu.sg

Abstract. We identify a network of sequential processes that communicate by synchronizing frequently on common actions. More precisely, we demand that there is a bound k such that if the process p executes k steps without hearing from process q—directly or indirectly—then it will never hear from q again. The non-interleaved branching time behavior of a system of connectedly communicating processes (CCP) is given by its event structure unfolding. We show that the monadic second order (MSO) theory of the event structure unfolding of every CCP is decidable. Using this result, we also show that an associated distributed controller synthesis problem is decidable for linear time specifications that do not discriminate between two different linearizations of the same partially ordered execution.

1 Introduction

Sequential systems can be represented as transition systems and their behaviors can be specified and verified using a variety of linear time and branching time logics. One can view the monadic second order (MSO) logic of 1-successor interpreted over strings as the canonical linear time logic and the MSO logic of n-successors interpreted over regular trees as the canonical branching time logic [12] for sequential systems. All other reasonable logics can be viewed as specializations of these two logics with expressive power often traded in for more efficient verification procedures.

In the case of concurrent systems the situation is similar in many respects. As for models, one can choose asynchronous transition systems or 1-safe Petri nets or some other equivalent formalism [15]. In the linear time setting, Mazurkiewicz traces—viewed as restricted labelled partial orders—constitute a nice generalization of sequences and the MSO logic of sequences can be smoothly extended to Mazurkiewicz traces [1]. In the branching time setting, it is clear that labelled event structures [15] are an appropriate extension of trees. Further, just as a transition system can be unwound into a (regular) tree, so can an asynchronous transition system or 1-safe Petri net be unwound into a (regular) labelled event structure [15]. One can also define a natural MSO logic for event structures in which the causality relation (a partial order) and the conflict relation are the

R. Ramanujam and S. Sen (Eds.): FSTTCS 2005, LNCS 3821, pp. 201–212, 2005.

non-logical predicates and quantification is carried out over individual and subsets of events. But at this stage, the correspondence between the sequential and concurrent settings breaks down.

One can say that the MSO theory—of the branching time behavior—of a transition system is the MSO theory of the tree obtained as its unwinding. According to Rabin's famous result [11], the MSO theory of *every* finite state transition system is decidable. In the concurrent setting, it is natural to say that the MSO theory—of the non-interleaved branching time behavior—of a finite asynchronous transition system is the MSO theory of the event structure obtained as its event structure unfolding. The trouble is, it is *not* the case that the MSO theory of every finite asynchronous transition system is decidable. Hence an interesting question is: what is the precise subclass of finite asynchronous transition systems for which the MSO theory is decidable?

We provide a partial answer to this question by exhibiting a subclass of finite asynchronous transition systems called, for want of a better term, Connectedly Communicating Processes (CCPs), whose MSO theories are decidable. As the name suggests, in a CCP, processes communicate with each other frequently. More precisely, there is a bound k such that if process p executes k steps without hearing from process q either directly or indirectly and reaches a state s, then starting from s it will never hear from q again, directly or indirectly. This class of systems *properly includes* two subclasses of 1-safe net systems that we know of, which have decidable MSO theories. These two subclasses are: the sequential net systems that do not exhibit any concurrency and dually, the conflict-free net systems which do not exhibit any branching—due to choices—in their behavior.

One motivation for studying branching time temporal logics in a non-interleaved setting has to do with distributed controller synthesis. More specifically, for distributed systems, where one is interested in strategies that are not dependent on global information—and hence can be synthesized in turn as a distributed controller—one needs to look at partial order based branching time behaviors. This is the case even if the controller must satisfy just a linear time specification. Here, as an application of our main result, we establish the decidability of a distributed controller synthesis problem where the plant model is based on a CCP and the specification is a robust (trace-closed) ω-regular language. By a robust language we mean one that does not discriminate between two different interleavings of the same partially ordered execution.

The communication criterion we impose is motivated by results in undecidability of distributed control. Most undecidability proofs in distributed control rely on the undecidability of *multi-player games with partial information* where the players (in our case processes) have an unbounded loss of information on the status of other players. Our restriction ensures that the processes communicate often enough so that this partial information stays bounded.

Our proof technique consists of extracting a regular tree from the event structure induced by a CCP with the nodes of this tree corresponding to the events of the event structure such that the causality relation is definable in the MSO theory of trees. This representation is obtained directly and broadly preserves the structure of the event structure. Similar ideas have been used in other—tenuously related—settings [3, 4].

Turning to more directly related work, a variety of branching time logics based on event structures have been proposed in the literature (see for instance [9] and the references therein) but few of them deal directly with the generalization of Rabin's result. In this context, a closely related work is [5] where it is shown, in present terms, that the MSO theories of *all* finite asynchronous transition systems are decidable *provided* set quantification is restricted to *conflict-free* subsets of events. It is however difficult to exploit this result to solve distributed controller synthesis problems.

Following the basic undecidablity result reported in [10], positive results in restricted settings are reported in [7, 8, 14]. However, [7] considers processes communicating via buffers as also [14] in a more abstract form. On the other hand, [8] imposes restrictions on communication patterns that are much more severe than the property we demand here. Our notion of strategies considered in this paper are local in the sense that each process's strategy is based on its local view of the global history, consisting of its own sequence of actions as well as the sequence of actions executed by other agents that it comes to know about through synchronizations. The work in [6] also considers view-based strategies, and shows that for simulations, the problem is undecidable. A more recent study that uses view-based strategies is [2]. This work is also based on asynchronous transition systems, but the restrictions placed on the plants concerned is in terms of the trace alphabet associated with the plant rather than the communication patterns. As a result, this subclass is incomparable with the subclass of CCPs. Finally, decentralized controllers have also been studied (see for instance [13] and its references) where the plant is monolithic but one looks for a set of controllers each of which can control only a subset of the controllable actions.

In the next section we formulate our model and in section 3 we show that the MSO theory of every CCP is decidable. We use this result in section 4 to solve a distributed controller synthesis problem. We discuss a number of possible extensions in the concluding part of the paper. Due to lack of space, many proofs are omitted and can be found in the technical report at www.comp.nus.edu.sg/~thiagu/fsttcs05.

2   Connectedly Communicating Processes

We fix a finite set of processes $\mathcal{P}$ and let p, q, range over $\mathcal{P}$. For convenience, we will often write a $\mathcal{P}$-indexed family $\{X_p\}_{p \in \mathcal{P}}$ simply as $\{X_p\}$. A distributed alphabet over $\mathcal{P}$ is a pair (Σ, loc) where Σ is a finite alphabet of actions and $loc : \Sigma \to 2^{\mathcal{P}} \setminus \{\emptyset\}$ identifies for each action, a nonempty set of processes (locations) that take part in each execution of the action. Σ_p is the set of actions that p participates in and it is given by $\{a \mid p \in loc(a)\}$. Fix such a distributed alphabet for the rest of the paper.

We will formulate our model in terms of deterministic asynchronous transition systems. We impose determinacy only for convenience. All our results will go through, with minor complications, even in the absence of determinacy. An *asynchronous transition system* (ATS) over (Σ, loc) is a structure $\mathcal{A} = (\{S_p\}, s_{in}, \{\delta_a\}_{a \in \Sigma})$ where S_p is a finite set of p-states for each p and $s_{in} \in \prod_{p \in \mathcal{P}} S_p$. Further, $\delta_a \subseteq \prod_{p \in loc(a)} S_p \times \prod_{p \in loc(a)} S_p$ for each a. The ATS $\mathcal{A}$ is deterministic if for each a, $(s_a, s'_a), (s_a, s''_a) \in \delta_a$ implies $s'_a = s''_a$. From now on we will implicitly assume that the ATSs we encounter are deterministic. Members of $\prod_{p \in \mathcal{P}} S_p$ are referred to as global states. It will be convenient to view the global state s as a map from $\mathcal{P}$ into $\bigcup S_p$ such that $s(p) \in S_p$ for every p. For the global state s and $P \subseteq \mathcal{P}$, we will let s_P denote the map s restricted to P. An example of an asynchronous transition system is shown in figure 1(i), where the locations of an action is assumed are the components in which it appears as a label of a local transition.

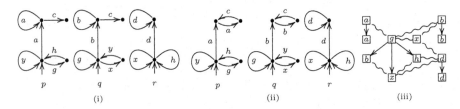

Fig. 1.

The dynamics of $\mathcal{A}$ is given by a transition system $TS_{\mathcal{A}} = (RS_{\mathcal{A}}, s_{in}, \Sigma, \rightarrow_{\mathcal{A}})$ where $RS_{\mathcal{A}} \subseteq \prod_{p \in \mathcal{P}} S_p$, the set of reachable global states, and $\rightarrow_{\mathcal{A}} \subseteq RS_{\mathcal{A}} \times \Sigma \times RS_{\mathcal{A}}$ are least sets satisfying: Firstly, $s_{in} \in RS_{\mathcal{A}}$. Secondly, suppose $s \in RS_{\mathcal{A}}$ and $s' \in \prod_{p \in \mathcal{P}} S_p$ such that $(s_P, s'_P) \in \delta_a$ and $s_Q = s'_Q$ where $P = loc(a)$ and $Q = \mathcal{P} \setminus P$. Then $s' \in RS_{\mathcal{A}}$ and $s \xrightarrow{a}_{\mathcal{A}} s'$. We extend $\rightarrow_{\mathcal{A}}$ to sequences in Σ^* in the obvious way. We define $L(\mathcal{A}) = \{\sigma \in \Sigma^* \mid \exists s. \, s_{in} \xrightarrow{\sigma}_{\mathcal{A}} s\}$.

We shall use (Mazurkiewicz) trace theory to capture the notion of connectedly communicating. It will also come in handy for defining the event structure semantics of asynchronous transition systems. We first recall that a trace alphabet is a pair (Γ, I) where Γ is a finite alphabet set and $I \subseteq \Gamma \times \Gamma$ is an irreflexive and symmetric relation called the *independence relation*. The trace alphabet (Σ, I) induced by the distributed alphabet (Σ, loc) is given by : $a \, I \, b$ iff $loc(a) \cap loc(b) = \emptyset$. Clearly I is irreflexive and symmetric. We let $D = (\Sigma \times \Sigma) \setminus I$ denote the dependency relation. The independence relation is extended to Σ^* via: $\sigma \, I \, \sigma'$ iff $a \, I \, b$ for every letter a that appears in σ and every letter b that appears in σ'. In what follows, we let σ, σ' range over Σ^*. As usual, $\sim_I$ is the least equivalence relation contained in $\Sigma^* \times \Sigma^*$ such that $\sigma a b \sigma' \sim_I \sigma b a \sigma'$ whenever $a \, I \, b$. We let $\sigma \upharpoonright p$ be the Σ_p-projection of σ. It is the sequence obtained by erasing from σ all appearances of letters that are not in Σ_p. We define $|\sigma|_p = |\sigma \upharpoonright p|$ where $|\tau|$ denotes the length of the sequence τ. In what follows, we will often write $\sim$ instead of $\sim_I$.

We say that two processes p and q are *separated in* σ if there exist $\tau, \tau' \in \Sigma^*$ such that $\sigma \sim \tau \tau'$ and $\tau \, I \, \tau'$ and $|\tau|_q = |\tau'|_p = 0$. Thus in the execution represented by σ there can be no flow of information from q to p or conversely. The asynchronous transition system $\mathcal{A}$ is k-*communicating* if for every $s \in RS_{\mathcal{A}}$ and every p, q, the following condition is satisfied: Suppose $s \xrightarrow{\sigma}_{\mathcal{A}} s'$ and $|\sigma|_p \geq k$ and $|\sigma|_q = 0$. Then p and q are separated in σ' for any $s' \xrightarrow{\sigma'}_{\mathcal{A}} s''$.

We shall say that $\mathcal{A}$ is *connectedly communicating* iff it is k-communicating for some k. Clearly $\mathcal{A}$ is connectedly communicating iff it is K-communicating where K is at most $|RS_{\mathcal{A}}|$. Furthermore, one can effectively determine whether $\mathcal{A}$ is connectedly communicating. From now on we will often refer to a finite deterministic connectedly communicating ATS as a CCP. The ATS shown in figure 1(ii) is a CCP while the one shown in figure 1(i) is not. Note that the two ATSs are based on the same distributed alphabet.

3   Decidability

We wish to prove that the MSO theory of the unfolding of every CCP is decidable. To formulate this result we begin with a brief account of event structures.

An event structure (often called a prime event structure) is a triple $ES = (E, \leq, \#)$ where $(E, \leq)$ is a poset such that for every $e \in E$, $\downarrow e = \{e' \in E \mid e' \leq e\}$ is a finite set. And $\# \subseteq E \times E$ is an irreflexive and symmetric relation such that, for every e_1, e_2 and e_3, if $e_1 \# e_2$ and $e_2 \leq e_3$, then $e_1 \# e_3$. E is the set of events, $\leq$ the causality relation and $\#$ the conflict relation. The minimal causality relation $\lessdot$ is defined as: $e \lessdot e'$ iff $e < e'$ and for every e'', if $e \leq e'' \leq e'$, then $e'' = e$ or $e'' = e'$. A Σ-labelled event structure is a structure $(E, \leq, \#, \lambda)$ where $(E, \leq, \#)$ is an event structure and $\lambda : E \to \Sigma$ a labelling function.

The non-interleaved branching time behavior of $\mathcal{A}$ is naturally given by its event structure unfolding [15]. This Σ-labelled event structure denoted $ES_{\mathcal{A}}$ is obtained as follows. We first note that $L(\mathcal{A})$ is a trace-closed subset of Σ^* in the sense if $\sigma \in L(\mathcal{A})$ and $\sigma \sim \sigma'$ then $\sigma' \in L(\mathcal{A})$ as well. For a non-null sequence $\sigma \in \Sigma^*$, let $last(\sigma)$ denote the last letter appearing in σ. In the present context, we shall view a (Mazurkiewicz) trace as a $\sim$-equivalence class of strings and denote the $\sim$-equivalence class containing the string σ as $[\sigma]_{\sim}$ and often drop the subscript $\sim$. The partial ordering relation $\sqsubseteq$ over traces is given by : $[\sigma] \sqsubseteq [\sigma']$ iff there exists σ'' in $[\sigma']$ such that σ is a prefix of σ''. A trace $[\sigma]$ is *prime* iff σ is non-null and for every σ' in $[\sigma]$, $last(\sigma) = last(\sigma')$. Thus for a prime trace $[\sigma]$, we can set $last([\sigma]) = last(\sigma)$. Now, $ES_{\mathcal{A}}$ is defined to be the structure $(E, \leq, \#, \lambda)$ where

- $E = \{[\sigma] \mid \sigma \in L(\mathcal{A})$ and $[\sigma]$ is prime$\}$.
- $\leq$ is $\sqsubseteq$ restricted to $E \times E$.
- $\#$ is given by: $e \# e'$ iff there does *not* exist $\sigma \in L(\mathcal{A})$ such that $e \sqsubseteq [\sigma]$ and $e' \sqsubseteq [\sigma]$, for every $e, e' \in E$.
- $\lambda(e) = last(e)$, for every $e \in E$.

It is easy to check that $ES_{\mathcal{A}}$ is a Σ-labelled event structure. In fact, the labelling function λ will respect the dependency relation D in the sense that if $\lambda(e) D \lambda(e')$ then it will be the case that $e \leq e'$ or $e' \leq e$ or $e \# e'$. And this will endow $ES_{\mathcal{A}}$

with a great deal of additional structure. In particular, it will let us define its MSO theory using just the $\prec$ relation and the labelling function as it will turn out below. In what follows, we will often write ES_A as just ES.

In figure 1(iii) we show an initial fragment of the event structure unfolding of the system shown in figure 1(ii). As usual, directed arrows represent members of the $\prec$ relation and the squiggly edges represent the "minimal" members of the $\#$ relation. The relations $\leq$ and $\#$ are to be deduced using the transitivity of $\leq$ and the conflict inheritance axiom satisfied by an event structure.

We now define the syntax of the MSO logic over ES_A as:

$$MSO(ES_A) ::= R_a(x) \mid x \prec y \mid x \in X \mid \exists x\,(\varphi) \mid \exists X(\varphi) \mid \sim \varphi \mid \varphi_1 \vee \varphi_2 \ ,$$

where $a \in \Sigma$, $x, y, \ldots$ are individual variables and $X, Y, \ldots$ are set variables. An interpretation $\mathcal{I}$ assigns to every individual variable an event in E and every set variable, a subset of E. The notion of ES satisfying a formula φ under an interpretation $\mathcal{I}$, denoted $ES \models_{\mathcal{I}} \varphi$, is defined in the obvious way. For example, $ES \models_{\mathcal{I}} R_a(x)$ iff $\lambda(\mathcal{I}(x)) = a$; $ES \models_{\mathcal{I}} x \prec y$ iff $\mathcal{I}(x) \prec \mathcal{I}(y)$.

It is a standard observation that $\leq$ can be defined in terms of $\prec$ in the presence of set quantification. We next observe that the conflict relation of ES_A admits an alternative characterization. Let the relation $\#_D$ be given by: $e \,\#_D\, e'$ iff $e \not\leq e'$ and $e' \not\leq e$ and $\lambda(e)\, D\, \lambda(e')$. Next define $\widehat{\#}$ as: $e\, \widehat{\#}\, e'$ iff there exist $e1$ and $e1'$ such that $e1 \,\#_D\, e1'$ and $e1 \leq e$ and $e1' \leq e'$. It is easy to verify that $\widehat{\#} = \#$ and that $\widehat{\#}$ is definable.

The MSO theory of ES is the set of sentences (formulas that do not have free occurrences of individual or set variables) given by: $\{\varphi \mid ES \models \varphi\}$. The MSO theory of ES is said to be decidable if there exists an effective procedure that determines for each sentence φ in $MSO(ES)$, whether $ES \models \varphi$. Finally, by the MSO theory of $\mathcal{A}$ we shall mean the MSO theory of ES_A. It is not difficult to show that the MSO theory of the asynchronous transition system in figure 1(i) is undecidable (as easily shown in our technical report). Our main result is:

Theorem 1. *Let $\mathcal{A}$ be a CCP. Then the MSO theory of $\mathcal{A}$ is decidable.*

Through the rest of this section, we assume $\mathcal{A}$ is k-communicating where $k \leq |RS_A|$. Let $TR = (\Sigma^*, \{succ_a\}_{a \in \Sigma})$ be the infinite Σ-tree, where $succ_a = \{(u, ua) \mid u \in \Sigma^*\}$. In what follows, we shall denote the standard MSO logic of n-successors $(|\Sigma| = n)$ interpreted over TR as $MSO(TR)$. Its syntax is:

$$MSO(TR) ::= succ_a(x, y) \mid x \in X \mid \exists x\,(\varphi) \mid \exists X(\varphi) \mid \sim \varphi \mid \varphi_1 \vee \varphi_2 \ .$$

The semantics is the standard one [12]. We shall show that the structure $(E, \prec, \lambda)$ can be embedded in TR and that this embedding can be defined in $MSO(TR)$. This will at once yield theorem 1 by the result that $MSO(TR)$ is decidable [11].

Through the rest of the paper, we fix a total order lex on Σ. Often, we refer to this order implicitly, for example, by speaking of a being less than b. Clearly lex induces a total order over Σ^* which we shall refer to as the lexicographic order. For an event e in E with $e = [\sigma]$, we let $lin(e)$ be the lexicographically least member in $[\sigma]$. Set $LEX_A = \{lin(e) \mid e \in E\}$. In what follows, we will write LEX_A as just LEX. Clearly $LEX \subseteq \Sigma^*$ and hence members of LEX can be looked upon as distinguished nodes in the tree TR. A pleasant fact is that LEX is definable in $MSO(TR)$.

Lemma 2. *One can effectively construct a formula $\varphi_{LEX}(x)$ with one free individual variable x such that for any interpretation $\mathcal{I}$, $TR \models_{\mathcal{I}} \varphi_{LEX}(x)$ iff $\mathcal{I}(x) \in LEX$.*

Proof. It is easy to show that $L_{events} = \{\sigma \mid [\sigma] \in E\}$ is a regular trace-closed subset of Σ^* and is hence a regular trace language. It is known that the collection $\widehat{L}_{lex}$ obtained by picking the lexicographically least member of each $\sim$-equivalence class of a regular trace language $\widehat{L}$ is, in turn, a regular language [1]. Thus LEX is a regular subset of Σ^* and we can effectively construct from $\mathcal{A}$, a deterministic finite state automaton accepting LEX. Further, one can describe the successful runs of this automaton in the form of a formula $\varphi_{LEX}(x)$. □

Define now the relation $<_{LEX} \subseteq LEX \times LEX$ by: $\sigma <_{LEX} \sigma'$ iff $[\sigma] < [\sigma']$ in ES_A. Define also the map λ_{LEX} as $\lambda_{LEX}(\sigma) = last(\sigma)$ for every $\sigma \in LEX$. It now follows that $(LEX, <_{LEX}, \lambda_{LEX})$ is isomorphic to the structure $(E, <, \lambda)$. Hence if we show that $<_{LEX}$ is definable in $MSO(TR)$ then we are done. In this light, the following result is crucial.

Lemma 3. *There exists a constant K (which can be effectively computed from $\mathcal{A}$) with the following property: Suppose $w = a_1 \ldots a_m, w' = b_1 \ldots b_n \in LEX$. Suppose further, $w <_{LEX} w'$ and w is not a prefix of w'. Then $|a_i a_{i+1} \ldots a_m| \leq K$, where i is the least index such that $a_i \neq b_i$.*

Proof. Let $e = [w]$ and $e' = [w']$ so that $e < e'$. It follows from the definition of ES that $w' \sim w\tau$ for some τ in Σ^+. Hence b_i is less than a_i. We show that $b_i \ I \ a_i a_{i+1} \ldots a_m$. This will easily yield that $|a_i a_{i+1} \ldots a_m| \leq k|\mathcal{P}|$, following the facts that $\mathcal{A}$ is k-communicating and $[w']$ is prime and $w' \sim wb_i\tau'$ for some τ' in Σ^+. Now suppose $b_i \ I \ a_i a_{i+1} \ldots a_m$ does not hold. Let j ($i \leq j \leq m$) be the least index such that $a_j \ D \ b_i$. A basic property of traces is that if $a \ D \ b$ then the $\{a, b\}$-projection of $\sigma 1$ is identical to the $\{a, b\}$-projection of $\sigma 2$ whenever $\sigma 1 \sim \sigma 2$. It follows that $a_j = b_i$. But then b_i being less than a_i would imply that $\widehat{w} = a_1 \ldots a_{i-1} b_i a_i \ldots a_{j-1} a_{j+1} \ldots a_m \sim w$ and clearly $\widehat{w}$ is lexicographically less than w, a contradiction. □

We can now show that $<_{LEX}$ is expressible in $MSO(TR)$.

Lemma 4. *One can effectively construct a formula $\varphi_<(x, y)$ in $MSO(TR)$ with two free individual variables x and y such that, for any interpretation $\mathcal{I}$, $TR \models_{\mathcal{I}} \varphi_<(x, y)$ iff $\mathcal{I}(x), \mathcal{I}(y) \in LEX$ and $\mathcal{I}(x) <_{LEX} \mathcal{I}(y)$.*

Proof. Let $w, w' \in LEX$. Consider the condition $C1$ given by:

C1: w is a proper prefix of w' and $last(w) \ D \ last(w')$
and $last(w) \ I \ w''$ where $w' = ww''$.

It is easy to see that if $C1$ is satisfied then $w \prec_{LEX} w'$ and moreover, $C1$ is definable in $MSO(TR)$. Let K be the constant established in lemma 3. Now consider the following conditions:

$$C2.1 : w = w_0 a_1 a_2 \ldots a_l \text{ with } l \leq K \text{ and}$$
$$w' = w_0 w'_1 a_1 w'_2 a_2 \ldots w'_l a_l w'_{l+1} \, last(w').$$
$$C2.2 : w'_i \ I \ a_j \text{ for } 1 \leq i \leq j \leq l \text{ and } a_l \ I \ w'_{l+1}.$$
$$C2.3 : a_l \ D \ last(w').$$

Let $C2$ be the conjunction of $C2.1$, $C2.2$ and $C2.3$. It is easy to see that if $C2$ is satisfied then $w \prec_{LEX} w'$ and also that $C2$ is definable in $MSO(TR)$. What takes some work is showing that if $w \prec_{LEX} w'$ then $C1$ or $C2$ is satisfied. This can however be achieved by faithfully applying the definitions of LEX and $\prec_{LEX}$.

□

We can now establish theorem 1. Define the map $\|\cdot\|$ from $MSO(ES_{\mathcal{A}})$ into $MSO(TR)$ inductively: $\|R_a(x)\| = \exists y \, succ_a(y, x)$ and $\|x < y\| = \varphi_\prec(x, y)$ where $\varphi_\prec(x, y)$ is the formula established in lemma 4. Next we define $\|x \in X\| = x \in X$. Further, $\|\exists x (\Psi)\| = \exists x (\varphi_{LEX}(x) \wedge \|\Psi\|)$ and $\|\exists X (\Psi)\| = \exists X ((\forall x \in X \varphi_{LEX}(x)) \wedge \|\Psi\|)$ where $\varphi_{LEX}(x)$ is the formula established in lemma 2 . Finally, $\|\sim \Psi\| = \sim \|\Psi\|$ and $\|\Psi 1 \vee \Psi 2\| = \|\Psi 1\| \vee \|\Psi 2\|$. It is now easy to show that $ES_{\mathcal{A}} \models \Psi$ iff $TR \models \|\Psi\|$ for each sentence Ψ. It is also easy to see that our decision procedure for determining the truth of the sentence Ψ in $MSO(ES_{\mathcal{A}})$ is non-elementary in the size of Ψ but not in k.

4   Controller Synthesis

Our goal here is to define a distributed plant model based on deterministic ATSs and show the decidability of the controller synthesis problem for CCPs.

A plant is a structure $\mathcal{A} = (\{S_p^{env}\}, \{S_p^{sys}\}, s_{in}, \Sigma^{env}, \Sigma^{sys}, \{\delta_a\}_{a \in \Sigma})$ where $(\{S_p\}, s_{in}, \{\delta_a\}_{a \in \Sigma})$ is a deterministic ATS over (Σ, loc), called the underlying ATS of $\mathcal{A}$ with $S_p = S_p^{env} \cup S_p^{sys}$ and $S_p^{env} \cap S_p^{sys} = \emptyset$ for each p. Further, $\{\Sigma^{env}, \Sigma^{sys}\}$ is a partition of Σ such that for each a in Σ^{env}, $|loc(a)| = 1$. Finally, suppose $(s_a, s'_a) \in \delta_a$ and $p \in loc(a)$. Then $s_a(p) \in S_p^{env}$ iff $a \in \Sigma^{env}$ and hence $loc(a) = \{p\}$.

The sets S_p^{env}, S_p^{sys} are respectively the p-environment and p-system states. The sets Σ^{env} and Σ^{sys} are the environment (uncontrollable) and system (controllable) actions respectively. Each component interacts with its local environment and these interactions are enabled only when the component is in one of its environment states. We note that although the underlying ATS is deterministic, in general, a menu of controllable actions involving different processes will be available for the controller at each stage as the plant evolves. This will be the case even for the local strategies we define below. Through the rest of the section, we fix a plant $\mathcal{A}$ as above. When talking about the behavioral aspects of $\mathcal{A}$, we shall identify it with its underlying ATS and will often drop the subscript $\mathcal{A}$. We will also say the plant is a CCP in case its underlying ATS is.

Members of $L(\mathcal{A})$ are referred to as *plays*. The set of infinite plays $L^\omega(\mathcal{A})$ is defined in the obvious way. We are interested in distributed strategies obtained by piecing together local strategies and the local views of a play will be instrumental in determining local strategies.

Let $\sigma = a_1 \ldots a_n$ be a play in $L(\mathcal{A})$. The *p-view* of σ denoted $\downarrow^p (\sigma)$ is the subsequence $a_{h_1} \ldots a_{h_m}$ such that $H = \{h_1, h_2, \ldots, h_m\}$ is the least subset of $\{1, 2, \ldots, n\}$ which satisfies: Firstly, h_m is the largest index in $\{1, 2, \ldots, n\}$ such that $p \in loc(a_{h_m})$. Secondly, if $i \in H$ and $j < i$ and $a_j \, D \, a_i$, then $j \in H$. In other words, $\downarrow^p (\sigma)$ is the maximum amount of the current play that p knows about where this knowledge is gathered by its participation in the actions that have occurred in the play *and* the information it acquires as a result of synchronizations with other agents.

It will be convenient to define the set of actions that can potentially occur at a local state. For $u \in S_p$ we let $act(u)$ be the set given by: $a \in \Sigma_p$ is in $act(u)$ iff there exists (s_a, s'_a) in δ_a with $s_a(p) = u$. A *p-strategy* is a function $f : L(\mathcal{A}) \to 2^{\Sigma_p}$ which satisfies: Suppose $\sigma \in L(\mathcal{A})$ and $s_{in} \xrightarrow{\sigma} s$ with $s(p) = u$. Then $f(\sigma) \subseteq act(u)$ and moreover $f(\sigma) = act(u)$ in case $u \in S_p^{env}$. Thus a p-strategy recommends a subset of the structurally possible Σ_p-actions at the current p-state. It does so without restricting in any way the environment's choices.

The p-strategy f is said to be *local* if it satisfies: for every $\sigma, \sigma' \in L(\mathcal{A})$, $\downarrow^p (\sigma) \sim \downarrow^p (\sigma')$ implies $f(\sigma) = f(\sigma')$. Hence a local p-strategy depends only on the (partially ordered!) p-view of the play.

We now define a distributed strategy $Str = \{Str_p\}$ to be a family of local p-strategies, one for every p. From now, unless otherwise stated, we shall say "p-strategy" to mean "local p-strategy" and "strategy" to mean a distributed strategy.

Let $Str = \{Str_p\}$ be a strategy. The set of plays according to Str denoted $L(Str)$ is defined inductively by: Firstly, $\varepsilon \in L(Str)$. Secondly, if $\sigma \in L(Str)$ and $\sigma a \in L(\mathcal{A})$ such that $a \in Str_p(\sigma)$ for every $p \in loc(a)$, then $\sigma a \in L(Str)$. That is, an action a is allowed to execute only when it is recommended by every process taking part in a. In what follows, we will assume without loss of generality that $TS_\mathcal{A}$ has no deadlocks; more precisely, every reachable global state has a successor state reachable via a transition. Thus if a play according to a strategy cannot be extended it is only due to the local strategies not being able to agree on executing any system action. We will say that a strategy Str is *non-blocking* in case every play in $L(Str)$ can be extended to a longer play in $L(Str)$. This notion does not rule out the possibility of a play being extended indefinitely by just the execution of environmental actions. However one can rule out such plays by choosing the specification suitably.

To define specifications, we first define the set of infinite plays according to the strategy Str denoted $L^\omega(Str)$ in the obvious way. A *specification* is an ω-regular subset of Σ^ω which is assumed to be presented in a finite way, say, as a Büchi automaton. Let L_{spec} be a specification. A strategy Str is winning for L_{spec} iff Str is non-blocking and $L^\omega(Str) \subseteq L_{spec}$. A winning strategy for L_{spec}

is called a *controller* for the pair $(\mathcal{A}, L_{spec})$. The controller synthesis problem we wish to solve is: given a pair $(\mathcal{A}, L_{spec})$ where $\mathcal{A}$ is a CCP, determine whether there exists a controller for L_{spec}. We will be mainly interested in showing here that this problem is effectively solvable if the specification is *robust*.

To pin down robustness, we extend $\sim$ to Σ^ω. This can be done in a number of equivalent ways. For our purposes it will do to define it as follows: Suppose $\sigma, \sigma' \in \Sigma^\omega$. Then $\sigma \sim \sigma'$ iff $\sigma \restriction p = \sigma' \restriction p$ for every p. We say that the specification L_{spec} is *robust* iff for every $\sigma, \sigma' \in \Sigma^\omega$, if $\sigma \in L_{spec}$ and $\sigma \sim \sigma'$, then $\sigma' \in L_{spec}$.

We can now state:

Theorem 5. *Given a CCP plant $\mathcal{A}$ and a robust specification L_{spec}, one can effectively determine whether there exists a controller for $(\mathcal{A}, L_{spec})$.*

In fact we can say much more as we point out in remarks following the proof of theorem 5.

4.1   Proof of Theorem 5

Throughout this subsection, we assume $\mathcal{A}$ is a CCP and L_{spec} is robust. We shall show that the existence of a controller for $(\mathcal{A}, L_{spec})$ can be asserted in $MSO(ES_{\mathcal{A}})$. The required result will then follow at once from theorem 1.

In what follows, we let $ES_{\mathcal{A}} = (E, \leq, \#, \lambda)$ and often write ES instead of $ES_{\mathcal{A}}$. A *configuration* of ES is a subset $c \subseteq E$ such that $\downarrow c = c$ (where $\downarrow c = \cup_{e \in c}(\downarrow e)$) and $(c \times c) \cap \# = \emptyset$. Let c be a finite configuration. Then it is well-known that the Σ-labelled poset $(c, \leq_c, \lambda_c)$ where $\leq_c$ and λ_c are the obvious restrictions, represents a trace in the following sense. The set of linearizations of $(c, \leq_c)$ (subjected to the point-wise application of λ_c) will be a trace, viewed as a $\sim$-equivalence class of strings. In fact finite and infinite configurations on the one hand and finite and infinite traces on the other hand, represent each other. It is not difficult to see that in $MSO(ES)$ one can construct a formula $infinite(X)$ with one free set variable X which asserts that X is an infinite set of events. Consequently, in $MSO(ES)$ one can define a formula $fin\text{-}conf(X)$ $(inf\text{-}conf(X))$ asserting that X is a finite (infinite) configuration.

Next we define, for $E' \subseteq E$, the p-view of E' denoted $p\text{-}view(E')$ to be the set of events given by: $e' \in p\text{-}view(E')$ iff there exists $e'' \in E'$ such that $e' \leq e''$ and $p \in loc(\lambda(e''))$. Again it is easy to see that we can define a formula $p\text{-}view(X, Y)$ asserting that Y is the p-view of X.

Now let Str be a strategy. From the definitions, it follows that $L(Str)$ is trace-closed. Hence for each $\sigma \in L(Str)$ we will have $[\sigma] \subseteq L(Str)$ and moreover, by the observation above, there will be a unique finite configuration in ES that corresponds to $[\sigma]$. We will say that E_{Str} is the *set of Str-events* and define it to be the set given by: $e \in E$ is in E_{Str} iff there exists $\sigma \in L(Str)$ such that $e = [\sigma]$. We will say that E' is *good* in case there exists a strategy Str such that E' is the set of Str-events. We can construct a formula $Good(X)$ which will assert that X is good. For arguing this, it will be convenient to assume the transition relation $\Rightarrow \subseteq C_{fin} \times E \times C_{fin}$ where C_{fin} is the set of finite configurations of ES

and $\Rightarrow$ is given by: $c \overset{e}{\Rightarrow} c'$ iff $e \notin c$ and $c' = c \cup \{e\}$. The formula $Good(X)$ will be a conjunction of the following properties all of which are easily definable in $MSO(ES)$.

- X is a nonempty set and for every finite configuration Y contained in X, if $Y \overset{e}{\Rightarrow} Y'$ and $\lambda(e) \in \Sigma^{env}$ then $Y' \subseteq X$.
- If Y is a finite configuration contained in X then there exists a finite configuration Y' such that $Y \subset Y' \subseteq X$.
- Suppose Y is a finite configuration contained in X, and $Y \overset{e}{\Rightarrow} Y'$. Suppose that for every p in $loc(a)$, where $a = \lambda(e)$, there exists $Y_p \subseteq X$ such that the p-view of Y_p is identical to the p-view of Y and $Y_p \overset{e1}{\Rightarrow} Y_p'$ with $\lambda(e1) = a$ and $Y_p' \subseteq X$. Then $Y' \subseteq X$.

All we need now is to argue that we can assert that every infinite play belonging to a good set meets the specification. But this is easy to do since L_{spec} is robust. It follows that L_{spec} in fact is an ω-regular trace language and is hence definable in the Monadic Second Order logic of infinite traces interpreted over the set of infinite traces generated by our trace alphabet (Σ, I) [1]. Denoting this logical language by $MSO(\Sigma, loc)$, we can assume, without loss of generality, that its syntax is *exactly* that of $MSO(ES)$ *but* interpreted over infinite traces represented as Σ-labelled partial orders. In particular, the $<$ refers to the partial order of the trace rather than the positional order of a linearization of the trace.

Now let Φ_{spec} be a sentence in $MSO(\Sigma, loc)$ such that the ω-regular trace language defined by it is precisely L_{spec}. We can now assert in $MSO(ES)$ that there exists X such that X is a good set and moreover, for every infinite configuration Y contained in X, the trace corresponding to Y satisfies Φ_{spec}. It is routine to show that this sentence, say $\Psi_{controller}$, is satisfiable in $MSO(ES)$ iff there exists a controller for $(\mathcal{A}, L_{spec})$.

5 Discussion

Here we informally sketch a number of additional results that one can derive for our ATSs. To start with, theorem 5 can be considerably strengthened. In case a controller exists then there exists a finite state one which can be effectively computed and synthesized as a (finite deterministic) CCP over (Σ, loc). This controller will synchronize with the plant on common actions and the resulting controlled behavior will meet the specification. Developing this result however requires additional work and machinery. It also requires us to work with TR, the tree representation of ES, rather than with ES itself. By adapting the arguments developed in [10] we can also show quite easily that the controller synthesis problem is undecidable for CCP plants in case the specification is allowed to be non-robust.

Clearly we can assume the specification for the controller synthesis problem to be given as a sentence in $MSO(ES)$ and our argument for decidability will extend smoothly. One can also assume that the plant itself is not a CCP but require, for robust specifications, the controller be a CCP. More precisely, we say that the strategy Str is k-*communicating* iff for every $\sigma \in L(Str)$, if $\sigma\sigma' \in L(Str)$ and $|\sigma'|_p \geq k$ and $|\sigma'|_q = 0$, then for every $\sigma\sigma'\sigma'' \in L(Str)$, p, q are separated in σ''. We say Str is *connectedly communicating* iff Str is k-communicating for some integer k. We conjecture that the k-communicating controller synthesis problem for a given k is decidable and in case such a controller exists, a finite state one exists as well and it can be effectively synthesized. It is also interesting to determine if the connectedly communicating controller synthesis problem is decidable. In other words, given a plant and a robust specification determine if there exists a k-communicating controller for some k. We conjecture that this problem is undecidable.

References

[1] V. Diekert and G. Rozenberg, editors. *The Book of Traces*. World Scientific, Singapore, 1995.

[2] P. Gastin, B. Lerman, and M. Zeitoun. Distributed games with causal memory are decidable for series-parallel systems. In *FSTTCS '04, LNCS 3328*, pages 275–286. Springer, 2004.

[3] D. Kuske. Regular sets of infinite message sequence charts. *Information and Computation*, 187:80–109, 2003.

[4] P. Madhusudan. Reasoning about sequential and branching behaviours of message sequence graphs. In *ICALP '00, LNCS 2076*, pages 396–407. Springer, 2000.

[5] P. Madhusudan. Model-checking trace event structures. In *LICS '03*, pages 371–380. IEEE Press, 2003.

[6] P. Madhusudan and P.S. Thiagarajan. Controllers for discrete event systems via morphisms. In *CONCUR '98, LNCS 1466*, pages 18–33. Springer, 1998.

[7] P. Madhusudan and P.S. Thiagarajan. Distributed control and synthesis for local specifications. In *ICALP '01, LNCS 2076*, pages 396–407. Springer, 2001.

[8] P. Madhusudan and P.S. Thiagarajan. A decidable class of asynchronous distributed controllers. In *CONCUR '02, LNCS 2421*, pages 145–160. Springer, 2002.

[9] W. Penczek. Model-checking for a subclass of event structures. In *TACAS '97, LNCS 1217*, pages 146–164. Springer, 1997.

[10] A. Pnueli and R. Rosner. Distributed reactive systems are hard to synthesize. In *FOCS '90*, pages 746–757. IEEE Press, 1990.

[11] M. Rabin. Decidability of second order theories and automata on infinite trees. *Trans. of AMS*, 141:1–35, 1969.

[12] W. Thomas. Automata on infinite objects. In *Handbook of Theoretical Comp. Sci., Vol. B*. Elsevier, 1990.

[13] S. Tripakis. Decentralized control of discrete event systems with bounded or unbounded delay communication. *IEEE Trans. on Automatic Control*, 49:1489–1501, 2004.

[14] I. Walukiewicz and S. Mohalik. Distributed games. In *FSTTCS '03, LNCS 2914*, pages 338–351. Springer, 2003.

[15] G. Winskel and M. Nielsen. Models for concurrency. In *Handbook of Logic in Comp. Sci., Vol. 3*. Oxford University Press, 1994.

Reachability of Hennessy-Milner Properties for Weakly Extended PRS

Mojmír Křetínský, Vojtěch Řehák, and Jan Strejček

Faculty of Informatics, Masaryk University, Brno, Czech Republic
{kretinsky,rehak,strejcek}@fi.muni.cz

Abstract. We examine the problem whether a given weakly extended process rewrite system (wPRS) contains a reachable state satisfying a given formula of Hennessy–Milner logic. We show that this problem is decidable. As a corollary we observe that the problem of strong bisimilarity between wPRS and finite-state systems is decidable. Decidability of the same problem for wPRS subclasses, namely PAN and PRS, has been formulated as an open question, see e.g. [Srb02]. We also strengthen some related undecidability results on some PRS subclasses.

1 Introduction

Current software systems often exhibit an evolving structure and/or operate on unbounded data types. Hence automatic verification of such systems usually requires to model them as infinite-state ones. Various modeling formalisms suited to different kinds of applications have been developed with their respective advantages and limitations.

Here we employ the classes of infinite-state systems defined by term rewrite systems and called *Process Rewrite Systems* (PRS) as proposed by Mayr [May00]. PRS subsume a variety of the formalisms studied in the context of formal verification. *Petri nets* (PN), *pushdown processes* (PDA), and process algebras like BPA, BPP, or PA all serve to exemplify this. The relative expressive power of various process classes has been studied, especially with respect to strong bisimulation; see [BCS96, Mol96] and [May00] showing the strictness of the PRS hierarchy. Their relevance for modeling and analysing programs is shown e.g. in [Esp02], for automatic verification see e.g. surveys [BCMS01, KJ02, Srb02].

Expressiveness of (most of) the PRS classes can be increased by adding a finite-state control unit to the PRS rewriting mechanism, which results in so-called state-extended PRS (sePRS) classes, see e.g. [JKM01, HM01]. We have extended the PRS hierarchy by the sePRS classes and refined this extended hierarchy by introducing PRS equipped with a weak finite-state unit (wPRS, inspired by weak automata [MSS92]) [KŘS04b, KŘS04a].

Research on the expressive power of process classes has been accompanied by exploring algorithmic boundaries of various verification problems. In this paper we mainly focus on model checking some (fragments of) simple branching time logics, namely EF and EG, on the process classes mentioned above.

R. Ramanujam and S. Sen (Eds.): FSTTCS 2005, LNCS 3821, pp. 213–224, 2005.

First, we note that the *reachability problem*, i.e. to decide whether a given state is reachable from the initial one, is decidable for the classes of PRS [May00] and wPRS [KŘS04a], while it is undecidable for sePA [BEH95]. All the problems mentioned below remain undecidable on the sePA class due to its Turing power.

A *reachability property problem*, for a given system Δ and a given formula φ, is to decide whether $\mathsf{EF}\varphi$ holds in the initial state of Δ. Hence, these problems are parametrized by the class to which the system Δ belongs, and by the type of the formula φ. In most of practical situations, φ specifies error states and the reachability property problem is a formalization of a natural verification problem whether some error state is reachable in a given system.

We recall that the (full) EF logic is decidable for PAD [May98] (PAD subsumes both PA and PDA). It is undecidable for PN [Esp94]; an inspection of the proof moves this undecidability border down to seBPP (also known as *multiset automata*, MSA). If we consider the *reachability HM property problem*, i.e. the reachability property problem where φ is a formula of Hennessy–Milner logic (HM formula), then this problem has been shown to be decidable for the classes of PN [JM95] and PAD [JKM01]. We lift the decidability border for this problem to the wPRS class. This results also moves the decidability border for the *reachability simple property problem*, i.e. the reachability property problem where φ is a HM formula without any nesting of modal operators $\langle a \rangle$, as the problem has been know to be decidable for PRS [May00] so far.

Let us recall that the (full) EG logic is decidable for PDA (a consequence of [MS85] and [Cau92]), whilst undecidability has been obtained for its $\mathsf{EG}\varphi$ fragment on (deterministic) BPP [EK95], where φ is a HM formula. We show that this problem remains undecidable on (deterministic) BPP even if we restrict φ to a HM formula without nesting of modal operators $\langle a \rangle$.

As a corollary of our main result, i.e. decidability of the reachability HM property problem for wPRS, we observe that the problem of strong bisimilarity between wPRS systems and finite-state ones is decidable. As PRS and its subclasses are proper subclasses of wPRS, it follows that we positively answer the question of the reachability HM property problem for the PRS class and hence the questions of bisimilarity checking the PAN and PRS processes with finite-state ones, which have been open problems, see for example [Srb02]. Their relevance to program specification and verification is advocated, for example, in [JKM01, KS04].

The outline of the paper is as follows. In the next section we recall some basic notions including syntax and semantics of (extended) PRS. In Section 3 we show that the problem of reachability HM property is decidable for wPRS. Some consequences and further results are discussed in Section 4.

2   Preliminaries

2.1   PRS and Its Extensions

Let $Const = \{X, \ldots\}$ be a set of *process constants*. The set of *process terms* (ranged over by $t, \ldots$) is defined by the abstract syntax $t ::= \varepsilon \mid X \mid t.t \mid t\|t$, where ε is the *empty term*, $X \in Const$ is a process constant; and '.' and '$\|$' mean *sequential* and *parallel compositions* respectively. We always work with equivalence classes of terms modulo commutativity and associativity of '$\|$', associativity of '.', and neutrality of ε, i.e. $\varepsilon.t = t.\varepsilon = t\|\varepsilon = t$. We distinguish four *classes of process terms* as:

1 – terms consisting of a single process constant only, in particular $\varepsilon \notin 1$,
S – *sequential* terms - terms without parallel composition, e.g. $X.Y.Z$,
P – *parallel* terms - terms without sequential composition, e.g. $X\|Y\|Z$,
G – *general* terms - terms without any restrictions, e.g. $(X.(Y\|Z))\|W$.

Let $M = \{o, p, q, \ldots\}$ be a set of *control states* and $Act = \{a, b, c, \ldots\}$ be a set of *actions*. Let $\alpha, \beta \in \{1, S, P, G\}, \alpha \subseteq \beta$ be the classes of process terms. An (α, β)-*sePRS (state extended process rewrite system)* Δ is a tuple (R, p_0, t_0), where

- R is a finite set of *rewrite rules* of the form $(p, t_1) \xrightarrow{a} (q, t_2)$, where $t_1 \in \alpha$, $t_1 \neq \varepsilon$, $t_2 \in \beta$, $p, q \in M$, and $a \in Act$,
- a pair $(p_0, t_0) \in M \times \beta$ forms the distinguished *initial state* of the system.

Sets of control states and process constants occurring in rewrite rules or in the initial state of Δ are denoted by $M(\Delta)$ and $Const(\Delta)$ respectively.

An (α, β)-*sePRS* $\Delta = (R, p_0, t_0)$ represents a labelled transition system the states of which are pairs (p, t) such that $p \in M(\Delta)$ is a control state and $t \in \beta$ is a process term over $Const(\Delta)$. The transition relation $\longrightarrow$ is the least relation satisfying the following inference rules:

$$\frac{((p, t_1) \xrightarrow{a} (q, t_2)) \in \Delta}{(p, t_1) \xrightarrow{a} (q, t_2)} \qquad \frac{(p, t_1) \xrightarrow{a} (q, t_2)}{(p, t_1\|t_1') \xrightarrow{a} (q, t_2\|t_1')} \qquad \frac{(p, t_1) \xrightarrow{a} (q, t_2)}{(p, t_1.t_1') \xrightarrow{a} (q, t_2.t_1')}$$

Sometimes we use $\longrightarrow_\Delta$ or $\longrightarrow_R$ to emphasize that we mean the transition relation corresponding to Δ or the relation generated by a set of rules R, respectively. To shorten our notation we write pt in lieu of (p, t). The transition relation can be extended to finite words over Act in a standard way. A state qt_2 is *reachable from a state* pt_1, written $pt_1 \xrightarrow{*} qt_2$, if there is $\sigma \in Act^*$ such that $pt_1 \xrightarrow{\sigma} qt_2$. We say that a state is *reachable* if it is reachable from the initial state.

An (α, β)-*sePRS* where $M(\Delta)$ is a singleton is called (α, β)-*PRS (process rewrite system)*. In such systems we omit the single control state from rules and states. An (α, β)-*sePRS* Δ is called a *process rewrite system with weak finite-state control unit* or a *weakly extended process rewrite system*, written (α, β)-*wPRS*, if there exists a partial order $\leq$ on $M(\Delta)$ such that each rule $pt_1 \xrightarrow{a} qt_2$ of Δ satisfies $p \leq q$.

Some classes of (α, β)-PRS correspond to widely known models as *finite-state systems* (FS, $(1, 1)$-PRS), *basic process algebras* (BPA, $(1, S)$-PRS), *basic parallel processes* (BPP, $(1, P)$-PRS), *process algebras* (PA, $(1, G)$-PRS), *pushdown processes* (PDA, (S, S)-PRS, see [Cau92] for justification), and *Petri nets* (PN, (P, P)-PRS). The classes (S, G)-PRS, (P, G)-PRS and (G, G)-PRS were introduced and named as PAD, PAN, and PRS by Mayr [May00]. Instead of (α, β)-sePRS or (α, β)-wPRS we juxtapose prefixes 'se-' or 'w-' respectively with the acronym corresponding to the (α, β)-PRS class. For example, we use wBPP rather than $(1, P)$-wPRS.

The expressive power of a class is measured by the set of labelled transition systems that are definable (up to strong bisimulation equivalence [Mil89]) by the class. Details can be found in [KŘS04b, KŘS04a].

2.2 Logics and Studied Problems

In this paper we work with fragments of *unified system of branching-time logic* (UB) [BAPM83]. Formulae of UB have the following syntax:

$$\varphi ::= tt \mid \neg\varphi \mid \varphi_1 \wedge \varphi_2 \mid \langle a \rangle\varphi \mid \mathsf{EF}\varphi \mid \mathsf{EG}\varphi,$$

where $a \in Act$ is an action. Here, formulae are interpreted over states of sePRS systems. Validity of a formula φ in a state pt of a given sePRS system Δ, written $(\Delta, pt) \models \varphi$, is defined by induction on the structure of φ: tt is valid for all states; boolean operators have standard meaning; $(\Delta, pt) \models \langle a \rangle\varphi$ iff there is a state qt' such that $pt \xrightarrow{a} qt'$ and $(\Delta, qt') \models \varphi$; $(\Delta, pt) \models \mathsf{EF}\varphi$ iff there is a state qt' reachable from pt such that $(\Delta, qt') \models \varphi$; $(\Delta, pt) \models \mathsf{EG}\varphi$ iff there is a maximal (finite or infinite) transition sequence $p_1t_1 \xrightarrow{a_1} p_2t_2 \xrightarrow{a_2} p_3t_3 \xrightarrow{a_3} \ldots$ such that $pt = p_1t_1$ and all states in the sequence satisfy $p_it_i \models \varphi$. We write $\Delta \models \varphi$ if φ is valid in the initial state p_0t_0 of Δ. For each UB formula φ, $depth(\varphi)$ denotes a nesting depth of $\langle a \rangle$ operators in φ (see e.g. [Mil89] for this standard definition).

A UB formula φ is called

- an *EF formula* if it does not contain any EG operator;
- an *EG formula* if it does not contain any EF operator;
- a *Hennessy–Milner formula* (or *HM formula* for short) if it contains neither EG nor EF operators;
- a *simple formula* if it is an HM formula satisfying $depth(\varphi) = 1$.

In the following, we deal with six problems parametrized by a subclass of sePRS systems. Let Δ be a given system of the subclass considered. The problem to decide whether

- $\Delta \models \varphi$, where φ is a given EF formula, is called *decidability of EF logic*;
- $\Delta \models \mathsf{EF}\varphi$, where φ is a given HM formula, is called *reachability HM property*;
- $\Delta \models \mathsf{EF}\varphi$, where φ is a given simple formula, is called *reachability simple property*;
- $\Delta \models \varphi$, where φ is a given EG formula, is called *decidability of EG logic*;
- $\Delta \models \mathsf{EG}\varphi$, where φ is a given HM formula, is called *evitability HM property*;
- $\Delta \models \mathsf{EG}\varphi$, where φ is a given simple formula, is called *evitability simple property*.

3   Main Result

In this section, we study a *reachability HM property problem* for wPRS, i.e. the problem to decide whether a given wPRS Δ and a given HM formula φ satisfy $\Delta \models \mathsf{EF}\varphi$ or not. We prove that the problem is decidable. The proof reduces this problem to the *reachability problem* for wPRS, i.e. the problem to decide whether a given state of a given wPRS is reachable or not, which is decidable due to [KŘS04a].

Theorem 1 ([KŘS04a]). *The reachability problem for wPRS is decidable.*

For the rest of this section, let Δ be a fixed wPRS system, $D \notin Const(\Delta)$ be a fixed fresh process constant, and $\mathcal{C} = Const(\Delta) \cup \{D\}$. Further, let φ be a HM formula and $n = depth(\varphi)$. We assume that $n > 0$.

Definition 1. *A term t' is called n-equivalent to a state pt of Δ if and only if, for each HM formula ψ satisfying $depth(\psi) \leq n$, it holds:*

$$(\Delta, pt) \models \psi \iff (\Delta, pt') \models \psi$$

Our proof will proceed in two steps. In the first step we show that there exists a *finite* set T of terms such that, for each reachable state pt of Δ, the set T contains a term t' which is n-equivalent to pt. In the second step we enrich the system with rules allowing us to rewrite an arbitrary reachable state pt to a state $[p, t']\,D$, where the control state $[p, t']$ represents the original control state p and a term t' which is n-equivalent to pt. Finally, for each $p \in M(\Delta), t' \in T$ satisfying $(\Delta, pt') \models \varphi$ we add a rule $[p, t']\,D \xrightarrow{a} acc\,D$. Let us note that the validity of $(\Delta, pt') \models \varphi$ is decidable as wPRS systems are finitely branching. To sum up, φ is valid for some reachable state pt of Δ if and only if the state $acc\,D$ is reachable in the modified system.

First, we introduce some auxiliary terminology and notation. A nonempty proper subterm t' of a term t is called *idle* if t' is the right-hand-side component of some sequential composition in t (such that its left-hand-side component is nonempty), where sequential composition is considered to be left-associative. For example, a term $(X.Y.Z)\|(U.(V\|W))$ should be interpreted as $((X.Y).Z)\|(U.(V\|W))$ and its idle subterms are $Y, Z, V\|W$ but not $Y.Z$. By *IdleTerms* we denote a set of all idle terms occurring in the initial term or in terms on the right-hand sides of rewrite rules of Δ. Observe that each idle subterm of any reachable state of Δ is contained in *IdleTerms*.

We define a *length* of a term t, written $|t|$, as the number of all occurrences of process constants in the term. For example, $|X\|(X.Y)\|\varepsilon| = 3$. Further, for each $j \geq 0$, we define a set

$$SmallTerms(j) = \{t \mid t \text{ is a term over } \mathcal{C} \text{ and } 0 < |t| \leq j\}.$$

Definition 2. *Let $h > 0$ be an integer. We put $k = \max\{|t| \mid t \in IdleTerms\}$ and $H = h \cdot (h + k) \cdot |SmallTerms(h + k)|$. We define Rules(h) to be the set of rewrite rules of three types (see the proof of Lemma 1 for their respective roles):*

(1) $ps'.D \overset{del}{\hookrightarrow} pD$ for all $p \in M(\Delta)$ and $s' \in SmallTerms(H)$,

(2) $ps^{h+1} \overset{del}{\hookrightarrow} ps^h$ for all $p \in M(\Delta)$ and $s \in SmallTerms(H)$,

(3) $ps'.s \overset{del}{\hookrightarrow} pD$ for all $p \in M(\Delta)$, $s \in IdleTerms$, and
$s' \in SmallTerms(H) \smallsetminus SmallTerms(h)$,

where s^i denotes a parallel composition of i copies of term s.

Lemma 1. *For each $h > 0$ and for each reachable state pt of Δ it holds that $pt.D \overset{*}{\longrightarrow}_{Rules(h)} pD$.*

Proof. As every rule in $Rules(h)$ has its right-hand side shorter than its left-hand side and an application of a rule in $Rules(h)$ cannot produce any new idle subterm, it is sufficient to prove that, for each $p \in M(\Delta)$ and each term t over $\mathcal{C}$ with all idle subterms in $IdleTerms$, there is a rule of $Rules(h)$ applicable to $pt.D$. We assume the contrary and derive a contradiction. Let $p \in M(\Delta)$ be a control state and t be a term of the minimal length such that t satisfies the preconditions and no rule of $Rules(h)$ is applicable to $pt.D$. Then $|t| > H$ as in the other case a rule of type (1) is applicable to $pt.D$. There are two cases:

$t = u.v$ As $v \in IdleTerms$ we have $|v| \leq k$. Further, $|t| > H$ implies $|u| > H - k > h$. If $h < |u| \leq H$, then there is a rule of type (3) that can be applied to $pt.D$. Hence $|u| > H$. As no rule of $Rules(h)$ can be applied to $pt.D = pu.v.D$, no such rule can be applied to pu. The inequality $|u| > H$ gives us that a rule of type (1) is applicable to $pu.D$ if and only if it is applicable to pu. The same holds for rules of type (2) and (3) as well due to the shape of these rules and due to the fact that D does not occur in any term of $IdleTerms$. To sum up, no rule of $Rules(h)$ can be applied to $pu.D$ and thus u contradicts the minimality of t.

$t = u \| v$ As '$\|$' is associative and commutative, it can be seen as an operator with an unbounded arity. Thus, t can be seen as a parallel composition of several components which are nonempty sequential terms. The length of each of these components is less than or equal to H; a component u satisfying $|u| > H$ would contradict the minimality of t using the same arguments as in the previous case. Further, as no rule of type (3) can be applied, the length of each component is at most $h + k$. Moreover, as rules of type (2) are not applicable, we have that the parallel composition contains at most h copies of each component. Hence, $|t| \leq h \cdot (h + k) \cdot |SmallTerms(h + k)| = H$. This contradicts the relation $|t| > H$.   □

Definition 3. *Let l be the maximal length of a left-hand-side term of a rule in Δ. Lemma 1 implies that, for each reachable state pt of Δ, there exists a transition sequence $pt.D \overset{*}{\longrightarrow}_{Rules(nl)} pD$. By $MultiSet_{nl}(pt)$ (or just $MultiSet(pt)$ if no confusion can arise) we denote a multiset containing exactly all the subterms that are rewritten during this transition sequence and correspond to a subterm s' of rewrite rules of types (1) and (3). Further, for each multiset of terms $S = \{t_1, t_2, \ldots, t_j\}$, we define its characteristic term $t_S = (t_1.D)\|(t_2.D)\| \ldots \|(t_j.D)$.*

Lemma 2. *Let pt be a reachable state of Δ. Then $t_{MultiSet(pt)}$ is n-equivalent to pt.*

Proof. Let us fix a transition sequence $pt.D \xrightarrow{*}_{Rules(nl)} pD$ and the corresponding multiset $MultiSet(pt)$. The proof proceeds by induction on the number of transition steps in the transition sequence.

Let S_i denote a part of $MultiSet(pt)$ obtained in the first i transition steps and pu_i be the state reached by these steps. It is sufficient to prove that, for each i, $u_i \| t_{S_i}$ is n-equivalent to pt. We note that D cannot be rewritten by any rewrite rule of Δ – it is used to prevent unwanted rewriting.

The basic step is trivial as $u_0 = t$, $S_0 = \emptyset$, and thus $u_i \| t_{S_i} = t \| \varepsilon$. Now we assume that $u_i \| t_{S_i}$ is n-equivalent to pt and we prove that the same holds for $u_{i+1} \| t_{S_{i+1}}$. Let l be the maximal length of a left-hand-side term of a rule in Δ. There are three cases reflecting the type of the rewrite rule applied in a transition step $pu_i \xrightarrow{del}_{Rules(nl)} pu_{i+1}$:

type (1) We note that no rule in $Rules(nl)$ can introduce D on the right-hand side of a sequential composition. Thus, a rule $p\,s'.D \xrightarrow{del} pD$ of type (1) is applicable to pu_i iff $u_i = s'.D$. Therefore, $u_{i+1} = D$, $S_{i+1} = S_i \cup \{s'\}$, and $u_{i+1} \| t_{S_{i+1}} = D \| (s'.D) \| t_{S_i} = D \| u_i \| t_{S_i}$. As $u_i \| t_{S_i}$ is n-equivalent to pt, it is obvious that so is $u_{i+1} \| t_{S_{i+1}}$.

type (2) Let ψ be a HM formula such that $depth(\psi) \leq n$. Then its validity in a state depends only on the first n successive transitions performable from the state. At most nl process constants of the term t can be rewritten during n successive steps. Hence, at most nl parallel components can be rewritten during these steps. Thus, reducing of the number of identical parallel components from $nl + 1$ to nl does not affect the validity of ψ. To sum up, $u_{i+1} \| t_{S_{i+1}} = u_{i+1} \| t_{S_i}$ is n-equivalent to pt.

type (3) The term s' occurring in the applied rule satisfies $|s'| > nl$. Hence, the part of the term t corresponding to the subterm s of the rule is "too far" to be rewritten in the first n steps of any transition sequence. The term $s'.s$ in u_i is replaced by D in u_{i+1}. It is easy to see that $u_{i+1} \| t_{S_{i+1}} = u_{i+1} \| (s'.D) \| t_{S_i}$ is n-equivalent to pt. $\square$

Given a multiset of terms S, by $S{\downarrow}n$ we denote the largest subset of S containing at most n copies of each element. One can readily confirm that a characteristic term t_S is n-equivalent to some state of Δ if and only if $t_{S{\downarrow}n}$ is n-equivalent to this state.

To sum up, for each reachable state pt of Δ, we can construct a multiset $MultiSet(pt){\downarrow}n$ such that its characteristic term $t_{MultiSet(pt){\downarrow}n}$ is n-equivalent to pt. Moreover, there is a bound on the size of each such a multiset which depends on Δ and n only. More precisely, such a multiset contains at most n copies of terms $s' \in SmallTerms(nl \cdot (nl + k) \cdot |SmallTerms(nl + k)|)$, where l is the maximal length of a left-hand-side term of a rule in Δ and k the maximal length of a term in $IdleTerms$. We now present the reduction of the reachability HM property problem for wPRS to the reachability problem for wPRS.

Lemma 3. *Let Δ be a wPRS system and φ be a Hennessy–Milner formula. Then we can construct a wPRS Δ' with a state acc D such that*

$$\Delta \models \mathsf{EF}\varphi \iff acc\, D \text{ is reachable in } \Delta'.$$

Proof. Let n, D, $\mathcal{C}$, *IdleTerms*, *SmallTerms(j)*, and *MultiSet(pt)* have the same meanings as above.

Let k be the maximal length of a term in *IdleTerms*, l be the maximal length of a left-hand-side term in any rule from Δ, and $H = nl\cdot(nl+k)\cdot|SmallTerms(nl+k)|$. Further, let $\mathcal{MS}$ be a set of all multisets containing at most n copies of each term $s' \in SmallTerms(H)$.

The system Δ' uses control states of the original system, a distinguished control state $acc \notin M(\Delta)$, and control states of the form (p, S) where $p \in M(\Delta)$ and $S \in \mathcal{MS}$.

Let $p_0 t_0$ be the initial state of Δ. Then Δ' has the initial state $p_0 t_0.D$ and the following rules, where p and S range over $M(\Delta)$ and $\mathcal{MS}$ respectively. We omit labels as they are not relevant.

(1) $pt \hookrightarrow qt'$ for all $(pt \xrightarrow{a} qt') \in \Delta$

(2) $pX \hookrightarrow (p, \emptyset)\, X$ for all $X \in \mathcal{C}$

(3) $(p, S)\, s'.D \hookrightarrow (p, (S \cup \{s'\})\!\downarrow\! n)\, D$ for all $s' \in SmallTerms(H)$

(4) $(p, S)\, s^{nl+1} \hookrightarrow (p, S)\, s^{nl}$ for all $s \in SmallTerms(H)$

(5) $(p, S)\, s'.s \hookrightarrow (p, (S \cup \{s'\})\!\downarrow\! n)\, D$ for all $s \in IdleTerms$ and
  $s' \in SmallTerms(H) \setminus SmallTerms(nl)$

(6) $(p, S)\, D \hookrightarrow acc\, D$ whenever $(\Delta, pt_S) \models \varphi$

Intuitively, the rules of type (1) mimic the behaviour of Δ and allow Δ' to reach a state $p\,t.D$ if and only if pt is a reachable state of Δ. A rule of type (2) stops this mimic phase and starts a checking phase where only rules of types (3)–(6) are applicable. The rules of types (3), (4), and (5) correspond to the rules of type (1), (2), and (3) in *Rules(nl)*, respectively. Let $p\,t.D$ be a final state reached in the mimic phase. The rules of types (3)–(5) allow us to rewrite this state to the state $(p, MultiSet(pt)\!\downarrow\! n)\, D$. Finally, the control state $(p, MultiSet(pt)\!\downarrow\! n)$ can be changed to acc using a rule of type (6) if and only if $(\Delta, t_{MultiSet(pt)\downarrow n}) \models \varphi$. As $t_{MultiSet(pt)\downarrow n}$ is n-equivalent to pt, the control state can be changed to acc if and only if $(\Delta, pt) \models \varphi$. □

The following theorem is an immediate corollary of Lemma 3 and Theorem 1.

Theorem 2. *The reachability HM property problem is decidable for wPRS.*

4   Related Results

An interesting corollary of Theorem 2 arises in connection with one of the results of [JKM01].

Theorem 3 ([JKM01], Theorem 22). *If the model checking problem for simple EF formulae (i.e. reachability HM property problem) is decidable in a class K of transition systems, then strong bisimilarity is decidable between processes of K and finite-state ones.*

A combination of Theorem 2 and Theorem 3 yields the following corollary.

Theorem 4. *Strong bisimilarity is decidable between wPRS systems and finite-state ones.*

Remark 1. Theorem 2 also implies that reachability simple property problem is decidable for PRS. This result has been previously presented in [May98] under the name *reachable property* problem. However, the proof given there contains a nontrivial mistake which was not fixed in subsequent papers [MR98, May00]. The weak point is the proof showing a transformation of an arbitrary PRS onto a PRS in normal form. Considering a PRS $\Delta = (\{A\|(B.C) \stackrel{a}{\hookrightarrow} A\|(B.C)\}, A\|(B.C))$ that does not model a formula $\mathsf{EF}(\neg\langle a\rangle tt)$, one receives a transformed PRS in normal form that models this formula.

Remark 2. It is known that (full) EF logic is undecidable for PN [Esp94]. An inspection of the proof given in [Esp97] shows that this undecidability result is valid even for seBPP class (also known as *multiset automata*, MSA).

Remark 3. Esparza and Kiehn have proved that EG logic is undecidable for (deterministic) BPP [EK95]. In Appendix A we describe a modification of their proof showing that for (deterministic) BPP even the evitability simple property problem is undecidable.

5   Conclusion

In the paper we have shown that given any wPRS system Δ and any Hennessy–Milner formula φ, one can decide whether there is a state s of Δ reachable from the initial state of Δ such that s satisfies φ. Using Theorem 22 of [JKM01], our result implies that strong bisimilarity between wPRS and finite-state systems is decidable. Decidability of the same problem for some of the wPRS subclasses, namely PAN and PRS, has been formulated as an open question, see e.g. [Srb02].

The following table describes the current state of (un)decidability results regarding the six problems defined at the end of Section 2 for the classes of PRS hierarchy and their extended counterparts. The results established by this paper are typeset in bold.

problem	decidable for	undecidable for
decidability of EF logic	PAD [May98]	**seBPP**
reachability HM property	**wPRS**	sePA
reachability simple property	**wPRS**	sePA
decidability of EG logic	PDA [MS85, Cau92]	BPP [EK95]
evitability HM property	PDA [MS85, Cau92]	BPP [EK95]
evitability simple property	PDA [MS85, Cau92]	**BPP**

To sum up, the situation with (un)decidability of these six problems for all the considered classes is now clear with one exception: decidability of EF logic remains open for classes wBPP, wPA, and wPAD.

Regarding other decidability questions we note that the BPP class and its extensions form a strict (sub)hierarchy with respect to bisimulation,

$$\text{BPP} \subsetneq \text{wBPP} \subsetneq \text{MSA} \subsetneq \text{PN},$$

which is decidable (even PSPACE-complete [Jan03]) for BPP processes and undecidable for MSA ([HM01] using the techniques of [Jan95]). Decidability of bisimilarity remains open for the wBPP class and is a subject of our further research. We are motivated by the fact the strictness of the left-most inclusion can be proved (but is not shown here) even for language equivalence. The strictness of inclusion between wBPP and MSA on the language equivalence level is just our conjecture.

Acknowledgment. We thank Antonín Kučera for valuable suggestions and pointers. Authors have been partially supported as follows: M. Křetínský by the Grant Agency of the Czech Republic, grant No. 201/03/1161, V. Řehák by the research centre "Institute for Theoretical Computer Science (ITI)", project No. 1M0021620808, and J. Strejček by the Academy of Sciences of the Czech Republic, grant No. 1ET408050503.

References

[BAPM83]   M. Ben-Ari, A. Pnueli, and Z. Manna. The temporal logic of branching time. *Acta Informatica*, 20(3):207–226, 1983.

[BCMS01]   O. Burkart, D. Caucal, F. Moller, and B. Steffen. Verification on infinite structures. In *Handbook of Process Algebra*, pages 545–623. Elsevier, 2001.

[BCS96]   O. Burkart, D. Caucal, and B. Steffen. Bisimulation collapse and the process taxonomy. In *Proc. of CONCUR'96*, volume 1119 of *LNCS*, pages 247–262. Springer, 1996.

[BEH95]   A. Bouajjani, R. Echahed, and P. Habermehl. On the verification problem of nonregular properties for nonregular processes. In *Proc. of LICS'95*. IEEE, 1995.

[Cau92]   D. Caucal. On the regular structure of prefix rewriting. *Theor. Comput. Sci.*, 106:61–86, 1992.

[EK95]   J. Esparza and A. Kiehn. On the model checking problem for branching time logics and basic parallel processes. In *CAV*, volume 939 of *LNCS*, pages 353–366. Springer, 1995.

[Esp94]   J. Esparza. On the decidability of model checking for several mu-calculi and petri nets. In *CAAP*, volume 787 of *LNCS*, pages 115–129. Springer, 1994.

[Esp97]   J. Esparza. Decidability of model checking for infinite-state concurrent systems. *Acta Informatica*, 34(2):85–107, 1997.

[Esp02]   J. Esparza. Grammars as processes. In *Formal and Natural Computing*, volume 2300 of *LNCS*. Springer, 2002.

[HM01]   Y. Hirshfeld and F. Moller. Pushdown automata, multiset automata, and petri nets. *Theor. Comput. Sci.*, 256(1-2):3–21, 2001.

[Jan95]   P. Jančar. Undecidability of bisimilarity for Petri nets and some related problems. *Theor. Comput. Sci.*, 148(2):281–301, 1995.

[Jan03]   P. Jančar. Strong bisimilarity on basic parallel processes is PSPACE-complete. In *Proc. of 18th IEEE Symposium on Logic in Computer Science (LICS'03)*, pages 218–227. IEEE Computer Society, 2003.

[JKM01]   P. Jančar, A. Kučera, and R. Mayr. Deciding bisimulation-like equivalences with finite-state processes. *Theor. Comput. Sci.*, 258:409–433, 2001.

[JM95]   P. Jancar and F. Moller. Checking regular properties of petri nets. In *CONCUR*, volume 962 of *LNCS*, pages 348–362. Springer, 1995.

[KJ02]   A. Kučera and P. Jančar. Equivalence-checking with infinite-state systems: Techniques and results. In *Proc. SOFSEM'2002*, volume 2540 of *LNCS*. Springer, 2002.

[KŘS04a] M. Křetínský, V. Řehák, and J. Strejček. Extended process rewrite systems: Expressiveness and reachability. In *Proceedings of CONCUR'04*, volume 3170 of *LNCS*, pages 355–370. Springer, 2004.

[KŘS04b] M. Křetínský, V. Řehák, and J. Strejček. On extensions of process rewrite systems: Rewrite systems with weak finite-state unit. In *Proceedings of INFINITY'03*, volume 98 of *ENTCS*, pages 75–88. Elsevier, 2004.

[KS04]   A. Kučera and Ph. Schnoebelen. A general approach to comparing infinite-state systems with their finite-state specifications. In *CONCUR*, volume 3170 of *LNCS*, pages 371–386. Springer, 2004.

[May98]   R. Mayr. *Decidability and Complexity of Model Checking Problems for Infinite-State Systems*. PhD thesis, Technische Universität München, 1998.

[May00]   R. Mayr. Process rewrite systems. *Information and Computation*, 156(1):264–286, 2000.

[Mil89]   R. Milner. *Communication and Concurrency*. Prentice-Hall, 1989.

[Mol96]   F. Moller. Infinite results. In *Proc. of CONCUR'96*, volume 1119 of *LNCS*, pages 195–216. Springer, 1996.

[MR98]   R. Mayr and M. Rusinowitch. Reachability is decidable for ground AC rewrite systems. In *Proceedings of INFINITY'98 workshop*, 1998.

[MS85]   D. Muller and P. Schupp. The theory of ends, pushdown automata, and second-order logic. *Theor. Comput. Sci.*, 37:51–75, 1985.

[MSS92]   D. Muller, A. Saoudi, and P. Schupp. Alternating automata, the weak monadic theory of trees and its complexity. *Theor. Comput. Sci.*, 97(1–2):233–244, 1992.

[Srb02]   J. Srba. Roadmap of infinite results. *EATCS Bulletin*, (78):163–175, 2002. http://www.brics.dk/~srba/roadmap/.

A   Evitability Simple Property for Deterministic BPP

In this section, we show how to strengthen the result of undecidability the EG logic for BPP, a proof of which has been given by Esparza and Kiehn in [EK95]. As we just describe the necessary changes to be done within the proof, we use the same notation as introduced in [EK95]. The original proof is done by a reduction from the halting problem of a Minsky counter machine. A quick inspection of the reduction shows that it demonstrates undecidability of the *inevitability HM property problem* for the class of deterministic BPP systems. We note that it is not a proof of undecidability for the *inevitability simple property problem* due to the following reason. In the definition of $\widehat{EN}(a_1, \ldots, a_k)$, there is a subformula

$$\bigwedge_{i:=1}^{k} \neg \exists (a_i) EN(a_i) \text{ corresponding to } \bigwedge_{i=1}^{k} \neg \langle a_i \rangle \langle a_i \rangle tt \text{ in our notation}$$

which expresses that no sequence $a_i a_i$ is enabled. Omitting this subformula from $\widehat{EN}(a_1, \ldots, a_k)$, the construction produces a simple property formula.

In what follows, we present some other changes to be done within the construction in orded to keep its correctness for the case of the simple property formula as well. In other words, we prove than even the inevitability *simple* property problem remains undecidable for the deterministic BPP systems.

The following definitions of SM, M, and C_j are the same as in [EK95]:

$$\text{SM} \stackrel{\text{def}}{=} (\text{SQ}_1 \| \ldots \| \text{SQ}_{n+1}) \qquad \text{M} \stackrel{\text{def}}{=} \text{SM} \| Q_0 \qquad C_j \stackrel{\text{def}}{=} \text{dec}_j^1 \cdot \text{dec}_j^2 \cdot \text{dec}_j^3 \cdot 0$$

Without loss of generality, we assume that there is no self loop in the counter machine $\mathcal{M}$ (i.e., $k \neq i \neq k'$, for each transition rule of $\mathcal{M}$). Hence, it is not necessary to create a new parallel instance of a process constant Q_i from SQ_i as far as the rewriting on the existing instance of Q_i is not finished. In the following, we reformulate the definitions of SQ_i and Q_i to prevent sequences of the form $\text{out}_i^1 \text{out}_i^1$ or $\text{out}_i^2 \text{out}_i^2$.

The halting state definition is reformulated as follows.

$$\text{SQ}_{n+1} \stackrel{\text{def}}{=} \text{in}_{n+1}^1 \cdot Q_{n+1} \qquad\qquad Q_{n+1} \stackrel{\text{def}}{=} \text{halt} \cdot \text{SQ}_{n+1}$$

A state q_i of type II is modelled as follows.

$$\text{SQ}_i \stackrel{\text{def}}{=} \text{in}_i^1 \cdot Q_i \qquad\qquad Q_i \stackrel{\text{def}}{=} \text{out}_i^1 \cdot \text{out}_i^2 \cdot \text{SQ}_i$$

A state q_i of type I has to proceed to the state q_k. To prevent multiple occurrences of the process constant Q_k, we use the same technique as in the case of states of type II. Hence, SQ_i and Q_i are modelled as

$$\text{SQ}_i \stackrel{\text{def}}{=} \text{in}_i^1 \cdot Q_i \qquad\qquad Q_i \stackrel{\text{def}}{=} \text{out}_i^1 \cdot \text{out}_i^2 \cdot (\text{SQ}_i \| C_j)$$

and we add the following disjunct to the formula ϕ_h to guarantee a move to the state q_k in an honest run.

$$\widehat{EN}(\text{out}_i^1) \vee \widehat{EN}(\text{out}_i^2) \vee \widehat{EN}(\text{out}_i^2, \text{out}_k^1) \vee \widehat{EN}(\text{out}_k^1)$$

Hence, the multiple enabling of out_i^1 and out_i^2 is omitted by the construction. It remains to focus on the situation for dec_i^2 and dec_i^3. As the states where both dec_i^2 and dec_i^3 are enabled do not satisfy ϕ_h, each state satisfying $\exists (\text{dec}_i^2) EN(\text{dec}_i^2)$ has no continuation to make a honest run and each state satisfying $\exists (\text{dec}_i^3) EN(\text{dec}_i^3)$ is unreachable in any honest run.

Decision Procedures for Queues with Integer Constraints

Ting Zhang, Henny B. Sipma, and Zohar Manna[*]

Computer Science Department
Stanford University
{tingz,sipma,zm}@theory.stanford.edu

Abstract. Queues are a widely used data structure in programming languages. They also provide an important synchronization mechanism in modeling distributed protocols. In this paper we extend the theory of queues with a length function that maps a queue to its size, resulting in a combined theory of queues and Presburger arithmetic. This extension provides a natural but tight coupling between the two theories, and hence the general Nelson-Oppen combination method for decision procedures is not applicable. We present a decision procedure for the quantifier-free theory and a quantifier elimination procedure for the first-order theory that can remove a block of existential quantifiers in one step.

1 Introduction

Queues are a widely used data structure in programming languages. They also provide an important synchronization mechanism in modeling distributed protocols. To verify programs or protocols using queues we must be able to reason about this data structure. Single theory decision procedures, however, are usually not applicable, because programming languages often involve multiple data domains. A natural example of such "mixed" constraints are combinations of queues with integer constraints on the size of queues.

In this paper we extend the theory of queues with a length function that maps a queue to its size, resulting in a combined theory of queues and Presburger arithmetic (PA). The language is the set-theoretic union of the language of queues and that of PA. Formulae are formed from *atom*, *queue*, and *integer literals* using logical connectives and quantifiers. The two theories are connected by the length function $|\cdot| : Q \to \mathbb{N}$. With the expressive power of PA, we can express linear relations between sizes of queues. E.g., in a network with n input queues q_i, the property that the influx is bounded by B can be expressed as $\Sigma_{i=0}^{n-1}|q_i| < B$.

We present a decision procedure for the quantifier-free theory of queues. The method extracts accurate integer constraints from queue constraints. Thus, we

---

[*] This research was supported in part by NSF grants CCR-01-21403, CCR-02-20134, CCR-02-09237, CNS-0411363, and CCF-0430102, by ARO grant DAAD19-01-1-0723, and by NAVY/ONR contract N00014-03-1-0939.

R. Ramanujam and S. Sen (Eds.): FSTTCS 2005, LNCS 3821, pp. 225–237, 2005.
© Springer-Verlag Berlin Heidelberg 2005

can utilize decision procedures for queues and integers to derive the new decision procedure. We also present a quantifier elimination procedure for the first-order theory of queues with integers. The elimination procedure removes a block of existential quantifiers in one step. In all developments, we assume that the atom domain is finite; the decision problems in an infinite domain are considerably easier.

Related Work and Comparison. Presburger arithmetic (PA) was first shown to be decidable in 1929 by the quantifier elimination method [4]. Efficient algorithms were later discovered by [3] and further improved in [9].

[2] gave a decision procedure for the quantifier-free theory of queues with subsequence relations which consist of prefix, suffix and sub-queue relations. It also discussed the integer combination for the case of infinite atom domain without the subsequence relations. The decidability and the complexity of the first-order theory of queues were given by [10,11]. By the decidability of *WS1S* and a standard encoding, the theory of words with the prefix relation and the successor operator (i.e., a theory of queues) is decidable and admits quantifier elimination [1]. [1,12] studied theories of words with "equal length" predicate which can be viewed as special integer constraints.

This arithmetic extension provides a natural but tight coupling between the two theories, and hence the general Nelson-Oppen combination method [8] for decision procedures is not applicable. Recently [6] showed the decidability of a fragment of *WS1S* with cardinality constraints (*WS1S*^{card}) and the undecidability of *WS1S*^{card} for the fragments with alternation of second-order quantifiers. By a standard encoding (in which a queue is represented as sets of natural numbers), the theory of queues with integers can be interpreted in *WS1S*^{card}. Even the quantifier-free theory of queues with integers, however, is unlikely to be interpreted in the quantifier-free fragment of *WS1S*^{card}, because encoding a queue by sets of natural numbers necessarily involves quantification. Moreover, though interpretation in general renders elegant decidability results, it produces less efficient decision procedures in practice, especially if the host theory has high complexity (in our case even the existential *WS1S* is non-elementary).

In [13,14] we gave decision procedures for the theory of term algebras with integer constraints. The method relies on a key normalization process to extract integer constraints from term constraints. The normalization partitions terms into stratified clusters such that (i) each cluster consists of pairwise unequal terms (trees) of the same length, and (ii) disequalities between composite terms (proper trees) in a cluster are implied by disequalities in the clusters of lower ranks. Property (ii) allows the construction of a satisfying assignment in a bottom-up fashion, while providing integer constraints that express the satisfiability of the clusters. Thus, (i) and (ii) allow us to reduce the satisfiability of the original formula to the satisfiability of computable integer constraints. The decision procedure presented here relies on the same idea, but for queues disequalities cannot be normalized into stratified clusters, because queues are not uniquely generated. Consider, for example, the constraint

$$X \neq Y \ \wedge \ aX \neq Yb \ \wedge \ Xa \neq bY \ \wedge \ |X| = |Y|.$$

Infinitely many assignments of the form $\{X = (ba)^n b, Y = a(ba)^n\}$ satisfy $X \neq Y$, but neither $aX \neq Yb$ nor $Xa \neq bY$. Therefore, we cannot construct a satisfying assignment inductively. In this paper we present new normalization procedures that allow the computation of a *cut length* L_t for all queue variables: below L_t all satisfying assignments can be enumerated, above L_t integer constraints can be computed that are equisatisfiable with the original formula.

Paper Organization. Sec. 2 defines the language and structure of queues and presents some word properties. Sec. 3 describes a decision procedure for the quantifier-free theory of queues [2], the basis for our decision procedures. Sec. 4 introduces the theory of queues augmented with Presburger arithmetic and presents the technical machinery for the decision procedures. Sec. 5 presents the main contribution of this paper: it adapts the technique in [13,14] to derive a decision procedure for the extended theory of queues. Sec. 6 applies the technique to give a quantifier elimination procedure for the extended first-order theory of queues. Sec. 7 concludes with a discussion on complexity and some ideas for future work. Due to space limitation all proofs and some algorithms have been omitted. An extended version of this paper is available from the first author's webpage.

2   The Theory of Queues

We present a two-sorted language and structure of queues. For notation convenience, we do not distinguish syntactic terms in the language from semantic terms in the structure. The meaning should be clear from the context.

Definition 1. *The structure of queues* $\mathfrak{Q} : \langle Q; \mathcal{A}, C, S \rangle$ *consists of*

1. $\mathcal{A}$: *A finite set of atoms:* a, b, c, ... *We use* $\epsilon_{\mathcal{A}}$ *to denote the "phantom atom" whose only purpose is to keep functions on queues total.*
2. Q: *The domain of queues, consisting of sequences of atoms. We use* ϵ_Q *to denote the empty queue.*
3. C: *Two constructors: the* left insertion $\mathrm{la} : \mathcal{A} \times Q \to Q$ *and the* right insertion $\mathrm{ra} : \mathcal{A} \times Q \to Q$ *such that for* $\alpha \in Q$, $\mathrm{la}(\epsilon_{\mathcal{A}}, \alpha) = \mathrm{ra}(\epsilon_{\mathcal{A}}, \alpha) = \alpha$, *and for* $a \in \mathcal{A} \backslash \{\epsilon_{\mathcal{A}}\}$, $\langle s_1, \ldots, s_n \rangle \in Q$, $\mathrm{la}(a, \epsilon_Q) = \mathrm{ra}(a, \epsilon_Q) = \langle a \rangle$, *and* $\mathrm{la}(a, \langle s_1, \ldots, s_n \rangle) = \langle a, s_1, \ldots, s_n \rangle$, $\mathrm{ra}(a, \langle s_1, \ldots, s_n \rangle) = \langle s_1, \ldots, s_n, a \rangle$.
4. S: *Four selectors: the* left head $\mathrm{lh} : Q \to \mathcal{A}$, *the* left tail $\mathrm{lt} : Q \to Q$, *the* right head $\mathrm{rh} : Q \to \mathcal{A}$, *and the* right tail $\mathrm{rt} : Q \to Q$ *such that for* $\langle s_1, \ldots, s_n \rangle \in Q$, $\mathrm{lh}(\epsilon_Q) = \mathrm{rh}(\epsilon_Q) = \epsilon_{\mathcal{A}}$, $\mathrm{lt}(\epsilon_Q) = \mathrm{rt}(\epsilon_Q) = \epsilon_Q$, *and*

$$\mathrm{lh}(\langle s_1, \ldots, s_n \rangle) = s_1, \qquad \mathrm{lt}(\langle s_1, \ldots, s_n \rangle) = \langle s_2, \ldots, s_n \rangle,$$
$$\mathrm{rh}(\langle s_1, \ldots, s_n \rangle) = s_n, \qquad \mathrm{rt}(\langle s_1, \ldots, s_n \rangle) = \langle s_1, \ldots, s_{n-1} \rangle.$$

We use $\mathscr{L}_Q$ *for the language of queues.*

Queues are finite *words* constructed from *letters* in $\mathcal{A}$, i.e., $Q = \mathcal{A}^*$. We assume $|\mathcal{A}| > 1$ as queue constraints trivially reduce to integer constraints if $\mathcal{A}$

is a singleton. We use "word", "letter" in semantic discussions and use "queue", "atom" to refer to their counterparts in the formal language. For a word α, $|\alpha|$ denotes the length of α; $\alpha[i]$ ($1 \leq i \leq |\alpha|$) denotes the letter at position i; $\alpha[m..n]$ ($1 \leq m, n \leq |\alpha|$) denotes the consecutive fragment from position m to position n; α^m denotes the word obtained by concatenating m copies of α; α^* (α^+) denotes the set $\{\alpha^m \mid m \geq 0\}$ ($\{\alpha^m \mid m > 0\}$).

Because of finiteness of $\mathcal{A}$, we assume only constant atoms appear in formulas (i.e., no occurrences of atom variables). For clarity, $X, Y, Z, \ldots$ are reserved for queue variables, $a, b, c, \ldots$ for constant atoms and $\alpha, \beta, \gamma, \ldots$ for constant queues. We use concatenation $\circ$ to express constructor operations. For example, $a \circ X \circ b$ stands for either $\mathsf{ra}(b, \mathsf{la}(a, X))$ or $\mathsf{la}(a, \mathsf{ra}(b, X))$. Often we even omit $\circ$ unless necessary for clarity.

The expressive power of the constructor language (the language without selectors) is the same as that of $\mathcal{L}_Q$.

Proposition 1 (Elimination of Selectors). *For any φ in $\mathcal{L}_Q$, one can effectively compute an equivalent φ' such that (i) φ' contains no selectors, and (ii) if φ is quantifier-free, then φ' can be put into either $\exists_1$ or $\forall_1$ form.*

So in terms of satisfiability or validity, even in the quantifier-free fragment of $\mathcal{L}_Q$, selectors are dispensable without compromising expressiveness. From now on we assume $\mathcal{L}_Q$ is the constructor language except in Sec. 6 where selectors are used in quantifier elimination. In a constructor language, a queue variable can occur at most once in a term, and hence we can assume all terms of sort Q are in the form $\alpha X \beta$, where α, β are constant words and X is a queue variable.

The equations in $\mathcal{L}_Q$ can express certain "circular properties" on queues.

Definition 2 ([7]). *Two words α, β are conjugate if there exist words u, v ($v \neq \epsilon_Q$) such that $\alpha = uv$ and $\beta = vu$. In other words, α is obtained from β by circular shift, and vice versa. We say that α is k-conjugate with β if $|u| = k$.*

Let $\mathsf{ext}(\beta, m, k)$ denote $\beta^m \beta[1..k]$, $\mathsf{orb}(\beta, k)$ the set $\{\mathsf{ext}(\beta, m, k) \mid m \geq 0\}$, and $\mathsf{orb}(\beta)$ the set $\bigcup_{k \geq 0} \mathsf{orb}(\beta, k)$. Note that $\mathsf{orb}(\beta)$ is the orbit of all words of the form $\beta^* \beta[1..i]$ ($i < |\beta|$) and $\mathsf{orb}(\beta, k)$ is the subtrack of $\mathsf{orb}(\beta)$ ending with $\beta[1..k]$.

Example 1. Let $\beta = aba$. Then $\mathsf{ext}(\beta, 1, 2) = abaab$, $\mathsf{orb}(\beta)$ are words in one of the following forms $(aba)^*$, $(aba)^* a$, $(aba)^* ab$, which are $\mathsf{orb}(\beta, 0)$, $\mathsf{orb}(\beta, 1)$ and $\mathsf{orb}(\beta, 2)$.

Proposition 2 ([7]). *Two words α and β are conjugate if and only if there exists γ such that $\alpha \gamma = \gamma \beta$. Moreover, α and β are k-conjugate if and only if for all γ, $\alpha \gamma = \gamma \beta$ if and only if $\gamma \in \mathsf{orb}(\alpha, k)$.*

This proposition says that if $\alpha = u_1 u_2$, $\beta = u_2 u_1$, then the solution set of $\alpha X = X \beta$ is $(u_1 u_2)^* u_1$. As a consequence, we define $X \in \mathsf{orb}(\alpha, k)$ as "syntactic sugar" for $\alpha X = X \alpha[k+1..|\alpha|] \alpha[1..k]$; similarly $X \notin \mathsf{orb}(\alpha, k)$ for $\alpha X \neq X \alpha[k+1..|\alpha|] \alpha[1..k]$.

Definition 3 (Primitive Words). *A word β is primitive if $\beta \neq \alpha^n$ ($n \geq 1$) for any proper prefix α of β, and is strongly primitive if in addition $\beta \notin \mathsf{orb}(\alpha)$.*

Example 2. Consider $\alpha \equiv aba$, $\beta \equiv abab$ and $\gamma \equiv abb$. It is clear that β is non-primitive, α is primitive but not strongly primitive and γ is strongly primitive.

If β is non-primitive, then there exists α such that $\beta \in \alpha^*$. We call the shortest such α the *generator* of β, denoted by $\mathbf{gen}(\beta)$. It is easily seen that $\mathrm{orb}(\beta) = \mathrm{orb}(\mathbf{gen}(\beta))$, i.e., every orbit is uniquely generated. Thus, without loss of generality, we always assume the occurrences of β in $\mathrm{orb}(\beta, k)$ to be primitive.

Proposition 3 ([2,10]). *Let α, β be two distinct primitive words and γ a word of length n. Then $\gamma \in \mathrm{orb}(\alpha) \cap \mathrm{orb}(\beta)$ implies $n < |\alpha| + |\beta| - 1$.*

This proposition says that $X \in \mathrm{orb}(\alpha)$ and $X \in \mathrm{orb}(\beta)$ (where $\alpha \not\equiv \beta$), are *mutually exclusive* except for a finite number of cases which can be enumerated by comparing two orbits of α and β coordinate-wise up to $|\alpha| + |\beta| - 2$. We have

Proposition 4 ([2,10]). *A conjunction of literals of the form*

$$\bigwedge_{i=1}^{n} X \in \mathrm{orb}(\alpha_i) \;\wedge\; \bigwedge_{j=1}^{m} X \notin \mathrm{orb}(\beta_j) \tag{1}$$

can be simplified to a formula in which at most one of $X \in \mathrm{orb}(\alpha_i)$ appears, and if this happens, no $X \notin \mathrm{orb}(\beta_j)$ occurs. In addition, if $n > 1$, (1) simplifies to either false *or a finite set of solutions.*

Example 3. $X \in \mathrm{orb}(ab) \wedge X \in \mathrm{orb}(aba)$ simplifies to $X \in \{a, b, aba\}$, and $X \in \mathrm{orb}(ab) \wedge X \notin \mathrm{orb}(aba)$ simplifies to $X \in \mathrm{orb}(ab) \wedge X \notin \{a, b, aba\}$.

3   Decision Procedure for $\mathrm{Th}^{\vee}(\mathfrak{Q})$

The basis of the decision procedures for the combined theory is the decision procedure for the quantifier-free theory of queues, $\mathrm{Th}^{\vee}(\mathfrak{Q})$ [2]. This decision procedure is *refutation-based*; to determine the validity of a formula φ, it determines the unsatisfiability of $\neg\varphi$, which further reduces to determining the unsatisfiability of each disjunct in the *disjunctive normal form* of $\neg\varphi$. A key constituent of all decision procedures is *equality elimination*.

Definition 4 (Solved Form). *A set of equalities $\mathcal{E}$ is in* solved form *if every $E \in \mathcal{E}$ has the form $x = t(\bar{x})$ where x neither occurs in $\bar{x}$ nor in any other equations in $\mathcal{E}$.*

Obviously a set of equalities in solved form pose no restriction on the solution, and hence those equalities can be considered "virtually eliminated".

Definition 5 (Normal Form in $\mathfrak{Q}$). *A queue constraint Φ_Q is in* normal form *if (i) all equalities are in solved form, (ii) for each queue variable X there exists at most one literal $X \in \mathrm{orb}(\alpha, k)$, and (iii) disequalities are in the form $\alpha X \neq Y\beta$ for $X \not\equiv Y$.*

The following algorithm, a simplified version of [2], reduces a set of equalities and inequalities to normal form.

Algorithm 1 (Normalization in $\mathfrak{Q}$, cf. [2]). *Input* $\Phi_Q : \mathcal{E} \cup \mathcal{D}$ *where* $\mathcal{E}, \mathcal{D}$ *are sets of equalities and disequalities, respectively.*

1. *Reduce literals of the form* $\alpha X \beta = \alpha' Y \beta'$, $\alpha X \beta \neq \alpha' Y \beta'$, *where* $\alpha, \beta, \alpha', \beta'$ *are constant queues and* X, Y *are queue variables, to* $\alpha X = Y \beta$ *and* $\alpha X \neq Y \beta$ *by position-wise removing prefixes and suffixes. For example,* $abXcd = abcYdd$ *reduces to* false *and* $abXcd \neq abcYd$ *to* $Xc \neq cY$.
2. *Eliminate equalities of the form* $\alpha X = Y \beta$ *with* $X \not\equiv Y$. *For* $|X| < |\beta|$, $\alpha X = Y \beta$ *reduces to* $X = \beta[|\beta| - |X| + 1..|\beta|] \wedge Y = \alpha \beta[1..|\beta| - |X|]$. *For* $|X| \geq |\beta|$, $\alpha X = Y \beta$ *reduces to* $X = X' \beta \wedge Y = \alpha X'$, *where* X' *is a fresh queue variable.*
3. *Eliminate equalities of the form* $\alpha X = X \beta$. *By Prop. 2 if* α, β *are not conjugate, then* $\alpha X = X \beta$ *simplifies to* false. *If* α, β *are* k-*conjugate,* $\alpha X = X \beta$ *is replaced by* $X \in \mathrm{orb}(\alpha, k)$.
4. *Eliminate disequalities of the form* $\alpha X \neq X \beta$. *Again by Prop. 2, if* α, β *are not conjugate,* $\alpha X \neq X \beta$ *simplifies to* true. *If* α, β *are* k-*conjugate,* $\alpha X \neq X \beta$ *is replaced by* $X \notin \mathrm{orb}(\alpha, k)$.

Although the literals $X \in \mathrm{orb}(\alpha, k)$, $X \notin \mathrm{orb}(\alpha, k)$, introduced in steps 3 and 4, are implicit equalities (disequalities, resp.), Prop. 4 ensures that a set of such equalities is either inconsistent or a finite set of solutions can be computed, and that in the presence of $X \in \mathrm{orb}(\alpha, k)$, all occurrences $X \notin \mathrm{orb}(\alpha', k')$ can be eliminated.

We claim that a constraint in normal form is satisfiable: a satisfiable assignment can be constructed incrementally by assigning each queue variable a queue with length distinct from all previously assigned terms. This justifies the following algorithm.

Algorithm 2 ([2]). *Input:* $\Phi \equiv \mathcal{E} \cup \mathcal{D}$.

1. *Transform* Φ *to* $\Phi' : \mathcal{E}' \cup \mathcal{D}'$ *which is normal.*
2. *If inconsistency is discovered, return* FAIL; *otherwise, return* SUCCESS.

4   The Theory of Queues with Integers

Definition 6. *The structure of queues with integers is* $\mathfrak{Q}_{\mathbb{Z}} : \langle \mathfrak{Q}, \mathsf{PA}; | \cdot | \rangle$ *where* $\mathfrak{Q}$ *is the structure of queues,* PA *is Presburger arithmetic, and* $| \cdot | : Q \to \mathbb{N}$ *is the length function such that* $|X|$ *denotes the number of atoms in the queue* X.

We use subscripts Q and $\mathbb{Z}$ (or prefixes Q- and PA-) to denote notions related to queue sort and integer sort, respectively. For example, Φ_Q denotes a queue formula and $\mathcal{V}_Q$ denotes the collection of queue variables. We use integer terms $|t(X)|$ in two ways: as the function value of $t(X)$ when $t(X)$ is in discussion, and as purely syntactic integer variable (called *pseudo integer variable*). In the latter case, suppose $\Phi_{\mathbb{Z}}(\bar{X})$ is given, then $\Phi_{\mathbb{Z}}(\bar{z})$ is the formula obtained by substituting each pseudo integer variable $|X|$ ($X \in \bar{X}$) for a real integer variable z ($z \in \bar{z}$). $|\bar{X}| = \bar{z}$ denotes $\bigwedge_i |X_i| = z_i$. If σ is an assignment for $\mathcal{V}_Q$, then $|\sigma|$ denotes the corresponding assignment for pseudo integer variables.

In a combined constraint $\Phi_Q \wedge \Phi_Z$, Φ_Z restricts solutions to Φ_Q.

Example 4. The constraint Φ_Q: $Xba \neq abY \wedge Xab \neq baY \wedge Xaa \neq baY \wedge Xab \neq aaY$ is not satisfiable with $\Phi_Z : |X| = |Y| = 1$, in $\mathfrak{Q}_Z$ with $\mathcal{A} = \{a, b\}$. It can be easily verified by enumerating all four combinations. On the other hand, both Φ_Q and Φ_Z are obviously satisfiable in their respective domains.

A simple but crucial observation is that Φ_Q induces an "implicit" length constraint, in addition to the "explicit" constraint Φ_Z given in the input. For example, in Ex. 4, Φ_Q implies $\Phi_\Delta : |X| = |Y| \rightarrow |X| = |Y| \neq 1$ and thus Φ_Δ contradicts Φ_Z. If we can extract from Φ_Q the implicit Φ_Δ that exactly characterizes the solution set of Φ_Q, then the satisfiability of $\Phi_Q \wedge \Phi_Z$ reduces to the satisfiability of $\Phi_\Delta \wedge \Phi_Z$. As a consequence, we can derive decision procedures for the combined theory by utilizing the decision procedures for PA and queues.

Definition 7 (Length Constraint Completion (LCC)). *A formula $\Phi_\Delta(\bar{X})$ in $\mathcal{L}_Z$ is a* length constraint completion *(LCC) for $\Phi_Q(\bar{X})$ if the following formulae are valid:*

$$(\forall \bar{X} : Q) \left[\Phi_Q(\bar{X}) \rightarrow (\exists \bar{z} : Z)\left(\Phi_\Delta(\bar{z}) \wedge |\bar{X}| = \bar{z} \right) \right], \tag{2}$$

$$(\forall \bar{z} : Z) \left[\Phi_\Delta(\bar{z}) \rightarrow (\exists \bar{X} : Q)\left(\Phi_Q(\bar{X}) \wedge |\bar{X}| = \bar{z} \right) \right]. \tag{3}$$

(2) states that an LCC Φ_Δ for Φ_Q is *sound*: $|\cdot|$ maps a satisfying assignment in $\mathfrak{Q}$ to a satisfying assignment in PA. (3) states that Φ_Δ is *realizable*: any satisfying assignment in PA is an image under $|\cdot|$ of a satisfying assignment in $\mathfrak{Q}$. Given Φ_Q, let Φ_Δ be an LCC, $\Phi_{\Delta+}$ (resp. $\Phi_{\Delta-}$) be the formula (when substituted for Φ_Δ) satisfying (2) (resp. (3)). If we identify these constraints with their corresponding solution sets, we have $\Phi_{\Delta-} \subseteq \Phi_\Delta \subseteq \Phi_{\Delta+}$. Thus Φ_Δ is the exact projection of Φ_Q from $\mathfrak{Q}$ to PA, while $\Phi_{\Delta+}$, $\Phi_{\Delta-}$ are over and under approximations of Φ_Δ respectively.

Example 5. Consider Φ_Q in Ex. 4 and $\Phi_{\Delta+}$: true, $\Phi_{\Delta-}$: $|X| = |Y| = 2$, and Φ_Δ : $|X| \neq |Y| \vee (|X| = |Y| \wedge |X| \neq 1)$. $\Phi_{\Delta+}$ is not realizable by Φ_Q because the integer assignment σ_Δ:$\{|X| = |Y| = 1\}$ can not be realized. On the other hand, $\Phi_{\Delta-}$ is not sound because it does not satisfy the queue assignment σ_Q:$\{X = \epsilon_Q, Y = \epsilon_Q\}$. Finally, Φ_Δ is both sound and realizable w.r.t. Φ_Q and hence is an LCC for Φ_Q.

We have a decision procedure for Th($\mathfrak{Q}_Z$) if Φ_Δ can be computed from Φ_Q.

Theorem 1. *Let Φ_Δ be an LCC for Φ_Q. Then $\mathfrak{Q}_Z \models_\exists \Phi_Q \wedge \Phi_Z$ if and only if PA $\models_\exists \Phi_\Delta \wedge \Phi_Z$.*

To obtain an LCC, we need to normalize Φ_Q into an equivalent disjunction in which each disjunct is of the form $\Phi'_Q \wedge \theta'_Z$ with θ'_Z a newly generated integer constraint. We do not require the disjuncts to be mutually exclusive. First, we extend Def. 7 to deal with newly generated integer constraints in the normalization.

Definition 8 (Relativized Length Constraint Completion (RLCC)). *A formula* $\Phi_\Delta(\bar{X})$ *is a* length constraint completion *for* $\Phi_Q(\bar{X})$ relativized to $\theta_Z(\bar{X})$, *(in short,* $\Phi_\Delta(\bar{X})$ *is an RLCC for* $\Phi_Q(\bar{X})/\theta_Z(\bar{X})$), *if the following formulae are valid:*

$$(\forall \bar{X} : Q) \left[\Phi_Q(\bar{X}) \wedge \theta_Z(\bar{X}) \rightarrow (\exists \bar{z} : Z)\left(\Phi_\Delta(\bar{z}) \wedge |\bar{X}| = \bar{z}\right) \right], \tag{4}$$

$$(\forall \bar{z} : Z) \left[\Phi_\Delta(\bar{z}) \rightarrow (\exists \bar{X} : Q)\left(\Phi_Q(\bar{X}) \wedge \theta_Z(\bar{X}) \wedge |\bar{X}| = \bar{z}\right) \right]. \tag{5}$$

It is easily seen that an LCC is an RLCC with $\theta_Z \equiv$ true and RLCCs have the "additive" property.

Proposition 5. *If* Φ_Δ *is an RLCC for* Φ_Q/θ_Z, *then for any* θ'_Z, $\Phi_\Delta \wedge \theta'_Z$ *is also an RLCC for* $\Phi_Q/(\theta_Z \wedge \theta'_Z)$.

In particular, if $(\theta'_Z := \Phi_Z, \theta_Z :=$ true$)$, Φ_Δ is an LCC for Φ_Q, then $\Phi_\Delta \wedge \Phi_Z$ is an RLCC for Φ_Q/Φ_Z. So Thm. 1 is in fact a special case of the following theorem.

Theorem 2. *Let* Φ_Δ *be an RLCC for* Φ_Q/Φ_Z. *Then* $\mathfrak{Q}_Z \models_\exists \Phi_Z \wedge \Phi_Q$ *if and only if* PA $\models_\exists \Phi_\Delta$.

This theorem motivates the strategy of our decision procedures. In the normalization process, with introduction of auxiliary integer constraints, we partition the original search space for Φ_Q such that $\Phi_Q \leftrightarrow \bigcup_i \Phi_Q^{(i)} \wedge \theta_Z^{(i)}$, until we easily compute the RLCC $\Phi_\Delta^{(i)}$ for each $\Phi_Q^{(i)}/\theta_Z^{(i)}$. By Prop. 5, $\Phi_\Delta^{(i)} \wedge \Phi_Z$ is an RLCC for $\Phi_Q^{(i)}/(\theta_Z^{(i)} \wedge \Phi_Z)$. Then $\mathfrak{Q}_Z \models_\exists \Phi_Q \wedge \Phi_Z$ if and only if for some i, $\mathfrak{Q}_Z \models_\exists \Phi_Q^{(i)} \wedge \theta_Z^{(i)} \wedge \Phi_Z$, which, by Thm. 2 (set $\Phi_Q := \Phi_Q^{(i)}, \Phi_\Delta := \Phi_\Delta^{(i)} \wedge \Phi_Z$, $\Phi_Z := \Phi_Z \wedge \theta_Z^{(i)}$), reduces to determining whether PA $\models_\exists \Phi_\Delta^{(i)} \wedge \Phi_Z$ and $\mathfrak{Q} \models_\exists \Phi_Q$. This leads to the following generic decision procedure.

Algorithm 3 (Generic Decision Procedure). *Input:* $\Phi_Q \wedge \Phi_Z$.

1. *Return* FAIL *if* $\mathfrak{Q} \not\models_\exists \Phi_Q$.
2. *For each partition* $\Phi_Q^{(i)} \wedge \theta_Z^{(i)}$ *of* Φ_Q:
    (a) *Compute an RLCC* $\Phi_\Delta^{(i)}$ *for* $\Phi_Q^{(i)}/\theta_Z^{(i)}$.
    (b) *Return* SUCCESS *if* PA $\models_\exists \Phi_\Delta^{(i)} \wedge \Phi_Z$.
3. *Return* FAIL.

Example 6. Revisiting Ex. 5, we partition Φ_Q into $(\Phi_Q \wedge |X| \neq |Y|) \vee (\Phi_Q \wedge |X| = |Y|)$. The first disjunct simplifies to $|X| \neq |Y|$ as $|X| \neq |Y|$ implies Φ_Q. Now consider the second disjunct. It is clear that the RLCC for $\Phi_Q/(|X| = |Y|)$ is $|X| = |Y| \wedge |X| \neq 1$.

5   Decision Procedure for $\text{Th}^\vee(\mathfrak{Q}_{\mathbb{Z}})$

We partition the search space for Φ_Q in a series of steps. When $|X|$ is known to be bounded by a constant l, we can instantiate X with a constant queue of length l. As $\mathcal{A}$ is finite, there are only finitely many such queues.

First we assume $\Phi_Q \wedge \theta_{\mathbb{Z}}$ satisfies the following condition.

Definition 9 (Equality Completion). Φ_Q *is* equality complete *if* $t_1 \neq t_2 \in \Phi_Q$ *if and only if* $|t_1| = |t_2| \in \theta_{\mathbb{Z}}$.

To satisfy this condition, we first set $\theta_{\mathbb{Z}} := \emptyset$ and for each $t_1 \neq t_2$, add either $|t_1| = |t_2|$ or $|t_1| \neq |t_2|$ to $\theta_{\mathbb{Z}}$. In the latter case, $t_1 \neq t_2$ can be removed from Φ_Q.

Definition 10 (Normal Form in $\mathfrak{Q}_{\mathbb{Z}}$). Φ_Q *is in* normal form *in* $\mathfrak{Q}_{\mathbb{Z}}$ *if* Φ_Q *satisfies Def. 5 and satisfies (i) if* $\alpha X \neq Y\beta$ *occurs with either* $X \in \text{orb}(\alpha', k)$ *or* $Y \in \text{orb}(\beta', l)$, *then* $\alpha \equiv \epsilon_Q$; *(ii)* $\alpha X \neq Y\beta$ *does not occur with both* $X \in \text{orb}(\alpha', k)$ *and* $Y \in \text{orb}(\beta', l)$.

Algorithm 4 (Normalization in $\mathfrak{Q}_{\mathbb{Z}}$).

1. *Call Alg. 1 to normalize* Φ_Q.
2. *For all disequalities* $\alpha X \neq Y\beta$ *with* $|X| < |\beta|$ *or* $|Y| < |\alpha|$, *replace* X *and* Y *by instantiations. In the remaining steps we assume* $|X| \geq |\beta|$ *and* $|Y| \geq |\alpha|$.
3. *Consider each constraint of the form*
$$\alpha X \neq Y\beta \wedge X \in \text{orb}(\alpha', k) \wedge Y \in \text{orb}(\beta', l), \tag{6}$$
   which asserts that X *is of the form* $(\alpha')^*\alpha'[1..k]$ *and similar for* Y. *If* β *is not a prefix of* X *or* α *is not a prefix of* Y, $\alpha X \neq Y\beta$ *simplifies to* true. *Otherwise* $\alpha X \neq Y\beta$ *can be replaced by* $X = X'\beta \wedge Y = \alpha Y' \wedge X' \neq Y'$ *which can be further reduced to*
$$X' \in \text{orb}(\alpha', k') \wedge Y' \in \text{orb}(\beta'', l') \wedge X' \neq Y', \tag{7}$$
   where
$$k' = \Big(k + |\alpha'| - (|\beta| \bmod |\alpha'|)\Big) \bmod |\alpha'|,$$
$$\beta'' = \beta'[(|\alpha| \bmod |\beta'|) + 1..|\beta'|] \circ \beta'[1..(|\alpha| \bmod |\beta'|)],$$
$$l' = \Big(l + |\beta'| - (|\alpha| \bmod |\beta'|)\Big) \bmod |\beta'|.$$
   If $\alpha' = \beta''$, *then* $k' = l'$, *because* $|X'| = |Y'|$. *Thus* (7) *is* false *and so is* (6). *If* $\alpha' \neq \beta''$, *then there are only finitely many cases that* $X' = Y'$ *which can be computed and excluded.*
4. *Consider each constraint of the form* $\alpha X \neq Y\beta \wedge X \in \text{orb}(\alpha', k)$. *Guess a word* α'' *such that* $|\alpha''| = |\alpha|$ *and set* $Y = \alpha''Y'$. *For* $\alpha \not\equiv \alpha''$, *replace* $\alpha X \neq Y\beta$ *by* $Y = \alpha''Y'$, *otherwise, replace* $\alpha X \neq Y\beta$ *by* $Y = \alpha Y' \wedge X \neq Y'\beta$.
5. *Consider each constraint of the form* $\alpha X \neq Y\beta \wedge Y \in \text{orb}(\beta', l)$. *If* α *is not a prefix of* Y *(which has the form* $(\beta')^*\beta'[1..l]$), $\alpha X \neq Y\beta \wedge Y \in \text{orb}(\beta', l)$ *simplifies to* true. *Otherwise* $\alpha X \neq Y\beta$ *can be replaced by* $Y = \alpha Y' \wedge X \neq Y'\beta$, *which can be further simplified to* $Y' \in \text{orb}(\beta'', l') \wedge X \neq Y'\beta$, *with* β'' *and* l' *the same as in step 3.*

Algorithm 5 (Computation of $\Phi_{\Delta+}$). *Input: $\Phi_Q \wedge \theta_{\mathbb{Z}}$. Initially set $\Phi_{\Delta+} = \emptyset$. Add to $\Phi_{\Delta+}$: (1) $|t_1| = |t_2|$, if $t_1 \neq t_2$ or $t_1 = t_2$; (2) $|X| + |\alpha| = |\alpha X| = |X\alpha|$, if αX or $X\alpha$ occurs; (3) $|X| \equiv k(\bmod |\alpha|)$, if $X \in \mathrm{orb}(\alpha, k)$.*

Φ_Q can be satisfied by sufficiently long queues: there exists a *cutpoint* δ such that if $\mathfrak{Q} \models_\exists \Phi_Q$, then for any solution $(l_i)_n$ (i.e., $l_0, \ldots, l_n$) for $\Phi_{\Delta+}$ such that $l_i \geq \delta$, there exists a solution $(\alpha_i)_n$ for Φ_Q such that $|\alpha_i| = l_i$. Let $C_\Phi(\delta)$ denote $\bigwedge_{X \in V_Q(\Phi_Q)} |X| \geq \delta$. It is clear that $\Phi_{\Delta+} \wedge C_\Phi(\delta) \wedge \theta_{\mathbb{Z}}$ is an RLCC for $\Phi_Q / \theta_{\mathbb{Z}}$. It is not true, however, that δ is the smallest $max\{(\mu_i)_n\}$ such that $\mathfrak{Q}_{\mathbb{Z}} \models_\exists \Phi_Q \wedge \bigwedge_{i=1}^n |X_i| = \mu_i$ where $(X_i)_n$ enumerate $V_Q(\Phi_Q)$. Ex. 4 shows an anomaly where $\{X := \epsilon_Q, Y := \epsilon_Q\}$ is a solution for Φ_Q (with $|X| = |Y| = 0$), while there exists no solution for Φ_Q such that $|X| = |Y| = 1$. To avoid such anomalies we separate the search for a satisfying assignment into two cases. We compute a cut length $L_t \geq \delta$ and enumerate all assignments σ with $[\![|X|]\!]\sigma < L_t$, while for $[\![|X|]\!]\sigma \geq L_t$ satisfiability of the queue constraints is reduced to satisfiability of integer constraints as in [13,14].

The computation of L_t is based on the observation that an assignment σ is satisfying if every $[\![X]\!]\sigma$ includes a unique "marker" at the same, fixed, position. Such a marker can be constructed by concatenating a "shortest unused prefix" and a unique identifier for each queue variable. Let PRE_Φ denote the set of all words α such that αX or α is a proper term in Φ_Q. A word q is called a *delimiter* of Φ_Q if q is strongly primitive and $q \notin \mathrm{orb}(\alpha)$ for any $\alpha \in \mathrm{PRE}_\Phi$. Let d_p denote an arbitrary shortest delimiter (there can be more than one) and let $L_p = |d_p|$. Let L_c be the smallest number of letters necessary to create a unique identifying word, called a *color*, for each queue variable in Φ_Q. We claim that $L_c + L_p = L_t \geq \delta$.

Example 7 (Computation of L_t). Consider again Φ_Q in Ex. 4. Here $\mathrm{PRE}_\Phi = \{ab, ba, aa\}$; a shortest delimiter is aab, and thus $L_p = 3$. Φ_Q includes two queue variables, requiring one letter to identifying them with two letters in the alphabet. Thus, we need four letters to construct a unique identifying word, resulting in $L_t = 4$.

Proposition 6 (RLCC in $\mathfrak{Q}_{\mathbb{Z}}$). $\Phi_{\Delta+} \wedge C_\Phi(L_t) \wedge \theta_{\mathbb{Z}}$ *is an RLCC for $\Phi_Q / \theta_{\mathbb{Z}}$.*

Definition 11 (Length Configuration in $\mathfrak{Q}_{\mathbb{Z}}$). *A length configuration for Φ_Q (in $\mathfrak{Q}_{\mathbb{Z}}$) is a conjunction $\bigwedge_{X \in V_Q(\Phi_Q)} A_X$, where A_X is either $|X| = i$ (for some $i < L_t$) or $|X| \geq L_t$.*

Let $\mathcal{C}$ be the set of all configurations. Clearly $\mathcal{C}$ creates a finite partition of the search space that includes $C_\Phi(L_t)$. A partial assignment ∂ is *compatible* with a configuration C if for any variable X, $[\![X]\!]\partial$ is defined iff $|X| = i$ (for some $i < L_t$) occurs in C. The empty assignment is vacuously a satisfying partial assignment, the only one compatible with $C_\Phi(L_t)$. As a consequence of Prop. 6, we have

Algorithm 6 (Decision Procedures for $\mathfrak{Q}_{\mathbb{Z}}$). *Input: $\Phi_Q \wedge \theta_{\mathbb{Z}} \wedge \Phi_{\mathbb{Z}}$ where $\Phi_Q \wedge \theta_{\mathbb{Z}}$ denotes one of the partitions.*

1. *For each* $C \in \mathcal{C}$,
    (a) *Guess a satisfying ∂ compatible with C and update* $\Phi_{\Delta+}, C, \theta_{\mathbb{Z}}$ *and* $\Phi_{\mathbb{Z}}$.
    (b) *If succeed, return* SUCCESS *if* $PA \models_{\exists} \Phi_{\Delta+} \wedge C \wedge \theta_{\mathbb{Z}} \wedge \Phi_{\mathbb{Z}}$.
2. *Return* FAIL.

6   Quantifier Elimination for Th($\mathfrak{Q}_{\mathbb{Z}}$)

In this section we present a quantifier elimination for the first-order theory of queues with integers, Th($\mathfrak{Q}_{\mathbb{Z}}$). The procedure removes a block of quantifiers of the same type in a single step.

It is well-known that eliminating arbitrary quantifiers reduces to eliminating existential quantifiers from formulae in the form $(\exists \bar{x})[A_1(\bar{x}) \wedge \ldots \wedge A_n(\bar{x})]$, where $A_i(\bar{x})$ $(1 \le i \le n)$ are literals [5]. By parameters we mean the *implicitly universally quantified variables*. We use $\bar{Y}$ to denote a sequence of Q-parameters.

The elimination procedure consists of the following two subprocedures.

Elimination of Quantifiers on Integer Variables We assume formulas with quantifiers on integer variables are in the form

$$(\exists \bar{u} : \mathbb{Z}) \left[\Phi_Q(\bar{X}) \ \wedge \ \Phi_{\mathbb{Z}}(\bar{u}, \bar{v}, \bar{X}) \right], \tag{8}$$

where $\bar{X} \subseteq \mathcal{V}_Q$ and $\bar{v}, \bar{u} \subseteq \mathcal{V}_{\mathbb{Z}}$. Since $\Phi_Q(\bar{X})$ does not contain $\bar{u}$, we can move them out of the scope of $(\exists \bar{u})$, and then obtain

$$\Phi_Q(\bar{X}) \ \wedge \ (\exists \bar{u} : \mathbb{Z}) \, \Phi_{\mathbb{Z}}(\bar{u}, \bar{v}, \bar{X}). \tag{9}$$

Since in $\Phi_{\mathbb{Z}}(\bar{u}, \bar{v}, \bar{X})$, $\bar{X}$ occurs as pseudo integer variables, $(\exists \bar{u} : \mathbb{Z})\Phi_{\mathbb{Z}}(\bar{u}, \bar{v}, \bar{X})$ is essentially a Presburger formula and we can proceed to remove the quantifier using Cooper's method [3]. In fact we can defer the elimination until all other types of quantifiers are removed.

Elimination of Quantifiers on Queue Variables We assume formulas with quantifiers on queue variables are in the form

$$(\exists \bar{X} : Q) \left[\Phi_Q(\bar{X}, \bar{Y}) \ \wedge \ \Phi_{\mathbb{Z}}(\bar{u}, \bar{X}, \bar{Y}) \right], \tag{10}$$

where $\bar{X}, \bar{Y} \subseteq \mathcal{V}_Q$, $\bar{u} \subseteq \mathcal{V}_{\mathbb{Z}}$, and $\Phi_{\mathbb{Z}}(\bar{u}, \bar{X}, \bar{Y})$ can be an arbitrary Presburger formula (not necessarily quantifier-free). By Prop. 1, we can assume $\bar{X}$ does not occur in selectors. Though elimination of selectors in general adds more existential quantifiers of sort queue or atom, the newly added quantifiers will be removed together with the original ones.

We need to extend the notion of RLCC to deal with parameters.

Definition 12 (RLCC with parameters). *Consider* $(\exists \bar{X} : Q)\left[\Phi_Q(\bar{X}, \bar{Y}) \wedge \theta_{\mathbb{Z}}(\bar{X}, \bar{Y})\right]$, *where* $\bar{Y}$ *are parameters. Let* $\Phi_Q^{(2)}(\bar{Y})$ *be the maximum subset of* $\Phi_Q(\bar{X}, \bar{Y})$ *not containing* $\bar{X}$ *and* $\Phi_Q^{(1)}(\bar{X}, \bar{Y}) := \Phi_Q(\bar{X}, \bar{Y}) \setminus \Phi_Q^{(2)}(\bar{Y})$. *A formula*

$\Phi_\Delta(\bar{X}, \bar{Y})$ is an RLCC in $\bar{X}$ for $\Phi_Q(\bar{X}, \bar{Y})$ relativized to $\theta_{\mathbb{Z}}(\bar{X}, \bar{Y})$, (in short, $\Phi_\Delta(\bar{X}, \bar{Y})$ is an RLCC for $\Phi_Q(\bar{X}, \bar{Y})/\bar{X}/\theta_{\mathbb{Z}}(\bar{X}, \bar{Y}))$, if the following hold:

$$(\forall \bar{X}, \bar{Y} : Q)\left[\Phi_Q(\bar{X}, \bar{Y}) \wedge \theta_{\mathbb{Z}}(\bar{X}, \bar{Y}) \to (\exists \bar{z} : \mathbb{Z})\left(\Phi_\Delta(\bar{z}, \bar{Y}) \wedge |\bar{X}| = \bar{z}\right)\right], \quad (11)$$

$$(\forall \bar{Y} : Q)(\forall \bar{z} : \mathbb{Z})\left[\Phi_Q^{(2)}(\bar{Y}) \wedge \Phi_\Delta(\bar{z}, \bar{Y}) \right.$$
$$\left. \to (\exists \bar{X} : Q)\left(\Phi_Q(\bar{X}, \bar{Y}) \wedge \theta_{\mathbb{Z}}(\bar{X}, \bar{Y}) \wedge |\bar{X}| = \bar{z}\right)\right]. \quad (12)$$

We also need to update the notion of normal form for parameters.

Definition 13 (Normal Form in $\mathfrak{Q}_{\mathbb{Z}}$ with $\bar{Y}$). Φ_Q is in normal form in $\mathfrak{Q}_{\mathbb{Z}}$ (with parameters) if Φ_Q satisfies Def. 10 and the following condition: if $\alpha X \beta \neq t(Y)$ (where Y is a parameter) appears in Φ_Q, then $\alpha \equiv \beta \equiv \epsilon_Q$ and X does not occur in literals of the form $X \in \mathrm{orb}(\alpha, k)$.

We treat Q-terms of the form $t(Y)$ as distinct variables. Let L_c, L_p and L_t be as defined in Sec. 5 and we obtain $C_\Phi(L_t)$ and $\Phi_{\Delta+}(\bar{X}, \bar{Y})$ accordingly.

Proposition 7 (RLCC in $\mathfrak{Q}_{\mathbb{Z}}$ with $\bar{Y}$). $\Phi_{\Delta+}(\bar{X}, \bar{Y}) \wedge C_\Phi(L_t) \wedge \theta_{\mathbb{Z}}(\bar{X}, \bar{Y})$ is an RLCC for $\Phi_Q(\bar{X}, \bar{Y})/\bar{X}/\theta_{\mathbb{Z}}(\bar{X}, \bar{Y})$.

We guess and add a $C \in \mathcal{C}$ to (10). First we remove each X such that $|X| = i$ ($i < L_t$) occurs in C. For the variables left in $\bar{X}$, we have $|X| \geq L_t$ in C and so we can assume C is $C_\Phi(L_t)$ Then (10) is rewritten as

$$(\exists \bar{X} : Q)\left[\Phi_Q(\bar{X}, \bar{Y}) \wedge \theta_{\mathbb{Z}}(\bar{X}, \bar{Y}) \wedge \Phi_{\mathbb{Z}}(\bar{u}, \bar{X}, \bar{Y})\right], \quad (13)$$

which is equivalent to

$$\Phi_Q^{(2)}(\bar{Y}) \wedge (\exists \bar{v} : \mathbb{Z})\left[\Phi_{\Delta+}(\bar{v}, \bar{Y}) \wedge C_\Phi(L_t) \wedge \theta_{\mathbb{Z}}(\bar{v}, \bar{Y}) \wedge \Phi_{\mathbb{Z}}(\bar{u}, \bar{v}, \bar{Y})\right]. \quad (14)$$

7   Conclusion

We presented decision procedures for the theory of queues with integer constraints. Our method combines the extraction of integer constraints from queue constraints, and in case of the quantified theory, with a reduction of quantifiers on queue variables to quantifiers on integer variables.

Complexity Clearly $\mathrm{Th}^\vee(\mathfrak{Q}_{\mathbb{Z}})$ is NP-hard as it is a super theory of $\mathrm{Th}^\vee(\mathfrak{Q})$ and $\mathrm{Th}^\vee(\mathbb{Z})$, which are both NP-complete. Alg. 5 computes $\Phi_{\Delta+}$ in $O(n)$ and L_t, L_t^+ are also in $O(n)$. By the nondeterministic nature of our algorithms, we can show that each branch of computation in the normalization procedures and in Algs. 2, 3, 6 is in P. Therefore $\mathrm{Th}^\vee(\mathfrak{Q}_{\mathbb{Z}})$ is NP-complete and consequently, for $\mathrm{Th}(\mathfrak{Q}_{\mathbb{Z}})$, the elimination of a block of existential quantifiers, regardless of the size of the block, can be done in $O(2^n)$.

Future Work We plan to extend our results to the theory of queues in a more expressive signature, e.g., in the language with prefix, suffix and subqueue relation, and investigate decidability of the first-order theory of queues with integers and prefix or suffix relation. Note that for the first-order theory we cannot obtain decidability with both prefix and suffix relations, nor in a signature with prefix (or suffix) relation and all constructors, because both extensions are sufficiently expressive to interpret the theory of arrays.

References

1. Michael Benedikt, Leonid Libkin, Thomas Schwentick, and Luc Segoufin. A model-theoretic approach to regular string relations. In *Proceedings of 16th IEEE Symposium on Logic in Computer Science (LICS'01)*, pages 431–440. IEEE Computer Society Press, 2001.
2. Nikolaj S. Bjørner. *Integrating Decision Procedures for Temporal Verification*. PhD thesis, Computer Science Department, Stanford University, November 1998.
3. D. C. Cooper. Theorem proving in arithmetic without multiplication. In *Machine Intelligence*, volume 7, pages 91–99. American Elsevier, 1972.
4. H. B. Enderton. *A Mathematical Introduction to Logic*. Academic Press, 2001.
5. Wilfrid Hodges. *Model Theory*. Cambridge University Press, Cambridge, UK, 1993.
6. Felix Klaedtke and Harald Rueß. Monadic second-order logics with cardinalities. In *30th International Colloquium on Automata, Languages and Programming (ICALP'03)*, volume 2719 of *LNCS*. Springer-Verlag, 2003.
7. M. Lothaire. *Combinatorics on Words*. Addison-Wesley, Massachusetts, USA, 1983.
8. Greg Nelson and Derek C. Oppen. Simplification by cooperating decision procedures. *ACM Transaction on Programming Languages and Systems*, 1(2):245–257, October 1979.
9. C. R. Reddy and D. W. Loveland. Presburger arithmetic with bounded quantifier alternation. In *Proceedings of the 10th Annual Symposium on Theory of Computing (STOC'78)*, pages 320–325. ACM Press, 1978.
10. Tatiana Rybina and Andrei Voronkov. A decision procedure for term algebras with queues. In *Proceedings of 15th IEEE Symposium on Logic in Computer Science (LICS'00)*, pages 279 – 290. IEEE Computer Society Press, 2000.
11. Tatiana Rybina and Andrei Voronkov. Upper bounds for a theory of queues. In *Proceedings of 30th International Colloquium on Automata, Languages and Programming (ICALP'03)*, volume 2719 of *LNCS*, pages 714–724. Springer-Verlag, 2003.
12. Wolfgang Thomas. Infinite trees and automaton-definable relations over ω-words. *Theoretical Computer Science*, 103:143–159, 1992.
13. Ting Zhang, Henny B. Sipma, and Zohar Manna. Decision procedures for recursive data structures with integer constraints. In *the 2nd International Joint Conference on Automated Reasoning (IJCAR'04)*, volume 3097 of *LNCS*, pages 152–167. Springer-Verlag, 2004.
14. Ting Zhang, Henny B. Sipma, and Zohar Manna. Term algebras with length function and bounded quantifier alternation. In *the 17th International Conference on Theorem Proving in Higher Order Logics (TPHOLs'04)*, volume 3223 of *LNCS*, pages 321–336. Springer-Verlag, 2004.

The Directed Planar Reachability Problem

Eric Allender[1], Samir Datta[2], and Sambuddha Roy[3]

[1] Department of Computer Science, Rutgers University, Piscataway, NJ 08855
allender@cs.rutgers.edu
[2] Chennai Mathematical Institute, Chennai, TN 600 017, India
sdatta@cmi.ac.in
[3] Department of Computer Science, Rutgers University, Piscataway, NJ 08855
samroy@paul.rutgers.edu

Abstract. We investigate the s-t-connectivity problem for directed planar graphs, which is hard for L and is contained in NL but is not known to be complete. We show that this problem is logspace-reducible to its complement, and we show that the problem of searching graphs of genus 1 reduces to the planar case.

We also consider a previously-studied subclass of planar graphs known as *grid graphs*. We show that the directed planar s-t-connectivity problem reduces to the reachability problem for directed grid graphs.

A special case of the grid-graph reachability problem where no edges are directed from right to left is known as the "layered grid graph reachability problem". We show that this problem lies in the complexity class UL.

1 Introduction

Graph reachability problems play a central role in the study and understanding of subclasses of P. The s-t-connectivity problem for directed graphs (STCONN) is complete for nondeterministic logspace (NL); the restriction of this problem to undirected graphs, called USTCONN, has recently been shown to be complete for logspace (L) [Rei05]; thus this problem has the same complexity as the s-t-connectivity problem for graphs of outdegree 1 (and even for graphs of indegree and outdegree at most 1 [Ete97]).

Grid graphs are an important restricted class of graphs for which the reachability problem has significant connections to complexity classes. (The vertices in a grid graph are a subset of $\mathbb{N} \times \mathbb{N}$, and all edges are of the form $(i, j) \rightarrow (i + b, j)$ or $(i, j) \rightarrow (i, j + b)$, where $b \in \{1, -1\}$.) In most settings (and in particular in all of the results we will present in this paper) it is sufficient to restrict attention to grid graphs where the start vertex s lies in the first column, and the terminal vertex t lies in the final column. In [BLMS98], Barrington et al showed that the reachability problem in (directed or undirected) grid graphs of width k captures the complexity of depth k AC^0. Barrington also considered general grid graphs without the width restriction, calling this the Grid Graph Reachability problem (GGR) [Bar02]. The construction of [BLMS98, Lemma 13] shows that GGR reduces to its complement via uniform projections. (The problems STCONN and USTCONN also reduce to their complements via uniform projections, as a consequence of [Imm88, Sze88, Rei05, NTS95].) Reachability problems for grid graphs have proved easier to work with than the corresponding problems for general

R. Ramanujam and S. Sen (Eds.): FSTTCS 2005, LNCS 3821, pp. 238–249, 2005.

graphs. For instance, the reachability problem for *undirected* grid graphs was shown to lie in L in the 1970's [BK78], although more than a quarter-century would pass before Reingold proved the corresponding theorem for general undirected graphs.

Barrington also defined what we will refer to as the *layered* grid graph reachability problem LGGR, in which no edges are directed from right to left in the grid. (That is, there is no edge of the form $(i, j) \rightarrow (i, j - 1)$; we use the convention that vertex (i, j) refers to the point in row i and column j.) Barrington originally called these graphs "acyclic" grid graphs, because this is a simple syntactic condition guaranteeing that a grid graph will have no cycles. (However, this terminology was confusing because there are grid graphs without cycles that do not meet this syntactic criterion.) In personal communication, Barrington suggested the name "layered", with the following justification. It is shown in [Bar02] that this problem is equivalent to the special case where all edges are directed from left to right or from top to bottom. Thus without loss of generality, the start node is in the top left corner. If such a grid graph is rotated 45 degrees counterclockwise, one obtains a graph whose "columns" correspond to the diagonals of the original graph, where s is the only node in the first "column", and all edges in one column are directed "northeast" or "southeast" to their neighbors in the following column. This is consistent with the usual usage of the word "layered" in graph theory.

Barrington showed that GGR and LGGR are hard for NC^1 under uniform projections [Bar02], but the best upper bound that was identified by Barrington for these problems is NL.

Our focus in this paper is the restriction of STCONN to planar (directed) graphs PLANAR.STCONN. This problem is hard for L under uniform projections, as a consequence of [Ete97], and it lies in NL. Nothing else has been published regarding its computational complexity. Thus the class of problems $\leq_m^{\log}$-reducible to PLANAR.STCONN can be viewed as a complexity class lying between L and NL. We show that this class is closed under complement, by presenting a $\leq_m^{\log}$ reduction of PLANAR.STCONN to its complement; we do not know if this reduction can be accomplished by uniform projections or even by NC^1 reductions; in contrast to the case for STCONN, USTCONN, and GGR. We also show that this class contains the s-t-connectivity problem for graphs of genus 1; the generalization for graphs of higher genus remains open.

We have two separate proofs of closure under complement, but due to space limitations we will not present our direct proof. Instead, we will present only a reduction showing PLANAR.STCONN$\leq_m^{\log}$GGR. By [BLMS98, Lemma 13] (showing that GGR reduces to its complement) this is sufficient.

Our final technical contribution is to show that LGGR lies in the complexity class UL. This must be viewed as a slight improvement, since it is shown in [ARZ99] that NL = UL if there is any problem in DSPACE(n) that requires circuits of exponential size, and it is shown in [RA00] that NL/poly = UL/poly (unconditionally). We actually show that LGGR lies in UL∩coUL, although (in contrast to all of the other reachability problems we consider) it remains open if LGGR reduces to its complement. (Note also that it remains open if UL = coUL.) Some other examples of reachability problems in UL were presented by Lange [Lan97]; these problems are obviously in UL (in the sense that the positive instances consist of certain graphs that contain only one path from s to

t), and the main contribution of [Lan97] is to present a *completeness* result for a natural subclass of UL. In contrast, positive instances of LGGR can have many paths from s to t. We know of no reductions (in either direction) between LGGR and the problems considered in [Lan97].

Series-parallel graphs are an important and well-studied subclass of planar directed graphs. Jakoby, Liskiewicz, and Reischuk showed in [JLR01] that s-t-connectivity in series-parallel graphs can be computed in logspace (and in fact is complete for L). They also show the much stronger result that *counting* the number of paths between s and t can be computed in logspace for series-parallel graphs. Very recently, in joint work with David Mix Barrington and Tanmoy Chakraborty, we have identified some even larger classes of planar directed graphs for which s-t-connectivity can be solved in logspace; these results will be described in a subsequent paper.

2   Reduction to a Special Case

In this section we present a reduction showing that it is sufficient to consider the special case where the vertices s and t both lie on the external face of the planar graph. This was useful in our direct proof of closure under complement, but it is also useful in presenting our reduction to grid-graph reachability.

Let G be a directed graph. Testing if G is planar reduces to the undirected s-t-connectivity problem [AM04] and thus can be done in logarithmic space [Rei05]. Furthermore, if a graph is planar then a planar combinatorial embedding (i.e., a cyclic ordering of the edges adjacent to each vertex) can be computed in logarithmic space [AM04]. Given a combinatorial embedding, it is easy to check if two vertices lie on the same face. (The vertices on each face adjacent to a vertex v can be enumerated by starting at some (undirected) edge adjacent to v and starting a walk from v along that edge; each time a new vertex w is entered along some edge e the walk continues along the edge that succeeds e in the cyclic ordering of edges around w.) Thus in logspace we can check if s and t lie on the same face. If so, then the graph G is already in the desired form, since we can consider any face to be the "external" face in the embedding.

If s and t do not lie on the same face, then by use of the undirected connectivity algorithm we can determine if there is an undirected path from s to t. If there is no such path, then clearly there is no directed path, either. Otherwise (as observed in [AM04]) we can find a simple undirected path $\mathcal{P} = (s, v_1, v_2, \ldots, v_m, t)$ in logspace. First, we construct a new face with s and t on it, by "cutting" along the path $\mathcal{P}$. (That is, we replace each vertex v_i on $\mathcal{P}$ by vertices $v_{i,a}$ and $v_{i,b}$. For any vertex v_i on $\mathcal{P}$, let u and x be the vertices appearing before and after v_i on $\mathcal{P}$; that is, $u \in \{s, v_{i-1}\}$ and $x \in \{t, v_{i+1}\}$. Let $e_1, \ldots, e_{d_a}$ be the edges embedded "above" the edges connecting v_i to u and x in the cyclic ordering around v_i, and let $e'_1, \ldots, e'_{d_b}$ be the edges embedded "below" the edges between v_i and u and x. That is, if the undirected path from s to t moves from left to right, edges $e_1, \ldots, e_{d_a}$ appear on the left side of this path, and edges $e'_1, \ldots, e'_{d_b}$ appear on the right side. Let $\mathcal{L}$ be the set of all edges adjacent to $\mathcal{P}$ embedded on the left side, and let $\mathcal{R}$ be the set of all edges adjacent to $\mathcal{P}$ embedded on the right side. In the new graph, the edges in $\mathcal{L}$ that were connected to v_i are connected to $v_{i,a}$ and those in $\mathcal{R}$ are connected to $v_{i,b}$. Edges between v_i and $\{v_{i+1}, v_{i-1}$ are duplicated, with edges between $v_{i,c}$ and $\{v_{i+1,c}, v_{i-1,c}\}$ for $c \in \{a, b\}$. Similarly, edges between s and v_1 (and t and v_m) are duplicated, with edges between s and $v_{1,a}$ and $v_{1,b}$ (and edges between t and $v_{m,a}$ and $v_{m,b}$, respectively). This is illustrated in Figure 1.)

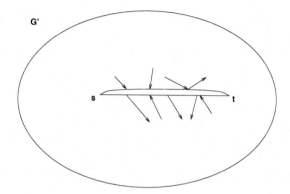

Fig. 1. Cutting along a st path

This new graph G' is planar, and has vertices s and t on the same face (the only new face created). Since we can embed any planar graph such that any specific face is the outer face, we re-embed our graph G' such that s and t are now on the outer face. From now on we assume G' has this embedding.

In the process of going from G to G' we have changed the connectivity of the graph; s and t might have been connected in G but they might not be connected in G'. In particular, any directed path in G from s to t that uses edges from *both* $\mathcal{L}$ and $\mathcal{R}$ is not replicated in G'. We solve this problem by pasting together copies of the graph G', as follows. The outer face of G' consists of two undirected paths from s to t: $s, v_{1,a}, v_{2,a}, \ldots, v_{m,a}, t$ and $s, v_{1,b}, v_{2,b}, \ldots, v_{m,b}, t$. The operation of "pasting" two copies of G' together consists of identifying the vertices $v_{1,a}, v_{2,a}, \ldots, v_{m,a}$ in one copy with the vertices $v_{1,b}, v_{2,b}, \ldots, v_{m,b}$ in the other copy. (Note that this amounts to "sewing together" two copies of the path that were "cut apart" in creating G' from G.) The graph G'' consists of $2n + 1$ copies of G' pasted together in this way: the "original copy" in the middle, and n copies pasted in sequence to the top boundary of the outer face, and n copies pasted in sequence to the bottom boundary.

G'' has (the original copies of) s and t on the outer face. A simple inductive argument shows that there is a directed path from s to t in G if and only there is a directed path from (the original copy of) s to one of the copies of t in G''. A pathological example showing that many copies of G' are needed is shown in Figure 2. To complete the reduction, we construct a graph H that consists of G'' along with a new vertex t'' with directed edges from each copy of t to t''. The vertices s and t'' appear on the external face of H, and there is a directed path from s to t in G if and only if there is a directed path from s to t'' in H.

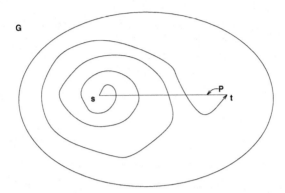

Fig. 2. A pathological case

3 Grid Graphs

In this section, we present a $\leq_m^{\log}$ reduction of PLANAR.STCONN to GGR.

Using the reduction of Section 2, we may assume that we are given a planar graph G with s and t on the external face. By applying the reachability algorithm on undirected graphs, we can merge all vertices that are joined by bidirected edges, and thus we can assume that all edges are unidirectional; note that the graph remains planar after this transformation. We may also assume without loss of generality that G has no vertex of degree (indegree + outdegree) greater than 3, and that s has degree two. (To see this, observe that if v is a vertex of degree $d > 3$, then we may replace v with d vertices arranged in a directed cycle, with each one adjacent to one of the d edges that were connected to v. In order to compute this transformation it is important to note that we can compute the planar embedding in logspace. If the vertex s has degree three, then an additional vertex of degree two can be inserted into this cycle, and re-named s.)

We can compute an (undirected) spanning tree T of G in logspace. The vertex s is a vertex of T, and we can consider it to be the root of T; without loss of generality s has two children in T. By our assumptions on G, the tree T is a binary tree; the planar embedding of G imposes an ordering on the children of each node in T. As observed in [AM04], we can compute the height $h(v)$ of each node v in T in logspace (by counting the number of vertices that are ancestors of v). For notational convenience, define the height of the root s to be 1, and if v has child u then $h(u) = h(v) + 1$.

At this point, we are ready to assign each vertex of G to a grid point. Our grid graph will consist of a "fine grid" and a "coarse grid". The coarse grid consists of points placed at the corners of large squares (of size $(4n + 1) \times (4n + 1)$) of the fine grid. (The fine grid will be used to route non-tree edges between vertices placed on the coarse grid.) For any node x, define $w(x)$ to be the number of leaves of T that appear strictly to the left of x; $w(x)$ can be computed easily in logspace by traversing T. Each vertex x is assigned to the point $(h(x), w(x) + 1)$ in the coarse grid; note that the root s is placed at the top left corner $(1, 1)$. If node x is at position (i, j) in the coarse grid, then the tree edge from x to its left child is embedded as a vertical path to point $(i + 1, j)$ in the coarse grid. If x also has a right child y, then this edge is embedded as a horizontal path to location $(i, w(y) + 1)$ followed by a vertical path to location $(i + 1, w(y) + 1)$ in the coarse grid. This is illustrated in Figure 3.

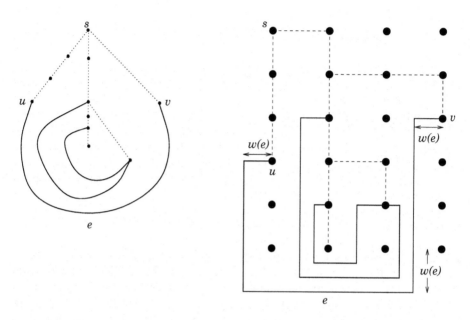

Fig. 3. Embedding a graph on the grid. Edges used in the spanning tree are shown as dashed lines; non-tree edges are solid.

For every non-tree edge e in the tree we can find the number $w(e)$ of non-tree edges enclosed by the unique cycle formed by adding e to the tree. (For edge $e = (u, v)$, $w(e)$ can be computed by finding the least common ancestor y of u and v and determining for each non-tree edge connected to a descendant of y if it is embedded to the right or left of the paths between y and u and v.) For any non-tree edge $e = (u, v)$, note that u and v have degree at most two in the tree T, and thus there is no tree edge attached horizontally adjacent to u or v. The embedding determines if the path representing e should be attached to the east or west sides of u and v. If the embedding goes around a leaf z of the tree T, then the path is routed horizontally from u to a location $w(e)$ fine grid points to the east or west of the column containing z, and vertically down to a point $w(e)$ fine grid points below the level of the leaf of maximum height, and from there horizontally to a point $w(e)$ fine grid points east or west of the column containing v, then vertically to the level of v, and then horizontally to attach to v. If the embedding does not go around a leaf, then a simpler path can be drawn: horizontally to a point $w(e)$ fine grid points east or west of v, then vertically to the level of v, and then horizontally to connect to v. It is easy to verify that no paths collide in this way. See Figure 3 for an example.

Thus we have the following theorem.

Theorem 3.1. PLANAR.STCONN$\leq_m^{\log}$GGR

We obtain the following corollary by appeal to [BLMS98, Lemma 13].

Corollary 3.2. PLANAR.STCONN $\leq_m^{\log}$-*reduces to its complement.*

4 More Closure Properties

Different types of logspace reductions were introduced and studied by Ladner and Lynch [LL76], who showed that logspace Turing and truth-table reducibilities coincided ($A\leq_T^{\log}B$ iff $A\leq_{tt}^{\log}B$). They also introduced a more restrictive version of logspace-computable truth-table reducibility, known as logspace Boolean formula reducibility $\leq_{bf-tt}^{\log}$. $A\leq_{bf-tt}^{\log}B$ if there is a logspace computable function f such that $f(x) = (q_1, q_2, \ldots, q_r, \phi)$ where each q_i is a query and ϕ is a Boolean formula with r variables $y_1, \ldots, y_r$, such that $x \in A$ if and only if ϕ evaluates to 1 when the variables y_i are assigned the truth value of the statement "$q_i \in B$". Additional results about this type of reducibility can be found in [BST93, BH91].

Corollary 4.1. $A\leq_m^{\log}$PLANAR.STCONN *if and only if* $A\leq_{bf-tt}^{\log}$PLANAR.STCONN.

Proof. One direction is trivial; thus assume that $A\leq_{bf-tt}^{\log}$PLANAR.STCONN. For a given input x, let $f(x) = (q_1, q_2, \ldots, q_r, \phi)$ be the result of applying the reduction to x. Without loss of generality, the formula ϕ has negation operations only at the leaves (since it is easy in logspace to apply DeMorgan's laws to rewrite a formula). Using closure under complementation, we can even assume that there are no negation operations at all in the formula. By the results of Section 2, we can assume that each graph q_i is a planar graph with s and t on the external face. Given two such graphs G_1, G_2, note that both G_1 and G_2 are in PLANAR.STCONN if and only if the graph with the terminal vertex of G_1 connected to the start vertex of G_2 is in PLANAR.STCONN, and thus it is easy to simulate an AND gate. Similarly, an OR gate can be simulated by building a new graph with start vertex s connected to the start vertices of both G_1 and G_2, and with edges from the terminal vertices of G_1 and G_2 to a new vertex t. These constructions maintain planarity, and they also maintain the property that s and t are on the external face. Simulating each gate in turn involves only a constant number of additional vertices and edges, and it is easy to see that this gives rise to a $\leq_m^{\log}$ reduction.

5 Higher Genus

In this section we prove that the s-t-connectivity problem for graphs of genus 1 reduces to the planar case. Throughout this section, we will assume that we are given an embedding Π of a graph G onto a surface of genus 1. (Unlike the planar case, it does not appear to be known if testing if a graph has genus $g > 0$ can be accomplished in logspace, even for $g = 1$ [MV00].) Given such an embedding, using [AM04], we can check in logspace if the minimal genus of the graph is 1.

We introduce here some terminology and definitions relating to graphs on surfaces. It will be sufficient to give informal definitions of various notions; the interested reader can refer to [MT01] for more rigorous definitions.

A *closed orientable* surface is one that can be obtained by adding handles to a sphere in 3-space. The genus of the resulting surface is equal to the number of handles added; see also the text [GT87]. Given a graph G, the genus of the graph is the genus of the (closed orientable) surface of least genus on which the graph can be embedded.

Given a graph G embedded on a closed orientable surface, and a cycle of the graph embedded on the surface, there are two (possibly intersecting) subgraphs, called the two *sides* of the cycle with respect to the embedding. Informally, a side of a cycle is the set of vertices of the graph that are path-connected (via a path in the graph, each edge of the graph being considered regardless of direction) to some vertex on the cycle, such that this path does not cross the cycle itself. (In the considerations below, we are concerned only with genus 1 graphs for which this notion of path-connectivity suffices.) A cycle thereby has two sides, which are called the *left* and the *right* sides. If the left and right sides of a cycle have nonempty intersection, then we call the cycle a *surface-nonseparating cycle*. Note that a graph embedded on a sphere (i.e., a planar graph) does not have any surface-nonseparating cycles. Also, it is easy to see that a *facial* cycle (one that forms the boundary of a face in the embedding of the graph on the surface) cannot be surface-nonseparating. Given a cycle C in an embedded graph, it is easy to check in logspace, if C is surface-nonseparating or not: merely check if there is a vertex $v \in G$, such that v is path-connected to both sides of C (on the embedding).

Lemma 5.1. *Let G be a graph of genus $g > 0$, and let T be a spanning tree of G. Then there is an edge $e \in E(G)$ such that $T \cup \{e\}$ contains a surface-nonseparating cycle.*

Proof. The proof follows ideas from [Tho90] which introduces the "3-path condition":

Definition 5.2. *Let $\mathcal{K}$ be a family of cycles of G as follows. We say that $\mathcal{K}$ satisfies the 3-path condition if it has the following property. If x, y are vertices of G and P_1, P_2, P_3 are internally disjoint paths joining x and y, and if two of the three cycles $C_{i,j} = P_i \cup P_j$ $(1 \leq i < j \leq 3)$ are not in $\mathcal{K}$, then also the third cycle is not in $\mathcal{K}$.*

We quote the following from [MT01].

Proposition 5.3. *(Proposition 4.3.1 of [MT01]) The family of Π-surface-nonseparating cycles satisfies the 3-path condition.*

Suppose, that $\forall e$, $(T \cup \{e\})$ does not have a surface-nonseparating cycle. We will prove that no cycle C in the graph G can be surface-nonseparating, by induction on the number k of non-tree edges in C. This contradicts the fact that every non-planar graph has a surface-nonseparating cycle ([MT01, Lemma 4.2.4 and the following discussion]) and thus suffices to prove the claim.

The basis ($k = 1$) follows from the above supposition.

For the inductive step from $k - 1$ to k, let a cycle C be given with k edges not in T.

Take any non-tree edge $e = (x, y)$ on C. Consider the tree path P between x and y. If P never leaves the cycle C, then C is a fundamental cycle and we are done by the assumption for $k = 1$. Otherwise, we can consider a maximal segment S of P not in C. Let S lie between vertices u and v of C. Now, we have three paths between u and v: the two paths between u and v on C (call these C_1, C_2), and path S. Note that both $S \cup C_1$ and $S \cup C_2$ have less than k non-tree edges. Hence they are not surface-nonseparating cycles by the induction assumption. So, by the 3-path condition, neither is $C = C_1 \cup C_2$.

This completes the induction, and the proof.

At this point we are able to describe how to reduce the s-t-connectivity problem for graphs of genus 1 to the planar case.

Given a graph G of genus 1 and an embedding Π of G onto the torus, construct an (undirected) spanning tree T of G. (It follows from [NTS95, Rei05] that spanning trees can be constructed in logspace.) For each edge e of G that is not in T, determine if the unique cycle C_e in $T \cup \{e\}$ is surface-nonseparating, as follows.

Let $C_e = \{v_1, v_2, \cdots, v_r\}$. Let G_e be the graph obtained from G by *cutting along* the cycle C_e (as described in [MT01, p. 105]). (For the purposes of visualization, it is useful to imagine cycles as embedded on an inner tube. Cutting along a surface-separating cycle amounts to cutting a hole in the inner tube (resulting in two pieces). In contrast, if C_e is surface-nonseparating, then it is embedded either like a ribbon tied around the tube, or like a whitewall painted on the inner tube. In the former case, cutting along C_e turns the inner tube into a bent cylinder with a copy of C_e on each end; in the latter case cutting along C_e results in a flat ring with one copy of C_e around the inside and one around the outside. In this latter case, the graph is again topologically equivalent to a cylinder with a copy of C_e on each side.) More formally, the graph G_e has two copies of each of the vertices $\{v_1, v_2, \cdots, v_r\}$, which we denote by $\{v_{1,1}, v_{2,1}, \cdots, v_{r,1}\}$, and $\{v_{1,2}, v_{2,2}, \cdots, v_{r,2}\}$. For every edge (u, v_j) (or (v_j, u)) on the right side of C_e (according to Π), G_e has the edge $(u, v_{j,1})$ $((v_{j,1}, u)$, respectively), and for every edge (u, v_j) $((v_j, u)$,respectively) on the left side of C_e we have the edge $(u, v_{j,2})$ (or $(v_{j,2}, u)$) in G_e. The graph G_e also has two copies of the cycle C_e, which we denote by $C_{e,1}$ and $C_{e,2}$. That is, we have edges between $v_{j,b}$ and $v_{j+1,b}$ for each $b \in \{1, 2\}$ and each $1 \leq j \leq r$, directed as in C_e. An important property of cutting along the cycle C_e is that if C_e was surface-nonseparating, then the resulting graph G_e is planar, and the the cycles $C_{e,1}$ and $C_{e,2}$ are *facial* cycles ([MT01, p. 106,Lemma 4.2.4]). (Otherwise, G_e will not be planar.) Thus in logspace we can determine if C_e is surface-nonseparating.

By Lemma 5.1, we are guaranteed to find a surface-nonseparating cycle by testing each edge e that is not in T. The graph G_e does not have the same connectivity properties as G; s and t might have been connected in G but not in G_e. In particular, any directed path in G from s to t that uses edges from *both* the right and left sides of C_e is not replicated in G_e. As in Section 2, we solve this problem by pasting together copies of the graph G_e, as follows. The operation of "pasting" two copies of G_e together consists of identifying the vertices $v_{1,1}, v_{2,1}, \ldots, v_{r,1}$ in one copy with the vertices $v_{1,2}, v_{2,2}, \ldots, v_{m,2}$ in the other copy. (Note that this amounts to "sewing together" two copies of the path that were "cut apart" in creating G_e from G.)

Now construct the graph G' consisting of $2n + 1$ copies of G_e pasted together in this way: the "original copy" in the middle, and n copies along each side, forming one long cylinder. Since this cylinder has genus zero, it is easy to see that G' is planar.

As in Section 2, a simple inductive argument shows that there is a directed path from s to t in G if and only there is a directed path from (the original copy of) s to one of the copies of t in G'. Thus we have presented a logspace-computable disjunctive truth-table reduction to the planar directed s-t-connectivity problem. We obtain a many-one reduction by appeal to Corollary 4.1 Thus we have proved the following theorem.

Theorem 5.4. *The s-t-connectivity problem for graphs of genus one is $\leq^{\log}_m$ reducible to the planar directed s-t-connectivity problem.*

6 Layered Grid Graphs

Theorem 6.1. LGGR $\in$ UL.

Proof. Let G be a layered $n \times n$ grid graph, with vertex s in column 1 and vertex t in column n. We define a weight function w on the edges of G as follows. If e is directed vertically (that is, from (i, j) to (i', j) for $i' \in \{i + 1, i - 1\}$), then e has weight zero. Otherwise, e is directed horizontally and is of the form $(i, j) \rightarrow (i, j + 1)$. In this case, the weight of e is i. This weight function induces a natural weight function on paths; the weight of a path is the sum of the weights of its edges. (It is a helpful approximation to think of the weight of a path as the number of boxes of the grid that lie above the path.)

The minimal-weight simple path from s to any vertex v is unique. This is because if there are two paths P_1 and P_2 from s to v that have the same weight, there must be some column in which P_1 is higher than P_2 and another column in which P_2 is higher than P_1. Since G is a layered grid graph, this means that there is some point in between these two columns in which the two paths intersect. The path from s to v that follows the two paths until they diverge, and then follows the path closer to the top of the grid until they next intersect, and continues in this way until v is reached, will have smaller weight than either P_1 or P_2, and thus they cannot have had minimal weight.

At this point, we are able to mimic the argument of [RA00].

Let C_k be the set of all vertices in column k that are reachable from s. Let $c_k = |C_k|$. Let Σ_k be the sum, over all $v \in C_k$ of the minimal weight path from s to v. Exactly as in [RA00], there is a UL algorithm that, given (G, k, c_k, Σ_k, v), can determine if there is a path from s to v *or not*. (We emphasize the words "or not"; if there is no path, the UL machine will determine this fact; the algorithm presented in [RA00] has this property.) Furthermore, this algorithm has the property that, if v is reachable from s, then the UL machine can compute the weight of the minimal-weight path from s to v. (Informally, the machine tries each vertex x in column k in turn, keeping a running tally of the number of vertices that have been found to be reachable, and the total weight of the guessed paths. For each vertex x, the machine guesses whether there is a path from s to x; if it guesses there is a path, then it tries to guess the path, and increments its running totals. If $x = v$, then it remembers the weight of the path that was guessed. At the end, if the running totals do not equal c_k and Σ_k, then the machine concludes that it did not make good guesses and aborts. By the properties of the weight function, there will be exactly one path that makes the correct guesses and does not abort.)

It suffices now to show that a UL machine can compute the values c_k and Σ_k. Observe first of all that c_1 is easy to compute (by simply walking up and down column 1 from s and counting how many vertices are reachable), and $\Sigma_1 = 0$.

Assuming that the values c_k and Σ_k are available, the numbers c_{k+1} and Σ_{k+1} can be computed as follows. Initialize c_{k+1} and Σ_{k+1} to zero. For each vertex v in column $k+1$, for each edge of the form $x \to y$ to a vertex y in column $k+1$ such that there is a path in column $k+1$ from y to v, if $x \in C_k$ via a minimal-weight path of weight w_x, then compute the weight w'_x of the path to v through x. Let w_v be the minimum of all such x. Increment c_{k+1} by one (to indicate that v is reachable) and increase Σ_{k+1} by w_v. (This algorithm is actually more general than necessary; it is easy to show that the minimal-weight path to v will always be given by the "topmost" vertex $x \in C_k$ for which there is an edge $x \to y$ to a vertex y that can reach v in column $k+1$.)

This completes the proof.

We observe that we have shown that a UL algorithm can also determine if there is *not* a path from s to t, and thus LGGR is in UL $\cap$ coUL.

Acknowledgments

We acknowledge many people for sharing with us their thoughts about what was already known about this problem, including David Mix Barrington, Til Tantau, Omer Reingold, Paul Beame, Pierre McKenzie, Jeff Edmunds, Anna Gal, Vladimir Trifonov, K.V. Subrahmanyam, Meena Mahajan, and Tanmoy Chakraborty. The first and third authors acknowledge the support of NSF Grant CCF-0514155. We also acknowledge the helpful comments provided to us by the program committee.

References

[AM04]   Eric Allender and Meena Mahajan. The complexity of planarity testing. *Information and Computation*, 189:117–134, 2004.

[ARZ99]   E. Allender, K. Reinhardt, and S. Zhou. Isolation, matching, and counting: Uniform and nonuniform upper bounds. *Journal of Computer and System Sciences*, 59(2):164–181, 1999.

[Bar02]   David A. Mix Barrington. Grid graph reachability problems. Talk presented at Dagstuhl Seminar on Complexity of Boolean Functions, Seminar number 02121, 2002.

[BH91]   Samuel R. Buss and Louise Hay. On truth-table reducibility to SAT. *Inf. Comput.*, 91(1):86–102, 1991.

[BK78]   Manuel Blum and Dexter Kozen. On the power of the compass (or, why mazes are easier to search than graphs). In *IEEE Symposium on Foundations of Computer Science (FOCS)*, pages 132–142, 1978.

[BLMS98]   David A. Mix Barrington, Chi-Jen Lu, Peter Bro Miltersen, and Sven Skyum. Searching constant width mazes captures the AC^0 hierarchy. In *15th International Symposium on Theoretical Aspects of Computer Science (STACS)*, number 1373 in Lecture Notes in Computer Science, pages 73–83. Springer, 1998.

[BST93]   Harry Buhrman, Edith Spaan, and Leen Torenvliet. The relative power of logspace and polynomial time reductions. *Computational Complexity*, 3:231–244, 1993.

[Ete97]   Kousha Etessami. Counting quantifiers, successor relations, and logarithmic space. *Journal of Computer and System Sciences*, 54(3):400–411, Jun 1997.

[GT87]   Jonathan Gross and Thomas Tucker. *Topological Graph Theory*. John Wiley and
            Sons, New York, 1 edition, 1987.

[Imm88]   N. Immerman. Nondeterministic space is closed under complementation. *SIAM
            Journal on Computing*, 17:935–938, 1988.

[JLR01]   A. Jakoby, M. Liskiewicz, and R. Reischuk. Space efficient algorithms for series-
            paralle graphs. In *18th International Symposium on Theoretical Aspects of Com-
            puter Science (STACS)*, number 2010 in Lecture Notes in Computer Science, pages
            339–352. Springer, 2001. To appear in J. Algorithms.

[Lan97]   Klaus-Jörn Lange. An unambiguous class possessing a complete set. In *14th Inter-
            national Symposium on Theoretical Aspects of Computer Science (STACS)*, number
            1200 in Lecture Notes in Computer Science, pages 339–350. Springer, 1997.

[LL76]   R. Ladner and N. Lynch. Relativization of questions about log space reducibility.
            Mathematical Systems Theory, 10:19–32, 1976.

[MT01]   Bojan Mohar and Carsten Thomassen. *Graphs on surfaces*. John Hopkins Univer-
            sity Press, Maryland, 1 edition, 2001.

[MV00]   Meena Mahajan and Kasturi R. Varadarajan. A new NC-algorithm for finding a
            perfect matching in bipartite planar and small genus graphs. In *ACM Symposium
            on Theory of Computing (STOC)*, pages 351–357, 2000.

[NTS95]   N. Nisan and A. Ta-Shma. Symmetric Logspace is closed under complement.
            Chicago Journal of Theoretical Computer Science, 1995.

[RA00]   K. Reinhardt and E. Allender. Making nondeterminism unambiguous. *SIAM Jour-
            nal of Computing*, 29:1118–1131, 2000.

[Rei05]   O. Reingold. Undirected st-connectivity in log-space. In *Proceedings 37th Sympo-
            sium on Foundations of Computer Science*, pages 376–385. IEEE Computer Society
            Press, 2005.

[Sze88]   R. Szelepcsényi. The method of forced enumeration for nondeterministic automata.
            Acta Informatica, 26:279–284, 1988.

[Tho90]   C. Thomassen. Embeddings of graphs with no short noncontractible cycles. *J.
            Comb. Theory Ser. B*, 48(2):155–177, 1990.

Dimensions of Copeland-Erdős Sequences

Xiaoyang Gu*, Jack H. Lutz*, and Philippe Moser**

Department of Computer Science, Iowa State University, Ames, IA 50011 USA
{xiaoyang,lutz,moser}@cs.iastate.edu

Abstract. The base-k *Copeland-Erdős sequence* given by an infinite set A of positive integers is the infinite sequence $\mathrm{CE}_k(A)$ formed by concatenating the base-k representations of the elements of A in numerical order. This paper concerns the following four quantities.

- The *finite-state dimension* $\dim_{\mathrm{FS}}(\mathrm{CE}_k(A))$, a finite-state version of classical Hausdorff dimension introduced in 2001.
- The *finite-state strong dimension* $\mathrm{Dim}_{\mathrm{FS}}(\mathrm{CE}_k(A))$, a finite-state version of classical packing dimension introduced in 2004. This is a dual of $\dim_{\mathrm{FS}}(\mathrm{CE}_k(A))$ satisfying $\mathrm{Dim}_{\mathrm{FS}}(\mathrm{CE}_k(A)) \geq \dim_{\mathrm{FS}}(\mathrm{CE}_k(A))$.
- The *zeta-dimension* $\mathrm{Dim}_\zeta(A)$, a kind of discrete fractal dimension discovered many times over the past few decades.
- The *lower zeta-dimension* $\dim_\zeta(A)$, a dual of $\mathrm{Dim}_\zeta(A)$ satisfying $\dim_\zeta(A) \leq \mathrm{Dim}_\zeta(A)$.

We prove the following.

1. $\dim_{\mathrm{FS}}(\mathrm{CE}_k(A)) \geq \dim_\zeta(A)$. This extends the 1946 proof by Copeland and Erdős that the sequence $\mathrm{CE}_k(\mathrm{PRIMES})$ is Borel normal.
2. $\mathrm{Dim}_{\mathrm{FS}}(\mathrm{CE}_k(A)) \geq \mathrm{Dim}_\zeta(A)$.
3. These bounds are tight in the strong sense that these four quantities can have (simultaneously) any four values in $[0,1]$ satisfying the four above-mentioned inequalities.

1 Introduction

In the early years of the twenty-first century, two quantities have emerged as robust, well-behaved, asymptotic measures of the finite-state information content of a given sequence S over a finite alphabet Σ. These two quantities, the *finite-state dimension* $\dim_{\mathrm{FS}}(S)$ and the *finite-state strong dimension* $\mathrm{Dim}_{\mathrm{FS}}(S)$ (defined precisely in section 3), are duals of one another satisfying $0 \leq \dim_{\mathrm{FS}}(S) \leq \mathrm{Dim}_{\mathrm{FS}}(S) \leq 1$ for all S. They are mathematically well-behaved, because they are natural effectivizations of the two most important notions of fractal dimension. Specifically, finite-state dimension is a finite-state version of classical Hausdorff dimension introduced by Dai, Lathrop, Lutz, and Mayordomo [10], while finite-state strong dimension is a finite-state version of classical packing dimension introduced by Athreya, Hitchcock, Lutz, and Mayordomo [3]. Both finite-state dimensions, $\dim_{\mathrm{FS}}(S)$ and $\mathrm{Dim}_{\mathrm{FS}}(S)$, are robust in

---

* This research was supported in part by National Science Foundation Grant 0344187.
** This research was supported in part by Swiss National Science Foundation Grant PBGE2–104820.

R. Ramanujam and S. Sen (Eds.): FSTTCS 2005, LNCS 3821, pp. 250–260, 2005.

that each has been exactly characterized in terms of finite-state gamblers [10,3], information-lossless finite-state compressors [10,3], block-entropy rates [5], and finite-state predictors in the log-loss model [14,3]. In each case, the characterizations of $\dim_{FS}(S)$ and $\text{Dim}_{FS}(S)$ are exactly dual, differing only in that a limit inferior appears in one characterization where a limit superior appears in the other. Hence, whether we think of finite-state information in terms of gambling, data compression, block entropy, or prediction, $\dim_{FS}(S)$ and $\text{Dim}_{FS}(S)$ are the lower and upper asymptotic information contents of S, as perceived by finite-state automata.

For any of the dimensions mentioned above, whether classical or finite-state, calculating the dimension of a particular object usually involves separate upper and lower bound arguments, with the lower bound typically more difficult. For example, establishing that $\dim_{FS}(S) = \alpha$ for some particular sequence S and $\alpha \in (0,1)$ usually involves separate proofs that α is an upper bound and a lower bound for $\dim_{FS}(S)$. The upper bound argument, usually carried out by exhibiting a particular finite-state gambler (or predictor, or compressor) that performs well on S, is typically straightforward. On the other hand, the lower bound argument, proving that *no* finite-state gambler (or predictor, or compressor) can perform better on S, is typically more involved.

This paper exhibits and analyzes a flexible method for constructing sequences satisfying given lower bounds on $\dim_{FS}(S)$ and/or $\text{Dim}_{FS}(S)$. The method is directly motivated by work in the first half of the twentieth century on Borel normal numbers. We now review the relevant aspects of this work.

In 1909, Borel [4] defined a sequence S over a finite alphabet Σ to be *normal* if, for every string $w \in \Sigma^{+}$,

$$\lim_{n \to \infty} \frac{1}{n} |\{i < n \,|\, S[i..i + |w| - 1] = w\}| = |\Sigma|^{-|w|},$$

where $S[i..j]$ is the string consisting of the ith through jth symbols in S. That is, S is normal (now also called *Borel normal*) if all the strings of each length appear equally often, asymptotically, in S. (Note: Borel was interested in numbers, not sequences, and defined a real number to be *normal in base k* if its base-k expansion is normal in the above sense. Subsequent authors mentioned here also stated their results in terms of real numbers, but we systematically restate their work in terms of sequences.)

The first explicit example of a normal sequence was produced in 1933 by Champernowne [7], who proved that the sequence

$$S = 123456789101112\cdots, \tag{1.1}$$

formed by concatenating the decimal expansions of the positive integers in order, is normal over the alphabet of decimal digits. Of course there is nothing special about decimal here, i.e., Champernowne's argument proves that, for any $k \geq 2$, the sequence (now called the base-k *Champernowne sequence*) formed by concatenating the base-k expansions of the positive integers in order is normal over the alphabet $\Sigma_k = \{0, 1, \ldots, k - 1\}$.

Champernowne [7] conjectured that the sequence

$$S = 235711131719232931\cdots, \tag{1.2}$$

formed by concatenating the decimal expansions of the prime numbers in order, is also normal. Copeland and Erdös [8] proved this conjecture in 1946, and it is the method of their proof that is of interest here. Given an infinite set A of positive integers and an integer $k \geq 2$, define the *base-k Copeland-Erdös sequence* of A to be the sequence $\mathrm{CE}_k(A)$ over the alphabet $\Sigma_k = \{0, 1, \ldots, k-1\}$ formed by concatenating the base-k expansions of the elements of A in order. The sequences (1.1) and (1.2) are thus $\mathrm{CE}_{10}(\mathbb{Z}^+)$ and $\mathrm{CE}_{10}(\mathrm{PRIMES})$, respectively, where $\mathbb{Z}^+$ is the set of all positive integers and PRIMES is the set of prime numbers. Say that a set $A \subseteq \mathbb{Z}^+$ satisfies the *Copeland-Erdös hypothesis* if, for every real number $\alpha < 1$, for all sufficiently large $n \in \mathbb{Z}^+$,

$$|A \cap \{1, 2, \ldots, n\}| > n^\alpha.$$

Copeland and Erdös [8] proved that *every* set $A \subseteq \mathbb{Z}^+$ satisfying the Copeland-Erdös hypothesis has the property that, for *every* $k \geq 2$, the sequence $\mathrm{CE}_k(A)$ is normal over the alphabet Σ_k. The normality of the sequence (1.2) – and of all the sequences $\mathrm{CE}_k(\mathrm{PRIMES})$ – follows immediately by the Prime Number Theorem [1,13], which says that

$$\lim_{n \to \infty} \frac{|\mathrm{PRIMES} \cap \{1, 2, \ldots, n\}| \ln n}{n} = 1,$$

whence PRIMES certainly satisfies the Copeland-Erdös hypothesis.

The significance of the Copeland-Erdös result for finite-state dimension lies in the fact that the Borel normal sequences are known to be precisely those sequences that have finite-state dimension 1 [16,5]. The Copeland-Erdös result thus says that the sequences $\mathrm{CE}_k(A)$ have finite-state dimension 1, provided only that A is "sufficiently dense" (i.e., satisfies the Copeland-Erdös hypothesis).

In this paper, we generalize the Copeland-Erdös result by showing that a parametrized version of the Copeland-Erdös hypothesis for A gives lower bounds on the finite-state dimension of $\mathrm{CE}_k(A)$ that vary continuously with – in fact, coincide with – the parameter. The parametrization that achieves this is a quantitative measure of the asymptotic density of A that has been discovered several times by researchers in various areas over the past few decades. Specifically, define the *zeta-dimension* of a set $A \subseteq \mathbb{Z}^+$ to be

$$\mathrm{Dim}_\zeta(A) = \inf \{s \,|\, \zeta_A(s) < \infty\},$$

where the *A-zeta function* $\zeta_A : [0, \infty) \to [0, \infty]$ is defined by

$$\zeta_A(s) = \sum_{n \in A} n^{-s}.$$

It is easy to see (and was proven by Cahen [6] in 1894; see also [2,13]) that zeta-dimension admits the "entropy characterization"

$$\mathrm{Dim}_\zeta(A) = \limsup_{n \to \infty} \frac{\log|A \cap \{1, \ldots, n\}|}{\log n}. \tag{1.3}$$

It is then natural to define the *lower zeta-dimension* of A to be

$$\dim_\zeta(A) = \liminf_{n\to\infty} \frac{\log|A \cap \{1,\ldots,n\}|}{\log n}. \tag{1.4}$$

Various properties of zeta-dimension and lower zeta-dimension, along with extensive historical references, appear in the recent paper [11], but none of this material is needed to follow our technical arguments in the present paper.

It is evident that a set $A \subseteq \mathbb{Z}^+$ satisfies the Copeland-Erdős hypothesis if and only if $\dim_\zeta(A) = 1$. The Copeland-Erdős result thus says that, for all infinite $A \subseteq \mathbb{Z}^+$ and $k \geq 2$,

$$\dim_\zeta(A) = 1 \implies \dim_{\mathrm{FS}}(\mathrm{CE}_k(A)) = 1. \tag{1.5}$$

Our main theorem extends (1.5) by showing that, for all infinite $A \subseteq \mathbb{Z}^+$ and $k \geq 2$,

$$\dim_{\mathrm{FS}}(\mathrm{CE}_k(A)) \geq \dim_\zeta(A), \tag{1.6}$$

and, dually,

$$\mathrm{Dim}_{\mathrm{FS}}(\mathrm{CE}_k(A)) \geq \mathrm{Dim}_\zeta(A). \tag{1.7}$$

Moreover, these bounds are tight in the following strong sense. Let $A \subseteq \mathbb{Z}^+$ be infinite, let $k \geq 2$, and let $\alpha = \dim_\zeta(A)$, $\beta = \mathrm{Dim}_\zeta(A)$, $\gamma = \dim_{\mathrm{FS}}(\mathrm{CE}_k(A))$, $\delta = \mathrm{Dim}_{\mathrm{FS}}(\mathrm{CE}_k(A))$. Then, by (1.6), (1.7), and elementary properties of these dimensions, we must have the inequalities

$$\begin{array}{ccc} \gamma & \leq & \delta \leq 1 \\ \mathrm{VI} & & \mathrm{VI} \\ 0 \leq \alpha & \leq & \beta. \end{array} \tag{1.8}$$

Our main theorem also shows that, for *any* α, β, γ, δ satisfying (1.8) and any $k \geq 2$, there is an infinite set $A \subseteq \mathbb{Z}^+$ such that $\dim_\zeta(A) = \alpha$, $\mathrm{Dim}_\zeta(A) = \beta$, $\dim_{\mathrm{FS}}(\mathrm{CE}_k(A)) = \gamma$, and $\mathrm{Dim}_{\mathrm{FS}}(\mathrm{CE}_k(A)) = \delta$. Thus the inequalities

$$\begin{array}{ccc} \dim_{\mathrm{FS}}(\mathrm{CE}_k(A)) & \leq & \mathrm{Dim}_{\mathrm{FS}}(\mathrm{CE}_k(A)) \leq 1 \\ \mathrm{VI} & & \mathrm{VI} \\ 0 \leq \quad \dim_\zeta(A) & \leq & \mathrm{Dim}_\zeta(A). \end{array} \tag{1.9}$$

are the *only* constraints that these four quantities obey in general.

The rest of this paper is organized as follows. Section 2 presents basic notation and terminology. Section 3 reviews the definitions of finite-state dimension and finite-state strong dimension and gives useful characterizations of zeta-dimension and lower zeta-dimension. Section 4 presents our main theorem. Most proofs are omitted from this conference version of the paper.

2   Preliminaries

We write $\mathbb{Z}^+ = \{1, 2, \ldots\}$ for the set of positive integers. For an infinite set $A \subseteq \mathbb{Z}^+$, we often write $A = \{a_1 < a_2 < \cdots\}$ to indicate that $a_1, a_2, \ldots$ is an enumeration of A in increasing numerical order. The quantifier $\exists^\infty n$ means "there exist infinitely many $n \in \mathbb{Z}^+$ such that ...", while the dual quantifier $\forall^\infty n$ means "for all but finitely many $n \in \mathbb{Z}^+$, ...".

We work in the alphabets $\Sigma_k = \{0, 1, \ldots, k-1\}$ for $k \geq 2$. The set of all (finite) *strings* over Σ_k is Σ_k^*, and the set of all (infinite) *sequences* over Σ_k is Σ_k^∞. We write λ for the empty string. Given a sequence $S \in \Sigma_k^\infty$ and integers $0 \leq i \leq j$, we write $S[i..j]$ for the string consisting of the ith through jth symbols in S. In particular, $S[0..n-1]$ is the string consisting of the first n symbols of S. We write $w \sqsubseteq z$ to indicate that the string w is a prefix of the string or sequence z.

We use the notation $\Delta(\Sigma_k)$ for the set of all probability measures on Σ_k, i.e., all functions $\pi : \Sigma_k \to [0, 1]$ satisfying $\sum_{a \in \Sigma_k} \pi(a) = 1$. Identifying each probability measure $\pi \in \Delta(\Sigma_k)$ with the vector $(\pi(0), \ldots, \pi(k-1))$ enables us to regard $\Delta(\Sigma_k)$ as a closed simplex in the k-dimensional Euclidean space $\mathbb{R}^k$. We write $\Delta_\mathbb{Q}(\Sigma_k)$ for the set of all rational-valued probability measures $\pi \in \Delta(\Sigma_k)$. It is often convenient to represent a positive probability measure $\pi \in \Delta_\mathbb{Q}(\Sigma_k)$ by a vector $\vec{a} = (a_0, \ldots, a_{k-1})$ of positive integers such that, for all $i \in \Sigma_k$, $\pi(i) = \frac{a_i}{n}$, where $n = \sum_{i=0}^{k-1} a_i$. In this case, $\vec{a}$ is called a *partition of* n. When $\vec{a}$ represents π in this way, we write $\pi = \frac{\vec{a}}{n}$.

The k-ary *Shannon entropy* [9] of a probability measure $\pi \in \Delta(\Sigma_k)$ is

$$\mathcal{H}_k(\pi) = \mathrm{E}_\pi \log_k \frac{1}{\pi(i)} = \sum_{i=0}^{k-1} \pi(i) \log_k \frac{1}{\pi(i)},$$

where E_π denotes mathematical expectation relative to the probability measure π and we stipulate that $0 \log_k \frac{1}{0} = 0$, so that $\mathcal{H}_k$ is continuous on the simplex $\Delta(\Sigma_k)$. The k-ary *Kullback-Leibler divergence* [9] between probability measures $\pi, \tau \in \Delta(\Sigma_k)$ is

$$\mathcal{D}_k(\pi \parallel \tau) = \mathrm{E}_\pi \log_k \frac{\pi(i)}{\tau(i)} = \sum_{i=0}^{k-1} \pi(i) \log_k \frac{\pi(i)}{\tau(i)}.$$

It is well-known that $\mathcal{D}_k(\pi \parallel \tau) \geq 0$, with equality if and only if $\pi = \tau$.

For $k \geq 2$ and $n \in \mathbb{Z}^+$, we write $\sigma_k(n)$ for the standard base-k representation of n. Note that $\sigma_k(n) \in \Sigma_k^*$ and that the length of (number of symbols in) $\sigma_k(n)$ is $|\sigma_k(n)| = 1 + \lfloor \log_k n \rfloor$. Note also that, if $A = \{a_1 < a_2 < \cdots\} \subseteq \mathbb{Z}^+$ is infinite, then the base-k Copeland-Erdös sequence of A is

$$\mathrm{CE}_k(A) = \sigma_k(a_1)\sigma_k(a_2) \cdots \in \Sigma_k^\infty.$$

Given a set $A \subseteq \mathbb{Z}^+$ and $k, n \in \mathbb{Z}^+$, we write $A_{=n} = \{a \in A \,|\, |\sigma_k(a)| = n\}$ in contexts where the base k is clear.

We write $\log n$ for $\log_2 n$.

3   The Four Dimensions

As promised in the introduction, this section gives precise definitions of finite-state dimension and finite-state strong dimension. It also gives a useful bound on the success of finite-state gamblers and useful characterizations of zeta-dimension and lower zeta-dimension.

Definition. A *finite-state gambler* (*FSG*) is a 5-tuple

$$G = (Q, \Sigma_k, \delta, \beta, q_0),$$

where Q is a nonempty, finite set of *states*; $\Sigma_k = \{0, 1, \ldots, k-1\}$ is a finite alphabet $(k \geq 2)$; $\delta : Q \times \Sigma_k \to Q$ is the *transition function*; $\beta : Q \to \Delta_\mathbb{Q}(\Sigma_k)$ is the *betting function*; and $q_0 \in Q$ is the *initial state*.

Finite-state gamblers have been investigated by Schnorr and Stimm [16], Feder [12], and others. The transition function δ is extended in the standard way to a function $\delta : Q \times \Sigma_k^* \to Q$. For $w \in \Sigma_k^*$, we use the abbreviation $\delta(w) = \delta(q_0, w)$.

Definition. ([10]). Let $G = (Q, \Sigma_k, \delta, \beta, q_0)$ be an FSG, and let $s \in [0, \infty)$. The *s-gale* of G is the function

$$d_G^{(s)} : \Sigma_k^* \to [0, \infty)$$

defined by the recursion

$$d_G^{(s)}(\lambda) = 1,$$

$$d_G^{(s)}(wa) = k^s d_G^{(s)}(w)\beta(\delta(w))(a) \tag{3.1}$$

for all $w \in \Sigma_k^*$ and $a \in \Sigma_k$.

Intuitively, $d_G^{(s)}(w)$ is the amount of money that the gambler G has after betting on the successive symbols in the string w. The parameter s controls the payoffs via equation (3.1). If $s = 1$, then the payoffs are fair in the sense that the conditional expected value of $d_G^{(1)}(wa)$, given that w has occurred and the symbols $a \in \Sigma_k$ are all equally likely to follow w, is precisely $d_G^{(1)}(w)$. If $s < 1$, then the payoffs are unfair.

We repeatedly use the obvious fact that $d_G^{(s)}(w) \leq k^{s|w|}$ holds for all s and w.

Definition. Let $G = (Q, \Sigma_k, \delta, \beta, q_0)$ be an FSG, let $s \in [0, \infty)$, and let $S \in \Sigma_k^\infty$.

1. G *s-succeeds* on S if

$$\limsup_{n \to \infty} d_G^{(s)}(S[0..n-1]) = \infty.$$

2. G *strongly s-succeeds* on S if

$$\liminf_{n\to\infty} d_G^{(s)}(S[0..n-1]) = \infty.$$

Definition. Let $S \in \Sigma_k^\infty$.

1. [10]. The *finite-state dimension* of S is

$$\dim_{\mathrm{FS}}(S) = \inf\{s \,|\text{there is an FSG that } s\text{-succeeds on } S\}.$$

2. [3] The *finite-state strong dimension* of S is

$$\mathrm{Dim}_{\mathrm{FS}}(S) = \inf\{s \,|\text{there is an FSG that strongly } s\text{-succeeds on } S\}.$$

It is easy to verify that $0 \leq \dim_{\mathrm{FS}}(S) \leq \mathrm{Dim}_{\mathrm{FS}}(S) \leq 1$ for all $S \in \Sigma_k^\infty$. More properties of these finite-state dimensions, including their relationships to classical Hausdorff and packing dimensions, respectively, may be found in [10,3].

It is useful to have a measure of the size of a finite-state gambler. This size depends on the alphabet size, the number of states, and the least common denominator of the values of the betting function in the following way.

Definition. The *size* of an FSG $G = (Q, \Sigma_k, \delta, \beta, q_0)$ is

$$\mathrm{size}(G) = (k+l)|Q|,$$

where $l = \min\{l \in \mathbb{Z}^+ \,|(\forall q \in Q)(\forall i \in \Sigma_k)l\beta(q)(i) \in \mathbb{Z}\}$.

Observation 3.1 *For each* $k \geq 2$ *and* $t \in \mathbb{Z}^+$, *there are, up to renaming of states, fewer than* $t^2(2t)^t$ *finite-state gamblers* G *with* $\mathrm{size}(G) \leq t$.

In general, an *s-gale* is a function $d : \Sigma_k^* \to [0, \infty)$ satisfying

$$d(w) = k^{-s} \sum_{a=0}^{k-1} d(wa)$$

for all $w \in \Sigma_k^*$ [15]. It is clear that $d_G^{(s)}$ is an s-gale for every FSG G and every $s \in [0, \infty)$. The case $k = 2$ of the following lemma was proven in [15]. The extension to arbitrary $k \geq 2$ is routine.

Lemma 3.2 ([15]). *If* $s \in [0, 1]$ *and* d *is an* s-*gale, then, for all* $w \in \Sigma_k^*$, $j \in \mathbb{N}$, *and* $0 < \alpha \in \mathbb{R}$, *there are fewer than* $\frac{k^{sj}}{\alpha}$ *strings* $u \in \Sigma_k^*$ *of length* j *for which* $d(u) > \alpha$.

The following lemma will be useful in proving our main theorem.

Lemma 3.3 *For each $s, \alpha \in (0, \infty)$ and $k, n, t \in \mathbb{Z}^+$ with $k \geq 2$, there are fewer than*

$$\frac{k^{2s} n^s t^2 (2t)^t}{\alpha(k^s - 1)}$$

integers $m \in \{1, \ldots, n\}$ for which

$$\max_{\text{size}(G) \leq t} d_G^{(s)}(\sigma_k(m)) \geq \alpha,$$

where the maximum is taken over all FSGs $G = (Q, \Sigma_k, \delta, \beta, q_0)$ with $\text{size}(G) \leq t$.

The zeta-dimension $\text{Dim}_\zeta(A)$ and lower zeta-dimension $\dim_\zeta(A)$ of a set A of positive integers were defined in the introduction. The following lemma gives useful characterizations of these quantities in terms of the increasing enumeration of A.

Lemma 3.4 *Let $A = \{a_1 < a_2 < \cdots\}$ be an infinite set of positive integers.*

1. $\dim_\zeta(A) = \inf\{t \geq 0 \,|\, (\exists^\infty n) a_n^t > n\} = \inf\{t \geq 0 \,|\, (\exists^\infty n) a_n^t \geq n\}$
   $= \sup\{t \geq 0 \,|\, (\forall^\infty n) a_n^t < n\} = \sup\{t \geq 0 \,|\, (\forall^\infty n) a_n^t \leq n\}$.
2. $\text{Dim}_\zeta(A) = \inf\{t \geq 0 \,|\, (\forall^\infty n) a_n^t > n\} = \inf\{t \geq 0 \,|\, (\forall^\infty n) a_n^t \geq n\}$
   $= \sup\{t \geq 0 \,|\, (\exists^\infty n) a_n^t < n\} = \sup\{t \geq 0 \,|\, (\exists^\infty n) a_n^t \leq n\}$.

4   Main Theorem

The proof of our main theorem uses the following combinatorial lemma.

Lemma 4.1 *For every $n \geq k \geq 2$ and every partition $\vec{a} = (a_0, \ldots, a_{k-1})$ of n, there are more than*

$$k^{n \mathcal{H}_k(\frac{\vec{a}}{n}) - (k+1) \log_k n}$$

integers m with $|\sigma_k(m)| = n$ and $\#(i, \sigma_k(m)) = a_i$ for each $i \in \Sigma_k$.

We now have all the machinery that we need to prove the main result of this paper.

Theorem 4.2 (main theorem). *Let $k \geq 2$.*

1. *For every infinite set $A \subseteq \mathbb{Z}^+$,*

$$\dim_{\text{FS}}(\text{CE}_k(A)) \geq \dim_\zeta(A) \tag{4.1}$$

   and

$$\text{Dim}_{\text{FS}}(\text{CE}_k(A)) \geq \text{Dim}_\zeta(A). \tag{4.2}$$

2. *For any four real numbers $\alpha, \beta, \gamma, \delta$ satisfying the inequalities*

$$
\begin{array}{c}
\gamma \leq \delta \leq 1 \\
\text{\tiny VI} \quad \text{\tiny VI} \\
0 \leq \alpha \leq \beta,
\end{array}
\tag{4.3}
$$

there exists an infinite set $A \subseteq \mathbb{Z}^+$ such that $\dim_\zeta(A) = \alpha$, $\mathrm{Dim}_\zeta(A) = \beta$, $\dim_{\mathrm{FS}}(\mathrm{CE}_k(A)) = \gamma$, and $\mathrm{Dim}_{\mathrm{FS}}(\mathrm{CE}_k(A)) = \delta$.

Proof. We prove part 1 here. Let $A = \{a_1 < a_2 < \cdots\} \subseteq \mathbb{Z}^+$ be infinite. Fix $0 < s < t < 1$, let

$$
J_t = \left\{ n \in \mathbb{Z}^+ \, \middle| \, a_n^t < n \right\},
$$

and let $G = (Q, \Sigma_k, \delta, \beta, q_0)$ be an FSG. Let $n \in \mathbb{Z}^+$, and consider the quantity $d_G^{(s)}(w_n)$, where

$$
w_n = \sigma_k(a_1) \cdots \sigma_k(a_n).
$$

There exist states $q_1, \ldots, q_n \in Q$ such that

$$
d_G^{(s)}(w_n) = \prod_{i=1}^{n} d_{G_{q_i}}^{(s)}(\sigma_k(a_i)),
$$

where $G_{q_i} = (Q, \Sigma_k, \delta, \beta, q_i)$. Let $B = \left\{ 1 \leq i \leq n \, \middle| \, d_{G_{q_i}}^{(s)}(\sigma_k(a_i)) \geq \frac{1}{k} \right\}$, and let $B^c = \{1, \ldots, n\} - B$. Then

$$
d_G^{(s)}(w_n) = \left(\prod_{i \in B} d_{G_{q_i}}^{(s)}(\sigma_k(a_i)) \right) \left(\prod_{i \in B^c} d_{G_{q_i}}^{(s)}(\sigma_k(a_i)) \right).
\tag{4.4}
$$

By our choice of B,

$$
\prod_{i \in B^c} d_{G_{q_i}}^{(s)}(\sigma_k(a_i)) \leq k^{|B|-n}.
\tag{4.5}
$$

By Lemma 3.3,

$$
|B| \leq \frac{ck^{2s+1} a_n^s}{k^s - 1},
\tag{4.6}
$$

where $c = \mathrm{size}(G)^2 (2\mathrm{size}(G))^{\mathrm{size}(G)}$. Since $d_{G_{q_i}}^{(s)}(u) \leq k^{s|u|}$ must hold in all cases, it follows that

$$
\prod_{i \in B} d_{G_{q_i}}^{(s)}(\sigma_k(a_i)) \leq k^{s|B||\sigma_k(a_n)|} \leq k^{s|B|(1 + \log_k a_n)}.
\tag{4.7}
$$

By (4.4), (4.5), (4.6), and (4.7), we have

$$
\log_k d_G^{(s)}(w_n) \leq \tau(1 + s + s\log_k a_n) a_n^s - n,
\tag{4.8}
$$

where $\tau = \frac{ck^{2s+1}}{k^s-1}$. If n is sufficiently large, and if $n+1 \in J_t$, then (4.8) implies that

$$
\begin{aligned}
\log_k d_G^{(s)}(w_n) &\le \tau(1+s+s\log_k a_n)a_n^s - 2(n+1)^{\frac{s+t}{2t}} \\
&\le \tau(1+s+s\log_k a_n)a_n^s - 2a_{n+1}^{\frac{s+t}{2}} \\
&\le \tau(1+s+s\log_k a_n)a_n^s - a_n^{\frac{s+t}{2}} - s(1+\log_k a_{n+1}) \\
&\le -s(1+\log_k a_{n+1}) \\
&\le -s|\sigma_k(a_{n+1})|.
\end{aligned}
$$

We have now shown that

$$
d_G^{(s)}(w_n) \le k^{-s|\sigma_k(a_{n+1})|} \tag{4.9}
$$

holds for all sufficiently large n with $n+1 \in J_t$.

To prove (4.1), let $s < t < \dim_\zeta(A)$. It suffices to show that $\dim_{\mathrm{FS}}(\mathrm{CE}_k(A)) \ge s$. Since $t < \dim_\zeta(A)$, Lemma 3.4 tells us that the set J_t is cofinite. Hence, for every sufficiently long prefix $w \sqsubseteq \mathrm{CE}_k(A)$, there exist n and $u \sqsubseteq \sigma_k(a_{n+1})$ such that $w = w_n u$ and (4.9) holds, whence

$$
d_G^{(s)}(w) \le k^{-s|\sigma_k(a_{n+1})|}k^{s|u|} \le 1.
$$

This shows that G does not s-succeed on $\mathrm{CE}_k(A)$, whence $\dim_{\mathrm{FS}}(\mathrm{CE}_k(A)) \ge s$.

To prove (4.2), let $s < t < \mathrm{Dim}_\zeta(A)$. It suffices to show that $\mathrm{Dim}_{\mathrm{FS}}(\mathrm{CE}_k(A)) \ge s$. Since $t < \mathrm{Dim}_\zeta(A)$, Lemma 3.4 tells us that the set J_t is infinite. For the infinitely many n for which $n+1 \in J_t$ and (4.9) holds, we then have $d_G^{(s)}(w_n) < 1$. This shows that G does not strongly s-succeed on $\mathrm{CE}_k(A)$, whence $\mathrm{Dim}_{\mathrm{FS}}(\mathrm{CE}_k(A)) \ge s$. □

Finally, we note that the Copeland-Erdös theorem is a special case of our main theorem.

Corollary 4.3 (Copeland and Erdös [8]). *Let $k \ge 2$ and $A \subseteq \mathbb{Z}^+$. If, for all $\alpha < 1$, for all sufficiently large $n \in \mathbb{Z}^+$, $|A \cap \{1,\ldots,n\}| > n^\alpha$, then the sequence $\mathrm{CE}_k(A)$ is normal over the alphabet Σ_k. In particular, the sequence $\mathrm{CE}_k(\mathrm{PRIMES})$ is normal over the alphabet Σ_k.*

Acknowledgment. We thank the referees for careful reading.

References

1. T. M. Apostol. *Introduction to Analytic Number Theory*. Undergraduate Texts in Mathematics. Springer-Verlag, 1976.
2. T. M. Apostol. *Modular Functions and Dirichlet Series in Number Theory*, volume 41 of *Graduate Texts in Mathematics*. Springer-Verlag, 1976.

3. K. B. Athreya, J. M. Hitchcock, J. H. Lutz, and E. Mayordomo. Effective strong dimension, algorithmic information, and computational complexity. *SIAM Journal on Computing*. To appear. Preliminary version appeared in *Proceedings of the 21st International Symposium on Theoretical Aspects of Computer Science*, pages 632–643, 2004.

4. E. Borel. Sur les probabilités dénombrables et leurs applications arithmétiques. *Rend. Circ. Mat. Palermo*, 27:247–271, 1909.

5. C. Bourke, J. M. Hitchcock, and N. V. Vinodchandran. Entropy rates and finite-state dimension. *Theoretical Computer Science*. To appear.

6. E. Cahen. Sur la fonction $\zeta(s)$ de Riemann et sur des fonctions analogues. *Annales de l'École Normale Supérieure*, 1894. (3) **11**, S. 85.

7. D. G. Champernowne. Construction of decimals normal in the scale of ten. *J. London Math. Soc.*, 2(8):254–260, 1933.

8. A. H. Copeland and P. Erdős. Note on normal numbers. *Bull. Amer. Math. Soc.*, 52:857–860, 1946.

9. T. M. Cover and J. A. Thomas. *Elements of Information Theory*. John Wiley & Sons, Inc., New York, N.Y., 1991.

10. J. J. Dai, J. I. Lathrop, J. H. Lutz, and E. Mayordomo. Finite-state dimension. *Theoretical Computer Science*, 310:1–33, 2004.

11. D. Doty, X. Gu, J. H. Lutz, E. Mayordomo, and P. Moser. Zeta-dimension. In *Proceedings of the Thirtieth International Symposium on Mathematical Foundations of Computer Science*, volume 3618 of *Lecture Notes in Computer Science*, pages 283–294, 2005.

12. M. Feder. Gambling using a finite state machine. *IEEE Transactions on Information Theory*, 37:1459–1461, 1991.

13. G. Hardy and E. Wright. *An Introduction to the Theory of Numbers*. Clarendon Press, 5th edition, 1979.

14. J. M. Hitchcock. Fractal dimension and logarithmic loss unpredictability. *Theoretical Computer Science*, 304(1–3):431–441, 2003.

15. J. H. Lutz. Dimension in complexity classes. *SIAM Journal on Computing*, 32:1236–1259, 2003.

16. C. P. Schnorr and H. Stimm. Endliche Automaten und Zufallsfolgen. *Acta Informatica*, 1:345–359, 1972.

Refining the Undecidability Frontier of Hybrid Automata

Venkatesh Mysore[1] and Amir Pnueli[1,2]

[1] Courant Institute of Mathematical Sciences, NYU, New York, NY, U.S.A.
{mysore,amir}@cs.nyu.edu
[2] The Weizmann Institute of Science, Rehovot, Israel

Abstract. Reachability becomes undecidable in hybrid automata (HA) that can simulate a Turing (TM) or Minsky (MM) machine. Asarin and Schneider have shown that, between the decidable 2-dim Piecewise Constant Derivative (PCD) class and the undecidable 3-dim PCD class, there lies the "open" class 2-dim Hierarchical PCD (HPCD). This class was shown to be equivalent to the class of 1-dim Piecewise Affine Maps (PAM). In this paper, we first explore 2-dim HPCD's proximity to decidability, by showing that they are equivalent to 2-dim PCDs with translational resets, and to HPCDs without resets. A hierarchy of intermediates also equivalent to the HPCD class is presented, revealing semblance to timed and initialized rectangular automata. We then explore the proximity to the undecidability frontier. We show that 2-dim HPCDs with zeno executions or integer-checks can simulate the 2-counter MM. We conclude by retreating HPCDs as PAMs, to derive a simple over-approximating algorithm for reachability. This also defines a decidable subclass 1-dim Onto PAM (oPAM). The novel non-trivial transformation of 2-dim HPCDs into "almost decidable" systems, is likely to pave the way for approximate reachability algorithms, and the characterization of decidable subclasses. It is hoped that these ideas eventually coalesce into a complete understanding of the reachability problem for the class 2-dim HPCD (1-dim PAM).

1 Introduction

Reachability – the problem of deciding whether a certain continuous state is reachable from a given initial state, becomes undecidable if the dynamical system specifications allow a Turing Machine (TM) to be simulated. This is because of Alan Turing's seminal proof, that the problem of deciding whether a given TM will halt on a given input is in general undecidable [20]. Another convenient formalization is the 2-counter Minsky Machine (MM) [13], which has been shown to be able to simulate a TM. Hence reachability is undecidable for an MM, and any dynamical system that can simulate an MM as well. Hybrid Automata (HA), which can have arbitrary discrete transitions and continuous flows, correspond to a class of immense computational power. HA very easily become undecidable for the reachability query, with only extremely stringent restrictions leading to decidability. Timed automata [2], multirate automata [1], initialized rectangular automata [16,7], controllable linear systems [18], some families of linear vector fields [11] and o-minimal HA [10] have been shown to be decidable for the reachability query.

The fundamental question continues to be: "What is the simplest class of dynamical systems for which reachability is undecidable ?". The conventional answers to this question have involved proving that a certain decidable class becomes undecidable, when given some additional computational power. For instance, 2-dimensional Piecewise Constant Derivative (PCD) systems [12] and Simple Planar Differential Inclusions (SPDIs) [5] are decidable, while 3-dimensional PCDs are undecidable [3]. This paper focuses on the 2-dim Hierarchical PCD (HPCD) class introduced by Asarin and Schneider [4]. This intermediate class, between decidable 2-dim PCDs and undecidable 3-dim PCDs, is not known to be provably decidable or undecidable! Asarin and Schneider proved that 2-dim HPCDs are *equivalent* to 1-dim Piecewise Affine Maps (PAM). Since the reachability problem for 1-dim PAMs is an open question [9], 2-dim HPCD-reachability is also open. They went a step further, and proved that the HPCD class, when endowed with a little additional computational power, becomes undecidable. Thus, the HPCD [3] class (and equivalently the PAM class) is clearly on the boundary between decidable and undecidable subclasses of HA.

This paper presents new developments in the analysis of the HPCD class, a sequel to Asarin and Schneider's work [4]. We begin this analysis of the proximity to decidability and undecidability in *Section 2*, with the definitions of the various subclasses of HA we will encounter in this paper. In *Section 3*, we present our main result: 2-dim PCDs with translational resets can simulate a PAM. We then construct several very interesting subclasses of HPCDs, which also simulate PAMs. Since PAMs have been shown to be equivalent to HPCDs [4], it proves that surprisingly, these subclasses are just as powerful as the HPCD class itself. This reveals the redundancy in the expressive power of the HPCD, and shows how even closer HPCDs are to decidable systems. In *Section 4*, we present some undecidable extensions of HPCDs, very different from Asarin and Schneider's constructions. They reveal new dimensions of the fineness of the line separating HPCDs from undecidability. We present a simple algorithm for over-approximating reachability in PAMs in *Section 5*, and show how decidable subclasses can be identified. We summarize our contributions in *Section 6* and discuss several open research questions.

2   Background: Hybrid Automata and Subclasses

An HA approximates a complicated non-linear system in terms of a model that is partly discrete and partly continuous [8,15]. An HA is a directed graph of discrete states and transitions, which allows arbitrary: (1) "invariant" expressions dictating when the system can be in this state; (2) differential equations in the

---

[3] Henceforth, "HPCD" refers to 2-dim HPCD, "PAM" to 1-dim PAM, and "decidability" to decidability of reachability, unless explicitly stated otherwise.

"flow" expressions, in each discrete state (continuous evolution with time); (3) conditions controlling when a transition can be taken, in the "guard"; (2) equations that change the values of the variables, in the "reset" expressions during each discrete state transition (instantaneous discrete evolution). A computation of an HA is a series of continuous evolution steps of arbitrary time-length each, interspersed with an arbitrary number of zero time-length discrete transition steps.

Before introducing the subclasses, we quickly review some terms frequently used to describe different restrictions. Let a, b, c, d stand for numerical constants, and p, q stand for the HA variables. A *rectangular guard* refers to an expression of the form $a < p < b$, while a *non-rectangular* or *comparative guard* is of the form $ap + bq + c < 0$. A *rectangular invariant* is of the form $a < p < b \wedge c < q < d$ i.e. the state represents a rectangular region in the $p - q$ plane. State invariants are said to be *non-overlapping* if the regions they represent in their variable-space do not intersect. A *constant reset* refers to $p' = c$, a *translational reset* refers to $p' = p + c$ and an *affine reset* to $p' = ap + b$. An "initialized" automaton is one where all variables, whose flow changes after a discrete state transition, are reset to a constant. An automaton is "timed" if all flow-derivatives are 1.

Among the several formalizations that simplify the reachability problem by curbing the computational power of the HA, we dwell on the PCD construct. A 2-dim PCD [12] is an HA in two continuous variables, where (1) All flow-derivatives are constants; (2) The guards are rectangular i.e. $p \in I$, where I is a numerical interval; (3) No variable can be reset during transitions i.e., $p' = p \wedge q' = q$; (4) The discrete states (invariants) correspond to *non-overlapping* rectangles in the real plane with non-empty interiors. The trajectories of a 2-dim PCD are restricted to be broken straight lines, with slopes changing only when a different polygonal region (new discrete state) is entered. Maler and Pnueli [12] used the property of planar systems to prove that reachability is decidable for 2-dim PCDs. 3-dim PCDs are the natural extension of 2-dim PCDs with a third dynamic variable (dimension). Asarin, Maler and Pnueli [3] proved that 3-dim PCDs are undecidable.

Subsequently, Asarin and Schneider set out to discover an "open" class in between 2-dim and 3-dim PCDs. They proceeded by studying HA that could simulate a known open problem - the 1-dim PAM. To understand their equivalence result, we first introduce PAMs, where computation is modeled as iterative function evaluation. A PAM [9] is of the form $f(x) = a_i x + b_i$, $x \in I_i$, $i = 1, 2, \cdots, n$, where all a_i, b_i and the ends of the non-overlapping intervals I_i are rational. f is closed i.e. $\forall x, i \ (x \in I_i) \Rightarrow (\exists j, \ f(x) \in I_j)$. Further, the intervals are in ascending order. In other words, there are n non-overlapping partitions of the real line (which may not cover it entirely). The current value of the variable x decides which interval I_i it falls in, and hence its next value $f(x)$ is uniquely defined. The reachability problem is also defined in the natural way: "Is the point x_f reachable from the point x_0 by repeated application of the piece-wise affine maps ?". Note that unlike HA, there is no non-determinism or choice – the starting point defines a unique trajectory.

Recall that a class A simulates a class B if every computational trajectory of B has a unique counterpart in A. Two classes are equivalent if they simulate each other: thus if the reachability problem is (un)decidable for one class, so it is for the other. Asarin and Schneider characterized the PCD extensions necessary to simulate a PAM, keeping in mind that the resulting HA subclass in turn needed to be expressible as a PAM. The result was the HPCD class which augmented a PCD, by allowing comparative guards and affine resets in overlapping regions of the plane. A 2-dim HPCD [4] is an HA in 2 continuous variables where, (1) All flow-derivatives are constants; (2) The guards are of the form $(ax + by + c = 0 \wedge x \in I \wedge y \in J)$ where I and J are intervals and a, b, c and the extremities of I and J are rational-valued; (3) The reset functions are affine functions: $x' = ax + b$; (4) The state invariant, which could overlap with other state invariants, is the negation of the union of the guards. The term hierarchical was used originally, to indicate that an HPCD could also be thought of as a PCD with overlapping state invariants, where each state was actually a PCD.

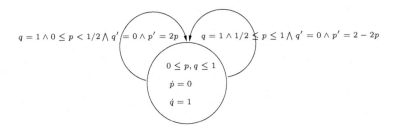

$q = 1 \wedge 0 \leq p < 1/2 \wedge q' = 0 \wedge p' = 2p$ $q = 1 \wedge 1/2 \leq p \leq 1 \wedge q' = 0 \wedge p' = 2 - 2p$

$0 \leq p, q \leq 1$

$\dot{p} = 0$

$\dot{q} = 1$

Fig. 1. One-State Tent Map HPCD

Example 1. Consider the PAM describing the Tent Map [19]:
$f(x) = 2x + 0, \ x \in [0, 1/2)(\equiv I_1)$
$f(x) = -2x + 2, \ x \in [1/2, 1](\equiv I_2)$
The HPCD simulating this PAM is shown in *Figure 1.*   □

We now summarize the results of Asarin and Schneider [4]. The HPCD class is equivalent to the PAM class. The restricted class $HPCD_{iso}$, with translational instead of affine resets, is also equivalent to the PAM class. The extended classes $HPCD_{1c}$ (with an additional counter), $HPCD_{\infty}$ (with infinite partitions) and $HPCD_x$ (origin-dependent rates) are undecidable, as they can simulate a TM.

3   Open HPCD Subclasses

Asarin and Schneider's results thus have two implications: (1) a PAM can capture an HPCD; (2) an HPCD can capture a PAM. Their first result is clearly the more significant one, also involving a non-trivial construction. It demonstrates that a 2-dim HPCD, which seems dramatically more complex than a 1-dim PAM, actually has no additional computational power ! Their second result seems simple in comparison, as HPCDs seem to have more expressivity than necessary, to capture a PAM. A PAM can be trivially captured by a PCD with just 1 state, with all computations done only using affine resets along self-loops (see for example, the Tent Map HPCD in *Figure* 1). Schneider has proved [17] that these affine resets can be made translational ($HPCD_{iso}$). However, that construction uses all the other enhancements. To summarize, PCDs with just *affine* resets can simulate a PAM. However, multiple states with overlapping invariants and comparative guards seem necessary, when only *translational* resets are allowed.

In this section, we first prove our main result: a 1-dim PAM can be simulated using a 2-dim PCD, with just translational resets of the form $x' = x + c_i$. Comparative guards and affine resets can be done away with by making the two PCD variables (p and q) take turns simulating the PAM variable (x), while non-overlapping state invariants become sufficient because the PCD variables are guaranteed to lie in a bounded region. We then show how 1-dim PAMs can be simulated by other simple subclasses of HPCDs, each revealing proximity to a different decidable HA subclass. The following lemma simplify the proof:

Lemma 1. *A 1-dim PAM is bounded.*   □

Lemma 2. *Every 1-dim PAM is equivalent to a 1-dim "positive" PAM where all intervals are positive.*   □

Now we are ready to prove our main result:

Theorem 1. *A 1-dim PAM can be simulated by a 2-dim PCD with translational resets.*

Proof. Consider an equivalent 1-dim positive PAM $f(x) = a_i x + b_i$, $x \in I_i (\equiv [l_i, r_i))$, $i = 1, 2, \cdots, n$. Let L be a number such that $L > r_n \wedge \forall i, L > b_i$. Corresponding to the i-th function of the PAM, we will have two states P_i and Q_i. In P_i, p flows from $p_0 = b_i$ to $x_{n+1} (\equiv b_i + a_i x_n)$ at the rate $\dot{p} = a_i$. q drops from $q_0 = x_n$ to 0 at the rate $\dot{q} = -1$. The guard $q = 0$ thus ensures that the system spends $t = q_0$ time in this state. This allows the affine term $a_i x_n$ to be computed, without using comparative guards or affine resets. In the "Q" states, the roles of p and q are reversed i.e., q uses p's value to grow to the next iterate, while p just drops to 0, effectively keeping track of time.

From P_i, there are transitions to each possible state Q_j. p retains the value it just computed, while q is reset to the constant portion (b_j) of the next iterate of x. In Q_j, q will accumulate the rest of its target value ($a_j \times x$) by flowing for time x (stored in p) at the rate a_j. Similarly, from Q_i, there are transitions to each possible state P_j, while there are no transitions within P-states or within Q-states.

The above expressions are adjusted, now assuming that each state is associated with a different large constant "base". In a state, all numbers are represented with respect to this base. Thus, x becomes $L_{S_i} + x$ in state S_i, where L_{S_i} is the base. Even if x increases or decreases to its maximum / minimum possible value,

p and q will not cross over to an adjoining state. This is because the different base constants are themselves very far apart. This base-adjustment creates the translational resets, when the current iterate needs to be remembered and passed on to a new state. It is to be noted that just constant resets suffice if the state invariants are allowed to overlap.

We now construct the PCD with translational resets and $2n$ states:

- Corresponding to the i-th function of the PAM, we have two states P_i and Q_i associated with the constants $L_{P_i} = 4iL - 3L$ and $L_{Q_i} = 4iL - L$.
- In P_i, p grows at rate $\dot{p} = a_i$ from $L_{P_i} + p_0(= b_i)$ to $a_i q_0(= x_n) + b_i + L_{P_i}$, while q drops from $q_0 + L_{P_i}$ to L_{P_i} at the rate $\dot{q} = -1$. q_0 denotes the unscaled previous iterate x_n, using which x_{n+1} is being computed by spending exactly $t = q_0$ time in this state.
- Q_i behaves exactly as above with p and q swapped i.e., this corresponds to the case where q grows to the next iterate, while p just drops to L_{Q_i}.
- In P_i and Q_i, the values of p and q are both bounded by $\{(L_{P_i/Q_i} - L, L_{P_i/Q_i} + L)\}$, which is equal to $\{(4iL - 4L, 4iL - 2L)\}$ in P_i and $\{(4iL - 2L, 4iL)\}$ in Q_i. Clearly, none of rectangular regions can overlap.
- From P_i, there are transitions to each possible state Q_j with guard $q = L_{P_i} \wedge p \in I_j$ i.e., "p has reached the next iterate of x" and "p is in the interval corresponding to the j-th PAM function". The reset (note: constant or translational) is $p' = p - L_{P_i} + L_{Q_j} \wedge q' = L_{Q_j} + b_j$ i.e., "p, which holds the current value of x, is translated to the range of the destination state (to prevent overlap)" and "q is reset to the constant portion (b_j) of the next iterate of x". The portion proportional to x_n ($a_j \times x_n$) will be gained by flowing for time x_n (stored in p) with slope a_j.
- Similarly, from Q_i, there are transitions to each possible state P_j. There are no transitions within P-states or within Q-states.

This PCD with translational resets simulates the PAM, as p and q take turns simulating x. It can be seen that x_f is reachable from x_0: (i) if $(p = x_f + L_{P_i}, q = L_{P_i})$ and $(p = x_f + L_{Q_j}, q = L_{Q_j} + b_j)$ are reachable; or (ii) if $(p = L_{Q_i}, q = x_f + L_{Q_i})$ and $(p = L_{P_j}, q = x_f + L_{P_j})$ are reachable. This needs to hold for some i and j, such that $x_f \in I_j$ and one of the pre-images of x_f lies in I_i. The "and" terms are necessary to eliminate intermediate points during continuous evolution from satisfying the query. The "or" term is necessary because p reaches only even iterates and q reaches only the odd iterates of x_0. The starting state is $(p = x_0 + L_{Q_k}, q = L_{Q_k} + b_k)$ (or $(p = L_{P_k} + b_k, q = L_{Q_k} + x_0)$), where $x_0 \in I_k$. □

Example 2. We will now construct a PCD with translational resets that simulates the Tent Map, in two variables p and q and $2 \times 2 = 4$ states. Setting $L = 3(> max(r_n, b_i) = 2)$, we get $L_{P_1} = 3, L_{Q_1} = 9, L_{P_2} = 15, L_{Q_2} = 21$. The result is presented in *Figure 2*.   □

Various other intermediates – subclasses of HPCDs, simulate a 1-dim PAM. We now present some of the interesting cases, which extend known decidable systems.

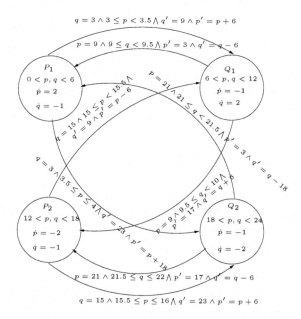

Fig. 2. PCD with Translational Resets simulating the Tent Map

Theorem 2. *A 1-dim PAM can be simulated by: (1) an HPCD with comparative guards, 3 different flows* $+1, -1, 0$ *and no resets; (2) an initialized PCD, with comparative guards; (3) an HPCD with rectangular guards i.e.* $p = 0 \wedge q \in I_i$, *when simple constant resets of the form* $q' = a_j \wedge p' = p$ *are allowed; (4) a PCD with just clocks, when translational resets and comparative guards are allowed; and (5) an HPCD with just clocks, when simple constant resets* $(p', q') = (0, q)$ *or* $(p, 0)$ *and comparative guards are allowed.*

Proof. All the proofs are based on the techniques demonstrated in the proof of *Theorem 1*. So, for brevity, we only give a flavor of results (1) and (4).

For result (1), we will construct an HPCD with $4n$ states of the form $P_j^{\pm}$ and $Q_j^{\pm}$ that simulates this PAM. We will now have p evolving from x_{n-1} to x_{n+1}, while q remains stationary at x_n. The affine guard condition $p = a_i q + b_i$ makes the HA jump to the next state at the correct time. Since x_{n+1} could be greater or less than x_{n-1}, the flow will need to be $+1$ or -1 respectively. Hence, each P (and Q) state now corresponds to two states: P^+ and P^-. In the state P_j^+, q flows from $q_0(\in$ some $I_i)$ to $q' = a_j p_0 + b_j$, with flow is $\dot{q} = +1$. In P_j^-, $q' > q_0$ and $\dot{q} = -1$. $\dot{p} = 0$ to ensure that q flows to the correct amount. The transitions are of the form $P_j^+ \to Q_k^{\pm}$, with the guard being $q = a_j p + b_j \wedge q \in I_k \wedge p < (b_k + a_k b_j)/(1 - a_j a_k)$. The last term will be $p \geq$ if we are jumping to Q_k^-. The $Q_j^{\pm}$ states are defined exactly as above, with p and q interchanged. Clearly, the above HPCD without resets simulates the given PAM. In particular, the reachability query "*Is* x_f *reachable from* x_0" is true *iff* $(p = x_f, q = x_{f-1})$ *or* $(p = x_{f-1}, q = x_f)$ *is reachable from* $(p = x_0, q = x_1)$, *where* x_{f-1} *is some pre-image of* x_f *and* x_1 *is the successor of* x_0.

For result (4), an HPCD with $2n$ states of the form P_j and Q_j can simulate the equivalent positive PAM. In state P_j, p flows from p_0 to $p_0 + a_j p_0 + b_j$ with $\dot{p} = +1$, while q flows from 0 to $a_j p_0 + b_j$ with $\dot{q} = +1$. The discrete transitions will be of the form $P_j \rightarrow Q_k$ with guard $a_j p - (1 + a_j)q + b_j = 0 \land q \in I_k$ and reset $p' = 0 \land q' = q$. $\square$

4   Undecidable HPCD Extensions

True to its "open" nature, the HPCD class does not present any direct mechanism to simulate a TM / MM. Asarin and Schneider [4] have shown that the HPCD class becomes undecidable when extended with one additional counter ($HPCD_{1c}$), with infinite partition ($HPCD_\infty$) and with origin-dependent rates ($HPCD_x$). In this section, we present a new set of extensions of HPCDs that manage to be undecidable. We proceed by simulating the MM with the least possible additional work. Recall that an MM uses two (positive) integer counters m and n. Incrementing and decrementing a counter, and branching based on equality to zero are the operations that need to be supported.

Any program over a 2-counter MM can be almost trivially captured as an HPCD, using just the discrete transitions without using the flows. Recall that a "zeno" system is one where one cannot bound the number of discrete transitions i.e. potentially all the computation could be done in the resets, in zero time. Thus:

Theorem 3. *Reachability over HPCDs with zeno-paths ($HPCD_{zeno}$) is undecidable.* $\square$

Alternatively, we can capture the value of both the counters m and n using just one continuous variable x as $x = p_1^m p_2^n$, where p_1 and p_2 are two prime numbers. Clearly, given the integer product x, there is exactly one way of factoring it and hence m and n can be extracted. The second variable y is now free to be used as a temporary variable for computations and to make the system non-zeno. Incrementing and decrementing the counter correspond respectively, to multiplying and dividing by the appropriate prime factor. The problem of simulating a 2-counter MM over a HPCD now reduces to the problem of checking if $m > 0$ given the numerical value of $x = p_1^m p_2^n$, and being able to recover the original value of x at the end of the procedure. One approach is to divide x by the prime number corresponding to the counter we wish to check for zero, and then check if the result of the division is an integer. *The problem of simulating a 2-counter MM over an HPCD thus reduces, to the problem of checking whether a given number is an integer (!) using the 2-dim HPCD infrastructure, and being able to recover the original number at the end of the procedure.* Surprisingly, there is no known way of doing this.

Theorem 4. *Reachability over the following HPCD-extensions are undecidable:*

1. *$HPCD_{fn-int}$, where the guard can include a function $integer(x)$ that returns* true *if the parameter x is an integer*
2. *$HPCD_{zeno-int}$, where the integer-check function is now simulated by a zeno execution of repeatedly subtracting 1 and checking if the number equals 0*   □

5   Understanding PAMs

Having refined the decidable and undecidable frontiers of the HPCD class, we explore one last avenue – treating HPCDs as PAMs, and subjecting them to a similar extend-restrain analysis. Just like we enhanced a 2-dim HPCD to make it undecidable, we present the flavor of a similar effort for PAMs.

Theorem 5. *1-dim PAMs that can check if a given number x can be expressed as p^{-i} (the class "PAM_{pow}"), where p is a given prime number and i is an unknown positive integer, can simulate an MM.*   □

We stop with this contrived extension, and move on to restricted subclasses.

The simplest PAM is one where every interval maps exactly on to another interval. Thus the mapping unwinds to a cyclical application of functions, possibly preceded by a linear sequence.

Definition 1. 1-dim oPAM   *A 1-dimensional Onto PAM (oPAM) is a 1-dim PAM where, for every interval I_i in the PAM definition, there is an interval I_j also in the definition such that $\{a_i x + b_i | x \in I_i\} = \{x | x \in I_j\}$.*   □

Next we prove a crucial lemma:

Lemma 3. *In a 1-dim oPAM with k intervals, every point has at most $2k$ unique successors.*

Proof. If interval I_i maps on to I_j, the end points (l_i, r_i) have to map on to (l_j, r_j) or to (r_j, l_j). No other mapping is possible because of our restriction, that the affine post-image of I_i has to exactly and completely overlap with I_j. Hence, there are only two possible equations linking x_j with x_i:

1. Direct $(l_i \rightarrow l_j, r_i \rightarrow r_j)$: $x_j = l_j + \frac{x_i - l_i}{r_i - l_i}(r_j - l_j)$
2. Flipped $(l_i \rightarrow r_j, r_i \rightarrow l_j)$: $x_j = l_j + \frac{r_i - x_i}{r_i - l_i}(r_j - l_j)$

In other words, if we define $d = \frac{x_0 - l_{x_0}}{r_{x_0} - l_{x_0}}$, only the points that are $l_j + d(r_j - l_j)$ or $l_j + (1 - d)(r_j - l_j)$ are ever reachable. Thus, every interval has only two possible reachable points from a given x_0. Since there are k intervals, after $2k$ iterations all possible successors would have been explored, and there will be a cycle of period $\leq 2k$ in the path.   □

Using this observation about exactly onto affine maps over linear intervals, we can prove that:

Theorem 6. *Reachability is decidable for 1-dim oPAMs.* □

Example 3. $f(x) = 2x + 1/3$, $x \in [0, 1/3](\equiv I_1)$ and $f(x) = 1/2 - x/2$, $x \in [1/3, 1](\equiv I_2)$ is a oPAM as $f([0, 1/3]) = [1/3, 1]$ and $f([1/3, 1]) = [0, 1/3]$. Thus, all points reachable from $x_0 = 1/4$ are given by $x_1 = 2/4 + 1/3 = 5/6, x_2 = 1/2 - 5/12 = 1/12, x_3 = 2/12 + 1/3 = 1/2, x_4 = 1/2 - 1/4 = 1/4 = x_0$ as expected. □

Reachability is easily semidecidable for PAMs: we just keep iterating x_0, $f(x_0)$, $f(f(x_0))$, $\cdots$ until x_f is reached. If x_f is not reachable, this algorithm will never converge. We now present a simple algorithm for over-approximating the reachable points (see box below). The idea is to repeatedly partition the intervals I_i of the PAM, until all the successors (post-images) of points in one interval map on to exactly one complete interval i.e. domain and range are fully covered (an extension of this idea was presented in [14]).

Over-Approximation of PAM Reachability

1. Let the initial set of partitions P be the set of PAM intervals $\{I_i\}$
2. Pick an interval P_i in P and calculate its post-image P_i'. Let P_i' span the intervals $P_l, P_{l+1}, \cdots, P_{r-1}, P_r$.
3. P_i' induces $r - l + 1$ partitions of P_i: $P_{i_1} \cdots P_{i_{r-l+1}}$ such that P_{i_j} maps on to P_{l+j-1}. It could also partition P_l and P_r in case it maps on to a sub-interval rather than covering the whole of P_l or P_r. In all, the total number of partitions can increase by 0 to $n + 1$.
4. Update P so it now holds the newly induced partitions as well.
5. Repeat steps $2-4$ until every interval P_i maps on to exactly one interval P_j already in P

By treating each interval as a node and connecting P_i and P_j if the post image of P_i is P_j, we get a graph representation of the PAM. Thus, x_f is reachable from x_0, if there is a path from P_{x_0} to P_{x_f} in this graph (where $x_i \in P_{x_i}$). □

Clearly, the algorithm is not guaranteed to converge. However, we can terminate after a reasonable number of steps and still use the resultant graph to approximately decide reachability. Also note that the graph needs to be constructed only once no matter how many different reachability queries we need to answer. A rewarding observation is that a 1-dim oPAM is obtained, if the above partitioning algorithm converges ! This concurs with the fact that they are decidable.

6   Discussion

In this paper, we refined the decidability frontier by exploiting the expressive redundancy of the HPCD class definition. We introduced the "taking-turns" idea, that the two PCD variables could alternately compute PAM iterations.

It was pointed out by one of the reviewers that a similar idea was used by Berard and Duford to prove that the emptiness query is undecidable for timed automata with four clocks and additive clock constraints [6]. We also showed how we could exploit the finite range of the PAM to construct non-overlapping state invariants. These ideas helped show that a 1-dim PAM can be simulated by a 2-dim PCD with translational resets. Further, resets can be disposed, if we allow overlapping invariants and comparative guards. We also demonstrated how decidable classes, like timed and initialized rectangular automata, can be extended into open problems. On the undecidability front, we showed that zeno HPCD executions can naturally capture MMs. More interestingly, the ability to check if a number is an integer was seen to be the computational ability, that separates an HPCD from universal Turing computability. A simple algorithm for over-approximating reachability was presented. It revealed that the problem is decidable, for those PAMs that converge during this iteration (oPAMs). The current understanding of this undecidability frontier of HA is summarized in *Figure* 3.

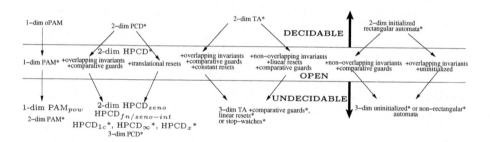

Fig. 3. Decidable, Open and Undecidable subclasses of HA ("*" indicates what was already known; unstarred results are contributions of this paper)

There are many related questions that need to be explored. Using the reductions of an HPCD to a PCD or initialized rectangular automaton with extensions, can we identify more interesting decidable subclasses and approximate reachability algorithms ? One suggestion we offer is to construct the "PCD-graph" of a 1-dim PAM, and then show how planarity can correspond to decidability. Using the construction in *Theorem 1*, we can build a graph with a set of nodes capturing each state. Different nodes can correspond to the different intervals, with an edge corresponding to each reset. We can then check whether it is possible to rearrange the given PCD-graph into a planar graph, by using the standard graph drawing literature. Another perspective to be explored is, how discrete chaotic dynamical systems (like the Tent Map) can have a say in the decidability of the PAM class. It is hoped that the ideas presented in this paper will aid the eventual "deciding" of the 1-dim PAM / 2-dim HPCD reachability problem.

References

1. R. Alur, C. Courcoubetis, N. Halbwachs, T. A. Henzinger, P.-H. Ho, X. Nicollin, A. Olivero, J. Sifakis, and S. Yovine. The Algorithmic Analysis of Hybrid Systems. *Theoretical Computer Science*, 138:3–34, 1995.
2. R. Alur and D.L. Dill. A Theory of Timed Automata. *TCS*, 126:183–235, 1994.
3. E. Asarin, O. Maler, and A. Pnueli. Reachability analysis of dynamical systems having piecewise-constant derivatives. *Theoretical Computer Science*, 138:35–65, 1995.
4. E. Asarin and G. Schneider. Widening the boundary between decidable and undecidable hybrid systems. In *CONCUR'2002, Brno, Czech Republic*, volume 2421 of *LNCS*, pages 193–208. Springer-Verlag, August 2002.
5. E. Asarin, G. Schneider, and S. Yovine. On the decidability of the reachability problem for planar differential inclusions. In *In: Hybrid Systems: Computation and Control*, pages 89–104. LNCS 2034, March 2001.
6. B. Berard and C. Dufourd. Timed automata and additive clock constraints. *Information Processing Letter*, 75(1-2):1–7, 2000.
7. T. Henzinger, P. W. Kopke, A. Puri, and P. Varaiya. What's Decidable about Hybrid Automata. In *Symposium on the Theory of Computing (STOC)*, pages 373–382, 1995.
8. Thomas A. Henzinger and Shankar Sastry. *Hybrid Systems-Computation and Control: Proceedings of the First International Workshop, HSCC '98. Lecture Notes in Computer Science 1386*. Springer-Verlag, 1998.
9. Pascal Koiran. My favourte problems. http://perso.ens-lyon.fr/pascal.koiran/problems.html, 1999.
10. G. Lafferiere, G. J. Pappas, and S. Sastry. O-minimal Hybrid Systems. *Mathematics of Control, Signals, and Systems*, 13(1):1–21, March 2000.
11. Gerardo Lafferriere, George J. Pappas, and Sergio Yovine. Symbolic reachability computation for families of linear vector fields. *J. Symb. Comput.*, 32(3):231–253, 2001.
12. O. Maler and A. Pnueli. Reachability analysis of planar multi-linear systems. In C. Courcoubetis, editor, *Computer Aided Verification: Proc. of the 5th International Conference CAV'93*, pages 194–209, Berlin, Heidelberg, 1993. Springer.
13. M.L. Minsky. Recursive unsolvability of post's problem of tag and other topics in theory of turing machines. *Ann. of Math.*, 74:437–455, 1961.
14. Venkatesh Mysore and Bud Mishra. Algorithmic Algebraic Model Checking III: Approximate Methods. In *Infinity*, 2005.
15. C. Piazza, M. Antoniotti, V. Mysore, A. Policriti, F. Winkler, and B. Mishra. Algorithmic Algebraic Model Checking I: The Case of Biochemical Systems and their Reachability Analysis. In *CAV*, 2005.
16. A. Puri and P. Varaiya. Decidebility of hybrid systems with rectangular differential inclusions. *Computer Aided Verification*, pages 95–104, 1994.
17. Gerardo Schneider. *Algorithmic Analysis of Polygonal Hybrid Systems. Ph.D. thesis*. VERIMAG - UJF, Grenoble, France, 2002.
18. Paulo Tabuada and George J. Pappas. Model checking ltl over controllable linear systems is decidable. *Hybrid Systems : Computation and Control, Lecture Notes in Computer Science*, 2623, April 2003.
19. Gerald Teschl. Ordinary differential equations and dynamical systems. Lecture Notes from http://www.mat.univie.ac.at/ gerald/ftp/book-ode/index.html, 2004.
20. Alan Turing. On computable numbers, with an application to the entscheidungs problem. *Proceedings of the London Mathematical Society*, 2(42):230–265, 1936.

When Are Timed Automata Weakly Timed Bisimilar to Time Petri Nets?

Beatrice Bérard[1], Franck Cassez[2], Serge Haddad[1], Didier Lime[3], and Olivier H. Roux[2]

[1] LAMSADE, Paris, France
{beatrice.berard | serge.haddad}@lamsade.dauphine.fr
[2] IRCCyN, Nantes, France
{Franck.Cassez | Olivier-h.Roux}@irccyn.ec-nantes.fr
[3] CISS, Aalbork, Denmark
Didier@cs.aau.dk

Abstract. In this paper, we compare Timed Automata (TA) with Time Petri Nets (TPN) with respect to weak timed bisimilarity. It is already known that the class of bounded TPNs is included in the class of TA. It is thus natural to try and identify the (strict) subclass $\mathcal{TA}^{wtb}$ of TA that is equivalent to TPN for the weak time bisimulation relation. We give a characterisation of this subclass and we show that the membership problem and the reachability problem for $\mathcal{TA}^{wtb}$ are $PSPACE$-complete. Furthermore we show that for a TA in $\mathcal{TA}^{wtb}$ with integer constants, an equivalent TPN can be built with integer bounds but with a size exponential w.r.t. the original model. Surprisingly, using rational bounds yields a TPN whose size is linear.

Keywords: Time Petri Nets, Timed Automata, Weak Timed Bisimilarity.

1 Introduction

Expressiveness of timed models. Adding explicit time to classical models was first done in the seventies for Petri nets [12,14]. Since then, timed models based on Petri nets and finite automata were extensively studied, and various tools were developed for their analysis. In this paper, we focus on two well known models: Timed Automata (TA) from [2] and Time Petri Nets (TPNs) from [12]. In [4], we studied the different semantics for TPNs w.r.t. weak timed bisimilarity. Here, we are interested in comparing the expressive power of TA and TPN for this equivalence. Recall that there are unbounded TPNs for which no bisimilar TA exists. This is a direct consequence of the following observation: the untimed language of a TA is regular which is not necessarily the case for TPNs. On the other hand, it was proved in [8] that bounded TPNs form a subclass of the class of timed automata, in the sense that for each bounded TPN $\mathcal{N}$, there exists a TA which is weakly timed bisimilar to $\mathcal{N}$. A similar result can be found in [11], where it is obtained by a completely different approach. In another line of work [10], Haar, Kaiser, Simonot and Toussaint compare Timed State Machines (TSM) and Time Petri Nets, giving a translation from TSM to TPN that preserves timed languages. In [5], we propose an extended translation between TA and TPNs with better complexity.

Our Contribution. In this work, we consider TPNs and label-free TA, *i.e.* where two different edges have different labels (and no label is ε) and we give a characterisation of the subclass $\mathcal{TA}^{wtb}$ of timed automata which admit a weakly timed bisimilar TPN. This non intuitive condition relates to the topological properties of the so-called region automaton associated with a TA. To prove that the condition is necessary, we introduce the notion of *uniform bisimilarity*, which is stronger than weak timed bisimilarity. Conversely, when the condition holds for a TA, we provide two effective constructions of bisimilar TPNs: the first one with rational constants has a size linear w.r.t. the TA, while the other one, which uses only integer constants has an exponential size. From this characterisation, we will deduce that given a TA, the problem of deciding whether there is a TPN bisimilar to it, is *PSPACE*-complete. Thus, we obtain that the membership problem is *PSPACE*-complete. Finally we also prove that the reachability problem is *PSPACE*-complete.

Outline of the paper. Section 2 recalls the semantics of TPNs and TA, and the notion of timed bisimilarity. Section 3 explains the characterisation while Section 4 is devoted to a sketch of its proof. We conclude in Section 5.

2   Time Petri Nets and Timed Automata

Notations. Let Σ be a finite alphabet, Σ^* (resp. Σ^ω) the set of finite (resp. infinite) words of Σ and $\Sigma^\infty = \Sigma^* \cup \Sigma^\omega$. We also use $\Sigma_\varepsilon = \Sigma \cup \{\varepsilon\}$ with ε (the empty word) not in Σ.

The sets $\mathbb{N}$, $\mathbb{Q}_{\geq 0}$ and $\mathbb{R}_{\geq 0}$ are respectively the sets of natural, non-negative rational and non-negative real numbers. We write $\mathbf{0}$ for the tuple $v \in \mathbb{N}^n$ such that $v(k) = 0$ for all $1 \leq k \leq n$. Let $g > 0$ in $\mathbb{N}$, we write $\mathbb{N}_g = \{\frac{i}{g} \mid i \in \mathbb{N}\}$. A tuple $v \in \mathbb{Q}^n$ belongs to the *g-grid* if $v(k) \in \mathbb{N}_g$ for all $1 \leq k \leq n$.

An interval I of $\mathbb{R}_{\geq 0}$ is a $\mathbb{Q}_{\geq 0}$-*interval* iff its left endpoint belongs to $\mathbb{Q}_{\geq 0}$ and its right endpoint belongs to $\mathbb{Q}_{\geq 0} \cup \{\infty\}$. We set $I^{\downarrow} = \{x \mid x \leq y \text{ for some } y \in I\}$, the *downward closure* of I and $I^{\uparrow} = \{x \mid x \geq y \text{ for some } y \in I\}$, the *upward closure* of I. We denote by $\mathcal{I}(\mathbb{Q}_{\geq 0})$ the set of $\mathbb{Q}_{\geq 0}$-intervals of $\mathbb{R}_{\geq 0}$.

Timed Transition Systems and Equivalence Relations. Timed transition systems describe systems which combine discrete and continuous evolutions. They are used to define and compare the semantics of TPNs and TA.

A *Timed Transition System (TTS)* is a transition system $S = (Q, q_0, \rightarrow)$, where Q is the set of configurations, $q_0 \in Q$ is the initial configuration and the relation $\rightarrow$ consists of either delay moves $q \xrightarrow{d} q'$, with $d \in \mathbb{R}_{\geq 0}$, or discrete moves $q \xrightarrow{a} q'$, with $a \in \Sigma_\varepsilon$. Moreover, we require standard properties for the relation $\rightarrow$:

Time-Determinism: if $q \xrightarrow{d} q'$ and $q \xrightarrow{d} q''$ with $d \in \mathbb{R}_{\geq 0}$, then $q' = q''$

0-delay: $q \xrightarrow{0} q$

Additivity: if $q \xrightarrow{d} q'$ and $q' \xrightarrow{d'} q''$ with $d,\ d' \in \mathbb{R}_{\geq 0}$, then $q \xrightarrow{d+d'} q''$

Continuity: if $q \xrightarrow{d} q'$, then for every d' and d'' in $\mathbb{R}_{\geq 0}$ such that $d = d' + d''$, there exists q'' such that $q \xrightarrow{d'} q'' \xrightarrow{d''} q'$.

With these properties, a *run* of S can be defined as a finite or infinite sequence of moves $\rho = q_0 \xrightarrow{d_0} q_0' \xrightarrow{a_0} q_1 \xrightarrow{d_1} q_1' \xrightarrow{a_1} \cdots q_n \xrightarrow{d_n} q_n' \cdots$ where discrete actions alternate with durations. We also write this run as $q \xrightarrow{d_0 a_0 \dots d_n \dots} q'$. The word *Untimed*$(\rho)$ in Σ^{∞} is obtained by the concatenation $a_0 a_1 \dots$ of labels in Σ_{ε} (so empty labels disappear), and *Duration*$(\rho) = \sum_{i=0}^{|\rho|} d_i$.

From a TTS, we define the relation $\dashrightarrow \subseteq Q \times (\Sigma \cup \mathbb{R}_{\geq 0}) \times Q$ for $a \in \Sigma$ and $d \in \mathbb{R}_{\geq 0}$ by:

- $q \xdashrightarrow{d} q'$ iff $\exists \rho = q \xrightarrow{w} q'$ with *Untimed*$(\rho) = \varepsilon$ and *Duration*$(\rho) = d$,
- $q \xdashrightarrow{a} q'$ iff $\exists \rho = q \xrightarrow{w} q'$ with *Untimed*$(\rho) = a$ and *Duration*$(\rho) = 0$.

Definition 1 (Weak Timed Bisimilarity). *Let $S_1 = (Q_1, q_0^1, \to_1)$ and $S_2 = (Q_2, q_0^2, \to_2)$ be two TTS and let $\approx$ be a binary relation over $Q_1 \times Q_2$. We write $q \approx q'$ for $(q, q') \in \approx$. The relation $\approx$ is a* weak timed bisimulation *between S_1 and S_2 iff $q_0^1 \approx q_0^2$ and for all $a \in \Sigma \cup \mathbb{R}_{\geq 0}$*
- *if $q_1 \xrightarrow{a}_1 q_1'$ and $q_1 \approx q_2$ then $\exists q_2 \xdashrightarrow{a}_2 q_2'$ such that $q_1' \approx q_2'$;*
- *conversely, if $q_2 \xrightarrow{a}_2 q_2'$ and $q_1 \approx q_2$ then $\exists q_1 \xdashrightarrow{a}_1 q_1'$ such that $q_1' \approx q_2'$.*
Two TTS S_1 and S_2 are weakly timed bisimilar*, written $S_1 \approx_{\mathcal{W}} S_2$, if there exists a weak timed bisimulation relation between them.*

Strong timed bisimilarity would require similar properties for transitions labeled by $a \in \Sigma \cup \mathbb{R}_{\geq 0}$, but with $\xrightarrow{a}$ instead of $\xdashrightarrow{a}$. Thus it forbids the possibility of a simulating a move by a sequence. On the other hand, weak timed bisimilarity is more precise than language equivalence and it is well-known to be central among equivalence relations between timed systems. In the rest of the paper, we abbreviate weak timed bisimilarity by bisimilarity and we explicitly name other equivalences when needed.

Time Petri Nets. Introduced in [12], and studied more recently in [13], Time Petri Nets (TPNs) associate a closed time interval with each transition.

Definition 2 (Labeled Time Petri Net). *A Labeled Time Petri Net $\mathcal{N}$ over Σ_{ε} is a tuple $(P, T, \Sigma_{\varepsilon}, {}^{\bullet}(.), (.)^{\bullet}, M_0, \Lambda, I)$ where P is a finite set of places, T is a finite set of transitions with $P \cap T = \emptyset$, ${}^{\bullet}(.) \in (\mathbb{N}^P)^T$ is the backward incidence mapping, $(.)^{\bullet} \in (\mathbb{N}^P)^T$ is the forward incidence mapping, $M_0 \in \mathbb{N}^P$ is the initial marking, $\Lambda : T \to \Sigma_{\varepsilon}$ is the labeling function and $I : T \mapsto \mathcal{I}(\mathbb{Q}_{\geq 0})$ associates with each transition a closed firing interval.*

A TPN $\mathcal{N}$ is a *g-TPN* if for all $t \in T$, the interval $I(t)$ has its bounds in $\mathbb{N}_g$. We also use ${}^{\bullet}t$ (resp. $t^{\bullet}$) to denote the set of places ${}^{\bullet}t = \{p \in P \mid {}^{\bullet}t(p) > 0\}$ (resp. $t^{\bullet} = \{p \in P \mid t^{\bullet}(p) > 0\}$) as is common is the literature.

A *configuration* of a TPN is a pair (M, ν), where M is a *marking* in the usual sense, *i.e.* a mapping in $\mathbb{N}^P$, with $M(p)$ the number of tokens in place

p. A transition t is *enabled* in a marking M iff $M \geq {}^\bullet t$. We denote by $En(M)$ the set of enabled transitions in M. The second component of the pair (M, ν) describes the values of clocks implicitly associated with transitions enabled in M: a *valuation* ν is a mapping in $(\mathbb{R}_{\geq 0})^{En(M)}$. For $d \in \mathbb{R}_{\geq 0}$, the valuation $\nu + d$ is defined by $(\nu + d)(t) = \nu(t) + d$ for each $t \in En(M)$. An enabled transition t can be fired if $\nu(t)$ belongs to the interval $I(t)$. The result of this firing is as usual the new marking $M' = M - {}^\bullet t + t^\bullet$. Moreover, some valuations are reset and we say that the corresponding transitions are newly enabled. Different semantics are possible for this operation. In this paper, we choose *persistent atomic semantics*, which is slightly different from the classical semantics [7,3], but equivalent when the net is bounded [4]. The predicate is defined by:

$$\uparrow enabled(t', M, t) = t' \in En(M - {}^\bullet t + t^\bullet) \wedge (t' \notin En(M)).$$

Thus, firing a transition is considered as an atomic step and the transition currently fired behaves like the other transitions ($\nu(t)$ need not be reset when t is fired). The set $ADM(\mathcal{N})$ of *(admissible) configurations* consists of the pairs (M, ν) such that $\nu(t) \in I(t)^\downarrow$ for each transition $t \in En(M)$. Thus time can progress in a marking only up to the minimal right endpoint of the intervals for all enabled transitions.

Definition 3 (Semantics of TPN). *The semantics of a TPN $\mathcal{N} = (P, T, \Sigma_\varepsilon, {}^\bullet(.), (.)^\bullet, M_0, \Lambda, I)$ is a TTS $S_\mathcal{N} = (Q, q_0, \rightarrow)$ where $Q = ADM(\mathcal{N})$, $q_0 = (M_0, \mathbf{0})$ and $\rightarrow$ is defined by:*

- either a delay move $(M, \nu) \xrightarrow{d} (M, \nu + d)$ iff $\forall t \in En(M), \nu(t) + d \in I(t)^\downarrow$,

- or a discrete move $(M, \nu) \xrightarrow{\Lambda(t)} (M - {}^\bullet t + t^\bullet, \nu')$ where $\forall t' \in En(M - {}^\bullet t + t^\bullet)$, $\nu'(t') = 0$ if $\uparrow enabled(t', M, t)$ and $\nu'(t') = \nu(t')$ otherwise, iff $t \in En(M)$ is such that $\nu(t) \in I(t)$.

We simply write $(M, \nu) \xrightarrow{w}$ to emphasise that a sequence of transitions w can be fired. If $Duration(w) = 0$, we say that w is an *instantaneous firing sequence*. A net is said to be k-bounded if for each reachable configuration (M, ν) and for each place p, $M(p) \leq k$.

Note that taking into account the enabling degree of transitions would require to add components to ν, which leads to awkward notations, although our result holds in the bounded case.

Timed Automata. First defined in [2], the model of timed automata (TA) associates a set of non negative real-valued variables called *clocks* with a finite automaton. Let X be a finite set of *clocks*. We write $\mathcal{C}(X)$ for the set of *constraints* over X, which consist of conjunctions of atomic formulas of the form $x \bowtie h$ for $x \in X$, $h \in \mathbb{Q}_{\geq 0}$ and $\bowtie \in \{<, \leq, \geq, >\}$.

Definition 4 (Timed Automaton). *A Timed Automaton $\mathcal{A}$ over Σ_ε is a tuple $(L, \ell_0, X, \Sigma_\varepsilon, E, Inv)$ where L is a finite set of locations, $\ell_0 \in L$ is the initial location, X is a finite set of clocks, $E \subseteq L \times \mathcal{C}(X) \times \Sigma_\varepsilon \times 2^X \times L$ is a finite set of edges and $Inv \in \mathcal{C}(X)^L$ assigns an invariant to each location. An edge $e = \langle \ell, \gamma, a, R, \ell' \rangle \in E$ represents a transition from location ℓ to location ℓ' with guard γ and reset set $R \subseteq X$. We restrict the invariants to conjunctions of terms of the form $x \bowtie h$ for $x \in X$, $h \in \mathbb{N}$ and $\bowtie \in \{<, \leq\}$.*

When we need to consider label-free automata, we simply assume that each edge has a unique label, different from ε.

A *valuation* v is a mapping in $\mathbb{R}_{\geq 0}^X$. For $R \subseteq X$, the valuation $v[R \mapsto 0]$ maps each variable in R to the value 0 and agrees with v over $X \setminus R$. Constraints of $\mathcal{C}(X)$ are interpreted over valuations: we write $v \models \gamma$ when the constraint γ is satisfied by v.

Definition 5 (Semantics of TA). *The semantics of a TA* $\mathcal{A} = (L, \ell_0, X, \Sigma_\varepsilon, E, Inv)$ *is a TTS* $S_\mathcal{A} = (Q, q_0, \rightarrow)$ *where* $Q = L \times (\mathbb{R}_{\leq 0})^X$, $q_0 = (\ell_0, \mathbf{0})$ *and* $\rightarrow$ *is defined by:*

- *either a delay move* $(\ell, v) \xrightarrow{d} (\ell, v + d)$ *iff* $v + d \models Inv(\ell)$,
- *or a discrete move* $(\ell, v) \xrightarrow{e} (\ell', v')$ *iff there exists some* $e = (\ell, \gamma, a, R, \ell') \in E$ *s.t.* $v \models \gamma$, $v' = v[R \mapsto 0]$ *and* $v' \models Inv(\ell')$.

Elementary zones of a TA. Recall [9,2] that, if m is the maximal constant appearing in atomic formulas $x \bowtie c$ of $\mathcal{A}$, an equivalence relation with finite index can be defined on clock valuations, leading to a partition $\mathcal{P}_m$ of $(\mathbb{R}_{\geq 0})^X$, with the following property: two equivalent valuations have the same behaviour under progress of time and reset operations, with respect to the constraints. Note that the same property holds for any partition which refines $\mathcal{P}_m$. This is the case in particular if we replace m by any $K \geq m$ instead of m, even with $K = +\infty$ (as depicted in Figure 1 on the left). Of course, a finite constant is needed for decidability results. Finally, we can also consider a g-grid, where all constants are of the form $\frac{i}{g}$, $0 \leq i \leq K \cdot g$ instead of $\{0, 1, \ldots, K\}$.

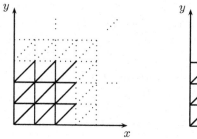 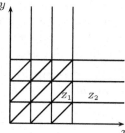

Fig. 1. Partitions of $(\mathbb{R}^+)^2$ with $K = +\infty$ and $K = 3$

In this paper, the elements of the partition are called *elementary zones* and we consider a slight variation for their definition: we take a constant $K \geq m + 1$ and with each clock $x \in X$, we associate an interval in the set $\{\{0\},]0, 1[, \{1\}, \ldots, \{K-1\},]K-1, K[, [K, +\infty[\}$, instead of keeping $\{K\}$ separately. As usual, we also specify the ordering on the fractional parts for all clocks x such that $x < K$. Such a partition is represented in Figure 1 (on the right) for the set of two clocks $X = \{x, y\}$ and $K = 3$. For this example, elementary zones Z_1 and Z_2 are described by the constraints: $Z_1 : (2 < x < 3) \wedge (1 < y < 2) \wedge (0 < frac(y) < frac(x))$ and $Z_2 : (x \geq 3) \wedge (1 < y < 2)$.

If Z and Z' are elementary zones, Z' is a time successor of Z, written $Z \leq Z'$, if for each valuation $v \in Z$, there is some $d \in \mathbb{R}_{\geq 0}$ such that $v + d \in Z'$. For each elementary zone Z, there is at most one elementary zone such that (i) Z' is a time successor of Z, (ii) $Z \neq Z'$ and (iii) there is no time successor Z'' different from Z and Z' such that $Z \leq Z'' \leq Z'$. When it exists, this elementary zone is called the immediate successor of Z and denoted by $succ(Z)$.

Standard topological notions on $(\mathbb{R}_{\geq 0})^X$ apply to elementary zones. Moreover, due to the particular form of the constraints, the topological closure of any elementary zone has a minimal element.

3   A Characterisation of TA Bisimilar to TPNs

Regions of a timed automaton. Since our results are mainly based on the *region automaton*, we recall its definition [2]. For a TA $\mathcal{A}$, a constant K and a granularity g, the region automaton $R(\mathcal{A})_{g,K}$ is a finite automaton with states of the form (ℓ, Z), where ℓ is a location of $\mathcal{A}$ and Z an elementary zone of $(\mathbb{R}_{\geq 0})^X$.

We call *region* a pair (ℓ, Z). The regions of $R(\mathcal{A})_{g,K}$ are built inductively from the initial one $(\ell_0, \mathbf{0})$ by the following transitions over the set of labels $\{succ\} \cup \Sigma_\varepsilon$: $(\ell, Z) \xrightarrow{succ} (\ell, succ(Z))$ if $succ(Z) \models Inv(\ell)$ and $(\ell, Z) \xrightarrow{a} (\ell', Z')$ if there is a transition $(\ell, \gamma, a, R, \ell') \in E$ such that $Z \models \gamma$ and $Z' = Z[R \mapsto 0]$, with $Z' \models Inv(\ell')$. Thus, only *reachable* regions appear in $R(\mathcal{A})_{g,K}$. A region $r = (\ell, Z)$ is said to be *maximal* in $R(\mathcal{A})_{g,K}$ with respect to ℓ if no *succ*-transition is possible from r. In the sequel, the topological properties of r are implicitly derived from those of Z. We write $\bar{r}$ for the topological closure of r, and we denote by min_r the minimal vector of $\bar{r}$.

We now give a definition which distinguishes time-closed and time-open descriptions for regions. It is equivalent to the original one but more convenient for our proofs and it fits both cases, whether K is finite or infinite.

Definition 6 (Region description for automaton $R(\mathcal{A})_{g,K}$).
A time-closed description of a region r is given by:
- *ℓ_r the location of r,*
- *$min_r \in \mathbb{N}_g^X$ with $\forall x$, $min_r(x) \leq K$, the minimal vector of the topological closure of r,*
- *$ActX_r = \{x \in X \mid min_r(x) < K\}$ the subset of relevant clocks,*
- *the number $size_r$ of different fractional parts for the values of relevant clocks in the $\mathbb{N}_g^{ActX_r}$ grid, with $1 \leq size_r \leq Max(|ActX_r|, 1)$ and the onto mapping $ord_r : X \mapsto \{1, \ldots, size_r\}$ giving the ordering of the fractional parts.*
By convention, $\forall x \in X \setminus ActX_r, ord_r(x) = 1$.
Then $r = \{(\ell_r, min_r + \boldsymbol{\delta}) \mid \boldsymbol{\delta} \in \mathbb{R}_{\geq 0}^X \wedge \forall x, y \in ActX_r[ord_r(x) = 1 \Leftrightarrow \boldsymbol{\delta}(x) = 0] \wedge \boldsymbol{\delta}(x) < 1/g \wedge [ord_r(x) < ord_r(y) \Leftrightarrow \boldsymbol{\delta}(x) < \boldsymbol{\delta}(y)]\}$
A time-open description of a region r is defined with the same attributes (and conditions) as the time-closed one with:
$r = \{(\ell_r, min_r + \boldsymbol{\delta} + d) \mid d \in \mathbb{R}_{>0} \wedge \forall x \in ActX_r, \boldsymbol{\delta}(x) + d < 1/g\}$.

The set $[X]_r$ is the set of equivalence classes of clocks w.r.t. their fractional parts, i.e. x and y are equivalent iff $ord_r(x) = ord_r(y)$.

Remark that $min_r \notin r$ except if there is a single class of clocks relative to r (for instance if the corresponding zone is a singleton). Of course, when $K = +\infty$, the part about *relevant* clocks, for which the value is less than K, can be omitted (since $ActX_r = X$). This hypothesis makes some proofs simpler, because the extremal case where a clock value is greater than K is avoided, and it can be lifted afterward. Furthermore when K is finite, some regions admit both time-open and time-closed descriptions (for instance a region associated with zone Z_2 in fig. 1), whereas when $K = +\infty$, a region admits a single description, so that time elapsing leads to an alternation of time-open regions (where time can elapse) and time-closed ones (where no time can elapse).

Reachability. For a reachable region r of $R(\mathcal{A})_{g,K}$, not all configurations of r are reachable. Nevertheless, by induction on the reachability relation, the following property can be shown: For any reachable region r, there is a region $reach(r)$ w.r.t. the g-grid and constant $K = \infty$ such that (i) $reach(r) \subset r$, (ii) each configuration of $reach(r)$ is reachable and (iii) if $reach(r)$ is a time-open region then r admits a time-open description else r admits a time-closed description. As a consequence, we have: $\forall x \in ActX_r, min_{reach(r)}(x) = min_r(x)$ and $\forall x \in X \setminus ActX_r, min_{reach(r)}(x) \geq K$ and ord_r restricted to $ActX_r$ is identical to $ord_{reach(r)}$.

Consider now the relation $\mathcal{R}$ defined by $(l, v)\ \mathcal{R}\ (l, v')$ iff $\forall x \in X, v'(x) = v(x) \vee (v(x) \geq K \wedge v'(x) \geq K)$. It is a strong timed bisimulation relation. From the previous observations, we note that each configuration of a reachable region is strongly timed bisimilar to a reachable configuration of this region. Thus speaking about reachability of regions is a slight abuse of notations.

We can now state our main results.

Theorem 1 (Characterisation of TA bisimilar to some TPN). *Let $\mathcal{A}$ be a (label-free) timed automaton and $R(\mathcal{A})_{1,K}$ its region automaton with a constant K strictly greater than any constant occurring in the automaton, then $\mathcal{A}$ is weakly timed bisimilar to a time Petri net iff for each region r of $R(\mathcal{A})_{1,K}$ and for each edge e from $\mathcal{A}$,*

(a) Every region r' such that $r' \cap \bar{r} \neq \emptyset$ is reachable
(b) $\forall (\ell_r, v) \in r$, if $(\ell_r, v) \xrightarrow{e}$ then $(\ell_r, min_r) \xrightarrow{e}$
(c) $\forall (\ell_r, v) \in \bar{r}$, if $(\ell_r, min_r) \xrightarrow{e}$ then $(\ell_r, v) \xrightarrow{e}$.

Furthermore, if these conditions are satisfied then we can build a 1-bounded 2-TPN bisimilar to $\mathcal{A}$ whose size is linear w.r.t. the size of $\mathcal{A}$ and a 1-bounded 1-TPN bisimilar to $\mathcal{A}$ whose size is exponential w.r.t. the size of $\mathcal{A}$.
We denote by $\mathcal{TA}^{wtb}$ the corresponding subclass of timed automata.

Theorem 2 (Complexity results). *Given a (label-free) timed automaton $\mathcal{A}$, deciding whether there is a TPN weakly timed bisimilar to $\mathcal{A}$ is PSPACE-complete. The reachability problem for the class $\mathcal{TA}^{wtb}$ is PSPACE-complete.*

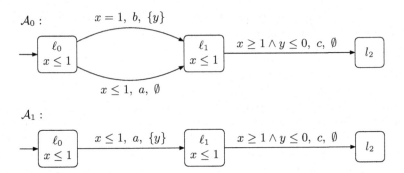

Fig. 2. Two automata with different behaviours w.r.t bisimulation with a TPN

The characterisation of Theorem 1 is closely related to the topological closure of reachable regions: it states that any region intersecting the topological closure of a reachable region is also reachable and that a discrete step either from a region or from the minimal vector of its topological closure is possible in the whole topological closure. Consider the two TA $\mathcal{A}_0$ and $\mathcal{A}_1$ in Figure 2. The automaton $\mathcal{A}_0$ admits a bisimilar TPN whereas $\mathcal{A}_1$ does not. Indeed, the region $r = \{(\ell_1, x = 1 \wedge 0 < y < 1\}$ is reachable. The guard of edge c is true in $min_r = (\ell_1, (1, 0))$ whereas it is false in r.

The next section is devoted to a sketch of the proof of Theorem 1. The proof of Theorem 2 is obtained from Theorem 1 and an adaptation of results in [1]. The complete proofs can be found in [6].

4   Proof of Theorem 1

4.1   Necessary Condition

From bisimulation to uniform bisimulation. As a first step, we prove that when a TPN and a TA are bisimilar, this relation can in fact be strengthened in what we call *uniform bisimulation*. We first need a lemma which points out the effect of time granularity on the behaviour of TPN.

Lemma 1. *Let (M, ν) and $(M, \nu + \delta)$ be two admissible configurations of a g-TPN with $\nu, \delta \in \mathbb{R}^{En(M)}_{\geq 0}$. Let w be an instantaneous firing sequence, then:*
(i) $(M, \nu) \xrightarrow{w}$ implies $(M, \nu + \delta) \xrightarrow{w}$
(ii) If $\nu \in \mathbb{N}_g^{En(M)}$ and $\delta \in [0, 1/g[^{En(M)}$ then $(M, \nu + \delta) \xrightarrow{w}$ implies $(M, \nu) \xrightarrow{w}$

Lemma 2 is the central point for the proof of necessity. It shows that bisimulation implies uniform bisimulation for the g-grid with $K = \infty$. Roughly speaking, uniform bisimulation means that a unique mechanism is used for every configuration of the topological closure of the region to obtain a bisimilar configuration of the net.

Lemma 2 (From bisimulation to uniform bisimulation). *Let $\mathcal{A}$ be a timed automaton bisimilar to some g-TPN $\mathcal{N}$ via some relation $\mathcal{R}$ and let $R(\mathcal{A})_{g,\infty}$ be a region automaton of $\mathcal{A}$. Then:*

- *if a region r belongs to $R(\mathcal{A})_{g,\infty}$ then $\bar{r}$ also belongs to $R(\mathcal{A})_{g,\infty}$;*
- *for each reachable region r, there exist a configuration of the net (M_r, ν_r) with $\nu_r \in \mathbb{N}_g^{En(M_r)}$ and a mapping $\phi_r : En(M_r) \to [X]_r$ such that:*
  - *If r is time-closed, then for each $\delta \in \mathbb{R}_{\geq 0}^X$ such that $(\ell_r, \min_r + \delta) \in \bar{r}$, $(\ell_r, \min_r + \delta) \; \mathcal{R} \; (M_r, \nu_r + proj_r(\delta))$,*
  - *If r is time-open, then for each $\delta \in \mathbb{R}_{\geq 0}^X$, $d \in \mathbb{R}_{\geq 0}$ such that $(\ell_r, \min_r + \delta + d) \in \bar{r}$, $(\ell_r, \min_r + \delta + d) \; \mathcal{R} \; (M_r, \nu_r + proj_r(\delta) + d)$,*
  where $proj_r(\delta)(t) = \delta(\phi_r(t))$.

Proof. First note that the choice of a particular clock x in the class $\phi_r(t)$ is irrelevant when considering the value $\delta(x)$. Thus the definition of $proj_r$ is sound. The proof is an induction on the transition relation in the region automaton. The basis case is straightforward with $\{(l_0, \mathbf{0})\}$ and $\{(M_0, \mathbf{0})\}$. The induction part relies on lemma 1, with 4 cases, according to the incoming or target region and to the nature of the step: 1. a time step from a time-closed region, 2. a time step from a time-open region, 3. a discrete step into a time-closed region, and 4. a discrete step into a time-open region.   □

Proof of Necessity. The fact that conditions *(a)*, *(b)* and *(c)* of Theorem 1 hold for $R(\mathcal{A})_{g,\infty}$ is straightforward:
(a) This assertion is included in the inductive assertions.
(b) Let r be a reachable region, let $(\ell_r, \min_r + \delta) \in r$ be a configuration with $\delta \in [0, 1/g[^X$, then $\exists (M, \nu) \; \nu \in \mathbb{N}_g^{En(M)}$ bisimilar to $(\ell_r, \min_r)$ and $(M, \nu + \delta')$ with $\delta' \in [0, 1/g[^{En(M)}$ bisimilar to $(\ell_r, \nu + \delta)$. Suppose that $(\ell_r, \min_r + \delta) \xrightarrow{e}$, then $(M, \nu + \delta') \xrightarrow{w}$ with w an instantaneous firing sequence and $label(w) = e$. Now by lemma 1-*(ii)*, $(M, \nu) \xrightarrow{w}$, thus $(\ell_r, \min_r) \xrightarrow{e}$.
(c) Let r be a region, and $(\ell_r, \min_r + \delta) \in \bar{r}$ with $\delta \in [0, 1/g]^X$ thus $\exists (M, \nu)$ bisimilar to $(\ell_r, \min_r)$ and $(M, \nu + \delta')$ with $\delta' \in [0, 1/g]^{En(M)}$ bisimilar to $(\ell_r, \min_r + \delta)$. Suppose that $(\ell_r, \min_r) \xrightarrow{e}$, then $(M, \nu) \xrightarrow{w}$ with w an instantaneous firing sequence and $label(w) = e$. By lemma 1-*(i)*, we have $(M, \nu + \delta') \xrightarrow{w}$, thus $(\ell_r, \min_r + \delta) \xrightarrow{e}$.

In order to complete the proof, we successively show that if the conditions are satisfied in $R(\mathcal{A})_{g,\infty}$ for some g, they also hold for $R(\mathcal{A})_{1,\infty}$, and finally that they are satisfied in $R(\mathcal{A})_{1,K}$, with a finite constant K sufficiently large.

4.2   Sufficient Condition

Starting from a TA $\mathcal{A}$ satisfying the conditions of Theorem 1, we build a 2-TPN bisimilar to $\mathcal{A}$. We describe the construction, the proof of correctness as well as the construction of a 1-TPN can be found in [6].

For this construction, all edges are weighted by 1. Omitted labels for transitions stand for ε. A firing interval $[0, 0]$ is indicated by a blackened transition and intervals $[0, \infty[$ are omitted. A double arrow between a place p and a transition t indicates that p is both an input and an output place for t.

W.l.o.g. we assume that an invariant never forbids to enter a state (by adding constraints to the input transitions). We then remark that $x < c$ occurring in an invariant of $\mathcal{A}$ may be safely omitted. If it would forbid the progress of time in some configuration, then the associated region would be a maximal time-open region r. Due to condition (a), $\bar{r}$ is reachable but since r is time-open, $\bar{r} \cap succ(r) \neq \emptyset$, so that $succ(r)$ is reachable which contradicts the maximality of r.

Clock constraints. The atomic constraints associated with a clock x are arbitrarily numbered from 1 to $n(x)$ where $n(x)$ is the number of such conditions. When $x \leq h$ occurs in at least one transition and in at least one invariant, we consider it as two different conditions. Then we add places $(Rtodo_i^x)_{i \leq n(x)+1}$ for the reset operations. We build a subnet for each atomic constraint $x \bowtie h$ occurring in a transition of the TA, and one for each condition $x \leq h$ occurring in an invariant. Figure 3 below shows the subnets corresponding to $x < h$ (with $h > 0$) on the left and $x \leq h$ on the right. Since constant $\frac{1}{2}$ appears in interval bounds, the resulting TPN is a 2-TPN.

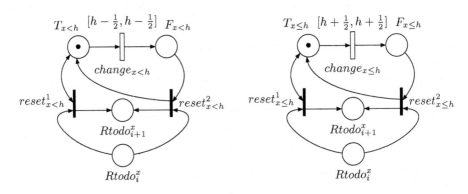

Fig. 3. The subnets for $x < h$ (with $h > 0$) and $x \leq h$

Locations and edges. With each location ℓ of the automaton, we associate an eponymous place ℓ. The place ℓ is initially marked iff the location ℓ is the initial one. The invariant $Inv(\ell)$ is tested with the subnets corresponding to its atomic constraints. To simulate an edge $(\ell, \gamma, a, R, \ell')$, we must test the atomic constraints from $\gamma = \gamma_1 \wedge \ldots \wedge \gamma_{m(e)}$, using the places corresponding to true in the associated subnets, and reset successively all the clocks in $R = \{x_1, \ldots, x_{n(e)}\}$ by instantaneous transitions. This is done by the subnet in Figure 4, which must be connected to some subsets like those of Figure 3.

This construction is illustrated in Figure 4.2 for the timed automaton $\mathcal{A}_0$ from Figure 2 with some simplifications related to this particular TA. Note that the subnet associated to the constraint $y \leq 0$ switches the condition to false (marking $F_{y \leq 0}$) when the implicit value of y maintained in the net reaches 1/2. This

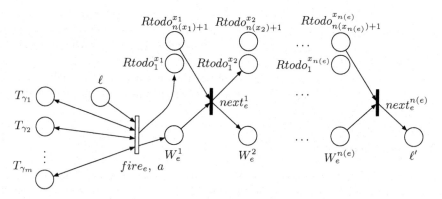

Fig. 4. The subnet for edge $e = (\ell, \gamma = \gamma_1 \wedge \ldots \wedge \gamma_{m(e)}, a, R = \{x_1, \ldots, x_{n(e)}\}, \ell')$

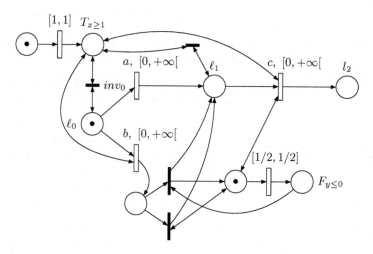

Fig. 5. A 2-TPN bisimilar to $\mathcal{A}_0$

translation thus seems less constrained than the original condition. However, conditions *(b)* and *(c)* ensure that the configurations where both constraints do not simultaneously hold are not reachable.

5   Conclusion

In this paper, we considered the (semantic) subclass $\mathcal{TA}^{wtb}$ of labeled-free TA such that a timed automaton $\mathcal{A}$ is in $\mathcal{TA}^{wtb}$ if and only if there is a TPN $\mathcal{N}$ weakly timed bisimilar to $\mathcal{A}$. We obtained a characterisation of this class, based on the region automaton associated with $\mathcal{A}$. To prove that our condition is necessary, we introduced the notion of uniform bisimulation between TA and TPNs. For the sufficiency, we proposed two constructions. From this characterisation, we have proved that for the class $\mathcal{TA}^{wtb}$, the membership problem and the reachability problem are $PSPACE$-complete. The techniques introduced here also lead to a similar characterisation for TA with diagonal constraints and to a simpler one for TA without strict or diagonal constraints (see [6]). These techniques also give some insight for use of the region automaton in order to obtain expressivity results. Further work would consist in finding a characterization for a larger class of intervals.

References

1. L. Aceto and F. Laroussinie. Is Your Model Checker on Time? On the Complexity of Model Checking for Timed Modal Logics. *Journal of Logic and Algebraic Programming*, volume 52-53, pages 7-51. Elsevier Science Publishers, august 2002.
2. R. Alur and D. Dill. A theory of timed automata. *Theoretical Computer Science B*, 126:183–235, 1994.
3. T. Aura and J. Lilius. A causal semantics for time Petri nets. *Theoretical Computer Science*, 243(1–2):409–447, 2000.
4. B. Bérard, F. Cassez, S. Haddad, D. Lime and O.H. Roux. Comparison of Different Semantics for Time Petri Nets. *ATVA'05, Taipei, Taiwan*, volume 3707 of *LNCS*, 2005, to appear.
5. B. Bérard, F. Cassez, S. Haddad, D. Lime and O.H. Roux. Comparison of the Expressiveness of Timed Automata and Time Petri Nets . *FORMATS'05, Uppsala, Sweden, LNCS*, 2005, to appear.
6. B. Bérard, F. Cassez, S. Haddad, D. Lime and O.H. Roux. Comparison of the Expressiveness of Timed Automata and Time Petri Nets. Research Report IRC-CyN R2005-2 available at http://www.lamsade.dauphine.fr/~haddad/publis.html 2005.
7. B. Berthomieu and M. Diaz. Modeling and verification of time dependent systems using time Petri nets. *IEEE Transactions on Software Engineering*, 17(3):259–273, March 1991.
8. F. Cassez and O. H. Roux. Structural Translation of Time Petri Nets into Timed Automata. In Michael Huth, editor, *Workshop on Automated Verification of Critical Systems (AVoCS'04)*, Electronic Notes in Computer Science. Elsevier, August 2004.
9. D. L. Dill. Timing assumptions and verification of finite-state concurrent systems. In Proc. Workshop on Automatic Verification Methods for Finite State Systems, Grenoble, volume 407 of *LNCS*, 1989.
10. S. Haar, F. Simonot-Lion, L. Kaiser, and J. Toussaint. Equivalence of Timed State Machines and safe Time Petri Nets. In *Proceedings of WODES 2002*, Zaragoza, Spain, pages 119–126.
11. D. Lime and O. H. Roux. State class timed automaton of a time Petri net. In *PNPM'03*. IEEE Computer Society, September 2003.
12. P. M. Merlin. *A study of the recoverability of computing systems*. PhD thesis, University of California, Irvine, CA, 1974.
13. M. Pezzé and M. Young. Time Petri Nets: A Primer Introduction. Tutorial presented at the Multi-Workshop on Formal Methods in Performance Evaluation and Applications, Zaragoza, Spain, september 1999.
14. C. Ramchandani. *Analysis of asynchronous concurrent systems by timed Petri nets*. PhD thesis, Massachusetts Institute of Technology, Cambridge, MA, 1974.

Subquadratic Algorithms for Workload-Aware Haar Wavelet Synopses

S. Muthukrishnan[*]

Dept. of Computer Science, Rutgers University, New Brunswick, NJ 08903
muthu@cs.rutgers.edu

Abstract. Given a signal $\mathbf{A}$ of N dimensions, the problem is to obtain a representation $\mathbf{R}$ for it that is a linear combination of vectors in the dictionary H of Haar wavelets. The quality of the representation $\mathbf{R}$ is determined by B, the number of vectors from H used, and δ, the error between $\mathbf{R}$ and $\mathbf{A}$. Traditionally, δ has been the sum squared error $\epsilon_{\mathbf{R}} = \sum_i (\mathbf{R}[i] - \mathbf{A}[i])^2$, in which case, Parseval's theorem from 1799 helps solve the problem of finding the $\mathbf{R}$ with smallest $\epsilon_{\mathbf{R}}$ in $O(N)$ time.

Recently, motivated by database applications, researchers have sought other notions of error such as

- workload-aware error, or $\epsilon_{\mathbf{R}}^{\pi} = \sum_i \pi[i](\mathbf{R}[i] - \mathbf{A}[i])^2$, where $\pi[i]$ is the workload or the weight for i, and
- maximum pointwise absolute error, eg., $\epsilon_{\mathbf{R}}^{\infty} = \max_i |\mathbf{R}[i] - \mathbf{A}[i]|$.

Recent results give $\Omega(N^2)$ time algorithms for finding $\mathbf{R}$ that minimize these errors.

We present subquadratic algorithms for versions of these problems. We present a near-linear time algorithm to minimize $\epsilon_{\mathbf{R}}^{\pi}$ when π is compressible. To minimize $\epsilon_{\mathbf{R}}^{\infty}$, we give an $O(N^{2-\epsilon})$ time algorithm. These algorithms follow a natural dynamic programming approach developed recently, but the improvements come from exploiting *local* structural properties of the Haar wavelet representations of signals we identify.

Sparse approximation theory is a mature area of Mathematics that has traditionally studied signal representations with Haar wavelets. It is interesting that the past few years have seen new problems in this area motivated by Computer Science concerns: we pose a few new additional problems and some partial results.

1 Introduction

We study the problem of representing signals via Haar wavelets.

Definition of Haar Basis. There are many kinds of wavelets. We work with one of the most popular and fundamental: Haar wavelets [16]. Let N be a power of 2. We define $N - 1$ proper wavelet functions on $[0, N - 1]$ as follows. For integer j, $0 \leq j < \log(N)$ and integer k, $0 \leq k < 2^j$, we define a *proper wavelet* by $\phi(x)[j, k] = -\sqrt{2^j/N}$ for $x \in [kN/2^j, kN/2^j + N/2^{j+1})$, $\phi(x)[j, k] = \sqrt{2^j/N}$ for

---

[*] Supported by NSF DMS 0354600.

R. Ramanujam and S. Sen (Eds.): FSTTCS 2005, LNCS 3821, pp. 285–296, 2005.

$x \in [kN/2^j + N/2^{j+1}, (k+1)N/2^j)$ and 0 otherwise. Additionally, we define a wavelet function ϕ, also known as a *scaling function*, that takes the value $+1/\sqrt{N}$ over the entire domain $[0, N)$. We number the $\phi(x)[j, k]$'s as $\psi_0, \psi_1, \ldots, \psi_{N-2}$ in some arbitrary order and ϕ as ψ_{N-1}. The *support* of a vector v, denoted supp(v), is $\{t : v(t) \neq 0\}$. Thus the support of a wavelet vector is either the entire interval $[0, N)$ or, recursively, the left half or right half of the support of some other wavelet. The wavelet ψ_{N-1} is constant on its entire support; each other wavelet is constant on the left half and right half of its support and takes values on its left and right halves that are negatives of each other. The set of possible supports of a wavelet is the set of dyadic intervals of length at least 2. (A *dyadic* interval is the whole space a power of two in length, or recursively, a dyadic interval comprising the left or right half. The intervals that x belong to in the definition above are dyadic.)

Haar Wavelet Synopsis for Signals. Wavelets can be used to represent signals. Consider a signal $\mathbf{A}[0...N - 1]$, where N is a power of 2 for convenience and $\mathbf{A}[i] \in \mathcal{R}$. The *wavelet coefficient* $c_i = \langle \mathbf{A}, \psi_i \rangle$. Since $H = \{\psi_0, \psi_1, \ldots, \psi_{N-1}\}$ is a basis for $\mathcal{R}^N$, any signal $\mathbf{A}$ is exactly recoverable using the wavelet basis, ie., $\mathbf{A} = \sum_i c_i \psi_i$. Typically, we are not interested in recovering the signal exactly using all the N wavelet coefficients; instead, we want to represent the signal using no more than B wavelet coefficients for some $B \ll N$. Say Λ is a set of wavelets of size at most B. Signal $\mathbf{A}$ can be represented as $\mathbf{R}$ using these coefficients as follows:

$$\mathbf{R} = \sum_{i \in \Lambda} c_i \psi_i.$$

Since $B \ll N$, $\mathbf{R}$ must necessarily be an approximation for worst case $\mathbf{A}$. The *best B-term representation* of $\mathbf{A}$ is the choice of Λ that minimizes the error $\epsilon_{\mathbf{R}}$ of representing $\mathbf{A}$ which is typically the sum-squared-error, i.e., $\epsilon_{\mathbf{R}} = ||\mathbf{R} - \mathbf{A}||_2^2 = \sum_i (\mathbf{R}[i] - \mathbf{A}[i])^2$. From a fundamental result of Parseval from 1799 [22,2], it follows that choosing the B largest $|c_i|$'s suffices to get an $\mathbf{R}$ that minimizes $\epsilon_{\mathbf{R}}$.

Recent Versions of Haar wavelet Representation Recently, researchers have identified two variations of the basic problem above.

Problem 1. Given signal $\mathbf{A}[0, \ldots, N - 1]$, N a power of 2, an integer $B \ll N$, and *workload* $\pi[0, \ldots, N - 1]$, determine set Λ of wavelets such that $|\Lambda| \leq B$, and $\epsilon_{\mathbf{R}}^{\pi} = \sum_i \pi[i](\mathbf{R}[i] - \mathbf{A}[i])^2$ is minimized.

Problem 2. Given signal $\mathbf{A}[0, \ldots, N - 1]$, N a power of 2, an integer $B \ll N$, and *workload* $\pi[0, \ldots, N - 1]$, determine set Λ of wavelets such that $|\Lambda| \leq B$, and *absolute error*[1] $\epsilon_{\mathbf{R}}^{\infty} = \max_i \pi[i]|\mathbf{R}[i] - \mathbf{A}[i]|$ is minimized.

---

[1] All our discussions here will apply to minimizing the relative error $\epsilon_{\mathbf{R}} = \max_i \pi[i]\frac{|\mathbf{R}[i] - \mathbf{A}[i]|}{\max\{|\mathbf{R}[i]|, 1\}}$ with minor changes.

Problem 1 appears in [18,12,20,13,14]. Problem 2 appears in [9,3,8,13,14], with uniform workload, that is, $\pi[i] = 1/N$ for all i, but it is a natural to generalize that to nonuniform $\pi[i]$'s. It is trivial to observe that the B i's with the largest $|c_i|$'s no longer form the best B-term representation and indeed can be arbitrarily far away from the optimal in specific instances for both the problems above. So, algorithmically the problems above are nontrivial.

Motivation. Consider how Haar wavelet synopses get used in databases and data analysis. A signal $\mathbf{A}$ ($\mathbf{A}[i]$ is the number of tuples in a table with attribute value—say age of a student—i) is represented using a B-term wavelet representation $\mathbf{R}$ which is used as the (succinct) approximation or the surrogate of $\mathbf{A}$. When the signal is queried using *point queries*, i.e., queries are of the form "$\mathbf{A}[i] =$?", the approximation $\mathbf{R}[i]$ is returned instead. *If all point queries are equally likely*, then average of the squared error in using $\mathbf{R}[i]$ rather than $\mathbf{A}[i]$ is precisely $\epsilon_{\mathbf{R}}$, thus, the traditional rationale to minimize $\epsilon_{\mathbf{R}}$.

Problems 1 and 2 arise in the same setting, but motivated by different practical aspects.

First, in practice, all point queries are *not* equally likely. In general, there is bias in how points are queried that depends on the application and the nature of the signal. So, there is a *workload* π, where $\pi[i]$ is the *probability* of i being queried. The uniform workload case is the one when $\pi[i] = 1/N$ for all i. In the general workload case then, one wants to minimize, analogous to the uniform workload case, the total squared-error over all i's, but now normalized for the probability of a point i being queried (equivalently the probability of incurring the error on i). More precisely, we wish to minimize $\epsilon_{\mathbf{R}}^{\pi} = \sum_i \pi[i] \, (\mathbf{R}[i] - \mathbf{A}[i])^2$. This is the Problem 1 above.

Second, in practice, averaging the error over the set of all points may not be appropriate. For example, [9] shows that errors can vary without bound and unpredictably, even for identical queries on nearly-identical values on different parts of the data with representations that minimize the total or average error. Hence, they propose to minimize error on individual points [9,8,3], leading to Problem 2 above.

Both these problems are fairly central to query optimization in databases. Databases [17] maintain workload information by profiling queries in a number of ways and would prefer to use representations that accurately reflects their cost for the given workload rather than ignore this information; similarly, optimizing per-query error estimates is of interest too. There has been several heuristic algorithms related to these problem [1,7,23,4].

Previous Results. In a key development, Garofalakis and Kumar [8] proposed a dynamic programming approach to solve these problems. Their method, applied to Problems 1 and 2, takes time $O(N^2 B \log B)$. Guha [12] improved this to $O(N^2 \log B)$ for Problem 1 and $O(N^2)$ time for Problem 2, where the author also made a crucial improvement in the space used from $O(NB)$ to $O(N)$—this has an impact in practice.

One of the outstanding questions is can one design improved algorithms for these problems. Besides the natural question of improving running times in general, this question is of relevance because part of the rationale for using wavelets over other summaries like histograms comes from the fact that in the traditional setting, wavelet transformation is highly efficient, working in $O(N)$ time while histograms have taken $O(N^2B)$ time [15]. Now with the two variants above, histogram algorithms still take $O(N^2B)$ time, but the known wavelet algorithms are not significantly more efficient. So, better wavelet constructions are needed to make a strong case for wavelet representations in nontraditional settings such as the ones above.

There are improved *approximation* results for Problems 1 and 2 [8,13,14], and a linear time result with a modified basis [18]. But no $o(N^2)$ time optimal algorithms are known for either variant for precisely minimizing the error with the Haar basis.

Our Results. We present $o(N^2)$ time exact algorithms for versions of both variants. More precisely,

- We consider *compressible* π's. In particular, a *k-flat* π for $k \ll N$ comprises k piecewise constant partition. That is, for $p_0 = 0 < p_1 \cdots < p_k = N$, we have for all i, $\pi[j] = \pi[j+1]$ where $j \in [p_i, p_{i+1} - 1)$. We present an $O(NkB^2 \log N)$ time algorithm in this case to minimize $\epsilon_{\mathbf{R}}^{\pi}$. This is nearly linear for choices of B (sparse representation) and k (compressible π's) of interest.

  In practice, π's are seldom arbitrary in real life. k-flat π's are natural in some situations. For example, if the domain were time, one can imagine different weights attached to several observations from different days (months) but equal weights for all observations of the same day (or month, respectively). Another natural setting is one in which N is very large and we do not associate $\pi[i]$ with all i's, but only with a handful of i's that are distinguished, and let the remainder be uniformly important. If there are k distinguished values, π is $2k - 1$-flat. Finally, if π were compressed by run length encoding or even wavelet representation, then it is $O(k)$-flat where k is the compressed size of π. So, this is a very interesting case in practice.

- For minimizing $\epsilon_{\mathbf{R}}^{\infty}$, we study its dual version: given an upper bound δ on the error, minimize the number B of wavelet vectors needed in $\mathbf{R}$ so that $\epsilon_{\mathbf{R}}^{\infty} \leq \delta$. We present an $O(N^2/\log N)$ algorithm, and another taking time roughly $O(N^{2-\epsilon}B^*)$ where B^* is the optimal answer, for some constant ϵ. Both algorithms take subquadratic time.

- We pose a few open problems in the larger context of representing signals via different dictionaries to optimize suitable errors. We also present few other (partial) results.

We believe the emerging Computer Science perspective to the area of Sparse Approximation Theory which is a mature area in Mathematics is interesting, and our results add to the growing body of work.

2 Problem 1

Recall that a k-flat π for $k \ll N$ comprises k piecewise constant partition, ie., for $p_0 = 0 < p_1 \cdots < p_k = N$, we have for all i, $\pi[j] = \pi[j+1]$ where $j \in [p_i, p_{i+1} - 1)$. We will solve Problem 1 for the case of k-flat π's in two steps. First, we will consider k-*dyadic-flats*, that is, the case where each interval $I_i = [p_i, p_{i+1})$ is dyadic. Later, we will consider the general case.

k-*dyadic-flat π's.* Consider the full binary tree T with $[0, N-1]$ as the leaves. Associate with each node u in T, the interval J_u spanned by the leaves in the subtree rooted at it. Since each I_i is dyadic, it is an interval J_u associated with some internal node u of T. Let the set of all nodes u in T that have an associated $J_u = I_i$ be denoted L; clearly $|L| = k$ and no two such nodes are the parents of each other since the k-flat intervals form a partition.

Definition 1. *Let t be the portion of tree T that includes the nodes in L and all their ancestors in T.*

Observe that since the k-dyadic-flat intervals form a partition, t is size at most $2k - 1$ (k of leaves and $k - 1$ internal nodes); this is crucial.

We will apply a dynamic programming approach to the internal nodes of t and a "local Parsevals" to the leaves of t.

Dynamic Programming. At any internal node u of t, we will consider J_u and determine $E(J_u, \ell, S)$ which is the least $\epsilon_\mathbf{R}^\pi$ for representing $\mathbf{A}[J_u]$ with any subset Λ_u of wavelets that have supports contained in J_u, $|\Lambda_u| \leq \ell$, together with the contribution for the set S of wavelets whose individual supports strictly contain J_u.

Our emphasis is on searching over the different sets S that impinge on J_u. Each dyadic interval I has a left half denoted I_L and a right half denoted I_R which are themselves dyadic intervals. With each interval I, we associate the wavelet vector ψ_I that is positive on I_L and is negative on I_R. There are two cases to consider while computing $E(I, k, S)$: ψ_I is included in the set of k wavelet terms or not. Either way, we will write $E(I, k, S)$ in terms of similar functions for I_R and I_L recursively. Say ψ_I is included in the set of k wavelet terms. Then,

$$E(I, k, S) = \min_{0 \leq k' \leq k-1} E(I_L, k', S \cup \psi_I) + E(I_R, k - 1 - k', S \cup \psi_I).$$

In the other case,

$$E(I, k, S) = \min_{0 \leq k' \leq k} E(I_L, k', S) + E(I_R, k - k', S).$$

Hence, $E(I, k, S)$ is the minimum of the two possibilities above. The boundary cases are easy to define, and $E(I, k, S)$ can be calculated using dynamic programming. The number of problems to solve by dynamic programming is $O(kB2^{\min\{k, \log N\}})$ since the number of different S can be bounded by either

$\log N$, the depth of T, or k, the number of internal nodes in t; each such problem can be computed in $O(B)$ time.

Local Search. Now we focus on the local search which is applied to intervals on the leaves of t. We will exploit the property of π that it is constant in such intervals, and be much more efficient than exploring the solution space by dynamic programming. Formally, consider computing $E(J_u, \ell, S)$ where $J_u = I_i$ for some i. Let $\mathbf{A}_u$ denote the signal in interval J_u. We make the following crucial observation:

Lemma 1. (Local Parseval's) *Let $\alpha_0, \alpha_1, \ldots, \alpha_{|J_u|-2}$ be the proper wavelet vectors of an interval $[0, |J_u| - 1]$ and $\alpha_{|J_u|-1}$ be the all "average" scaling vector. $E(J_u, \ell, S)$ is minimized by choosing the largest ℓ wavelet coefficients in magnitude from $\langle \mathbf{A}, \alpha_i \rangle$ for $i = 0, \ldots, |J_u| - 2$.*

Proof. The contribution of S to a $j \in J_u$ is $v[j] = (\sum_{\psi_i \in S} \langle \mathbf{A}, \psi_i \rangle \psi_i)[j]$. Since all ψ_i's in S have support that contains J_u, $v[j]$'s will be identical for all $j \in J_u$. So, we have a generic v to denote the value $v[j]$ for any $j \in J_u$ and $\mathbf{v}$ to denote the vector of all v's of size J_u. Observe that $E(J_u, \ell, S)$ is minimized by choosing the ℓ wavelet coefficients ψ_i with $\text{supp}(\psi_i) \in J_u$ for the signal $\mathbf{A}_u - \mathbf{v}$. Let $\mathbf{R}$ be such a representation. Observe that the ψ_i's with $\text{supp}(\psi_i) \in J_u$ have a one-to-one correspondence with $\alpha_0, \alpha_1, \ldots, \alpha_{|J_u|-2}$. The difference between picking amongst the best wavelet representation of $\mathbf{A}_u - \mathbf{v}$ from α_i's that form an orthonormal basis for it, and from amongst ψ_i with $\text{supp}(\psi_i) \in J_u$ is the presence of $\alpha_{|J_u|-1}$ in the orthonormal basis that is not available in determining $E(J_u, \ell, S)$ since it is not a wavelet vector for the signal $\mathbf{A}$ on $[0, N)$.

We now proceed with the proof of the lemma. We have $\mathbf{A}_u = \sum_i \langle \mathbf{A}, \alpha_i \rangle \alpha_i$ and $\mathbf{v} = \sum_i \langle \mathbf{v}, \alpha_i \rangle \alpha_i$ since α_i's are an orthonormal basis. Note further that $\langle \mathbf{v}, \alpha_i \rangle = 0$ for $i = 0, \ldots, |J_u| - 2$. We have $\mathbf{R} = \sum_{i \in \Lambda, |\Lambda| \leq \ell, \Lambda \in \{0, \ldots, |J_u|-2\}} c_i \alpha_i$ which we seek. Expanding and doing algebraic manipulations, one can conclude that (fix $\Lambda \in \{0, \ldots, |J_u| - 2\}$)

$$\|\mathbf{A}_u - \mathbf{v} - \mathbf{R}\|^2 = (\langle \mathbf{A}_u, \alpha_{|J_u|-1} \rangle - v)^2 + \sum_{i \in \Lambda}(c_i - \langle \mathbf{A}_u, \alpha_i \rangle)^2 + \sum_{i \notin \Lambda} \langle \mathbf{A}_u, \alpha_i \rangle^2$$

because all the other cross terms cancel out since $\alpha_i \perp \alpha_j$ for $i \neq j$. Now the lemma follows since last two summands do not depend on v. ∎

Local Parseval's has certain nontrivial aspects. For example, v in the proof may be positive or negative, and we do not pick the largest ℓ of the wavelet coefficients for the signal in the interval of interest, but rather the largest ℓ from those *except* the scaling vector. This form of Local Parseval's may have other applications.

The algorithm that uses the Local Parseval's for local search is simple and takes $O(|J_u|)$ time and therefore $O(N)$ over all u's that form the leaf of t. That completes the description of the algorithm for the k-dyadic-flat case.

Theorem 1. *Problem 1 can be solved in $O(N + kB^2 2^{\min\{k, \log N\}})$ time for k-dyadic-flat π's.*

Note that when k is small, say a constant, this algorithm takes time linear in N; for general k, the running time is $O(NkB^2)$ which is near-linear since $k, B \ll N$.

k-flat π's. When π is k-flat but not k-dyadic-flat, we can not directly follow the previous algorithm. Since any dyadic interval J_u in T may overlap *two* partitions of a k-flat π (one at either end), the dynamic programming and local search problems do not divide nicely into independent problems. Our approach here is to replace any k-flat π with $O(k \log N)$-dyadic-flat π' by replacing each constant partition in π using at most $O(\log N)$-sized partitions that are dyadic (in a straightforward way). We can conclude with a near-linear time algorithm again since $k, B \ll N$:

Theorem 2. *Problem 1 can be solved in time $O(NkB^2 \log N)$ for k-flat π's.*

3   Problem 2

Formally, we study the dual version below.

Problem 3. Given a bound δ, find the smallest B such that the optimal B-sized representation $\mathbf{R}$ satisfies, $\max_i \pi[i]|\mathbf{R}[i] - \mathbf{A}[i]| \leq \delta$.

We will outline our solution for the uniform π case (that is, all π's are equal, so they can be removed from the optimization criteria); extension to the nonuniform case is straightforward. Given an interval I and set S of wavelets whose individual supports strictly contain I, consider $B(I, \delta, S)$, the least number of wavelets from Λ_I needed for representing $\mathbf{A}[I]$ such that for each $i \in I$, $|\mathbf{R}[i] - a[i]| \leq \delta$. Say ψ_I is included in the set of k wavelet terms. Then,

$$B(I, \delta, S) = B(I_L, \delta, S \cup \psi_I) + B(I_R, \delta, S \cup \psi_I) + 1.$$

In the other case,

$$B(I, \delta, S) = B(I_L, \delta, S) + B(I_R, \delta, S).$$

Hence, $B(I, \delta, S)$ is the minimum of the two possibilities above. This dynamic programming method gives an algorithm that takes time $O(N^2)$.

Using local search, we will develop a more efficient algorithm. We need the key observation: we do not have to solve $B(I, \delta, S)$ for each possible S. Instead, *it suffices to keep the maximum and minimum absolute errors for each subset of wavelets in Λ_I.* This is because:

Lemma 2. *We have*

$$\min_{S, i \in 2^{\Lambda_I}} \max_{j \in I} |\delta_i^j - v_S|,$$

where δ_i^j is the error in $\mathbf{A}[j]$ due to set i of wavelets chosen from Λ_I and v_S is the contribution of S to each $i \in I$, is equal to

$$\min_{S, i \in 2^{\Lambda_I}} \max\{|(\max_{j \in I} \delta_i^j) - v_S|, |(\min_{j \in I} \delta_i^j) - v_S|\}.$$

As before, we run dynamic programming until we have intervals of size 2^j and following that, we run the local search above; the combined algorithm will take time $O(\frac{N}{2^j}\frac{N}{2^j}2^j + \frac{N}{2^j}2^{2^j})$, which, when balanced, reduces to $O(N^2/\log N)$. Details have been omitted, but they can be reconstructed with some work.

Another improvement is as follows. Say B^* is the optimal answer. It suffices to keep the maximum and minimum absolute errors over all B^*-sized subsets. Then in the local search phase, we will spend only time $O(|I|^{B^*})$. Then we can balance the two running times by choosing $2^j = n^{1/B^*+1}$ so the total running time is $O(N^{2-\frac{2}{B^*+1}}B^*)$. Both these improvements make the running time marginally subquadratic $o(N^2)$.

Theorem 3. *There is an $O(N^2/\log N)$ (or $O(N^{2-\frac{2}{B^*+1}}B^*)$, where B^* is the optimal number) time algorithm to solve Problem 3.*

This result for the dual problem is not only of independent interest, but also may be used to approximate the solution to the primal problem studied in [8] by binary searching with guesses of δ. Then, with $O(\log \delta^*)$ extra factor in the running time, one can solve the primal version as well.

4   Extensions

From a mathematical and algorithmic viewpoint, lot remains to be done with different π's and $\epsilon_\mathbf{R}$'s, despite the recent progress.

In what follows, we will list a set of open problems and provide some comments. We have chosen to discuss only those problems that we believe are relevant to understanding the role of π, and those that have some nontrivial intuition or challenge.

4.1   Foundational Open Problems

Problem 4. Consider some *compression measure* of π, ie., the size of π using a compression algorithm, denoted $C(\pi)$. Find fast algorithms for Problem 1 that adopt to $C(\pi)$.

The problem above is motivated by an interest to develop faster algorithms that exploit properties of the importance vector π. In particular, we would like to study the information content of π. The uniform $\pi = 1/N$ is most compressible and arbitrary π is incompressible; they lead to the classical wavelet representation problem solved via Parseval's, and the recent nonuniform problem studied in this paper, respectively. Problem 4 is an attempt to parameterize the complexity of the problem in terms of the information content of π as determined by a compression method. Two simple examples arise:

- If we used *run-length compression* to compress π, then π is piecewise constant with $C(\pi)$ disjoint pieces. Then our Theorem 2 solves it in near-linear time.

- If π can be summarized exactly using say k Haar wavelet coefficients, then π can be rewritten as piecewise constant functions on $O(k)$ *dyadic* pieces. Then our Theorem 1 solves it in nearly linear time.

But better compressors (such as Lempel-Ziv) are known and Problem 4 is open for those cases. Recently, this view was developed for weight hitogram construction algorithms [21], but they do not provide any insight into wavelet representation construction.

Problem 5. Say π is *periodic* with period p, ie., $\pi[j + p] = \pi[j]$ for all $j \in 0, \ldots, N - 1$. Solve Problem 1 under this assumption.

Again, this problem tries to exploit properties of π but from a different perspective from Problem 4. Periodic π's can be nicely compressed, but compressible π's are not strictly periodic. This problem brings out the difficulty in computing partial solutions at two disjoint portions of the signal which have identical weights, ie., for the same information content of π, what is the role of different signals on the complexity of Problem 1?

Problem 6. Given signal $\mathbf{A}[0, \ldots, N - 1]$, N a power of 2, an integer $B \ll N$, and importance $\pi[0, \ldots, N - 1]$, determine set Λ of wavelets with $|\Lambda| \leq B$ and coefficients d_i for $i \in \Lambda$ such that $\epsilon_{\mathbf{R}}^{\pi} = \sum_i \pi[i] \, (\mathbf{R}[i] - \mathbf{A}[i])^2$ is minimized where $\mathbf{R} = \sum_{i \in \Lambda} d_i \psi_i$.

The problem above is more general than Problem 1 because d_i is not necessarily chosen to be the wavelet coefficients $c_i = \langle \mathbf{A}, \psi_i \rangle$. In principle, choosing d_i's more effectively does not hurt the applications. First,

Theorem 4. *If the set Λ of wavelets were fixed, then the choice of d_i's to solve 6 can be computed using least-squares fit approach in time $O(N + B^3)$ in the worst case.*

But the problem above is to search simultaneously over the choice of wavelets ψ_i's as well as d_i's. Note that if π was uniform, then from the orthogonality of ψ_i's, it will follow that $d_i = \langle \mathbf{A}, \psi_i \rangle$. But that does not hold for arbitrary π's. We present the following partial result.

Theorem 5. *There is an algorithm that solves Problem 6 in time $O(nB^2 \log^2 N)$ and outputs a representation $\mathbf{R}$ of at most $B \log N$ wavelet vectors and error $\epsilon_{\mathbf{R}}^{\pi}$ no worse than the optimal error of any representation with B wavelet vectors.*

The result above is an augmented-resource result. We are able to obtain no worse error than we seek, but at the expense of larger number of buckets than the budget allows. The theorem above relies on the observation that any B vector representation can be converted into one with at most $B \log N$ vectors where the wavelet vectors are non-intersecting (for suitable choice of d_i's). Thereafter, we do a dynamic programming to pick the $B \log N$ nonoverlapping wavelet vectors in a straightforward way taking time claimed in the theorem. Again, details have been omitted. We can get an improved running time if we additionally assumed that π's are compressible as in Section 2, but this is of lesser concern than decreasing the $\log N$ factor in the number of wavelet vectors in the solution.

Finally, here is a gem.

Problem 7. Solve Problem 1 with the dictionary of Fourier basis.

We think this is a fairly basic question and surprisingly, perhaps because this problem was not formulated explicitly before, we do not know of an efficient algorithm for this problem from prior work.

4.2   Applied Open Problems

From an applied point of view, finally, experimental studies matter. For example, it will be interesting to evaluate different heuristics for optimal wavelets using experiments under realistic arbitrary workloads. An interesting question is what heuristics to study. In sparse approximation theory, when one deals with non-standard problems where Parseval's does not apply, it is common to (a) use greedy methods and sometimes they give provably good bounds, or (b) transform the problem so that Parseval's may be used. In our problem, for example, (b) can be applied as follows.

Heuristic. We have

$$\epsilon_{\mathbf{R}}^{\pi} = (\mathbf{A} - \mathbf{R})^T D(\mathbf{A} - \mathbf{R}),$$

where D is the diagonal matrix with $D[i,i] = \pi[i]$ and $D[i,j] = 0$ for $i \neq j$. We can rewrite this by setting $\mathbf{A}' = D^{1/2}\mathbf{A}$ and say its approximate representation is $\mathbf{R}'$. Then, we have

$$\epsilon_{\mathbf{R}}^{\pi} = (\mathbf{A}' - \mathbf{R}')^T(\mathbf{A}' - \mathbf{R}').$$

This is in the standard form of the error and hence we can directly apply Parseval's theorem and find the B largest Haar coefficients to get optimal $\mathbf{R}'$ for $\mathbf{A}'$. This whole procedure takes only $O(N)$ time. While this is optimal in error, using this transformation to represent $\mathbf{A}$ involves an inverse transformation that is not akin to Haar wavelet decoding (eg., it involves estimating $\mathbf{A}'[j]$ and scaling it by $1/\sqrt{\pi[j]}$ because even though $\mathbf{A}'$ is represented using the Haar wavelet basis (denote it by $\mathbf{\Psi}$), $\mathbf{A}$ is represented using a transformed basis (ie., $D^{-1/2}\mathbf{\Psi}$)). ∎

Recently, another nice heuristic has been suggested that too involves transforming the basis from Haar to a suitably different weighted version [18]. Also, there are heuristics to the Haar wavelet basis case based on greedy methods. Finally, some approximate algorithms have been proposed recently [13,14]. The open issue from an applied point of view is to compare these heuristics to each other and to our optimal results with Haar wavelets, and to explore the tradeoffs in practice.

5   Concluding Remarks

This brings us to the concluding thought, namely, why focus on representing a signal using the Haar basis and why not one of the transformed basis if it has suitable properties for fast coding and decoding. Adapting the standard Haar basis for coding signals and making it more suitable for the workload entails no changes in the *decoding* procedure of a signal using the wavelet representations. In fact, the decoding program does not need to know π. Hence, from a systems point of view, there is some preference to our approach. Of course from a technical point of view, our problem is of great interest because what appears to be a natural variation of the classical method from 1910 seems to pose new challenges and calls for new algorithmic strategies beyond the Parseval's theorem that has been the workhorse of sparse approximation theory since 1799. Also, this inspires the area of sparse approximation with nonuniform workloads and non-euclidean error metrics which we hope will develop into a theory with a clear understanding of the complexity of the problem in terms of the structure of π and $\mathbf{A}$.

6 Acknowledgements

Thanks to David Applegate for pointing me to the least squares fit method in Problem 6. Thanks to Suhas Diggavi for discussions about wavelet basis transformations. Thanks to Sudipto Guha for describing his recent results [12,13,14].

References

1. A. Aboulnaga and S. Chaudhuri. Self-tuning histograms: building histograms without looking at data. *Proc. SIGMOD*, 181–192, 1999.
2. K. G. Beauchamp. *Walsh functions and their applications*. 1975.
3. A. Deligiannakis, M. Garofalakis, and N. Roussopoulos. A fast approximation scheme for probabilistic wavelet synopses. *Proc. of SSDBM*, 2005.
4. A. Deligiannakis and N. Roussopoulos. Extended wavelets for multiple measures. *Proc. SIGMOD*, 2003.
5. R. Devore and G. Lorentz. *Constructive approximation*. Springer Verlag, 1991.
6. K. Egiazarian and J. Astola. Tree-structured Haar transforms. *Journal of Mathematical Imaging and Vision*, 16:269–279, 2002.
7. V. Ganti, M. Lee and R. Ramakrishnan. ICICLES: Self-tuning samples for approximate query answering. *VLDB Journal*, 176–187, 2000.
8. M. Garofalakis and A. Kumar. Deterministic wavelet thresholding for maximum error metrics. *Proc. PODS*, 2004.
9. M. Garofalakis and P. Gibbons. Wavelet Synopses with Error Guarantees. *Proc. of ACM SIGMOD*, 476–487, 2002.
10. A. Gilbert, S. Guha, P. Indyk, Y. Kotidis, S. Muthukrishnan and M. Strauss. Fast, small space algorithms for approximate histogram maintenance. *Proc. STOC*, 389–398, 2002.
11. A. Gilbert, S. Muthukrishnan and M. Strauss. Approximation of functions over redundant dictionaries using coherence. *Proc. ACM-SIAM SODA*, 2003.
12. S. Guha. Space Efficiency in Synopsis Construction Algorithms *Proc. VLDB*, 2005.
13. S. Guha, B. Harb. Wavelet Synopsis for Data Streams: Minimizing Non-Euclidean Error. *Proc. KDD*, 2005.
14. S. Guha, B. Harb. Approximation Algorithms for Wavelet Transform Coding of Data Streams. To appear in *Proc. ACM-SIAM SODA*, 2006.

15. H. Jagadish, N. Koudas, S. Muthukrishnan, V. Poosala, K. Sevcik, and T. Suel. Optimal Histograms with Quality Guarantees. *Proc. VLDB*, 275–286, 1998.
16. A. Haar. "Zur theorie der orthogonalen functionsysteme". *Math Annal.*, Vol 69, 331–371, 1910.
17. V. Markl, G. Lohman and V. Raman. LEO: An automatic query optimizer for DB2. *IBM Systems Journal*, Vol 42, No 1, 2003. Aloso, *Proc. VLDB*, 2002.
18. Y. Matias and D. Urieli. Optimal workload-based wavelet synopses. *Proc. Intl Conf on Database Technology*, 2004.
19. Y. Matias, J. Vitter and M. Wang. Wavelet-based histograms for selectivity estimation. *Proc. ACM SIGMOD*, 448–459, 1998.
20. S. Muthukrishnan. Workload-optimal wavelet synopsis. DIMACS Technical Report 2004-25, May 2004.
21. S. Muthukrishnan, M. Strauss and X. Zhang. Workload-aware histograms on streams. To appear in *Proc. ESA*, 2005. Also, DIMACS TR 2005.
22. M. Parseval. http://encyclopedia.thefreedictionary.com/Parseval's+theorem 1799.
23. R. Schmidt and C. Shahabi. How to evaluate multiple range-sum queries progessively. *Proc. PODS*, 2002.

Practical Algorithms for Tracking Database Join Sizes

Sumit Ganguly, Deepanjan Kesh, and Chandan Saha

Indian Institute of Technology, Kanpur

Abstract. We present novel algorithms for estimating the size of the natural join of two data streams that have efficient update processing times and provide excellent quality of estimates.

1 Introduction

The problem of accurately estimating the size of the natural join of two database tables is a classical problem[15,13,1,11,12], with fundamental applications to database query optimization and approximate query answering. Prior work in the '80s through the mid '90s largely focussed on the *stored data* model, where, the joining relations are either disk or memory-resident. *Sampling* emerged as a popular solution technique in this model [14,15,13].

The *streaming data model* [6,5,7,4] was proposed in the late '90's as a model for a class of monitoring applications, such as network management, RF-id based applications, sensor networks, etc. These applications are characterized by high volumes of rapidly and continuously arriving records. The monitoring applications can often tolerate approximate answers, provided, (a) the error probability and the approximation ratio are both guaranteed to be low, (b) the rate of processing is able to keep pace with the fast arrival rates without significantly degrading the quality of answers, and, (c) the space consumed is significantly smaller than that needed for exact computation. Existing streaming algorithms satisfy a majority of the above properties, and in addition, process the stream in an online fashion, (i.e., look once only).

Data Stream Model and Notation. A data stream is viewed as a sequence of updates of the form (i, v), where, i takes values from the domain $\mathcal{D} = \{0, 1, \ldots, N - 1\}$, and v is the change in the frequency of the items. If $v > 0$, then we can think of the tuple (i, v) as representing v insertions of i; correspondingly, if $v < 0$, then, (i, v) can be thought of as representing v deletions of i. The frequency of i, denoted by f_i, is the sum of the changes to the frequency of i since the inception of the stream, that is, $f_i = \sum_{(i,v) \text{ appears in stream}} v$. We denote by m_R the sum of the frequencies of the items in a stream R, that is, $m_R = \sum_{i \in \mathcal{D}} f_i$. In this paper, we consider the insert-only model of data streams (i.e., $v > 0$ for all updates) and the general update model of data streams (i.e., $v > 0$ or $v < 0$).

The self-join [2,3,1] of a stream R is denoted by $\mathrm{SJ}(R)$ and is defined as $\mathrm{SJ}(R) = \sum_{i \in \mathcal{D}} f_i^2$. For $r = 1, 2, \ldots, N$, let rank(r) be a (ranking) function that returns an item whose frequency is the rth largest frequency in f (ties are broken arbitrarily). The *residual self-join* [8] of a stream R, denoted by $\mathrm{SJ}^{res}(R, k)$ is defined as the self-join of

R. Ramanujam and S. Sen (Eds.): FSTTCS 2005, LNCS 3821, pp. 297–309, 2005.

R after the top-k ranked frequencies are removed, that is, $\mathrm{SJ}^{res}(R, k) = \sum_{r>k} f^2_{\mathrm{rank}(r)}$.
It is easily shown that $\mathrm{SJ}^{res}(R, k) \le \frac{m_R^2}{4k}$.

In this paper, we consider two data streams R and S, and denote the frequencies of an item i in streams R and S by f_i and g_i respectively. The size J of the natural join of R and S is defined as $J = |R \bowtie S| = \sum_{i \in \mathcal{D}} f_i \cdot g_i$. Following standard convention, we let $0 < \epsilon \le 1$ and $0 < \delta < 1$ denote user-specified accuracy and confidence parameters respectively. When referring to the join of R and S, we use m to denote $m_R + m_S$, SJ to denote $\mathrm{SJ}_R + \mathrm{SJ}_S$, and $\mathrm{SJ}^{res}(k)$ to denote $\mathrm{SJ}^{res}(R, k) + \mathrm{SJ}^{res}(S, k)$.

Previous work. The seminal work in [1,2,3] presents the product of sketches technique that estimates the join size using space $O(s \cdot (\log(mN)) \cdot \log \frac{1}{\delta})$ bits with additive error of $O(\frac{(\mathrm{SJ}(R)\mathrm{SJ}(S))^{1/2}}{\epsilon \sqrt{s}})$. The work in [1] also presents a space lower bound of $s = \Omega(\frac{m^2}{J})$ for approximating the join size J to within a constant confidence over general data streams. The product of sketches algorithm does not match the space lower bound for the problem, and, the time taken to process each stream update can be large ($O(s \cdot \log \frac{1}{\delta})$). The *Fast-AGMS* algorithm[10] is a time-efficient variant of the product of sketches technique, processing stream updates in time $O(\log \frac{1}{\delta})$, while providing the same space versus accuracy guarantees of the product of sketches algorithm.

COUNT-MIN sketches[9] presents an elegant technique for estimating the join size using space $O(s(\log N + \log m) \log \frac{1}{\delta})$ bits, time $O(\log \frac{1}{\delta})$ for processing each stream update and with additive estimation error of $O(\frac{m^2}{s})$. The cross-sampling algorithm [1] has similar properties; however, it is not applicable to streams with deletion operations and is known to be generally outperformed by sketch-based methods in practice. The skimmed-sketches algorithm [12] estimates the join size using space $O(s(\log N) \log(m \cdot N) \cdot \log \frac{(m \log N)}{\delta})$ bits, time $O(\log \frac{1}{\delta})$ for processing each stream update and with additive error of $O(\frac{m^2}{\epsilon s})$. The COUNT-MIN sketch and skimmed-sketch techniques match the worst-case lower bound for the problem. Their main drawback is that they often perform poorly in comparison with the simple product of sketches algorithm, since, the complexity term m^2 of [12] is in practice, much larger than the self-join sizes.

Contributions. In this paper, we present two novel, space-time efficient algorithms called REDSKETCH and REDSKETCH-A for estimating the size of the natural join of two data streams. The REDSKETCH algorithm estimates the join size using $O(s \cdot \log(mN) \cdot \log \frac{m}{\delta})$ bits, with additive error $= O(\frac{m \cdot (\mathrm{SJ}^{res}(s))^{1/2}}{\sqrt{s}})$. The REDSKETCH-A algorithm estimates the join size using space $O(s \cdot \log(mN) \cdot \log \frac{m}{\delta})$ bits and with additive estimation error of $O\left(\frac{J^{2/3} \cdot (\mathrm{SJ})^{1/6} \cdot (\mathrm{SJ}^{res}(s))^{1/6}}{s^{1/6}}\right)$. Both algorithms process each stream update in time $O(\log \frac{m}{\delta})$ and match the space lower bound of [1] (up to logarithmic factors). Our algorithms are practically effective, since the bounds are in terms of SJ and SJ^{res}_s, which are significantly less than m^2 and $\frac{m^2}{s}$, respectively, in practice.

Organization. The rest of the paper is organized as follows. In Section 2, we review basic data stream algorithms that we use later. Sections 3 and 4 present the REDSKETCH and the REDSKETCH-A algorithms respectively. We conclude in Section 5.

2   Review

In this section, we review sketches [2,3], the algorithm *CountSketch* [8] for approximately finding the top-k frequent items over R and the FAST-AGMS algorithm [10] for estimating binary join sizes.

Sketches and estimating self-join sizes. A sketch[2,3] X of the stream R is a random integer defined as $X = \sum_{i \in \mathcal{D}} f_i \cdot x_i$, where, for each $i \in \mathcal{D}$, x_i is chosen randomly from the set $\{-1, +1\}$ such that the family of random variables $\{x_i\}_{i \in \mathcal{D}}$ are four-wise independent. The family $\{x_i\}_{i \in \mathcal{D}}$ is called the *sketch basis*. Corresponding to a stream update of the form (i, v), the sketch is updated in time $O(1)$ as follows: $X := X + x_i \cdot v$. It can be shown that $E[X^2] = \text{SJ}$ and $\text{Var}[X^2] = O(\text{SJ}^2)$. An ϵ-accurate estimate of the self-join is obtained by taking the average of $O(\frac{1}{\epsilon^2})$ independent sketches. The confidence of the estimate is boosted to $1 - \delta$ by using the standard technique of returning the median of $O(\log \frac{1}{\delta})$ independently computed averages.

Algorithm CountSketch [8]. Sketches are used in [8] to design the *CountSketch* algorithm for finding the top-k frequent items in a data stream. The data structure called CSK consists of a collection of s hash tables, $T[1], \ldots, T[s]$, each consisting of A buckets. A pair-wise independent hash function $h_t : \mathcal{D} \to \{0, 1, \ldots, A - 1\}$ and a pair-wise independent sketch basis $\{x_{t,i}\}_{i \in \mathcal{D}}$ are associated with each hash table, $1 \leq t \leq s$. Each bucket, $T[t, b]$ keeps the sketch $X_{t,b} = \sum_{h_t(i)=b} f_i \cdot x_{t,i}$, of the sub-stream of the items that map to this bucket. In addition, an array capable of storing A pairs of the form $(i, \hat{f}_i)$ is kept and organized as a classical min-heap data structure. Corresponding to a stream update (i, v), the structure CSK is updated in time $O(s)$ as follows.

UPDATE$_{\text{CSK}}(i, v)$: **for** $t := 1$ **to** s **do** $X_{t,h_t(i)} := X_{t,h_t(i)} + v \cdot x_{t,i}$ **endfor**

Once all the hash tables are updated, the frequency f_i is estimated as

$$\hat{f}_i = \text{median}_{t=1}^s X_{t,h_t(i)} \cdot x_{t,i} \ . \tag{1}$$

If $\hat{f}_i$ exceeds the lowest value estimate in the heap H, then, the latter value is evicted and replaced by the pair $(i, \hat{f}_i)$. The estimation guarantees of the *CountSketch* algorithm are stated as a function Δ of the residual self-join and is summarized below.

$$\Delta(s, A) = 8 \left(\frac{\text{SJ}^{res}(s)}{A} \right)^{1/2} \tag{2}$$

Theorem 1 ([8]). *Let* $s = O(\log \frac{m}{\delta})$, $A \geq 8 \cdot k$, *and let* $\Delta = \Delta(\frac{A}{8}, A)$. *Then, for every item* i, $\Pr\left\{|\hat{f}_i - f_i| \leq \Delta\right\} \geq 1 - \frac{\delta}{2 \cdot m}$. *The space complexity is* $O(k \cdot \log \frac{m}{\delta} \cdot (\log(m \cdot N))$ *bits, and the time taken to process a stream update is* $O(\log \frac{m}{\delta})$. $\qquad\square$

The FAST-AMS *[16] and* FAST-AGMS *algorithms* [10]. The FAST-AGMS algorithm is a time-efficient variant of the product of sketches technique for estimating join sizes. The *CountSketch* based second moment estimator presented in [16] applies a similar optimization for reducing the processing time for estimating self-joins. The algorithm uses a pair of set of hash tables, $T_1, T_2, \ldots, T_s$ and $U_1, U_2, \ldots, U_s$ for streams R and S respectively, such that, each hash table consists of A buckets. The T and U hash tables are *parallel* in the sense that for $1 \leq t \leq s$, the tables T_t and U_t use the same random pair-wise independent hash function $h_t : \mathcal{D} \to \{0, 1, \ldots, A - 1\}$ and the same four-wise independent sketch basis $\{x_{t,i}\}$. The random bits used for different hash table indices are independent of each other. For $1 \leq t \leq s$ and $0 \leq b \leq A - 1$, each bucket $T_t[b]$ (resp. $U_t[b]$), contains a single sketch $X_{t,b}$ (resp. $Y_{t,b}$) of the sub-stream of items that hash to this bucket, that is, $X_{t,b} = \sum_{h_t(i)=b} f_i \cdot x_{t,i}$ (resp. $Y_{t,b} = \sum_{h_t(i)=b} g_i \cdot x_{t,i}$). Updates to the stream R or S are propagated to the corresponding data structure T or U appropriately, similar to the UPDATE$_{\text{CSK}}$ sub-routine given in Section 2. For each hash table index t, $1 \leq t \leq s$, an estimate $\hat{J}_t$ is obtained as follows: $\hat{J}_t = \sum_{b=0}^{A-1} X_{t,b} \cdot Y_{t,b}$. Finally, the median of these estimates is returned as the estimate of the join size, that is, $\hat{J} = \text{median}_{t=1}^s \hat{J}_t$. Lemma 1 summarizes the basic property of this algorithm.

Lemma 1 ([10,16]). $\mathrm{E}[\hat{J}_t] = J$ and $\mathrm{Var}[\hat{J}_t] \leq \frac{1}{A}(\text{SJ}(R) \cdot \text{SJ}(S) + J^2)$. In particular, if $R = S$, then, $\mathrm{E}[\hat{J}_t] = \text{SJ}(R)$ and $\mathrm{Var}[\hat{J}] < \frac{2(\text{SJ}(R))^2}{A}$.   □

3   Algorithm REDSKETCH for Join Size Estimation

In this section, we present the algorithm REDSKETCH for estimating the size of the join of data streams R and S for the insert-only stream model. The algorithm can be extended to insert-delete streams by using a variant of the CountSketch algorithm that can handle deletions.

The data structure used by the algorithm is a pair of *parallel* CountSketch structures denoted by CSK$_R$ and CSK$_S$, for streams R and S respectively. The structures CSK$_R$ and CSK$_S$ use a pair of *parallel* hash table sets, $T[1], \ldots, T[s]$ for CSK$_R$ and $U[1], \ldots, U[s]$ for CSK$_S$, respectively, each consisting of A buckets. The hash table sets in the sense that T_t and U_t use the same random pair-wise independent hash function h_t and the same four-wise independent sketch basis $x_{t,i}$. The updates to the structure are done as in the CountSketch algorithm.

A join value i from stream R (resp. S) is said to be *frequent* in R (resp. S) provided its estimate $\hat{f}_i$ obtained using the frequency estimation procedure of CountSketch(resp. $\hat{g}_i$) is among the top-k estimated frequencies in the stream R (resp. S).

Let F denote the set of join values that are frequent in either R or S. We decompose the join size J into two components as follows.

$$J_0 = \sum_{i \in F} f_i \cdot g_i, \quad \text{and} \quad J_1 = \sum_{i \notin F} f_i \cdot g_i.$$

The estimate $\hat{J}_0$ is obtained as $\hat{J}_0 = \sum_{i \in F} \hat{f}_i \cdot \hat{g}_i$. Next, we *reduce* the hash tables by deleting the estimated contribution of each frequent item $i \in F$ from the sketches contained in those buckets to which the item i hashes to.

$$X_{t,h_t(i)} := X_{t,h_t(i)} - \hat{f}_i \cdot x_{t,i} \, ; \quad Y_{t,h_t(i)} := Y_{t,h_t(i)} - \hat{g}_i \cdot x_{t,i} \quad \text{for } i \in F, 1 \leq t \leq s$$

We then multiply the corresponding buckets of the reduced hash table pair T_t and U_t and obtain an estimate for J_1 as the median of averages.

$$J'_t = \sum_{b=0}^{A-1} X_{t,b} \cdot Y_{t,b}, \quad \text{for } t = 1, 2, \ldots, s, \quad \text{and } \hat{J}_1 = \text{median}_{t=1}^s J'_t .$$

The join size is estimated as $\hat{J} = \hat{J}_0 + \hat{J}_1$. Theorem 2 presents the accuracy versus space guarantees of the algorithm.

Theorem 2. *For any* $0 < \delta < 1$, $A = 64k$, *and* $s = O(\log \frac{m}{\delta})$, $\mathbf{Pr}\{|\hat{J} - J| \leq E\} \geq 1 - \delta$, *where,* $E = \frac{4}{\sqrt{k}}(m_R \cdot (\text{SJ}^{res}(S,k))^{1/2} + m_S \cdot (\text{SJ}^{res}(R,k))^{1/2} + \frac{J}{4\sqrt{k}}$. $\quad\square$

If $A = 64k$, then, the space used by the algorithm is $O(k \cdot \log m \log \frac{m}{\delta})$ bits. The time taken to process each stream update is $O(\log \frac{m}{\delta})$ operations. We now prove Theorem 2.

Analysis. Let $\Delta_R = \Delta_R\left(\frac{A}{8}, A\right) = 8\left(\frac{(\text{SJ}^{res}(R, \frac{A}{8}))}{A}\right)^{1/2}$ and $\Delta_S = 8\left(\frac{\text{SJ}^{res}(S, \frac{A}{8})}{A}\right)^{1/2}$. Let $\Gamma = (m_R(\text{SJ}^{res}(S,k)^{1/2} + m_S(\text{SJ}^{res}(S,k))^{1/2})$.

Lemma 2. *Let* $A \geq 64k$. *Then,* (i) $(m_R\Delta_S + m_S\Delta_R) \leq \frac{2\Gamma}{\sqrt{k}}$,
(ii) $(\text{SJ}^{res}(R,k))^{1/2}(\text{SJ}^{res}(S,k))^{1/2} \leq \frac{\Gamma}{8\sqrt{2k}}$ *and* (iii) $k\Delta_R\Delta_S \leq \frac{\Gamma}{8\sqrt{2k}}$.

Proof. We use the property that $\text{SJ}^{res}(R,k) \leq \frac{m_R^2}{4k}$.

(i) $m_R\Delta_R \leq \frac{8m_R(\text{SJ}^{res}(R,\frac{A}{8}))^{1/2}}{\sqrt{A}} \leq \frac{m_R(\text{SJ}^{res}(R,k))^{1/2}}{\sqrt{k}}$, since, $A \geq 64k$. Similarly $m_S\Delta_S \leq \frac{m_S\text{SJ}^{res}(S,k)}{\sqrt{k}}$). Adding, we obtain part (i).

(ii) $(\text{SJ}^{res}(R,k))^{1/2}(\text{SJ}^{res}(S,k))^{1/2} \leq \frac{m_R}{4\sqrt{2k}}(\text{SJ}^{res}(S,k))^{1/2}$. Similarly, $(\text{SJ}^{res}(R,k))^{1/2}(\text{SJ}^{res}(S,k))^{1/2} \leq (\text{SJ}^{res}(R,k))^{1/2}\frac{m_S}{4\sqrt{2k}}$). Therefore, adding, we have, $2(\text{SJ}^{res}(R,k))^{1/2}(\text{SJ}^{res}(S,k))^{1/2} \leq \frac{\Gamma}{4\sqrt{2k}}$.

(iii) Since, $k \leq \frac{A}{64} < \frac{A}{8}$, $\text{SJ}^{res}(R, \frac{A}{8}) \leq \text{SJ}^{res}(R,k)$ and $\text{SJ}^{res}(S, \frac{A}{8}) \leq \text{SJ}^{res}(S,k)$. Thus, $k\Delta_R\Delta_S \leq \frac{64k}{A}(\text{SJ}^{res}(R,k)\text{SJ}^{res}(S,k))^{1/2} \leq \frac{\Gamma}{8\sqrt{2k}}$, by part(ii). $\quad\square$

Lemma 3. *Let* $A = 64k$. *Then,* $|\hat{J}_0 - J_0| \leq (2 + \frac{1}{4\sqrt{2}})\frac{\Gamma}{\sqrt{k}}$ *with probability* $1 - \frac{\delta}{4}$.

Proof. By Theorem 1, it follows that $|\hat{f}_i - f_i| \leq \Delta_R$, and $|\hat{g}_i - g_i| \leq \Delta_S$, with probability $1 - \frac{\delta}{8m}$. Since, $|F| \leq k + k = 2k$, therefore,

$$|\hat{J}_0 - J_0| \leq \sum_{i \in F}|\hat{f}_i\hat{g}_i - f_ig_i| \leq \sum_{i \in F}((f_i + \Delta_R)(g_i + \Delta_S) - f_ig_i)$$

$$= \sum_{i \in F}(f_i\Delta_S + g_i\Delta_R + \Delta_R\Delta_S) \leq m_R\Delta_S + m_S\Delta_R + |F|\Delta_R\Delta_S$$

$$\leq m_R\Delta_S + m_S\Delta_R + 2k\Delta_R\Delta_S \leq \left(\frac{2\Gamma}{\sqrt{k}} + \frac{\Gamma}{4\sqrt{2}\sqrt{k}}\right)$$

by Lemma 2, parts (i) and (iii). By union bound, the error probability is bounded by
$\frac{\delta|F|}{8m} \le \frac{\delta}{4}$. $\qquad\square$

Defining the reduced frequency vector f' as follows.

$$f'_i = \begin{cases} f_i & \text{if } i \notin F \text{ (i.e., } i \text{ is not a frequent item)} \\ f_i - \hat{f}_i & \text{otherwise.} \end{cases} \tag{3}$$

Lemma 4. *Let* $A = 64k$. *Then,* $\left|E\left[J'_t\right] - J_1\right| \le \frac{\Gamma}{4\sqrt{2k}}$, *with probability* $1 - \frac{\delta}{4}$.

Proof. By Lemma 1, $E\left[J'_t\right] = \sum_{i \in D} f'_i g'_i$. Thus,

$$\left|E\left[J'_t\right] - J_1\right| = \left|\sum_{i \in D} f'_i g'_i - \sum_{i \notin F} f_i g_i\right| \le \sum_{i \in F} |f_i - \hat{f}_i||g_i - \hat{g}_i| \le 2k\Delta_R \Delta_S \le \frac{\Gamma}{4\sqrt{2k}}$$

by Lemma 2, part(iii). The total error probability is bounded by $\frac{\delta|F|}{8m} \le \frac{\delta}{4}$. $\qquad\square$

We now present an upper bound on the self-join size of the reduced frequencies. Let H denote the set of top-k items of a stream (say R) in terms of estimated frequencies.

Lemma 5. *Let* $s_3 = O(\log \frac{m}{\delta})$. *Then,* $\sum_{i \notin H} f_i^2 \le SJ^{res}(k)\left(1 + 32\left(\frac{k}{A}\right)^{1/2} + 256\frac{k}{A}\right)$, *with probability at least* $1 - \frac{\delta}{16}$.

Proof. Let P be the set of the top-k items in terms of their true frequencies. Since P and H are sets of k values each, therefore, $|P - H| = |H - P|$ and we can map each value i of $P - H$ to a unique value i' of $H - P$ (arbitrarily). For any $i \in P - H$, $f_i \ge f_{i'}$ and $\hat{f}_i \le \hat{f}_{i'}$. Therefore, for any $i \in P - H$,

$$0 \le f_i - f_{i'} = (\hat{f}_{i'} - f_{i'}) + (f_i - \hat{f}_i) + (\hat{f}_i - \hat{f}_{i'}) \le (\hat{f}_{i'} - f_{i'}) + (\hat{f}_i - f_i) .$$

Taking absolute values, $|f_i - f_{i'}| \le |\hat{f}_{i'} - f_{i'}| + |\hat{f}_i - f_i| \le \Delta + \Delta = 2\Delta$, by Theorem 1 (with probability $1 - \frac{\delta}{8m}$ each). We therefore have,

$$\sum_{i \notin H} f_i^2 = \sum_{i \in P-H} f_i^2 + \sum_{i \notin (P \cup H)} f_i^2 \le \sum_{i' \in (H-P)} (f_{i'} + 2 \cdot \Delta)^2 + \sum_{i \notin (P \cup H)} f_i^2$$

$$= \sum_{j \notin P} f_j^2 + 4\Delta \sum_{i' \in (H-P)} f_{i'} + 4 \cdot |H - P| \cdot \Delta^2$$

$$= SJ^{res}(k) + 4\Delta|H - P|^{1/2} \sum_{i' \in H-P} f_{i'}^2 + 4k\Delta^2$$

$$\le SJ^{res}(k) + 4k^{1/2}\Delta(SJ^{res}(k))^{1/2} + 4k\Delta^2$$

$$< SJ^{res}(k)\left(1 + 32\left(\frac{k}{A}\right)^{1/2} + 256\frac{k}{A}\right) \qquad\square$$

Lemma 6. *Let* $A = 64k$. *Then,* $\sum_{i \in D} f_i'^2 < \frac{37}{4} SJ^{res}(R, k)$ *and* $\sum_{i \in D} g_i'^2 < \frac{37}{4} SJ^{res}(S, k)$ *with probability* $1 - \frac{\delta}{16}$.

Proof. Let F_R denote the top-k items in R in terms of estimated frequencies. Then,

$$\sum_{i \in D} f_i'^2 = \sum_{i \in F_R} (f_i - \hat{f}_i)^2 + \sum_{i \notin F_R} f_i^2$$
$$\leq k\Delta_R^2 + SJ^{res}(R, k)\left(1 + \frac{32\sqrt{k}}{\sqrt{A}} + \frac{256k}{A}\right), \text{ by Lemma 5}$$
$$= \frac{1}{4} SJ^{res}(R, k) + SJ^{res}(R, k)(1 + \frac{32\sqrt{k}}{\sqrt{64k}} + \frac{256k}{64k}) = \frac{37}{4} SJ^{res}(R, k) . \square$$

Lemma 7. *Let* $A = 64k$. *Then,* $|\hat{J}_1 - J_1| \leq \frac{\Gamma}{\sqrt{k}} + \frac{J_1}{4\sqrt{k}}$ *with probability* $1 - \frac{\delta}{4}$.

Proof. By Lemma 1, $\text{Var}[J_t'] \leq \frac{1}{A}\left((\sum_{i \in D} f_i'^2)(\sum_{i \in D} g_i'^2)\right) + \frac{1}{A}(\text{E}[J_t'])^2)$. Substituting from Lemma 6, we obtain that

$$\text{Var}[J_t'] \leq \frac{(37)^2}{16A} SJ^{res}(R, k)SJ^{res}(S, k) + \frac{1}{A}(\text{E}[J_t'])^2) \leq \frac{(37)^2 \Gamma^2}{(16)(64)(128)k} + \frac{(\text{E}[J_t'])^2}{64k}$$

by Lemma 2, part(ii) and substituting $A = 64k$. Therefore, $(\text{Var}[J_t'])^{1/2} \leq \frac{37\Gamma}{256\sqrt{2k}} + \frac{\text{E}[J_t']}{8\sqrt{k}}$. By Lemma 4, $\text{E}[J_t'] \leq J_1 + \frac{\Gamma}{4\sqrt{2k}}$. Adding, we have, $(\text{Var}[J_t'])^{1/2} < \frac{37\Gamma}{256\sqrt{2k}} + \frac{\Gamma}{32k\sqrt{2}} + \frac{J_1}{8\sqrt{k}}$. By Chebychev's inequality $\Pr\left\{|J_t' - \text{E}[J_t']| \leq 2(\text{Var}[J_t'])^{1/2}\right\} \geq \frac{3}{4}$, or that $\Pr\left\{|J_t' - J_1|\right\} \leq 2(\text{Var}[J_t'])^{1/2} + \frac{\Gamma}{4\sqrt{2k}}$, with probability $\frac{3}{4}$. By a standard argument of boosting the confidence of taking medians, we obtain the statement of the lemma. $\square$

Proof (Of Theorem 2.). Adding the errors given by Lemmas 3 and 7 and the error probabilities , we obtain that $|\hat{J} - J| \leq (2 + \frac{1}{4\sqrt{2}})\frac{\Gamma}{\sqrt{k}} + \frac{\Gamma}{\sqrt{k}} + \frac{J_1}{4\sqrt{k}} < \frac{4\Gamma}{\sqrt{k}} + \frac{J}{4\sqrt{k}}$ with probability $1 - \frac{\delta}{2}$. $\square$

4   Algorithm REDSKETCH-A

In this section, we present a variant of the REDSKETCH algorithm for estimating join sizes. The data structure used by the REDSKETCH-A algorithm is identical to that of the REDSKETCH algorithm; hence the space and the time complexity of algorithm REDSKETCH-A is the same as that of the REDSKETCH algorithm. Additionally, the REDSKETCH-A algorithm uses an estimator for the residual self-join size $SJ^{res}(R, k)$ for any stream R which is presented below.

4.1   Estimating $SJ^{res}(k)$

The estimator for $SJ^{res}(k) = SJ^{res}(R, k)$ uses a *CountSketch* data structure CSK consisting of $s_3 = O(\log \frac{m}{\delta})$ independent hash tables, $T[1], \ldots, T[s_3]$, each consisting of $A = O(\frac{k}{\epsilon^2})$ buckets, as explained in Section 2. Let H denote the set of the top-k items in terms of the estimated frequencies. First, the contributions of the top-k estimated frequencies are removed from the corresponding sketches contained in the hash tables, that is, $X_{t,h_t(i)} := X_{t,h_t(i)} - \hat{f}_i \cdot x_{t,i}$, for every $i \in H$ and $1 \leq t \leq s_3$. Next, we obtain an estimate Z_t from each hash table index t as follows: $Z_t = \sum_{b=0}^{A-1} X_{t,b}^2$. Finally, we return the estimate $\hat{SJ}^{res}(k)$ as the median of the Z_t's, that is, $\hat{SJ}^{res}(k) = \text{median}_{t=1}^{s_3} Z_t$. The accuracy guarantees are given by Theorem 3. The algorithm uses space $O\left(\frac{k}{\epsilon^2} \cdot \log \frac{m}{\delta} \cdot \log m\right)$ bits and processes each stream update in time $O(\log \frac{m}{\delta})$.

Theorem 3. *If* $\epsilon \leq \frac{1}{8}$, $A \geq \frac{1600k}{\epsilon^2}$ *and* $s_3 = O(\log \frac{m}{\delta})$ *then,* $|\hat{SJ}^{res}(R,k) - SJ^{res}(k)| \leq \epsilon SJ^{res}(k)$, *with probability* $1 - \delta$.

Proof. Let $f_i' = (f_i - \hat{f}_i)$, if $i \in H$, and $f_i' = f_i$, for $i \notin H$. Define $SJ^{\text{suffix}}(k) = \sum_i f_i'^2$. Note that the estimator $\hat{SJ}^{res}$ returns an approximation of $SJ^{\text{suffix}}(k)$ using the FAST-AMS algorithm. Let $\Delta = \Delta_R$. By property of *CountSketch* algorithm, $|\hat{f}_i - f_i| \leq \Delta$, with probability $1 - \frac{\delta}{8m}$.

$$SJ^{\text{suffix}}(k) = \sum_{i \in H}(f_i - \hat{f}_i)^2 + \sum_{i \notin H} f_i^2 \leq k \cdot \Delta^2 + \sum_{i \notin H} f_i^2$$

$$\leq SJ^{res}(k)\left(1 + \frac{32\sqrt{k}}{\sqrt{A}} + \frac{320k}{A}\right), \text{ by Lemma 5.}$$

Further, $SJ^{\text{suffix}} \geq \sum_{i \notin H} f_i^2 \geq \sum_{i \notin P} f_i^2 \geq SJ^{res}(k)$.

By Lemma 1, $E[Z_t] = SJ^{\text{suffix}}(k)$ and $\text{Var}[Z_t] \leq \frac{2}{A}(SJ^{\text{suffix}}(k))^2$. Therefore, Chebychev's inequality, $|Z_t - SJ^{\text{suffix}}(k)| \leq \frac{2}{\sqrt{A}} SJ^{\text{suffix}}(k)$ occurs with probability at least $\frac{3}{4}$. Therefore, by boosting the confidence by returning the median $\hat{SJ}^{res}(k)$ of the Z_t's, we have, $\hat{SJ}^{res}(k) \in (1 \pm \frac{2}{\sqrt{A}}) SJ^{\text{suffix}}(k)$. Therefore, $\left(1 - \frac{2}{\sqrt{A}}\right) SJ^{res}(k) \leq \hat{SJ}^{res}(k) \leq SJ^{res}(k)\left(1 + \frac{32\sqrt{k}}{\sqrt{A}} + \frac{320k}{A}\right)\left(1 + \frac{2}{\sqrt{A}}\right) SJ^{res}(k)$. Substituting $A \geq \frac{1600}{\epsilon^2}$ and $\epsilon \leq \frac{1}{8}$ gives $(1 - \epsilon)SJ^{res}(k) \leq \hat{SJ}^{res}(k) \leq (1 + \epsilon)SJ^{res}(k)$. $\square$

4.2   Estimating Join Size Using Algorithm REDSKETCH-A

The REDSKETCH-A algorithm first estimates $SJ^{res}(R,k)$ and $SJ^{res}(S,k)$ as $\hat{SJ}^{res}(R,k)$ and $\hat{SJ}^{res}(S,k)$ respectively, to within factors of $1 \pm \frac{1}{8}$ with probability $1 - \frac{\delta}{32}$, each, using the algorithm given above. Let $\hat{\Delta}_R$ denote $8\left(\frac{\hat{SJ}^{res}(R,\frac{A}{8})}{A}\right)^{1/2}$ and $\hat{\Delta}_S$ denote $8\left(\frac{\hat{SJ}^{res}(S,\frac{A}{8})}{A}\right)^{1/2}$. The algorithm uses the following notion of frequent items.

Definition 1. *A join value* i *from the stream* R *(resp.* S*) is said to be frequent in* R *(resp.* S*), provided, (a)* $\hat{f}_i \geq \gamma \hat{\Delta}_R$ *(resp.* $\hat{g}_i \geq \gamma \hat{\Delta}_S$*), and, (b)* $\hat{f}_i$ *is among the top-k estimated frequencies in the stream* R *(resp.* S*), where,* $\gamma = \frac{6}{5}\left(1 + \frac{2}{\epsilon}\right)$. $\square$

The value of ϵ used in Definition 1 is a parameter. Let F_R (resp. F_S) denote the set of join values that are frequent in R (resp. S) and let F denote $F_R \cup F_S$. Following the paradigm of the bifocal method [13], we decompose the join size J into four components, namely, $J = J_{d,d} + J_{d,s} + J_{s,d} + J_{s,s}$, where, $J_{d,d} = \sum_{i \in F_R \cap F_S} f_i g_i$, $J_{s,s} = \sum_{i \notin (F_R \cup F_S)} f_i g_i$, $J_{d,s} = \sum_{i \in F_R - F_S} f_i g_i$ and $J_{s,d} = \sum_{i \in F_S - F_R} f_i g_i$. The estimate $\hat{J}_{d,d}$ for $J_{d,d}$ is obtained as usual: $\hat{J}_{d,d} = \sum_{i \in F_R \cap F_S} \hat{f}_i \cdot \hat{g}_i$. Next, we *reduce* the hash table structure as follows. For every hash table index t, $1 \le t \le s_3$, we perform the following operations.

$$X_{t,h_t(i)} := X_{t,h_t(i)} - \hat{f}_i \cdot x_{t,i}, \quad \text{for each } i \in F_R, \text{ and}$$
$$Y_{t,h_t(i)} := Y_{t,h_t(i)} - \hat{g}_i \cdot x_{t,i}, \quad \text{for each } i \in F_S$$

We then obtain the estimates $\hat{J}_{d,s,t}$ and $\hat{J}_{s,d,t}$ from each hash table index t, $1 \le t \le s_3$, as follows.

$$\hat{J}_{d,s,t} = \sum_{b=0}^{A-1} Y_{t,b} \cdot \Big(\sum_{i \in F_R : h_t(i)=b} \hat{f}_i \cdot x_{t,i} \Big), \quad \hat{J}_{s,d,t} = \sum_{b=0}^{A-1} X_{t,b} \cdot \Big(\sum_{i \in F_S : h_t(i)=b} \hat{g}_i \cdot x_{t,i} \Big)$$

The estimates $\hat{J}_{d,s}$ and $\hat{J}_{s,d}$ are obtained as the medians of the estimates $\hat{J}_{d,s,t}$ and $\hat{J}_{s,d,t}$ respectively. That is,

$$\hat{J}_{d,s} = \text{median}_{t=1}^{s_3} \hat{J}_{d,s,t}, \quad \text{and} \quad \hat{J}_{s,d} = \text{median}_{t=1}^{s_3} \hat{J}_{s,d,t} \ .$$

The estimates $\hat{J}_{s,s,t}$, $1 \le t \le s_3$ and the median estimate $\hat{J}_{s,s}$ is obtained in a manner identical to J'_t and $\hat{J}_1$ in the REDSKETCH algorithm, as follows.

$$\hat{J}_{s,s,t} = \sum_{b=0}^{A-1} X_{t,b} \cdot Y_{t,b}, \ 1 \le t \le s_3, \quad \text{and} \quad \hat{J}_{s,s} = \text{median}_{t=1}^{s_3} \hat{J}_{s,s,t}$$

Finally, the estimate $\hat{J}$ for the join size is obtained as the sum of the estimates, that is, $\hat{J} = \hat{J}_{d,d} + \hat{J}_{d,s} + \hat{J}_{s,d} + \hat{J}_{s,s}$. The space versus accuracy properties of the algorithm is stated in Theorem 4 and proved below. $\Lambda = (\text{SJ}(R)\text{SJ}^{res}(S,k))^{1/2} + (\text{SJ}^{res}(R,k)\text{SJ}(S))^{1/2}$.

Theorem 4. *Let $A \ge 64k$. Then,* $\Pr\Big\{|\hat{J} - J| \le E\Big\} \ge 1 - \delta$, *where,* $E = \min\Big(\frac{32\Lambda}{\sqrt{k}} + \frac{J}{2} + \frac{J}{\sqrt{k}}\Big), \ 2J^{2/3}\Big(\frac{2\Lambda}{\sqrt{k}}\Big)^{1/3}\Big)$. $\qquad\square$

Analysis. Let $\gamma = \frac{6}{5}\big(1 + \frac{2}{\epsilon}\big)$ (as given by Definition 1), $\gamma_1 = \frac{5}{6}\gamma$ and $\gamma_2 = \frac{6}{5}\gamma$. Since, $\hat{\text{SJ}}^{res}(R,k) \ge \frac{3}{4}\text{SJ}^{res}(R,k)$, with probability $1 - \frac{\delta}{8m}$, therefore, $\big(\frac{3}{4}\big)^{1/2}\Delta(R,k) \le \hat{\Delta}(R,k) \le \big(\frac{4}{3}\big)^{1/2}\Delta(R,k)$, which implies that, $\gamma_1\Delta(R,k) \le \hat{\Delta}(R,k) \le \gamma_2\Delta(R,k)$. Similarly, $\gamma_1\Delta(S,k) \le \hat{\Delta}(S,k) \le \gamma_2\Delta(S,k)$, each with probability $1 - \frac{\delta}{8m}$.

Lemma 8. *Suppose i is a frequent item in R. Then, $\hat{f}_i \ge (\gamma_1 - 1)\Delta_R$ and $|\hat{f}_i - f_i| \le \epsilon f_i$, with probability $1 - \frac{\delta}{8m}$. Otherwise, $\hat{f}_i < (\gamma_2 + 1)\Delta(R,k)$, with probability $1 - \frac{\delta}{8m}$.*

Proof. By Definition 1, $\hat{f}_i \ge \gamma_1\Delta_R$. Therefore, with probability $1 - \frac{\delta}{8m}$, $\hat{f}_i \ge (\gamma_1 - 1)\Delta_R$. Further, $\frac{|\hat{f}_i - f_i|}{f_i} \le \frac{\Delta_R}{\gamma_1 - 1} \le \epsilon$. If $i \notin F_R$, then, $\hat{f}_i < \gamma_1\hat{\Delta}(R,k) \le \gamma_2\Delta(R,k)$. Therefore, with probability $1 - \frac{\delta}{8m}$, $\hat{f}_i < (\gamma_2 + 1)\Delta(R,k)$. $\qquad\square$

Lemma 9. *Let $\epsilon \leq 1$. Then, $|\hat{J}_{d,d} - J_{d,d}| \leq \frac{5\epsilon}{4} J_{d,d}$, with probability $1 - \frac{\delta}{8}$.*

Proof. $|\hat{J}_{d,d} - J_{d,d}| \leq \sum_{i \in F_R \cap F_S} |\hat{f}_i \hat{g}_i - f_i g_i| \leq \sum_{i \in F_R \cap F_S} f_i g_i ((1 + \frac{\epsilon}{2})^2 - 1) \leq \frac{5\epsilon}{4} J_{d,d}$. Since, $|F_R \cap F_S| \leq k$, the total error probability, is at most $\frac{\delta k}{8m} \leq \frac{\delta}{8}$. $\square$

The reduced frequencies are defined as before, namely: $f_i' = f_i$ if $i \notin F_R$, and $f_i' = f_i - \hat{f}_i$, otherwise; and analogously for S: $g_i' = g_i$ if $i \notin F_S$, and $g_i' = g_i - \hat{g}_i$, otherwise.

Lemma 10. $|\mathrm{E}[\hat{J}_{d,s,t}] - J_{d,s}| \leq \frac{\epsilon}{2} J_{d,s} + \frac{9\epsilon}{16} J_{d,d}$ *and* $|\mathrm{E}[\hat{J}_{s,d,t}] - J_{s,d}| \leq \frac{\epsilon}{2} J_{s,d} + \frac{9\epsilon}{16} J_{d,d}$, *each with probability* $1 - \frac{\delta}{8}$.

Proof. $J_{d,s} = \sum_{i \in F_R - F_S} f_i g_i$. By Lemma 1, $\mathrm{E}[\hat{J}_{d,s,t}] = \sum_{i \in F_R} \hat{f}_i g_i'$. Therefore,

$$|\mathrm{E}[\hat{J}_{d,s,t}] - J_{d,s}| = |\sum_{i \in F_R} \hat{f}_i g_i' - \sum_{i \in F_R - F_S} f_i g_i| = |\sum_{i \in F_R \cap F_S} \hat{f}_i g_i' + \sum_{i \in F_R - F_S} (\hat{f}_i - f_i) g_i|$$

If $i \in F_R \cap F_S$, then, $|\hat{f}_i - f_i| \leq \frac{\epsilon f_i}{2}$, by Lemma 8, and $|g_i'| \leq |\hat{g}_i - g_i| \leq \frac{\epsilon g_i}{2}$, by Lemma 8. Adding, $|\sum_{i \in F_R \cap F_S} \hat{f}_i g_i'| \leq \sum_{i \in F_R \cap F_S} (1 + \frac{\epsilon}{2}) \frac{\epsilon}{2} f_i g_i \leq \frac{9\epsilon}{16} J_{d,d}$. If $i \in F_R - F_S$, then, $|\hat{f}_i - f_i| \leq \frac{\epsilon f_i}{2}$, by Lemma 8. Therefore, $|\sum_{i \in F_R - F_S} (\hat{f}_i - f_i) g_i| \leq \sum_{i \in F_R - F_S} \frac{\epsilon f_i}{2} g_i = \frac{\epsilon}{2} J_{d,s}$. Adding, we obtain the statement of the lemma. The proof for $J_{s,d}$ is analogous. $\square$

Lemma 11. $|\mathrm{E}[\hat{J}_{s,s,t}] - J_{s,s}| \leq \epsilon^2 J_{d,d} + \epsilon(J_{d,s} + J_{s,d})$, *with probability* $1 - \frac{\delta}{4}$.

Proof. $|\mathrm{E}[\hat{J}_{s,s,t}] - J_{s,s}| = |\sum_{i \in D} f_i' g_i' - \sum_{i \notin (F_R \cup F_S)} f_i g_i|$

$\leq \sum_{i \in F_R \cap F_S} |f_i - \hat{f}_i||g_i - \hat{g}_i| + \sum_{i \in F_R - F_S} |f_i - \hat{f}_i| g_i + \sum_{i \in F_S - F_R} f_i |g_i - \hat{g}_i|$

$\leq \epsilon^2 J_{d,d} + \epsilon(J_{d,s} + J_{s,d})$. $\square$

Lemma 12. *If $A = 64k$, then, $\sum_{i \in F_R} \hat{f}_i^2 \leq \frac{9}{4} \mathrm{SJ}(R)$ and $\sum_{i \in F_S} \hat{g}_i^2 \leq \frac{9}{4} \mathrm{SJ}(S)$.*

Proof. Using $(a + b)^2 \leq 2(a^2 + b^2)$, we have,

$$\sum_{i \in F_R} \hat{f}_i^2 \leq \sum_{i \in F_R} (f_i + \Delta_R)^2 \leq 2 \sum_{i \in F_R} f_i^2 + 2k\Delta_R^2$$

$$\leq 2\mathrm{SJ}(R) + \frac{16k}{A} \mathrm{SJ}^{res}(R, \frac{A}{8}) \leq \frac{5}{2} \mathrm{SJ}(R). \quad \square$$

Lemma 13. *If $A \geq 64k$ and $\epsilon \leq \frac{1}{4}$, then, $\sum_{i \in D} f_i'^2 \leq \frac{5}{4\epsilon^2} \mathrm{SJ}^{res}(R, k)$ and $\sum_{i \in D} g_i'^2 \leq \frac{5}{4\epsilon^2} \mathrm{SJ}^{res}(S, k)$, with high probability $(1 - \frac{\delta}{8})$.*

Proof. Suppose that $|F_R| = l$. Consider the item whose rank is $l+1$. This item must have frequency at most $\gamma \hat{\Delta}_R + \Delta_R \le (\gamma_2 + 1)\Delta_R$, otherwise, its estimate would have crossed the frequent item threshold $\gamma \hat{\Delta}_R$ (with probability $1 - \frac{\delta}{8m}$), and it, along with the l higher ranked items would all have been included in the frequent item set F_R. This would make $|F_R| \ge l+1$. Thus,

$$\mathrm{SJ}^{res}(R, l) \le (k-l)((\gamma_2 + 1)\Delta_R)^2 + \mathrm{SJ}^{res}(R, k)$$

$$\le \frac{10(k-l)}{\epsilon^2}\Delta_R^2 + \mathrm{SJ}^{res}(R, k) \le \left(1 + \frac{5(k-l)}{4\epsilon^2 k}\right)\mathrm{SJ}^{res}(R, k)$$

$\sum_{i \in D} f_i'^2 = \sum_{i \in F_R}(f_i - \hat{f}_i)^2 + \sum_{i \notin F_R} f_i^2 \le l\Delta_R^2 + \sum_{i \notin F_R} f_i^2 \le \frac{l}{8k}\mathrm{SJ}^{res}(R, k) + \sum_{i \notin F_R} f_i^2$, with probability at least $1 - \frac{l\delta}{8m}$. By Lemma 5, $\sum_{i \notin F_R} f_i^2 \le \mathrm{SJ}^{res}(R, l)\left(1 + \frac{32\sqrt{l}}{\sqrt{A}} + \frac{256l}{A}\right)$. Adding,

$$\sum_{i \in D} f_i'^2 \le \mathrm{SJ}^{res}(R, k)\left(\frac{l}{8k} + \left(1 + \frac{5(k-l)}{4\epsilon^2 k}\right)\left(1 + \frac{32\sqrt{l}}{\sqrt{A}} + \frac{256l}{A}\right)\right) \le \frac{5}{4\epsilon^2}\mathrm{SJ}^{res}(R, k) \quad \square$$

Recall that $A = (\mathrm{SJ}(R)\mathrm{SJ}^{res}(S, k))^{1/2} + (\mathrm{SJ}^{res}(R, k)\mathrm{SJ}(S))^{1/2}$.

Proof (Of Theorem 4). By Lemma 1, $\mathrm{Var}[\hat{J}_{d,s,t}] \le \frac{1}{A}(\sum_{i \in F_R}\hat{f}_i^2)(\sum_{i \in D} g_i'^2) + \frac{1}{A}(\mathrm{E}[J_{d,s,t}])^2$. By Lemmas 12 and 13, $\frac{1}{A}(\sum_{i \in F_R}\hat{f}_i^2)(\sum_{i \in D} g_i'^2) \le \frac{45}{16\epsilon^2 A}\mathrm{SJ}(R) \cdot \mathrm{SJ}^{res}(S, k) \le \frac{A^2}{20\epsilon^2 k}$. By Lemma 10, $\mathrm{E}[\hat{J}_{d,s,t}] \le (J_{d,s} + \frac{9\epsilon}{16}(J_{d,d} + J_{d,s}))$. By Chebychev's inequality, $|\hat{J}_{d,s,t} - \mathrm{E}[J_{d,s,t}]| \le 3(\mathrm{Var}[\hat{J}_{d,s,t}])^{1/2}$ with probability at least $\frac{8}{9}$. The median $\hat{J}_{d,s}$ satisfies the same relation with probability $1 - \frac{\delta}{4}$. Therefore, using triangle inequality,

$$|\hat{J}_{d,s} - J_{d,s}| \le 3(\mathrm{Var}[\hat{J}_{d,s,t}])^{1/2} + |\mathrm{E}[\hat{J}_{d,s,t}] - J_{d,s}|$$

$$\le \frac{3A}{\epsilon\sqrt{20}} + \frac{3J_{d,s}}{8\sqrt{k}} + \frac{9\epsilon}{16}\left(1 + \frac{3}{8\sqrt{k}}\right)(J_{d,d} + J_{d,s})$$

Analogously, it can be shown that

$$|\hat{J}_{s,d} - J_{s,d}| \le \frac{3A}{\epsilon\sqrt{20}} + \frac{3J_{s,d}}{8\sqrt{k}} + \frac{9\epsilon}{16}\left(1 + \frac{3}{8\sqrt{k}}\right)(J_{d,d} + J_{s,d}) .$$

By Lemma 1, $\mathrm{Var}[\hat{J}_{s,s,t}] \le \frac{1}{A}(\sum_{i \in D} f'^2)(\sum_{j \in D} g'^2) + \frac{1}{A}(\mathrm{E}[\hat{J}_{s,s,t}])^2$. Using Lemmas 13 and 11 and following a similar reasoning as above, it can be shown that $\mathrm{Var}[\hat{J}_{s,s,t}] \le \frac{A^2}{40\epsilon^4 k} + \frac{(\mathrm{E}[\hat{J}_{s,s,t}])^2}{64k}$, and therefore, the median $\hat{J}_{s,s}$ satisfies

$$|\hat{J}_{s,s} - J_{s,s}| \le \frac{A}{\sqrt{40}\epsilon^2 k} + (\epsilon^2 J_{d,d} + \epsilon(J_{d,s} + J_{s,d}))\left(1 + \frac{3}{8\sqrt{k}}\right) + \frac{2J_{s,s}}{8\sqrt{k}}$$

with probability $1 - \frac{\delta}{8}$. By Lemma 9, $|\hat{J}_{d,d} - J_{d,d}| \le \frac{5\epsilon}{4}J_{d,d} \le \frac{5\epsilon}{4}J$, with probability $1 - \frac{\delta}{8}$. Adding the errors and error probabilities, and using that $\epsilon \le \frac{1}{4}$, we have, $|\hat{J} - J| \le \frac{A}{2\epsilon^2\sqrt{k}} + (4\epsilon + \frac{2}{\sqrt{k}})J$, with probability $1 - \frac{\delta}{2}$.

The above property holds for all values of $\epsilon \leq \frac{1}{4}$. Therefore, we can find the value of ϵ that minimizes the above function. Doing so, we obtain $\epsilon = \left(\frac{\Lambda}{4J\sqrt{k}}\right)^{1/3}$ and substituting this value yields the statement of the theorem. □

5   Conclusions

In this paper, we present novel, space and time efficient algorithms for estimating the join size of two data streams consisting of general insertion and deletion operations.

References

1. Noga Alon, Phillip B. Gibbons, Yossi Matias, and Mario Szegedy. "Tracking Join and Self-Join Sizes in Limited Storage". In *Proceedings of the Eighteenth ACM SIGACT-SIGMOD-SIGART Symposium on Principles of Database Systems*, Philadeplphia, Pennsylvania, May 1999.
2. Noga Alon, Yossi Matias, and Mario Szegedy. "The Space Complexity of Approximating the Frequency Moments". In *Proceedings of the 28th Annual ACM Symposium on the Theory of Computing STOC, 1996*, pages 20–29, Philadelphia, Pennsylvania, May 1996.
3. Noga Alon, Yossi Matias, and Mario Szegedy. "The space complexity of approximating frequency moments". *Journal of Computer Systems and Sciences*, 58(1):137–147, 1998.
4. A. Arasu, B. Babcock, S. Babu, J. Cieslewicz, M. Datar, K. Ito, R Motwani, U. Srivastava, and J. Widom. "STREAM: The Stanford Data Stream Management System". In *Data Stream Management Processing High-Speed Data Streams Series: Data-Centric Systems and Applications,* Minos Garofalakis, Johannes Gehrke and Rajeev Rastogi *(Eds.) 2006, ISBN: 3-540-28607-1, Springer.*
5. Ron Avnur and Joseph M. Hellerstein. "Eddies: Continuously Adaptive Query Processing". In *Proceedings of the 2000 ACM SIGMOD International Conference on Management of Data*, Dallas, Texas, USA, 2000.
6. Brian Babcock, Shivnath Babu, Mayur Datar, Rajeev Motwani, and Jennifer Widom. "Models and Issues in Data Stream Systems". In *Proceedings of the Twentysecond ACM SIGACT-SIGMOD-SIGART Symposium on Principles of Database Systems*, Madison, Wisconsin, USA, 2002.
7. Donald Carney, Ugur Çetintemel, Mitch Cherniack, Christian Convey, Sangdon Lee, Greg Seidman, Michael Stonebraker, Nesime Tatbul, and Stanley B. Zdonik. "Monitoring Streams - A New Class of Data Management Applications". In *Proceedings of the 28th International Conference on Very Large Data Bases*, Hong Kong, China, 2002.
8. Moses Charikar, Kevin Chen, and Martin Farach-Colton. "Finding frequent items in data streams". In *Proceedings of the 29th International Colloquium on Automata Languages and Programming*, 2002.
9. G. Cormode and S. Muthukrishnan. "An improved data stream summary: The Count-Min sketch and its applications". In *Proceedings of the 6th Latin American Symposium on Informatics LATIN, Lecture Notes in Computer Science 2976 Springer 2004, ISBN 3-540-21258-2*, pages 29–38, Buenos Aires, Argentina, April 2004.
10. Graham Cormode and Minos Garofalakis. "Sketching Streams Through the Net: Distributed Approximate Query Tracking". In *Proceedings of the 31st International Conference on Very Large Data Bases*, September 2005.

11. Alin Dobra, Minos N. Garofalakis, Johannes Gehrke, and Rajeev Rastogi. "Processing complex aggregate queries over data streams". In *Proceedings of the 2002 ACM SIGMOD International Conference on Management of Data*, Madison, Wisconsin, USA, 2002.

12. Sumit Ganguly, Minos Garofalakis, and Rajeev Rastogi. "Processing Data Stream Join Aggregates using Skimmed Sketches". In *Proceedings of the Ninth International Conference on Extending Database Technology*, Herkailon, Crete, Greece, March 2004.

13. Sumit Ganguly, Phil Gibbons, Yossi Matias, and Avi Silberschatz. "Bifocal Sampling for Skew-Resistant Join Size Estimation". In *Proceedings of the 1996 ACM SIGMOD International Conference on Management of Data*, Montreal, Quebec, June 1996.

14. Wen-Chi Hou, Gultekin Ozsoyoglu, and Baldeo K. Taneja. "Statistical estimators for relational algebra expressions". In *Proceedings of the Seventh ACM SIGACT-SIGMOD-SIGART Symposium on Principles of Database Systems*, pages 276–287, Philadelphia, Pennsylvania, March 1988.

15. Richard Lipton, Jeffrey Naughton, and Donovan Schneider. "Practical Selectivity Estimation Through Adaptive Sampling". In *Proceedings of the 1990 ACM SIGMOD International Conference on Management of Data*, Atlantic City, NJ, 1990.

16. Mikkel Thorup and Yin Zhang. "Tabulation based 4-universal hashing with applications to second moment estimation". In *Proceedings of the Fifteenth ACM SIAM Symposium on Discrete Algorithms*, pages 615–624, New Orleans, Louisiana, USA, January 2004.

On Sampled Semantics of Timed Systems

Pavel Krčál[1*] and Radek Pelánek[2**]

[1] Uppsala University, Sweden
pavelk@it.uu.se
[2] Masaryk University Brno, Czech Republic
xpelanek@fi.muni.cz

Abstract. Timed systems can be considered with two types of semantics – dense time semantics and discrete time semantics. The most typical examples of both of them are *real* semantics and *sampled* semantics (i.e., discrete semantics with a fixed time step ϵ). We investigate the relations between real semantics and sampled semantics with respect to different behavioral equivalences. Also, we study decidability of reachability problem for stopwatch automata with sampled semantics. Finally, our main technical contribution is decidability of non-emptiness of a timed automaton ω-language in some sampled semantics (this problem was previously wrongly classified as undecidable). For the proof we employ a novel characterization of reachability relations between configurations of a timed automaton.

1 Introduction

In this paper we are concerned with formal verification of timed systems. As models of timed systems we consider mainly timed automata (TA) [1]; some results are also shown for stopwatch automata (SWA) [12] — an extension of timed automata which allows clocks to be stopped in some locations.

The semantics of these models can be defined over various time domains. The usual approach is to use *dense* time semantics, particularly *real* time semantics (time domain is $\mathbb{R}_0^+$). From many points of view, this semantics is very plausible. One does not need to care about the granularity of time during the modeling phase. This semantics leads to an uncountable structure with a finite quotient (for timed automata) and thus it is amenable to verification with finite state methods. Moreover, theoretical and also practical complexity of problems for dense time semantics is usually the same as for various discrete semantics.

Discrete semantics, particularly *sampled* semantics with fixed time step $\epsilon \in \mathbb{Q}_{>0}^+$ (time domain is $\{k \cdot \epsilon \mid k \in \mathbb{Z}_0^+\}$), is also often considered, e.g. in [6, 5]. One of the advantages is that with the sampled time domain we have a wider choice of representations for sets of clock valuations, e.g., explicit representation or symbolic representation using decision diagrams. Another important issue is

* Partially supported by the European Research Training Network GAMES.
** Partially supported by the Grant Agency of Czech Republic grant No. 201/03/0509 and by the Academy of Sciences of Czech Republic grant No. 1ET408050503.

R. Ramanujam and S. Sen (Eds.): FSTTCS 2005, LNCS 3821, pp. 310–321, 2005.
© Springer-Verlag Berlin Heidelberg 2005

implementability, e.g., discussed in [20, 18]. If a system is realized on a hardware then there is always some granularity of time (e.g., clock cycle, sampling period). Therefore, sampled semantics is closer to the implementation then more abstract dense time semantics.

Dense time semantics can even give us misleading verification results. Assume that we have a model of a timed system such that it satisfies some property in dense time semantics. Now the question is whether there is an implementation (realized on a discrete time hardware) such that it preserves this property. Dense time semantics allows behaviors which are not realizable in any real system. If satisfaction of the property depends on these behaviors then there might not be an implementation satisfying the property.

Verification problems can be stated as the (ω-)language non-emptiness. By verification of a model A with respect to sampled semantics we mean answering the question whether there exists ϵ such that the (ω-)language of A is empty in sampled semantics with ϵ as the sampling period. We show that this problem is decidable for timed automata and that one can also synthesize such ϵ. This problem for ω-languages was previously wrongly classified as undecidable [2]. The same problem was studied in the control setting with slightly different sampled behavior in [7]. In this setting, an automaton is a model of a controller with a periodic control loop which reacts on input data by a control action. Therefore, an automaton has to perform an action at *every* sampled time point which makes the problem undecidable even for (finite word) language non-emptiness.

Our proof uses a novel characterization of reachability relations in timed automata. Representations of reachability relations were studied before: using additive theory of real numbers [8] and $2n$-automata [9]. Our novel representation is based on simple linear (in)equalities (comparisons of clock differences). This representation is of an independent interest, since it is simpler and more specific then previously considered characterizations and it gives a better insight into reachability relations.

We also systematically study relations between dense time semantics and sampled semantics for different timed systems. We study these relations in terms of behavioral equivalences, as it is well known which verification results are preserved by which equivalence. These results are summarized in Table 1. For sampled semantics, a given result means that there exists an ϵ such that a given equivalence is guaranteed. All considered equivalences are "untimed" – the only important information for an equivalence are actions performed and not the precise time points at which these actions are taken. There has been a considerable amount of work related to discretization issues and verifying dense time properties using discrete time methods, e.g. [13, 15, 16, 10, 3]. The main difference is that usually a fixed sampling rate and trace equivalence are considered.

Finally, we summarize the (un)decidability of the reachability problem in timed systems (Table 1.). Particularly, we provide a new undecidability proof for the reachability problem in sampled semantics for stopwatch automata with diagonal constraints and one stopwatch. One stopwatch suffices for all undecidability results.

Table 1. The first table gives a summary of the equivalences: each field gives the relation to real semantics. The second table gives a summary of decidability results for the reachability problem.

equivalences	closed TA	TA	SWA
rational semantics	bisimilar	bisimilar	trace eq.
sampled semantics	similar	reachability eq.	reachability eq.

reachability	TA	diagonal-free SWA	SWA
dense semantics	PSPACE-complete	undecidable	undecidable
sampled semantics	PSPACE-complete	PSPACE-complete	undecidable

2   Preliminaries

In this section we define syntax and semantics of the automata. We define a stopwatch automaton and a timed automaton as a special case of the stopwatch automaton. Semantics is defined as a labeled transition system (LTS). We also define usual behavioral equivalences on LTSs and equivalences on valuations. Note that all languages and equivalences that we consider are untimed (this is sometimes denoted as $untime(L(A))$ and time abstracted equivalences in the literature).

Labeled Transition Systems An LTS is a tuple $T = (S, Act, \rightarrow, s_0)$ where S is a set of states, Act is a finite set of actions, $\rightarrow \subseteq S \times Act \times S$ is a transition relation, $s_0 \in S$ is an initial state. A *run* of T over a trace $w \in Act^* \cup Act^\omega$ is a sequence of states $\pi = q_0, q_1, \ldots$ such that $q_0 = s_0$ and $q_i \xrightarrow{w(i)} q_{i+1}$. The set of finite (resp. infinite) traces of the transition system is $L(T) = \{w \in Act^* \mid$ there exists a run of T over $w\}$ (resp. $L_\omega(T) = \{w \in Act^\omega \mid$ there exists a run of T over $w\}$).

Equivalences Let $T_1 = (S_1, Act, \rightarrow_1, s_0^1)$, $T_2 = (S_2, Act, \rightarrow_2, s_0^2)$ be two labeled transitions systems. A relation $R \subseteq S_1 \times S_2$ is a *simulation relation* iff for all $(s_1, s_2) \in R$ and $s_1 \xrightarrow{a}_1 s_1'$ there is s_2 such that $s_2 \xrightarrow{a}_2 s_2'$ and $(s_1', s_2') \in R$. System T_1 is simulated by T_2 if there exists a simulation R such that $(s_0^1, s_0^2) \in R$. A relation R is a *bisimulation relation* iff R is a symmetric simulation relation. A *bisimulation* $\sim$ is the largest bisimulation relation. A set of *reachable actions* $RA(T)$ is the set $\{a \in Act \mid s_0 \rightarrow^* s_n \xrightarrow{a} s_{n+1}\}$. Systems T_1, T_2 are:

- *reachability equivalent* iff $RA(T_1) = RA(T_2)$,
- *trace equivalent* iff $L(T_1) = L(T_2)$,
- *infinite trace equivalent* iff $L_\omega(T_1) = L_\omega(T_2)$,
- *simulation equivalent* iff T_1 simulates T_2 and vice versa,
- *bisimulation equivalent* (bisimilar) iff $s_0^1 \sim s_0^2$.

Syntax Let $\mathcal{C}$ be a set of non-negative real-valued variables called *clocks*. The set of guards $G(\mathcal{C})$ is defined by the grammar $g := x \bowtie c \mid x - y \bowtie c \mid g \wedge g$ where $x, y \in \mathcal{C}, c \in \mathbb{N}_0$ and $\bowtie \in \{<, \leq, \geq, >\}$. A *stopwatch automaton* is a tuple $A = (Q, Act, \mathcal{C}, q_0, E, stop)$, where:

- Q is a finite set of locations,
- $\mathcal{C}$ is a finite set of clocks,
- $q_0 \in Q$ is an initial location,
- $E \subseteq Q \times Act \times G(\mathcal{C}) \times 2^{\mathcal{C}} \times Q$ is a set of edges labeled by an action name, a guard, and a set of clocks to be reset,
- $stop : Q \to 2^{\mathcal{C}}$ assigns to each location a set of clocks that are stopped at this location.

A clock $x \in \mathcal{C}$ is called a *stopwatch* clock if $\exists q \in Q : x \in stop(q)$. We use the following special types of stopwatch automata:

- a *timed automaton* is a stopwatch automaton such that there are no stopwatch clocks (i.e., $\forall q \in Q : stop(q) = \emptyset$),
- a *closed* automaton uses only guards with $\{\leq, \geq\}$,
- a *diagonal-free* automaton uses only guards defined by $g := x \bowtie c \mid g \wedge g$.

We also consider combinations of these types, e.g., closed timed automaton.

Semantics Semantics is defined with respect to a given time domain D. We suppose that time domain is a subset of real numbers which contains 0 and is closed under addition. A *clock valuation* is a function $\nu : \mathcal{C} \to D$. If $\delta \in D$ then a valuation $\nu + \delta$ is such that for each clock $x \in \mathcal{C}$, $(\nu + \delta)(x) = \nu(x) + \delta$. If $Y \subseteq \mathcal{C}$ then a valuation $\nu[Y := 0]$ is such that for each clock $x \in \mathcal{C} \setminus Y$, $\nu[Y := 0](x) = \nu(x)$ and for each clock $x \in Y$, $\nu[Y := 0](x) = 0$. The satisfaction relation $\nu \models g$ for $g \in G(\mathcal{C})$ is defined in the natural way.

The semantics of a stopwatch automaton $A = (Q, Act, \mathcal{C}, q_0, E, stop)$ with respect to the time domain D is an LTS $[\![A]\!]_D = (S, Act, \to, s_0)$ where $S = Q \times D^{\mathcal{C}}$ is the set of states, $s_0 = (q_0, \nu_0)$ is the initial state, $\nu_0(x) = 0$ for all $x \in \mathcal{C}$. Transitions are defined with the use of two types of basic steps:

- time step: $(q, \nu) \xrightarrow{delay(\delta)} (q, \nu')$ if $\delta \in D, \forall x \in stop(q) : \nu'(x) = \nu(x), \forall x \in \mathcal{C} \setminus stop(q) : \nu'(x) = \nu(x) + \delta$,
- action step: $(q, \nu) \xrightarrow{action(a)} (q', \nu')$ if there exists $(q, a, g, Y, q') \in E$ such that $\nu \models g, \nu' = \nu[Y := 0]$.

The transition relation of $[\![A]\!]_D$ is defined by concatenating these two types of steps: $(q, \nu) \xrightarrow{a} (q', \nu')$ iff there exists (q'', ν'') such that $(q, \nu) \xrightarrow{delay(\delta)} (q'', \nu'') \xrightarrow{action(a)} (q', \nu')$.

We consider the following time domains: $\mathbb{R}_0^+, \mathbb{Q}_0^+, \{k \cdot \epsilon \mid k \in \mathbb{Z}_0^+\}$. The semantics with respect to the last domain is denoted $[\![A]\!]_\epsilon$ (also called *sampled semantics*). We use the following shortcut notation: $L(A) = L([\![A]\!]_{\mathbb{R}_0^+}), L_\omega(A) = L_\omega([\![A]\!]_{\mathbb{R}_0^+}), L^\epsilon(A) = L([\![A]\!]_\epsilon), L_\omega^\epsilon(A) = L_\omega([\![A]\!]_\epsilon)$.

Equivalences on Valuations For any $\delta \in \mathbb{R}$, $\text{int}(\delta)$ denotes the integral part of δ and $\text{fr}(\delta)$ denotes the fractional part of δ. Let k be an integer constant. We define the following relations on the valuations. The equivalence $\cong_k$ is a standard region equivalence (its equivalence classes are regions), the equivalence $\sim_k$ is an auxiliary relation which allows us to forget about the clocks whose values are above k.

- $\nu \cong_k \nu'$ iff all the following conditions hold:
  - for all $x \in \mathcal{C} : \text{int}(\nu(x)) = \text{int}(\nu'(x))$ or $\nu(x) > k \wedge \nu'(x) > k$,
  - for all $x, y \in \mathcal{C}$ with $\nu(x) \leq k$ and $\nu(y) \leq k : \text{fr}(\nu(x)) \leq \text{fr}(\nu(y))$ iff $\text{fr}(\nu'(x)) \leq \text{fr}(\nu'(y))$,
  - for all $x \in \mathcal{C}$ with $\nu(x) \leq k : \text{fr}(\nu(x)) = 0$ iff $\text{fr}(\nu'(x)) = 0$;
- $\nu \sim_k \nu'$ iff for all $x \in \mathcal{C} : \nu(x) = \nu'(x)$ or $\nu(x) > k \wedge \nu'(x) > k$.

Note that $\sim_k$ is refinement of $\cong_k$, $\cong_k$ has a finite index for all semantics, $\sim_k$ has a finite index for sampled semantics. Let A be a diagonal-free timed automaton and K be a maximal constant which occurs in some guard in A. For each location $l \in Q$ and two valuations $\nu \cong_K \nu'$ it holds that (l, ν) is bisimilar to (l, ν').

3   Dense Vs. Sampled Semantics

In this section, we present a set of results about relations between dense time semantics and sampled semantics of timed systems showing the limits of using discrete time verification methods for the dense time. We start with relations between real and rational semantics as it creates a connection between dense and sampled semantics. For timed automata, real and rational semantics are clearly bisimilar. This follows directly from the region construction since each region contains at least one rational valuation. For stopwatch automata, however, we can guarantee only trace equivalence — we show that there exists a SWA which has infinite traces realizable in real semantics, but not in rational one.

Lemma 1. *Let A be an SWA. Then $[\![A]\!]_{\mathbb{Q}_0^+}$ is trace equivalent to $[\![A]\!]_{\mathbb{R}_0^+}$.*

Proof. Let us consider a run π in $[\![A]\!]_{\mathbb{R}_0^+}$. We can consider the delays on this run as parameters $\delta_1, \ldots, \delta_n$. The set of values of these parameters, which enable execution through the same sequence of location and over the same trace is described by a system of linear inequalities in $\delta_1, \ldots, \delta_n$ — these inequalities are obtained by substituting sums of $\delta_1, \ldots, \delta_n$ for $\nu(x)$ in guards. The set of solutions of this system of linear inequalities is a non-empty convex polyhedron and it has a rational solution. Therefore, there exists a run π' in $[\![A]\!]_{\mathbb{Q}_0^+}$ over the same trace as π. □

Lemma 2. *There exist an SWA A such that $[\![A]\!]_{\mathbb{Q}_0^+}$ is not infinite trace equivalent to $[\![A]\!]_{\mathbb{R}_0^+}$.*

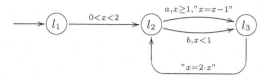

Fig. 1. Stopwatch automaton for binary expansion. Clock x is stopped in l_2, l_3.

Proof (sketch). A skeleton of the example illustrating this observation is given in Fig. 1. The operations $x = x - 1$ and $x = 2 \cdot x$ are not valid operations of SWA, but can be simulated using several locations and (stopwatch) clocks (see e.g., [12]). The automaton in the first step nondeterministically chooses a value between 0 and 2 and then it accepts the sequence of a, b corresponding to binary expansion of the chosen value. Note, that for this automaton, there is no countably branching LTS which would be infinite trace equivalent to $[\![A]\!]_{\mathbb{R}_0^+}$. $\square$

Now we study relations between dense time and sampled semantics. We show that for a closed TA we can guarantee the simulation equivalence (i.e., that there is an ϵ such that $[\![A]\!]_{\mathbb{R}_0^+}$ is simulation equivalent to $[\![A]\!]_\epsilon$), but not bisimilarity. For general TA (as well as for SWA) the best what we can guarantee is the reachability equivalence (i.e., that there is an ϵ such that $[\![A]\!]_{\mathbb{R}_0^+}$ is reachability equivalent to $[\![A]\!]_\epsilon$).

Lemma 3. *Let A be a closed TA and ϵ is the greatest common divisor of constants in A. Then $[\![A]\!]_\epsilon$ is simulation equivalent to $[\![A]\!]_{\mathbb{R}_0^+}$.*

Proof. See [14] for the proof.

Lemma 4. *There exits a closed TA A such that $[\![A]\!]_{\mathbb{R}_0^+}$ is not bisimilar to $[\![A]\!]_\epsilon$ for any ϵ.*

Proof. Fig. 2 shows an automaton for which there is no ϵ such that dense time and sampled semantics are bisimilar. For the proof we use a characterization of bisimulation in terms of a game between Challenger and Defender [19]. Consider the following play of the bisimulation game. Let Challenger plays with the sampled semantics, delays for $1 - \epsilon$ and then takes a transition. Defender can delay for $0 \leq \delta < 1$ and then take a transition. If Defender delays for 1 time unit then Challenger will take e transition, which Defender cannot take.

Now Challenger plays with dense time semantics, delays for $(1 - \delta)/2$ and then takes b transition. Defender can either delay for 0 or for ϵ and then take b transition. Challenger plays with sampled semantics again in the next step, delays for 0 and takes a transition according to the previous move of Defender. If Defender delayed for 0 then Challenger takes d transition, otherwise he takes c transition. Defender has no answer. $\square$

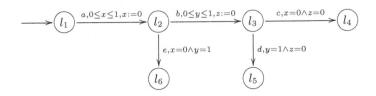

Fig. 2. An automaton for which there is no ϵ such that discrete and dense semantics are bisimilar.

Lemma 5. *Let A be an SWA. Then there exists ϵ such that $[\![A]\!]_{\mathbb{R}_0^+}$ is reachability equivalent to $[\![A]\!]_\epsilon$.*

Proof. From Lemma 1 we have that for each reachable action a there is a finite run π_a which contains action a and which has only rational delays. Let ϵ_a be the greatest common divisor of all delays on π_a. Let ϵ be the greatest common divisor of all ϵ_a where a is a reachable action. Then, clearly, each action is reachable in $[\![A]\!]_\epsilon$ if and only if it is reachable in $[\![A]\!]_{\mathbb{R}_0^+}$.   □

Lemma 6. *There exists a TA A such that $[\![A]\!]_{\mathbb{R}_0^+}$ is not trace equivalent to $[\![A]\!]_\epsilon$ for any ϵ.*

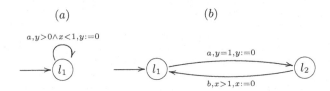

Fig. 3. Difference between dense and sampled semantics (example (b) is taken from [2]).

Such an automaton could be easily obtained by enabling *zeno* behavior (arbitrary number of events in finite time), see Fig. 3(a). Zeno behavior cannot be obtained in the sampled semantics. But there are also non-zeno automata which are not trace equivalent in dense and sampled domains, see Fig. 3(b).

All results are summarized in Table 1. For the sampled semantics, a given result means that there exists an ϵ such that the given equivalence is guaranteed. In a case of closed TA, such ϵ can be easily constructed from the syntax of the automaton (as the greatest common divisor of all constants). For general TA, such ϵ can be constructed, but it requires to explore the region graph corresponding to the automaton. For SWA, such ϵ cannot be constructed algorithmically (because we do not know which actions are reachable).

4   Reachability Problem for Stopwatch Automata in Sampled Semantics

The reachability problem is to determine, for a given automaton A and an action a, whether a is reachable in $[\![A]\!]$ (for a given semantics). This is a fundamental problem, because verification of the most common type of properties (safety properties) can be reduced to the reachability problem. It is well-known that for timed automata the problem is PSPACE-complete and that the complexity depends neither on the time domain which we use nor on the choice of the type of constraints (diagonal-free, non-strict) [1]. The type of constraints becomes important if we allow more general updates in the reset operation [4].

Here we show that for stopwatch automata the choice of the time domain and the type of constraints are important. With dense semantics, the problem is known to be undecidable even for diagonal-free constraints and one stopwatch [12]. We show that in sampled semantics, the problem is decidable for diagonal-free constraints. However, if we allow diagonal constraints, the reachability problem is again undecidable. We have to use a different reduction than in the dense case, but, surprisingly, only one stopwatch suffices even in the case of sampled semantics.

Lemma 7. *Let A be a diagonal-free SWA and ϵ a given sampling period. Then the reachability problem in sampled semantics $[\![A]\!]_\epsilon$ is PSPACE-complete.*

Proof. We use a standard 'normalization' approach — it is easy to check that the relation $\sim_K$ induces bisimulation on $[\![A]\!]_\epsilon$ (K is the largest constant occurring in guards) for a diagonal-free SWA. We can easily obtain unique representative of each bisimulation class (by 'normalizing' all clock values larger than K to value $K+1$) and thus we can easily perform the search over the bisimulation collapse.

Complexity: PSPACE-membership follows from the algorithm (search in an exponential graph can be done in polynomial space), PSPACE-hardness follows from PSPACE-hardness for timed automata.   □

Lemma 8. *Let A be an SWA with one stopwatch. Then the reachability problem in sampled semantics $[\![A]\!]_\epsilon$ is undecidable.*

Proof. We show the undecidability by reduction from the halting problem for a two counter machine M. Since this is usual approach in this area (see e.g., [12, 7, 4]), we just describe the main idea — how to encode counter values and perform increment/decrement.

The value of a counter i is represented as the difference of two clocks: $x_i - y_i$. Before the start of the simulation of M the simulating SWA nondeterministically guesses the maximal value c of counters during a computation of M and sets the stopwatch to the value $c+1$. From this moment on the stopwatch is stopped for the rest of the computation with the value $c+1$.

Values of clocks are kept in the interval $[0, c+1]$ all the time. Whenever the value of a clock reaches $c+1$, the clock is reseted. Testing the value of a counter for zero is straightforward: just testing $x_i = y_i$. Decrementing a counter i is performed by postponing the reset of a clock x_i by 1 time unit. Incrementing a counter i is performed by postponing the reset of a clock y_i by 1 time unit. During the increment we have to check for an 'overflow' — if the difference $x_i - y_i$ equals to c and we should perform increment then it means that the initial nondeterministic guess was wrong and the simulation should not continue.

Note that the stopwatch is used in a very limited fashion: it is stopped once and then it keeps a constant value.   □

5   Non-emptiness of ω-Language in Sampled Semantics

Examples in Fig. 3 demonstrate that there are timed automata such that $L_\omega(A)$ is non-empty whereas for all ϵ the language $L_\omega^\epsilon(A)$ is empty. Non-emptiness is an important problem, because verification of liveness properties can be reduced to checking non-emptiness of an ω-language. Non-emptiness implies existence of a behavior which violates a given liveness property. But as examples in Fig. 3 demonstrate, it may happen that all infinite traces are non-realizable. Therefore, the property would be satisfied on a real system.

What we really want is non-emptiness of $L_\omega^\epsilon(A)$ for some ϵ instead of non-emptiness of $L_\omega(A)$. We show that the problem of deciding whether such an ϵ exists is decidable. This problem was considered in a survey paper [2], where it is claimed that the problem is undecidable, with a reference to [7]. The work [7], however, deals with a slightly different problem: it is required that the timed automaton performs action step after *every* discrete time step (this requirement is motivated by control theory).

Theorem 1. *Let A be a timed automaton. The problem of deciding whether* $\bigcup_\epsilon L_\omega^\epsilon(A) \neq \emptyset$ *is decidable.*

Our proof is based on the classical region construction [1] (for the definition of region graph and for technical aspects of the proof see [14]). The region graph can be directly used for ω-language emptiness checking in dense semantics — the ω-language is non-empty if and only if there is a cycle in the region graph. This is, however, not true for sampled semantics, as illustrated by examples in Fig. 3.

Intuitively, the problem is the following. Existence of a cycle in the region graph from a region (l, D) to itself means that there exists some valuations $\nu, \nu' \in D$ such that $(l, \nu) \rightarrow^+ (l, \nu')$. These valuations may be constrained, e.g., in example in Fig. 3(b) the constraint on paths from state $(l_1, [x = 0, 0 < y < 1])$ to itself is that $1 > \nu'(y) > \nu(y) > 0$. In dense semantics we can have an infinite run which satisfies this constraint, but in sampled semantics we cannot. In sampled semantics we need a path $(l, \nu) \rightarrow^+ (l, \nu')$ such that $\nu \sim_k \nu'$ (valuations may differ only in clocks above constants).

To formalize this intuition, we need a notion of reachability relation, which describes exactly which valuations can be reached from a given valuation. Let $(l, D), (l, D')$ be two states in region graph. Then *reachability relation* of the pair

$(l, D), (l, D')$ is a relation on valuations $C_{(l,D)(l',D')} \subseteq D \times D'$ such that for each $\nu \in D, \nu' \in D'$:

$$(\nu, \nu') \in C_{(l,D)(l',D')} \iff \exists \nu'' \sim_K \nu' : (l, \nu) \to^+ (l, \nu'')$$

We present a simple representation for reachability relations. The fact that such simple (in)equalities are sufficient to capture the reachability relations and that these relations can be computed effectively is rather interesting.

Clock difference relations (CDR) structure over a set of clocks $\mathcal{C}$ is a set of (in)equalities of the following form:

- $x' - y' \bowtie u - v$
- $x' - y' \bowtie 1 - (u - v)$

where $\bowtie \in \{<, >, =\}$, $x, y, u, v \in \mathcal{C}$. The semantics of a CDR B is defined as follows:

- if $x' - y' \bowtie u - v \in B$ then $\mathsf{fr}(\nu'(x)) - \mathsf{fr}(\nu'(y)) \bowtie \mathsf{fr}(\nu(u)) - \mathsf{fr}(\nu(v))$,
- if $x' - y' \bowtie 1 - (u - v) \in B$ then $\mathsf{fr}(\nu'(x)) - \mathsf{fr}(\nu'(y)) \bowtie 1 - (\mathsf{fr}(\nu(u)) - \mathsf{fr}(\nu(v)))$,

Theorem 2. *Reachability relations $C_{(l,D)(l',D')}$ are effectively definable as a finite unions of clock difference relations.*

The proof of this theorem is based on the following key facts:

- If there is an immediate transition $(l, D) \to (l', D')$ then the reachability relation can be directly expressed as a CDR.
- If $(l, D) \to^+ (l'', D'') \to (l', D')$ and the reachability relation over (l, D), (l'', D'') is expressed as a union of CDRs then the reachability relation over (l, D), (l', D') can be expressed as a union of CDRs as well.
- Using these two steps, reachability relations can be computed by a standard dynamic programming algorithm; termination is guaranteed, because there is only a finite number of CDRs over a fixed set of clocks; correctness is proved by induction with respect to the length of a path between (l, D) and (l', D').

Lemma 9. *There exists an ϵ such that $L_\omega^\epsilon(A)$ is non-empty if and only if there exists a reachable state (l, D) in the region graph of A such that the following condition is satisfiable:*

$$\exists \nu, \nu' \in D : (\nu_0, \nu) \in C_{(l_0,D_0)(l,D)} \wedge (\nu, \nu') \in C_{(l,D)(l,D)} \wedge \nu \sim_K \nu'$$

Proof. At first, suppose that the condition is satisfiable. Due to Theorem 2, the condition can be expressed as boolean combination of linear inequalities. The set of solutions is an union of convex polyhedrons and therefore there must exist a rational solution ν, ν'. From the definition of reachability relations we get that there exists $\nu'' \sim_K \nu$ such that $(l_0, \nu_0) \to^+ (l, \nu) \to^+ (l, \nu'')$ in the real semantics. Since real and rational semantics are bisimilar, there exists such a path in rational semantics as well. We take ϵ as the greatest common divisor of time steps on this path. Thus the path $(l_0, \nu_0) \rightarrow^+ (l, \nu) \rightarrow^+ (l, \nu'')$ is executable in $[\![A]\!]_\epsilon$ and since ν'' is bisimilar to ν (because $\nu \sim_K \nu''$) we can construct an infinite run. Therefore, $L_\omega^\epsilon(A)$ is non-empty.

On the other hand, if $L_\omega^\epsilon(A)$ is non-empty then there exists an infinite run $(l_0, \nu_0) \rightarrow (l_1, \nu_1) \rightarrow (l_2, \nu_2) \rightarrow \dots$. Since $\sim_K$ has a finite index (over sampled semantics) there must exists i, j such that $l_i = l_j, \nu_i \sim_K \nu_j$. These valuation demonstrate the satisfiability of the condition. $\qquad\square$

With the use of Theorem 2 and Lemma 9 it is now quite straightforward to prove Theorem 1 (see [14] for technical details).

6   Future Work

Sampled semantics gives natural under-approximations of timed systems, where the choice of sampling period ϵ can nicely tune the size of the state space of an under-approximation. This makes sampled semantics plausible as a base for under-approximation refinement scheme. This scheme starts with coarse-grained under-approximation of the systems and refines it until an error is found or the approximation is exact [11, 17]. This approach is suitable particularly for falsification (defect detection).

From a theoretical point of view, a successful application of the under-approximation refinement scheme based on sampled semantics has many obstacles. Complexity (decidability) of verification problems remains usually the same for sampled semantics as it is for dense semantics. Moreover, it is even not possible to efficiently decide whether ϵ-sampled and dense semantics are equivalent. Nevertheless, we believe that for practical examples this approach can give better results than classical complete methods (at least for defect detection). One possible direction for future work is an experimental evaluation of this approach on practical case studies.

Another direction for future work is provided by the decidability result for non-emptiness of ω-language in some sampled semantics. The result leads to standard questions about complexity of the problem and about the existence of a practically feasible algorithm.

Acknowledgments. We thank Wang Yi and Ivana Černá for their comments on previous drafts of this paper.

References

[1] R. Alur and D. L. Dill. A theory of timed automata. *Theoretical Computer Science*, 126(2):183–235, 1994.

[2] R. Alur and P. Madhusudan. Decision problems for timed automata: A survey. In *Formal Methods for the Design of Real-Time Systems*, volume 3185 of *LNCS*, pages 1–24. Springer, 2004.

[3] E. Asarin, O. Maler, and A. Pnueli. On discretization of delays in timed automata and digital circuits. In *Proc. of Conference on Concurrency Theory (CONCUR'98)*, volume 1466 of *LNCS*, pages 470–484. Springer, 1998.

[4] P. Bouyer, C. Dufourd, E. Fleury, and A. Petit. Are timed automata updatable? In *Proc. of Computer Aided Verification (CAV 2000)*, volume 1855 of *LNCS*, pages 464–479. Springer, 2000.

[5] M. Bozga, O. Maler, A. Pnueli, and S. Yovine. Some Progress in the Symbolic Verification of Timed Automata. In *Proc. of Computer Aided Verification (CAV'97)*, volume 1254 of *LNCS*, pages 179–190. Springer, June 1997.

[6] M. Bozga, O. Maler, and S. Tripakis. Efficient verification of timed automata using dense and discrete time semantics. In *Proc. of Charme'99*, volume 1703 of *LNCS*, pages 125–141. Springer, 1999.

[7] F. Cassez, T. A. Henzinger, and J.-F. Raskin. A comparison of control problems for timed and hybrid systems. In *Proc. of the Hybrid Systems: Computation and Control*, volume 2289 of *LNCS*, pages 134–148. Springer, 2002.

[8] H. Comon and Y. Jurski. Timed automata and the theory of real numbers. In *Proc. of Conference on Concurrency Theory (CONCUR'99)*, volume 1664 of *LNCS*, pages 242–257. Springer, 1999.

[9] C. Dima. Computing reachability relations in timed automata. In *Proc. of Symp. on Logic in Computer Science (LICS 2002)*, pages 177–188. IEEE Computer Society Press, 2002.

[10] A. Gollu, A. Puri, and P. Varaiya. Discretization of timed automata. In *Proc. of Conferene on Decision and Control*, pages 957–958, 1994.

[11] O. Grumberg, F. Lerda, O. Strichman, and M. Theobald. Proof-guided underapproximation-widening for multi-process systems. In *Proc. of Principles of programming languages (POPL'05)*, pages 122–131. ACM Press, 2005.

[12] T. A. Henzinger, P. W. Kopke, A. Puri, and P. Varaiya. What's decidable about hybrid automata? In *Proc. of ACM Symposium on Theory of Computing (STOC'95)*, pages 373–382. ACM Press, 1995.

[13] T. A. Henzinger, Z. Manna, and A. Pnueli. What good are digital clocks? In *Proc. of Colloquium on Automata, Languages and Programming (ICALP'92)*, volume 623 of *LNCS*, pages 545–558. Springer, 1992.

[14] P. Krčál and R. Pelánek. Reachability relations and sampled semantics of timed systems. Technical Report FIMU-RS-2005-09, Masaryk University Brno, 2005.

[15] K. G. Larsen and W. Yi. Time-abstracted bisimulation: Implicit specifications and decidability. *Information and Computation*, 134(2):75–101, 1997.

[16] J. Ouaknine and J. Worrell. Revisiting digitization, robustness, and decidability for timed automata. In *Proc. of IEEE Symp. on Logic in Computer Science (LICS 2003)*, pages 198–207. IEEE Computer Society Press, 2003.

[17] C. Pasareanu, R. Pelánek, and W. Visser. Concrete search with abstract matching and refinement. In *Proc. of Computer Aided Verification (CAV 2005)*, LNCS. Springer, 2005. To appear.

[18] Anuj Puri. Dynamical properties of timed automata. *Discrete Event Dynamic Systems*, 10(1-2):87–113, 2000.

[19] C. Stirling. Local model checking games. In *Proc. of Conference on Concurrency Theory (CONCUR'95)*, volume 962 of *LNCS*, pages 1–11. Springer, 1995.

[20] M. De Wulf, L. Doyen, and J.-F. Raskin. Almost ASAP semantics: From timed models to timed implementations. In *Proc. of Hybrid Systems: Computation and Control (HSCC'04)*, volume 2993 of *LNCS*, pages 296–310. Springer, 2004.

Eventual Timed Automata

Deepak D'Souza and M. Raj Mohan

Department of Computer Science and Automation,
Indian Institute of Science, Bangalore 560012, India
{deepakd,raj}@csa.iisc.ernet.in

Abstract. We study the class of timed automata called *eventual timed automata* (ETA's) obtained using guards based on the operator $\Diamond$. In this paper we show that ETA's form a decidable class of timed automata via a flattening to non-recursive ETA's followed by a reduction to 1-clock alternating timed automata. We also study the expressiveness of the class of ETA's and show that they compare favourably with other classes in the literature. Finally we show that class obtained using the dual operator $\diamondsuit$ is also decidable, though the two operators together lead to an undecidable class of languages.

1 Introduction

The timed automata of Alur and Dill [AD94] are a popular model of time dependent systems. While they are very expressive and have a decidable emptiness problem, they suffer from the fact that they are not closed under complement and have an undecidable language inclusion problem. As a result of non-closure under complementation, they also do not admit natural monadic second order logic characterizations. In an attempt to describe a robust class of timed automata which are closed under boolean operations and which have more robust logical properties, the generic class of Input Determined Automata (IDA's) were identified in [DT04]. In contrast to a timed automaton, an IDA does not have explicit clocks but uses distance operators whose meaning is determined solely by the given timed word and a position in it. These generic classes of automata have several desirable properties. They are determinizable, closed under boolean operations, admit natural monadic second order logic characterizations, and have expressively complete timed temporal logics.

In this paper we focus on the class of IDA's based on the input determined operator $\Diamond$, and call it *eventual timed automata* or ETA's. The operator $\Diamond_a$, where a is a letter of the alphabet, identifies a set of distances to future positions in the timed word which are labeled a. An eventual timed automaton can use guards of the form $(\Diamond_a \in I)$ which is then true at a point in a timed word provided there is a position in the future where an a occurs and the distance to that point lies in the interval I. In general, the class of *recursive* ETA's can make use of operators of the form $\Diamond_{\mathcal{B}}$, where $\mathcal{B}$ is in turn such an ETA which accepts timed words *at* a designated position in them.

R. Ramanujam and S. Sen (Eds.): FSTTCS 2005, LNCS 3821, pp. 322–334, 2005.
© Springer-Verlag Berlin Heidelberg 2005

The class of recursive ETA's are an interesting class of timed automata for reasons other than that they inherit the useful properties of generic IDA's listed above. The well known timed temporal logic Metric Temporal Logic (MTL) [Koy90, AFH96, OW05] corresponds to the first order fragment of recursive ETA's. That is, MTL is expressively equivalent to the first order fragment of the timed MSO which characterizes recursive ETA's [DT04]. Further, they form an orthogonal class of timed languages with respect to Alur-Dill timed automata, since they can express some languages not expressible by timed automata [DT04]. However nothing much was known about decision procedures for this class of languages.

In this paper we address this issue and show that recursive ETA's form a decidable class of timed languages. We do this in two steps. We first show that recursive ETA's can be "flattened" to a non-recursive one over an extended alphabet. We then show that the emptiness problem for ETA's can be decided by showing how they can be simulated by 1-clock alternating timed automata which were recently shown to be decidable [LW05, OW05].

We also study the expressiveness of this class more closely, and show that it is indeed incomparable with the class of timed automata in that there is also a language which timed automata can express but a recursive ETA cannot. The class of recursive ETA's can also be seen to be strictly more expressive than the class of recursive Event Predicting Automata [AFH94, HRS98] which are another class with robust logical properties [DT04]. This, together with the properties described above, make the class of recursive ETA's one of the most expressive classes of timed automata of its kind in the literature.

Finally we show that the class of automata obtained by considering the dual operator $\diamond$ is also decidable. We do this by reducing its emptiness problem to that of ETA's. However, the two operators taken together lead to an undecidable class of automata.

Some proofs are omitted due to lack of space and can be found in the full version of this paper [DM05].

2   Eventual Timed Automata

For an alphabet A we use A^* to denote the set of finite words over A, and $|w|$ to denote the length of a word w. The set of non-negative and positive real numbers will be denoted by $\mathbb{R}_{\geq 0}$ and $\mathbb{R}_{>0}$ respectively.

A (finite) *timed word* over an alphabet Σ is an element of $(\Sigma \times \mathbb{R}_{>0})^*$ of the form $\sigma = (a_0, t_0)(a_1, t_1) \cdots (a_n, t_n)$, satisfying $t_i < t_{i+1}$ for all $i \in \{0, \ldots, n-1\}$. Wherever convenient, we will also use the representation of the timed word σ above as (w, τ) where $w = a_0 \cdots a_n$ and $\tau = t_0 \cdots t_n$. We denote the set of all timed words over Σ by $T\Sigma^*$.

We will use rational bounded intervals to specify timing constraints. These intervals can be open or closed, and we allow ∞ as an open right end. These intervals denote a subset of reals in the usual manner – for example $[2, \infty)$ denotes the set $\{t \in \mathbb{R}_{\geq 0} \mid 2 \leq t\}$. The set of all intervals is denoted $\mathcal{I}_{\mathbb{Q}}$.

An eventual timed automaton is essentially a timed automaton which has no explicit clocks, but uses atomic guards of the form "$\Diamond_a \in I$", which assert that with respect to the current position in a timed word there is an occurrence of an action a at some point in the future, such that the distance to that point lies in the interval I. To define these automata more formally, we begin by defining the guards used by them. For an alphabet Σ, we use $\mathcal{G}(\Sigma)$ to denote the set of guards given by the syntax $g ::= \top \mid \Diamond_a \in I \mid \neg g \mid g \vee g \mid g \wedge g$, where $a \in \Sigma$ and $I \in \mathcal{I}_{\mathbb{Q}}$. The guards are interpreted at the "action points" in a timed word σ (we call these *positions* and denote them by natural numbers between 0 and $|\sigma| - 1$). Let $\sigma = (a_0, t_0) \cdots (a_n, t_n)$ and $i \in \{0, \ldots, |\sigma| - 1\}$. Then σ at position i satisfies the guard $\Diamond_a \in I$, written $\sigma, i \models \Diamond_a \in I$, iff there exists $j \geq i$ such that $a_j = a$ and $t_j - t_i \in I$. The guard $\top$ is always true, and the boolean operators are interpreted in the expected manner.

An *eventual timed automaton (ETA)* over Σ is of the form $\mathcal{A} = (Q, s, \delta, F)$ where Q is a finite set of states, $s \in Q$ is the start state, δ is the transition relation and is a finite subset of $Q \times \Sigma \times \mathcal{G}(\Sigma) \times Q$, and $F \subseteq Q$ is a set of final states. A run of $\mathcal{A}$ on a timed word $\sigma = (a_0, t_0) \cdots (a_n, t_n)$ is a sequence of states $q_0, \ldots, q_{n+1}$ satisfying

- $q_0 = s$,
- for each $i \in \{0, \ldots, n\}$ there exist guards g_i such that $(q_i, a_i, g_i, q_{i+1}) \in \delta$ and $\sigma, i \models g_i$.

The run is accepting if $q_{n+1} \in F$. The language of timed words accepted by $\mathcal{A}$ is denoted $L(\mathcal{A})$ and defined to be the set of all timed words in $T\Sigma^*$ on which $\mathcal{A}$ has an accepting run.

The figure below shows an example of a simple ETA with a single state that is both the start and the final state. It accepts the language L_0 of all timed words of a's in which there are no two a's at a distance of 1 time unit apart.

$$a, \neg(\Diamond_a \in [1,1])$$

Fig. 1. An example ETA

It will be convenient to recall the general class of input determined automata (IDA) defined in [DT04]. An IDA over an alphabet Σ has a structure similar to an ETA except that it is parameterized by a set of "input determined" operators Op. Each operator $\Delta \in Op$ has a semantic function $[\![\Delta]\!]$ which we assume in this paper associates a set of distances with a given timed word σ and a position i in it. Thus $[\![\Delta]\!](\sigma, i) \subseteq \mathbb{R}_{\geq 0}$. The atomic guards in an IDA are now of the form $(\Delta \in I)$ and the truth of the guard at position i in a timed word σ is given by $\sigma, i \models \Delta \in I$ iff $[\![\Delta]\!](\sigma, i) \cap I \neq \emptyset$. The timed language accepted by an IDA $\mathcal{A}$

over an alphabet Σ and a set of operators Op is denoted $L(\mathcal{A})$ and is defined as for ETA's, with the guards interpreted as described above.

Thus the class of ETA's over an alphabet Σ defined above is nothing but the class of IDA's corresponding to the set of operators $\{\Diamond_a \mid a \in \Sigma\}$ (we denote this class by IDA($\Diamond$)) with the semantic function $[\![\Diamond_a]\!]$ given by

$$[\![\Diamond_a]\!](\sigma, i) = \{\tau(j) - \tau(i) \mid \sigma = (w, \tau),\ j \geq i,\ \text{and}\ w(j) = a\}.$$

We now introduce the *recursive* version of ETA's. The main idea is to index the $\Diamond$ operator with an *automaton* $\mathcal{B}$ and use the operator $\Diamond_{\mathcal{B}}$ to mean the set of distances to the points in the future where the automaton $\mathcal{B}$ "accepts". To make this notion more precise, we first introduce the notion of a *floating* language. A *floating language* over Σ is a set of *floating timed words* over Σ which in turn are pairs of the form (σ, i) where σ is a timed word over Σ and i is a position in σ. We will represent a "floating" word (σ, i) as a timed word over the extended alphabet $\Sigma \times \{0, 1\}$. Thus a timed word ν over $\Sigma \times \{0, 1\}$ represents the floating word (σ, i), iff $\nu = (w, v, \tau)$, with $v \in \{0, 1\}^*$ with a *single* 1 in the i-th position, and $\sigma = (w, \tau)$. We use fw to denote the (partial) map which given a timed word ν over $\Sigma \times \{0, 1\}$ returns the floating word (σ, i) corresponding to ν, and extend it to apply to timed languages over $\Sigma \times \{0, 1\}$ in the natural way.

We can now define recursive ETA's and the timed languages they accept as follows. The class of *recursive eventual timed automata* (recursive ETA's) over the alphabet Σ is the union of the classes of level i recursive eventual timed automata over Σ (for $i \geq 0$) which are defined inductively below:

- A *level 0 recursive ETA* over Σ is an ETA $\mathcal{A}$ over Σ that uses only the guard $\top$. It accepts the language $L(\mathcal{A})$ as defined for ETA's.
- Similarly, a *level 0 recursive floating ETA* over Σ is an ETA $\mathcal{B}$ over the alphabet $\Sigma \times \{0, 1\}$ that uses only the guard $\top$. It accepts the floating language $L^f(\mathcal{B})$ defined to be $fw(L(\mathcal{B}))$.
- Let D be a finite collection of recursive floating ETA of level i or less over Σ, and consider the set of operators $Op = \{\Diamond_{\mathcal{B}} \mid \mathcal{B} \in D\}$. We define the semantics of $\Diamond_{\mathcal{B}}$ in Op by:

$$[\![\Diamond_{\mathcal{B}}]\!](\sigma, i) = \{\tau(j) - \tau(i) \mid \sigma = (w, \tau),\ j \geq i,\ \text{and}\ (\sigma, j) \in L^f(\mathcal{B})\}.$$

  A *level $i + 1$ recursive ETA* over Σ is then an IDA $\mathcal{A}$ over (Σ, Op), and accepts the language $L(\mathcal{A})$ as defined for IDA's. We also require that $\mathcal{A}$ should use at least one operator of the form $\Diamond_{\mathcal{B}}$ for a recursive floating ETA $\mathcal{B}$ of level i.
- To define level $i + 1$ recursive floating ETA's, let D be a finite collection of recursive floating ETA's of level i or less over Σ, and consider the set of operators $Op = \{\Diamond_{\mathcal{B}} \mid \mathcal{B} \in D\}$. For floating automata the operator $\Diamond$ works slightly differently in that it ignores the extended part of the alphabet. We define the semantics of $\Diamond_{\mathcal{C}}$ when used in a floating automaton as follows. Let σ' be a timed word over $\Sigma \times \{0, 1\}$. Then

$$[\![\Diamond_{\mathcal{C}}]\!](\sigma', i) = \{\tau(j) - \tau(i) \mid \sigma' = (w, v, \tau),\ j \geq i,\ \text{and}\ ((w, \tau), j) \in L^f(\mathcal{C})\}.$$

A *level $i+1$ recursive floating ETA* over Σ is then an IDA $\mathcal{B}$ over $(\Sigma \times \{0,1\}, Op)$, and accepts the floating language $L^f(\mathcal{B})$ defined to be $fw(L(\mathcal{B}))$. Once again we require that $\mathcal{B}$ should use at least one operator of the form $\diamondsuit_{\mathcal{C}}$ for a recursive floating ETA $\mathcal{C}$ of level i.

Below we give an example of a recursive ETA over the alphabet $\{a, b, c\}$.

Fig. 2. A level 2 recursive ETA.

Fig. 2 shows a level 2 recursive ETA $\mathcal{A}$ which uses a level 1 floating automaton $\mathcal{B}$, which in turn calls a level 0 floating automaton $\mathcal{C}$. $\mathcal{A}$ accepts timed words σ which start with an a at some time t, followed eventually by a b at time t' such that $t' - t \in [1, 2]$, and a c at time $t'' = t' + 1$. For example, the timed word $(a, 0.2)(a, 1.2)(b, 1.4)(c, 2.4)$ satisfies all the conditions given above and therefore belongs to $L(\mathcal{A})$.

Before we close this section, we recall some of the results of [DT04] specialized to the case of recursive ETA's. We recall briefly the timed monadic second order logic rec-TMSO(Σ) based on the operator $\diamondsuit$, which characterizes the class of timed languages defined by recursive ETA's. The syntax of the logic is given by

$$\varphi ::= Q_a(x) \mid \diamondsuit_\psi(x) \in I \mid x \in X \mid x < y \mid \neg\varphi \mid (\varphi \vee \varphi) \mid \exists x \varphi \mid \exists X \varphi.$$

In the predicate $\diamondsuit_\psi(x) \in I$, we require ψ to be a rec-TMSO(Σ) formula with a single free variable z, x a first-order variable, and $I \in \mathcal{I}_{\mathbb{Q}}$.

The logic is interpreted over timed words in $T\Sigma^*$. For formulas with free variables we use an interpretation $\mathbb{I}$ which maps variables to positions in a timed word. The semantics of the predicate "$\diamondsuit_\psi(x) \in I$" is defined inductively as follows. If ψ is a formula which uses no $\diamondsuit$ predicates, then the satisfaction relation $\sigma, \mathbb{I} \models \psi$ is defined as for standard MSO. Inductively, assuming the semantics of ψ has already been defined, $\diamondsuit_\psi$ is interpreted as an input determined operator as follows:

$$[\![\diamondsuit_\psi]\!](\sigma, i) = \{\tau(j) - \tau(i) \mid \sigma = (w, \tau), \ j \geq i, \text{ and } \sigma, [j/z] \models \psi\}.$$

Then we say:

$$\sigma, \mathbb{I} \models \diamondsuit_\psi(x) \in I \quad \text{iff} \quad [\![\diamondsuit_\psi]\!](\sigma, \mathbb{I}(x)) \cap I \neq \emptyset.$$

A sentence φ in rec-TMSO(Σ) defines the language $L(\varphi) = \{\sigma \in T\Sigma^\omega \mid \sigma \models \varphi\}$.

Theorem 1 ([DT04]). *The class of recursive ETA's over an alphabet Σ satisfies the following properties:*

1. *They are determinizable and closed under boolean operations.*
2. *The timed monadic second order logic rec-TMSO(Σ) is expressively equivalent to them.*
3. *The timed temporal logic MTL is expressively equivalent to the first order fragment of rec-TMSO(Σ).*   □

3 Deciding Emptiness for ETA's

In this section we give a decision procedure for the language emptiness problem for ETA's. We do this by showing how to translate an ETA to a 1-clock alternating timed automaton, the emptiness problem for which has been shown to be decidable [LW05, OW05].

We first recall the definition of a 1-clock alternating timed automaton. Let $\mathcal{G}_x$ denote the set of guards over the clock x given by the following syntax: $g ::= \top \mid x \in I \mid \neg g \mid g \vee g$. A valuation for the clock x, $d \in \mathbb{R}_{\geq 0}$, satisfies $x \in I$, written $d \models x \in I$, iff $d \in I$. The other guards are interpreted in the expected manner. For $X \subseteq \{x\}$, we use $d[0/X]$ to denote the valuation d or 0, depending on whether $X = \emptyset$ or $\{x\}$.

A 1-clock *alternating timed automaton* (ATA) over an alphabet Σ is of the form $\mathcal{T} = (Q, s, \Delta, F)$ where Q is a finite set of states, $s \in Q$ is the initial state, $\Delta \subseteq Q \times \Sigma \times \mathcal{G}_x \times (2^{\{\emptyset, \{x\}\} \times Q} - \{\emptyset\})$ is the transition relation, and $F \subseteq Q$ is the set of final states.

An *extended state* of $\mathcal{T}$ is a pair of the form (q, d) where $q \in Q$ and $d \in \mathbb{R}_{\geq 0}$ is a valuation for x. A *configuration* of $\mathcal{T}$ is a finite collection of extended states. To describe a run of the ATA over a timed word it is convenient to first define a consecution relation between configurations. Let $C = \{(q_0, d_0), \ldots, (q_k, d_k)\}$ be a configuration of $\mathcal{T}$. Let $t \in \mathbb{R}_{\geq 0}$ and $a \in \Sigma$. Then a configuration D is an (a, t)-successor of C iff D is the union of configurations $D_0, \ldots, D_k$ which satisfy: there exist guards g_i and sets of reset-state pairs $T_i = \{(r_0^i, p_0^i), \ldots, (r_{n_i}^i, p_{n_i}^i)\}$ such that

- $(q_i, a, g_i, T_i) \in \Delta$,
- $d_i + t \models g_i$, and
- $D_i = \{(p_j^i, (d_i + t)[0/r_j^i]) \mid j \in \{0, \ldots, n_i\}\}$.

An accepting run of $\mathcal{T}$ over a timed word $\sigma = (a_0, t_0) \cdots (a_n, t_n)$ is a sequence of configuration $C_0, \ldots, C_{n+1}$ satisfying:

1. $C_0 = \{(s, 0)\}$
2. For each $i \in \{0, \ldots, n\}$, the configuration C_{i+1} is an $(a_i, t_i - t_{i-1})$-successor of C_i. (We use the convention that $t_{-1} = 0$.)
3. C_{n+1} contains only final states – i.e. $C_{n+1} \subseteq F \times \mathbb{R}_{\geq 0}$.

The timed language accepted by $\mathcal{T}$, denoted $L(\mathcal{T})$, is the set of timed words over Σ on which $\mathcal{T}$ has an accepting run.

As an example, the timed language over $\{a, b\}$ in which every a is followed by a b exactly one time unit later is accepted by the ATA $\mathcal{T}$ shown in the diagram below. The transition relation Δ of $\mathcal{T}$ is depicted by using an arc covering the edges corresponding to an "And" transition. For example the state s has two entries in Δ corresponding to its two outgoing transitions: $(s, b, \top, \{(\emptyset, s)\})$ and $(s, a, \top, \{(\emptyset, s), (\{x\}, t)\})$.

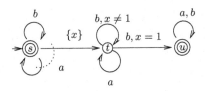

Fig. 3. An alternating timed automaton $\mathcal{T}$

We recall here the recent result of Lasota-Walukiewicz and Ouaknine-Worell:

Theorem 2 ([LW05, OW05]). *The emptiness problem of one-clock alternating timed automata over finite words is decidable.* $\square$

We now show how to translate a given ETA to a language-equivalent 1-clock ATA. The idea is fairly simple: for every guarded transition in the ETA we spawn off a copy of the automaton which verifies a literal guard of the form $\Diamond_a \in I$ or $\neg\Diamond_a \in I$. The translation is depicted in Fig. 4.

More precisely, let $\mathcal{A} = (Q, s, \delta, F)$ be an ETA over the alphabet Σ. We construct an ATA $\mathcal{T} = (Q', s', \Delta, F')$ as follows. The set of states Q' of $\mathcal{T}$ consists of the original states Q of $\mathcal{A}$, a new state u, and a new state p_c for each literal guard c (i.e. of the form $\Diamond_a \in I$ or $\neg\Diamond_a \in I$) in $\mathcal{A}$. The initial state s' is the initial state s of $\mathcal{A}$. The transition relation Δ contains the following transitions:

1. For each transition (p, a, g, q) of $\mathcal{A}$ we have the following transition in Δ. Without loss of generality let $g = c_0 \wedge \cdots \wedge c_k$ be a conjunction of literal guards c_i. Then

$$(p, a, g, \{(\emptyset, q)\} \cup \{(\{x\}, p_{c_i}) \mid 0 \le i \le k\}) \in \Delta$$

2. For each positive literal c of the form $\Diamond_a \in I$ we have the transitions

$$(p_c, b, \top, \{(\emptyset, p_c)\}) \qquad \in \Delta \text{ (for each } b \in \Sigma),$$
$$(p_c, a, x \in I, \{(\emptyset, u)\}) \in \Delta.$$

3. For each negative literal c of the form $\neg\Diamond_a \in I$ we have the transitions

$$(p_c, b, \top, \{(\emptyset, p_c)\}) \qquad \in \Delta \text{ (for each } b \neq a\text{)},$$
$$(p_c, a, \neg(x \in I), \{(\emptyset, p_c)\}) \in \Delta.$$

4. $(u, a, \top, \{(\emptyset, u)\}) \in \Delta$.

The set of final states F' is given by

$$F' = F \cup \{u\} \cup \{p_c \mid c \text{ is a negative literal in } \mathcal{A}\}.$$

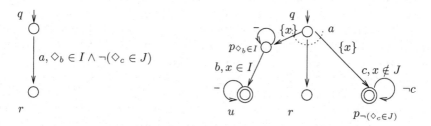

Fig. 4. Translation of an ETA transition

It is not difficult to check that $L(\mathcal{A}) = L(\mathcal{T})$. Using Theorem 2, we conclude that:

Theorem 3. *The emptiness problem for ETA's is decidable.* □

4 Deciding Recursive ETA's

In this section we show how we can decide the emptiness problem for recursive ETA's by showing how they can be simulated by non-recursive ETA's, though over an extended alphabet.

To explain the idea of our "flattening" construction, consider a recursive ETA $\mathcal{A}$ that uses the floating recursive ETA's $\mathcal{B}_0, \ldots, \mathcal{B}_k$ in its guards. We can then consider a timed word over the extended alphabet $\Sigma \times \{0, 1\}^{k+1}$ which represents the positions where the automata B_i accept the underlying timed word. Thus if $\sigma = (a_0, t_0) \cdots (a_n, t_n)$ is a timed word over Σ, the canonical extension of σ (wrt $\mathcal{B}_0, \ldots, \mathcal{B}_k$) is the timed word $\bar{\sigma}$ which we represent as $((a_0, v_0), t_0) \cdots ((a_n, v_n), t_n)$ where for each $i \in \{0, \ldots, n\}$ and $j \in \{0, \ldots, k\}$, $v_i[j] = 1$ iff $\mathcal{B}_j$ accepts (σ, i). The figure below shows the canonical extension of the timed word $(a, 0.2)(a, 1.2)(b, 1.4)(c, 2.4)$ with respect to the recursive ETA of Fig. 2.

T	0.2	1.2	1.4	2.4
Σ	a	a	b	c
$\mathcal{B}$	0	0	1	0
$\mathcal{C}$	0	0	0	1

Now the idea is essentially to run a modified version of $\mathcal{A}$, which we call $\hat{\mathcal{A}}$, over the extended timed words, and replace each atomic guard of the form $\Diamond_{\mathcal{B}_j} \in I$ in $\mathcal{A}$ by an appropriate non-recursive guard of the form $\Diamond_{(a,v)} \in I$ where $a \in \Sigma$ and v is such that $v[j] = 1$. We must further make sure that $\hat{\mathcal{A}}$ does not accept "bad" extended words in which some 0 and 1 guesses are incorrect. For this we use ETA's $\hat{\mathcal{B}}_j^0$ and $\hat{\mathcal{B}}_j^1$ which verify that the 0 entries (respectively the 1 entries) in the j-th row are correct.

The ETA $\hat{\mathcal{B}}_j^0$ which verifies that the 0 entries in the j-th row are correct, works by maintaining two components in its state: the first a state of $\mathcal{B}_j$ and the second a subset of states of $\mathcal{B}_j$. Whenever it gets an (a, v) with $v[j] = 0$ it pretends it has received a 1 entry instead, and pushes the resulting state to its second component. Apart from this, it runs its second component similar to a subset construction, assuming all entries are 0. Thus, if the extended word contained a 0 entry that should have been a 1, at the end of the word $\hat{\mathcal{B}}_j^0$ will have a *final* state of $\mathcal{B}_j$ and it will reject the extended word.

We now give the formal construction of the flattened ETA. Let $\mathcal{A} = (Q, s, \delta, F)$ be a recursive ETA over the alphabet Σ, and let it make use of the recursive floating ETA's $\mathcal{B}_0, \ldots, \mathcal{B}_k$, listed in the order of increasing levels. Without loss of generality (cf. Theorem 1) we assume that each $\mathcal{B}_j$ is deterministic. Let each $\mathcal{B}_j$ have the structure $(Q_j, s_j, \delta_j, F_j)$.

The required flattened ETA $\mathcal{A}'$ over the extended alphabet $\Sigma' = \Sigma \times \{0, 1\}^{k+1}$ is defined to be the intersection of the following ETA's as below:

$$\mathcal{A}' = \hat{\mathcal{A}} \cap \bigcap_{j=0}^{k} \hat{\mathcal{B}}_j^0 \cap \bigcap_{j=0}^{k} \hat{\mathcal{B}}_j^1.$$

The ETA $\hat{\mathcal{A}}$ has the same structure as $\mathcal{A}$ and is defined to be $(Q, s, \hat{\delta}, F)$ where the transition relation $\hat{\delta}$ is given as follows. For a guard g in $\mathcal{A}$, we denote by $\hat{g}$ the guard obtained by replacing each occurrence of an atomic guard of the form $\Diamond_{\mathcal{B}_j} \in I$ by the guard

$$\bigvee_{a \in \Sigma, v[j]=1} (\Diamond_{(a,v)} \in I).$$

Now let $(p, a, g, q) \in \delta$. Then we have the transition $(p, (a, v), \hat{g}, q)$ in $\hat{\delta}$ for all v.

The automaton $\hat{\mathcal{B}}_j^0$ is defined as follows. $\hat{\mathcal{B}}_j^0 = (\hat{Q}_j^0, \hat{s}_j^0, \hat{\delta}_j^0, \hat{F}_j^0)$, where:

- $\hat{Q}_j^0 = Q_j \times 2^{Q_j}$
- $\hat{s}_j^0 = (s_j, \emptyset)$
- $\hat{\delta}_j^0$ is given as follows. Let (q, S) be a state of $\hat{\mathcal{B}}_j^0$, with $S = \{q_0, \ldots, q_m\}$. Let $(a, v) \in \Sigma'$ with $v[j] = 0$. Then we have the transition $((q, S), (a, v), h, (r, T))$ in $\hat{\delta}_j^0$ provided the following conditions are satisfied:
  - There exists g such that $(q, (a, 0), g, r) \in \delta_j$.
  - There exists g' such that $(q, (a, 1), g', t) \in \delta_j$.
  - There exist $g_0, \ldots, g_m$ such that $(q_i, (a, 0), g_i, r_i) \in \delta_j$

- $h = \hat{g}_0 \wedge \cdots \wedge \hat{g}_m \wedge \hat{g} \wedge \hat{g}'$, and,
- $T = \{r_0, \ldots, r_m\} \cup \{t\}$.

If $(a, v) \in \Sigma'$ with $v[j] = 1$, then we have the transition $((q, S), (a, v), h, (r, T))$ in $\hat{\delta}_j^0$ provided:

- There exists g such that $(q, (a, 0), g, r) \in \delta_j$.
- There exist $g_0, \ldots, g_m$ such that $(q_i, (a, 0), g_i, r_i) \in \delta_j$
- $h = \hat{g}_0 \wedge \cdots \wedge \hat{g}_m \wedge \hat{g}$, and,
- $T = \{r_0, \ldots, r_m\}$.

- $\hat{F}_j^0 = Q_j \times 2^{Q_j - F_j}$.

The ETA $\hat{\mathcal{B}}_j^1$ is defined in a similar manner, except that we now verify the 1's instead of the 0 entries.

To reason about the correctness of the construction, it is convenient to use the notion of a "projection" of an extended word to a standard timed word. Let σ' be a timed word over the extended alphabet Σ'. Let us represent σ' as (w, β, τ) where $w \in \Sigma^*$, $\beta \in (\{0, 1\}^{k+1})^*$, and $\tau \in (\mathbb{R}_{>0})^*$. Then the projection of σ' to Σ, denoted $\sigma' \!\restriction\! \Sigma$, is defined to be the timed word (w, τ). We extend the projection operator to work on timed languages over Σ' in the expected way.

Theorem 4. *The recursive ETA $\mathcal{A}$ accepts the projection of the language accepted by the ETA $\mathcal{A}'$, i.e $L(\mathcal{A}) = L(\mathcal{A}') \!\restriction\! \Sigma$.*

Proof (Sketch). The proof involves two arguments. The first that the ETA over the extended alphabet $\hat{\mathcal{A}}$ accepts precisely the canonical extensions of timed words accepted by $\mathcal{A}$, *provided* we restrict ourselves to only canonical extended timed words. That is, if σ is a timed word over Σ and $\bar{\sigma}$ is its canonical extension wrt $\mathcal{B}_0, \ldots, \mathcal{B}_k$, then $\sigma \in L(\mathcal{A})$ iff $\bar{\sigma} \in L(\hat{\mathcal{A}})$. This is easy to see once we observe that

$$\sigma, i \models g \text{ iff } \bar{\sigma}, i \models \hat{g}.$$

The second part of the argument is to show that the intersection of the ETA's $\hat{\mathcal{B}}_j^0$ and $\hat{\mathcal{B}}_j^1$ together ensure that $\mathcal{A}'$ accepts only canonical extensions wrt $\mathcal{B}_0, \ldots, \mathcal{B}_k$. To prove this it is sufficient to argue that if σ' is an extended timed word such that for a particular j all rows below it have "correct" 0's and 1's, then $\hat{\mathcal{B}}_j^0$ (and symmetrically $\hat{\mathcal{B}}_j^1$) accepts it iff all 0 entries (respectively 1 entries) in the j-th row are correct. This is fairly routine to prove using the fact that the $\mathcal{B}_j$'s are time deterministic. □

5   Expressiveness of ETA's

In this section we compare the expressiveness of the class of recursive ETA's with a couple of well known classes of timed automata in the literature. We show that recursive ETA's are incomparable in expressiveness with Alur-Dill timed automata, and that they are strictly more expressive than the class of recursive Event Predicting Automata (EPA's) of [HRS98].

The timed language L_0 of section 2 was shown to to be definable by an ETA whereas it is not definable by an Alur-Dill timed automaton. Conversely, consider the language L_{ni} (for "no insertions") over the alphabet $\{a, b\}$, in which for any two consecutive a's the corresponding time period translated by one time unit contains no events. The complement of this language is definable by a non-deterministic timed automaton. However, as shown in [DP05], the language L_{ni} is not definable by a 1-clock alternating timed automaton (and hence neither is its complement, since this class is closed under complement). Recursive ETA's can be seen to be a subclass of 1-clock ATA's, using Theorem 4 and the fact that 1-clock ATA's are closed under projection. It then follows that recursive ETA's cannot define the complement of L_{ni} either. Thus the class of recursive ETA's is incomparable to the class of Alur-Dill timed automata.

The class of recursive Event Predicting Automata [AFH96, HRS98] can be seen to be strictly contained in the class of recursive ETA's. Recall that EPA's use an input determined operator $\triangleright_a$ which measures the distance to the *next* a event. The EPA guard $\triangleright_a \in I$ can be simulated by the ETA guard $(\Diamond_a \in I) \wedge \neg(\Diamond_a \in I')$, where the interval I' is of the form $(0, l)$ if $I = [l, r)$, and $(0, l]$ if $I = (l, r\rangle$ (here '$\rangle$' is either ')' or ']'). A recursive EPA can also be simulated by a recursive ETA by inductively replacing guards in a similar manner. A recursive EPA can be flattened to a projection equivalent non recursive EPA which runs over an extended alphabet. The class of non recursive EPA is shown to be a subclass of Alur-Dill timed automata [AFH94]. Since timed automata are closed under projection there exists a timed automaton which accepts the language accepted by the recursive EPA. Therefore the class of EPA's is strictly contained in the of ETA's. The figure below summarizes the arguments of this section.

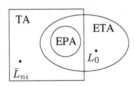

Fig. 5. Expressiveness of recursive ETA's, EPA's and timed automata

6   Decision Procedures for the Dual of $\Diamond$

In this section we consider the class of IDA's obtained by considering the dual operator $\diamondsuit$. The semantics of the operator is given as follows:

$$[\![\diamondsuit_a]\!](\sigma, i) = \{\tau(i) - \tau(j) \mid \sigma = (w, \tau), \ j \leq i, \text{ and } w(j) = a\}.$$

We denote this class IDA($\diamondsuit$). We prove that the emptiness problem of the class of IDA($\diamondsuit$) over finite words is decidable by reducing it to the emptiness problem of ETA's.

We now define the *reverse* of a timed word. Let $\sigma = (a_0, t_0) \cdots (a_n, t_n)$ be a timed word. We define the set of reversed timed words σ^R corresponding to σ as follows: $\sigma^R = \{(a_n, d - t_n) \cdots (a_0, d - t_0) \mid d > t_n\}$. For a timed language $L \subseteq T\Sigma^*$ we define $L^R = \bigcup_{\sigma \in L} \sigma^R$.

Let g be a $\Diamond\!\!\!\cdot$-guard, and let us denote by g^R the $\Diamond$-guard obtained from g by replacing each atomic guard $\Diamond\!\!\!\cdot_a \in I$ in g by the atomic guard $\Diamond_a \in I$. Then the following can be easily verified: Let σ and σ' be such that $\sigma' \in \sigma^R$. Then (a) if $\sigma, i \models g$ then $\sigma', (n - i) \models g^R$, and (b) if $\sigma, i \models g^R$ then $\sigma', (n - i) \models g$.

We now construct an ETA $\mathcal{A}^R$ from the given IDA($\Diamond\!\!\!\cdot$) $\mathcal{A}$ by replacing every guard g in $\mathcal{A}$ with the guard g^R, reversing the direction of all the edges, and interchanging the start and the final states. For convenience we allow $\mathcal{A}^R$ to have multiple start states. It is then easy to verify that if $\sigma' \in \sigma^R$ then $\sigma \in L(\mathcal{A})$ implies $\sigma' \in L(\mathcal{A}^R)$, and $\sigma \in L(\mathcal{A}^R)$ implies $\sigma' \in L(\mathcal{A})$. Thus $\mathcal{A}^R$ preserves the language emptiness of $\mathcal{A}$. In general, the language accepted by $\mathcal{A}^R$ can be seen to be $L(\mathcal{A})^R$.

Since the emptiness problem for ETA's is decidable we conclude that:

Theorem 5. *The emptiness problem for IDA($\Diamond\!\!\!\cdot$) is decidable.* $\qquad\square$

It is easy to see that recursive IDA($\Diamond\!\!\!\cdot$) can be flattened in a similar manner to ETA's. Hence we can conclude that:

Theorem 6. *The emptiness problem for recursive IDA($\Diamond\!\!\!\cdot$) is decidable.* $\qquad\square$

Finally, we point out that the class of IDA's with both operators $\Diamond$ and $\Diamond\!\!\!\cdot$ becomes undecidable. One can give a reduction from the halting problem of a 2-counter machine to the emptiness problem for this class, in a similar manner as done in [AD94]. More details can be found in [DM05].

Theorem 7. *The emptiness problem for IDA($\Diamond, \Diamond\!\!\!\cdot$) is undecidable.* $\qquad\square$

References

[AD94]   R. Alur and D. Dill: A theory of timed automata, *Theoretical Computer Science* **126**, Elsevier, 183–235 (1994).

[AFH96]   R. Alur, T. Feder and T.A. Henzinger: The benefits of relaxing punctuality, *J. ACM* **43**, 116–146 (1996).

[AFH94]   R. Alur, L. Fix and T. A. Henzinger: Event-clock automata: a determinizable class of timed automata, *Proc. 6th CAV*, LNCS **818**, 1–13, Springer-Verlag (1994).

[DM05]   D. D'Souza and Raj Mohan M: Eventual Timed Automata, IISc-CSA-TR-2005-8, Technical Report, Indian Institute of Science, Bangalore (2005).

[DP05]   D. D'Souza and P. Prabhakar: On the expressiveness of MTL in the pointwise and continuous semantics, IISc-CSA-TR-2005-7, Technical Report, Indian Institute of Science, Bangalore (2005).

[DT04]   D. D'Souza and N. Tabareau: On timed automata with input-determined guards, *Proc. FORMATS-FTRTFT*, LNCS **3253** (2004).

[HRS98]   T. Henzinger, J. Raskin and P. Schobbens: The regular real-time languages, *Proc. 25th ICALP*, LNCS **1443**, 580–591 (1998).

[Koy90]   R. Koymans: Specifying real-time properties with metric temporal logic, *Real Time Systems*, Vol. **2**, No.4, 255–299 (1990).

[LW05]   S. Lasota and I. Walukiewicz: Alternating timed automata, *Proc. FOS-SACS 2005* (2005).

[OW05]   J. Ouaknine and J. Worrell: On the decidability of metric temporal logic, *Proc. LICS 2005* (2005).

Causal Closure for MSC Languages

Bharat Adsul, Madhavan Mukund, K. Narayan Kumar, and
Vasumathi Narayanan

Chennai Mathematical Institute, Chennai, India
{abharat,madhavan,kumar,vasumathi}@cmi.ac.in

Abstract. Message sequence charts (MSCs) are commonly used to specify interactions between agents in communicating systems. Their visual nature makes them attractive for describing scenarios, but also leads to ambiguities that can result in incomplete or inconsistent descriptions.

One such problem is that of implied scenarios—a set of MSCs may imply new MSCs which are "locally consistent" with the given set. If local consistency is defined in terms of local projections of actions along each process, it is undecidable whether a set of MSCs is closed with respect to implied scenarios, even for regular MSC languages [3].

We introduce a new and natural notion of local consistency called *causal closure*, based on the causal view of a process—all the information it collects, directly or indirectly, through its actions. Our main result is that checking whether a set of MSCs is closed with respect to implied scenarios modulo causal closure is decidable for regular MSC languages.

1 Introduction

Message Sequence Charts (MSCs) [10] are an appealing visual formalism that are used in a number of software engineering notational frameworks such as SDL [15] and UML [4, 8]. A collection of MSCs is used to capture the scenarios that a designer might want the system to exhibit (or avoid).

A standard way to generate a set of MSCs is via Hierarchical (or High-level) Message Sequence Charts (HMSCs) [12]. Without losing expressiveness, we consider only a subclass of HMSCs called Message Sequence Graphs (MSGs). An MSG is a finite directed graph in which each node is labelled by an MSC. An MSG defines a collection of MSCs by concatenating the MSCs labelling each path from an initial vertex to a terminal vertex.

Though the visual nature of MSGs makes them attractive for describing scenarios, it also leads to ambiguities that can result in incomplete or inconsistent descriptions. An important issue is the presence of implied scenarios [2, 3]. An MSC M is (weakly) implied by an MSC language $\mathcal{L}$ if the local actions of each process p along M agree with its local actions along some good MSC $M_p \in \mathcal{L}$.

Implied scenarios are naturally tied to the question of *realizability*—when is an MSG specification implementable as a set of communicating finite-state machines? In a distributed model with local acceptance conditions, it is natural to expect the specification to be closed with respect to local projections. Thus,

R. Ramanujam and S. Sen (Eds.): FSTTCS 2005, LNCS 3821, pp. 335–347, 2005.

a language is said to be weakly realizable if all weakly implied scenarios are included in the language. Unfortunately, weak realizability is undecidable, even for regular MSC languages [3].

Weak implication presumes that the only information a process can maintain locally about an MSC is the sequence of actions that it participates in. However, we can augment the underlying message alphabet of an MSC by tagging auxiliary information to each message. Using this extra information, processes can maintain a bounded amount of information about the global state of the system [13]. With this, we arrive at a stronger notion of implied scenario that we call causal closure, based on the local view that each process has of an MSC from the information it receives, directly or indirectly, about the system.

Our main result is that causal closure preserves regularity for MSC languages, in contrast to the situation with weak closure. From this it follows that causal realizability is effectively checkable for regular MSC languages, both in the case of implementations with deadlocks and for *safe*, or deadlock-free, implementations.

Our result also allows us to interpret MSGs as incomplete specifications whose semantics is given in terms of the causal closure. Thus, we can retain relatively simple visual specifications without compromising on the completeness and consistency of verification.

The paper is organized as follows. We begin with some basic definitions regarding MSCs, message sequence graphs and message-passing automata. In the next section, we recall the results for weakly implied scenarios. In Section 4, we define the notion of causal closure and establish our main result, that causal closure preserves regularity for MSC languages. Finally, in Section 5, we examine the feasibility of using causal closure as a semantics for MSGs.

2   Preliminaries

2.1   Message Sequence Charts

Let $\mathcal{P} = \{p, q, r, \ldots\}$ be a finite set of processes (agents) that communicate with each other through messages via reliable FIFO channels using a finite set of message types $\mathcal{M}$. For $p \in \mathcal{P}$, let $\Sigma_p = \{p!q(m), p?q(m) \mid p \neq q \in \mathcal{P}, m \in \mathcal{M}\}$ be the set of communication actions in which p participates. The action $p!q(m)$ is read as p *sends the message m to q* and the action $p?q(m)$ is read as p *receives the message m from q*. We set $\Sigma_p = \bigcup_{p \in \mathcal{P}} \Sigma_p$. We also denote the set of *channels* by $Ch = \{(p, q) \mid p \neq q\}$. Whenever the set of processes $\mathcal{P}$ is clear from the context, we write Σ instead of $\Sigma_{\mathcal{P}}$, etc.

Labelled posets A Σ-labelled poset is a structure $M = (E, \leq, \lambda)$ where $(E, \leq)$ is a poset and $\lambda : E \to \Sigma$ is a labelling function. For $e \in E$, let $\downarrow e = \{e' \mid e' \leq e\}$. For $X \subseteq E$, $\downarrow X = \bigcup_{e \in X} \downarrow e$. We call $X \subseteq E$ a *prefix* of M if $X = \downarrow X$.

For $p \in \mathcal{P}$ and $a \in \Sigma$, we set $E_p = \{e \mid \lambda(e) \in \Sigma_p\}$ and $E_a = \{e \mid \lambda(e) = a\}$, respectively. For each $(p, q) \in Ch$, we define the relation $<_{pq}$ as follows:

$$e <_{pq} e' \iff \lambda(e) = p!q(m), \ \lambda(e') = q?p(m) \text{ and } |\!\downarrow e \cap E_{p!q(m)}| = |\!\downarrow e' \cap E_{q?p(m)}|$$

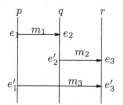

Fig. 1. An MSC over $\{p, q, r\}$.

The relation $e <_{pq} e'$ says that channels are FIFO with respect to each message—if $e <_{pq} e'$, the message m read by q at e' is the one sent by p at e.

Finally, for each $p \in \mathcal{P}$, we define the relation $\leq_{pp} = (E_p \times E_p) \cap \leq$, with $<_{pp}$ standing for the largest irreflexive subset of $\leq_{pp}$.

Definition 1. *An MSC (over $\mathcal{P}$) is a finite Σ-labelled poset $M = (E, \leq, \lambda)$ that satisfies the following conditions.*

1. *Each relation $\leq_{pp}$ is a linear order.*
2. *If $p \neq q$ then for each $m \in \mathcal{M}$, $|E_{p!q(m)}| = |E_{q?p(m)}|$.*
3. *If $e <_{pq} e'$, then $|{\downarrow}e \cap (\bigcup_{m \in \mathcal{M}} E_{p!q(m)})| = |{\downarrow}e' \cap (\bigcup_{m \in \mathcal{M}} E_{q?p(m)})|$.*
4. *The partial order $\leq$ is the reflexive, transitive closure of the relation $\bigcup_{p,q \in \mathcal{P}} <_{pq}$.*

The second condition ensures that every message sent along a channel is received. The third condition says that every channel is FIFO across all messages.

In diagrams, the events of an MSC are presented in *visual order*. The events of each process are arranged in a vertical line and messages are displayed as horizontal or downward-sloping directed edges. Fig. 1 shows an example with three processes $\{p, q, r\}$ and six events $\{e_1, e_1', e_2, e_2', e_3, e_3'\}$ corresponding to three messages—m_1 from p to q, m_2 from q to r and m_3 from p to r.

For an MSC $M = (E, \leq, \lambda)$, we let $\text{lin}(M) = \{\lambda(\pi) \mid \pi$ is a linearization of $(E, \leq)\}$. For instance, $p!q(m_1)\ q?p(m_1)\ q!r(m_2)\ p!r(m_3)\ r?q(m_2)\ r?p(m_3)$ is one linearization of the MSC in Fig. 1.

MSC languages An *MSC language* is a set of MSCs. We can also regard an MSC language $\mathcal{L}$ as a word language L over Σ consisting of all linearizations of the MSCs in $\mathcal{L}$. For an MSC language $\mathcal{L}$, we set $\text{lin}(\mathcal{L}) = \bigcup\{\text{lin}(M) \mid M \in \mathcal{L}\}$.

Definition 2. *An MSC language $\mathcal{L}$ is said to be a regular MSC language if the word language $\text{lin}(\mathcal{L})$ is a regular language over Σ.*

2.2   Message Sequence Graphs

Message sequence graphs (MSGs) are finite directed graphs with designated initial and terminal vertices. Each vertex in an MSG is labelled by an MSC. The edges represent (asynchronous) MSC concatenation, defined as follows.

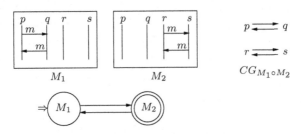

Fig. 2. A message sequence graph

Let $M_1 = (E_1, \leq^1, \lambda_1)$ and $M_2 = (E_2, \leq^2, \lambda_2)$ be a pair of MSCs such that E_1 and E_2 are disjoint. The *(asynchronous) concatenation* of M_1 and M_2 yields the MSC $M_1 \circ M_2 = (E, \leq, \lambda)$ where $E = E_1 \cup E_2$, $\lambda(e) = \lambda_i(e)$ if $e \in E_i$, $i \in \{1, 2\}$, and $\leq = (\bigcup_{p,q \in \mathcal{P}} <_{pq})^*$, where $<_{pp} = <_{pp}^1 \cup <_{pp}^2 \cup \{(e_1, e_2) \mid e_1 \in E_1, e_2 \in E_2, \lambda(e_1) \in \Sigma_p, \lambda(e_2) \in \Sigma_p\}$ and for $(p, q) \in Ch$, $<_{pq} = <_{pq}^1 \cup <_{pq}^2$.

A *Message Sequence Graph* is a structure $\mathcal{G} = (Q, \rightarrow, Q_{in}, F, \Phi)$, where Q is a finite and nonempty set of states, $\rightarrow \subseteq Q \times Q$, $Q_{in} \subseteq Q$ is a set of initial states, $F \subseteq Q$ is a set of final states and Φ labels each state with an MSC.

A *path* π through an MSG $\mathcal{G}$ is a sequence $q_0 \rightarrow q_1 \rightarrow \cdots \rightarrow q_n$ such that $(q_{i-1}, q_i) \in \rightarrow$ for $i \in \{1, 2, \ldots, n\}$. The MSC generated by π is $M(\pi) = M_0 \circ M_1 \circ M_2 \circ \cdots \circ M_n$, where $M_i = \Phi(q_i)$. A path $\pi = q_0 \rightarrow q_1 \rightarrow \cdots \rightarrow q_n$ is a *run* if $q_0 \in Q_{in}$ and $q_n \in F$. The language of MSCs accepted by $\mathcal{G}$ is $L(\mathcal{G}) = \{M(\pi) \mid \pi \text{ is a run through } \mathcal{G}\}$.

An example of an MSG is depicted in Fig. 2. The initial state is marked $\Rightarrow$ and the final state has a double line. The language $\mathcal{L}$ defined by this MSG is *not* regular: $\mathcal{L}$ projected to $\{p!q(m), r!s(m)\}^*$ consists of $\sigma \in \{p!q(m), r!s(m)\}^*$ such that $|\sigma\!\restriction_{p!q(m)}| = |\sigma\!\restriction_{r!s(m)}| \geq 1$, which is not a regular string language.

In general, it is undecidable whether an MSG describes a regular MSC language [9]. However, a sufficient condition for the MSC language of an MSG to be regular is that the MSG be *locally synchronized*.

Communication graph For an MSC $M = (E, \leq, \lambda)$, let CG_M, the *communication graph of M*, be the directed graph $(\mathcal{P}, \mapsto)$ where:

- $\mathcal{P}$ is the set of processes of the system.
- $(p, q) \in \mapsto$ iff there exists an $e \in E$ with $\lambda(e) = p!q(m)$.

M is said to be *com-connected* if CG_M consists of one nontrivial strongly connected component and isolated vertices.

Locally synchronized MSGs The MSG $\mathcal{G}$ is *locally synchronized* [14] (or *bounded* [1]) if for every loop $\pi = q \rightarrow q_1 \rightarrow \cdots \rightarrow q_n \rightarrow q$, the MSC $M(\pi)$ is com-connected. In Fig. 2, $CG_{M_1 \circ M_2}$ is not com-connected, so the MSG is not locally synchronized. We have the following result for MSGs [1].

Theorem 3. *If $\mathcal{G}$ is locally synchronized, $L(\mathcal{G})$ is a regular MSC language.*

2.3   Message-Passing Automata

Message-passing automata are natural recognizers for MSC languages.

Definition 4. *A* message-passing automaton (MPA) *over Σ is a structure $\mathcal{A} = (\{\mathcal{A}_p\}_{p \in \mathcal{P}}, \Delta, s_{in}, F)$ where:*

- *Δ is a finite alphabet of* auxiliary messages.
- *Each component $\mathcal{A}_p$ is of the form $(S_p, \rightarrow_p)$ where S_p is a finite set of p-local states and $\rightarrow_p \subseteq S_p \times \Sigma_p \times \Delta \times S_p$ is the p-local transition relation.*
- *$s_{in} \in \prod_{p \in \mathcal{P}} S_p$ is the global initial state.*
- *$F \subseteq \prod_{p \in \mathcal{P}} S_p$ is the set of global final states.*

The local transition relation $\rightarrow_p$ specifies how the process p sends and receives messages. The transition $(s, p!q(m), x, s')$ says that in state s, p can send the message m to q tagged with auxiliary information x and move to state s'. Similarly, the transition $(s, p?q(m), x, s')$ signifies that at state s, p can receive the message m from q tagged with information x and move to state s'.

A global state of $\mathcal{A}$ is an element of $\prod_{p \in \mathcal{P}} S_p$. For a global state s, s_p denotes the pth component of s. A *configuration* is a pair (s, χ) where s is a global state and $\chi : Ch \rightarrow (\mathcal{M} \times \Delta)^*$ is the *channel state* describing the message queue in each channel c. The *initial configuration* of $\mathcal{A}$ is $(s_{in}, \chi_\varepsilon)$ where $\chi_\varepsilon(c)$ is the empty string ε for every channel c. The set of *final configurations* of $\mathcal{A}$ is $F \times \{\chi_\varepsilon\}$.

The set of reachable configurations of $\mathcal{A}$, $Conf_\mathcal{A}$, is defined in the obvious way. The initial configuration $(s_{in}, \chi_\varepsilon)$ is in $Conf_\mathcal{A}$. If $(s, \chi) \in Conf_\mathcal{A}$ and $(s_p, p!q(m), x, s'_p) \in \rightarrow_p$, then there is a global move $(s, \chi) \stackrel{p!q(m)}{\Longrightarrow} (s', \chi')$ where for $r \neq p$, $s_r = s'_r$, for each $r \in \mathcal{P}$, $\chi'((p, q)) = \chi((p, q)) \cdot (m, x)$, and for $c \neq (p, q)$, $\chi'(c) = \chi(c)$. Similarly, if $(s, \chi) \in Conf_\mathcal{A}$ and $(s_p, p?q(m), x, s'_p) \in \rightarrow_p$, then there is a global move $(s, \chi) \stackrel{p?q(m)}{\Longrightarrow} (s', \chi')$ where for $r \neq p$, $s_r = s'_r$, for each $r \in \mathcal{P}$, $\chi((q, p)) = (m, x) \cdot \chi'((q, p))$, and for $c \neq (q, p)$, $\chi'(c) = \chi(c)$.

Let $prf(\sigma)$ denote the set of prefixes of a word $\sigma \in \Sigma^*$. A run of $\mathcal{A}$ over σ is a map $\rho : prf(\sigma) \rightarrow Conf_\mathcal{A}$ such that $\rho(\varepsilon) = (s_{in}, \chi_\varepsilon)$ and for each $\tau a \in prf(\sigma)$, $\rho(\tau) \stackrel{a}{\Longrightarrow} \rho(\tau a)$. The run ρ is *accepting* if $\rho(\sigma)$ is a final configuration.

We define $L(\mathcal{A}) = \{\sigma \mid \mathcal{A}$ has an accepting run over $\sigma\}$. $L(\mathcal{A})$ corresponds to the set of linearizations of an MSC language. To simplify notation, we write $L(\mathcal{A}) = \mathcal{L}$, where $\mathcal{L}$ is an MSC language, rather than $L(\mathcal{A}) = \lim(\mathcal{L})$.

For $B \in \mathbb{N}$, we say that a configuration (s, χ) of $\mathcal{A}$ is B-*bounded* if $|\chi(c)| \leq B$ for every channel $c \in Ch$. We say that $\mathcal{A}$ is a B-bounded automaton if every reachable configuration $(s, \chi) \in Conf_\mathcal{A}$ is B-bounded.

The MPA $\mathcal{A}$ in Fig. 3 has two components, p and q, with initial state (s_1, t_1) and only one final state, (s_2, t_3). A typical MSC in $L(\mathcal{A})$ is displayed at the right.

Deterministic Message-Passing Automata We say that $\mathcal{A}$ is *deterministic* if the transition relation $\rightarrow_p$ for each component satisfies the following conditions:

- $(s, p!q(m), x', s') \in \rightarrow_p$ and $(s, p!q(m), x'', s'') \in \rightarrow_p$ imply $x' = x''$, $s' = s''$.
- $(s, p?q(m), x, s') \in \rightarrow_p$ and $(s, p?q(m), x, s'') \in \rightarrow_p$ imply $s' = s''$.

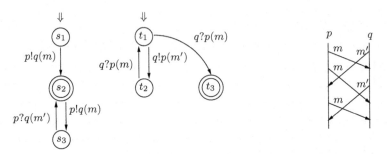

Fig. 3. A message-passing automaton.

For deterministic MPAs, the global state at the end of an MSC is independent of the choice of linearization.

Proposition 5. *Let $\mathcal{A}$ be a deterministic MPA, $M = (E, \leq, \lambda)$ an MSC and $E' \subseteq E$ a prefix of M. Let w and w' be linearizations of E' and let ρ and ρ' be the runs of $\mathcal{A}$ on w and w', respectively. Then, $\rho(w) = \rho(w')$.*

If $\mathcal{A}$ is deterministic, for any prefix E' of an MSC M, we can unambiguously write $\rho(E')$ to denote the unique run of $\mathcal{A}$ on E'. In particular, the unique run of $\mathcal{A}$ on M can be written as $\rho(M)$. The following theorem characterizes regular MSC languages in terms of message-passing automata [9].

Theorem 6. *An MSC language $\mathcal{L}$ is regular iff there is a deterministic B-bounded MPA $\mathcal{A}$ such that $L(\mathcal{A}) = \mathcal{L}$.*

3   Implied Scenarios: The Weak Case

When we use MSC languages to specify sets of scenarios, it is important to identify whether the specification is complete. A natural requirement is that the language be closed with respect to local views—for an MSC M, if every process locally believes that M belongs to the language $\mathcal{L}$, M should in fact be in $\mathcal{L}$.

One way to formalize closure with respect to local views is in terms of local projections [2, 3].

Definition 7.   – *Let $M = (E, \leq, \lambda)$ be an MSC and $p \in \mathcal{P}$ a process. The projection of M onto p, $M{\restriction}_p$, is the Σ-labelled partial order $(E_p, \leq_p, \lambda_p)$, where $\leq_p = \leq \cap (E_p \times E_p)$ is a total order and $\lambda_p = \lambda{\restriction}_{E_p}$.*
 – *An MSC M is said to be weakly implied by $\mathcal{L}$ if for every process $p \in \mathcal{P}$ there is an MSC $M_p \in \mathcal{L}$ such that $M_p{\restriction}_p = M{\restriction}_p$.*
 – *The weak closure of $\mathcal{L}$ is the collection of MSCs*
$$WeakCl(\mathcal{L}) \stackrel{\triangle}{=} \{M \mid M \text{ is weakly implied by } \mathcal{L}\}.$$

Unfortunately, the weak closure of a language can admit unbounded channels even when every channel in the original language is uniformly bounded. An example is shown in Fig. 4—all messages are labelled m and labels are omitted.

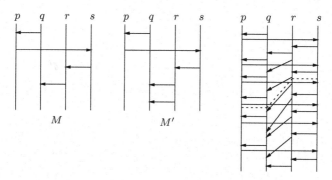

Fig. 4. A regular MSC language whose weak closure has unbounded buffers

Both M and M' are com-connected, so the MSC language consisting of arbitrary concatenations of M and M' is regular. However, for every natural number k, the weak closure of this language contains the MSC M_k in which the actions of p and q correspond to the sequence $M^{2k} \circ M'^k$ while the actions of r and s match the sequence $M'^k \circ M^{2k}$. In M_k, the buffer from p to s contains k messages at the global state where p and q make the transition from M to M' and r and s make the transition from M' to M. The figure shows the case $k = 2$. The dotted line marks the global cut where the channel from p to s has maximum capacity.

Implied scenarios have a close link to implementability, or *realizability*. An MSC language recognized by a communicating finite-state machine with a local acceptance condition must be closed with respect to local views. We say that an MSC language $\mathcal{L}$ is *weakly realizable* if $\mathcal{L} = WeakCl(\mathcal{L})$. We have the following negative result [3], which arises from the fact that the weak closure of a regular MSC language may have unbounded buffers.

Theorem 8. *Let $\mathcal{G}$ be a locally synchronized MSG. It is undecidable if $L(\mathcal{G})$ is weakly realizable.*

To overcome this negative result, a more restrictive notion of realizability is proposed in [2, 11]. An MSC language is said to be *safely realizable* if it admits a deadlock-free implementation—a *deadlock* is a global state from which no accepting state is reachable. In a safe implementation, it turns out that all implied scenarios must have bounded buffers, yielding the following result [3].

Theorem 9. *Let $\mathcal{G}$ be a locally synchronized MSG. It is decidable if $L(\mathcal{G})$ is safely realizable.*

4   Causal Closure for Regular MSC Languages

Weak closure assumes that the only information that a process can maintain locally about the current MSC is the sequence of actions that it participates in. However, as we have observed when characterizing regular MSC languages in terms of MPAs, we can tag each underlying message with extra data using which

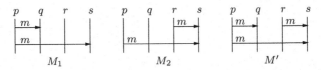

Fig. 5. Illustrating the difference between weak and causal closure

processes can maintain a bounded amount of information about the global state of the system. This leads us to a stronger notion of local view called causal view.

We begin by defining p-views. For an MSC $M = (E, \leq, \lambda)$ and $p \in \mathcal{P}$, let $\max_p(M)$ denote the maximum event from E_p in M—since all p events in M are linearly ordered by $\leq_{pp}$, $\max_p(M)$ is well-defined whenever $E_p \neq \emptyset$.

Definition 10. *Let $M = (E, \leq, \lambda)$ be an MSC and $p \in \mathcal{P}$ a process. The p-view of M, $\partial_p(M)$, is the Σ-labelled partial order $(E', \leq', \lambda')$ where $E' = \{e \mid e \leq \max_p(M)\}$, $\leq' = \leq \cap (E' \times E')$ and $\lambda' = \lambda \restriction_{E'}$. If $E_p = \emptyset$, $\partial_p(M) = (\emptyset, \emptyset, \emptyset)$.*

It is easy to observe that $\partial_p(M)$ is always a prefix of M. Causal realizability captures the intuition that each process p can keep track of the events in $\partial_p(M)$.

Definition 11. *Let $\mathcal{L}$ be an MSC language.*

- *An MSC M is said to be* causally implied *by $\mathcal{L}$ if for every process $p \in \mathcal{P}$ there is an MSC $M_p \in \mathcal{L}$ such that $\partial_p(M) = \partial_p(M_p)$.*
- *The* causal closure *of $\mathcal{L}$ is the collection of MSCs*

$$CausalCl(\mathcal{L}) \triangleq \{M \mid M \text{ is causally implied by } \mathcal{L}\}.$$

- *The language $\mathcal{L}$ is said to be* causally realizable *if $\mathcal{L} = CausalCl(\mathcal{L})$.*

An MSC language is causally realizable if each local process can recognize whether an MSC belongs to the language based purely on its causal view of the MSC. Observe that we always have $\mathcal{L} \subseteq CausalCl(\mathcal{L})$. Thus, $\mathcal{L}$ is not causally realizable iff there is an MSC $M \in CausalCl(\mathcal{L})$ such that $M \notin \mathcal{L}$.

We also have the inclusion $CausalCl(\mathcal{L}) \subseteq WeakCl(\mathcal{L})$. In general, $CausalCl(\mathcal{L}) \neq WeakCl(\mathcal{L})$—for instance, the implied MSCs in Fig. 4 are not in the causal closure of the language. Fig. 5 illustrates the difference between weak and causal closure. Here M' is in the weak closure of $\{M_1, M_2\}$ but not in the causal closure, because the causal view of process s includes information about whether or not p has sent a message to q.

Every regular MSC language $\mathcal{L}$ is recognized by a deterministic B-bounded MPA $\mathcal{A}_\mathcal{L}$. To construct an MPA for $CausalCl(\mathcal{L})$, we simulate $\mathcal{A}_\mathcal{L}$ and make each process go into a local accepting state if its current history is consistent with some accepting run of $\mathcal{A}_\mathcal{L}$. To achieve this, we make use of a bounded time-stamping protocol for B-bounded MPA, described in [13], by which each process can maintain the latest known state of every other process and channel. Using this protocol, we can derive the following result.

Theorem 12. *Let $\mathcal{A} = (\{\mathcal{A}_p\}_{p \in \mathcal{P}}, \Delta, s_{in}, F)$ be a deterministic B-bounded MPA. We can augment $\mathcal{A}$ with time-stamping information to get a deterministic B-bounded MPA $\mathcal{A}_\tau = (\{\mathcal{A}_p^\tau\}_{p \in \mathcal{P}}, \Delta^\tau, s_{in}^\tau, F^\tau)$ such that:*

- *For each process p, let $\mathcal{A}_p = (S_p, \rightarrow_p)$ and $\mathcal{A}_p^\tau = (S_p^\tau, \rightarrow_p^\tau)$ be the p components of $\mathcal{A}$ and $\mathcal{A}_\tau$, respectively. Then:*
  - S_p^τ *is of the form $S_p \times \Gamma$, where Γ contains a bounded amount of time-stamped data about all the processes and channels in the system.*
  - $\rightarrow_p^\tau$ *is such that for every MSC $M = (E, \leq, \lambda)$ and for every prefix E' of M, the unique run $\rho_\tau(E')$ of $\mathcal{A}_\tau$ on E' corresponds to the unique run $\rho(E')$ of $\mathcal{A}$ on E' in the sense that $\rho(E')$ matches the first component of $\rho_\tau(E')$.*
- $s_{in}^\tau = \prod_{p \in \mathcal{P}}(s_p, \gamma_p^0)$ *where $s_{in} = \prod_{p \in \mathcal{P}} s_p$ and $\prod_{p \in \mathcal{P}} \gamma_p^0$ is a fixed set of initial time-stamps.*
- $F^\tau = \left\{ \prod_{p \in \mathcal{P}}(s_p, \gamma_p) \mid \prod_{p \in \mathcal{P}} s_p \in F \right\}.$
- *Let $M = (E, \leq, \lambda)$ be an MSC. For each $p \in \mathcal{P}$, from the p-state (s_p, γ_p) assigned by $\rho_\tau(\partial_p(M))$ we can recover the configuration (s, χ) reached by $\mathcal{A}$ at the end of $\partial_p(M)$.*

When we augment a deterministic MPA $\mathcal{A}$ with time-stamping data to obtain $\mathcal{A}_\tau$, after any sequence of actions w, the local state of p in $\mathcal{A}_\tau$ allows us to recover the global configuration reached by $\mathcal{A}$ after processing all actions in the p-view of w. Thus, incrementally each process can keep track of the global configuration of the automaton $\mathcal{A}$ for the portion of the MSC that it has seen so far.

Theorem 13. *Let $\mathcal{L}$ be a regular MSC language. Then, its causal closure $CausalCl(\mathcal{L})$ is also a regular MSC language.*

Proof. Since $\mathcal{L}$ is a regular MSC language, by Theorem 6 there is a deterministic B-bounded MPA $\mathcal{A}$ such that $L(\mathcal{A}) = \mathcal{L}$.

We apply Theorem 12, to obtain a new automaton $\mathcal{A}_\tau$ that augments $\mathcal{A}$ with time-stamped information. For each process p, we define a subset of *local* final states $F_p^\tau \subseteq S_p^\tau$ as follows. A state (s_p, γ_p) belongs to F_p^τ iff, starting from the configuration (s, χ) of $\mathcal{A}$ that we recover from (s_p, γ_p), $\mathcal{A}$ can reach a configuration (f, χ_ε), where $f \in F$, without performing any actions involving process p. Notice that the sets F_p^τ are effectively computable.

In $\mathcal{A}_\tau$, we replace the set of global final states F^τ by the product of local final states $\prod_{p \in \mathcal{P}} F_p^\tau$ and call this modified MPA $\mathcal{A}_\tau^{Cl}$.

Claim $L(\mathcal{A}_\tau^{Cl}) = CausalCl(\mathcal{L})$.

Proof of claim ($\Leftarrow$) Suppose that $M \in CausalCl(\mathcal{L})$. Then, for every process p, there is an MSC $M_p \in \mathcal{L}$ such that $\partial_p(M) = \partial_p(M_p)$. Fix $p \in \mathcal{P}$ and let (s_p, γ_p) be the state of p in the run ρ_τ of $\mathcal{A}_\tau$ on $\partial_p(M)$. The configuration (s, χ) recorded in (s_p, γ_p) is the configuration reached by $\mathcal{A}$ at the end of $\partial_p(M) = \partial_p(M_p)$. Since $M_p \in \mathcal{L}$, $\mathcal{A}$ can reach a configuration (f, χ_ε), $f \in F$, starting from (s, χ), without performing any actions involving p. Thus, $(s_p, \gamma_p) \in F_p^\tau$. Since p does not make any moves outside $\partial_p(M)$, the state of p in $\rho_\tau(M)$ also belongs to F_p^τ. Since every process p reaches a state in F_p^τ at the end of M, $M \in L(\mathcal{A}_\tau^{Cl})$.

($\Rightarrow$) Suppose that $M \in L(\mathcal{A}_\tau^{Cl})$. Fix a process p, and let $(s_p, \gamma_p) \in F_p^\tau$ be the state of p in the accepting run $\rho_\tau(M)$ of $\mathcal{A}_\tau^{Cl}$ on M. Since p does not participate in any action outside $\partial_p(M)$, the state of p in $\rho_\tau(\partial_p(M))$ must also be (s_p, γ_p).

Let (s, χ) be the configuration of $\mathcal{A}$ that we recover from (s_p, γ_p)—by Theorem 12, (s, χ) is the configuration reached by $\mathcal{A}$ at the end of $\partial_p(M)$. From the definition of F_p^τ, we know that $\mathcal{A}$ can reach a configuration (f, χ_ε) from (s, χ), where $f \in F$, without perfoming any actions involving p. Let w_p be linearization of $\partial_p(M)$ and let w be the sequence of actions processed by $\mathcal{A}$ when going from the configuration (s, χ) to the configuration (f, χ_ε). All messages sent during w_p but not received in w_p must be received in w since all channels are empty in the final configuration. It is not difficult to see that $w_p w$ corresponds to the linearization of an MSC M_p. By construction, $\mathcal{A}$ has an accepting run on M_p, so $M_p \in \mathcal{L}$, with $\partial_p(M) = \partial_p(M_p)$.

Thus, whenever p reaches a state in F_p^τ after M, there is an MSC $M_p \in \mathcal{L}$ such that $\partial_p(M) = \partial_p(M_p)$. If M is in $L(\mathcal{A}_\tau)$, then we find such a witness M_p for every $p \in \mathcal{P}$, so $M \in CausalCl(\mathcal{L})$.   □

Since we can construct a B-bounded MPA recognizing $CausalCl(\mathcal{L})$ for any regular MSC language $\mathcal{L}$, we can effectively check whether $\mathcal{L} = CausalCl(\mathcal{L})$. Thus, we have the following.

Corollary 14. *For any regular MSC language $\mathcal{L}$ (respectively, locally synchronized MSG $\mathcal{G}$), it is decidable if $\mathcal{L}$ (respectively, $L(\mathcal{G})$) is causally realizable.*

Every regular MSC language is recognized by a deterministic MPA. Our construction for the causal closure preserves determinacy. We can check this deterministic MPA for deadlocked states, which immediately yields the following.

Corollary 15. *Let $\mathcal{L}$ be a regular MSC language. It is decidable if $\mathcal{L}$ is causally realizable and admits a deadlock-free implementation.*

Not all regular MSC languages are MSG-definable. A regular MSC language is MSG-definable precisely when it is *finitely generated*—that is, there is a finite set of MSCs $Atoms = \{M_1, M_2, \ldots, M_k\}$ such that every MSC in the language can be written out as a sequence $M_{i_1} \circ M_{i_2} \circ \cdots \circ M_{i_\ell}$ where each $M_{i_j} \in Atoms$ [9].

Proposition 16. *There exist regular MSC languages $\mathcal{L}$ such that $\mathcal{L}$ is MSG-definable but $CausalCl(\mathcal{L})$ is not.*

Proof. The MSG in Fig. 6 is locally synchronized and hence defines a regular MSC language. In the same figure is shown a family of MSCs $\{M_n\}_{n \in \mathbb{N}}$, each of which is causally implied by the language of this MSG. However, observe that each M_n is an *atomic* MSC that cannot be written as the asynchronous concatenation $M_1 \circ M_2$ of two nontrivial MSCs. Thus, the causal closure of this MSG language is regular but not MSG-definable.   □

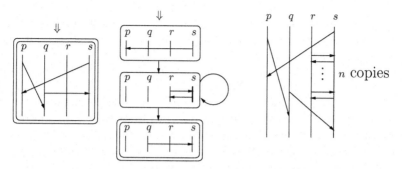

Fig. 6. MSG definability and causal closure

Moving to arbitrary MSGs takes us into the realm of undecidability. We have the following results, whose proofs are omitted.

Theorem 17. *For an arbitrary MSG $\mathcal{G}$, it is undecidable whether $L(\mathcal{G})$ is causally realizable. It is also undecidable whether the causal closure of $L(\mathcal{G})$ is a regular MSC language.*

5   MSGs as Partial Specifications

The realizability question for MSGs asks whether the set of scenarios represented by an MSG corresponds exactly to the language of a suitably defined MPA. To ensure that a specification is realizable, we need to impose severe restrictions on the structure of the MSG. This leads to an explosion in the complexity of the MSG and detracts significantly from the main motivation for using this notation, which is to have a transparent and visually appealing formalism to describe the behaviour of communicating systems.

An alternative is to view MSGs as partial specifications and interpret them modulo the closure conditions required by distributed implementations. This approach was studied in the context of Petri nets in [5]. For MPAs, we cannot use weak closure as the semantics of MSGs because weak closure does not preserve regularity. However, since the causal closure does preserve regularity, it is feasible to use this as a semantics for MSGs.

Under the exact interpretation, locally synchronized MSGs correspond to the class of finitely-generated regular MSC languages [9]. If we interpret MSGs modulo causal closure, an MSG can represent languages that are not finitely generated (like the example in Fig. 6). This increases the expressive power of the MSG notation. Another advantage is that we can sensibly analyze less complicated MSG specifications, making the notation more usable.

MSC languages can also be used to specify desirable properties of communicating systems. Two interpretations are possible: positive scenarios are those that the system must be able to exhibit, while negative scenarios should be avoided.

Suppose we use MSC languages both to specify the communicating system as well as to describe the scenarios that the system should exhibit. To verify that a set of positive scenarios P is included in the set of system behaviours S, it is important that both P and S are causally closed to avoid missing out some scenarios when checking this inclusion.

When model checking a negative property, it is again important to use the causal closure of the property. We have argued that reasonable implementations are causally closed. If the property is not causally closed, the implementation may exhibit an implied scenario that is forbidden, but this fact could go undetected.

In [7], it is shown that model checking of positive and negative scenarios under the exact interpretation can be performed for existentially bounded MSC languages—there is at least one linearization for each MSC in the language for which all channels are uniformly bounded. This is in contrast to regular MSC languages, where channels are universally bounded across *all* linearizations. The properties of existentially bounded MSC languages are further elaborated in [6]. Unfortunately, the causal closure of an existentially bounded MSC language need not be existentially bounded. It would be interesting to identify when the causal closure of an existentially bounded MSC language remains existentially bounded so that the results of [7] can be applied modulo causal closure.

References

[1] Alur, R., Yannakakis, M.: Model checking of message sequence charts. *Proc. CONCUR 1999)*, Springer Lecture Notes in Computer Science **1664** (1999) 114–129.

[2] Alur, R., Etessami, K., Yannakakis, M.: Inference of message sequence graphs. *IEEE Trans. Software Engg* **29(7)** (2003) 623–633.

[3] Alur, R., Etessami, K., Yannakakis, M.: Realizability and Verification of MSC Graphs. *Theor. Comput. Sci.* **331(1)** (2005) 97–114.

[4] Booch, G., Jacobson, I., Rumbaugh, J.: *Unified Modeling Language User Guide.* Addison-Wesley (1997).

[5] Caillaud, B., Darondeau, P., Hélouët, L. and Lesventes, G.: HMSCS as partial specifications . . . with PNs as completions. In *Modeling and Verification of Parallel Processes, 4th Summer School, MOVEP 2000*, Nantes, France (2000).

[6] Genest, B., Muscholl, A., and Kuske, D.: A Kleene Theorem for a Class of Communicating Automata with Effective Algorithms. *Proc DLT 2004*, Springer Lecture Notes in Computer Science **3340** (2004) 30–48.

[7] Genest, B., Muscholl, A., Seidl, H. and Zeitoun, M.: Infinite-State High-Level MSCs: Model-Checking and Realizability. *Proc ICALP 2002*, Springer Lecture Notes in Computer Science **2380** (2002) 657–668.

[8] Harel, D., Gery, E.: Executable object modeling with statecharts. *IEEE Computer*, July 1997 (1997) 31–42.

[9] Henriksen, J.G., Mukund, M., Narayan Kumar, K., Sohoni, M., and Thiagarajan, P.S.: A Theory of Regular MSC Languages. *Inf. Comp.*, **202(1)** (2005) 1–38.

[10] ITU-TS Recommendation Z.120: *Message Sequence Chart (MSC)*. ITU-TS, Geneva (1997).

[11] Lohrey, M.: Safe Realizability of High-Level Message Sequence Charts. *Proc CONCUR 2002*, Springer Lecture Notes in Computer Science **2421** (2002) 177–192.

[12] Mauw, S., Reniers, M. A.: High-level message sequence charts, *Proc SDL'97*, Elsevier (1997) 291–306.

[13] Mukund, M., Narayan Kumar, K., Sohoni, M.: Bounded time-stamping in message-passing systems. *Theor. Comput. Sci.*, **290(1)** (2003) 221–239.

[14] Muscholl, A., Peled, D.: Message sequence graphs and decision problems on Mazurkiewicz traces. *Proc. MFCS 1999)*, Springer Lecture Notes in Computer Science **1672** (1999) 81–91.

[15] Rudolph, E., Graubmann, P., Grabowski, J.: Tutorial on message sequence charts. In *Computer Networks and ISDN Systems — SDL and MSC* **28** (1996).

Reachability Analysis of Multithreaded Software with Asynchronous Communication

Ahmed Bouajjani[1], Javier Esparza[2], Stefan Schwoon[2], and Jan Strejček[2,*]

[1] LIAFA, University of Paris 7, abou@liafa.jussieu.fr
[2] Institute for Formal Methods in Computer Science, University of Stuttgart
{esparza,schwoosn,strejcek}@informatik.uni-stuttgart.de

Abstract. We introduce *asynchronous dynamic pushdown networks* (ADPN), a new model for multithreaded programs in which pushdown systems communicate via shared memory. ADPN generalizes both CPS (concurrent pushdown systems) [7] and DPN (dynamic pushdown networks) [5]. We show that ADPN exhibit several advantages as a program model. Since the reachability problem for ADPN is undecidable even in the case without dynamic creation of processes, we address the *bounded* reachability problem [7], which considers only those computation sequences where the (index of the) thread accessing the shared memory is changed at most a fixed given number of times. We provide efficient algorithms for both forward and backward reachability analysis. The algorithms are based on automata techniques for symbolic representation of sets of configurations.

1 Introduction

In recent years a number of formalisms have been proposed for modelling and analyzing procedural multithreaded programs. A well-known result states that, if recursion is allowed, checking assertions for these programs is undecidable, even if all variables are boolean (see for instance [8]).

Due to this undecidability result, approximate analysis techniques have been considered. While [3, 4] deal with overapproximations of the set of reachable states, [7] presents the first nontrivial technique to compute underapproximations. In this paper we build on the ideas of [7], which we now describe in some more detail. Qadeer and Rehof introduce *concurrent pushdown systems* (CPS) as a model of multithreaded programs. A CPS is a set of stacks with a global finite control; at each step, the CPS reads the current control state and the topmost symbol of (exactly) one of the stacks, can change the control state and replace the stack symbol by a word, like in a pushdown automaton. A *dynamic* CPS (or DCPS) can also create a new stack as the result of a transition. Each stack of a CPS corresponds to a thread. Communication between threads is modelled through the common set of global control states. A *context* is defined as a computation in which all transitions act *on the same stack*. In [7] it is shown how to compute, given a fixed number k, the set of states that can be reached by k-*bounded* computations, i.e., by computations consisting of the concatenation of at most k contexts. Obviously, this set constitutes an underapproximation of the set of all reachable states.

---

* The co-author has been partially supported by GAČR, grant No. 201/03/1161.

R. Ramanujam and S. Sen (Eds.): FSTTCS 2005, LNCS 3821, pp. 348–359, 2005.
© Springer-Verlag Berlin Heidelberg 2005

In this paper, we show that with the help of a refined model it is possible to generalize and improve the results of [7] in a number of ways. We propose a generalization of CPS called *asynchronous pushdown networks* (APN); we also introduce the dynamic version of the model, called ADPN. Loosely speaking, the stacks of an APN have an additional set of local control states, different from the common global finite control; transitions are either local (dependent only on the local control), or global (depending on both the global and local control states). We also propose a new, more liberal, definition of context: a context is now a computation in which all *global* transitions act on the same stack, possibly interspersed with local transitions acting on arbitrary stacks.

In the first part of the paper (Section 2) we observe that, while the APN and CPS formalisms are equally expressive, APN can model programs more succinctly than CPS. In the dynamic case we show that, while ADPN can naturally model value passing from a called procedure to its caller, DCPS cannot.

In the second part of the paper (Section 3), we study the forward and backward k-bounded reachability problem for APN. Comparing [7], we propose a more general and asymptotically faster algorithm for forward reachability. We introduce a backward reachability algorithm as well.

In the third part of the paper (Sections 4 and 5), we consider the k-reachability problem for the ADPN model. We show that, due to the more liberal notion of context, the set of configurations of an ADPN reachable by k-bounded computations may be non-regular, contrary to the case of DCPSs. Using results of [5], we show that the set is always context-free and provide an algorithm to compute a context-free grammar that generates it. We then observe that the set of backwards k-bounded reachable configurations is regular, and, relying on results from [6], provide an efficient algorithm to compute it.

2   The Model

2.1   Asynchronous Dynamic Pushdown Networks

An *asynchronous dynamic pushdown network (ADPN)* is a tuple $\mathcal{N} = (G, P, \Gamma, \Delta_l, \Delta_g)$, where G is a finite set of *global states*, P is a finite set of *local states*, Γ is a finite *stack alphabet*, and

- Δ_l is a finite set of *local rules* of the form $p\gamma \hookrightarrow p_1 w_1$ or $p\gamma \hookrightarrow p_1 w_1 \rhd p_2 w_2$, where $p, p_1, p_2 \in P$, $\gamma \in \Gamma$, and $w_1, w_2 \in \Gamma^*$.
- Δ_g is a finite set of *global rules* of the form $(g, p\gamma) \hookrightarrow (g', p_1 w_1)$ or $(g, p\gamma) \hookrightarrow (g', p_1 w_1) \rhd p_2 w_2$, where $g, g' \in G$, $p, p_1, p_2 \in P$, $\gamma \in \Gamma$, and $w_1, w_2 \in \Gamma^*$.

The rules with a suffix of the form $\rhd p_2 w_2$ are called *dynamic*. A *configuration* of an ADPN is a pair $(g, \alpha) \in G \times (P\Gamma^*)^+$ of a global state g and a word $\alpha = p_1 w_1 p_2 w_2 \ldots p_n w_n$, where each subword $p_i w_i \in P\Gamma^*$ represents a configuration of (a pushdown corresponding to) one *component*. A word $p_i w_i$ is called *component configuration*. The set of all configurations is denoted by C.

The transition relation $\to \subseteq C \times C$ is defined as follows: $(g, u) \to (g', v)$ if there is

- $p\gamma \hookrightarrow p_1 w_1$ in Δ_l such that $u = u_1 p\gamma u_2$, $v = u_1 p_1 w_1 u_2$, and $g = g'$, or
- $p\gamma \hookrightarrow p_1 w_1 \rhd p_2 w_2$ in Δ_l such that $u = u_1 p\gamma u_2$, $v = u_1 p_2 w_2 p_1 w_1 u_2$, and $g = g'$, or

- $(g, p\gamma) \hookrightarrow (g', p_1 w_1)$ in Δ_g such that $u = u_1 p\gamma u_2$ and $v = u_1 p_1 w_1 u_2$, or
- $(g, p\gamma) \hookrightarrow (g', p_1 w_1) \triangleright p_2 w_2$ in Δ_g such that $u = u_1 p\gamma u_2$ and $v = u_1 p_2 w_2 p_1 w_1 u_2$,

where $u_1 \in (P\Gamma^*)^*$ and $u_2 \in \Gamma^*(P\Gamma^*)^*$. We say that the transition has been performed by the component whose local state changes from p to p_1. The transitions generated by global and local rules are called *global* and *local transitions* respectively. A dynamic rule creates a new component starting in component configuration $p_2 w_2$.

2.2   Subclasses of ADPNs

ADPNs are an extension of several other models. An ADPN with only global states and global rules is a *dynamic concurrent pushdown systems* (DCPS). Formally, a DCPS is an ADPN $(G, P, \Gamma, \Delta_l, \Delta_g)$ satisfying $|P| = 1$ and $\Delta_l = \emptyset$. The DCPS model is studied in [7]. The subclasses of ADPN and DCPS without dynamic rules are called APN and CPS, respectively. Notice that in an APN or CPS all configurations reachable from an initial configuration have the same number of components. Finally, both APNs and CPSs are extensions of pushdown systems (PDS). Formally, a PDS is a CPS in which the initial configuration only has one component.

An ADPN without global variables or global rules is called a DPN. DPNs have been introduced and studied in [5]. Notice that in a DPN there is no communication between different threads.

2.3   Reachability and Bounded Reachability

Given an ADPN $\mathcal{N}$ and a set $S \subseteq C$, we denote by $post^*_{\mathcal{N}}(S)$ and $pre^*_{\mathcal{N}}(S)$ the sets of forward and backward reachable configurations from S. The *forward* and *backward reachability problem* consists of, given sets I and F of initial and final configurations, determining if $post^*_{\mathcal{N}}(I) \cap F = \emptyset$ or $pre^*_{\mathcal{N}}(F) \cap I = \emptyset$, respectively. Both problems are undecidable, even when I and F are singletons. This is a consequence of the fact that APNs (even without dynamic rules) are Turing powerful. For instance, it is straightforward to encode a 2-counter Minsky machine into an APN.

Following [7], we define a notion of bounded reachability. A *context* is a transition sequence where all global transitions are performed by the same component. We say that this component *controls* the context. Notice that within a context local transitions can be performed by arbitrary components. For $k \geq 1$, a sequence of transitions is *k-bounded* if it is a concatenation of at most k contexts. We denote by $post^*_{k, \mathcal{N}}(S)$ the set of all configurations reachable from S by k-bounded sequences. By analogy, $pre^*_{k, \mathcal{N}}(S)$ denotes the set of all configurations from which a configuration from S is reachable by a k-bounded sequence. We talk about *forward* and *backward k-bounded reachability*, respectively. Further, by $post^*_{0, \mathcal{N}}(S)$ and $pre^*_{0, \mathcal{N}}(S)$ we denote the sets of configurations that are forward and backward reachable only by local transitions, respectively.

2.4   APN as Program Model

The following example illustrates how to model programs with APNs (for simplicity, we omit thread creation here). We consider a program with procedures $m, n, lock, unlock$

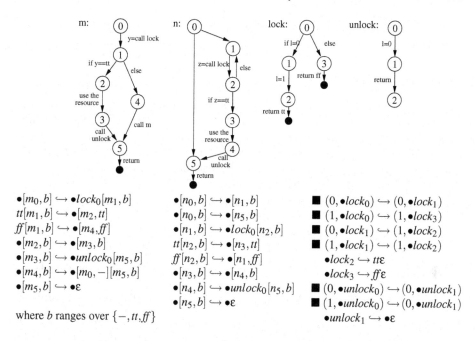

Fig. 1. A program with four procedures and two threads.

described by the flow graphs of Figure 1; y and z are local variables of the procedures m and n, respectively, and can take the values undefined ($-$), true (tt), or false (ff). The procedures m and n call procedures *lock* and *unlock* to get exclusive access to a shared resource. The *lock* action is nonblocking; it returns true if it succeeds to lock the resource, false otherwise. The variable l occurring in the procedures *lock* and *unlock* is global and ranges over $\{0,1\}$. The system consists of two concurrent threads, one starting with the execution of m, the other with the execution of n.

We model this program by the APN $\mathcal{N} = (G, P, \Gamma, \Delta_l, \Delta_g)$ as follows: Global states model the value of the global variable l, i.e. $G = \{0,1\}$. Local states are used to pass a potential return value from a callee back to the caller: The callee stores the value in the local state of the thread, from where it is read by the caller.[3] As a procedure cannot return the undefined value ($-$), we set $P = \{tt, ff, \bullet\}$, where tt and ff are used to return the corresponding values, and $\bullet$ is used elsewhere. The set Γ of stack symbols contains all program locations (p_l denotes the symbol for location l of procedure p), together with the actual values of the local variables for procedures m, n. The local and global rules corresponding to each procedure are given directly in the figure; global rules (marked with ■) correspond to transitions dealing with the global variable l.

The techniques developed in the next sections can show that the program does not satisfy its basic specification: exclusive access to the resource. More precisely, they

---

[3] In general, local states can be also used to hold values of variables that are global to a thread (if such a variable type is supported in the modeled system).

show that the program can reach a configuration of the form $(0, \bullet[m_2, b]w_1 \bullet [n3, b']w_2)$ from the initial configuration $(0, \bullet[m_0, -] \bullet [n_0, -])$, and in fact within 3 contexts.

2.5   A(D)PN Versus (D)CPS

As we have seen, local states are used to model value-passing from a callee to its caller. In the CPS model there is no notion of local state of a thread, and so value passing must be simulated through a global variable. Clearly, this amounts to simulating an APN by a CPS. We show that this is possible, but involves a blow-up in size. Moreover, the translation has to fix the number n of components that the CPS can work upon. Let $\mathcal{N} = (G, P, \Gamma, \Delta_l, \Delta_g)$ be an APN. We construct a CPS $\mathcal{N}' = (G', \Gamma', \Delta'_g)$ such that the configuration graphs of $\mathcal{N}$ and $\mathcal{N}'$, defined in the usual way, are isomorphic. We take $G' = G \times P^n$, $\Gamma' = \Gamma \times \{1, \ldots, n\}$, and add to Δ'_g rules

$$((g_1, p_1, \ldots, p_{i-1}, p, p_{i+1}, \ldots, p_n), q(\gamma, i)) \hookrightarrow ((g_2, p_1, \ldots, p_{i-1}, p', p_{i+1}, \ldots, p_n), q[w, i])$$

for every $(g_1, p\gamma) \hookrightarrow (g_2, p'w)$ in Δ_g, $1 \le i \le n$, $p_1, \ldots, p_{i-1}, p_{i+1}, \ldots, p_n \in P$, and rules

$$((g, p_1, \ldots, p_{i-1}, p, p_{i+1}, \ldots, p_n), q(\gamma, i)) \hookrightarrow ((g, p_1, \ldots, p_{i-1}, p', p_{i+1}, \ldots, p_n), q[w, i])$$

for every $p\gamma \hookrightarrow p'w$ in Δ_l, $g \in G$, $1 \le i \le n$, and $p_1, \ldots, p_{i-1}, p_{i+1}, \ldots, p_n \in P$. Here, q is the only local state of $\mathcal{N}'$. Further, for $w = w_1 w_2 \ldots w_m$, $[w, i]$ stands for $(w_1, i)(w_2, i) \ldots (w_m, i)$. Observe that the size of $\mathcal{N}'$ may be larger than that of $\mathcal{N}$ by a factor of $n \cdot |G| \cdot |P|^{n-1}$.

Observe also that the transformation APN $\rightarrow$ CPS cannot be naturally extended to a transformation ADPN $\rightarrow$ DCPS. The straightforward idea of taking $G \times P^*$ as set of global states does not work, and not only because this set is infinite, but also because in order to simulate a change of local state a stack has to know its position in the current state $(g, p_1 p_2 \ldots p_n)$, which now changes as the computation proceeds because of thread creation. Currently we do not know if an ADPN can be translated into an equivalent DCPS, and we do not see any elegant way of modelling value-passing and thread creation in the DCPS formalism.

We finish with an advantage of our more liberal notion of context. In a k-bounded computation, at most k components can execute global transitions, and this has the following consequence when comparing ADPN and DCPS: While a k-bounded computation of a DCPS can create an arbitrary number of components, at most k of them can execute a transition at all. For ADPN the constraint is weaker: arbitrarily many processes can execute transitions, but at most k of them can execute global transitions. So an algorithm for exploring k-bounded computations of ADPN searches 'deeper' as the same algorithm for DCPS.

3   Reachability Analysis for APN

We now consider k-bounded reachability for the APN model, i.e. the restriction of ADPN to non-dynamic rules. Let us fix an APN $\mathcal{N} = (G, P, \Gamma, \Delta_l, \Delta_g)$ and $k \in \mathbb{N}$ for the rest of this section. We investigate the case where the initial or final configurations are given by so-called aggregates:

Definition 1. *An* aggregate *is a tuple* $M = (g, C_1, \ldots, C_n)$, *where* $g \in G$, $n \geq 1$ *is the number of concurrent processes, and* $C_1, \ldots, C_n \subseteq P \times \Gamma^*$ *are* regular *sets of component configurations.* M *is used to denote the set* $\{g\} \times (C_1. \cdots .C_n)$, *where . is the concatenation of the component configurations.*

We now fix an aggregate $M = (g, C_1, \ldots, C_n)$ for the rest of the section, and we will present solutions for computing $post^*_{k, \mathcal{N}}(M)$ as well as $pre^*_{k, \mathcal{N}}(M)$.

For the CPS model, k-bounded reachability was considered in [7]. The algorithms presented in this section follow the same general idea as the solutions in [7] (but applied to APN). Moreover, the new solution has these benefits:

- Our algorithm avoids repeating partial computations of reachable component configurations. Even if we consider only CPSs, the algorithm runs asymptotically faster than the one presented in [7].
- The APN model distinguishes between local and global states, and our algorithm exploits this difference. Therefore, it is faster than a translation of a given APN to CPS (see Section 2.5) followed by the application of an algorithm for CPS.
- Some details in our algorithm are different from [7] and would lead to time and memory savings in an implementation. These are discussed in Section 3.3.
- We provide algorithms for both forward and backwards reachability, whereas [7] only covered forward reachability. The two algorithms are fairly similar – in fact we will present them as one algorithm – but their complexity analysis is a little more involved. The algorithm makes use of a procedure called CLOSURE, which stands for the $post^*$ or pre^* procedure on PDSs [6] in case of forward and backwards reachability, respectively.

3.1 Reordering of Transitions

Our algorithms are based on the following observation: Let c be a configuration reachable from $M = (g, C_1, \ldots, C_n)$ by a k-bounded computation, and let σ be this computation. Then the transitions in σ can be rearranged to another k-bounded computation σ' that also leads from M to c. Moreover, σ' can be partitioned into $n + k$ phases, where in each phase all rules are applied to the same component:

- In the i-th phase, $1 \leq i \leq n$, component i executes all its *local* steps in σ up to, but not including, its first global step (or all steps, if it never executes a global rule).
- In the $n + i$-th phase, $1 \leq i \leq k$, the component controlling the i-th context executes the first *global* step of the i-th context in σ, followed by all its *global* and *local* steps up to, but not including, the first global step in the next context controlled by the same component (all its remaining steps, if it does not control any more contexts).

Notice that this rearrangement only requires to swap the ordering of local transitions of some component with local or global transitions of other components; but as the application of a local rule does not depend on the global state, these reorderings do not alter the final configuration of the computation.

3.2 Reduction to PDS

We now show that all $n + k$ phases reduce to reachability problems on PDS. In the following, $\text{CLOSURE}_{\mathcal{P}}(C)$ denotes the set $post_{\mathcal{P}}^*(C)$ or $pre_{\mathcal{P}}^*(C)$, depending on whether forward or backward reachability is of interest.

– Let $\mathcal{P}_{\mathcal{N}}^1 := (P, \Gamma, \Delta_l)$, i.e. $\mathcal{P}_{\mathcal{N}}^1$ simulates the local moves of $\mathcal{N}$. Thus, the results of the first n phases are obtained by $\text{CLOSURE}_{\mathcal{P}_{\mathcal{N}}^1}(C_i)$ for $i = 1, \ldots, n$.

– For the remaining phases, we create a PDS in which the global and local states are merged. Let $\mathcal{P}_{\mathcal{N}}^2 = (G \times P, \Gamma, \Delta')$, where Δ' contains all $(g_1, p_1)\gamma \hookrightarrow (g_2, p_2)w$ such that either $(g_1, p_1\gamma) \hookrightarrow (g_2, p_2w)$ in Δ_g, or $p_1\gamma \hookrightarrow p_2w$ in Δ_l and $g_1 = g_2$. Thus, $\mathcal{P}_{\mathcal{N}}^2$ computes the possible operations of one component in a single context. More precisely, we define $\text{LIFT}(g, C) := \{((g, p), w) \mid (p, w) \in C\}$ and $\text{RESTRICT}(C, g) := \{(p, w) \mid ((g, p), w) \in C\}$. Now, if a component starts a context in global state g and with component configurations C, the reachable configurations within this context that end in global state g' are $\text{RESTRICT}(\text{CLOSURE}_{\mathcal{P}_{\mathcal{N}}^2}(\text{LIFT}(g, C)), g')$.

Recall that the initial sets $C_1, \ldots, C_n$ are regular and can be represented by finite automata. Regular sets are closed under the CLOSURE operation, and algorithms for these have been provided in [6]. It is easy to see that LIFT and RESTRICT can also be implemented as operations on finite automata.

3.3 The Algorithm

Figure 2 shows our algorithm, which directly implements the ideas outlined before. Line 2 computes the local phases $1, \ldots, n$ of the computations, whereas the lines from line 3 onwards implement phases $n + 1, \ldots, n + k$. Essentially, the algorithm explores a 'tree' of depth k, where each node corresponds to an aggregate, and its successors are the aggregates reachable by executing one context. Each iteration of the while loop picks an aggregate and computes its successors. As hinted at before, the operations on the sets of component configurations are carried out by operations on finite automata. The algorithm uses the following data structures:

todo is a list with information on those aggregates whose successors still need to be computed. The first part of each entry in *todo* indicates the depth of the aggregate in the tree, the second is the index of the component that has controlled the previous context; the rest is the aggregate itself.

aut is a hash table. An entry $aut[g, B]$ remembers the result of applying the closure on $\text{LIFT}(g, B)$. The motivation for this table is that, for a pair (g, B), the computation of $\text{CLOSURE}_{\mathcal{P}_{\mathcal{N}}^2}(\text{LIFT}(g, B))$ may be required in multiple branches of the 'tree'; therefore we would like to reuse the result. Notice that actually hashing over (an automaton accepting) the language B could be very time consuming. In order to achieve the desired time-saving effect, it suffices to approximate this effect, e.g. by giving a unique identifier to each automaton that arises from an application of CLOSURE.

reachable collects the aggregates that represent reachable configurations.

Input: An APN $\mathcal{N}$, an aggregate $M = (g, C_1, \ldots, C_n)$, and $k \in \mathbb{N}$
Output: The set $post^*_{k,\mathcal{N}}(M)$ (or $pre^*_{k,\mathcal{N}}(M)$) given by union of the aggregates in *reachable*.

```
1   reachable ← ∅;
2   todo ← {(0,0,g,CLOSURE_{P¹_N}(C₁),...,CLOSURE_{P¹_N}(Cₙ))};
3   while todo ≠ ∅ do
4       pop (level,last,g,B₁,...,Bₙ) with minimal level from todo;
5       if level = k then
6           reachable ← reachable ∪ {(g,B₁,...,Bₙ)};
7       else
8           for all i = 1,...,n such that i ≠ last do
9               if aut[g,Bᵢ] undefined then
10                  aut[g,Bᵢ] ← CLOSURE_{P²_N}(LIFT(g,Bᵢ));
11              for all g' ∈ G do
12                  todo←todo∪{(level+1,i,g',B₁,...,Bᵢ₋₁,RESTRICT(aut[g,Bᵢ],g'),Bᵢ₊₁,...,Bₙ)};
```

Fig. 2. Algorithm computing k-bounded reachability on APN.

The basic idea of exploring a tree of depth k is similar to the CPS algorithm in [7]. However, the algorithm in Figure 2 also contains some improvements:

– When adding a new item to *todo*, the algorithm reuses all previous local automata except for B_i (unlike [7], where all n automata are changed in every step). This makes the algorithm more memory-efficient, because the automata that have not changed from one context to another can be shared.
– Using *aut* allows to reuse results of computations made in other parts of the tree.
– A trivial improvement is that no component is allowed to execute two contexts in a row (the second context would yield nothing new due to closure properties).
– Another simple, but important optimization (not shown) is that line 11 should only be executed for those global states g' such that $aut[g, B_i]$ accepts at least one configuration of the form $\langle g', w \rangle$ for some $w \in \Gamma^*$.

3.4 Complexity Analysis

We now state the complexity of our algorithm for both directions. The proofs can be found in [2]. Let $A_1, \ldots, A_n$ be automata representing $C_1, \ldots, C_n$.

Theorem 1. *Let $M = (g, C_1, \ldots, C_n)$ be an aggregate of an APN $\mathcal{N} = (G, P, \Gamma, \Delta_l, \Delta_g)$ and let $k \in \mathbb{N}$ be a number. Then there exist aggregates $M_0, \ldots, M_m$ such that $post^*_{k,\mathcal{N}}(M)$ (or $pre^*_{k,\mathcal{N}}(M)$, resp.) has the form $M_0 \cup M_1 \cup \ldots \cup M_m$ and all these aggregates are effectively computable. Moreover,*

(a) *computing $post^*_{k,\mathcal{N}}(M)$ takes $O(n^k \cdot |G|^k + n \cdot |G|^k \cdot |P| \cdot (d + |\Delta| \cdot k \cdot q + |\Delta|^2 \cdot k^2))$ time, where $|\Delta| = |G| \cdot |\Delta_l| + |\Delta_g|$ and q, d are the largest numbers of non-initial states and transitions leading out of non-initial states in $A_1, \ldots, A_n$, respectively;*

(b) $pre^*_{k,\mathcal{N}}(M)$ *can be computed in time* $O(n^k \cdot |G|^k + n \cdot |G|^{k-1} \cdot (q + k \cdot |P| \cdot |G|)^2 \cdot |\Delta|)$
where $|\Delta| = |G| \cdot |\Delta_l| + |\Delta_g|$ *and* q *is the maximal number of states in* $A_1, \ldots, A_n$.

Note that the complexity given for k-bounded forward CPS reachability in [7] has (among others) the factors k^3 and $|G|^{k+5}$. Seeing as APNs are an extension of CPSs, Theorem 1 provides a better upper bound for k-bounded reachability even on CPSs.

4 Forward Reachability Analysis of ADPN

Even in the DPN case, the $post^*$ image of a regular set of configurations is not always regular [5]. However, it can be shown that this image is always context-free, and [5] provides a construction that, given a DPN and an initial configuration $p_0\gamma_0$, computes a context-free grammar G such that $L(G) = post^*(p_0\gamma_0)$.

In this paper we show how to compute $post^*_{k,\mathcal{N}}(c_0)$ for an ADPN $\mathcal{N}$, a configuration $c_0 = (g_0, p_0\gamma_0)$ and an arbitrary $k \geq 0$. (The algorithm can be extended from one configuration c_0 to a regular set of configurations.) The key of the result is a construction which, given a sequence $\sigma = g_0 \ldots g_{k-1}$ of global states of $\mathcal{N}$, constructs a DPN $\mathcal{N}_\sigma$, a configuration c, a regular set S, and a regular transduction π (as we shall see, S, c, and π are independent from σ) such that $post^*_{k,\mathcal{N}}(c_0) = \pi(S \cap \bigcup_{\sigma \in G^k} post^*_{\mathcal{N}_\sigma}(c))$. By the result of [5], the sets $post^*_{\mathcal{N}_\sigma}(c)$ are effectively context-free, and so $post^*_{k,\mathcal{N}}(c_0)$ is effectively context-free as well.

Informally, given $\sigma = g_0 \ldots g_{k-1}$ the DPN $\mathcal{N}_\sigma$ is able to simulate those execution sequences of $\mathcal{N}$ in which, for every $1 \leq i < k$, the i-th context-switch occurs at a configuration of $\mathcal{N}$ with global state g_i. During the simulation, each pushdown component of $\mathcal{N}_\sigma$ maintains a guess about the index of the current context. (Notice that, due to the lack of communication between components of a DPN, a component cannot know how many context-switches have occurred). The component can at any point increase its guess, but cannot decrease it. A wrong guess leads to an unfaithful simulation (see below how to 'filter them away'). Moreover, the component can at any point decide to control the current context (more precisely, the context it guesses is the current one). In such a case, the current global state is mantained as a part of the corresponding local state. Since components cannot communicate, this may lead to an unfaithful simulation, where zero, two or more different components claim to control the same context.

The problem of the unfaithful simulations is solved with the help of the set S and the homomorphism π. We define $\mathcal{N}_\sigma$ so that if a component completes the simulation of a context it claims to have controlled, then it must create an inactive 'marker' (a new component that can do nothing) witnessing this claim. At the end of the simulation we can inspect the inactive markers, and check if every context was indeed controlled by one and at most one component. If this is so, the simulation is faithful, otherwise it is unfaithful. The set S is the set of configurations where every marker appears exactly once, and so intersection with S 'filters out' all the configurations reached by faithful simulations. The transduction π is used to 'clean up' the configurations so obtained by disposing of the markers and other auxiliary symbols used along the simulation, and to move the global state (stored in the local state of the process controlling the last context) to the front of the configuration.

For details of the construction of $\mathcal{N}_G$ we refer to [2]. The construction gives rise to the following theorem:

Theorem 2. *Let $\mathcal{N} = (G, P, \Gamma, \Delta_l, \Delta_g)$ be an ADPN and let $c_0 = (g_0, p_0 \gamma_0)$ be a configuration of $\mathcal{N}$. The set $post^*_{k,\mathcal{N}}(c_0)$ is context-free. A context-free grammar generating it can be constructed in time $O(k^3 \cdot |G|^{k+3} \cdot |P|^3 \cdot (|\Delta_l| + |\Delta_g|))$*

5   Backward Reachability Analysis of ADPN

We consider here the problem of constructing the pre^*_k images of a regular set of configurations, under the assumption of at most k contexts. We provide a reduction of this problem to the problem of computing pre^* images in the case of DPNs (or in other words to the problem of computing pre^*_1 images), and we provide and efficient algorithm for solving the latter problem. This algorithm improves the complexity of the basic saturation-based procedure proposed in [5] for symbolic backward reachability analysis of DPN.

5.1   Regular Symbolic Representations

Our algorithms use a class of automata-based representations for regular sets of configurations (mass configurations) which have been introduced in [5] for DPN analysis. These representations are finite-state automata in a *special form* defined below.

Let $\mathcal{N} = (G, P, \Gamma, \Delta_l, \Delta_g)$ be an ADPN. Then, a finite-state automaton $A = (Q, \Sigma, \delta, q_0, F)$ is called $\mathcal{N}$-*automaton* if and only if it satisfies the following conditions:

- $\Sigma = P \cup \Gamma$,
- Q can be partitioned into three mutually disjoint subsets Q_0, Q_1, Q_2 such that for all $q \in Q_0, p \in P$ there exists a unique state $q_p \in Q_1$,
- transition relation δ can be partitioned into three disjoint relations $\delta_0, \delta_1, \delta_2$ such that $\delta_0 = \{(q, p, q_p) \mid q \in Q_0, p \in P, q_p \in Q_1\}$, $\delta_1 \subseteq (Q_1 \cup Q_2) \times \Gamma \times Q_2$, and $\delta_2 \subseteq (Q_1 \cup Q_2) \times \{\varepsilon\} \times Q_0$,
- $q_0 \in Q_0$, and $F \subseteq Q_1 \cup Q_2$.

An automaton in the above special form is schematically depicted in Figure 3. Notice that $\mathcal{N}$-automata recognize languages which are regular subsets of $(P\Gamma^*)^+$. It is easy to see that, conversely, every finite-state automaton over the alphabet $\Sigma = P \cup \Gamma$ recognizing a language included in $(P\Gamma^*)^+$ can be transformed into a language equivalent $\mathcal{N}$-automaton. Notice also that this definition depends obviously on the model

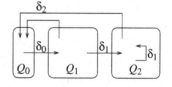

Fig. 3. An automaton in special form.

$\mathcal{N}$ under consideration, but only on his set of control states P and his stack alphabet Γ and not on the fact whether global variables and rules are considered.

Following the common habit, we write $q \xrightarrow{a}_\delta q'$ meaning $(q, a, q') \in \delta$. We also extend this notation to finite words in standard way: for every $q, q' \in Q, a \in \Sigma$ and $u \in \Sigma^*$ we set $q \xrightarrow{\varepsilon}_\delta q$ and $q \xrightarrow{au}_\delta q'$ iff there is $q'' \in Q$ such that $q \xrightarrow{a}_\delta q''$ and $q'' \xrightarrow{u}_\delta q'$.

5.2   Computing pre^* Images for DPN

Let $\mathcal{N} = (P, \Gamma, \Delta)$ be a DPN and $A = (Q, \Sigma, \delta, q_0, F)$ be an $\mathcal{N}$-automaton. We describe a simple procedure proposed in [5] for computing a finite-state automaton A_{pre^*} satisfying $L(A_{pre^*}) = pre^*_{\mathcal{N}}(L(A))$. The automaton is defined as $A_{pre^*} = (Q, \Sigma, \delta', q_0, F)$, where δ' is the smallest relation $\delta' \supseteq \delta$ satisfying the following two conditions.

- If $p\gamma \hookrightarrow p_1 w_1 \in \Delta$ and $q \xrightarrow{p_1 w_1}_{\delta'} q'$ for $q, q' \in Q$ then $(q_p, \gamma, q') \in \delta'$.
- If $p\gamma \hookrightarrow p_1 w_1 \rhd p_2 w_2 \in \Delta$ and $q \xrightarrow{p_2 w_2 p_1 w_1}_{\delta'} q'$ for $q, q' \in Q$ then $(q_p, \gamma, q') \in \delta'$.

The construction of the automaton A_{pre^*} terminates since it corresponds to adding iteratively new transitions to the original automaton A without modifying the number of its states. The construction can be proved to be sound and complete [5].

It can be seen that this construction is polynomial but a naive implementation of it can be of a prohibitive cost, similarly to the basic algorithm of [1] for pushdown systems with respect to its efficient implementation of [6]. Following the principles used in [6], we define an efficient algorithm implementing the saturation-based procedure above (see [2]). We have the following result:

Theorem 3. *Given a DPN $\mathcal{N} = (P, \Gamma, \Delta)$ and an $\mathcal{N}$-automaton $A = (Q, \Sigma, \delta, q_0, F)$, it is possible to construct in $O(|Q|^3 \cdot |\Delta|)$ time and $O(|Q|^2 \cdot |\Delta|)$ space an automaton A_{pre^*} such that $L(A_{pre^*}) = pre^*(L(A))$.*

5.3   Computing pre_k^* Images for ADPN

Let $\mathcal{N} = (G, P, \Gamma, \Delta_l, \Delta_g)$ be an ADPN, and let $k \geq 1$. Roughly speaking, the computation of a $pre^*_{k,\mathcal{N}}$ image is decomposed into k successive steps of $pre^*_{1,\mathcal{N}}$ image computation, each of them consisting basically in a pre^* image computation in a (suitably defined) DPN. To define in more details the construction, we need some notations and definitions. A *mass configuration* is a pair $M = (g, A)$. It represents the set of configurations (g, u) where $u \in L(A)$. Given a mass configuration $M = (g, A)$, let $local(M)$ denote the automaton A. We generalize this notation to finite collections of mass configurations by taking the union of their $\mathcal{N}$-automata.

Then, given a mass configuration (g, A), the computation of $pre^*_{k,\mathcal{N}}(g, A)$ is performed as follows: first we compute the set $pre^*_{1,\mathcal{N}}(g, A)$ corresponding to all predecessors of (g, A) without context switch. For every global state g', let (g', A') be the set of all configurations in $pre^*_{1,\mathcal{N}}(g, A)$ having g' as global state. Then, the second step constists in computing the $pre^*_{1,\mathcal{N}}$ images of all the pairs (g', A'), for all global states g', and so on. More precisely, given an $\mathcal{N}$-automaton A and a sequence of global states $\sigma \in G^+$, we define inductively the set $\text{REACH}_\sigma(A)$:

$$\text{REACH}_g(A) = pre^*_{1,\mathcal{N}}(g, A)$$
$$\text{REACH}_{g_1 g_2 \sigma'}(A) = \text{REACH}_{g_2 \sigma'}(local(\text{REACH}_{g_1}(A) \cap (g_2, (P\Gamma^*)^+)))$$

where $g, g_1, g_2 \in G$ and $\sigma' \in G^*$. Then, the following fact holds.

Lemma 1. *Given an ADPN $\mathcal{N}$, a global state g, an $\mathcal{N}$-automaton A, and an integer $k \geq 1$, we have $pre^*_{k,\mathcal{N}}(g,A) = \bigcup_{g_1,\ldots,g_{k-1} \in G^{k-1}} \text{REACH}_{gg_1\cdots g_{k-1}}(A)$.*

Therefore, we only have to show how to construct $pre^*_{1,\mathcal{N}}$ images. For that, we can actually use our algorithm of Theorem 3 which allows to perform backward analysis for DPN. Given an $\mathcal{N}$-automaton A and a global state g, we proceed as follows:

- we construct an automaton $\widehat{A}$ such that for every word u of component configurations which is accepted by A, the automaton $\widehat{A}$ accepts all words arising from u by embedding the global state g into a local state of one of the components. More precisely, $\widehat{A}$ accepts a word w if and only if there is a word $u_1 p u_2 \in L(A)$ such that $u_1 \in (P\Gamma^*)^*$, $p \in P$, $u_2 \in \Gamma^*(P\Gamma^*)^*$, and $w = u_1(g,p)u_2$.
- we transform the sets Δ_l and Δ_g into a set of *local rules* Δ which are applicable to local states (with an embedded global state). The set of obtained rules has a size $O(|G| \cdot |\Delta_l| + |\Delta_g|)$.
- we use the algorithm for DPN of Theorem 3 to build an automaton $\widehat{A}_{pre^*}$.
- then,

$$pre^*_{1,\mathcal{N}}(g,A) = \bigcup_{g' \in G} (g', \{w \in (P\Gamma^*)^+ \ : \ w = upu' \text{ and } \exists u(g',p)u' \in L(\widehat{A}_{pre^*})\}).$$

An automata-based representation for this set can be straightforwardly obtained from $\widehat{A}_{pre^*}$ using intersection and projection. Then we have the following (see [2]).

Theorem 4. *Given an ADPN $\mathcal{N} = (G,P,\Gamma,\Delta_l,\Delta_g)$, $k \geq 1$, $g \in G$, and an $\mathcal{N}$-automaton $A = (Q,\Sigma,\delta,q_0,F)$, it is possible to construct a finite-state automata-based representation of the set $pre^*_{k,\mathcal{N}}(g,A)$ in $O(k^4 \cdot |Q|^3 \cdot (|G|^k \cdot |\Delta_l| + |G|^{k-1} \cdot |\Delta_g|))$ time.*

References

1. A. Bouajjani, J. Esparza, and O. Maler. Reachability analysis of pushdown automata: Application to model-checking. In *Proceedings of CONCUR'97*, LNCS 1243, pages 135–150, 1997.
2. A. Bouajjani, J. Esparza, S. Schwoon, and J. Strejček. Reachability analysis of multithreaded software with asynchronous communication. Technical Report 2005/06, Universität Stuttgart, 2005. A full version of this paper.
3. A. Bouajjani, J. Esparza, and T. Touili. A generic approach to the static analysis of concurrent programs with procedures. In *Proceedings of POPL'2003*, pages 62–73. ACM Press, 2003.
4. A. Bouajjani, J. Esparza, and T. Touili. Reachability analysis of synchronized PA-systems. In *Proceedings of Infinity 2004*, 2004. To appear.
5. A. Bouajjani, M. Müller-Olm, and T. Touili. Regular symbolic analysis of dynamic networks of pushdown processes. In *Proceedings of CONCUR 2005*, LNCS 3653, pages 473–487, 2005.
6. J. Esparza, D. Hansel, P. Rossmanith, and S. Schwoon. Efficient algorithms for model checking pushdown systems. In *Proceedings of CAV'2000*, LNCS 1855, pages 232–247, 2000.
7. S. Qadeer and J. Rehof. Context-bounded model checking of concurrent software. In *Proceedings of TACAS'2005*, LNCS 3440, pages 93–107, 2005.
8. G. Ramalingam. Context-sensitive synchronisation-sensitive analysis is undecidable. *ACM Transactions on Programming Languages and Systems*, 22:416–430, 2000.

Probabilistic Analysis for a Multiple Depot Vehicle Routing Problem

Andreas Baltz[1], Devdatt Dubhashi[2], Libertad Tansini[2], Anand Srivastav[1], and Sören Werth[1]

[1] Institut für Informatik und Praktische Mathematik, Christian-Albrechts-Universität zu Kiel, Christian-Albrechts-Platz 4, 241098 Kiel, Germany
{aba,asr,swe}@numerik.uni-kiel.de
[2] Department of Computing Science,
Chalmers University, SE 412 96 Göteborg, Sweden
{dubhashi,libertad}@cs.chalmers.se

Abstract. We give the first probabilistic analysis of the Multiple Depot Vehicle Routing Problem(MDVRP) where we are given k depots and n customers in $[0,1]^2$. The optimization problem is to find a collection of disjoint TSP tours with minimum total length such that all customers are served and each tour contains exactly one depot(not all depots have to be used). In the random setting the depots as well as the customers are given by independently and uniformly distributed random variables in $[0,1]^2$. We show that the asymptotic tour length is $\alpha_k \sqrt{n}$ for some constant α_k depending on the number of depots. If $k = o(n)$, α_k is the constant $\alpha(TSP)$ of the TSP problem. Beardwood, Halton, and Hammersley(1959) showed $0.62 \leq \alpha(TSP) \leq 0.93$. For $k = \lambda n$, $\lambda > 0$, one expects that with increasing λ the MDVRP tour length decreases. We prove that this is true exhibiting lower and upper bounds on α_k, which decay as fast as $(1 + \lambda)^{-\frac{1}{2}}$.
A heuristics which first clusters customers around the nearest depot and then does the TSP routing is shown to find an optimal tour almost surely.

1 Introduction

An important and practically relevant generalization of the classical Traveling Salesman Problem (TSP) is the Multiple Depot Vehicle Routing Problem (MD-VRP). Given are several depots and a set of customers who must be served from these depots, the problem is to both (a) assign the customers to a depot and (b) find optimal service tours. It is known that the MDVRP is NP-hard [10]. On the other hand, there is PTAS for the MDVRP [16] in the line of Arora's [1] PTAS for the TSP. Since it is inefficient for real world applications, one usually resorts to heuristics to solve the problem. There is a wide body of literature describing the application of various heuristics, tested with various benchmark instances [5,4,13,7]. We are unaware of any rigorous theoretical results complementing these experimental works. In particular, to our best knowledge there is no probabilistic analysis for the multiple depot vehicle routing problem in the literature.

R. Ramanujam and S. Sen (Eds.): FSTTCS 2005, LNCS 3821, pp. 360–371, 2005.

We study the MDVRP problem on random instances, where the depots as well as the customers are given by independently and uniformly distributed random variables in $[0,1]^2$.

Let $k, n \in \mathbb{N}$ and $D = \{D_1, \ldots, D_k\}$ resp. $P = \{P_1, \ldots, P_n\}$ be sets of points in $[0,1]^2$. The D_i's are called depots and the P_i's points. A multiple depot vehicle routing tour is a set of disjoint cycles such that all points are covered and each cycle contains exactly one depot, but not all depots have to be used. The goal is to find a tour of minimum length with respect to the Euclidean metric. The length of an optimal MDVRP tour is denoted by $L(D, P)$.

Related Work: In the celebrated paper of Beardwood, Halton, and Hammersley [3] it was shown that for n independently and identically distributed random variables $P_1, \ldots, P_n$ in $[0,1]^2$, the optimal TSP tour length $L_{TSP}(P_1, \ldots, P_n)$ is asymptotically $\sqrt{n}$, more precisely there is a constant $\alpha(TSP) > 0$ such that $\lim_{n \to \infty} L_{TSP}(P_1, \ldots, P_n)/\sqrt{n} = \alpha(TSP)$ almost surely. This motivated a large body of research on the probabilistic analysis of Euclidean optimization problems like minimum spanning tree, minimum perfect matching, etc. Today, there is a good understanding of the general structure that underlies the asymptotic behavior of these problems. A good overview on the history and main developments in this area is given in the books of Yukich [17] and Steele [15]. In the MDVRP the numbers of points and depots have to be considered both, so this is a first step to extend the typical average case analysis of Euclidean functionals to two-sets problems.

Karp, resp. Karp and Steele [8,9] showed that the stochastic version of an NP-hard optimization problem allows a tight approximation in polynomial time almost surely by introducing a polynomial time partitioning heuristics which for every $\varepsilon > 0$, constructs a TSP tour of length at most $(1 + \varepsilon)L_{TSP}(P_1, \ldots, P_n)$ for n independently and identically distributed random points in $[0,1]^2$. Later, it was shown that the heuristics can be extended to other classic Euclidean optimization problems, see [17].

Our results: We recall the notion of complete convergence of random variables: let $(Y_n)_{n \geq 1}$ be a sequence of random variables and let Y be a random variable in some probability space $(\Omega, \mathcal{F}, \mathbb{P})$. We say $Y_n \to Y$ completely, written $\lim_{n \to \infty} Y_n \to Y$ c.c., if $\sum_{n=1}^{\infty} \mathbb{P}[|Y_n - Y| > \varepsilon] < \infty$ for all $\varepsilon > 0$. One can show that complete convergence implies almost surely convergence.

In Section 2 we analyze the asymptotic behavior of the optimal MDVRP tour length for random depot and point sets in $[0,1]^2$. Intuitively, we can expect the k tours to take up (roughly) each cell of a $\sqrt{k}$ by $\sqrt{k}$ grid. And then we can simply use the TSP result and use the fact that (roughly) there would be n/k points in each tour and totalized over all the tours we get k times $\sqrt{n/k}/\sqrt{k}$, that is $\sqrt{n}$. We distinguish two cases:

(a) If $k = \lambda n$ for a constant $\lambda > 0$, then $L(D, P)/\sqrt{n} \to \alpha_k$ for $n \to \infty$ c.c., where α_k is a positive constant. In this case the MDVRP shows the $\sqrt{n}$ asymptotics of the TSP, but the constant α_k depends on the number of depots. We show that $\frac{2\alpha(TSP)}{\sqrt{1+\lambda}} \geq \alpha_k \geq \frac{1}{2\sqrt{1+\lambda}}\left(1 + \frac{1}{4(1+\lambda)}\right)$ and thus exhibit the quantitative decay of the MDVRP tour length compared to the TSP tour length as λ increases.

(b) If $k = o(n)$, $L(D,P)/\sqrt{n} \to \alpha(TSP)$ for $n \to \infty$ c.c. Thus, for "small" numbers of depots, the MDVRP behaves asymptotically exactly like the TSP.
In Section 3 we present an analysis of an algorithm which first assigns points to the nearest depot (clustering phase) and then computes a TSP tour for each cluster by adapting Karp's partitioning heuristics [8] for the routing phase of the MDVR problem. We prove that this 2-phase algorithm computes a solution with cost at most $(1 + o(1))OPT$ for random instances (as defined above) for $k = o(n)$ almost surely.

This result is the first rigorous analysis of a heuristics for the MDVRP in a natural probabilistic setting. The analysis involves a clustering lemma of independent interest which is proved using results on the complexities of the Voronoi diagram of points distributed uniformly and independently at random in the unit square.

2   Probabilistic Analysis

Our main result considers the asymptotic behavior of $L(D,P)$:

Theorem 1. *Let $D = \{D_1, \ldots, D_k\}$ and $P = \{P_1, \ldots, P_n\}$ be depots and points in $[0,1]^2$ given by independent uniformly distributed random variables. The optimal length $L(D,P)$ of an MDVRP tour through D and P satisfies*

(i) $\lim_{n \to \infty} \frac{L(D,P)}{\sqrt{n}} = \alpha_k$ *c.c., if $k = \lambda n$ for a constant $\lambda > 0$,*

(ii) $\lim_{n \to \infty} \frac{L(D,P)}{\sqrt{n}} = \alpha(TSP)$ *c.c., if $k = o(n)$,*

where $\alpha(TSP)$ is the constant for the TSP and α_k is a positive constant.

Upper and lower bounds for α_k are presented in Theorem 3.

2.1   The Case $k = \lambda n$ for a Constant $\lambda > 0$

In contrast to the TSP tour length, the MDVRP tour length is not monotone if we add depots. Such a lack of monotonicity has challenged the development of the theory of Euclidean boundary functionals which approximate the original functional, and are accessible for probabilistic analysis. For a detailed description of this approach we refer to Yukich [17] and Redmond and Yukich [12].

First of all, we list some general properties of a length function F that is defined for an Euclidean optimization problem on two finite subsets of $\mathbb{R}^2$. Let F be a function $F : \mathcal{S} \times \mathcal{S} \to \mathbb{R}^+$, where $\mathcal{S}$ is the set of finite subsets of $\mathbb{R}^2$. F fulfills the *translation invariance* property if for all $y \in \mathbb{R}^2$ and finite subsets $D, P \subset \mathbb{R}^2$,

$$F(D,P) = F(D + y, P + y),$$

the *homogeneity*, if for all $\alpha > 0$ finite subsets $D, P \subset \mathbb{R}^2$,

$$F(\alpha D, \alpha P) = \alpha F(D,P),$$

and *normalization* property, if $F(\emptyset, \emptyset) = 0$. F is called a *Euclidean functional* if it satisfies these properties.

F is called *subadditive* if for all rectangles $R \subset \mathbb{R}^2$, all finite subsets $D, P \subset R$ and all partitions of R into R_1 and R_2,

$$F(D, P) \leq F(D \cap R_1, P \cap R_1) + F(D \cap R_2, P \cap R_2) + C(R),$$

with a constant C depending only on the diameter of R.

A major difference between the MDVRP functional L and most classic functionals is that L is not subadditive, a counterexample is given in Figure 1. Normally,

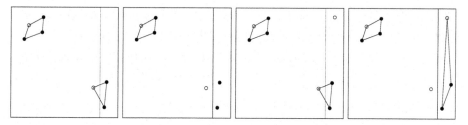

Fig. 1. The first two figures show that L is not subadditive, and the remaining that L is not superadditive.

the subadditivity is used to express the global graph length as a sum of local components. This can also be done via superadditivity, a functional F is called *superadditive*, if for all rectangles $R \subset \mathbb{R}^2$, all finite subsets $D, P \subset R$ and all partitions of R into R_1 and R_2

$$F(D, P) \geq F(D \cap R_1, P \cap R_1) + F(D \cap R_2, P \cap R_2).$$

The MDVRP functional is not superadditive, see Figure 1. The boundary modification introduced by Redmond and Yukich [12] helps to overcome the lack of sub- and superadditivity. The boundary modification of the total edge length function of the MDVRP is the total edge length function of the least expensive depot tour, where the cost of traveling along the boundary is zero, and the paths connected to the boundary do not have to contain a depot. The formal definition for the boundary functional of the MDVRP follows: for all rectangles $R \subset \mathbb{R}^2$, finite point sets $D, P \subset R$ and points a, b on the boundary of R let $L(\emptyset, P, \{a, b\})$ denote the length of the shortest path through all points of P with endpoints a and b. The *boundary functional* L_B is defined by

$$L_B(D, P) := \min \left\{ L(D, P), \ \inf \left\{ L(D, P_1) + \sum_{i>1} L(\emptyset, P_i, \{a_i, b_i\}) \right\} \right\},$$

where the infimum ranges over all sequences $(a_i, b_i)_{i \geq 1}$ of points on the boundary of R and all partitions $(P_i)_{i \geq 1}$ of P.

Fig. 2. An optimal MDVRP tour and an optimal boundary MDVRP tour.

We have the following lemma for the MDVRP boundary functional, the proof is straightforward and will appear in the full paper.

Lemma 1. *Let L be the functional of the MDVRP and L_B the boundary functional. L_B is superadditive and for $D \neq \emptyset$ and a constant $C > 0$*

$$|L(D, P) - L_B(D, P)| \leq C.$$

In addition to superadditivity we need another property of the boundary functional, the smoothness. A Euclidean functional F is *smooth* if there is a constant $C > 0$ such that for all finite sets $D_1, D_2, P_1, P_2 \subset \mathbb{R}^2$,

$$|F(D_1 \cup D_2, P_1 \cup P_2) - F(D_1, P_1)| \leq C\sqrt{|D_2| + |P_2|}.$$

So the smoothness describes the variation of F when points and depots are added and deleted.

Lemma 2. *The boundary functional L_B of the MDVRP is smooth.*

Proof. Let $D_1, D_2, P_1, P_2 \subset [0,1]^2$ be sets containing depots respectively points. To see that $L_B(D_1 \cup D_2, P_1 \cup P_2) - L_B(D_1, P_1) \leq C\sqrt{|D_2| + |P_2|}$ consider an optimal solution for D_1 and P_1 and add a traveling salesman tour through all elements of D_2 and P_2. This is a feasible solution for the boundary MDVRP if $D_2 \neq \emptyset$. If $D_2 = \emptyset$, we transform the cycle into a path starting and ending at the border of $[0,1]^2$. The tour/path together with the graph associated to $L_B(D_1, P_1)$ yields a feasible solution for the problem on $D_1 \cup D_2$ and $P_1 \cup P_2$ of length at most $L_B(D_1, P_1) + C\sqrt{|D_2| + |P_2|}$.

Once we show $L_B(D_1, P_1) \leq L_B(D_1 \cup D_2, P_1 \cup P_2) + C\sqrt{|D_2| + |P_2|}$ the smoothness of L_B follows. We start with a graph G associated to $L_B(D_1 \cup D_2, P_1 \cup P_2)$, see Figure 3, and remove all elements of D_2 and P_2. Let B denote the set of points where the graph meets the boundary of $[0,1]^2$, we add B to the graph, see Figure 4. In the following, we do not consider unmodified components in G. The deletion of D_2 and P_2 generates at most $2(|D_2| + |P_2|)$ connected components, since the elements of D_2 and P_2 are either in a path connected to the border or they are in a closed cycle.

The resulting components are either paths or isolated vertices. So the total number of vertices with degree 1 is even, and the overall number of vertices with degree 1 and 0 is at most $4(|D_2| + |P_2|)$. We add a traveling salesman tour through the points of degree one and zero and a minimal perfect matching of the points with degree one, see Figure 5. The length of tour is at most $C\sqrt{|D_2| + |P_2|}$ with a constant C, the same holds for the matching.

Adding the TSP tour and the matching yields a connected graph. Every vertex has an even degree so that there exists a Eulerian tour. We shortcut the Eulerian tour into a traveling salesman tour. If the tour contains a depot, it is a feasible cycle, otherwise we delete an edge and connect the remaining path to the border. Together with the unmodified cycles in G we get a feasible solution for D_1 and P_1, Figure 6, so it follows that $L_B(D_1, P_1) \leq L_B(D_1 \cup D_2, P_1 \cup P_2) + C\sqrt{|D_2| + |P_2|}$.

□

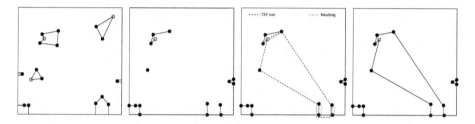

Fig. 3. The bound- **Fig. 4.** P_2 and D_2 **Fig. 5.** Tour and **Fig. 6.** The result-
ary MDVRP tour.   deleted, B added.   matching added.   ing tour.

Since L_B is a Euclidean, superadditve and smooth functional, we can show the asymptotic behavior of the mean of L_B via typical methods, refer [17].

Lemma 3. *Let* $k = \lambda n$, $\lambda > 0$ *constant. Then there exists a constant* $\alpha_k > 0$ *such that*

$$\lim_{n \to \infty} \frac{\mathbb{E}\left[L_B(D_1 \ldots, D_{\lambda n}, P_1 \ldots, P_n)\right]}{\sqrt{n}} = \alpha_k.$$

Proof. Set $\Phi(k, n) := \mathbb{E}\left[L_B(D_1, \ldots, D_k, P_1, \ldots, P_n)\right]$. The number of depots resp. points that fall into a given subcube of $[0, 1]^2$ of volume m^{-2} is given by a binomial random variable $B(k, m^{-2})$ resp. $B(n, m^{-2})$. We divide $[0, 1]^2$ into m^2 identical cubes R_i of volume m^{-2}. With the superadditivity and homogeneity of L_B we have

$$\Phi(k, n) \geq \sum_{i=1}^{m^2} \Phi(B(k, m^{-2}) \cap R_i, B(n, m^{-2}) \cap R_i)$$

$$\geq \frac{1}{m} \sum_{i=1}^{m^2} \Phi(B(k, m^{-2}) \cap [0, 1]^2, B(n, m^{-2}) \cap [0, 1]^2).$$

Via the smoothness of L_B and Jensen's inequality for concave functions one can show that

$$\Phi(k, n) \geq m\Phi(km^{-2}, nm^{-2}) - Ck^{\frac{1}{4}}m^{\frac{1}{2}} - Cn^{\frac{1}{4}}m^{\frac{1}{2}}.$$

Dividing by $k^{\frac{1}{4}}n^{\frac{1}{4}}$ and replacing n by nm^2 and k by km^2, we get for the case $k = \lambda n$

$$\frac{\Phi(\lambda nm^2, nm^2)}{(nm^2)^{\frac{1}{2}}} \geq \frac{\Phi(\lambda n, n)}{n^{\frac{1}{2}}} - \frac{C\lambda^{\frac{1}{4}}}{n^{\frac{1}{4}}} - \frac{C}{n^{\frac{1}{4}}}.$$

Set $\alpha := \alpha(L_B) := \limsup_{n\to\infty} \frac{\Phi(\lambda n, n)}{n^{\frac{1}{2}}}$. The smoothness of L_B guarantees $\alpha < \infty$. For all $\varepsilon > 0$, choose n_0 such that for all $n \geq n_0$ we have $\frac{C}{n^{\frac{1}{4}}} < \varepsilon$, $\frac{C\lambda^{\frac{1}{4}}}{n^{\frac{1}{4}}} < \varepsilon$ and $\frac{\Phi(\lambda n_0, n_0)}{n_0^{\frac{1}{2}}} > \alpha - \varepsilon$. Thus, for all $m \geq 1$ it follows that $\frac{\Phi(\lambda n_0 m^2, n_0 m^2)}{(n_0 m^2)^{\frac{1}{2}}} > \alpha - 3\varepsilon$.

Now we use an interpolation argument and the smoothness of the functional. For an arbitrary integer t determine the unique integer m such that $n_0 m^2 < t \leq n_0(m+1)^2$. Then holds $|n_0 m^2 - t| \leq C' n_0 m$ and by smoothness we get

$$\frac{\Phi(\lambda t, t)}{t^{\frac{1}{2}}} \geq \frac{\Phi(\lambda n_0 m^2, n_0 m^2)}{(n_0(m+1)^2)^{\frac{1}{2}}} - \frac{C'(n_0 m)^{\frac{1}{2}}}{(n_0(m+1)^2)^{\frac{1}{2}}} - \frac{C'(\lambda n_0 m)^{\frac{1}{2}}}{(n_0(m+1)^2)^{\frac{1}{2}}}$$

$$\geq (\alpha - 3\varepsilon)\left(\frac{m}{m+1}\right) - \frac{C' m^{\frac{1}{2}}}{m+1} - \frac{C'(\lambda m)^{\frac{1}{2}}}{m+1}.$$

Since the last two terms go to zero as m goes to infinity, $\liminf_{t\to\infty} \frac{\Phi(\lambda t, t)}{t^{\frac{1}{2}}} \geq \alpha - 3\varepsilon$. For ε tending to zero we see that the $\liminf$ and the $\limsup$ of the sequence $\frac{\Phi(\lambda t, t)}{t^{\frac{1}{2}}}, t \geq 1$, coincide, and we may define

$$\alpha_k := \lim_{t\to\infty} \frac{\Phi(\lambda t, t)}{t^{\frac{1}{2}}}.$$

It remains to show that $\alpha_k > 0$. For a set of independent random variables $\mathcal{X} := \{X_1, \ldots, X_{n+\lambda n}\}$ with uniform distribution in $[0,1]^2$, there is a $c > 0$ such that $\mathbb{E}\left[\min\{|X_i - X_j| : X_i, X_j \in \mathcal{X}\}\right] > \frac{c}{\sqrt{n+\lambda n}}$. Since $\frac{c}{\sqrt{n+\lambda n}} > \frac{c'}{\sqrt{n}}$ for a $c' > 0$, and a depot tour through n points contains at least $n+1$ edges, we have $\Phi(\lambda n, n, [0,1]^2) > c'\sqrt{n}$. Consequently, α is positive. $\qquad\square$

The following isoperimetric inequality by Rhee shows that, except for a small set with polynomially small probability, the boundary functional and its mean are close.

Theorem 2 ([14]). *Let $X_1, \ldots, X_n$ be independent identically distributed random variables with values in $[0,1]^2$ and let $L(X_1, \ldots, X_n)$ be a smooth Euclidean functional. Then there are constants C, C' and C'' such that for all $t > 0$:*

$$\mathbb{P}\left[|L(X_1, \ldots, X_n) - \mathbb{E}\left[L(X_1, \ldots, X_n)\right]| > t\right] \leq C e^{-\frac{(t/C')^4}{C'' n}}.$$

Proof (Proof of Theorem 1 (i)). The boundary functional is Euclidean and smooth, so we can apply the theorem directly to L_B, i.e. in [17]. Since L approximates L_B, Lemma 1, it is sufficient to show Theorem 1 (i) for L_B. $\qquad\square$

2.2   Bounds for α_k for $k = \lambda n$

For $\lambda \leq \frac{1}{p}$ our lower bound equals the lower bound of the TSP constant in [3] which is $\frac{5}{8}$ and decreases with increasing λ. The upper bound is also decreasing with increasing λ, but for $\lambda < 3$, the TSP tour through all points is a better upper bound. We have:

Theorem 3.

$$\min\left\{\alpha(TSP), \frac{2\alpha(TSP)}{\sqrt{1+\lambda}}\right\} \geq \alpha_k \geq \frac{1}{2\sqrt{1+\lambda}}\left(1 + \frac{1}{4(1+\lambda)}\right).$$

Proof. For the lower bound we consider an arbitrary point $p \in P$. Let $O = P \setminus \{p\} \cup D$. Let o_i denote the distance from p the i-nearest object of O. In the optimal tour p is either connected with two edges to a depot or it is connected to two different objects in O. So the length of one edge is bounded by o_1. The length of the second edge is bounded by o_1, too, if the nearest neighbor is a depot or by o_2 if the nearest neighbor is a point. Let z_1 and z_2 be random variables denoting the length of the first and second edge used, thus, $\mathbb{P}[z_1 = o_1] = 1$, $\mathbb{P}[z_2 = o_1] = \frac{k}{n+k-1}$ and $\mathbb{P}[z_2 = o_2] = \frac{n-1}{n+k-1}$. So we consider a slightly different setting. We have $n + k - 1$ random variables with uniform distribution in $[0, 1]^2$. After the objects are placed, we choose a random subset of k elements which we consider as depots. This is equivalent to the original situation with n random variables for the points and k for the depots. We have $2\mathbb{E}[L(D, P)] \geq n\mathbb{E}[z_1 + z_2]$. To determine the probability that the nearest neighbor has a distance of at least r, we consider the probability that there is no point in a circle around p with radius r. Thus,

$$\mathbb{E}[L(D, P)] \geq \frac{n}{2}\mathbb{E}[z_1 + z_2] = \frac{n}{2}\left(\mathbb{E}(o_1) + \frac{k}{n+k-1}\mathbb{E}(o_1) + \frac{n-1}{n+k-1}\mathbb{E}(o_2)\right)$$

$$\geq \frac{n}{2}\left(1 + \frac{k}{n+k-1}\right)\int_0^\infty \mathbb{P}[o_1 > r]dr + \frac{n-1}{n+k-1}\int_0^\infty \mathbb{P}[o_2 > r]dr$$

$$\geq \frac{n}{2}\left(\left(1 + \frac{k}{n+k-1}\right)\int_0^{\frac{1}{\sqrt{\pi}}}(1 - \pi r^2)^{n+k-1}dr\right.$$

$$\left. + \frac{n-1}{n+k-1}\int_0^{\frac{1}{\sqrt{\pi}}}(1 - \pi r^2)^{n+k-1} + (n+k-1)\pi r^2(1-\pi)^{n+k-2}dr\right)$$

$$\geq \frac{n}{2\sqrt{\pi}}\left(\int_0^1 z^{\frac{-1}{2}}(1-z)^{n+k-1}dz + \frac{(n-1)(n+k-1)}{2(n+k-1)}\int_0^1 z^{\frac{1}{2}}(1-z)^{n+k-2}dz\right).$$

In the last step we substituted $z = \pi r^2$. Using $\int_0^1 t^{x-1}(1-t)^{y-1}dt = \frac{\Gamma(x)\Gamma(y)}{\Gamma(x+y)}$, $x\Gamma(x) = \Gamma(x+1)$ and $\Gamma(\frac{1}{2}) = \sqrt{\pi}$, one can calculate

$$\mathbb{E}[L(D, P)] \geq \frac{n}{2}\frac{\Gamma(n+k)}{\Gamma(n+k+\frac{1}{2})}\left(1 + \frac{n-1}{4(n+k)}\right) \geq \frac{n}{2\sqrt{n+k}}\left(1 + \frac{n-1}{4(n+k)}\right).$$

For the last inequality consider $a_l = \frac{\Gamma(l)\sqrt{l}}{\Gamma(l+\frac{1}{2})}$. Since $\frac{a_l}{a_{l+1}} = \left(1+\frac{1}{l}\right)^{-\frac{1}{2}}\left(1+\frac{1}{2l}\right) \geq 1$ and $a_l \to 1$ for $l \to \infty$, we get the last inequality for $l = n+k$. Thus, for $k = \lambda n$, we have asymptotically $\mathbb{E}[L(D,P)] \geq \sqrt{n}\frac{1}{2\sqrt{1+\lambda}}\left(1 + \frac{1}{4(1+\lambda)}\right)$.

For the upper bound, we consider the TSP tour of length $\alpha(TSP)\sqrt{n+k}$ through all points and depots. We start with an arbitrary point and follow the tour, duplicating all edges starting at a point and deleting all edges starting at a depot. So we use $\frac{2n}{n+k}$ of the edges of the TSP tour. Each of the resulting connected components is turned into a feasible depot tour solution by shortcuts. Thus, the length of the constructed depot solution is $\frac{\alpha(TSP)\sqrt{n+k}2n}{n+k} = \frac{2\alpha(TSP)\sqrt{n}}{\sqrt{1+\lambda}}$.   □

2.3   The Case $k = o(n)$

For $k = o(n)$ the MDVRP behaves asymptotically exactly like the TSP. In the following lemma we show that the lengths of optimal solutions for the MDVRP and the TSP are very close if $k = o(n)$. Let $L_{TSP}(P)$ denote the length of an optimal TSP tour through a point set $P \subset [0,1]^2$.

Lemma 4. *Let $D, P \subset [0,1]^2$. If $|D| = o(|P|)$, then $|L_{TSP}(P) - L(D,P)| = o(\sqrt{|P|})$.*

Proof. Let $D, P \subset [0,1]^2$ with $|D| = o(|P|)$. Then $L(D,P) \leq L_{TSP}(P) + 2\sqrt{2}$, because we get a feasible multiple depot tour if we connect an optimal TSP tour to a depot. It remains to show that $L_{TSP}(P) - L(D,P) = O(\sqrt{|D|})$. Given an optimal multiple depot tour of length $L(D,P)$, we add a traveling salesman tour through D of length $O(\sqrt{|D|})$. The resulting graph is connected and all vertices have even degree, so there is a Eulerian tour. Short-cutting the Eulerian tour yields a traveling salesman tour through P of length at most $L(D,P)+O(\sqrt{|D|})$.   □

So the influence of the depots on the length of an optimal MDVRP tour is small in this case and we get Theorem 1 (ii):

Proof (Proof of Theorem 1 (ii)). Let $|P| = n$ and $|D| = o(n)$. We show that $\frac{L(D,P)}{\sqrt{n}}$ converges completely to $\alpha(TSP)$: let $\varepsilon > 0$,

$$\sum_{n=1}^{\infty} \mathbb{P}\left[\left|\frac{L(D,P)}{\sqrt{n}} - \alpha(TSP)\right| > \varepsilon\right]$$

$$\leq \sum_{n=1}^{\infty} \mathbb{P}\left[\left|\frac{L(D,P) - L_{TSP}(P)}{\sqrt{n}}\right| > \frac{\varepsilon}{2}\right] + \mathbb{P}\left[\left|\frac{L_{TSP}(P)}{\sqrt{n}} - \alpha(TSP)\right| > \frac{\varepsilon}{2}\right].$$

With Lemma 4 $|L_{TSP}(P) - L_{MD}(D,P)| = o(\sqrt{|P|})$ holds, and the length of the TSP functional converges completely to $\alpha(TSP)$, refer [17], hence the above sum is finite. Thus, we have complete convergence.   □

3   Probabilistic Analysis of a Nearest Neighbor Heuristics

We describe and analyze an algorithm for the multiple depot routing problem that combines a depot clustering heuristics with approximation algorithms for solving a TSP problem.

Two step scheme:

1. *Cluster* the points around the depots.
2. *Route* the points in each cluster to the corresponding depot with a TSP tour.

This is a widespread approach to solve the problem practically [6,7], but to our best knowledge there is no theoretical analysis. We give a first analysis for the case that the clustering step is implemented by the *nearest neighbor* heuristics: assign each point to its nearest depot. The second routing step is implemented by the fixed dissection heuristics of Karp[9].

Let $\mathcal{C}$ denote a clustering i.e. an assignment of points to depots. Let $\mathcal{C}^N$ denote the clustering produced by applying the nearest neighbor rule and let $\mathcal{C}^*$ denote the clustering in an optimal tour. For a clustering $\mathcal{C}$, let $T^*(\mathcal{C})$ denote the optimal tours for the clustering $\mathcal{C}$, i.e. the union of the optimal TSP tours for each cluster $C \in \mathcal{C}$. Let $T^K(\mathcal{C})$ denote the union of the TSP tours produced by applying the fixed dissection heuristics of Karp to each cluster $C \in \mathcal{C}$ separately. Our objective is to compare $T^K(\mathcal{C}^N)$ to $T^*(\mathcal{C}^*)$. We bound two approximation errors separately, that due to using the nearest neighbor clustering instead of an optimal clustering and that due to applying the Karp heuristics instead of an optimal TSP solver:

$$T^K(\mathcal{C}^N) \le T^*(\mathcal{C}^N) + E_1 \le T^*(\mathcal{C}^*) + E_1 + E_2$$

Lemma 5 (Clustering Approximation Lemma). *Let the points and depots be given by independent and uniformly distributed random variables. The nearest neighbor clustering rule satisfies*

$$T^*(\mathcal{C}^N) \le T^*(\mathcal{C}^*) + O(\sqrt{k}),$$

with high probability. If $k = o(n)$, the error term is $o(\sqrt{n})$ with high probability.

Proof. Consider the Voronoi partition V corresponding to the depots in the unit square. Take the optimal tour T^* corresponding to the optimal clustering $\mathcal{C}^*$ and modify it to respect the partition V. This is accomplished by "stitching in" a tour along one of the sides of a Voronoi region and connecting it to a possible inner tour, see Figure 7 and 8. This means to cut of the optimal tours keeping only the portions within the Voronoi region and connecting these portions along the sides of the polygon. In order to obtain a true TSP tour, the inner tour that contains the depot inside the region has to be connected to the outer tour.

To analyze the resulting tour, we use the following two geometric results, for more details see [2,11]: the sum of the lengths of all sides of the Voronoi diagram is $O(\sqrt{k})$ and the distance of a point to its closest depot is $O(1/\sqrt{k})$. The first fact implies that the sum of the stitched tours along the sides of the Voronoi diagram is at most $O(\sqrt{k})$, and the second that the sum of the lengths of the connections to the inner tours in all cells is at most $k \cdot O(1/\sqrt{k}) = O(\sqrt{k})$. Overall, the increase in the length due to the "stitching" operations is $O(\sqrt{k})$. Since the optimal routing in each region will give shorter tours than the ones constructed above the error is at most $O(\sqrt{k})$.   □

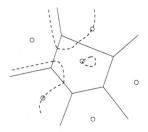

Fig. 7. Six depots with Voronoi diagram, the optimal tour shown as dashed line

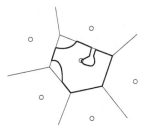

Fig. 8. The stitched tour of the central depot as a bold line

Lemma 6 (Tour Approximation Lemma). *For any clustering $\mathcal{C}$ of n points and k depots, we have:*

$$T^K(\mathcal{C}) \leq T^*(\mathcal{C}) + o\left(\sqrt{n+k}\right).$$

Proof. The analysis of Karp's fixed dissection heuristics shows by simple scaling that the approximation error for n uniformly distributed points in a square of side ℓ is $O(\ell\sqrt{n/s})$ where $s = \log n / \log\log n$. Suppose the clustering $\mathcal{C}$ has m clusters, each in a box of length ℓ_j and containing n_j points for $j \in [m]$. Note that $\sum_j n_j \leq n + k$ (some depots may have no points alloted to them) and $\sum_j \ell_j^2 = O(1)$. Applying the approximation bound for Karp's heuristics separately to each cluster, we have an absolute approximation error of $\sum_j \ell_j \sqrt{n_j/s_j} \leq \sqrt{\sum_j \ell_j^2} \sqrt{\sum_j \frac{n_j}{s_j}} O(1) \cdot \frac{\sqrt{n+k}}{\frac{\log n}{\log\log n}}$ if we take $s_j = \frac{\log n}{\log\log n}$ for each $j \in [m]$.   □

Note that the analysis in this lemma is *deterministic*. Putting both lemmas together, we get:

Theorem 4. *The two step algorithm with nearest neighbor clustering and Karp's fixed dissection TSP heuristics computes a $(1+o(1))OPT$ approximation for MD-VRP with n points and $k = o(n)$ depots uniformly and independently distributed in the unit square almost surely.*

Acknowledgments: We thank Luc Devroye and Mordecai Golin for comments which helped to improve the paper.

References

1. S. Arora. Polynomial time Approximation Schemes for Euclidean TSP and other Geometric problems. *J. ACM*, 45(5): 753–782, 1998.
2. F. Avram and D. Bertsimas. On Central Limit Theorems in Geometrical Probability. *The Annals of Applied Probability*, 3(4): 1033–1046, 1993.
3. J. Beardwood, J.H. Halton, and J. M. Hammersley. The shortest path through many points. In *Proc. Cambridge Philos. Soc.*, 55, 299–327, 1959.
4. I. M. Chao, B. L. Golden and E. Wasil. A new heuristic for the multi-depot vehicle routing problem that improves upon best-known solutions. *American Journal of Mathematical and Management Sciences* 13: 371–406, 1993.
5. J. F. Cordeau, M. Gendreau, and G. Laporte. A Tabu Search Heuristic for Periodic and Multi-Depot Vehicle Routing Problems. *Networks*, 30: 105–119, 1997.
6. M. L. Fisher and R. Jaikumar. A Generalized Assignment Heuristic for Vehicle Routing. *Networks,* 11:109-124, 1981.
7. D. Giosa, L. Tansini and O. Viera. New Assignment Algorithms for the Multi-Depot Vehicle Routing Problem. *Journal of the Operational Research Society* 53(9): 977–984, 2002.
8. R. Karp. Probabilistic Analysis of Partitioning Algorithms for the Travelling Salesman Problem in the Plane. *Math. of Operations Research* 2, 1977.
9. R. Karp and J. M. Steele. Probabilistic Analysis of Heuristics. In Lenstra et al. (ed) *The Travelling Salesman Problem*, John Wiley 1985.
10. J. Lenstra and A. Rinnooy Kan. Complexity of vehicle routing and scheduling problems. *Networks* 11, 221–227, 1981.
11. M. Penrose and J. Yukich. Central Limit Theorems for some Graphs in Computational Geometry. *Annals of Applied Prob.*, 11:4, 1005–1041, 2001.
12. C. Redmond and J. E. Yukich. Limit theorems and rates of convergence for Euclidean functionals. *Ann. Appl. Probab.*, 4(4):1057–1073, 1994.
13. J. Renaud, G. Laporte and F. F. Boctor. A tabu search heuristic for the multi-depot vehicle routing problem. *Computers and Operations Research*, 23: 229–235, 1996.
14. W. T. Rhee. A matching problem and subadditive Euclidean functionals. *Ann. Appl. Probab.*, 3(3):794–801, 1993.
15. J. M. Steele. *Probability theory and combinatorial optimization*, volume 69 of *CBMS-NSF Regional Conference Series in Applied Mathematics*. Society for Industrial and Applied Mathematics (SIAM), Philadelphia, PA, 1997.
16. L. Tansini. PhD Thesis, to appear.
17. J. E. Yukich. *Probability theory of classical Euclidean optimization problems*, volume 1675 of *Lecture Notes in Mathematics*. Springer-Verlag, Berlin, 1998.

Computing the Expected Accumulated Reward and Gain for a Subclass of Infinite Markov Chains

Tomáš Brázdil* and Antonín Kučera**

Faculty of Informatics, Masaryk University,
Botanická 68a, 60200 Brno, Czech Republic
{brazdil,kucera}@fi.muni.cz

Abstract. We consider the problem of computing the expected accumulated reward and the average gain per transition in a subclass of Markov chains with countable state spaces where all states are assigned a non-negative reward. We state several abstract conditions that guarantee computability of the above properties up to an arbitrarily small (but non-zero) given error. Finally, we show that our results can be applied to probabilistic lossy channel systems, a well-known model of processes communicating through faulty channels.

1 Introduction

Methods for qualitative and quantitative analysis of stochastic systems have been rapidly gaining importance in recent years. Stochastic systems are used for modeling systems that exhibit some kind of uncertainty caused by, e.g., unpredictable errors, randomness, or underspecification. The semantics of stochastic systems is usually defined in terms of Markov chains or Markov decision processes [19,22]. So far, problems related to formal verification of stochastic systems have been studied mainly for finite-state systems [24,11,6,12,19,10]. Only recently, some of these results were extended to certain classes of infinite-state systems, in particular to probabilistic pushdown automata [13,9,14,7], recursive Markov chains [16,15], and probabilistic lossy channel systems [2,3,5,4,18,23].

A more abstract approach has been adopted in [1], where the problems of qualitative and quantitative reachability are studied for a subclass of Markov chains with a finite attractor. In [1], it is shown that the problems of qualitative reachability and qualitative repeated reachability are decidable in the considered subclass, and that the quantitative variants of these problems can be solved up to an arbitrarily small given error. These abstract results are then applied to probabilistic lossy channel systems. Moreover, in the same paper it is shown that the exact probability of (repeated) reachability is not expressible in first order

---

* Supported by the Czech Science Foundation, grant No. 201/03/1161.
** Supported by the research centre Institute for Theoretical Computer Science (ITI), project No. 1M0021620808.

R. Ramanujam and S. Sen (Eds.): FSTTCS 2005, LNCS 3821, pp. 372–383, 2005.

theory of the reals for probabilistic lossy channel systems (unlike for probabilistic pushdown automata or recursive Markov chains [13,9,16,15]).

Our contribution: In this paper we adopt an abstract approach similar to the one of [1]. We identify an abstract class of infinite Markov chains where the expected accumulated reward between two given states and the average reward per transition can be effectively approximated up to a given precision. Our results are applicable to a similar class of systems as the results of [1], in particular to various versions of probabilistic lossy channel systems. These problems have previously been considered and solved for probabilistic pushdown automata by showing that these parameters are effectively expressible in first order theory of the reals [14]. However, this approach cannot be used for any class of Markov chains that subsumes probabilistic lossy channel systems; by adapting the results of [1], one can easily show that these values are (provably) not expressible in first order theory of the reals.

The problem of computing the expected accumulated reward can be roughly formulated as follows: assume that each state of a given Markov chain is assigned a rational *reward*, which is collected when the state is visited. We are interested in the expected reward accumulated when going from a given state s to another given state t. In particular, if the reward function returns 1 for every state, then the expected accumulated reward corresponds to the expected number of transitions between s and t, and can also be interpreted as the expected termination time. Another important parameter which is well-known from general theory of Markov chains is the *gain*, i.e., the average reward per transition along a given infinite run. The gain (computed w.r.t. various reward functions) plays an important role in performance analysis and can be used to evaluate various long-run system properties (such as the expected throughput, expected service time, etc.)

Since the expected accumulated reward and the average gain can take irrational values, the best we can hope for is to compute rational lower and upper approximations that are arbitrarily close. Our approach is similar to the one of [21] used for approximating the probability of reaching a given state t from another given state s. Roughly speaking, the algorithm successively computes the probability p_n^- of reaching t from s in at most n steps. This yields a sequence of lower approximations $p_1^-, p_2^-, \ldots$ of p. It holds (without any additional assumptions) that $\lim_{n \to \infty} p_n^-$ equals the probability p of reaching t from s, and that $p_1^- \leq p_2^- \leq \ldots \leq p$. However, it is not clear which p_n^- is "close enough" to p in the sense that $p - p_n^- \leq \varepsilon$ for a given precision $\varepsilon > 0$. Therefore, one also computes the probabilities d_n of reaching a "dead" state in at most n steps (a state s' is dead if t is not reachable from s'). Putting $p_i^+ = 1 - d_i$ for every $i \in \mathbb{N}$, we obtain a sequence of upper approximations $p_1^+ \geq p_2^+ \geq \cdots$ of p. If the Markov chain contains a finite attractor, then $\lim_{n \to \infty} p_n^- = p = \lim_{n \to \infty} p_n^+$, and it suffices to compute a sufficiently large n such that $p_n^+ - p_n^- \leq \varepsilon$.

We use a similar approach for computing the expected accumulated reward and the average gain by showing that there are effectively computable sequences $E_1^+, E_2^+, \ldots$ and $E_1^-, E_2^-, \ldots$ of upper and lower approximations which converge to the value of the considered parameter. For the expected accumulated reward, the sequence of lower approximations is easy to find, using a similar technique as in the case of reachability. In Section 3 we show how to construct the sequence of upper approximations for a subclass of Markov chains that satisfy certain abstractly formulated conditions. We show that an infinite Markov chain M of this class can be effectively approximated with a sequence of finite-state Markov chains so that the expected accumulated rewards computed in these approximations converge to the expected accumulated reward in M. In order to prove this convergence, we use results of perturbed Markov chains theory [17]. The problem of computing the expected gain is solved along similar lines, but the problem (and hence also the techniques involved) become more complicated. In particular, there is no simple method for constructing a sequence of lower approximations as in the case of the expected accumulated reward, and we have to compute both lower and upper approximating sequences using the sequence of finite-state Markov chains mentioned above.

Due to space constraints, all proofs are omitted. These can be found in a full version of this paper [8].

2   Preliminaries

In the paper we use $\mathbb{Q}$, $\mathbb{R}$, and $\mathbb{R}^+$ to denote the sets of rational numbers, real numbers, and non-negative real numbers, respectively. We also use $\mathbb{Q}_\infty$ and $\mathbb{R}^+_\infty$ to denote the set $\mathbb{Q} \cup \{\infty\}$ and $\mathbb{R}^+ \cup \{\infty\}$, respectively. The symbol ∞ is treated according to the standard conventions.

Definition 1. *A (discrete) Markov chain is a triple $M = (S, \to, Prob)$ where S is a finite or countably infinite set of states, $\to \subseteq S \times S$ is a transition relation, and Prob is a function which to each transition $s \to t$ of M assigns its probability $Prob(s \to t) \in (0, 1]$ so that for every $s \in S$ we have $\sum_{s \to t} Prob(s \to t) = 1$.*

In the rest of this paper we write $s \xrightarrow{x} t$ instead of $Prob(s \to t) = x$. A *path* in M is a finite or infinite sequence $w = s_0, s_1, \ldots$ of states such that $s_i \to s_{i+1}$ for every i. We say that a state t is *reachable* from a state s if there is a path from s to t. We say that a Markov chain M is *irreducible*, if for all states s, t of M there is a path from s to t in M. The *length* of a given path w is the number of transitions in w. In particular, the length of an infinite path is ∞, and the length of a path s, where $s \in S$, is zero. We also use $w(i)$ to denote the state s_i of w (by writing $w(i) = s$ we implicitly impose the condition that the length of w is at least i). The prefix $s_0, \ldots, s_i$ of w is denoted by w^i. A *run* is an infinite path. The sets of all finite paths and all runs of M are denoted *FPath* and *Run*, respectively. Similarly, the sets of all finite paths and runs that start with a given $w \in FPath$ are denoted $FPath(w)$ and $Run(w)$, respectively. In particular, $Run(s)$, where $s \in S$, is the set of all runs initiated in s.

We are interested in probabilities of certain events that are associated with runs. To every $s \in S$ we associate the probabilistic space $(Run(s), \mathcal{F}, \mathcal{P})$ where $\mathcal{F}$ is the σ-field generated by all *basic cylinders* $Run(w)$ where $w \in FPath(s)$, and $\mathcal{P} : \mathcal{F} \to [0,1]$ is the unique probability function such that $\mathcal{P}(Run(w)) = \Pi_{i=0}^{m-1} x_i$ where $w = s_0, \cdots, s_m$ and $s_i \xrightarrow{x_i} s_{i+1}$ for every $0 \le i < m$ (if $m = 0$, we put $\mathcal{P}(Run(w)) = 1$).

For every $s \in S$ and every $A \subseteq S$, we use $\mathcal{P}[s, A]$ to denote the probability of reaching A from s. Formally, $\mathcal{P}[s, A] = \mathcal{P}(\{w \in Run(s) \mid \exists i \ge 0 : w(i) \in A\})$. We write $\mathcal{P}[s, t]$ instead of $\mathcal{P}[s, \{t\}]$.

Definition 2. *A set $A \subseteq S$ is recurrent if for all $s \in A$ we have that $s \to t$ implies $\mathcal{P}[t, A] = 1$.*

Note that whenever a run leaves a recurrent set A, then it almost surely (i.e., with probability one) returns back to A in the future.

A *reward function* is a function $f : S \to \mathbb{R}^+$. We extend f to finite paths by putting $f(s_0, \ldots, s_n) = \sum_{i=0}^{n} f(s_i)$. Thus, f assigns to each path its *accumulated reward*. The special reward function which assigns 1 to every $s \in S$ is denoted $\mathbf{1}$ (i.e., $\mathbf{1}(s) = 1$ for each $s \in S$).

3 Computing the Expected Accumulated Reward and Gain

In this section we show how to compute certain quantitative properties in certain classes of Markov chains up to an arbitrarily small $\varepsilon > 0$. More precisely, we show that these properties are *effectively approximable* in the following sense:

Definition 3. *Let $\mathcal{O}$ be a class of objects, and let $P : \mathcal{O} \to \mathbb{R}_\infty^+$. We say that P is effectively approximable if there is an algorithm which, for a given $o \in \mathcal{O}$, enumerates two sequences $E_1^+, E_2^+, \ldots$ and $E_1^-, E_2^-, \ldots$ where $E_i^+, E_i^- \in \mathbb{Q}_\infty$ such that for all $i \ge 1$ we have $E_i^- \le P(o) \le E_i^+$ and $\lim_{i \to \infty} E_i^+ = \lim_{i \to \infty} E_i^-$.*

The sequences $E_1^+, E_2^+, \ldots$ and $E_1^-, E_2^-, \ldots$ are called the upper/lower *approximating sequences of $P(o)$, respectively.*

If P is effectively approximable, then the value of $P(o)$ can effectively be approximated up to an arbitrarily small $\varepsilon > 0$ by enumerating the upper and lower sequences simultaneously until they become sufficiently close.

3.1 The Expected Accumulated Reward

For the rest of this subsection, let us fix a Markov chain $M = (S, \to, Prob)$, two states $s_{in}, s_{fin} \in S$, and a reward function $f : S \to \mathbb{R}^+$. Moreover, we assume that given a state $s \in S$, the set $\{(s, x, t) \mid s \xrightarrow{x} t\}$ of all transitions from s is effectively denumerable.

We define a random variable $R : Run(s_{in}) \to \mathbb{R}_\infty^+$ that counts the reward accumulated between s_{in} and s_{fin}. Formally, given a run $w \in Run(s_{in})$, we define

$$R(w) = \begin{cases} f(w(0), \ldots, w(n-1)) & \exists n : w(n) = s_{fin}, w(i) \neq s_{fin} \text{ for } 1 \le i \le n-1; \\ \infty & \text{otherwise.} \end{cases}$$

The expected value of R is denoted $\mathcal{E}(M, f)$ (the reason why we write $\mathcal{E}(M, f)$ and not just $E(R)$ is that in our proofs we consider various modifications of the chain M and various reward functions, keeping s_{in}, s_{fin} fixed).

Our aim is to show that the function which to a given tuple (M, f, s_{in}, s_{fin}) assigns the value $\mathcal{E}(M, f)$ is effectively approximable (cf. Definition 3) if M and f satisfy certain abstractly formulated conditions. To simplify our notation, we formulate these conditions directly for the previously fixed M and f, and show how to compute the sequences $E_1^+, E_2^+, \ldots$ and $E_1^-, E_2^-, \ldots$ if these conditions are satisfied.

First, let us realize that the lower approximating sequence $E_1^-, E_2^-, \ldots$ can be computed without any additional assumptions about M and f, because

- one can effectively compute a sequence $P_1, P_2, \ldots$ of *finite* sets of finite paths such that $P_i \subseteq P_{i+1}$ for each $i \geq 1$, and $\bigcup_{i=1}^{\infty} P_i$ is exactly the set of all finite paths w where $w(0)=s_{in}$, $w(k)=s_{fin}$ for some k, and $w(j) \neq s_{fin}$ for all $0 \leq j < k$;
- E_i^- can be defined as $\sum_{w \in P_i} \mathcal{P}(Run(w)) \cdot f(w)$

However, the upper approximating sequence $E_1^+, E_2^+, \ldots$ cannot be effectively constructed for general M and f. In order to formulate the promised sufficient conditions, we need to state one auxiliary definition.

Definition 4. *Let $h : S \to \mathbb{R}^+$ be a reward function, $A \subseteq S$, and $s \in A$. We define a random variable $O_s^{h,A} : Run(s) \to \mathbb{R}^+$ that counts the reward accumulated "before hitting the set A" as follows:*

$$O_s^{h,A}(w) = \begin{cases} h(w(1), \ldots, w(n-1)) & \exists n : w(n) \in A, w(1), \ldots, w(n-1) \notin A; \\ \bot & otherwise. \end{cases}$$

The symbol $\mathcal{E}O_s^{h,A}$ denotes either the conditional expectation $E(O_s^{h,A} \mid O_s^{h,A} \neq \bot)$ or 0, depending on whether $\mathcal{P}(O_s^{h,A} \neq \bot)$ is positive or zero, respectively.

The sufficient conditions which (as we shall see) enable an effective construction of $E_1^+, E_2^+, \ldots$ are the following:

1. there is an effectively computable sequence $A_0 \subseteq A_1 \subseteq \cdots$ of finite recurrent sets such that $\bigcup_{i=0}^{\infty} A_i = S$;
2. there is an effectively computable number $\varXi \in \mathbb{R}^+$ such that for all $i \geq 0$ and all $s \in A_i$ we have $\mathcal{E}O_s^{f,A_i} \leq \varXi$ and $\mathcal{E}O_s^{1,A_i} \leq \varXi$ (remember that $\mathbf{1}$ is the reward function which assigns 1 to each state);
3. given a finite set $A \subseteq S$ and $s, t \in A$, it is decidable whether there is a finite path of the form $s=s_0, \ldots, s_n=t$ where $s_i \notin A$ for all $0 < i < n$ (i.e., whether s can reach t without visiting any state of A in the middle).

As we shall see, these conditions are satisfied by, e.g., Markov chains generated by various variants of probabilistic lossy channel systems. The intuitive meaning of these conditions is explained at appropriate places below. Note that we can safely assume that $s_{in}, s_{fin} \in A_0$.

For the rest of this subsection, let us assume that the conditions 1–3 are satisfied and $s_{in}, s_{fin} \in A_0$. First, let us deal with the case when $\mathcal{P}[s_{in}, s_{fin}] < 1$.

Then clearly $\mathcal{E}(M, f) = \infty$. Moreover, one can easily prove that $\mathcal{P}[s_{in}, s_{fin}] < 1$ if and only if there is a state $s \in A_0$ such that s is reachable from s_{in}, and s_{fin} is *not* reachable from s (we use the fact that A_0 is recurrent and finite). Hence, using condition 3 we can effectively check whether $\mathcal{P}[s_{in}, s_{fin}] < 1$. If this is the case, then $\mathcal{E}(M, f) = \infty$.

Now let us assume that $\mathcal{P}[s_{in}, s_{fin}] = 1$. We show that conditions 1–3 suffice for computing the upper approximating sequence $E_1^+, E_2^+, \ldots$ Loosely speaking, the algorithm computes a sequence of finite-state Markov chains that "approximate" the Markov chain M, and the expected reward accumulated between s_{in} and s_{fin} in these chains "approximates" $\mathcal{E}(M, f)$.

We start with some auxiliary definitions. Given a set $A \subseteq S$ and two states $s, t \in A$, we define the set $Out(A, s, t) \subseteq Run(s)$ of runs that reach t without visiting A in the middle:

$$Out(A, s, t) = \{w \in Run(s) \mid \exists n : w(n) = t, w(1), \ldots, w(n-1) \notin A\}$$

We put $Out(A, s) = \{w \in Run(s) \mid w(1) \notin A\}$, and for all $i \geq 0$ define a Markov chain $M_i = (S_i, \to_i, Prob_i)$, where $S_i = A_i \cup \{\bar{s} \mid s \in A_i, \mathcal{P}(Out(A_i, s)) > 0\}$ and the transitions are determined as follows:

- if $s, t \in A_i$, then $s \xrightarrow{x}_i t$ iff $s \xrightarrow{x} t$;
- if $s \in A_i$ and $\bar{s} \in S_i$, then $s \xrightarrow{x}_i \bar{s}$ iff $x = \mathcal{P}(Out(A_i, s))$;
- if $s, t \in A_i$ and $\bar{s} \in S_i$, then $\bar{s} \xrightarrow{x}_i t$ iff $x = \mathcal{P}(Out(A_i, s, t) \mid Out(A_i, s)) > 0$.

Note that M_i has finitely many states. Now we define a reward function $f_i : S_i \to \mathbb{R}^+$ where $f_i(s) = f(s)$ and $f_i(\bar{s}) = \mathcal{E}O_s^{f, A_i}$ for every $s \in A_i$. The following (crucial) lemma states that each (M_i, f_i) is a faithful abstraction of (M, f) with respect to the expected reward accumulated between s_{in} and s_{fin}.

Lemma 1. *For all $i \geq 0$ we have that $\mathcal{E}(M, f) = \mathcal{E}(M_i, f_i)$.*

Note that if we were able to compute (M_i, f_i) for some i, we would be done, because the expected accumulated reward can easily be computed for finite-state Markov chains using standard methods. Unfortunately, we cannot compute the transition probabilities of M_i precisely (the transitions of the form $\bar{s} \xrightarrow{x}_i t$ cause the problem), and the definition of f_i is not effective either. However, we can use condition 2 to design a reward function f_i^+ that approximates f_i — for every $i \geq 0$ and every $s \in A_i$ we define $f_i^+(s) = f(s)$ and $f_i^+(\bar{s}) = \Xi$. Condition 2 implies that $f_i \leq f_i^+$ for all $i \geq 0$, hence $\mathcal{E}(M_i, f_i) \leq \mathcal{E}(M_i, f_i^+)$. The following lemma states that the difference between $\mathcal{E}(M_i, f_i)$ and $\mathcal{E}(M_i, f_i^+)$ approaches 0 as i grows.

Lemma 2. *For each $\varepsilon > 0$ there is $i \geq 0$ s.t. $0 \leq \mathcal{E}(M_j, f_j^+) - \mathcal{E}(M_j, f_j) \leq \varepsilon$ for every $j \geq i$.*

The only problem left is that we are not able to compute transition probabilities in the chains M_i. This is overcome by showing that, for a given $\delta > 0$, one can effectively approximate the transition probabilities of M_i and compute a finite-state Markov chain $M_i^\delta = (S_i, \to_i, Prob_i^\delta)$ with the transition matrix P_i^δ

so that $\|P_i - P_i^\delta\|_\infty \leq \delta$ (the norm $\|\cdot\|_\infty$ of a matrix $P = \{p_{ij}\}$ is defined as $\|P\|_\infty = \max_i \sum_j |p_{ij}|$). Then, we show that for every M_i^δ there is an effectively computable number $c_\delta \in \mathbb{R}^+$ such that $|\mathcal{E}(M_i^\delta, f_i^+) - \mathcal{E}(M_i, f_i^+)| \leq c_\delta \cdot \delta$. Moreover, the number c_δ approaches a *bounded* value as δ goes to zero. Here we employ results of perturbed Markov chains theory and develop some new special tools that suit our purposes. In this way, we obtain the following lemma:

Lemma 3. *For every $i \geq 0$ and every $\varepsilon > 0$ there is an effectively computable $\delta > 0$ such that $|\mathcal{E}(M_i^\delta, f_i^+) - \mathcal{E}(M_i, f_i^+)| \leq \varepsilon$.*

Note that since the definition of M_i^δ is effective, we can compute $\mathcal{E}(M_i^\delta, f_i^+)$ by standard methods for finite-state Markov chains.

Now we can define the upper approximating sequence $E_1^+, E_2^+, \ldots$ of $\mathcal{E}(M, f)$ as follows: For each $i \geq 1$ we put $E_i^+ = \mathcal{E}(M_i^{\delta_i}, f_i^+) + \frac{1}{2^{i+1}}$, where $\delta_i > 0$ is the δ of Lemma 3 computed for the considered i and $\varepsilon = \frac{1}{2^{i+1}}$. Now it is easy to see that $0 \leq E_i^+ - \mathcal{E}(M_i, f_i^+) \leq \frac{1}{2^i}$. By combining this observation together with Lemma 1 and Lemma 2, we obtain that $\lim_{i \to \infty} E_i^+ = \mathcal{E}(M, f)$ and $E_i^+ \geq \mathcal{E}(M, f)$ for all $i \geq 1$. Moreover, the approximations $E_1^+, E_2^+, \ldots$ are effectively computable. Thus, we obtain our first theorem:

Theorem 1. *For every $\varepsilon > 0$ there is an effectively computable number x such that $|\mathcal{E}(M, f) - x| \leq \varepsilon$.*

3.2   The Average Gain

Similarly as in Section 3.1, we fix a Markov chain $M = (S, \to, Prob)$, a state $s_{in} \in S$, and a reward function $f : S \to \mathbb{R}^+$, such that for each $s \in S$ the set $\{(s, x, t) \mid s \xrightarrow{x} t\}$ is effectively denumerable.

We define a function $\mathcal{G}(M, f) : Run(s_{in}) \to \mathbb{R}_\infty^+$ as follows

$$\mathcal{G}(M, f)(w) = \begin{cases} \lim_{n \to \infty} \frac{f(w^n)}{n} & \text{if the limit exists;} \\ \bot & \text{otherwise.} \end{cases}$$

Hence, $\mathcal{G}(M, f)(w)$ corresponds to the *gain* (i.e., "average reward per transition"), which is a standard notion in stochastic process theory (see, e.g., [20]). As we shall see in Section 3.3, the gain can be used to compute other interesting characteristics which reflect long-run properties of a given system.

Note that $\mathcal{G}(M, f)(w)$ can be undefined for some $w \in Run(s_{in})$. As we shall see, for Markov chains that satisfy conditions 1–3 of Section 3.1, the total probability of all such runs is zero. Since $\mathcal{G}(M, f)(w)$ can take infinitely many values, a standard problem of stochastic process theory is to compute $E(\mathcal{G}(M, f))$, the expected value of $\mathcal{G}(M, f)$. However, one should realize that the information provided by $E(\mathcal{G}(M, f))$ is relevant only in situations when a system is repeatedly restarted and runs "sufficiently long" so that the average reward per transition approaches its limit. In our setup, we can provide a bit more detailed information about the runs of $Run(s_{in})$, which is not reflected in the "ensemble average"

$E(\mathcal{G}(M, f))$. We show that in the subclass of Markov chains that satisfy conditions 1–3, the variable $\mathcal{G}(M, f)$ can take *only finitely many values with a positive probability*, and we give an algorithm which approximates these values as well as the associated probabilities up to an arbitrarily small $\varepsilon > 0$. Thus, we obtain a "complete picture" about possible limit behaviours of runs initiated in s_{in}. Note that $E(\mathcal{G}(M, f))$ can be effectively approximated simply by taking the weighted sum of the finitely many admissible values of $\mathcal{G}(M, f)$. It is worth noting that similar results have recently been achieved for an incomparable class of Markov chains generated by probabilistic pushdown automata [7] by using completely different methods.

The class of Markov chains considered in this subsection is the same as in Section 3.1, i.e., we assume that the previously fixed chain M satisfies conditions 1–3 (cf. Section 3.1). We also assume (without restrictions) that $s_{in} \in A_0$. Since the constructions and techniques employed in this section are hard to explain at an intuitive level, we only state our main theorem and refer to [8] for missing details.

Theorem 2. *There are finitely many pairwise disjoint sets* $\mathcal{R}_1, \ldots, \mathcal{R}_n \subseteq Run(s_{in})$ *and numbers* $x_1, \ldots, x_n \in \mathbb{R}^+$ *such that*

- $Prob(\bigcup_{i=1}^n \mathcal{R}_i) = 1$, *and* $Prob(\mathcal{R}_i) > 0$ *for every* $1 \le i \le n$;
- *for every* $1 \le i \le n$ *and every* $w \in \mathcal{R}_i$ *we have* $\mathcal{G}(M, f)(w) = x_i$;
- *for every* $\varepsilon > 0$ *and every* $1 \le i \le n$, *there is an effectively computable number* y_i *such that* $|x_i - y_i| \le \varepsilon$;
- *for every* $1 \le i \le n$, *it is decidable whether* $Prob(\mathcal{R}_i) = 1$; *moreover, for every* $\varepsilon > 0$ *and every* $1 \le i \le n$, *there is an effectively computable number* r_i *such that* $|Prob(\mathcal{R}_i) - r_i| \le \varepsilon$.

3.3 The Average Ratio

The gain can be used to define some interesting characteristics of Markov chains, like, e.g., the frequency of visits to a distinguished family of states along an infinite run. In performance analysis, one is also interested in features that cannot be directly specified as gains, but as limits of *fractions* of two reward functions.

Let us start with a simple motivating example. Let $M = (S, \rightarrow, Prob)$ be a Markov chain, $s_{in} \in S$ an initial state, $f : S \rightarrow \mathbb{R}^+$ a reward function, and $T \subseteq S$ a set of *triggers*. Intuitively, a trigger is a state initiating a finite "service" of a certain request. Hence, each run with infinitely many triggers can be seen as an infinite sequence of finite services, where each service corresponds to a finite path between two consecutive occurrences of a trigger. What we are interested in is the average accumulated reward per service. Formally, the average accumulated reward per service can be defined as follows: we fix another reward function g where $g(s)$ returns 1 if $s \in T \cup \{s_{in}\}$, and 0 otherwise. Now we define a random variable $R : Run(s_{in}) \rightarrow \mathbb{R}_\infty^+$ as follows:

$$R(w) = \begin{cases} \lim_{n \to \infty} \frac{f(w^n)}{g(w^n)} & \text{if the limit exists;} \\ \bot & \text{otherwise.} \end{cases}$$

It is easy to see that $R(w)$ indeed corresponds to the average accumulated reward per service in the run w. For the reasons which have been discussed at the beginning of Section 3.2, we are interested not only in $E(R)$ (the expected average accumulated reward per service), but in a complete classification of admissible values of R and their associated probabilities. Of course, this is possible only under some additional assumptions about the chain M; as we shall see, conditions 1–3 are sufficient.

Now we move from the above example to a general setup. For the rest of this section, we fix a Markov chain $M = (S, \to, Prob)$, a state $s_{in} \in S$, and two reward functions $f, g : S \to \mathbb{R}^+$. In order to simplify our presentation, we assume that $g(s_{in}) > 0$. We define the *average ratio* $\mathcal{R}_g^f : Run(s_{in}) \to \mathbb{R}_\infty^+$ as follows.

$$\mathcal{R}_g^f(w) = \begin{cases} \lim_{n \to \infty} \frac{f(w^n)}{g(w^n)} & \text{if the limit exists;} \\ \bot & \text{otherwise.} \end{cases}$$

First we observe that the average ratio can be expressed in terms of gains.

Lemma 4. *Let* $w \in Run(s_{in})$ *be a run. If both* $\mathcal{G}(M, f)(w)$ *and* $\mathcal{G}(M, g)(w)$ *are defined and finite, and if* $\mathcal{G}(M, f)(w) + \mathcal{G}(M, g)(w) > 0$, *then*

$$\mathcal{R}_g^f(w) = \frac{\mathcal{G}(M, f)(w)}{\mathcal{G}(M, g)(w)}$$

Here we use the convention that $c/0 = \infty$ *for* $c > 0$.

For the rest of this section, we assume that the chain M satisfies conditions 1–3 of Section 3.1. First, let us consider the special case when the chain M_0 is irreducible. It follows from Theorem 2 that $\mathcal{G}(M, f)$ and $\mathcal{G}(M, g)$ are constant almost everywhere and finite. Moreover, the values $\mathcal{G}(M, f)$ and $\mathcal{G}(M, g)$ can be effectively approximated up to a given $\varepsilon > 0$. The case when $\mathcal{G}(M, g) = 0$ requires some attention.

Lemma 5. $\mathcal{G}(M, g) = 0$ *iff for all* $s \in S$ *reachable from* s_{in} *we have that* $g(s)=0$.

Now we consider the general case when M_0 is not necessarily irreducible. We obtain that the values of $\mathcal{G}(M, g)$ are determined by the bottom strongly connected components of the underlying transition system $\mathcal{T}_{M_0}$ of M_0. The value associated with a given component C is 0 iff all states $s \in S$ that are reachable from a state of $C \cap A_0$ satisfy $g(s) = 0$ iff for all runs $w \in Run(s_{in})$ that enter a state of $C \cap A_0$ there is $k \geq 0$ such that for all $j \geq k$ we have $g(w(j)) = 0$. Thus, we obtain the following generalization of Theorem 2.

Theorem 3. *Let us assume that for each* $s \in A_0$ *it is decidable whether there is* $t \in S$ *reachable from* s *such that* $g(t) > 0$, *and the same for the reward function* f. *Then there are finitely many pairwise disjoint sets* $\mathcal{Z}_f, \mathcal{Z}_g, \mathcal{Z}_{f,g}, \mathcal{R}_1, \ldots, \mathcal{R}_n \subseteq Run(s_{in})$ *and numbers* $x_1, \ldots, x_n \in \mathbb{R}^+$ *such that*

- $Prob(\bigcup_{i=1}^{n} \mathcal{R}_i \cup \mathcal{Z}_f \cup \mathcal{Z}_g \cup \mathcal{Z}_{f,g}) = 1$, and
  - $\mathcal{R}_g^f(w) = x_i > 0$ for all $w \in \mathcal{R}_i$ and all $1 \leq i \leq n$;
  - $\mathcal{R}_g^f(w) = 0$ for all $w \in \mathcal{Z}_f$;
  - $\mathcal{R}_g^f(w) = \infty$ for all $w \in \mathcal{Z}_g$.
- for all $w \in \mathcal{Z}_{f,g}$ there is $k \geq 0$ such that $j \geq k$ implies $f(w(j)) = g(w(j)) = 0$.
- for every $\varepsilon > 0$ there are effectively computable $y_1, \ldots, y_n$ such that $|x_i - y_i| \leq \varepsilon$ for $1 \leq i \leq n$;
- the probabilities $Prob(\mathcal{R}_i)$ for $1 \leq i \leq n$, $Prob(\mathcal{Z}_f)$, $Prob(\mathcal{Z}_g)$, and $Prob(\mathcal{Z}_{f,g})$ can be effectively approximated up to a given $\varepsilon > 0$; moreover, for each of these probabilities, it is decidable whether the probability is equal to 1 or not.

4   Probabilistic Lossy Channel Systems

Lossy channel systems (LCS) [2] have been proposed as a model for processes communicating via faulty communication channels. A lossy channel system consists of a finite-state control unit and a finite set of FIFO channels. A *configuration* of LCS consists of the current control state and the current contents of the channels. A computational step from a given configuration consists of adding/removing one message to/from a channel, and possibly changing the control state. Moreover, during each transition, one or more messages can be lost from the channels.

A probabilistic lossy channel system (PLCS) is a probabilistic variant of LCS. In PLCS, transitions and message losses are chosen randomly according to a given probability distribution. There are several models of PLCS that differ mainly in the treatment of message losses. The model considered in [18] assumes that each step of a system is either a message loss or a "perfect" step that is performed consistently with transition function. There is a fixed probability $\lambda > 0$ that the next step will be a message loss. This model is called a global-fault model in [23]. Another variant of PLCS was considered in [5], where it is assumed that each message can be lost independently of the other messages with some given probability $\lambda > 0$. Then each step of a system consists of a perfect step followed by a loss of (zero or more) messages, where each message is lost with the probability λ, independently of the other messages. This model is also called a local-fault model. See [23] for a deeper explanation of the above models of PLCS.

We show that the abstract results of Section 3 are applicable both to the global-fault and the local-fault variant of PLCS. In our discussion, we use the following result for one-dimensional random walks: For each $0 < \lambda < 1$ we define a Markov chain $M_\lambda = (\mathbb{N}_0, \rightarrow, Prob)$ where the transitions are defined as follows. For all $n \geq 0$ we put $n \xrightarrow{1-\lambda} n+1$, for all $n \geq 1$ we put $n \xrightarrow{\lambda} n-1$, and we also put $0 \xrightarrow{\lambda} 0$. It is easy to prove that if $\lambda > \frac{1}{2}$, then the expected number of transitions needed to reach 0 from 1 equals $\frac{1}{2\lambda-1}$.

Let $\mathcal{L}$ be a PLCS, and let us assume that f is a reward function that assigns a rational reward to configurations of $\mathcal{L}$. Moreover, let us assume that f is effectively bounded, i.e., there is an effectively computable constant ξ such that for every configuration s we have $f(s) \leq \xi$.

Let us first consider the global-fault model. We argue that if $\lambda > \frac{1}{2}$, then the conditions 1–3 of Section 3.1 are satisfied, and hence Theorems 1, 2, and 3 apply. For all $i \geq 0$ we define the set A_i consisting of all configurations where the total number of messages stored in the channels is bounded by i. Since at most one message can be added into channels during a perfect step and each step is lossy with probability λ, we obtain that the expected time to reach A_i after leaving A_i is bounded from above by the expected number of transitions needed to reach 0 from 1 in M_λ. Hence, condition 2 is satisfied because f is effectively bounded. Condition 3 can be proved using similar arguments as in Theorem 8 in [1].

In the local-fault model, the probability of a message loss converges to 1 as the number of stored messages increases. In particular, there is $n \in \mathbb{N}$ such that for each configuration where the total number of stored messages exceeds n we have that the probability of losing at least two messages in the next step is greater than $\frac{1}{2}$ (since at most one message can be added to channels in a single step, the number of messages stored in the next configuration decreases with probability greater than $\frac{1}{2}$). It is easy to see that the number n is computable from λ. Hence, if we define A_i to be the set of all configurations where the number of stored messages is less than or equal to $n + i$, we obtain that conditions 2 and 3 are satisfied, using the same argument as for the global-fault model above. Hence, the general results of Theorems 1, 2, and 3 apply.

References

1. P. Abdulla, N.B. Henda, and R. Mayr. Verifying infinite Markov chains with a finite attractor or the global coarseness property. In *Proceedings of LICS 2005*, pp. 127–136. IEEE, 2005.
2. P. A. Abdulla and B. Jonsson. Verifying programs with unreliable channels. *I&C*, 127(2):91–101, 1996.
3. P.A. Abdulla and A. Rabinovich. Verification of probabilistic systems with faulty communication. In *Proceedings of FoSSaCS 2003*, vol. 2620 of *LNCS*, pp. 39–53. Springer, 2003.
4. C. Baier and B. Engelen. Establishing qualitative properties for probabilistic lossy channel systems: an algorithmic approach. In *Proceedings of 5th International AMAST Workshop on Real-Time and Probabilistic Systems (ARTS'99)*, vol. 1601 of *LNCS*, pp. 34–52. Springer, 1999.
5. N. Bertrand and Ph. Schnoebelen. Model checking lossy channel systems is probably decidable. In *Proceedings of FoSSaCS 2003*, vol. 2620 of *LNCS*, pp. 120–135. Springer, 2003.
6. A. Bianco and L. de Alfaro. Model checking of probabalistic and nondeterministic systems. In *Proceedings of FST&TCS'95*, vol. 1026 of *LNCS*, pp. 499–513. Springer, 1995.
7. T. Brázdil, J. Esparza, and A. Kučera. Analysis and prediction of the long-run behavior of probabilistic sequential programs with recursion. In *Proceedings of FOCS 2005*. IEEE, 2005. To appear.

8. T. Brázdil and A. Kučera. Computing the expected accumulated reward and gain for a subclass of infinite markov chains. Technical report FIMU-RS-2005-10, Faculty of Informatics, Masaryk University, 2005.

9. T. Brázdil, A. Kučera, and O. Stražovský. On the decidability of temporal properties of probabilistic pushdown automata. In *Proceedings of STACS'2005*, vol. 3404 of *LNCS*, pp. 145–157. Springer, 2005.

10. C. Courcoubetis and M. Yannakakis. Verifying temporal properties of finite-state probabilistic programs. In *Proceedings of FOCS'88*, pp. 338–345. IEEE, 1988.

11. C. Courcoubetis and M. Yannakakis. The complexity of probabilistic verification. *JACM*, 42(4):857–907, 1995.

12. L. de Alfaro, M.Z. Kwiatkowska, G. Norman, D. Parker, and R. Segala. Symbolic model checking of probabilistic processes using MTBDDs and the Kronecker representation. In *Proceedings of TACAS 2000*, vol. 1785 of *LNCS*, pp. 395–410. Springer, 2000.

13. J. Esparza, A. Kučera, and R. Mayr. Model-checking probabilistic pushdown automata. In *Proceedings of LICS 2004*, pp. 12–21. IEEE, 2004.

14. J. Esparza, A. Kučera, and R. Mayr. Quantitative analysis of probabilistic pushdown automata: Expectations and variances. In *Proceedings of LICS 2005*, pp. 117–126. IEEE, 2005.

15. K. Etessami and M. Yannakakis. Algorithmic verification of recursive probabilistic systems. In *Proceedings of TACAS 2005*, vol. 3440 of *LNCS*, pp. 253–270. Springer, 2005.

16. K. Etessami and M. Yannakakis. Recursive Markov chains, stochastic grammars, and monotone systems of non-linear equations. In *Proceedings of STACS'2005*, vol. 3404 of *LNCS*, pp. 340–352. Springer, 2005.

17. E. Cho G and C. D. Meyer. Markov chain sensitivity measured by mean first passage times. *Linear Algebra and its Applications*, 316(1–3):21–28, 2000.

18. S.P. Iyer and M. Narasimha. Probabilistic lossy channel systems. In *Proceedings of TAPSOFT'97*, vol. 1214 of *LNCS*, pp. 667–681. Springer, 1997.

19. M.Z. Kwiatkowska. Model checking for probability and time: from theory to practice. In *Proceedings of LICS 2003*, pp. 351–360. IEEE, 2003.

20. M. Puterman. *Markov Decision Processes*. John Wiley and Sons, 1994.

21. A. Rabinovich. Quantitative analysis of probabilistic lossy channel systems. In *Proceedings of ICALP 2003*, vol. 2719 of *LNCS*, pp. 1008–1021. Springer, 2003.

22. J. Rutten, M. Kwiatkowska, G. Norman, and D. Parker. *Mathematical Techniques for Analyzing Concurrent and Probabilistic Systems*, vol. 23 of *CRM Monograph Series*. American Mathematical Society, 2004.

23. Ph. Schnoebelen. The verification of probabilistic lossy channel systems. In *Validation of Stochastic Systems: A Guide to Current Research*, vol. 2925 of *LNCS*, pp. 445–465. Springer, 2004.

24. M. Vardi. Automatic verification of probabilistic concurrent finite-state programs. In *Proceedings of FOCS'85*, pp. 327–338. IEEE, 1985.

Towards a CTL* Tableau

Mark Reynolds

The University of Western Australia, Perth, Australia
mark@csse.uwa.edu.au

Abstract. We present a sound, complete and relatively straightforward tableau method for deciding valid formulas in the propositional version of the bundled (or suffix and fusion closed) computation tree logic BCTL*. This proves that BCTL* is decidable. It is also moderately useful to have a tableau available for a reasonably expressive branching time temporal logic. However, the main interest in this should be that it leads us closer to being able to devise a tableau-based technique for theorem-proving in the important full computational tree logic CTL*.

1 Introduction

CTL*, or full computation tree logic, was introduced in [4] and [8]. It extends both the simple branching logic, CTL, of [3], and the standard linear temporal logic, PLTL of [17].

The language of CTL*, which is a propositional temporal language, is built recursively from the atomic propositions using the next X and until U operators of PLTL, and the universal path switching modality A of CTL as well as classical connectives. This language is appropriate for describing properties of all paths of states through a transition structure, or applications which can be modelled as such. This standard semantics for CTL* is called the semantics over R-generable models.

The main uses of CTL* in computer science are for developing and checking the correctness of complex reactive systems. See [10] for a survey. CTL* is also used widely as a framework for comparing other languages more appropriate for specific reasoning tasks of this type. These include the purely linear and purely branching sub-languages as well as languages which allow a limited amount of interplay between these two aspects.

In this paper we will mainly be concerned with a variant semantics which gives a slightly different logic. In [23], this is called ∀LTFC and it allows us to restrict the use of the path quantifier to a given subset of all of the paths through the transition structure. The only requirements are that the chosen set of paths is closed under taking suffixes (i.e. it is suffix closed) and is closed under putting together a finite prefix of one path with the suffix of any other path such that the prefix ends at the same state as the suffix begins (i.e. the set is fusion closed). This logic lacks the so called *limit closure* property of the standard CTL* semantics (see section 2.3 below).

R. Ramanujam and S. Sen (Eds.): FSTTCS 2005, LNCS 3821, pp. 384–395, 2005.
© Springer-Verlag Berlin Heidelberg 2005

The alternative name of BCTL*, or *bundled* CTL*, for ∀LTFC comes from the term *bundle* which is used in philosophical accounts of branching time tense logics, when only certain selected branches of time play a role in the semantics (see for example [1]). Such a variation on the semantics gives us a different set of valid formulas in BCTL* when compared to standard CTL*: we give some details in section 2.3. Every valid formula in BCTL* is a valid formula in CTL*. There are possible applications for BCTL* (as distinct from CTL*) where only certain of the possible infinite paths through a transition structure are counted as legitimate computations. For example, there may be fairness constraints on the repeated choice amongst branching alternatives. BCTL* also has played a role as a technically simpler variant of CTL*, giving a basis on which to work towards handling standard CTL*. See [19] and [23]. This is how we use it here.

Validity of formulas of CTL* is known to be decidable. This was proved in [8] using an automata-theoretic approach. [7] makes use of the specific form of some linear automata to give a decision procedure of deterministic double exponential time complexity in the length of the formula. This agrees with the lower bound found in [24].

As with other temporal logics and despite these conclusive results, the search for other reasoning methods has been a major undertaking. Even for the basic task of deciding validity (or equally satisfiability), of a CTL* formula, there is interest in finding approaches which are more straightfoward, or more traditional, or more amenable to human understanding, or yield meaningful intermediate steps, etc. In this vein, there is a complete Hilbert-style axiomatization for CTL* in [19] using an unusual and unorthodox rule of inference and a perfectly orthodox axiomatization of an extension of CTL* with past-time operators in [20].

Tableaux are another popular style of modal reasoning technique and there has been a substantial amount of work on applying them to temporal logics: see [12] and [18] for surveys. They can be presented in an intuitive way, they are often suitable for automated reasoning and it is often not hard to prove complexity results for their use. Tableaux were used for modal logics in [15] and [11] and there has been much work since on tableaux for temporal logics [25,13,5,6,21].

Despite all the interest in tableaux for temporal logic and for reasoning with CTL*, tableaux do not exist for deciding validity in CTL*. However, it should be noted that tableau-style elements appear in the somewhat intricate CTL* model-checking systems in [22] and [16]. Model-checking is a distinct task from deciding validity: it involves checking whether a given formula holds of a given system, and is used for the verification of implementations. Validity deciders can be used to model-check but model-checkers can not in general decide validity: model-checking is an "easier" or less computationally complex reasoning task. In [22] there is a tableau system for model-checking with predicate CTL*. In [16] there is a complete deductive system for model-checking formulas in predicate CTL* and some of the derivation steps look similar to tableau-building steps.

There are good reasons to try to devise a not too complicated tableau-style system for deciding validity in CTL*. Even though there is the seriously inconvenient double exponential lower bound on the complexity, there are reasons to believe that experienced tableau practitioners will be able to use a range of techniques to make fast implementations capable of delivering results for a wide range of practical reasoning problems. A general CTL* tableau can be the basis for searching for more practical sublanguages, and for assisting with human-guided derivations on bigger tasks. It can be the basis of proofs of correctness for alternative reasoning techniques like resolution or rewrite systems. It may assist with model-checking and program synthesis tasks. It may be extended to cope with some predicate reasoning.

In this paper we do not deliver a CTL* tableau. However, we do describe a simple, sound and complete tableau system for BCTL*. This can be used directly for BCTL* reasoning, and thus for showing the validity of many CTL* formulas.

It also seems that our result gives the first explicit proof of decidability of BCTL*. However, it should be noted that the same fact can be deduced from a result (theorem 10) in [14], and possibly from one in [2], concerning decidability for bundled tree logics with more general semantics.

The main reason for this paper, however, is to lay the basis for a future tableau system for standard propositional CTL*.

The tableau construction we describe for BCTL* is of the graph rather than the tree form. To decide the validity of ϕ, we build a graph with the nodes built from sets of formulas from a finite closure set defined from ϕ. There is then a pruning process. A novel aspect is the fact that the nodes in the initial tableau graph are built from sets of sets of formulas. We use certain sets of formulas called hues, and then put together sets of hues called colours. This notation reflects some similar ideas in the CTL* axiomatic completeness proof in [19]. The proof of correctness is an interesting mixture of techniques from linear and branching temporal logic, and it has some subtleties.

In section 2 we give a formal definition of BCTL* and CTL* and give some example valid formulas. In section 3 we describe the tableau and the following section sketches the proof of correctness. Complexity and implementation issues are discussed briefly in section 5 before a conclusion.

2   Syntax and Semantics

The language of (propositional) CTL* is used to describe several different types of structures and so there are really several different logics here. In the background in our paper is the logic of R-generable sets of paths on transition structures. In most papers it is this logic which is referred to as CTL*: this is the standard CTL* logic.

We will, however, be proving results for a different logic, BCTL*, which uses the same language but has fewer valid formulas. In this section we introduce BCTL* first and then CTL*.

2.1   BCTL*

We fix a countable set $\mathcal{L}$ of atomic propositions.

Definition 1. *A transition frame is a pair (S, R) where:*
S is the non-empty set of states
R is a total binary relation $\subseteq S \times S$
    i.e. for every $s \in S$, there is some $t \in S$ such that $(s, t) \in R$.

A transition frame could equally be called a *Kripke* frame as in standard modal logic except that a Kripke frame's accessibility relation, R, is not necessarily assumed to be total.

Formulas are defined along ω-long sequences of states. A *fullpath* in (S, R) is an infinite sequence $\langle s_0, s_1, s_2, ... \rangle$ of states such that for each i, $(s_i, s_{i+1}) \in R$. For the fullpath $b = \langle s_0, s_1, s_2, ... \rangle$, and any $i \geq 0$, we write b_i for the state s_i and $b_{\geq i}$ for the fullpath $\langle s_i, s_{i+1}, s_{i+2}, ... \rangle$.

BCTL* allows the semantics to be defined with respect to a predefined set of fullpaths, not necessarily all possible fullpaths. However there are restrictions. We say that a set B of fullpaths through (S, R) is *suffix closed* iff for all $b \in B$, for all $i \geq 0$, $b_{\geq i} \in B$.

We say that B is *fusion closed* if we can switch from one path to another at any common state. That is, if $b, c \in B$ and $i, j \geq 0$ and $b_i = c_j$, then $\langle b_0, b_1, ..., b_{i-1}, c_j, c_{j+1}, c_{j+2}, ... \rangle$ (which is a fullpath, of course) is also in B.

A non-empty set of fullpaths (through (S, R)) will be called a *bundle* (on (S, R)) if it is both suffix and fusion closed.

Formulas of BCTL* are evaluated in *bundled structures*:

Definition 2. *A bundled (transition) structure is a triple $M = (S, R, B, g)$ where:*
(S, R) is a transition frame;
$g : S \rightarrow \wp(\mathcal{L})$ is a labelling of the states with sets of atoms; and
B is a bundle.

The formulas of BCTL* are built from the atomic propositions in $\mathcal{L}$ recursively using classical connectives $\neg$ and $\wedge$ as well as the temporal connectives X, U and A: if α and β are formulas then so are $X\alpha$, $\alpha U \beta$ and $A\alpha$. As well as the standard classical abbreviations, **true**, $\vee$, $\rightarrow$, $\leftrightarrow$, we have linear time abbreviations $F\alpha \equiv \textbf{true} U \alpha$ and $G\alpha \equiv \neg F \neg \alpha$, and we have the path switching modal diamond $E\alpha \equiv \neg A \neg \alpha$.

We shall write $\psi \leq \phi$ if ψ is a subformula of ϕ.

Truth of formulas is evaluated at bundled fullpaths in bundled structures. We write $M, b \models \alpha$ iff the formula α is true of the fullpath $b \in B$ in the structure $M = (S, R, B, g)$. This is defined recursively by:

$M, b \models p$ iff $p \in g(b_0)$, any $p \in \mathcal{L}$
$M, b \models \neg\alpha$ iff $M, b \not\models \alpha$
$M, b \models \alpha \wedge \beta$ iff $M, b \models \alpha$ and $M, b \models \beta$
$M, b \models X\alpha$ iff $M, b_{\geq 1} \models \alpha$
$M, b \models \alpha U \beta$ iff there is some $i \geq 0$ such that $M, b_{\geq i} \models \beta$
                 and for each j, if $0 \leq j < i$ then $M, b_{\geq j} \models \alpha$
$M, b \models A\alpha$ iff for all fullpaths $b' \in B$ such that $b_0 = b'_0$ we have $M, b' \models \alpha$

We say that α is *valid* in BCTL* iff for all bundled transition structures M, for all fullpaths b in M, we have $M, b \models \alpha$. Let us write $\models_B \alpha$ in that case.

We say that α is *satisfiable* in BCTL* iff for some bundled transition structure M and for some fullpath b in M, we have $M, b \models \alpha$. Clearly α is satisfiable (in BCTL*) iff $\not\models_B \neg\alpha$.

2.2   CTL*

The standard version of CTL*, the full computation tree logic of R-generable structures uses the same language as defined above for BCTL*. However, the semantics is different and, as we will see below (subsection 2.3), there are some extra valid formulas.

There are two slightly different but ultimately equivalent ways of defining the semantics of CTL*. In terms of the definitions above for BCTL* both involve a further restriction on the sets we allow as bundles B in structures (S, R, B, g). One alternative is to only allow B to be exactly the set of all fullpaths through (S, R).

The other alternative way of introducing CTL* semantics is to impose an extra closure condition called *limit closure*. Limit closure is the requirement that if a sequence of prefixes of fullpaths from the bundle is strictly increasing then the fullpath which is their limit is also in the bundle. The set of all fullpaths is limit closed. Full details about the relationship between limit closure of sets of paths and equivalence results can be found in [9] and [19]. We do not need to go into details here.

A (transition) structure is just (S, R, g) where (S, R) is a transition frame and g is a labelling of the states with sets of atoms. Let $FB(S, R)$ be the set of all fullpaths through (S, R). Note that $FB(S, R)$ is a bundle.

Truth of formulas in CTL* is evaluated at fullpaths in transition structures. Using our definitions above we just put $(S, R, g), b \models \alpha$ iff $(S, R, FB(S, R), g), b \models \alpha$.

We say that α is *valid* in CTL* iff for all transition structures M, for all fullpaths b in M, we have $M, b \models \alpha$. Let us write $\models_C \alpha$ in that case.

We say that α is *satisfiable* in CTL* iff for some transition structure M and for some fullpath b in M, we have $M, b \models \alpha$. Clearly α is satisfiable in CTL* iff $\not\models_C \neg\alpha$.

2.3   Examples: BCTL* Versus CTL*

Many interesting valid formulas in our two logics can be gained from the axiomatizations in [23] and [19].

Formulas which appear in these axiom systems and which are valid in both BCTL* and CTL* include all the valid formulas of PLTL such as $\theta_1 = G(\alpha \rightarrow \beta) \rightarrow (G\alpha \rightarrow G\beta)$, $\theta_2 = G\alpha \rightarrow (\alpha \wedge X\alpha \wedge XG\alpha)$, $\theta_3 = (\alpha U \beta) \leftrightarrow (\beta \vee (\alpha \wedge X(\alpha U \beta)))$ and $\theta_4 = (\alpha U \beta) \rightarrow F\beta$. There are also S5 axioms such as $\theta_5 = \alpha \rightarrow AE\alpha$ and $\theta_6 = A\alpha \rightarrow AA\alpha$. The main interaction between the path switching and the linear time modalities is the valid formula $\theta_7 = AX\alpha \to XA\alpha$. There is also a special axiom saying that atomic propositions only depend on states: $\theta_8 = p \to Ap$ (for atom p).

Now we list three more interesting valid formulas of BCTL* and CTL*:

$$\theta_9 = E(pU(E(pUq))) \to E(pUq)$$
$$\theta_{10} = (AG(p \to qUr) \wedge qUp) \to qUr$$
$$\theta_{11} = G(EFp \to XFEFp) \to (EFp \to GFEFp).$$

We leave it to the reader to verify the validity of these examples using semantic arguments.

It is immediate that, as $FB(S, R)$ is a bundle in (S, R), every valid formula in BCTL* is a valid formula in CTL*.

The literature includes a few examples of the extra valid formulas of CTL*, that is formulas which are valid in CTL* but not in BCTL*. The negations of these formulas are satisfiable in BCTL* but not in CTL*.

A simple example is the limit closure axiom from CTL,

$$\theta_{12} = AG(p \to EXp) \to (p \to EGp).$$

A basic induction shows that this is valid in CTL*: if $M, b \models AG(p \to EXp) \wedge p$ then we can find, for all $n \geq 0$, a finite sequence $\langle s_0, s_1, ..., s_n \rangle$ such that $s_0 = b_0$ and for any fullpath σ, if $\sigma_0 = s_n$ then $M, \sigma \models AG(p \to EXp) \wedge p$. Then we have a fullpath satisfying Gp and we are done.

To see that the negation of θ_{12} is satisfiable in BCTL* consider the structure in figure 1. Let $S = \{u, v\}$, $R = \{(u, u), (u, v), (v, v)\}$, $g(u) = \{p\}$, $g(v) = \{\}$ and $B = \{b | \exists i \; b_i = v\}$. The reader can verify that (S, R, B, g) is a bundled model of $\neg\theta_{12}$.

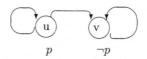

Fig. 1. $\neg\theta_{12}$ is satisfiable

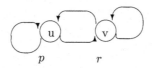

Fig. 2. $\neg\theta_{14}$ is satisfiable

The LC (limit closure) axiom schema from [19] gives us other examples:

$$\theta_{13} = AG(E\alpha \rightarrow EX((E\beta)U(E\alpha))) \rightarrow (E\alpha \rightarrow EG((E\beta)U(E\alpha))).$$

There is a (semantic) proof of the soundness of this scheme in [19]. In BCTL*
this is not generally valid. As a simple example take $\alpha = p$ and $\beta = \textbf{true}$. To
see that its negation is satisfiable in BCTL* use the bundled structure from the
previous example.

Another example from [19]:

$$\theta_{14} = (AG(p \rightarrow EXr) \wedge AG(r \rightarrow EXp)) \rightarrow (p \rightarrow EG(Fp \wedge Fr)).$$

This is proved to be valid in CTL* using the axiom system in [19]. To see that
its negation is satisfiable in BCTL* consider the structure in figure 2. Let the
bundle only contain those fullpaths which eventually remain in the same state
from some time onwards.

3   The Tableau for BCTL*

Most of the work on temporal tableaux involves a move away from the traditional tree-shaped tableau building process of other modal logics. The standard
approach for temporal logics is to start with a graph and repeatedly prune away
nodes, according to certain removal rules, until there is nothing more to remove
(success) or some failure condition is detected. This approach is seen for the
linear PLTL in [25] and [13] and for the simple branching CTL in [5] and [6].
The PLTL tableau in [21] is interesting because of the return to a tree shape.

We want to use a tableau approach to decide validity of a formula in BCTL*.
We will start with a formula ϕ and determine whether ϕ is satisfiable in BCTL*
or not. To decide validity simply determine satisfiabilty of the negation.

As in the usual graph-style tableau processes for linear time temporal logics,
we start with a graph of these nodes and repeatedly "prune" away (i.e. remove)
nodes until we either reach a failure condition or a successful stabilization.

The main difference here is that the nodes in our graph will be sets of sets of
formulas rather than just sets of formulas. Obviously there is a risk of getting a
very large graph to deal with. We discuss complexity and implementation issues
briefly in section 5 below.

From the closure set for ϕ, which is just the subformulas and their negations,
we will define a certain set of subsets of the closure set called the *hues* of ϕ. The
colours of ϕ will be certain sets of hues of ϕ. The nodes in our tableau graph
will be colours of ϕ: each colour will be at most one node. The hue and colour
terminology relects some similar notions in the axiomatic completeness proof for
CTL* in [19]. Edges in the tableau will be determined by certain conditions on
the formulas in the hues at each end of the edge.

3.1   Hues and Colours

Fix the formula ϕ whose satisfiability we are interested in.

Definition 3 (closure set). *The closure set for ϕ is* $\mathbf{cl}\phi = \{\psi, \neg\psi | \psi \leq \phi\}$.

Definition 4 (MPC). *Say that $a \subseteq \mathbf{cl}\phi$ is* maximally propositionally consistent *(MPC) iff for all $\alpha, \beta \in \mathbf{cl}\phi$,*
M1) if $\beta = \neg\alpha$ then ($\beta \in a$ iff $\alpha \notin a$); and
M2) if $\alpha \wedge \beta \in \mathbf{cl}\phi$ then ($\alpha \wedge \beta \in a$ iff both $\alpha \in a$ and $\beta \in a$).

A hue is supposed to (approximately) capture a set of formulas which could all hold together of one fullpath.

Definition 5 (Hue). *$a \subseteq \mathbf{cl}\phi$ is a* hue *for ϕ iff all these conditions hold:*
H1) a is MPC;
H2) if $\alpha U \beta \in a$ and $\beta \notin a$ then $\alpha \in a$;
H3) if $\alpha U \beta \in \mathbf{cl}\phi \setminus a$ then $\beta \notin a$;
H4) if $A\alpha \in a$ then $\alpha \in a$.

Let H_ϕ be the set of hues of ϕ.
The usual temporal successor relation plays a role:

Definition 6 (r_X). *For hues a and b, put $a \, r_X \, b$ iff the following four conditions all hold.*
R1) $X\alpha \in a$ implies $\alpha \in b$.
R2) $\neg X\alpha \in a$ implies $\neg\alpha \in b$.
R3) $\alpha U \beta \in a$ and $\neg\beta \in a$ implies $\alpha U \beta \in b$.
R4) $\neg(\alpha U \beta) \in a$ and $\alpha \in a$ implies $\neg(\alpha U \beta) \in b$.

The next relation aims to tell whether two hues correspond to fullpaths starting at the same state:

Definition 7 (r_A). *For hues a and b, put $a \, r_A \, b$ iff the following two conditions both hold:*
A1) $A\alpha \in a$ iff $A\alpha \in b$; and
A2) for all $p \in \mathcal{L}$, $p \in a$ iff $p \in b$

Now we move up from the level of hues to the level of colours. Could a set of hues be exactly the hues corresponding to all the fullpaths starting at a particular state?

Definition 8 (Colour). *$c \subseteq H_\phi$ is a* colour *(of ϕ) iff the following two conditions hold. For all $a, b \in c$,*
C1) $a r_A b$
C2) if $a \in c$ and $\neg A\alpha \in a$ then there is $b \in c$ such that $\neg\alpha \in b$.

Let C_ϕ be the set of colours of ϕ.
We define a successor relation R_X between colours. It is defined in terms of r_X between the component hues. Note that colours will in general have a non-singleton range of successors.

Definition 9 (R_X). *For all $c, d \in C_\phi$, put $c \, R_X \, d$ iff for all $b \in d$ there is $a \in c$ such that $a \, r_X \, b$.*

The initial tableau graph will be (C_ϕ, R_X).

3.2   Pruning the Tableau

Start with the set S' of colours being equal to C_ϕ and repeatedly remove colours from S' according to the following two rules, applied in any order to the colours left in S'.

Removal rule 1: Remove c from S' if its succession can not be completely covered, i.e. if there is $a \in c$ and there is no $b \in d \in S'$ such that $c \, R_X \, d$ and $a \, r_X \, b$. Thus each hue in c must have an r_X successor in some R_X successor of c still in S'.

Removal rule 2: Remove c from S' if it contains an unfulfillable eventuality. This is defined in several steps. An *eventuality* in a hue a is any formula of the form $\alpha U \beta \in a$. An eventuality in a colour c is just some eventuality in a hue in c. A *fulfillment* of the eventuality $\alpha U \beta \in a \in c \in S'$ is a finite sequence $\langle (c_0, h_0), (c_1, h_1), (c_2, h_2), ..., (c_n, h_n) \rangle$ of colour-hue pairs such that: $n \geq 0$, $h_0 = a$, $c_0 = c$, each $h_i \in c_i \in S'$, each $c_i \, R_X \, c_{i+1}$, each $h_i \, r_X \, h_{i+1}$ and $\beta \in h_n$. (Note that here we need not require α in each h_i as that follows from the definition of r_X.) Remove c if it contains an eventuality which does not have a fulfillment. Note that this may be implemented by spreading fulfillment backwards from hue to hue along r_X within R_X.

Halt and Fail condition: If at any stage there is no colour containing a hue containing ϕ left in S' then we can stop and say that ϕ is unsatisfiable in BCTL*.

Halt and Succeed: Otherwise, it is clear that we will eventually stop finding colours to remove. Then we halt and say that ϕ is satisfiable in BCTL*.

4   Soundness and Completeness

Call the above algorithm BCTL*-TAB.

Theorem 1. *BCTL*-TAB, which clearly always terminates, is sound and complete for deciding satisfiability in BCTL*.*

This follows from lemmas 1 and 3.

Lemma 1. *BCTL*-TAB is sound, that is, if it halts and succeeds on ϕ then ϕ is satisfiable in BCTL*.*

Here we give a brief sketch of the proof.

Say that the algorithm terminates with the set $S' \subseteq C_\phi$ of colours remaining. Say $\phi \in a_0 \in e_0 \in S'$.

Define a bundled structure (S', R_X, B, g) as follows. The transition structure is just (S', R_X).

The bundle B of fullpaths is built from examining sequences of colour-hue pairs from S'. Call an ω-sequence of colour-hue pairs $\langle (c_0, h_0), (c_1, h_1), (c_2, h_2), ... \rangle$ a *thread* through S' iff: each $h_i \in c_i \in S'$, each $c_i \, R_X \, c_{i+1}$, and each $h_i \, r_X \, h_{i+1}$. Say that this thread is a *fulfilling* thread iff for all $i \geq 0$, for all formulas of the form $\alpha U \beta \in h_i$, there is some $j \geq i$ such that $\beta_j \in h_j$. We include the fullpath

$\sigma = \langle c_0, c_1, c_2, ... \rangle$ in B iff there is a fulfilling thread $\langle (c_0, h_0), (c_1, h_1), (c_2, h_2), ... \rangle$, and then we say that this thread *justifies* σ being in B.

Using the definition of R_X we can show that B is a bundle.

Finally define $g : S' \rightarrow \wp(\mathcal{L})$, the labelling of the states with sets of atoms, by $p \in g(c)$ iff there is some $a \in c$ with $p \in a$.

Now find some sequence $\langle (c_0, h_0), (c_1, h_1), (c_2, h_2), ... \rangle$ of colour-hue pairs such that: each $h_i \in c_i \in S'$, each $c_i \ R_X \ c_{i+1}$, each $h_i \ r_X \ h_{i+1}$, every eventuality in any h_i is fulfilled, and $\phi \in h_0$. Let π^0 be $\langle c_0, c_1, ... \rangle$.

Now we claim $(S', R_X, B, g), \pi^0 \models \phi$. In fact we show

Lemma 2. *For all $\alpha \in \mathbf{cl}(\phi)$, for all threads $\mu = \langle (c_0, h_0), (c_1, h_1), ... \rangle$ justifying $\sigma = \langle c_0, c_1, ... \rangle \in B$ we have $(S', R_X, B, g), \sigma \models \alpha$ iff $\alpha \in h_0$.*

That proves soundness. Now the converse.

Lemma 3. *BCTL*-TAB is complete, that is, if ϕ is satisfiable in BCTL* then it halts and succeeds on ϕ.*

Here we give a brief sketch of the proof. Suppose that ϕ is satisfiable, say that $(K, R, B, g), \pi^0 \models \phi$. For each $\pi \in B$ define a hue $h(\pi)$ containing exactly those $\alpha \in \mathbf{cl}\phi$ such that $(K, R, B, g), \pi \models \alpha$. Define a map $\rho : K \rightarrow C_\phi$, by $\rho(s) = \{h(\pi) | \pi \in B, \pi_0 = s\}$. Define $S_0 = \rho(K) \subseteq C_\phi$.

We can show that during the running of the algorithm we do not ever remove any element of S_0 from S'. As ϕ appears in $h(\pi^0) \in \rho(\pi_0^0) \in S_0$, the algorithm must halt with the correct answer as required.

Corollary 1. *BCTL* is decidable.*

5   Complexity and Implementation Issues

Say that the length of ϕ is $|\phi| = l$. Thus ϕ has $\leq l$ subformulas and $\mathbf{cl}\phi$ contains at most $2l$ formulas. Since each hue contains, for each $\alpha \leq \phi$ at most one of α or $\neg\alpha$, there are at most $\leq 2^l$ hues. Thus there are less than 2^{2^l} colours.

The process of constructing the initial tableau and determining the R_X relation is thus double exponentially complex in time and space usage. Each round of the pruning process takes time bounded above by the size of the graph in terms of colour-hue pairs. There are less than 2^{2^l+l} such pairs. Each round (except possibly the last) removes at least one colour so there are at most 2^{2^l} rounds. Overall we have a double exponential upper bound on time and space usage.

No lower bound on deciding validity in BCTL* is known although the reductions in [24] showing a exponential space lower bound for CTL* will probably go through for BCTL* as well.

The implementation of BCTL*-TAB is relatively straightforward (but no version robust enough for public release has yet been constructed).

A prototype implementation written by the author shows that for many interesting, albeit relatively small, formulas, the actual performance is nowhere near as bad as the the theoretical upper bounds above. All but one of the 14 example formulas are easily decided by this prototype implementation. Only θ_{14} is too expensive. The size of the initial tableau is the limiting factor: pruning the tableau rarely takes more than a few rounds.

6   Conclusion

We have provided a simple, sound and complete tableau system for the bundled (or suffix and fusion closed) variant, here called BCTL*, of the propositional full computational tree logic CTL*.

This seems to be the first account of a decision procedure for BCTL*. There is potential for BCTL* reasoning applications with an identified set of acceptable computation paths.

However, the standard propositional CTL* logic is even more useful. Our system for BCTL* should be of some importance as it lays the groundwork for possible attempts to devise a tableau system for CTL*. Future work will concentrate on trying to identify CTL* models in the final BCTL* tableau. In the literature, there is a wide range of existing expertise in making fast tableaux and we will also be trying to apply that.

Even though there is an existing decision procedure for CTL* (based on automata) there are many potential uses of tableaux systems for CTL*. We can often extract counter-models and formal proofs from tableaux. They could be a base for developing, or proving correctness of, other techniques such as tree-shaped tableaux, resolution or term rewriting. They may give indications of simpler more reasonable sub-languages. Tableaux help manual proofs of validity. They can be extended to help with reasoning in the predicate case, for example for software verification.

References

1. J. P. Burgess. Logic and time. *J. Symbolic Logic*, 44:566–582, 1979.
2. J. P. Burgess. Decidability for Branching Time. *Studia Logica*, 39:203–218, 1980.
3. E. Clarke and E. Emerson. Synthesis of synchronization skeletons for branching time temporal logic. In *Proc. IBM Workshop on Logic of Programs, Yorktown Heights, NY*, pages 52–71. Springer, Berlin, 1981.
4. E. Clarke, E. Emerson and A. Sistla, Automatic verification of finite state concurrent system using temporal logic specifications: a practical approach. In *Proc. 10th ACM SIGACT-SIGPLAN Symposium on Principles of Programming Languages*, pages 117–126. 1983.
5. E. Emerson and E. C. Clarke. Using branching time temporal logic to synthesise synchronisation skeletons. *Sci. of Computer Programming*, 2, 1982.
6. E. Emerson and J. Halpern. Decision procedures and expressiveness in the temporal logic of branching time. *J. Comp and Sys. Sci*, 30(1):1–24, 1985.
7. E. Emerson and C. Jutla. Complexity of tree automata and modal logics of programs. In *29th IEEE Foundations of Computer Science, Proceedings*. IEEE, 1988.

8. E. Emerson and A. Sistla. Deciding full branching time logic. *Information and Control*, 61:175 – 201, 1984.
9. E. Emerson. Alternative semantics for temporal logics. *Theoretical Computer Science*, 26:121–130, 1983.
10. E. Emerson. Temporal and modal logic. In J. van Leeuwen, editor, *Handbook of Theoretical Computer Science*, volume B. Elsevier, Amsterdam, 1990.
11. M. Fitting. *Proof methods for modal and intuitionistic logics.* Reidel, 1983.
12. R. Goré. Tableau methods for modal and temporal logics. In M. D'Agostino, D. Gabbay, R. Hähnle, and J. Posegga, editors, *Handbook of Tableau Methods*, pages 297–396. Kluwer Academic Publishers, 1999.
13. G. Gough. Decision procedures for temporal logics. Technical Report UMCS-89-10-1, Department of Computer Science, University of Manchester, 1989.
14. I. Hodkinson and F. Wolter and M. Zakharyaschev. Decidable and undecidable fragments of first-order branching temporal logics. In *LICS 2002*, Proceedings of 17th Annual IEEE Symp. on Logic in Computer Science,pages 393–402. IEEE, 2002.
15. G. Hughes and M. Cresswell. *An Introduction to Modal Logic.* Methuen, 1968.
16. A. Pnueli and Y. Kesten. A deductive proof system for CTL*. In L. Brim, P. Jancar, M. Kretínský, and A. Kucera, editors, *CONCUR 2002*, volume 2421 of *Lecture Notes in Computer Science*, pages 24–40. Springer, 2002.
17. A. Pnueli. The temporal logic of programs. In *Proceedings of 18th Symp. on Foundations of Computer Science*, pages 46–57, 1977. Providence, RI.
18. M. Reynolds and C. Dixon. Theorem-proving for discrete temporal logic. In M. Fisher, D. Gabbay, and L. Vila, editors, *Handbook of Temporal Reasoning in Artificial Intelligence*, pages 279–314. Elsevier, 2005.
19. M. Reynolds. An axiomatization of full computation tree logic. *J. Symbolic Logic*, 66(3):1011–1057, 2001.
20. M. Reynolds. An axiomatization of PCTL*. *Information and Computation*, 201:72–119, 2005.
21. S. Schwendimann. A new one-pass tableau calculus for PLTL. In H. de Swart, editor, *Proceedings of International Conference, TABLEAUX 1998, Oisterwijk*, LNAI 1397, pages 277–291. Springer, 1998.
22. C. Sprenger. *Deductive Local Model Checking.* PhD thesis, Swiss Federal Institute of Technology, Lausanne, Switzerland, 2000.
23. C. Stirling. Modal and temporal logics. In S. Abramsky, D. Gabbay, and T. Maibaum, editors, *Handbook of Logic in Computer Science, Volume 2*, pages 477–563. OUP, 1992.
24. M. Vardi and L. Stockmeyer. Improved upper and lower bounds for modal logics of programs. In *17th ACM Symp. on Theory of Computing, Proceedings*, pages 240–251. ACM, 1985.
25. P. Wolper. The tableau method for temporal logic: an overview. *Logique et Analyse*, 28:110–111, June–Sept 1985.

Bisimulation Quantified Logics: Undecidability

Tim French

The University of Western Australia
tim@csse.uwa.edu.au

Abstract. In this paper we introduce a general semantic interpretation for propositional quantification in all multi-modal logics based on bisimulations (bisimulation quantification). Bisimulation quantification has previously been considered in the context of isolated modal logics, such as PDL (D'Agostino and Hollenberg, 2000), intuitionistic logic (Pitts, 1992) and logics of knowledge (French 2003). We investigate the properties of bisimulation quantifiers in general modal logics, particularly the expressivity and decidability, and seek to motivate the use of bisimulation quantified modal logics. This paper addresses two important questions: when are bisimulation quantified logics bisimulation invariant; and do bisimulation quantifiers always preserve decidability? We provide a sufficient condition for bisimulation invariance, and give two examples of decidable modal logics which are undecidable when augmented with bisimulation quantifiers. This is part of a program of study to characterize the expressivity and decidability of bisimulation quantified modal logics.

1 Introduction

In this paper we introduce a general semantic interpretation for propositional quantification in modal logic. This interpretation is based on the notion of *bisimulation* [11,10]. We use *bisimulation quantifiers* [3] to quantify over the interpretation of propositional atoms in all bisimilar models. Bisimulation quantifiers were introduced in [8] and [14] and have been defined in logics based on PDL [3], intuitionistic logics [12] and logics of knowledge [6].

Modal logics find use in great variety of applications, such as temporal reasoning, reasoning about the correctness of programs, and reasoning about knowledge [4]. The variety of modal logics is achieved by restricting the structures (or models) of the logics to various classes. When applying bisimulation quantifiers to these logics we do not quantify over the entire bisimulation class of a structure, rather we quantify over the intersection of that bisimulation class with the class of structures that defines the logic.

In the context of modal logic, bisimulation quantifiers are a natural extension which have some nice properties which we discuss in Section 3. We would like bisimulation quantification to preserve our intuitions regarding propositional quantification, particularly the axioms of *existential introduction* and *existential elimination*. We define a class of logics, the *safe* logics, for which these axioms are sound.

In 1970 Kit Fine [5] investigated the decidability of propositional quantifiers in modal logics. The standard propositional quantifiers were highly expressive and often undecidable (for example, in the cases of **K** and **S4**). Bisimulation quantifiers quantify over the interpretation of propositions in all bisimilar models and are consequently

R. Ramanujam and S. Sen (Eds.): FSTTCS 2005, LNCS 3821, pp. 396–407, 2005.

less expressive. In fact the logic **K** augmented with bisimulation quantifiers is no more expressive than **K** itself.

D'Agostino and Hollenberg have shown the decidability of **BQL** [3], which is effectively the dynamic modal logic, **PDL**, augmented with bisimulation quantifiers, and in [6] the decidability of logics of knowledge with bisimulation quantifiers is shown. Unfortunately it is not always the case that augmentation with bisimulation quantifiers preserves decidability. In this paper we show two decidable modal logics: **S5** × **S5** and **LTL** × **S5**, are undecidable when augmented with bisimulation quantifiers.

2   Syntax and Semantics

We let $L_{\mathcal{C}}$ be a multi-modal logic consisting of k modalities, where $\mathcal{C}$ represents the class of frames over which the logic is defined. Given a modal logic $L_{\mathcal{C}}$, we will let $QL_{\mathcal{C}}$ be an extension of $L_{\mathcal{C}}$ including *bisimulation quantifiers* (defined below).

Let $\mathcal{V}$ be a set of atomic propositions. We recursively define the formulas of $L_{\mathcal{C}}$ as follows:

$$\alpha ::= x \mid \neg\alpha \mid \alpha_1 \vee \alpha_2 \mid \Diamond_i\alpha \tag{1}$$

where $x \in \mathcal{V}$ and $i = 1, ...k$. The syntax for $QL_{\mathcal{C}}$ includes the recursion $\exists x\alpha$, where $x \in \mathcal{V}$. We let the abbreviations $\wedge$, $\rightarrow$, $\leftrightarrow$, $\top$, $\bot$ and $\forall$ be defined as usual and let $\Box_i\alpha$ abbreviate $\neg\Diamond_i\neg\alpha$.

We will first give the semantics for an arbitrary modal logic without bisimulation quantifiers.

Definition 1. *A k-frame, F, is given by the tuple $(S, R_1, ..., R_k)$ where S is a set of* worlds *and for each i, $R_i \subseteq S \times S$. A k-model, M, is given by the tuple $(S, R_i, ..., R_k, \pi, s)$ where $s \in S$ and $\pi : S \longrightarrow \wp(\mathcal{V})$*

We let $\overline{R}$ abbreviate $R_1, ..., R_k$, and for $s' \in S$ we let $M_{s'} = (S, \overline{R}, \pi, s')$. Given a k-model, $M = (S, \overline{R}, \pi, s)$, the semantic interpretation of propositional atoms and modalities is given by:

$$M \models x \iff x \in \pi(s) \tag{2}$$
$$M \models \Diamond_i\alpha \iff \exists(s, t) \in R_i, M_t \models \alpha \tag{3}$$

and the propositional operators have their usual meaning. If a formula is true in every k-model it is referred to as a validity, and if it is true in some k-model it is satisfiable. The set of valid formulas in this language is referred to as K_k (the fusion of k unrestricted modalities, see [7]). However the usefulness of modal logic comes from placing restrictions on modalities. For example specifying a modality to be transitive, irreflexive and antisymmetric allows it to represent properties of time, and specifying a modality to be reflexive, symmetric and transitive allows it to represent properties of knowledge [4].

For a given k, we let $\mathcal{C}$ be a class of k-frames.

Definition 2. *Given a set of k-frames, $\mathcal{C}$, we say $(S, \overline{R})$ is a $\mathcal{C}$-frame if $(S, \overline{R}) \in \mathcal{C}$ and we define a $\mathcal{C}$-model to be the tuple $M = (S, \overline{R}, \pi, s)$ where $\pi : S \longrightarrow \wp(\mathcal{V})$, $s \in S$ and $(S, \overline{R}) \in \mathcal{C}$.*

The set of valid formulas in the language $L_\mathcal{C}$ is defined by restricting the logic to the class of $\mathcal{C}$-frames, so that a formula is valid for $L_\mathcal{C}$ if and only if it is true for all $\mathcal{C}$-frames. To define propositional quantification we will require some additional definitions, based on the concept of a bisimulation [10] [11].

Definition 3. *Given the $\mathcal{C}$-models $M = (S, \overline{R}, \pi, s)$ and $N = (T, \overline{P}, \lambda, t)$, and given $\Theta \subseteq \mathcal{V}$ we say the models M and N are Θ-bisimilar (written $M \cong_\Theta N$) if there is some relation $B \subseteq S \times T$ such that:*

1. $(s, t) \in B$ *and for all* $(s, t) \in B$, $\pi(s) \backslash \Theta = \lambda(t) \backslash \Theta$;
2. *for all* $(s, t) \in B$, *for all* $u \in S$, *if* $(s, u) \in R_i$ *then there exists some* $(u, v) \in B$ *such that* $(t, v) \in P_i$;
3. *for all* $(s, t) \in B$, *for all* $v \in T$ *if* $(t, v) \in P_i$ *then there exists some* $(u, v) \in B$ *such that* $(s, u) \in R_i$.

We call such a relation B a Θ-bisimulation[1] from M to N. If $M \cong_\emptyset N$ we say they are bisimilar *(written $M \cong N$), and if $M \cong_{\{x\}} N$ we say M and N are x-bisimilar (written $M \cong_x N$).*

We are now able to give the semantic interpretation of bisimulation quantification in $QL_\mathcal{C}$:

$$M \models \exists x \alpha \text{ if and only if there is some } \mathcal{C}\text{-model, } N \text{ such that } M \cong_x N \text{ and } N \models \alpha.$$

We note that the meaning of $\models$ is now dependent on $\mathcal{C}$. In the case that $\mathcal{C}$ is not clear from context, we will write $\models_\mathcal{C}$.

3   Properties of Bisimulation Quantification

Bisimulations have been investigated in the context of modal logics for many years. The following results are well-known:

Lemma 1. *For all $\Theta \subset \mathcal{V}$, Θ-bisimulation is an equivalence relation.*

Lemma 2. *For all pure modal formulas ϕ not containing atoms from Θ, for all models, M and N, if $M \models \phi$ and M is Θ-bisimilar to N, then $N \models \phi$.*

Bisimulation quantifiers are a natural extension to modal logic. They allow us to achieve some powers of monadic second-order logic whilst retaining many of the intuitions of pure modal logic. The semantics can appear daunting, since every occurrence of a quantifier in a formula requires us to consider all possible bisimulations of a given model (this complexity is apparent in Section 4.1). However there is a good argument for studying bisimulation quantifiers further. Several bisimulation quantified modal logics, such as BQL [3], are expressively equivalent to the modal μ-calculus. Reasoning

---

[1] Note, in some previous work (e.g. [3]), a Θ-bisimulation refers to what we would denote a $\mathcal{V} \backslash \Theta$-bisimulation. The current notation is more convenient in the context of propositional quantification.

in the μ-calculus is relatively efficient (EXPTIME), and μ-automata [9] allow us to effectively represent bisimulation quantifiers (the construction is effectively equivalent to the projection operation in binary tree automata). In such a case we can avoid much of the complexity involved in bisimulations, whilst still enjoying the ability to express higher order properties.

The action of bisimulation quantifiers is also worth investigating in its own right, rather than as a simple tool to gain greater expressivity. Given any structure, M, in any pure modal logic, $\mathcal{C}$, let $\mathcal{L}$ be set of formulas ϕ such that $M \models \phi$. We will refer to the set $\mathcal{L}$ as the *facts* of M, whilst $\mathcal{C}$ is the context of M. We can suppose that an agent reasoning about M knows the context of M (for example if $\mathcal{C}$ was a temporal system, we would expect an agent would know time is transitive), and knows all the facts of M. Importantly the agent does not know about the structure of M, which is really just a tool to facilitate the set $\mathcal{L}$. So if the agent were to reason about alternative interpretations for an atom, x, we would expect the agent to consider any model that is firstly, an element of $\mathcal{C}$, and secondly agrees with $\mathcal{L}$ on all pure modal formulas not containing x. This process can be applied recursively to motivate any number of nestings of bisimulation quantifiers. This argument is not precise: there are cases where two non-bisimilar models can satisfy the same set of pure modal formulas. However it does give some philosophical motivation for studying bisimulation quantifiers. The relationship between bisimulations and non-well-founded sets is explored in [2].

The final reason for examining bisimulation quantifiers is that they give us some power for describing the logic itself. For example, $\forall x(x \rightarrow \Diamond_i x)$ is equivalent to saying "the modality, $\Diamond_i$, is reflexive". However this is not a statement about any particular structure. It says that in every model in the class $\mathcal{C}$ the modality $\Diamond_i$ is reflexive, so $x \rightarrow \Diamond_i x$ is a validity. Being able to express validities as validities, rather than simply as satisfied formulas, does not change the expressivity of the logic, but it certainly could be significant in providing axiomatizations, or allowing meta-logical reasoning.

As the properties definable in modal logic are bisimulation invariant [13], the application of bisimulation quantifiers does not affect the interpretation of pure modal formulas. However we would also like the semantic interpretation of bisimulation quantifiers to preserve the intuitions of propositional quantification. Particularly, it should satisfy the standard axioms for propositional quantifiers:

1. If $\phi \rightarrow \psi$ is a validity and ψ does not contain the variable x, then for every model that $\exists x\phi \rightarrow \psi$ should also be a validity. This is referred to as *existential elimination*.

2. Suppose α is a formula such that β is free for x in α. Then $\alpha[x\backslash\beta] \rightarrow \exists x\alpha$ is a validity. This is referred to as *existential introduction*.

Here $\alpha[x\backslash\beta]$ is the formula α with every free occurrence of the variable x replaced by the formula β, and β is *free for x in α* if and only if for every free variable, y, of β the variable x is not in the scope of a quantifier, $\exists y$, in α.

Unfortunately these axioms will not hold for all logics, $QL_{\mathcal{C}}$. However these axioms are sound for all *safe* logics, defined below [2]:

---

[2] The author thanks Giovanna D'Agostino and Giacomo Lenzi for improving this definition

Definition 4. *We say the class of frames* $\mathcal{C}$ *is* safe *if and only if for any* $\Theta_1, \Theta_2 \subset \mathcal{V}$, *for any* $\mathcal{C}$-*models* M *and* N *such that* $M \cong_{\Theta_1 \cup \Theta_2} N$, *there is some* $\mathcal{C}$-*model,* K *such that* $M \cong_{\Theta_1} K$ *and* $N \cong_{\Theta_2} K$.

Lemma 3. *Suppose that* $\mathcal{C}$ *is safe and* M, N *are* $\mathcal{C}$-*models such that* $M \cong_\Theta N$. *Then for all formulas,* α, *not containing free atoms from* Θ, $M \models \alpha$ *if and only if* $N \models \alpha$.

Proof. This is shown by induction over the complexity of formulas. The cases for propositional atoms and propositional operators are trivial. Suppose that for some α not containing atoms from Θ, for all $\mathcal{C}$-models, M and N with $M \cong_\Theta N$ we have $M \models \alpha$ if and only if $N \models \alpha$.

Let $M = (S, \overline{R}, \pi, s)$ and $N = (T, \overline{P}, \mu, t)$ be $\mathcal{C}$-models. If $M \cong_\Theta N$ and $M \models \Diamond_i \alpha$, then there is some $s' \in S$ such that $(s, s') \in R_i$ and $(S, \overline{R}, \pi, s') \models \alpha$. Since $M \cong_\Theta N$, there is some $t' \in T$ such that $(t, t') \in P_i$ and $(S, \overline{R}, \pi, s') \cong_\Theta (T, \overline{P}, \mu, t')$. By the induction hypothesis, $(T, \overline{P}, \mu, t') \models \alpha$, and thus $N \models \Diamond_i \alpha$.

Now suppose that M and N are $\mathcal{C}$-models such that $M \cong_\Theta N$ and $M \models \exists x \alpha$. Then there is some model M' such that $M \cong_x M'$ and $M' \models \alpha$. Therefore N and M' are $\{x\} \cup \Theta$-bisimilar, (by Lemma 1). Since $\mathcal{C}$ is safe, there must be a $\mathcal{C}$-frame, K such that $K \cong_\Theta M'$ and $K \cong_{\{x\}} N$. By the induction hypothesis, $K \models \alpha$, and thus $N \models \exists x \alpha$. As the converse for these inductions is symmetric this is sufficient to prove the lemma.

Lemma 4. *Given* $\mathcal{C}$ *is safe, the axioms* existential elimination *and* existential introduction *are sound for* $\mathrm{QL}_\mathcal{C}$.

Proof. To show existential elimination is sound, suppose that for all $\mathcal{C}$-models, $\alpha \to \beta$ is a validity, and for some $\mathcal{C}$-model, M, we have $M \models \exists x \alpha$, where x is not a variable of β. Thus there is some $\mathcal{C}$-model, N, such that $M \cong_x N$ and N models α. Since $\alpha \to \beta$ is a validity, we have $N \models \beta$. Since $M \cong_x N$, it follows from Lemma 3 that $M \models \beta$. Therefore existential elimination is sound.

To show existential introduction suppose that $M = (S, \overline{R}, \pi, s)$ is a $\mathcal{C}$-model such that $M \models \alpha[x \backslash \beta]$ where β is free for x in α. We define the model $N = M_{\beta \to x} = (S, \overline{R}, \rho, s)$ where ρ is such that for all $t \in S$, $\pi(t) \backslash \{x\} = \rho(t) \backslash \{x\}$ and $x \in \rho(t)$ if and only if $M_t \models \beta$. In the first instance we will assume that x is not a free variable of β. For all subformulas, γ of α, let $\gamma' = \gamma[x \backslash \beta]$. We show for all $t \in S$, $M_t \models \gamma'$ if and only if $N_t \models \gamma$ by induction over the complexity of formulas. As the base cases of the induction we have $M_t \models \gamma'$ if and only if $N_t \models \gamma$ where γ is an atomic proposition. Now assume for any γ we have $M_t \models \gamma'$ if and only if $N_t \models \gamma$. It follows directly that

1. $N_t \models \neg\gamma \iff M_t \models (\neg\gamma)'$.
2. $N_t \models \gamma_1 \vee \gamma_2 \iff M_t \models (\gamma_1 \vee \gamma_2)'$.
3. $N_t \models \Diamond_i \gamma \iff M_t \models (\Diamond_i \gamma)'$.

Now suppose that $N_t \models \exists y \gamma$. Therefore there is some $\mathcal{C}$-model $K = (U, \overline{P}, \rho, u)$ such that $K \cong_{\{y\}} N_t$ (so $K \cong_{\{x,y\}} M_t$) and $K \models \gamma$. By the safety of $\mathcal{C}$ there is some $\mathcal{C}$-model, L such that $L \cong_x K$ and $L \cong_y M_t$. If x does not occur free in γ, then by Lemma 3 we have $L \models \gamma$, and $\gamma = \gamma'$, so the induction follows. If x does occur in γ, then β does not contain the atom y, since x is free for β in α. Since x does not occur in β, we have for all $v \in U$, $K_v \models x \leftrightarrow \beta$. Therefore $K = K_{\beta \to x}$ so we can apply this construction inductively to derive $K \models \gamma'$. It follows from Lemma 3 that $L \models \gamma'$ and therefore $M_t \models \exists y \gamma'$.

Conversely suppose that $M_t \models \exists y \gamma'$. There is some $\mathcal{C}$-model, $K = (U, \overline{P}, \rho, u)$ such that $K \cong_{\{y\}} M_t$ (so $K \cong_{\{x,y\}} N_t$) and $K \models \gamma'$. By the safety of $\mathcal{C}$ there is some model $L = (V, \overline{Q}, \eta, v)$ such that $L \cong_{\{y\}} N_t$ and $L \cong_{\{x\}} K$. If γ does not contain x the result follows from Lemma 3. If γ does contain x, then β cannot contain y, so for all $w \in V$, $L_w \models \beta \leftrightarrow x$ (since L is y-bisimilar to N_t). As $K \models \gamma'$, it follows from Lemma 3 that $L \models \gamma'$. Since $L = L_{\beta \to x}$ we can again apply this construction inductively to derive $L \models \gamma$ and therefore $N_t \models \exists y \gamma$.

To complete this proof we need to generalize to the case where x may be a variable of β. Let α' be the formula with every free occurrence of x replaced by y, where y does not occur in α nor β. As x is free for β in α, y is free for β in α' (since y does not occur in α). Clearly $\alpha'[y \backslash \beta]$ is the same as $\alpha[x \backslash \beta]$ and as y does not occur in β the above induction applies. Thus

$$\alpha[x \backslash \beta] \longrightarrow \exists y \alpha' \qquad (4)$$

is a validity. As x does not occur free in α' from the semantic definition of existential quantification and Lemma 3 we have $\exists y \alpha' \to \exists x \alpha$ is also a validity and hence existential introduction is valid.

To see the value of the lemma above it is worthwhile looking and a class of frames which is not safe. Later we will see a logic $\mathbf{S5} \times \mathbf{S5}$ which does not enjoy this property, but first we will consider a simpler logic. Let **Three** be the set of all frames, $F = (S, R)$ where $|S| = 3$ and $R = S \times S$. We can define two **Three**-models which demonstrate existential elimination is not sound. Particularly, let

- $M = (S, R, \pi, a)$ where $S = \{a, b, c\}$, $R = S \times S$, $\pi(a) = \{y, z\}$, $\pi(b) = \{y\}$ and $\pi(c) = \{x\}$.
- $N = (T, P, \rho, d)$ where $T = \{d, e, f\}$, $P = T \times T$, $\rho(d) = \{y\}$, $\rho(e) = \{x, w\}$ and $\rho(f) = \{x\}$.

Now $M \cong_{\{w,z\}} N$ via the bisimulation, $B = \{(a, d), (b, d), (c, e), (c, f)\}$ but there is no **Three**-model, $K = (U, Q, \eta, u)$ such that $M \cong_{\{w\}} K$ and $N \cong_{\{z\}} K$. To see this we note that any such model must contain some state $g \in U$, with $\eta(g) = \{y, z\}$, some state $h \in U$ with $\eta(h) = \{y\}$, some state $i \in U$ with $\eta(i) = \{x, w\}$ and some state $j \in U$ with $\eta(j) = \{x\}$. That is, K cannot be a **Three**-model. Therefore $M \models_{\textbf{Three}} \exists z \exists w (\diamond (x \wedge w) \wedge \diamond (x \wedge \neg w))$, but $M \not\models_{\textbf{Three}} \exists w (\diamond (x \wedge w) \wedge \diamond (x \wedge \neg w))$

This example exploits a simple counting property to invalidate existential elimination. The $\mathbf{S5} \times \mathbf{S5}$ example below shows how more complex structural properties can make a class of frames unsafe.

4 Undecidable Logics

Here we will briefly examine some logics which are decidable, but whose bisimulation quantified extension is undecidable. The logics we will describe are PLTL $\times$ **S5** and

S5 × S5. The decidability of both of these logics is described in [7]. Both undecidability proofs will make use of tiling problems, which is a common technique for proving the undecidability of modal logics.

The tiling problem is as follows: We are given a finite set $\Gamma = \{\gamma_i | i = 1, ..., m\}$ of tiles. Each tile γ_i has four coloured sides: left, right, top and bottom, written γ_i^l, γ_i^r, γ_i^t, and γ_i^b. Each side can be one of n colours c_j for $j = 1, ..., n$. Given any set of these tiles, we would like to know if we can cover the plane $\mathbb{N} \times \mathbb{N}$ with these tiles such that adjacent sides share the same colour. Formally, given some finite set of tiles Γ we would like to decide if there exists a function $\lambda : \mathbb{N} \times \mathbb{N} \longrightarrow \Gamma$ such that for all $(x, y) \in \mathbb{N} \times \mathbb{N}$

1. $\lambda(x, y)^r = \lambda(x + 1, y)^l$
2. $\lambda(x, y)^t = \lambda(x, y + 1)^b$

where $\lambda(x, y)^t$ is the colour of the top side of the tile on (x, y), and likewise for the other sides. As shown by Berger [1], this problem is undecidable.

4.1   S5 × S5

The logic **S5 × S5** is defined to be the cross-product of two **S5** frames. The syntax is given by $\alpha ::= x | \alpha \vee \alpha | \neg \alpha | \Diamond_1 \alpha | \Diamond_2 \alpha$. The logic is defined over the set of all frames specified as follows: $F = (S, R_1, R_2)$ where

- $S = S_1 \times S_2$ where S_1 and S_2 are arbitrary non-empty sets.
- $((a, b), (c, d)) \in R_1$ if and only if $a = c$.
- $((a, b), (c, d)) \in R_2$ if and only if $b = d$.

By an abuse of notation, we will also refer to the class of **S5 × S5** frames as **S5 × S5**.

Lemma 5. *The class of frames,* **S5 × S5**, *is not safe.*

Proof. We will prove this lemma with an example. In Figure 4.1 there are two **S5 × S5**-models, M and N. One modality corresponds to the vertical axis, and one modality corresponds to the horizontal access. The propositions true at each state are marked, and we let the starting state for each model be the bottom left state. We can see the two models $\{x, y\}$-bisimilar, via a bisimulation which relates states with the same propositions (excepting x and y). Note that when we ignore x and y, the two models are almost identical, except the central four states are transposed.

Now suppose for contradiction that there is some **S5 × S5**-model K such that $K \cong_{\{y\}} M$ and $K \cong_{\{x\}} N$. Therefore the starting state for K must be labeled with the propositions, c, x and y. Since K is y bisimilar to M, by Lemma 2 for every pure modal formula, ϕ, not containing y K satisfies ϕ if and only if M satisfies ϕ (and likewise for N and x). Let

$$\phi(w, z) = \Box_1(d \rightarrow \Box_2(w \rightarrow \Box_1(g \rightarrow \Box_2(c \rightarrow \neg z)))).$$

We can see $M \models \phi(b, x)$ and $N \models \phi(a, y)$, so $K \models \phi(b, x) \wedge \phi(a, y)$. However since K is an **S5 × S5**-model, $\{x, y\}$-bisimilar to both M and N, there must be states h, i, j, k is K where:

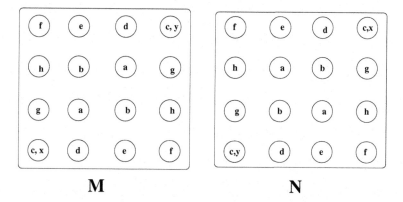

Fig. 1. An example where **S5** × **S5** is not safe. The two modalities correspond to the horizontal and vertical axis respectively.

1. h is the starting state, labeled with c, x, y;
2. i is some state such that $(h, i) \in R_1$ and i is labeled with d;
3. j is some state such that $(h, j) \in R_2$ and j is labeled with g;
4. k is defined such that $(i, k) \in R_2$ and $(j, k) \in R_1$.

By observing M and N we can see that the state k must be labeled with either a or b. However the relations R_1 and R_2 are symmetric, so if k was labeled by a we would have $K \models \neg\phi(a, y)$, and if k was labeled by b we would have $K \models \neg\phi(b, x)$, giving the necessary contradiction.

As **S5** × **S5** is not safe we must proceed with caution as our usual intuitions regarding the behavior of quantification will not necessarily hold. However we can see from the proof above that bisimulation invariance still applies to pure modal formulas.

We encode the tiling problem by defining propositional atoms u and v such that they allow us to linearly order the horizontal and vertical axis. In particular we would like the following properties to hold:

1. if u is true at any state (a, b) in the model, then there is exactly one state (a, c) in the model such that $c \neq b$ where v is true.
2. if v is true at any state (a, b) in the model, then there is exactly one state (c, b) in the model such that $c \neq a$ where u is true.

We will refer to such properties as the *step* properties. Such a configuration is given in Figure 4.1.

In general bisimulation quantifiers do not allow us to define such strict properties, but we will see that we can "simulate" such properties in the scope of quantifiers.

For each $\gamma \in \Gamma$ we suppose that there is a unique propositional atom in $\mathcal{V}$, which we also refer top as γ (where its meaning shall be clear from context). We encode the tiling problem in several stages: Let

$$step(x, y) = x \wedge \Box_2 \neg y \wedge \Box_1 \Box_2 ((x \rightarrow \Diamond_1 y) \wedge (y \rightarrow \Diamond_2 x)).$$

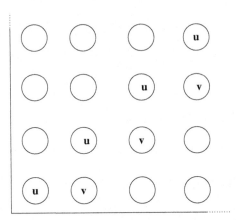

Fig. 2. u and v define the step property in **S5** $\times$ **S5**, which allows us to discretize and order the horizontal and vertical axis.

This states that x and y satisfy the step properties except for the uniqueness constraints. Next we define

$$step(x, y, u, v) = u \wedge \Box_2 \neg v \wedge \Box_1 \Box_2 ((u \to (x \wedge \Diamond_1 v)) \wedge (v \to (y \wedge \Diamond_2 u))).$$

Finally assuming the u and v satisfy the step properties we can encode the tiling problem as follows:

$$right = \Box_1 \Box_2 \left(\bigwedge_{\gamma \in \Gamma} (\gamma \to \forall z(z \to \Box_2(u \to \Box_1(v \to \Diamond_2(\Diamond_1 z \wedge \bigvee_{\gamma^r = \delta^l} \delta))))) \right)$$

$$up = \Box_1 \Box_2 \left(\bigwedge_{\gamma \in \Gamma} (\gamma \to \forall z(z \to \Box_1(v \to \Box_2(u \to \Diamond_1(\Diamond_2 z \wedge \bigvee_{\gamma^t = \delta_b} \delta))))) \right)$$

$$unique = \Box_1 \Box_2 \left(\left(\bigvee_{\gamma \in \Gamma} \gamma \right) \wedge \left(\bigwedge_{\gamma \in \Gamma} \gamma \to \bigwedge_{\delta \in \Gamma - \gamma} \neg \delta \right) \right)$$

We now give the complete formula as

$$Tile_\Gamma = unique \wedge step(x, y) \wedge \forall u \forall v (step(x, y, u, v) \to (right \wedge up)).$$

We note that the alternation in quantifier is similar to a least fixed point. If $Tile_\Gamma$ is true then there must be some uv-bisimulation which satisfies the step properties, and if $Tile_\Gamma$ is false, then it must be false for some xy-bisimulation where x and y satisfy the step properties (and hence u and v satisfy the step properties up to bisimulation equivalence).

Lemma 6. $Tile_\Gamma$ *is satisfiable if and only if Γ can tile the plane.*

Proof. First, let us suppose that there is a tiling, λ, of the plane with the tiles in Γ. We show that there is a model, $M = (S, R_1, R_2, \pi, s)$, satisfying $Tile_\Gamma$. We let:

1. $S = \omega \times \omega$
2. $R_1 = \{((a, b), (c, b)) | a, b, c \in \omega\}$
3. $R_2 = \{((a, b), (a, c)) | a, b, c \in \omega\}$
4. $\gamma \in \pi(a, b) \Leftrightarrow \gamma = \lambda(a, b)$, $x \in \pi(a, b) \Leftrightarrow a = b$ and $y \in \pi(a, b) \Leftrightarrow a = b + 1$.
5. $s = (0, 0)$.

As λ is a function it follows that $M \models unique$, and by the construction of M we also have $M \models step(x, y)$. The remaining part of the formula, $Tile_\Gamma$ is in the scope of universal quantifiers which makes things more complicated. It is especially complicated in the case of $\mathbf{S5} \times \mathbf{S5}$ as the logic is not safe. However we have constructed a model where every state can be uniquely identified by a formula, and we will use these "unique" formulas to show that $Tile_\Gamma$ is satisfied. The unique formulas are defined recursively by

$$\eta_0 = x \wedge \Box_2 \neg y$$
$$\eta_{i+1} = x \wedge \Diamond_2(y \wedge \Diamond_1 \eta_i)$$
$$\eta(a, b) = \Diamond_2 \eta_a \wedge \Diamond_1 \eta_b.$$

We can see $M_t \models \eta_a$ if and only if $t = (a, a)$, and thus for all $t \in S$, $M_t \models \eta(a, b)$ if and only if $t = (a, b)$. Consequently, for any $(a, b) \in S$, we have $M \models \eta(a, b) \rightarrow \lambda(a, b)$. By a result of van Benthem, pure modal formulas are bisimulation invariant, so for any model N where $N \cong_{u,v} M$ we will have $N \models \Box_1 \Box_2(\eta((a, b) \rightarrow \lambda(a, b))$. Let $N = (S', R_1', R_2', \pi', s')$ be any $\{u, v\}$-bisimulation of M, such that N is an $\mathbf{S5} \times \mathbf{S5}$-model and $N \models step(x, y, u, v)$. For any state $t \in S'$, there is a unique (a, b) such that $N_t \models \eta(a, b)$ and thus $N_t \models \lambda(a, b)$. Suppose that $\lambda(a, b) = \gamma$. To show that the subformula $right$ is satisfied by N we must show

$$N_t \models \forall z(z \rightarrow \Box_1(v \rightarrow \Box_2(u \rightarrow \Diamond_1(\Diamond_2 z \wedge \bigvee_{\gamma^t = \delta_b} \delta)))) \tag{5}$$

For any z-bisimulation $N' = (T, P_1, P_2, \rho, t')$ of N_t where $N' \models z$, we will have $N' \models \Box_2(u \rightarrow \eta(a, a))$ (since $u \rightarrow x$). Since $N \models step(x, y, u, v)$, there is some state $e \in T$ such that $N_e' \models u$ where $(t', e) \in P_2$. By the definition of the step function we also have $N' \models \Box_2(u \rightarrow \Box_1(v \rightarrow \eta(a + 1, a)))$, (since $u \rightarrow x$ and $v \rightarrow y$ in N'). Let $f \in T$ be any state such that $N_f' \models v$ and $(e, f) \in P_1$. Since N is a $\mathbf{S5} \times \mathbf{S5}$ frame there is some unique state $g \in T$ such that $(f, g) \in P_2$ and $(t', g) \in P_1$. Also since $N_f' \models \Diamond_2 \eta_{a+1}$ and $N_{t'}' \models \Diamond_1 \eta_b$, we have $N_g' \models \eta(a + 1, b)$ and hence $N_g' \models \lambda(a + 1, b) \wedge \Diamond_1 z$. Therefore we have shown (5) to be true, and as t was chosen arbitrarily it follows that $N \models right$. The case for showing that $N \models up$ is symmetric. As N is an arbitrary $\{u, v\}$-bisimulation of M satisfying $step(x, y, u, v)$ it follows that $M \models \forall u \forall v(step(x, y, u, v) \rightarrow (right \wedge up))$.

Conversely, suppose that $M \models Tile_\Gamma$, where $M = (S, R_1, R_2, \pi, s)$. Since $M \models Tile_\Gamma$ for every $\{u, v\}$-bisimulation, N of M we have $N \models unique \wedge step(x, y) \wedge step(x, y, u, v) \rightarrow (right \wedge up)$. Clearly there is some such $\{u, v\}$-bisimulation $N =$

(T, P_1, P_2, ρ, t) of M such that $N \models step(x, y, u, v)$. We define a function $\phi : \omega \times \omega \longrightarrow T$ inductively by

1. $\phi(0, 0) = t$. We note that as $N \models step(x, y, u, v)$ we have $N_{\phi(0,0)} \models u \wedge \Diamond_1 v$.
2. Given $a \in \omega$ such that $\phi(a, a) = t'$ and $N_{\phi(a,a)} \models u \wedge \Diamond_1 v$ we choose some $r \in T$ such that $u \in \rho(r)$ and for some $r' \in T$, $v \in \rho(r')$, $(t', r') \in P_1$ and $(r', r) \in P_2$. We let $\phi(a + 1, a + 1) = r$, and note that $N_{\phi(a+1,a+1)} \models u \wedge \Diamond_1 v$ (since $N \models step(x, y, u, v)$). Thus for all $a \in \omega$ we can define $\phi(a, a)$.
3. For any $(a, b) \in \omega \times \omega$ where $a \neq b$, we define $\phi(a, b)$ to be the unique element r of T, such that $(\phi(a, a), r) \in P_1$ and $(\phi(b, b), r) \in P_2$

It follows from the definitions of up and $right$, that λ is a tiling of the plane where $\lambda(a, b) = \gamma$ if and only if $\gamma \in \rho(\phi(a, b))$.

Corollary 1. $\mathrm{QL_{S5 \times S5}}$, *the bisimulation quantified extension of* **S5** $\times$ **S5**, *is undecidable.*

4.2   LTL $\times$ S5

In the previous section we saw a complicated bisimulation quantified logic which was neither safe nor decidable. We might hope that bisimulation quantifiers preserve the decidability of all safe logics, but this is not the case. **LTL** $\times$ **S5** is a safe logic which is also undecidable when augmented with bisimulation quantifiers.

The syntax for **LTL** $\times$ **S5** is as follows:

$$\alpha ::= x | \alpha \vee \alpha | \neg \alpha | X \alpha | F \alpha | \Box \alpha$$

where $G\alpha$ is the dual of $F\alpha$.

The logic **LTL** $\times$ **S5** is defined over structures specified by $F \subset \mathcal{F} = \{\sigma | \sigma : \mathbb{N} \longrightarrow \wp(\mathcal{V})\}$ The states of F are represented by the tuple, σ, i, where $\sigma \in F$ and $i \in \mathbb{N}$. The semantics are:

$$(F, \sigma, j) \models x \Leftrightarrow x \in \sigma(j), \text{ for all } x \in \mathcal{V}.$$
$$(F, \sigma, j) \models X\alpha \Leftrightarrow (F, \sigma, j + 1) \models \alpha.$$
$$(F, \sigma, j) \models G\alpha \Leftrightarrow \forall k \geq j, (F, \sigma, k) \models \alpha.$$
$$(F, \sigma, j) \models \Box \alpha \Leftrightarrow \forall \sigma', (F, \sigma', j) \models \alpha$$

where $\vee$ and $\neg$ have there usual meaning.

This logic has been shown to be decidable (see [7]). We note that the set **LTL** $\times$ **S5** models can easily be translated to define a class of frames in the notation of Section 2. This allows us to provide the semantics for bisimulation quantifiers. We give the following lemmas.

Lemma 7. LTL $\times$ **S5** *is safe.*

Proof. Suppose that $M = (F, \sigma, 0)$ and $N = (G, \eta, 0)$ are $\Theta \cup \Lambda$-bisimilar models, via the bisimulation Z. We define a **LTL** $\times$ **S5** model $K = (H, \phi, 0)$ such that $K \cong_\Theta M$ and $K \cong_\Lambda N$ as follows: We let $H = \{a' | a = (\tau_a, \mu_a) \in Z\}$ where for all i, $a'(i) = (\tau_a(i) \backslash \Theta) \cup (\mu_a(i) \backslash \Lambda)$. It follows that the relation $X = \{(a', \tau_a) | a = (\tau_a, \mu_a) \in Z\}$ is a Θ-bisimulation from K to M and $Y = \{(a', \mu_a) | a = (\tau_a, \mu_a) \in Z\}$ is a Λ-bisimulation from K to N. Therefore **LTL** $\times$ **S5** is safe, and hence preserves existential elimination.

Given that **LTL** $\times$ **S5** is safe it is easier to encode a tiling problem, since we can assume that existential introduction and elimination are sound.

Lemma 8. *The bisimulation quantified extension of* **LTL** $\times$ **S5** *is undecidable.*

This can be shown in a similar manner to Lemma 6. The proof is slightly easier since the X operator can be used to identify vertically adjacent states. For horizontally adjacent states we can again use the step properties and bisimulation quantified atoms to define a formula $Tile_\Gamma^2$ that is satisfiable if and only if Γ can tile the plane.

5   Conclusion

In this paper we have examined a generalized definition for bisimulation quantified modal logics. We have also introduced the notion of *safe* frames, which satisfy the axioms of existential elimination and existential introduction. We have shown that there are decidable modal logics which are not safe and undecidable. However, the decidability of $QL_{\mathbf{LTL} \times \mathbf{S5}}$ shows that safety alone is not enough to guarantee that extension by bisimulation quantification will preserve decidability. It is an interesting problem to characterize the modal logics for which are decidable when augmented with bisimulation quantification. While this paper provides several negative results, we hope to soon provide a positive decidability result for a general class of safe modal logics.

References

1. R. Berger. The undecidability of the dominoe problem. *Mem. Amer. Math. Soc.*, 66, 1966.
2. G. D'Agostino. *Modal logic and non-well-founded set theory: translation, bisimulation, interpolation.* PhD thesis, University of Amsterdam, 1998.
3. G. D'Agostino and M. Hollenberg. Logical questions concerning the mu-calculus: interpolation, Lyndon and Los-Tarski. *The Journal of Symbolic Logic*, 65(1):310–332, 2000.
4. R. Fagin, J. Halpern, Y. Moses, and M. Vardi. *Reasoning About Knowledge*. MIT Press, 1995.
5. K. Fine. Propositional quantifiers in modal logic. *Theoria*, 36:336–346, 1970.
6. T. French. Decidability of propositionally quantified logics of knowledge. In *Proc. 16th Australian Joint Conference on Artificial Intelligence*, 2003.
7. D. Gabbay, A. Kurucz, F. Wolter, and M. Zakharayashev. *Many Dimensional Modal Logics: Theory and Applications.* Elsevier, 2003.
8. S. Ghilardi and M. Zawadowski. A sheaf representation and duality for finitely presented heyting algebras. *Journal of Symbolic Logic*, 60:911–939, 1995.
9. D. Janin and I. Walukiewicz. Automata for the modal mu-calculus and related results. *Lecture Notes in Computer Science*, 969:552–562, 1995.
10. R. Milner. A calculus of communicating systems. *Lecture Notes in Computer Science*, 92, 1980.
11. D. Park. Concurrency and automata on infinite sequences. *Lecture Notes in Computer Science*, 104:167–183, 1981.
12. A. Pitts. On the interpretation of second-order quantification in first-order intuitionistic propositional logic. *Journal of Symbolic Logic*, 57:33–52, 1992.
13. J. van Benthem. Correspondence theory. *Handbook of Philosophical Logic*, 2:167–247, 1984.
14. A. Visser. Uniform interpolation and layered bisimulation. In *Godel '96*, volume 6 of *Lecture Notes Logic*, pages 139–164, 1996.

Logarithmic-Time Single Deleter, Multiple Inserter Wait-Free Queues and Stacks

Prasad Jayanti and Srdjan Petrovic

Department of Computer Science, Dartmouth College,
Hanover, New Hampshire, USA
{prasad,spetrovic}@cs.dartmouth.edu

Abstract. Despite the ubiquitous need for shared FIFO queues in parallel applications and operating systems, there are no sublinear-time wait-free queue algorithms that can support more than a single enqueuer and a single dequeuer. Two independently designed algorithms—David's recent algorithm [1] and the algorithm in this paper—break this barrier. While David's algorithm is capable of supporting multiple dequeuers (but only one enqueuer), our algorithm can support multiple enqueuers (but only one dequeuer). David's algorithm achieves $O(1)$ time complexity for both enqueue and dequeue operations, but its space complexity is infinite because of the use of infinite sized arrays. The author states that he can bound the space requirement, but only at the cost of increasing the time complexity to $O(n)$, where n is the number of dequeuers. A significant feature of our algorithm is that its time and space complexities are both bounded and small: enqueue and dequeue operations run in $O(\lg n)$ time, and the space complexity is $O(n + m)$, where n is the number of enqueuers and m is the actual number of items currently present in the queue. David's algorithm uses *fetch&increment* and *swap* instructions, which are both at level 2 of Herlihy's Consensus hierarchy, along with *queue*. Our algorithm uses the LL/SC instructions, which are universal. However, since these instructions have constant time wait-free implementation from CAS and restricted LL/SC that are widely supported on modern architectures, our algorithms can run efficiently on current machines. Thus, in applications where there are multiple producers and a single consumer (e.g., certain server queues and resource queues), our algorithm provides the best known solution to implementing a wait-free queue. Using similar ideas, we can also efficiently implement a stack that supports multiple pushers and a single popper.

1 Introduction

In parallel systems, *shared data objects* provide the means for processes to communicate and cooperate with each other. Atomicity of these shared data objects has traditionally been ensured through the use of locks. Locks, however, limit parallelism and cause processes to wait on each other, with several consequent drawbacks, including deadlocks, convoying, priority inversion, and lack of fault-tolerance to process crashes. This sparked off extensive research on the design

R. Ramanujam and S. Sen (Eds.): FSTTCS 2005, LNCS 3821, pp. 408–419, 2005.

of *wait-free* data objects, which ensure that every process completes its operation on the data object in a bounded number of its steps, regardless of whether other processes are slow, fast or have crashed [2]. We refer to this bound (on the number of steps that a process executes to complete an operation on the data object) as the *time complexity* (of that operation).

Early research sought to demonstrate the feasibility of implementing wait-free data objects, culminating in Herlihy's universal construction [2,3], which transforms *any* sequential implementation $\mathcal{A}$ of a data object into a wait-free shared implementation $\mathcal{B}$ of that data object. However, the worst-case time complexity of performing an operation on the data object $\mathcal{B}$ is $\Omega(n)$, where n is the number of processes sharing $\mathcal{B}$. In fact, it has been proved later that this linear dependence of time complexity on n is unavoidable with any universal construction [4]. Thus, if *sublinear time* wait-free data objects are our goal, it is imperative that algorithms exploit the semantics of the specific object (e.g., counter, queue, stack) being implemented. In recent years, this approach has indeed led to sublinear time wait-free algorithms for implementing a variety of shared data objects, e.g., the class of closed objects (which include counters and swap objects) [5], f-arrays [6], and LL/SC objects [7,8,9].

A *shared FIFO queue* is one of the most commonly used data objects in parallel applications and operating systems. Not surprisingly, a number of algorithms have been proposed for implementing queues. However, most of these algorithms are only nonblocking[1] and not wait-free. With the exception of a recent algorithm by David [1], which we will discuss shortly, wait-free queue algorithms either had excessive time complexity of $\Omega(n)$ [3,7,10,11], or implemented a queue in the restricted case when there is only one enqueuer and one dequeuer [12,13]. Specifically, until recently, no sublinear time wait-free queue algorithm was discovered, despite the ubiquitous need for queues. When we considered why there has been so little success in designing efficient wait-free queue algorithms, we found a plausible explanation, which we now describe. Normally, we represent a queue as a (linear) linked list of elements with variables *front* and *rear* holding the pointers to the first and the last elements of the list. To enqueue an element e, a process p must perform a sequence of steps: first it must read *rear* to locate the currently last element, then adjust that element to point to the new element e and, finally, adjust *rear* to point to e. If p stops after performing only a few of these steps, other processes (that need to enqueue elements into the queue) have no option but to help p (otherwise the implementation won't be wait-free). Thus, if k processes are concurrently performing enqueue operations, the last process to complete the enqueue may have to help all other processes, resulting in $\Omega(k)$ time complexity for its enqueue operation. In the worst case, k may be as high as n, the maximum number of processes sharing the queue. Hence, the worst-case time complexity of an enqueue operation is linear in n.

---

[1] A nonblocking queue is strictly weaker than a wait-free queue: when multiple processes attempt to execute operations on a nonblocking queue, all but one process may starve.

The above informal reasoning suggests that any wait-free queue algorithm, if it aspires to break the linear time barrier, must necessarily be based on a more creative data structure than a linear linked list. This paper proposes one such novel data structure where a queue is represented as a binary tree whose leaves are linear linked lists. Based on this data structure, we design an efficient wait-free queue algorithm, but it has one limitation: the algorithm does not allow concurrent dequeue operations. In other words, our algorithm requires that the dequeue operations be executed one after the other, but allows the dequeue to be concurrent with any number of enqueue operations. The significant features of our algorithm are:

1. Sublinear Time Complexity: The worst-case time complexity of an *enqueue* or a *dequeue* operation is $O(\lg n)$, where n is the maximum number of processes for which the queue is implemented.
2. Space Efficiency: At any time t, the algorithm uses $O(m + n)$ space, where m is the actual number of items present in the queue at time t.

Our algorithm uses LL/SC instructions which act like read and conditional-write, respectively. More specifically, the LL(X) instruction by process p returns the value of the location X, while the SC(X, v) instruction by p checks whether some process updated the location X since p's latest LL, and if that isn't the case it writes v into X and returns *true*; otherwise, it returns *false* and leaves X unchanged. Although these instructions are not directly supported in hardware, they have constant time and space wait-free implementation from CAS and restricted LL/SC, which are widely supported on modern architectures [7,8,9]. Consequently, our algorithms can run efficiently on current machines. In applications where there are multiple producers and a single consumer (e.g., certain server queues and resource queues), our algorithm provides the best known solution to implementing a wait-free queue.

Concurrently with our research and independently, David designed a sublinear-time wait-free queue algorithm [1] that imposes a different limitation than ours: his algorithm does not allow concurrent enqueue operations (but allows an enqueue operation to run concurrently with any number of dequeue operations). In contrast, our algorithm does not allow concurrent dequeue operations, but allows a dequeue to run concurrently with any number of enqueue operations. In the following we describe David's result and contrast it with ours.

David's algorithm implements a wait-free *single enqueuer, multiple dequeuer* queue while our algorithm implements a *multiple enqueuer, single dequeuer* queue. His algorithm uses *fetch&increment* and *swap* instructions while ours uses LL/SC instructions. The enqueue and dequeue operations run in $O(1)$ time in his algorithm while they run in $O(\lg n)$ time in our algorithm. David's result is interesting because (1) it shows for the first time that it is possible to implement a sublinear-time, non-trivial, wait-free queue (i.e., a queue that supports more concurrent operations than just a single enqueue and a single dequeue) from objects of the same power as the queue itself,[2] and (2) it achieves the best possible running time of $O(1)$ for enqueue and dequeue operations. His algorithm, however, is not practical: it uses arrays of infinite length and therefore has an infinite space complexity. The author states that it is possible to bound the space complexity of his algorithm, but at the cost of increasing the time complexity of the algorithm to $O(n)$. In contrast, our algorithm, besides achieving sublinear time complexity, is also space efficient: its space complexity is $O(n + m)$, where n is the total number of processes sharing the queue and m is the actual number of items currently present in the queue.

The ideas introduced in this paper have a more general applicability than for just implementing queues: they have proved useful in designing a wait-free *multiple pusher, single popper* stack with the same time and space complexities as for queue, and seem to have potential for efficiently implementing priority queues (which we are currently exploring).

1.1 Algorithmic Ideas in a Nutshell

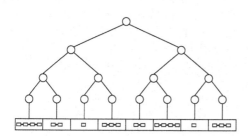

Fig. 1. Main data structure for the multiple enqueuer, single dequeuer queue.

The key idea behind our algorithm is to distribute the "global" queue Q (that we wish to implement) over n "local" queues, where n is the maximum number of processes sharing Q. More specifically, the algorithm keeps one local queue at each process. To enqueue an element e, a process p first obtains a time stamp t and then inserts the pair (e, t) into its local queue. (Processes that concurrently attempt to get time stamps are allowed to get the same time stamp, which makes it possible to obtain a time stamp in just two machine instructions, as we will see later.) Thus, the local queue at p contains only the elements inserted by p, in the order of their insertion. The front element of the *global* queue is the earliest of the front elements of the local queues (*i.e.*, an element with the smallest time stamp over all local queues). The naive strategy to locate this earliest element would be to examine the front elements of all of the local queues, which leads to $O(n)$ running time for the dequeue operation. We use a cleverer strategy that views the front elements of the local queues as the leaves of a binary tree (see Figure 1) and, using ideas first proposed by Afek, Dauber and Touitou [14], propagate the minimum of these elements to the root of the tree. Significantly, even though many processes might be acting concurrently, this propagation works correctly and takes only $O(\lg n)$ time. The dequeuer reads the root to determine the local queue that has the earliest element, removes that element from the local queue, and finally propagates the new front element of that local queue towards the root (to ensure that the root reflects the new minimum element).

---

[2] By the power of an object we mean its level in the Herlihy's Consensus Hierarchy [2]. All of *fetch&increment*, *swap*, and *queue* are at level 2 of the consensus hierarchy, and are thus equally powerful by this measure.

In the above strategy, the local queue at process p is accessed (possibly concurrently) by at most two processes—the enqueuer (namely, process p) and the lone dequeuer. The enqueuer executes either an *enqueue* operation or a *read-front* operation, which returns the front element without affecting the state of the queue. The dequeuer executes either a *dequeue* operation or a *read-front* operation. The *read-front* operation is needed because, in order to propagate the front element of the local queue towards the root of the binary tree, the enqueuer and the dequeuer need the means to determine what the front element of the local queue is. In Section 2 we describe how to implement a local queue supporting these operations using only *read* and *write* operations on shared variables. Then, in Section 3, we describe how to implement a global queue from the local queues, using the strategy described in the previous paragraph.

2   Single Enqueuer, Single Dequeuer Queue

In this section we present an important building block for our main queue implementation, namely, a *single enqueuer, single dequeuer queue object* that supports three operations—*enqueue(v)*, *dequeue()*, and *readFront()*. The *enqueue(v)* operation inserts an element v into the queue. The *dequeue()* operation removes and returns the front element of the queue. The *readFront()* operation reads the value of the front element without removing that element from the queue. If the queue is empty, both *dequeue()* and *readFront()* return $\perp$.

A single enqueuer, single dequeuer queue can be accessed by two processes: the *enqueueing process*, which can invoke an *enqueue()* or a *readFront()* operation, and a *dequeuing process*, which can invoke a *dequeue()* or a *readFront()* operation. To distinguish between the *readFront()* operations performed by an enqueuer and a dequeuer, we refer to the two operations as $readFront_e$ and $readFront_d$, respectively.

Figure 2 presents an implementation of a single enqueuer, single dequeuer queue. This algorithm is similar to the two-lock queue algorithm by Michael and Scott [15], except that it additionally supports the *readFront()* operation. (We need this operation for our main queue algorithm, presented in the next section.) As we will shortly see, the presence of the *readFront()* operation significantly complicates the algorithm design.

The queue is represented as a singly linked list terminated by a dummy node. Variables First and Last point, respectively, to the first and the last node in the list. Enqueueing and dequeueing elements from the queue consists of inserting and removing nodes from the linked list in a way similar to a sequential linked-list implementation of a queue. In particular, to enqueue the value v into the queue, process p performs the following steps. First, p creates a new node (Line 1). Next, p locates the last node in the list, i.e., the dummy node (Line 2) and writes the value v into that node (Line 3). Finally, p completes its operation by inserting a new (dummy) node to the end of the list (Lines 4 and 5). To dequeue an item from the queue, process p first checks whether the list contains only a single node (Lines 6 and 7). If it does, then that node is a dummy node and

Types

    valuetype = Any type

    nodetype = **record** *val*: valuetype; *next*: **pointer to** nodetype **end**

Shared variables

    First, Last, Announce, FreeLater: **pointer to** nodetype

    Help: valuetype

Initialization

    First = Last = **new** *Node*()

    FreeLater = **new** *Node*()

procedure enqueue(v)

1:   *newNode* = **new** *Node*()

2:   *tmp* = Last

3:   *tmp.val* = v

4:   *tmp.next* = *newNode*

5:   Last = *newNode*

procedure readFront$_e$()

           returns valuetype

17: *tmp* = First

18: **if** (tmp == Last) **return** $\perp$

19: Announce = *tmp*

20: **if** ($tmp \neq$ First)

21:     *retval* = Help

22: **else** *retval* = *tmp.val*

23: **return** *retval*

procedure dequeue()

           returns valuetype

6:   *tmp* = First

7:   **if** (tmp == Last) **return** $\perp$

8:   *retval* = *tmp.val*

9:   Help = *retval*

10: First = *tmp.next*

11: **if** (tmp == Announce)

12:     tmp' = FreeLater

13:     FreeLater = *tmp*

14:     free(tmp')

15: **else** free(tmp)

16: **return** *retval*

procedure readFront$_d$()

           returns valuetype

24: *tmp* = First

25: **if** (tmp == Last) **return** $\perp$

26: **return** *tmp.val*

Fig. 2. Implementation of the single enqueuer, single dequeuer queue object from *read/write* registers.

so p returns $\perp$ (Line 7). Otherwise, p reads the value stored at the front node (Line 8), removes that node from the list (Line 10), and frees up memory used by that node (Lines 14 or 15). Finally, p completes its operation by returning the value it read from the front node (Line 16).

    Observe that in the above algorithm, the enqueue and dequeue operations work on separate parts of the list, namely, its front and back. Hence, there is no contention between the two operations, which is why the above algorithm is so simple. However, if we add a *readFront()* operation to our set of operations, we have a problem: both *readFront$_e$()* and *dequeue()* now operate on the same node of the list, namely, its front node. This contention on the first element of the list complicates the design of the two operations, as we describe below.

    To perform a *readFront$_e$* operation, process p first reads the pointer to the front node in the list (Line 17) and then checks whether the list contains only a single node (Line 18). If it does, then that node is a dummy node and so p

returns $\bot$ (Line 18). Otherwise, at the time when p read the pointer to the front node, the front node indeed contained a valid value for p's operation to return. However, it is quite possible that after p's reading of the pointer a dequeue operation deleted the front node and freed up the memory used by it. Thus, p cannot even attempt to read the value at the front node since it may result in a memory access to a memory that has already been freed.

So, instead of reading the value at the front node, p first writes the pointer to the front node into the variable Announce (Line 19), notifying a dequeuing operation that it is interested in the front node and asking it not to free that node from the memory. Next, p reads the pointer to the front node again (Line 20). If the pointer is the same as before, then p knows that a dequeuer has not yet removed the front node from the queue. (Notice that the front node could not have been removed and re-inserted into the queue because $readFront_e$ is executed by the enqueuer and hence no insertions take place during that operation.) More importantly, p can be certain that a dequeuer will notice p's announcement (at Line 11) and as a result will not free up that node from memory. (Instead, a dequeuer will store the pointer to the front node into the FreeLater variable, and will free it up only after p changes its announcement—Lines 12–14.) Hence, p simply reads and returns the value stored at the front node (Lines 22 and 23). If, on the other hand, the pointer to the front node has changed, then a dequeuer has already removed the front node from the queue and potentially freed up that node from memory. So, p must obtain a valid value for its operation to return by other means, and it does so with help from a dequeuing operation, which, prior to removing the front node from the list, first writes the value stored at the front node into the variable Help (Line 9). When p notices that the pointer to the front node has changed, it knows that some dequeuing operation removed the front node from the list and has therefore written into Help the value at that node. Hence, by simply reading the variable Help, p can obtain a valid value for its operation to return. In particular, p will obtain either the value stored at the original front node, or, if multiple nodes have been removed, it will obtain a value stored at a node that was at the front of the list at some point during p's operation. Hence, p reads and returns the value stored in Help (Lines 21 and 23) and terminates its operation.

The algorithm for $readFront_d$ is very simple: process p first checks whether the list contains only a single node (Lines 24 and 25). If it does, then that node is a dummy node, and so p returns $\bot$ (Line 25). Otherwise, p returns the value stored at the front node of the list (Line 26). The reason why $readFront_d$ is much simpler than $readFront_e$ is that the former operation never overlaps with a $dequeue()$ operation (since they are both executed by the same process). Hence, when p reads the pointer to the front node, p knows that the front node will not be removed or freed before it reads the value stored at that node. Therefore, p is guaranteed to return the valid value.

Based on the above, we have the following theorem.

Theorem 1. *The algorithm in Figure 2 is a linearizable [16] wait-free implementation of the single enqueuer, single dequeuer queue from read/write regis-*

ters. The time complexities of enqueue, dequeue, readFront$_e$, *and* readFront$_d$ *operations are 5, 10, 6, and 3, respectively. The space consumption of the algorithm at any time t is $O(m)$, where m is the number of elements in the queue at time t.*

3   Multiple Enqueuer, Single Dequeuer Queue

In this section we present our main result, namely, the wait-free implementation of a *multiple enqueuer, single dequeuer queue object* with time complexity of $O(\lg n)$. The high-level intuition for this algorithm was presented in Section 1.1; the reader should consult that section before proceeding further.

We begin by a formal definition of this object. An *n*-process multiple enqueuer, single dequeuer queue object supports two operations—*enqueue(p,v)* and *dequeue(p)*. The *enqueue(p,v)* operation enables process *p* to insert an element *v* into the queue. The *dequeue(p)* operation enables process *p* to remove the front element from the queue. Multiple processes are allowed to execute the *enqueue()* operation concurrently. However, at any point in time, at most one process can be executing the *dequeue()* operation. The *dequeue()* operation can overlap with any number of *enqueue()* operations.

The algorithm is presented in Figure 3. It maintains two data structures: an array Q of size *n*, holding one single enqueuer, single dequeuer queue for each process, and a complete binary tree T of size *n* built on top of that array. To remove any ambiguity, the algorithm refers to the enqueue and dequeue operations on the single enqueuer, single dequeuer queues by the names *enqueue2* and *dequeue2*, respectively.

To enqueue an element *v* into the queue, process *p* first obtains a new time stamp by reading the variable counter (Line 1). Next, *p* increments counter by adding 1 to the time stamp it has obtained and SC-ing the result back into counter (Line 2). Notice that by the end of this step, the value in counter is strictly greater than *p*'s time stamp, regardless of whether *p*'s SC on counter succeeds or not. (This is because even if *p*'s SC fails, some other process must have performed a successful SC and has therefore incremented the counter.) Notice also that it is quite possible for two different processes to obtain the same time stamp. To ensure that all time stamps are unique, a process adds its process id to the back of its time stamp.

After constructing the time stamp, process *p* inserts the element *v* along with the time stamp into its local queue (Line 3). Notice that, since *p* increments the variable counter during each enqueue operation, successive enqueue operations by *p* obtain time stamps in a strictly increasing order. Consequently, the time stamps of the elements in *p*'s local queue are ordered as follows: the front element has the smallest time stamp, the next element has a higher time stamp, and so on. The front element of the *global* queue is the earliest of the front elements of all the local queues, i.e., an element with the smallest time stamp over all local queues. To help a dequeuer locate this earliest element quickly, process *p* propagates the time stamp at the front element of its local queue toward the

Types

    valuetype = Any type

    queue2type = Single enqueuer, single dequeuer queue

    treetype = Complete binary tree with n leaves

Shared variables

    counter: integer (counter supports LL and SC operations)

    Q: **array** $[1..n]$ **of** queue2type

    T: treetype

Initialization

    counter = 0

procedure enqueue(p, v)

1:   $tok = $ LL(counter)

2:   SC(counter, $tok + 1$)

3:   enqueue2(Q$[p]$, $(v, (tok, p))$)

4:   propagate(Q$[p]$)

procedure dequeue(p) returns valuetype

11: $[t, q] = read($root$(T))$

12: **if** $(q == \bot)$ **return** $\bot$

13: $ret = $ dequeue2(Q$[q]$)

14: propagate(Q$[q]$)

15: **return** $ret.val$

procedure propagate(Q)

5:    $currentNode = Q$

6:   **repeat**

7:     $currentNode = $
               parent($currentNode$)

8:     **if** ¬refresh()

9:       refresh()

10: **until**($currentNode == $root$(T))$

procedure refresh() returns boolean

16: LL($currentNode$)

17: read time stamps in $currentNode$'s children
     Let $minT$ be the smallest time stamp read

18: **return** SC($currentNode, minT$)

Fig. 3. Implementation of the n-process multiple enqueuer, single dequeuer queue object from LL/SC variables and *read/write* registers.

---

root of the binary tree (Line 4). At each internal tree node s that p visits, it makes sure that the following invariant holds:

Invariant: Let s be any node in the binary tree. Let $E(s)$ be the set of all elements in the local queues located at the leaves of the subtree rooted at s whose time stamps have been propagated up to s. Then, at any point in time, s contains the smallest time stamp among all elements in $E(s)$.

We will describe shortly how the above Invariant is maintained. For now, we assume that the Invariant holds and look at how it impacts the implementation of the dequeue operation.

To dequeue an element from the queue, process p first reads the time stamp stored at the root node (Line 11). If the time stamp is $\bot$, it means that the queue is empty and so p returns $\bot$ (Line 12). Otherwise, by the Invariant, the time stamp $[t, q]$ that p reads at the root is the smallest time stamp among all elements in the local queues that have been propagated to the root. Furthermore, the element with that time stamp must be located at the front of q's local queue.

Therefore, to obtain the front element a of the global queue, p simply visits q's local queue and removes the front element from it (Line 13). Since the smallest time-stamped element has been removed from q's local queue, some of the nodes in the binary tree need to be updated in order to reflect this change (and maintain the Invariant). Hence, p propagates the new front element to the root, updating each node along the way (Line 14). At the end, p returns the element a that it dequeued from q's local queue (Line 15).

Notice that, at the time when p reads the root, it is possible that there exists another element b with a smaller time stamp than a that hasn't yet been propagated to the root. In this case, p is in fact not returning the element with the smallest time stamp among all local queues. However, the fact that (1) b has a smaller time stamp than a, and (2) b hasn't been propagated to the root, implies that the enqueue operations that inserted elements a and b overlap. Thus, we can assume that the operation that inserted a has taken effect (i.e., was linearized) before the operation that inserted b, and hence p was correct in returning a.

We now describe the mechanism by which nodes in the tree are updated to maintain the Invariant. More specifically, we describe the manner in which a process p propagates the change at the front of some local queue $Q[q]$ to all the nodes on the path from $Q[q]$ to the root, thereby ensuring that the Invariant holds at each node on that path. (Notice that the other tree nodes are unaffected by the change and for that reason do not need to be updated.) This propagation step is similar to the way propagation is handled in Afek, Dauber, and Touitou's universal construction [14]. It is captured by a procedure propagate(), described below.

Process p starts at the local queue $Q[q]$ (Line 5). During the next $\lg n$ iterations, p repeatedly performs the following steps. First, p sets its current node to be the parent of the old current node (Line 7). Next, p attempts to update the minimum time stamp at the current node by a call to refresh() (Line 8). If refresh() returns $true$, it means that p's attempt to update the current node has succeeded. If p's attempt fails, p simply calls refresh() again (Line 9). The interesting feature of the algorithm is that, by the end of this call, the current node is sure to have an updated minimum time stamp, regardless of whether the second refresh() fails or not. To see why that is so, we must look at how the refresh() procedure is implemented.

During each refresh() call, p performs the following steps. First, p LL's the current node s (Line 16). Next, p reads the time stamps from all the children of s (Line 17). (If the current node is a leaf, then reading of the children consists of reading the time stamp of the first element of the local queue.) Then, p finds the smallest time stamp t among all the time stamps it read. Observe that, since the time stamps at the children (by the Invariant) contain the smallest time stamps among all elements in their respective subtrees that have been propagated to those nodes, t is guaranteed to be the smallest time stamp among all elements in the subtree rooted at s that have been propagated to s. So, p installs the value t into s by performing an SC on s (Line 18). If p's SC succeeds, time stamp t

is installed into s (thus ensuring that the Invariant holds) and p returns *true*. Otherwise, p's attempt to install t into the current node has failed (due to some other process performing a successful SC between p's LL at Line 16 and its SC at Line 18) and p returns *false* (Line 18).

We now justify an earlier claim that, after p calls refresh() twice, the current node is sure to have an updated minimum time stamp, even if both refresh() calls fail. Observe that if the first refresh() call fails, then some process q had performed a successful SC operation on the current node during that call. Similarly, if the second refresh() call fails, then some process r had performed a successful SC operation on the current node during that call. Since r's SC succeeded, r must have LL-ed the current node after q performed its successful SC. Consequently, r must have also read the time stamps at current node's children after q performed its successful SC and before r performed its successful SC. Hence, r reads the time stamps during the time interval of p's two calls to refresh(). So, the time stamps that r reads from the current node's children are the time stamps that p would have also read from current node's children. Therefore, r's successful SC installs the correct minimum time stamp into the current node. As a result, by the end of p's second refresh() call, the current node is sure to have an updated minimum time stamp, thus ensuring that the Invariant holds.

We now analyze the time and space complexities for the above algorithm. First, observe that the tree updating process takes $O(\lg n)$ time. Hence, the time complexity for both dequeue and enqueue operations is $O(\lg n)$. Second, by Theorem 1, the space complexity of a local queue is proportional to the actual number of elements in the queue. Therefore, if m is the total number of items in the global queue at time t, then the space used by all local queues at time t is $O(m)$. Since the tree uses $O(n)$ space at any time, the space consumption for the queue algorithm at time t is $O(m + n)$.

Notice that the algorithm stores at each node in the tree a time stamp consisting of an unbounded integer and a process id. Since these two values are stored together in the same machine word, it means that if the length of the machine word is b, $b - \lg n$ bits are left for the unbounded integer. Since the value of the unbounded integer is proportional to the number of enqueue operations invoked on the queue, it follows that the algorithm allows at most $2^b/n$ enqueue operations to be performed. This restriction is not a limitation in practice. For instance, on most modern architectures, we have $b = 64$. Hence, even if the number of processes accessing the algorithm is as large as 16,000, the algorithm allows for at least 2^{50} enqueue operations to be performed. If there are a million enqueue operations performed each second, the algorithm can thus safely run for more than 35 years!

The following theorem summarizes the above discussion.

Theorem 2. *Let b be the length of the machine word, and n be the number of processes. Under the assumption that at most $2^b/n$ enqueue operations are invoked, the algorithm in Figure 3 is a linearizable wait-free implementation of the multiple enqueuer, single dequeuer queue from LL/SC words and registers.*

The time complexity for both the dequeue and enqueue operations is $O(\lg n)$. The space consumption of the algorithm at any time t is $O(m + n)$ machine words, where m is the number of elements in the queue at time t.

Acknowledgments

We thank the anonymous referees for their valuable comments on an earlier version of this paper.

References

1. David, M.: A single-enqueuer wait-free queue implementation. In: Proceedings of the 18th International Conference on Distributed Computing. (2004) 132–143
2. Herlihy, M.: Wait-free synchronization. ACM TOPLAS **13** (1991) 124–149
3. Herlihy, M.: A methodology for implementing highly concurrent data structures. ACM Transactions on Programming Languages and Systems **15** (1993) 745–770
4. Jayanti, P.: A lower bound on the local time complexity of universal constructions. In: Proceedings of the 17th Annual Symposium on Principles of Distributed Computing. (1998)
5. Chandra, T., Jayanti, P., Tan, K.Y.: A polylog time wait-free construction for closed objects. In: Proceedings of the 17th Annual Symposium on Principles of Distributed Computing. (1998)
6. Jayanti, P.: f-arrays: implementation and applications. In: Proceedings of the 21st Annual Symposium on Principles of Distributed Computing. (2002) 270 – 279
7. Anderson, J., Moir, M.: Universal constructions for large objects. In: Proceedings of the 9th International Workshop on Distributed Algorithms. (1995) 168–182
8. Jayanti, P., Petrovic, S.: Efficient and practical constructions of LL/SC variables. In: Proceedings of the 22nd ACM Symposium on Principles of Distributed Computing. (2003)
9. Moir, M.: Practical implementations of non-blocking synchronization primitives. In: Proceedings of the 16th Annual ACM Symposium on Principles of Distributed Computing. (1997) 219–228
10. Afek, Y., Weisberger, E., Weisman, H.: A completeness theorem for a class of synchronization objects. In: Proceedings of the 12th Annual Symposium on Principles of Distributed Computing. (1993) 159–170
11. Li, Z.: Non-blocking implementation of queues in asynchronous distributed shared-memory systems. Master's thesis, University of Toronto (2001)
12. Lamport, L.: Specifying concurrent program modules. ACM Transactions on Programming Languages and Systems **5** (1983) 190–222
13. Michael, M., Scott, M.: Simple, fast, and practical non-blocking and blocking concurrent queue algorithms. In: Proceedings of the 15th Annual ACM Symposium on Principles of Distributed Computing. (1996) 267–276
14. Afek, Y., Dauber, D., Touitou, D.: Wait-free made fast. In: Proceedings of the 27th Annual ACM Symposium on Theory of Computing. (1995) 538–547
15. Michael, M., Scott, M.: Nonblocking algorithms and preemption-safe locking on multiprogrammed shared memory multiprocessors. Journal of Parallel and Distributed Computing (1998) 1–26
16. Herlihy, M., Wing, J.: Linearizability: A correctness condition for concurrent objects. ACM TOPLAS **12** (1990) 463–492

Monitoring Stable Properties in Dynamic Peer-to-Peer Distributed Systems

Sathya Peri and Neeraj Mittal

Department of Computer Science, The University of Texas at Dallas,
Richardson, TX 75083, USA
sathya.p@student.utdallas.edu, neerajm@utdallas.edu

Abstract. Monitoring a distributed system to detect a stable property is an important problem with many applications. The problem is especially challenging for a *dynamic* distributed system because the set of processes in the system may change with time. In this paper, we present an efficient algorithm to determine whether a stable property has become true in a system in which processes can join and depart the system at any time. Our algorithm is based on maintaining a spanning tree of processes that are currently part of the system. The spanning tree, which is dynamically changing, is used to periodically collect local states of processes such that: (1) all local states in the collection are *consistent* with each other, and (2) the collection is *complete*, that is, it contains all local states that are necessary to evaluate the property and derive meaningful inferences about the system state.

Unlike existing algorithms for stable property detection in a dynamic environment, our algorithm is general in the sense that it can be used to evaluate *any* stable property. Further, it does not assume the existence of any permanent process. Processes can join and leave the system while the snapshot algorithm is in progress.

1 Introduction

One of the fundamental problems in distributed systems is to detect whether some stable property has become true in an ongoing distributed computation. A property is said to be stable if it stays true once it becomes true. Some examples of stable properties include "system is in terminated state", "a subset of processes are involved in a circular wait" and "an object is a garbage". The stable property detection problem has been well-studied and numerous solutions have been proposed for solving the general problem (*e.g.*, [1,2,3]) as well as its special cases (*e.g.*, [4,5,6,7,8,9,10]). However, most of the solutions assume that the system is *static*, that is, the set of processes is fixed and does not change with time.

With the advent of new computing paradigms such as grid computing and peer-to-peer computing, *dynamic* distributed systems are becoming increasingly popular. In a dynamic distributed system, processes can join and leave the on-going computation at anytime. Consequently, the set of processes in the system may change with time. Dynamic distributed systems are especially useful for solving *large-scale problems* that require vast computational power. For example, distributed.net [11] has undertaken several projects that involve searching a

R. Ramanujam and S. Sen (Eds.): FSTTCS 2005, LNCS 3821, pp. 420–431, 2005.

large state-space to locate a solution. Some examples of such projects include RC5-72 to determine a 72-bit secret key for the RC5 algorithm, and OGR-25 to compute the Optimal Golomb Ruler with 25 and more marks.

Although several algorithms have been proposed to solve the stable property detection problem in a dynamic environment, they suffer from one or more of the following limitations. First, to the best of our knowledge, all existing algorithms solve the detection problem for special cases such as property is either termination [12,13,14] or can be expressed as conjunction of local predicates [15]. Second, most of the algorithms assume the existence of permanent processes that never leave the system [13,15,14]. Third, some of the algorithms assume that processes can join but cannot leave the system until the detection algorithm has terminated [12,14]. Fourth, the algorithm by Darling and Mayo [15] assumes that processes are equipped with local clocks that are weakly synchronized.

In this paper, we describe an algorithm to detect a stable property for a dynamic distributed system that does not suffer from any of the limitations described above. Our approach is based on maintaining a spanning tree of all processes currently participating in the computation. The spanning tree, which is dynamically changing, is used to collect local snapshots of processes periodically. Processes can join and leave the system while a snapshot algorithm is in progress. We identify sufficient conditions under which a collection of local snapshots can be safely used to evaluate a stable property. Specifically, the collection has to be consistent (local states in the collection are pair-wise consistent) and *complete* (no local state necessary for correctly evaluating the property is missing from the collection). We also identify a condition that allows the current root of the spanning tree to detect termination of the snapshot algorithm even if the algorithm was initiated by an "earlier" root that has since left the system. Due to lack of space, formal description of our algorithm and proofs of various lemmas and theorems have been omitted and can be found in [16].

2   System Model and Notation

2.1   System Model

We assume an asynchronous distributed system in which processes communicate with each other by exchanging messages. There is no global clock or shared memory. Processes can join and leave the system at any time. We do not assume the existence of any permanent process. We, however, assume that there is at least one process in the system at any time and processes are reliable. For ease of exposition, we assume that a process can join the system at most once. If some process wants to join the system again, it joins it as a different process. This can be ensured by using incarnation numbers.

When a process sends a message to another process, we say that the former process has an *outgoing channel* to the latter process. Alternatively, the latter process has an *incoming channel* to the former process. We make the following assumptions about channels. First, any message sent to a process that never leaves the system is eventually delivered. This holds even if the sender of the message leaves the system after sending the message but before the message is delivered. Second, any message sent by a process that never leaves the system to a process that leaves the system before the message is delivered is eventually returned to the sender with an error notification. Third, all channels are FIFO. Specifically, a process receives a message from another process only after it has received all the messages sent to it earlier by that process. The first two assumptions are similar to those made by Dhamdhere *et al* [13].

We model execution of a process as an alternating sequence of *states* and *events*. A process changes its state by executing an event. Additionally, a send event causes a message to be sent and a receive event causes a message to be received. Sometimes, we refer to the state of a process as *local state*. To avoid confusion, we use the letters a, b, c, d, e and f to refer to events and the letters u, v, w, x, y and z to refer to local states.

Events on a process are totally ordered. However, events on different processes are only partially ordered by the Lamport's *happened-before* relation [17], which is defined as the smallest transitive relation satisfying the following properties:

1. if events e and f occur on the same process, and e occurred before f in real time then e happened-before f, and
2. if events e and f correspond to the send and receive, respectively, of a message then e happened-before f.

For an event e, let $process(e)$ denote the process on which e is executed. Likewise, for a local state x, let $process(x)$ denote the process to which x belongs. We define $events(x)$ as the set consisting of all events that have to be executed to reach x. Intuitively, $events(x)$ captures the causal past of x.

A state of the system is given by the set of events that have been executed so far. We assume that existence of fictitious events $\perp$ that initialize the state of the system. Further, every collection (or set) of events we consider contains these initial events. Clearly, a collection of events E corresponds to a valid state of the system only if E is closed with respect to the happened-before relation. We refer to such a collection of events as *comprehensive cut*. Formally,

$$E \text{ is a comprehensive cut } \triangleq (\perp \subseteq E) \wedge \langle \forall e, f :: (f \in E) \wedge (e \rightarrow f) \Rightarrow e \in E \rangle$$

Sometimes, it is more convenient to model a system state using a collection of local states instead of using a collection of events, especially when taking a snapshot of the system. Intuitively, a comprehensive state is obtained by executing all events in a comprehensive cut. In this paper, we use the term "comprehensive cut" to refer to a collection of events and the term "comprehensive state" to refer to a collection of local states. To avoid confusion, we use the letters A, B, C, D, E and F to refer to a collection of events and the letters U, V, W, X, Y and X to refer to a collection of local states.

For a collection of local states X, let $processes(X)$ denote the set of processes whose local state is in X. Also, let $events(X)$ denote the set of events that have to be executed to reach local states in X.

Two local states x and y are said to be *consistent* if, in order to reach x on $process(x)$, we do not have to advance beyond y on $process(y)$, and vice versa.

Definition 1 (consistent collection of local states). *A collection of local states is said to be consistent if all local states in the collection are pair-wise consistent.*

Note that, for a collection of local states to form a comprehensive state, the local states should be pair-wise consistent. However, not every consistent collection of local states forms a comprehensive state. This happens when the collection is missing local states from certain processes. Specifically, a collection of local states X corresponds to a comprehensive state if the following two conditions hold: (1) X is consistent, and (2) X contains a local state from every process that has at least one event in $events(X)$.

For a consistent collection of local states X, let $CS(X)$ denote the system state obtained by executing all events in $events(X)$. Clearly, $X \subseteq CS(X)$ and, moreover, $CS(X)$ corresponds to a comprehensive state.

For a static distributed system, a system state is captured using the notion of consistent global state. A collection of local states forms a *consistent global state* if the collection is consistent and it contains one local state from every process in the system. For a dynamic distributed system, however, the set of processes may change with time. As a result, the term "every process in the system" is not well-defined. Therefore, we use a slightly different definition of system state, and, to avoid confusion, we use the term "comprehensive state" instead of the term "consistent global state" to refer to it.

2.2   Stable Properties

A property maps every comprehensive state of the system to a boolean value. Intuitively, a property is said to be stable if it stays true once it becomes true. For two comprehensive states X and Y, we say that Y lies in the future of X, denoted by $X \preccurlyeq Y$, if $events(X) \subseteq events(Y)$. Then, a property ϕ is stable if for every pair of comprehensive states X and Y,

$$(\phi \text{ holds for } X) \wedge (X \preccurlyeq Y) \quad \Rightarrow \quad \phi \text{ holds for } Y$$

We next describe an algorithm to detect a stable property in a dynamic distributed system.

3   Our Algorithm

3.1   The Main Idea

A common approach to detect a stable property in a *static* distributed system is to repeatedly collect a consistent set of local states, one from each process. Such a collection is also referred to as a *(consistent) snapshot* of the system. The property is then evaluated for the snapshot collected until it evaluates to true. The problem of collecting local states, one from each process, is relatively easier for a static distributed system than for a dynamic distributed system. This is because, in a static system, the set of processes is fixed and does not change with time. In a dynamic system, however, the set of processes may change with time. Therefore it may not always be clear local states of which processes have to be included in the collection.

In our approach, we impose a logical spanning tree on processes that are currently part of the system. The spanning tree is used to collect local states of processes currently attached to the tree. Observe that, to be able to evaluate the property, the collection has to at least include local states of all processes that are currently part of the application. Therefore we make the following two assumptions. First, a process attaches itself to spanning tree *before* joining the application. Second, a process leaves the application *before* detaching itself from the spanning tree.

A process joins the spanning tree by executing a *control join protocol* and leaves the spanning tree by executing a *control depart protocol*. Likewise, a process joins the application by executing an *application join protocol* and leaves the application by executing an *application depart protocol*.

We associate a status with every process, which can either be OUT, JOINING, IN, TRYING, DEPARTING. Intuitively, status captures the state of a process *with respect to the spanning tree*. A process that is not a part of the system (that is, before it starts executing the control join protocol or after it has finished executing the control depart protocol) has status OUT. When a process starts executing its control join protocol, its status changes to JOINING. The status changes to IN once the join protocol finishes and the process has become part of the spanning tree. When a process wants to leave the spanning tree, it begins executing the control depart protocol, which consists of two parts. In the first part, the process tries to obtain permission to leave from all its neighboring processes. In the second part, it actually leaves the spanning tree. But, before leaving the system, it ensures that the set of processes currently in the system remain connected. During the former part of the depart protocol, its status is TRYING and, during the latter part, its status is DEPARTING.

Typically, for evaluating a property, state of a process can be considered to consist of two components. The first component captures values of all program variables on a process; we refer to it as *core* state. The second component is used to determine state of a channel (*e.g.*, the number of messages a process has sent to another process); we refer to it as *non-core* state. We assume that, once a process has detached itself from the application its core state is no longer needed to evaluate the property. However, its non-core state may still be required to determine the *state of an outgoing channel* it has with another process that is still part of the application. For example, consider a process p that leaves the application soon after sending an application message m to process q. In this case, m may still be in transit towards q after p has left the application. If q does not know about the departure of p when it receives m and it is still part of the application, then it has to receive and process m. This may cause q's core state to change, which, in turn, may affect the value of the property. In this example, even though p has left the application, its non-core state is required to determine the state of the channel from p to q, which is non-empty.

We say that an application message is *irrelevant* if either it is never delivered to its destination process (and is therefore returned to the sender with error notification) or when it is delivered, its destination process is no longer part of the application; otherwise the message is *relevant*. In order to prevent the aforementioned situation from arising, we make the following assumption about an application depart protocol:

Assumption 1. *Once a process has left the application, none of its outgoing channels, if non-empty, contain a relevant application message.*

The above assumption can be satisfied by using acknowledgments for application messages. Specifically, a process leaves the application only after ensuring that, for every application message it sent, it has either received an acknowledgment for it or the message has been returned to it with error notification. Here, we assume that a process that is no longer a part of the application, on receiving an application message, still sends an acknowledgment for it. It can be verified that this scheme implements Assumption 1.

Assumption 1 is useful because it enables a process to evaluate a property using local states of only those processes that are currently part of the spanning tree. Specifically, to evaluate the property, a process does not need information about states of processes that left the system before the snapshot algorithm started.

Now, to understand local states of which processes need to be recorded in a snapshot, we define the notion of *completeness*. We call a process *active* if its status is IN and *semi-active* if its status is either IN or TRYING. Further, for a collection of local states X, let $active(X)$ denote the set of local states of all those processes whose status is IN in X. We can define $semi\text{-}active(X)$ similarly.

Definition 2 (complete collection of local states). *A consistent collection of local states Y is said to be* complete *with respect to a comprehensive state X with $Y \subseteq X$ if Y includes local states of all those processes whose status is IN in X. Formally,*

$$Y \text{ is complete with respect to } X \quad \triangleq \quad active(X) \subseteq Y$$

From Assumption 1, to be able to evaluate a property for a collection of local states, it is sufficient for the collection to be complete; it need not be comprehensive. This is also important because our definition of comprehensive state includes local states of even those processes that are no longer part of the system. As a result, if a snapshot algorithm were required to return a comprehensive state, it will make the algorithm too expensive. As we see later, our snapshot algorithm returns a collection that contains local states of *all semi-active processes* of some comprehensive state (and not just all active processes).

3.2   Spanning Tree Maintenance Algorithm

Processes may join and leave the system while an instance of the snapshot algorithm is in progress. Therefore spanning tree maintenance protocols, namely control join and depart protocols, have to designed carefully so that they do not "interfere" with an ongoing instance of the snapshot algorithm. To that end, we maintain a set of invariants that we use later to establish the correctness of the snapshot algorithm.

Each process maintains information about its parent and its children in the tree. Initially, before a process joins the spanning tree, it does not have any parent or children, that is, its parent variable is set to nil and its children-set is empty. Let x be a local state of process p. We use $parent(x)$ to denote the parent of p in x and $children(x)$ to denote the set of children of p in x. Further, p is said to be *root* in x if $parent(x) = p$. For a collection of local states X and a process $p \in processes(X)$, we use $X.p$ to denote the local state of p in X.

Now, we describe our invariants. Consider a comprehensive state X and let p and q be two processes in X. The first invariant says that if the status of a process is either IN or TRYING, then its parent variable should have a non-nil value. Formally,

$$status(X.p) \in \{\text{IN}, \text{TRYING}\} \quad \Rightarrow \quad parent(X.p) \neq nil \tag{1}$$

The second invariant says that if a process considers another process to be its parent then the latter should consider the former as its child. Moreover, the parent variable of the latter should have a non-nil value. Intuitively, it means that child "relationship" is maintained for a longer duration than parent "relationship". Further, a process cannot set its parent variable to nil as long as there is at least one process in the system, different from itself, that considers it to be its parent. Formally,

$$\begin{aligned}(parent(X.p) = q) \wedge (p \neq q) &\Rightarrow \\ (p \in children(X.q)) &\wedge (parent(X.q) \neq nil)\end{aligned} \tag{2}$$

The third invariant specifically deals with the departure of a root process. To distinguish between older and newer root processes, we associate a *rank* with every root process. The rank is incremented whenever a new root is selected. This invariant says that if two processes consider themselves to be root of the spanning tree, then there cannot be a process that considers the "older" root to be its parent. Moreover, the status of the "older" root has to be DEPARTING. Formally,

$$\begin{aligned}root(X.p) \wedge root(X.q) \wedge (rank(X.p) < rank(X.q)) &\Rightarrow \\ \langle \nexists r : r \in processes(X) \setminus \{p\} : parent(X.r) = p \rangle &\wedge \\ (status(X.p) = \text{DEPARTING})\end{aligned} \tag{3}$$

We now describe our control join and depart protocols that maintain the invariants (1)–(3).

Joining the Spanning Tree: A process attaches itself to the spanning tree by executing the control join protocol. Our control join protocol is quite simple. A process wishing to join the spanning tree first obtains a list of processes that are currently part of the spanning tree. This, for example, can be achieved using a name server. It then contacts the processes in the list, one by one, until it finds a process that is willing to accept it as its child. We assume that the process is eventually able to find such a process, and, therefore, the control join protocol eventually terminates successfully.

Leaving the Spanning Tree: A process detaches itself from the spanning tree by executing the control depart protocol. The protocol consists of two phases. The first phase is referred to as *trying* phase and the status of process in this phase is TRYING. In the trying phase, a departing process tries to obtain permission to leave from all its tree neighbors (parent and children). To prevent neighboring processes from departing at the same time, all departure requests are assigned timestamps using logical clock. A process, on receiving departure request from its neighboring process, grants the permission only if it is not departing or its depart request has larger timestamp than that of its neighbor. This approach is similar to Ricart and Agrawala's algorithm [18] modified for drinking philosopher's problem [19]. Note that the neighborhood of a departing process may change during this phase if one of more of its neighbors are also trying to depart. Whenever the neighborhood of a departing process changes, it sends its departure request to all its new neighbors, if any. A process wishing to depart has to wait until it has received permission to depart from its *current* neighbors.

We show in [16] that the first phase of the control depart protocol eventually terminates. Once that happens, the process enters the second phase. The second phase is referred to as *departing* phase and the status of process in this phase is DEPARTING. The protocol of the departing phase depends on whether the departing process is a root process. If the departing process is not a root process, then, to maintain the spanning tree, it attaches all its children to its parent. On the other hand, if it is a root process, then it selects one its children to become the new root. It then attaches all its other children to the new root. The main challenge is to change the spanning tree without violating any of the invariants.

Case 1 (when the departing process is not the root): In this case, the departing phase consists of the following steps:
- **Step 1:** The departing process asks its parent to inherit all its children and waits for acknowledgment.
- **Step 2:** The departing process asks all its children to change their parent to its parent and waits for acknowledgment from all of them. At this point, no process in the system considers the departing process to be its parent.
- **Step 3:** The departing process terminates all its neighbor relationships. At this point, the parent of the departing process still considers the process to be its child.
- **Step 4:** The departing process asks its parent to remove it from its set of children and waits for acknowledgment.

Case 2 (when the departing process is the root): In this case, the departing phase consists of the following steps:
- **Step 1:** The departing process selects one of its children to become the new root. It then asks the selected child to inherit all its other children and waits for acknowledgment.
- **Step 2:** The departing process asks all its other children to change their parent to the new root and waits for acknowledgment from all of them. At this point, only the child selected to become the new root considers the departing process to be its parent.
- **Step 3:** The departing process terminates child relationships with all its other children. The child relationship with the child selected to become the new root cannot be terminated as yet.
- **Step 4:** The departing process asks the selected child to become the new root of the spanning tree and waits for acknowledgment. At this point, no process in the system considers the departing process to be its parent.
- **Step 5:** The departing process terminates all its neighbor relationships.

To ensure liveness of the snapshot algorithm, we require the departing process to "transfer" the latest set of local states it has collected so far (which may be empty) to another process, after it has detached itself from the spanning tree but before leaving the system permanently. The process to which the collection has to be "transfered" is the parent of the departing process in the first case and the new root of the spanning tree in the second case. In both cases, the process to which the collection is "transfered" has to wait until it has received the collection from all processes it is supposed to before it can itself enter the departing phase.

3.3   The Snapshot Algorithm

As discussed earlier, it is sufficient to collect a *consistent* set of local states that is *complete* with respect to some comprehensive state. We next discuss how consistency and completeness can be achieved. For convenience, when a process records it local state, we say that it has taken its snapshot.

Achieving Consistency   To achieve consistency, we use Lai and Yang's approach for taking a consistent snapshot of a static distributed system [2]. Each process maintains the *instance number* of the latest snapshot algorithm in which it has participated. This instance number is piggybacked on every message it sends—application as well as control. If a process receives a message with an instance number greater than its own, it first records its local state before delivering the message. It can be verified that:

Theorem 3 (consistency). *Two local states belonging to the same instance of the snapshot algorithm are consistent with each other.*

Achieving Completeness   As explained earlier in Sect. 3.1, to be able to evaluate a property for a collection of local states, it is sufficient for the collection to be complete with respect to some comprehensive state. The main problem is: *"How does the current root of the spanning tree know that its collection has become complete?"* To solve this problem, our approach is to define a *test property* that can be evaluated *locally* for a collection of local states such that once the test property evaluates to true then the collection has become complete. To that end, we define the notion of f-*closed* collection of local states.

Definition 4 (f-closed collection of local states). *Let f be a function that maps every local state to a set of processes. A consistent collection of local states X is said to be f-closed if, for every local state x in X, X contains a local state from every process in $f(x)$. Formally,*

$$X \text{ is } f\text{-closed} \quad \triangleq \quad \langle \forall x \in X :: f(x) \subseteq processes(X) \rangle$$

Intuitively, f denotes a neighborhood function. For example, f may map a local state x to $children(x)$. We consider two special cases for function f. For a local state x, let $\rho(x)$ be defined as the set containing the parent of $process(x)$ in local state x, if it exists. Further, let $\kappa(x)$ be defined as the set of children of $process(x)$ in local state x, that is, $\kappa(x) = children(x)$. We show that, under certain condition, if the collection is $(\rho \cup \kappa)$-closed, then it is also complete. To capture the condition under which this implication holds, we define the notion of f-path as follows:

Definition 5 (f-path). *Let f be a function that maps every local state to a set of processes. Consider a comprehensive state X and two distinct processes p and q in $processes(X)$. We say that there is an f-path from p to q in X, denoted by f-path(p, q, X), if there exists a sequence of processes $s_i \in processes(X)$ for $i = 1, 2, \ldots, m$ such that:*

1. *$s_1 = p$ and $s_m = q$*
2. *for each i, $1 \leq i < m$, $s_i \neq s_{i+1}$ and $s_{i+1} \in f(X.s_i)$*

Using the notion of f-path, we define the notion of an f-connected state as follows:

Definition 6 (f-connected state). *Let f be a function that maps every local state to a set of processes. A comprehensive state X is said to be f-connected if there is a f-path between every pair of distinct processes in semi-active(X). Formally, X is f-connected if*

$$\langle \forall p, q \in processes(X) : p \neq q : \{p, q\} \subseteq semi\text{-}active(X) \ \Rightarrow \ f\text{-}path(p, q, X) \rangle$$

Using the invariants (1)–(3), we show that every comprehensive state is actually $(\rho \cup \kappa)$-connected. We first prove an important property about the spanning tree maintained by our algorithm.

Theorem 7. *The directed graph induced by parent variables of a comprehensive state is acyclic (except for self-loops).*

The following theorem can now be proved:

Theorem 8. *Every comprehensive state is $(\rho \cup \kappa)$-connected.*

The main idea behind the proof is to show that each semi-active process has a ρ-path to the current root of the spanning tree. This, in turn, implies that there is a κ-path from the current root to each semi-active process in the system. We now provide a sufficient condition for a collection of local states to be complete.

Theorem 9 (f-closed and f-connected $\Rightarrow$ complete). *Let f be a function that maps every local state to a set of processes. Consider a consistent collection of local states X. If (1) X is f-closed, (2) semi-active$(X) \neq \emptyset$, and (3) $CS(X)$ is f-connected, then X is complete with respect to $CS(X)$.*

Therefore it suffices to ensure that the set of local states collected by the snapshot algorithm is $(\rho \cup \kappa)$-closed. We now describe our snapshot algorithm. After recording its local state, a process waits to receive local states of its children in the tree until its collection becomes κ-closed. As soon as that happens, it sends the collection to its (current) parent in the spanning tree unless it is a root. In case it is a root, it uses the collection to determine whether the property of interest (*e.g.*, termination) has become true. A root process initiates the snapshot algorithm by recording its local state provided its status is either IN or TRYING. This ensures that the collection contains a local state of at least one semi-active process. (Note that the snapshot algorithm described above does not satisfy liveness. We describe additions to the basic snapshot algorithm to ensure its liveness later.) The next theorem establishes that the collection of local states returned by an instance of the snapshot algorithm is not only κ-closed but also $(\rho \cup \kappa)$-closed.

Theorem 10. *The collection of local states returned by the snapshot algorithm is consistent and $(\rho \cup \kappa)$-closed.*

It follows from Theorem 3, Theorem 9, Theorem 8 and Theorem 10 that:

Corollary 11 (safety). *The collection of local states returned by the snapshot algorithm is (1) consistent and (2) complete with respect to some comprehensive state.*

The liveness of the snapshot algorithm is only guaranteed if the system becomes permanently quiescent eventually (that is, the set of processes does not change). Other algorithms for property detection make similar assumptions to achieve liveness [13,15]. Without this assumption, the spanning tree may continue to grow forcing the snapshot algorithm to collect local states of an ever increasing number of processes. To ensure liveness under this assumption, we make the following enhancements to the basic snapshot algorithm. First, whenever a process records its local state, it sends a marker message containing the current instance number to all its neighbors. In addition, it sends a marker message to any new neighbor whenever its neighborhood set changes. Second, whenever its parent changes, it sends its collection to the new parent if the collection has become κ-closed. Third, just before leaving the system, a process transfers its collection to one of its neighbors as explained earlier. Once the system becomes permanently quiescent, the first modification ensures that all processes in the tree eventually record their local states and the second modification ensures that the collection at the root eventually becomes κ-closed. It can be proved that:

Theorem 12 (liveness). *Assuming that the system eventually becomes permanently quiescent (that is, the set of processes does not change), every instance of the snapshot algorithm terminates eventually.*

4   Conclusion and Future Work

In this paper, we present an efficient algorithm to determine whether a stable property has become true in a dynamic distributed system in which processes can join and leave the system at any time. Our approach involves periodically collecting local states of processes that are currently part of the system using a (dynamically changing) spanning tree.

There are several interesting problems that still need to be addressed. The depart protocol described in the paper has relatively high worst-case time-complexity. Specifically, a process may stay in the trying phase for a long period of time (because of other processes joining and leaving the system) before it is able to enter the departing phase. An interesting problem is to design a depart protocol that has low worst-case time-complexity. Also, in our current approach, control neighbors of a process may be completely different from its application neighbors, which may be undesirable in certain cases. Finally, in this paper, we assume that processes are reliable and they never fail. It would be interesting to investigate this problem in the presence of failures.

References

1. Chandy, K.M., Lamport, L.: Distributed Snapshots: Determining Global States of Distributed Systems. ACM Transactions on Computer Systems **3** (1985) 63–75
2. Lai, T.H., Yang, T.H.: On Distributed Snapshots. Information Processing Letters (IPL) **25** (1987) 153–158
3. Alagar, S., Venkatesan, S.: An Optimal Algorithm for Recording Snapshots using Casual Message Delivery. Information Processing Letters (IPL) **50** (1994) 311–316
4. Dijkstra, E.W., Scholten, C.S.: Termination Detection for Diffusing Computations. Information Processing Letters (IPL) **11** (1980) 1–4
5. Francez, N.: Distributed Termination. ACM Transactions on Programming Languages and Systems (TOPLAS) **2** (1980) 42–55
6. Ho, G.S., Ramamoorthy, C.V.: Protocols for Deadlock Detection in Distributed Database Systems. IEEE Transactions on Software Engineering **8** (1982) 554–557
7. Chandy, K.M., Misra, J., Haas, L.M.: Distributed Deadlock Detection. ACM Transactions on Computer Systems **1** (1983) 144–156
8. Marzullo, K., Sabel, L.: Efficient Detection of a Class of Stable Properties. Distributed Computing (DC) **8** (1994) 81–91
9. Schiper, A., Sandoz, A.: Strong Stable Properties in Distributed Systems. Distributed Computing (DC) **8** (1994) 93–103
10. Atreya, R., Mittal, N., Garg, V.K.: Detecting Locally Stable Predicates without Modifying Application Messages. In: Proceedings of the 7th International Conference on Principles of Distributed Systems (OPODIS). (2003) 20–33
11. distributed.net: http://www.distributed.net/projects.php (2005)
12. Lai, T.H.: Termination Detection for Dynamic Distributed Systems with Non-First-In-First-Out Communication. Journal of Parallel and Distributed Computing (JPDC) **3** (1986) 577–599
13. Dhamdhere, D.M., Iyer, S.R., Reddy, E.K.K.: Distributed Termination Detection for Dynamic Systems. Parallel Computing **22** (1997) 2025–2045
14. Wang, X., Mayo, J.: A General Model for Detecting Termination in Dynamic Systems. In: Proceedings of the 18th International Parallel and Distributed Processing Symposium (IPDPS), Santa Fe, New Mexico (2004)
15. Darling, D., Mayo, J.: Stable Predicate Detection in Dynamic Systems. Submitted to the Journal of Parallel and Distributed Computing (JPDC) (2003)
16. Peri, S., Mittal, N.: Monitoring Stable Properties in Dynamic Peer-to-Peer Distributed Systems. Technical Report UTDCS-27-05, Department of Computer Science, The University of Texas at Dallas, Richardson, TX, 75083, USA (2005)
17. Lamport, L.: Time, Clocks, and the Ordering of Events in a Distributed System. Communications of the ACM (CACM) **21** (1978) 558–565
18. Ricart, G., Agrawala, A.K.: An Optimal Algorithm for Mutual Exclusion in Computer Networks. Communications of the ACM (CACM) **24** (1981) 9–17
19. Chandy, K.M., Misra, J.: The Drinking Philosophers Problem. ACM Transactions on Programming Languages and Systems (TOPLAS) **6** (1984) 632–646

On the Expressiveness of **TPTL** and **MTL**

Patricia Bouyer, Fabrice Chevalier, and Nicolas Markey

LSV – CNRS & ENS de Cachan – France
{bouyer,chevalie,markey}@lsv.ens-cachan.fr

Abstract. TPTL and MTL are two classical timed extensions of LTL. In this paper, we positively answer a 15-year-old conjecture that TPTL is strictly more expressive than MTL. But we show that, surprisingly, the TPTL formula proposed in [4] for witnessing this conjecture can be expressed in MTL. More generally, we show that TPTL formulae using only the **F** modality can be translated into MTL.

1 Introduction

Temporal logics. Temporal logics [19] are a widely used framework in the field of specification and verification of (models of) reactive systems. In particular, Linear-time Temporal Logic (LTL) allows to express properties about the executions of a model, such as the fact that *any occurrence of a problem eventually raises the alarm*. LTL has been extensively studied, both about its expressiveness [14,11] and for model checking purposes [21,23].

Timed temporal logics. At the beginning of the 90s, real-time constraints have naturally been added to temporal logics [15,2], in order to add quantitative constraints to temporal logic specifications of timed models. The resulting logics allow to express, *e.g.*, that any occurrence of a problem in a system will raise the alarm *in at most 5 time units.*

When dealing with dense time, we may consider two different semantics for timed temporal logics, depending on whether the formulae are evaluated over *timed words* (*i.e.* over a discrete sequence of timed events; this is the *pointwise semantics*) or over *timed state sequences* (*i.e.*, roughly, over the continuous behavior of the system; this is the *interval-based semantics*). We refer to [6,12] for a survey on linear-time timed temporal logics and to [20] for more recent developments on that subject.

Expressiveness of TPTL *and* MTL. Two interesting timed extensions of LTL are MTL (Metric Temporal Logic) [15,7] and TPTL (Timed Propositional Temporal Logic) [8]. MTL extends LTL by adding subscripts to temporal operators: for instance, the above property can be written in MTL as

$$\mathbf{G}\,(\texttt{problem} \Rightarrow \mathbf{F}_{\leq 5}\,\texttt{alarm}).$$

TPTL is "more temporal" [8] in the sense that it uses real clocks in order to assert timed constraints. A TPTL formula can "reset" a formula clock at some

R. Ramanujam and S. Sen (Eds.): FSTTCS 2005, LNCS 3821, pp. 432–443, 2005.

point, and later compare the value of that clock to some integer. The property above would then be written as

$$\mathbf{G}\,(\texttt{problem} \Rightarrow x.\mathbf{F}\,(\texttt{alarm} \wedge x \leq 5))$$

where "$x.\varphi$" means that x is reset at the current position, before evaluating φ. This logic also allows to easily express that, for instance, within 5 t.u. after any problem, the system rings the alarm and then enters a failsafe mode:

$$\mathbf{G}\,(\texttt{problem} \Rightarrow x.\mathbf{F}\,(\texttt{alarm} \wedge \mathbf{F}\,(\texttt{failsafe} \wedge x \leq 5))). \tag{1}$$

While it is clear that any MTL formula can be translated into an equivalent TPTL one, [6,7] state that there is no intuitive MTL equivalent to formula (1). It has thus been conjectured that TPTL would be strictly more expressive than MTL [6,7,12], formula (1) being proposed as a possible witness not being expressible in MTL.

Our contributions. We consider that problem for two standard semantics (viz. the *pointwise* and the *interval-based* semantics). We prove that

- the conjecture *does* hold for both semantics;
- for the pointwise semantics, formula (1) witnesses the expressiveness gap, *i.e.* it cannot be expressed in TPTL;
- for the interval-based semantics, formula (1) *can* be expressed in MTL, but we exhibit another TPTL formula (namely, $x.\mathbf{F}\,(a \wedge x \leq 1 \wedge \mathbf{G}\,(x \leq 1 \Rightarrow \neg b))$, stating that the last atomic proposition before time point 1 is an a) and prove that it cannot be expressed in MTL.

As side results, we get that MTL is strictly more expressive under the interval-based semantics than under the pointwise one, as recently and independently proved in [10], and that, for both semantics, MTL+Past and MITL+Past (where the past-time modality "Since" is used [3]) are strictly more expressive than MTL and MITL, resp. We also get that the branching-time logic TCTL with explicit clock [13] is strictly more expressive than TCTL with subscripts [2], which had been conjectured in [1,24].

Finally, we prove that, under the interval-based semantics, the fragment of TPTL where only the $\mathbf{F}$ modality is allowed (we call it the *existential fragment* of TPTL) can be translated into MTL. This generalizes the fact that formula (1) can be expressed in MTL.

Related work. Over the last 15 years, many researches have focused on expressiveness questions for timed temporal logics (over both integer and real time). See [5,7,8,3] for original works, and [12,20] for a survey on that topic.

MTL and TPTL have also been studied for the purpose of verification. If the underlying time domain is discrete, then MTL and TPTL have decidable verification problems [7,8]. When considering dense time, verification problems (satisfiability, model checking) become much harder: [3] proves that the satisfiability problem for MTL is undecidable when considering the interval-based semantics. This result of course carries on for TPTL. It has recently been proved that MTL model checking and satisfiability *are* decidable over finite words under the pointwise semantics [18], while it is still undecidable for TPTL [8]. Note that our expressiveness result concerning TPTL$_\mathbf{F}$ yields an NP decision procedure for that fragment under the pointwise semantics (see Corollary 11).

MTL and TPTL have also been studied in the scope of monitoring and path model checking. [22] proposes an (exponential) monitoring algorithm for MTL under the pointwise semantics. [17] shows that, in the interval-based semantics, MTL formulae can be verified on lasso-shaped timed state sequences in polynomial time, while TPTL formulae require at least polynomial space.

Some proofs are omitted due to lack of space. They can be found in [9].

2   Timed Linear-Time Temporal Logics

Basic definitions. In the sequel, AP represents a non-empty, countable set of atomic propositions. Let $\mathbb{R}$ denote the set of reals, $\mathbb{R}^+$ the set of nonnegative reals, $\mathbb{Q}$ the set of rationals and $\mathbb{N}$ the set of nonnegative integers. An *interval* is a convex subset of $\mathbb{R}$. Two intervals I and I' are said to be *adjacent* when $I \cap I' = \emptyset$ and $I \cup I'$ is an interval. We denote by $\mathcal{I}_\mathbb{R}$ the set of intervals, and by $\mathcal{I}_\mathbb{Q}$ the set of intervals whose bounds are in $\mathbb{Q}$.

Given a finite set X of variables called *clocks*, a *clock valuation* over X is a mapping $\alpha \colon X \to \mathbb{R}^+$ which assigns to each clock a time value in $\mathbb{R}^+$.

Timed state sequences and timed words. A *timed state sequence* over AP is a pair $\kappa = (\overline{\sigma}, \overline{I})$ where $\overline{\sigma} = \sigma_1 \sigma_2 \ldots$ is an infinite sequence of elements of 2^{AP} and $\overline{I} = I_1 I_2 \ldots$ is an infinite sequence of intervals satisfying the following properties:

- *(adjacency)* the intervals I_i and I_{i+1} are adjacent for all $i \geq 1$, and
- *(progress)* every time value $t \in \mathbb{R}^+$ belongs to some interval I_i.

A timed state sequence can equivalently be seen as an infinite sequence of elements of $2^{\mathsf{AP}} \times \mathcal{I}_\mathbb{R}$.

A *time sequence* over $\mathbb{R}^+$ is an infinite non-decreasing sequence $\tau = \tau_0 \tau_1 \ldots$ of nonnegative reals satisfying the following properties:

- *(initialization)* $\tau_0 = 0$,
- *(monotonicity)* the sequence is nondecreasing: $\forall\, i \in \mathbb{N}\ \tau_{i+1} \geq \tau_i$,
- *(progress)* every time value $t \in \mathbb{R}^+$ is eventually reached: $\forall t \in \mathbb{R}.\exists i.\ \tau_i > t$.

A *timed word* over AP is a pair $\rho = (\sigma, \tau)$, where $\sigma = \sigma_0 \sigma_1 \ldots$ is an infinite word over AP and $\tau = \tau_0 \tau_1 \ldots$ a time sequence over $\mathbb{R}^+$. It can equivalently be seen as an infinite sequence of elements $(\sigma_0, \tau_0)(\sigma_1, \tau_1) \ldots$ of $(\mathsf{AP} \times \mathbb{R})$. We force timed words to satisfy $\tau_0 = 0$ in order to have a natural way to define initial satisfiability in the semantics of MTL. This involves no loss of generality since it can be obtained by adding a special action to the alphabet.

Note that a timed word can be seen as a timed state sequence: for example the timed word $(a, 0)(a, 1.1)(b, 2) \ldots$ corresponds to the timed state sequence $(\{a\}, [0, 0])(\emptyset,]0, 1.1[)(\{a\}, [1.1, 1.1])(\emptyset, [1.1, 2[)(\{b\}, [2, 2]) \ldots$

2.1   Clock Temporal Logic (TPTL)

The logic TPTL [8,20] is a timed extension of LTL [19] which uses extra variables (clocks) explicitly in the formulae. Below, we define the syntax and semantics of TPTL+Past. The logic TPTL is the fragment of TPTL+Past not using the operator **S**.

Formulae of TPTL+Past are built from atomic propositions, boolean connectives, "until" and "since" operators, clock constraints and clock resets:

$$\text{TPTL+Past} \ni \varphi ::= p \mid \varphi_1 \wedge \varphi_2 \mid \neg\varphi \mid \varphi_1 \, \mathbf{U} \, \varphi_2 \mid \varphi_1 \, \mathbf{S} \, \varphi_2 \mid x \sim c \mid x.\varphi$$

where $p \in \text{AP}$ is an atomic proposition, x is a clock variable, $c \in \mathbb{Q}$ is a rational number and $\sim \, \in \{\leq, <, =, >, \geq\}$. There are two main semantics for TPTL, the *interval-based* semantics which interprets TPTL over timed state sequences, and the *pointwise* semantics, which interprets TPTL over timed words. This last semantics is less general as (as we will see below) formulae can only be interpreted at points in time when actions occur.

In the literature, these two semantics are used interchangeably, but results highly depend on the underlying semantics. For example, a recent result [18] states that MTL (a subset of TPTL, see below) is decidable under the pointwise semantics, whereas it is known to be undecidable for finite models under the interval-based semantics [3].

Interval-based semantics. In this semantics, models are time state sequences κ, and are evaluated at a date $t \in \mathbb{R}^+$ with a valuation $\alpha : X \to \mathbb{R}^+$ (where X is the set of clocks for formulae of TPTL+Past). The satisfaction relation (denoted with $(\kappa, t, \alpha) \models_i \varphi$) is defined inductively as follows (we omit the standard semantics of boolean operators):

$$
\begin{aligned}
(\kappa, t, \alpha) \models_i p \quad &\text{iff} \quad p \in \kappa(t) \\
(\kappa, t, \alpha) \models_i x \sim c \quad &\text{iff} \quad t - \alpha(x) \sim c \\
(\kappa, t, \alpha) \models_i x.\varphi \quad &\text{iff} \quad (\kappa, t, \alpha[x \mapsto t]) \models_i \varphi \\
(\kappa, t, \alpha) \models_i \varphi_1 \, \mathbf{U} \, \varphi_2 \quad &\text{iff} \quad \exists t' > t \text{ such that } (\kappa, t', \alpha) \models_i \varphi_2 \\
&\qquad \text{and } \forall t < t'' < t', \, (\kappa, t'', \alpha) \models_i \varphi_1 \vee \varphi_2{}^1 \\
(\kappa, t, \alpha) \models_i \varphi_1 \, \mathbf{S} \, \varphi_2 \quad &\text{iff} \quad \exists t' < t \text{ such that } (\kappa, t', \alpha) \models_i \varphi_2 \\
&\qquad \text{and } \forall t' < t'' < t, \, (\kappa, t'', \alpha) \models_i \varphi_1 \vee \varphi_2
\end{aligned}
$$

We write $\kappa \models_i \varphi$ when $(\kappa, 0, \mathbf{0}) \models_i \varphi$ where $\mathbf{0}$ is the valuation assigning 0 to all clocks. Following [20], we interpret "$x.\varphi$" as a reset operator. Note also that the semantics of **U** is strict in the sense that, in order to satisfy $\varphi_1 \, \mathbf{U} \, \varphi_2$, a time state sequence is not required to satisfy φ_1. In the following, we use classical shorthands: $\top$ stands for $p \vee \neg p$, $\varphi_1 \Rightarrow \varphi_2$ holds for $\neg\varphi_1 \vee \varphi_2$, $\mathbf{F} \, \varphi$ holds for $\top \, \mathbf{U} \, \varphi$ (and means that φ eventually holds at a future time), and $\mathbf{G} \, \varphi$ holds for $\neg(\mathbf{F} \, \neg\varphi)$ (and means that φ always holds in the future).

---

[1] Following [20] we use $\varphi_1 \vee \varphi_2$ to handle open intervals in timed models.

Pointwise semantics. In this semantics, models are timed words ρ, and satisfiability is no longer interpreted at a date $t \in \mathbb{R}$ but at a position $i \in \mathbb{N}$ in the timed word. For a timed word $\rho = (\sigma, \tau)$ with $\sigma = (\sigma_i)_{i \geq 0}$ and $\tau = (\tau_i)_{i \geq 0}$, we define the satisfaction relation $(\rho, i, \alpha) \models_p \varphi$ inductively as follows (where α is a valuation for the set X of formula clocks):

$$
\begin{aligned}
(\rho, i, \alpha) \models_p p \quad &\text{iff} \quad \sigma_i = p \\
(\rho, i, \alpha) \models_p x \sim c \quad &\text{iff} \quad \tau_i - \alpha(x) \sim c \\
(\rho, i, \alpha) \models_p x.\varphi \quad &\text{iff} \quad (\rho, i, \alpha[x \mapsto \tau_i]) \models_p \varphi \\
(\rho, i, \alpha) \models_p \varphi_1 \, \mathbf{U} \, \varphi_2 \quad &\text{iff} \quad \exists j > i \text{ s.t. } (\rho, j, \alpha) \models_p \varphi_2 \\
&\qquad\quad \text{and } \forall i < k < j \; (\rho, k, \alpha) \models_p \varphi_1 \\
(\rho, i, \alpha) \models_p \varphi_1 \, \mathbf{S} \, \varphi_2 \quad &\text{iff} \quad \exists j < i \text{ s.t. } (\rho, j, \alpha) \models_p \varphi_2 \\
&\qquad\quad \text{and } \forall j < k < i \; (\rho, k, \alpha) \models_p \varphi_1
\end{aligned}
$$

We write $\rho \models_p \varphi$ whenever $(\rho, 0, \mathbf{0}) \models_p \varphi$.

Example 1. Consider the timed word $\rho = (a, 0)(a, 1.1)(b, 2) \ldots$ which, as already mentioned, can be viewed as the time state sequence

$$\kappa = (\{a\}, [0])(\emptyset, (0, 1.1))(\{a\}, [1.1, 1.1])(\emptyset, (1.1, 2))(\{b\}, [2, 2]) \ldots$$

If $\varphi = x.\mathbf{F} \, (x = 1 \wedge y.\mathbf{F} \, (y = 1 \wedge b))$, then $\rho \not\models_p \varphi$ whereas $\kappa \models_i \varphi$. This is due to the fact that there is no action at date 1 along ρ.

2.2   Metric Temporal Logic (MTL)

The logic MTL [15,7] extends the logic LTL with time restrictions on "until" modalities. Here again, we first define MTL+Past:

$$\text{MTL+Past} \ni \varphi ::= p \mid \varphi_1 \wedge \varphi_2 \mid \neg\varphi \mid \varphi_1 \, \mathbf{U}_I \, \varphi_2 \mid \varphi_1 \, \mathbf{S}_I \, \varphi_2$$

where p ranges over the set AP of atomic propositions, and I an interval in $\mathcal{I}_{\mathbb{Q}}$. MTL is the fragment of MTL+Past not using the operator $\mathbf{S}$. We also define MITL and MITL+Past as the fragments of MTL and MTL+Past in which intervals cannot be singletons.

For defining the semantics of MTL+Past, we view MTL+Past as a fragment of TPTL+Past: $\varphi_1 \, \mathbf{U}_I \, \varphi_2$ is then interpreted as $x.(\varphi_1 \, \mathbf{U} \, (x \in I \wedge \varphi_2))$ and $\varphi_1 \, \mathbf{S}_I \, \varphi_2$ as $x.(\varphi_1 \, \mathbf{S} \, (x \in I \wedge \varphi_2))$. As for TPTL, we will thus consider both the interval-based (interpreted over time state sequences) and the pointwise (interpreted over timed words) semantics. For both semantics, it is clear that TPTL is at least as expressive as MTL, which in turn is at least as expressive as MITL.

We omit the constraint on modality $\mathbf{U}$ when $[0, \infty)$ is assumed. We write $\mathbf{U}_{\sim c}$ for $\mathbf{U}_I$ when $I = \{t \mid t \sim c\}$. As previously, we use classical shorthands such as $\mathbf{F}_I$ or $\mathbf{G}_I$.

Example 2. In MTL, the formula φ of Example 1 can be expressed as $\mathbf{F}_{=1} \, \mathbf{F}_{=1} \, b$. In the interval-based semantics, this formula is equivalent to $\mathbf{F}_{=2} \, b$, and this is **not** the case in the pointwise semantics.

3   TPTL Is Strictly More Expressive than MTL

3.1   Conjecture

It has been conjectured in [6,7,12] that TPTL is strictly more expressive than MTL, and in particular that a TPTL formula such as

$$\mathbf{G}\,(a \Rightarrow x.\mathbf{F}\,(b \wedge \mathbf{F}\,(c \wedge\ x \leq 2)))$$

can not be expressed in MTL. The following proposition states that this formula is not a witness for proving that TPTL is strictly more expressive than MTL.

Proposition 1. *The* TPTL *formula* $x.\mathbf{F}\,(b \wedge \mathbf{F}\,(c \wedge\ x \leq 2))$ *can be expressed in* MTL *for the interval-based semantics.*

Proof. Let Φ be the TPTL formula $x.\mathbf{F}\,(b \wedge \mathbf{F}\,(c \wedge\ x \leq 2))$. This formula expresses that, along the time state sequence, from the current point on, there is a b followed by a c, and the delay before that c is less than 2 t.u. For proving the proposition, we write an MTL formula Φ' which is equivalent to Φ over time state sequences. Formula Φ' is defined as the disjunction of three formulae $\Phi' = \Phi'_1 \vee \Phi'_2 \vee \Phi'_3$ where:

$$\begin{cases} \Phi'_1 = \mathbf{F}_{\leq 1}\, b \wedge \mathbf{F}_{[1,2]}\, c \\ \Phi'_2 = \mathbf{F}_{\leq 1}\,(b \wedge \mathbf{F}_{\leq 1}\, c) \\ \Phi'_3 = \mathbf{F}_{\leq 1}\,(\mathbf{F}_{\leq 1}\, b \wedge \mathbf{F}_{=1}\, c) \end{cases}$$

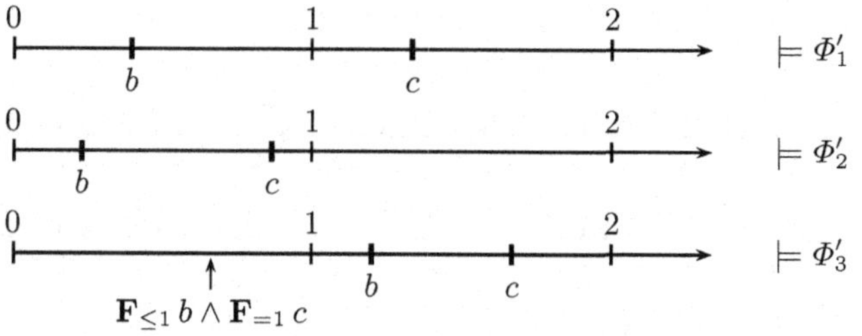

Fig. 1. Translation of TPTL formula Φ in MTL

Let κ be a time state sequence. If $\kappa \models_i \Phi'$, it is obvious that $\kappa \models_i \Phi$. Suppose now that $\kappa \models_i \Phi$, then there exists $0 < t_1 < t_2 \leq 2$ such that[2] $(\kappa, t_1) \models_i b$ and $(\kappa, t_2) \models_i c$. If $t_1 \leq 1$ then κ satisfies Φ'_1 or Φ'_2 (or both) depending on t_2 being smaller or greater than 1. If $t_1 \in (1, 2]$ then there exists a date t' in $(0, 1]$ such that $(\kappa, t') \models_i \mathbf{F}_{\leq 1}\, b \wedge \mathbf{F}_{=1}\, c$ which implies that $\kappa \models_i \Phi'_3$. We illustrate the three possible cases on Fig. 1.   □

---

[2] Here we abstract away the value for clock x as it corresponds to the date.

From the proposition above we get that the TPTL formula $\mathbf{G}\,(a \Rightarrow \Phi)$ is equivalent over time state sequences to the MTL formula $\mathbf{G}\,(a \Rightarrow \Phi')$. This does not imply that the conjecture is wrong, and we will now prove two results:

- $x.\mathbf{F}\,(b \wedge \mathbf{F}\,(c \wedge\ x\ \le\ 2))$ can not be expressed in MTL for the pointwise semantics (thus over timed words)
- the more involved TPTL formula $x.\mathbf{F}\,(a \wedge x \le 1 \wedge \mathbf{G}\,(x \le 1 \Rightarrow \neg b))$ can not be expressed in MTL for the interval-based semantics.

This implies that TPTL is indeed strictly more expressive than MTL for both pointwise and interval-based semantics, which positively answers the conjecture of [6,7,12].

3.2   Pointwise Semantics

We now show that the formula $\Phi\ =\ x.(\mathbf{F}\,(b \wedge \mathbf{F}\,(c \wedge x\ \le\ 2)))$ cannot be expressed in MTL for the pointwise semantics. This gives another proof of the strict containment of MTL with pointwise semantics in MTL with interval-based semantics [10].

We note $\mathrm{MTL}_{p,n}$ for the set of MTL formulae whose constants are multiple of p and whose temporal height (maximum number of nested modalities) is at most n. We construct two families of timed words $(\mathcal{A}_{p,n})_{p\in\mathbb{Q},n\in\mathbb{N}}$ and $(\mathcal{B}_{p,n})_{p\in\mathbb{Q},n\in\mathbb{N}}$ such that:

- $\mathcal{A}_{p,n} \models_\mathrm{p} \Phi$ whereas $\mathcal{B}_{p,n} \not\models_\mathrm{p} \Phi$ for every $p \in \mathbb{Q}$ and $n \in \mathbb{N}$,
- for all $\varphi \in \mathrm{MTL}_{p,n-3}$, $\mathcal{A}_{p,n} \models_\mathrm{p} \varphi \iff \mathcal{B}_{p,n} \models_\mathrm{p} \varphi$.

The two families of models are presented in Fig. 2. Note that there is no action between dates 0 and $2 - p$. It is obvious that $\mathcal{A}_{p,n} \models_\mathrm{p} \Phi$ whereas $\mathcal{B}_{p,n} \not\models_\mathrm{p} \Phi$.

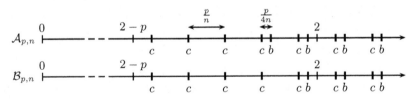

Fig. 2. Models $\mathcal{A}_{p,n}$ and $\mathcal{B}_{p,n}$

We now give a sketch of the expressiveness proof:

- we first prove that given any integer n, models $\mathcal{A}_{p,n+3}$ and $\mathcal{B}_{p,n+3}$ can not be distinguished by $\mathrm{MTL}_{p,n}$ formulae after date $2 - p$. This result holds both in the pointwise and the interval-based semantics.
- we then use the fact that there are no actions between 0 and $2 - p$ in the models; in the pointwise semantics, a formula cannot point a date before $2 - p$. This enables us to prove that the two models $\mathcal{A}_{p,n+3}$ and $\mathcal{B}_{p,n+3}$ can not be initially distinguished by any $\mathrm{MTL}_{p,n}$ formula in the pointwise semantics. This result does not hold in the interval-based semantics.

– assume Φ has an MTL equivalent Ψ. We define the granularity P as follows: $P = \prod_{a/b\in\Psi} 1/b$. Let N be its temporal height. Then the models $\mathcal{A}_{P,N+3}$ and $\mathcal{B}_{P,N+3}$ cannot be distinguished by Ψ, according to the above result, which contradicts that Ψ is equivalent to Φ.

Theorem 2. TPTL *is strictly more expressive than* MTL *under the pointwise semantics.*

Since the MITL+Past formula $\mathbf{F}_{<2}(c \wedge \top\, \mathbf{S}\, b)$ also distinguishes between the families of models $(\mathcal{A}_{p,n})_{p\in\mathbb{Q},n\in\mathbb{N}}$ and $(\mathcal{B}_{p,n})_{p\in\mathbb{Q},n\in\mathbb{N}}$, we get the corollary:

Corollary 3. MTL+Past *(resp.* MITL+Past*) is strictly more expressive than* MTL *(resp.* MITL*) for the pointwise semantics.*

Note that the above result is a main difference between the timed and the untimed framework where it is well-known that past does not add any expressiveness to LTL [14,11]. This had already been proved in [6] for MITL.

3.3   Interval-Based Semantics

As we have seen, the formula which has been used for the pointwise semantics can not be used for the interval-based semantics. We will instead prove the following proposition:

Proposition 4. *The* TPTL *formula* $\Phi = x.\mathbf{F}(a \wedge x \le 1 \wedge \mathbf{G}(x \le 1 \Rightarrow \neg b))$ *has no equivalent* MTL *formula over time state sequences.*

Proof. Assume some formula $\Psi \in$ MTL is equivalent to Φ over time state sequences. Let P be its granularity. W.l.o.g., we may assume that Ψ only uses constraints of the form $\sim P$, with $\sim\, \in \{<,=,>\}$. Let N be the temporal height of this formula. We write $\mathrm{MTL}^-_{p,n}$ for the fragment of MTL using only $\sim p$ constraints, and with temporal height at most n. Thus $\Psi \in \mathrm{MTL}^-_{P,N}$.

Now, we build two different families of time state sequences $\mathcal{A}_{p,n}$ and $\mathcal{B}_{p,n}$, such that Φ holds initially in the first one but not in the second one. We will then prove that they cannot be distinguished by any formula in $\mathrm{MTL}^-_{p,n-3}$.

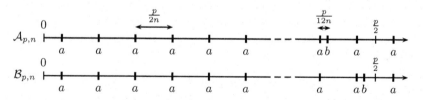

Fig. 3. Two timed paths $\mathcal{A}_{p,n}$ and $\mathcal{B}_{p,n}$

Let us first define $\mathcal{A}_{p,n}$. Along that time state sequence, atomic proposition a will be set to true exactly at time points $\frac{p}{4n} + \alpha\frac{p}{2n}$, where α may be any nonnegative integer. Atomic proposition b will hold exactly at times $(\alpha+1)\cdot\frac{p}{2} - \frac{4p}{6n}$, with $\alpha \in \mathbb{N}$. As for $\mathcal{B}_{p,n}$, it has exactly the same a's, and b holds exactly at time points $(\alpha + 1) \cdot \frac{p}{2} - \frac{p}{6n}$, with $\alpha \in \mathbb{N}$. The portion between 0 and $\frac{p}{2}$ of both time state sequences is represented on Fig. 3. Both time state sequences are in fact periodic, with period $\frac{p}{2}$. The following lemma is straightforward since, for each equivalence, the suffixes of the paths are the same.

Lemma 5. *For any positive p and n, for any nonnegative real x, and for any* MTL *formula φ,*

$$\mathcal{A}_{p,n}, x \models_i \varphi \qquad \Longleftrightarrow \qquad \mathcal{B}_{p,n}, x + \frac{p}{2n} \models_i \varphi \qquad (2)$$

$$\mathcal{A}_{p,n}, x \models_i \varphi \qquad \Longleftrightarrow \qquad \mathcal{A}_{p,n}, x + \frac{p}{2} \models_i \varphi \qquad (3)$$

$$\mathcal{B}_{p,n}, x \models_i \varphi \qquad \Longleftrightarrow \qquad \mathcal{B}_{p,n}, x + \frac{p}{2} \models_i \varphi \qquad (4)$$

We can then prove (by induction, see [9]) the following lemma:

Lemma 6. *For any $k \leq n$, for any $p \in \mathbb{Q}^+$, for any $\varphi \in \mathsf{MTL}^-_{p,k}$, for any $x \in \left[0, \frac{p}{2} - \frac{(k+2)p}{2(n+3)}\right)$, for any nonnegative integer α, we have*

$$\mathcal{A}_{p,n+3}, \alpha\frac{p}{2} + x \models \varphi \qquad \Longleftrightarrow \qquad \mathcal{B}_{p,n+3}, \alpha\frac{p}{2} + x \models \varphi$$

As a corollary of the lemma, when $n = N = k$, $p = P$ and $\alpha = x = 0$, we get that any formula in $\mathsf{MTL}^-_{P,N}$ cannot distinguish between models $\mathcal{A}_{P,N+3}$ and $\mathcal{B}_{P,N+3}$. This is in contradiction with the fact that Ψ is equivalent to Φ, since Ψ holds initially along $\mathcal{A}_{P,N+3}$ but fails to hold initially along $\mathcal{B}_{P,N+3}$. □

We can now state our main theorem:

Theorem 7. TPTL *is strictly more expressive than* MTL *for the interval-based semantics.*

As a side result we get that TPTL under the pointwise semantics is strictly more expressive than MTL under the interval-based semantics (assuming that the latter is restricted to timed words). Also note that the formula Φ does not use the **U** modality. However, it needs both **F** and **G**, as the fragment of TPTL using only the **F** modality can be translated into MTL (see Section 4).

Since the MTL+Past formula $\mathbf{F}_{=1}(\neg b \, \mathbf{S} \, a)$ distinguishes between the two families of models $(\mathcal{A}_{p,n})_{p \in \mathbb{Q}, n \in \mathbb{N}}$ and $(\mathcal{B}_{p,n})_{p \in \mathbb{Q}, n \in \mathbb{N}}$, we get the following corollary:

Corollary 8. MTL+Past *is strictly more expressive than* MTL *for the interval-based semantics.*

The more involved MITL+Past formula[3] $\mathbf{F}_{\geq 1}(\neg a \wedge \mathbf{F}^{-1}_{\geq -1}(\mathbf{G}^{-1} \neg a) \wedge \neg b \, \mathbf{S} \, a)$ also distinguishes between the two families, so that we also get:

Corollary 9. MITL+Past *is strictly more expressive than* MITL *for the interval-based semantics.*

To our knowledge, these are the first expressiveness result for timed linear-time temporal logics using past modalities under the interval-based semantics.

---

[3] Note that $\mathbf{F}^{-1}_{\geq -1} \varphi$ holds when φ held at some point in the last time unit.

4   On the Existential Fragments of **MTL** and **TPTL**

TPTL$_\mathbf{F}$ is the fragment of TPTL which only uses the $\mathbf{F}$ modality and which does not use the general negation but only negation of atomic propositions. Formally, TPTL$_\mathbf{F}$ is defined by the following grammar:

$$\text{TPTL}_\mathbf{F} \ni \varphi ::= p \mid \neg p \mid \varphi_1 \vee \varphi_2 \mid \varphi_1 \wedge \varphi_2 \mid \mathbf{F}\,\varphi \mid x \sim c \mid x.\varphi.$$

An example of a TPTL$_\mathbf{F}$ formula is $x.\mathbf{F}\,(b \wedge \mathbf{F}\,(c \wedge x \leq 2))$ (see Subsection 3.1). Similarly we define the fragment MTL$_\mathbf{F}$ of MTL where only $\mathbf{F}$ modalities are allowed:

$$\text{MTL}_\mathbf{F} \ni \varphi ::= p \mid \neg p \mid \varphi_1 \vee \varphi_2 \mid \varphi_1 \wedge \varphi_2 \mid \mathbf{F}_I\,\varphi.$$

From Subsection 3.2, we know that, under the pointwise semantics, TPTL$_\mathbf{F}$ is strictly more expressive than MTL$_\mathbf{F}$, since formula $x.\mathbf{F}\,(b \wedge \mathbf{F}\,(c \wedge x \leq 2))$ has no equivalent in MTL (thus in MTL$_\mathbf{F}$). On the contrary, when considering the interval-based semantics, we proved that this TPTL$_\mathbf{F}$ formula can be expressed in MTL$_\mathbf{F}$ (see Subsection 3.1). In this section, we generalize the construction of Subsection 3.1, and prove that TPTL$_\mathbf{F}$ and MTL$_\mathbf{F}$ are in fact equally expressive for the interval-based semantics.

Theorem 10. *TPTL$_\mathbf{F}$ is as expressive as MTL$_\mathbf{F}$ for the interval-based semantics.*

Sketch of proof. From a TPTL$_\mathbf{F}$ formula φ, we construct a *system of difference inequations* $\mathcal{S}_\varphi$ which recognizes the same models. Such a system has a finite number of free variables corresponding to dates, these dates are constrained by difference inequations, and propositional variables must be satisfied at some dates. Here is an example of the system constructed for the formula of section 3.1.

Example 3. For the formula $x.\mathbf{F}\,(a \wedge \mathbf{F}\,(b \wedge x \leq 2))$, we obtain:

$$\mathcal{S} = \begin{cases} V : y_1 \mapsto a, \ y_2 \mapsto b \\ \mathcal{J} = \{y_2 \leq 2, y_2 > y_1, y_1 > 0\} \end{cases}$$

We explain now how to construct a MTL formula for such systems:

- if all variables of the system are sorted ($r_1 < y_1 < \cdots < y_p < r_2$ with $r_1, r_2 \in \mathbb{Q}$), we generalize the technique used in proposition 1 to construct a corresponding MTL formula.
- if all variables are bounded in the system, it can be obtained by an union of previous systems using a region construction.
- a general system can be decomposed in bounded systems as follows:

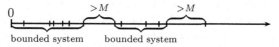

Each point on the line represents a variable, and a part denoted by "bounded system" gathers variables whose differences are bounded. Two variables in different bounded systems are separated by at least M t.u.

Note that this construction from $\mathsf{TPTL_F}$ to $\mathsf{MTL_F}$ is exponential due to the ordering of variables and the region construction.

It is known [3] that the satisfiability problem for TPTL and MTL is undecidable for the interval-based semantics, whereas it has been proved recently that the satisfiability problem for MTL is decidable but non primitive recursive for the pointwise semantics [18]. As a corollary of the previous proof, we get:

Corollary 11. *The satisfiability problem for* $\mathsf{TPTL_F}$ *(and thus* $\mathsf{MTL_F}$*) is NP-complete for the interval-based semantics.*

5   Conclusion

In this paper we have proved the conjecture (first proposed in [4]) that the logic TPTL is strictly more expressive than MTL. However we have also proved that the TPTL formula $\mathbf{G}\,(a \rightarrow x.\mathbf{F}\,(b \wedge \mathbf{F}\,(c \wedge x \leq 1)))$, which had been proposed as an example of formula which could not be expressed in MTL, has indeed an equivalent formula in MTL for the interval-based semantics. We have thus proposed another formula of TPTL which can not be expressed in MTL. We have also proved that the fragment of TPTL which only uses the $\mathbf{F}$ modality can be translated in MTL.

As side results, we have obtained that $\mathsf{MTL+Past}$ and $\mathsf{MITL+Past}$ are strictly more expressive than MTL and MITL, resp., which is a main difference with the untimed framework where past modalities do not add any expressive power to LTL [14,11].

Linear models we have used for proving above expressiveness results can be viewed as special cases of branching-time models. Our results thus apply to the branching-time logic TCTL (by replacing the modality $\mathbf{U}$ with the modality $\mathbf{AU}$), and translate as: TCTL with explicit clocks [13] is strictly more expressive than TCTL with subscripts [2], as conjectured in [1,24].

As further developments, we would like to study automata formalisms equivalent to both logics TPTL and MTL. Several existing works may appear as interesting starting points, namely [6,16,18,10].

References

1. R. Alur. *Techniques for Automatic Verification of Real-Time Systems.* PhD thesis, Stanford Univ., Stanford, CA, USA, 1991.
2. R. Alur, C. Courcoubetis, and D. Dill. Model-checking in dense real-time. *Information and Computation*, 104(1):2–34, 1993.
3. R. Alur, T. Feder, and T. A. Henzinger. The benefits of relaxing punctuality. *Journal of the ACM*, 43(1):116–146, 1996.
4. R. Alur and T. A. Henzinger. Real-time logics: Complexity and expressiveness. In *Proc. 5th Ann. Symp. Logic in Computer Science (LICS'90)*, pages 390–401. IEEE Comp. Soc. Press, 1990.
5. R. Alur and T. A. Henzinger. Back to the future: towards a theory of timed regular languages. In *Proc. 33rd Ann. Symp. Foundations of Computer Science (FOCS'92)*, pages 177–186. IEEE Comp. Soc. Press, 1992.

6. R. Alur and T. A. Henzinger. Logics and models of real-time: A survey. In *Real-Time: Theory in Practice, Proc. REX Workshop 1991*, volume 600 of *LNCS*, pages 74–106. Springer, 1992.

7. R. Alur and T. A. Henzinger. Real-time logics: Complexity and expressiveness. *Information and Computation*, 104(1):35–77, 1993.

8. R. Alur and T. A. Henzinger. A really temporal logic. *Journal of the ACM*, 41(1):181–204, 1994.

9. P. Bouyer, F. Chevalier, and N. Markey. About the expressiveness of TPTL and MTL. Research Report LSV-05-05, LSV, ENS Cachan, France, 2005.

10. D. D'Souza and P. Prabhakar. On the expressiveness of MTL in the pointwise and continuous semantics. Technical Report IISc-CSA-TR-2005-7, Indian Institute of Science, Bangalore, India, 2005.

11. D. M. Gabbay, A. Pnueli, S. Shelah, and J. Stavi. On the temporal analysis of fairness. In *Conf. Record 7th ACM Symp. Principles of Programming Languages (POPL'80)*, pages 163–173. ACM Press, 1980.

12. T. A. Henzinger. It's about time: Real-time logics reviewed. In *Proc. 9th Int. Conf. Concurrency Theory (CONCUR'98)*, volume 1466 of *LNCS*, pages 439–454. Springer, 1998.

13. T. A. Henzinger, X. Nicollin, J. Sifakis, and S. Yovine. Symbolic model-checking for real-time systems. *Information and Computation*, 111(2):193–244, 1994.

14. J. A. Kamp. *Tense Logic and the Theory of Linear Order*. PhD thesis, UCLA, Los Angeles, CA, USA, 1968.

15. R. Koymans. Specifying real-time properties with metric temporal logic. *Real-Time Systems*, 2(4):255–299, 1990.

16. S. Lasota and I. Walukiewicz. Alternating timed automata. In *Proc. 8th Int. Conf. Foundations of Software Science and Computation Structures (FoSSaCS'05)*, volume 3441 of *LNCS*, pages 250–265. Springer, 2005.

17. N. Markey and J.-F. Raskin. Model checking restricted sets of timed paths. *Theoretical Computer Science*, 2005. To appear.

18. J. Ouaknine and J. B. Worrell. On the decidability of metric temporal logic. In *Proc. 19th Ann. Symp. Logic in Computer Science (LICS'05)*, pages 188–197. IEEE Comp. Soc. Press, 2005.

19. A. Pnueli. The temporal logic of programs. In *Proc. 18th Ann. Symp. Foundations of Computer Science (FOCS'77)*, pages 46–57. IEEE Comp. Soc. Press, 1977.

20. J.-F. Raskin. *Logics, Automata and Classical Theories for Deciding Real-Time*. PhD thesis, Univ. Namur, Namur, Belgium, 1999.

21. A. P. Sistla and E. M. Clarke. The complexity of propositional linear temporal logics. *Journal of the ACM*, 32(3):733–749, 1985.

22. P. Thati and G. Rosu. Monitoring algorithms for metric temporal logic specifications. In *Proc. 4th International Workshop on Runtime Verification (RV'04)*, volume 113 of *ENTCS*, pages 145–162. Elsevier, 2005.

23. M. Y. Vardi and P. Wolper. An automata-theoretic approach to automatic program verification. In *Proc. 1st Ann. Symp. Logic in Computer Science (LICS'86)*, pages 322–344. IEEE Comp. Soc. Press, 1986.

24. S. Yovine. *Méthodes et outils pour la vérification symbolique de systèmes temporisés*. PhD thesis, INPG, Grenoble, France, 1993.

Modal Strength Reduction in Quantified Discrete Duration Calculus

Shankara Narayanan Krishna[1] and Paritosh K. Pandya[2]

[1] Indian Institute of Technology, Bombay, India
krishnas@cse.iitb.ac.in
[2] Tata Institute of Fundamental Research, India
pandya@tifr.res.in

Abstract. QDDC is a logic for specifying quantitative timing properties of reactive systems. An automata theoretic decision procedure for QDDC reduces each formula to a finite state automaton accepting precisely the models of the formula. This construction has been implemented into a validity/model checking tool for QDDC called DCVALID. Unfortunately, the size of the final automaton as well as the intermediate automata which are encountered in the construction can some times be prohibitively large. In this paper, we present some validity preserving transformations to QDDC formulae which result into more efficient construction of the formula automaton and hence reduce the validity checking time. The transformations can be computed in linear time. We provide a theoretical as well as an experimental analysis of the improvements in the formula automaton size and validity checking time due to our transformations.

1 Introduction

Various logics have emerged as useful formalisms for the specification of desired behaviour of systems. The temporal logics have proved especially useful in the specification of properties of reactive systems. The connection between logics and automata provides an important foundation for many validity and model checking algorithms. For example, logic S1S, Monadic second order logic over finite words and Linear Temporal logic can all be decided using automata theoretic techniques [1,2]. Leading model checking tools such as MONA, SPIN and NuSMV make use of these logic-to-automata translations.

Quantified Discrete-time Duration Calculus (QDDC) [11,12,3,13] is a highly expressive logic for specifying properties of finite sequences of states (behaviours). It is well suited to specifying quantitative timing properties of synchronous programs such as response time and latency [5]. QDDC is closely related to the Interval Temporal Logic of Moszkowski [10] and Duration Calculus of Zhou *et al* [16]. (See [11,15] for their relationship.)

QDDC provides novel interval based modalities for describing behaviours. For example, the formula $\square(\lceil P\rceil^0 \frown \lceil\lceil\neg Q\rceil \frown \lceil Q\rceil^0 \Rightarrow (\Sigma R \leq 3))$ holds for a behaviour σ provided for all fragments σ' of σ which have (a) P true in the

R. Ramanujam and S. Sen (Eds.): FSTTCS 2005, LNCS 3821, pp. 444–456, 2005.

beginning, (b) Q true at the end, and (c) no occurrences of Q in between, the number of occurrences of states in σ' where R is true is at most 3. Here, $\square$ modality ranges over all fragments of a behaviour. Operator $\frown$ is like concatenation (fusion) of behaviour fragments and $\lceil\lceil\neg Q\rceil$ states invariance of $\neg Q$ over the behaviour fragment. Finally, ΣR counts number of occurrences of R within a behaviour fragment. A precise definition of the syntax and semantics of QDDC is given in Section 2.

The validity (and model checking) of QDDC formulae is decidable. An automata theoretic decision procedure allows construction of a finite state automaton $A(D)$ for each formula D such that the models of D are precisely the words accepted by $A(D)$ [11]. This construction is implemented into a tool DCVALID [11,12] which can be used to check validity/satisfiability of a QDDC formula and for model checking. The tool DCVALID is built on top of MONA [7,8].

It must be noted that the lower bound on the size of $A(D)$ is non-elementary in general. However, this complexity is not frequently observed in practice and we have been able to check validity of many large formulae with our tool DCVALID [11,13]. On the other hand, we have also encountered several formulae where the automaton construction becomes prohibitively expensive.

In this paper, we present some validity preserving transformations of QDDC formulae. These transformations replace the temporal operators $\square, \diamond, \frown$ with suitable quantification, and in some cases they can eliminate these quantifiers while preserving validity. Hence, we call our transformation as *modal strength reduction* (MSR). The objective of this transformation is to come up with formulae which result in more efficient construction of the formula automaton.

In the paper, we provide a theoretical analysis to show that the MSR transformation can lead to an exponential reduction in the size of the formula automaton. The transformation takes only linear time to compute. We also carry out detailed experimental analysis to profile the effect our transformation on the final and the intermediate automata sizes and on the time taken to compute validity of QDDC formulae. We show a very significant improvement in the performance of our tool DCVALID on some formulae of interest by using the MSR transformation. Thus, the proposed transformation has practical utility and it will be incorporated in next release of the DCVALID tool.

2   Quantified Discrete-Time Duration Calculus (QDDC)

Let *Pvar* be a finite set of propositional variables representing some observable aspects of system state. $VAL(Pvar) \overset{\text{def}}{=} Pvar \rightarrow \{0, 1\}$ be the set of valuations assigning truth-value to each variable. We shall identify behaviours with finite, nonempty sequences of valuations, i.e. $VAL(Pvar)^+$. Given such a nonempty finite sequence of valuations $\sigma \in VAL^+$, we denote the satisfaction of a QDDC formula D over σ by $\sigma \models D$.

Syntax of QDDC Formulae Let p range over propositional variables, P, Q over propositions, c over positive integers and D, D_1, D_2 over QDDC formulae. Propositions are constructed from variables *Pvar* and constants 0, 1 (denoting *true*, *false* resp.) using boolean connectives $\wedge$, $\neg$ etc. as usual. The syntax of QDDC is as follows.

$$\lceil P \rceil^0 \mid \lceil\lceil P \rceil\rceil \mid D_1 \,^\frown D_2 \mid D_1 \wedge D_2 \mid \neg D \mid \exists p.D \mid$$
$$\eta \; op \; c \mid \Sigma P \; op \; c \quad \text{where} \quad op \in \{<, \leq, =, \geq, >\}$$

Let $\sigma \in VAL(Pvar)^+$ be a behaviour. Let $\#\sigma$ denote the length of σ and $\sigma[i]$ the i'th element. Let $dom(\sigma) = \{0, 1, \ldots, \#\sigma - 1\}$ denote the set of positions within σ. The set of intervals in σ is $Intv(\sigma) = \{[b, e] \in dom(\sigma)^2 \mid b \leq e\}$.

Let $\sigma, i \models P$ denote that proposition P evaluates to true at position i in σ. We omit this obvious definition. We inductively define the satisfaction of QDDC formula D for behaviour σ and interval $[b, e] \in Intv(\sigma)$ as follows.

$$\begin{aligned}
\sigma, [b, e] &\models \lceil P \rceil^0 \quad &\textbf{iff} \quad & b = e \text{ and } \sigma, b \models P \\
\sigma, [b, e] &\models \lceil\lceil P \rceil\rceil \quad &\textbf{iff} \quad & b < e \text{ and } \sigma, i \models P \text{ for all } i : b \leq i < e \\
\sigma, [b, e] &\models \neg D \quad &\textbf{iff} \quad & \sigma, [b, e] \not\models D \\
\sigma, [b, e] &\models D_1 \wedge D_2 \quad &\textbf{iff} \quad & \sigma, [b, e] \models D_1 \text{ and } \sigma, [b, e] \models D_2 \\
\sigma, [b, e] &\models D_1 \,^\frown D_2 \quad &\textbf{iff} \quad & \text{for some } m : b \leq m \leq e : \\
& & & \sigma, [b, m] \models D_1 \text{ and } \sigma, [m, e] \models D_2
\end{aligned}$$

Entities η and ΣP are called *measurements*. Term η denotes the length of the interval whereas ΣP denotes the count of number of times P is true within the interval $[b, e]$ (we treat the interval as being left-closed right-open). Formally,

$$eval(\eta, \sigma, [b, e]) \stackrel{\text{def}}{=} e - b$$
$$eval(\Sigma P, \sigma, [b, e]) \stackrel{\text{def}}{=} \sum_{i=b}^{e-1} \left\{ \begin{array}{ll} 1 & if \ \sigma, i \models P \\ 0 & otherwise \end{array} \right\}$$

Then, $\sigma, [b, e] \models t \; op \; c$ **iff** $eval(t, \sigma, [b, e]) \; op \; c$ for a measurement t.

Call a behaviour σ' to be p-variant of σ provided $\#\sigma = \#\sigma'$ and for all $i \in dom(\sigma)$ and for all $q \neq p$, we have $\sigma(i)(q) = \sigma'(i)(q)$. Then, let

$\sigma, [b, e] \models \exists p.D$ **iff** $\sigma', [b, e] \models D$ for some p-variant σ' of σ.

Finally, $\sigma \models D$ **iff** $\sigma, [0, \#\sigma - 1] \models D$. The modality $\Diamond D \stackrel{\text{def}}{=} true \,^\frown D \,^\frown true$ holds provided D holds for some subinterval, and its dual $\Box D \stackrel{\text{def}}{=} \neg\Diamond\neg D$ holds provided D holds for all subintervals. For more details on logic QDDC, see [11].

Notation Consider a formula D over propositional variables $Pvar$. A pair $\sigma, [b, e]$ is called a model and $\sigma, [b, e] \models D$ is as before. Let MOD denote the set of all models over $Pvar$. For $M \subseteq MOD$, define $M \models D$ **iff** $\forall \, m \in M, \, m \models D$.

Definition 1. *Let $D(D')$ denote an occurrence of D' in D. Define D' to be* **modally free** *if D' is not in scope of any modality $^\frown, \Box, \Diamond$ or quantifier $\forall, \exists$. Let $B^+(D)$ denote a modally free occurrence of the subformula D where D occurs in scope of an even number of negations (i.e. positively). Similarly, $B^-(D)$ denotes that D occurs modally freely and negatively. Let $D(D') \equiv D(D'')$ abbreviate the equivalence $D(D') \equiv D[D''/D']$ where $D[D''/D']$ denotes the formula obtained by replacing in D the occurrence D' by D''.* $\square$

Definition 2 (Validity Equivalence). *Let* $D_1 \equiv_e D_2 \overset{\text{def}}{=} \forall m \in MOD.m \models$
D_1 *iff* $m \models D_2$. *Also,* $D_1 \equiv_v D_2 \overset{\text{def}}{=} \models D_1$ *iff* $\models D_2$. $\qquad\qquad\square$

Proposition 1. *(a)* $\forall p D(p) \equiv_v D(p)$, *(b) If* $D_1 \equiv_e D_2$ *and* D_1 *occurs in* D, *then* $D(D_1) \equiv_e D(D_2)$, *(c)* $B^+(\forall p.D(p)) \equiv_v B^+(D(p))$, *and (d)* $B^-(\exists p.D(p)) \equiv_v B^-(D(p))$ *provided that variables* p *do not occur elsewhere in* B^+ *or* B^-. $\qquad\square$

Decidability of QDDC The following theorem characterizes the sets of models of a QDDC formula D over propositional variables $Pvar(D)$.

Theorem 1. *For every QDDC formula* D, *we can effectively construct a finite state automaton* $A(D)$ *over the alphabet* $VAL(Pvar(D))$ *such that for all* $\sigma \in VAL(Pvar(D))^*$, *we have* $\sigma \models D$ *iff* $\sigma \in L(A(D))$. *Hence, satisfiability (validity) of QDDC formulae is decidable [11].* $\qquad\qquad\square$

DCVALID The reduction from formulae of QDDC to finite state automata as stated in Theorem 1 has been implemented into a tool called DCVALID, which also checks for the validity of formulae (see [11]). This tool is built on top of tool MONA [7].

In the next section we consider how to transform formulae of the form $D_1 \frown \ldots \frown D_n$ and its negation to a form which leads to more efficient automaton construction. We then specialize these transformations to the derived operators $\square D$ and $\diamond D$.

3   Modal Strength Reduction

Consider a formula of the formula $DD = D_1 \frown \ldots \frown D_n$ over $Pvar$. Then, $\sigma, [b, e] \models DD$ iff $\exists m_1, \ldots, m_{n-1}$ such that taking $m_0 = b$ and $m_n = e$ we have $m_{i-1} \le m_i$ and $\sigma, [m_{i-1}, m_i] \models D_i$ for $1 \le i \le n$. To capture this chopping of interval $[b, e]$ into n parts at points m_i, we shall introduce fresh witness propositions, $p_1, \ldots, p_{n-1}$ such that first occurrence of p_i within $[b, e]$ records the position m_i. We shall also define a formula $\alpha_n(i, D_i)$ which states that the first occurrence of p_{i-1} is not later than the first occurrence of p_i and between these two positions the formula D_i holds. Then $D_1 \frown \ldots \frown D_n$ can be reformulated using the witness propositions as the formula $\bigwedge_{i=1}^n \alpha(i, D_i)$. This is formalized below.

Definition 3. *Let* $\lceil\lceil P \rceil\rceil^- \overset{\text{def}}{=} \lceil\lceil P \rceil\rceil \vee \lceil\ \rceil$ *which is true provided that* P *holds for all points of the (point or extended) interval except possibly the end point. Define*

$$\alpha_n(1, D_1) \overset{\text{def}}{=} (\lceil\lceil \neg p_1 \rceil\rceil^- \wedge D_1) \frown \lceil p_1 \rceil^0 \frown true$$
$$\alpha_n(n, D_n) \overset{\text{def}}{=} \lceil\lceil \neg p_{n-1} \rceil\rceil^- \frown \lceil p_{n-1} \rceil^0 \frown D_n$$
$$\alpha_n(i, D_i) \overset{\text{def}}{=} \lceil\lceil \neg p_{i-1} \wedge \neg p_i \rceil\rceil^- \frown \lceil p_{i-1} \rceil^0 \frown (\lceil\lceil \neg p_i \rceil\rceil^- \wedge D_i) \frown \lceil p_i \rceil^0 \frown true$$

Formula $Order_n$ states that first occurrences of propositions $p_1, \ldots, p_{n-1}$ are in the order 1 to n, i.e. $Order_n \overset{\text{def}}{=} \bigwedge_{i=1}^{n} \alpha_n(i, true)$.

1. Let $\widehat{Pvar} = Pvar \cup \{p_1, \ldots p_{n-1}\}$. Let $\widehat{VAL} = \widehat{Pvar} \rightarrow \{0, 1\}$ be the set of valuations of $\widehat{Pvar}$. Let $\widehat{\sigma}$ denote behaviours with finite non-empty sequence of valuations over $\widehat{VAL}$ and let $\widehat{MOD}$ denote the set of all models over $\widehat{Pvar}$.
2. Let $\widehat{OMOD} = \{\widehat{\sigma}, [b, e] \mid \widehat{\sigma}, [b, e] \models Order_n\}$ be the set of models over $\widehat{Pvar}$ satisfying formula $Order_n$.
3. Define $h : \widehat{MOD} \rightarrow MOD$ such that $h(\widehat{\sigma}, [b, e]) = \widehat{\sigma} \downarrow Pvar, [b, e]$.
4. Let $f : MOD \rightarrow 2^{\widehat{MOD}}$ be such that $f(\sigma, [b, e]) = \{\widehat{\sigma}, [b, e] \in \widehat{MOD} \mid \widehat{\sigma} \downarrow Pvar = \sigma \ \wedge \ \widehat{\sigma}, [b, e] \models Order_n\}$.
5. Functions f and h can be extended to sets of models in point wise manner, i.e. we can define $f(M)$ and $h(M')$ for $M \subseteq MOD$ and $M' \subseteq \widehat{MOD}$.

Every element of $\widehat{OMOD}$ encodes a way of chopping $[b, e]$ into n-parts.

Proposition 2. $f(MOD) = \widehat{OMOD}$.   □

Proposition 3. *For all $m \in MOD, m' \in \widehat{OMOD}$, we have $m' \in f(m)$ iff $m = h(m')$. Hence, $f(h(M')) = M'$ and $M \subseteq h(f(M))$.*   □

The following formulae shall play an important role in the paper.

$$\hat{\alpha}_n^+(D_1, \ldots, D_n) \overset{\text{def}}{=} Order_n \wedge \bigwedge_{i=1}^{n} \alpha_n(i, D_i) \tag{1}$$

$$\hat{\alpha}_n^-(D_1, \ldots, D_n) \overset{\text{def}}{=} Order_n \Rightarrow \left(\bigvee_{i=1}^{n} \alpha_n(i, \neg D_i) \right) \tag{2}$$

In the rest of the paper, we shall omit the subscript n from $Order_n$, α_n and β_n.

Proposition 4. $\models \bigwedge_{i=1}^{n} \alpha(i, D_i) \Rightarrow Order$.
Hence, $\hat{\alpha}^+(D_1, \ldots, D_n) \equiv_e \bigwedge_{i=1}^{n} \alpha(i, D_i)$.   □

We now relate the truth of formula $D_1 \frown \ldots \frown D_n$ to the truth of the formula $\hat{\alpha}^+(D_1, \ldots, D_n)$. The following important theorem proves the correctness this encoding. Its proof relies on the proposition following it. We omit the proofs which can be found in the full version of the paper [9].

Theorem 2. $\sigma, [b, e] \models D_1 \frown D_2 \frown \ldots \frown D_n$
iff $\widehat{\sigma}, [b, e] \models \hat{\alpha}^+(D_1, \ldots, D_n)$ for some $\widehat{\sigma}, [b, e] \in f(\sigma, [b, e])$ □

Proposition 5. *Let $\widehat{\sigma}, [b, e] \in \widehat{OMOD}$. Define $\pi_i(\widehat{\sigma}, [b, e])$ as the position of first occurrence of p_i for $1 \leq i < n - 1$. Also define $\pi_0(\widehat{\sigma}, [b, e]) = b$ and $\pi_n(\widehat{\sigma}, [b, e]) = e$. Then, for $1 \leq i \leq n$ and some QDDC formula D we have*
$$\widehat{\sigma}, [\pi_{i-1}(\widehat{\sigma}, [b, e]), \pi_i(\widehat{\sigma}, [b, e])] \models D \quad \textbf{iff} \quad \widehat{\sigma}, [b, e] \models \alpha_n(i, D).$$ □

Corollary 1. $\sigma, [b, e] \models D_1 \frown D_2 \frown \ldots \frown D_n$
iff $\sigma, [b, e] \models \exists p_1 \ldots \exists p_{n-1}.\ \hat{\alpha}^+(D_1, \ldots, D_n)$.   □

We now consider the formula $\neg(D_1 \frown \ldots \frown D_n)$ and its relation to $\hat{\alpha}^-(D_1, \ldots, D_n)$.

Proposition 6. *(a)* $\models (Order \Rightarrow ((\neg\alpha(i, D)) \Leftrightarrow \alpha(i, \neg D)))$.
(b)Hence, $\neg\ \hat{\alpha}^+(D_1, \ldots, D_n) \equiv_e \hat{\alpha}^-(D_1, \ldots, D_n)$.   □

Theorem 3. $\sigma, [b, e] \models \neg(D_1 \frown D_2 \frown \ldots \frown D_n)$ *iff*
$\sigma, [b, e] \models \forall p_1 \ldots \forall p_{n-1}.\ \hat{\alpha}^-(D_1, \ldots, D_n)$.   □

3.1   MSR Transformations

Below, we list the equivalences which can be used to transform QDDC formulae. The equivalences **Tr A**, **Tr B** follow immediately from the Corollary 1 and Theorem 3. The equivalence **Tr C** follow from **Tr B** using the proposition 1(a). The equivalences **Tr D**, **Tr E** follow from **Tr A**, **Tr B** using the proposition 1(c,d).

- **(Tr A)** $D_1 \frown \ldots \frown D_n \equiv_e \exists p_1 \ldots \exists p_{n-1}.\ \hat{\alpha}^+(D_1, \ldots, D_n)$.
- **(Tr B)** $\neg(D_1 \frown \ldots \frown D_n) \equiv_e \forall p_1 \ldots \exists p_{n-1}.\ \hat{\alpha}^-(D_1, \ldots, D_n)$.
- **(Tr C)** $\neg(D_1 \frown \ldots \frown D_n) \equiv_v \hat{\alpha}^-(D_1, \ldots, D_n)$.
- **(Tr D)** $B^+(\neg(D_1 \frown \ldots \frown D_n)) \equiv_v B^+(\hat{\alpha}^-(D_1, \ldots, D_n))$.
- **(Tr E)** $B^-(D_1 \frown \ldots \frown D_n) \equiv_v B^-(\hat{\alpha}^+(D_1, \ldots, D_n))$.

Note that $\Diamond D \stackrel{\text{def}}{=} true \frown D \frown true$ and $\Box D \stackrel{\text{def}}{=} \neg(true \frown D \frown true)$. Using these, we can specialize the above equivalences as follows.

- **(Tr F)** $\Diamond D \equiv_e \exists p_1, p_2.\ \alpha_3(2, D)$.
- **(Tr G)** $\Box D \equiv_e \forall p_1, p_2.\ (Order \Rightarrow \alpha_3(2, D))$.
- **(Tr H)** $\Box D \equiv_v Order \Rightarrow \alpha_3(2, D)$.
- **(Tr I)** $B^+(\Box D) \equiv_v B^+(Order \Rightarrow \alpha_3(2, D))$.
- **(Tr J)** $B^-(\Diamond D) \equiv_v B^-(\alpha_3(2, D))$.

Applying the above equivalences left-to-right eliminates modal operators by introducing suitable quantifiers over temporal variables. Transformations **A,B, F,G** can be applied to any subformula due to Proposition 1(b).

The application of transformations **C,D,E** and **H,I,J** eliminates all modally free positive occurrences of $\Box$ and $\neg\frown$ operators as well as negative occurrences of $\Diamond$ and $\frown$ operators without introducing quantifiers. Note that the introduced witness variables $p_1, \ldots, p_n$ must be fresh. With this precaution, the transformations can be recursively applied to resulting formulae. We shall denote the result of repeated application of transformations **C,D,E** and **H,I,J** to a formula D as $MSR(D)$. *Observe that $MSR(D)$ can computed in time linear in the size of D.*

Example 1. The gas burner problem is fully described in the full version of this paper [9]. To prove its correctness, we must establish the validity of a formula $G(winlen, leakbound)$ which has the form $G = (\Box F_1 \wedge \Box F_2) \Rightarrow \Box F_3$. Here the top level modal sub-formulae $\Box F_1$ and $\Box F_2$ occur negatively. Hence, MSR transformation cannot be applied to them. However, $\Box F_3$ occurs positively. Hence applying **Tr D**, we get validity equivalent formula $MSR(G) = (\Box F_1 \wedge \Box F_2) \Rightarrow (Order_3 \Rightarrow \alpha_3(2, F_3))$. Using the definitions of $Order$ and α_3, this reduces to:
$$(\Box F_1 \wedge \Box F_2) \Rightarrow (([\![\neg p_1 \wedge \neg p_2]\!]^- \frown \lceil p_1 \rceil^0 \frown [\![\neg p_2]\!]^- \frown \lceil p_2 \rceil^0 \frown true)$$
$$\Rightarrow ([\![\neg p_1 \wedge \neg p_2]\!]^- \frown \lceil p_1 \rceil^0 \frown ([\![\neg p_2]\!]^- \wedge F_3) \frown \lceil p_2 \rceil^0 \frown true))$$

Complexity We now study the effect of the transformations on the formula automaton size. Given a formula D let $A(D)$ denote the minimal, deterministic automaton for the formula as in Theorem 1. Let $|A(D)|$ denote the size of this automaton in number of states. Hence, $|A(D)| = |A(\neg D)|$. Below, we characterize the size of the automaton for $\hat{\alpha}^-(D_1, \ldots, D_n)$. Note that due to Proposition 6 this size is same as the size for $\hat{\alpha}^+(D_1, \ldots, D_n)$.

Theorem 4. $|A(\hat{\alpha}^-(D_1, \ldots, D_n))| \leq \sum_{i=1}^n |A(D_i)| + n$ □

Proof. Let us denote $\hat{\alpha}^-(D_1, \ldots, D_n)$ by $\hat{\alpha}^-$. Given DFAs $A(\neg D_i)$ over the alphabet $VAL(Pvar)$, we can construct a DFA $A(\hat{\alpha}^-)$ for $\hat{\alpha}^-$ having requisite number of states. This automaton has alphabet $VAL(\widehat{Pvar})$. Figure 1 illustrates the construction of $\hat{\alpha}^-(D_1, D_2, D_3, D_4)$. Each edge of $A(\hat{\alpha}^-)$ is labeled with a label from $A(D_i)$ (such as a, b, c) augmented with a column vector giving values of witness propositions $\langle p_1, p_2, p_3 \rangle$. The automaton $A(\hat{\alpha}^-)$ is basically the union of $A(\neg D_i)$ with some additional nodes and edges (we denote these fragments as $B(\neg D_i)$). Automaton $A(\hat{\alpha}^-)$ functions as follows.
1. Beginning with the initial state of $B(\neg D_1)$, the automaton enters $B(\neg D_i)$ when $p_{i-1} = 1$ for the first time. It stays within $B(\neg D_i)$ mimicking $A(\neg D_i)$ while $p_i = \ldots = p_{n-1} = 0$. Such transitions are drawn with solid arrows in Figure 1.
2. If input occurs violating $Order$, then $A(\hat{\alpha}^-)$ accepts by transiting to state q_f. In Figure 1 such transitions are drawn with dash-dot-dash lines.
3. A new state fin_i is added to $B(\neg D_i)$ as the unique final state within it. Thus any final state q_{f_i} in $A(\neg D_i)$ is made non-final within $B(\neg D_i)$. While mimicking $A(\neg D_i)$, if final state q'_{f_i} of $A(\neg D_i)$ is entered simultaneously with $p_i = 1$ then $B(\neg D_i)$ transits to the accepting state fin_i. This is because between the first occurrences of p_{i-1} and p_i we have found behaviour satisfying $\neg D_i$, i.e. $\alpha(i, \neg D_i)$ holds for the full input sequence. On the other hand, if final state q'_{f_i} of $A(\neg D_i)$ is entered while mimicking $A(\neg D_i)$ with condition $p_i = 0$, the automaton $B(\neg D_i)$ goes to non-accepting state q_{f_i} and continues mimicking $A(\neg D_i)$.
4. If while mimicking a transition labeled d of $A(\neg D_i)$ we encounter $p_i = 1$, and the transition does not lead to a final state of $A(\neg D_i)$, then $B(\neg D_i)$ is exited. $A(\hat{\alpha}^-)$ then enters $B(\neg D_{i+1})$. Such transitions are drawn with dashed arrows in Figure 1. The state entered is one which would arise by mimicking $A(\neg D_{i+1})$ on input d. For example see the transition from q_{02} to q_{13} (and the more complex one from q_{02} to q_{14} when both p_i and p_{i+1} become true simultaneously).

5. Since we have added one additional state fin_i for each $B(\neg D_i)$ except the last one $B(\neg D_n)$, and we have also used one additional state q_f for violation of *Order*, the total number of states is $\sum_{i=1}^{n} |A(D_i)| + n$.   □

Proposition 7. *(a)* $|A(D_1 \frown \ldots \frown D_n)|$ *can be of the order of* $2^{max(|A(D_i)|)}$ *where* $1 \leq i \leq n$. *(b)* $|A(\Diamond D)|$ *and* $|A(\Box D)|$ *can be of the order of* $2^{|A(D)|}$.

Proof. (a) Consider the formula $DD_1 = (true \frown \lceil p \rceil^0 \frown \eta = (l-1))$ for any value of l. This defines a language over $\{0,1\}$ where the lth letter from the right is 1. It is well-known that any deterministic automaton recognizing this will have at least 2^l states. Now consider the formula $DD_2 = D_1 \frown \ldots \frown D_n$ with $D_i = (\lceil p \rceil^0 \frown \eta = l \frown \lceil p \rceil^0)$ for some fixed $i \neq 1$ and $D_j = true$ for all $j \neq i$. It is easy to show as a variation of the first case that the size of any deterministic automaton for this formula will be exponential in l. However, the size of the automaton for the component D_i is only l. Part (b) follows by noting that $\Diamond D = true \frown D \frown true$.   □

The above theorem 4 and the proposition 7 show that transformations **Tr C** and **Tr F** can give rise to an exponential reduction in the size (number of states) of the automaton of a formula, while preserving validity.

4   Experimental Results

We apply the modal strength reduction transformations to some formulae to study their effects on automata size and validity checking time. The validity checking time is proportional to the sum of the formula automaton construction time and the automaton size.

When the transformations **Tr B** or **Tr G** are applied to a formula D, we denote the resulting formula by $TrBG(D)$. Instead, when transformations **Tr C** or **Tr H** are applied to the formula D, we denote the resulting formula by $TrCH(D)$. Note that $D \equiv_e TrBG(D)$ and $D \equiv_v TrCH(D)$.

Table 1 gives the improvement in the automata sizes and their computation times due to $TrBD$ and $TrCH$ transformations on several examples. In each case, we record (a) the time taken to compute the formula automaton, (b) the size (number of state) of the final automaton, (c) a pair giving the maximum size of the intermediate automata and the maximum number of BDD nodes for representing the intermediate automata. In all tables a ↓ denotes that the automaton construction could not be completed due to excessive BDD size ($>$ 16777216 nodes).

The experiments are conducted using the tool DCVALID V1.4 [11] on a Linux i686 dual processor PC having 1GB physical memory, 1 GB swap memory, clock speed 1GHz and cache size 256 kb for both processors. The following artificially created formulae are used in the experiments.

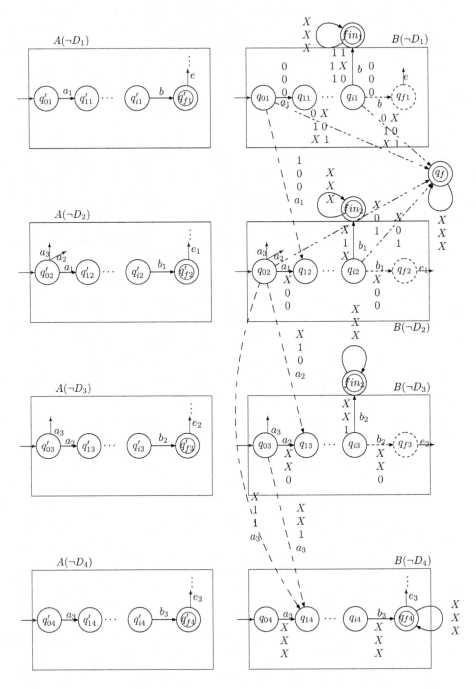

Fig. 1. The automata $A(\neg D_i)$ on the left, and $A(\hat{\alpha}^-(D_1, D_2, D_3, D_4))$, on the right

$$F_1(i,j) = (\Sigma \ P \leq i \wedge \eta \leq j), \qquad F_2 = (\eta = 25 \Rightarrow \Sigma P \leq 4),$$
$$F_3 = \lceil\lceil P \rceil \cap \lceil\lceil \neg P \rceil \cap \lceil\lceil R \rceil \cap \lceil\lceil \neg R \rceil \cap \lceil\lceil Q \rceil \cap \lceil\lceil \neg Q \rceil \Rightarrow \ (\eta = 8 \cap \eta = 2 \cap \eta \geq 3),$$
$$F_4(i) = ((\lceil\lceil P \rceil\rceil \Rightarrow \lceil\lceil Q \rceil\rceil) \Rightarrow \Sigma R \leq i).$$

Table 1. Effect of Transformations B,C,G & H on Automata Sizes

F				$TrCH(F)$			$TrBG(F)$		
	Time	Final Size	Max. Size	Time	Final Size	Max. Size	Time	Final Size	Max. Size
$\Box F_1(3,12)$	00.17s	43	(3434, 9198)	00.07s	45	(173, 772)	00.12s	43	(1719, 4601)
$\Box F_2$	02m	65802	(594046, 1675874)	00.17s	130	(517, 2321)	01m	65802	(363817, 1027689)
$\neg(F3 \cap F1(6,7))$	02m	16	(968971, 3058671)	00.16s	139	(280, 1887)	02m	16	(835219, 2601408)
$\neg[F3 \cap F4(20) \cap F1(2,4)]$	13m	3	(1766509, 6739628)	00.37s	156	(717, 4269)	05m	3	(1187634, 3811428)

In order to profile the improvement in validity checking time, we applied the full $MSR(D)$ transformations as outlined in Section 3.1 to some benchmark QDDC examples drawn from the literature. These examples include (a) the Gas Burner problem, (b) the Lift controller problem, (c) the jobshop scheduling problem, and (d) the delay-insensitive oscillator (see [11]). In Table 2, we report the times taken to check the validity of the gas burner formula G versus the validity of $MSR(G)$ using the tool DCVALID (see Example 1). Similar tables for the other problems can be found in the full version of the paper [9].

5 Discussion

In this paper, we have proposed some modal strength reduction (MSR) transformations for QDDC formulae. These transformations preserve the validity of formulae while reducing the size of the finite state automaton accepting the models of the formula. In Proposition 7, we have shown that the construct $\neg(D_1 \cap \ldots \cap D_n)$ can give rise to an exponential blowup in the size of the formula automaton. Compared with this, Theorem 4 shows that the automaton for the validity equivalent formula $\hat{a}^-(D_1, \ldots, D_n)$ is only linear in the size of its component automata. Thus, theoretically the $MSR(D)$ transformation can give rise to up to an exponential reduction in size (number of states) of the formula automaton. Note that computing $MSR(D)$ takes time which is linear in the size of D. The $MSR(D)$ transformation introduces auxiliary variables. Hence, The reduction in the automaton state size is achieved at the cost of increasing the alphabet size of the automaton. However, due to the use of efficient BDD-based data structure for representing the transition table, this does not create proportionate increase in the computation time in tool DCVALID. Hence, our technique leads to improvement in the validity checking time for QDDC formulae.

In order to evaluate the practical significance of the MSR transformations, we have carried out experiments measuring the improvement due to MSR in the size of the formula automaton, the time taken for computing the formula automaton as well as the validity checking time for many formulae. Some of these results are presented in Tables 1, 2, and the rest can be found in the full version of the paper [9]. These results show a tremendous improvement (of 3-4 orders of magnitude) in the automaton size and validity computation time for many formulae of interest. The MSR transformations allow us to handle significantly larger instances of the benchmark Gas Burner and the Jobshop scheduling problems. Hence, the MSR transformations are of practical importance and they will be incorporated in the next release of the DCVALID tool.

In other examples, such as the lift controller and delay intensive oscillator, the validity checking time reduces only to to 50% to 70% of the original using MSR. These examples contain a large boolean combination of many small formulae leading to the construction of product of a large number of small automata causing state space explosion. It is our observation that MSR transformations are most effective when the complexity of the automaton construction is due to modal operators such as $\neg(D_1 \frown \ldots \frown D_n)$ or $\Box D_i$ and where the sub-formula D_i contains the duration construct $\sum P \sim k$ with moderately large constant k. Such formulae occur when specifying schedulability and performance constraints.

One interesting new feature is allowing explicit declaration of "singleton" (or first-order) variables within the logic QDDC. Such variables are constrained to be true exactly at one position within any behaviour. The tool DCVALID allows the use of such variables and modalities are in fact modelled internally as quantification over such singleton variables. Singleton variables are handled efficiently using special techniques (e.g. guidance [8]) in the underlying tool MONA on which DCVALID is built.

The MSR transformations introduce auxiliary variables in the validity equivalent formula. One potential optimization is to replace these variables by singleton variables. However, a quick examination of the automaton for $\hat{a}^-(D_1, \ldots, D_n)$ in Theorem 4 and the lower bound on the size of the automaton for $\neg(D_1 \frown \ldots \frown D_n)$ in Proposition 7 show that the resultant automata sizes are not changed by reformulation using singleton variables. Hence, using singleton variables does not affect the size reduction due to MSR transformations. Our experiments with the DCVALID tool indicate that using singleton auxiliary variables in the MSR transformation actually increases the validity checking time. This is due to the additional need for ensuring singleton-ness during the formula automaton construction.

Related Work Hansen [6] and Skakkebaek [14] were the first to investigate the automata based tools for checking validity of Discrete Duration Calculus. MONA [7,8] is a sophisticated tool for the construction of automata recognizing the models of formulae of the monadic second order logic over finite words. Many sophisticated techniques [8] are used in the construction of the formula automaton in MONA. Our tool DCVALID [11] is built on top of MONA, and it benefits from all these optimizations. Our transformations lead to further improvements in the MONA automaton construction. Gonnord *et al* [5] have investigated the translation of QDDC to symbolic automata. Franzle [4] has independently profiled the performance of DCVALID checker on the gas burner problem and some scheduling problems. Franzle has shown that bounded model checking using SAT solving can be more efficient on instances of such problems where short counter examples exist. But, with MSR transformations we obtain several orders of magnitude improvement in validity checking of the gas burner and the jobshop scheduling problems which makes DCVALID comparable with the BMC approach of Franzle [4]. Thus, in our view, both techniques have their applicability. Recently, Chakravorty and Pandya [3,13] have proposed a digitization approach to validity checking of dense-time duration calculus by reducing it to discrete time validity checking in QDDC. The resulting QDDC formulae are particularly benefitted by the MSR transformations (see Sharma *et al* [13]).

Table 2. Effect of MSR on Checking Validity of Gas Burner

Parameters	G	MSR(G)
	Time taken	
winlen = 30, leakbound = 3	13.26s	00.24s
winlen = 45, leakbound = 3	03m 15.88s	00.53s
winlen = 60, leakbound = 3	01h 02m 55s	00.93s
winlen = 1000, leakbound = 40	↓	01h11m24s
winlen = 2000, leakbound = 100	↓	13h36m59.99s

References

1. J.R. Buchi, Weak second-order arithmetic and finite automata, *Z. Math. Logik Grundl. Math.* **6**, 1960.
2. C.C. Elgot, Decision problems of finite automata design and related arithmetics, *Trans. Amer. Math. Soc.* **98**, 1961.
3. Chakravorty, G. and P.K. Pandya, Digitizing Interval Duration Logic, in *Proceedings of CAV 2003*, LNCS 2725, pp 167-179, 2003.
4. M. Fränzle and C. Herde, Efficient SAT engines for concise logics: Accelerating proof search for zero-one linear constraint systems, In *Proceedings of LPAR 2003*, LNCS 2850, pp 300-314, 2003.
5. L. Gonnord, N. Halbwachs and P. Raymond, From Discrete Duration Calculus to Symbolic Automata, in *ENTCS Proceedings of SLAP'04*, Barcelona, Spain, 2004.
6. M.R. Hansen, Model-Checking Duration Calculus, *Formal Aspects of Computing*, 1994.
7. J. G. Henriksen, J. Jensen, M. Jorgensen, N. Klarlund, B. Paige, T. Rauhe, and A. Sandholm, Mona: Monadic Second-Order Logic in Practice, in *Proceedings of TACAS'95*, LNCS 1019, Springer-Verlag, 1996.

8. N. Klarlund, A. Møller and M. I. Schwartzbach, MONA Implementation Secrets, *Proceedings of CIAA 2000*, LNCS 2088, pp 182-194, 2001.
9. S. N. Krishna and P. K. Pandya, Modal Strength Reduction in QDDC, Technical Report, 2005 (www.cse.iitb.ac.in/~krishnas/fsttcstr.ps).
10. B. Moszkowski, A Temporal Logic for Multi-Level Reasoning about Hardware, in *IEEE Computer*, **18**(2), 1985.
11. P. K. Pandya, Specifying and Deciding Quantified Discrete-time Duration Calculus Formulae using DCVALID: An Automata Theoretic Approach, in *Proceedings of RTTOOLS'2001*, Denmark, 2001.
12. P. K. Pandya, Model checking CTL*[DC], in *Proceedings of TACAS 2001*, LNCS 2031, pp 559-573, 2001.
13. B. Sharma, P.K. Pandya and S. Chakraborty, Bounded Validity Checking of Interval Duration Logic, *Proceedings of TACAS 2005*, LNCS 3440, pp 301-316, 2005.
14. J.U. Skakkebaek and P. Sestoft, Checking Validity of Duration Calculus Formulas, *Technical Report ID/DTH JUS 3/1*, Department of Computer Science, Technical University of Denmark, 1994.
15. Zhou Chaochen and M.R. Hansen, *Duration Calculus: A formal approach to real-time systems*, Springer, 2004.
16. Zhou Chaochen, C.A.R. Hoare and A.P. Ravn, A Calculus of Durations, *Info. Proc. Letters*, **40**(5), 1991.

Comparing Trees Via Crossing Minimization

Henning Fernau[1,2], Michael Kaufmann[1], and Mathias Poths[1]

[1] Univ. Tübingen, WSI für Informatik, Sand 13, 72076 Tübingen, Germany
{fernau/mk/poths}@informatik.uni-tuebingen.de
[2] Univ. Hertfordshire, Comp. Sci., College Lane, Hatfield, Herts AL10 9AB, UK

Abstract. Two trees with the same number of leaves have to be embedded in two layers in the plane such that the leaves are aligned in two adjacent layers. Additional matching edges between the leaves give a one-to-one correspondence between pairs of leaves of the different trees. Do there exist two planar embeddings of the two trees that minimize the crossings of the matching edges? This problem has important applications in the construction and evaluation of phylogenetic trees.

1 Introduction

The comparison of trees has applications in various areas like text data bases, bioinformatics, compiler construction etc. Various algorithms for different models for comparisons have been proposed. Keywords are tree matching, tree alignment, tree editing [12,13,14,15,16], a nice overview being [3]. Motivated by discussions with researchers from bioinformatics like D. Huson and D. Bryant, we propose to compare two tree structures by finding two most similar left-to-right orderings of their leaves. The ordering of the leaves can be made best visible by drawing one tree downward from the root and aligning all the leaves on a horizontal line. The leaves of the other tree are also aligned parallel to the first line and the corresponding tree structure is drawn from the leaves upside downward to the root. Corresponding leaves from the two trees are connected by matching edges.

Let $L(T)$ denote the leaves of a tree T. A linear order $<$ on $L(T)$ is called *suitable* if T can be embedded into the plane such that $L(T)$ is mapped onto a straight line (*layer*) in the order given by $<$. A *two-tree* $(T_1, T_2; M)$ is given by a pair of rooted binary trees (T_1, T_2) with perfect matching $M \subseteq L(T_1) \times L(T_2)$, where the matching is given by a bijective labeling $\lambda_i : L(T_i) \to \Lambda$ with $(\ell_1, \ell_2) \in M$ iff $\lambda_1(\ell_1) = \lambda_2(\ell_2)$. A *drawing* of $(T_1, T_2; M)$ is given by two suitable linear orders $<_1$ and $<_2$ on $L(T_1)$ and $L(T_2)$, respectively. We assume that a drawing is *realized* by embedding $L(T_1)$ and $L(T_2)$ into two parallel lines L_1 and L_2, so that all nodes of T_i lie within one of the half-planes described by L_{3-i}. Hence, only matching edges may cross. The number of crossings is independent of the chosen realization. Let $cr(T_1, T_2, M, <_1, <_2)$ denote the number of crossings in the drawing of $(T_1, T_2; M)$ given by $<_1$ and $<_2$. A two-tree $(T_1, T_2; M)$ is called *drawable* if $cr(T_1, T_2, M, <_1, <_2) = 0$ for some linear orders $<_1$ and $<_2$.

R. Ramanujam and S. Sen (Eds.): FSTTCS 2005, LNCS 3821, pp. 457–469, 2005.
© Springer-Verlag Berlin Heidelberg 2005

Very simple non-drawable two-trees are shown in Fig. 2. These are the smallest examples of non-drawable two-trees: all two-trees with three leaves are drawable.

Let $cr(T_1, T_2, M, <_1, \cdot)$ denote the minimum value of $cr(T_1, T_2, M, <_1, <_2)$ for all suitable orders $<_2$, and $cr(T_1, T_2, M, \cdot, \cdot)$ denote the minimum value of $cr(T_1, T_2, M, <_1, <_2)$ for all suitable orders $<_1$ and $<_2$. An instance of TWO-TREE CROSSING MINIMIZATION (TTCM) is given by a two-tree $(T_1, T_2; M)$, and the parameter, a positive integer k. Question: Is $cr(T_1, T_2, M, \cdot, \cdot) \leq k$? An instance of ONE-TREE CROSSING MINIMIZATION (OTCM) is given by a two-tree $(T_1, T_2; M)$, a suitable fixed order $<_1$ on $L(T_1)$, and the parameter, a positive integer k. Question: Is $cr(T_1, T_2, M, <_1, \cdot) \leq k$?

A possible application from bioinformatics for the variant ONE-TREE CROSSING MINIMIZATION is that for a known species tree different gene trees should be compared to the species tree. The more general variant TWO-TREE CROSSING MINIMIZATION supports tasks like: Compare different construction methods for phylogenetic trees for some data set or compare multiple gene trees [11].

A related important problem from graph drawing [4] is the TWO-SIDED CROSSING MINIMIZATION problem (TSCM) for bipartite graphs, where the vertices within each layer are connected only to vertices of the other layer. The main differences are that the vertices might have more than one incident edge and that no trees restrict the possible orderings. TWO-SIDED CROSSING MINIMIZATION is $\mathcal{NP}$-complete, and the problem remains $\mathcal{NP}$-complete even if the order of one of the layers is fixed [8] (ONE-SIDED CROSSING MINIMIZATION(OSCM)). Both problems are fixed-parameter tractable. In the case of a binary tree with n leaves, there are exactly 2^{n-1} different leaf orders implied by different orderings of the subtrees. This is in contrast to the $n!$ permutations which are possible in OSCM.

Similarly related is the problem of finding an embedding of a graph in the plane that minimizes the number of crossings; this problem remains $\mathcal{NP}$-complete even if the degree of the graph is bounded by three. Notice that a two-tree (plus matching edges) obeys this degree bound. Moreover, in that case, the crossing minimization problem is known to be fixed-parameter tractable [9].

Since we like to talk about left and right subtrees and these notions usually depend on the parent's position, let us fix the following convention: We assume that all our trees are drawn either downwards (the *upper tree*) or upwards (the *bottom tree*); then, "left" and "right" refers to how an observer would name these relative directions when viewing such a drawing. More specifically, in a two-tree (T_1, T_2), T_1 is the upper and T_2 is the bottom tree. In a tree $T = (V, E)$ with root r, the notion of a *least common ancestor* $lca(X)$ of a non-empty set $X \subseteq V$ is well-defined. Given $X \subseteq V$, let the *ancestral tree* $T \langle X \rangle = (V', E')$ be the given by $V' = X \cup lca(X)$ and $xy \in E'$ iff there is a path P from x to y in T and no other vertex $z \in V'$ is on P. Conversely, for $x \in V$, the *descendants tree* $T[x]$ is the graph induced by all vertices y of T such that the path from y to the root r contains x. Furthermore, we may talk about the *left* and the *right child* of an inner node x, written l_x and r_x, respectively.

Results. (1) We improve on the dynamic programming approach exhibited in [6] to solve OTCM in time $\mathcal{O}(n \log^2 n)$. (2) We give an linear-time algorithm for the drawability test. (3) We prove $\mathcal{NP}$-completeness for TTCM. (4) We show in the main part that TTCM is fixed-parameter tractable.

2   The OTCM Problem

Let $(T_1, T_2; M)$ be a two-tree with a fixed suitable order $<_1$ on $L(T_1)$. The task is to find a suitable order $<_2$ on $L(T_2)$ that minimizes the number of crossings of matched edges. We are going to give a dynamic programming solution to OTCM. Therefore, notice that any inner node v of T_2 defines a subproblem in the following sense: let L be the leaves from T_1 that are matched to leaves from $L(T_2[v])$; then, consider the two-tree $(T_1, T_2)[v] = (T_1 \langle L \rangle, T_2[v], M \cap (L \times L(T_2[v])))$, with the order $<_1$ restricted to L. For an inner node v of T_2, $cr(T_2(l_v, r_v))$ denotes the number of pairwise crossings of the matching edges incident with leaves from $L(T_2[l_v])$ and $L(T_2[r_v])$. Note that the total number of crossings for a certain embedding can be expressed as $\sum_v cr(T_2(l_v, r_v))$. Hence, we can express the minimum crossing number by the following recursion:

$$cr((T_1, T_2)[v], <_1, \cdot) = cr((T_1, T_2)[l_v], <_1, \cdot) + cr((T_1, T_2)[r_v], <_1, \cdot)$$
$$+ \min\{cr(T_2(l_v, r_v)), cr(T_2(r_v, l_v))\}$$

This recursion can be solved in a naive way in time $O(n^2)$. We give a sketch of the proof and show how to improve this time complexity.

Firstly, we show how to compute $cr(T_2(l_v, r_v))$. $cr(T_2(l_v, r_v))$ can be expressed as the sum over all $\ell \in L(T_2[l_v])$, where each term gives the number of $r \in L(T_2[r_v])$ to the left of ℓ; we call this number the *rank* of ℓ. This sum can be determined by a simple sweep in time linear in $|L(T_2[v])|$. Since the subtrees $T_2[l_v]$ and $T_2[r_v]$ are disjoint, the total time complexity is $O(n^2)$, where n is the number of leaves.

Alternatively, we can keep the leaves in a balanced search tree. We have to determine the rank of the leaves in $L(T_2[r_v])$ within $L(T_2[l_v])$. For each single leaf in $L(T_2[r_v])$ this can be done in time $\mathcal{O}(\log n)$. Hence, it takes $\mathcal{O}(|L(T_2[r_v])| \log n)$ time. Vice-versa we can compute the ranks of the leaves from $L(T_2[l_v])$ within $L(T_2[r_v])$ in time $\mathcal{O}(|L(T_2[l_v])| \log n)$. Since both sums are of the same type, we can choose the cheaper alternative and solve the recursion in time $T(|L(T_2[v])|) = T(|L(T_2[l_v])|) + T(|L(T_2[r_v])|) + \min\{|L(T_2[l_v])|, |L(T_2[r_v])|\} \log n$. By induction, we can easily prove that $T(n) = \mathcal{O}(n \log^2 n)$.

Theorem 1. *In time $\mathcal{O}(n \log^2 n)$, we can solve the* OTCM *problem, where n is the number of leaves.*

3   An Efficient Algorithm for the Non-crossing Case

Theorem 2. *Given a two-tree $(T_1, T_2; M)$, its drawability can be decided in linear time.*

Proof. The two input trees together with the matching edges can be naturally directed upward having the two roots as single source and sink respectively. Then, we can directly apply the linear time algorithm for upward planarity of acyclic digraphs with a single source [2]. ∎

4   The General Case

Theorem 3. TWO-TREE CROSSING MINIMIZATION *is $\mathcal{NP}$-complete.*

Proof. Membership in $\mathcal{NP}$ is clear. Next, we give a reduction of the MAXCUT problem with unit weights. The MAXCUT problem is to partition the vertex set V into V_1 and V_2 for a given graph $G = (V, E)$, such that $|\{e = (v, w) \in E$ with $v \in V_1$ and $w \in V_2\}|$ is maximized.

So, let $G = (V, E)$ with $V = \{1, \ldots, n\}$ be an instance of MAXCUT. From G, we construct an instance of the TWO-TREE CROSSING MINIMIZATION problem, so that we have a 'backbone'-path $a_1, b_1, \ldots, a_n, b_n, C$ in both of the trees T_1, T_2, which, with the leaf-layers, partitions the drawing area into four parts that later give us the membership of each vertex to V_1 or V_2, respectively. Let a_1 be the root in each tree, C is one of the leaves. For each vertex $v \in V$, we connect two representative nodes a'_v, b'_v to the corresponding backbone nodes a_v, b_v in each tree. Moreover, to each of those representative nodes a'_v, b'_v, we have to connect further representatives in the leaf-layer, say A_v, B_v; A_v-leaves shall be matched to the B_v-leaves of the other tree and vice versa with n^5 edges for each $v = 1, \ldots, n$. For each edge $e = \{v, w\} \in E$, we create leaf-vertices $a_{v,w}$ and $a_{w,v}$ and connect both pairwise by matching edges. Furthermore, we connect a'_v with the leaf nodes $a_{v,w}$ for all $e = \{v, w\} \in E$. We also connect the two C leaves of the backbone to each other via n^7 edges. To make the trees binary, every vertex that is connected to more than one other vertex is substituted by a small binary subtree with an appropriate number of leaves. We can observe the following facts:

1. In any optimum solution, there is no crossing between edges adjacent to C-nodes and $(A_v - B_v)$-edges.
2. In any optimum solution, the a'_v- and b'_v- vertices are on different sides of the backbone in both trees. The side for a'_v in T_1 is different from that in T_2.
3. In any optimum solution, the number of edges $(a_{v,w}, a_{w,v})$ crossing the backbone connection is minimized, and the number of edges $(a_{v,w}, a_{w,v})$ which do not cross the backbone is maximized.

Now, we define $V_1 = \{i \mid a_v$ is on the left-hand side of the backbone in $T_1\}$ and $V_2 = \{i \mid a_v$ is on the right-hand side of the backbone in $T_1\}$ for splitting V into two disjoint sets V_1 and V_2. From our observations, we can see that this is an optimal solution for the MAXCUT problem. Obviously, this construction can be built in polynomial time. Hence the reduction of MAXCUT to TTCM is completed. ∎

Parameterized complexity and algorithmics is now an established way of dealing with hard problems that have a natural parameter in its definition. The idea is that, for small parameter values, we can get away with a polynomial-time algorithm, where the degree of the polynomial is independent of the parameter. This is the approach we take in the next section.

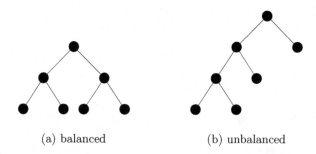

(a) balanced   (b) unbalanced

Fig. 1. The two types of trees to be analyzed.

5 Fixed-Parameter Tractability

A *parameterized problem* P is a subset of $\Sigma^* \times \mathbb{N}$, where Σ is a fixed alphabet and $\mathbb{N}$ is the set of all non-negative integers. Therefore, each instance of the parameterized problem P is a pair (I, k), where the second component k is called the *parameter*. The language $L(P)$ is the set of all **YES**-instances of P. We say that the parameterized problem P is *fixed-parameter tractable* [5] if there is an algorithm that decides whether an input (I, k) is a member of $L(P)$ in time $f(k)|I|^c$, where c is a fixed constant and $f(k)$ is a recursive function independent of the overall input length $|I|$. The class of all fixed-parameter tractable problems is denoted by $\mathcal{FPT}$. Ignoring the polynomial part of a parameterized algorithm, we write $\mathcal{O}^*(f(k))$ to indicate the non-polynomial running time estimate.

5.1 Quadruple Trees

To establish our results, we need a complete analysis of what happens if we restrict ourselves to the case of two trees T_1 and T_2 each having four leaves labeled a, b, c, d. We will also refer to such small trees as *quadruple trees* and the four leaf labels are then called a *quadruple*. Since our trees $T = T_i$ are binary, we can have only two different cases: T has depth two and is hence *balanced*; T has depth three and is *unbalanced*, see Fig 1. We will show that there are only two types of non-drawable quadruple trees as depicted in Fig. 2.

Let us first analyze the balanced trees. If we assume a labeling a, b, c, d in this sequence along the leaves of a balanced tree (in the sequence as shown in

Fig. 1), then let [abcd] denote the different labelings of leaves that can be obtained by different drawings of that particular tree, i.e., by redefining (swapping) the left/right child relations in that tree. We can observe the following possibilities, where $B_1 \cap B_2 = B_1 \cap B_3 = B_2 \cap B_3 = \emptyset$:

- $B_1 = [abcd] = \{abcd, abdc, bacd, badc, cdab, cdba, dcab, dcba\}$,
- $B_2 = [acbd] = \{acbd, acdb, bdac, bdca, cabd, cadb, dbac, dbca\}$, and
- $B_3 = [adbc] = \{adbc, adcb, bcad, bcda, cbad, cbda, dabc, dacb\}$.

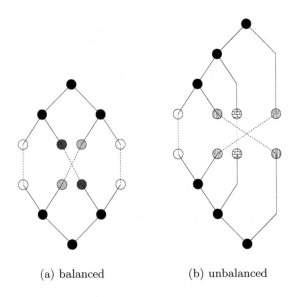

(a) balanced   (b) unbalanced

Fig. 2. The two types of contradicting quadruple two-trees.

Lemma 1. B_1, B_2, B_3 *are the three mutually disjoint equivalence classes of leaf labelings for balanced trees that together exhaust all 24 permutations of a, b, c, d.*

If we assume that both T_1 and T_2 are balanced quadruple trees, then we can conclude from Lemma 1:

Corollary 1. *Let T_1 and T_2 be balanced quadruple trees. Let L_i^1 (L_i^2, resp.) be the two two-element label sets that label leaves reachable from the first (second, resp.) child of the root of T_i. Then, the pair (T_1, T_2) can be drawn without crossings iff $L_1^1 = L_2^1$ or $L_1^1 = L_2^2$. Hence, non-drawability in the balanced quadruple tree case means that, with $L_1^1 = \{x, y\}$, $x \in L_2^1$ and $y \in L_2^2$.*

The unbalanced quadruple trees can be also treated with a case-by-case analysis.

Corollary 2. *Let T_1 and T_2 be unbalanced quadruple trees. Assume (w.l.o.g.) that T_1 and T_2 are drawn as in Fig. 1 (of course, T_2 must be flipped to get the* *root at the bottom), with labels a, b, c, d attached to the leaves of T_1 in that order. Then, the pair (T_1, T_2) is drawable iff either the third leaf of T_2 is not labeled c or the last leaf of T_2 is not labeled with one of the first two labels of T_1.*

Hence, such a pair cannot be drawn iff the third leaf coincides and the last leaf of T_2 is among the first two leaves of T_1. Comparing the classes of unbalanced trees with those of balanced trees, one can see:

Corollary 3. *Let T_1 and T_2 be quadruple trees, where T_1 is balanced and T_2 is unbalanced (or vice versa). Then, the pair (T_1, T_2) is drawable.*

5.2 Quadruples Are All About Inconsistencies

The following theorem shows that the drawability of a two-tree only depends on the drawability of the induced quadruple trees.

Theorem 4. *Let $(T_1, T_2; M)$ be a two-tree with labelings $\lambda_i : L(T_i) \to \Lambda$. If $cr(T_1, T_2, M, \cdot, \cdot) > 0$, then there exists a quadruple $Q = \{a, b, c, d\} \subseteq \Lambda$ such that $cr\left(T_1 \langle \lambda_1^{-1}(Q) \rangle, T_2 \langle \lambda_2^{-1}(Q) \rangle, M \cap (\lambda_1^{-1}(Q) \times \lambda_2^{-1}(Q)), \cdot, \cdot\right) > 0$.*

We will present a recursive algorithm which either finds such an quadruple, or it provides a drawing of the two-tree. This algorithm will not only prove this structural result that gives a characterization of drawable two-trees in terms of forbidden substructures, but also provides the backbone of two $\mathcal{FPT}$ algorithms that are presented in the following.

Proof. Let $(T_1, T_2; M)$ be the two-tree and Λ the set of labels associated to the leaves. W.l.o.g., $|\Lambda| > 1$.

We assume that each inner node provides links to its two children and in addition permanent and temporary information attached to each such link. The permanent information $p(\ell)$ attached to link ℓ is either L, R or $*$, meaning:

L	This link leads to the left child.
R	This link leads to the right child.
$*$	It is not yet determined if this link leads to the left or to the right child.

The permanent information indicates a commitment how the links are to be drawn (either forced or without loss of generality) in order to obtain a crossing-free embedding of the two-tree; once fixed, it will not be changed in later stages of the algorithm. The temporary information is only used to either produce further evidence that allows to make further commitments of the permanent information or to provide a contradictory quadruple.

In the initialization phase of our algorithm, we (arbitrarily) set $p(\ell_1) = L$ and $p(\ell_2) = R$ for the two links emanating from the root of T_2. All other permanent information is set to $*$. This defines the function p (that we use both for T_1 and for T_2). Thus initiated, we call embed(T_1, T_2, p). The way how the permanent information is initiated and updated shows that the following is always true:

Claim 1: Let $\mathfrak{n}$ be an inner node with emanating links ℓ_1 and ℓ_2. Then, $p(\ell_1) = L$ iff $p(\ell_2) = R$, and $p(\ell_1) = R$ iff $p(\ell_2) = L$.

The temporary information $t(\ell)$ attached to link ℓ is either l, r or m, meaning:

l	All links ℓ' below (i.e., in direction to the leaves) satisfy $t(\ell') = l$.
r	All links ℓ' below satisfy $t(\ell') = r$.
m	Mixed case: some links below are marked l and some are marked r.

The temporary information is processed bottom-up as follows:

1. As described in Alg. 1 in detail, the links leading to the leaves of the tree to be processed are assigned either l or r.
2. Let $\mathfrak{n}$ be an inner node (besides the root) where to both links ℓ_1 and ℓ_2 emanating to its two children, the temporary information has been assigned, such that the previous situation does not apply. Then, to the link ℓ that leads to $\mathfrak{n}$ we assign $t(\ell)$ according to the following table:

$t(\ell_1)$	l	l	l	r	r	r	m	m	m
$t(\ell_2)$	l	r	m	l	r	m	l	r	m
$t(\ell)$	l	m	m	m	r	m	m	m	e

Here, e signals an error case: we have found a quadruple situation corresponding to the balanced tree case in Fig. 2. Hence, there is no way of finding a crossing-free embedding of the two-trees, and we can abort here.

Interestingly, we can also update the permanent information of two siblings. Let $\mathfrak{n}$ be an inner node where to both links ℓ_1 and ℓ_2 emanating to its two children, the temporary information has been assigned. We update $p(\ell_1)$ and $p(\ell_2)$ according to the following table:

$t(\ell_1)$	l	l	l	l	l	l	l	l	l
$t(\ell_2)$	l	l	l	r	r	r	m	m	m
$p(\ell_1)$	L	R	$*$	L	R	$*$	L	R	$*$
$p(\ell_2)$	R	L	$*$	R	L	$*$	R	L	$*$
$p(\ell_1)$	L	R	$*$	L	E	L	L	E	L
$p(\ell_2)$	R	L	$*$	R	E	R	R	E	R

Observe that there are more cases for assigning temporary information, with the roles of ℓ_1 and ℓ_2 being interchanged. Furthermore, notice that the list of cases of assignments to ℓ_1 and ℓ_2 is complete with respect to the permanent information because of Claim 1. The table should be read as follows: the first four lines give the current values of t and p on the two links. The last two lines give the updated values of p. Here, an E signals that we found a contradictory situation; more specifically (as we will see below), we have found a quadruple situation corresponding to the unbalanced tree case in Fig. 2 Hence, there is no way of finding a crossing-free embedding of the two-trees, and we can abort here.

Claim 2: Observe that the graph that is induced by the edges (links) to which non-$*$ permanent information has been attached to is a tree before and after each complete bottom-up tree processing (as described above). Moreover, if this induced tree is non-empty, then it also contains the root.

How to actually use the bottom-up processing of the temporary and permanent information is explained in Alg. 1. Observe that the roles of the trees alternate. We will make use of the following property of our algorithm:

<u>Claim 3:</u> Each time that it is again say the upper tree's turn to get new temporary labels, the former root of that tree (and possibly more nodes) will no longer be taken into consideration.

We still have to show that the two aborts (error cases) described above are indeed based on finding a contradictory quadruple two-tree as explained in Fig. 2. The (omitted) proofs of the following claims show the details of this construction.

Algorithm 1 Procedure "embed-TT"

Require: A two-tree $(T_1, T_2; M)$ and a permanent link information function p.
Ensure: YES iff a crossing-free drawing of $(T_1, T_2; M)$ respecting p can be obtained. Moreover, either (implicitly) a crossing-free drawing of $(T_1, T_2; M)$ respecting p is found or a contradictory quadruple two-tree is produced.

    Let r be the root of T_2.
    if $(T_1, T_2; M)$ has at most four leaves **then**
        return answer by table look-up (produced according to Subsec. 5.1)
    else if r has only one child **then**
5:     Delete r to produce T_2'.
        Modify p and M accordingly, yielding p' and M'.
        return embed-TT(T_1, T_2', M', p');
    else
        {Let ℓ_1 and ℓ_2 be the two links emanating from the root x of T_2.}
10:    **if** $p(\ell_1) = *$ **then**
           $p(\ell_1) := L$ and $p(\ell_2) := R$ (without loss of generality).
        end if
        {Let $\ell_L = xy_L$ with $p(\ell_L) = L$ and $\ell_R = xy_R$ with $p(\ell_R) = R$.}
        Let $L_L := L(T_2[y_L])$ and $L_R := L(T_2[y_R])$.
15:    Let $L_l = \{u \in L(T_1) \mid \exists u' \in L_L : (u, u') \in M\}$ and $L_r = L(T_1) \setminus L_l$.
        for all links $\ell = uv$ of T_1 where v is closer to the root than u **do**
           if $u \in L(T_1)$ **then**
               $t(\ell) := z \in \{l, r\}$ such that $u \in L_z$.
           else
20:         $t(\ell) := *$
           end if
        end for
        Update the temporary and permanent information within T_1 as in the proof.
        if contradiction is reached **then**
25:     Report contradictory quadruple two-tree (see the proof).
           return NO
        else
           Let p_L be the permanent information p updated to cover the two-tree $(T_2[y_L], T_1 \langle L_l \rangle ; M_L)$ with $M_L^{-1} = M \cap (L_l \times L_L)$; similarly, define p_R, M_R.
           return embed-TT$(T_2[y_L], T_1 \langle L_l \rangle, M_L, p_L)$ $\wedge$embed-TT$(T_2[y_R], T_1 \langle L_r \rangle, M_R, p_R)$
30:    **end if**
    end if

<u>Claim 4:</u> Whenever an error occurs within the temporary label information update, we can exhibit a balanced quadruple two-tree.

<u>Claim 5:</u> Whenever a contradiction is found between the temporary label information and the already existent permanent label information, we can exhibit an unbalanced quadruple two-tree. ∎

Theorem 4 shows an immediate result for the following problem that is closely related to TTCM: An instance of TWO-TREE DRAWING BY DELETING EDGES (TTDE) is given by a two-tree $(T_1, T_2; M)$, and the parameter, a positive integer k. Question: Is there a set $M' = L_1' \times L_2' \subseteq M$ with $|M'| \leq k$ such that the two-tree $(T_1 \langle L(T_1) \setminus L_1' \rangle, T_2 \langle L(T_1) \setminus L_2' \rangle)$ is drawable? Namely, we can translate any TWO-TREE DRAWING BY DELETING EDGES instance into 4-HITTING SET: simply cycle through all $\mathcal{O}(n^4)$ possible quadruple two-trees (given a concrete two-tree (T_1, T_2) with n leaves): If a quadruple two-tree is contradictory, then it corresponds to a hyperedge with four vertices, the leaf labels forming that quadruple. All n leaf labels together are the vertices of the hypergraph. Using known parameterized algorithms for 4-HITTING SET, see [10], we can thus show:

Corollary 4. TTDE *is solvable in* $\mathcal{O}^*(3.115^k)$ *time.*

Let us mention that we can similarly translate the variant ONE-TREE DRAWING BY DELETING EDGES of TTDE where one tree is fixed into 3-HITTING SET.

6   TWO-TREE CROSSING MINIMIZATION Is in $\mathcal{FPT}$

This result is heavily based on the structural results of the previous section. More precisely, we will sketch a parameterized algorithm that branches on small contradicting structures (primarily, at contradicting quadruples) as long as these incur new crossings. In a second phase, we attempt at drawing the remaining two-tree with using a variant of the algorithm embed, possibly finding new small contradicting structures. The validity of this approach relies on the fact that we are able to separate contradicting structures from the rest of the two-tree by attachment links that are described as follows.

Let u be a node in a tree T. The parent link $\mathfrak{p}(u)$ is the unique edge leading to u in T; if u is the root, then there is no parent link to u. Let $V' \subseteq V(T)$. The set of all parent links of V' is $\mathfrak{P}(V') = \{\mathfrak{p}(u) \mid u \in V'\}$. The set of *attachment links* of a subgraph G of T is $\mathfrak{A}(G) = \mathfrak{P}(lca(V(G)))$.

As above, we work with the permanent information $p(\ell)$ attached to an edge ℓ, initialized with $p = *$ and later gradually updated to either L or R. Sometimes, it is more convenient to think of this labeling information being attached to the inner nodes in the sense that a bit (called *flip*) is associated with each inner node that tells, when defined, which child is to the left and which is to the right.

Given a two-tree $(T_1, T_2; M)$ with labelings λ_i, our algorithm will basically branch on all possible settings of p to either L or R on the attachment links $\mathfrak{A}(G_i)$ (that do not contradict earlier settings $\neq *$) for the subgraphs $G_i = T_i \langle \lambda_i^{-1}(Q) \rangle$ of T_i for all possible contradicting quadruples Q. Observe that whenever a parent link of some node is assigned L, then the parent link of its sibling will be assigned R for reasons of consistency (and vice versa).

The problem we are facing is that we have to ensure that the natural parameter of this problem, i.e., the given budget k of tolerable crossings, is decremented in each branching step. So, our strategy will be to only branch at contradicting structures if this gives us a gain in each branch. To simplify matters, we assume that only those leaves that participated in those contradicting structures we earlier branched on have been accounted for in the branching process.

As *contradicting structures*, we will view contradicting quadruples (as before) and contradicting pairs, i.e., pairs of labels a, b where say the upper tree fixes $a < b$ and the lower tree fixes $b < a$ (due to the flips that are fixed in both trees).

Algorithm 2 Sketch of procedure "embed-TTCM"

Require: A two-tree $(T_1, T_2; M)$; permanent link information p; a parameter k.
Ensure: YES iff $(T_1, T_2; M)$ can be drawn with $\leq k$ crossings so that p is respected.

    if $k < 0$ **then**
      return NO
    else if $k = 0$ **then**
      return embed-TT(T_1, T_2, M, p) {see to Alg. 1}
5: **else**
      if there is a small contradicting structure S **then**
        branch on all possible flips for $\mathfrak{A}(T_i \langle S \rangle)$ with recursive calls on embed-TTCM,
        where S is deleted from the new instances and M, p are accordingly modified.
      else
        return embed-TT$'(T_1, T_2, M, p, k)$
10:       {k is only needed if embed-TT$''$ recursively calls embed-TTCM.}
      end if
    end if

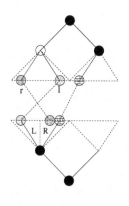

To fully understand Alg. 2, we still have to explain what to do when there are no longer contradicting quadruples or pairs to be found (line 9): we will then start a procedure very similar to embed-TT. The only difference is that it will not find any of the contradictions described in the proof of Theorem 4 (since there are no contradicting quadruples). Now, a temporary labeling could contradict the already established permanent labeling. In that case, the permanent labeling would already exist upon first calling embed-TT$'$, so that we face the situation depicted in the figure to the left. This figure is understood as follows: the white inner node indicates a flip that has been determined.

As the labels L and R indicate, this flip would go the other way round according to the temporary link information propagation. The permanent labeling must have a reason (otherwise, we could just interchange the meaning of L and R):

namely, there must be a third leaf (the brick-pattern label) that is residing some-where in the "right branch" of the upper tree but in the "left branch" in the bottom tree (on a previous level of recursion). Hence, we also get a crossing if we draw the left part of bottom tree coherently with the "white flip." Upon finding such an erroneous situation, we would consider the depicted leaves as a con-tradicting structure and branch on all attachment points as before, recursively calling embed-TTCM again.

Theorem 5. TWO-TREE CROSSING MINIMIZATION *is in* $\mathcal{FPT}$. *More precisely, the problem can be solved in time* $\mathcal{O}^*(c^k)$ *for some constant c.*

Unfortunately, the constant c is still quite huge (about 2^{10}) due to the many attachment links whose combinations must be tested. We can see our result therefore as a preliminary one, mainly providing a classification of the problem.

7   Conclusion

We have considered two-layer crossing minimization problems for the purpose of comparing two unordered trees. We derived $\mathcal{NP}$-completeness results and ef-ficient polynomial-time algorithms as well as $\mathcal{FPT}$-algorithms. The following open problems are worthwhile to consider: (1) Determine the (parameterized) complexity of the maximum planar submatching variant TTDE and prove $\mathcal{NP}$-completeness. (2) Extend the techniques to d-ary trees. From the first sight, an additional factor of $d!$ shows up. This problem has clustering applications, see [1]. (3) Consider the weighted version of TTCM, where the crossings have higher weights if they occur between edges of larger different subtrees. (4) The connections to HITTING SET we exhibited for TTDE provides a factor-4 approx-imation; we do not see any constant-factor approximation for TTCM.

Acknowledgment: Thanks to G. Liotta and D. Huson for motivation and help.

References

1. Z. Bar-Joseph, D. Gifford, and T. Jaakkola. Fast optimal leaf ordering for hierar-chical clustering. *Bioinformatics*, 17:22–29, 2001.
2. P. Bertolazzi, G. DI Battista, G. Liotta and C. Mannino. Optimal upward planarity testing of single-source digraphs. *SIAM Journal of Computing*, 27:132-169, 1998.
3. P. Bille. A survey on tree edit distance and related problems. *Theoretical Computer Science*, 337:217–239, 2005.
4. G. Di Battista, Eades P., Tamassia R. and I. G. Tollis. *Graph Drawing: Algorithms for the Visualization of Graphs*. Prentice Hall, 1999.
5. R. G. Downey and M. R. Fellows. *Parameterized Complexity*. Springer, 1999.
6. T. Dwyer and F. Schreiber. Optimal leaf ordering for two and a half dimensional phylogenetic tree visualisation. In: *Proc. Australasian Symp. on Information Vi-sualisation (InVis.au 2004)*, CRPIT 35:109–115, 2004.
7. P. Eades and S. Whitesides. Drawing graphs in two layers. *Theoretical Computer Science*, 13:361–374, 1994.

8. P. Eades and N. Wormald. Edge crossings in drawings of bipartite graphs. *Algorithmica*, 10:379–403, 1994.

9. M. R. Fellows. The Robertson-Seymour theorems: a survey of applications. *Contemp. Math.*, 89:1–18, 1989.

10. H. Fernau. *Parameterized Algorithmics: A Graph-Theoretic Approach*. Habilitationsschrift, Universität Tübingen, Germany, 2005. Submitted.

11. D. Huson. Private Communication, 2005.

12. T. Jiang, L. Wang, and K. Zhang. Alignment of trees—an alternative to tree edit. *Theoretical Computer Science*, 143:137–148, 1995.

13. P. Kilpeläinen and H. Mannila. Ordered and unordered tree inclusion. *SIAM Journal of Computing*, 24:340-356, 1995.

14. P. Klein, S. Tirthapura, D. Sharvit, and B. Kimia. A tree-edit-distance algorithm for comparing simple, closed shapes. In: *Proc. of 11th ACM-SIAM Symposium on Discrete Algorithms (SODA)*, 696–704, 2000.

15. R. Ramesh and I. Ramakrishnan. Nonlinear pattern matching in trees. *Journal of the ACM*, 39:295-316, 1992.

16. K. Zhang and D. Shasha. Simple fast algorithms for the edit distance between trees and related problems *SIAM Journal of Computing*, 18:1245-1262, 1989.

On Counting the Number of Consistent Genotype Assignments for Pedigrees

Jiří Srba*

BRICS**, Department of Computer Science, Aalborg University
Fredrik Bajersvej 7B, 9220 Aalborg East, Denmark
srba@brics.dk

Abstract. Consistency checking of genotype information in pedigrees plays an important role in genetic analysis and for complex pedigrees the computational complexity is critical. We present here a detailed complexity analysis for the problem of counting the number of complete consistent genotype assignments. Our main result is a polynomial time algorithm for counting the number of complete consistent assignments for non-looping pedigrees. We further classify pedigrees according to a number of natural parameters like the number of generations, the number of children per individual and the cardinality of the set of alleles. We show that even if we assume all these parameters as bounded by reasonably small constants, the counting problem becomes computationally hard (#P-complete) for looping pedigrees. The border line for counting problems computable in polynomial time (i.e. belonging to the class FP) and #P-hard problems is completed by showing that even for general pedigrees with unlimited number of generations and alleles but with at most one child per individual and for pedigrees with at most two generations and two children per individual the counting problem is in FP.

1 Introduction

Pedigrees are fundamental structures used in genetics. A pedigree describes family relations among generations of individuals. Genealogists study pedigrees in connection with the genotype information associated to the individuals at a particular locus. A genotype of a given individual is a pair of alleles in its genome (allele is one of the possible forms a gene may have). Due to different reasons, for a given pedigree the genotype information of its individuals can be known only partially. In order to complete the missing genotype information or to filter out erroneous input data, genealogists need to verify that the given partial information is consistent with the classic Mendelian laws of inheritance (see e.g. [5]), which means that every individual in the pedigree has to inherit exactly one

---

* The author is supported in part by the research center ITI, project No. 1M0021620808.
** Basic Research in Computer Science,
Centre of the Danish National Research Foundation.

R. Ramanujam and S. Sen (Eds.): FSTTCS 2005, LNCS 3821, pp. 470–482, 2005.

allele from each of its parents. This process is called *consistency checking* and as argued in [9], in many real-life cases a manual consistency check is very difficult, time-consuming and sometimes unsuccessful. For an accessible overview of further biological aspects we refer the reader to [1].

To the best of our knowledge only algorithmic issues of consistency and likelihood checking for pedigrees have been studied in the literature so far (see e.g. [6,10,12,2,1]). In this paper we shall focus on a more general problem of *counting* the total number of complete genotype assignments consistent with the input data. This approach can provide a deeper insight and generalize the algorithms already developed for pure consistency checking. Moreover, knowing the total number of complete genotype assignments consistent with the input data can answer several additional questions. For example the fact that the number of assignments is 1 tells us that the missing information can be uniquely reconstructed from the available data. On the other hand, knowing that there are too many possibilities how to interpret the input data indicates that more genotype sampling is needed in order to reduce uncertainty.

Our contribution. We introduce characterization of pedigrees according to a number of natural parameters that describe their shapes. Apart for the standard notion of looping/non-looping pedigrees we further distinguish the number of generations, number of children per individual and the cardinality of the set of alleles. We describe a polynomial time algorithm that counts the number of complete genotype information for a given partial genotype data in non-looping pedigrees. We use this result to show that the counting problems for general pedigrees with at most 2 generations and 2 children per individual and for pedigrees with at most 1 child per individual are also solvable in polynomial deterministic time. We complete the results by demonstrating two parsimonious reductions (i.e. reductions that preserve the number of solutions) from #Bpos-2Sat to the counting problems for pedigrees with (i) 3 generations, 2 children per individual and 2 alleles, and (ii) 2 generations, 3 children per individual and 2 alleles. Together with an obvious containment in #P this proves #P-completeness of the problems.

Related work. For the case of pure consistency checking the following results are known. The problem for non-looping pedigrees is decidable in polynomial time using a *genotype elimination* algorithm proposed by Lange and Goradia [7] and further optimized and extended by O'Connell and Weeks [10], and Du and Hoeschele [2]. For general pedigrees there is a recent work by Aceto et al. [1] showing that consistency checking is NP-complete for pedigrees with marriage loops. They prove the result by reduction from 3SAT, however, their reduction is not parsimonious (does not preserve the number of solutions). It also works only for pedigrees with at least 5 generations, 3 children per individual and 3 alleles but under the assumption that there is either a complete or no knowledge about the genotype of single individuals. Another related result is NP-completeness of marginal probability and maximum likelihood by Piccolboni and Gusfield [12].

As discussed in [1], although the problems are closely connected to consistency checking, they cannot be used to imply hardness results for our problem.

Full version will appear as a technical report in BRICS research series.

2   Basic Definitions

2.1   Pedigrees and Genotype Information

In order to reason about pedigrees and the genotype information that they contain, we need to introduce a formal model. Several formalizations of the notion of pedigree have been presented in the literature on computational genetics (see e.g. [1,8,12]). The definition that we provide is equivalent to the ones mentioned above.

Definition 1 (Pedigree). *A* pedigree *is a triple* $P = (M, F, \phi)$ *where*

- *M and F are finite disjoint sets of* male, *resp.* female, *individuals,*
- *$\phi : M \times F \longrightarrow 2^{(M \cup F)}$ is a function called* family function *satisfying:*
    1. *$\phi(f) \cap \phi(f') = \emptyset$ for all $f, f' \in M \times F$ such that $f \neq f'$,*
    2. *the transitive closure of the* parental relation *$\prec \subseteq (M \cup F) \times (M \cup F)$ is irreflexive, where $\prec$ is defined by $u \prec v$ iff there is a $w \in M \cup F$ such that $u \in \phi(v, w)$ if $v \in M$, or $u \in \phi(w, v)$ if $v \in F$.*

We define a set of families *in P given by ϕ as $\mathcal{F}(\phi) \stackrel{\text{def}}{=} \{f \in M \times F \mid \phi(f) \neq \emptyset\}$. Let us also define $p(f) \stackrel{\text{def}}{=} \{u, v\}$ for any family $f = (u, v) \in \mathcal{F}(\phi)$; we call u and v the* parents *in the family f.*

Here is an informal explanation of the definition. Given a male $u \in M$ and a female $v \in F$, $\phi(u, v)$ is the set of all children they have. Condition 1. says that every child belongs to exactly one family and condition 2. guarantees that no individual can be its own ancestor.

The maximal elements from $M \cup F$ w.r.t. $\prec$ are called *founders* of the pedigree. Individuals that are not founders are called *non-founders*. The length of a longest chain (counting the number of nodes) w.r.t. $\prec$ is called the number of *generations*. The *set of children* of an individual $u \in M \cup F$ is defined by $\bigcup_{f \in \mathcal{F}(\phi), u \in p(f)} \phi(f)$ and the number of *children per individual* is the largest cardinality of this set over all individuals in the pedigree.

Example 1. Let $M \stackrel{\text{def}}{=} \{x, y, z\}$ and $F \stackrel{\text{def}}{=} \{u, v, w\}$. We define a pedigree P by $\phi(x, u) \stackrel{\text{def}}{=} \{v\}$ and $\phi(y, v) \stackrel{\text{def}}{=} \{w, z\}$. In all other cases $\phi(\_, \_) \stackrel{\text{def}}{=} \emptyset$. This is graphically depicted as follows (male individuals are represented by squares, female individuals by circles and families with parental relation by lines).

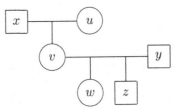

The founders of the pedigree are the individuals x, u and y. The pedigree has 3 generations and 2 children per individual. □

For each individual $u \in M \cup F$ we define a *community* $C(u)$ as a collection of all families where u is a parent, i.e., $C(u) \stackrel{\text{def}}{=} \{f \in \mathcal{F}(\phi) \mid u \in p(f)\}$. *Maximal community size* is the largest cardinality over all communities in the pedigree, i.e., $\max_{u \in M \cup F} |C(u)|$.

Remark 1. In any pedigree, the number of children per individual is at least the maximal community size.

We shall now introduce formal definitions of a mating graph and (non-)looping pedigrees. The following definitions are equivalent to the ones in [10] and [1].

Definition 2 (Mating Graph, Connected Pedigrees). *Let $P = (M, F, \phi)$ be a pedigree. We define an undirected bipartite graph $G(P) \stackrel{\text{def}}{=} (M \cup F, \mathcal{F}(\phi), \leftrightarrow)$, also called the* mating graph *of P, by stating that for all $u \in M \cup F$ and for all $f \in \mathcal{F}(\phi)$ we have $\{u, f\} \in \leftrightarrow$ iff $u \in p(f)$, or $u \in \phi(f)$. We say that a pedigree P is* connected *iff $G(P)$ is a connected graph.*

From now on we shall consider only non-empty and connected pedigrees. All results presented in the paper can be extended also to unconnected pedigrees in a straightforward manner.

Definition 3 ((Non-)Looping Pedigree). *We say that a pedigree P is* looping *if there is a loop in the mating graph $G(P)$. Otherwise we call P a* non-looping *pedigree.*

Consistency checking of a pedigree is based on its associated genotype information; intuitively, the pedigree defines the structure of the family relationships that are being modelled, and the genotype information is the data which must be consistent with the structure. Let $\mathcal{A}$ be a finite and non-empty set of *alleles*. A particular genotype information associated to every individual is represented by an element from $\mathcal{A}^2$ modulo the least equivalence on $\mathcal{A}^2$ satisfying $xy \equiv yx$ (the order of alleles in a genotype does not play any role).

Definition 4 ((Partial) Genotype Information). *Let $P = (M, F, \phi)$ be a pedigree. A (partial) genotype information for P is a function $\mathcal{G} : M \cup F \longrightarrow 2^{\mathcal{A}^2}$ that associates a set of possible genotype data to the individuals in the pedigree, s.t. $\mathcal{G}(u) \neq \emptyset$ for all $u \in M \cup F$.*

The intuition is that $\mathcal{G}(u) = \{AB\}$ means that the genotype of the individual u is known to be exactly AB. If e.g. $\mathcal{G}(u) = \{AB, AC\}$ then we have only a partial information about the individual u (we know that its genotype can be either AB or AC). If only one allele (let us say A) from the pair is know then we model it by $\mathcal{G}(u) = \{AX \mid X \in \mathcal{A}\}$. In case that nothing is known about the genotype of u then $\mathcal{G}(u) = \mathcal{A}^2$.

Definition 5 (Specialization). *Let $\mathcal{G}$ and $\mathcal{G}'$ be two partial genotype informa-tion. We say that $\mathcal{G}$ specializes into $\mathcal{G}'$ iff $\mathcal{G}'(u) \subseteq \mathcal{G}(u)$ for all $u \in M \cup F$.*

Definition 6 (Complete Genotype Information). *A genotype information $\mathcal{G}$ is called* complete *if $|\mathcal{G}(u)| = 1$ for every $u \in M \cup F$, i.e., every individual is assigned exactly one genotype.*

Verifying the consistency for a specific gene amounts to checking whether the pedigree and the genotype information are consistent according to the Mendelian law of segregation (see e.g. [5]). The law of segregation implicitly defines the following constraint on consistent genotype assignments:

Each individual inherits exactly one allele from both of its parents.

Our order of business will now be to formalize this constraint, and what it means that a genotype information is consistent with respect to a pedigree. Given two genotypes AB and CD, we define $zygote(AB, CD) \stackrel{\text{def}}{=} \{AC, AD, BC, BD\}$ as the set of all possible combinations of the given genotypes. Note that due to the commutativity introduced on $\mathcal{A}^2$ we get that e.g. $zygote(AB, AB) = \{AA, AB, BB\}$ and $zygote(AA, AB) = \{AA, AB\}$.

Definition 7 (Consistent Genotype Information).

1. *A complete genotype information $\mathcal{G}$ is* consistent *if for all $(u, v) \in \mathcal{F}(\phi)$ such that $\mathcal{G}(u) = \{AB\}$, $\mathcal{G}(v) = \{CD\}$ for some $A, B, C, D \in \mathcal{A}$ and for all $w \in \phi(u, v)$ it is the case that $\mathcal{G}(w) \subseteq zygote(AB, CD)$.*
2. *A partial genotype information $\mathcal{G}$ is* consistent *if there is a complete consistent genotype information $\mathcal{G}'$ such that $\mathcal{G}$ specializes into $\mathcal{G}'$.*

Let P be a pedigree and $\mathcal{G}$ a genotype information for P. By $\#(P, \mathcal{G})$ we denote the number of complete and consistent genotype information into which $\mathcal{G}$ specializes (or simply the number of solutions). A natural algorithmic problem is that of computing $\#(P, \mathcal{G})$ and we call it the *counting problem* for a pedigree P and a genotype information $\mathcal{G}$.

2.2   Counting Problems and Complexity Classes FP and #P

The complexity classes FP and #P for counting problems play a similar role as the complexity classes P and NP in case of decision problems. Let R be a polynomially balanced ($(x, y) \in R$ implies $|y| \leq |x|^k$ for some constant $k > 0$) and polynomial time decidable binary relation [11]. The counting problem $\#R$ is for a given input x to count how many different y there are such that $(x, y) \in R$. To provide the answer to such a problem is generally considered as a hard computational task. #P is the class of all such problems. Alternatively, #P can be defined as the class of functions that can be computed by counting the number of accepting paths of a polynomial time nondeterministic Turing machine. On the other hand, the complexity class FP is the class of functions that are computable by a deterministic Turing machine in polynomial time (also called the class of feasible functions, i.e., those solvable by computers). We can easily notice that FP $\subseteq$ #P and it is widely conjectured that the inclusion is strict.

In order to show #P-hardness of a counting problem, we often use the notion of *parsimonious reduction*. Let #R and #S be two counting problems. We say that there is a parsimonious reduction from #R to #S if there is a polynomial time transformation f from the instances of #R to the instances of #S which preserves the number of solutions, i.e., for all x we have that $|\{y \mid (x, y) \in R\}| = |\{y \mid (f(x), y) \in S\}|$.

Remark 2. This notion of reduction is little too restrictive so sometimes one defines that #R reduces to #S if there is a polynomial time algorithm for #R given an oracle that solves #S. Nevertheless, all the reductions presented in this paper are parsimonious.

As noted in [11] p. 439: "Even in cases in which the decision problem is polynomial, counting the solutions may be highly nontrivial." An example of such a problem is e.g. counting the number of perfect matchings in a bipartite graph. This is a #P-complete problem, while the decision variant of the problem is in P. On the other hand, showing that a counting problem is in FP immediately gives a polynomial time algorithm for the corresponding decision problem. Hence proving that the counting problem for a certain subclass of pedigrees (e.g. non-looping pedigrees) is in FP provides a stronger claim than only showing that the decision problem of consistency checking is in P.

3   Pedigrees with the Counting Problem in FP

In this section we demonstrate that for an arbitrary non-looping pedigree P and a given genotype information $\mathcal{G}$, the number $\#(P, \mathcal{G})$ can be computed in polynomial time on a deterministic Turing machine. Hence we generalize the result by Lange and Goradia [7] where they showed that the decision version of the problem is solvable in polynomial time using a genotype elimination algorithm. In our approach, we provide a different solution which exploits dynamic programming and enables us to count (and list if necessary) the total number of complete and consistent genotype information. We also show how to count in polynomial time the number of consistent pedigree assignments for pedigrees with 2 generations and maximal community size 2, and for pedigrees with at most one child per individual.

Let us consider a pedigree $P = (M, F, \phi)$ with a partial genotype information $\mathcal{G}$ over the alleles from $\mathcal{A}$. When counting $\#(P, \mathcal{G})$ we will use the techniques of dynamic programming and store the intermediate results in the following table.

$$T : (M \cup F) \times \mathcal{A}^2 \to \mathbb{N}$$

We shall often denote a table element $T(u, XY)$ where $u \in M \cup F$ and $XY \in \mathcal{A}^2$ by $T^u(XY)$. The main idea of the algorithm is that we shall process all families (and the corresponding individuals) of the pedigree in a particular order such that the number assigned to the table position $T^u(XY)$ stands for the number of solutions in a subpedigree that was already processed and is connected to u, all under the assumption that the genotype information of u is fixed to XY.

The procedure **initialize** in Figure 1 initializes the table T for all individuals from $M \cup F$.

Let $(x, y) \in \mathcal{F}(\phi)$, $u \in M \cup F$ s.t. $u \leftrightarrow (x, y)$ and $XY \in \mathcal{G}(u)$. The function **update** in Figure 1 returns the number of solutions in the already processed subpedigree connected (in the mating graph) to the individual u, under the assumption that the genotype information for u is fixed to XY and that the table T^v is fully computed for all the individuals v connected to the family (x, y) except for u.

Finally, the function **count** in Figure 1 computes the number $\#(P, \mathcal{G})$ where the notion of a mediator for $f \in \mathcal{F}(\phi)$ and $Z \subseteq \mathcal{F}(\phi)$ is defined as follows: an individual $u \in M \cup F$ is a *mediator* for f w.r.t. Z iff $u \leftrightarrow f$ and there is some $f' \in Z$ such that $f \neq f'$ and $u \leftrightarrow f'$. In other words a mediator is an individual that connects two different families in the mating graph. The function **count** first initializes the table T to its initial values and creates a set Z, which represents the set of families to be processed. It then removes the families from Z one by one in a particular order which ensures that the table T^u for a mediator u can be easily computed. Finally, when Z contains only one family, the final number of solutions is computed and returned.

Theorem 1. *The counting problem for non-looping pedigrees is in FP.*

Proof. (Sketch) It is easy to see that the algorithm runs in polynomial time. We have to argue that for a given pedigree P and a genotype information $\mathcal{G}$ the function **count**$(P, \mathcal{G})$ returns the number $\#(P, \mathcal{G})$. The requirement that P is non-looping (and connected) ensures that we can always select a family $f \in Z$ with exactly one mediator u with respect to Z. Moreover, whenever a value is assigned to $T^u(XY)$ the following assertion holds: "$T^u(XY)$ is the number of solutions in the subpedigree generated by u and the families in $\mathcal{F}(\phi) \setminus Z$ (together with their children) that are connected to u in the mating graph". □

Example 2. We shall demonstrate the algorithm for counting the number of solutions on the following pedigree.

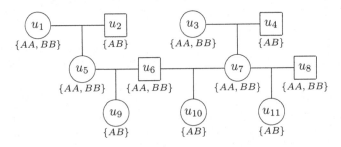

initialize =
for all $v \in M \cup F$ **do**
  for all $XY \in \mathcal{A}^2$ **do**
    $T^v(XY) := \begin{cases} 1 & \text{if } XY \in \mathcal{G}(v) \\ 0 & \text{otherwise} \end{cases}$
  end for
end for

update$((x,y), u, XY)$:int =
if $u = x$ **then**
  *** u is a male parent in the family ***
  let $\{w_1, \ldots, w_\ell\} = \phi(x,y)$ be all children in the family (x,y)
  return $\displaystyle\sum_{\substack{AB \in \mathcal{G}(y) \\ X_1Y_1, \ldots, X_\ell Y_\ell \in zygote(XY, AB)}} T^y(AB) \cdot T^{w_1}(X_1Y_1) \cdot \cdots \cdot T^{w_\ell}(X_\ell Y_\ell)$
else if $u = y$ **then**
  *** u is a female parent in the family ***
  let $\{w_1, \ldots, w_\ell\} = \phi(x,y)$ be all children in the family (x,y)
  return $\displaystyle\sum_{\substack{AB \in \mathcal{G}(x) \\ X_1Y_1, \ldots, X_\ell Y_\ell \in zygote(AB, XY)}} T^x(AB) \cdot T^{w_1}(X_1Y_1) \cdot \cdots \cdot T^{w_\ell}(X_\ell Y_\ell)$
else
  *** $u \in \phi(x,y)$ is a child in the family ***
  let $\{w_1, \ldots, w_\ell\} = \phi(x,y) \setminus \{u\}$ be all the children except for u
  return $\displaystyle\sum_{\substack{AB \in \mathcal{G}(x) \text{ and } CD \in \mathcal{G}(y) \\ \text{s.t. } XY \in zygote(AB, CD) \\ X_1Y_1, \ldots, X_\ell Y_\ell \in zygote(AB, CD)}} T^x(AB) \cdot T^y(CD) \cdot T^{w_1}(X_1Y_1) \cdot \cdots \cdot T^{w_\ell}(X_\ell Y_\ell)$
end if

count$(P = (M, F, \phi), \mathcal{G} : M \cup F \to 2^{\mathcal{A}^2})$:int =
$Z := \mathcal{F}(\phi)$
initialize
while $|Z| > 1$ **do**
  select $f \in Z$ s.t. f has exactly one mediator u w.r.t. Z
  for all $XY \in \mathcal{G}(u)$ **do**
    $T^u(XY) := T^u(XY) \cdot$**update**(f, u, XY)
  end for
  $Z := Z \setminus \{f\}$
end while
let $f = (x,y)$ where $\{f\} = Z$;
let $\{w_1, \ldots, w_\ell\} = \phi(x,y)$ be all children in the family (x,y)
return $\displaystyle\sum_{\substack{AB \in \mathcal{G}(x) \text{ and } CD \in \mathcal{G}(y) \\ X_1Y_1, \ldots, X_\ell Y_\ell \in zygote(AB, CD)}} T^x(AB) \cdot T^y(CD) \cdot T^{w_1}(X_1Y_1) \cdot \cdots \cdot T^{w_\ell}(X_\ell Y_\ell)$

Fig. 1. Algorithm for computing the number $\#(P, \mathcal{G})$

The pedigree consists of 11 individuals $u_1, \ldots, u_{11}$ and 5 families (u_2, u_1), (u_4, u_3), (u_6, u_5), (u_6, u_7) and (u_8, u_7). The genotype information for each individual is depicted in the picture (e.g. $\mathcal{G}(u_5) = \{AA, BB\}$ and $\mathcal{G}(u_2) = \{AB\}$).

During the call of the function **count** we first for all individuals initialize the table T to either 0 and 1 according to the given genotype information. Next we start eliminating the families in the pedigree. Let us assume that the first selected family in the while-loop is (u_2, u_1) and the mediator u is equal to u_5. As u_5 is a child in the family (u_2, u_1) we compute $T^{u_5}(AA) = 1 \cdot 1 = 1$ and $T^{u_5}(BB) = 1 \cdot 1 = 1$ according to the third case in the function **update**. The family (u_2, u_1) is then removed from Z. Next assume that the second selected family is (u_6, u_5) with a mediator u_6 and we compute $T^{u_6}(AA) = T^{u_6}(BB) = 1 \cdot 1 = 1$ by using the first case in the function **update**. The family (u_6, u_5) is removed from Z. Assume that the third selected family is (u_4, u_3) where u_7 is the mediator and we compute $T^{u_7}(AA) = T^{u_7}(BB) = 1 \cdot 1 = 1$. The family (u_4, u_3) is removed from Z. Now we can select e.g. the family (u_8, u_7) with the mediator u_7 and compute $T^{u_7}(AA) = T^{u_7}(BB) = 1 \cdot 1 = 1$ while removing (u_8, u_7) from Z. Finally, only the family (u_6, u_7) remains in Z and we return the final value

$$T^{u_6}(AA) \cdot T^{u_7}(BB) \cdot T^{u_{10}}(AB) + T^{u_6}(BB) \cdot T^{u_7}(AA) \cdot T^{u_{10}}(AB) = 1 + 1 = 2.$$

Indeed, there are exactly two possibilities for the assignment of a genotype to u_1 and this uniquely determines the assignments in the rest of the pedigree. In particular, one can see that u_3 has to be assigned exactly the same genotype as u_1 in order to preserve consistency.   □

Theorem 2. *If a pedigree* $P = (M, F, \phi)$ *has at most one child per individual then it is non-looping.*

Corollary 1. *The counting problem for pedigrees with at most one child per individual is in FP.*

Let us now consider pedigrees with 2 generations only and the maximal community size at most 2. We can demonstrate that the counting problem for this subclass is also in FP by applying the observations about "loop-breakers" from [4].

Theorem 3. *The counting problem for pedigrees with 2 generations and maximal community size 2 (and an arbitrary number of alleles) is in FP.*

Corollary 2. *The counting problem for pedigrees with 2 generations and at most two children per individual (and an arbitrary number of alleles) is in FP.*

Proof. Directly from Theorem 3 and Remark 1.   □

4   Pedigrees with #P-Complete Counting Problem

In this section we shall argue that the counting problems in all other pedigrees except for those considered in Section 3 are computationally hard. We will demonstrate #P-hardness (with respect to parsimonious reduction) for pedigrees with 3 generations, 2 children per individual and 2 alleles, and for pedigrees with 2 generations, 3 children per individual and 2 alleles. Even for general pedigrees one can easily see that the problems are in #P, which together with the hardness results implies #P-completeness. This completes the full picture of the computational complexity of counting problems for pedigrees.

Let us consider the #Bpos-2Sat counting problem [3]. We are given two disjoint sets of variables $\{x_1, \ldots, x_n\}$ and $\{y_1, \ldots, y_m\}$ and a formula $C_1 \wedge C_2 \wedge \ldots \wedge C_k$ where for every ℓ, $1 \leq \ell \leq k$, the clause C_ℓ is of the form $x_i \vee y_j$ such that $1 \leq i \leq n$ and $1 \leq j \leq m$. Counting the number of satisfying truth assignments of such a formula is a #P-complete problem [3]. Note that the corresponding decision problem is trivial as any #Bpos-2Sat formula is satisfiable.

We shall reduce #Bpos-2Sat to the counting problem for pedigrees of particular shapes such that the reduction preserves the number of solutions (i.e. it is a parsimonious reduction). In our reductions we shall use only two alleles $\mathcal{A} \stackrel{\text{def}}{=} \{A, B\}$ such that AA represents *true* and BB represents *false*.

Theorem 4. *The counting problem for pedigrees with 3 generations, 2 children per individual and 2 alleles is #P-complete.*

Proof. (Sketch) Containment in #P is easy. We shall argue for #P-hardness of the problem. Let $C_1 \wedge C_2 \wedge \ldots \wedge C_k$ be a given instance of #Bpos-2Sat. We shall construct a pedigree P as follows.

First, for every variable x_i, $1 \leq i \leq n$, we create k of its copies by constructing the following pedigree part.

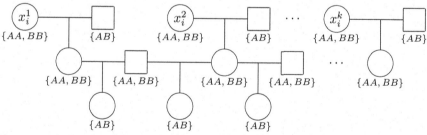

Next we create a similar structure for every variable y_j, $1 \leq j \leq m$.

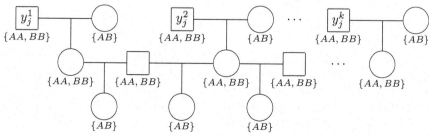

As argued in Example 2, we can now see that the pedigrees for x_i (resp. y_j) have exactly two solutions so that $x_i^1, \ldots, x_i^k$ (resp. $y_j^1, \ldots, y_j^k$) can simultaneously take the assignment AA or BB, hence representing the truth value true or false.

Now for every ℓ, $1 \leq \ell \leq k$, such that $C_\ell \equiv x_i \vee y_j$ we will add the following pedigree part where the individuals x_i^ℓ and y_j^ℓ are identified with the corresponding nodes in the pedigrees above.

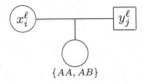

We can now easily verify that at least one of x_i^ℓ and y_j^ℓ has to be set to true (i.e. takes the value AA) in order to achieve a consistent assignment. It is a routine exercise to check that the number of satisfying truth assignments of the formula is the same as the number of complete genotype information for the constructed pedigree. The construction ensures that the pedigree has 3 generations, at most 2 children per individual and uses only 2 alleles. □

Theorem 5. *The counting problem for pedigrees with 2 generations, 3 children per individual and 2 alleles is #P-complete.*

Proof. (Sketch) As in the previous proof, the reduction goes from #Bpos-2Sat. We modify the way in which we generate the truth assignments. We shall use only 2 generation pedigrees at the expense of 3 children per individual.

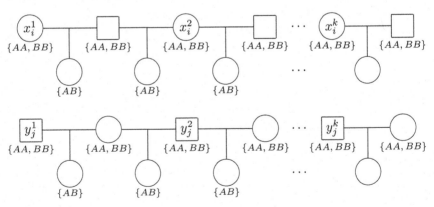

It is easy to see that $x_i^1, \ldots, x_i^k$ (resp. $y_j^1, \ldots, y_j^k$) can simultaneously take the assignment AA or BB and after adding the pedigree parts for all clauses C_ℓ as in the construction above, the reduction preserves the number of solutions. The final pedigree has 2 generations and at most 3 children per individual. As before, the containment in #P is easy. □

5 Conclusion

We have studied counting problems for genotype assignments in pedigrees and found a delicate borderline between tractable and intractable instances of the problem. The following table summarizes the main results achieved in the paper.

type	# generations	# children	# alleles	complexity
non-looping	∞	∞	∞	in FP (Thm. 1)
looping	∞	∞	1	in FP (trivial)
looping	1	∞	∞	in FP (trivial)
looping	∞	1	∞	in FP (Cor. 1)
looping	2	2	∞	in FP (Cor. 2)
looping	3	2	2	#P-complete (Thm. 4)
looping	2	3	2	#P-complete (Thm. 5)

The table provides a complete characterization of the computational complexity of counting problems with respect to the selected parameters. Moreover, the hardness results use only marriage loops [12] and contain no inbreeding loops.

In [1] it is shown that consistency checking for general pedigrees with 2 alleles only is in P, provided that for each individual we either know precisely his/her genotype information or we know nothing at all, i.e., for every individual u we have either $|\mathcal{G}(u)| = 1$ or $\mathcal{G}(u) = \mathcal{A}^2$. It would be interesting to see whether the counting problem is in FP under this restriction. The future research will also focus on investigating possible ways of tackling the counting problem for pedigrees with loops (here some ideas from [10] seem to be applicable) and on the complete complexity characterization of the consistency checking problems.

References

1. L. Aceto, J.A. Hansen, A. Ingólfsdóttir, J. Johnsen, and J. Knudsen. The complexity of checking consistency of pedigree information and related problems. *J. of Computer Science and Technology*, 19(1):42–59, 2004.
2. F.X. Dua and I. Hoeschele. A note on algorithms for genotype and allele elimination in complex pedigrees with incomplete genotype data. *Genetics*, 156:2051–2062,2000.
3. M.O. Ball J.S. Provan. The complexity of counting cuts and of computing the probability that a graph is connected. *SIAM J. on Comp.*, 12(4):777–788, 1983.
4. K. Lange K and R.C. Elston. Extensions to pedigree analysis i. likehood calculations for simple and complex pedigrees. *Human Heredity*, 25(2):95–105, 1975.
5. William S. Klug and Michael R. Cummings. *Concepts of Genetics*. Prentice Hall, 5th edition, 1997.
6. K. Lange and T. Goradia. An algorithm for automatic genotype elimination. *American J. of Human Genetics*, 40:250–256, 1987.
7. Kenneth Lange and Tushar Madhu Goradia. An algorithm for automatic genotype elimination. *American J. of Human Genetics*, 40:250–256, 1987.
8. Jing Li and Tao Jiang. Efficient rule-based haplotyping algorithms for pedigree data. In *Proceedings of RECOMB'03*, pages 197–206. ACM, 2003.

9. J.R. O'Connell and D.E. Weeks. Pedcheck: A program for identification of genotype incompatibilities in linkage analysis. *Am. J. of Human Genetics*, 63:259–266, 1998.

10. J.R. O'Connell and D.E. Weeks. An optimal algorithm for automatic genotype elimination. *American J. of Human Genetics*, 65:1733–1740, 1999.

11. Ch.H. Papadimitriou. *Computational Complexity*. Addison-Wesley, 1994.

12. A. Piccolboni and D. Gusfield. On the complexity of fundamental computational problems in pedigree analysis. *J. of Computational Biology*, 10(5):763–773, 2003.

Fixpoint Logics on Hierarchical Structures

Stefan Göller and Markus Lohrey

FMI, Universität Stuttgart, Germany
{goeller,lohrey}@informatik.uni-stuttgart.de

Abstract. Hierarchical graph definitions allow a modular description of graphs using modules for the specification of repeated substructures. Beside this modularity, hierarchical graph definitions allow to specify graphs of exponential size using polynomial size descriptions. In many cases, this succinctness increases the computational complexity of decision problems. In this paper, the model-checking problem for the modal μ-calculus and (monadic) least fixpoint logic on hierarchically defined graphs is investigated. In order to analyze the modal μ-calculus, parity games on hierarchically defined graphs are studied.

1 Introduction

Hierarchical graph definitions specify a graph via modules, where every module is a graph that may refer to modules of a smaller hierarchical level. In this way, large structures can be represented in a modular and succinct way. Hierarchical graph definitions were introduced in [14] in the context of VLSI design. Formally, hierarchical graph definitions can be seen as hyperedge replacement graph grammars [6] that generate precisely one graph. Specific algorithmic problems (e.g. reachability, planarity, circuit-value, 3-colorability) on hierarchically defined graphs are studied in [12,13,14,18].

In this paper we consider the complexity of the model-checking problem for *least fixpoint logic* (LFP) and its fragments *monadic least fixpoint logic* (MLFP) and the *modal μ-calculus*. LFP is the extension of classical first-order logic that allows the definition of least fixpoints of arbitrary arity [15]. MLFP is the fragment of LFP where only monadic fixpoints can be defined. The modal μ-calculus is the fragment of MLFP that is obtained from classical modal logic extended by a monadic fixpoint operator. The model-checking problem for a certain logic asks whether a given sentence from that logic is true in a given finite structure (e.g. a graph). Usually, the structure is given explicitly, for instance by listing all tuples in each of the relations of the structure. In this paper, input structures will be given in a hierarchical form via *straight-line programs*. Straight-line programs are equivalent to hierarchical graph definitions [16] w.r.t. succinctness, but are more convenient for our purpose.

LFP and its fragments MLFP and the modal μ-calculus found many applications in data base theory, finite model theory, and verification, see e.g. [15]. It is therefore not surprising that the model-checking problem for these logics on explicitly given input structures is a very well-studied problem. Let us just mention a few references: [2,4,5,9,10,11,21,22]. Concerning hierarchically defined graphs, in [1] the complexity of the temporal logics LTL and CTL over hierarchical state machines was investigated.

R. Ramanujam and S. Sen (Eds.): FSTTCS 2005, LNCS 3821, pp. 483–494, 2005.

Hierarchical state machines can be seen as a restricted form of hierarchical graph definitions that are tailored towards the modular specification of large reactive systems. Since LTL and CTL can be efficiently translated into the modal μ-calculus, our work is a natural extension of [1]. Moreover, our work continues the previous paper [17] of the second author, where the model-checking problem of first-order logic, monadic second-order logic, and full second-order logic over hierarchically defined graphs was studied.

Our investigation of model-checking problems follows Vardi's methodology from [21]. For a logic $\mathcal{L}$ and a class of structures $\mathcal{C}$, Vardi introduced three different ways of measuring the complexity of the model-checking problem for $\mathcal{L}$ and $\mathcal{C}$: (i) One may fix a formula $\varphi \in \mathcal{L}$ and consider the complexity of verifying for a given structure $A \in \mathcal{C}$ whether $A \models \varphi$; thus, only the structure belongs to the input (data complexity or structure complexity). (ii) One may fix a structure $A \in \mathcal{C}$ and consider the complexity of verifying for a given formula $\varphi \in \mathcal{L}$, whether $A \models \varphi$; thus, only the formula belongs to the input (expression complexity). (iii) Finally, both the structure and the formula may belong to the input (combined complexity). In the context of hierarchically defined structures, expression complexity does not lead to new results. Having a fixed hierarchically defined structure is the same as having a fixed explicitly given structure. Thus, we only consider data and combined complexity for hierarchically defined structures.

Section 2 introduces the necessary concepts. In Section 3 we show that the winner of a *parity game* on a hierarchically defined graph can be determined in PSPACE. Since the classical reduction of the model-checking problem for the modal μ-calculus to parity games [3,4] can be extended to hierarchically defined graphs (Thm. 3), we obtain PSPACE-completeness of the model-checking problem for the modal μ-calculus on hierarchically defined graphs. The upper bound generalizes a corresponding result for CTL/LTL from [1]. For a restricted class of hierarchically defined graphs we obtain the better upper bound of NP $\cap$ coNP for parity games, which leads to the same upper bound for the data complexity of the modal μ-calculus. In Section 5 we study least fixpoint logic (LFP) and its fragment monadic least fixpoint logic (MLFP) over hierarchically defined input structures. MLFP is still more expressive than the modal μ-calculus. It turns out that in most cases the complexity of the model-checking problem over hierarchically defined input structures becomes EXP. Our results are collected in Table 1 in Section 2. Proofs that are omitted due to space restrictions can be found in the full version [7].

2   Preliminaries

General notations Let $\equiv$ be an equivalence relation on a set A. For $a \in A$, $[a]_\equiv = \{b \in A \mid a \equiv b\}$ is the equivalence class containing a. With $[A]_\equiv$ we denote the set of all equivalence classes. With $\pi_\equiv : A \rightarrow [A]_\equiv$ we denote the function with $\pi_\equiv(a) = [a]_\equiv$ for all $a \in A$. For a function $f : A \rightarrow B$ let $\mathrm{ran}(f) = \{b \in B \mid \exists a \in A : f(a) = b\}$. For $C \subseteq A$ we define the restriction $f{\restriction}_C : C \rightarrow B$ by $f{\restriction}_C(c) = f(c)$ for all $c \in C$. For functions $f : A \rightarrow B$ and $g : B \rightarrow C$ we define the composition $g \circ f : A \rightarrow C$ by $(g \circ f)(a) = g(f(a))$ for all $a \in A$. For $n \in \mathbb{N}$ we denote by $\mathrm{id}_{\{1,\dots,n\}}$ the identity function over $\{1, \dots, n\}$.

Complexity theory We assume some basic background in complexity theory [20]. In particular, we assume that the reader is familiar with the classes P (deterministic polynomial time), NP (nondeterministic polynomial time), coNP (complements of problems in NP), PH (the polynomial time hierarchy), PSPACE (polynomial space), and EXP (deterministic exponential time). We will use alternating Turing-machines, see [20] for more details. An *alternating Turing-machine* M is a nondeterministic Turing-machine, where the set of states Q is partitioned into three sets: $Q_\exists$ (existential states), $Q_\forall$ (universal states), and F (accepting states). A configuration C with current state q is accepting, if (i) $q \in F$, or (ii) $q \in Q_\exists$ and there exists a successor configuration of C that is accepting, or (iii) $q \in Q_\forall$ and every successor configuration of C is accepting. An input word w is accepted by M if the corresponding initial configuration is accepting. It is well known that PSPACE equals the class of all problems that can be solved on an alternating Turing-machine in polynomial time.

Relational structures and straight-line programs A *signature* is a finite set $\mathcal{R}$ of relational symbols, where each relational symbol $r \in \mathcal{R}$ has an associated arity n_r. A *(relational) structure* over the signature $\mathcal{R}$ is a tuple $\mathcal{A} = (A, (r^{\mathcal{A}})_{r \in \mathcal{R}})$, where A is a set (the universe of $\mathcal{A}$) and $r^{\mathcal{A}}$ is a relation of arity n_r over the set A, which interprets the relational symbol r. Usually, we denote the relation $r^{\mathcal{A}}$ with r as well. The size $|\mathcal{A}|$ of $\mathcal{A}$ is $|A| + \sum_{r \in \mathcal{R}} n_r \cdot |r^{\mathcal{A}}|$. For an equivalence relation relation $\equiv$ on A we define the quotient $\mathcal{A}/{\equiv} = ([A]_\equiv, (\{(\pi_\equiv(a_1), \ldots, \pi_\equiv(a_{n_r})) \mid (a_1, \ldots, a_{n_r}) \in r^{\mathcal{A}}\})_{r \in \mathcal{R}})$. For $n \geq 0$, an n-pointed structure is a pair $(\mathcal{A}, \tau)$, where $\mathcal{A}$ is a structure with universe A and $\tau : \{1, \ldots, n\} \to A$ is injective. The elements in $\operatorname{ran}(\tau)$ (resp. $A \setminus \operatorname{ran}(\tau)$) are also called *contact nodes* (resp. *internal nodes*). Let $G_i = (\mathcal{A}_i, \tau_i)$ be an n_i-pointed structure ($i \in \{1, 2\}$) over the signature $\mathcal{R}$, where A_i is the universe of $\mathcal{A}_i$ and $A_1 \cap A_2 = \emptyset$. We define the disjoint union $G_1 \oplus G_2$ as the $(n_1 + n_2)$-pointed structure $((A_1 \cup A_2, (r^{\mathcal{A}_1} \cup r^{\mathcal{A}_2})_{r \in \mathcal{R}}), \tau)$, where $\tau : \{1, \ldots, n_1 + n_2\} \to A_1 \cup A_2$ with $\tau(i) = \tau_1(i)$ for all $1 \leq i \leq n_1$ and $\tau(i + n_1) = \tau_2(i)$ for all $1 \leq i \leq n_2$. Now let $G = (\mathcal{A}, \tau)$ be an n-pointed structure, where A is the universe of $\mathcal{A}$. For a permutation $f : \{1, \ldots, n\} \to \{1, \ldots, n\}$ define $\operatorname{rename}_f(G) = (\mathcal{A}, \tau \circ f)$. If $n \geq 1$, then $\operatorname{forget}(G) = (\mathcal{A}, \tau \restriction \{1, \ldots, n-1\})$. Finally, if $n \geq 2$, then $\operatorname{glue}(G) = (\mathcal{A}/{\equiv}, (\pi_\equiv \circ \tau) \restriction \{1, \ldots, n-1\})$, where $\equiv$ is the smallest equivalence relation on A which contains the pair $(\tau(n), \tau(n-1))$. Note that the combination of rename_f and glue (resp. forget) allows to glue (resp. forget) arbitrary contact nodes.

Straight-line programs offer a succinct representation of large structures. A *straight-line program (SLP)* $\mathcal{S} = (X_i := t_i)_{1 \leq i \leq l}$ is a sequence of definitions, where every right hand side t_i is either an n-pointed *finite* structure (for some n) or an expression of the form $X_j \oplus X_k$, $\operatorname{rename}_f(X_j)$, $\operatorname{forget}(X_j)$, or $\operatorname{glue}(X_j)$ with $j, k < i$ and $f : \{1, \ldots, n\} \to \{1, \ldots, n\}$ a permutation. Here, X_i is a formal variable. For every variable X_i, $\operatorname{type}(X_i)$ is inductively defined as follows: (i) if t_i is an n-pointed structure, then $\operatorname{type}(X_i) = n$, (ii) if $t_i = X_j \oplus X_k$, then $\operatorname{type}(X_i) = \operatorname{type}(X_j) + \operatorname{type}(X_k)$, (iii) if $t_i = \operatorname{rename}_f(X_j)$, then $\operatorname{type}(X_i) = \operatorname{type}(X_j)$, and (iv) if $t_i = \operatorname{op}(X_j)$ for $\operatorname{op} \in \{\operatorname{forget}, \operatorname{glue}\}$, then $\operatorname{type}(X_i) = \operatorname{type}(X_j) - 1$. The $\operatorname{type}(X_i)$-pointed finite structure $\operatorname{eval}(X_i)$ is inductively defined by: (i) if t_i is an n-pointed structure, then $\operatorname{eval}(X_i) = t_i$, (ii) if $t_i = X_j \oplus X_k$, then $\operatorname{eval}(X_i) = \operatorname{eval}(X_j) \oplus \operatorname{eval}(X_k)$, and (iii) if $t_i = \operatorname{op}(X_j)$ for $\operatorname{op} \in \{\operatorname{rename}_f, \operatorname{forget}, \operatorname{glue}\}$, then $\operatorname{eval}(X_i) = \operatorname{op}(\operatorname{eval}(X_j))$. We define $\text{eval}(\mathcal{S}) = \text{eval}(X_l)$. The SLP $\mathcal{S}$ is *c-bounded* ($c \in \mathbb{N}$) if $\text{type}(X_i) \leq c$ for all $1 \leq i \leq l$. Finally, the *size* $|\mathcal{S}|$ of $\mathcal{S}$ is l plus the size of all explicit n-pointed structures that appear as a right-hand side t_i. In [17] we used *hierarchical graph definitions* for the specification of large structures. A hierarchical graph definition can be translated in polynomial time into an SLP defining the same structure [7,16].

Fixpoint logics Fix a signature $\mathcal{R}$. *First-order (FO) formulas* over the signature $\mathcal{R}$ are built from atomic formulas of the form $x = y$ and $r(x_1, \ldots, x_{n_r})$ (where $r \in \mathcal{R}$ and $x, y, x_1, \ldots, x_{n_r}$ are first-order variables ranging over elements of the universe) using boolean connectives and (first-order) quantifications over elements of the universe. *Least fixpoint logic* (LFP) extends FO by the definition of least fixpoints. For this, let us take a countably infinite set of *fixpoint variables*. Each fixpoint variable R has an associated arity n and ranges over n-ary relations over the universe. Fixpoint variables will be denoted by capital letters. Syntactically, LFP extends FO by the following formula building rule: Let $\varphi(\bar{x}, R, \bar{P}, \bar{y})$ be a formula of LFP. Here, $\bar{x}$ and $\bar{y}$ are repetition-free tuples of first-order variables, $\bar{P}$ is a repetition-free tuple of fixpoint variables, the arity of the fixpoint variable R is $|\bar{x}|$ (the length of the tuple $\bar{x}$), and R only occurs positively in φ (i.e., within an even number of negations). Then also $\text{lfp}_{\bar{x}, R}\ \varphi(\bar{x}, R, \bar{P}, \bar{y})$ is a formula of LFP. The semantics of the lfp-operator is the following: Let $\bar{b} \in A^{|\bar{y}|}$ and let $\bar{S}$ be a tuple of relations that is interpreting the tuple $\bar{P}$ of fixpoint variables. Since R only occurs positively in $\varphi(\bar{x}, R, \bar{P}, \bar{y})$, the function F_φ that maps $T \subseteq A^{|\bar{x}|}$ to $\{\bar{a} \in A^{|\bar{x}|} \mid \mathcal{A} \models \varphi(\bar{a}, T, \bar{S}, \bar{b})\}$ is monotonic. Hence, by the Knaster-Tarski fixpoint theorem, the smallest fixpoint $\text{fix}(F_\varphi)$ exists. Now for $\bar{a} \in A^{|\bar{x}|}$ we have $\mathcal{A} \models [\text{lfp}_{\bar{x}, R}\ \varphi(\bar{x}, R, \bar{S}, \bar{b})](\bar{a})$ if and only if $\bar{a} \in \text{fix}(F_\varphi)$. The greatest fixpoint operator can be defined as $\text{gfp}_{\bar{x}, R}\ \varphi(\bar{x}, R, \bar{P}, \bar{y}) = \neg\text{lfp}_{\bar{x}, R}\ \neg\varphi(\bar{x}, \neg R/R, \bar{P}, \bar{y})$, it defines the greatest fixpoint of F_φ.

Monadic least fixpoint logic (MLFP) is the fragment of LFP that only contains unary (i.e., monadic) fixpoint variables. The modal μ-calculus can be defined as a fragment of MLFP that is defined as follows. Formulas of the *modal μ-calculus* are interpreted over special relational structures that are called transition systems. Let $\mathcal{P}$ be a finite set of *atomic propositions*. A *transition system* (over $\mathcal{P}$) is a tuple $T = (Q, R, \lambda)$, where Q is a finite set of states, $R \subseteq Q \times Q$, and $\lambda : Q \to 2^{\mathcal{P}}$. Note that a state may be labeled with several atomic propositions. Clearly, T can be identified with the relational structure $\mathcal{A}_T = (Q, R, (\{q \in Q \mid p \in \lambda(q)\})_{p \in \mathcal{P}})$. This allows us to use SLPs in order to construct large transition systems. The set of *formulas* $\mathcal{F}_\mu(\mathcal{P})$ over $\mathcal{P}$ of the modal μ-calculus is defined by the following EBNF, where $p \in \mathcal{P}$ and X is a unary fixpoint variable: $\varphi ::= p \mid \neg p \mid X \mid \varphi_1 \wedge \varphi_2 \mid \varphi_1 \vee \varphi_2 \mid \Diamond\varphi \mid \Box\varphi \mid \mu X.\varphi \mid \nu X.\varphi$ We define the semantics of a formula $\varphi \in \mathcal{F}_\mu(\mathcal{P})$ by translating it to an MLFP-formula $\|\varphi\|(x)$ over the signature $\{R\} \cup \mathcal{P}$, where R has rank 2, every $p \in \mathcal{P}$ has rank 1, and x is a first-order variable. The translation is done inductively:

$$\|(\neg)p\|(x) = (\neg)p(x) \qquad\qquad \|X\|(x) = X(x)$$
$$\|\varphi \wedge \psi\|(x) = \|\varphi\|(x) \wedge \|\psi\|(x) \qquad \|\varphi \vee \psi\|(x) = \|\varphi\|(x) \vee \|\psi\|(x)$$
$$\|\Box\varphi\|(x) = \forall y : R(x, y) \Rightarrow \|\varphi\|(y) \qquad \|\Diamond\varphi\|(x) = \exists y : R(x, y) \wedge \|\varphi\|(y)$$
$$\|\mu X.\varphi\|(x) = [\text{lfp}_{x, X}\|\varphi\|(x)](x) \qquad \|\nu X.\varphi\|(x) = [\text{gfp}_{x, X}\|\varphi\|(x)](x)$$

Table 1. Data and combined complexity for fixpoint logics

		explicit [4,9,21]	c-bounded SLP	unrestricted SLP
μ-calc.	data	P	P $\cdots$ NP $\cap$ coNP	
	combined	P $\cdots$ NP $\cap$ coNP	PSPACE	
MLFP	data	P	P $\cdots$ PH	
	combined	EXP		
LFP	data	P	EXP	
	combined			

For a transition system $T = (Q, R, \lambda)$, a state $q \in Q$, and a formula $\varphi \in \mathcal{F}_\mu(\mathcal{P})$, we write $(T, q) \models \varphi$ if $\mathcal{A}_T \models \|\varphi\|(q)$.

The model checking problem for a logic $\mathcal{L}$ asks whether for a structure $\mathcal{A}$ and a sentence $\varphi \in \mathcal{L}$ we have $\mathcal{A} \models \varphi$. As already explained in the introduction, we will be interested in combined complexity (both, the formula and the structure belong to the input) and data complexity (the formula is fixed and only the structure belongs to the input), where the structure is represented via an SLP. Table 1 collects the known results as well as our new results concerning the (data and combined) complexity of the model-checking problem for the logics LFP, MLFP, and the modal μ-calculus. Only for the data complexity of MLFP and the modal μ-calculus on structures defined by c-bounded SLPs (for some fixed $c \in \mathbb{N}$) we do not obtain matching lower and upper bounds.

Parity games The modal μ-calculus has a close relationship to *parity games*, which are played between two players, called Adam and Eve, on a particular kind of relational structure, called a game graph. Let $C = \{0, \ldots, k\}$ ($k \in \mathbb{N}$) be a finite set of *priorities*. A *game graph* G over C is a tuple $G = (V, E, \rho)$ s.t. V is a finite set of nodes, $E \subseteq V \times C \times V$ is the set of labeled edges, and $\rho : V \to \{\text{Eve}, \text{Adam}\}$ assigns to every node v a player $\rho(v)$. Its *size* is defined by $|G| = |V| + |E|$. We define $\overline{\text{Eve}} = \text{Adam}$ and $\overline{\text{Adam}} = \text{Eve}$. The set of successor nodes of a given node $v \in V$ is $vE = \{u \in V \mid \exists c \in C : (v, c, u) \in E\}$. Note that we diverge from common conventions as in [4,8,19] since priorities are assigned to edges instead to nodes. This is no restriction when considering parity games. A sequence $\pi = v_0, c_0, v_1, c_1, \ldots \in V(CV)^\omega$ (resp. $\pi = v_0, c_0, v_1, \ldots, c_{n-1}, v_n \in V(CV)^*$) is an *infinite path* (resp. *finite path*) in G if for all $i \geq 0$ (resp. $0 \leq i \leq n - 1$) we have $(v_i, c_i, v_{i+1}) \in E$. A finite path π is called *empty* if $\pi = v$ for some $v \in V$. The set of priorities occurring in π is denoted by $\text{Occ}(\pi)$. For an infinite path π we denote with $\text{Inf}(\pi) \subseteq \text{Occ}(\pi)$ the set of those priorities that occur infinitely many times in the path π. Clearly, the game graph $G = (V, E, \rho)$ can be identified with the relational structure $(V, (\{(u, v) \mid (u, c, v) \in E\})_{c \in C}, \rho^{-1}(\text{Eve}), \rho^{-1}(\text{Adam}))$. This allows us to generate large game graphs using SLPs. Here we have to be careful with the glue-operation. If (G, τ) is an n-pointed relational structure, where G is the game graph $G = (V, E, \rho)$ — we call such a structure an n-*game graph* — then glue(G, τ) is an $(n - 1)$-game graph only if $n \geq 2$ and

$\rho(\tau(n-1)) = \rho(\tau(n))$, i.e., the two nodes that are glued belong to the same player. Thus, glue is only a partial operation on n-game graphs.

Let $G = (V, E, \rho)$ be a game graph over the priorities $C = \{0, \dots, k\}$ ($k \in \mathbb{N}$). A *play* is either an infinite path in G or a finite path in G that ends in a node v with $vE = \emptyset$ (i.e., a dead end). Eve (resp. Adam) *wins* an infinite play π if and only if $\max(\mathrm{Inf}(\pi)) \equiv 0 \mod 2$ (resp. $\max(\mathrm{Inf}(\pi)) \equiv 1 \mod 2$). Player $\sigma \in \{\text{Eve}, \text{Adam}\}$ *wins* a finite play π if and only if $\rho(v) = \overline{\sigma}$ for the last node v of π, i.e., the dead end, where π ends, belongs to player $\overline{\sigma}$. It is an important question whether Eve/Adam has the possibility to force the game to a play which she/he can win, i.e., if she/he has a winning-strategy. For parity games, so called memoryless strategies suffice. A *memoryless strategy* for player $\sigma \in \{\text{Eve}, \text{Adam}\}$ is a map $\mathscr{S}_\sigma : \{v \mid \rho(v) = \sigma, vE \neq \emptyset\} \to V$ s.t. $\mathscr{S}_\sigma(v) \in vE$ for all $v \in \{v \mid \rho(v) = \sigma, vE \neq \emptyset\}$. We say that a finite play $\pi = v_0, c_0, v_1, \dots c_{n-1}, v_n$ (resp. an infinite play $\pi = v_0, c_0, v_1, \dots$) is $\mathscr{S}_\sigma$-*confirm* w.r.t. a memoryless strategy $\mathscr{S}_\sigma$ if for all $0 \leq i \leq n-1$ (resp. for all $i \geq 0$) we have $\mathscr{S}_\sigma(v_i) = v_{i+1}$ whenever $\rho(v_i) = \sigma$. For $v \in V$ we call the memoryless strategy $\mathscr{S}_\sigma$ a *memoryless winning strategy for player σ from the node v* if player σ wins every $\mathscr{S}_\sigma$-confirm play which starts in v. The question whether a memoryless strategy $\mathscr{S}_\sigma$ for player σ is a winning strategy can be answered in deterministic polynomial time. With PARITY we denote the set of all triples (G, v, σ), where G is a game graph, v is a node of G, $\sigma \in \{\text{Eve}, \text{Adam}\}$, and there exists a memoryless winning strategy for player σ from v. The determinacy theorem for parity games [4] states that $(G, v, \sigma) \in$ PARITY if and only if $(G, v, \overline{\sigma}) \notin$ PARITY. It implies that PARITY belongs to NP$\cap$coNP. By a result of [3,4], the model-checking problem for the modal μ-calculus can be reduced to PARITY.

3   Parity Games over SLP-defined Graphs

In this section we will prove a PSPACE upper bound for parity games over game graphs that are given via SLPs. Our construction is inspired by [19], where parity games on graphs of bounded tree width are examined. For the following considerations, let us fix a set $C = \{0, \dots, k\}$ ($k \in \mathbb{N}$) of priorities and let $G = (H, \tau)$ be an n-game graph over C with $H = (V, E, \rho)$.

Strategy reducts   Let $W \subseteq \rho^{-1}(\text{Eve}) \cap \mathrm{ran}(\tau)$ be a set of contact nodes that belong to Eve. An n-game graph G' is a *strategy reduct* of G w.r.t. W if G' can be obtained from G by (i) removing all outgoing edges for all $w \in W$, and (ii) keeping exactly one outgoing edge for all $w \in \rho^{-1}(\text{Eve}) \setminus (W \cup \{v \mid vE = \emptyset\})$. Thus, a strategy reduct of G is the remainder of G by restricting G to a given strategy and making certain Eve-nodes to dead ends. Note that a strategy reduct is always defined w.r.t. a subset W of Eve-nodes and is not unique in general. The reason for making an Eve-node u to a dead end in G is the fact that u is a contact node which will be glued with another contact node u' from another n'-game graph G' in an SLP, and for u' an outgoing edge (as a part of the strategy for Eve on G') has already been guessed.

The reward function   For a guessed strategy reduct G' of the potentially exponentially large n-game graph G we only store a polynomial amount of relevant information. More precisely for each pair of contact nodes $\tau(i)$ and $\tau(j)$ we only store the maximal priority along an optimal path for Adam from $\tau(i)$ to $\tau(j)$. In order to define this formally, we introduce the function reward $: 2^C \setminus \{\emptyset\} \to C$, see also [19]. Let $B \subseteq C$, $B \neq \emptyset$:

$$\text{reward}(B) = \begin{cases} \max(B \cap \{2n+1 \mid n \in \mathbb{N}\}) & \text{if } B \cap \{2n+1 \mid n \in \mathbb{N}\} \neq \emptyset \\ \min(B) & \text{else} \end{cases}$$

Intuitively, reward(B) is the best priority among B for Adam: if there is an odd priority in B, then the largest odd priority is the best for Adam. If there are only even priorities in B, then the smallest priority in B causes the smallest harm for Adam. For a set $\Pi \neq \emptyset$ of finite paths in G let reward$(\Pi) = $ reward$(\{ \max(\text{Occ}(\pi)) \mid \pi \in \Pi \})$. The intuition behind this definition is the following: If G' is a strategy reduct of G, then it is only Adam who can freely choose the next outgoing edge in G'. Hence, if Π is the set of all paths in G' between two contact nodes $\tau(i)$ and $\tau(j)$, then, if Adam is smart, he will choose a path $\pi \in \Pi$ with $\max(\text{Occ}(\pi)) = \text{reward}(\Pi)$ when going from $\tau(i)$ to $\tau(j)$. Hence, we can replace the set of paths Π by a single edge from $\tau(i)$ to $\tau(j)$ with priority reward(Π). For technical reasons we only put paths into Π that do not visit any contact nodes except its start and end node. We call such paths $\tau\tau$-internal paths.

$(\tau)\tau$-internal paths For two contact nodes $v_0, v_n \in \text{ran}(\tau)$ we call a *non-empty* finite path $\pi = v_0, c_0, v_1, \ldots, c_{n-1}, v_n$ a $\tau\tau$-*internal path* from v_0 to v_n if $v_1, \ldots, v_{n-1} \notin \text{ran}(\tau)$. Note that $v_0 = v_n$ is allowed. We call a *non-empty play* π (i.e., either π is an infinite path or it ends in a dead end but is non-empty) a τ-*internal path* if its first node is a contact node but it never visits a contact node again. We will be only interested in τ-internal paths, which player Adam wins. For $1 \leq i, j \leq n$ we denote with $\Pi^\tau_{i,j}(G)$ the set of all $\tau\tau$-internal paths in G from $\tau(i)$ to $\tau(j)$. Note that an arbitrary path between two contact nodes can be split up into consecutive $\tau\tau$-internal paths. Similarly an arbitrary maximal path that begins in a contact node consists of a sequence of $\tau\tau$-internal paths possibly followed by a τ-internal path. Hence, we do not lose any information by only considering $(\tau)\tau$-internal paths.

The reduce operation Assume that G' is a strategy reduct of the n-game graph G. Then it is only player Adam who can choose any path in G'. Of course, there is no reason for player Adam to move from contact node $\tau(i)$ to contact node $\tau(j)$ along a path which is not optimal for him. Hence we can replace the set $\Pi^\tau_{i,j}(G)$ of all $\tau\tau$-internal paths from $\tau(i)$ to $\tau(j)$ by a single edge with priority reward$(\Pi^\tau_{i,j}(G))$. The operation reduce is doing this for every pair of contact nodes. We define the reduce-operation on arbitrary n-game graphs, but later we will only apply it to strategy reducts: reduce(G) is the game graph $(\{1, \ldots, n\}, F, \varrho)$, where $\varrho(i) = \rho(\tau(i))$ for all $1 \leq i \leq n$ and $(i, p, j) \in F$ if and only if $\Pi^\tau_{i,j}(G) \neq \emptyset$ and reward$(\Pi^\tau_{i,j}(G)) = p$. We identify reduce(G) with the n-game graph $((\{1, \ldots, n\}, F, \varrho), \text{id}_{\{1,\ldots,n\}})$.

Lemma 1. *The operation* reduce *is polynomial time computable.*

Interfaces and realizability For a given variable X_i of an SLP $\mathcal{S}$, the type(X_i)-game graph eval(X_i) may have exponential size in $|\mathcal{S}|$, and the same is true for some strategy reduct G' of eval(X_i). We will store all the relevant information about G' in a so called n-interface of G', which can be stored in polynomial space. An n-*interface* S over the priorities C is a tuple $S = (\{1, \ldots, n\}, F, \varrho, I, U)$ s.t. (i) $(\{1, \ldots, n\}, F, \varrho)$ is a game graph over the priorities C, (ii) $I \subseteq \{1, \ldots, n\}$, and (iii) $U \subseteq \varrho^{-1}(\text{Eve})$ is a subset of the nodes which belong to Eve. The notion of an interface is inspired by the notion of a border from [19]. The n-interface S is *realized* by the n-game graph $G = (H, \tau)$ if there is a strategy reduct $G' = (H', \tau)$ of G w.r.t. $\tau(U)$ s.t. (i) $(\{1, \ldots, n\}, F, \varrho) =$ reduce(G'), and (ii) $i \in I$ if and only if there is a τ-internal path π in G' which begins at $\tau(i)$ and which player Adam wins (recall that π has to be non-empty). We also say that G' is a *witness* that S is realized by G. By first guessing a strategy reduct and then applying Lemma 1, we obtain:

Lemma 2. *The problem of checking, whether a given n-interface is realized by a given n-game graph, belongs to* NP.

Example 1. The following figure shows a 3-game graph G together with a strategy reduct G' w.r.t. $\{\tau(2)\}$ (node $\tau(i)$ is labeled with i and ♦-labeled (resp. ■-labeled) nodes belong to Eve (resp. Adam). The interface $S = (\{1, 2, 3\}, F, \varrho, I, U)$ with $I = \{1\}$ and $U = \{2\}$ is realized by G, and G' is a witness for this.

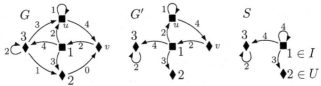

We have $1 \in I$, because the infinite τ-internal path $\tau(1), 2, (u, 1)^\omega$ starts in node $\tau(1)$ in G' and Adam wins this path. The loop with priority 4 at node 1 in S exists due to the $\tau\tau$-internal path $\tau(1), 2, u, 4, v, 2, \tau(1)$ in G'.

Operations on interfaces Our PSPACE-algorithm will only manipulate n-interfaces instead of whole n-game graphs. In order to do this, we have to extend the operations $\oplus$, rename$_f$, forget, and glue on interfaces. The crucial correctness property is formalized in this section for arbitrary operations. In the following we restrict to n-game graphs $G = (H, \tau)$ such that every contact node $\tau(i)$ has at least one outgoing edge. This can be ensured by adding for a contact node $\tau(i)$ without outgoing edges an outgoing edge to a new internal node v, which is a dead end and which belongs to the same player as $\tau(i)$. This new edge has no influence on the winner of a parity game.

Let op be a partial operation, mapping a k-tuple $(G_1, \ldots, G_k)$, where G_i is an n_i-game graph, to an n-game graph op$(G_1, \ldots, G_k)$. We say that op has a *faithful polynomial implementation (briefly FPI) on interfaces*, if there exists a partial *polynomial time computable* operation op^s, mapping a k-tuple $(S_1, \ldots, S_k)$, where S_i is an n_i-interface, to an n-interface op$(S_1, \ldots, S_k)$ s.t. the following is true: Whenever $G = \text{op}(G_1, \ldots, G_k)$, where G_i is an n_i-game graph and G is an n-game graph, and S is an n-interface, then G realizes S if and only if there exist n_i-interfaces S_i ($1 \leq i \leq k$) s.t. $S = \text{op}(S_1, \ldots, S_k)$ and G_i realizes S_i.

Lemma 3. *The operations* $\oplus$, *rename$_f$, forget, and glue have FPIs on interfaces.*

Proof. The operations $\oplus^s$ and rename^s_f are straight-forward: $\oplus^s$ builds the disjoint union of two interfaces, and rename^s_f renames the contact nodes according to the permutation f. Let us now describe the operation glue^s, the operation forget^s can be defined similarly. Let $S = (\{1, \ldots, n\}, F, \varrho, I, U)$ be an n-interface. Then $\text{glue}^s(S)$ is only defined if (i) $n \geq 2$, (ii) $\varrho(n) = \varrho(n-1)$ (thus, node $n-1$ and n belong to the same player and can actually be glued), and (iii) if $\varrho(n) = \varrho(n-1) = $ Eve then $n-1 \in U$ or $n \in U$. Then $\text{glue}^s(S) = (\{1, \ldots, n-1\}, F', \varrho', I', U')$, where:

- $(\{1, \ldots, n-1\}, F', \varrho') = \text{reduce}(\text{glue}(\{1, \ldots, n\}, F, \varrho))$.
- $I' = I \setminus \{n\} \cup \{n-1\}$ if $(n-1 \in I$ or $n \in I)$, otherwise $I' = I$.
- $U' = U \setminus \{n\}$ if $n-1, n \in U$, otherwise $U' = U \setminus \{n-1, n\}$.

The intuition behind this definition is the following. Assume that the n-interface S is realized by an n-game graph $G = (H, \tau)$ and let G' be a witness for this. We want to define $\text{glue}^s(S) = (\{1, \ldots, n-1\}, F', \varrho', I', U')$ in such a way that $\text{glue}^s(S)$ is realized by $\text{glue}(G)$ and moreover $\text{glue}(G')$ is a witness for this. Note that by assumption (i)–(iii), $\text{glue}(G')$ is in fact a strategy reduct of $\text{glue}(G)$. In order to determine the maximal priority of an optimal path for Adam from $\tau(i)$ to $\tau(j)$ in $\text{glue}(G')$, it suffices to look at the $(n-1)$-game graph $K = \text{glue}(\{1, \ldots, n\}, F, \varrho)$, i.e., to calculate $\text{reduce}(K)$. This graph will be therefore $(\{1, \ldots, n-1\}, F', \varrho')$. Note that in K, there may be more than one edge between two contact nodes. By applying reduce to K we select the optimal edge for player Adam between two contact nodes. Finally, if $n-1 \in I$ or $n \in I$, i.e., there exists a τ-internal path in G' that starts in $\tau(n-1)$ or in $\tau(n)$ and which player Adam wins, then we can be sure that there exists a τ-internal path in $\text{glue}(G')$ that starts in $\tau(n-1)$ and which player Adam wins. Here it is important that τ-internal paths are non-empty. Hence, we put $n-1$ into I'. □

Parity games over SLP-defined graphs We are now ready to prove an upper bound of PSPACE for the parity game problem on graphs that are represented by SLPs:

Theorem 1. *For a given SLP $\mathcal{S} = (X_i := t_i)_{1 \leq i \leq l}$, where $\text{eval}(\mathcal{S}) = (G, \tau)$ is a 1-game graph, we can decide in PSPACE, whether $(G, \tau(1), \text{Eve}) \in \text{PARITY}$.*

Proof. W.l.o.g. we can assume that node $\tau(1)$ belongs to Eve and that $\tau(1)$ has no incoming edge; this property can be easily enforced by adding a new node. Due to this convention, we have $(G, \tau(1), \text{Eve}) \in \text{PARITY}$ if and only if $\text{eval}(G)$ realizes the interface $S_l = (\{1\}, \emptyset, [1 \mapsto \text{Eve}], \emptyset, \emptyset)$. We present the algorithm in form of the following procedure $\mathcal{P}$, which works on a polynomial time bounded alternating Turing machine; $(Q_\forall)$ (resp. $(Q_\exists)$) indicates that the machine branches universally (resp. existentially). Procedure $\mathcal{P}$ has two parameters, the current line i of the SLP and a $\text{type}(X_i)$-interface S_i, and it returns $\texttt{true}$ if and only if S_i is realized by $\text{eval}(X_i)$. At the beginning we call $\mathcal{P}$ with the parameter (l, S_l).

```
procedure  P(i ∈ {1,...,l}, Sᵢ) return boolean is
    if tᵢ is a type(Xᵢ)-game graph then return (tᵢ realizes Sᵢ)        (∗)
    elseif tᵢ = op(Xᵢ₁,...,Xᵢₖ) then
        (Q∃): for 1 ≤ j ≤ k guess type(Xᵢⱼ)-interfaces Sᵢⱼ s.t. Sᵢ = opˢ(Sᵢ₁,...,Sᵢₖ)
        (Q∀): return ⋀₁≤ⱼ≤ₖ P(iⱼ, Sᵢⱼ)
    endif
```

The correctness of the algorithm follows easily by induction on the index $i \in \{1, \ldots, l\}$. For the alternating polynomial time bound note that: (i) the test whether t_i realizes S_i in line $(*)$ is in NP by Lemma 2 and (ii) each of the operations op^s is computable in polynomial time by Lemma 3 and the definition of an FPI.   □

By the following theorem, we can improve the PSPACE upper bound from Thm. 1 to NP ∩ coNP, when we restrict to c-bounded SLPs for some fixed constant c.

Theorem 2. *Let $c \in \mathbb{N}$ be a fixed constant. The problem of checking $(G, \tau(1), \text{Eve}) \in$ PARITY for a given c-bounded SLP $\mathcal{S} = (X_i := t_i)_{1 \le i \le l}$, where $\mathrm{eval}(\mathcal{S}) = (G, \tau)$ is a 1-game graph, belongs to NP ∩ coNP.*

Proof. By the determinacy theorem it suffices to prove membership in NP. The main idea is to guess for all $1 \le i \le l$ a set of type(X_i)-interfaces M_i. Note that for the representation of a single interface $c^2 \log |C| + 2c$ bits suffice, where C is the set of priorities used in the SLP $\mathcal{S}$. Thus, every M_i contains at most $|C|^{c^2} 2^{2c}$ many interfaces. Hence, since c is a constant, we can guess in polynomial time the set $\bigcup_{1 \le i \le l} M_i$ of interfaces. Then we check whether for all $1 \le i \le l$ the set M_i is a subset of the set of interfaces which are realized by $\mathrm{eval}(X_i)$. In case t_i is an n-game graph we can do this in NP by Lemma 2. If $t_i = \mathrm{op}(X_{i_1}, \ldots, X_{i_k})$, then one has to check, whether for every $S_i \in M_i$ there are $S_{i_j} \in M_{i_j}$ $(1 \le j \le k)$ s.t. $S_i = \mathrm{op}^s(S_{i_1}, \ldots, S_{i_k})$.   □

4   The Modal μ-Calculus over SLP-defined Graphs

In this section, we show that both the data and combined complexity of the modal μ-calculus over transition systems that are represented by SLPs is PSPACE-complete. The upper bound extends [1, Thm. 9] concerning CTL. Note that a translation of the modal μ-calculus into MSO and an application of the MSO-model-checking algorithm from [17] leads to a higher upper bound, namely within the exponential time hierarchy (already for data complexity). For c-bounded SLPs we obtain an upper bound of NP ∩ coNP for the data complexity, whereas the combined complexity remains PSPACE. For the upper bounds we use a reduction to parity games, which is analogous to the corresponding reduction for explicitly given input graphs [3,4]:

Theorem 3. *The following problem can be calculated in polynomial time:*
INPUT: A c-bounded SLP $\mathcal{S}_t$ defining a transition system $\mathrm{eval}(\mathcal{S}_t)$, a state q of $\mathrm{eval}(\mathcal{S}_t)$, and a sentence φ of the modal μ-calculus having exactly k subformulas.
OUTPUT: A $(c \cdot k)$-bounded SLP $\mathcal{S}_g$ defining a game graph $\mathrm{eval}(\mathcal{S}_g)$ and a node v of $\mathrm{eval}(\mathcal{S}_g)$ s.t. $(\mathrm{eval}(\mathcal{S}_t), q) \models \varphi$ if and only if $(\mathrm{eval}(\mathcal{S}_g), v, \text{Eve}) \in$ PARITY.

Corollary 1. *The following problem is PSPACE-complete:*
INPUT: An SLP $\mathcal{S}$ defining a transition system $\mathrm{eval}(\mathcal{S})$, a state q of $\mathrm{eval}(\mathcal{S})$, and a sentence φ of the modal μ-calculus.
QUESTION: $(\mathrm{eval}(\mathcal{S}), q) \models \varphi$?
Moreover: (i) the above problem is already PSPACE-complete when restricted to c-bounded SLPs (for a suitably large c), and (ii) there exists already a fixed sentence of the modal μ-calculus for which the above problem is PSPACE-complete.

Proof. The upper bound follows from Thm. 1 and 3. For the lower bounds, we use two results from [1]: The combined complexity of CTL for hierarchical state machines is PSPACE-complete [1, Thm. 9]; recall that CTL is a fragment of the modal μ-calculus. It is easy to see that the hierarchical state machines from the proof of [1, Thm. 9] can be generated by a 5-bounded SLP, which gives us (i). Moreover, there is already a fixed CTL-sentence s.t. the model-checking problem for hierarchical state machines (and thus SLPs) is PSPACE-complete [1, Thm. 11]. This implies (ii).   □

When we restrict both to c-bounded SLPs and to a fixed sentence φ, then we obtain a better upper bound:

Corollary 2. *Let* $c \in \mathbb{N}$ *be a fixed constant and* φ *be a fixed sentence of the modal* μ*-calculus. The problem of checking* $(\mathrm{eval}(\mathcal{S}_t), q) \models \varphi$ *for a given* c*-bounded SLP* $\mathcal{S}_t$ *(s.t.* $\mathrm{eval}(\mathcal{S}_t)$ *is a transition system) and a state* q *of* $\mathrm{eval}(\mathcal{S}_t)$ *belongs to* NP ∩ coNP.

Proof. If φ has k many subformulas, then the SLP $\mathcal{S}_g$ from Thm. 3 is $(c \cdot k)$-bounded. Since φ and φ are fixed, $c \cdot k$ is a fixed constant. The corollary follows from Thm. 2.   □

5   LFP and MLFP over SLP-defined Graphs

In this section we state our results concerning MLFP and LFP. An upper bound for the most general case (combined complexity of LFP) is given by the next theorem; recall that EXP is also the combined complexity of LFP for explicitly given structures.

Theorem 4. *It can be checked in* EXP, *whether* $\mathrm{eval}(\mathcal{S}) \models \varphi$ *for a given SLP* $\mathcal{S}$ *and a given LFP-sentence* φ.

Only for the data complexity of MLFP we obtain a better upper bound. MLFP is a fragment of MSO (monadic second order logic). Since for every fixed MSO-sentence φ and every fixed constant c the model-checking problem for φ on structures represented by c-bounded SLPs belongs to the polynomial time hierarchy PH [17, Thm. 6.3], we obtain:

Theorem 5. *For every fixed MLFP sentence* φ *and every fixed constant* $c \in \mathbb{N}$, *the problem of checking* $\mathrm{eval}(\mathcal{S}) \models \varphi$ *for a given* c*-bounded SLP* $\mathcal{S}$ *belongs to* PH.

Finally, we state several EXP lower bounds. Together with Thm. 4 we get the EXP completeness results in Table 1. We start with the data complexity of LFP:

Theorem 6. *There is a fixed LFP-sentence* φ *s.t. it is* EXP-*hard to check whether* $\mathrm{eval}(\mathcal{S}) \models \varphi$ *for a given* 4-*bounded SLP* $\mathcal{S}$.

If we do not restrict to c-bounded hierarchical graph definitions, then an EXP lower bound can be also shown for the data complexity of MLFP:

Theorem 7. *There exists a fixed MLFP-sentence* φ *s.t. it is* EXP-*hard to check whether* $\mathrm{eval}(\mathcal{S}) \models \varphi$ *for a given SLP* $\mathcal{S}$.

For the combined complexity of MLFP, we can derive an EXP lower bound also for the c-bounded case:

Theorem 8. *It is* EXP-*hard to check* $\mathrm{eval}(\mathcal{S}) \models \varphi$ *for a given* 3-*bounded SLP* $\mathcal{S}$ *and a given MLFP-sentence* φ.

References

1. R. Alur and M. Yannakakis. Model checking of hierarchical state machines. *ACM Trans. Program. Lang. Syst.*, 23(3):273–303, 2001.
2. S. Dziembowski. Bounded-variable fixpoint queries are PSPACE-complete. In *Proc. CSL'96*, LNCS 1258, pages 89–105. Springer, 1996.
3. E. A. Emerson and C. S. Jutla. Tree automata, mu-calculus and determinacy (extended abstract). In *Proc. FOCS'91*, pages 132–142. IEEE Computer Society Press, 1991.
4. E. A. Emerson, C. S. Jutla, and A. P. Sistla. On model checking for the μ-calculus and its fragments. *Theor. Comput. Sci.*, 258(1-2):491–522, 2001.
5. E. A. Emerson and C.-L. Lei. Efficient model checking in fragments of the propositional mu-calculus (extended abstract). In *Proc. LICS'86*, pages 267–278. IEEE Computer Society Press, 1986.
6. J. Engelfriet. Context-free graph grammars. In G. Rozenberg and A. Salomaa, editors, *Handbook of Formal Languages, Volume 3: Beyond Words*, pages 125–213. Springer, 1997.
7. S. Göller and M. Lohrey. Fixpoint logics on hierarchical structures. Tech. Rep. 2005/3, University of Stuttgart, Germany, 2005. ftp.informatik.uni-stuttgart.de/pub/library/ncstrl.ustuttgart_fi/TR-2005-04/.
8. E. Grädel, W. Thomas, and T. Wilke. *Automata, Logics, and Infinite Games*. LNCS 2500. Springer, 2002.
9. N. Immerman. Relational queries computable in polynomial time. *Inf. Control*, 68(1–3):86–104, 1986.
10. M. Jurdziński. Deciding the winner in parity games is in UP and co-UP. *Inf. Process. Lett.*, 68(3):119–124, 1998.
11. M. Jurdziński. Small progress measures for solving parity games. In *Proc. STACS 2000*, LNCS 1770, pages 290–301. Springer, 2000.
12. T. Lengauer. Hierarchical planarity testing algorithms. *J. Assoc. Comput. Mach.*, 36(3):474–509, 1989.
13. T. Lengauer and K. W. Wagner. The correlation between the complexities of the nonhierarchical and hierarchical versions of graph problems. *J. Comput. Syst. Sci.*, 44:63–93, 1992.
14. T. Lengauer and E. Wanke. Efficient solution of connectivity problems on hierarchically defined graphs. *SIAM J. Comput.*, 17(6):1063–1080, 1988.
15. L. Libkin. *Elements of Finite Model Theory*. Springer, 2004.
16. M. Lohrey. Model-checking hierarchical graphs. Tech. Rep. 2005/1, University of Stuttgart, Germany, 2005. ftp.informatik.uni-stuttgart.de/pub/library/ncstrl.ustuttgart_fi/TR-2005-1/.
17. M. Lohrey. Model-checking hierarchical structures. In *Proc. LICS 2005*, pages 168–177. IEEE Computer Society Press, 2005.
18. M. V. Marathe, H. B. Hunt III, R. E. Stearns, and V. Radhakrishnan. Approximation algorithms for PSPACE-hard hierarchically and periodically specified problems. *SIAM J. Comput.*, 27(5):1237–1261, 1998.
19. J. Obdržálek. Fast mu-calculus model checking when tree-width is bounded. In *CAV'03*, LNCS 2725, pages 80–92. Springer, 2003.
20. C. H. Papadimitriou. *Computational Complexity*. Addison Wesley, 1994.
21. M. Y. Vardi. The complexity of relational query languages (extended abstract). In *Proc. STOC 1982*, pages 137–146. ACM Press, 1982.
22. M. Y. Vardi. On the complexity of bounded-variable queries. In *Proc. PODS 1995*, pages 266–276. ACM Press, 1995.

The Equivalence Problem for Deterministic MSO Tree Transducers Is Decidable

Joost Engelfriet[1] and Sebastian Maneth[2]*

[1] LIACS, Leiden University, The Netherlands
engelfri@liacs.nl
[2] Faculté I & C, EPFL, Switzerland
sebastian.maneth@epfl.ch

Abstract. It is decidable for deterministic MSO definable graph-to-string or graph-to-tree transducers whether they are equivalent on a context-free set of graphs.

1   Introduction

It is well known that the equivalence problem for nondeterministic (one-way) finite state transducers is undecidable, even when they cannot read or write the empty string [Gri68]. In contrast, equivalence *is* decidable for deterministic finite state transducers, even for two-way transducers [Gur82]. The question arises whether these results can be generalized from strings to transducers working on more complex structures like, e.g., trees or graphs. There is no accepted notion of finite state transducer working on graphs; instead, it is believed that transductions expressed in monadic second-order logic (MSO) are the natural counterpart of finite state transductions on graphs. The idea is to define an output graph by interpreting fixed MSO formulas on a given input graph. In fact, if the input and output graphs of such an MSO graph transducer are strings, then the resulting transductions (in the deterministic case) are precisely the deterministic two-way finite state transductions [EH01]. Hence, by the above, equivalence is decidable for deterministic MSO string transducers. A nondeterministic MSO graph transducer can easily simulate a nondeterministic finite state transducer that cannot read the empty string; hence, equivalence is undecidable. Actually, even for deterministic MSO graph transducers equivalence is undecidable. This is due to the fact that MSO is undecidable for graphs (Propositions 5.2.1 and 5.2.2 of [Cou97]); cf. end of Section 3 for more details. The question remains whether deterministic MSO tree transducers have a decidable equivalence problem. Recently, these transducers have been characterized by certain attribute grammars [BE00] and macro tree transducers [EM99]. However, for both models it is unknown whether equivalence is decidable. Here we give an affirmative answer: equivalence of deterministic MSO tree transducers is decidable. This result has several applications; for instance, it implies that XML queries of linear size increase have decidable equivalence, by the results of [MSV03], [EM03a], [EM03b], [Man03], and [MBPS05]. Our proof generalizes the one of [Gur82] (see also [Iba82]): it is based on the fact that certain sets are semilinear. It proceeds roughly as follows: two transducers M_1, M_2 are equivalent if there is no input s and position n such that the symbol at

---

* Present address: National ICT Australia Ltd. sebastian.maneth@nicta.com.au

R. Ramanujam and S. Sen (Eds.): FSTTCS 2005, LNCS 3821, pp. 495–504, 2005.

position n of M_1's output on s is different from the symbol at position n of M_2's output on s. Hence, we must test whether there exists an n and distinct symbols a, b such that (n, n) is contained in the set $S^{a,b}$ of all pairs (i, j) where M_1's output at position i is a and M_2's output at position j is b, for some input s. The set $S^{a,b}$ is semilinear which implies that the existence of such an n is decidable. Semilinearity of $S^{a,b}$ is proved using known results from the theory of MSO graph transducers, by coding the pair (i, j) as a discrete graph with i a-labeled nodes and j b-labeled nodes.

2 Preliminaries

The reader is assumed to be familiar with MSO on graphs and with MSO graph transducers, see, e.g., the survey papers [Cou97, Cou94].

A graph alphabet is a pair (Σ, Γ) of alphabets of node and edge labels, respectively. A graph over (Σ, Γ) is a tuple (V, E, λ) where V is the finite set of nodes, $E \subseteq V \times \Gamma \times V$ is the set of edges, and $\lambda : V \to \Sigma$ is the node labeling function. The set of all graphs over (Σ, Γ) is denoted $\mathrm{GR}(\Sigma, \Gamma)$. The language $\mathrm{MSO}(\Sigma, \Gamma)$ of monadic second-order (MSO) formulas over (Σ, Γ) uses node variables $x, y, \ldots$ and node-set variables $X, Y, \ldots$; both can be quantified with $\exists$ and $\forall$. It has atomic formulas $\mathrm{lab}_\sigma(x)$ for $\sigma \in \Sigma$, denoting that x is labeled σ, $\mathrm{edg}_\gamma(x, y)$ for $\gamma \in \Gamma$, denoting that there is a γ-labeled edge from x to y, and $x \in X$ denoting that x is in X. For $g \in \mathrm{GR}(\Sigma, \Gamma)$ and a closed formula ψ in $\mathrm{MSO}(\Sigma, \Gamma)$ we write $g \models \psi$ if g satisfies ψ; similarly, if ψ has free variables x or x, y and u, v are nodes of g, then we write $(g, u) \models \psi$ or $(g, u, v) \models \psi$ if g satisfies ψ with $x = u$ or with $x = u, y = v$, respectively.

Let $(\Sigma_1, \Gamma_1), (\Sigma_2, \Gamma_2)$ be graph alphabets. A *deterministic MSO graph transducer* M *(from* (Σ_1, Γ_1) *to* (Σ_2, Γ_2)) is a tuple $(C, \varphi_{\mathrm{dom}}, \Psi, X)$ where C is a finite set of *copy names*, $\varphi_{\mathrm{dom}} \in \mathrm{MSO}(\Sigma_1, \Gamma_1)$ is the closed *domain formula*, $\Psi = \{\psi_{c,\sigma}(x)\}_{c \in C, \sigma \in \Sigma_2}$ is a family of *node formulas*, i.e., MSO formulas $\psi_{c,\sigma}(x)$ over (Σ_1, Γ_1) with one free variable x, and $X = \{\chi_{c,c',\gamma}(x, y)\}_{c,c' \in C, \gamma \in \Gamma_2}$ is a family of *edge formulas*, i.e., MSO formulas $\chi_{c,c',\gamma}(x, y)$ over (Σ_1, Γ_1) with two free variables x, y.

The purpose of the node formulas of an MSO graph transducer is twofold: (1) they define which (copies of) nodes of the input graph are used, and they define their labels. As can be seen easily, it is no loss of generality to require that, for every $c \in C$, the formulas $\psi_{c,\sigma}(x)$ are mutually exclusive.

Given $g \in \mathrm{GR}(\Sigma_1, \Gamma_1)$, the graph $h = \tau_M(g) \in \mathrm{GR}(\Sigma_2, \Gamma_2)$ is defined if $g \models \varphi_{\mathrm{dom}}$, and then $V_h = \{(c, u) \mid c \in C, u \in V_g,$ there is exactly one $\sigma \in \Sigma_2$ such that $(g, u) \models \psi_{c,\sigma}(x)\}$, $E_h = \{((c, u), \gamma, (c', u')) \mid (c, u), (c', u') \in V_h, \gamma \in \Gamma_2,$ and $(g, u, u') \models \chi_{c,c',\gamma}(x, y)\}$, and $\lambda_h = \{((c, u), \sigma) \mid (c, u) \in V_h, \sigma \in \Sigma_2,$ and $(g, u) \models \psi_{c,\sigma}(x)\}$. Hence, τ_M is a partial function from $\mathrm{GR}(\Sigma_1, \Gamma_1)$ to $\mathrm{GR}(\Sigma_2, \Gamma_2)$ with $\mathrm{dom}(\tau_M) = \{g \in \mathrm{GR}(\Sigma_1, \Gamma_1) \mid g \models \varphi_{\mathrm{dom}}\}$.

In the sequel we often identify a transducer M with its transduction τ_M, and simply write, e.g., $M(g)$ in place of $\tau_M(g)$.

A *(nondeterministic) MSO graph transducer* is obtained from a deterministic one by allowing all formulas to use fixed free node-set variables $Y_1, Y_2, \ldots$, called *parameters*. For each valuation of the parameters (by sets of nodes of the input graph) that satisfies the domain formula, the other formulas define the output graph as before. Hence each such valuation may lead to a different output graph for the given input graph. Thus, $\tau_M \subseteq \mathrm{GR}(\Sigma_1, \Gamma_1) \times \mathrm{GR}(\Sigma_2, \Gamma_2)$.

For an alphabet Δ and $a_1, \ldots, a_n \in \Delta$, $n \geq 0$, we identify the string $w = a_1 a_2 \cdots a_n$ with the graph in $\mathrm{GR}(\{\#\}, \Delta)$ that has $\#$-labeled nodes $v_1, \ldots, v_{n+1}$ and, for $1 \leq i \leq n$, an a_i-labeled edge from v_i to v_{i+1}. For $1 \leq i \leq n$, we denote by w/i the i-th letter a_i of w.

Let Σ be a ranked alphabet, i.e., an alphabet Σ together with a mapping $\mathrm{rank}_\Sigma : \Sigma \to \mathbb{N}$. Let m be the maximal rank of symbols in Σ. A *tree* (*over* Σ) is an acyclic, connected graph in $\mathrm{GR}(\Sigma, \{1, \ldots, m\})$, with exactly one node that has no incoming edges (the root), and, for $\sigma \in \Sigma$, every σ-labeled node has exactly $\mathrm{rank}_\Sigma(\sigma)$ outgoing edges, labeled $1, 2, \ldots, \mathrm{rank}_\Sigma(\sigma)$, respectively. The set of all trees over Σ is denoted by T_Σ.

Let M be an MSO graph transducer and let X, Y be sets of graphs. Then M is called an MSO X-to-Y transducer, if $\mathrm{dom}(M) \subseteq X$ and $\mathrm{range}(M) \subseteq Y$, and it is an MSO X transducer if additionally $Y = X$. Thus, as an example, an MSO tree-to-string transducer translates trees into strings.

Convention: All lemmas stated in this paper are *effective*.

Example 1. (i) Let Σ be the ranked alphabet consisting of the binary symbol σ and the nullary symbol a. Consider the deterministic MSO tree-to-string transducers M_1, M_2 that translate trees s over Σ into strings b^n, where $n = i + j + k - 1$, i is the number of binary nodes on the left-most path in s, j is the number of leaves in s, and k is the number of binary nodes on the right-most path in s. Let us denote n by $\mathrm{outer}(s)$. Roughly, the transducer M_1 realizes the translation by doing a depth-first

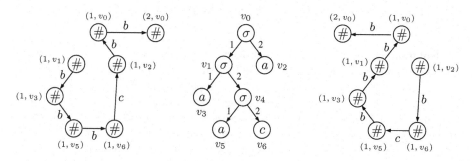

Fig. 1. The tree $s = \sigma(\sigma(a, \sigma(a, c)), a)$ in the center, $M_3(s) = bbbcbb$ on the left, and $M_4(s) = bcbbbb$ on the right.

left-to-right traversal through s, while M_2 does a depth-first right-to-left traversal. Let $M_1 = (\{1, 2\}, \varphi_{\text{tree}}, \{\psi_{1,\#}(x), \psi_{2,\#}(x)\}, \{\chi_{c,c',b}(x, y)\}_{c,c' \in \{1,2\}})$ where φ_{tree} is an MSO formula expressing that a graph is a tree, and

$$\psi_{1,\#}(x) \quad \equiv \mathrm{lab}_a(x) \vee (\exists y)(\mathrm{root}(y) \wedge (\mathrm{edg}_1^*(y,x) \vee \mathrm{edg}_2^*(y,x)))$$
$$\psi_{2,\#}(x) \quad \equiv \mathrm{root}(x)$$
$$\chi_{1,1,b}(x,y) \equiv \neg\mathrm{root}(x) \wedge (\mathrm{edg}_1(x,y) \vee \mathrm{yield}(x,y) \vee \mathrm{edg}_2(y,x))$$
$$\chi_{1,2,b}(x,y) \equiv \mathrm{root}(x)$$
$$\chi_{2,1,b}(x,y) \equiv \chi_{2,2,b}(x,y) \equiv \mathrm{false}.$$

Here, $\mathrm{root}(y)$ denotes that y is the root node, $\mathrm{yield}(x,y)$ denotes that x is a leaf and y is the next leaf in pre-order, and $\mathrm{edg}_1^*(x,y)$ denotes the transitive closure of edg_1 (similarly edg_2^*); all these can easily be expressed in MSO. The transducer M_2 is defined as M_1 with the only difference that $\chi_{1,1,b}(x,y) \equiv \neg\mathrm{root}(x) \wedge (\mathrm{edg}_2(x,y) \vee \mathrm{yield}(y,x) \vee \mathrm{edg}_1(y,x))$.

(ii) Next, consider the transducers M_3, M_4, obtained from M_1, M_2 as follows. We now take input trees over Σ' that additionally contains the nullary symbol c which is translated into c. Hence, M_3 becomes

$$\psi_{1,\#}(x) \quad \equiv \mathrm{lab}_a(x) \vee \mathrm{lab}_c(x) \vee (\exists y)(\mathrm{root}(y) \wedge (\mathrm{edg}_1^*(y,x) \vee \mathrm{edg}_2^*(y,x)))$$
$$\psi_{2,\#}(x) \quad \equiv \mathrm{root}(x)$$
$$\chi_{1,1,b}(x,y) \equiv \neg\mathrm{root}(x) \wedge \neg\mathrm{lab}_c(x) \wedge (\mathrm{edg}_1(x,y) \vee \mathrm{yield}(x,y) \vee \mathrm{edg}_2(y,x))$$
$$\chi_{1,1,c}(x,y) \equiv \neg\mathrm{root}(x) \wedge \mathrm{lab}_c(x) \wedge (\mathrm{edg}_1(x,y) \vee \mathrm{yield}(x,y) \vee \mathrm{edg}_2(y,x))$$
$$\chi_{1,2,b}(x,y) \equiv \mathrm{root}(x) \wedge \neg\mathrm{lab}_c(x)$$
$$\chi_{1,2,c}(x,y) \equiv \mathrm{root}(x) \wedge \mathrm{lab}_c(x)$$
$$\chi_{2,1,b}(x,y) \equiv \chi_{2,2,b}(x,y) \equiv \chi_{2,1,c}(x,y) \equiv \chi_{2,2,c}(x,y) \equiv \mathrm{false}.$$

Consider the input tree $s = \sigma(\sigma(a, \sigma(a,c)), a))$. Then, as can be seen in Fig. 1, M_3 generates as output the string $M_3(s) = bbbcbb$ and M_4 generates $M_4(s) = bcbbbb$.

The following lemma contains a basic fact about MSO definable graph transductions; see, e.g., Proposition 3.2 in [Cou94].

Lemma 2. *The (deterministic) MSO graph transductions are closed under composition.*

Notation. Let $M_1; M_2$ denote a transducer M for which $\tau_M = \tau_{M_2} \circ \tau_{M_1}$; note that M is deterministic, if M_1 and M_2 are. By Lemma 2, $M_1; M_2$ effectively exists.

A *discrete graph* (dgraph, for short) is a graph without edges. Let g be a dgraph over $(\Sigma, \varnothing)$ with $\Sigma = \{\sigma_1, \ldots, \sigma_k\}$. Define $\mathrm{Par}(g)$ as the vector $(n_1, \ldots, n_k)$ in $\mathbb{N}^k$ such that, for $1 \leq i \leq k$, n_i is the number of σ_i-labeled nodes in g. Similarly, for a string $w \in \Sigma^*$, $\mathrm{Par}(w)$ is the vector in $\mathbb{N}^k$ such that the i-th component is the number of σ_i's in w. We denote by $\mathrm{dgr}(w)$ the (unique) dgraph g such that $\mathrm{Par}(g) = \mathrm{Par}(w)$. For a set S of dgraphs or strings, $\mathrm{Par}(S)$ is the set of all $\mathrm{Par}(g)$ for $g \in S$. A set $P \subseteq \mathbb{N}^k$ is *semilinear* if there exists a regular language R such that $P = \mathrm{Par}(R)$, cf. [Par66, GS64, Gin66] for the more usual definition of semilinearity. The set S is *Parikh* if $\mathrm{Par}(S)$ is semilinear. Note that since $\mathrm{Par}(R) = \varnothing$ iff $R = \varnothing$, emptiness of semilinear sets is decidable.

A set of graphs is *NR* if it is generated by a context-free node replacement graph grammar, see, e.g., [Eng97, Cou94]; it is also called C-edNCE or VR. Such grammars have productions of the form $X \to (g, C)$ where X is a nonterminal, g is a graph, and

C is a finite set of connection instructions. The application of $X \to (g, C)$ to an X-labeled node v of a sentential form works as follows. First v (and edges to and from it) is removed, g is disjointly added, and then edges from the former neighbors of v to nodes in g are established, according to the connection instructions. A connection instruction is of the form $(\sigma, \beta, \gamma, x, d)$ where σ is a node label, β, γ are edge labels, x is a node of g, and $d \in \{\text{in}, \text{out}\}$. For $d = \text{out}$ it means that if there was a β-labeled edge from v to a σ-labeled neighbor w of v, then a γ-labeled edge from x to w is generated. Similarly, for "in", edges from a w to x are generated. The derivation relation of the grammar should satisfy a certain confluence requirement, see Definition 4.6 of [Eng97].

Lemma 3. *(Theorem 7.1 of [Cou94]) The images of NR sets of graphs under MSO graph-to-dgraph transductions are Parikh.*

In fact, the class of NR sets of graphs is closed under MSO graph transductions (see Theorem 4.2(3) of [Cou94], or Section 5 of [Eng97]) and NR sets of graphs are Parikh (see Proposition 4.11 of [Eng97]).

A useful property of semilinear sets is their (effective) closure under intersection. It implies the following lemma.

Lemma 4. *It is decidable for a semilinear set $S \subseteq \mathbb{N}^2$ whether there exists an $n \in \mathbb{N}$ such that $(n, n) \in S$.*

Proof. Let $P = \{(n, n) \mid n \in \mathbb{N}\} = \text{Par}((ab)^*)$. The lemma holds because $S \cap P$ is semilinear [GS64, Gin66] and semilinear sets have a decidable emptiness problem. □

Note that Lemma 4 can alternatively be proved without using the fact that semilinear sets are closed under intersection: let R be a regular language with $\text{Par}(R) = S$ and let C be the context-free language containing all strings over $\{a, b\}$ that have an equal number of a's and b's. Then $C' = R \cap C$ is context-free and hence $\text{Par}(C')$ is semilinear by Parikh's Theorem [Par66].

3   Main Result

The main result of this paper (Theorem 8) is that it is decidable for deterministic MSO graph-to-string or graph-to-tree transducers whether they are equivalent on an NR set of graphs, cf. the Abstract.

Recall from the Preliminaries that for a string w, w/i denotes the i-th letter of w.

Lemma 5. *Let Δ be an alphabet and $a \in \Delta$. There exists an MSO string-to-dgraph transducer N_Δ^a such that for every $w \in \Delta^*$,*

$$N_\Delta^a(w) = \{\text{dgr}(a^n) \mid w/n = a\}.$$

Proof. The transducer N_Δ^a uses one parameter Y_1 to nondeterministically choose a node v that has an outgoing a-labeled edge (if there is one). It copies v and all input nodes to the left of v, and labels them a. There are no edge formulas because dgraphs have no edges. Define $N_\Delta^a = (\{1\}, \varphi_{\text{dom}}(Y_1), \psi_{1,a}(x, Y_1), \varnothing)$ with

$$\varphi_{\text{dom}}(Y_1) \equiv \varphi_{\text{string}} \wedge \text{singleton}(Y_1) \wedge (\exists x)(\exists y)(\text{edg}_a(x, y) \wedge x \in Y_1)$$
$$\psi_{1,a}(x, Y_1) \equiv (\exists y)(x \preceq y \wedge y \in Y_1)$$

where φ_{string} expresses that a graph is a string, $\text{singleton}(Y_1)$ expresses that Y_1 is a singleton, and $x \preceq y$ that there is a path from x to y.   □

We denote the disjoint union of graphs h_1 and h_2 by $h_1 \uplus h_2$.

Lemma 6. *Let M_1, M_2 be MSO graph transducers. There exists an MSO graph transducer M, denoted $M_1 \uplus M_2$, such that for every graph g,*

$$M(g) = \{h_1 \uplus h_2 \mid h_1 \in M_1(g), h_2 \in M_2(g)\}.$$

Proof. Let $M_1 = (C_1, \varphi_1, \Psi_1, X_1)$ and $M_2 = (C_2, \varphi_2, \Psi_2, X_2)$. We may assume w.l.o.g. that C_1 is disjoint from C_2 and that the parameters of M_1 are disjoint from those of M_2. Then $M = (C_1 \cup C_2, \varphi_1 \wedge \varphi_2, \Psi_1 \cup \Psi_2, X_1 \cup X_2 \cup X)$ realizes the desired transduction, where all edge formulas in X are set to false, i.e., $\chi_{c,c',\gamma}(x, y) \equiv$ false for all $(c, c') \in (C_1 \times C_2) \cup (C_2 \times C_1)$.   □

Lemma 7. *Let M_1, M_2 be MSO graph-to-string transducers and let a, b be distinct symbols. There exists an MSO graph-to-dgraph transducer $M^{a,b}$ such that for every graph g,*

$$M^{a,b}(g) = \{\text{dgr}(a^m b^n) \mid \exists h_1 \in M_1(g), h_2 \in M_2(g) : h_1/m = a \text{ and } h_2/n = b\}.$$

Proof. Let M_i be from (Σ_i, Γ_i) to $(\{\#\}, \Delta_i)$ for $i \in \{1, 2\}$. If $a \notin \Delta_1$ or $b \notin \Delta_2$ then let $M^{a,b} = (\varnothing, \text{false}, \varnothing, \varnothing)$. Otherwise define $M^{a,b} = (M_1; N_{\Delta_1}^a) \uplus (M_2; N_{\Delta_2}^b)$ according to Lemmas 2, 5, and 6.   □

For a relation $R \subseteq A \times B$ and a set $D \subseteq A$, denote by $R|_D$ the restriction of R to D, i.e., $R|_D = \{(a, b) \in R \mid a \in D\}$.

Theorem 8. *It is decidable for deterministic MSO graph-to-string or graph-to-tree transducers M_1, M_2 and an NR set D of graphs whether $\tau_{M_1}|_D = \tau_{M_2}|_D$.*

Proof. We start with the graph-to-string case. For $i \in \{1, 2\}$ let $D_i = \text{dom}(M_i) \cap D$. We first show that it is decidable whether $D_1 = D_2$. Clearly, $D_1 = D_2$ if and only if $\text{Par}(E(D)) = \varnothing$, where E is the deterministic MSO graph-to-dgraph transducer that removes the edges of all graphs in the symmetric difference of $\text{dom}(M_1)$ and $\text{dom}(M_2)$: $E = (\{1\}, \neg(\varphi_1 \leftrightarrow \varphi_2), \{\psi_{1,\sigma}(x)\}_{\sigma \in \Sigma}, \varnothing)$ where φ_i is the domain formula of M_i for $i \in \{1, 2\}$, Σ is the node alphabet of D, and $\psi_{1,\sigma}(x) = \text{lab}_\sigma(x)$ for $\sigma \in \Sigma$. By Lemma 3, $\text{Par}(E(D))$ is effectively semilinear, and hence its emptiness can be decided. If $D_1 \neq D_2$ then we are finished and know that $\tau_{M_1}|_D \neq \tau_{M_2}|_D$. Assume now that $D_1 = D_2$.

Let M_i have output edge alphabet Δ_i, for $i \in \{1, 2\}$, and let \$ be a symbol not in $\Delta = \Delta_1 \cup \Delta_2$. We define deterministic MSO graph-to-string transducers $M_i^\$ = M_i; N$ such that $M_i^\$(g) = M_i(g)\$$ for all $g \in \mathrm{dom}(M_i)$. Here N is the deterministic MSO string transducer $(C, \mathrm{true}, \{\psi_{1,\#}(x), \psi_{2,\#}(x)\}, \{\chi_{c,c',\delta}(x, y)\}_{c,c' \in C, \delta \in \Delta \cup \{\$\}})$ such that $C = \{1, 2\}$, $\psi_{1,\#}(x) \equiv \mathrm{true}$, $\psi_{2,\#}(x) \equiv \chi_{1,2,\$}(x, y) \equiv \neg(\exists z) \bigvee_{\delta \in \Delta} \mathrm{edg}_\delta(x, z)$ and, for $\delta \in \Delta$, $\chi_{1,1,\delta}(x, y) \equiv \mathrm{edg}_\delta(x, y)$; all other edge formulas are set to false.

Since now all output strings end on the special marker \$, $\tau_{M_1}|_D \neq \tau_{M_2}|_D$ iff

$$\exists a \exists b : (d(a, b) \wedge \exists n \exists g : (g \in D_1 \wedge M_1^\$(g)/n = a \wedge M_2^\$(g)/n = b))$$

where $d(a, b)$ denotes the statement $a, b \in (\Delta \cup \{\$\}) \wedge a \neq b$. For given a, b, let $M^{a,b}$ be the transducer of Lemma 7 for $a, b, M_1^\$, M_2^\$$. Then the statement displayed above holds if and only if

$$\exists a \exists b : (d(a, b) \wedge \exists n : \mathrm{dgr}(a^n b^n) \in M^{a,b}(D)))$$
$$\mathrm{iff}\ \exists a \exists b : (d(a, b) \wedge \underbrace{\exists n : (n, n) \in \mathrm{Par}(M^{a,b}(D))))}_{P(a,b)}$$

By Lemma 3, $\mathrm{Par}(M^{a,b}(D))$ is effectively semilinear. By Lemma 4 this means that $P(a, b)$ is decidable. Since there are only finitely many a, b with $d(a, b)$, the statement is decidable.

We now reduce the graph-to-tree case to the graph-to-string case. Let Δ be a ranked alphabet and let m be the maximal rank of its elements. There is a deterministic MSO tree-to-string transducer M_Δ that translates every tree t over Δ into the string $\mathrm{pre}(t)$ of its node labels in pre-order. Clearly, if we associate with a deterministic MSO graph-to-tree transducer M (from (Σ, Γ) to $(\Delta, \{1, \ldots, m\})$) the deterministic MSO graph-to-string transducer $\widehat{M} = M; M_\Delta$, then M_1 is equivalent to M_2 on D if and only if $\widehat{M_1}$ is equivalent to $\widehat{M_2}$ on D. Let $M_\Delta = (\{1, 2\}, \mathrm{true}, \{\psi_{1,\#}, \psi_{2,\#}\}, \{\chi_{c,c',\delta}\}_{c,c' \in \{1,2\}, \delta \in \Delta})$ with $\psi_{1,\#} \equiv \mathrm{true}$, $\psi_{2,\#} \equiv \mathrm{root}(x)$, where $\mathrm{root}(x)$ expresses that x is the root node. Further, for $\delta \in \Delta$, $\chi_{1,1,\delta} \equiv \mathrm{lab}_\delta(x) \wedge \pi(x, y)$ and $\chi_{1,2,\delta} \equiv \mathrm{lab}_\delta(x) \wedge \mathrm{root}(y) \wedge \neg(\exists z) \pi(x, z)$ where $\pi(x, y)$ expresses that y is the successor of x in the pre-order. □

Note that it is essential in Theorem 8 that the transductions are restricted to an NR set of graphs. The set of all graphs (over a given alphabet) is *not* NR. In fact, equivalence of deterministic MSO graph (or graph-to-string, or graph-to-tree) transducers is undecidable when taking all graphs as input. This follows from the fact that, as mentioned in the Introduction, MSO is undecidable for graphs (Propositions 5.2.1 and 5.2.2 of [Cou97]); i.e., given an MSO formula ϕ, it is undecidable whether ϕ holds for all graphs. It is easy to construct MSO graph-to-string transducers M_1, M_2 that take as input the disjoint union h of an arbitrary graph g and the string \$, such that M_1 translates h into \$ if g satisfies ϕ (and is undefined otherwise), and M_2 translates h into \$. Clearly, M_1 is equivalent to M_2 if and only if ϕ holds for all graphs g. The proof for the graph-to-tree case is analogous.

Example 9. (i) Let M_1, M_2 (and Σ, Σ') be as in Example 1(i). We now want to follow the proof of Theorem 8 to test whether M_1 is equivalent to M_2. We take $D = T_\Sigma$. First, construct $M_1^\$$ and $M_2^\$$. Then construct $M^{b,\$}$ and $M^{\$,b}$. Clearly, for every tree

s over Σ, $M^{b,\$}(s) = \{\mathrm{dgr}(b^m\$^n) \mid 1 \le m \le \mathrm{outer}(s), n = \mathrm{outer}(s) + 1\}$ and $M^{\$,b}(s) = \{\mathrm{dgr}(\$^m b^n) \mid m = \mathrm{outer}(s) + 1, 1 \le n \le \mathrm{outer}(s)\}$. The sets $M^{b,\$}(D)$ and $M^{\$,b}(D)$ are Parikh. Clearly, $\mathrm{Par}(M^{b,\$}(T_\Sigma)) = \{(m, n) \mid 1 \le m < n, n = 2 \text{ or } n = 4 \text{ or } n \ge 6\}$ which implies that its intersection with $P = \{(n, n) \mid n \in \mathbb{N}\}$ is empty. Similarly, $\mathrm{Par}(M^{b,\$}(T_\Sigma)) \cap P = \varnothing$, which proves that indeed M_1 is equivalent to M_2.

(ii) Consider now the transducers M_3, M_4 of Example 1(ii). If we again follow the proof of Theorem 8, then it turns out that the set $\mathrm{Par}(M^{b,c}(T_{\Sigma'})$ contains, e.g., the pair $(2, 2)$ and hence M_3 is *not* equivalent to M_4. To see this, consider the input tree $s = \sigma(\sigma(a, \sigma(a, c)), a)))$. Then $M_3(s) = bbbcbb$ and $M_4(s) = bcbbbb$, and therefore $\mathrm{dgr}(bbcc) \in M^{b,c}(s)$.

4   String and Tree Transductions

Clearly, Theorem 8 also holds if we restrict the input graphs to strings or trees. In particular, deterministic MSO X-to-Y transducers have decidable equivalence for all $X, Y \in \{\text{string}, \text{tree}\}$, because the set of all strings and the set of all trees (over given alphabets) are NR. For string transducers this reproves the decidability result of [Gur82] (through [EH01]). For trees we obtain the following new decidability result (see the title of this paper).

Corollary 10. *The equivalence problem is decidable for deterministic MSO tree transducers.*

Of course, even stronger statements hold; namely, given an NR set D of strings or trees, it is decidable if two deterministic MSO X-to-Y transducers are equivalent when restricted to D. For string transducers this means the following.

Corollary 11. *It is decidable whether two deterministic two-way finite state transducers are equivalent on an NR set of strings.*

As discussed in Section 6 of [Eng97], the NR sets of strings are the same as the ranges of deterministic tree-walking tree-to-string transducers. They properly contain, for instance, the context-free languages and the ranges of deterministic two-way finite state transducers. Since the NR sets of strings form a full AFL of Parikh languages, Corollary 11 is in fact a special case of the general decidability result for deterministic two-way finite state transducers in Theorem 5 of [Iba82]. It is incomparable to the decidability of equivalence of two such transducers on an NPDT0L language [CK87].

Our results also imply that equivalence of deterministic tree-walking tree-to-string transducers [AU71] is decidable: by Lemma 4.4 and Theorem 4.7 of [ERS80] such transducers can be simulated by deterministic finite-copying top-down tree-to-string transducers with regular look-ahead, which, in turn, realize exactly the same translations as deterministic MSO tree-to-string transducers by Theorem 7.7 of [EM99].

Corollary 12. *It is decidable whether two deterministic tree-walking tree-to-string transducers are equivalent.*

The two statements of the next corollary follow from the characterizations of deterministic MSO tree transductions in [BE00] and [EM03b], respectively. Note that a tree transducer is of linear size increase if the size of the output tree is at most linear in the size of the input tree. An attributed tree transducer is essentially an attribute grammar which translates trees over a ranked alphabet (instead of derivation trees of a context-free grammar) into trees; the only allowed semantic operation is top-concatenation of trees. An attribute grammar (or attributed tree transducer) is said to be single-use restricted if each attribute is used at most once in every local set of semantic rules. The single-use restriction implies that the corresponding dependency graphs are trees (instead of DAGs, for unrestricted grammars/transducers). For more information on tree transducers see [FV98].

Corollary 13. *The equivalence problem is decidable*
(1) for single-use restricted attributed tree transducers and
(2) for deterministic macro tree transducers of linear size increase.

This result is incomparable with the decidability of the equivalence problem for

(1) deterministic bottom-up tree transducers [Zac80],
(2) deterministic top-down tree transducers [Ési79], and
(3) deterministic nonnested separated attributed/macro tree transducers [CF82].

Note that (2) is included in the more general (3), and that all transducers mentioned in (1) – (3) can be simulated by deterministic macro tree transducers. It remains open since 1979 [Eng80] whether the equivalence problem is decidable for attributed tree transducers and for deterministic macro tree transducers.

In both [MSV03] and [MBPS05] formal models of XML queries are introduced (the pebble tree transducer and the transformation language TL, respectively). In the deterministic case these can be simulated by compositions of deterministic macro tree transducers [EM03a, MBPS05]. Hence we call such compositions *deterministic XML queries*. If they are of linear size increase, then they are MSO definable [Man03].

Corollary 14. *The equivalence problem is decidable for deterministic XML queries of linear size increase.*

References

[AU71]   A. V. Aho and J. D. Ullman. Translations on a context-free grammar. *Inform. and Control*, 19:439–475, 1971.

[BE00]   R. Bloem and J. Engelfriet. A comparison of tree transductions defined by monadic second order logic and by attribute grammars. *J. Comp. Syst. Sci.*, 61:1–50, 2000.

[CF82]   B. Courcelle and P. Franchi-Zannettacci. On the equivalence problem for attribute systems. *Inform. and Control*, 52:275–305, 1982.

[CK87]   K. Culik II and J. Karhumäki. The equivalence problem for single-valued two-way transducers (on NPDT0L languages) is decidable. *SIAM J. Comput.*, 16:221–230, 1987.

[Cou94] B. Courcelle. Monadic second-order definable graph transductions: a survey. *Theoret. Comput. Sci.*, 126:53–75, 1994.

[Cou97]   B. Courcelle. The expression of graph properties and graph transformations in monadic second-order logic. In *Handbook of graph grammars and computing by graph transformation, Volume 1*, pages 313–400. World Scientific, 1997.

[EH01]   J. Engelfriet and H. J. Hoogeboom. MSO definable string transductions and two-way finite-state transducers. *ACM Transactions on Computational Logic*, 2:216–254, 2001.

[EM99]   J. Engelfriet and S. Maneth. Macro tree transducers, attribute grammars, and MSO definable tree translations. *Inform. and Comput.*, 154:34–91, 1999.

[EM03a]   J. Engelfriet and S. Maneth. A comparison of pebble tree transducers with macro tree transducers. *Acta Informatica*, 39:613–698, 2003.

[EM03b]   J. Engelfriet and S. Maneth. Macro tree translations of linear size increase are MSO definable. *SIAM J. Comput.*, 32:950–1006, 2003.

[Eng80]   J. Engelfriet. Some open questions and recent results on tree transducers and tree languages In *Formal language theory; perspectives and open problems*, Academic Press, 1980.

[Eng97]   J. Engelfriet. Context-free graph grammars. In G. Rozenberg and A. Salomaa, editors, *Handbook of Formal Languages, Volume 3*, chapter 3. Springer-Verlag, 1997.

[ERS80]   J. Engelfriet, G. Rozenberg, G. Slutzki. Tree transducers, L systems, and two-way machines. *J. Comp. Syst. Sci.*, 20:150–202, 1980.

[Ési79]   Z. Ésik. Decidability results concerning tree transducers I. *Acta Cybern.*, 5:1–20, 1980.

[FV98]   Z. Fülöp and H. Vogler. *Syntax-Directed Semantics – Formal Models based on Tree Transducers*. EATCS Monographs in Theoretical Computer Science (W. Brauer, G. Rozenberg, A. Salomaa, eds.). Springer-Verlag, 1998.

[Gin66]   S. Ginsburg. *The Mathematical Theory of Context-Free Languages*. McGraw-Hill, 1966.

[Gri68]   T. V. Griffiths. The unsolvability of the equivalence problem for Λ-free nondeterministic generalized machines. *J. ACM*, 15:409–413, 1968.

[GS64]   S. Ginsburg and E. H. Spanier. Bounded Algol-like languages. *Trans. Amer. Math. Soc.*, 113:333–368, 1964.

[Gur82]   E. M. Gurari. The equivalence problem for deterministic two-way sequential transducers is decidable. *SIAM J. Comput.*, 11(3):448–452, 1982.

[Iba82]   O. H. Ibarra. 2DST mappings on languages and related problems. *Theoret. Comput. Sci.*, 19:219–227, 1982.

[Man03]   S. Maneth. The macro tree transducer hierarchy collapses for functions of linear size increase. In *Proc. FSTTCS 2003*, LNCS 2556, pages 326–337, Springer-Verlag, 2003.

[MBPS05] S. Maneth, A. Berlea, T. Perst, H. Seidl. XML type checking with macro tree transducers. In *Proc. PODS 2005*, pages 283–294, ACM Press, 2005.

[MSV03]   T. Milo, D. Suciu, and V. Vianu. Typechecking for XML transformers. *J. Comp. Syst. Sci.*, 66:66–97, 2003.

[Par66]   R. J. Parikh. On context-free languages. *J. ACM*, 13:570–581, 1966.

[Zac80]   Z. Zachar. The solvability of the equivalence problem for deterministic frontier-to-root tree transducers. *Acta Cybern.*, 4:167–177, 1980.

Market Equilibrium for CES Exchange Economies: Existence, Multiplicity, and Computation*

Bruno Codenotti[1], Benton McCune[2], Sriram Penumatcha[3], and Kasturi Varadarajan[2]

[1] IIT-CNR, Pisa, Italy
bruno.codenotti@iit.cnr.it
[2] Department of Computer Science, The University of Iowa,
Iowa City IA 52242
[bmccune,kvaradar]@cs.uiowa.edu
[3] Department of Mathematics, Arizona State University, Tempe AZ 85287
sriram@mathpost.la.asu.edu

Abstract. We consider exchange economies where the traders' preferences are expressed in terms of the extensively used *constant elasticity of substitution* (CES) utility functions. We show that for any such economy it is possible to say in polynomial time whether an equilibrium exists. We then describe a convex formulation of the equilibrium conditions, which leads to polynomial time algorithms for a wide range of the parameter defining the CES utility functions. This range includes instances that do not satisfy weak gross substitutability. As a byproduct of our work, we prove the uniqueness of equilibrium in an interesting setting where such a result was not known.

The range for which we do not obtain polynomial-time algorithms coincides with the range for which the economies admit multiple disconnected equilibria.

1 Introduction

An *exchange economy* consists of a collection of goods, initially distributed among a number of traders. The preferences of the traders for the bundles of goods are expressed by a utility function. Each trader wants to maximize her utility, subject to her budget constraint.

An equilibrium is a set of prices at which there are allocations of goods to traders such that two conditions are simultaneously satisfied: each trader's allocation maximizes her utility subject to the budget constraint, and the market clears.

---

* Part of the first author's work was done when visiting the Toyota Technological Institute at Chicago. The work by the last three authors was in part supported by NSF CAREER award CCR-0237431. This paper is an expanded and revised version of an unpublished paper that was presented at a DIMACS Workshop on Large Scale Games in April, 2005.

R. Ramanujam and S. Sen (Eds.): FSTTCS 2005, LNCS 3821, pp. 505–516, 2005.

Existence. An early and fundamental triumph of Mathematical Economics was the 1954 result by Arrow and Debreu [1] that, even in a more general situation which includes the production of goods, subject to mild sufficient conditions, there is an equilibrium. However, given a set of traders, each endowed with a concave utility function and a nonnegative vector of initial endowments, an equilibrium does not need to exist.

Thus the problem arises of determining whether a given exchange economy has an equilibrium. In this paper, we show that this problem can be solved in polynomial time, whenever the utility functions are of the form $u(x_1, \ldots, x_n) = \left(\sum_{j=1}^{n} c_j x_j^{\rho} \right)^{\frac{1}{\rho}}$, for $-\infty < \rho < 1$ and $\rho \neq 0$, i.e., for constant elasticity of substitution (CES) utility functions [27].

This result generalizes methods of Gale [13], who analyzed the existence of equilibria for linear utility functions, and Eaves [12], who analyzed the existence of positive equilibrium prices for Cobb-Douglas utility functions. (See also Jain [17], who employs a sufficient condition for the existence of positive price equilibria for linear utility functions.) Our result is in contrast with the NP-hardness result of [7], which applies to Leontief utility functions. As described below, linear, Cobb-Douglas, and Leontief utility functions are limiting cases of CES utility functions.

Computation. The problem of computing equilibrium prices for exchange economies has attracted a lot of attention since the 1960s. In recent years, theoretical computer scientists have become interested in the polynomial-time solvability of the problem. Several results [25] seem to indicate that in order for the problem to admit polynomial time algorithms, certain restrictions should be satisfied by the market.

Two well studied restrictions are *gross substitutability* – GS (see [22], p. 611) and the *weak axiom of revealed preferences* – WARP (see [22], Section 2.F). Although restrictive, these conditions are useful and model some realistic scenarios. A utility function satisfies GS (resp., weak GS – WGS) if increasing the prices of some of the goods while keeping the other prices and the income fixed causes the increase (resp., does not cause the decrease) in demand for the goods whose price is fixed. Roughly speaking, WARP means that the aggregate behavior of the market fulfills a fundamental property satisfied by the choices made by any rational individual trader.

It is well known that GS implies that the equilibrium prices are unique up to scaling ([28], p. 395), and that WGS and WARP both imply that the set of equilibrium prices is convex ([22], p. 608). When the set of equilibria is convex, it is enough to add a non-degeneracy assumption (which is almost always satisfied) to get the uniqueness of the equilibrium up to scaling [9].

Most of the polynomial-time algorithms developed so far apply to exchange economies where either WGS or WARP hold. In this paper we present a convex characterization of the equilibrium conditions which applies to exchange economies with CES functions such that $-1 \leq \rho < 0$. Note that these economies do not fall into either WGS or WARP. Also, the methods of [24,17], which work when each utility function $u(x_1, \ldots, x_n)$ has the property that $\log(\frac{u(x)}{\partial u(x)/\partial x_j})$ is a concave function for every j, do not apply here.

Multiplicity. Besides its algorithmic contribution, our work allows us to conclude that, for CES functions with $-1 \leq \rho < 0$, the equilibria are connected, and are thus essentially unique. This was not known by economists. Indeed it turns out that an exchange economy with traders endowed with CES utility functions such that $-1 \leq \rho < 0$ is not covered by any of the known conditions that ensure that there are no multiple disconnected equilibria, such as the *Super Cobb-Douglas Property* of Mas-Colell [21], and thus our result also provides an original contribution to the theory of equilibrium. Combined with a result by Gjerstad [16], who showed that multiple disconnected equilibria can arise in economies where traders have CES functions with any $\rho < -1$, our work leads to a characterization of the values of ρ for which the CES exchange economies equilibrium sets must be connected.

Related Work. In a series of papers which started with linear utility functions, polynomial time algorithms have been developed to compute equilibria for more and more general settings [10,11,18,14,17,29,3,15,6,4]. However, the corresponding market satisfies one of the two conditions discussed above (WGS or WARP) (see [5] for a review).

The technical tool used in some of these results is to reformulate the problem in terms of mathematical programming in a way that a polynomial time algorithm (or approximation scheme – in general the equilibrium point is not a vector of rationals) can be obtained by known optimization techniques. In particular, *convex programming* has been proven to be a particularly useful tool [24,17,29,6,4].

Organization. In Section 2, we formally describe the model of an exchange economy, introduce CES functions, and hint at their economic relevance. Section 3 is devoted to a detailed discussion of the demand function of traders with CES utility functions. In Section 4, we characterize the problem of existence of an equilibrium for CES exchange economies, in terms of a graph property that can be verified in polynomial time. In Section 5 we show that equilibrium prices and allocations for an exchange economy, where the traders are endowed with CES functions with $-1 \leq \rho < 0$, can be computed by solving a feasibility problem, defined in terms of explicitly given convex constraints.

2   Background

We now describe the exchange market model. Let us consider m economic agents who represent traders of n goods. Let $\mathbf{R}_+^n$ (resp. $\mathbf{R}_{++}^n$) denote the subset of $\mathbf{R}^n$ where the coordinates are nonnegative (resp. strictly positive). The j-th coordinate in $\mathbf{R}^n$ will stand for the good j. Each trader i has a concave utility function $u_i : \mathbf{R}_+^n \to \mathbf{R}_+$, which represents her preferences for the different bundles of goods, and an initial endowment of goods $w_i = (w_{i1}, \ldots, w_{in}) \in \mathbf{R}_+^n$. At given prices $\pi \in \mathbf{R}_+^n$, the i-th trader will sell her endowment, and get the bundle of goods $x_i = (x_{i1}, \ldots, x_{in}) \in \mathbf{R}_+^n$ which maximizes $u_i(x)$ subject to the budget constraint[4] $\pi \cdot x \leq \pi \cdot w_i$. The budget constraint restricts the choice to bundles that cost no more than $\pi \cdot w_i$, the *income* of trader i. If the utility maximization is well-defined, such a bundle x_i is called the *demand* of trader i at price π, and is denoted by $x_i(\pi)$. If the utility has no maximum over the set of feasible bundles, we say that the demand is not well-defined. (The feasible region is always non-empty, since the origin is in it.)

An equilibrium is a nonnegative vector of prices $\pi = (\pi_1, \ldots, \pi_n) \in \mathbf{R}_+^n$ at which there is a bundle $\bar{x}_i = (x_{i1}, \ldots, x_{in}) \in \mathbf{R}_+^n$ of goods for each trader i such that the following two conditions hold:

1. For each trader i, the demand is well-defined at price π and $\bar{x}_i$ is a demanded bundle.
2. For each good j, $\sum_i \bar{x}_{ij} \leq \sum_i w_{ij}$.

Under the assumption that for each i and every bundle $x \in \mathbf{R}_+^n$, there is a bundle $y \in \mathbf{R}_+^n$ such that $u_i(y) > u_i(x)$, it can be shown that for any good with positive price, equality must hold in (2). The already mentioned result of Arrow and Debreu [1] implies that, under some mild assumptions, such an equilibrium exists. The above described market model is usually called an *exchange economy*.

A special (and analytically more tractable) case of the exchange model, known as Fisher's model, arises when the economic agents are buyers, endowed with fixed incomes, competing for goods, which are available in fixed quantities. Note that Fisher's model can be seen as a special case of an exchange economy, obtained by assuming that the initial endowments are *proportional*, i.e., $w_i = \delta_i w$, $\delta_i > 0$, so that the relative incomes of the traders are independent of the prices.

CES utility functions. The most popular family of utility functions is given by CES (constant elasticity of substitution) functions, which have been introduced in [27]. We refer the reader to the book by Shoven and Whalley [26] for a sense of their pervasiveness in applied general equilibrium models. A CES function ranks the trader's preferences over bundles of goods $(x_1, \ldots, x_n)$ according to the value of $u(x_1, \ldots, x_n) = \left(\sum_{j=1}^n c_j x_j^\rho \right)^{\frac{1}{\rho}}$. where $-\infty < \rho < 1$, but $\rho \neq 0$.

The success of CES functions is due to the useful combination of their mathematical tractability with their expressive power, which allows for a realistic modeling of a wide range of consumer preferences. Indeed, one can model markets with very different characteristics in terms of preference towards variety, substitutability versus complementarity, and multiplicity of price equilibria, by changing the values of ρ and of the utility parameters c_j.

CES functions have been thoroughly analyzed in [2], where it has also been shown how to derive, in the limit, their special cases, i.e., linear, Cobb-Douglas, and Leontief functions (see [2], p. 231). Let $\sigma = \frac{1}{1-\rho}$. The parameter σ is called the *elasticity of substitution*. For $\sigma \to \infty$ ($\rho \to 1$), CES take the linear form, and the goods are perfect substitutes, so that there is no preference for variety. For

---

[4] Given two vectors x and y, we use the notation $x \cdot y$ to denote their inner product.

$\sigma > 1$ $(\rho > 0)$, the goods are partial substitutes, and different values of σ in this range allow us to express different levels of preference for variety. For $\sigma \to 1$ $(\rho \to 0)$, CES become Cobb-Douglas functions, and express a perfect balance between substitution and complementarity effects. Indeed it is not difficult to show that a trader with a Cobb-Douglas utility spends a fixed fraction of her income on each good.

For $\sigma < 1$ $(\rho < 0)$, CES functions model markets with significant complementarity effects between goods. This feature reaches its extreme (*perfect complementarity*) as $\sigma \to 0$ $(\rho \to -\infty)$, i.e., when CES takes the form of Leontief functions. In the latter case, the *shape* of the optimal bundle demanded by the consumer does not depend at all on the prices of the goods, but is fully determined by the parameters defining the utility function.

Whenever the relative incomes of the traders are independent of the prices, CES functions give rise to a market which satisfies WARP. This happens for instance in the Fisher model, a very special case of the exchange model. On the other hand, CES functions satisfy WGS if and only if $\rho \geq 0$, whereas, if $\rho < -1$, they allow for multiple disconnected equilibria.

3   Demand of CES Consumers

In this section, we characterize the demand function of traders with CES utility functions. Consider a setting where trader i has an initial endowment $w_i = (w_{i1}, \ldots, w_{in}) \in \mathbf{R}_+^n$ of goods, and the CES utility function $u_i(x_{i1}, \ldots, x_{in}) = \left(\sum_{j=1}^n \alpha_{ij} x_{ij}^{\rho_i} \right)^{\frac{1}{\rho_i}}$, where $\alpha_{ij} \geq 0$, and $-\infty < \rho_i < 1$, but $\rho_i \neq 0$.

We assume throughout that each trader i *owns* some good j, that is, $w_{ij} > 0$ for some j. We also assume that each trader i *wants* some good j, that is, $\alpha_{ij} > 0$ for some j. If trader i does not want good j, it is easy to see that the utility of a bundle $x_i \in \mathbf{R}_+^n$ is independent of x_{ij}. We adopt the convention that $\alpha_{ij} x_{ij}^{\rho_i} = 0$ when $\alpha_{ij} = 0$ and $x_{ij} = 0$. If $\rho_i < 0$, we define $u_i(x_{i1}, \ldots, x_{in}) = 0$ if there is a j such that i wants j and $x_{ij} = 0$. Note that this ensures that u_i is continuous over $\mathbf{R}_+^n$.

Consider a case where $\rho_i > 0$. Evidently, if we start with any bundle $x_i \in \mathbf{R}_+^n$ and add to it an arbitrarily small amount of a good that i wants, we get a bundle with more utility. From this, it follows that the demand of the trader is well-defined at a given price if and only if each of the goods that the trader wants has a strictly positive price.

Now consider the case where $\rho_i < 0$. A bundle $x_i \in \mathbf{R}_+^n$ has a strictly positive utility if and only if it has a strictly positive amount of each of the goods that the trader wants. Evidently, if we start with any bundle $x_i \in \mathbf{R}_+^n$ that has strictly positive utility and add to it an arbitrarily small amount of a good that i wants, we get a bundle with more utility. Let π be a price at which the income $\pi \cdot w_i$ is positive. Since the trader can afford a bundle with positive utility, we conclude that the demand is well-defined at π if and only if each of the goods that the trader wants has a strictly positive price. Now let π be a price at which the income $\pi \cdot w_i$ is zero. We see that the demand is well-defined if and only if *at least one* of the goods that the trader wants is positively priced.

Irrespective of whether ρ_i is positive or negative, traders with positive income demand a positive amount of each good they want. Such positive income traders are also *non-satiable* on all goods they want which means that demand is not well-defined if any good they want is priced zero.

Also irrespective of whether ρ_i is positive or negative, the demand is well-defined at any strictly positive price vector $\pi \in \mathbf{R}^n_{++}$. It is in fact unique and is given by the expression

$$x_{ij}(\pi) = \frac{\alpha_{ij}^{1/1-\rho_i}}{\pi_j^{1/1-\rho_i}} \times \frac{\sum_k \pi_k w_{ik}}{\sum_k \alpha_k^{1/1-\rho_i} \pi_k^{-\rho_i/1-\rho_i}}. \tag{1}$$

The formula above is folklore and is derived using the Kuhn-Tucker conditions.

4   Existence of an Equilibrium

The celebrated paper of Arrow and Debreu [1] had a much weaker set of assumptions sufficient for the existence of equilibrium than earlier work. However, the assumptions were still somewhat restrictive. Indeed, Arrow and Debreu themselves called the assumptions for their first existence theorem "clearly unrealistic" and immediately proceeded to weaken the sufficient conditions for their second theorem. See the introduction to Maxfield [23] for a discussion of the work on showing existence of equilibrium under progressively weaker assumptions. In general, it is NP-hard to determine whether a market possesses an equilibrium or not [7].

Gale [13] provided a very simple two trader example of a market that does not possess an equilibrium. Gale's example was for the linear exchange model, but it also serves as an example for the CES case with $\rho > 0$. Suppose trader one possesses both apples and oranges, but only wants apples. Trader two wants both apples and oranges, but owns only oranges. This simple market has no equilibrium. If oranges are priced at zero, then the demand of trader two is not well-defined. If oranges have a positive price, then trader one will want to sell all of her oranges to buy more apples even though she already owns all the apples present in the market. Gale's example will not work for the CES with $\rho < 0$ case though because that actually has an equilibrium with a positive price for apples and zero price for oranges.

In this section, we characterize the existence of equilibrium for an exchange economy where the traders have CES utility functions. The characterization immediately implies a polynomial time algorithm to decide whether the economy has an equilibrium. As before, we assume that each trader wants at least one good and owns at least one good. We also assume that each good is owned by some trader.

We assume in the remainder of this section that each trader has a positive amount of precisely one good. This assumption is without loss of generality: we may replace a trader with positive amounts of k different goods with k traders, each with the same utility function and a positive amount of one good. A straightforward argument that employs the homogeneity of the CES utility functions shows that this transformation preserves the equilibria.

It is easy to see, but nonetheless worth noting, that the traders with positive income will be precisely those traders whose single good is positively priced.

Definition 1. *There is a vertex v_i for each consumer i. We have an arc from v_i to v_k when trader i possesses a good which trader k wants. The resulting directed graph is called an economy graph.*

The following existence theorem is the main result we use from Maxfield [23].

Theorem 1. *If the economy graph is strongly connected, an equilibrium exists. Moreover, all goods are positively priced at any equilibrium.*

Proof. This follows from Theorem 2 of Maxfield [23] who obtains this result using strong connectivity and general results on the existence of a *quasi-equilibrium* ([22], Chapter 17).   □

Definition 2. *We say that a strongly connected component is on (at a given price) if every trader within it has a positive income. If no trader in a strongly connected component has a positive income, then we say that that component is off.*

Lemma 1. *At equilibrium, every strongly connected component in an economy graph is either on or off.*

Proof. Suppose not. Suppose that at equilibrium price π, there is a component that is neither on or off. In that case, there must be a trader with positive income that desires a good from a trader with no income. That means the zero income trader's good must have a price of zero. Since the trader with positive income is non-satiable on the zero priced good, demand is not well-defined for that good and therefore, π is not an equilibrium. This provides a contradiction.   □

Consider a strongly connected component C of the economy graph that has no incoming arcs from traders outside C. We claim that a good held by any trader i in C is also desired by some trader i' in C. If C consists simply of the node v_i, then since there are no incoming arcs from outside, it must be that i desires his own good. If C consists of more than one node, the claim follows from strong connectivity.

Furthermore, it now follows that a good held by a trader in C is not held by any trader outside C. Otherwise, C would have an incoming arc.

Lemma 2. *At equilibrium, a strongly connected component of an economy graph is on if and only if it has no incoming arcs.*

Proof. Suppose the economy has an equilibrium price π. Suppose a strongly connected component C_1 is on. We will show that C_1 can have no incoming arcs. If C_1 has an incoming arc, that means some trader t in C_1, wants some good g held by a trader in another component C_2. If C_2 is off, then g has price zero. But t has positive income since C_1 is on. Since t wants g, t's demand is undefined, thus contradicting the assumption of equilibrium. Thus, at equilibrium C_2 must be on. If C_2 has any incoming arcs, then we can make an identical argument to show that the components providing the incoming arcs must also be on. Following this chain, we arrive at two components C_1' and C_2' that are on, C_1' has an incoming arc from a trader in C_2', and C_2' has no incoming arcs. So a trader t in C_1', who has positive income, will demand a positive amount of a good g that is held by some trader in C_2'. Since C_2' has no incoming arcs, g is owned only by traders in C_2', as we have already established. Since C_2' has no incoming arcs, the traders in C_2' form a subeconomy for which π is seen to be an equilibrium. Since the price of all goods held by traders in C_2' is positive (C_2' is on), it holds that for all such goods, including g, the demand within C_2' equals the supply within C_2'. But this means that the demand for g in the bigger economy exceeds the supply: t, who is outside C_2', demands a positive amount of it, but only traders in C_2' own it. Thus, π is not an equilibrium which is a contradiction.

Suppose the economy has an equilibrium price π. Suppose further that a component, C, has no incoming arcs. We show that C must be on. Suppose C is off. Consider any trader in C. He wants some goods; all of these are owned only by traders in C, since C has no incoming arc. All goods in C are free (C is off), so the trader's demand is undefined. Therefore, π is not an equilibrium. We have a contradiction and the lemma is proven.   □

There is an important distinction, which bears repeating, between CES utility functions with $\rho > 0$ and those with $\rho < 0$. Traders with $\rho > 0$ will have positive utility as long as they have a positive amount of some good that they desire. Traders with $\rho < 0$ will only have positive utility if they have a positive amount of all goods they desire. Moreover, traders with $\rho > 0$ with zero income have undefined demands if any of their desired goods are priced at zero. Zero income traders with $\rho < 0$ only have undefined demand if all of their desired goods are free.

The following theorem is the main result of this section.

Theorem 2. *An equilibrium exists if and only if for every vertex v in a strongly connected component with incoming arcs, either (a) v has a CES utility function with $\rho > 0$ and all its incoming arcs are from vertices in strongly connected components without incoming arcs, or (b) v has a CES utility function with $\rho < 0$ and has at least one incoming arc from a strongly connected component without incoming arcs.*

Proof. Suppose an equilibrium price π exists. Then by Lemma 2, the strongly connected components that are on are precisely those that have no incoming arcs. And it is precisely the goods that are held by traders in such components that have positive price. Let C_1 be a strongly connected component with incoming arcs (if none exist, then this direction of the theorem is trivially true). Suppose there is a vertex i with a CES utility function with $\rho > 0$, and it has an incoming arc from a vertex that is in a strongly connected component with incoming arcs. Then i wants a good with price zero and so her demand is not defined, contradicting the assumption that π is an equilibrium price. Now suppose that there is a vertex i with a CES utility function with $\rho < 0$, and none of its incoming arcs are from a vertex in a strongly connected component with no incoming arcs. This means that trader i desires only zero priced goods and thus has undefined demand contradicting the assumption that π is an equilibrium price.

We now establish the other direction of the theorem. Each strongly connected component with no incoming arcs can be considered as an economy unto itself, and has an equilibrium with positive prices by Maxfield's theorem. For each good in a component with no incoming arcs we assign a price identical to its equilibrium price in the subeconomy. As no good in one of these strongly connected components is owned outside the component, this assignment of prices is well-defined.

For each good held by a trader in a component with incoming arcs, we assign a price of zero. By the argument above, we know that none of these goods are the same as those that were priced positively so this assignment is well defined. We claim that this price π is an equilibrium price.

For a trader in a component without incoming arcs, we assign the bundle that is the same as the one she gets in the equilibrium for the corresponding subeconomy. Clearly, this is a valid demand.

Consider a trader in a component with incoming arcs. Her income is 0. We claim that her demand is well-defined and that the zero bundle is a valid demand vector. This is because she is either a CES trader with $\rho > 0$ and all the goods that she wants are in components with no incoming arcs and hence positively priced, or she is a CES trader with $\rho < 0$ and at least one of the goods that she wants is positively priced, and thus the best utility she can afford is 0.

We now verify that condition (2) in the definition of an equilibrium holds, that is, the demand is at most the supply. For a good held by a trader in a component with no incoming arc, this follows from the equilibrium conditions of the corresponding subeconomy, and the fact that any trader outside the subeconomy demands 0 units of the good. For a good held by a trader in a component with incoming arcs, the net demand is 0, so condition (2) trivially holds.   □

We conclude by noting that besides yielding a polynomial time algorithm for checking the existence of equilibrium, the above characterization provides a polynomial-time reduction of the computation of an equilibrium for the original economy to the computation of positive price equilibria for sub-economies.

5   Efficient Computation by Convex Programming

In this section, we consider an economy in which each trader i has a CES utility function with $-1 \leq \rho_i < 0$. We show that the positive price equilibria of such an economy can be characterized as the solutions of a convex feasibility problem. The results of the previous section show that the computation of an equilibrium for an economy can be reduced to the computation of a positive price equilibrium for a sub-economy. This reduction, together with the fact that the convex feasibility problem can be solved (approximately) in polynomial time lead to a polynomial time algorithm for computing an approximate equilibrium. The notion of approximate equilibrium that we use corresponds to the strong approximate equilibrium defined by Codenotti et al.[6]; here, the condition (2) in the definition of an equilibrium is relaxed so that it holds approximately. Our algorithm will be polynomial not only in the input parameters but also in the number of bits used in the standard encoding of the rational number representing the approximation parameter. (We postpone a detailed discussion of this to a fuller version.) Whenever the solution can be irrational, such an algorithm is considered equivalent to an exact algorithm.

Since the demand of every trader is well-defined and unique at any positive price, we may write the positive price equilibria as the set $\pi \in \mathbf{R}_{++}$ such that for each good j, we have $\sum_i x_{ij}(\pi) \leq \sum_i w_{ij}$. Let $\rho = -1$, and note that $\rho \leq \rho_i$, for each i. Let $f_{ij}(\pi) = \pi_j^{1/(1-\rho)} x_{ij}(\pi)$. Let $\sigma_j = \pi_j^{1/(1-\rho)}$. In terms of the σ_j's, we obtain the set of $\sigma = (\sigma_1, \ldots, \sigma_n) \in \mathbf{R}_{++}$ such that for each good j,

$$\sum_i f_{ij}(\sigma) \leq \sigma_j \left(\sum_i w_{ij}\right).$$

We argue that this is a convex feasibility program. Since the right hand side of each inequality is a linear function, it suffices to argue that the left hand side is a convex function. The latter is established via the following proposition.

Proposition 1. *The function $f_{ij}(\sigma)$ is a convex function over $\mathbf{R}_{++}$.*

Proof. If $\alpha_{ij} = 0$, f_{ij} is zero over the domain and the proposition follows. Otherwise, f_{ij} is positive at each point of the domian. It therefore suffices to show that the constraint $f_{ij} \leq t$ defines a convex set for positive t. Using the formula (1) for the demand, this constraint is

$$\frac{\alpha_{ij}^{\frac{1}{1-\rho_i}}}{\sigma_j^{\frac{\rho_i-\rho}{1-\rho_i}}} \times \frac{\sum_k \sigma_k^{1-\rho} w_{ik}}{\sum_k \alpha_{ik}^{\frac{1}{1-\rho_i}} \sigma_k^{\frac{-\rho_i(1-\rho)}{1-\rho_i}}} \leq t.$$

Rewriting, and raising both sides to the power $1/(1-\rho)$, we obtain

$$\alpha_{ij}^{\frac{1}{(1-\rho)(1-\rho_i)}} \times \left(\sum_k \sigma_k^{1-\rho} w_{ik}\right)^{\frac{1}{1-\rho}} \leq t^{\frac{1}{1-\rho}} \sigma_j^{\frac{\rho_i-\rho}{(1-\rho_i)(1-\rho)}} v_i^{\frac{-\rho_i}{1-\rho_i}}, \tag{2}$$

where

$$v_i = \left(\sum_k \alpha_{ik}^{\frac{1}{1-\rho_i}} \sigma_k^{\frac{-\rho_i(1-\rho)}{1-\rho_i}}\right)^{\frac{1-\rho_i}{-\rho_i(1-\rho)}}. \tag{3}$$

The left hand side of inequality 2 is a convex function, and the right hand side is a concave function that is non-decreasing in each argument when viewed as a function of t, σ_j, and v_i, since the exponents are non-negative and add up to one. Since $0 < \frac{-\rho_i(1-\rho)}{1-\rho_i} \leq 1$, the right hand side of equality 3 is a concave function, in fact a CES function. It follows that the right hand side of inequality 2 remains a concave function when v_i is replaced by the right hand side of equality 3. This completes the proof.

The convex feasibility formulation derived in this section highlights an independently useful property of the demand, encapsulated by Proposition 1. As we will show in a fuller version of this paper, a similar approach works for CES functions with $\rho > 0$, as well as for some other utility functions. The tools developed here for exchange economies also find some use in an extension to production [19].

Acknowledgements. We wish to acknowledge some fruitful exchanges with Andreu Mas-Colell on the state-of-the-art in the area of uniqueness of equilibrium. We wish to thank Janos Simon for many useful suggestions on early versions of this paper, and Steve Gjerstad for valuable feedback.

References

1. K.J. Arrow and G. Debreu, Existence of an Equilibrium for a Competitive Economy, Econometrica 22 (3), pp. 265–290 (1954).
2. K.J. Arrow, H.B. Chenery, B.S. Minhas, R.M. Solow, Capital-Labor Substitution and Economic Efficiency, The Review of Economics and Statistics, 43(3), 225–250 (1961).
3. N. Chen, X. Deng, X. Sun, and A. Yao, Fisher Equilibrium Price with a Class of Concave Utility Functions, ESA 2004.
4. B. Codenotti, B. McCune, K. Varadarajan, Market Equilibrium via the Excess Demand Function, STOC 2005.
5. B. Codenotti, S. Pemmaraju, K. Varadarajan, Algorithms Column: The Computation of Market Equilibria. SIGACT News Vol. 35(4), December 2004.
6. B. Codenotti, S. Pemmaraju, K. Varadarajan, On the Polynomial Time Computation of Equilibria for certain Exchange Economies. SODA 2005.
7. B. Codenotti, A. Saberi, K. Varadarajan, Y. Ye, Leontief Economies Encode Nonzero Sum Two-Player Games. Electronic Colloquium on Computational Complexity, Report TR05-055. To appear in SODA 06.
8. B. Codenotti, K. Varadarajan, Efficient Computation of Equilibrium Prices for Markets with Leontief Utilities, ICALP 2004.
9. G. Debreu, Economies with a Finite Set of Equilibria. Econometrica, vol. 38(3), pp. 387-92 (1970).
10. X. Deng, C. H. Papadimitriou, M. Safra, On the Complexity of Equilibria, STOC 02.
11. N. R. Devanur, C. H. Papadimitriou, A. Saberi, V. V. Vazirani, Market Equilibrium via a Primal-Dual-Type Algorithm. FOCS 2002, pp. 389-395.
12. B. C. Eaves, Finite Solution of Pure Trade Markets with Cobb-Douglas Utilities, Mathematical Programming Study 23, pp. 226-239 (1985).

13. D. Gale, The Linear Exchange Model, Journal of Mathematical Economics (3), 205–209, 1976.
14. R. Garg and S. Kapoor, Auction Algorithms for Market Equilibrium. In *Proc. STOC*, 2004.
15. R. Garg, S. Kapoor, and V. V. Vazirani, An Auction-Based Market Equilibrium Algorithm for the Separable Gross Substitutibility Case, APPROX 2004.
16. S. Gjerstad. Multiple Equilibria in Exchange Economies with Homothetic, Nearly Identical Preference, University of Minnesota, Center for Economic Research , Discussion Paper 288, 1996.
17. K. Jain, A polynomial time algorithm for computing the Arrow-Debreu market equilibrium for linear utilities, Proc. FOCS 2004.
18. K. Jain, M. Mahdian, and A. Saberi, Approximating Market Equilibria, Proc. APPROX 2003.
19. K. Jain and K. Varadarajan. Equilibria for Economies with Production: Constant-Returns Technologies and Production Planning Constraints. To appear in SODA 06.
20. O. L. Mangasarian. Nonlinear Programming, McGraw-Hill, 1969.
21. A. Mas-Colell, On the Uniqueness of Equilibrium Once Again, in: Equilibrium Theory and Applications, W. Barnett, B. Cornet, C. DAspremont, J. Gabszewicz, andA. Mas-Colell (eds). Cambridge University Press (1991).
22. A. Mas-Colell, M.D. Whinston, and J.R. Green, Microeconomic Theory, Oxford University Press (1995).
23. R. R. Maxfield, General Equilibrium and the Theory of Directed Graphs, Journal of Mathematical Economics 27, 23-51 (1997).
24. E. I. Nenakov and M. E. Primak. One algorithm for finding solutions of the Arrow-Debreu model, Kibernetica 3, 127–128 (1983). (In Russian.)
25. C.H. Papadimitriou, On the Complexity of the Parity Argument and other Inefficient Proofs of Existence, Journal of Computer and System Sciences 48, pp. 498-532 (1994).
26. J. B. Shoven and J. Whalley. Applying General Equilibrium, Cambridge University Press (1992).
27. R. Solov, A Contribution to the Theory of Economic Growth, Quarterly Journal of Economics 70, pp. 65-94 (1956).
28. H. Varian, Microeconomic Analysis, New York: W.W. Norton, 1992.
29. Y. Ye, A Path to the Arrow-Debreu Competitive Market Equilibrium. To appear in Mathematical Programming.

Testing Concurrent Systems: An Interpretation of Intuitionistic Logic

Radha Jagadeesan[1], Gopalan Nadathur[2], and Vijay Saraswat[3]

[1] School of CTI, DePaul University
[2] Digital Technology Center and Department of CSE, University of Minnesota
[3] IBM T.J. Watson Research Center

Abstract. We present a natural confluence of higher-order hereditary Harrop formulas (HH formulas), Constraint Logic Programming (CLP, [JL87]), and Concurrent Constraint Programming (CCP, [Sar93]) as a fragment of (intuitionistic, higher-order) logic. This combination is motivated by the need for a simple executable, logical presentation for static and dynamic semantics of modern programming languages. The power of HH formulas is needed for higher-order abstract syntax, and the power of constraints is needed to naturally abstract the underlying domain of computation. Underpinning the combination is a sound and complete operational interpretation of a two-sided sequent presentation of (a large fragment of) intuitionistic logic in terms of *behavioral testing of concurrent systems*. Formulas on the left hand side of a sequent style presentation are viewed as a system of concurrent agents, and formulas on the right hand side as *tests* against this evolving system. The language permits recursive definitions of agents and tests, allows tests to augment the system being tested and allows agents to be contingent on the success of a test. We present a condition on proofs, *operational derivability* (OD), and show that the operational semantics generates only operationally derivable proofs. We show that a sequent in this logic has a proof iff it has an operationally derivable proof.

1 Introduction

The investigations in this paper are driven by an interest in logical frameworks for program manipulation. This interest has a twofold motivation.

First, the recent emergence of extremely successful program development environments such as Eclipse [ecl], has highlighted the power of advanced program manipulation techniques (such as refactorings, [FTK04]), particularly for modern, concurrent, object-oriented programming languages such as JAVA. At the same time the complexity of internal programming APIs in Eclipse – and the brittleness in extending them to languages other than JAVA – has highlighted the importance of developing a coherent conceptual framework for programs that manipulate programs. The holy grail of this work is to make it possible for end-users to define their own refactorings. This requires that there be a simple declarative framework in which the user can compose the refactoring, and there be a way to determine if the proposed refactoring is semantics-preserving.

A second motivation for such a framework is to ease the task of writing and extending compilers. Object-oriented (OO) compiler frameworks such as Polyglot [NCM03]

R. Ramanujam and S. Sen (Eds.): FSTTCS 2005, LNCS 3821, pp. 517–528, 2005.

ease some of the burden of compiler-writing for new OO languages. A compiler-writer has to provide a parser for the new language, define new Abstract Syntax Tree (AST) nodes to represent the parsed program, and implement different passes for various compiler tasks such as disambiguation, type-checking, translation to an intermediate representation (IR), static analysis and code-generation. Several of these passes can be thought of as generating and checking constraints on the AST. However this structure is hidden in the current conceptualization in terms of *procedural* code to implement "visitors" that build up the context for a node as they traverse the path from the root to the node, and rewrite the AST based on this context. Thus, it becomes difficult to extend the underlying IR and perform new analyses for new programming constructs. Similar difficulties have been reported in other frameworks that aim to make it easy for programmers to specify and plug new optimization rules into a compiler, while guaranteeing that these rules preserve program correctness [LMRC05].

This leads us to enunciate the following desiderata for the kind of framework we investigate. Below we will find it convenient to distinguish the (hypothetical) *object language* $\mathcal{O}$ and the programming language $\mathcal{F}$ to be used to write programs that manipulate $\mathcal{O}$-programs.

Programs as data. $\mathcal{F}$ should be able to express programs in modern languages (e.g. Java, Co-Array Fortran, Prolog) as data in such a way that object programs can be decomposed into their constituent parts and new object programs can be created from program parts, while respecting scoping constructs. A central requirement is that $\mathcal{O}$ scoping constructs (such as method parameter declaration, local variable introduction) subject to "alpha renaming" should in fact be represented by $\mathcal{F}$ scoping constructs so that the programmer does not have to worry about the book-keeping involved in explicitly implementing alpha renaming, substitution, generating "new" constants etc. This is the idea of *higher-order abstract syntax* [PE88].

Constraint-based. There is a large body of work establishing the centrality of constraints to the static and dynamic analysis of programs e.g. [Hei92, OSW99, Pal95, PS94], [Aik99, PW98, RMR01]. Thus, the framework should support the compositional generation of constraints from program structures. Constraints may be simple (no embedded quantifiers) or polymorphic (universally and existentially quantified). Programs should be able to query these constraints and take further action (such as generating more constraints or checking more constraints), based on the success or failure of such a query. Furthermore, we demand *extensibility*. It should be possible to extend the constraint system with analysis-specific constraints with the same ease with which new analyses can be written.

Declarative. It should be possible to view $\mathcal{F}$ programs as logical formulas so that properties of these programs (such as: they preserve the semantics of the object program they are manipulating) can be established through logical reasoning involving other $\mathcal{F}$ programs (e.g. representing the static and dynamic semantics of $\mathcal{O}$). The declarative framework should be expressive enough to allow the static and dynamic semantics of $\mathcal{O}$ to be expressed (and implemented) in terms of declarative rules over program structures in $\mathcal{F}$.

2 Basic Paradigm

In searching for a programming language framework for dealing with programs, it is natural to start with λProlog, and its underlying conceptual basis, higher-order hereditary Harrop formulas [MNPS91] (henceforth called HH). Consider the basic syntactic structure of definite clause programs. Starting with the base

$$\textbf{(Agent)}\ D ::= \texttt{true} \mid D \wedge D \mid \forall x\, D$$
$$\textbf{(Test)}\ G ::= \texttt{true} \mid G \wedge G \mid G \vee G \mid \exists x\, G \tag{1}$$

we may obtain definite clause logic programming LP by adding

$$D ::= G \supset A \qquad\qquad G ::= A \tag{2}$$

That is, a program is formulated in terms of universally quantified implications, whose head contains an atom and whose body contains *goals*, which may be atomic or conjunctive, disjunctive or existential formulas. We assume a higher-order language so the arguments of atomic formulas may be (typed) lambda terms. To keep matters simple, we exclude quantification over predicates; this condition may be relaxed as in λProlog.

To LP, HH adds the notion of *universal* and *implicational goals*:

$$G ::= D \supset G \mid \forall x\, G \tag{3}$$

Computationally, implicational goals or *extensible tests* permit the extension of the current database of programs before answering a specific query. Universal goals permit the introduction of *scoped constants*. These additional constructs complement the use of typed lambda-calculus to represent object level binding notions with devices for realizing recursion over such structure [NM98]. The practical benefits of these capabilities in syntax manipulation have been discussed in several places in the literature.

A limitation of λProlog for the applications of interest is the absence of a treatment of constraints; as we have noted earlier, constraint systems find many uses in static and dynamic analyses over program structure. This leads us to the integration of constraint programming with HH. The addition of constraints to goals and agents has been proposed by [FFL03, GDN04, LNRA01] through the further syntax rules:

$$D ::= c \qquad\qquad G ::= c \tag{4}$$

An implicational goal (e.g. $c \supset G$) can be used to add constraints to the *store* (the LHS); a constraint goal c may check that a constraint follows from the store.

The language with syntax described by rules (1)–(4) still has a shortcoming: it does not permit (recursive) computations on the LHS of a sequent. For example, consider the computation of the goal $D \supset (G_1 \wedge G_2)$ in the context of an LHS given by Λ. Solving this goal requires the addition of D to Λ. In HH, the consequences that emerge from the addition of D to Λ must be computed separately while solving G_1 and G_2. Permitting recursive computation in the LHS could eliminate this redundancy: the consequences can then be computed once, and used in showing both G_1 and G_2. The following excerpt from the type checking of Java programs in the context of a class hierarchy is an example of the utility of this idea.

Example 1 (Java type checking). The type checking of a method body in a JAVA program must be done in the context of type assertions generated by examining the classes referenced in the code. These assertions are built using predicates such as *extends* between class names that captures the subtype relationship. It is desirable that the parsing of referenced classes and the elaboration of type assertions (based on the inheritance hierarchy, method signatures, field signatures, etc) be done only once. Thus, conceptually, one wishes to define:

$$\forall ClassName \; \forall Code$$
$$(((parse \; ClassName \; Code) \wedge$$
$$((referencedClassTypes \; Code) \supset (typed\_code \; Code)))$$
$$\supset (typed\_class \; ClassName))$$

The definition of the predicate for *typed_code* assumes that the type information for each referenced class is already available in the store and may simply be queried (e.g. using the constraint subType):

$$\forall LExp \; \forall RExp \; \forall LT \; \forall RT$$
$$((isType \; RExp \; RT) \wedge (isType \; LExp \; LT) \wedge (subType \; RT \; LT))$$
$$\supset (typed \; (assign \; LExp \; RExp))).$$

Thus, we expect *referencedClassTypes* to be a user-defined (agent) predicate here that operates on the LHS of a sequent and that walks the AST *Code*, determining referenced classes and for each such class generating type assertions based on the type hierarchy. Running the agent *referencedClassTypes Code* to quiescence on the LHS would thus elaborate the type information in *Code* once and for all, sharing this computation among all subsequent RHS queries.

This motivates us to take the fundamental step underlying this paper: combining the power of HH with CCP. CCP is organized around the notion of (deterministic) agents working together in parallel to produce constraints on a shared store.

$$\textbf{(Agent)} \; D ::= \textbf{true} \mid c \mid D \wedge D \mid E \mid G \supset D \mid E \supset D \mid \exists x \; D$$
$$\textbf{(Test)} \; G ::= \textbf{true} \mid c \mid G \wedge G$$

One views true as the vacuous agent, c as the agent which adds the constraint c to the *store*, $D_1 \wedge D_2$ as the parallel composition of D_1 and D_2, E (an atomic formula) as a recursively defined agent, (whose rules of behavior are specified by the formulas $E \supset D$), $G \supset D$ as a *deep guard ask agent* which checks whether the store entails G, and if so, reduces to D, and $\exists x \; D$ as the agent that introduces a new local variable x and then behaves like D. [LS93] has shown that the logical view of CCP (in the subcase of flat guards $c \supset D$) corresponds to *computation on the left* in a sequent based presentation. Conceptually the purpose of the computation is to determine the (strongest) set of constraints c (on the variables in D) that follow from D. Thus on termination we have a c and a proof tree for $D \vdash c$ such that for any other c_1, if $D \vdash c_1$ then $c \vdash c_1$.

This motivates us to add to the syntax rules (1)–(4) the rules:

$$D ::= E \mid G \supset D \mid E \supset D \mid \exists x \; D \qquad (5)$$

We call the resulting language framework λRCC (RCC for the sub-language with first-order terms). Notice that the second rule should be thought of as permitting fully recursive asks ("deep guards" in concurrent logic programming terminology), thus allowing a symmetric interplay between goals and agents (cf the production $G ::= D \supset G$).

An important restriction in λRCC is that the vocabulary of predicate names used for goals, agents and constraints are pairwise disjoint—we refer to this as the *Disjoint Vocabulary* condition. The Rules (1)–(5) can be consolidated as:

$$\begin{array}{ll}\textbf{(Agent)} & D ::= \texttt{true} \mid c \mid E \mid D \wedge D \mid G \supset A \mid G \supset D \mid E \supset D \mid \exists x\, D \mid \forall x\, D \\ \textbf{(Test)} & G ::= \texttt{true} \mid c \mid A \mid G \wedge G \mid D \supset G \mid G \vee G \mid \exists x\, G \mid \forall x\, G\end{array} \qquad (6)$$

Clearly this includes LP, HH, CLP and CCP. The results of this paper may be extended to support disjunctive agents as well; but we omit their treatment for lack of space.

3   Operational Semantics for λRCC

How should we understand computation in λRCC? We propose that *behavioral testing of concurrent systems* provides a suitable framework. Let us think of a configuration in our system as being given by a multiset of *predications* of the form (Λ, G) in which Λ is a multiset of D (agent) formulas. Informally, we would like to view such a pair as posing the question "Does the concurrent system Λ pass the test G?" We expect the operational semantics of the language to be described by a transition relation $\longrightarrow$ on configurations that allows us to address such a question in an incremental fashion. To indicate success, we introduce the configuration ϵ; thus the question (Λ, G) is considered to be one that has a successful answer iff $(\Lambda, G) \xrightarrow{\ *\ } \epsilon$.

The testing notion is behavioral in the sense that it merely examines the behavior, i.e. the potential to produce certain results, treating the structure of the system as opaque. Even simple structural queries such as "Does the system contain the agent A?" are not permitted (thanks to the Disjoint Vocabulary condition). Permitting such queries would interfere with the understanding of goal-predicates and agent-predicates as recursive procedure calls. One would have to account for the possibility that a query A can be answered not only by unrolling A into the body G of a clause defining A but by the mere presence of the atom A on the LHS. Similarly, there is no possibility of formulating a query which is able to decompose the system into the parallel composition of two agents A_1 and A_2 and ask whether A_1 satisfies G_1 and A_2 satisfies G_2 (cf bunched implication logics [OP99]).

3.1   The Underlying Intuitions

Let us write $\Lambda \Vdash G$ (read: "Λ passes G" or "Λ has the potential to answer G") to represent the condition $(\Lambda, G) \xrightarrow{\ *\ } \epsilon$.

Structural principles. A question to ask is: When should $\Lambda \Vdash c$ succeed? The operational interpretation of CCP suggests a natural answer: it should succeed iff it is possible for Λ to evolve in such a way that the resulting store entails c. Thus the question being asked is: does Λ have the *potential* to generate c? Even before we get specific about the evolution process, the viewpoint that it only serves to "actualize" potential leads to certain structural principles that our operational semantics should satisfy:

Potential preservation $(\Lambda, c) \xrightarrow{*} (\Lambda', c)$ and $\Lambda \Vdash c$ implies $\Lambda' \Vdash c$.
Structural Rules $\Lambda \Vdash c'$ and $\Lambda, c' \Vdash c$ implies $\Lambda \Vdash c$; $\Lambda, D, D \Vdash c$ if $\Lambda, D, D \Vdash c$;
$\Lambda, D_1, D_2 \Vdash c$ if $\Lambda, D_2, D_1 \Vdash c$; and $\Lambda, D \Vdash c$ if $\Lambda \Vdash c$.

Agent combinators. To address the issue of evolution itself, when should Λ, D pass a test c? This should happen if (a) Λ passes the test by itself or (b) D interacts with Λ in such a way that the system reaches a state in which c can be answered. To specify this precisely, we need *agent interaction rules*:

Vacuous agent $\Lambda, \mathtt{true} \Vdash c$ iff $\Lambda \Vdash c$.
Parallel agent $\Lambda, D_1 \wedge D_2 \Vdash c$ iff $\Lambda, D_1, D_2 \Vdash c$.
Recursive agent $\Lambda, E \Vdash c$ iff $\Lambda \Vdash c$ or there is a Λ' and a rule $E \supset D \in \Lambda'$ s.t.
   $((\Lambda, E), c) \xrightarrow{*} ((\Lambda', E), c)$ and $\Lambda', E, D \Vdash c$.
Deep guard agent $\Lambda, G \supset D \Vdash c$ iff for some Λ': $((\Lambda, G \supset D), c) \xrightarrow{*} ((\Lambda', G \supset D), c)$, and (i) $\Lambda' \Vdash c$ or (ii) $\Lambda', G \supset D \Vdash G$ and $\Lambda', D \Vdash c$.
Existential agent $\Lambda, \exists x\, D \Vdash c$ iff $\Lambda, D[i/x] \Vdash c$ for some new parameter i.
Universal agent $\Lambda, \forall x\, D \Vdash c$ iff $\Lambda, \forall x\, D, D[t/x] \Vdash c$.

The first two rules have already been discussed in conjunction with CCP. For recursive agents, Λ, E passes the test c if Λ passes the test by itself or if Λ can evolve to Λ' in which a rule $E \supset D$ is revealed such that Λ', E, D passes the test. The agent $\exists x\, D$ interacts with Λ by producing a previously unknown instance of D that it runs in parallel. The case for $\forall x\, D$ keeps $\forall x\, D$ around to produce other instances that might be needed. Finally, $G \supset D$ interacts with Λ by testing whether Λ passes G (using $G \supset D$ as a resource if needed) and, if so, by running D in parallel with Λ. Thus we require $\Lambda, G \supset D \Vdash c$ iff for some Λ': $((\Lambda, G \supset D), c) \xrightarrow{*} ((\Lambda', G \supset D), c)$, and (i) $\Lambda' \Vdash c$ or (ii) $\Lambda', G \supset D \Vdash G$ and $\Lambda', D \Vdash c$. Notice that, in contrast to E, G functions as a deep guard in this kind of agent formula. Further, the evolution of $((\Lambda, G \supset D), c)$ may itself involve a recursive use of $G \supset D$, but this time in the context of establishing G' for a different $G' \supset D'$ in the current configuration.

Test combinators. Of course, tests may themselves have a complex, non-primitive structure and the operational semantics must specify behavior with respect to such structure as well. Here we rely on the usual interpretation of atomic goals A as recursively defined tests and of $G_1 \wedge G_2$ (resp. $G_1 \vee G_2$, $D \supset G$, $\forall x\, G$) should be viewed as a conjunctive (resp. disjunctive, conditional, generic) test, consistent with their "search reading" formalized by uniform proofs [MNPS91]. There is, however, a subtle difference in the interpretation of existential tests: While the test $\exists x\, G$ succeeds when there is some term t such that the test $G[t/x]$ succeeds, existential agents are allowed to evolve and introduce new constants that can be used to construct t.

Vacuous query $\Lambda \Vdash \mathtt{true}$ always holds.
Recursive query $\Lambda \Vdash A$ iff there is some Λ' s.t. $(\Lambda, A) \xrightarrow{*} (\Lambda', A)$, and there is a
   $G \supset A \in \Lambda'$ and $\Lambda' \Vdash G$.
Conjunctive query $\Lambda \Vdash G_1 \wedge G_2$ iff $\Lambda \Vdash G_1$ and $\Lambda \Vdash G_2$.
Disjunctive query $\Lambda \Vdash G_1 \vee G_2$ iff $\Lambda \Vdash G_1$ or $\Lambda \Vdash G_2$.
Extensible query $\Lambda \Vdash D \supset G$ iff $\Lambda, D \Vdash G$.

Universal query $\Lambda \Vdash \forall x\, G$ iff $\Lambda \Vdash G[i/x]$ for some new parameter i.
Existential query $\Lambda \Vdash \exists x\, G$ iff there is some Λ' s.t. $(\Lambda, \exists x\, G) \xrightarrow{*} (\Lambda', \exists x\, G)$ and $\Lambda' \Vdash G[t/x]$, for some t built using the constants in Λ', G.

From a programmer's point of view, the notion of behavioral testing of a concurrent system provides an account of the operational behavior of various combinators. λRCC can be thought of as building on the basic query of the underlying constraint system, $c_0, \ldots, c_n \vdash c$, by permitting complex, recursively defined agents on the LHS of the $\vdash$, and complex recursively defined queries on the RHS. The purpose of the complex formulas on the LHS and RHS in this context is to construct appropriate queries of the underlying constraint system (which may be viewed as a replacement for the axiom case in the usual inference systems).

3.2   A Formal Presentation

We formalize these ideas via a transition system specified in the tradition of Plotkin's SOS. The transition relation builds on some unknown but fixed underlying constraint system $\mathcal{C}$ satisfying the properties described in [Sar92, PSSS92] that formalizes a derivability relation of the form $c_0, \ldots, c_k \vdash_{\mathcal{C}} c$. In particular, the properties include the admissibility of CUT, i.e., if $c_0, \ldots, c_{k-1} \vdash_{\mathcal{C}} c_k$ and $c_0, \ldots, c_k \vdash_{\mathcal{C}} c$ then $c_0, \ldots, c_{k-1} \vdash_{\mathcal{C}} c$, the admissibility of *Contraction*, i.e., if $\Gamma, c, c \vdash_{\mathcal{C}} c'$ then $\Gamma, c \vdash_{\mathcal{C}} c'$, and closure under substitution for parameters, i.e., if $\Gamma \vdash_{\mathcal{C}} c$ and Γ' and c' result from Γ and c by replacing a parameter i by a term t then $\Gamma' \vdash_{\mathcal{C}} c'$. We augment $\mathcal{C}$ with the inference rule CONST

$$\frac{c_0, \ldots, c_k \vdash_{\mathcal{C}} c}{\Lambda, c_0, \ldots, c_k \vdash_{\mathcal{C}} c}(\text{CONST}) \tag{7}$$

in which Λ ranges over multisets of D-formulas. The configurations of the machine are multisets Γ of predications (Λ, G). We use ϵ for the empty multiset. The inference rules of the transition system are:

$$((\Lambda, E, E \supset D), G) \longrightarrow ((\Lambda, E, D), G) \text{ (FC)} \qquad \frac{\Lambda \vdash_{\mathcal{C}} c}{(\Lambda, c) \longrightarrow \epsilon}(\text{C})$$

$$\frac{((\Lambda, G \supset D), G) \xrightarrow{*} \epsilon}{((\Lambda, G \supset D), G') \longrightarrow ((\Lambda, D), G')}(\text{DG}) \qquad (\Lambda, G \vee G') \longrightarrow (\Lambda, G) \text{ (R-OR-1)}$$

$$((\Lambda, D \wedge D'), G) \longrightarrow ((\Lambda, D, D'), G) \text{ (L-AND)} \qquad (\Lambda, G \vee G') \longrightarrow (\Lambda, G') \text{ (R-OR-2)}$$

$$((\Lambda, \exists x\, D), G) \longrightarrow ((\Lambda, D[i/x]), G) \text{ (L-E(*))} \qquad (\Lambda, D \supset G) \longrightarrow ((\Lambda, D), G) \text{ (R-IMP)}$$

$$((\Lambda, \forall x\, D), G) \longrightarrow ((\Lambda, \forall x\, D, D[t/x]), G) \text{ (L-U)} \qquad (\Lambda, \exists x\, G) \longrightarrow (\Lambda, G[t/x]) \text{ (R-E)}$$

$$(\Lambda, \text{true}) \longrightarrow \epsilon \text{ (R-TRUE)} \qquad (\Lambda, (\forall x)G) \longrightarrow (\Lambda, G[i/x]) \text{ (R-U(*))}$$

$$((\Lambda, G \supset A), A) \longrightarrow ((\Lambda, G \supset A), G) \text{ (BC)} \qquad \frac{(\Lambda, G) \xrightarrow{*} \Gamma'}{\Gamma, (\Lambda, G) \longrightarrow \Gamma, \Gamma'}(\text{STRUC})$$

$$(\Lambda, G \wedge G') \longrightarrow (\Lambda, G), (\Lambda, G') \text{ (R-AND)}$$

The symbol "," is used to denote multiset union in these rules. In determining the applicability of any rule to a given configuration, we assume that a notion of equality modulo the rules of λ-conversion is used. In the rules L-E and R-U, i must be a parameter that does not already appear in the predication on the LHS of the transition rule.

The semantics described above accurately models *successful termination* leveraging don't know non-determinism inherent in the application of BC (which of many applicable rules should be chosen?), R-Or-1/2 (which branch should be chosen?), and R-E (when the rule should be used and with which term?). (See Theorem 8 which establishes that the nondeterminism in the application of the remaining rules is don't care.) The first two can be handled via or-parallel search or backtracking in the usual Prolog style. Once the point of use of the R-E rule has been determined, the actual instantiation for the quantifier may be incrementally generated, using techniques such as those described in [Sha92] to encode quantifier dependency information that constrains the instantiation. A more detailed operational semantics could also replace the "coarse step" evaluation of deep guards above with an incremental evaluation based on maintaining and propagating partial state (cf AKL [HJ90]). Such a detailed operational semantics is beyond the scope of this paper and will be presented in subsequent work.

The proof of the following theorem relies on Theorem 3, Theorem 7, and known properties of intuitionistic derivability.

Theorem 2 (Operational Characterization). *The operational semantics formalized above validates the structural principles and the agent and test combinator conditions described in Section 3.1.*

4   Proof-Theoretic Semantics for λRCC

We show the declarative semantics of λRCC to be given by provability in intuitionistic logic augmented by a fixed constraint system $\mathcal{C}$ of the kind described in Section 3. Specifically we assume that the derivability relation is characterized by a standard sequent system that may additionally use as axioms

$$\frac{}{\Lambda \vdash c}(\text{Const})$$

whenever $\Lambda \vdash_{\mathcal{C}} c$ is a valid judgement. We differentiate these axioms from the usual ones in a sequent calculus below by annotating the latter as (ID).

4.1   Operational Derivability

We are interested in (cut-free) proofs of sequents of the form $\Lambda \vdash G$ where Λ is a multiset of D formulas. Observe that if Ξ is any sequent that appears in a proof, then the LHS of Ξ contains only D and A formulas and the RHS of Ξ contains either a G or an E formula. One consequence of this observation is that we do not have a need for the ∨-L rule in constructing proofs for the sequents under consideration. We would also like to restrict the use of the ⊃-L rule as follows.

Chaining condition: Every instance of ⊃-L in which the principal formula is $G \supset A$ (resp. $E \supset D$) is of the form on the left (resp. right):

$$\frac{\overline{\Lambda, G \supset A \vdash G} \qquad \frac{}{\Lambda, A \vdash A}(\text{Id})}{\Lambda, G \supset A \vdash A}(\supset\text{-L}) \qquad \frac{\frac{}{\Lambda, E, E \supset D \vdash E}(\text{Id}) \qquad \overline{\Lambda, E, D \vdash G}}{\Lambda, E, E \supset D \vdash G}(\supset\text{-L})$$

Constraint-condition: Every instance of $\supset$-L in which the principal formula is $c \supset D$ is of the form:

$$
\cfrac{\cfrac{}{\Lambda, c \supset D \vdash c}(\text{Const}) \qquad \cfrac{\begin{array}{c}\Pi' \\ \vdots \\ \Lambda, D \vdash G\end{array}}{}}{\Lambda, c \supset D \vdash G}(\text{L-Imp})
$$

There are no restrictions on the use of $\supset$-L on $G \supset D$ formulas where G is not c.

We say that a sequent $D \vdash G$ is *operationally derivable* iff it has a proof in which the $\lor$-L rule is not used and each occurrence of the $\supset$-L rule satisfies the above restrictions. We indicate the existence of such a proof by writing $D \vdash_o G$. In such proofs, goal rules are used only to determine what to do next when trying to prove an atomic goal (thus goal rules define the behavior of goal-predicates); agent rules are used only to determine which agents follow from atomic agents (thus agent rules define the behavior of agent-predicates); a constraint query can be proven only if sufficiently powerful constraints are explicitly present in the constraint store. In particular, operational derivability forces proofs to have a "straight line" structure. In a proof the only nodes which have two deep subtrees (i.e. subtrees of depth > 1) and which correspond to the application of a left rule are those whose principal formula is $(G \supset D)$ (where G is not c).

Operational derivability corresponds to the transition system of Section 3.

Theorem 3 (Faithfulness Theorem). $\Lambda \vdash_o G$ iff $(\Lambda, G) \xrightarrow{\ \ *\ \ } \epsilon$

The proof in one direction proceeds by induction on the size of a derivation and in the other by induction on the length of the transition sequence.

4.2 Correspondence with Intuitionistic Logic

Operational derivability is intended as a bridge between the transition semantics and intuitionistic provability. In one direction, the connection is immediate since operational proofs are intuitionistic proofs with additional structure.

Theorem 4 (Soundness Theorem). $D \vdash_o G$ *implies* $D \vdash G$.

For the other direction, we have to show that the provability relation is unaltered even though we may lose some proofs. We proceed towards this goal via a couple of lemmas. The first lemma is modelled on results in Dyckhoff [Dyc92]. Call a proof *sensible* if whenever $A \supset B$ is the principal formula of an $\supset$-L rule in an intuitionistic derivation and A is atomic, then A also appears on the LHS of the lower sequent. Then the following holds for Intuitionistic Logic (with constraints, as developed in this paper):

Lemma 5. *A proof exists for a sequent if and only if a sensible proof exists.*

Proof. (Sketch) Associate with a proof an *insensibility* measure that counts the number of places where $\supset$-L is applied in a way that violates the notion of sensibility, i.e., where it pertains to a formula of the form $A \supset B$ where A is atomic and A does not appear in the antecedent. We then prove the lemma by induction on the insensibility measure, essentially showing that the first occurrence of such a rule in the derivation along any path starting from the leaves (axioms) can be eliminated.

Lemma 5 shows that we can restrict attention to intuitionistic derivations satisfying the forward chaining condition. By a similar argument, we can show also that the constraint condition can be respected without loss of completeness. We now want to show that if the RHS of the sequent is an atom then we can require it to be proved by backchaining. Define a *clause instance* based on the structure of a D formula as follows:

(1) Any clause instance of $D'[i/x]$ for a new constant i is a clause instance of $\exists x\, D'$.
(2) Any clause instance of $D'[t/x]$, for a closed term t is a clause instance of $\forall x\, D'$.
(3) Any clause instance of D_1 or D_2 is a clause instance of $D_1 \wedge D_2$.
(4) Let $D = G \supset D$: If $G' \supset A$ is a clause instance of D then $((G \wedge G') \supset A$ is a clause instance of D.

Lemma 6. *If A is an atomic formula and Λ is a multiset of D formulas, then $\Lambda \vdash A$ has a derivation if and only if there is a clause instance $G \supset A$ of some D formula in Λ such that $\Lambda \vdash G$ has a derivation.*

Proof. (Sketch) The proof proceeds by induction on the height of the derivation. The last rule in the derivation must pertain to the LHS. The definition of clause instances is modelled to address the non-trivial cases, namely $\exists$-L, $\forall$-L and $\supset$-L.

Lemmas 5 and 6 provide the basis for the proof of the desired result:

Theorem 7 (Completeness Theorem). $D \vdash G$ *implies* $D \vdash_o G$.

The results of this section show that entailment in intuitionistic logic provides an alternative semantics for λRCC. Apart from underpinning the declarative semantics of this language, this property also allows us to use known properties of the intuitionistic calculus to understand characteristics of our transition relation. As one example, known permutation properties for this calculus reveal that some aspects of non-determinism in the transition relation are inconsequential:

Theorem 8 (Local Confluence Theorem). *Let $(\Lambda, A) \longrightarrow (\Lambda_1, A_1)$ by any rule except R-OR-2, R-OR-1, R-E or BC. Let $(\Lambda, A) \longrightarrow (\Lambda_2, A_2)$ by any rule. Then there exists a Λ_3 such that $(\Lambda_1, A_1) \overset{*}{\longrightarrow} (\Lambda_3, A')$ and $(\Lambda_2, A_1) \overset{*}{\longrightarrow} (\Lambda_3, A')$.*

5   Conclusions

This paper establishes the semantic foundations for a logical approach to program manipulation, λRCC, which satisfies the desiderata laid out in Section 1. λRCC endows a very rich subset of intuitionistic logic with a (complete) computational interpretation based on testing determinate concurrent systems. Operationally, the programmer may use recursive agents to generate constraints from a representation of an object program, and recursive queries to test these constraints.

From a practical point of view, we are currently developing a concrete extension of λProlog along these lines. We intend to develop an integration of such a language into JAVA-like languages along the lines of jcc[SJG03], and use it as the basis for AST-rewrites in Polyglot and Eclipse.

On the theoretical front, extending the basic conception of this paper to sub-structural logics such as linear logic remains open. In contrast to LolliMon [LPPW05] that associates backward (resp. forward) chaining with asynchronous (resp. synchronous) connectives of linear logic, this paper explores forward and backward chaining mostly (except existentials) in the asynchronous fragment. The detailed integration of these seemingly different approaches remains open to further investigations.

Acknowledgements. We gratefully acknowledge discussions with Robert Fuhrer and Mandana Vaziri on the topic of logical representation of program refactorings. Radha Jagadeesan was supported in part by NSF 0430175. Gopalan Nadathur has received support for this work from NSF Grant CCR-0429572 and the Digital Technology Center and the Department of Computer Science at the University of Minnesota.

References

[Aik99]   Alexander Aiken. Introduction to set constraint-based program analysis. *Sci. Comput. Program.*, 35(2-3):79–111, 1999.

[Dyc92]   Roy Dyckhoff. Contraction-free sequent calculi for intuitionistic logic. *The Journal of Symbolic Logic*, 57(3), September 1992.

[ecl]   The eclipse project. www.eclipse.org.

[FFL03]   Stacy E. Finkelstein, Peter Freyd, and James Lipton. A new framework for declarative programming. *Theor. Comput. Sci.*, 300(1-3):91–160, 2003.

[FTK04]   Robert Fuhrer, Frank Tip, and Adam Kiezun. Advanced refactorings in eclipse. In *OOPSLA '04: Companion to the 19th annual ACM SIGPLAN conference on Object-oriented programming systems, languages, and applications*, pages 8–8, New York, NY, USA, 2004. ACM Press.

[GDN04]   Miguel Garcia-Diaz and Susana Nieva. Providing declarative semantics for hh extended constraint logic programs. In *PPDP '04: Proceedings of the 6th ACM SIGPLAN international conference on Principles and practice of declarative programming*, pages 55–66, New York, NY, USA, 2004. ACM Press.

[Hei92]   Nevin Charles Heintze. *Set based program analysis*. PhD thesis, Carnegie Mellon University, Pittsburgh, PA, USA, 1992.

[HJ90]   S. Haridi and S. Janson. Kernel andorra Prolog and its computation model. In David H. D. Warren and Peter Szeredi, editors, *Proceedings of the Seventh International Conference on Logic Programming*, pages 31–46, Jerusalem, 1990. The MIT Press.

[JL87]   J. Jaffar and J.-L. Lassez. Constraint Logic Programming. In *Proceedings of the 14th Annual ACM Symposium on Principles of Programming Languages (POPL'87), Munich, Germany*, pages 111–119. ACM Press, New York (NY), USA, 1987.

[LMRC05]   Sorin Lerner, Todd Millstein, Erika Rice, and Craig Chambers. Automated soundness proofs for dataflow analyses and transformations via local rules. In *POPL '05: Proceedings of the 32nd ACM SIGPLAN-SIGACT symposium on Principles of programming languages*, pages 364–377, New York, NY, USA, 2005. ACM Press.

[LNRA01]   Javier Leach, Susana Nieva, and Mario Rodrguez-Artalejo. Constraint logic programming with hereditary harrop formulas. *Theory Pract. Log. Program.*, 1(4):409–445, 2001.

[LPPW05]   Pablo López, Frank Pfenning, Jeff Polakow, and Kevin Watkins. Monadic concurrent linear logic programming. In Pedro Barahona and Amy P. Felty, editors, *PPDP*, pages 35–46. ACM, 2005.

[LS93]   Patrick Lincoln and Vijay Saraswat. Proofs as concurrent processes. Technical report, PARC, 1993.

[MNPS91]   Dale Miller, Gopalan Nadathur, Frank Pfenning, and Andre Scedrov. Uniform proofs as a foundation for logic programming. *Annals of Pure and Applied Logic*, 51:125–157, 1991.

[NCM03]   Nathaniel Nystrom, Michael R. Clarkson, and Andrew C. Myers. Polyglot: An extensible compiler framework for java. In *Proceedings of the Conference on Compiler Construction (CC'03)*, pages 1380–152, April 2003.

[NM98]   Gopalan Nadathur and Dale Miller. Higher-order logic programming. In C. Hogger D. Gabbay and A. Robinson, editors, *Handbook of Logic in Artificial Intelligence and Logic Programming*, volume 5, pages 499–590. Oxford University Press, 1998.

[OP99]   P.W. O'Hearn and D. J. Pym. The logic of bunched implications. *Bulletin of Symbolic Logic*, 5(2):215–244, 1999.

[OSW99]   Martin Odersky, Martin Sulzmann, and Martin Wehr. Type inference with constrained types. *Theor. Pract. Object Syst.*, 5(1):35–55, 1999.

[Pal95]   Jens Palsberg. Closure analysis in constraint form. *ACM Trans. Program. Lang. Syst.*, 17(1):47–62, 1995.

[PE88]   Frank Pfenning and Conal Elliott. Higher-order abstract syntax. In *Proceedings of the ACM-SIGPLAN Conference on Programming Language Design and Implementation*, pages 199–208. ACM Press, June 1988.

[PS94]   Jens Palsberg and Michael I. Schwartzbach. *Object-oriented type systems*. John Wiley and Sons Ltd., Chichester, UK, UK, 1994.

[PSSS92]   Prakash Panangaden, Vijay A. Saraswat, P. J. Scott, and R. A. G. Seely. A hyperdoctrinal view of concurrent constraint programming. In J. W. de Bakker, Willem P. de Roever, and Grzegorz Rozenberg, editors, *REX Workshop*, volume 666 of *Lecture Notes in Computer Science*, pages 457–476. Springer, 1992.

[PW98]   William Pugh and David Wonnacott. Constraint-based array dependence analysis. *ACM Trans. Program. Lang. Syst.*, 20(3):635–678, 1998.

[RMR01]   Atanas Rountev, Ana Milanova, and Barbara G. Ryder. Points-to analysis for java using annotated constraints. In *OOPSLA '01: Proceedings of the 16th ACM SIGPLAN conference on Object oriented programming, systems, languages, and applications*, pages 43–55, New York, NY, USA, 2001. ACM Press.

[Sar92]   Vijay A. Saraswat. The category of constraint systems is cartesian closed. In *Proceedings of the IEEE Symposium on Logic in Computer Science*, 1992.

[Sar93]   V. Saraswat. *Concurrent Constraint Programming*. Doctoral Dissertation Award and Logic Programming. MIT Press, 1993.

[Sha92]   Natarajan Shankar. Proof search in the intuitionistic sequent calculus. In Deepak Kapur, editor, *Automated Deduction – CADE-11*, number 607 in Lecture Notes in Computer Science, pages 522–536. Springer Verlag, June 1992.

[SJG03]   V Saraswat, R Jagadeesan, and V Gupta. jcc: Integrating timed default concurrent constraint programming into Java. Number 2902 in Lecture Notes in Computer Science, pages 156–170. Springer Verlag, 2003.

Proofs of Termination of Rewrite Systems for Polytime Functions

Toshiyasu Arai[1] and Georg Moser[2]

[1] Kobe University, Graduate School of Science and Technology
arai@kurt.scitec.kobe-u.ac.jp
[2] University of Innsbruck, Computational Logic
georg.moser@uibk.ac.at

Abstract. We define a new path order $\prec_{\text{POP}}$ so that for a finite rewrite system R compatible with $\prec_{\text{POP}}$, the *complexity* or *derivation length function* Dl_R^f for each function symbol f is guaranteed to be bounded by a polynomial in the length of the inputs. Our results yield a simplification and clarification of the results obtained by Beckmann and Weiermann (Archive for Mathematical Logic, 36:11–30, 1996).

Keywords: Termination, term rewriting characterisation, derivation length, complexity theory.

1 Introduction

Suppose $\mathcal{C}$ denotes an inductively defined class of recursive number-theoretic functions and suppose each $f \in \mathcal{C}$ is defined via an equation (or more generally a system of equations) of the form

$$f(\mathbf{x}) = t(\lambda \mathbf{y}.f(\mathbf{y}), \mathbf{x}) , \tag{1}$$

where t may involve previously defined functions. In a term-rewriting context these defining equations are oriented from left to right and the canonical *term-rewriting characterisation* $R_{\mathcal{C}}$ of $\mathcal{C}$ can be defined as follows: The signature Σ of $R_{\mathcal{C}}$ includes for each function f in $\mathcal{C}$ a corresponding function symbol f. In order to represent natural numbers Σ includes a constant 0 and a unary function symbol S. I.e. numbers are represented by their numerals. (Later we represent natural numbers in the form of binary strings.) For each function $f \in \mathcal{C} - \{0, S\}$, defined by (1), the rule

$$f(\mathbf{x}) \rightarrow t(\lambda \mathbf{y}.f(\mathbf{y}), \mathbf{x}) ,$$

is added to $R_{\mathcal{C}}$. In all non-pathological cases the term rewrite system (TRS) $R_{\mathcal{C}}$ is terminating and confluent. $R_{\mathcal{C}}$ is best understood as a constructor TRS, where the constructors are 0 and S. Hence $R_{\mathcal{C}}$ may be conceived as a *functional program* implementing the functions in $\mathcal{C}$.

Term-rewriting characterisations have been studied e.g. in [1,2,3,4]. The analysis of $R_{\mathcal{C}}$ provides insight into the structure of $\mathcal{C}$ or renders us with a delineation

R. Ramanujam and S. Sen (Eds.): FSTTCS 2005, LNCS 3821, pp. 529–540, 2005.

of a class of rewrite systems whose complexity (measured by the length of derivations) is guaranteed to belong to the class $\mathcal{C}$. Term-rewriting characterisations turn the emphasis form the *definition* of a function f to its *computation*. An essential property of term-rewriting characterisations $R_{\mathcal{C}}$ is its *feasibility*: $R_{\mathcal{C}}$ is called *feasible*, if for each n-ary function $f \in \mathcal{C}$, there exists a function symbol g in the signature of $R_{\mathcal{C}}$ such that $g(\overline{m}_1, \ldots, \overline{m}_n)$ computes the value of $f(m_1, \ldots, m_n)$ and the derivation length of this computation is bounded by a function from $\mathcal{C}$.

We study *term-rewriting characterisations* of the complexity class **FP**. In particular, our starting point is a clever characterisation R'_B of **FP** introduced by Beckmann and Weiermann. In [1] the feasibility of R'_B is established and conclusively shown that any reduction strategy for R'_B yields an algorithm for $f \in$ **FP** that runs in polytime. We provide a slight generalisation of the fact that R'_B is feasible. Moreover, we flesh out the crucial ingredients of the TRS R'_B by defining a *path order for* **FP**, denoted as $\prec_{\text{POP}}$. We show that for a finite TRS R, compatible with $\prec_{\text{POP}}$, the *derivation length function* Dl_R^f is bounded by a polynomial in the length of the inputs for any defined function symbol f. Furthermore $\prec_{\text{POP}}$ is *complete* in the sense that for any function $f \in$ **FP**, there exists a TRS R computing f such that termination of R can be shown by $\prec_{\text{POP}}$.

2   A Rewrite System for FP

In the following we need some notions from term rewriting and assume (at least nodding) acquaintance with term rewriting. (For background information, please see [5].) Let $\mathcal{V}$ denote a countably infinite set of variables and Σ a signature. The set of terms over Σ and $\mathcal{V}$ is denoted as $T(\Sigma, \mathcal{V})$, while the set of ground terms is written as $\mathcal{T}(\Sigma)$. The rewrite relation induced by a rewrite system R is denoted as $\rightarrow_R$, and its transitive closure by $\rightarrow_R^*$. We write $\tau(t)$ to denote the *size* of a term t, i.e. the number of symbols in t.

Conventions: Terms are denoted by r, s, t, possibly extended by subscripts. We write **t**, to denote sequences of terms $t_1, \ldots, t_k \in T(\Sigma, \mathcal{V})$ and **g** to denote sequences of function symbols $g_1, \ldots, g_k$, respectively. The letters i, j, k, l, m, n, possible extended by subscripts will always refer to natural numbers. The set of natural numbers is denoted as usual by $\mathbb{N}$.

We consider the class **FP** of *polytime computable functions*, i.e. those functions computable by a deterministic Turing machine M, such that M runs in time $\leq p(n)$ for all inputs of length n, where p denotes a polynomial. We consider equivalent formulations of the class of polytime computable functions in terms of recursion schemes.

Recursion schemes such as *bounded recursion* due to Cobham [6] generate exactly the functions computable in polytime. In contrast to this, Bellantoni-Cook [7] introduce certain *unbounded* recursion schemes that distinguish between arguments as to their position in a function. This separation of variables gives rise to the following definition of the *predicative recursive functions* $\mathcal{B}$; for further details see [7]. We fix a suitable signature of *predicative recursive function symbols* B.

Definition 1. *For $k, l \in \mathbb{N}$ we define $B^{k,l}$ inductively.*

- $S_i^{0,1} \in B^{0,1}$, *where* $i \in [0,1]$.
- $O^{k,l} \in B^{k,l}$.
- $U_r^{k,l} \in B^{k,l}$, *for all* $r \in [1, k+l]$.
- $P^{0,1} \in B^{0,1}$.
- $C^{0,3} \in B^{0,3}$.
- *If* $f \in B^{k',l'}$, $g_1, \ldots, g_{k'} \in B^{k,0}$, *and* $h_1, \ldots, h_{l'} \in B^{k,l}$,
  then $\mathrm{SUB}_{k',l'}^{k,l}[f, \mathbf{g}, \mathbf{h}] \in B^{k,l}$.
- *If* $g \in B^{k,l}$, $h_0, h_1 \in B^{k+1,l+1}$, *then* $\mathrm{PREC}^{k+1,l}[g, h_1, h_2] \in B^{k+1,l}$.

Set $B := \bigcup_{k,l \in \mathbb{N}} B^{k,l}$.

To simplify notation we usually drop the superscripts, when denoting predicative recursive function symbols. Occasionally, we even write SUB (, PREC), instead of $\mathrm{SUB}^{k,l}[f, \mathbf{g}]$ (,$\mathrm{PREC}^{n+1}[g, h]$). No confusion will arise from this.

The binary successor function $m \mapsto 2m + i$, $i \in \{0,1\}$ is denoted as S_i. Every natural number can be buildt up from 0 with repeated applications of S_i. The binary length of a number m is defined as follows: $|0| := 0$ and $|S_i(m)| := |m| + 1$.

We write $\mathbb{N}^{k,l}$ for $\mathbb{N}^k \times \mathbb{N}^l$ and for $f \colon \mathbb{N}^{k,l} \to \mathbb{N}$, write $f(m_1, \ldots, m_k; n_1, \ldots, n_l)$ instead of $f(\langle m_1, \ldots, m_k \rangle, \langle n_1, \ldots, n_l \rangle)$. The arguments occurring to the left of the semi-colon are called *normal*, while the arguments to the right are called *safe*.

We define the following functions: $S_i^{0,1}$, $i \in \{0,1\}$ denotes the function $\langle ; m \rangle \mapsto 2m + i$. $O^{k,l}$ denotes the function $\langle \mathbf{m}; \mathbf{n} \rangle \mapsto 0$. $U_r^{k,l}$ denotes the function $\langle m_1, \ldots, m_k; m_{k+1}, \ldots, m_{k+l} \rangle \mapsto m_r$. $P^{0,1}$ denotes the unique number-theoretic function satisfying the following equations: $f(; 0) = 0$, $f(; S_i(m)) = m$. $C^{0,3}$ denotes the unique function satisfying: $f(; 0, m_0, m_1) = m_0$, $f(; S_i(m), m_0, m_1) = m_i$.

If $f \colon \mathbb{N}^{k',l'} \to \mathbb{N}$, $g_i \colon \mathbb{N}^{k,0} \to \mathbb{N}$ for $i \in [1, k']$, $h_j \colon \mathbb{N}^{k,l} \to \mathbb{N}$ for $j \in [1, l']$, then $\mathcal{SUB}_{k',l'}^{k,l}[f, \mathbf{g}, \mathbf{h}]$ denotes the function $\langle \mathbf{m}; \mathbf{n} \rangle \mapsto f(g_1(\mathbf{m};), \ldots, g_{k'}(\mathbf{m};); h_1(\mathbf{m}; \mathbf{n}), \ldots, h_{l'}(\mathbf{m}; \mathbf{n}))$.

If $g \colon \mathbb{N}^{k,l} \to \mathbb{N}$, $h_i \colon \mathbb{N}^{k+1,l+1} \to \mathbb{N}$ for $i \in [0,1]$ then $\mathcal{PREC}^{k+1,l}[g, h_1, h_2]$ denotes the unique number-theoretic function f satisfying: $f(0, \mathbf{m}; \mathbf{n}) = g(\mathbf{m}; \mathbf{n})$ and $f(S_i(m), \mathbf{m}; \mathbf{n}) = h_i(m, \mathbf{m}; \mathbf{n}, f(m, \mathbf{m}; \mathbf{n}))$.

Definition 2. *For $k, l \in \mathbb{N}$ we define $\mathcal{B}^{k,l}$ inductively.*

- $S_i^{0,1} \in \mathcal{B}^{0,1}$, *where* $i \in [0,1]$.
- $\mathcal{O}^{k,l} \in \mathcal{B}^{k,l}$.
- $\mathcal{U}_r^{k,l} \in \mathcal{B}^{k,l}$, *for all* $r \in [1, k+l]$.
- $\mathcal{P}^{0,1} \in \mathcal{B}^{0,1}$.
- $\mathcal{C}^{0,3} \in \mathcal{B}^{0,3}$.
- *If* $f \in \mathcal{B}^{k',l'}$, $g_1, \ldots, g_{k'} \in \mathcal{B}^{k,0}$, *and* $h_1, \ldots, h_{l'} \in \mathcal{B}^{k,l}$, *then* $\mathcal{SUB}_{k',l'}^{k,l}[f, \mathbf{g}, \mathbf{h}] \in \mathcal{B}^{k,l}$.
- *If* $g \in \mathcal{B}^{k,l}$, $h_0, h_1 \in \mathcal{B}^{k+1,l+1}$, *then* $\mathcal{PREC}^{k+1,l}[g, h_1, h_2] \in \mathcal{B}^{k+1,l}$.

The set of predicative recursive functions *is defined as* $\mathcal{B} = \bigcup_{k,l} \mathcal{B}^{k,l}$.

Table 1. A Feasible Term-Rewriting Characterisation of the Predicative Recursive Functions

$O^{k,l}(\mathbf{x}; \mathbf{a}) \to 0$,   [zero]

$U^{k,l}(x_1, \ldots, x_k; x_{k+1}, \ldots, x_{k+l}) \to x_r$,   [projection]

$P^{0,1}(; 0) \to 0$,   [predecessor]

$P^{0,1}(; S_i(; a)) \to a$,

$C^{0,3}(; 0, a_0, a_1) \to a_0$,   [conditional]

$C^{0,3}(; S_i(; a), a_1, a_0) \to a_{2-i}$,

$\mathrm{SUB}^{k,l}[f, \mathbf{g}, \mathbf{h}](\mathbf{x}; \mathbf{n}) \to f(\mathbf{g}(\mathbf{x};); \mathbf{h}(\mathbf{x}; \mathbf{n}))$,   [safe composition]

$\mathrm{PREC}^{k+1,l}[g, h_1, h_2](0, \mathbf{x}; \mathbf{n}) \to g(\mathbf{x}; \mathbf{n})$,   [predicative recursion

$\mathrm{PREC}^{k+1,l}[g, h_1, h_2](S_i(; b), \mathbf{x}; \mathbf{n}) \to$ on notation]

$\quad \to h_i(b, \mathbf{x}; \mathbf{n}, \mathrm{PREC}^{k+1,l}[g, h_1, h_2](b, \mathbf{x}; \mathbf{n}))$.

We use the following notation: $i \in [0, 1]$ and $r \in [1, k + l]$.

It follows from the definitions that for each $f \in \mathcal{B}$, there exists a unique predicative recursive function $f^{\mathcal{B}}$; the latter is called the *interpretation* of f in $\mathcal{B}$. For every number m we define its *numeral* $\overline{m} \in T(B, \mathcal{V})$ as follows: $\overline{0} := 0$, $\overline{S_i(; m)} := S_i(; m)$ for $i \in [0, 1]$. We write $\overline{\mathbf{m}}$ to denote a sequence of numerals $\overline{m}_1, \ldots, \overline{m}_k$. Now the polytime computable functions **FP** can be defined as follows, see [7]:

$$\mathbf{FP} = \bigcup_k \mathcal{B}^{k,0} .$$

In [1] a clever *feasible* term-rewriting characterisation R'_B of the predicative recursive functions $\mathcal{B}$ is given. By Bellantoni's result this yields a feasible term-rewriting characterisation of the class of polytime computable functions **FP**. The (infinite) TRS is given in Table 1.

The TRS R'_B is terminating and confluent. Termination follows by recursive path order (RPO). Confluence is a consequence of the fact that R'_B is orthogonal. Note the restriction in the rewrite rules for *safe composition* and *predicative recursion*. These rules only apply if all *safe* arguments are numerals, i.e. in normal-form. This peculiar restriction is necessary as the canonical term-rewriting characterisation R_B of $\mathcal{B}$, admits exponential lower-bounds, hence R_B is *non-feasible*, compare. [1].

Let R denote a TRS. A *derivation* is a sequence of terms t_i, $i \in \mathbb{N}$, such that for all i, $t_i \to_R t_{i+1}$. The $(i + 1)^{th}$ element of a sequence a is denoted as $(a)_i$. We write $\frown$ for the concatenation of sequences and define the length $|a|$ of a sequence a as usually. We define a partial order $\subseteq$ on pairs of sequences. $a \subseteq b$, if b is an *extension* of a, i.e. $|a| \leq |b|$ and for all $i < |a|$ we have $(a)_i = (b)_i$. A derivation d with $(d)_0 = t$ is called *derivation starting with*

t. The *derivation tree* $\mathcal{T}_R(t)$ of t is defined as the structure $(T(t), \subseteq)$, where $T(t) := \{d \mid d$ is a derivation starting with $t\}$. The root of $\mathcal{T}_R(t)$ is denoted by t (instead of (t)).

We measure the *complexity* or *derivation length* of the computation of $f(\overline{\mathbf{m}})$ by the *height* of $\mathcal{T}_R(f(\overline{\mathbf{m}}))$; more concisely we define the *derivation length function* $\mathrm{Dl}_R^f : \mathcal{T}(\Sigma) \to \mathbb{N}$:

$$\mathrm{Dl}_R^f(\overline{\mathbf{m}}) := \max\{n \mid \exists\, t_0, \ldots, t_n \in \mathcal{T}(\Sigma)\, (t_n \leftarrow_R \cdots \leftarrow_R t_0 = f(\overline{\mathbf{m}}))\}\,.$$

Based on these definitions we make the notion of *feasible* term-rewriting characterisation precise. A term-rewriting characterisation $R_\mathcal{C}$ of a function class $\mathcal{C}$ is called *feasible*, if for each n-ary function $f \in \mathcal{C}$, there exists a function symbol g in the signature of $R_\mathcal{C}$ such that $g(\overline{m}_1, \ldots, \overline{m}_n)$ computes the value of $f(m_1, \ldots, m_n)$ and $\mathrm{Dl}_{R_\mathcal{C}}^f$ is bounded by a function from $\mathcal{C}$. For the rewrite system R_B' we have the following proposition.

Proposition 1. *For every $f \in \mathcal{B}$, $\mathrm{Dl}_{R_B'}^f$ is bounded by a monotone polynomial in the length of the normal inputs. Specifically for each f we can find a number $\ell(f)$ so that $\mathrm{Dl}_{R_B'}^f(\overline{\mathbf{m}}; \overline{\mathbf{n}}) \leq (2 + |\mathbf{m}|)^{\ell(f)}$, where $|\mathbf{m}|$ denotes the sum of the length normal inputs m_i.*

Proof. See [8] for a proof, essentially we employ the observation that the derivation trees $\mathcal{T}_{R_B'}(f(\mathbf{m}; \mathbf{n}))$ are *isomorphic* no matter how the safe input numerals $\mathbf{n}$ vary, to drop the dependency on the length of the normal inputs.   □

3   A Path Ordering for FP

To extend the above results and to facilitate the study of the polytime computable functions in a term-rewriting framework, we introduce in this section a new *path order for* **FP**, which is a *miniaturisation* of the recursive path order, cf. [5], see also [9].

In the definition we make use of an auxiliary varyadic function symbol 'list' of arbitrary, but finite arity, to denote sequences $s_0, \ldots, s_n$ of terms. Instead of $\mathrm{list}(s_0, \ldots, s_n)$ we write $(s_0, \ldots, s_n)$. We write $a \frown b$ for sequences $a = (s_0, \ldots, s_n)$, $b = (s_{n+1}, \ldots, s_{n+m})$ to denote the concatenation $(s_0, \ldots, s_{n+m})$ of a and b.

Let Σ be a signature. We write $T^*(\Sigma, \mathcal{V})$ to denote the set of all finite sequences of terms in $T(\Sigma, \mathcal{V})$. To ensure that $T(\Sigma, \mathcal{V}) \subset T^*(\Sigma, \mathcal{V})$, any term is identified with the sequence $\mathrm{list}(t) = (t)$. We denote sequences by a, b, c, both possible extended with subscripts. Sometimes we write fa as abbreviations of $f(t_0, \ldots, t_n)$, if $a = (t_0, \ldots, t_n)$.

We suppose a partial well-founded relation on S, the *precedence*, denoted as $<$. We write $f \sim g$ if $(f \lesssim g) \wedge (g \lesssim f)$ and we write $f > g$ and $g < f$ interchangeably. Further, we suppose that the signature Σ contains two unary symbols S_0, S_1 of lowest rank in the precedence. I.e. $\Sigma = \{S_0, S_1\} \cup \Sigma'$ and

$S_0 \sim S_1$ and for all $f \in \Sigma'$, $S_0, S_1 < f$. Moreover, we define $0 := ()$. For every number m we define its *numeral* $\overline{m} \in T(\Sigma, \mathcal{V})$ as follows: $\overline{0} := ()$; $\overline{S_i(m)} := S_i(\overline{m})$ for $i \in [0, 1]$.

The definition of the path order for **FP** (POP) $\prec_{\mathrm{POP}}$ (induced by $<$) is based on an auxiliary order $\sqsubseteq$. The separation in two orders is necessary to break the strength of the recursive path order that induces primitive recursive derivation length, cf. [10].

Definition 3. *Inductive definition of $\sqsubseteq$ induced by $<$.*

1. $\exists j \in [1, n]\, (s \sqsubseteq t_j) \Longrightarrow s \sqsubset f(t_1, \ldots, t_n)$,
2. $t = f(t_1, \ldots, t_n)\ \&\ s = g(s_1, \ldots, s_m)$ *with* $g < f\ \&\ \forall i \in [1, m]\, (s_i \sqsubset t)$
   $\Longrightarrow s \sqsubset t$.

Definition 4. *Inductive definition of $\prec_{\mathrm{POP}}$ induced by $<$; $\prec_{\mathrm{POP}}$ is based on $\sqsubseteq$.*

1. $s \sqsubset t \Longrightarrow s \prec_{\mathrm{POP}} t$,
2. $\exists j \in [1, n]\, (s \preceq_{\mathrm{POP}} t_j) \Longrightarrow s \prec_{\mathrm{POP}} f(t_1, \ldots, t_n)\ \&\ s \prec_{\mathrm{POP}} (t_1, \ldots, t_n)$,
3. $t = f(t_1, \ldots, t_n)\ \&\ (m = 0\ or\ (\exists i_0\, (\forall i \neq i_0\, (s_i \sqsubset t)\ \&\ s_i \prec_{\mathrm{POP}} t))$
   $\Longrightarrow (s_1, \ldots, s_m) \prec_{\mathrm{POP}} t$,
4. $t = f(t_0, \ldots, t_n)\ \&\ s = g(s_0, \ldots, s_m)$ *with* $f \sim g\ \&\ (s_0, \ldots, s_m) \prec_{\mathrm{POP}}$
   $(t_0, \ldots, t_n)$
   $\Longrightarrow s \prec_{\mathrm{POP}} t$,
5. $a \approx a_0 \frown \cdots \frown a_n\ \&\ \forall i \leq n\, (a_i \preceq_{\mathrm{POP}} b_i)\ \&\ \exists i \leq n\, (a_i \prec_{\mathrm{POP}} b_i)$
   $\Longrightarrow a \prec_{\mathrm{POP}} (b_0, \ldots, b_n)$ *if* $n \geq 1$,

   $a \approx a_0 \frown \cdots \frown a_n$ *denotes the fact that the sequence a of terms is obtained from the concatenated $a_0 \frown \cdots \frown a_n$ by permutation.*

Note that due to rule 3 $()\prec_{\mathrm{POP}} a$ for any sequence $a \in T^*(\Sigma, \mathcal{V})$. Further, we write $s \succ_{\mathrm{POP}} t$ for $t \prec_{\mathrm{POP}} s$. It is not difficult to argue that $\prec_{\mathrm{POP}}$ is a reduction order. A number of relations are missing; we mention only the following:

$-\ t = f(t_1, \ldots, t_n)\ \&\ s = g(s_1, \ldots, s_m)$ with $g < f\ \&\ \forall i \in [1, m]\, (s_i \prec_{\mathrm{POP}} t) \Longrightarrow s \prec_{\mathrm{POP}} t$.

We indicate the reasons for the omission of this clause.

Example 1. Consider the following TRS, where Σ contains additionally the symbols a, g, h, f with precedence $a, h < f$, $g < h$.

$$f(0) \to a \qquad f(S_i(x)) \to h(f(x)) \qquad h(x) \to g(x, x).$$

It is easy to see that $\prec_{\mathrm{POP}}$ cannot handle the TRS in the example, but would if rule above is included. However, note that the TRS admits an *exponential lower-bound* on the derivation length function.

We introduce suitable *approximations* $\prec_k$ of $\prec_{\mathrm{POP}}$.

Definition 5. *Inductive definition of $\sqsubset_k^l$ induced by $<$; we write $\sqsubset_k$ to abbreviate $\sqsubset_k^k$.*

1. $\exists j \in [1,n] \; (s \sqsubseteq_k^l t_j) \Longrightarrow s \sqsubset_k^l f(t_0, \ldots, t_n)$,
2. $t = f(t_0, \ldots, t_n) \; \& \; s = g(s_0, \ldots, s_m)$ with $g < f \; \& \; m < k \; \& \; \forall i \, (s_i \sqsubseteq_k^l t)$
   $\Longrightarrow s \sqsubset_k^{l+1} t$.

Definition 6. *Inductive definition of $\prec_k$ induced by $<$; $\prec_k$ is based on $\sqsubset_k$.*

1. $s \sqsubset_k t \Longrightarrow s \prec_k t$,
2. $\exists j \in [1,n] \; (s \preceq_k t_j) \Longrightarrow s \prec_k f(t_1, \ldots, t_n)$,
3. $t = f(t_1, \ldots, t_n) \; \& \; (m = 0 \text{ or } \exists i_0 \in [1,m] \, (\forall i \neq i_0 \, (s_i \sqsubseteq_k t) \; \& \; s_{i_0} \prec_k t))$
   $\& \; m < k \Longrightarrow (s_1, \ldots, s_m) \prec_k t$,
4. $t = f(t_0, \ldots, t_n) \; \& \; s = g(s_0, \ldots, s_m)$ with $f \sim g \; \& \; (s_0, \ldots, s_m) \prec_k$
   $(t_0, \ldots, t_n) \; \& \; m < \max\{k, n\} \Longrightarrow s \prec_k t$,
5. $a \approx a_0 \frown \cdots \frown a_n \; \& \; \forall i \leq n \, (a_i \preceq_k b_i) \; \& \; \exists i \leq n \, (a_i \prec_k b_i) \Longrightarrow a \prec_k$
   $(b_0, \ldots, b_n)$ if $n \geq 1$.

In the following we prove that if for a finite rewrite system R, $R \subseteq \prec_{\text{POP}}$, then it even holds that $\to_R \subseteq \prec_k$, where k depends on R only.

Lemma 1. *If $s \prec_k t$ and $k < l$, then $s \prec_l t$.*

We introduce the auxiliary measure $|.|: T^*(\Sigma, \mathcal{V}) \to \mathbb{N}$: (i) $|x| := 1$, $x \in \mathcal{V}$, (ii) $|(s_1, \ldots, s_n)| := \max\{n, |s_1|, \ldots, |s_n|\}$, (iii) $|fa| := |a| + 1$.

Lemma 2. *If $s \prec_{\text{POP}} t$, then for any substitution σ, $s\sigma \prec_{|s|} t\sigma$.*

Lemma 3. *If $t = f(t_1, \ldots, v, \ldots, t_n)$, $s = f(t_1, \ldots, u, \ldots, t_n)$ with $u \prec_k v$, where $k \geq \max\{\text{ar}(f): f \in \Sigma\}$, then $s \prec_k t$.*

Recall that $\prec_{\text{POP}}$ is a reduction order. Hence the assumption $R \subseteq \prec_{\text{POP}}$ implies $\to_R \subseteq \prec_{\text{POP}}$.

Lemma 4. *If $t \to_R s$, then $s \prec_k t$, where $k = \max\{\max\{\tau(r) | (l \to r) \in R\}, \max\{\text{ar}(f) | f \in S\}\}$.*

We set

$$G_k(\sigma) := \max\{n \in \mathbb{N} \mid \exists (a_0, \ldots, a_n) \, (a_n \prec_k \cdots \prec_k a_0 = a)\} \,,$$
$$F_{k,p}(n) := \max\{G_k(fa): \text{rk}(f) = p \; \& \; G_k(a) \leq n\} \,,$$

where $\text{rk}(f): \Sigma \to \mathbb{N}$ is defined inductively: $\text{rk}(f) := \max\{\text{rk}(g) + 1: g \in \Sigma \wedge g \prec f\}$. We collect some properties of the function G_k in the next lemma.

Lemma 5. *1. $G_k((s_0, \ldots, s_n)) = \sum_{i=0}^n G_k(a_i)$.*
2. $G_k(\overline{m}) = |m|$ for any natural number m.

Lemma 6. *Inductively we define $d_{k,0} := 2$ and $d_{k,p-1} := (d_{k,p})^k + 1$. Then there exists a constant c (depending only on k and p) such that $F_{k,p}(n) \leq c \cdot n^{d_{k,p}} + c$.*

Proof. The lemma is proven by main induction on p and side induction on σ.

Set $a := (t_0, \ldots, t_n)$ and let $w \prec_k f(t_0, \ldots, t_n) =: t$, $\mathrm{rk}(f) = p$ and w maximal. By assumption $G_k(a) \leq n$. We prove

$$G_k(w) < cn^{d_{k,p}} \quad \text{for almost all } n \ ,$$

by case-distinction on the definition of $\prec_k$. It suffices to consider the case $w = (r_0, \ldots, r_m)$.

CASE. $p = 0$ and $\forall i \leq m \ (r_i \sqsubset_k t)$. By definition of $\prec_{\mathrm{POP}}$ we have $\forall i \leq m \ \exists j \leq n \ (r_i \preceq_k t_j)$. Then $G_k(w) \leq G_k(a) = n$. Hence

$$G_k(w) \leq kn < cn^2 \ ,$$

where we set $c := k$.

CASE. $p = 0$, $\forall i \neq i_0 \ (r_i \sqsubset_k t)$, and $r_{i_0} \prec_k t$. By definition of $\prec_{\mathrm{POP}}$ we have $\forall i \leq m \ \exists j \leq n \ (r_i \preceq_k t_j)$ and $r_{i_0} = f(s_0, \ldots, s_l)$, $\mathrm{rk}(f) = 0$, with $(s_0, \ldots, s_l) \prec_k a$. Hence by induction hypothesis (IH) on a, there exists a constant c, such that $G_k(r_{i_0}) \leq c(n-1)^2$ a.e. Employing Lemma 5.1 we obtain:

$$G_k(w) = G_k((r_0, \ldots, r_m)) = \sum_{i=0}^{m} G_k(r_i) \leq c(n-1)^2 + (k-1)n < cn^2 \ ,$$

as we can assume $c > k$.

CASE. $p > 0$ and $\forall i \leq m \ (r_i \sqsubset_k t)$. Let i be arbitrary. We can assume $r_i = g(s_0, \ldots, s_l)$, $g \prec f$, and $\forall i \leq l \ (s_i \sqsubset_k^{k-1} t)$. Otherwise, if $r_i = g(s_0, \ldots, s_l)$ with $g \succ f$ s.t. there $\exists j \leq n \ (r_i \sqsubseteq t_j)$ we proceed as in the first case. By IH there exists c and $d = d_{k,p}$ s.t. $F_{k,p}(n) \leq cn^d$ a.e.

We show the existence of a constant c' s.t. $F_{k,p+1}(n) \leq c'n^{d'}$, where $d' = d_{k,p+1}$. We define $f(a) := ca^d$ and $g^{(0)}(a) := a$, $g^{(l+1)}(a) = f(g^{(l)}(a) \cdot k)$; we obtain:

$$s \sqsubset_k^l t \implies G_k(s) \leq g^{(l)}(n) \text{ a.e.} \tag{$\star$}$$

To see $(\star)$ we show by induction on l, that $s \sqsubset_k^l t$ implies $G_k(s) \leq g^{(l)}(n)$, where $g^{(l)}(n) = c_0 a^{d^{(l)}}$ with $c_0 = c^{\sum_{i=0}^{l-1} d^i} k^{\sum_{i=1}^{l} d^i}$. Suppose $l > 0$, then we obtain by IH on the claim and $F_{k,p}(n) \leq cn^d$ we obtain:

$$G_k(s) \leq c[(c_0 n^{d^l}) \cdot k]^d = c_1 n^{d^{l+1}} \text{ a.e.} \ ,$$

where $c_1 = c^{\sum_{i=0}^{l} d^i} k^{\sum_{i=1}^{l+1} d^i}$. This accomplishes the claim.

Now the upper-bound for $G_k(w)$ follows:

$$G_k(w) \leq kg^{(k)}(n) < c'n^{d'} \text{ a.e.} \ ,$$

where $c' = c^{\sum_{i=0}^{k-1} d^i} k^{\sum_{i=0}^{k} d^i}$ and $d' = d^{k+1} + 1 = d_{k,p+1}$.

CASE. $p > 0$, $\forall i \neq i_0$ $(r_i \sqsubset_k t)$, and $r_{i_0} \prec_k t$. By definition $\forall i \leq m \,\exists j \leq n$ $(r_i \preceq_k t_j)$, and $r_{i_0} = f(s_0, \ldots, s_l)$ so that $(s_0, \ldots, s_l) \prec_k a$. Let c, c', d' be defined as above. By IH on σ we obtain $G_k(r_{i_0}) \leq c'(n-1)^{d'}$ and thus

$$G_k(w) \leq c'(n-1)^{d'} + (k-1) \cdot c \cdot n^{d^k} < c' n^{d'} \ .$$

$\square$

Recall the definition of the derivation length function:

$$\mathrm{Dl}_R^f(\overline{m}) = \max\{l \mid \exists\, t_0, \ldots, t_n \in \mathcal{T}(\Sigma)\,(t_n \leftarrow_R \ldots \leftarrow_R t_0 = f(\overline{m}))\}$$

We have established the following theorem.

Theorem 1. *If for a finite TRS R defined over $\mathcal{T}(\Sigma, \mathcal{V})$, $R \subseteq \prec_{\mathrm{POP}}$ then for each $f \in \Sigma$, Dl_R^f is bounded by a monotone polynomial in the sum of the binary length of the inputs.*

Proof. Let R be a finite TRS defined over $\mathcal{T}(\Sigma, \mathcal{V})$, such that for every rule $(l \to r) \in R$, $r \prec_{\mathrm{POP}} l$ holds. This implies that for any two terms t, s, $t \to_R s$ implies $s \prec_{\mathrm{POP}} t$. Hence by Lemma 4 there exists $k \in \mathbb{N}$, s.t. $\leftarrow_R \subseteq \prec_k$. Suppose f is an n-ary function symbol and set $t := f(\overline{m}_1, \ldots, \overline{m}_n)$. By definition it follows that

$$\mathrm{Dl}_R^f(\overline{m}_1, \ldots, \overline{m}_n) \leq G_k(f(\overline{m}_1, \ldots, \overline{m}_n)) \ .$$

By Lemma 6 there exists a polynomial p, depending only on k and the rank of f, s.t.

$$G_k(f(\overline{m}_1, \ldots, \overline{m}_n)) \leq p(G_k((\overline{m}_1, \ldots, \overline{m}_n)) \ .$$

Employing with Lemma 5, we obtain $\mathrm{Dl}_R^f(\overline{m}_1, \ldots, \overline{m}_n) \leq p(\sum_{i=1}^n |m_i|)$. $\square$

4 Predicative Recursion and POP

In the previous section we have shown that if for a finite TRS R, defined over $\mathcal{T}^*(\Sigma, \mathcal{V})$, $R \subseteq \prec_{\mathrm{POP}}$, then the derivation length function Dl_R^f is bounded by a monotone polynomial in the binary length of the inputs. As an application of Theorem 1, we prove in this section that $\mathrm{Dl}_{R_B'}^f$ is bounded by a monotone polynomial in the binary length of the normal inputs. I.e. we give an alternative proof of Prop. 1. As R_B' exactly characterises the functions in **FP** this yields that $\prec_{\mathrm{POP}}$—via the mapping S defined below—exactly characterises the class of polytime computable functions **FP**.

It suffices to define a mapping $\mathrm{S}\colon T(B) \to T^*(\Sigma)$, such that S is a monotone interpretation such that $\mathrm{S}(l\sigma) \succ_{\mathrm{POP}} \mathrm{S}(r\sigma)$ holds for all $(l \to r) \in R_B'$. We suppose the signature Σ is defined such that for any function symbol $f \in B^{k,l}$ there is a function symbol $f' \in \Sigma$ of arity k. Moreover, Σ includes two constants S_0, S_1 and a varyadic function symbol $\bullet$ of lowest rank. We need a few auxiliary notions: $\mathrm{sn}(\overline{n}) := n$ for numerals $\overline{n}$; $\mathrm{sn}(f(\mathbf{t}; \mathbf{s})) = \sum_j (\mathrm{sn}(s_j))$, otherwise. For every number m we define its representation $\widehat{m} \in T(\Sigma, \mathcal{V})$ as follows: $\widehat{0} :=$ $\bullet$; $\widehat{S_i(m)} := \bullet(S_i) * \widehat{m}$ for $i \in [0,1]$, where $\bullet(s_0, \ldots, s_i) * \bullet(s_{i+1}, \ldots, s_n) :=$ $\bullet(s_0, \ldots, s_n)$. We define S: $T(B) \to T^*(\Sigma)$ by mutual induction together with the interpretation N: $T(B) \to T^*(\Sigma)$.

Definition 7.

- $S(\overline{n}) := ()$ and $S(S_i(;t)) := (S_i) \frown S(t)$ for $t \not\equiv \overline{n}$ (i.e. t is not a numeral).
- For $f \neq S_i$, define $S(f(\mathbf{t}; \mathbf{s})) := (f(N(t_0), \ldots, N(t_n)), S(s_0), \ldots, S(s_m))$.
- $N(t) := \bullet \, S(t) * \widehat{sn(t)}$.

First we show that for $Q \in \{S, N\}$, $Q(l\sigma) \succ_{\text{POP}} Q(r\sigma)$. More precisely we show the following lemma.

Lemma 7. Let $(l \to r) \in R'_B$, σ a ground substitution, such that $l\sigma, r\sigma \in T(B)$. Then there exists k, depending on the rule $(l \to r)$, such that $Q(r\sigma) \prec_k Q(l\sigma)$.

Proof. Let $(l \to r)$ and σ as in the assumptions of the lemma. We sketch the proof by considering the rule:

$$\text{PREC}^{p+1,q}[g, h_1, h_2](S_i(;t), \mathbf{t}; \mathbf{n}) \to h_i(t, \mathbf{t}; \mathbf{n}, \text{PREC}[g, h_1, h_2](t, \mathbf{t}; \mathbf{n})) \,.$$

We abbreviate $F := \text{PREC}^{p+1,q}[g, h_1, h_2]$ and set $k := 1 + \max\{3, p+1, q+1\}$. Let $\text{lh}(f)$, $f \in B$ be defined as follows: $\text{lh}(f) := 1$, for $f \in \{S_i, O, U, P\}$. $\text{lh}(\text{SUB}[f, \mathbf{g}, \mathbf{h}]) := 1 + \text{lh}(f) + \text{lh}(g_1) + \cdots + \text{lh}(g_{k'}) + \text{lh}(h_1) + \cdots + \text{lh}(h_{l'})$. $\text{lh}(\text{PREC}[g, h_1, h_2]) := 1 + \text{lh}(g) + \text{lh}(h_1) + \text{lh}(h_2)$. Then we define the precedence $<$ over Σ compatible with lh, i.e. $f' < g'$ if $\text{lh}(f) < \text{lh}(g)$. For $Q = S$, we employ the following sequence of comparisons:

$$\begin{aligned}
&S(F(S_i(;t), \mathbf{t}; \mathbf{n})) \\
&= (F'(N(S_i(;t)), N(t_1), \ldots, N(t_p)), S(\overline{n}_1), \ldots, S(\overline{n}_q)) \\
&= F'(N(S_i(;t)), N(t_1), \ldots, N(t_p)) \\
&= F'(\bullet(S_i) * N(t), N(t_1), \ldots, N(t_p)) \,.
\end{aligned}$$

By definition $S(\overline{n}_i) = ()$ and for each $t \in T(\Sigma, \mathcal{V})$, $t = (t)$. Moreover it is a direct consequence of the definitions that $N(S_i(;t)) = \bullet(S_i) * N(t)$. Further:

$$\begin{aligned}
&F'(\bullet(S_i) * N(t), N(t_1), \ldots, N(t_p)) \\
&\succ_k (h'_i(N(t), N(t_1), \ldots, N(t_p)), F'(N(t), N(t_1), \ldots, N(t_p))) \,,
\end{aligned}$$

By Definition 6.4 we obtain $\bullet(S_i) * N(t) \succ_k N(t)$. This yields by rules 6.4 and 6.5 using $k > p+1$: $F'(\bullet(S_i) * N(t), N(t_1), \ldots, N(t_p)) \succ_k F'(N(t), N(t_1), \ldots, N(t_p))$. Finally applying Definition 6.3 together with rule 6.2 and 5.2 yields the inequality. In these rule applications we employ $k > q+1$ and $F' > h'_i$.

$$\begin{aligned}
&(h'_i(N(t), N(t_1), \ldots, N(t_p)), F'(N(t), N(t_1), \ldots, N(t_p))) \\
&= (h'_i(N(t), N(t_1), \ldots, N(t_p)), S(n_1), \ldots, S(n_l), F'(N(t), N(t_1), \ldots, N(t_p))) \\
&= S(h_i(t, \mathbf{t}; \mathbf{n}, F(t, \mathbf{t}; \mathbf{n}))) \,.
\end{aligned}$$

Finally, it is easy to see that $N(F(S_i(;t), \mathbf{t}; \mathbf{n})) \succ_k N(h_i(t, \mathbf{t}; \mathbf{n}, F(t, \mathbf{t}; \mathbf{n}))$. We established the lemma for the rule $F(S_i(;t), \mathbf{t}; \mathbf{n}) \rightarrow h_i(t, \mathbf{t}; \mathbf{n}, F(t, \mathbf{t}; \mathbf{n}))$. The other rules follow similar.

Note that the definition of k in all cases depends on the arity-information encoded in the head function symbol on the left-hand side. Moreover at most 3 iterated applications of $\sqsubset_k$ are necessary. □

The next lemma establish monotonicity for the interpretations S, N.

Lemma 8. *For $k \in \mathbb{N}$ and for $u, v \in T(\Sigma)$, $Q(u) \prec_k Q(v)$ for $Q \in \{S, N\}$. Suppose $f \in B^{p,q}$ and $\bar{t}, \bar{s} \in T(\Sigma)$. Then*

- $Q(f(t_1, \ldots, u, \ldots, t_p; \bar{s}) \prec_k Q(f(t_1, \ldots, v, \ldots, t_p; \bar{s})$ *for $Q \in \{S, N\}$, and*
- $Q(f(\bar{t}; s_1, \ldots, u, \ldots, s_q) \prec_k Q(f(\bar{t}; s_1, \ldots, v, \ldots, s_q))$ *for $Q \in \{S, N\}$.*

We define the derivation length function $\mathrm{Dl}^f_{R'_B}$ over the ground term-set $T(\Sigma)$:

$$\mathrm{Dl}^f_{R'_B}(\overline{\mathbf{m}}; \overline{\mathbf{n}}) := \max\{n \mid \exists\, t_0, \ldots, t_n \in T(B) \left(t_n \leftarrow_{R'_B} \cdots \leftarrow_{R'_B} t_0 = f(\overline{\mathbf{m}}; \overline{\mathbf{n}})\right)\}.$$

Recall the definition of the derivation tree $\mathcal{T}_{R'_B}$. Note that for each $t \in T(B, \mathcal{V})$, $\mathcal{T}_{R'_B}(t)$ is finite. This follows from the fact that R'_B is terminating and $\mathcal{T}_{R'_B}(t)$ is finitely branching. The latter is shown by well-founded induction on $\rightarrow_{R'_B}$. Let $f \in B$ be a fixed predicative recursive function symbol. As the derivation tree $\mathcal{T}_{R'_B}(f(\overline{\mathbf{m}}; \overline{\mathbf{n}}))$ is finite only finitely many function symbols occur in $\mathcal{T}_{R'_B}(f(\overline{\mathbf{m}}; \overline{\mathbf{n}}))$. This allows to define a finite subset $F \subset B$, such that all terms occurring in $\mathcal{T}_{R'_B}(f(\overline{\mathbf{m}}; \overline{\mathbf{n}}))$ belong to $T(F)$. We define

$$k := 1 + \max(\{3\} \cup \{p, q + 1 | f^{p,q} \in B \text{ occurs in } \mathcal{T}_{R'_B}(f(\overline{\mathbf{m}}; \overline{\mathbf{n}}))\}).$$

Let R' denote the restriction of R'_B to $T(F)$. Then, we have $\mathrm{Dl}^f_{R'_B}(\overline{\mathbf{m}}; \overline{\mathbf{n}}) = \mathrm{Dl}^f_{R'}(\overline{\mathbf{m}}; \overline{\mathbf{n}})$. From these observations together with Lemma 7 and 8 we conclude

Lemma 9. *Let $s, t \in T(F)$ such that $t \rightarrow_R s$. Then $S(s) \prec_k S(t)$.*

In summary we obtain, by following the pattern of the proof of Thm. 1:

Theorem 2. *For every $f \in B$, $\mathrm{Dl}^f_{R'_B}(\overline{m}_1, \ldots, \overline{m}_p; \overline{n}_1, \ldots, \overline{n}_q)$ is bounded by a monotone polynomial in the sum of the length of the normal inputs $m_1, \ldots, m_p$.*

5   Conclusion

The main contribution of this paper is the definition of a *path order for* **FP**, denoted as $\prec_{\mathrm{POP}}$. This path order has the property that for a finite TRS R compatible with $\prec_{\mathrm{POP}}$, the *derivation length function* Dl^f_R is bounded by a polynomial in the length of the inputs for any defined function symbol f in the signature of R. Moreover $\prec_{\mathrm{POP}}$ is *complete* in the sense that for a function $f \in \mathbf{FP}$, there exists a TRS R computing f such that such that termination of R follows by $\prec_{\mathrm{POP}}$. Another feature of $\prec_{\mathrm{POP}}$ is, that its definition is devoid of the separation of normal and safe arguments, present in the definition of the predicative recursive functions and therefore in the definition of the term-rewriting characterisation R'_B.

We briefly relate our findings to the notion of the *light multiset path order*, denoted as $\prec_{\mathrm{LMPO}}$, introduced by Marion in [11]. It is possible to define a variant of $\prec_{\mathrm{POP}}$—denoted as $\prec_{\mathrm{POPV}}$—such that Theorem 1 remains true for $\prec_{\mathrm{POPV}}$ when suitably reformulated. While Definition 3 and 4 are based on an arbitrary signature, the definition of $\prec_{\mathrm{POPV}}$ assumes that normal and safe arguments are separated as in Section 2. It is easy to see that $\prec_{\mathrm{POPV}} \subset \prec_{\mathrm{LMPO}}$ and this inclusion is strict as $\prec_{\mathrm{LMPO}}$ proves termination of the non-feasible rewrite system R_B, while $\prec_{\mathrm{POPV}}$ clearly does not. On the other hand let R be a functional program (i.e. a constructor TRS) computing a number-theoretic function f. A termination proof of R via $\prec_{\mathrm{LMPO}}$ guarantees the existence of a polytime algorithm for f. However, a termination proof of R via or the introduced path order $\prec_{\mathrm{POPV}}$ (or $\prec_{\mathrm{POP}}$) guarantees that R itself is already a polytime algorithm for f. It seems clear to us that the latter property is of more practical value.

Acknowledgments. We would like to thank Arnold Beckmann who uncovered an embarrassing error in an earlier version of this paper.

References

1. Beckmann, A., Weiermann, A.: A term rewriting characterization of the polytime functions and related complexity classes. Archive for Mathematical Logic **36** (1996) 11–30
2. Cichon, E.A., Weiermann, A.: Term rewriting theory for the primitive recursive functions. Annals of Pure and Applied Logic **83** (1997) 199–223
3. Oitavem, I.: A term rewriting characterization of the functions computable in polynomal space. Archive for Mathematical Logic **41** (2002) 35–47
4. Bonfante, G., Marion, J.Y., Moyen, J.Y.: Quasi-intepretations and small space bounds. In: Proceedings of RTA'2005. (2005) 150–164
5. Baader, F., Nipkow, T.: Term Rewriting and All That. Cambridge Univeristy Press (1998)
6. Cobham, A.: The intrinsic computational difficulty of functions. In Bar-Hillel, Y., ed.: Logic, Methodology and Philosophy of Science, proceedings of the second International Congress, Jerusalem, 1964, North-Holland (1965)
7. Bellantoni, S., Cook, S.: A new recursion-theoretic characterization of the polytime functions. Comput. Complexity **2** (1992) 97–110
8. Arai, T., Moser, G.: A note on a term rewriting characterization of PTIME. In: Proc. of WST'2004. (2004) 10–13 Extended Abstract.
9. Buchholz, W.: Proof-theoretical analysis of termination proofs. Annals of Pure and Applied Logic **75** (1995) 57–65
10. Hofbauer, D.: Termination proofs by multiset path orderings imply primitive recursive derivation lengths. TCS **105** (1992) 129–140
11. Marion, J.: Analysing the implicit complexity of programs. Information and Computation **183** (2003) 2–18

On the Controller Synthesis for Finite-State Markov Decision Processes

Antonín Kučera* and Oldřich Stražovský**

Faculty of Informatics, Masaryk University,
Botanická 68a, 60200 Brno, Czech Republic
{kucera,strazovsky}@fi.muni.cz

Abstract. We study the problem of effective controller synthesis for finite-state Markov decision processes (MDPs) and the class of properties definable in the logic PCTL extended with long-run average propositions. We show that the existence of such a controller is decidable, and we give an algorithm which computes the controller if it exists. We also address the issue of "controller robustness", i.e., the problem whether there is a controller which still guarantees the satisfaction of a given property when the probabilities in the considered MDP slightly deviate from their original values. From a practical point of view, this is an important aspect since the probabilities are often determined empirically and hence they are inherently imprecise. We show that the existence of robust controllers is also decidable, and that such controllers are effectively computable if they exist.

1 Introduction

The controller synthesis problem is one of the fundamental research topics in the area of system design. Loosely speaking, the task is to modify or limit some parts of a given system so that a given property is satisfied. The controller synthesis problem is well understood for discrete systems [11], and the scope of this study has recently been extended also to timed systems [2,5] and probabilistic systems [1].

In this paper, we concentrate on a class of probabilistic systems that can be modelled by finite-state Markov decision processes. Intuitively, Markov decision processes (MDPs) are finite-state systems where each state has several outgoing transitions leading to probability distributions over states. Thus, Markov decision processes combine the paradigms of non-deterministic/probabilistic choice, and this combination turns out to be very useful in system modelling. Quantitative properties of MDPs can be defined only after resolving nondeterminism by assigning probabilities to the individual transitions. Similarly as in [1], we distinguish among four natural types of strategies for resolving nondeterminism, depending on whether

---

* Supported by the research center Institute for Theoretical Computer Science (ITI), project No. 1M0021620808.
** Supported by the Czech Science Foundation, grant No. 201/03/1161.

R. Ramanujam and S. Sen (Eds.): FSTTCS 2005, LNCS 3821, pp. 541–552, 2005.
© Springer-Verlag Berlin Heidelberg 2005

- the transition is chosen deterministically (D) or randomly (R);
- the choice does or does not depend on the sequence of previously visited states (Markovian (M) and history-dependent (H) strategies, respectively).

Thus, one obtains the four basic classes of MD, HD, MR, and HR strategies. In addition, we assume that the states of a given MDP are split into two disjoint subsets of *controllable* and *environmental* states, depending on whether the nondeterminism is resolved by a controller or by the environment, respectively. Hence, in our setting the controller synthesis problem is specified by choosing the type of strategy for controller and environment, and the class of properties that are to be achieved. The task is to find, for a given MDP and a given property, a controller strategy such that the property is satisfied for every strategy of the environment. In [1], it was shown that this problem is **NP**-complete for MD strategies and PCTL properties, and elementary for HD strategies and LTL properties.

For linear-time properties, the problem of finding a suitable controller strategy can also be formulated in the terms of stochastic games on graphs [12]. Controller and environment act as two players who resolve the non-deterministic choice in controllable and environmental states, resp., and thus produce a "play". The winning conditions are defined as certain properties of the produced play. In many cases, it turns out that the optimal strategies for both players are memoryless (i.e., Markovian in our terms). However, in the case of branching-time properties that are considered in this paper, optimal strategies are not necessarily memoryless and the four types of strategies mentioned above form a strict hierarchy [1].

Our contribution: In this paper we consider the controller synthesis problem for MR strategies and the class of properties definable in the logic PCTL extended with long-run average propositions defined in the style of [4]. The resulting logic is denoted PCTL+LAP. The long-run average propositions allow to specify long-run average properties such as the average service time, the average frequency of visits to a distinguished subset of states, etc. In the logic PCTL+LAP, one can express properties such as:

- the probability that the average service time for a request does not exceed 20 seconds is at least 98%;
- the system terminates with probability at least 80%, and at least 98% of runs have the property that the percentage of time spent in "dangerous" states does not exceed 3%.

A practical relevance of PCTL+LAP properties is obvious.

The controller synthesis problem for PCTL+LAP properties and MD strategies is trivially reducible to the satisfaction problem for finite-state Markov chains and PCTL+LAP properties. This is because there are only finitely many MD strategies for a given MDP, and hence one can try out all possibilities. For MR strategies, a more sophisticated approach is required because the total number of MR strategies is infinite (and in fact not countable). This is overcome by encoding the existence of a MR-controller in $(\mathbb{R}, +, *, \leq)$, the first-order theory of reals, which is known to be decidable [10]. The encoding is not simple and includes several subtle tricks. Nevertheless, the size of the resulting formula is polynomial in the size of a given MDP and a given PCTL+LAP property, and the number of quantifier alternations is fixed. Hence, we obtain the **EXPTIME** upper complexity bound by applying the result of [6].

Another problem addressed in this paper is controller robustness [8]. Since the probabilities of events that are modelled in MDPs are often evaluated empirically, they are inherently imprecise. Hence, it is important to know whether the constructed controller still works if the probabilities in the considered MDP slightly deviate from their original values. We say that a controller is ε-robust if the property in question is still satisfied when probability distributions in the considered MDP change at most by ε in each component (here we do not allow for changing the probabilities from zero to non-zero (and vice versa), because this corresponds to changing from "impossible" to "possible"). Similarly, we can also wonder whether the constructed controller is "fragile" in the sense that it stops working if the computed strategy changes a little bit. We say that a controller is δ-*free* if every other controller obtained by changing the strategy by at most δ is again a correct controller. We show that the problem whether there is an ε-robust and δ-free controller for given MDP, PCTL+LAP property, and $\varepsilon, \delta \geq 0$, is in **EXPTIME**. Moreover, we also give an algorithm which effectively estimates the maximal achievable level of controller robustness for given MDP and PCTL+LAP property (i.e., we show how to compute the maximal ε, up to a given precision, such that there is an ε-robust controller for given MDP and PCTL+LAP property). Finally, we show how to construct an ε-robust controller for a given MDP and PCTL+LAP property, provided that an ε-robust and δ-free controller exists and $\delta > 0$.

2   Basic Definitions

We start by recalling basic notions of probability theory. A σ-*field* over a set X is a set $\mathcal{F} \subseteq 2^X$ that includes X and is closed under complement and countable union. A *measurable space* is a pair $(X, \mathcal{F})$ where X is a set called *sample space* and $\mathcal{F}$ is a σ-field over X. A measurable space $(X, \mathcal{F})$ is called *discrete* if $\mathcal{F} = 2^X$. A *probability measure* over measurable space $(X, \mathcal{F})$ is a function $\mathcal{P} : \mathcal{F} \to \mathbb{R}^{\geq 0}$ such that, for each countable collection $\{X_i\}_{i \in I}$ of pairwise disjoint elements of $\mathcal{F}$, $\mathcal{P}(\bigcup_{i \in I} X_i) = \sum_{i \in I} \mathcal{P}(X_i)$, and moreover $\mathcal{P}(X) = 1$. A *probabilistic space* is a triple $(X, \mathcal{F}, \mathcal{P})$ where $(X, \mathcal{F})$ is a measurable space and $\mathcal{P}$ is a probability measure over $(X, \mathcal{F})$. A probability measure over a discrete measurable space is called a *discrete measure*. We also refer to discrete measures as *distributions*. The set of all discrete measures over a measurable space $(X, 2^X)$ is denoted $Disc(X)$.

Markov Decision Processes. A *Markov decision process* (MDP) $\mathcal{M}$ is a triple (S, Act, P) where S is a finite or countably infinite set of *states*, Act is a finite set of *actions*, and $P : S \times Act \times S \to [0, 1]$ is a (total) *probabilistic function* such that for every $s \in S$ and every $a \in Act$ we have that $\sum_{t \in S} P(s, a, t) \in \{0, 1\}$. We say that $a \in Act$ is *enabled* in $s \in S$ if $\sum_{t \in S} P(s, a, t) = 1$. The set of all actions that are enabled in a given $s \in S$ is denoted $Act(s)$. For technical convenience, we assume that each state $s \in S$ has at least one enabled action. We say that $\mathcal{M}$ is *finite* if S is finite. A *path* in $\mathcal{M}$ is a nonempty finite or infinite alternating sequence of states and actions $\pi = s_1 a_1 s_2 a_2 \ldots a_{n-1} s_n$ or $\pi = s_1 a_1 s_2 a_2 \ldots$ such that $P(s_i, a_i, s_{i+1}) > 0$ for all $1 \leq i < n$ or $i \in \mathbb{N}$, resp. The *length* (i.e., the number of actions) of a given π is denoted $|\pi|$, where $|\pi| = \infty$ if π is infinite. For every $1 \leq i \leq |\pi|+1$, the symbol $\pi(i)$ denotes the i-th state of π (which is s_i). A *run* is an infinite path. The sets of all finite paths and all runs of $\mathcal{M}$ are denoted *FPath* and *Run*, respectively. Sometimes we write $FPath_{\mathcal{M}}$ and $Run_{\mathcal{M}}$ if $\mathcal{M}$ is not clear from the context. Similarly, the sets of all finite paths and runs that start in a given $s \in S$ are denoted $FPath(s)$ and $Run(s)$, respectively. For finite paths, $last(\pi) = \pi(|\pi|+1)$ denotes the last state of π.

For the rest of this section, we fix a MDP $\mathcal{M} = (S, Act, P)$.

Strategies, Adversaries, and Policies for MDPs. Let $S_0 \subseteq S$ be nonempty subset of *controllable* states. The states of $S \setminus S_0$ are *environmental*. A *strategy* is a function D that resolves nondeterminism for the controllable states of $\mathcal{M}$. Similarly as in [1], we distinguish among four basic types of strategies for $(\mathcal{M}, S_0)$, according to whether they are deterministic (D) or randomized (R), and Markovian (M) or history-dependent (H).

– A *MD-strategy* is a function $D : S_0 \to Act$ such that $D(s) \in Act(s)$ for all states $s \in S_0$.
– A *MR-strategy* is a function $D : S_0 \to Disc(Act)$ such that $D(s) \in Disc(Act(s))$ for all states $s \in S_0$.
– A *HD-strategy* is a function $D : FPath \to Act$ such that $D(\pi) \in Act(last(\pi))$ for all finite paths $\pi \in FPath$ where $last(\pi) \in S_0$, otherwise $D(\pi) = \bot$.
– A *HR-strategy* is a function $D : FPath \to Disc(Act)$ such that $D(\pi) \in Disc(Act(last(\pi)))$ for all finite paths $\pi \in FPath$ where $last(\pi) \in S_0$, otherwise $D(\pi) = \bot$.

MD, MR, HD, and HR *adversaries* are defined in the same way as strategies of the corresponding type; the only difference is that adversaries range over environmental states. A *policy* is a pair $H = (D, E)$ where D is a strategy and E an adversary. Slightly abusing notation, we write $H(s)$ to denote either $D(s)$ or $E(s)$, depending on whether $s \in S_0$ or not, respectively.

Markov Chains Induced by Policies. A *Markov chain* is a MDP with only one action, i.e., without nondeterminism. Formally, a Markov chain $\mathcal{MC}$ is a pair (S, P) where $(S, \{a\}, P)$ is a MDP. The (only) action a can safely be omitted, and so the probabilistic function is restricted to the set $S \times S$, and a path in $\mathcal{MC}$ is a (finite or infinite) sequence of states $s_1 s_2 s_3 \ldots$.

Each $\pi \in FPath_{\mathcal{MC}}$ determines a *basic cylinder* $Run(\pi)$ which consists of all runs that start with π. To every $s \in S$ we associate the probabilistic space

$(Run(s), \mathcal{F}, \mathcal{P})$ where $\mathcal{F}$ is the σ-field generated by all basic cylinders $Run(\pi)$ where π starts with s (i.e., $\pi(1) = s$), and $\mathcal{P} : \mathcal{F} \to [0,1]$ is the unique probability measure such that $\mathcal{P}(Run(\pi)) = \Pi_{i=1}^{|\pi|} P(\pi(i), \pi(i+1))$ (if $|\pi| = 0$, we put $\mathcal{P}(Run(\pi)) = 1$).

Let $\mathcal{M} = (S, Act, P)$ be a MDP. Each policy H for $\mathcal{M}$ induces a Markov chain $\mathcal{MC}_H = (S_H, P_H)$ in the following way:

- If H is a Markovian (MD or MR) policy, then $S_H = S$.
- If H is a history-dependent (HD or HR) policy, then $S_H = FPath_{\mathcal{M}}$.

The function P_H is determined as follows:

- If H is a MD-policy, then $P_H(s_i, s_j) = P(s_i, H(s_i), s_j)$.
- If H is a MR-policy, then $P_H(s_i, s_j) = \Sigma_{a \in Act(s_i)} \mu(a).P(s_i, a, s_j)$ where $\mu = H(s_i)$.
- If H is a HD-policy, then $P_H(\pi, \pi') = P(last(\pi), H(\pi), s)$ if $\pi' = \pi.H(\pi).s$, and $P_H(\pi, \pi') = 0$ otherwise.
- If H is a HR-policy, then $P_H(\pi, \pi') = \mu(a).P(last(\pi), a, s)$ where $\mu = H(\pi)$, if $\pi' = \pi.a.s$, and $P_H(\pi, \pi') = 0$ otherwise.

The Logics PCTL and PCTL+LAP. Let $Ap = \{p, q, \dots\}$ be a countably infinite set of *atomic propositions*. The syntax of PCTL *state* and *path* formulae is given by the following abstract syntax equations:

$$\Phi ::= \mathbf{tt} \mid p \mid \neg\Phi \mid \Phi_1 \wedge \Phi_2 \mid \mathcal{P}^{\sim \varrho} \varphi \qquad \varphi ::= \mathcal{X}\Phi \mid \Phi_1 \mathcal{U} \Phi_2$$

Here p ranges over Ap, $\varrho \in [0,1]$, and $\sim \in \{\le, <, \ge, >\}$.

Let $\mathcal{MC} = (S, P)$ be a Markov chain, and let $\nu : Ap \to 2^S$ be a *valuation*. The semantics of PCTL is defined below. State formulae are interpreted over S, and path formulae are interpreted over Run.

$$s \models^{\nu} \mathbf{tt}$$
$$s \models^{\nu} p \qquad \text{iff} \quad s \in \nu(p)$$
$$s \models^{\nu} \neg\Phi \qquad \text{iff} \quad s \not\models^{\nu} \Phi$$
$$s \models^{\nu} \Phi_1 \wedge \Phi_2 \quad \text{iff} \quad s \models^{\nu} \Phi_1 \text{ and } s \models^{\nu} \Phi_2$$
$$s \models^{\nu} \mathcal{P}^{\sim \varrho} \varphi \quad \text{iff} \quad \mathcal{P}(\{\pi \in Run(s) \mid \pi \models^{\nu} \varphi\}) \sim \varrho$$

$$\pi \models^{\nu} \mathcal{X}\Phi \qquad \text{iff} \quad \pi(2) \models^{\nu} \Phi$$
$$\pi \models^{\nu} \Phi_1 \mathcal{U} \Phi_2 \quad \text{iff} \quad \exists j \ge 1 : \pi(j) \models^{\nu} \Phi_2 \text{ and } \pi(i) \models^{\nu} \Phi_1 \text{ for all } 1 \le i < j$$

The logic PCTL+LAP is obtained by extending PCTL with long-run average propositions (in the style of [4]). Intuitively, we aim at modelling systems which repeatedly service certain requests, and we are interested in measuring the average costs of servicing a request along an infinite run. The states where the individual services start are identified by (the validity of) a dedicated atomic proposition, and each service corresponds to a finite path between two consecutive occurrences of marked states.

Definition 1. *A* long-run average proposition *is a pair* $[p, f]$ *where* p *is an atomic proposition and* $f : S \rightarrow \mathbb{R}^{\geq 0}$ *a reward function* that assigns to each $s \in S$ a reward $f(s)$.

The reward assigned to a given $s \in S$ corresponds to some costs which are "paid" when s is visited. For example, $f(s)$ can be the expected average time spent in s, the amount of allocated memory, or simply a binary indicator specifying whether s is "good" or "bad". The proposition p is valid in exactly those states where a new service starts. Note that in this setup, a new service starts immediately after finishing the previous service. This is not a real restriction, because the states which precede/follow the actual service can be assigned zero reward.

The syntax of PCTL+LAP formulae is obtained by modifying the syntax of PCTL path formulae as follows:

$$\varphi ::= \mathcal{X}\Phi \mid \Phi_1 \mathcal{U} \Phi_2 \mid \xi \qquad \xi ::= [p, f]^{\sim b} \mid \neg\xi \mid \xi_1 \wedge \xi_2$$

Here $[p, f]$ ranges over long-run average propositions, $b \in \mathbb{R}^{\geq 0}$, and $\sim \in \{\leq, <, \geq, >\}$.

Let $\mathcal{MC} = (S, P)$ be a Markov chain, $[p, f]$ a long-run average proposition, and $\nu : Ap \rightarrow 2^S$ a valuation. Let $\pi \in Run$ be a run along which p holds infinitely often, and let $\pi(i_1), \pi(i_2), \ldots$ be the sequence of all states in π where p holds. Let $\pi[j]$ denote the subword $\pi(i_{j-1} + 1), \cdots, \pi(i_j)$ of π, where $i_0 = 0$. Hence, $\pi[j]$ is the subword of π consisting of all states in between the $j-1^{th}$ state satisfying p (not included) and the jth state satisfying p (included). Intuitively, $\pi[j]$ corresponds to the jth service. Slightly abusing notation, we use $f(\pi[j])$ to denote the total reward accumulated in $\pi[j]$, i.e., $f(\pi[j]) = \sum_{k=i_{j-1}+1}^{i_j} f(\pi(k))$. Now we define the average reward per service in π (with respect to $[p, f]$) as follows:

$$A[p, f](\pi) = \begin{cases} \lim_{n \to \infty} \frac{\sum_{j=1}^{n} f(\pi[j])}{n} & \text{if the limit exists;} \\ \bot & \text{otherwise.} \end{cases}$$

If $\pi \in Run$ contains only finitely many states satisfying p, we put $A[p, f](\pi) = \bot$. Now we define

$$\pi \models^{\nu} [p, f]^{\sim b} \quad \text{iff} \quad A[p, f](\pi) \neq \bot \text{ and } A[p, f](\pi) \sim b$$

The semantics of negation and conjunction of long-run average propositions is defined in the expected way.

3   Controller Synthesis

In this section we examine the controller synthesis problem for finite MDPs, PCTL+LAP properties, and MR policies.

Since the probabilities used in MDPs are often evaluated empirically (and hence inherently imprecise), it is important to analyze the extent to which a given result about a given MDP is "robust" in the sense that its validity is not influenced by small probability fluctuations. This is formalized in our next definitions:

Definition 2. *Let* $\mathcal{M} = (S, Act, P)$ *be a MDP, and let* $\varepsilon \in [0, 1]$. *We say that a MDP* $\mathcal{M}' = (S, Act, P')$ *is an* ε-*perturbation of* $\mathcal{M}$ *if for all* $(s, a, t) \in S \times Act \times S$ *the following two conditions are satisfied:*

- $P(s, a, t) = 0$ *iff* $P'(s, a, t) = 0$,
- $|P(s, a, t) - P'(s, a, t)| \leq \varepsilon$.

Note that Definition 2 also applies to Markov chains.

Definition 3. *Let* $\mathcal{M} = (S, Act, P)$ *be a MDP,* $\varepsilon \in [0, 1]$, $s_i \in S$, *and Prop some property of* s_i. *We say that Prop is* ε-*robust if for every MDP* $\mathcal{M}'$ *which is an* ε-*perturbation of* $\mathcal{M}$ *we have that if* $s_i \models Prop$ *in* $\mathcal{M}$, *then* $s_i \models Prop$ *in* $\mathcal{M}'$.

Examples of 1-robust properties are qualitative LTL and qualitative PCTL properties of states in finite Markov chains, whose (in)validity depends just on the "topology" of a given chain [3]. On the other hand, the property of "being bisimilar to a given state" (here we consider a probabilistic variant of bisimilarity [9]) is generally 0-robust, because even a very small change in probability distribution can spoil the bisimilarity relation.

In a similar fashion we also define a δ-perturbation of a randomized strategy.

Definition 4. *Let* $\mathcal{M} = (S, Act, P)$ *be a MDP,* $S_0 \subseteq S$ *a nonempty set of controllable states, D a randomized (i.e., MR or HR) strategy, and* $\delta \in [0, 1]$. *We say that a strategy D' is a* δ-*perturbation of D if D' is of the same type as D and for all* $a \in Act$:

- *MR case: for all* $s \in S_0$: $|D(s)(a) - D'(s)(a)| \leq \delta$ *and* $D(s)(a) = 0 \Leftrightarrow D'(s)(a) = 0$
- *HR case: for all* $\pi \in FPath$ *where* $last(\pi) \in S_0$: $|D(\pi)(a) - D'(\pi)(a)| \leq \delta$ *and* $D(\pi)(a) = 0 \Leftrightarrow D'(\pi)(a) = 0$

Let $\mathcal{M} = (S, Act, P)$ be a MDP, $S_0 \subseteq S$ a nonempty set of controllable states, $s_i \in S$, and *Prop* some property of s_i. Let $T \in \{MD, MR, HD, HR\}$. A *T-controller* for $\mathcal{M}$ and *Prop* is a *T*-strategy D such that $s_i \models Prop$ in $MC_{(D,E)}$ for every *T*-environment E. We say that the controller D is

- ε-robust for a given $\varepsilon \in [0, 1]$ if the property "D is a controller for $\mathcal{M}$ and *Prop*" is ε-robust. In other words, D is a valid controller for *Prop* even if the probabilities in $\mathcal{M}$ are slightly (i.e., at most by ε) changed.
- ε-robust and δ-free for given $\varepsilon, \delta \in [0, 1]$ if every D' which is a δ-perturbation of D is an ε-robust controller for $\mathcal{M}$ and *Prop*.

In the rest of this section we consider the problem of MR-controller synthesis for a given MDP $\mathcal{M} = (S, Act, P)$, a set of controllable states $S_0 \subseteq S$, a state $s_i \in S$, a PCTL+LAP formula φ, and a valuation ν. For notation simplification, we do not list these elements in our theorems explicitly, although they are always a part of a problem instance.

Theorem 5. *Let $\varepsilon, \delta \in [0,1]$. The problem whether there is an ε-robust and δ-free MR-controller is in* ***EXPTIME***.

Proof. We construct a closed formula of $(\mathbb{R}, *, +, \leq)$ which is valid iff an ε-robust and δ-free MR-controller exists. The formula has the following structure:

$$\exists D \; \forall D' \; (D' \; \delta\text{-pert. of } D) \Rightarrow (\forall E \; \forall P' \; (P' \; \varepsilon\text{-pert. of } P) \Rightarrow (\exists Y \; (Y_\varphi^{s_i} {=} 1)))$$

Intuitively, the formula says "there is an MR-strategy D such that for every strategy D', which is a δ-perturbation of D, every environment E, and every chain (an ε-perturbation of $\mathcal{M}$) with probabilities P', there is a consistent validity assumption Y (which declares each subformula of φ to be either true or false in every state of S) such that Y sets the formula φ to true in the state s_i". Now we describe these parts in greater detail.

Let $X_a^s, X_a'^s$ be fresh first-order variables for all $s \in S_0$ and $a \in Act(s)$. These variables are used to encode the strategies D, D'. Intuitively, X_a^s and $X_a'^s$ carry the probability of choosing the action a in the state s in D and D', respectively. The

$$\exists D \; \forall D' \; (D' \; \delta\text{-pert. of } D)$$

part can then be implemented as follows:

$$\exists \{X_a^s \mid s \in S_0, a \in Act(s)\} : \bigwedge_{X_a^s} (0 \leq X_a^s \leq 1) \wedge \bigwedge_{s \in S_0} (\sum_{a \in Act(s)} X_a^s = 1) \wedge$$

$$\forall \{X_a'^s \mid s \in S_0, a \in Act(s)\} : (\bigwedge_{X_a'^s} (0 \leq X_a'^s \leq 1) \wedge \bigwedge_{s \in S_0} (\sum_{a \in Act(s)} X_a'^s = 1) \wedge$$

$$\bigwedge_{X_a^s} ((X_a^s = 0 \Leftrightarrow X_a'^s = 0) \wedge (|X_a^s - X_a'^s| \leq \delta))$$

Similarly,

- for all $s \in S \setminus S_0$ and $a \in Act(s)$ we fix fresh first-order variables $X_a'^s$ that encode the environment E (from a certain point on, we do not need to distinguish between the probabilities chosen by D' and E);
- for all $s, t \in S$ and $a \in Act(s)$ we fix a fresh variable $P_a^{s,t}$ that encodes the corresponding probability of P';
- for every $\phi \in cl(\varphi)$ (here $cl(\varphi)$ is the set of all subformulas of φ) and every $s \in S$ we fix a variable Y_ϕ^s that carries either 1 or 0, depending on whether s satisfies ϕ or not, respectively. As we shall see, the value of Y_ϕ^s is first "guessed" and then "verified".

The $\forall E \; \forall P' \; (P' \; \varepsilon\text{-pert. of } P) \Rightarrow (\exists Y \; (Y_\varphi^{s_i} {=} 1))$ part can now be implemented as follows:

$$\forall\{X_a'^s \mid s \in S \setminus S_0, a \in Act(s)\} : \bigwedge_{X_a'^s} (0 \le X_a'^s \le 1) \wedge \bigwedge_{s \in S \setminus S_0} (\sum_{a \in Act(s)} X_a'^s = 1) \Rightarrow$$

$$\forall\{P_a^{s,t} \mid s,t \in S, a \in Act(s)\} :$$

$$\bigwedge_{P_a^{s,t}} ((P(s,a,t) = 0 \Leftrightarrow P_a^{s,t} = 0) \wedge (|P(s,a,t) - P_a^{s,t}| \le \varepsilon)) \Rightarrow$$

$$\exists\{Y_\phi^s \mid \phi \in cl(\varphi), s \in S\} :$$

$$\bigwedge_{Y_\phi^s} ((Y_\phi^s = 0 \vee Y_\phi^s = 1) \wedge (Y_\phi^s = 1 \Leftrightarrow \psi_\phi^s)) \wedge (Y_\varphi^{s_i} = 1)$$

The tricky part of the construction is the formula ψ_ϕ^s, which is defined inductively on the structure of ϕ. Intuitively, ψ_ϕ^s says that s satisfies ϕ, where we assume that this has already been achieved for all subformulae of ϕ (hence, by justifying all steps in our inductive definition we also yield a correctness proof for our construction):

- $\phi \equiv p$. If $s \in \nu(p)$, then $\psi_\phi^s \equiv \mathtt{tt}$, otherwise $\psi_\phi^s \equiv \mathtt{ff}$.
- $\phi \equiv \neg\phi'$. Then $\psi_\phi^s \equiv (Y_{\phi'}^s = 0)$.
- $\phi \equiv \phi_1 \wedge \phi_2$. Then $\psi_\phi^s \equiv (Y_{\phi_1}^s = 1) \wedge (Y_{\phi_2}^s = 1)$.
- $\phi \equiv \mathcal{P}^{\sim\varrho}\mathcal{X}\phi'$. Then $\psi_\phi^s \equiv \left(\sum_{a \in Act(s), t \in S} X_a'^s \cdot P_a^{s,t} \cdot Y_{\phi'}^t\right) \sim \varrho$.

The case when $\phi \equiv \mathcal{P}^{\sim\varrho}\phi_1 \mathcal{U} \phi_2$ is slightly more complicated. The probabilities $\{Z^r \mid r \in S\}$, where Z^r is the probability that a run initiated in r satisfies the path formula $\phi_1 \mathcal{U} \phi_2$, form the least solution (in the interval $[0,1]$) of a system of recursive linear equations constructed as follows (where Z^r should be seen as "unknowns"; cf. [7,3]):

- if $Y_{\phi_2}^r = 1$, we put $Z^r = 1$;
- if $Y_{\phi_1}^r = 0$ and $Y_{\phi_2}^r = 0$, we put $Z^r = 0$;
- if $Y_{\phi_1}^r = 1$ and $Y_{\phi_2}^r = 0$, we put $Z^r = \left(\sum_{a \in Act(s), t \in S} X_a'^r \cdot P_a^{r,t} \cdot Z^t\right)$.

So, the formula ψ_ϕ^s for the case when $\phi \equiv \mathcal{P}^{\sim\varrho}\phi_1 \mathcal{U} \phi_2$ looks as follows:

$$\exists\{Z^r \mid r \in S\} : \bigwedge_{r \in S} (0 \le Z^r \le 1) \wedge \{Z^r\} \text{ is a solution } \wedge Z^s \sim \varrho \wedge$$

$$\left(\forall\{Z'^r \mid r \in S\} : (\bigwedge_{r \in S} (0 \le Z'^r \le 1) \wedge \{Z'^r\} \text{ is solution }) \Rightarrow (\bigwedge_{r \in S} Z^r \le Z'^r)\right)$$

Here "$\{Z^r\}$ is a solution" means that the variables $\{Z^r\}$ satisfy the above system of recursive linear equations, which can be easily encoded in $(\mathbb{R}, +, *, \le)$.

Finally, we analyze the most complicated case when $\phi \equiv \mathcal{P}^{\sim\varrho}[p,f]^{\approx b}$. In order to check long-run average propositions, we need to analyze the structure of the Markov chain induced by the current values of the $X_a'^r$ variables and find bottom strongly connected components (BSCC) of this chain.

We start by computing the probabilities $Prob_r^t$ of reaching the state t from the state r. The set $\{Prob_r^t \mid r, t \in S\}$ forms the least solution (in the interval $[0,1]$) of the following system of recursive linear equations, where $Prob_r^t$ should be interpreted as "unknowns":

- if $r = t$, we put $Prob_r^t = 1$;
- if $r \neq t$, we put $Prob_r^t = \sum_{u \in S} \left(\sum_{a \in Act(r)} X_a^{\prime r} \cdot P_a^{r,u} \right) \cdot Prob_u^t$.

So, the formula which "computes" all $Prob_r^t$ looks as follows:

$$\exists \{Prob_r^t \mid r, t \in S\} : \bigwedge_{r,t \in S} (0 \leq Prob_r^t \leq 1) \wedge \{Prob_r^t\} \text{ is solution} \wedge$$

$$\left(\forall \{Prob_r^{\prime t} \mid r, t \in S\} : (\bigwedge_{r,t \in S} (0 \leq Prob_r^{\prime t} \leq 1) \wedge \{Prob_r^{\prime t}\} \text{ is solution}) \Rightarrow \right.$$

$$\left. (\bigwedge_{r,t \in S} Prob_r^t \leq Prob_r^{\prime t}) \right)$$

Now we introduce predicates $SCC_{r,t}$ and $BSCC_r$, where $SCC_{r,t}$ means that r, t are in the same strongly connected component, and $BSCC_r$ means that r is in a bottom strongly connected component.

$$SCC_{r,t} ::= (Prob_r^t > 0 \wedge Prob_t^r > 0)$$

$$BSCC_r ::= \bigwedge_{t \in S} (Prob_r^t > 0 \Rightarrow Prob_t^r > 0)$$

The next step is to compute the (unique) invariant distribution for each $BSCC$. Recall that the invariant distribution in a finite strongly connected Markov chain is the (unique) vector Inv of numbers from $[0,1]$ such that the sum of all components in Inv is equal to 1 and $Inv * T = Inv$ where T is the transition matrix of the considered Markov chain.

For each BSCC (represented by a given $t \in S$), the following formula "computes" its unique invariant distribution $\{Inv_r^t \mid r, t \in S\}$. More precisely, Inv_r^t is either zero (if r does not belong to the BSCC represented by t), or equals the value of the invariant distribution in r (otherwise). We also need to ensure that the representative t is chosen uniquely, i.e., the values of all $Inv_r^{t'}$, where t' is in the same SCC as t, is zero:

$$\exists \{Inv_r^t \mid r, t \in S\} :$$

$$\bigwedge_{r,t \in S} \left(\quad (0 \leq Inv_r^t \leq 1) \wedge ((\neg BSCC_r \vee \neg BSCC_t \vee \neg SCC_{r,t}) \Rightarrow Inv_r^t = 0) \right.$$

$$\wedge ((BSCC_r \wedge BSCC_t \wedge SCC_{r,t}) \Rightarrow$$

$$\left. Inv_r^t = \sum_{u \in S} (Inv_u^t \cdot \sum_{a \in Act(u)} X_a^{\prime u} \cdot P_a^{u,r})) \right) \wedge$$

$$\bigwedge_{t \in S} \left(BSCC_t \Rightarrow \left(\sum_{r \in S} Inv_r^t = 1 \wedge \bigwedge_{t' \in S, t' \neq t} (SCC_{t,t'} \Rightarrow \sum_{r \in S} Inv_r^{t'} = 0) \right) \vee \right.$$

$$\left. \left(\sum_{r \in S} Inv_r^t = 0 \wedge \bigvee_{t' \in S, t' \neq t} (SCC_{t,t'} \wedge \sum_{r \in S} Inv_r^{t'} = 1) \right) \right)$$

According to ergodic theorem, almost all runs (i.e., with probability one) end up in some BSCC, and then "behave" according to the corresponding invariant distribution (i.e., the "percentage of visits" to each state is given by the invariant distribution). From this one can deduce that the average reward per service is the same for almost all runs that hit a given BSCC. Hence, for each $t \in S$ we can "compute" a value Rew_t which is equal to 1 iff

- t represents some BSCC and
- at least one state in this BSCC satisfies p (and hence p is satisfied infinitely often in almost all runs that hit this BSCC) and
- the average reward per service associated with this BSCC is "good" with respect to the long-run average proposition $[p, f]^{\approx b}$.

Note that the average reward per service can be computed as the ratio between the average reward per state and the percentage of visits to states where the service starts. Thus, we obtain the formula

$$\exists \{Rew_t \mid t \in S\} : \bigwedge_{t \in S} (Rew_t = 0 \vee Rew_t = 1) \wedge$$

$$\left(Rew_t = 1 \Leftrightarrow \left(\sum_{r \in S} Inv_r^t \cdot Y_p^r > 0 \right) \wedge \left(\frac{\sum_{r \in S} Inv_r^t \cdot f(r)}{\sum_{r \in S} Inv_r^t \cdot Y_p^r} \approx b \right) \right)$$

Finally, the formula ψ_ϕ^s "checks" whether the "good" BSCCs are reachable with a suitable probability:

$$\psi_\phi^s ::= \left(\sum_{t \in S} Prob_s^t \cdot Rew_t \right) \sim \varrho$$

Although the whole construction is technically complicated, none of the above considered subcases leads to an exponential blowup. Hence, we can conclude that the size of the resulting formula is *polynomial* in the size of our instance. Moreover, a closer look reveals that the quantifiers are alternated only to a fixed depth. Hence, our theorem follows by applying the result of [6]. □

The technique used in the proof of Theorem 5 can easily be adapted to prove the following:

Theorem 6. *For every $\varepsilon \in [0, 1]$, if there is an ε-robust MR-controller which is δ-free for some $\delta > 0$, then an ε-robust MR-controller is effectively constructible.*

Proof. First, realize that the problem whether there is an ε-robust MR-controller which is δ-free for some $\delta > 0$ is in **EXPTIME**. We use the formula constructed in the proof of Theorem 5, where the constant δ is now treated as first-order variable, and the whole formula is prefixed by "$\exists \delta > 0$". If the answer is positive (i.e., there is a controller with a non-zero freedom), one can effectively find some δ' for which there is an ε-robust and δ'-free controller by trying smaller and smaller δ'. As soon as we have such a δ', there are only finitely many candidates for a suitable MR-strategy D. Intuitively, we divide the interval $[0, 1]$ into finitely many pieces of length δ', and from each such subinterval we test only one value. This suffices because the controller we are looking for is δ'-free. More precisely, we successively try to set each of the variable $\{X_a^s\}$ to values

$$\left\{ \frac{n}{|Act(s)|} + m\delta' \text{ where } n, m \in \mathbb{Z}, 0 \leq n \leq |Act(s)|, -\left\lceil \frac{1}{\delta'} \right\rceil \leq m \leq \left\lceil \frac{1}{\delta'} \right\rceil \right\}$$

so that $0 \leq X_a^s \leq 1$ and $\sum_{a \in Act(s)} X_a^s = 1$ for each $s \in S$. For each choice we check if it works (using the formula of Theorem 5 where the $\{X_a^s\}$ variables are replaced with their chosen values and δ is set to zero). One of these finitely many options is guaranteed to work, and hence a controller is eventually found.   □

Similarly, we can also approximate the maximal ε for which there is an ε-robust MR-controller (this maximal ε is denoted ε_m):

Theorem 7. *For a given $\theta > 0$, one can effectively compute a rational number κ such that $|\kappa - \varepsilon_m| \leq \theta$.*

Since our algorithm for computing an ε-robust MR-controller works only if there is at least one such controller with a non-zero freedom, it makes sense to ask what is the maximal ε for which there is an ε-robust MR-controller with a non-zero freedom. Let us denote this maximal ε by ε_m'.

Theorem 8. *For a given $\theta > 0$, one can effectively compute a rational number κ such that $|\kappa - \varepsilon_m'| \leq \theta$.*

References

1. C. Baier, M. Größer, M. Leucker, B. Bollig, and F. Ciesinski. Controller synthesis for probabilistic systems. In *Proceedings of IFIP TCS'2004*. Kluwer, 2004.
2. P. Bouyer, D. D'Souza, P. Madhusudan, and A. Petit. Timed control with partial observability. In *Proceedings of CAV 2003*, vol. 2725 of *LNCS*, pp. 180–192. Springer, 2003.
3. C. Courcoubetis and M. Yannakakis. The complexity of probabilistic verification. *JACM*, 42(4):857–907, 1995.
4. L. de Alfaro. How to specify and verify the long-run average behavior of probabilistic systems. In *Proceedings of LICS'98*, pp. 454–465. IEEE, 1998.
5. L. de Alfaro, M. Faella, T. Henzinger, R. Majumdar, and M. Stoelinga. The element of surprise in timed games. In *Proceedings of CONCUR 2003*, vol. 2761 of *LNCS*, pp. 144–158. Springer, 2003.
6. D. Grigoriev. Complexity of deciding Tarski algebra. *Journal of Symbolic Computation*, 5(1–2):65–108, 1988.
7. H. Hansson and B. Jonsson. A logic for reasoning about time and reliability. *Formal Aspects of Computing*, 6:512–535, 1994.
8. A. Nilim and L. El Ghaoui. Robustness in markov decision problems with uncertain transition matrices. In *Proceedings of NIPS 2003*. MIT Press, 2003.
9. R. Segala and N.A. Lynch. Probabilistic simulations for probabilistic processes. *NJC*, 2(2):250–273, 1995.
10. A. Tarski. *A Decision Method for Elementary Algebra and Geometry*. Univ. of California Press, Berkeley, 1951.
11. W. Thomas. Infinite games and verification. In *Proceedings of CAV 2003*, vol. 2725 of *LNCS*, pp. 58–64. Springer, 2003.
12. U. Zwick and M. Paterson. The complexity of mean payoff games on graphs. *TCS*, 158(1&2):343–359, 1996.

Reasoning About Quantum Knowledge

Ellie D'Hondt[1] and Prakash Panangaden[2]

[1] Vrije Universiteit Brussel, Belgium
Ellie.DHondt@vub.ac.be
[2] McGill University, Canada
prakash@cs.mcgill.ca

Abstract. We construct a formal framework for investigating epistemic and temporal notions in the context of distributed quantum computation. While we rely on structures developed in [1], we stress that our notion of quantum knowledge makes sense more generally in any agent-based model for distributed quantum systems. Several arguments are given to support our view that an agent's possibility relation should not be based on the reduced density matrix, but rather on local classical states and local quantum operations. In this way, we are able to analyse distributed primitives such as superdense coding and teleportation, obtaining interesting conclusions as to how the knowledge of individual agents evolves. We show explicitly that the knowledge transfer in teleportation is essentially classical, in that eventually, the receiving agent knows that its state is equal to the initial state of the sender. The relevant epistemic statements for teleportation deal with this correlation rather than with the actual quantum state, which is unknown throughout the protocol.

1   Introduction

The idea of developing formal models to reason about knowledge has proved to be very useful for distributed systems [2,3,4]. Epistemic logic provides a natural framework for expressing the knowledge of agents in a network, allowing one to make quite complex statements about what agents know, what they know that other agents know, and so on. Moreover, combining epistemic with temporal logic, one can investigate how knowledge evolves over time in distributed protocols, which is useful both for program analysis as well as formal verification.

The standard approach to knowledge representation in multi-agent systems is based on the *possible worlds* model. The idea is that there exists a set of worlds such that an agent may consider several of these to be possible. An agent *knows* a fact if it is true in all the worlds it considers possible; this is expressed by epistemic modal operators acting on some basic set of propositions. The flexibility of this approach lies in the fact that there are many ways in which one can specify possibility relations. In a distributed system, worlds correspond to global configurations occurring in a particular protocol, and *possible* worlds are determined by an equivalence relation over these configurations. Typically,

R. Ramanujam and S. Sen (Eds.): FSTTCS 2005, LNCS 3821, pp. 553–564, 2005.

global network configurations are considered equivalent by an agent if its local state in these configurations is identical.

Quantum computation is a field of research that is rapidly acquiring a place as a significant topic in computer science [5]. Logic-based investigations in quantum computation are relatively recent and few. Recently there have been some endeavours in describing quantum programs in terms of predicate transformers [6,7,8]. These frameworks, however, aim at modelling traditional algorithms that establish an input-output relation, a point of view which is not appropriate for distributed computations. A first attempt to define knowledge for quantum distributed systems is found in [9]. Therein, two different notions of knowledge are defined. First, an agent i can *classically* know a formula θ to hold, denoted $K_i^c\theta$; in this case the possibility relation is based on equality of local classical states. Second, an agent can *quantumly* know a formula to hold, denoted $K_i^q\theta$. For the latter, the possibility relation is based on equality of reduced density matrices for that agent. The authors argue that K_i^q is an information-theoretic idealisation of knowledge, in that the reduced density matrix embodies what an agent, in principle, could determine from its local quantum state. However, there are two main problems with this approach. The first is that one cannot assume that the reduced density matrix is always known, because in quantum mechanics, observing a state alters it irreversibly. So, quantum knowledge does not consist of possession of a quantum state: it is not because an agent has a qubit in its lab that the agent knows anything about it. Indeed, consider the situation where a qubit has just been sent from **A** to **B**. Then **B** knows nothing about its newly acquired qubit – it is possible, even, that **A** knows more about it than **B** does. The second problem with the above approach is that one loses information on correlations between agents by considering only the reduced density matrix, a crucial ingredient in distributed quantum primitives.

What we need is a proper notion of quantum knowledge, which captures the information an agent can obtain about its quantum state. This includes the following ingredients: first, an agent knows states that it has prepared; second, an agent knows a state when it has just measured it; and third, an agent may obtain knowledge by classical communication of one of the above. While knowledge of preparation states is automatically contained in the description of the protocol, our notion of equivalence precisely captures the latter two items. As we shall see below, in doing this we find a similar notion as $K_i^c\theta$. Our main argument, then, is that there is no such thing as quantum knowledge in the sense of $K_i^q\theta$; rather quantum knowledge is about classically knowing facts about quantum systems.

The structure of this paper is as follows. In Sec. 2 we construct a framework for reasoning about knowledge in quantum distributed systems. Next, we investigate the important distributed primitives of superdense coding and teleportation in our epistemic framework in Sec. 3, investigating how agents' knowledge is updated as each protocol proceeds. We conclude in Sec. 4.

This paper assumes some familiarity with quantum computation – for the reader not familiar with the domain, we refer to the excellent [5]. The present paper is also a continuation of earlier work by the authors [10,1]. However, most of the material presented here can be understood independently of the latter.

2   Knowledge in Quantum Networks

In this section, we develop the notion of knowledge for distributed quantum systems. The equivalence relation for agents, on the basis of which quantum knowledge is defined, is established in Sec. 2.1. Next, temporal operators are defined in Sec. 2.2, where we also briefly discuss how temporal and epistemic operators combine.

We phrase our results below in the context of *quantum networks*, an agent-based model for distributed quantum computation elaborated in [1]. We stress, however, that our notion of quantum knowledge is model-independent. That is to say, any agent-based model for distributed quantum computation would benefit from quantum knowledge as defined below, or slight adaptations thereof. Due to space limitations, only a short overview is given here; for more detailed explanations, we refer the reader to [1,11].

A *network of agents* $\mathcal{N}$ is defined by a set of concurrently acting agents together with a shared quantum state, that is

$$\mathcal{N} = \mathbf{A}_1 : Q_1.\mathcal{E}_1 \mid \ldots \mid \mathbf{A}_m : Q_m.\mathcal{E}_m \parallel \sigma = |_i \mathbf{A}_i(\mathbf{i}_i, \mathbf{o}_i) : Q_i.\mathcal{E}_i \parallel \sigma , \qquad (1)$$

where σ is the network quantum state, $\mid$ denotes parallel composition, and for all i, $\mathbf{A}_i$ is an agent with local qubits Q_i and event sequence $\mathcal{E}_i$. The network state σ in the definition is the initial entanglement resource which is distributed among agents. Local quantum inputs are added to the network state σ during initialisation; in this way we keep initial shared entanglement as a first-class primitive in our model. Note that agents in a network need to have different names, since they correspond to different parties that make up the distributed system. In other words, concurrency comes *only* from distribution; we do not consider parallel composition of processes in the context of one party. Events consist of local quantum operations A, classical communication c? and c!, and quantum communication qc? and qc!. Quantum operations are denoted in the style of [10], that is we have entanglement operators E, measurements M and Pauli corrections X and Z. All of this is much clarified in the applications in Sec. 3.

A network determines a set of configurations $\mathcal{C}_{\mathcal{N}}$ that can potentially occur during execution of $\mathcal{N}$. Configurations are written

$$C = |\sigma\rangle, |_i \Gamma_i, \mathbf{A}_i : Q_i.\mathcal{E}_i , \qquad (2)$$

where Γ_i is each agent's local (classical) state, which is where measurement outcomes and classical messages are stored. $\mathcal{C}_{\mathcal{N}}$ consists of all configurations encountered in those paths a protocol can take. More formally, $\mathcal{C}_{\mathcal{N}}$ is obtained by following the rules for the small-step operational semantics of networks, denoted by transitions $\Longrightarrow$ and elaborated in [1].

Before we can actually define modal operators for knowledge or time, we need to clarify what the propositions are that these act upon. It is not our intention to define a full-fledged language for primitive propositions; rather, we define these abstractly. An *interpretation* of $\mathcal{N}$ is a truth-value assignment for configurations in $\mathcal{C}_{\mathcal{N}}$ for some basic set of primitive propositions θ. Writing $I(C, \theta)$ for the interpretation of fact θ in configuration C, we then have,

$$C, \mathcal{N} \vDash \theta \iff I(C, \theta) = \text{true} . \tag{3}$$

The primitive propositions considered usually depend on the network under study, and are specified individually for each application encountered below. Composite formulas can be constructed from primitive propositions and the logical connectives $\wedge$, $\vee$ and $\neg$ in the usual way. However, the formulas encountered in the applications below are usually about equality For example, θ may be of the form $x = v$, meaning that the classical variable x has the value v, or $q_1 = q_2$, meaning that the states of qubits q_1 and q_2 are identical. We also allow functions *init* and *fin* for taking the initial and final values of a variable or quantum state. These formulas are currently defined in an ad-hoc manner.

2.1   Knowledge

In order to define quantum knowledge, we need to define an equivalence relation on configurations for each of the agents, embodying what an agent knows about the global configuration from its own information only. We deliberately do not say *local* information here, as, via the network preparation, an agent may also have non-local information, under the form of correlations, at its disposal. By considering only configurations in $\mathcal{C}_{\mathcal{N}}$ we model that agents know which protocol they are executing.

In a quantum network, each agent's equivalence relation has to reflect what an agent knows about the network state, the execution of the protocol and the results of measurements. All classical information an agent has is stored in its local state Γ; this includes classical input values, measurement outcomes, and classical values passed on by other agents. Just like in classical distributed systems, an agent can certainly differentiate configurations for which the local state is different. As for quantum information, an agent knows which qubits it owns, what local operations it applies on these qubits, and, moreover, what (non-local) preparation state it starts out with, i.e. what entanglement it shares with other agents initially. It can also have information on its local quantum inputs, though this is not necessarily so, as we have explained in the above. All of the above information is in fact captured by an agent's event sequence in a particular configuration, together with its local state. Therefore, we obtain the following definition.

Definition 1. *Given a network $\mathcal{N}$ and configurations $C = \sigma; |_i \Gamma_i, \mathbf{A}_i : Q_i . \mathcal{E}_i$ and $C' = \sigma'; |_i \Gamma_i', \mathbf{A}_i : Q_i' . \mathcal{E}_i'$ in $\mathcal{C}_{\mathcal{N}}$, we say that agent $\mathbf{A}_i$ considers C and C' to be* equivalent, *denoted $C \sim_i C'$, if $\Gamma_i = \Gamma_i'$ and $\mathcal{E}_i = \mathcal{E}_i'$. For each agent $\mathbf{A}_i$*

the relation $\sim_i$ is an equivalence relation on $\mathcal{C}_\mathcal{N}$, called the possibility relation *of* $\mathbf{A}_i$.

Via possibility relations we can now define what it means for an agent $\mathbf{A}_i$ to know a fact θ in a configuration C in the usual way,

$$C, \mathcal{N} \models K_i\theta \iff \forall C' \sim_i C : C' \models \theta . \qquad (4)$$

Our choice of equivalence embodies that agents cannot distinguish configurations if they only differ in that other agents have applied local operations to their qubits; neither can they if other agents have exchanged messages with each other. While the global network state does change as a result of local operations, an agent not executing these has no knowledge of this, and no way of obtaining it. This is precisely what we capture with the relation $\sim_i$.

Special attention needs to be given to the matter of quantum inputs. Agents distinguish configurations corresponding to different values of their classical input via their local state, in which these input values are stored. Essentially, for each set of possible input values there is a group of corresponding configurations in $\mathcal{C}_\mathcal{N}$. However, this is not something we can do for quantum inputs, since these occupy a continuous space. Hence we choose to let configurations be parameterised by these inputs, writing $C(|\psi\rangle)$ whenever we want to stress this. But then what about an agent's possibility relation? Basically, either a quantum input is known, in which case it is just a local preparation state such that there is only one possible initial configuration. If a quantum input for agent $\mathbf{A}$ is truly arbitrary, or the agent knows nothing about it – as is the case for teleportation – then all values of $|\psi\rangle$, and hence all configurations in the set $\{C(|\psi\rangle), |\psi\rangle \in I_\mathbf{A}\}$, are considered equivalent by $\mathbf{A}$. If $\mathbf{A}$ does know some properties of its input, then we model this by only allowing a certain set of input states. We do not explicitly mention the equivalence related to unknown quantum inputs in the examples below, for the simple reason that we are interested only in logical statements that hold for *all* quantum inputs. That is, we compare only configurations resulting from the same quantum inputs, and derive knowledge-related statements that are independent of this input. Nevertheless, whenever a configuration $C(|\psi\rangle)$ is written, it should be interpreted as a *set* of states, all considered equivalent by all agents of the network.

From this one can construct more complicated statements, such as for example $C \models K_\mathbf{A} K_\mathbf{B}\theta$ for "agent $\mathbf{A}$ knows that agent $\mathbf{B}$ knows that θ holds in configuration C".

2.2 Time

One typically also wants to investigate how knowledge *evolves* during a computation, for example due to communication between agents. Thus, one also needs a proper formalisation of *time*. This is usually done by allowing a set of *temporal modal operations*, operating on the same set of propositions. The area of temporal logics is itself an active field of research, with applications in virtually all aspects of concurrent program design; for an overview see for example [12].

We use the approach of *computational tree logic* (CTL) to formalise time-related logical statements, providing state as well as path modal operators. The reason for this is that, due to the fact that quantum networks typically have a branching structure, we need to be able to express statements concerning *all* paths as well as those pertaining to *some* paths. Typically, we want to say things such as "for all paths, agent **A** always knows θ", or "there exists a path for which **A** eventually knows θ". We can of course express this by placing restrictions on the paths we are considering in a particular statement – this is, in fact, precisely what we do in the definition of modal path operators. Introducing these is more appealing since in this way we can abstract away from actual path definitions, which are determined by the formal semantics for networks elaborated in [1], and denoted abstractly as $\Longrightarrow$ below.

Concretely, we introduce the traditional temporal state operators $\Box$ ("always") and $\Diamond$ ("eventually") into our model, and combine these with the path operators A ("for all paths") and E ("there exists a path"), as follows[3]

$$C, \mathcal{N} \vDash A\Box\theta \iff \forall\gamma, \forall C' \text{ with } C \overset{\gamma}{\Longrightarrow} C' : C' \vDash \theta \tag{5}$$

$$C, \mathcal{N} \vDash E\Box\theta \iff \exists\gamma, \forall C' \text{ with } C \overset{\gamma}{\Longrightarrow} C' : C' \vDash \theta \tag{6}$$

$$C, \mathcal{N} \vDash A\Diamond\theta \iff \forall\gamma, \exists C' \text{ with } C \overset{\gamma}{\Longrightarrow} C' : C' \vDash \theta \tag{7}$$

$$C, \mathcal{N} \vDash E\Diamond\theta \iff \exists\gamma, \exists C' \text{ with } C \overset{\gamma}{\Longrightarrow} C' : C' \vDash \theta . \tag{8}$$

Obviously, we have that any formula with A implies the corresponding one with E, and likewise any formula with $\Box$ implies the corresponding ones with $\Diamond$ and $\bigcirc$.

When investigating knowledge issues in a distributed system, one naturally arrives at situations where one needs to describe formally how knowledge evolves as the computation proceeds. This can be done adequately by combining knowledge operators K_i with the temporal operators defined above. As usual, one needs to proceed with caution when doing this, since it is not always intuitively clear what the meaning of each of these different combinations is. For example, it is generally *not* the case that the formula $A\Box K_i\theta$ is equivalent to $K_i A\Box\theta$. Typically, we want to prove things that are eventually known by an agent, no matter what branch the protocol follows; this is embodied by the former.

3   Applications

With epistemic and temporal notions for quantum networks in place, we are ready to evaluate the distributed primitives superdense coding [13] and teleportation [14] from a knowledge-based perspective. That is, instead of investigating how the global network evolves by deriving a network's semantics, we now use

---

[3] $\overset{\gamma}{\Longrightarrow}$ is the closure of the small-step transition relation $\Longrightarrow$ mentioned above. That is, we have $C \overset{\gamma}{\Longrightarrow} C'$ if C' can be reached form C by a series of consecutive small-step transitions, specified by the path γ.

this semantics, or rather, the configurations encountered therein, to analyse how the knowledge of individual agents evolves. We start with superdense coding, which is simpler to analyse because it is deterministic and does not depend on quantum inputs. We move on to teleportation in Sec. 3.2. We note that an analysis of the quantum leader election protocol [15] was also carried out in [11].

3.1   Superdense Coding

The aim of superdense coding is to transmit two classical bits from one party to the other with the aid of one entangled qubit pair or ebit. The network for this task is defined as follows,

$$SC = \mathbf{A} : \{1\}.[(\mathsf{qc}!1)X_1^{x_2}Z_1^{x_1}] \mid \mathbf{B} : \{2\}.[M_{12}^{0,0}(\mathsf{qc}?1)] \parallel E_{12} \ , \qquad (9)$$

Here $x_1 x_2$ are $\mathbf{A}$'s classical inputs, subscripts stand for qubits on which events operate, X and Z are Pauli operations, $\mathsf{qc}!$ and $\mathsf{qc}?$ stand for a quantum rendezvous, $M_{12}^{0,0}$ is a Bell measurement on qubits 1 and 2, and E_{12} is an ebit. In the first step of the protocol Alice transforms her half of the entangled pair, in a different way for each of the four possible classical inputs. Next, she sends Bob her qubit, who then measures the entangled pair. At the end of the protocol the measurement outcomes, denoted s_1 and s_2, are equal to $\mathbf{A}$'s inputs.

The configurations in $\mathcal{C}_{SC}$ are the following [11],

$$C_1^{j_1 j_2} = E_{12}; [x_1, x_2 \mapsto j_1, j_2], \mathbf{A} : \{1\}.[(\mathsf{qc}!1)X_1^{x_2}Z_1^{x_1}] \mid \varnothing, \mathbf{B} : \{2\}.[M_{12}^{0,0}(\mathsf{qc}?1)]$$

$$C_2^{j_1 j_2} = X_1^{x_2}Z_1^{x_1}E_{12}; [x_1, x_2 \mapsto j_1, j_2], \mathbf{A} : \{1\}.(\mathsf{qc}!1) \mid \varnothing, \mathbf{B} : \{2\}.[M_{12}^{0,0}(\mathsf{qc}?1)]$$

$$C_3^{j_1 j_2} = X_1^{x_2}Z_1^{x_1}E_{12}; [x_1, x_2 \mapsto j_1, j_2], \mathbf{A} \mid \varnothing, \mathbf{B} : \{1,2\}.M_{12}^{0,0}$$

$$C_4^{j_1 j_2} = \mathbf{0}; [x_1, x_2 \mapsto j_1, j_2]\mathbf{A} \mid [s_1, s_2 \mapsto j_1, j_2], \mathbf{B} \ ,$$

where $j_1 j_2$ is equal to the input values 00,01,10 or 11.

The equivalence relation for both of the agents for configurations in $\mathcal{C}_{SC}$ is represented in Fig. 1, with arrows for computation paths, boxes for $\mathbf{A}$'s equivalence classes and dashed boxes for $\mathbf{B}$'s equivalence classes. Obviously, $\mathbf{A}$ distinguishes the 4 possible configurations at each time step – we refer to this below as *horizontally* – because $\mathbf{A}$'s local state $[x_1, x_2 \mapsto j_1, j_2]$ is different for each input value. *Vertically*, that is with respect to the evolution of time, configurations at the first three steps differ because $\mathbf{A}$'s event sequence has changed. However, we find that configurations at the third and fourth level are equivalent for $\mathbf{A}$, since from between both steps $\mathbf{B}$ has applied a local operation, which is not observable by $\mathbf{A}$.

The possibility relation for $\mathbf{B}$ is quite different. We find that that all configurations occurring at the first two steps are considered equivalent by $\mathbf{B}$. Furthermore, all configurations C_3 are equivalent to each other, though they are not equivalent to the previous ones because the event sequence of $\mathbf{B}$ has changed. Configurations C_4 differ from the previous ones because here $\mathbf{B}$ applies a local operation, and furthermore, here $\mathbf{B}$ finally distinguishes states horizontally via its local state $[s_1, s_2 \mapsto j_1, j_2]$.

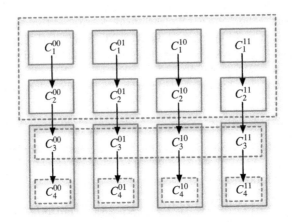

Fig. 1. Possibility relations for the superdense coding network.

The possibility relations of both agents allow us to derive several epistemic statements. First of all, however, let us note that the SC network is correct, since we have

$$\forall j_1, j_2 : C_1^{j_1 j_2}, SC \vDash A\Diamond(s_1 s_2 = j_1 j_2) ,\qquad(10)$$

or, if we want to stress that this occurs in the last step, we use $C_3(j_1 j_2), SC \vDash A\bigcirc(s_1 s_2 = j_1 j_2)$. Note that, since there is no branching in the protocol, we may replace A by E in the above.

Next, we trivially have that $C, SC \vDash K_A(x_1 x_2 = j_1 j_2)$ for all $C \in \mathcal{C}_{SC}$, that is, A always knows its input values – in fact, agents always know their own input values in any protocol. We can also state this by saying that for all input values $C_1^{j_1 j_2}, SC \vDash A\square K_A(x_1 x_2 = j_1 j_2)$. On the other hand, it is only in the last step that B knows A's input values, that is

$$\forall j_1, j_2 : C_4^{j_1 j_2}, SC \vDash K_B(s_1 s_2 = j_1 j_2) ,\qquad(11)$$

while

$$\forall j_1, j_2, s < 4 : C_s^{j_1 j_2}, SC \vDash \neg K_B(s_1 s_2 = j_1 j_2) .\qquad(12)$$

Interestingly, A never knows that B knows A's input values eventually,

$$\forall j_1, j_2 : C_1^{j_1 j_2}, SC \vDash \neg A\Diamond K_A K_B(s_1 s_2 = j_1 j_2) .\qquad(13)$$

The reason for this is that A cannot distinguish between configurations at the last two time steps, that is, A does not know whether B has applied its local measurement yet, and therefore A never knows if B knows that $s_1 s_2 = j_1 j_2$.

Other statements that can be made about the SC network, for example one can play around with temporal operators to highlight when exactly the quantum message is sent. However, the essential features of the protocol are captured above.

3.2   Teleportation

The goal of the teleportation network is to transmit a qubit from one party to another with the aid of an ebit and classical resources. The network achieving this is defined as follows,

$$TP = \mathbf{A} : \{1,2\}.[(\mathsf{c}!s_2s_1).M_{12}^{0,0}] \mid \mathbf{B} : \{3\}.[X_3^{x_2}Z_3^{x_1}.(\mathsf{c}?x_2x_1)] \parallel E_{23} , \qquad (14)$$

where $\mathsf{c}!$ and $\mathsf{c}?$ stand for a classical message rendezvous. In the first step of the protocol Alice executes a Bell measurement on her qubits. Next, Alice sends Bob her measurement outcomes, after which Bob applies Pauli corrections to his qubit dependent on these outcomes. The result is that Bob's qubit ends up in the same state as Alice's input qubit.

In this case, we have branching due to the Bell measurement. Moreover, configurations are parameterised by the quantum input $|\psi\rangle$. As explained above, we do not explicitly show that configurations for different quantum inputs are equivalent for all agents. This feature is usually expressed by saying that $|\psi\rangle$ is an unknown quantum state, that is, $\mathbf{A}$ (nor $\mathbf{B}$) know anything about it. We repeat the configurations occurring throughout the execution of the protocol explicitly here, labelling configurations by measurement outcomes obtained in the first step of the computation.

$$C_1(|\psi\rangle) = |\psi\rangle E_{23}; \varnothing, \mathbf{A} : \{1,2\}.[(\mathsf{c}!s_2s_1).M_{12}^{0,0}] \mid \varnothing, \mathbf{B} : \{3\}.[X_3^{x_2}Z_3^{x_1}.(\mathsf{c}?x_2x_1)]$$

$$C_2^{j_1j_2}(|\psi\rangle) = X^{j_2}Z^{j_1}|\psi\rangle; [s_1,s_2 \mapsto j_1,j_2], \mathbf{A}.(\mathsf{c}!s_2s_1)|\varnothing, \mathbf{B} : \{3\}.[X_3^{x_2}Z_3^{x_1}.(\mathsf{c}?x_2x_1)]$$

$$C_3^{j_1j_2}(|\psi\rangle) = X^{j_2}Z^{j_1}|\psi\rangle; [s_1,s_2 \mapsto j_1,j_2], \mathbf{A} \mid [x_1,x_2 \mapsto j_1,j_2], \mathbf{B} : \{3\}.X_3^{x_2}Z_3^{x_1})$$

$$C_4^{j_1j_2}(|\psi\rangle) = |\psi\rangle; [s_1,s_2 \mapsto j_1,j_2], \mathbf{A} \mid [x_1,x_2 \mapsto j_1,j_2], \mathbf{B} : \{3\} .$$

The equivalence relation for both agents for the set of configurations $\mathcal{C}_{TP}$ is represented in Fig. 2. We find that $C_1(|\psi\rangle)$ is equivalent only to itself for agent $\mathbf{A}$– once more, in effect we have a set $\{C_1(|\psi\rangle), |\psi\rangle \in \mathbb{C}^2\}$ of equivalent configurations with respect to $\sim_{\mathbf{A}}$. After the measurement $\mathbf{A}$ distinguishes (sets of) configurations horizontally at all time steps via its outcome map. Just as for SC, and for the same reason, $\mathbf{A}$ considers configurations at the last two steps to equivalent.

Again, the situation for agent $\mathbf{B}$ is quite different. We find that that configurations at the first two levels are considered to be equivalent, while all other configurations are distinguished, horizontally via $\mathbf{B}$'s local state, and vertically by the change in $\mathbf{B}$'s event sequence.

The correctness of the TP network is stated in logical terms as follows,

$$C_1, TP \models A\Diamond(\mathrm{fin}(q_3) = \mathrm{init}(q_1)) , \qquad (15)$$

where we have left out the parameterisation because the statement holds for all $|\psi\rangle$. In other words, the final state of $\mathbf{B}$'s qubit q_3 is identical to the initial value of $\mathbf{A}$'s qubit q_1[4]. Interestingly, neither of the agents know the actual quantum state at *any* point of the computation, that is

---

[4] We refer to the qubit named q_i as qubit i in semantical derivations.

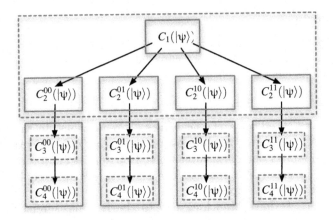

Fig. 2. Possibility relations for the teleportation network.

$$C_1(|\psi\rangle), TP \vDash \neg K_\mathbf{A}(q_1 = |\psi\rangle) \wedge \neg K_\mathbf{B}(q_1 = |\psi\rangle) \tag{16}$$

$$C_1(|\psi\rangle), TP \vDash \neg E \Diamond K_\mathbf{A}(q_3 = |\psi\rangle) \wedge \neg E \Diamond K_\mathbf{B}(q_3 = |\psi\rangle) , \tag{17}$$

that is to say, initially nobody knows that q_1 is in the state $|\psi\rangle$, and there is no future point in the protocol at which either **A** or **B** knows that q_3 is in the state $|\psi\rangle$. The basic reason for this is of course that for all input states $|\psi\rangle$ configurations $C(|\psi\rangle)$ are considered equivalent by all agents, and therefore they can conclude nothing about properties $|\psi\rangle$ may have. Apart from statements about classical message passing, in TP the only knowledge transfer deals with the *correlation* between initial and final states of the network, *not* with the actual form of the quantum input. To be more precise, we have that

$$C_1, TP \vDash A \Diamond K_\mathbf{B}(q_3 = \text{init}(q_1)) , \tag{18}$$

since at the last step of the computation **B** knows that it must have the original input state. However, since **A** cannot distinguish the last two time steps, we also have that

$$C_1, TP \vDash \neg E \Diamond K_\mathbf{A}(q_3 = \text{init}(q_1)) . \tag{19}$$

The latter two statements may seem odd in that we are talking about states that the agents know nothing about. However, even without knowing a state, one may still have information about how it compares with other states. There is nothing strange about this, as this sort of thing happens with classical correlations too. What it does show, however, is that there is no actual quantum knowledge transfer in the TP network – there was no quantum knowledge about the input to begin with! We can only say something about the relation of the initial to final quantum states.

Note that our analysis is in stark contrast with the one found in [9], which is jointly in terms of K_i^c and K_i^q. As mentioned above, the latter is based upon equality of reduced density matrices. Next to our objections to this approach mentioned earlier, such an analysis becomes increasingly awkward when applied to the teleportation protocol, since the basis of TP is that the initial state is *unknown*. In fact, the authors themselves note that their analysis leads to difficulties. Concretely, in their framework the conclusion is that initially **A** has quantum knowledge of $|\psi\rangle$ – i.e. **A** knows its initial reduced density matrix, which is just $|\psi\rangle\langle\psi|$ – while **B** does not, and that eventually **B** knows the initial state $|\psi\rangle$, i.e. the same reduced density matrix. However, if Alice teleports a single qubit to Bob she absolutely has not transmitted a continuum of information. Indeed, Bob needs many such qubits to determine, via statistical analysis, which quantum state has been teleported. Moreover, as pointed out by the authors themselves, their notion of knowledge allows **B** to distinguish the four possible network states even *before* **A** has sent the measurement results through, i.e. at the second step of the computation. This is not the case: in fact the classical message passing is *crucial* for the success of the protocol, as without this information Bob's state is given by the maximally mixed state. All these arguments just strengthen our point: analysing teleportation from an epistemic point of view has nothing to do with quantum states, but rather with the relationship between them. Our point is that, although quantum mechanics can be used to transmit information in unexpected ways, there is no such thing as quantum knowledge; it is all classical knowledge, albeit about quantum systems.

4   Conclusion

We have developed a formal framework for investigating epistemic and temporal notions in the context of distributed quantum systems. While we rely on structures developed in prior work, our notion of quantum knowledge makes sense more generally in any agent-based model of quantum networks. Several arguments are given to support our view that an agent's possibility relation should not be based on the reduced density matrix, but rather on local classical states and local quantum operations. In this way, we are able to analyse distributed primitives from a knowledge-based perspective. Concretely, we investigated superdense coding and teleportation, obtaining interesting conclusions as to how the knowledge of individual agents evolves. We have explicitly shown that the knowledge transfer in teleportation is essentially classical, in that eventually, the receiving agent only knows that its state is equal to the initial state of the sender. The relevant epistemic statements for teleportation deal with this correlation rather than with the actual quantum state, which is unknown throughout the protocol.

References

1. Danos, V., D'Hondt, E., Kashefi, E., Panangaden, P.: Distributed measurement-based quantum computation. In Selinger, P., ed.: Proceedings of the 3rd Workshop on Quantum Programming Languages (QPL05). (2005)

2. Hintikka, J.: Knowledge and belief - An introduction to the logic of the two notions. Cornell University Press, Ithaca, N.Y. (1962)
3. Halpern, J.Y.: Reasoning about knowledge: a survey. In: Handbook of Logic in Artificial Intelligence and Logic Programming. Volume 4. Oxford University Press (1995) 1–34
4. Fagin, R., Halpern, J.Y., Moses, Y., Vardi, M.Y.: Reasoning about knowledge. MIT Press (1995)
5. Nielsen, M.A., Chuang, I.: Quantum computation and quantum information. Cambridge university press (2000)
6. Baltag, A., Smets, S.: Quantum dynamic logic. In Selinger, P., ed.: Proceedings of the 2nd Workshop on Quantum Programming Languages (QPL04), Turku, Finland, Turku Centre for Computer Science, TUCS General Publication No 33 (2004)
7. Baltag, A., Smets, S.: LQP: the dynamic logic of quantum information. Unpublished (2005)
8. van der Meyden, R., Patra, M.: A logic for probability in quantum systems. In: Proc. Computer Science Logic and 8th Kurt Gödel Colloquium, Vienna, Austria (2003) 427–440
9. van der Meyden, R., Patra, M.: Knowledge in quantum systems. In: Proceedings of the 9th conference on Theoretical aspects of rationality and knowledge, Bloomington, Indiana (2003) 104–117
10. Danos, V., Kashefi, E., Panangaden, P.: The measurement calculus. quant-ph/0412135 (2004)
11. D'Hondt, E.: Distributed quantum computation – A measurement-based approach. PhD thesis, Vrije Universiteit Brussel (2005) In preparation.
12. Emerson, E.A.: Temporal and modal logic. In: Handbook of Theoretical Computer Science, Volume B: Formal Models and Sematics (B). MIT Press (1990) 995–1072
13. Bennett, C.H., Wiesner, S.J.: Communication via one- and two-particle operators on Einstein-Podolsky-Rosen states. Phys. Rev. Lett. (1992) 2881–2884
14. Bennett, C.H., Brassard, G., Crépeau, C., Jozsa, R., Peres, A., Wootters, W.: Teleporting an unknown quantum state via dual classical and EPR channels. Phys. Rev. Lett. **70** (1993) 1895–1899
15. D'Hondt, E., Panangaden, P.: The computational power of the W and GHZ states. Journal on Quantum Information & Computation (2005) To appear.

Author Index

Lecture Notes in Computer Science

For information about Vols. 1–3708

please contact your bookseller or Springer

Vol. 3760: R. Meersman, Z. Tari (Eds.), On the Move to Meaningful Internet Systems 2005: CoopIS, DOA, and ODBASE, Part I. XXVII, 921 pages. 2005.

Vol. 3759: G. Chen, Y. Pan, M. Guo, J. Lu (Eds.), Parallel and Distributed Processing and Applications - ISPA 2005 Workshops. XIII, 669 pages. 2005.

Vol. 3758: Y. Pan, D.-x. Chen, M. Guo, J. Cao, J.J. Dongarra (Eds.), Parallel and Distributed Processing and Applications. XXIII, 1162 pages. 2005.

Vol. 3757: A. Rangarajan, B. Vemuri, A.L. Yuille (Eds.), Energy Minimization Methods in Computer Vision and Pattern Recognition. XII, 666 pages. 2005.

Vol. 3756: J. Cao, W. Nejdl, M. Xu (Eds.), Advanced Parallel Processing Technologies. XIV, 526 pages. 2005.

Vol. 3754: J. Dalmau Royo, G. Hasegawa (Eds.), Management of Multimedia Networks and Services. XII, 384 pages. 2005.

Vol. 3753: O.F. Olsen, L.M.J. Florack, A. Kuijper (Eds.), Deep Structure, Singularities, and Computer Vision. X, 259 pages. 2005.

Vol. 3752: N. Paragios, O. Faugeras, T. Chan, C. Schnörr (Eds.), Variational, Geometric, and Level Set Methods in Computer Vision. XI, 369 pages. 2005.

Vol. 3751: T. Magedanz, E.R. M. Madeira, P. Dini (Eds.), Operations and Management in IP-Based Networks. X, 213 pages. 2005.

Vol. 3750: J.S. Duncan, G. Gerig (Eds.), Medical Image Computing and Computer-Assisted Intervention – MICCAI 2005, Part II. XL, 1018 pages. 2005.

Vol. 3749: J.S. Duncan, G. Gerig (Eds.), Medical Image Computing and Computer-Assisted Intervention – MICCAI 2005, Part I. XXXIX, 942 pages. 2005.

Vol. 3748: A. Hartman, D. Kreische (Eds.), Model Driven Architecture – Foundations and Applications. IX, 349 pages. 2005.

Vol. 3747: C.A. Maziero, J.G. Silva, A.M.S. Andrade, F.M.d. Assis Silva (Eds.), Dependable Computing. XV, 267 pages. 2005.

Vol. 3746: P. Bozanis, E.N. Houstis (Eds.), Advances in Informatics. XIX, 879 pages. 2005.

Vol. 3745: J.L. Oliveira, V. Maojo, F. Martín-Sánchez, A.S. Pereira (Eds.), Biological and Medical Data Analysis. XII, 422 pages. 2005. (Subseries LNBI).

Vol. 3744: T. Magedanz, A. Karmouch, S. Pierre, I. Venieris (Eds.), Mobility Aware Technologies and Applications. XIV, 418 pages. 2005.

Vol. 3740: T. Srikanthan, J. Xue, C.-H. Chang (Eds.), Advances in Computer Systems Architecture. XVII, 833 pages. 2005.

Vol. 3739: W. Fan, Z.-h. Wu, J. Yang (Eds.), Advances in Web-Age Information Management. XXIV, 930 pages. 2005.

Vol. 3738: V.R. Syrotiuk, E. Chávez (Eds.), Ad-Hoc, Mobile, and Wireless Networks. XI, 360 pages. 2005.

Vol. 3735: A. Hoffmann, H. Motoda, T. Scheffer (Eds.), Discovery Science. XVI, 400 pages. 2005. (Subseries LNAI).

Vol. 3734: S. Jain, H.U. Simon, E. Tomita (Eds.), Algorithmic Learning Theory. XII, 490 pages. 2005. (Subseries LNAI).

Vol. 3733: P. Yolum, T. Güngör, F. Gürgen, C. Özturan (Eds.), Computer and Information Sciences - ISCIS 2005. XXI, 973 pages. 2005.

Vol. 3731: F. Wang (Ed.), Formal Techniques for Networked and Distributed Systems - FORTE 2005. XII, 558 pages. 2005.

Vol. 3729: Y. Gil, E. Motta, V. R. Benjamins, M.A. Musen (Eds.), The Semantic Web – ISWC 2005. XXIII, 1073 pages. 2005.

Vol. 3728: V. Paliouras, J. Vounckx, D. Verkest (Eds.), Integrated Circuit and System Design. XV, 753 pages. 2005.

Vol. 3726: L.T. Yang, O.F. Rana, B. Di Martino, J.J. Dongarra (Eds.), High Performance Computing and Communications. XXVI, 1116 pages. 2005.

Vol. 3725: D. Borrione, W. Paul (Eds.), Correct Hardware Design and Verification Methods. XII, 412 pages. 2005.

Vol. 3724: P. Fraigniaud (Ed.), Distributed Computing. XIV, 520 pages. 2005.

Vol. 3723: W. Zhao, S. Gong, X. Tang (Eds.), Analysis and Modelling of Faces and Gestures. XI, 4234 pages. 2005.

Vol. 3722: D. Van Hung, M. Wirsing (Eds.), Theoretical Aspects of Computing – ICTAC 2005. XIV, 614 pages. 2005.

Vol. 3721: A.M. Jorge, L. Torgo, P.B. Brazdil, R. Camacho, J. Gama (Eds.), Knowledge Discovery in Databases: PKDD 2005. XXIII, 719 pages. 2005. (Subseries LNAI).

Vol. 3720: J. Gama, R. Camacho, P.B. Brazdil, A.M. Jorge, L. Torgo (Eds.), Machine Learning: ECML 2005. XXIII, 769 pages. 2005. (Subseries LNAI).

Vol. 3719: M. Hobbs, A.M. Goscinski, W. Zhou (Eds.), Distributed and Parallel Computing. XI, 448 pages. 2005.

Vol. 3718: V.G. Ganzha, E.W. Mayr, E.V. Vorozhtsov (Eds.), Computer Algebra in Scientific Computing. XII, 502 pages. 2005.

Vol. 3717: B. Gramlich (Ed.), Frontiers of Combining Systems. X, 321 pages. 2005. (Subseries LNAI).

Vol. 3716: L. Delcambre, C. Kop, H.C. Mayr, J. Mylopoulos, Ó. Pastor (Eds.), Conceptual Modeling – ER 2005. XVI, 498 pages. 2005.

Vol. 3715: E. Dawson, S. Vaudenay (Eds.), Progress in Cryptology – Mycrypt 2005. XI, 329 pages. 2005.

Vol. 3714: H. Obbink, K. Pohl (Eds.), Software Product Lines. XIII, 235 pages. 2005.

Vol. 3713: L.C. Briand, C. Williams (Eds.), Model Driven Engineering Languages and Systems. XV, 722 pages. 2005.

Vol. 3712: R. Reussner, J. Mayer, J.A. Stafford, S. Overhage, S. Becker, P.J. Schroeder (Eds.), Quality of Software Architectures and Software Quality. XIII, 289 pages. 2005.

Vol. 3711: F. Kishino, Y. Kitamura, H. Kato, N. Nagata (Eds.), Entertainment Computing - ICEC 2005. XXIV, 540 pages. 2005.

Vol. 3710: M. Barni, I. Cox, T. Kalker, H.J. Kim (Eds.), Digital Watermarking. XII, 485 pages. 2005.

Vol. 3709: P. van Beek (Ed.), Principles and Practice of Constraint Programming - CP 2005. XX, 887 pages. 2005.